CRIMINAL INTELLIGENCE FOR THE 21ST CENTURY

Richard Wright, Managing Editor

Bob Morehouse, Marilyn B. Peterson, and Lisa Palmieri, Editors

Published by

Association of
Law Enforcement Intelligence Units (LEIU)
&
International Association of Law Enforcement Intelligence Analysts (IALEIA)

ISBN 978-0-615-39038-3
© 2011
Reprinted December 2021

I

Criminal Intelligence for the 21ST Century

PERMISSIONS

TABLE OF CONTENTS

FORWARD

In 2000, the International Association of Law Enforcement Intelligence Analysts (IALEIA) and the Association of Law Enforcement Intelligence Units (LEIU) published *Intelligence 2000: Revising the Basic Elements.* It was a comprehensive collection of articles written by practitioners for readers interested in the craft of intelligence. It focused on updating the 1971 and 1976 editions of the *Basic Elements of Intelligence.*

Now, 10 years later, IALEIA and LEIU are pleased to present an updated, revised and expanded publication titled, *Criminal Intelligence for the 21st Century.* Although some articles are updates to the originals published in 2000, most articles are new. This book addresses the numerous changes that have occurred in the field of law enforcement intelligence over the past decade. It includes 27 articles by subject experts on different aspects of the intelligence field, including the basic functions, various applications and programs.

This book could not have been completed without the voluntary dedicated effort of its numerous authors. We thank them for their willingness to share their expertise. Special thanks goes to Michele Panages, LEIU's Recording Secretary, and Ann Hewitt, a Criminal Intelligence Specialist with the California Department of Justice for their review, formatting, and final editing.

We sincerely hope that you, the reader, will benefit from the accumulated knowledge contained in this edition and that it will assist you in enhancing public safety for your jurisdiction.

Sincerely,

Ritchie Martinez, President
International Association of
Law Enforcement Intelligence Analysts

Van Godsey, General Chairman
Association of Law Enforcement
Intelligence Units

The Role of Criminal Intelligence in Law Enforcement
By Bob Morehouse

INTRODUCTION

The role of criminal intelligence in law enforcement is a pivotal one and in great demand, particularly since September 11, 2001. The effective use of the intelligence process can mean the difference between success and failure for an agency. Intelligence can support a broad range of activities within each agency, from municipal to federal to international. Particularly now when information is plentiful—some would say information overload—and often confusing or contradictory, intelligence can point the way to effective policing.

As we enter the second decade of what was previously referred to as the "new millennium" the law enforcement community is again provided with an opportunity to update its view of the intelligence process. The original source of guidelines for intelligence in law enforcement was the *Basic Elements of Intelligence* written by E. Drexel Godfrey and Don R. Harris in 1971 and published by the Law Enforcement Assistance Administration. That work was revised in 1976 by Harris. In 2000, the Association of Law Enforcement Intelligence Units (LEIU) and the International Association of Law Enforcement Intelligence Analysts (IALEIA) combined resources to write *Intelligence 2000: Revising the Basic Elements (referred to as Intelligence 2000)*. Marilyn Peterson was the managing editor and Richard Wright and Bob Morehouse served as associate editors. Intelligence 2000, with chapters written by intelligence officers and analysts from three continents, provides an update and expansion of the concepts embodied in the *Basic Elements of Intelligence*. This current effort builds upon that expansion. This first chapter provides an overview of the history of intelligence and its gradual acceptance by law enforcement. Brief discussions are also included on the value of criminal intelligence, the need for a mission statement, tactical and strategic intelligence, and a short description of the intelligence process.

WHAT INTELLIGENCE MEANS

The effective use of a criminal intelligence unit is crucial to a law enforcement agency's ability to understand the criminal environment and combat criminal groups. An intelligence unit provides the agency with the knowledge and recommendations to allow effective management of its resources. With appropriate tasking, an intelligence unit will assist in developing strategic plans to prepare for future challenges.

Criminal intelligence is a process involving planning and direction, collection, evaluation, collation, analysis, dissemination, and re-evaluation of information on suspected criminals and/or organizations (Harris 1976:1-8). Criminal intelligence provides knowledge that allows law enforcement authorities to establish a pro-active response to crime (Aumond 1998:35-36). It enables law enforcement agencies to identify and understand criminal groups operating in their areas. Once criminal groups are identified and their habits known, law enforcement authorities may begin to assess current trends in crime and to forecast, and possibly prevent, future criminal activities. Criminal intelligence also provides the knowledge on which to base decisions and select appropriate targets (subjects, criminal groups, or businesses) for investigations. Although criminal intelligence may be used to assist in investigations, surveillance operations, and the prosecution of cases, it also provides law enforcement agencies with the ability to effectively manage resources, budget, and meet their responsibility to forecast community threats in order to prevent crime.

Just after the dawn of the last century, "organized crime" was synonymous with La Cosa Nostra (LCN) or Mafia. Today's organized crime picture, however, includes many new criminal groups. Many of these new groups, with well developed organizational structures, are—like the LCN—established for obtaining power and wealth. These criminal groups include outlaw motorcycle gangs, criminal organizations based on nationality or ethnicity, narcotics cartels, and a myriad of street gangs. There are also various criminal extremist groups that include white supremacy, animal rights, militia, and anti-government groups.

All of the criminal groups are involved in one or more of the continuing criminal ventures of gambling, prostitution, theft, drug trafficking, extortion, fraud, and murder. Some are using sophisticated technology to support their criminal activities. The explosion of Internet resources in the last several years opened up new opportunities for financial gain for criminals and the escalation in high-technology crime remains a challenging arena for law enforcement.

Criminal intelligence has an important role in law enforcement as it is a proven tool in ascertaining criminal activities in the community and leading to informed judgments and measures for crime prevention (Wright 1998:9-10). Criminal organizations and subjects continue to evolve in their sophistication. The challenge for law enforcement is to be prepared for this increasing sophistication in order to reduce the impact of criminal activities on our communities or, as our ultimate goal, preventing crimes from happening at all.

In order to accomplish this, law enforcement agencies will need aggressive, comprehensive strategies to counteract the threat of organized crime groups. Criminal intelligence, when tasked and used effectively, is a major weapon in the law enforcement arsenal. The collection, analysis, and dissemination of criminal intelligence will arm law enforcement with essential knowledge needed to reduce or prevent crime.

HISTORICAL FOCUS OF POLICE INTELLIGENCE IN THE UNITED STATES

Intelligence originated as a tool for the military. The ancient Chinese used it as did the military in biblical times. In the United States, George Washington used it during the Revolutionary War to make use of information gathered on British troop movements. In the time since the Revolutionary War, numerous U.S. governmental agencies have used intelligence to gain knowledge about other governments' intelligence (CIA 2000a and 2000b).

Prior to World War II, military intelligence in the United States was gathered by different federal agencies who worked independently of each other. During World War II, it became obvious that intelligence needed to be collected and processed on a coordinated government-wide basis. To reduce the duplication of effort and conflicting information among the many different governmental departments' intelligence components, the Joint Army Navy Intelligence Studies (JANIS) was formed to fulfill this coordination function (CIA 2000a and 2000b).

Prior to Pearl Harbor, President Franklin D. Roosevelt was concerned with United States' intelligence deficiencies and asked William J. Donovan, a New York lawyer, to formulate a proposal for an intelligence service. The Office of Strategic Services (OSS), a result of Donovan's proposal, was established in June 1942 and supplied policymakers with intelligence. The OSS was abolished in October 1945 with the State and War departments taking over OSS responsibilities. Donovan then proposed an organization that would provide intelligence, determine national intelligence objectives, and correlate intelligence from all government agencies. However, this proposal was greatly criticized by government agencies who wanted to keep military and civilian intelligence separate. After considering Donovan's proposal and the government agencies' concerns, President Harry S. Truman established the Central Intelligence Group in 1946. Under the direction of the National Intelligence Authority, it was a means of coordinating existing departments' intelligence. The Group's main function was to supplement existing departments' efforts. The Group was in existence only a short time and was abolished in September 1947 (CIA 2000a and 2000b).

After World War II, there was a need for a continuing coordinated intelligence collection effort, but on a more comprehensive, worldwide basis for both military and political purposes. The Central Intelligence Agency (CIA) was formed in July 1947 and began operations in September 1947. Most of the CIA's responsibilities were established by the National Security Act, which closely followed the Presidential directive that created the Central Intelligence Group and Donovan's proposal. In October 1947, responsibility for the Joint Army Navy Intelligence Studies (JANIS) program was moved to the CIA where the JANIS program was replaced by the National Intelligence Survey program for peacetime intelligence (CIA 2000a and 2000b). The CIA is just one of the many federal agencies that collect intelligence information. Another agency, the Bureau of Intelligence and Research (INR), established in 1946 is the State Department's primary source for interpretive analysis of global developments. The INR, drawing on all-source intelligence, provides value-added independent analysis of events to State Department policymakers, ensures that intelligence activities support foreign policy and national security purposes; and serves as the focal point in the Department for ensuring policy review of sensitive counterintelligence and law enforcement activities. INR's primary mission is to harness intelligence to serve U.S. diplomacy. The bureau also analyzes geographical and international boundary issues. Part of INR's purpose is to provide the Secretary of State with timely, objective assessments, free of policy prescription or preferences. INR's mandate is to tell policymakers what they need to know, not what they want to hear.

Law Enforcement Intelligence Develops

Civilian law enforcement use of intelligence is a fairly recent development. It was not until the beginning of the 1900s that law enforcement authorities began developing criminal intelligence. Law enforcement authorities were slow to accept the usefulness of criminal intelligence in countering criminal groups. Gradually, criminal intelligence gained acceptance as an effective tool in fighting crime. It took most of the 20th century for criminal intelligence to gain widespread acceptance. From the 1900s to the 1950s, criminal intelligence was only in use on a very limited basis. More acceptances developed in the second half of the century when criminal intelligence was shown to be an effective law enforcement tool to combat organized crime.

CHAPTER 1

The Role of Criminal Intelligence in Law Enforcement

One of the first and among the most well-known uses of intelligence by law enforcement was against the "Black Hand Society" (New York City Police Dept. 2000a and 2000b). Criminal intelligence was instrumental in solving the "Black Hand" murders of Italian immigrants in New York in the early 1900s. The "Black Hand Society," a loosely knit criminal organization, operated in the New York City area and extorted money from immigrant Italians. Members of the Society included individuals in both the United States and Italy. New York City Police Department Lieutenant Guiseppe Petrosino pursued an investigation of the "Black Hand" from 1905 to 1909, which resulted in the deportation of 500 people and the arrest of thousands of others. Crimes against Italian immigrants were reduced by half. Unfortunately, Lieutenant Petrosino was later murdered in Palmero, Italy, while gathering additional information on

Lieutenant Petrosino

"Black Hand" members (New York City Police Department 2000a and 2000b).

In the 1920s and 1930s, criminal intelligence was used on a limited basis by American and Canadian law enforcement agencies. By the 1940s and 1950s, law enforcement agencies and governmental officials became more motivated to establish intelligence units to counter the advancement of organized crime. The 1950 Kefauver hearings made the "Mafia" a household word and further emphasized the need for intelligence to counter the Mafia's criminal enterprises (Peterson 1994:1-11).

Criminals began to travel more widely and engage in their criminal pursuits wherever they traveled. The Association of Law Enforcement Intelligence Units (LEIU) was formed by 26 local and state law enforcement agencies in 1956 as an organization whose members exchanged confidential criminal information concerning organized, traveling criminals. Today, with approximately 240 member agencies in 3 countries, LEIU remains the only organization of its kind to promote the professional trust, training, integrity, and communication required to facilitate the lawful and ethical sharing and use of criminal intelligence information among law enforcement agencies.

- **Trust** - Trust is a critical requirement for sharing confidential information. LEIU promotes a trusting relationship among its members by screening applicants, maintaining legal and ethical standards, providing networking opportunities at conferences, and coordinating criminal investigations on subjects of common interest.

- **Training** - LEIU holds annual training seminars, hosts local and regional training classes, publishes books and articles on pertinent subjects, and offers assistance to members for developing or evaluating their criminal intelligence units.

- **Communication** - LEIU facilitates the communication of criminal intelligence by providing members with established dissemination standards, membership rosters with individual contact numbers for member personnel assigned to organized crime, gangs, and terrorism, and a computerized database accessible via RISS.net.

- **Integrity** – LEIU maintains that integrity is a key component of all criminal intelligence unit operations. Without integrity, there can be no trust between agencies or with the public constituencies they serve.

LEIU has established professional standards for the collection, maintenance, and dissemination of criminal intelligence among law enforcement agencies and is a leader in advocating a balance between the needs of law enforcement and the constitutional rights of individuals. Its mission is to provide leadership and promote professionalism in the criminal intelligence community in order to protect public safety and constitutional rights. The California Department of Justice has functioned as the Central Coordinating Agency since the inception of LEIU.

Rico's Impact on Intelligence

In the late 1960s, intelligence units began to appear in local law enforcement. The President's 1967 Commission on Organized Crime supported the use of criminal intelligence in law enforcement (Peterson 1994:1-11). The Commission's work was the basis for the development of federal legislation entitled Racketeering Influenced and Corrupt Organization (RICO). Passage of this legislation in 1970 was a major milestone in recognizing the extent and impact of organized crime in business and that current federal countermeasures were ineffective in the fight against organized crime. The power of the RICO statute was not fully understood after its passage and was not used for nearly ten years after its inception. However, as both federal law enforcement authorities and prosecutors began to recognize its far-reaching potential, its impact has been enormous.

In the early 1980s, the RICO statute was first used to successfully convict organized crime individuals and deliver a crippling blow to their organizations. This is significant because organized crime differs from individual crime in that it has the power to affect economic and political life to a much greater extent than individual crime. RICO's power lies in how it targets organized crime through identifying and prosecuting illegal organizations and their economic base as well as the individual criminals. This is a very effective tool in controlling organized crime (Pennsylvania Crime Commission 1990:17-19).

To exert this type of control, a method of investigation called enterprise theory was developed (Pennsylvania Crime Commission 1990:17-19). The enterprise approach was first used by the Federal Bureau of Investigation in the early 1980s and later used by other law enforcement agencies. The approach looks for a pattern of criminal acts over time and not just a single act by an individual at a single moment in time. It is the total range of criminal acts and the size and scope of the organization that is investigated. The goal of the enterprise approach is threefold. First, the business or "enterprise" of the organization is targeted and not just the individuals that run the organization. The intent is to disrupt the organization's business to the extent that the business is destroyed or greatly incapacitated. Second, the organization's leadership is targeted as well as those who participate in the business or profit from the business dealings. Third, the profit is removed from the criminal enterprises by identifying the assets realized from the criminal enterprise and seizing them.

It was in the 1980s that law enforcement authorities first used the power of RICO as a prosecutorial weapon. To effectively use RICO, law enforcement agencies needed to understand the structure and business activities of organized crime organizations. From the passage of RICO in 1970 to the early 1980s, law enforcement had established the criminal intelligence foundation and expertise necessary to obtain convictions. This understanding is crucial in proving that a pattern of criminal enterprise exists within an organization, to identify responsible individuals, and to seize the assets.

The 1980s landmark RICO case was against the Mafia Commission (Lindberg 2000). The heads of five Mafia families were convicted in 1986 for conducting a pattern of racketeering that violated the federal RICO statutes. The Commission was greatly weakened by having five of its members imprisoned. While the Commission still exists, it does not continue to exercise its former influence. The combination of successful prosecutions and the forfeiture of assets delivered a disabling blow to this organized crime organization from which it has not fully recovered.

Today, RICO remains the single most powerful weapon enabling federal law enforcement authorities to effectively attack organized crime organizations and not just the gangsters involved in the criminal activities. RICO means that it is no longer necessary to convict individuals on specific crimes or their activity in the crime; prosecutors are able to obtain convictions by only proving a pattern of racketeering activity in the operation of a business.

Intelligence Infrastructure

In 1971, the first version of **the *Basic Elements of Intelligence*** was produced. Shortly after, the California Department of Justice and the New Jersey State Police began employing analytical techniques in their intelligence programs. In 1976, *Basic Elements* was revised. Analytical training began to be offered across the United States. Law enforcement managers and analysts learned the basics of association, telephone, event, financial, and visual investigative analysis as well as other tools used for analysis. By the 1980s, analysis was more widely known and began to be used in cases at the federal, state, and local levels. Computers began to be used in the compilation of information (with the development of user-friendly computer programs) allowing for rapid information processing, storage, and retrieval (Peterson 1994:1-11).

Criminal intelligence continued to evolve in the law enforcement community. This was out of the need to both forecast and prevent the activities of organized crime groups. Officials needed information that forewarned of future criminal trends and activities so decisions could be made to counter the actions of a community's criminal groups. Based on decision-makers' needs and the need to maintain law and order, criminal intelligence became a widely used and effective tool against criminal organizations.

The federally funded Regional Information Sharing System (RISS) assisted in bringing analysis into greater use beginning in 1973 with the Regional Organized Crime Information Center. RISS programs offered analysis as a service and used sophisticated computer programs to assist in the analysis information and offer analytical reports to law enforcement authorities. RISS is composed of six regional centers, each of which selects its own target crimes and range of services to provide to members (Bureau of Justice Assistance 1999: v). Most members are municipal and county agencies, but they also include local offices of state and federal agencies. Membership by the end of 2009 included more than 8,500 agencies. Once law enforcement authorities discovered the usefulness of the analytical products the regional centers produced, more began establishing their own intelligence units. (See also Chapter 17 "Networks, Organizations, and Resources")

In 1981, the International Association of Law Enforcement Intelligence Analysts (IALEIA) formed for the purpose of enhancing the understanding, professionalism, and use of intelligence. In 2010, this organization has more than 2,000 members in over 50 countries.

IALEIA members include analysts, sworn law enforcement officers, law enforcement executives, intelligence officers, military personnel, fusion center and homeland security personnel, students, professors, and practitioners from securities, fraud, customs, and border agencies. Members are brought together to achieve the following objectives:

- **Advocacy** - IALEIA unites members and advances public and official understanding of criminal intelligence analysis and its role as a profession.

- **Training** - IALEIA devises concepts, standards, and curricula for training, and offers basic analyst training for analysts worldwide.

- **Certification** - IALEIA has qualification standards and indices of competence for the profession, and administers a professional international certification program. In 1991, through partnership with the Society of Certified Criminal Analysts (SCCA), a certification program for law enforcement analysts was created. Since then, IALEIA has adapted and adopted SCCA's certification process. The IALEIA Analyst Certification Program is structured to encourage continuing education, measure knowledge and skills, and recognize excellence though experience.

- **Networking** - Regular meetings, training, and speakers are arranged by the numerous regional IALEIA chapters worldwide. By providing timely, relevant information to members on opportunities and issues affecting the field, IALEIA promotes well-informed career analysts. In addition, IALEIA's website (www.ialeia.org) is available in several languages to facilitate international networking opportunities.

- **Professionalism** - IALEIA reinforces the concepts of professionalism, dedication to service, and integrity among practitioners of criminal intelligence analysis.

- **Research** - IALEIA encourages research about criminal intelligence analysis and the analytic process, and identifies funding for such research.

There remains a vital need for criminal intelligence to advance to an international level for combating crime organizations, which now operate worldwide. Organized crime has truly gone global. As stated in a 1993 report by Roy Godson and William Olson of the National Strategy Information Center, these groups are an international security threat and a major ingredient in growing global ungovernability (1993:i).

Today, criminal intelligence is a linchpin in efforts to counter the organized activities of the various crime groups operating in communities across the nation and, indeed, around the world. These groups operate in secret, are increasingly sophisticated in their methods and practices, and seek both power and financial rewards. As a result, criminal intelligence professionals will need to keep pace with an ever-evolving technology and the increased demand to properly interpret intelligence to prevent crimes and forecast the future trends that will enable decision-makers to properly manage their resources.

NATIONAL CRIMINAL INTELLIGENCE SHARING PLAN (NCISP)

The need for a NCISP ("Plan") was recognized as critical after the tragic events of September 11, 2001, when nearly 3,000 innocent lives were lost as a result of terrorist attacks against the United States. This event initiated a concerted effort by American law enforcement agencies to correct the inadequacies and barriers that impede information and intelligence sharing—so that future tragedies could be prevented.

CHAPTER 1

The Role of Criminal Intelligence in Law Enforcement

In spring 2002, law enforcement executives and intelligence experts attending the International Association of Chiefs of Police (IACP) Criminal Intelligence Sharing Summit recognized that local, state, tribal, and federal law enforcement agencies and organizations that represented them must work towards common goals—gathering information and producing intelligence within their agency and sharing that intelligence with other law enforcement and public safety agencies. Summit participants called for the creation of a nationally coordinated criminal intelligence coordinating council that would develop and oversee a national intelligence plan. In response to this crucial need, the U.S. Department of Justice's Global Justice Information Sharing Initiative (Global) Intelligence Working Group (GIWG) was formed. Local, state, and tribal law enforcement representatives were key participants in the development of the NCISP.

Many state law enforcement agencies and all federal agencies with intelligence gathering and assessment responsibilities have established intelligence functions within their organizations. However, approximately 75 percent of the law enforcement agencies in the United States have less that 24 sworn officers, and more often than not, these agencies do not have staff dedicated to intelligence functions. Officers in these smaller, local agencies interact with the public in the communities they patrol on a daily basis. Providing local agencies with the tools and resources necessary for developing, gathering, accessing, receiving, and sharing intelligence information is critically important to improving public safety and homeland security.

In 2003, (then) President George W. Bush pledged to make information sharing an important tool in the nation's war on terror. "All across our country we'll be able to tie our terrorist information to local information banks so that the front line of defeating terror becomes activated and real, and those are the local law enforcement officials. We expect them to be part of our effort; we must give them the tools necessary so they can do their job." The NCISP is a key tool that law enforcement agencies can employ to support their crime-fighting and public efforts. The following is a quote from then U.S. Attorney General John Ashcroft at the NCISP National Kick-off Event in May 2004: "This Plan represents law enforcement's commitment to take it upon itself to ensure that the dots are connected, be it in crime or terrorism. The Plan is the outcome of an unprecedented effort by law enforcement agencies, with the strong support of the Department of Justice, to strengthen the nation's security through better intelligence analysis and sharing." (Executive Summary: National Criminal Intelligence Sharing Plan; Revised August 2005). The Executive Summary of the Plan can be seen in the Appendix.

CREATION OF THE U.S. DEPARTMENT OF HOMELAND SECURITY

The Homeland Security Act of 2002 (signed by former President George W. Bush in November 2002) created the U.S. Department of Homeland Security (DHS) with cabinet–level standing. This Department's mission is to prevent terrorist attacks within the United States, reduce the vulnerability of the United States to terrorism, minimize the damage, and assist in the recovery from terrorist attacks that do occur in the United States. Several existing Federal agencies were merged into the DHS including the United States Customs and Border Protection, United States Immigration and Customs Enforcement, Transportation Security Administration, Federal Emergency Management Administration, United States Coast Guard, the United States Secret Service, and several others. Created within DHS was the Office of Intelligence and Analysis (I&A) which serves as a bridge between state and local law enforcement (and other homeland security partners) and the U.S. Intelligence Community. DHS I&A has intelligence officers deployed across the country to support not only intelligence needs nationwide, but also to provide training and guidance in support of the intelligence cycle.

Fusion Centers

One of the major recommendations contained in the NCISP was the creation of a group to provide long-term oversight and assistance in its implementation. The Criminal Intelligence Coordinating Council (CICC) was formally established in May 2004 with the purpose of advising the U.S. Congress, the U.S. Attorney General, and the Secretary of the U.S. Department of Homeland Security on the best use of criminal intelligence to keep our country safe. Staying consistent with the idea of local involvement, it was important that the CICC consist of representatives from local, state, tribal, and federal agencies and national law enforcement organizations.

As agencies began the process implementing the NCISP, it became apparent that joint efforts allowed for quicker information sharing and could allow for leveraging of resources. As these joint homeland security initiatives continued to mature and develop, the phrase "**Fusion Center**" was adopted. In 2004 and 2005 several states and larger cities embarked on the development of fusion centers. As more and more centers were created across the nation it was obvious that some structure or format should be put in place to assist in consistent and efficient operations.

As part of a joint effort between the Bureau of Justice Assistance, Office of Justice Programs, U. S. Department of Justice, U. S. Department of Justice's Global Justice Information Sharing Initiative (Global), U. S. Department of Homeland Security and numerous law enforcement experts from local, state, tribal, and federal agencies fusion center guidelines were developed. In August 2006, the guidelines were distributed. (See Chapter 12, Section 2 "Fusion Centers" for details on the history, development, and status of the Fusion Center concept).

THE MISSION OF CRIMINAL INTELLIGENCE

The general mission of criminal intelligence is to develop knowledge about individuals or groups who are involved in criminal conspiracies and to understand how they function, describe their current activities, and forecast future actions they may undertake. To guide the intelligence professional in collecting intelligence information, the intelligence unit requires a defined mission. A mission statement helps focus the scope and contents of the information that intelligence personnel are collecting and analyzing. Thus, a defined mission encourages the development of *useful* intelligence information. (See Chapter 4 "Management of the Intelligence Unit" for more information)

Supporting the Chief

An important part of the intelligence mission is to support the decision-making activities of the chief executive officer (CEO) of the agency (Harris 1976:1-8). The ultimate goal of any law enforcement agency is to prevent crime; and, to do this, the CEO must know the full picture of the criminal groups within his/her jurisdiction. The CEO must know their numbers, strength, influence, criminal pursuits, and possible future activities. He/she should also be aware of what organizations are susceptible to future infiltration by criminal organizations. Additionally, the CEO should be aware of, and plan for, preventing future criminal enterprises. To accomplish this, the CEO needs to ensure that intelligence products flow smoothly to him/her; and he/she must clearly communicate his/her needs to the intelligence unit and support its efforts. The intelligence cycle cannot be successfully implemented without the decision maker positively engaged in the process. Since few agencies are resourced to produce intelligence on a myriad of issues, the CEO must take the lead in setting priorities and focusing the intelligence unit based on realistic expectations.

The CEO must think systematically about responsibilities and resources. Objectives should be planned and used to set priorities. The criminal intelligence function should be used to assist with planning, resource focus, and deployment. Law enforcement agencies that use their intelligence resources wisely have assessed the threat of various crime groups in their jurisdictions and are thus able to effectively place resources.

THE INTELLIGENCE PROCESS

What is intelligence?

It is generally conceded that intelligence consists of pieces of raw information that when collected, evaluated, collated, and analyzed form meaningful and useful judgments that are both accurate and timely. Taking this raw information and turning it into intelligence requires a sequential process. The following depicts the step-by-step process described by Harris:

Collection $\rightarrow$ Collation $\rightarrow$ Evaluation $\rightarrow$ Analysis $\rightarrow$ Dissemination $\rightarrow$ Re-Evaluation

Later, the "Planning and Direction" step was added to the process as a critical first step. Before the collection phase, the collectors/analyst must have an idea about what they want to collect (and how/where) and the process requires direction from the CEO (Harris, 1974:4). However, the intelligence process is cyclic. The steps are interconnected and often the boundaries blur. Each step of the process needs to be understood to produce intelligence reports that are timely and accurate.

Planning and direction is the responsibility of the CEO, manager, and the analyst/investigator. It is the critical first step before engaging in data collection. Without this planning and direction, information collection will be unfocused and valuable time will be wasted. As was stated in the previous page this particular step needs the engagement of the CEO. He/she must define priorities so tasking can be focused and meaningful.

The collection part of the process is simply the collecting of individual pieces of information. Information may be gathered from many sources: criminal intelligence reports, reports from field officers, newspapers, magazines, public documents in government, informants, etc. (See Chapter 6 "Collection")

Evaluation is the examination of the information's validity and reliability. (See Chapter 7 "Collating and Evaluating Data")

Collation is usually the combining and storage of the information. Information is sorted, and the relevant information is arranged so relationships can be discerned. (See Chapter 7 "Collating and Evaluating Data")

The next step is the analysis of the information: compiling, summarizing, comparing, and organizing into meaningful relationships regarding the criminal and criminal organizations. Analysis is the portion of the intelligence process that transforms the raw data into a product that is useful. It provides the "what," which is an understanding of what is, the "so what," context regarding why it is important, and sometimes even the "now what," which can include recommended mitigation or solutions. This is also the function that separates "information" from "intelligence." It is the "valued added" part of the process. It is this vital function that makes the collection effort pay-off. Without this portion of the process, we are left with disjointed pieces of information about which no meaning or relevance has been attached. The goal is to develop a product where the information has been analyzed in a logical and valid manner to produce intelligence that contains valid judgments based on information analyzed. (See Chapter 8 "Analysis and Synthesis")

Dissemination is also a vital part of the process. Without disseminating the intelligence developed, it is pointless to produce it. The intelligence disseminated must be timely and credible to be useful. Dissemination must also be evaluated based on a "right-to-know" and the "need to know." The "right-to-know" means the recipient has the legal authority to obtain the information pursuant to court order, statute, or decisional law. The "need-to-know" means the requested information is pertinent and necessary in order to execute official responsibilities. (See Chapter 9 "Dissemination") This dissemination can be through written or oral reports; some written report examples and formats are seen in Chapter 10 "Report Writing Principles."

The final step in the process is re-evaluation. The need for feedback and evaluation of the efforts of intelligence units may have received less attention than the other steps, but this step reflects the results-oriented policing of today and is equally critical.

TACTICAL AND STRATEGIC INTELLIGENCE

There are two basic ways to use criminal intelligence: tactical and strategic (Aumond 1998:35-36). Each may be based on the same raw data and they generally complement each other. Both are important. The more tactical intelligence generated, the more strategic intelligence can be generated. Strategic tasking may lead to the development of more tactical intelligence.

Tactical information is usually factual data collected during case investigations and surveillance operations. The information may act as an investigative lead; or it may simply consist of a list of the subject's associations; provide locations of hang outs, listing of business associations, or describe criminal tendencies. This information gives law enforcement authorities a basic understanding of the criminals and their activities. Tactical intelligence is used to develop methods to counteract immediate criminal threats and is usually directed at a specific crime or criminal entity. It may be in reaction to an incident or used to prevent a crime.

Tactical intelligence consists of this data in a compiled and analyzed form: names, addresses, identifiers, criminal associates, and other identifying information. Tactical intelligence may take on many forms, but it is primarily the collection of facts to form a file on a targeted subject with a view toward an investigation or prosecution. This tactical intelligence is produced on an ongoing basis and should be readily available as an effective and valuable resource for investigators working on criminal investigations. Finally, tactical intelligence can provide the pieces of information that are the building blocks on which intelligence professionals build their strategic analysis.

The following are examples of tactical intelligence:

- On June 15, 2000, John Doe was seen at 2300 Main Street visiting a friend, Jack Doe. On three subsequent Thursdays, he was also seen at this address. John had also been seen on the preceding Wednesday evenings at Sloan's Bar & Grill and exited that location at approximately 2 a.m. carrying a black sports bag. A bag of that description was seen being carried by him to Jack Doe's residence on Thursday mornings; and, when John exited those premises, he was not carrying it. Thus, John Doe may be a courier for unknown items, possibly cash, being relayed from Sloan to John Doe. This may indicate a previously unknown connection between Jack Doe and Sloan's Bar and Grill.

- Mickey Jones, a well-known bookmaker and loan shark, has been observed at the Cozy Café on Gott Street several times from January thru March 2000. On a majority of occasions, Jones met with Rick Float and Tom Bottoms. Occasionally, a package was provided by Jones to Float. Float is suspected of involvement in money laundering and is a partner in the Lucky Draw Casino. Bottoms is Float's longtime associate. These meetings may indicate Jones has been allowed to make book or loan shark at the casino with Float's permission. The package may be a payoff for that permission. Jones may also be attempting to buy into the casino as a silent partner. Additional surveillance should be conducted to determine if Jones frequents the casino and what role he assumes. If no significant information develops, Float should be interviewed by licensing agents to determine his relationship with Jones and his subsequent suitability for a gaming license.

Strategic intelligence provides a broader view of the abilities, strengths, weaknesses, and trends of criminal enterprises. It is an informed judgment on which conclusions are drawn about future criminal endeavors. It calls on analysis that is used for long-range planning; discusses possible law enforcement impact; and enables law enforcement officials to make informed decisions on budgets, resources, and policy.

The ultimate goal of all intelligence – in particular, strategic intelligence – is to prevent crimes. However, drawing conclusions on "soft" data which necessarily constitutes criminal intelligence, may lend a degree of uncertainty to these judgments. Intelligence is not a certainty and must be viewed as a tool for decision-makers, not the final word.

The Role of Criminal Intelligence in Law Enforcement

The following provides some examples of strategic intelligence:

- The threat which organized crime poses to Middle County was analyzed to determine which crime groups are of greatest concern. It was seen that the Dirty Rotten Scoundrels Motorcycle Club presents the greatest threat due to its methamphetamine trafficking, propensity for violence, prostituting of its female companions, and its move to establish a clubhouse in Middle County. This group should be targeted by a multi-jurisdictional task force to reduce its influence in the Middle County area. If left unchecked, both the city and county can expect increases in assaults, prostitution, and narcotics violations. Citizen groups and much of the educational community will likely demand action be taken to reduce this activity. In fact, eliciting their support in this endeavor should be evaluated.

- The Tabletop Police Department conducted a study of the major criminal elements operating within its borders and determined there were three major criminal groups that require close monitoring to deter or prevent their criminal activities. A multi-jurisdictional task force comprised of agents and officers from city, county, state, and federal agencies will target the groups to check their criminal activities. Specific investigative plans, including resources requirements, will be developed by a working group of representatives from the agencies involved. The goal of the task force will be a significant reduction in the operations of these groups by the end of 2012.

CHAPTER 1

The Role of Criminal Intelligence in Law Enforcement

SUMMARY

The basics of intelligence are planning and direction, collecting, collating, evaluating, analyzing, disseminating data, and re-evaluating. The proper completion of these steps ensures that the data used are managed appropriately and within the legal constraints regarding privacy and the rights of all our citizens. Each law enforcement agency with an intelligence function should have this handbook on site for their staff to access when intelligence questions arise.

REFERENCES

Aumond, Karen, Tactical and Strategic Intelligence, *Issues of Interest to Law Enforcement, Criminal Intelligence: A Vital Police Function.* Law Enforcement Intelligence Unit (LEIU), February 1998.

California Peace Officers' Association Committee (1998) *Criminal Intelligence Program for the Smaller Agency.* California Peace Officers' Association.

Central Intelligence Agency (2000a) *A Factbook on Intelligence: Genesis of the CIA,* at: *<www.cia.gov/publications/facttell/genesis.htm>* CIA Website, (5/11).

Central Intelligence Agency (2000b) *A World Factbook: 1999 History of the World Factbook,* at: *<www.cia.gov/publications/factbook/history.html>,* CIA Website (3/6).

Godfrey, E. Drexel and Harris, Don R. (1971) *The Basic Elements of Intelligence.* Washington DC: Law Enforcement Assistance Administration.

Godson, Roy and William Olsen (1993) *International Organized Crime: Emerging Threat to US Security.* Washington DC: National Strategy Information Center 1993: i.

Harris, Don R. (1976) *Basic Elements of Intelligence - Revised.* Washington, DC: Law Enforcement Assistance Administration 1-8. September.

Lindberg, Richard, *Origins and History of the Mafia Commission*, at: *<www.search-international.com/Articles/crime/mafiaorigins.htm>,* (5/18/2000).

McDowell, Don, *Strategic Intelligence: A Handbook for Practitioners, Managers and Users - Revised Edition.* Scarecrow Press, Inc. ISBN *0-8108-6184-4*2009.

New York City Police Department (2000a) *A History: Shadows of the Past,* at: *<www.ci.nyc.ny.us/html/nypd/db/history.html>,* New York City Police Dept web site. (3/17).

-------------------- (2000b) *Lieutenant Petrosino,* at: *<www.ci.nyc.ny.us/html/nypd/html/3100/retro-22.html>,* New York City Police Dept web site. (3/17).

Pennsylvania Crime Commission, 1990 Report, *Organized Crime In Pennsylvania: A Decade of Change.* 1991.

Peterson, Marilyn B. *Applications in Criminal Analysis, A Source Book*, Greenwood Press, Westport, Connecticut, 1994.

Wright, Richard, Mission Statements, *Issues of Interest to Law Enforcement, Criminal Intelligence: A Vital Police Function.* Law Enforcement Intelligence Unit (LEIU), February 1998.

Wright, Richard, (1998) *Guidelines for the Criminal Intelligence Function*, Simi Valley Police Department, September 1998.

Bureau of Justice Assistance (1999) Regional *Information Sharing System, The RISS Program: 1998.* Washington, DC: U.S. Department of Justice, March.

Legal Issues in U.S. Criminal Intelligence: An Overview
By John Gordnier

INTRODUCTION

This chapter will focus on legal issues which relate to local and state criminal intelligence efforts. There is not a great deal of law identified as "intelligence law" for the state and local law enforcement community. As will be demonstrated, the law controlling criminal intelligence is found in various other legal areas.

Since September 11, 2001, initiatives at all levels of government have emphasized increased sharing of criminal intelligence in support of national security intelligence efforts. However, the reality is that criminal intelligence and national security intelligence are very different. Put another way, federal laws which predominate in the national security intelligence arena do not, for the most part, apply to state and local criminal intelligence efforts.

Certain initiatives such as fusion centers and the collection of Suspicious Activity Reports have brought state and local agencies more into the national security intelligence arena. The legal implications of these efforts are only now beginning to develop. At the present time the best course of action for a state/local agency to pursue is to have a firm understanding of the established rules governing criminal intelligence and to follow those rules.

There are three components to create and maintain an effective, legally compliant, criminal intelligence function.

- The first component is <u>the sworn officer</u>. While many agencies provide legal training to those specifically assigned to the criminal intelligence unit there is often little training at the management/supervisory level. Also, it can be the case that there is no "cultural" development that helps sworn personnel in other assignments appreciate how important their observations and accurate reporting are to the criminal intelligence function.

- The second component is <u>the trained, professional intelligence analyst</u>. These persons must be well versed in the legal constraints which are imposed by privacy concepts and the controlling legal authorities. The analytical products generated by this component will often be the basis for both tactical and strategic decisions by an agency. They will be carefully reviewed for legal flaws by the civil liberties community and must be grounded in a sound understanding of appropriate legal concepts.

- The last component is <u>a knowledgeable legal advisor</u>. Generally, advice to an agency is provided by the attorney representing the municipal or county government of which the agency is a part. Often these attorneys are not familiar with laws specific to criminal intelligence or with the application of general laws in the criminal intelligence context. Further, criminal discovery which implicates intelligence information will be addressed by prosecuting attorneys who are not generally familiar with intelligence related authorities.

Ideally the legal advisor will be well versed in all the controlling legal aspects and will be able to apply them in all contexts.

There are three general legal controlling concepts which impact criminal intelligence: 1) gathering, processing, and retention of information concepts; 2) "open records" concepts; and 3) litigation concepts. Each of these concepts has as its basis the need for a criminal intelligence system to be "utilized in conformance with the privacy and constitutional rights of individuals."

THE GENERAL CONTROLLING CONCEPTS

The criminal justice process is predicated on the concept that it is appropriate for society to limit the rights of some of its citizens when those citizens pose an unacceptable level of risk to the rest of society. We permit the incarceration of persons to whom we have proved criminal conduct *beyond a reasonable doubt.* Searches of person(s) or property are permitted when *probable cause* exists to believe a crime has been committed by a specific person(s). The process of gathering information, analyzing that information, and creating a criminal intelligence file as the product of that analysis involves the concepts of *legitimate law enforcement purpose* and *reasonable suspicion.* These criminal intelligence concepts constitute significantly lesser invasions of privacy and constitutional rights. They also require less certainty and potentially allow for more subjectivity.

From the legal point of view, criminal intelligence efforts are the process through which law enforcement intrudes – in an appropriately limited manner – on the rights of association and privacy of some of the citizens it is sworn to protect in order to better provide for the safety of all of the citizens who reside in a given jurisdiction. Criminal intelligence is the gathering, analyzing, and compiling of information in an attempt to anticipate criminal conduct before it happens, solve a crime more quickly when it happens, and defeat criminal organizations.

Such intrusions create tension between the legitimate needs for accumulating criminal intelligence and the rights of citizens. This tension is addressed by legal concepts embodied in rules that govern the different "phases" of the criminal intelligence process.

The two primary sources of rules for state and local agencies' criminal intelligence efforts are the Association of Law Enforcement Intelligence Units (LEIU) Criminal Intelligence File Guidelines and the Code of Federal Regulations, Title 28, Part 23 (28 CFR). The LEIU Guidelines are not statutory and are not mandatory for any agency. The provisions of 28 CFR are statutory, but technically apply only to agencies accepting federal funds pursuant to the Omnibus Crime and Safe Streets Act for the purpose of creating or sustaining an intelligence operation. The National Criminal Intelligence Sharing Plan advocates that these two rule sets should be adopted by all state/local (and, for that matter, federal) criminal intelligence operations regardless of whether they are mandatory. The reason is simple, during the time these rules have existed they consistently have proven to strike the proper balance between law enforcement needs and individuals' privacy and constitutional rights.

A second set of legal issues impacting criminal intelligence efforts is rooted in the concept that citizens in a democracy have the right to access records created and maintained by government entities. Criminal intelligence information does not reach the level of probable cause. Because it could be incomplete or erroneous, law enforcement authorities have an obligation to prevent public disclosure of criminal intelligence information because of the potential damage to reputations that could result from such disclosure. So-called "open records" provisions are different from state to state and provide greater or lesser protection from disclosure depending on the jurisdiction. Again, the federal rules (the Freedom of Information Act and the Privacy Act) do not generally apply at the state and local level.

Third, litigation discovery rules are predicated on concepts of fair trial and due process. They will have an impact on the ability to shield criminal intelligence information from disclosure. Like both privacy and "open records" rules, discovery rules vary from jurisdiction to jurisdiction.

And, as if having 50 different sets of state rules isn't enough of a challenge, it must be pointed out that in some jurisdictions there will be county and/or city rules that may well have an impact on criminal intelligence efforts. Typically these local rules address specific matters such as records retention, handling of public demonstrations, law enforcement oversight, or similar matters. There are simply too many such local rules to be addressed in this chapter. What needs to be taken from this chapter is the need to be certain that these local rules have been identified and considered.

THE LEGAL "PHASES" OF THE INTELLIGENCE PROCESS

There are, in the author's opinion, five distinct "phases" of legal concern in the process of obtaining and using information to develop criminal intelligence and then using that intelligence. The legal concepts which will apply in each will be different or, at least, have different emphases. These five "phases" are:

1. **Pre-reasonable suspicion** – In this phase, law enforcement personnel are involved in the process of making decisions about where (on specific persons, groups, organizations, or associations) the agency needs to focus its attention and resources in connection with gathering information.

2. **Post-reasonable suspicion** – This phase occurs after the information gathered in the pre-reasonable suspicion phase has been analyzed for the existence of a "criminal predicate." When such a predicate has been established a criminal intelligence file can legally be opened.

3. **Criminal intelligence file maintenance** – This is the most straightforward of the legal phases. It is concerned with the necessary security measures that must be taken to ensure that the criminal intelligence information is isolated from the general records system(s) in the agency. It is further concerned with the audit function which must be applied to criminal intelligence files.

4. **Dissemination/Access** – In many ways this is the most legally complex of the phases. One aspect, dissemination, is a combination of rules that govern how voluntary sharing amongst law enforcement entities should occur. A second aspect, non-law enforcement dissemination, is whether and how law enforcement entities can voluntarily share criminal intelligence with other public entities. A third aspect is a legal framework that governs involuntary access to criminal intelligence information by persons or entities outside of the public sector who are exercising "open records" rights. The fourth aspect involves a legal framework that governs involuntary access by persons exercising litigation discovery rights.

5. **Purging of criminal intelligence files** – What might seem to be the simplest of the phases, destruction of files, is often the phase which generates a significant number of problems for law enforcement entities.

Compliance with the legal requirements relating to each of these phases will result in a legally acceptable criminal intelligence effort.

PRE-REASONABLE SUSPICION

"Although the police unquestionably pursue a legitimate interest in gathering information to forestall future criminal acts, the identification of that legitimate interest is...the beginning point of analysis...not...the conclusion. The inherent legitimacy of the police 'intelligence gathering' function does not grant the police the unbridled power to pursue that function by any and all means. In this realm...the permissible limits of governmental action are circumscribed by the federal Bill of Rights and the comparable protections of our state Constitution." (*White v. Davis* (1975) 13 Cal. 3rd. 757, 766)

When combined with that same court's further observation that "the information gathered by the undercover police officers pertains to no illegal activity or acts" this finding by the California Supreme Court is a generally accurate description of the elements of the pre-reasonable suspicion phase. The only exception the author would make is that the court mixed two separate concepts; specifically, that information and criminal intelligence are the same creature. It is the gathering of information for analysis that is at the heart of the pre-reasonable suspicion phase.

So what exactly are the lessons of *White*?

- First, that it is a necessary and appropriate function of law enforcement to gather information that will help prevent crime.

- Second, that merely asserting that criminal intelligence is being gathered will not justify the process used.

- Third, that the ultimate boundaries governing when and how this information may be collected are set by the federal Bill of Rights and, in some instances, state law provisions.

- Fourth, that information can be gathered only when there is some nexus to criminal activity.

Information may be collected only for a *legitimate law enforcement purpose*. When information has been properly collected, the LEIU Guidelines allow it to be maintained for no more than one year to determine if there is a criminal predicate. Information so collected is referred to as "developmental," "temporary," or "working" files.

The difficulty in this area is that the First Amendment allows an individual to articulate unpopular views and associate with unpopular causes. Such conduct is not criminal. This means that such conduct without more does not support gathering information on the individual or organization. This was the issue in _White_. A professor was presenting ideas in a way which some deemed subversive, but doing nothing more than expressing ideas.

If on the other hand, an individual engages in acts or incites persons to engage in acts that endanger public safety or is knowingly part of aiding or abetting such persons it is appropriate to gather information. In such situations there is a _legitimate law enforcement purpose_ which supports the information gathering activity. Needless to say, this is an area in which there is much room for disagreement. Information collection which has the following components is the better practice:

- A very clear understanding of the reason(s) for focus on a particular subject, potential endangerment – either through direct action or conduct tantamount to aiding and abetting – of public safety is a good standard

- The ability to clearly articulate the "legitimate law enforcement purpose" for focus on the subject

- A specific plan for gathering the information which includes a timeline

- Executive level or designated management/supervisory approval for the effort

- Close supervision of the execution of the effort with regular briefings to the executive/manager/supervisor approving the effort

- Accurate, complete documentation of the effort from beginning to end

It is in this area, the "pre-reasonable suspicion" phase that involvement of state/local agencies as part of the national security intelligence effort creates some controversy. Certainly there is nothing wrong with enlisting the eyes and ears of state and local law enforcement in the national security effort, but when suspicious activities are described in terms which seem to include merely articulating unpopular points of view there is danger that one has crossed the line clearly drawn in _White_. Thus, while it is totally appropriate and desirable for criminal intelligence efforts to work closely with national security intelligence efforts, the basic criminal intelligence legal rules must still be observed. Put another way, a state or local agency cannot set aside the _legitimate law enforcement purpose standard_ on the basis that it is gathering national security intelligence.

POST- REASONABLE SUSPICION

The legal standard which governs this phase of the criminal intelligence process is the standard of _criminal predicate._ When a criminal predicate has been properly established, a criminal intelligence file may be opened, maintained, added to, and shared. In this phase the sharing of the file may be done through computerized systems which allow direct access to the information.

The key legal concept is that of criminal predicate. A criminal predicate is a reasonable suspicion based on legally obtained facts that a person or group of persons is planning to engage in or is engaging in definable criminal activity. There are a number of components to this concept:

- The facts relied upon must have been obtained through legal means. As an example, reliance on information gathered by a search subsequently ruled to have been unlawful would not be proper. It is the responsibility of an agency using facts to verify that they were legally obtained.

- The predicate information must be relevant to the identity of the subject(s) and/or to the criminal activity reasonably suspected. Indeed, 28 CFR expressly prohibits consideration of such matters as "…political, religious or social views, associations or activities of any individual or any group, association, corporation, business, partnership, or other organization unless such information directly relates to criminal conduct or activity and there is reasonable suspicion that the subject of the information is or may be involved in criminal conduct or activity." In this connection, 28 CFR also prohibits harassment of or interference with any lawful political activities.

- The criminal activity must be "definable." It is not sufficient to create a criminal intelligence file on the basis that the subject(s) may be up to something which is probably criminal.

This leaves the final issue. What are the legal requirements for making the determination that reasonable suspicion of definable criminal activity exists? These have been articulated by the United States Supreme Court in _United States v. Arvizu_, 534 U.S. 266 (2002). In _Arvizu_ the court articulated four standards which apply to the reasonable suspicion determination:

1. Reasonable suspicion is not subject to "formulaic" analysis. By this the court determined each situation had to be separately evaluated on the specific facts of that particular situation.

2. Reasonable suspicion is determined from the totality of the circumstances known to the person (either a sworn officer or an analyst) making the decision. Indeed, one of the elements of the Arvizu decision was rejection of the lower court's approach of isolating each known element and testing whether it supported reasonable suspicion standing alone.

3. The totality of the circumstances must also consider and credit the experience, training and specialized knowledge of the person making the determination. This would allow an experienced criminal intelligence officer or analyst to be given credit for conclusions reached based on his/her expertise. A contemporary example would be the expert opinion that an individual is a gang member.

4. The determination that reasonable suspicion exists does not require that the possibility of innocent conduct be eliminated. Put in another way, it is not necessary to prove that there could be no other explanation except criminal conduct; one need only support the criminal conduct conclusion.

When these four standards have been met, reasonable suspicion is established. The person making the determination has an obligation to document the basis for his/her finding. This documentation must include determinations of the levels of confidence the determining officer/analyst has in both the source and content of the information. This requirement presents a good example of how the LEIU Guidelines and 28 CFR work together. While 28 CFR imposes the requirement that levels of confidence be established within a criminal intelligence operation, it does not outline or explain the concept. The LEIU Guidelines, however, provide a detailed template.

INTELLIGENCE FILE MAINTENANCE

Both pre-reasonable suspicion and post-reasonable suspicion files must be kept in a secure location not available to persons outside the criminal intelligence function. Security measures must prevent the unauthorized destruction, modification of, or access to the files. The two types of files must be separated within this secure location. The reason for this separation is that the pre-reasonable suspicion files have not yet met the criminal predicate standard and cannot be comingled with files that have met that standard.

This need for separation has its genesis in the historic fact that the 28 CFR guidelines were promulgated in part because of the ability to use computers to transmit information rapidly and widely. Where the reasonable suspicion threshold has been met it is appropriate for the file contents to be shared over a secure network. Where the threshold has not yet been met it is better to employ a "pointer" system. A "pointer" system allows agencies to make name queries and be referred to agencies which have pre-reasonable suspicion information, but does not allow direct file content access. As to both pre-reasonable suspicion and post-reasonable suspicion files there are specific requirements as to the materials which must be present:

- Information about the source of the data which is in the file which includes the basis for concluding it was legally obtained

- An audit trail which records who has received the information, when it was given, and why it was given

- Levels of sensitivity and confidence must be assigned to the information and the source(s) of the information must be disclosed (or, if confidential, identified in an appropriate manner), and the date of receipt of the information should be present

- If the information has been analyzed, the name of the person(s) who performed the analysis and the documentation for the findings made

A critical part of the file maintenance structure is the creation of written policies and procedures which are approved by the agency executive and which address all of the legal requirements. It is important to note that 28 CFR requires that there be written guidelines that provide for screening and related employment limitations as to those persons who have direct access to the files.

DISSEMINATION/ACCESS

In the author's view, these are best described as the process of voluntarily sharing information (dissemination) and the process of properly responding to legal efforts by non-law enforcement entities to obtain information (access).

Legal Issues in U.S. Criminal Intelligence: An Overview

The basic rule, as stated in 28 CFR, is in two parts:

1. "A project or authorized recipient shall disseminate criminal intelligence information only where there is a need-to-know and a right-to-know the information in the performance of a law enforcement activity." and

2. "… a project shall disseminate criminal intelligence information only to law enforcement authorities who shall agree to follow procedures …which are consistent with these principles."

An exception to this basic rule allows for the dissemination of an assessment of the criminal intelligence information to any government official or other individual when necessary to avoid imminent danger to life or property.

It is in this dissemination context that the creation of homeland security efforts after the 9/11 events can complicate the legal framework. Clearly, 28 CFR contemplates sharing in emergencies. The difficulty arises when there is a desire to disseminate to non-law enforcement public agencies in non-emergency situations. The federal homeland security laws addressed this matter by giving law enforcement status to certain critical persons in that agency thus facilitating routine criminal intelligence access provided the need-to-know requirement was met. Many state and local agencies do not have such status. This means that if routine sharing is deemed desirable, careful examination of the applicable laws must be made to guarantee that a desirable step does not compromise the confidentiality of the criminal intelligence.

Before dissemination can occur, even to another law enforcement authority, it is the responsibility of the agency disseminating to examine the policies and procedures of the recipient agency. If these are not "consistent with" 28 CFR, then sharing should not occur until satisfactory standards are in place. This also underscores the need for an agency to have current written policies and procedures which meet or exceed 28 CFR standards. These policies and procedures should include the pre-reasonable suspicion area.

Once this initial part of the basic rule is met, the right-to-know (agency personnel, sworn, or analytical) and the need-to-know in connection with a law enforcement purpose must be established. It must be underscored that merely being a sworn officer or agency analyst is not enough by itself to provide a need-to-know. Need-to-know is a function of the job and/or case assignment of the individual.

Lastly, before dissemination can occur, is the need to comply with the "third party rule." This rule requires an agency which has received information from another source to check with that source before it disseminates the information to a third agency. The rule does not exist to preclude sharing, it exists to ensure that the source agency is not going to have an investigation or a step in an investigation compromised. The other advantage derived from the "third party" rule is that the original source agency will learn of the interest of and any information uniquely known to the third party agency. When these various legal requirements are satisfied, voluntary dissemination can and should occur.

As previously noted, so-called "open records" laws provide legal leverage for non-governmental entities to seek access to government documents including pre-reasonable suspicion and post-reasonable suspicion files. These laws vary greatly from state-to-state. The extremes range from laws which would not permit any disclosure of law enforcement records except those relating to cases that have been filed in court to laws which make virtually every law enforcement document except those specific to active investigations public. Thus, as an example, an agency from a state which permits strong protection for its criminal intelligence files may have concerns about sharing of its information with an agency in a state which has nearly no protections.

Such concerns do not mean that sharing should not occur, but do require careful thought be given to what is shared and how it is shared. The practical result of the existence of these 50 different "open records" laws is that they add another inquiry that must be made before voluntary sharing occurs.

Another layer of duty added by the "open records" laws relates to the need for criminal intelligence operations to be prepared to deal with the law applicable in its jurisdiction. In general terms this means the agency has a duty to understand how and to what extent it is able to prevent disclosure of criminal intelligence files. Agencies must work from the premise that the right to intrude on privacy to compile criminal intelligence files carries an obligation to protect the privacy of the subjects of those files. Further, agencies need to recognize that the likely source of most "open records" requests will be communications mediums which will be prepared to litigate their requests aggressively.

Finally, the last form of access which must be of concern to criminal intelligence operations is the litigation discovery process. While it is most likely that the criminal prosecutions discovery process will have the greatest impact on criminal intelligence systems, it is certainly the case that civil litigation could also be an issue. Litigation discovery will typically be statutory in the civil context, but may often not be statutory in the criminal context.

The seminal criminal discovery case is _Brady v. Maryland_, 373 U.S. 10 (1973). _Brady_ imposes a duty on the prosecution team to provide any and all exculpatory evidence or information which could lead to exculpatory evidence in its possession to the defendant. A critical issue with respect to criminal intelligence is the fact that it is based on reasonable suspicion. This means that, as previously noted, it may or may not contain conclusions that rise to the level of probable cause. Indeed, it is typically the case that even where criminal intelligence files provided "leads" the facts which generated probable cause were generated by independent investigation.

There are two issues with respect to criminal intelligence as discoverable material: (1) whether it was collected with respect to the particular case in litigation; and (2) whether it is specific enough to the litigation to be relevant. Each prosecutor will be concerned about the existence of criminal intelligence information which pertains to a person being prosecuted because of his/her _Brady_ obligations. The best approach, in the author's opinion – absent any jurisdictionally specific statutory or case law – is to let the prosecutor know when criminal intelligence information played a role in the case and encourage him/her to seek an _in camera_ ruling whether and to what extent discovery ought to be granted.

The "good news" with respect to both open records and litigation access efforts is the existence of the _in camera_ hearing process. All states have some form of this process which will permit law enforcement authorities to make a showing without the requesting party present. This showing is typically subjected to a balancing test which usually evaluates the value of the information to the party seeking access against the harm that could come from it being made public. Generally, the result is favorable to maintaining the secrecy of the criminal intelligence file.

PURGING INTELLIGENCE FILES

"All projects shall adopt procedures to assure that all information…retained…has relevancy and importance. Such procedures shall provide for the periodic review of information and the ***destruction*** (emphasis added) of any information which is misleading, obsolete or otherwise unreliable…" (28 CFR 23)

The key concept here is the ***destruction*** of files which no longer satisfy these requirements. The provision goes on to state that in no case shall files which lack relevancy and importance be maintained beyond five years. It is to be noted that pre-reasonable suspicion files which do not result in establishment of a criminal predicate within one year must be destroyed as well.

This requirement does not mean that at the end of five years a file must be destroyed. What it does mean is that the file must reflect that the reasonable suspicion conclusion remains current and supportable. If a file reflects current support (within the five year period) for the criminal predicate or for additional criminal predicates related to the same subject then it may be maintained for another five year period. The new period begins from the date of the most recent substantive entry; merely adding non-predicate information (information which rises only to the level of personal identifying or location data) does not support additional time. However, confirmation that the subject(s) remains active in his/her criminal actions is sufficient. There must be an affirmative, fact-based showing of this continued activity.

When a supportable, current and relevant criminal predicate no longer exists the file must be destroyed. Destruction is not satisfied by any means other than eliminating all of the contents of the file. Regrettably there are a number of highly publicized cases over the years in which agencies made an effort to get around the destruction requirement; simply put, they all ended badly for the agency. Destroy means destroy, period! You can, however, make reference to the destroyed records – in a fashion which eliminates any information identifying the subject of the obsolete files – to keep track of your files both for audit purposes and to avoid questions whether a record has been lost, misfiled, or destroyed.

An additional duty which applies to both pre-reasonable suspicion and post-reasonable suspicion files is the notification duty. The provisions of 28 CFR impose the requirement that all persons who have been given access to a file be notified of its destruction or of any "changes which involve errors or corrections."

This final phase completes the legal cycle and ensures that outdated information will no longer be circulated as current and valid. This protects the file subject's privacy and reputation. Correctly executed completion of these phases will demonstrate the agency's commitment to properly conducting its criminal intelligence operations.

CLOSING COMMENTS

The legal structure provided by the LEIU Guidelines and 28 CFR should be imposed on all state/local intelligence operations. Some modifications will be necessary to accommodate state/local legal standards.

There is one simple, convincing reason this action ought to be taken--both the law enforcement community and the civil liberties community benefit. The years have demonstrated to both communities that the two standards strike the appropriate balance between individual rights and the duty to provide for collective safety. This is most recently illustrated by the response to a revision of 28 CFR proposed in 2008 by the Office of Justice Planning. Almost all groups responding to the proposal reached the same conclusion: **do not fundamentally change the requirements**. The proposal was withdrawn.

Simply put, the LEIU Guidelines and 28 CFR create trust because they satisfy basic legal requirements.

REFERENCES

Global Justice Information Sharing Initiative. (2003). *National Criminal Intelligence Sharing Plan.*

9/11 Commission (nd). *The 9/11 Commission Report.* Washington, DC: The 9/11 Commission.

Association of Law Enforcement Intelligence Units. (2005). *LEIU File Guidelines.*

U.S. Department of Justice Executive Order #12291. *Criminal Intelligence Systems Operating Policies 28 CFR Part 23.*

Staffing the Intelligence Unit
By Ian Wells

INTRODUCTION

Any supervisor setting out to fill a critical and sensitive position in an organization asks two basic questions: (1) "Is the person I am considering for the position capable of doing the job?" and, (2) "Can other staff members work with this officer effectively?" In the intelligence units of law enforcement organizations, as well as in many other occupations, a third question addresses the security aspect of intelligence: "Can the person I am considering be trusted?" A further question from the point of view of intelligence asks, "Can the officer think analytically, assemble and structure pieces of information, and ultimately find solutions to the problems posed?"

In the context of an intelligence unit, personnel requirements can be divided into four general categories: unit manager, intelligence officer, intelligence analyst, and support staff. The most important position is the unit manager. In a multi-jurisdictional law enforcement environment, selecting a unit manager can be complicated by the need to meet the requirements of a number of member agencies. The intelligence officer category poses a different selection problem. In law enforcement intelligence officers are often sworn officers transferred to an intelligence unit. In addition to being able to collect intelligence, the intelligence officer must be able to work on a team with intelligence analysts; develop new approaches to the increasingly sophisticated illegal enterprises of criminals; and, at the same time, draw satisfaction from pursuing intelligence objectives without focusing on arrests and prosecutions.

Another critical category is that of the intelligence analyst. This chapter will put considerable emphasis on intelligence analysts since they comprise an essential component of the intelligence unit. Increasingly, they are professionals employed from outside the organization specifically to analyze information collected by others. As a consequence, it is easier to set specific requirements for analysts when the unit manager has final say over the assessment and employment of individuals. The selection of intelligence officers and intelligence analysts is often viewed as a common problem, with some agencies treating the functions as interchangeable and, to a great extent, requiring the same level of intellectual equipment. While this latter point is to some degree valid, this approach can promote the unrealistic view that good intelligence officers are by definition good intelligence analysts and vice versa.

The fourth category considered by this chapter is support staff. While this group poses no unique recruitment problems, support staff contributes significantly to the outcome of the unit and can even be considered as a useful entry point for future analysts. This group will be addressed briefly later in the chapter.

TERMINOLOGY

Before proceeding, there is a need to clarify the terminology used in this chapter. Within the international law enforcement community, it is possible to identify a number of job descriptions that are used interchangeably for officers doing the same work. "Intelligence officer," for example, is sometimes used interchangeably with "intelligence analyst" to describe officers undertaking analytical work. Within the

United States, it tends to be used interchangeably with "investigator." For the purposes of this chapter, the following terms have been adopted and used consistently throughout.

- **Unit Manager** - The manager or commander of the intelligence unit. The officer can be a civilian or a sworn law enforcement officer.

- **Intelligence Officer** - An officer whose primary function is to collect information as needed, in accordance with a collection plan as well as the analytic function, in support of the intelligence cycle.

- **Intelligence Analyst** - A staff member trained to analyze information from multiple sources and effectively communicate the results to support consumers of intelligence.

- **Support Staff** - A staff member employed to provide administrative and logistical support to the unit.

- **Officer** - A sworn or badge member of a law enforcement agency.

- **Civilian** - A civilian employee employed on a full- or part-time basis.

These terms are not mutually exclusive and are intended only to assist the reader using this text.

THE UNIT MANAGER

An intelligence group's unit manager can be a civilian or a sworn officer. In some law enforcement organizations, the position of intelligence unit manager does not require the individual to have law enforcement authority. The position of unit manager is of such importance that a flexible approach needs to be taken to ensure that only a candidate of the highest quality is appointed. Choosing a unit manager requires a positive answer to all the selection questions mentioned at the beginning of the chapter. A unit manager must demonstrate the highest levels of integrity, an ability to work effectively with the agency management group, and conceptual and analytical skills sufficient to address the most complex intelligence problems. In addition, the unit manager must have very strong leadership and communication skills. The unit manager must be able to provide clear direction to all personnel in the unit and ensure that intelligence is communicated clearly and concisely to the unit's customers. The best intelligence in the world is wasted if it does not get to those who can use it most effectively.

The basic criteria for the selection of a unit manager should be developed along the lines of the following:

- Appropriate educational qualifications, with postgraduate studies not essential but viewed favorably
- Proven management skills
- Excellent oral and written communication skills
- Demonstrated conceptual and analytical skills
- Relevant experience at a management level in an intelligence environment

Staffing the Intelligence Unit

The selection of a unit manager is not always left to the judgment of a selection panel chaired by the direct supervisor of the area. All sorts of limits, which are familiar to any bureaucracy, are built into the system of choosing a unit manager. Where a number of agencies work together, the position may rotate between agencies. The choices may also be limited by the availability of suitable staff and organizational priorities if internal transfer or appointment fills the unit manager position. Ultimately, it is for individual organizations to decide on the selection process. It must be emphasized, however, that the position of unit manager is critical to the success or failure of the unit; and, in an environment of intelligence-led policing, can impact significantly on the success of decisions made based on the intelligence provided. As such, where a suitable candidate is not available, agencies should consider the viability of training and grooming a current employee, either an analyst or officer, for the position.

The selection panel may also find themselves with imperfect choices. As they analyze the qualifications of what may already be a smaller list of candidates than they would have wished, there may be a temptation to weigh analytic or information gathering skills above management and team building capabilities. Depending on the needs of the unit, each required skill must be weighed against the needs of the unit. Above all, the unit manager must have impeccable integrity credentials. To a large extent, the unit manager will set the tone for the unit. The actions of the unit manager must reflect a concern for transparency, integrity, and operational security. There is no room for compromise on this point.

GENERAL CRITERIA FOR STAFF SELECTION

Much of the criteria applied to the selection of a unit manager will apply in recruiting the balance of the unit staff. There is, of course, a need to make appropriate adjustment to reflect the roles played by personnel at differing levels. This is not to say that the unit manager should seek to fill his office exclusively with subordinates who think in the same way. A strong intelligence unit is made up of intelligence analysts, intelligence officers, and other staff who bring different perspectives to each intelligence question. The unit will need a range of individuals who can look at intelligence problems from a variety of perspectives; both in terms of their analytical discipline and general personality type (see Myers & Myers 1980:83-116 and Kroeger & Thuesen 1992:46-57 for discussion of personality types in teams). Regardless of their individual views and skills, they must have a strong sense of integrity and high intellectual capabilities. A unit manager will benefit more from personnel who will not hesitate to suggest an unorthodox approach and challenge traditional assumptions than from a collection of agreeable, think-alike types (Colwill & Birchall 1992:168).

A search for bright, tough-minded personnel can present difficulties. The unit manager should take care to avoid candidates who, though they may be impressive at first acquaintance, lack the flexibility for sound intelligence work. The officer with a mind made up on most issues (no matter how polished that mind is) may have difficulty dealing with the unexpected. Flexibility is a critical characteristic of an intelligence analyst. While a guiding hypothesis is an integral part of the intelligence research process, too close an adherence to one hypothesis can contribute to a tendency, in complex cases, to overlook evidence that begins to suggest a contrary hypothesis. The officer may have more confidence in intuition than in facts. At the worst, such personality types may single-mindedly pursue objectives they have identified for themselves, with little regard for the obligations of the unit or even the law enforcement agency as a whole. It may occasionally be possible to harness such a person to a specific and narrow specialty where a burning, uninterrupted interest in the subject can be an asset, but this is seldom the case. Moreover, as organizations change in response to economic and technological pressures, job descriptions also change and staff needs to be flexible to respond effectively (Nankervis & Compton 1996:149).

CHAPTER 3

Staffing the Intelligence Unit

One approach to intelligence personnel and specifically intelligence analyst recruitment is to begin by focusing on graduate entry programs. This type of program aims to recruit university graduates into training programs designed to develop analytical ability. This type of approach can result in a high quality analytical staff but requires effective training and development of programs as well as clearly defined career paths for new staff. Direct employment of experienced analytical staff to the unit is also beneficial to the effectiveness of the analytical effort. Intelligence is a mind-stretching business; its targets change, its methodologies are improving constantly, and it requires more and more innovative ideas to cope with the growing sophistication of crime. This is an aspect of intelligence work that can be used as an appealing temptation to suitable candidates. Overall, unit managers need a balanced recruitment program to ensure that the intelligence unit has a good cross section of personalities, experience and skills.

There is a general process for recruitment that can be applied effectively to the staffing of an intelligence unit (Colwill & Birchall 1992:165-166). This process is only intended to provide guidance and is not intended to be exclusive.

- **Identify the Need for Recruitment** - Does the job really need to be done; can you get the job accomplished any other way?

- **Identify the Nature of the Job** - The qualities of the person to be recruited and what the job is worth to the organization – can the job be filled by one person? Will they need to be experienced or can training be provided? What are the costs of not filling the job?

- **Identify the Resources Available to Attract Recruits** - Can you afford to recruit? Can you offer a salary that will attract the person you need?

- **Identify the Source of Likely Recruits** - From inside or outside the organization? Are they locally available or will they need to be brought in from elsewhere?

- **Identify How to Most Readily Reach the Potential Recruits** - Will you advertise in the newspaper, on a bulletin board, on radio or in professional journals?

- **Identify the First Stage of the Filtering Process** - You can save a lot of trouble by using an effective filtering process, but you should ensure that the filters are relevant to the job (salary, educational qualifications, experience etc).

- **Determine the Method You Will Use to Screen Applicants** - What type of applications will you accept? Will you use a private recruitment organization for initial screening?

- **Decide How You Will Interview** - How many will you interview? Will applicants be required to demonstrate any skills at interview? Will you use an assessment center or employment agency? Will you use pre-employment tests?

- **Identify Who Will Conduct the Interviews** - The selection panel should be balanced in terms of gender, skills, personality type, etc.

- **Decide on the Person for the Job** - Follow through on the above process, and make the final selection.

The Interview

Interviews remain a critical part of any staff selection process. A refined interview technique sometimes accomplishes what a written test can rarely do. It allows the quality of a candidate's mind and disposition toward intelligence analysis to be assessed objectively. The most fruitful interview is that which is planned carefully by the selection panel and prepared for by the candidate. Where candidates have not been asked to submit a written application, a useful requirement is for the candidate to submit (in advance) brief curriculum vitae, usually no more than two pages, which should contain at least one statement about career expectations.

This requirement has several advantages, as it:

- Discourages frivolous applications

- May inform the panel of claims the candidate may have for the position which were not revealed in personnel files

- May provide an early glimpse of a candidate's capacity for written articulation

- Impresses on the candidate the special nature of an assignment to an intelligence unit

- Provides the interviewer with conversation leads with the candidate

The selection panel must, of course, do more than read the application or curriculum vitae. They should, as carefully as possible, compare the application or curriculum vitae with the contents of the candidate's preliminary background investigation or personnel file. Moreover, when dealing with an internal candidate, the panel should make clear that the expectations of an intelligence officer are very different from patrol or investigations. Anyone applying for the job thinking he/she will be working undercover with the primary goal of making arrests needs to be dissuaded of that belief prior to any commitments being made.

Obviously, any good interview will explore a candidate's motivations. This is especially important for intelligence work where the rewards are more often the satisfaction of unraveling a problem than either monetary reward or the satisfaction of direct participation in pursuit of the criminal. There are also other qualities to probe for that few people openly display. Foremost among these is meticulousness or scrupulous attention to detail. Without this quality, a good intelligence discipline can quickly dissipate; analytic studies can founder; and the intelligence product can fail to meet its objectives. A law enforcement officer who has had investigative experience should be asked to bring in a copy or copies of field reports he/she has written. In a subsequent or follow-up interview, these reports can be used as the basis for a discussion of personal work habits, collection techniques, thoroughness in following up leads, etc. For larger scale recruitment, some law enforcement agencies are already using private recruiting organizations to administer tests to establish the first cut of candidates. Where analysts have previous employment in an intelligence environment, reference checks are an important part of establishing a candidate's skills.

CHAPTER 3

Staffing the Intelligence Unit

Candidate Testing

If, after the initial interview, a prospective intelligence officer or intelligence analyst shows promise, it may be wise to involve the individual in a structured problem. Such tests require careful preparation if they are to reveal useful or new information about the participant.

The problem should be focused on the discipline of the position being filled. It may be appropriate to set a simple, non-interrogative problem for a candidate intelligence officer involving some passive surveillance, address and automobile license checks, public library research, an examination of official records or similar. The candidate would be obliged to fill out two written statements at the conclusion of the problem: (1) a standard intelligence officer's report, provided at the start of the exercise; and (2) a complementary form recording a log of activities with explanatory notes on moves from one investigative point to the next. There should be no one solution to such a problem, but good discipline would require a fixed timetable for completion of the exercise.

Clearly, the two written reports would be products of great interest to the selectors. They would, if the exercise were well-designed, indicate the candidate's capability for advance planning; for careful handling of time; for thoroughness; clarity; attention to detail; etc. A good field exercise report would also reveal something of the candidate's imaginativeness and flexibility.

For a candidate intelligence analyst, the problem should be desk-based. The nature of the problem is not important and could be as straightforward as examining journal articles and identifying issues of concern for the agency. The principal issue for the selectors' concern will be the candidate's answers to the questions posed and the logic of the candidate's manner of tackling problems. What answers the candidate comes up with, of course, are less significant at this point than how they were handled and what ingenuity was shown in shaping them. Unless a seasoned intelligence analyst or intelligence officer from another law enforcement agency is under consideration, it is not experience that is being tested in the circumstances described above, but imaginativeness, resourcefulness, thoroughness, logical use of research tools and self-discipline.

The Selection Process

If the performance of two or more candidates in any or all of the scenarios described above can be measured against one another, it is relatively simple to decide who should fill the vacancy. However, this may not always be possible. Candidates may appear one at a time or irregularly throughout the year so that satisfactory comparisons cannot be made directly. Unit managers then have to develop appropriate standards and apply them consistently. The momentary need to support an overtaxed staff should not be used as an excuse to lower the entry threshold for new candidates. An unsuitable intelligence officer or intelligence analyst will, in the long run, put a greater burden on the unit than if a vacancy remained unfilled until a qualified candidate was available to fill the position.

A problem of a different nature arises when there are several equally qualified candidates but only one or two places to fill. On the surface, this is an enviable condition for the intelligence unit. The unit manager can hardly go wrong because whoever is selected will probably become a sound member of the team, but there will be concern that the best candidate may not be selected. Obviously, in this case, the selection panel is doing the unit no service at all by looking for reasons to eliminate qualified candidates rather than pinpointing the best.

Staffing the Intelligence Unit

Selecting the best of a highly qualified group of candidates is no easy matter. Very often, the choice will have to be made on the basis of fine details. One of the candidates may have a range of attributes more suitable to the particular opening than his competitors. If this is not the case, however, the selection becomes more complicated. The selection panel can at this point start searching for qualities that were not necessarily qualifiers at the beginning of the process.

The following qualities are mentioned here because they are in themselves, important attributes for good staff at all levels:

- A broad range of interests, because this may signify a flexible mind with a wider than average social interest

- Personal candor because this is a good gauge of innate honesty and integrity

- A capacity to clearly identify important issues, because successful intelligence depends on getting at the core of a problem no matter how dense the trivia surrounding it

INTELLIGENCE OFFICERS

For now, the majority of intelligence officers are sworn law enforcement officers. This may not always be the case as law enforcement agencies increasingly adopt more flexible approaches to recruitment. Notably, in some countries, civilian intelligence officers are seen as a legitimate alternative to sworn officers in intelligence units where law enforcement powers are not necessarily a requirement. Nevertheless, under normal circumstances, the intelligence officer will be transferred into the unit from within the organization. The officer will have already gained experience in the more traditional modes of investigative work and will also be part of the broader investigative career structure, looking forward to further promotion. This may mean that the officer will not want to stay too long in the intelligence unit and this may cause some conflict between the needs of the intelligence unit and the career expectations of the intelligence officer. The unit manager will have to select from among the best candidates in the agency and attempt to keep these officers for at least an agreed upon period of time. If no one in the agency meets the requirements of the intelligence unit, the intelligence unit manager may need to obtain the right to recruit from outside.

The intelligence unit should look for trained intelligence officers. In many circumstances, the unit will be relatively small and will have little time to train intelligence officers on the job. The difficult nature of organized crime investigations, for example, demands experienced personnel. Intelligence officers should preferably already know the geographic area and, at least, the street-level operations of organized crime and the main areas of such activity. Hopefully, they will have served in one or more of the precincts that are major operating areas for the organized criminal.

However, seeking the trained intelligence officer can present a problem in the selection process. The best target is an intelligence officer who has done well at routine work but is not satisfied. The officer should respond positively when more complex investigative work, such as that involved in fighting organized crime, is discussed. The successful candidate should take direction and have sufficient initiative to develop avenues of approach to a problem over and above that suggested by a supervisor. This means that the trained intelligence officer who seeks only the rapid arrest should be avoided. This type of

Staffing the Intelligence Unit

intelligence officer, while often very effective in other areas is unlikely to be able to work well in a world where an intelligence project might last for months and does not necessarily culminate in an arrest.

An intelligence officer must be able to take the lead from an intelligence analyst who may or may not have previous experience as an intelligence officer. The intelligence officer must be able to work in a team environment with the intelligence analyst, with each respecting the role of the other. The intelligence officer must be factually correct in his reporting but must also be able to develop a capacity for at least "first-cut" analysis and interpretation of the meaning of findings. In fact, the ideal intelligence officer should embrace and relish this aspect of intelligence work.

INTELLIGENCE ANALYSTS

Since the introduction of professional analysts to criminal intelligence work, there has been considerable debate as to the skills and qualifications required to make an effective intelligence analyst. Often, the debate is influenced by the desire of some unit managers to ensure that a degree of interchangeability exists between staff in the unit. At least in theory, the interchangeability of at least some of the staff greatly increases the flexibility of what is normally a small staff. Personnel can be shifted to investigation when cases are in their early stages and then to analysis as the information begins to accumulate. Nevertheless, while some interchangeability is beneficial to the management of the unit, the skills of intelligence officers and intelligence analysts are not totally interchangeable. Intelligence officers are unlikely to have the depth of analytical skill of a professional analyst, and professional analysts are unlikely to have the skills of an experienced intelligence officer. To be fully effective, the majority of intelligence analysts in an intelligence unit should be professional intelligence analysts that do not require prior investigative experience.

In 1998, the Federal Bureau of Investigation distributed a list of "Analyst's Core Competencies," which it felt provided an underlying standard for all analysts, regardless of their assignment. The skill areas included: analysis; judgment; research; written communication; oral communication; computer skills; professionalism/liaison; flexibility/adaptability; capacity to learn; initiative/motivation; organizing; planning and prioritizing; knowledge of current events; and coaching skills (Cromwell 1998).

Today, the majority of intelligence analysts in law enforcement are civilian; many have little or no experience as law enforcement officers. Despite the potential friction that comes from mixing sworn officers with civilian analysts, the benefits far outweigh the costs. Few law enforcement agencies have sworn officers with the skills that would enable them to combat organized crime. Civilian analysts add skills to an intelligence unit that can lead the unit into fields of investigation previously untouched by traditional police officers. Even more importantly, it can turn the focus of an intelligence unit away from exclusively assisting investigators, toward direct support of the agency's mission.

Notwithstanding the theoretical benefits that accrue as a result of employing intelligence officers and intelligence analysts who are able to operate cooperatively, there are significantly more benefits in ensuring that the information collected is well served by analysts with considerable expertise (Martens 1990:15-16). Law enforcement agencies now recruit analysts to address specific unit needs, such as military intelligence backgrounds for counterterrorism, or individuals with graduate degrees to address the needs for advanced analytic skills. Increasingly, law enforcement agencies are recognizing the need to employ staff with particular expertise, which means that agencies must be more flexible in their approach to recruitment.

CHAPTER 3

Staffing the Intelligence Unit

What would such specialists be able to do for an intelligence unit? Which skill fits a particular problem area? There are no easy answers to these questions, but it is possible to make some generalizations that may serve as guidance for unit managers.

The Generalist Analyst

Most law enforcement agencies to do not have the luxury of employing an analytic cadre which can staff specialized "desks" similar to how the intelligence community operates. Ideally, analysts would specialize in such complex areas as financial crimes, street gangs, or whatever major organized crime groups have the most impact on their jurisdiction. Instead, the most common situation is that an analyst must focus on developing analytical skills and supporting the priorities of the agency, regardless of what they are. By their nature, analysts should be quick studies, and be able to learn the subject matter and apply their analytic skills to each problem as appropriate.

The Specialist Analyst

Some criminal activities require more than a general analyst's expertise due to the complex nature of the crimes. That is not to say that a "generalist" could not work to provide intelligence on these subjects, but it would not be a casual undertaking in addition to other responsibilities. Intelligence analysis dealing with crimes such as business frauds, securities manipulation, money laundering, and accounting arrangements for otherwise legal businesses would require an analyst with specialized training and/or experience. For example, highly skilled specialists – such as forensic accountants and computer forensics professionals – may have to be called upon to interpret information and provide intelligence on sophisticated criminal networks. A unit manager must determine if he/she has the resources in house for this level of analysis, or if there is a need to leverage analysts from other agencies specializing in these areas. The effectiveness of this approach will depend on the nature of the analysis needed. A viable option may be to use personnel on loan from another law enforcement agency or to share a full-time financial analyst on an ongoing basis with another agency. Regional solutions may also be useful; if several agencies participate in entities such as a fusion center or a Regional Information Sharing System (RISS), then analysts who are knowledgeable in specific areas could more efficiently support not only the intelligence needs of several departments, but also provide investigative support when needed. Specialized areas involving technology and finance demand access to expertise which is not affordable on a small scale. Investment in more regional approaches for smaller agencies is the most likely to succeed, in that the specialist is more likely to be gainfully employed in the service of multiple agencies, and by serving multiple agencies, could be fairly compensated at a lesser cost to each. Keeping such a specialist challenged and well compensated is the key to the success of this approach.

A variant of the retainer relationship is the use of contract employees or consultants to address a specific project requiring expertise not available in a law enforcement agency. Much depends, of course, on the rigidity of local laws governing the letting of such contracts and hiring temporary employees. Generally speaking, this kind of arrangement is most satisfactory when there is a specific objective that either requires special skills unavailable within the agency; or that, if tackled by the existing staff of the agency, would seriously disrupt normal working routines over an extended period of time. Some examples are:

- A study of international financial transactions in order to identify indicators of money laundering

- A long-range study of travel patterns of leading criminal figures as a means of determining the nature of illegal activities

- A survey of real estate ownership transactions in a given section of a major city plagued by arson

- An assessment of the use of computer technology in fraud and other white-collar crimes

- Statistical comparison of medical billing practices in a geographic area to determine the "norm" and identify abnormalities to provide indicators of insurance fraud

There is also the kind of research and analysis that may not be directly related to criminal acts but is needed to provide strategies for countering organized crime. For example, a study of the effectiveness of different loan shark statutes in other jurisdictions might have more long-range impact for a state or municipality than many activities more traditional to intelligence units. Such a study might productively be done by an attorney or graduate student under contract or on a consulting basis with the intelligence unit.

Use of the Academic Community

While the academic community can provide a tremendous value to an intelligence unit, three issues must be addressed prior to any arrangements which would provide analytic support: security, accountability, and objectivity. Any compromise of these issues could cause problems for all involved.

First, the intelligence manager must deal with security. Regardless of the sensitivity of the project, the individual should be subject to a background investigation. The depth of any investigation should be commensurate with the sensitivity of the information to which the person will have access. While some candidates may be up to the analytic challenge, issues with prior arrests or even academic cheating must be uncovered prior to accessing sensitive facilities or having access to information not available to the general public. Non-disclosure agreements should be a standard requirement of anyone working in an intelligence unit at a law enforcement agency, regardless of affiliation.

The second issue is accountability. If a professor or student agrees to provide their analytic expertise in support of an intelligence unit, it must be made clear at the outset what is expected by the intelligence unit as far as a timeline when school is in session. The intelligence unit must try to adhere to these timelines as well, regardless of unforeseen issues which often plague the efficient execution of the intelligence cycle. Aside from agreements regarding expectations on both sides, the intelligence unit must understand that it has no operational control over someone from an academic environment and this has to be taken into consideration before entering into any such agreement. The best-case scenario to ensure accountability would be to have a student or professor support a project which could be published, to their benefit, while still supporting the needs of the unit, or for which they would be paid upon completion.

The third issue is objectivity. There are academicians who have built reputations on previous work establishing a certain view of a particular topic. An intelligence unit must be aware of past work which might influence or affect the analysis. Honest discussions and dialogue can certainly minimize any biases but it is a fact that, in the intelligence world, confronting bias is a very difficult thing for someone to do in a vacuum. It is important that the professor or student understand the various methodologies for addressing possible bias, such as the Analysis of Competing Hypotheses, which can be used to support the objectivity of the analysis. This is not an argument against developing this type of a relationship with academe, but one that needs to be addressed in order to ensure that the work done is of value to the unit.

In order to develop a mutually beneficial relationship with members of the academic community, whether it is with students or professors, there must be an opportunity for gain on both sides. This might limit this relationship to less sensitive intelligence projects, as in order to receive credit for work, a student or professor will likely seek to publish their methods and findings. If it is possible to arrange for college credit for an intern without such a publication, or with the stipulation that certain issues not be discussed, that may be a way around this issue. As long as the parameters of a project are outlined in advance and there is something to be gained by both the intelligence unit and supporting academic participant, much can be gained by this relationship. If appropriate, other benefits to both parties, such as the granting of national security clearances for particular projects, or a conditional job offer upon completion, may be negotiated. Valuable "real world" experience pertaining to their chosen field can be very attractive to those working in academe, and should be marketed as a benefit to this relationship. It would be useful to keep in mind that while this arrangement may appear to be a win-win situation, the agency would not have operational control over a professor or student, and therefore cannot guarantee a successful outcome on any particular project. Also, a complete background check and non-disclosure agreement must be completed regarding any individual outside of agency control who is provided access to sensitive records or information.

SUPPORT STAFF

Intelligence support staff makes a significant contribution to the activities of an intelligence unit. Most of the selection criteria set out in earlier sections of the chapter are equally applicable to intelligence support staff. Although, clearly, the intelligence support staff is not expected to have the same level of analytical skills as the intelligence analyst or the investigative skills of the intelligence officer, the general criteria still apply. The primary focus for selecting intelligence support staff should be on meticulousness, industry, and integrity. In many intelligence units, the support staff enjoys a wider range of access to classified material than even the intelligence analysts who tend to be focused on one or two specific projects. As a consequence, the issue of integrity is of particular importance.

Intelligence unit managers should take a balanced approach to recruiting intelligence support staff. The support staff is a critical point of continuity within a unit so the unit manager should seek candidates who best meet the selection criteria and who are likely to remain satisfied in the support staff role and, consequently, stay with the unit. In addition and subject to the resources available, the intelligence unit manager can also use support staff positions to recruit staff who are seeking experience in a law enforcement environment while undertaking studies. These staff will ultimately aspire to move on to more responsible positions – not necessarily within the same agency but will, in the interim, provide a useful analytical resource for the unit.

CAREER PATHS

Developing career paths for intelligence personnel, whether they are sworn officers or civilian analysts, has been a significant challenge for managers of intelligence units for years. In most U.S. police agencies, there is no structured career track for intelligence officers or analysts as there is for more traditional assignments.

CHAPTER 3

Staffing the Intelligence Unit

Expertise in the field of intelligence, or building knowledge regarding the criminal environment, is in some agencies considered a diversion from "real" police work, and long term assignments to an intelligence unit may stifle an officer's promotional potential. To underscore the peripheral nature of intelligence in the current policing environment, there is no requirement in most U.S. police academies for intelligence training. Some agencies are just now requiring some understanding of intelligence for promotional examinations but, in general, it is still not considered a well accepted or properly understood area of policing. In many instances, sworn officers are placed in intelligence units with no previous training, and are expected to learn skills on the job. However, by the time they understand their role and the responsibilities of an intelligence unit; they are frequently transferred or promoted to another assignment.

Civilian analysts in police agencies face additional challenges in that units are generally small, and leadership and management positions in these units are almost exclusively held by sworn officers. A civilian analyst may excel in his/her position for ten years without a promotion, while sworn officers, some new to the concept of intelligence, are rotated in and out of management and leadership positions every two or three years. As a result, some analysts move on to larger and more structured intelligence units, whether they are with government agencies or private sector intelligence units in which promotional potential and pay levels are not so limited.

There are no easy answers to developing career paths in intelligence units for all staff members. Agencies can be creative, allowing for more participation in management decisions for senior analysts and officers and providing a commensurate pay scale or promotional opportunities. But the structure in law enforcement agencies generally restricts the options for career progression of intelligence personnel. Professionalization and standardization of intelligence units as well as the skills and capabilities of the personnel assigned may help to change the status quo. For the time being, this will be a challenge for which flexibility and creativity of management and leadership will be the only solution.

The actual relationship between the detailed work of the intelligence officer or analyst and the ultimate unraveling of an organized criminal network or the indictment of a gang leader is seldom evident. Intelligence activity, in other words, may rarely have a recognizable outcome that is personally satisfying and rewarding to the professional. Instead, small pieces of information are pieced together to make a portion of a larger picture. Other officers or law enforcement agencies may contribute other portions of the picture until there is enough for a warrant, an arrest, or an indictment. The arrests and indictments are almost always made by somebody else, usually at a time and place unknown to the intelligence professional. Intelligence is often an anonymous business, and it certainly is a business where success is difficult to measure statistically by headlines or by the awarding of medals of valor. Three months spent on a study of racketeering in the wholesale laundry business has little glamour potential compared to the highly expert and highly publicized detective work which leads to the apprehension of an axe murderer. To compensate for this, the unit manager needs to be a conduit for communication between the intelligence unit and the rest of the agency – keeping the unit informed of successes which have flowed from the unit's work and promoting the unit's role in those same successes in the agency.

The unit manager may also discover that the experienced intelligence officers and intelligence analysts under his/her command are so specialized that any advancement in the agency may be jeopardized. In many agencies, they can be caught between two conflicting bureaucratic imperatives. First, to advance significantly in the agency, an officer must have a variety of career experiences – such as patrol, traffic, narcotics, planning, etc. Second, intelligence work is unique and those officers with an aptitude for the work are usually encouraged to stay in the unit. For the civilian analyst, of course, movement from one division to another in an agency may be an impossibility altogether.

A unit manager should have an aggressive personnel policy, even if it must operate under different conditions from the rest of the agency. Despite the short-term cost to the intelligence unit, suitable sworn officers should be encouraged to press for an occasional assignment or promotion out of intelligence. An intelligence officer promoted out of the unit is likely to be a supporter of intelligence elsewhere in the agency and subsequently have a positive effect on the intelligence unit's impact on an agency-wide basis.

There are two basic things the unit manager can and should do for subordinates. First, the unit manager must strive to establish high ranks or advanced pay grade positions in the unit. Here, the case must rest on the abilities of the men and women involved. It cannot rest on arrest statistics or even the numbers of organized crime leaders apprehended in the jurisdiction. It has to rest on the reality that the officers and analysts involved are an exceptionally talented group and could possibly be doing much better for themselves elsewhere in the agency or in other professions. To use this argument with any effective impact, selection policies must produce an exceptional team.

Second, the unit manager must ensure that, within the intelligence unit, the career of an officer or a civilian analyst is as varied as possible. An officer who has done several long investigations on gambling can be switched to a narcotics problem. The desk-bound civilian analyst who has mapped a large conspiracy for months or even years can be sent to participate in the training of middle-level officers from all elements the agency. Intelligence analysts and intelligence officers, regardless of rank, can also be given the opportunity to manage project teams for projects in the individual's area of expertise. Depending on the size of the unit, the opportunities for flexible deployment of intelligence professionals are there. It is up to the unit manager to exploit those opportunities.

EVALUATING STAFF

One of the most challenging issues facing the intelligence unit regarding staffing is performance evaluations. Because intelligence production is more qualitative then quantitative, it does not lend itself to the usual evaluation criteria in police agencies. Like all evaluation processes, it is essential that expectations of analysts and officers be provided well in advance of an evaluation period. Realistic and achievable expectations are the key to successful performance of intelligence staff. One possible method by which to evaluate staff would be to base part of it on the individual responsibilities for specific aspects of the intelligence cycle.

Planning and Direction

While, ideally, this step would be the function of executives or decision makers and executed by the intelligence unit manager, the reality is that the intelligence unit often identifies a problem which they will work to address. The evaluation of this step would be applicable to managers and/or supervisors of an intelligence unit since this falls within their realm of responsibility. An example would be: an intelligence manager overseeing several projects involving street gang issues notices a common theme in that more female gang members are becoming involved with violent crimes. This leads her/him to define a problem: how and why are these girls being recruited, why is the level of violence increasing, and how can the department have an impact on the issue? Encouraging intelligence staff to get out in front of problems before they have manifested themselves should be something upon which an intelligence unit manager should be evaluated.

CHAPTER 3

Staffing the Intelligence Unit

Collection

There are many facets to successful collection of information. Some aspects are more relevant to officers and others to analysts. For intelligence officers, successful collection can be based on interpersonal communication, which encompasses liaison with other agencies as well as developing covert sources of information. The use of informants and mastery of surveillance techniques support the collection efforts in the field. Report writing in a clear and concise manner is essential to the collection effort; since an incomplete or difficult to understand report will significantly hamper any analysis based upon it.

For analysts, collection may involve different techniques. Knowing where information can be obtained electronically, which government agency controls what information and how it can be legally obtained is extremely important. With the explosion of databases now available to intelligence analysts, these skills are a necessity. Understanding how the data is stored and how it can be most effectively queried is of tremendous value to an intelligence unit.

Privacy concerns and other legal issues are of the utmost importance in the collection phase of the intelligence cycle, and officers and analysts alike must be evaluated on an understanding of these principals. For example, collection of information which is irrelevant to the criminal activity being addressed (for example, that the person attends a certain church, or that he holds unpopular political views) puts the intelligence unit at risk. Ensuring that the unit is trained on these issues is criteria which can be used to evaluate the effectiveness of the unit manager as well.

There are also criteria regarding the analytic phase of the intelligence cycle which could be applied to officers and analysts to a different degree. To some extent, briefing and writing skills and evaluation of the credibility and reliability of information would apply to both. However, evaluation criteria for the intelligence analyst should be more complex based on the expectations of the unit. To develop such criteria, the manager would have to be trained to evaluate intelligence writing and briefing as well as analytic methodologies and rigor. One of the current challenges to effective evaluation of intelligence analysts is that most managers are not familiar with what they should expect and what core competencies they need to train their analysts to achieve.

Dissemination and Feedback are more applicable to the intelligence unit manager. Ensuring that the collection and analysis have an impact on the criminal environment by influencing decision makers is the bread and butter of the unit. It is not easy to continuously identify all the consumers who could benefit from certain intelligence, but management is the appropriate place to assign this task and evaluate performance on achieving it.

Performance evaluations for an intelligence unit will be unique based on the mission and capabilities of the individual staff members and the unit as a whole, but as illustrated above, the intelligence cycle can provide a basic structure on which to base more individualized performance plans. Beyond the skills needed to execute the mission of the intelligence unit, other considerations should be covered, including:

- Personal and professional integrity
- Motivation, perseverance, ability to work with a minimum of supervision, tenacity
- Ability to work on a team
- Ability to rise above personal bias and think critically and creatively

- Willingness to make judgments based on information available

While performance evaluation for intelligence staff may be difficult, it will provide a more qualitative basis for the promotion and evaluation of the unit as a whole.

Overall, the staffing of an intelligence unit within a law enforcement agency should focus on setting high standards. The recruitment and retention of personnel should be based upon those standards. The intelligence unit will be judged on the quality of its outcomes and this is inextricably tied to the quality of its staff.

REFERENCES

Carter, D.L., (1990), *Law Enforcement Intelligence Operations: Concepts, Issues, Terms*, Michigan: Michigan State University Press.

Colwill, J., and Birchall, G., (1992*), Practical Management: An Introduction to Management Skills*, Melbourne, Longman.

Cromwell, Robert. "Analyst's Core Competencies" presentation at IALEIA Conference, October 1998.

Kroeger, O., and Thuesen, J.M., (1992), *Type Talk at Work*, New York, Delacorte.

Makridakis, S.G., (1990), *Forecasting, Planning and Strategy for the 21ˢᵗ Century*, New York, MacMillan.

Martens, F.T., (1990), 'The Intelligence Function', in Andrews, P.P., and Peterson, M.B., (eds), *Criminal Intelligence Analysis*, Loomis, Ca: Palmer Enterprises, pp1-20.

Myers, I.B., and Myers, P.B., (1980), *Gifts Differing*, Palo Alto, Ca: Consulting Psychology Press.

Nankervis, A., Compton, R., and McCarthy, T., (1996), *Strategic Human Resources Management*, 2ⁿᵈ ed, Melbourne: Nelson.

Management of the Intelligence Unit
By Richard Wright

INTRODUCTION

The term "management" has been defined as the control and direction of organizational resources to achieve defined goals. Traditionally, managers have been tasked with the functions of planning, directing, staffing, training, budgeting, coordinating, reporting, providing public information and obtaining appropriate equipment. All of these functions are familiar to law enforcement managers. This chapter, however, will be focusing on those unique managerial challenges that occur when a law enforcement manager assumes the role of managing a criminal intelligence unit. When that occurs, the manager's role becomes more complex; and there are a number of issues that must be recognized and considered.

CHALLENGES

The primary issue for the new intelligence manager involves understanding the proactive concept of criminal intelligence and how the process works. Harris called the management of the police intelligence unit, "Perhaps the most difficult assignment that can be given to a supervisor in a police department" (Harris 1976:53). Part of this difficulty is because many law enforcement managers have had little exposure to intelligence, and an assignment as an intelligence unit manager will be their first opportunity to understand and work with the concept. Most law enforcement managers learned policing from the street up and have been trained throughout their careers to deal with problems in a reactive mode. Criminal intelligence requires a new mindset since it is an effort to change the perspective from a reactive approach to a proactive one. In essence, intelligence attempts to learn of criminal activity before it occurs and prepares the agency to deal with specific crime issues when they are small and can be managed with minimal resources. After a crime problem takes root, it becomes more difficult to manage and requires additional resources.

Simply stated, a properly managed criminal intelligence function can have a tremendous impact on a law enforcement agency and the community it serves. However, the key words in that sentence are "properly managed." It is not an easy task to properly manage this multidimensional task. It requires a trained staff that is provided appropriate direction and has the support of the agency, the political body that governs the agency, and the community it serves. This support might be easier to obtain if the understanding and perception of the word "intelligence" were not impacted by such a negative law enforcement history.

During the 1970s and 1980s, a small but highly visible number of sophisticated and experienced law enforcement agencies across the United States received a great deal of notoriety as a result of their criminal intelligence operations. The problems generally resulted from operating a criminal intelligence unit without appropriate guidelines or effective management. Specifically, agencies were accused of utilizing improper collection procedures, storage of non-crime related information, and the infiltration of non-criminal organizations.

CHAPTER 4

Management of the Intelligence Unit

A brief historical overview helps to understand how this situation developed and how it has changed over the last four decades. In the late 1960s, when the domestic tranquility of the United States was under siege by subversive organizations and widespread riots, many law enforcement agencies responded by using undercover officers to infiltrate suspected groups and obtain information on suspicious individuals and their organizations. This information was subsequently placed into intelligence files.

Law enforcement's efforts were obviously designed to alleviate the criminal behavior and help settle the unrest that was sweeping the country. However, at that time in our history, there were no guidelines or criminal intelligence standards in place to balance law enforcement's need for information with an individual's "right to privacy."

In fact, there had only been one United States Supreme Court case up to that point which had upheld the concept of "the right to privacy" (*Griswold vs. Connecticut, 381 U.S. 479 (1965)*). The Griswold case centered on marital privacy and its eventual impact on law enforcement intelligence was not recognized at that time.

The subsequent events of the early 1970s, including Watergate and the FBI's Cointelpro scandals, aggravated a growing distrust of government by some segments of society and brought on a number of lawsuits against law enforcement agencies for violating individual privacy rights during the course of accumulating criminal intelligence.

As a result, in 1972, California voters approved changing Article 1, Section 1, of the California Constitution so that "privacy" was added to the list of inalienable rights. Many other states followed suit. Legislatures also stepped into the fray and passed legislation on the issue, such as the Federal Privacy Act in 1974 and the California Information Practices Act in 1977. In more recent years it has been reported that 48 of the 50 states have some type of legislation that protects an individual's "right to privacy."

In the mid-1970s, several agencies and organizations, including the California Department of Justice, the New Jersey State Police, the FBI, and the Association of Law Enforcement Intelligence Units (LEIU), acknowledged the privacy rights issue by establishing standards for the criminal intelligence function. The most critical standard required that collected intelligence data had to relate to criminal activity. Other new standards addressed the proper storage and appropriate dissemination of intelligence products. Over the succeeding decades, these standards have been accepted by most law enforcement agencies and by the organizations which led the effort to provide for individual privacy rights.

Thus, today's law enforcement administrators can now benefit from a professionally managed criminal intelligence unit, with appropriate guidelines and standards, without being overly concerned about the threat of adverse litigation. The difficulty in this scenario, however, relates to the fact that much of the public is unaware of the professional standards now in place for criminal intelligence and may still have a negative view of government and the intelligence function. Therefore, on the local level, it falls to the unit manager and the agency's chief executive officer to sell the importance and legitimacy of the criminal intelligence function to community wide audiences including the agency's governing body.

This can be accomplished with an ongoing educational effort to inform politicians and citizens about criminal intelligence and its value to the safety of the jurisdiction. It needs to be well known that criminal intelligence is a proactive crime prevention effort and a viable part of community oriented policing. The educational effort can be supplemented with periodic reports to the involved city council or county board of supervisors, which reinforces the function's legal status and capabilities and identifies in general terms the existing criminal threats to the jurisdiction.

Another challenge in today's intelligence environment concerns the impact that demographics can play in identifying criminal threats within a jurisdiction. Every ethnic or cultural group usually has an organized criminal component that tends to prey upon their own ethnic group. This issue is a difficult one since waves of immigrants from various parts of the world have consistently taken up residence in this country. California, for example, currently has a population of 38 million people, with approximately 25 percent of the state's residents being born in a foreign country. California is a leader in this regard, but it is indicative of a trend that has significance for law enforcement agencies all across the country.

Many of these immigrants reside with their own ethnic groups in enclaves where they speak their native language, maintain their own cultures and tend to distrust American law enforcement agencies based upon their experience in their former countries. This distrust extends to the point that they do not inform law enforcement authorities of ongoing criminal activity. This allows criminal groups to exert a great deal of power and fear within their ethnic communities.

It is particularly difficult for a criminal intelligence unit to determine or predict criminal threats to their jurisdiction if sources do not exist for all segments of the community. Unless the intelligence unit possesses an officer or reliable source that speaks the language and understands the culture, there is little ability to learn of criminal activity. The most likely solution for this problem resides with the effective use of community-oriented policing (COP). The COP concept, which incorporates the use of criminal intelligence and encourages open communication with citizens, can provide positive interaction between the law-abiding members of these ethnic communities and law enforcement.

CRIMINAL INTELLIGENCE RESPONSIBILITIES

One of the first considerations for an agency is the extent of responsibilities that it intends to accept concerning the criminal intelligence function. Obviously, this is a local decision; but conditions regarding size of the agency and criminal issues within the area should dictate the need, mission and resources of the unit.

In 1973, the National Advisory Commission on Criminal Justice Standards and Goals recommended that any police agency with at least 75 sworn personnel should employ a full-time criminal intelligence officer (Police Standard 9.11). This guideline may be a starting point for an agency, but might not satisfy an agency's need for criminal intelligence. Organized crime and terrorist activity is seldom overt and certainly does not recognize jurisdictional boundaries. Many times, an agency will need to perform a threat assessment to learn the extent of its crime problems in order to determine the appropriate level of resources that need to be assigned to the intelligence function.

What the National Advisory Commission did not address is the need for smaller agencies, with less than 75 sworn, to be involved in the effort to identify and pursue organized criminal threats in their communities. While smaller agencies may not be able to devote a full-time position to the criminal intelligence function, there are things that can be done to address criminal threats. A small agency needs to understand the proactive concept of criminal intelligence and recognize that most law enforcement agencies, regardless of size, are susceptible to criminal activity that may extend beyond its jurisdictional boundaries. Their personnel should be trained to recognize and report indications of organized crime, gangs, criminal extremist, and terrorist activity.

This information should then be shared with intelligence-trained personnel from neighboring agencies, the sheriff's department, regional intelligence centers or appropriate state law enforcement agencies. Often, small pieces of information which may appear inconsequential by themselves can be a significant part of a larger picture pertaining to a criminal enterprise. This type of effort by members of smaller agencies would be an important step in allowing for criminal activity to be analyzed and evaluated on a larger scale, either countywide, regionally or statewide.

Medium-sized agencies with 75 to 250 sworn officers and large agencies with over 250 sworn officers should have a criminal intelligence function. The size of the unit would depend upon local crime conditions and the scope of the unit's mission. Agencies with only one or two officers assigned to the unit may have an issue regarding the availability of sufficient resources for accomplishing all of the functions required by the intelligence process.

A viable option for reducing the intelligence workload for a medium-sized agency is to enter into a networking or mutual aid criminal intelligence agreement. These agreements can be either formal or informal, with any number of surrounding law enforcement jurisdictions. Conceivably, neighboring agencies have common problems that can be approached with shared resources. This type of agreement allows an agency to assign limited personnel to work with intelligence officers from surrounding jurisdictions on combined investigations.

This concept can be expanded to the point where one lead agency within a region maintains the responsibility for keeping the intelligence file while other member agencies provide the investigative personnel. Member agencies would have access to the file for both input and dissemination purposes.

The pooling of resources from several agencies is also a tremendous asset in the area of training new or inexperienced criminal intelligence officers. Another benefit to this type of arrangement is that individual agencies do not lose all of their criminal intelligence expertise if an officer retires, promotes or transfers from the criminal intelligence position. Instead, there is a pool of experienced personnel to service the combined areas.

Another critical issue for a small unit involves having access to a trained analyst. The intelligence process requires analysis, and some medium-size agencies have addressed this issue by cross-training their crime analysts as intelligence analysts. This effort can prove to be both efficient and cost effective.

Specific responsibilities for criminal intelligence units include the following:

1. Initiate inquiries and conduct information searches to obtain criminal intelligence information relating to specific criminal activities designated by the chief executive officer

2. Develop and maintain a system for collecting, reviewing, evaluating, storing, collating, retrieving, and disseminating information relating to designated criminal activities

3. Develop analytical capability to provide useful criminal intelligence products, both strategic and tactical

4. Maintain the integrity and security of all information entrusted to the unit

5. Adhere to legal and ethical procedures in obtaining information

6. Develop methods to evaluate the effectiveness of the unit in accomplishing its law enforcement goals and in safeguarding the privacy of all individuals about whom the unit has information

7. Establish and maintain liaison with law enforcement agencies at all levels in order to foster a meaningful exchange of information on criminal matters

ORGANIZATIONAL STRUCTURE

The criminal intelligence function is a separate and distinct activity that requires special consideration when positioning it within an agency's organizational structure.

Depending on the size of the unit, the criminal intelligence officer, supervisor or unit manager, needs direct access to the chief executive officer. This direct access is imperative since the unit's primary function is to provide the chief executive officer (CEO) with timely strategic intelligence that will allow for appropriate planning and decision making to meet developing criminal trends. Members of the organization must recognize the need for the intelligence officer to report directly to the CEO. This reporting procedure, which circumvents the normal chain of command, is used to eliminate communication filters and to ensure the confidentiality of criminal intelligence information.

Ideally, the criminal intelligence unit should be located in its own secure office with appropriate equipment. It should not be combined with other investigative units such as narcotics, vice, detectives, or internal affairs.

Intelligence differs considerably from investigations, and it is important to understand why these legitimate law enforcement functions must be treated differently. Basically, criminal intelligence is a proactive effort designed to prevent crime by providing the CEO with knowledge of criminal events that may occur in his or her jurisdiction. If performed properly, this allows the CEO time to make decisions to counter potential criminal activity. Frequently, the criminal intelligence process involves "soft" information, which is not designed for use in court. "Soft" information can include hearsay information from rumors, suggestions, and beliefs for the building of files. In collecting initial raw data, intelligence officers often go to sources that criminal investigators would seldom contact for their investigative needs. In addition to surveillance observations and materials selected from public databases, intelligence officers may note anonymous comments about people who they believe may be planning a crime or listen to others they feel might be in a position to know. Their specialty is the nurturing of this type of soft data with appropriate verification into refined and useful criminal intelligence.

This type of information collection involves careful evaluation and analysis and requires that the needs of law enforcement are balanced against the individual's "right to privacy." This right of privacy requires that the dissemination of criminal intelligence information be treated carefully and in conjunction with established "right-to-know" and "need-to-know" standards. As a result, intelligence files require a high level of security. This level of protection is greater than that required for most other law enforcement files.

Conversely, the investigation of specific crimes is strictly a reactive function designed to arrest and prosecute the involved offender. This effort is directed toward identifying suspects and witnesses, recovering stolen property and contraband, and procuring viable evidence for use in court. Its focus is toward "hard" or provable information, which is designed for prosecution purposes.

The difference between the two disciplines is significant. Intelligence files need to be kept in a separate location from investigative files and the functions need to be assigned to different units. This separation will help to ensure that professional standards are maintained in each area of expertise.

THE ROLE OF THE CHIEF EXECUTIVE OFFICER

The Chief Executive Officer of a law enforcement agency has critical responsibilities regarding the intelligence function. A starting point for understanding this role for an uninformed CEO would be to initially review the National Criminal Intelligence Sharing Plan (NCISP). This plan was endorsed in 2003 by U.S. Attorney General John Ashcroft and the U.S. Department of Justice and includes model policies, standards and guidelines for developing a local law enforcement intelligence function. It provides recommendations for implementation issues and methods for sharing critical information.

Once a CEO has a basic understanding of the intelligence function, he/she will realize that criminal intelligence is really a simple and realistic concept; that information properly collected and analyzed can lead to better informed and more cost effective decisions and actions regarding; strategic assessments, tactics, the selection of criminal targets, crime prevention, and the proper allocation of resources. Ultimately, it leads to a safer community.

Once the function is initiated the CEO specifically needs to accept his/her role and responsibilities in producing the strategic and tactical products that will enhance public safety. Those responsibilities include establishing the intelligence unit's mission, setting its priorities and providing ongoing direction and support. Additionally, the CEO will need to ensure that the function has the active support of the whole department and the necessary resources to accomplish its mission. And finally, the CEO has an obligation to appropriately act on the recommendations that are the product of finished intelligence.

Another issue for the CEO, that has not generally been addressed, is the need for community support for the intelligence function. Criminal intelligence is a subject, particularly in light of potential terrorist threats, that needs to be explained to the public by the CEO and/or upper management. The public should understand that the criminal intelligence process is a legitimate crime prevention tool that requires their participation to prevent crime and create a safer community. Most local agencies currently employ some form of Community Oriented Policing and the sharing of crime-related information between community members and law enforcement is an important aspect of that process.

AGENCY SUPPORT

Agency support of the intelligence effort is crucial to a successful program. That support must encompass all personnel from the chief executive to the line officers. The necessary support can be obtained once staff understands the objectives of the program, and how they can assist with the effort.

CHAPTER 4

Management of the Intelligence Unit

Frequently, the perception of the criminal intelligence unit has been a problem with some agencies. In some instances, the intelligence mission is not clear to those outside the unit. The function, role, objectives, and the mission of the unit need to be shared with others in the organization. The established guidelines for the release of information from the unit and the modification of the traditional chain of command should be explained to avoid misconceptions that a "secret squad" exists. Some of the mystery concerning intelligence is stripped away once the process is explained and the legal aspect of privacy rights and need for confidentiality is recognized. Most informed employees will subsequently accept the manner in which intelligence must operate and will assist in the effort.

On a daily basis, support for the intelligence function includes the consideration of the communication flow of both formal and informal crime-related information within the agency. All personnel need to be aware of intelligence priorities, and encouraged to keep intelligence needs in mind when they review or handle reports or discuss crime-related issues. Those items that fall within the intelligence unit's mission or have value for intelligence purposes need to be forwarded to the intelligence unit in a timely manner.

UNIT MISSION

Determining the criminal intelligence unit's mission is another important concern. The criminal intelligence function, like other specialized law enforcement assignments, requires appropriate direction and focus. Specific parameters are necessary so that the criminal intelligence effort will not lose its perspective and will retain its ability to consistently deliver a useful product. Mission statements help provide that direction. They should indicate the agency's expectations of its criminal intelligence unit so that unit personnel, as well as the rest of the agency, understand the function.

Mission statements should address three different components:

1. The first portion of the mission statement should describe the criminal intelligence "process" of collecting, evaluating, collating, analyzing, and disseminating information related to criminal activities.

2. The second component of the mission statement requires the agency to identify the type or scope of criminal activity that the criminal intelligence unit will be addressing. In crafting this portion of the statement, it is important to determine what crime problems or issues are threatening the concerned jurisdiction. Each community or area has its own unique challenges and the mission statement should reflect those issues. For example, if a jurisdiction's prevailing crime problem involves criminal street gangs or "emerging organized crime groups," then the mission statement should identify those concerns as the unit's focus.

   In determining the focus of the criminal intelligence unit, it is also important to identify an objective that can realistically be accomplished by the personnel and resources assigned to the unit. It is counter productive to the unit to design the mission in such broad terms that the assigned personnel cannot adequately perform the job.

3. The final portion of the mission statement should describe the results that are expected to be obtained by the unit. If the primary function of the criminal intelligence unit is to provide strategic intelligence to the chief executive officer, this portion of the mission

statement should indicate that the information provided will allow the CEO to make rational choices regarding unanticipated criminal threats and the deployment of the agency's resources.

The following is a "sample" mission statement:

"The Department's Criminal Intelligence Unit will collect, evaluate, collate, analyze and disseminate information on individuals and groups who are suspected of being involved in (criminal problems of concern to the jurisdiction) and will provide this information to the Chief Executive Officer for crime prevention and decision making purposes."

TRAINING

State of the art training in criminal intelligence is available and should be made available for members of the agency. In order to maximize the benefits to be derived from a criminal intelligence unit, the department's training commitment should start with the chief executive officer. The CEO needs to understand how the unit operates and what it can produce. Of particular interest for the CEO is how strategic intelligence products can help the agency prevent crime, properly allocate resources and budget for emerging crime problems. The agency's managers and supervisors must also understand the concept of intelligence and how it can help reduce crime. Their support will greatly enhance the coordination of the collection effort.

Line personnel are a significant resource for the intelligence unit. They must understand that they are the eyes and ears of the agency. They are present in the community 24 hours a day, 7 days a week interacting with individuals and observing activities. It is critical that they understand their ability to contribute to the intelligence effort. In return, intelligence personnel should provide them with tactical information that will help keep them safe and assist them in recognizing threats in the community. Patrol personnel also need to understand the legal issue of individual privacy rights and the reason dissemination rules for intelligence information are so stringent. Proper training of line personnel will assist them in understanding the strategic need for the intelligence unit's close relationship to the CEO. (See Chapter 14 "Training and the Intelligence Unit")

It is also important that the city manager or county administrator be advised of the presence and purpose of the criminal intelligence function. These administrators are ultimately responsible to the community for the services of their governments and must be fully aware of the crime prevention aspects of the unit and the legal constraints within which it operates.

Training the agency's legal advisor prior to any legal issues arising also has its benefits. It provides an opportunity for the attorneys to understand the unit's policies, procedures, and the legal constraints with which the intelligence unit must operate. Although legal actions against criminal intelligence units have drastically diminished in recent years, the unit's legal advisor needs to be cognizant of the unit's operational guidelines prior to receiving subpoenas or lawsuits.

MANAGING THE PROCESS

Criminal intelligence units require proper direction, appropriate guidelines and consistent oversight. The seven-step "intelligence process" of planning and direction, collection, evaluation, collation, analysis, dissemination, and re-evaluation will not prove valuable for an agency unless ongoing coordination exists throughout the process. The objective of the process is to provide both strategic and tactical products for the agency.

The management, supervision and direction of a criminal intelligence unit will differ according to the size and composition of the unit. In every case, however, the direction of the intelligence effort is critical. Every intelligence project requires a focus. That focus and specific direction has to be of value to the agency. Many agencies have collected volumes of criminal intelligence information that has never been put to use. This obviously filled file cabinets and computer space but failed to provide a useful product for the agency. Properly identifying targets can resolve this issue and provide useful products to help ensure the safety of the community.

Effective direction starts with the CEO providing general guidance and broad objectives. The unit manager will subsequently select the targets or identify the specific goals. Once a specific intelligence project is identified, the planning for the methods and procedures for the collection of information must be considered and implemented. This "collection plan" is often the Achilles heel of the process. If a proper plan is not devised and carried out, then the objective is frequently not obtained.

Criminal intelligence personnel can be deployed in a number of different ways depending upon the project. Intelligence personnel can be assigned by criminal subject, criminal organization, geographic area, ethnic organized crime type or by criminal activity. This decision usually depends on the type of specific information gathering effort being undertaken.

Once a criminal intelligence project is initiated, the manager needs to meet with his staff to determine what methods and resources will be used to obtain the required information. Data can be gathered through or from surveillance, undercover operatives, data banks, criminal informants and law enforcement or citizen sources. A method that should not be ignored is the use of overt intelligence personnel being assigned to monitor known criminal subjects. Once the habits of these suspects are established, intelligence officers can create appropriate opportunities to interview or converse with the criminal suspects in public places. This type of contact can be very effective. Many times, criminal subjects will willingly converse with police investigators in public. Even those subjects who will not voluntarily speak with known intelligence officers can be influenced by observing intelligence officers in public locations where the suspect expects to conduct either social or business meetings with criminal associates. The psychological impact of this type of contact in restaurants, bars, hotels, and other public places will generally impede the suspect's activity and, undoubtedly, make them concerned that the officers are aware of their criminal intentions.

In addition to specific intelligence projects that are undertaken by the unit, regular sources of information must be cultivated and established by the unit to keep abreast of criminal activities within the jurisdiction. This stream of information would also include the review of selected crime and arrest reports, newspaper articles, search warrants, special publications and items from law enforcement contacts or community sources.

All of this raw data must subsequently be reviewed and evaluated for mission relatedness and, if deemed appropriate, considered for file input. "The unit commander must establish an effective filing system. It should be one that minimizes clerical work to the greatest extent possible while providing the analyst with an effective tool. A second major requirement for the filing system is that retrieval of information be easy. Finally, the system must be as simple as possible to enhance accuracy of filing so that there is assurance that all information relative to a particular subject is made available." (Harris 1976:54)

"In order to provide guidance, and at the same time ensure the legality of files, the unit commander must develop specific guidelines that determine what material can be entered into the files, how it is to be organized, and finally how information that is no longer deemed essential is to be purged from the files." (Harris 1976:54)

The analysis step has been accurately described as the "heart" of the intelligence process. Without this part of the process, intelligence is just an information-gathering function that will not enable the agency the benefit of extracting appropriate meaning from the collected data. This step of the process involves the need for management to ensure there is ongoing communication between the analysts and the data collectors. Their efforts need to be coordinated to ensure that appropriate data is available to the analyst for the current project.

The next step in the process involves the dissemination of the intelligence product. The consumers include the CEO, the agency and other law enforcement agencies. The unit manager needs to ensure that dissemination rules of "need to know", "right to know" and the third-party rule (no original document that has been obtained from an outside agency is to be released to a third agency) are followed. Additionally, appropriate guidelines need to be in place for release approval and to document the requests and release of information to consumers. "The unit commander must decide how the unit is to disseminate its output. In all cases, the intelligence unit should adopt an affirmative program, disseminating information, and output as widely as possible within the constraints of sensitivity…information in an intelligence file that is not used is worthless." (Harris: 1976:56)

The last step in the process, re-evaluation, involves obtaining the necessary feedback from the consumer to ensure that the intelligence product was useful and met its objectives.

Every intelligence unit should be evaluated on a regular basis. The unit manager should ensure that the unit is meeting its stated objectives. An informal evaluation should ask the following questions:

1. Is the unit staying within its guidelines?
2. Is the unit focused on its defined mission?
3. Is unit training needed?
4. Is the unit meeting its objectives?
5. Is it producing analytical products?
6. Does the unit provide the agency with both tactical and strategic products?
7. Are the unit's products valuable to the agency?

SUPERVISION

One of the keys to proper supervision is ensuring that all members are aware of the unit's objectives and focused on their individual roles. This requires ongoing communication among members of the unit. Frequent meetings are necessary so that a team effort is established in reaching unit objectives.

The unit as a whole needs to know the targets, the ongoing activities of the unit and the information needs being sought. This sharing of information and ideas for obtaining essential data is necessary as tenured intelligence officers tend to have a variety of sources from which to access items of information. Close coordination between the field collectors and the analysts must occur so that an accurate and complete picture of the criminal issue is developed.

Clear and concise unit guidelines are essential for the smooth and efficient operation of an intelligence unit. Assigned personnel need to understand the rules and procedures under which they must operate. The guidelines for unit operations should address issues, such as policy; mission; responsibilities; privacy rights; reporting procedures; file criteria and maintenance; information evaluation and classification; purge procedures; and dissemination. Additional guidelines must exist for the use of informants, unit security and the use of special funds. "The unit commander is also responsible for establishing guidelines that will inform investigators of targets they may cover and under what conditions… the commander then has the follow-on task of insuring that the investigators, in fact, observe the guidelines." (Harris 1976:54)

STAFFING

The issue of staffing is addressed more fully in Chapter 3; however, the unit manager should keep in mind that criminal intelligence personnel must possess a wide range of abilities to ensure their success in this assignment. Some of the more obvious include integrity, high intellectual capacity and analytical ability, initiative, and the ability to communicate effectively, both verbally and in writing. Another consideration is the ability to establish rapport with diverse individuals, from law enforcement personnel to the various members of the community. This ability is crucial and will ultimately determine an officer's capability to obtain information from a wide range of sources. Other important characteristics are an officer's judgment and his ability to anticipate what may occur in any given situation. Obviously, there are many individual skills to consider, but the success of the unit ultimately will depend on the talents of the assigned personnel.

The rotation of personnel is a subject that many CEOs feel is important in today's management environment. The argument in favor of a regular rotation of assignments relates primarily to the prevention of corruption in sensitive positions and to providing agency personnel a wider range of knowledge and experience. While rotation may be appropriate for many, if not most, assignments within a law enforcement agency, criminal intelligence is a specialty assignment that should not be rotated on a routine basis. The primary reasons for this perspective include the length of time it takes for an intelligence officer to learn the assignment and be effective, the skill development and training investment required, and the law enforcement contacts and other valuable contacts that have to be established. For these reasons, any rotation of intelligence personnel should be based on an evaluation of the quantity and quality of the intelligence products received from the assigned individual, and the suitability of the individual for this specialized assignment.

LIAISON

An ongoing need exists for the sharing and coordination of criminal information between law enforcement agencies at all levels of government. In many instances, pertinent criminal intelligence data relating to one's own jurisdiction is first obtained from adjacent agencies. This sharing of data on a regular basis allows for a more comprehensive review of criminal activities which impact more than one jurisdiction. Local agencies should be networking on a regional basis and on a regular schedule. Pertinent information should also be shared with state and federal authorities. It is recommended that all intelligence units have membership in the Regional Information Sharing System (RISS) and the Association of Law Enforcement Intelligence Units (LEIU) as well as regional task forces and fusion centers. Professional investigative associations also offer valuable contacts and training opportunities. (See Chapter 17 "Networks, Organizations, and Resources")

SUMMARY

The 21st century has arrived, and it is appropriate that law enforcement recognize criminal intelligence as the "Ultimate Management Tool for Law Enforcement." Crime prevention and suppression is law enforcement's business, and the criminal intelligence function allows police agencies to be proactive in addressing the criminal threats in their communities. As a critical component of Community-Oriented Policing or Intelligence Led Policing, criminal intelligence needs to be the approach that police agencies embrace to achieve an optimum level of public safety.

10 STEPS TO ESTABLISHING A SUCCESSFUL CRIMINAL INTELLIGENCE PROGRAM

1. Create a proper environment
    - Obtain the active support of the agency's chief executive officer
    - Gain the political and budgetary support from the appropriate elected officials
    - Educate the agency and the community concerning the benefits of having a criminal intelligence function

2. Establish the criminal intelligence unit as a proactive crime prevention operation, which supports the concept of community oriented policing

3. Design a unit mission statement focused toward specific criminal activities and disseminate it to the entire agency

4. Select qualified personnel, including a trained analyst, to staff the unit

5. Obtain separate, secure quarters for the unit

6. Implement and enforce professional guidelines for:
    - Unit operations
    - File procedures
    - Security

- Special expense funds
- Informant control

7. Provide training for:
    - The chief executive officer
    - Appropriate elected officials
    - Criminal intelligence managers and supervisors
    - Criminal intelligence officers and analysts
    - The remainder of the agency's personnel
    - Legal advisor

8. Liaison and neighboring agencies and participate in regional and state criminal intelligence networks. Join The Regional Information Sharing System (RISS) and the Association of Law Enforcement Intelligence Units (LEIU)

9. Require both strategic and tactical products from the unit and evaluate its operations on a regular schedule

10. Ensure the chief executive officer meets regularly with the criminal intelligence unit supervisor to provide appropriate direction

REFERENCES

Griswold v. Connecticut 381 U.S. 479 (1965).

Harris, Don R. (1976) *Basic Elements of Intelligence - Revised.* Washington, DC: Law Enforcement Assistance Administration, September.

Report on Police, National Advisory Commission on Criminal Justice Standards and Goals, 1973. Commissioned by the Law Enforcement Assistance Administration (LEAA) on October 20, 1971 to formulate national criminal justice standards and goals for crime reduction and prevention at the state and local level.

Wright, Richard (1998) *Ten Steps to Establishing a Criminal Intelligence Unit,* Issues of Interest to Law Enforcement Criminal Intelligence: A Vital Police Function. Marilyn B. Peterson, ed. Sacramento CA: Law Enforcement Intelligence Unit.

The National Criminal Intelligence Sharing Plan U.S. Department of Justice – 2003.

Planning and Direction
By Doug Larm

THE INTELLIGENCE PROCESS

"The intelligence process or cycle begins with questions – the answers to which inevitably lead to more questions. So, essentially, the end of the cycle is the beginning of the next cycle."[1]

The intelligence process is a dynamic and systematic approach for obtaining answers to questions. The process is wide-ranging and underlies the development of national security policies, law enforcement strategies, and competitive business decisions. The means and methods may differ between the government, law enforcement, and corporate domains but the end result is the same. The intelligence process seeks to fill in knowledge gaps in order to support decision-making.

The intelligence cycle is the most common visualization for this process. The cycle is a conceptual model indicating a continuous flow of actionable steps taken to transform information and data into finished intelligence for the decision-maker. Each step has a purpose or an output. The output links to the next step thereby continuing the sequential linkage between steps. The cycle repeats when decision-makers provide feedback and in turn new requirements are generated.

While there is no absolute consensus on the number of steps inherent within the intelligence cycle,[2] all of the conceptual models share a common viewpoint—provide decision-makers with relevant, accurate, and timely intelligence.

The number of steps defining the intelligence process is not important. All of the conceptual models agree on describing the intelligence process as interrelated activities for adding value to information. The intelligence cycle serves to illustrate a fundamental approach used in government, law enforcement, and corporate domains to identify, collect, process, and disseminate intelligence.

---

[1] *United States Intelligence Community-What We Do* at: *<http://www.intelligence.gov/2-business.shtml>* accessed March 2009.

[2] Descriptions illustrating an intelligence cycle range from a four and five to a six-step model. For example, one business intelligence model outlines a four-step cycle to gather, process, report and disseminate actionable intelligence for corporate consumers (White Paper-Intelligence Cycle, Tech-Writer.net at: *<http://www.tech-writer.net/Intelligence_Cycle.pdf>* accessed March 2009). The Central Intelligence Agency (CIA) follows a five-step intelligence cycle process (*<https://www.cia.gov/news-information/featured-story-archive/2007-featured-story-archive/what-is-intelligence.html>* accessed March 2009). The National Criminal Intelligence Sharing Plan (NCISP at: *<http://www.iir.com/global/products/NCISP_Plan.pdf>*, page 7 accessed March 2009), the Federal Bureau of Investigation (FBI, Intelligence Cycle, at *<http://www.fbi.gov/intelligence/di_cycle.htm>* accessed March 2009) and the Department of Defense (Joint Publication 2-01, Joint and National Intelligence Support to Military Operations, 7 October 2004, at *<http://www.dtic.mil/doctrine/new_pubs/jp2_01.pdf>* accessed March 2009) categorize the intelligence cycle as a six-step process.

In practice, the actual process is "multidimensional, multidirectional, and – most importantly – interactive and iterative."[3] This does not mean depicting a circular nature—a continuous flow of actionable steps— for the intelligence process is oversimplified or outdated. On the contrary, despite existing criticisms[4] the intelligence cycle remains an effective mental model for police executives and an agency's chief executive officer (CEO). With consideration for the need to understand and visualize a process for adding value to data and information, the intelligence cycle represents law enforcement's approach for decision-making, planning, criminal targeting, and crime prevention.

PLANNING AND DIRECTION WITHIN THE INTELLIGENCE PROCESS

"When asked what he would do if given 1 hour to save the world, Albert Einstein reportedly replied that he would spend 55 minutes to understand and formulate the problem and 5 minutes to execute the solution."[5]

The National Criminal Intelligence Sharing Plan (NCISP) acknowledges "criminal intelligence results from a process involving planning and direction, information collection, processing/collation, analysis, dissemination, and reevaluation (feedback) of information on suspected criminals and/or organizations. This sequential process is commonly referred to as the intelligence process."[6]

While the NCISP establishes planning and direction as part of a sequence of events, planning and direction is also evident throughout the entire intelligence process. It is more than a beginning or an end. As the FBI indicates on its Directorate of Intelligence website, planning and direction is *management of the entire effort.*[7]

From an organizational perspective, planning and direction is done at every level of criminal intelligence support to law enforcement. Planning and direction is the wellspring from which all other operational tasks or organizational actions resulting from the intelligence process gain relevance, prioritization, and authorization.

At department, unit, section, or squad level—the output from planning and direction identifies needs and requirements. This continuous output swirls and gains momentum throughout the intelligence process as

---

[3] Douglas H. Dearth, *National Intelligence: Profession and Process*, in Strategic Intelligence: Theory and Application, eds. Douglas H. Dearth and R. Thomas Goodden, 2d ed. (Washington, DC: Joint Military Intelligence Training Center, 1995), page 17.

[4] Kristan J. Wheaton, *The Coming Revolution in Intelligence Affairs*, in an editorial on International Relations and Security Network at:
<http://www.isn.ethz.ch/isn/Current-Affairs/Special-Reports/The-Revolution-in-Intelligence-Affairs/Editorial>
accessed March 2009; and Arthur S. Hulnick, *What's Wrong with the Intelligence Cycle,* in Intelligence and National Security, Routledge Publishing (Vol 21, Issue 6 December 2006) at:
<http://www.informaworld.com/10.1080/02684520601046291> accessed March 2009.

[5] K.R. Ravi, *Thinking About Thinking,* Jaico Book House (Mumbai, 2008) at:
<http://www.flipkart.com/thinking-ravi-kr/8179925161-5v23fal06f#previewbook> accessed March 2009, page 131.

[6] Bureau of Justice Assistance, US Department of Justice, *The Rationale for the National Intelligence Criminal Intelligence Sharing Plan,* National Criminal Intelligence Sharing Plan (Version 1.0, October 2003) at:
<http://www.iir.com/global/products/NCISP_Plan.pdf> accessed March 2009, page 16

[7] Federal Bureau of Investigation, US Department of Justice, Directorate of Intelligence at:
<http://www.fbi.gov/intelligence/di_cycle.htm> accessed March 2009

higher-level organizational questions are elaborated, progressively narrowed, and information gaps bridged. The answers to the questions build knowledge in order to generate tailored, timely, and actionable criminal intelligence.

One method for police executives to identify with the intelligence cycle's planning and direction vortex is to understand the key attributes defining *management of the entire effort.* Successful planning and direction—*management of the entire effort*—needs police executives (especially the agency's CEO) to facilitate and actively participate in the intelligence process by advocating five key performance attributes: strategic management, leadership, collaboration, agility, and action (in the form of a collection plan.)

Strategic management provides the foundation for planning and direction and frames the organizational commitment. It is the process by which organizations identify mission and vision; determine purpose and objectives; and formulate the plans, policies, or actions to achieve organizational objectives.[8] The NCISP, for example, emphasizes the criticality for law enforcement CEO's to adopt a strategic management process.[9]

Leadership is not necessarily the same as effective management. Leadership orchestrates change and involves unique processes that are distinguishable from managing day-to-day complexities of organizations.[10] Although the NCISP does not specifically label leadership as an essential element for intelligence sharing, the concepts of promoting new direction, shared vision, enhanced professional judgment, trust, and performance—the context of leadership[11]—are identified throughout the recommendations of the NCISP.[12] As such, the NCISP distinguishes leadership as a multifaceted performance characteristic needed for successful planning and direction of the intelligence process.

On its Directorate of Intelligence website, the FBI graphically portrays the importance of collaboration to the intelligence process by labeling *active collaboration* in the center of the cycle.[13] The FBI graphic illustrates that collaboration touches every aspect of the intelligence process at all organizational levels. Thus, it is multidimensional. Collaboration is also interactive and therefore it is multidirectional.

[8] John L. Thompson and Frank Martin, *Strategic Management: Awareness and Change*, 5th ed. (Cengage Learning EMEA, 2005), pages 9-10.

[9] Bureau of Justice Assistance, US Department of Justice, *The Rationale for the National Criminal Intelligence Sharing Plan,* National Criminal Intelligence Sharing Plan (Version 1.0, October 2003) at: <*http://www.iir.com/global/products/NCISP_Plan.pdf*> accessed March 2009, page 8.

[10] Thomas S. Bateman and Scott A. Snell, *Management: The New Competitive Landscape*, 6th ed. (McGraw-Hill Irwin, 2004), page 368.

[11] An excellent primer on context of leadership is "On Leadership: The Context of Leadership", an article in a series of leadership articles by Michael L. Venn, Ph.D., and B. Keith Simerson, Ed.D., on Tradewinds Consulting, LLC at: <*http://www.tradewindsconsulting.com/publications.htm*> accessed March 2009.

[12] NCISP recommendation 1 focuses on the intelligence process and includes elements of management and supervision; recommendation 7 recognizes communication and collaboration; recommendation 8 promotes outreach to publicize concepts for intelligence sharing; recommendation 10 highlights Criminal Intelligence Model Policy (2003 revision) as a guide for implementing the intelligence function; recommendation 12 supports the enhancement of professional judgment; recommendation 14 seeks to foster trust; recommendation 15 promotes effective accountability measures; recommendation 16 encourages justice leaders and practitioners to use noted privacy guidelines; and recommendations 20-25 solicit agencies to support new directions for communications, data systems, file sharing interoperability, and security.

[13] Federal Bureau of Investigation, US Department of Justice, Directorate of Intelligence at: <*http://www.fbi.gov/intelligence/di_cycle.htm*> accessed March 2009.

CHAPTER 5

Planning and Direction

Successful performance of and support for collaboration within an organization empowers internal and external sharing of knowledge. The NCISP, for example, recommends law enforcement agencies facilitate sharing of knowledge (internally and externally) to other law enforcement agencies, first responders, public safety, and others engaged in the broad homeland security mission.[14]

In the business world, agility means action—it implies capacity and capability to act.[15] In the intelligence process, agility in planning and direction results in organizational flexibility. This refers to the speed in which an organization can effectively adapt to changing requirements should it choose to do so. Not all changing requirements need to be confronted by organizational action, but all changing requirements do require awareness by everyone throughout the organization. Police executives, led by the agency's CEO, need to clearly articulate the conditions, circumstances, and influences requiring organizational action. Agility in planning and direction leads to timely, operationally effective, and cost-efficient responses.

Action, in the form of a collection plan, is the framework organizational executives use to determine, document, and evaluate intelligence needs. For law enforcement agencies, International Association of Law Enforcement Intelligence Analysts (IALEIA) defines a collection plan as "a plan that directs the collection of data on a particular topic with a specific objective, a list of potential sources of that data, and an estimated time frame."[16]

Within the intelligence process, the basic intent for a collection plan is to identify information desired or questions that need answers. The answers to such questions support a decision at the organizational level generating the questions. The format for a collection plan may be short and simple or lengthy and involved—depending on the methods or sources used to collect information. The range of sources extends from an organization's file records, investigative reports, personnel interviews, to a plethora of online information websites. For more complex sources such as informants, undercover investigators, and technical surveillance missions, a collection plan frames active investigative tasks and reflects the diversity of methods and depth of resources leveraged to achieve organizational objectives. The collection plan becomes a blueprint for building knowledge and generating actionable criminal intelligence. Consequently, action—in the form of a collection plan—focuses an organization to develop specific information about specific things at specific times to accomplish specific effects.

The intelligence cycle's planning and direction can be done in a deliberate or rapid response decision-making environment. The collection plan, as part of crisis management, can be as simple as a mental process for quickly identifying knowledge gaps during a time-sensitive situation. As well, when time is not a critical factor, the collection plan can result from a deliberate, not necessarily slow, cyclic, and continuous process.

---

[14] Bureau of Justice Assistance, US Department of Justice, *National Criminal Intelligence Sharing Plan,* (Version 1.0, October 2003) at: *<http://www.iir.com/global/products/NCISP_Plan.pdf>* accessed March 2009, pages 31 and 34.

[15] Michael Schrage, "The Struggle to Define Agility", a September 2004 article posted to CIO at: *<http://www.cio.com.au/article/185655/struggle_define_agility>* accessed March 2009.

[16] IALEIA, *Law Enforcement Analytic Standards*, November 2004, at: *<http://www.it.ojp.gov/documents/law_enforcement_analytic_standards.pdf>* accessed March 2009, page 39.

CHAPTER 5

Planning and Direction

IDENTIFYING PRIORITY INTELLIGENCE REQUIREMENTS

"If you ask the wrong question, of course, you get the wrong answer...it's much more important and difficult to ask the right question. Once you do that, the right answer becomes obvious."[17]

Successful management of the entire effort requires consistent application of all key attributes. Otherwise, incomplete work processes result in situations such as an engineer attempting to construct a building without the benefit of architectural blueprints or a postal carrier attempting to deliver mail without address labels. Successful intelligence cycle planning and direction requires input from others and the application of activities and processes to create the output—a collection plan to guide the development of knowledge.

Criminal intelligence analysts perform a significant role in the development of organizational knowledge. The analysts use questions as a tool in the search for understanding. The answers to effective questions build organizational knowledge. Further, the analyst can exert a positive influence on organizational decision-making by understanding the priorities and resource decisions faced by executives and the agency's CEO. Having such insight invests the analyst with a clearer understanding for the organizational implications that stem from decisions made on the basis of the answers developed. The analysts' interaction with the CEO and other police executives is paramount to the intelligence process for establishing and defining responsibilities, identifying and refining work activities, and outlining organizational needs.

The driving force for this interaction involves integrating two organizational processes—one business and the other military. The business application is an adaptation from project management's progressive elaboration or decomposition process.[18] This involves decomposing or subdividing significant but generic information needs, articulated by the CEO at department or agency level as a question, into smaller, more manageable situational conditions, a collaborative and iterative work process for decomposing and identifying known and unknown information. The military application is an adaptation of Priority Intelligence Requirements (PIR).[19] PIR are key questions regarding a situation, circumstance, or condition. While PIR is not uniquely a military application, the Department of Homeland Security mirrors similar intelligence requirements applications termed Standing Information Needs and Priority Information Needs along with the intelligence identifier PIR.[20] It is most closely associated as a military

---

[17] Business quote attributed to Amory Lovins, Rocky Mountain Institute Chairman and Chief Scientist, posted at: <http://www.woopidoo.com/business_quotes/authors/amory-lovins/index.htm> accessed March 2009
[18] Project Management Institute, *A Guide to the Project Management Body of Knowledge*, 2000 ed. (PMI, 2000), pages 57-59.
[19] Joint Publication 2-0, *Joint Intelligence*, Department of Defense, (Joint Chiefs of Staff), 22 June 2007, pages I-8 – I-10.
[20] While PIR is closely linked to military intelligence operations, the FBI uses the term in similar manner with regard to bureau intelligence products (FBI, Today's FBI: Intelligence, at: <http://www.fbi.gov/facts_and_figures/intelligence.htm> accessed September 2009). Some law enforcement operations have begun to incorporate PIR as a term of reference for the collection of material for intelligence reports (Frank S. Root, Law Enforcement Intelligence Critical Elements, at: <http://www.lawenforcementintelligence.com/glossary.htm#p_list> accessed September 2009). Further, DHS uses PIR as a term of reference for focusing intelligence operations activity within the Department and within the Intelligence Community. See DHS, Office of Intelligence and Analysis, *Information Sharing Strategies,* Robert C.

term of reference for identifying anticipated or stated priority requirements within an organizational hierarchy. Consequently, within the military, national security, and law enforcement environment the answers to the key questions—whether termed as Standing Information Needs, Priority Information Needs, or Priority Intelligence Requirements—provide information or knowledge required to support organizational decision-making, planning, and operations.

Combining the two processes—progressive elaboration and PIR—and integrating criminal intelligence analysts with the decision-makers in the organizational hierarchy allows the decomposition process to subdivide PIR into smaller, more manageable conditional questions. In turn, the decomposition process continues until conditional questions are elaborated or condensed into an intelligence indicator.

An intelligence indicator is evidentiary consideration in the form of a question. An intelligence indicator is positive or negative evidence of suspected criminal activity or any characteristic of a person, place, or thing that could point toward vulnerabilities, capacities, or capabilities posing a threat or as a public safety risk. Intelligence indicators facilitate identifying specific information gaps that must be bridged in order to reduce uncertainties or to determine the relevancy of conditional questions and ultimately PIR.

For law enforcement, the progressive elaboration of PIR enhances an organization's investigative plan. The creation of a collection plan is a methodical and deliberate output of the intelligence process and compels an organization to break down known and unknown information into conditional questions and ultimately into intelligence indicators. The intelligence indicators act as guideposts and assist analysts and investigators in focusing, coordinating, and stabilizing the investigative process.

For example, assume a simulated scenario in a hypothetical city. The police agency CEO has prioritized the city's conditions, circumstances, and influences into a list of key questions or PIR. One of the PIR reflects a CEO question "what events garner organized crime interest in the city?" The stated PIR is generic in nature and overly broad, however, at agency level the question indicates a priority concern for two elements voiced by the agency's CEO—*events* and *organized crime.*

The agency's executives, investigators, and analysts collaborate and decompose or subdivide the CEO PIR into conditional questions. The conditional questions focus on identifying what is known, and unknown, on city events and organized crime. In the scenario, progressive elaboration reveals an upcoming diamond buyer's meeting. One of the conditional questions could reflect "will the upcoming diamond buyer's meeting attract criminal 'alliances of opportunity' or extremist's pursuing criminal intent?" The conditional question identifies one constituent component of the PIR or key question voiced by the CEO—an event—the diamond buyer's meeting. The remaining element—organized crime—remains unknown in significance and purpose and requires further decomposition.

Decomposing or subdividing conditional questions into smaller situational questions is an iterative process. In the scenario, city law enforcement officers and analysts collaborate on breaking down their informational needs for determining causes, significance, and purpose that could relate to organized crime's interest in the diamond buyer's meeting.

The decomposition process continues until intelligence indicators are developed. The answers from the intelligence indicators, questions seeking positive or negative evidence, reflect the outcome of specific,

Riegle, State and Local Government Program Manager, DHS presentation at:
<*www.agpartnership.org/documents/Riegle_1.ppt*> accessed September 2009.

task-oriented work packages. The work packages are not in lieu of investigative tasks, but compliment the agency's investigative work with criminal intelligence analyst's support.

Both analyst and investigator seek answers to questions. Work packages reflect answers to potential questions such as:

- What is the characterization of local, national, and international media coverage on the upcoming diamond buyer's meeting?

- Are there recent reports indicating systemic or disciplined incidents, suspicious in nature, that cannot be easily dismissed or misinterpreted as inquisitive or as naïve acts manifesting around the site designated for the upcoming diamond buyer's meeting?

- Have any known gang members or their associates outside of the city recently inquired or traveled to or near the diamond buyer's meeting site?

As depicted in the simulated scenario, the output from PIR decomposition are specific, task-oriented work packages. Completing such tasks, whether identified in an investigative plan or supplemented by the intelligence process collection plan, provide information or answers to questions. Much like the intelligence cycle, the decomposition of PIR, from agency executive level down to the actionable work effort, is an iterative and interactive process. The process seeks answers to specific questions by answering subsequent questions and identifying conditions, circumstances, and influences surrounding the intelligence need.

The active involvement of the CEO is crucial for developing a strategy in prioritizing PIRs. An organization cannot answer every PIR and all subsequent conditional questions. Often organizations face the problem of too little time and not enough resources. In the intelligence process, the interaction between the CEO, executives, investigators, and analysts determine what knowledge is urgently important to the organization. Prioritizing an organization's key questions, or PIR, identifies for executives and analysts what needs to be done now and what could be done later, if at all.

As the analysts, executives, and other organizational members complete work tasks and provide informational updates, operational adjustments, and analytical valuations—information gaps are bridged and knowledge structure is built. Ultimately, the analytical outcome of the intelligence process is to mature an organization's situational awareness towards situational understanding.[21]

---

[21] The military terms "situational understanding" and "situational awareness" derive from US Army operations and are sometimes used interchangeably. However, the US Army differentiates between the two, as does this chapter. In the context of integrating business and military organizational processes, this chapter defines situational awareness as maintaining a clear mental image of relevant information pertaining to an event, condition, circumstance, or influence. This chapter defines situational understanding as the knowledge product from analysis, collaboration and judgment and facilitates decision-making throughout the organization by identifying operational opportunities, operational risks and information gaps. For further elaboration of situational awareness and situational understanding within the military context, see US Army Field Manual 3-20.96, *Cavalry Squadron (RSTA)*, (US Army Armor Center), December 2002, pages 1-2 and 2-3.

IMPLEMENTING PLANNING AND DIRECTION—*MANAGEMENT OF THE ENTIRE EFFORT*—WITHIN AN ORGANIZATION

"The process of seeking greatness cannot help but improve a policing agency. ...But for each chief and each sheriff, any efforts to find the path to greatness surely will lead to some improvements. And in policing, even a small success can be immeasurably large."[22]

The NCISP provides recommendations for managing the intelligence function within an agency. The essential element of the plan is as a blueprint for agencies to follow for enhancing or building an intelligence system. The NCISP promotes intelligence-led policing as the business model for developing, gathering, accessing, receiving, and sharing information and data to improve crime fighting, public safety, and homeland security.[23]

The NCISP recommendations serve as action steps that can be taken immediately by almost any agency. Implementing the intelligence process is an effective and efficient means for improving an organization's strategic value and quality of work. The plan recognizes the need to leverage existing efforts and build-on—not reinvent—successful information sharing practices currently in place.[24] Consequently, an agency's "buy-in" is not measured in terms of reorganizing, restructuring, or spending but rather in terms of commitment, alignment, and operational measures.

Implementing the intelligence cycle's planning and direction requires commitment in the form of advocacy and action by the agency's CEO. The CEO is responsible for applying the intelligence process in a manner consistent with its purpose and design and to put the intelligence process into practice throughout the organization. Only by supporting, emulating, and instituting the five key performance attributes—in word and through deed—does the CEO transform planning and direction from an actionable step in a sequence of management activities to *management of the entire effort.*

The intelligence process seeks information to bridge knowledge gaps. Using a disciplined, systematic approach aligns the organization's goals and objectives to performance and quality of work. The intelligence cycle's planning and direction provides vision, purpose, and focus for a law enforcement agency's executives, analysts, and officers to collaborate throughout the intelligence process—decomposing questions, identifying situational conditions and intelligence indicators, determining information and knowledge gaps, and developing follow-on questions and strategies or work packages for bridging the gaps. Consequently, organizational alignment harnesses work performance throughout an agency and focuses everyone on contributing to strategic value and quality of work.

---

[22] Chuck Wexler, Mary Ann Wycoff, Craig Fisher, Office of Community Oriented Policing Services, US Department of Justice, Police Executive Research Forum, "'Good to Great' Policing: Application of Business Management Principles in the Public Sector", (Washington DC, June 2007) at: <*http://www.cops.usdoj.gov/files/RIC/Publications/good_to_great.pdf*> accessed March 2009, page 60

[23] Bureau of Justice Assistance, US Department of Justice, *The Rationale for the National Criminal Intelligence Sharing Plan,* National Criminal Intelligence Sharing Plan (Version 1.0, October 2003) website at <*http://www.iir.com/global/products/NCISP_Plan.pdf*> accessed March 2009, page 15

[24] Ibid, page 16.

CHAPTER 5

Planning and Direction

Operational measures refer to a performance management tool for determining the effectiveness of an organization's alignment in accomplishing strategic value. As a management tool, operational measures enable an agency to consistently communicate its strategy in operational terms. As a result, everyone in an organization can understand how and why department, unit, section, or squad level work actions contribute to strategic goals and objectives.

A common method to visualize operational measures is a status board. A status board, whether in electronic (web-based) or paper format, is a communication tool. It identifies and provides current status of work. Organization executives can disaggregate the status board for maintaining need-to-know and right-to-know for specific work activities. However, the agency should consider an aggregate level within the organization in order to comprehensively view and determine alignment of all work performance.

There are different ways for displaying status. One method reflects a decision-tree format. A PIR shows associated conditional questions as branches. Subsequent decomposition of conditional questions continues branching out into work packages. Another method reflects an indentation format. Each PIR has conditional questions indented. Subsequent iteration of decomposition is indented further conveying a structure or hierarchy, much like the decision-tree format, linking a PIR down to work packages.

Regardless of format, the status board needs to effectively and consistently display work progress. One method is to use a red, amber, and green color status. For example, a red status reflects the PIR, conditional question, or work package has not been answered, or has not been assigned for work. An amber status reflects the answer is not verifiable by a reliable source or the answer does not demonstrate current relevance to the PIR. A green status indicates information obtained is current and the answer is by a reliable source. Analysts roll-up the status of conditional questions and work packages in order to determine the overall status of the PIR. While the roll-up is subjective, it is linked to the analyst's or investigator's expert judgment to assess the overall status.

CHAPTER 6

Collection
By Paul Coambs

INTRODUCTION

The data collection portion of the Intelligence Cycle is the "lifeblood of the intelligence process" and contains a variety of components designed to provide relevant data for analysis.

The collection of information to support the intelligence function should be guided by a collection plan predicated upon specific priorities determined by the agency leadership. Despite the fact that the intelligence function is not a new phenomenon within law enforcement, many executives and managers lack full understanding regarding their specific responsibilities pertaining to the law enforcement intelligence mission.

Police executives need to embrace the intelligence function, since that attitude ultimately pervades the rest of the agency and effectively supports the free flow of information to the intelligence unit. Intelligence personnel can facilitate an increased understanding of the intelligence function by consistently exposing non-intelligence personnel to the intelligence concepts and mission. One good method is to gain access to new hires and provide appropriate training during their orientation period.

In many ways, the intelligence function and accordingly the intelligence collection process, is a foreign concept to much of law enforcement. Fortunately, current evidence suggests that the Federal Bureau of Investigation has transformed itself from a primarily prosecutorial organization into an effective intelligence organ relative to fulfilling its function as the lead domestic law enforcement agency charged with combating terrorism. Many state and local law enforcement agencies actively partner their intelligence units in the national effort to combat terrorism.

Regrettably, there are shortsighted local law enforcement agencies which are not joining in the effort. Police executives who do not embrace the intelligence function are shortchanging their constituencies and increasing community vulnerability in this age of terrorism, espionage, and worldwide and cross-jurisdictional criminal enterprises. Agencies which fail to train their personnel in the active gathering and forwarding of tips and leads to an intelligence unit and/or the regional information centers are creating gaps in the national effort to detect and thwart inevitable future terrorist attacks. Additionally, police agencies electing to not participate with the law enforcement intelligence community are placing other jurisdictions at greater risk by not fully pursuing cross-jurisdictional criminals residing within their own community.

The comprehensiveness of the intelligence data collection process is governed by need immediacy and the specific type of intelligence product desired. Tactical intelligence products facilitate actionable operations in the short term and require an in-depth collection directly affecting operational parameters. Strategic intelligence products are much broader than tactical products and have the specific purpose of informing in support of policy formulation.

The law enforcement criminal intelligence function exceeds the formal collection of data toward an intelligence analysis of a pre-determined target exhibiting a criminal predicate. Unless the criminal intelligence unit is stringently focused upon a single mission, the unit, as a whole, must actively strive to be current and relatively conversant in a wide variety of topics beyond the realm of their current delineated criminal intelligence investigations. A wide peripheral vision on both historical and current conditions allows the unit to anticipate and recognize key indicators suggesting potential new or renewed issues of interest.

The gathering and compilation of intelligence data by a governmental agency can be an intrusive act necessitated by law enforcement's mandate to ensure public safety. A balanced view of privacy and governmental responsibility to protect America's safety is expressed by the Markle Foundation Task Force in, "*Protecting America's Freedom in the Information Age.*"

"To protect freedom, America's physical safety is essential. Protecting freedom also requires securing the values that define America, including the civil liberties and rights to privacy that make our country special. Rights go together with responsibilities in preserving the public order in which our values can flourish. When Americans feel they must start trading fundamental rights in return for more security, we will know our national security policies are failing. The rule of law is our strength."

The invasion of privacy and the misuse of collected personal data by the government and private companies can lead to a systematic erosion of civil rights. The collection of personal data within the United States is a topic of considerable concern. A leading oppositional voice is the American Civil Liberties Union (ACLU).

Jay Stanley and Barry Steinhardt wrote in the ACLU's January 2003 publication, *Bigger Monster, Weaker Chains: The Growth of an American Surveillance Society*, "Privacy and liberty in the United States are at risk. A combination of lightning-fast technological innovation and the erosion of privacy protections threaten to transform Big Brother from an oft-cited but remote threat into a very real part of American life. We are at risk of turning into a Surveillance Society."

There is a certain degree of truth in the ACLU's assertion given the human baser inclination to self-aggrandizement through the misuse of power. Historically, the federal government, state, and municipal law enforcement agencies engaged in incidents of "spying" activities, which judged by today's standards, were clearly unlawful. Today's prohibitions on the storage of domestic information without a criminal predicate, especially data of a political, sexual, or racial nature, are the ground rules for the protection of civil rights.

In terms of established legitimate governmental function, opponents to governmental intelligence activity frequently fail to distinguish the difference between observing public activity and private activity. There are vast differences when law enforcement authorities attend public functions in a surveillance mode, access information in the public domain, or otherwise lawfully obtain information, as opposed to collecting and retaining unlawful data. Again from the ACLU's Stanley and Steinhardt, "In May 2002, Attorney General John Ashcroft issued new guidelines on domestic spying that significantly increase the freedom of federal agents to conduct surveillance on American individuals and organizations. Under the new guidelines, FBI agents can infiltrate "any event that is open to the public" from public meetings and demonstrations to political conventions to church services to 12-step programs."

The protection of civil rights requires that today's domestic law enforcement intelligence programs must be governed by strict regulations supported by ongoing training.

CHAPTER 6

Collection

INFORMATION COLLECTION PROCESS
FOR THE CRIMINAL INTELLIGENCE PRODUCT

The collection of raw data for the purpose of creating formal law enforcement intelligence products requires a frame of reference different and expanded upon beyond that of the prosecution oriented criminal investigation. In the United States, the criminal intelligence investigator is, in many ways, unfettered by the restrictions of prosecutorial criminal investigations as long as the intelligence investigation has a criminal predicate, privacy laws are not violated, and the information is collected lawfully and in compliance with Part 23, Section 28, Code of Federal Regulations (28 CFR Part 23).

Adhering to both written collection criteria and criminal intelligence file criteria will ensure that information collected for the intelligence purpose is gathered and stored lawfully.

The intelligence data collection process requires the development of a collection plan to keep the procedure focused with an efficient flow of data from the collector to the analyst. Answering the questions: Why is the intelligence wanted? What sort of decision will be made from the intelligence? How will the intelligence information be used? will lead to specific goals to be met or modified to facilitate the evolving analysis.

A collection plan must address a series of organizational key points:

- Are all criminal intelligence personnel trained in legal applications, laws pertaining to data collection and the right to privacy?

- Are any non-criminal intelligence personnel involved in the investigation?

- Do the intelligence personnel have the necessary skills to undertake the project?

- If informants are to be used, are informant guidelines in place?

- Is there a written collection plan?

- Does the collection plan specify what data is required?

- Is there a time-line for the collection of data?

- Does the collection plan comply with case law and local, state, and federal statutes?

- Does the collection plan focus on criminal activity?

- Are all known sources of information to be utilized?

- Are the collection plan's objectives and requirements communicated to all personnel involved in the collection?

- Does the collection plan facilitate the close working relationship between analysts and collection investigators?

- Does the collection plan stipulate a hierarchy of responsibility?

- Does the collection plan estimate the difficulty and probability of completing a successful collection using all of the available resources?

- Are all of the specific collection goals identified and hierarchically arranged?

Specific generalized anticipated collection plan results:

- Determine the motivation of the target criminal group, i.e. revenue production and/or personal/political agendas

- Identify the participants of a criminal group and determine the intra-group relationships

- Identify the individual and collective criminal activities of the criminal group members

- Identify the target's decision making process

- Develop an in-depth biographical background on the target's key leaders, decision makers, and advisors

- Identify and delineate the geographic locations of the criminals and their activity

- Determine the intra-group mechanisms used to control members of the group

- Determine the relationships among competitive and non-competitive criminal groups with the target group

- Determine the relationship of the target criminal group with non-criminal groups

SOURCES OF INFORMATION

Information collected for intelligence purposes is primarily gathered from law enforcement investigative reports, surveillance and undercover operational reports, interviews and interrogations, photographs, electronic intercepts, search warrants, law enforcement professional contacts, public records, and open sources. While the collection of data from various written format is invaluable, the heart of intelligence work is the overt and covert gathering of information from human sources.

The sharing of insightful information by law enforcement intelligence colleagues is the hallmark of successful networking predicated upon the development of personal relationships nurtured by professionalism and mutual trust. The overt sharing of information with an intelligence collector can be as a result of a multitude of motivations requiring a diligent effort to determine both the truthfulness of the human source and the validity and usefulness of the information.

Overt information, sources, and leads may be developed as a result of active involvement in Community Oriented Policing. An unlimited source of informants and relevant information may be mined from the

Neighborhood Watch and the Terrorism Liaison Officer's community outreach programs or through educational presentations to public service and business groups either directly by intelligence gatherers or through the auspices of the police personnel running the programs.

Overt contacts by intelligence personnel with the community entail a certain amount of risk threatening the exposure of the investigation. Inquiries into bona fide terrorism and organized crime groups may well result in the target collecting the business and personal information of the intelligence personnel. There are rare examples of intelligence personnel targeted for retribution, which suggests that intelligence personnel should be trained in counter-surveillance techniques.

The covert gathering of information from human sources takes the form of physical surveillance and undercover operations wherein the intelligence collector disguises his/her purpose and/or identity.

Physical surveillance, with or without the aid of electronic surveillance equipment, is personnel intensive requiring a sufficient number of highly trained operatives properly equipped with and access to the following:

- Airplanes and Helicopters
- Covert Vehicles
- Binoculars
- Global Positioning System (GPS) Tracking Devices for Target Vehicles
- In-Car GPS Units
- Cameras
- Radios
- Cell Phones
- Tape Recorders
- Covert Video and Audio Recorders
- Night Vision Devices
- Miscellaneous Supporting Equipment and Clothing

Both overt and covert methods of human information collection share the same problems of assuring whether or not the information collected is valid or is disinformation and whether or not the sources and activities reveal the existence of the investigation to the targets.

Sources and techniques used for data collection include:

- Conducting briefings and presentations to public groups
- Covert physical surveillance
- Develop a professional relationship with business and community leaders
- Develop a relationship with law enforcement patrol officers and detectives
- Electronic surveillance in the form of (GPS) tracking, phone tolls, pen register, and wire taps
- Interviews of informants, citizens, and public officials
- Mining public and private hardcopy and electronic stored databases and records
- Monitoring Internet social networks
- Networking with law enforcement agencies and law enforcement topic specific groups
- Participating in joint task forces

- Photographic surveillance
- Postal mail covers
- Discarded documents obtained from trash collection bins sometimes referred to as a "Trash Grab"

Data may be obtained from:

Public Records

- Bankruptcy
- County Clerk's Office
- Divorce and Legal Separation
- Licensing Bureaus

- Property Assessor's Office
- Real Estate Records
- Wage and Income Statements

Financial Institutions and Reports

- Banks
- Bonding Companies
- Casino CTR
- Casino SAR
- Credit Reporting Agencies
- Currency and Monetary Transaction Report
- Currency Transaction Report CTR

- Exempt Person Report
- Foreign Bank Account Report
- Money Service Business SAR
- Securities and Futures SAR
- Stock Brokers
- Suspicious Activity Report SAR
- Western Union

Business Records

- Inventories
- Journals
- Ledgers
- Legal Documents

- Private Postal Box Subscriber Ledger
- Sales Receipts

City and County Hall

- Assessor
- Auditor
- Building Department
- Civil Defense
- Clerk
- Code Enforcement
- Coroner
- Court, Municipal and Superior
- District Attorney
- Fire Marshal
- Welfare

- Garbage Department
- Police Department
- Public Defender
- Public Library
- Recorder
- Recreation Department
- Sanitation Department
- Street Department
- Tax Collector
- Voter Registrar

CHAPTER 6

Collection

<u>Public Utilities</u>

- Electric and Natural Gas Companies
- Water Company

- Telephone Company
- Western Union

<u>Delivery and Transportation</u>

- Auto Rental Companies
- Delivery Companies
- Moving Companies

- Taxicab and Limousine Companies
- Travel Agencies

THE DIGITAL WORLD

The world is increasingly embracing the digital world, especially young people brought up in that environment. Law enforcement authorities, especially the intelligence community, must recognize and utilize the digital medium to remain professionally relevant.

An example of the youthful acceptance and utilization of the digital world was detailed in a recent New York Times article entitled, "Letting Our Fingers Do the Talking." The report stated that teenagers between 13 and 17 years of age receive an average of 1742 text messages on their cell phones a month.

The young are equally driving the phenomena of social networking on the Internet.

THE INTERNET

The Internet is the new world library providing as near to an instantaneous information resource as possible. Digital sources of information are relegating the print media to the dust bins of antiquity. A vast amount of information is only a few keyboard strokes away.

Individuals, businesses, private organizations, and governmental entities are establishing a presence on the Internet with their own official websites.

A word of caution: just because an information source is established in print or digital format is not a guarantee of balanced, accurate, or reliable reporting. Propaganda in the form of misinformation and undisclosed information is rampant. An analysis based solely upon single source information can be suspect.

The mainstream media in some countries is often controlled by the nation-state in which the media organ physically resides. What is not published can be more significant than what is published.

Accessing the Internet for information is an art in its own right and requires the collector to continually question its authenticity and reliability.

Internet sites appear, disappear, or have address changes without warning. Absent a specific web address, Internet search engines are efficient mechanisms to locate Internet resources.

Internet sites with either public or restricted access may provide raw data, analysis, links to other sources of information, or contact information to specialists in the area of interest.

Growing out of the original commercial and governmental oriented Internet websites is the posting of individual or group maintained websites known as weblogs or blogs. Those who post on blogs are known as bloggers. Bloggers may be either professional or amateur writers and write on every imaginable topic. There are some very good blogs offering original information and analysis, but it takes some effort to find them.

Amanda Lenhart, author of a PEW Research Center for the People and the Press survey on teen use of the Internet, states, "A social networking site is an online location where a user can create a profile and build a personal network that connects him or her to other users. In the past five years, such sites have rocketed from a niche activity into a phenomenon that engages tens of millions of internet users."

The January 2007 survey by PEW found that 55% of all online American youth between the ages of 12-17 use online social networking sites. The Internet social networking sites MySpace and Facebook, once the province of young adults and teenagers, are extremely popular.

Businesses, government, political parties, and other entities recognize that joining the newest iterations of the Internet allows an access to a larger and growing segment of the population. As an example, the California Department of Motor Vehicles has both a MySpace web site *http://www.myspace.com/californiadmv* and a traditional website *http://dmv.ca.gov/*.

The latest social networking phenomenon is Twitter, a cross between a Blog and instant messaging or text messaging. The Twitter website allows anyone to post an Internet message on *http://twitter.com/*, limited to 140 characters at a time, and the rest of the Internet world is allowed to select any Twitter poster and follow the postings at will.

See the Appendix III for a list of digital resources.

CONCLUSION

The collection and preservation of data, whether for the intended use as institutional knowledge or in either intelligence or a non-intelligence product, is governed by specific rules. The dangers to the freedom and liberties of a free country by the illegal obtaining and/or misuse of data are inestimable. Only the strictest adherence to laws protecting privacy will ensure that the law enforcement intelligence community serves the higher needs of society while at the same time battling the forces that would prey upon the wellbeing of that society.

REFERENCES

Basic Elements of Criminal Intelligence. (1990). Advanced Training Center, California Department of Justice.

Buccino, Bob. (1998). "The Collection of Information." *Issues of Interest to Law Enforcement: Intelligence-Criminal Intelligence A Vital Police Function.* Sacramento, CA Association of Law Enforcement Intelligence Units, February.

Carter, David L. (2004). *Law Enforcement Intelligence: A Guide for State, Local, and Tribal Law Enforcement Agencies.* Michigan State University.

Criminal Intelligence Program for the Smaller Agency (1998). Organized Crime Committee, California Peace Officers' Association.

"Instructor Guide." Foundations of Intelligence Analysis Training (FIAT). National White Collar Crime Center. Jan 2004.

Intelligence 2000: Revising the Basic Elements Law Enforcement Intelligence Unit and International Association of Law Enforcement Intelligence Analysts.

Krattenmaker, Jeffrey L. (1999). "A Model of Open Source Information." *Intelligence Models and Best Practices.* International Association of Law Enforcement Intelligence Analysis.

"LEIU Criminal Intelligence Unit Management Guidelines." Association of Law Enforcement Intelligence Units. Sacramento. July 2005.

Lenhart, Amanda. (2007). "Social Networking Websites and Teens: An Overview." PEW Internet & American Life Project. *<http://www.pewinternet.org/pdfs/PIP_SNS_Data_Memo_Jan_2007.pdf>*

Mindlin, Alex. (2008). "Letting Our Fingers Do the Talking" New York Times *<http://www.nytimes.com/2008/09/29/technology/29drill.html>*

Peterson, Marilyn B. (2003). "Strategic Analysis Workshop." Attorney General's Conference on Organized Crime.

"Protecting America's Freedom in the Information Age." Markle Foundation Task Force. October 2002.

Ray, Don. (1989). *A Public Records Primer and Investigator's Handbook.*

Stanley, Jay and Steinhardt, Barry. (2003). "Bigger Monster, Weaker Chains: The Growth of an American Surveillance Society." Information Awareness Office. American Civil Liberties Union. New York. January.

Sources of Information: Post Criminal Investigation. Chapman University. Orange CA.
Taplin, B. Clinton (1995) "Sources of Information in Developing Intelligence Assessments" *Issues of Interest to Law Enforcement: Intelligence-Into the 21ˢᵗ Century.* Sacramento, CA Association of Law Enforcement Intelligence Units, November

Weinberg, Steven (1996) *The Reporter's Handbook: An Investigator's Guide To Documents and Techniques.* St. Martins Press

Wright, Dick (1998) "Guidelines for the Criminal Intelligence Function" Simi Valley Police Department.

Collating and Evaluating Data
By Marilyn B. Peterson

INTRODUCTION

In the 1970s and early 1980s, criminal intelligence files of police departments were considered storehouses for criminals' names (Harris 1976:16). File cabinets housed index card after index card on which names and case numbers were shown—possibly cross-referenced to an alias and/or a type of criminal activity. The index card was the primary tool of the intelligence officer and analyst. These were shuffled and re-shuffled in an attempt to find the patterns and clues in the investigation.

Even in those days, good intelligence units had ways to measure and evaluate the reliability and validity of the data on those cards. Harris noted in 1976 "Without a **high quality (emphasis added)** store of readily retrievable information, meaningful analysis cannot take place (1976:16)."

Collating and evaluating the information that feeds the intelligence process are critical functions. This chapter provides an updated view of the standards that are used in these areas.

COLLATION

Collation was defined by Harris as information review, indexing, and filing (1976:16). Much of the discussion about collation of data in the earlier *Basic Elements* books covered the necessity of having a master name index and cross-indexing data (names to addresses, vehicles, phone numbers, criminal activity types, etc.). Today, that discussion is virtually pointless as most agencies have their data computerized and they are able to be searched and cross-indexed in a number of ways.

Of all the portions of the intelligence process, the most progress has been made in the collation of data. Where a few hundred records would have stymied any but the largest agencies 20 years ago, now agencies' computers routinely scan hundreds of thousands of records at a time. This means that agencies are able to tackle larger, more sophisticated cases than ever before.

Today, right-to-privacy concerns make it even more imperative that the information collected, stored, and used to create intelligence must meet the highest standards of relevancy. The cardinal rule is that information which has been collected, but cannot be verified (or at least supported by another source), should not be kept in the files for more than one year. The same holds true for unidentified subjects who have met the criteria for file entry. These files are sometimes referred to as "temporary files."

Information collected that does not meet file entry criteria (no criminal predicate) can be retained for a short period of time to ascertain if the subject(s) are criminally involved. The timeframe these files are kept will vary from agency to agency, but generally will be from 90 days to 1 year. These files are generally referred to as "working files." Information from these files should not be disseminated to outside agencies. These files should be actively worked.

Collation has been viewed as the sifting out of useless, non-relevant and incorrect information, and the orderly arrangement of the remaining information so relationships between apparently disconnected

Collating and Evaluating Data

elements can be established (California DOJ 1993:8). The key points in this statement are "orderly arrangement" and "relationships." Even though data is computerized, the format used for that computerization needs to be carefully planned so that the most effective way of arranging the data for its ease of retrievability and its analytic "massaging" is attained. However, in the new century, lines have blurred on what is relevant and what is not. For example, where one went to school or type of professional license one has obtained may have been considered irrelevant in the last century. But we now see that people gain associations and forge criminal relationships during a variety of contacts with others. Thus, we cannot dismiss, out of hand, associations that may be innocuous (or not).

Collation also reveals information gaps, guides further collection and analysis, and provides a framework for selecting and organizing additional information (Mathams 1995:85-86)." In today's environment, analysts are asked more often to provide ongoing direction to collectors regarding what should be collected. Requests for information are generated by analysts and sent to the collectors so they may fill gaps in their intelligence.

The organization of intelligence information is of critical importance. Data can be organized around specific categories, such as crime groups or networks (e.g., traditional organized crime or motorcycle gangs), criminal specialties (e.g., drug trafficking or loan sharking), modus operandi, or geographic territory (Schneider 1995:5). Through this categorization of data, patterns and trends may become more obvious. These patterns or trends should then be used to stimulate a more intensive data collection effort directed at an above-mentioned category that may raise a new set of questions that deserve further investigation (Martens 1987:133).

Examples of collation include "filing documents, condensing information (i.e., gisting) by categories, relationships and employing electronic databases to store, sort, and arrange large quantities or information....(Krizan 1999:26)." In some instances, it is of equal importance how something has been collated as this provides more or less ready access to the data by analysts and others who may want to use it.

INFORMATION REQUIREMENTS

Harris noted that "the flow of information is the lifeblood of the intelligence process (Harris 1976:9)." In order to determine how best to collate the data coming into an intelligence unit, determinations must be made regarding the criminal priorities of the agency and the purposes for which the data is be used.

If the agency is street-oriented, the bulk of the day-to-day requirements are for information to be used in tactical operations (Harris 1976:19). Most tactical information requests to an analytic unit will require a simple search of the data by name, other identifiers, etc. But if the agency is responsible for sophisticated criminal investigations, then inquiries may require the culling and analysis of data from diverse sources as agency files, centralized government sources (e.g., FinCEN), the Internet, regional databases (the Regional Information Sharing Systems), private sources (e.g., the Association of Law Enforcement Intelligence Units (LEIU)), etc. The "simple" request becomes a report of certain volume and weight as linkages and connections are tracked and highlighted.

At an even higher level, the requirements of the intelligence unit file system arise from requests for information by enforcement units of the department and other user agencies and for strategic analyses by the chief (Harris 1976:19).

The informational needs of the analysts in the intelligence unit are more demanding (Harris 1976:19). To be effective, the analysts must have access not only to agency files, but also to a broad range of research materials, commercial databases, the Internet, previous analytic assessments, and other materials. The analysts also need the appropriate computer hardware and software that will allow for the collation of those materials. This means that analysts become collectors in their own right. Thus, they must be able to apply evaluation standards to the data they find on the Internet and in other public record searches. In doing so, they should be aware of the possibility of hidden bias in all media. For example, if a photograph with an article is unflattering to the subject of the article, it is likely that it is a negative article (rather than an objective one).

STRUCTURING THE FILES

Selecting the best file structure depends on the needs of the unit. The filing system is the storage of data without which the intelligence function is meaningless (Harris 1976:20).

Criminal intelligence files are defined by the California Department of Justice as follows:

A criminal intelligence file consists of stored information on the activities and associations of individuals and groups known or suspected to be involved in criminal acts or in the threatening, planning, organizing, or financing of criminal acts. More specifically, this information relates to:

A. Individuals who:

- Are currently involved in or suspected of being involved in the planning, organizing, financing, or commission of criminal activities; or who are suspected of having threatened, attempted, planned, or performed criminal acts; or

- Have an established association with known or suspected crime figures

B. Organizations and businesses which:

- Are currently involved in or suspected of being involved in the planning, organizing, financing, or commission of criminal activities; or which have threatened, attempted, planned, or performed criminal acts; or

- Are operated, controlled, financed, infiltrated, or illegally used by crime figures (National Committee on Criminal Justice Standards and Goals 1976:130)

PERMANENT, TEMPORARY, AND WORKING FILES

Permanent files may include individuals, groups, businesses, and organizations which have been positively identified by one or more distinguishing characteristics and criminal involvement and the crime is mission-related. The retention period is five years, after which the information is evaluated for its file acceptability (Arizona DPS 1995:57-4).

Temporary files may include individuals, groups, businesses, and organizations which have not been positively identified by one or more distinguishing characteristics, or whose criminal involvement is questionable. They are given temporary file status when the subject is unidentifiable because there are no identification numbers or descriptors available and their involvement in a criminal group is questionable and the reliability of the source or validity of the information is not able to be determined, but the information appears to be significant and to warrant storage. This information is kept for one year without corroboration and is then purged and destroyed (Arizona DPS 1995:57-4 &5).

LEIU File Guidelines describe "temporary files" as information that does not meet the criteria for permanent storage, but may be pertinent to an investigation involving one of the categories listed below should be given "temporary" status. It is recommended the retention of temporary information not exceed one year unless a compelling reason exists to extend this time period. An example of a compelling reason is if several pieces of information indicate that a crime has been committed, but more than a year is needed to identify a suspect. During this period, efforts should be made to identify the subject/entity or validate the information so that its final status may be determined. If the information is still classified temporary at the end of the one year period, and a compelling reason for its retention is not evident, the information should be purged. An individual, organization, business, or group may be given temporary status in the following cases:

- **Subject/entity is Unidentifiable** - Subject/entity (although suspected of being engaged in criminal activities) has no known physical descriptors, identification numbers, or distinguishing characteristics available

- **Involvement is Questionable** - Involvement in criminal activities is suspected by a subject/entity which has either:

    o **Possible Criminal Associations** - Individual, organization, business, or group (not currently reported to be criminally active) associates with a known criminal and appears to be jointly involved in illegal activities

    o **Criminal History** - Individual, organization, business, or group (not currently reported to be criminally active) that has a history of criminal conduct, and the circumstances currently being reported (i.e., new position or ownership in a business) indicates they may again become criminally active

- **Reliability/Validity Unknown** - The reliability of the information sources and/or the validity of the information cannot be determined at the time of receipt; however, the information appears to be significant and merits temporary storage while verification attempts are made (LEIU File Guidelines Revised November 2008:4)

Working files consist of copies of reports, copies of enclosures, notes and other documents which are used as investigative tools during investigative/criminal intelligence inquiries. Although they are considered official files, these files should not be disseminated to outside agencies or individuals unless a criminal predicate can be established. The working file is the receiving point of newly acquired raw data. The retention will vary from agency to agency but generally will be from 90 days to 1 year. Noted exceptions may include pen register operations, wire interceptions, and telephone toll analysis data.

FILE ROOM PROCEDURES AND OPERATIONS

Too often a casual attitude toward filing procedures results in poor organization and breaches of file security as well as inadequate facilities and understaffing. On the other hand, if filing procedures are too tightly controlled, the file room becomes little more than a resting place for carefully kept, but seldom used records (Harris 1976:16).

Certain elements are necessary to a successful criminal intelligence unit filing system:

- Guidelines and specifically assigned responsibility for determining the kinds of information that shall be kept in the files, the method of reviewing the material for continued usefulness and relevance, and the method of disposing of material purged from the files considered to be no longer useful or relevant

- A systematic flow of pertinent and reliable information

- A uniform procedure for evaluating, cross-indexing, and storing information

- A system capable of rapid and efficient retrieval of all information

- Explicit guidelines for disseminating information from the files

- Security procedures (Harris 1976:16)

Harris further noted that the criminal intelligence unit, even more than other police units, must be scrupulous in collecting, storing, and disseminating information to avoid violation of the right to privacy (1976:16). The law enforcement accreditation group also presents a standard relative to keeping intelligence data:

"51.1.2 A written directive governs procedures for the safeguarding of intelligence information and the secure storage of intelligence records separate from all other records." (CALEA 1999:51-2)

Incoming information needs to be reviewed by the unit supervisor to be sure it relates to the intelligence unit's targeted crime areas. If the document does not relate to the crime areas and did not originate from a regional office it should be either destroyed or forwarded to an appropriate bureau. After approval by the supervisor, criminal intelligence specialists are responsible for preparing the document for indexing, storage, and retrieval (California DOJ 1993:22).

A system for routine purging of the files according to fixed guidelines will further ensure reliable data collection and retention. Reviewing and purging files should be done on a systematic time schedule, according to established guidelines, and under the supervision of the intelligence unit commander or designated senior personnel (Harris1976:16).

The Criminal Intelligence System Operating Policies (28 CFR 23.20) provide the following guideline for review and purge of intelligence information:

"(h) All projects shall adopt procedures ... (which) shall provide for the periodic review of information and the destruction of any information which is misleading, obsolete or otherwise unreliable and shall require that any recipient agencies be advised of such changes which involve errors or corrections. All information retained as a result of this review must reflect the name of the reviewer, date of the review, and explanation of decision to retain. Information retained in the system must be reviewed and validated for continuing compliance with system submission criteria before the expiration of its retention period, which in no event shall be longer than five years (www.iir.com/Publications/28cfr23.htm)."

A final consideration in a criminal intelligence system is audit trailing. It is critical to have logs generated—automatically or manually—regarding who has accessed what piece of data and when. An audit trail will allow the system owner to not only check for security reasons, but also to advise those who have accessed a piece of data if there is a change in the data.

The Criminal Intelligence System Operating Policies note that "A project maintaining criminal intelligence information shall ensure that administrative, technical, and physical safeguards (including audit trails) are adopted to insure against unauthorized access and against intentional or unintentional damage." (28 CFR 23.20(h))

INFORMATION EVALUATION

The data is evaluated because, in the world of criminal intelligence, not all data is created equal. Information received from an informant should not carry the same weight or reliability as that received from another agency's police file. Sworn statements are generally considered more reliable than those spoken in casual interviews. "Official" records might be considered more reliable than spoken information.

The Commission on Accreditation for Law Enforcement Agencies (CALEA) notes in its Criminal Intelligence standard that:

"If an agency performs an intelligence function, procedures must be established to ensure the legality and integrity of its operations to include:

- Procedures for ensuring information collected is limited to criminal conduct and relates to activities that present a threat to the community

- Descriptions of the types or quality of information that may be included in the system

- Methods for purging out-of-date or incorrect information

- Procedures for the utilization of intelligence personnel and techniques." (CALEA 1999:51-1)

Those in the criminal intelligence field understand the requirement for evaluating data, however, it must be restated here for those who may be coming into the field and are not aware of its importance. Following are some of the key components to data evaluation and reliability. This compendium of evaluation requirements are taken from standard intelligence system policies, such as LEIU and 28 *Code of Federal Regulations* 23, both of which are seen in their entirety in Appendix I.

AXIOMS OF DATA EVALUATION

Seven axioms for data evaluation have been developed. They are each seen below, along with their codification references and some explanations.

1. **Data Must Be Relevant** - Before information goes into a criminal intelligence system, it should be reviewed to see what specific relevancy it has to the suspected criminal activity at hand. (28 *CFR* 23.20(a)) For example, an individual known to be involved in criminal activity may perform a number of non-criminal actions and have certain non-criminal associations. Information relating to those activities and associations should not be included in a criminal intelligence system. It should be noted that in some situations, associations that appear non-criminal on the surface may, in fact, be facilitating criminality. These potentially criminal associations should not be ignored. Further research is required to determine the exact nature of the associations.

2. **Data Must Be Reliable** - An understanding of the reliability of information is also essential to protect the privacy of individuals. The criminal intelligence unit must be wary of circulating information of doubtful validity. However, if the material must be circulated, the criminal intelligence unit must state its reservations clearly in the report. An example of the need for care in handling such material is an allegation received regarding criminal acts of politicians or civil servants. Such reports must be treated with special care because they may have been made for political reasons (Harris 1976:23).

    Typically, a four-category reliability system is used, rating the source of the information. Harris illustrated four-categories in 1976 as are seen below:

SOURCE	RATING
1. Law Enforcement Officer	A
2. Source known and reliable in past	B
3. Source known, but not always reliable	C
4. Reliability of source unknown (Harris 1976:23)	D

A four-category system is also used by the Association of Law Enforcement Intelligence Units and the California Department of Justice. The differences are found in the definitions:

Reliable – Source's reliability is unquestioned or has been well-tested in the past.	A
Usually Reliable – Source's reliability can usually be relied upon as factual. The majority of past information has proven to be reliable.	B
Unreliable – Source's reliability as been sporadic.	C
Unknown – Source's reliability cannot be judged. Authenticity or trustworthiness has not been determined by either experience or investigation. (California DOJ 1993:9)	D

3. **Data Must Be Valid** - The information contained in the system must be as valid as possible. Thus, reports must be graded for validity as well as reliability. Similar to the previous categories, there are four generally accepted grades of validity:

REPORT CONTENT	VALIDITY
Factual	1
Probably True	2
Possibly True	3
Factuality Unknown	4

In this instance, Harris used only three categories in 1976; LEIU now uses four. The missing category in Harris is "possibly true." (Harris 1976:23) The California Department of Justice definitions for those categories are seen below:

Confirmed – The information has been corroborated.	1
Probable – The information is consistent with past accounts.	2
Doubtful – The information is inconsistent with past accounts.	3
Cannot be Judged – The information cannot be evaluated (1993:10)	4

1. **Data Must Not Include Information On Group Membership Unless It Is Relevant To The Criminal Activity** - Criminal intelligence information should not be collected or maintained "about the political, religious, or social views, associations, or activities of any individual or any group, association, corporation, business, partnership, or other organization unless such information directly relates to the criminal conduct or activity or there is reasonable suspicion that the subject of the information is or may be involved in criminal conduct or activity." (28 CFR 23.20(b)) Thus, only if the group is engaged in criminal activity or is being used as a front for criminal activity should it be included.

2. **Data Must Only Be Included On Those Reasonably Suspected Of Being Involved In Criminal Activity** - Federal intelligence guidelines state that data shall only be collected

and maintained on an individual only if there is "reasonable suspicion that the individual is involved in criminal conduct or activity (28 CFR 23.20(a))." That reasonable suspicion is established "when information exists which establishes sufficient facts to give a trained law enforcement or criminal investigative agency officer, investigator, or employee a basis to believe there is a reasonable possibility that an individual or organization is involved in a definable criminal activity or enterprise (28 CFR 23.20(c))."

LEIU guidelines limit inclusion to individuals, organizations, businesses, and groups that are suspected of being or having been involved in the actual or attempted planning, organizing, financing, or commission of criminal acts; are suspected of being or having been involved in criminal activities with known or suspected crime figures, or are suspected of being or having been illegally operated, controlled, financed, or infiltrated by known or suspected crime figures (LEIU 1999:1).

3. **Data Must Not Be Gathered Illegally** - No information which has been obtained in violation of any applicable federal, state, or local law or ordinance may be maintained (28 CFR 23.20(d)). In most cases, it is the responsibility of the owner of the intelligence system to insure that the data being submitted is not in violation of this provision. The owners of the intelligence system can do this through having submitters affirm that the data is legal and/or through periodic review and audit of submitters' files.

4. **Data Should Be Graded For Sensitivity Levels** - The need to mark information to indicate its sensitivity is often overlooked in intelligence systems. While most intelligence units tend to be overcautious in "holding closely" material from a sensitive source, the report is not necessarily marked in any way to inform future readers. Moreover, the sensitivity of information relates to both its source and its content. For example, information that could only have come from a source close to the inner circle of a criminal group would be sensitive because, should any group member learn that the police possessed the information, the informant could be identified. At the same time, information on the groups might indicate that they were engaged in certain activities which, were the initial information to leak, could cancel the future enforcement action against this group of criminals (Harris 1976:22).

Defining degrees of sensitivity is sometimes difficult. In large measure, this difficulty is because all information that enters the intelligence system is considered confidential. Thus, ordination information in the system may be classified as either "confidential" or "sensitive," meaning it must be controlled by the unit commander and not circulated through normal channels. This confidentiality is necessary to protect the integrity of the system (Harris 1976:22-23).

Harris suggested two sensitivity levels for data: Sensitive (SS) and Confidential (SC). Sensitive information must be closely held to avoid jeopardizing the source or the initiation of an important investigation. The material should be stamped as sensitive and stored in a locked file under direct control of the unit commander or his/her designee. (Harris 1976:23) Confidential information may be circulated in and outside of the department to law enforcement officers with a need and right to know (see Chapter 10 "Report Writing Principles"). Standard procedures for handling this other data should be established by the unit commander and approved by the chief of the department (Harris 1976:23).

The International Association of Chiefs of Police (IACP) intelligence policy includes three levels of sensitivity: restricted, confidential, and unclassified. "Restricted" intelligence files are those that could adversely affect an ongoing investigation, create safety hazards for officers, informants or others and/or compromise their identities. "Confidential" intelligence is less sensitive, while "unclassified" intelligence contains information from public sources." (IACP 1998:3)

DATABASES

Databases are the primary building blocks to the criminal intelligence system. Godfrey and Harris used several paragraphs describing the varied indexes (1971 and 1976) that could be kept (name, alias, criminal activity, vehicle, location, etc.), but in today's environment, databases and computer programs are discussed instead. A section on computerized databases is found in Chapter 16.

For the purpose of this chapter on collation and evaluation, it is sufficient to say that appropriately constructed databases are the key to maintaining a criminal intelligence system that is in compliance with regulations and guidelines, allows data to be easily retrieved, supports analysis, and allows for the automatic audit trailing of access to and dissemination from its files.

It is also important to remember, when building a database, it is only as good as the data entered. Certain procedures for data entry, including standardized entry (use and placement of name variations, etc.) must be determined so that retrievability can be accurate. Additionally, a 'quality control' mechanism for checking data that has been entered for accuracy is also encouraged.

REFERENCES

Arizona Department of Public Safety. (1995). Policy Fifty-Seven – Criminal Intelligence Phoenix, AZ: Arizona Department of Public Safety.

Bureau of Justice Assistance. (1993). "Criminal Intelligence Systems Operating Policies" *28 Code of Federal Regulations*. Part 23.20. >www.iir.com/Publications/23cfr.htm<

California Department of Justice (1993). The *Bureau of Intelligence Operations Manual*. Sacramento, CA: California Department of Justice.

Commission on Accreditation for Law Enforcement Agencies, Inc. *Standards for Law Enforcement Agencies, Fourth Edition.* Fairfax, VA: Commission on Accreditation for Law Enforcement Agencies, Inc.

Harris, Don R. (1976). *Basic Elements of Intelligence.* Washington, DC: Law Enforcement Assistance Administration.

International Association of Chiefs of Police. (1998). *Criminal Intelligence Model Policy.* Alexandria, VA: International Association of Chiefs of Police.

-------------- (1985). *Law Enforcement Policy on the Management of Criminal Intelligence.* Gaithersburg, VA: International Association of Chiefs of Police.

Krizan, Lisa. (1999). *Intelligence Essentials for Everyone.* Washington, DC: Joint Military Intelligence College.

Mathams, R.H. (1995). "The Intelligence Analysts' Notebook*". Strategic Intelligence: Theory and Applications.* Douglas H. Dearth and Thomas Goodden. 2nd ed. Washington, DC: Joint Military Intelligence Training Center.

Martens, Frederick T. (1987). "The Intelligence Function". *Major Issues in Organized Crime Control.* Herbert Edelhertz. ed. Washington, DC: U.S. Department of Justice.

National Committee on Criminal Justice Standards and Goals. (1976). *Report of the Task Force on Organized Crime.* Washington, DC: Government Printing Office.

Schneider, Stephen. (1995). "The Criminal Intelligence Function: Toward a Comprehensive and Normative Model. IALEIA. *Journal,* Vol. 9, No. 2. June.

Analysis and Synthesis
By Marilyn B. Peterson

INTRODUCTION

Godfrey and Harris called analysis "the heart of the intelligence process." (1971: 4) They stated that without it, the intelligence function was merely a set of files. What they meant was that information is just information, but *analyzed* information is intelligence. While 'intelligence' on the national security side has been defined as information that has been gathered by clandestine means, Lowenthal corrected that misunderstanding in the community by stating that intelligence was, in fact, processed information, rather than raw data (2006:1-2) and did not have to be secret to be intelligence.

The "analysis" portion of the intelligence process is comprised of four sub-sections: problem statement or issue development, analysis, synthesis, and conclusions/recommendations. The problem statement or issue development portion of analysis is often assumed to automatically occur, but requires some thought. It is the most critical state as, without it, the wrong issue may be addressed (Directorate of Intelligence 2008:5). In the analysis portion, the data are reviewed individually, in comparison or in contrast to one another, to gain a greater understanding for their meaning. In the synthesis portion, the data are reformulated into a coherent whole that can be understood by the audience. The conclusions are derived from this synthesis of the facts and the recommendations are based on the conclusions and the facts. In each of these areas, techniques have been adapted or developed to deal with the data.

Heuer noted that "Analysts sometimes describe their work procedure as immersing themselves in the data without fitting the data into any preconceived pattern." (1999:40) Others might say that they let the data 'speak' to them and tell them how it must be arranged. Either way, analysis is a journey of discovery.

This chapter looks at analysis: its role, underlying analytic skills and traits, analysts' duties, critical thinking, types of analysis and standards for analysis and analysts. It is not meant to guide the reader through doing a particular analysis, but rather to make the audience aware of what analysis is and what it can do.

THE ROLE OF ANALYSIS

Analysis is used in law enforcement investigation and intelligence sections. During investigations, evidence (information) is gathered and reviewed to reconstruct the crime. Analysis is the logical thought process that is applied to the data (Harris 1976:27). Within intelligence sections, analysis is used to complete tactical and strategic assessments of the threat posed by varied criminal actors or activities. It is also used to develop target packages to initiate investigations.

A case should begin by establishing the information needed and planning how to obtain it; by asking questions or by executing a search warrant, for example. At the same time, ideas or hypotheses should be constantly developed about who committed the crime and how it was committed. Such hypotheses are the basic tools of the intelligence process as well (Harris 1976:27). This collection planning and analytic approach to investigations places analysts in the role of information or case managers. Indeed, the preference in criminal intelligence would be to collect information regarding criminal organizations that pose a threat and develop a preventative approach to negating their impact.

In 1976, analysis was "that activity whereby meaning, actual or suggested, is derived through organizing and systematically examining diverse information" (Harris 1976:30). The three steps to completing analysis were shown as: summarizing the relevant information, comparing the summary with expectations derived from an initial hypothesis, and explaining the results of this comparison (Anderson and Zeldidch, quoted in Harris 1976:30).

Today, we view analysis as a process which begins with identifying a problem or violation developing alternate hypotheses as to what may have occurred or will occur, summarizing and analyzing what information is held, and detailing what additional data (evidence) is needed; repeating those steps until the hypothesis is proven (or disproven), the problem is solved, or the investigation is concluded.

Analysis is the key to giving information direction and meaning, or uncovering its meaning. This is not always an easy task. For example, new criminals or criminal activities may not fit known, normal patterns (Harris 1976:30). Indeed, if we contrast the current criminal environment with that of 20 or 30 years ago, a prime difference is the emergence of many crime groups committing many crimes.

The distinctions between analysis and other phases of the intelligence process are not absolute. For example, an intelligence report is the direct result of the analysis of a particular body of information. However, the same report can also indicate (or state) a requirement for information which leads to a collection activity. Thus, it may seem part of the planning process. Similarly, the difference between analysis and collation is not always distinct. Collation (placing data into formats to assist in their analysis) and analysis are often performed simultaneously.

The role of analysis varies from department to department. In some, cases are opened and immediately assigned to analysts to query databases, make summaries of known facts, and develop investigative plans for investigators to follow. These might be termed "analysis-driven investigations." In other agencies, analysts provide strategic assessments of unfolding and/or anticipated problems which give direction to policy and management. These might be termed "analysis/intelligence-driven agencies." In still others, analysis is used only after investigators have gathered substantial amounts of data and the analysts are used to review that data and pass leads back to the investigation. These might be termed "analysis-supported investigations." Some agencies use analysts only for charts and graphs (although it is generally accepted that this approach is not really analysis—without the corresponding hypotheses and conclusions. Others have analysis done to support "expert testimony" in court. Perhaps because of this diversity and the underlying skills it represents, analysis has become a critical part of most major law enforcement not only in the United States but in Europe, Canada, Australia, and other jurisdictions. What is clear is that agencies that use analysis the most get the greatest return from it.

One model of overall analytic assignment is seen in the figure on page 92.

UNDERLYING ANALYTIC SKILLS

Although there is a broad range of analytic techniques and products that reflect analysis, these have certain underlying skills as their basis. There are a handful of skills which underpin the analytic process. They include logical thought processes, research, and writing skills, computer literacy, and visualization skills (IALEIA 1997:6) as well as thinking critically. Analytic traits include persistence, independent work habits, flexibility, and willingness to make judgments (IALEIA 1997:6). Other intellectual traits that have been suggested include integrity, accuracy, clarity, precision, depth, breadth, logic, significance, and relevance (Paul and Elder 2006: 7). The United States Office of the Director of National Intelligence (ODNI) has developed analytic competencies including:

- objectivity
- independence of political considerations
- timeliness
- all-source intelligence basis tradecraft standards indicating that the analytic product properly:
  o describes quality and reliability of underlying sources
  o caveats and expresses uncertainties or confidence in analytic judgments
  o distinguishes between underlying intelligence and analysts' assumptions and judgments
  o incorporates alternative analysis where appropriate
  o demonstrates the relevance of the product to U.S. national security
  o uses logical argumentation
  o exhibits consistency of analysis over time, or highlights changes and explains rationale
  o makes accurate judgments and assessments (ODNI 2007)

Logical Thought Processes

The ability to think logically, see trends, and forecast a possible future is critical to an analyst. Conversely, those who cannot organize data and "learn" from them will not excel in analysis. Logical thinking may come easier to some than others, but it can be taught. Sharpening one's logic skills can take place through puzzling through clues in literature or in puzzle books, as well as through more intellectual pursuits. Logical argumentation is a key ingredient to not only analysis but to writing and speaking well (Govier 2005).

Critical Thinking

Critical thinking is thinking about what is being read, or written, or thought (Paul and Elder 2006). In many cases, people perform their jobs unthinkingly—that is, taking the same approach to different problems—and then wonder why the problems are not solved.

Godfrey and Harris said that the intelligence process is "sometimes physical but always intellectual." (1971:2) What they meant by that is that the thought process always needs to be applied to the data, whether it has been gone out and retrieved or it has been on hand all the while. It is just this thinking process that is being spoken of when 'critical thinking' is mentioned.

There are varied approaches to critical thinking. One, from the Critical Thinking Foundation (**www.criticalthinking.org**) suggests that eight questions be asked of the data at hand:

1. What is the point of view of the writer?
2. What is the purpose of the writing?
3. What are the key questions in what has been written?
4. What are the assumptions underlying the writing?
5. What concepts underlie the writing?

6. What evidence is provided to support the inferences drawn?
7. What inferences are drawn?
8. What are the implications that follow the inferences drawn? (Paul & Elder 2006:28)

Another, from Browne and Keeley, says we should ask:

1. What are the issues and the conclusions?
2. What are the reasons?
3. Which words or phrases are ambiguous?
4. What are the value conflicts and assumptions?
5. What are the descriptive assumptions?
6. Are there any fallacies in the reasoning?
7. How good is the evidence?
8. Are there rival causes?
9. Are the statistics deceptive?
10. What significant information is omitted?
11. What reasonable conclusions are possible? (Browne and Keeley 2007:13)

Applying critical thinking to a situation makes one look at it from other perspectives. Other possible explanations could also exist. Interpreting the data without looking at all the possibilities may cause an inaccurate analysis. Inaccurate analysis of a situation can be a fatal mistake.

Communication Skills

The ability to communicate in writing or orally is key to producing understandable analytic products. Intelligence is worthless if it is not shared with others. It may be easy to explain a complex case to those closest to it; analysts must be able to explain it simply to those who know nothing of it.

 Good writing is 65 percent good organization and 35 percent concise and clear writing. Analysts are required to read and assimilate data from a variety of sources, summarizing them as needed. This is part of every analyst's day. The same is true of oral briefings, although presentation skills are added in there as well. (See Chapter 10 "Report Writing Principles")

POSSIBLE ANALYTIC BUREAU ASSIGNMENTS

Support to Decision-Making - The bureau shall develop products and briefings in support of decision making by mid and upper-level managers and executives. These will include alternative outcomes and recommendations that are well-supported and timely.

Strategic Targeting - The bureau shall identify indicators of criminal activity and criminal capabilities to recommend targeting particular individuals and crime groups for investigation and prosecution. This will include the development of threat assessments and premonitories.

Investigative Planning - The bureau shall work with attorneys and investigators to develop investigative plans at the initiation of an investigation. The bureau's participation in the process will include a preliminary summary of all known data (including materials gleaned from public, government and commercial databases) a listing of leads that could be fruitful to follow and a preliminary assessment of the viability of the investigation.

Supporting Investigations - The bureau shall assign an appropriate analyst to each priority investigation including:

- Developing Computerized Databases to Assist in Compiling Case Data
- Link Analysis
- Telephone Record Analysis
- Financial Analysis
- Flow Analysis
- Business Record Analysis
- Specialized Record Analysis
- Summary and Expert Testimony

Analysts may also be assigned to joint investigations with other state, county, or federal agencies as requested.

Training - The bureau shall provide analytic and related training through the academy and other locations as requested. To support the use of analysis in the agency, every professional employee should have at least a one-day seminar on analysis.

Liaison - The bureau shall pursue opportunities to collaborate and coordinate with analysts in other law enforcement organizations through formal or informal groups, conferences, and outside training sessions. Liaison to the academic community should also be affected.

Special Projects - The bureau will help identify the need for and parameters of data mining to provide early detection and crime prevention systems. Analytic support software testing may also be done by the section as needed. Other special projects may include the development of resource manuals for the department.

CHAPTER 8

Analysis and Synthesis

Computer Literacy

It is difficult to do analysis in today's environment without using the computer. Whether the analyst is searching for public information over the Internet; preparing a written report in a word processing program; using a shelf-software spreadsheet or database to compile data; using a data mining, or visualization, or mapping program, computers are the fourth-most important skill for law enforcement analysis.

While most colleges and universities today require computer literacy for graduation, applicants are still arriving at law enforcement agencies without understanding of the concepts of relational databases, geo-coding, and other important computer activities. Computer literacy should be a 'must' for analysts.

Visualization Skills

Turning data into a visual can be integral to having people understand the data. For some, analysis is viewed as a set of visual depictions, although analysts know that this is only one product of the analytic process. Visuals allow us to gain new insights into the data and the analysis of the visual can further our quest for well-supported inferences.

Charting allows a clear view of a group, transaction, or process. The simplicity of the chart is often a product of the analysts' complete understanding of the data such that it can be reduced to only the visual elements necessary to explain the data. This involves not only an ability to create visuals, but the use of analytic judgment to determine what is important and what can be omitted. While visualization software has become commonplace in the analytic field and is an excellent tool, the analyst still needs to exercise judgment in using that tool to construct visualizations.

Analytic Traits

There are also some key traits which analysts should have to be the best analysts. Stated above, more detail on each is shown here.

- **Independent Work Habits** - Analysts need to be able to work independently without constant supervision. They must be self-motivating and self-determining; that is, they need to see a problem and figure out how to deal with it. This is particularly true in smaller departments where supervisors have no experience with analysis. In these cases, the analyst must make their job and make themselves indispensable to the supervisor.

- **Flexibility** - Analysts need to be able to move with change. Analysts often function at the 'cutting edge' of law enforcement. Thus, they must be able to adapt themselves to changes around them while being a catalyst for change themselves.

- **Persistence** - Analysts must be persistent in their efforts to pursue leads and work as an agent of change. In the criminal world, perpetrators count on investigators giving up before catching them. Persistence is what allows us to complete our goals when they seem unreachable.

- **Willingness to Make Judgments** - Analysts must take stands about their conclusions as the 'experts' on the data they have researched and analyzed. While previous use of analysts may have asked them to limit their comments to factual reporting, today managers need informed input to their decision-making from analysts. The inability (or unwillingness) to come to a conclusion about the data does not serve the analytic process or the law enforcement agency.

Paul and Elder's Intellectual Traits (2006) can also be applied to analysts:

- **Integrity** – Analysts need to be able to stand up for what they believe to be true and to defend their judgments to peers and supervisors. They should be aware of the other influences on decision-makers but should not allow themselves to be influenced.

- **Accuracy** – Above all, analytic products must be accurate and analysts must do everything possible to ensure their accuracy.

- **Clarity** – Analysts must strive to make their products as clear as possible.

- **Precision** – Analysts should be precise in their products and communications. This involves a level of specificity in addition to accuracy.

- **Depth** – Analysts should take a deep view of the issue they are analyzing. This incorporates looking at all facets of the issue before them.

- **Breadth** – Analysts must look at the context of their issue, taking into consideration the environment in which the issue occurs, not just the issue itself.

- **Logic** - Analysts should present their thoughts in a logical sequence that allows the person to whom those thoughts are presented is able to follow the argument from start to conclusion.

- **Significance** – Analysts should address issues that have significance for their audience such that the audience grasps the import of the issue and the value of the analysis.

- **Relevance** – The analyst should view all data that are relevant to the issue at hand, taking care to view both pro and con data relating to the issue.

A longer listing of "core competencies" for analysts was prepared by the Federal Bureau of Investigation and is seen in Chapter 3 "Staffing the Intelligence Unit."

DUTIES OF THE INTELLIGENCE ANALYST

Harris stated that it is the analyst's responsibility to review reports, daily newspapers, and other periodicals, to indicate how the report should be indexed and prepare abstracts of longer reports (1976:28). He also said that analysts should develop and maintain lists of names, sources of information, association charts, tentative hypotheses, operating assumptions that help him/her keep up to date on trends and new developments in his/her area of responsibility. The analyst was also responsible for identifying information requirements, performing research and analysis, and preparing intelligence reports (Harris 1976:29).

CHAPTER 8

Analysis and Synthesis

Overall, the activities of an intelligence analyst are as diverse as the number and types of agencies which use them. Analysts work for intelligence, investigative, and regulatory agencies. They also work in the private sector in law firms, in investigative sections of consulting firms, or in an anti-fraud, security, or political risk capacity.

In the past, the investigator provided the analyst with raw information while the analyst processed the raw information and developed suggested avenues of approach to the investigator. The analyst looked beyond specific cases to ascertain the similarities and differences among many different cases (Harris 1976:30). Today, the analyst has a world of information, through on-line commercial databases and other Internet resources, at his or her fingertips. Analysts can do a significant amount of research themselves, without having to leave their desks.

Today's analyst is responsible for performing a wide variety of tasks relating to the processing of new and existing information. These duties may include tactical, operational and strategic analysis products, database design, responding to requests for information, Internet and database research, and other support to investigations and policy making.

It is important to remember that the role of analysts is not as in-house graphic artists. Analytic charts and graphs are not pictures to be drawn as a graphic artist might draw them. Analytic charts and graphs are products of a thorough analysis of a data set and represent an accurate and clear analytic portrayal of data according to generally accepted analytic standards. Thus, it is unwise to ask an analyst to put a chart together without his/her thorough review of the facts.

Key duties for an analyst in an intelligence unit are:

- Developing Collection Plans
- Performing Research
- Completing Strategic Analysis
- Remaining Current in their Area of Specialty
- Preparing Reports
- Recommending Legislative Change

More advanced analysts would probably be more involved in strategic analysis, training and investigative planning, while the newer analyst might be more involved in tactical products and reports. Specialist analysts with more thorough computer backgrounds would be more involved in creating databases in support of analysis.

ANALYTIC TECHNIQUES

In carrying out the general functions of analysis in the intelligence process discussed above, the analyst can expect to be called upon to bring some specialized techniques to bear on the problem (Harris 1976:30).

The comparison of data is the critical step in analysis since, through this activity, meaning is derived. The data the analyst has organized and summarized are compared to a set of expectations derived from an initial hypothesis. In addition to imposing a general structure on the analysis, the hypothesis is the source of criteria that determines the significance of observed data. In this stage, statistics may be used. Similarities or regularities in geographic distribution might also be observed. During this step, analysts should always be aware of the differences among the data under examination (Harris 1976:30).

In the comparison step the analyst asks what is significant. The analyst should determine:

- Whether the data exhibit significant relationships
- The meaning of the relationships or lack of them in terms of the purpose of the analysis
- The larger meaning of these findings in terms of intelligence unit
- Larger meaning from the findings
- Requirements for additional information or further analysis (Harris 1976:31)

In the past, three general types of analysis were detailed but the distinctions among them have been viewed by some as arbitrary. However, the audience for the analytic products may be the easiest way to differentiate among the analysis done in law enforcement. The types are: crime analysis, investigative analysis, and strategic analysis (Sommers 1986: 26). Crime analysis is done most often for a local or county police agency and looks at criminal incidents or crime statistics to determine ways to prevent or deter future crime or identify and arrest its perpetrator(s). Thus, its audience is often patrol management.

Investigative analysis is done for all levels of government and focuses on a particular violation or crime, seeking to provide products that will assist in the violator's arrest and successful prosecution. Thus, the audience for this type of analysis is detective supervisors and attorneys. Strategic analysis looks at overviews of crime groups or criminal activities and seeks to measure the threat that those groups and activities pose to the jurisdiction, now and in the future. Recommendations are made to lessen that threat, often through policy changes. Its audience is police management. This is not to say that crime analysis data might not be used to recommend policy changes, or that investigative analysis products might not assist in crime reduction. All these are possible. In many small agencies, analysts are full-service analysts and carry the burden of whatever analysis is needed, regardless of its "type."

It is also important to differentiate between an analytic technique and an analytic product. For example, a link analysis might include a link chart, a set of biographic data on the subjects of the chart, a summary of known data, conclusions, and recommendations. The link chart is just one product of the process of link analysis, not an end to itself.

Heuer provides further insight into what we know about intelligence analysis by devising taxonomy of analytic types. He stated that there are four general categories of methods used in intelligence analysis:

1. Quantitative methods using empirical data (in law enforcement, an example might be analyzing telephone call data)

2. Quantitative methods using expert-generated data (analysis using models that others have generated based on research)

3. Unaided judgment (individual analytic intuition)

4. Structured analysis (step-by-step accepted processes used to analyze data) (Heuer 2008:4)

Analysis and Synthesis

Below is a listing of over two dozen basic types of analysis that have been used in law enforcement. It should be noted that there a several dozen more types of analytic products that are not included here. Heuer's latest work may include over 50 (Heuer 2008:6).

Activity Flow Analysis

Activity flow analysis is used to provide a generic view of a set of criminal actions, or modus operandi to determine what the key actions were and provide an overview of a crime. It looks at the process of an activity and can then assemble to necessary components of the crime to explain a complex crime simply. This activity flow analysis process can also be used to compare to other crimes, to see if there may be a connection between them.

Analysis of Competing Hypotheses (ACH)

This technique, developed by Richards Heuer in the 1980s, allows analysts to look at different potential hypotheses and compare them to the evidence gathered to determine the least unlikely hypothesis. It provides a means by which analysts can test their hypotheses against that which is known (Heuer 1999).

Association Analysis

Association, or link, or network analysis looks at the relationships among individuals, businesses, locations, groups, and other entities involved in a crime and how those relationships impact on, or are impacted by, the criminal activity. It is also called network or link analysis. The products of an association analysis may include charts, biographical profiles, chart summaries, conclusions and recommendations for further action (IALEIA:1996:3).

Bank Record Analysis

Bank record analysis encompasses any review or analysis of bank records for any purpose (Peterson 1998:8). It provides not only a review of activity in an account or set of accounts, but also looks at why the payments were made or received and what indicators of illegal activity may be present.

Bank Secrecy Act Data Analysis

Bank Secrecy Act data include Currency Transaction (CTR) and Suspicious Activity Reports (SAR) generated in compliance with a country's anti-money laundering or counter threat finance regulations. Analyzing this data allows the analyst to track illegal gains or funds used to support criminality from its source to its eventual destination (Peterson 2002).

Business Record Analysis

Business record analysis is the review of varied business records to compare and contrast them and look for inconsistencies in the records or for other indications of criminal activity. Business records may be generic (e.g., journals, ledgers, invoices, orders, tax filings, etc.) or specific (patient records, inventories, travel records, etc.).

CHAPTER 8

Analysis and Synthesis

Case Analysis (UK)

Sometimes also known as 'decision tree analysis,' Case Analysis examines the cycle of data-decision-action-new data-new decision that is the essence of any investigative management. Unlike Visual Investigative Analysis which seeks to 'map' the whole investigation, Case Analysis focuses upon the decisions that were made and the data upon which they were made. With many investigations subject to rigorous review, both internally by organizations and through cross-examination in Court, this technique provides a useful resource for detailing the 'what, when and why' of management decisions, and thus justifying every stage of the process and policy of an investigation.

Case Analysis (US)

Case analysis is an approach used to manage the analysis of varied data in support of current or historical investigations. It involves analytic decision-making to determine the appropriate analytic technique to use (Peterson 1990:22-27).

Content Analysis

Content analysis is the analysis of the oral or written communication to determine the meaning of that communication. Another term, used by Rabon, is "investigative discourse analysis" and is defined by him as "the close and systematic study of basic linking components of spoken or written communications in order to determine process...occurrence...descriptions...individuals involved...evaluation... relationships...reason for specific word selections...truthfulness and deception" (Rabon 1999:11-12).

Commodity Flow Analysis

Commodity flow analysis looks at the flow of goods or services among people, businesses, and locations to determine the meaning of that activity. It may give insights into the nature of a conspiracy, a hierarchy of a group, or the workings of a distribution network (Peterson 1994:37). It can show the final beneficiary of the criminal act or the final location of assets purchased on his or her behalf.

Crime Pattern Analysis (Incidents/Perpetrators/Crimes)

Crime pattern analysis is looking at the components of crimes to discern similarities among them. It is used at the local, state, and federal level when a series of crimes have occurred. The patterns involved can be based on time, geography, perpetrators, victims, modus operandi, criminal signatures, criminal rewards, or other factors. Within time, the date and day of the week are considered, along with the number of days between incidents and the times of day the incidents occurred. The geography can include the locations, the types of activity at the location (residential, commercial, industrial), urban, suburban, or rural, elevation, proximity to other inhabited (or non-inhabited) buildings, etc. It may also be used to draw conclusions about the victimology of the crimes. See also "Geographic Distribution Analysis" on page 99.

CHAPTER 8

Analysis and Synthesis

Descriptive Analysis

Descriptive analysis is the written summarization of an event, activity, group or person which imparts data of an evaluative nature and from which conclusions and recommendations can be drawn (Peterson 1994:44). It is used most frequently on information collected through surveillance, interviews, and written or oral statements.

Estimates

Estimates tell us what to expect as a result of a past or current activity, such as a projection of the amount of drugs to be available based on current illicit crop production. They can be used to project what the future territory, or size, or influence a crime group will have. They usually involve specific numbers or other data.

Event Flow Analysis

Event flow analysis incorporates event flow and timelines and looks at activities over time. While the traditional look at flow analysis has focused on flow charting, these charts are interim products to assist the analyst in determining what is known and what is missing from the activities or transactions.

Forecasts

Forecasts are a prediction of the future based on an analysis of past and current trends. Forecasting can be done on both numeric and descriptive data. Forecasts are different from estimates in that they can be general, rather than quantitative.

Geographic Distribution Analysis

Geographic Distribution Analysis looks at the occurrence of something over a particular geographic area to determine what can be concluded about the activity or area (Peterson 1994:46). In crime analysis, "hot spots" are targeted after their identification through geographic distribution analysis.

Geographic Profiling

"Geographic profiling is an investigative methodology that uses locations of a connected series of crimes to determine the most probable area of offender residence. It is applied in cases of serial murder, rape, arson, robbery and bombing…" (Rossmo 1999:1).

Indicator Analysis

Indicator analysis involves the compilation, review, and analysis of the activities which occur around a particular activity to develop a model of what occurrences may be used to predict the presence of that activity in other locations (Peterson 1994:47).

Market Profiles (UK)

Market profiles are assessments of the state of the criminal market around a commodity or service such as drugs, stolen vehicles, prostitution, etc. (Atkin 1999:31).

CHAPTER 8

Analysis and Synthesis

Matrix Analysis

Matrices provide a useful format to arrange data so that it can be more easily analyzed. One use of matrix analysis is to look at potential targets for terrorist attack and what a terror group's motivation would be to do an attack against them.

Net Worth/Source and Application of Funds Analysis

Net Worth Analysis and Source and Application of Funds Analysis both include a financial profile of the individual or business and compare those profiles (which are based on slightly different views of the data) to what the individual or business reported as legal income. The difference between the figures is considered as possibly illegal income. Its initial purpose was to "determine taxpayers' income tax liabilities, primarily in those instances where no books or records of income and expenses have been maintained by taxpayers from which a determination of tax liability could be made." (Nossen & Norvelle 1993:1) Its use expanded to non-tax financial crimes.

Multi-Dimensional Analysis

The analysis of a set of data using temporal, geographic, associational and/or other aspects of the data and layering the results upon each other to have a more contextual view of the information (See Bodnar, 2003).

Pattern Analysis

Pattern analysis is completed on data, often over time, to see recurrences of activity or other factors involved in the activity. For example, if crimes are committed between 10 am and 2 pm, it would most likely be in residences where the occupants are out of the residence.

Premonitories

Premonitories are short term looks at crime groups or criminal activity with the purpose of preparing to initiate an investigation into that group or activity.

Results Analysis

Results analysis is assessing the impact of patrol strategies, reactive investigation, proactive investigation, crime reduction methods, and techniques and policies (Atkin 1999:30).

Social Network Analysis (SNA)

Social Network Analysis is a more complex form of link analysis in which all connections among a set of targets are analyzed to determine their strength, longevity, and connectedness. Key individuals who play interconnecting roles and/or centralized roles are identified. As currently applied, the networks are not limited to criminal networks as they are in traditional network analysis, but include all associations of targeted individuals.

CHAPTER 8

Analysis and Synthesis

Statistical Analysis

Statistical analysis is the review of numerical data to summarize it and to draw conclusions about its meaning. It incorporates a number of different techniques including frequency distribution (Peterson 1994:53).

Telephone Record Analysis

Telephone record (also called telephone toll) analysis looks at phone call data to determine associations as well as the activity it encompasses. This has been considered the 'bread and butter' of analysis and is used in support of probable cause to obtain an electronic intercept. It can also show the geographic range of a conspiracy and can uncover additional participants in the criminal activity (IALEIA 1996:4). The advent of cell phone records which include locations along with call time and number data have given added depth to these analyses.

Timeline Analysis

Constructing a timeline is often a useful initial step in an analysis in that it helps 'tell the story' of what occurred. Analyzing that timeline for gaps, patterns, anomalies, causal relationships, etc. can further aid the analysis.

Visual Investigative Analysis (VIA)

Visual Investigative Analysis is the analysis of the steps taken, or necessary to be taken, in the course of an investigation or in the course of a criminal act. Using VIA, case managers can track the deployment of personnel, see the status of leads and identify what needs to be done next in the investigation (Peterson 1994:38).

Warnings/Vulnerability and Threat Assessments

Warnings may tell of some impending activity that will be a danger to society. Threat assessments are used to evaluate a criminal activity and its impact on society. Vulnerability assessments look at an area, or individual, or event in terms of what its vulnerabilities are to criminal activity. An example of an event that would have this type of treatment is the Olympics.

STANDARDS FOR ANALYSIS

One key role in the acceptance of analysis by law enforcement is the understanding of analysis by law enforcement executives, managers, and supervisors. This understanding usually comes from experience by the law enforcement personnel which, in part, come from knowing what to expect from the analytic group.

There have been several attempts to determine standards for analysis since 2000. The primary standards for law enforcement analysts are seen in the document, Law Enforcement Analytic Standards, developed by IALEIA and the Global Intelligence Working Group. The following shows these standards for analysis.

CHAPTER 8

Analysis and Synthesis

- **Planning** – Analysts shall understand the objective of their assignment, define the problem, and plan for the necessary resources. This shall be done through the use of a collection or investigative plan or through intelligence requirement. Specific steps to be taken to complete the assignment, including potential sources of information and a projected timeline, shall be included. The needs of the client (requirements) shall be reflected in the plan (IALEIA 2004: 15).

- **Direction** – Analysts shall be involved in planning and direction. Law enforcement agencies shall use analytic expertise to develop both short- and long-term investigative priorities and plans. Analytic expertise may also be used to develop intelligence requirements as a driving force to determine investigative priorities and for incorporation into investigative plans to drive operation (IALEIA 2004:16). It should be noted, however, that while analysts are involved in the planning and direction phase, executives and managers are as well; otherwise, the intelligence cycle is not supporting established executive priorities.

- **Collection** – Analytic research shall be thorough and use all available sources. An analytic product shall contain all relevant data available through sources and means available to the analyst (IALEIA 2004:17).

- **Collection Follow-Up** – In the course of collection by investigators and others, analysts shall evaluate the progress of the collection to determine if the collection plan/requirements are being met and shall identify additional sources of information, as well as identify information that may be useful to other cases or activities. Where possible, analysts shall relay that information to an appropriate body for follow-up (IALEIA 2004:18).

- **Legal Constraints** – Raw data that has been obtained in violation of any applicable local state or federal law or ordinance shall not be incorporated into an analytic product (IALEIA 2004:19).

- **Evaluation** – Information collected from all sources shall be evaluated and designated for source reliability, content validity, and relevancy. Effective evaluation is important not only to the validity of the intelligence product but also to officer safety, investigative effectiveness, and solidity of evidence in prosecutions (IALEIA 2004: 19).

- **Collation** – Raw data shall be organized and formatted so the analyst can retrieve; sort; identify patterns, anomalies and information gaps; and store the data. When possible, this shall be done in a computerized format using the most appropriate software available to the analyst (IALEIA 2004:20).

- **Analytic Accuracy** – An analytic product shall be an accurate representation of the data. In cases where exculpatory data has been found along with proofs, both should be included (IALEIA 2004:21).

- **Computerized Analysis** – Analyses shall utilize the best and most current computerized visualization and analytic tools available to the analyst (IALEIA 2004:22).

- **Analytic Product Content** – Analytic products shall always include analysis, assessments, integrated data, judgments, conclusions, and recommendations. Forecasts, estimates, and models shall be developed, where appropriate (IALEIA 2004:23).

- **Analytic Outcomes** – Analyses shall include alternative scenarios and avoid single-solution outcomes where appropriate, especially when the outcomes could have significant consequences. Analyses shall indicate the most likely hypothesis, but this hypothesis shall be arrived at through the analysis of competing hypotheses. Those hypotheses not chosen shall also be noted (IALEIA 2004: 24).

- **Dissemination Plan** – Analysts shall develop a dissemination plan to encourage sharing of the product with applicable agencies. This plan shall indicate the security level of the document. It shall be reviewed and approved by supervisory personnel (IALEIA 2004:25).

- **Analytic Report** – Reports shall be written clearly and facts documented thoroughly. A precise, analytic bottom line should be provided. A tight—logical—organization of facts shall show how the analyst arrived at conclusions. Objective and dispassionate language shall be used, emphasizing brevity and clarity of expression (IALEIA 2004:25).

- **Analytic Product Format Standard** – Analytic product formats shall be tailored to the consumer's need. Products shall include, but are not limited to:

  - Strategic and Tactical Assessments
  - Problem and Target Profiles
  - Crime-Pattern Analysis
  - Criminal Business Profiles
  - Network Analysis
  - Demographic/Social Trend Analysis
  - Risk analysis
  - Market Profiles
  - Results Analysis
  - Communication Analysis
  - Flow Analysis
  - Financial Analysis
  - Indicator Analysis
  - Geographic Analysis (IALEIA 2004:26)

- **Analytic Testimony** – Analysts shall be capable of giving testimony as fact/summary and expert witnesses. They shall be able to present and defend their qualifications as witnesses and explain and defend the material they present (IALEIA 2004:27).

- **Data Source Attribution** – Every intelligence product shall clearly distinguish which contents are public domains or general unclassified information, what information is restricted or classified, and what contents are the judgments or opinions of analysts and/or other professionals (IALEIA 2004:28).

- **Analytic Feedback** – The analytic product shall be reviewed, if appropriate, by peers and evaluated by customers. Peer review may be limited to factual content accuracy or may encompass collaborative comments concerning content and recommendations (IALEIA 2004:28).

- **Analytic Product Evaluation** – Analytic products shall be evaluated based on the standards set forth in this document (above) (IALEIA 2004:29).

STANDARDS FOR ANALYSTS

Analysts have developed standards and criteria by which they can be judged through their professional organizations. Godfrey suggested that there were two types of analysts: non-specialists and specialists. The former often came into the field as recent Liberal Arts graduates. These analysts were to be intelligent precise and anxious to explore new areas and would "soon make important contributions to criminal analysis." (Harris 1976:42) Specialist analysts, on the other hand, might be academics on retainer or people from other agencies which could assist on a specific investigation.

The intervening years since has shown law enforcement that specialist analysts can be developed and trained through a combination of education and experience within the law enforcement framework. For example, a person with a business or accounting degree could be hired for financial analysis if that was deemed to be appropriate and then trained in the finer points of analysis over straight accounting (or forensic accounting). Analysts with computer degrees or post-college courses might be best for jobs requiring a lot of database development. Analysts with language specialties are popular in narcotics units and on the international intelligence scene.

The general standards for analysts are summarized below.

Education

A number of agencies now require a four-year degree for beginning analysts; some require four year degrees for beginning police officers. IALEIA requires two or four year degrees for certification, depending upon the level of that certification (regular or lifetime). It is hoped that an analyst who is regular certified with a two-year degree will go on to get a four-year degree before applying for lifetime certification.

The General Counterdrug Intelligence Plan released in February, 2000 by the Center for Narcotics Control in the U.S. stated that analysts should have four- year college degrees (Harris 1976:42). In several countries, undergraduate and graduate degree programs in intelligence and analysis are being developed. Some of the graduate programs do not require a previous four-year degree for admission, but are taking experience in the field in lieu of educational qualifications.

Civilian vs. Non-Civilian

While the general consensus seems to be that civilians, without prior law enforcement officer training, make the best analysts, sworn intelligence officers are used in a number of settings, in and outside the United States. Until recently, for example, all Australian analysts were sworn intelligence officers. In Canada, the RCMP uses a mix of sworn and non-sworn analysts.

In the United States there are a number of sworn officers who are filling the role of crime analyst for their department, particularly in areas where it is difficult to hire non-sworn employees above the clerical support ranks. While in general, most agencies in the United States hire civilians as analysts, some agencies hire retired police officers to fill this role, believing that their previous enforcement experience will aid their performance of analysis. Others would frown on this supposition, believing that police officers' former training will not provide them with the flexibility and creativity to approach each diverse intelligence problem.

In 2004, IALEIA created a set of analytic standards working with the Global Intelligence Working Group. Those standards for analysts are seen below.

ANALYST STANDARDS

Education – Analysts hired should have four-year college degree or commensurate experience. Commensurate experience is defined as no less than five years of previous research/analysis/intelligence-oriented experience with a two-year degree, or no less than ten years of previous research/analysis/intelligence-oriented experience with less than a two-year degree. This experience can come from the private, public, or military sector. The experience can be documented through job descriptions and/or examples of work products. Appropriate college degree areas include those with research and writing components, including social sciences, English, journalism, and criminal justice. The areas may also include business or science degrees if the knowledge gained will assist in the types of analysis needed to be completed (IALEIA 2004:5).

Training – Initial analytic training shall be a minimum of 40 hours and shall be provided by instructors with law enforcement analytic experience. Training shall incorporate, but not necessarily be limited to, the following topics:

- Intelligence Cycle/Process
- Intelligence Led Policing
- NCISP
- File Management
- Information Evaluation
- Critical thinking
- Logic
- Inference and Recommendation Development
- Collection Plans
- Research Methods and Sources
- Crime-Pattern Analysis
- Association/Network Analysis
- Telephone Record Analysis/Communication Analysis
- Flow Analysis
- Spatial/Geographic Analysis
- Financial Analysis
- Strategic Analysis
- Analytic Writing
- Presentation Skills

- Statistics
- Graphical Techniques
- Computerized Programs to Assist Analysis
- Ethics
- Professionalism
- Courtroom Testimony (IALEIA 2004:6-7)

Continuing Education – Continuing analytic education of at least eight hours per year shall be received by those performing the analytic function, to be accomplished through a combination of formal education, training classes, distance learning, or self-directed study efforts. The training provider should have professional association or academic credentials in the subject matter. Continuing education may include topics listed in the previous standard (IALEIA 2004:10).

Professional Development – Analysts shall maintain a program of professional development throughout their career and be supported in this process by their employer. Employers should ensure that analysts provide maximum benefits to operations by implementing professional development programs for their analytic staff, whether analysts or sworn officers are performing the intelligence duties (IALEIA, 2004:11).

Certification – Analysts should be certified by an agency or organization (governmental, professional association, or institution of higher learning) specifically developed for intelligence analysts. These analytic certification programs shall reflect experience, education, training, and proficiency testing (IALEIA 2004:12).

Professional Liaison – Analysts and their organizations shall be encouraged to maintain links to and seek available support from recognized professional bodies and associations (IALEIA 2004:13).

Analytic Attributes – Analysts shall be hired and evaluated based on their work and attributes, including strong:

- Subject Matter Expertise
- Analytic Methodologies
- Customer-Service Ethics
- Information Handling and Processing Skills
- Communication Skills
- Critical-Thinking Skills
- Computer Literacy
- Objectivity and Intellectual Honesty (IALEIA 204:14)

AXIOMS FOR AN INTELLIGENCE ANALYST

1. **Believe in your own professional judgment.** - You are the expert, believe in your work and stand your ground if the intelligence supports your position.

2. **Be a risk taker.** - Do not be afraid to forecast trends or events or of being wrong.

3. **It is better to be mistaken.** - Admit to yourself and others when you are incorrect and be able to change your position when the facts call for it.

4. **Avoid mirror imaging at all costs.** - Mirror imaging – projecting your thought process or value system onto someone else – can be dangerous. Your targets do not think like you. They are different so you must think like them.

5. **Intelligence is of no value if it is not disseminated.** - You must clearly and effectively communicate the intelligence and your assessment to the consumer in a timely manner.

6. **When everyone agrees on an issue, something probably is wrong.** - It is rare when everyone in the intelligence community agrees on an analytic judgment. When these instances do occur, it is time to worry.

7. **Consumers do not care how much you know; just tell them what is important.** - Superfluous details merely serve to obscure the important facts.

8. **Form is never more important than substance.** - Although a professional appearance and correct formats are important, they do not outweigh substance. Consumers want to know what intelligence means, and they want it when they need it.

9. **Aggressively pursue collection of the information you need.** - If you are examining a problem and there is no intelligence available or the available intelligence is insufficient, be aggressive in pursuing collection and energizing collectors.

10. **Do not take the editing process personally.** - If editorial changes do not alter the meaning of what you are trying to say, accept them. If they alter the meaning, speak up.

11. **Know your intelligence community counterparts and talk to them.** - Find out what your counterparts are doing, and tell them what you are doing. Do not just talk to them when you need something.

12. **Do not take your job, or yourself, too seriously.** - Keep things in perspective; take care of yourself and your family.

(Wantanabe 2000)

REFERENCES

Andrews, Jr., Paul P. and Marilyn B. Peterson. (1990). Criminal Intelligence Analysis. Loomis, CA: Palmer Press.

Atkin, Howard N. (1999) "A New National Intelligence Model for the UK" *Intelligence Models and Best Practices*. Lawrenceville, NJ: International Association of Law Enforcement Intelligence Analysts.

Bodnar, John (2003) *Warning Analysis for the Information Age*. Washington DC: Joint Military Intelligence College.

Browne, M. Neil and Stuart M. Keeley (2007) Asking *the Right Questions A Guide to Critical Thinking Eighth Edition*. Upper Saddle River, NJ: Pearson/Prentice Hall.

Directorate of Analysis (2008) A *Tradecraft Primer: Basic Structured Analytic Techniques*. Washington, DC: Defense Intelligence Agency.

Godfrey, E. Drexel and Don R. Harris. (1976) *The Basic Elements of Intelligence*. Washington, DC: Law Enforcement Assistance Administration.

Govier, Trudy (2005) *A Practical Study of Argument Sixth Edition*. Belmont, CA: Thompson Wadsworth.

Harris, Don R. (1976) *The Basic Elements of Intelligence, 2nd Edition*. Washington, DC: Law Enforcement Assistance Administration.

Heuer, Jr., Richards. (1999) *The Psychology of Intelligence Analysis*. Washington, DC: Center for the Study of Intelligence.

--------------- (2008) Taxonomy of Structured Analytic Techniques. Paper presented at IAFIE 2008 Annual Convention, Monterey, CA.

International Association of Law Enforcement Intelligence Analysts (1996) Successful *Law Enforcement Using Analytic Methods*. Lawrenceville, NJ: IALEIA.

--------------- (1997) Guidelines *for Starting an Analytic Unit*. Lawrenceville, NJ: IALEIA

--------------- (2004) *Law Enforcement Analytic Standards*. Richmond, VA: International Association of Law Enforcement Intelligence Analysts and Global Justice Information Sharing Initiative.

Lowenthal, Mark (2006) Intelligence*: From Secrets to Policy*. Washington, DC: CQ Press.

Nossen, Richard and Joan Norvelle. (1993*) The Detection, Investigation and Prosecution of Financial Crimes, 2nd edition*. Richmond, VA: Thoth Publications.

Office of the Director of National Intelligence (2007) *Intelligence Community Directive 203*. Washington, DC: Office of the Director of National Intelligence. (June 21)

Paul, Richard and Linda Elder (2006) *A Miniature Guide to Analytic Thinking.* Berkeley, CA: The Critical Thinking Foundation.

Peterson, Marilyn B. (1994) Applications *in Criminal Analysis: A Sourcebook.* Westport, CT: Greenwood Press.

--------------- (1999) "Critical Thinking*" Intersec* magazine, pp.

--------------- (1998) *A Guide to the Financial Analysis of Personal and Corporate Bank Records.* Richmond, VA: National White Collar Crime Center.

--------------- (2002) A Guide to Understanding and Analyzing Bank Secrecy Act Data. Electronically published on "Big Money" CD Rom; Federal Bureau of Investigation and National White Collar Crime Center.

--------------- (1990) "The Context of Analysis – From Analysis to Synthesis Exploring the Context of Law Enforcement Analysis" *Criminal Intelligence Analysis,* Paul P. Andrews, Jr. and Marilyn B. Peterson, editors. Loomis, CA: Palmer Enterprises.

Rabon, Don. (1999) *Discourse Analysis.* University North Carolina.

Regali, Joseph (1999) Visual Investigative Analysis: An Underutilized Case Management Tool," *IALEIA Journal*, Vol. 12, No. 1, February.

Sommers, Marilyn (Peterson). (1986) "Criminal Intelligence: A New Look*" International Journal of Intelligence and Counterintelligence*, Vol. No.

Wantanabe, Frank. (undated) *Fifteen Axioms for Intelligence Analysts,*
<*www.cia.gov/csi/studies/97unclass/axioms.html*>, CIA Website, (7/12/2000).

Dissemination
By Robert D. Fowler

INTRODUCTION

Since the release of the first edition of *The Basic Elements of Intelligence* in 1971, there has always been a chapter that discussed the dissemination of law enforcement intelligence products.

However, the tragic events of September 11, 2001, showcased the importance of this aspect of the intelligence process. Former CIA Director George Tenet stated in testimony before the 9/11 Commission, "...the system was blinking red during the summer of 2001...Yet no one working on these late leads connected the case in his or her inbox to the threat reports." Although individuals will argue as to how much intelligence information there was prior to the attacks of that day, everyone seems to agree that the information possessed was not necessarily disseminated as readily as it should have been.

While some looked at intelligence information as something that needed to be tightly controlled and guarded from release, the new vision seems to be that information should be released whenever possible and to the lowest levels of the intelligence "chain" as possible. Most intelligence personnel do not want to be the one caught "holding" information which could have potentially prevented tragedy. In his address to the nation on June 6, 2002, then President George W. Bush stated, "Information must be fully shared so we can follow every lead to find the one that may prevent tragedy."

While this approach is clearly the most appropriate one today, it is still important that certain standards and rules for dissemination be followed so intelligence products are handled in such a way that the right intelligence gets to the right people, while still insuring sensitive information remains secure.

RIGHT-TO-KNOW

Once criminal intelligence information has been collected, collated, and analyzed, it is usually ready for dissemination. But to whom should it be disseminated? While this largely depends on the subject and sensitivity of the intelligence possessed, there are some standard guidelines common within the intelligence community.

The first of these is the doctrine of "right-to-know." In other words, when one possesses criminal intelligence information, they must determine if the person or entity that will receive the criminal intelligence has the "right-to-know." Do they possess the proper authoritative/legal clearance?

While these may seem like simple questions, when viewed at a national or possibly even international level, they can become overwhelmingly confusing. Who defines clearances and what does that allow you to release to an individual who possesses it? The term "sworn" may have different definitions from state to state, from state to federal, and from country to country. For example, intelligence analysts, who perform the same functions within different agencies can be sworn in one and non-sworn in another. Also, some non-governmental organizations work directly with governmental agencies and collect and possess intelligence data.

CHAPTER 9

Dissemination

The bottom line with the right-to-know doctrine is that the individual who is to receive the information must have the valid authority to receive the information. This should be based on predetermined policies and procedures that the releasing entity is bound by or agrees to honor.

NEED-TO-KNOW

Commonly attached to and many times seen as inseparable from the right-to-know, is the "need-to-know." The foundation of this doctrine is that an individual who is to receive information must have a valid official reason for receiving it.

Many individuals have the right to know information. As an example, thousands of individuals have top-secret clearances to receive national security related information. However, does every one of these individuals need every piece of top-secret information that is available? Not only is it unrealistic to do so, it could jeopardize the integrity of the information.

It is important to note that intelligence information is different from information received from public, commonly seen sources. This does not mean that important information is not received from these sources. Many times this is the place where the basic information is derived. However, once it is collated with other information and analyzed (a key component) -- intelligence is created.

This newly created intelligence information needs to be distributed to individuals and groups that can use it to take some sort of lawful action to prevent or deter criminal activity. Questions such as: "What can they do with the information? How will it help them in their official duties?" should be asked when seeking to determine if intelligence information should be released to particular individuals.

AUTHORITY TO RELEASE

There is another component involving the dissemination of intelligence information that is often not discussed. While most people think of having the right-to-know and the need-to-know as components of the dissemination process, the authority to release the information is often forgotten.

There are many reasons why individuals within an organization will come to possess intelligence information. They may have the absolute right and need to have the information, but many times they do not necessarily have the authority to release that information to others.

In general, the author of the intelligence information, be it an individual or organization, will disseminate intelligence information with specific markings that will tell the reader or receiver how the information is to be "handled." In the absence of specific markings, which will be discussed in the next section, it is generally understood that the originator of the intelligence product retains authority over its distribution unless stated otherwise in the document. In such cases, the possessor of the information needs to contact the originator in order to receive approval for its further distribution (sometimes referred to as the Third Party Rule). When in doubt, the possessor should call and find out.

CHAPTER 9

Dissemination

Within individual organizations, policies and procedures will generally define who distributes what intelligence information and under what circumstances. However, these policies and procedures need to be understood by all employees in order to avoid the unauthorized release of intelligence information.

MARKINGS

Previously, we discussed the fact that many pieces of intelligence information are "marked" with specific dissemination instructions. These instructions are meant to tell the possessor how they are to handle a specific piece of information. On the surface, this would seem like a perfect process for controlling the dissemination of intelligence information. Problems arise however when you realize that among only 20 federal agencies in the U.S. alone, there are over 100 unique markings currently in use, with over 130 handling and/or labeling processes. As stated, this is only for these 20 federal agencies. With over 18,000 state, local, and tribal (SLT) law enforcement agencies, this number has the potential to be overwhelming. The federal system is discussed here because, in that system, there are some statutory guidelines that can be referenced. Currently, there are no "across the board" standards by which SLT agencies can operate.

When someone receives intelligence information today, there is a good chance that they will see one or more of the following markings on it:

- ECI – Export Controlled Information
- FOUO – For Official Use Only
- LES – Law Enforcement Sensitive
- SBU – Sensitive But Unclassified
- SSI – Sensitive Security Information

These are just five examples of markings that exist. What do these markings actually mean to the individual who sees them? Who can receive the information? Who can it be distributed to? These are just some of the questions that frankly, cannot necessarily be answered easily.

Again, under the federal system, each of these markings can be on a document distributed to other federal or SLT agencies. Because each agency has its own rules and regulations for the handling of information, the recipient is responsible for handling the information following those guidelines. This problem is exacerbated by the fact many agencies do not have clear guidelines as to how their information is to be handled by others. Unfortunately, to make matters worse, many documents will be marked, but will not have originating agency information on them. Therefore, even if someone had access to each federal agency's handling and dissemination policy as it relates to a certain marking, they would not be able to handle it properly since they could not determine the origin of the intelligence.

Under the Intelligence Reform and Terrorism Prevention Act of 2004, the President was required to take action to facilitate the sharing of terrorism information. As a result, in December of 2005, President George Bush issued a Memorandum to the Heads of the Executive Departments and Agencies, in which he directed the Program Manager of the Information Sharing Environment to begin a process of standardizing the handling of Sensitive But Unclassified (SBU) information.

CHAPTER 9

Dissemination

In May 2008, President George Bush issued another Memorandum to the Heads of the Executive Departments and Agencies, in which he instituted Controlled Unclassified Information (CUI) as the single designation for SBU information. CUI--as defined in the President's Memorandum is:

> A categorical designation that refers to unclassified information that does not meet the standards for National Security Classification but is pertinent to the national interests of the United States or important to interests of entities outside the Federal Government, and under law or policy requires protection from unauthorized disclosure, special handling safeguards, or prescribed limits on exchange or dissemination.

In most circumstances, this is the information most intelligence personnel deal with each and every day. Simply put, it is intelligence information that does not rise to the level of needing to be classified, but its release needs to be controlled.

The federal government's attempt to standardize the sharing of intelligence information goes a long way toward improving the system and making it more accessible to all. In May 2009, President Barack Obama issued a Memorandum to the Heads of the Executive Departments and Agencies, in which he further expanded the CUI implementation process.

Although this is a federal project, SLT agency participation and input is being sought throughout the process. The goal is that SLT agencies will accept and implement the same guidelines once established, much like most SLT agencies have adopted the criminal information sharing provisions described in U.S. 28 Code of Federal Regulations (CFR), Part 23.

METHODS OF DISSEMINATION

As stated previously, prior to the events of September 11, 2001, methods of dissemination for intelligence information were limited and ad hoc. In general, information was distributed from person to person at the local level or through bulletins that were generally distributed via fax or electronic means through systems such as the Regional Information Sharing Systems (RISS) Network.

Additionally, specialized groups formed for the specific purpose of sharing information at the state and local level, when it was believed that the federal agencies were not sharing information as much as was felt was necessary. The Association of Law Enforcement Intelligence Units (LEIU) was one such group that formed in 1956 for the specific purpose of exchanging intelligence information on organized crime activity.

After 9/11, the strong need for the expansion and formalization of the intelligence process emerged. As a result, numerous SLT intelligence groups formed to exchange information on local, regional, state, and even national levels. Other federal agencies began or expanded similar programs. As a result, intelligence information began to flow more freely, although problems still exist.

Today, one of the primary resources for the exchange of intelligence information is the fusion center.

Fusion centers are defined as:

> A collaborative effort of two or more agencies that provide resources, expertise, and/or information to the center with the goal of maximizing the ability to detect, prevent, investigate, apprehend, and respond to criminal and terrorist activity.

Operationally, a fusion center is a physical location that houses personnel from different agencies and operates with a common purpose of promoting an intelligence function. Personnel can come from federal, state, regional, and local agencies. Those personnel usually include field intelligence analysts, and other support staffing. Fusion centers may also house representatives from key private sector organizations as well. Overall operational responsibility can be handled by one agency (usually the largest member agency) or a co-management relationship can be established.

The primary role of the fusion center is to collect, analyze, and disseminate intelligence information to member agencies and other fusion centers. Many federal agencies now participate in fusion center operations although SLT entities remain in overall control of these operations.

With today's technological advancements, intelligence personnel can retrieve personnel information from several official resources including fusion center bulletins. Personnel can also utilize electronic intelligence resources such as Law Enforcement Online, RISS, and the Homeland Security Information Network. These computer-based initiatives provide a resource for intelligence personnel to receive information from and communicate with other intelligence personnel.

DISSEMINATION ISSUES

While significant advances have been made in improving the exchange of intelligence information since September 11, 2001, there are still barriers that exist today. For years, many federal agencies have worked with national security information classified as Confidential, Secret, and Top Secret. This information must be handled, stored, and controlled in accordance with strict federal laws. On the other hand, SLT law enforcement entities do not classify information in this way and have traditionally operated under right-to-know and need-to-know doctrines. The result is that in many cases, SLT agencies may want to pass information that does not correlate with the national security classification standards. The CUI initiative discussed above is working towards facilitating the release of more information at a broader level, but its implementation remains a distant goal and its success remains uncertain.

Another issue facing intelligence units and their personnel is the potential for claims of "privacy rights" violations. There have been historical mistakes by law enforcement targeting First Amendment protected speech. Training has helped to mitigate this issue, but challenges on what to collect and disseminate remain. While this topic is more appropriately discussed in the realm of collecting intelligence, it is important to note that intelligence that should not be collected, should not be disseminated. While this seems obvious, it is important to understand the dissemination of inappropriately collected intelligence is damaging not only to the agency collecting it, but can endanger investigations that use this information as a basis for further, possibly unrelated investigations.

CHAPTER 9

Dissemination

While the growth of fusion centers has helped institute proper dissemination policies regarding intelligence information, there are still intercommunication issues that can be confusing to intelligence personnel. For example, when a local agency representative receives information that needs to be shared, to whom does the representative share it and what are the most appropriate means of dissemination? Should this information be sent to the local FBI-Joint Terrorism Task Force (JTTF)? Should it be sent to the nearest fusion center? Is it the representative's responsibility to pass the information to these groups or does he/she pass it through his agency's Terrorism Liaison Officer?

All of these are questions that need to be discussed and procedures determined in advance. Each agency must develop policy and procedures that are supported by resources available to each individual agency. Many agencies now have intelligence liaison officer programs to connect them with fusion centers. Some agencies have concluded that all intelligence information will flow through these liaison officers, while other agencies want dissemination to be handled by an intelligence unit. Many agencies have neither of these functions and therefore anyone can contact a local fusion center, JTTF, or other intelligence gathering entity. Suspicious Activity Report programs have emerged in many areas and are expanding daily. In any case, these procedures need to be determined in advance.

In conclusion, it is important to understand that intelligence is not effective or of any value if it is not shared with those that need to have it. The key is to develop rules and procedures for dissemination in advance. Therefore, when a product is disseminated; it will go to the right people for the right reasons by the right methods.

While there are still dissemination issues that need to be addressed, steps are being taken across the nation at the federal, state, and local levels to improve the systems and streamline the flow of information in the future. For now it is important that each person who handles intelligence information understands how to properly disseminate it, based on local standards already be in place.

CHAPTER 9

Dissemination

***

REFERENCES

Bureau of Justice Assistance. (2009). *<www.riss.net>*

Bush, George W. (2002). *Address to the Nation.* Washington, DC. June 6, 2002.

Bush, George W. (2005). *Presidential Memorandum: Guidelines and Requirements in Support of the Information Sharing Environment.* Washington, DC. December 16, 2005.

Bush, George W. (2008). *Presidential Memorandum: Designation and Sharing of Controlled Unclassified Information (CUI).* Washington, DC. May 9, 2008.

Federal Bureau of Investigations. (2009). *<www.leo.gov>*

German, Michael. (2007). *What's Wrong With Fusion Centers.* Washington, DC: American Civil Liberties Union.

House of Representatives. (2004). *Terrorism Prevention Act of 2004.* Washington, DC: U.S. Government Printing Office.

LEIU. (2002). *Criminal Intelligence File Guidelines.* Sacramento, CA: Association of Law Enforcement Intelligence Units.

McNamara, Thomas E. (2007). *Statement for the Record before House Committee on Homeland Security.* Washington, DC. April 26, 2007.

McNamara, Thomas E. (2008). *Information Sharing Environment Administrative Memorandum.* Washington, DC. September 5, 2008.

National Commission on Terrorist Attacks. (2004). *The 9/11 Commission Report.* New York, NY: W.W. Norton & Company.

Obama, Barack H. (2009). *Presidential Memorandum: Classified Information and Controlled Unclassified Information.* Washington, DC. May 27, 2009.

Office of Justice Programs. (2003). *National Criminal Intelligence Sharing Plan.* Washington, DC: U.S. Government Printing Office.

Office of Justice Programs. (2006). *Fusion Center Guidelines.* Washington, DC: U.S. Government Printing Office.

U.S. Department of Homeland Security. (2009). *<www.dhs.gov>*

Report Writing Principles
"A Guide for Intelligence Professionals"
By David Cariens Jr.

INTRODUCTION

For the purposes of this chapter, the author defines all aspects and all levels of police writing as intelligence writing because the underlying principles used in intelligence writing—such as precision of language, clarity of thought, and correct English sentence structure—apply whether a person is writing the initial crime scene report or preparing a piece of finished intelligence for a senior manager. Furthermore, there are several issues that are common throughout all aspects of the law enforcement/intelligence profession: First, you may never have all the evidence you need to feel 100 percent certain about your judgments; second, the chances of being wrong are possible; and third, sooner or later you may be wrong. These concerns underscore the imperative of not only careful thought and analysis, but the need for precision in observation, analysis, and writing at all times—at every step—from the initial investigation to the final report.

When an officer writes observations of a crime scene, he/she is making intelligence judgments—the first step in solving a crime is taking place. Every step of the way careful attention needs to be paid to accuracy in writing. All police officers should remember that he/she will not be in the room to explain what a sentence, word, or phrase means. There is a Murphy's law that if there is ambiguity in a written product, whatever the writer meant to say is not the interpretation that the reader will take away from the document.

THE NITTY-GRITTY OF INTELLIGENCE WRITING

Intelligence writing is one of the most exacting and demanding forms of writing, requiring a high degree of skill and precise use of English. Sworn personnel and analysts, at all levels, must take complicated problems and investigations and put them into a form of English that can be readily understood by both the specialist and generalist. Decisions are made on what is written—at every stage of the investigation.

Intelligence reports, whether at the crime scene or in the finished products, may be based on fragmentary evidence. If you have all the evidence and all the information, you are writing history, not intelligence. It is the intelligence officer/analyst's task to bring some sort of meaning and order to problems and situations that, on the surface, may defy logic and understanding.

Whether the threat is from al-Qa'ida, organized crime, street gangs, foreign intelligence services, or drug cartels, the stakes are too high to give short shrift to writing.

Following the tragedy of September 11, 2001, the need for all members of the intelligence and law enforcement communities to communicate using the same writing principles reached paramount importance. Different templates are used by different members of the intelligence/law enforcement communities (at the federal and state levels), but these templates are, for the most part, based on the same writing principles. Where differences do exist, once they are understood, personnel can easily adjust their writing.

Failure to understand the basic writing principles, as well as the variations on those principles, can and does lead to misunderstandings and confusion. One of the basic differences centers on the use of active voice versus passive voice. Most of the non-law enforcement members of the community insist on active voice. Some writing templates at the FBI and in the state and local police forces, however, emphasize passive voice sentence.

Passive voice allows for greater interpretation and from the law enforcement perspective these sentences make a great deal of sense. Who are primary consumers of the FBI and police reports—lawyers. Lawyers prefer passive voice because passive voice sentences allow greater flexibility in courtroom argumentation. Other members of the Intelligence Community (IC) prefer active voice. Active voice is a clearer and more direct form of written communication. Active voice in its purist form leaves little to doubt. Analysts throughout the IC must be well versed in both active and passive voice sentences; they must know when and how to use them.

Readers of this chapter may understand the difference between the two types of sentences, but let's take a moment to review both.

Here is a passive voice sentence: *Prime Minister Schmidt was wounded today during a military parade, but a coup does not appear to be in progress.* The sentence is passive voice, raising the question of who wounded the prime minister? You could rewrite the sentence to say: *Prime Minister Schmidt was wounded today by members of a radical right-wing group, but a coup does not appear to be in progress.* The problem is you still have a passive construction because you identify the actor after the verb. To turn this sentence into active voice construction you need to put the actor ahead of the verb: *A member of a radical right-wing group wounded Prime Minister Schmidt today, but a coup does not appear to be in progress.*

The decision to use active or passive voice may well depend on your audience—even within the same organization. The director of the FBI wants his intelligence in concise, active voice sentences. However, Department of Justice lawyers who want to use the intelligence reports as part of the prosecution of a criminal probably want passive sentences.

In some cases, FBI and law enforcement officers may have to write two separate reports on the same subject, the main difference being active or passive voice. An officer may have to craft an active voice paragraph or two to go to senior management. For example, an officer may have to write the synopsis of a longer report (crime investigation) in active voice pulling out the main conclusions and facts, while the report itself is written in passive voice.

In the case of the active voice report, the key thing to remember is to begin with a strong topic sentence telling the reader the main point or the "so-what." Think of it this way, if the primary recipient only reads the topic sentence you need to tell him/her the most important thing you want him/her to know.

This principle of conceptualizing what you want to say in one sentence should be basic to all officers'/analysts' writing, no matter what the format. You should be able to tell someone verbally or in writing, (one sentence), the main point you want the listener or reader to take away. This applies whether

Report Writing Principles

you are writing 1 paragraph or 100 pages. This conceptualization is difficult, but it will make your writing easier and clearer.

This need for conceptualization applies when the law enforcement officer is writing a more traditional enforcement report using passive voice sentences and building the case—walking the reader through the investigation point by point. It is not enough just to throw ideas and facts down—taking the time to conceptualize before putting fingers to keyboard or pen to paper will help the drafter construct a logical case.

Active voice sentences are the overwhelming choice of most senior intelligence officers and managers. Here, the topic sentence with the "what" and "so-what" is mandatory. Much of the detail and the bits of evidence that were critical for you in making your judgments will lie on the editorial floor. By the way, this direct, active voice, concise way of writing is the preferred style of the Office of the Director for National Intelligence (ODNI).

Some of you reading this chapter are probably throwing your hands up in horror and saying, "I have spent my whole career just putting the facts down on paper in passive voice sentences, are you telling me this is wrong?" No, this is not wrong. You will continue to do that. However, if you are required to write a series of facts or observations, you should take the time to conceptualize in your mind what all these things mean—even if you do not put that in your report. There should be some order and thought in your writing. Furthermore, for those of you with an attachment to passive voice, let's take a look at reasons to use passive voice so that it is clear when, where, and why we should use those sentences:

- Use a passive voice sentence when you don't know who the actor is—that is just common sense.

- Use a passive voice sentence when you want to emphasize something else other than the actor. For example: *A bumper crop of wheat was grown by the Russians.*

- Use a passive voice sentence when your main audience consists of lawyers. Passive voice allows them greater argumentation and interpretation.

- Use a passive voice sentence when you intentionally want to obscure the actor. This type of passive construction is the life blood of politicians, who during elections, want to give the impression they are coming clean with the electorate. For example: *"Mistakes were made!"* Yes! By whom? Tell us so we can vote the culprits out of office! In law enforcement, intelligence officers and analysts always need to be clear and accurate. The intelligence profession—across the board—puts a high premium on correct English usage. Most of the errors found in intelligence officers'/analysts' writing center on four parts of English:

1. **Verbs** – Writers need to consider all aspects of the verbs they use ranging from tenses, through verb selection, and subject-verb agreement.

2. **Prepositions** – *One must be care*ful in using prepositions since English, unlike other languages, uses prepositions to change the meaning of sentences. Additionally, English complicates the problem because prepositions are 100 percent idiomatic—***there are no rules***.

CHAPTER 10

Report Writing Principles

3. **Pronouns** – One should minimize the use of pronouns in intelligence writing. Other forms of writing encourage the use of pronouns as a way of adding variety, but with that variety comes the danger of ambiguity. What or who does the pronoun refer to? If you use a pronoun make sure that the antecedent of the pronoun is clear. The pronouns "this, that, these, and those" are frowned upon in intelligence writing. They are the demonstrative pronouns and are considered crutches. For example, if you begin a topic sentence with "This means ...," what or who does the "this" refer to? If you use the demonstrative pronouns make sure you identify what you are referring to: "This decision…" or "That rule change …."

4. **Sentence Structure and Grammar** – The writer should remember that intelligence writing puts a high premium on short declarative sentences with little or no internal punctuation. If you have trouble with English, you have found the right profession. Be careful of commas. An English sentence can be correct with or without a comma. For example:

- *I hereby leave all my earthly belongings to the first of my children who lives a good life.* Message: The first of my eleven off-springs to shape up and live a good life gets the loot.

- *I hereby leave all my earthly belongings to the first of my children, who lives a good life.* Message: I am leaving the family fortune to my first born because I am rewarding the child for living a good life.

There is also a rule in commas that runs counter to other forms of writing. In intelligence writing, you must have a comma in a series of three or more just before the "and." For example:

I hereby leave all my earthly belongings to Sally, Paul and Grace. What is Sally's reaction? "I knew dad loved me the best. I get 50% of the estate." The IC at both the state and federal level has adopted the legal standard—the failure to have the comma after Paul's name means that he and Grace are equal to Sally. To be correct, if you want all three to share equally in the estate, the sentence must be written: *I hereby leave all my earthly belongings to Sally, Paul, and Grace.*

THE ENGLISH SENTENCE

The revolution in technology has taken a toll on the use of correct English—nowhere is this more evident than in the use of correct English sentences. All of us, all intelligence officers/analysts, need to remind ourselves periodically of what an English sentence is. Every day we speak in sentence fragments, but in spoken English much of the communication comes through voice, tone, body language, gestures, and facial expressions. In writing you have none of these crutches to help fill in the missing pieces—you just have your sentences.

Everyone reading this section has fallen into bad habits when it comes to English sentences. If you text message or dash out an e-mail, you take short cuts. You probably abbreviate or write in sentence fragments when you write an e-mail to a friend. These bad habits chip away at your recognition of and ability to use a correct English sentence. You need to use the articles (the, a, and an) correctly. If you leave something out of your sentences you invite the reader to fill in and in intelligence writing that invitation can have dire consequences. In a courtroom, a defense attorney can have a field day with poorly written or obscure sentences in reports. Therefore, the use of complete English sentences is critical to intelligence writing. Let's take a moment and review the three types of sentences that should make up the majority of your written product.

Every English sentence has three essential elements: **a subject, a verb,** and **a complete thought**. If there is a subject and a verb, but the words do not express a complete thought—no sentence exists. Without the complete thought, you have a sentence fragment.

As for the intelligence sentences themselves, keep them short. Shorter sentences are easier for the reader to visually digest. If you use shorter sentences, you also reduce the chances of misunderstanding and add to both the precision and clarity of your writing. The bulk of intelligence writing should be in the following:

- Simple sentences using active voice: *Two witnesses saw the suspect near the crime.*

- Complex sentences (a simple sentence with a dependant clause): *The source asserted, "The terrorists plan to blow-up the Brooklyn Bridge."*

- Compound sentences (two simple sentences joined by a conjunction—don't forget to put a comma in front of the conjunction): *We tailed the suspect to the train station, and then we followed him to the bus station.*

CONCEPTUALIZATION

We need to return to the subject of conceptualization, of thinking, because it is so important. No matter what form of writing is involved, conceptualization is the necessary first step. The intelligence officer/analyst needs to know the format, objectives, and goals of what she/he is writing. What is the report intended to do, give crime scene observations and analysis? Analyze a possible threat? Indicate where and what terrorists may target next?

Taking the time to conceptualize at every step of an investigation will also pay added dividends. The conceptualization process will help you identify gaps in your knowledge. It is not a bad idea to make a list of the gaps at each stage of the investigation and as you turn out your written products. This list of gaps can be invaluable in helping to direct and guide sources.

Clarity and accuracy trump everything in intelligence writing. All the best ideas, crime scene analysis, and intelligence judgments are not worth the paper they are written on if they are not clear and readily understandable. The intelligence officers/analysts reports must be logical, accurate, and complete. Police and law enforcement writing must be logical and the intelligence officer/analyst should ask how does my written product help the reader understand? It is the job of the intelligence professional to present his/her conclusions clearly so they can be understood on the first reading. The reader should not have to ponder this or that.

Remember, writing is thinking on paper and if an individual's words are muddled, confused, or riddled with poor English, his/her credibility suffers. If written English is a main tool of communication and you cannot use that tool, what impression is given? What are you saying about yourself as a law enforcement/intelligence officer/analyst? Furthermore, the nation's police forces, the Department of Homeland Security (DHS), DIA, CIA, FBI, and all members of the Intelligence Communities must be able to communicate with each other through written products.

Before we move on, it is worthwhile to clear up a problem in intelligence writing that comes up in several venues. Someone will ask, "What is the difference between analysis and opinion? Aren't you just asking us to give an opinion, when you ask us to draft a topic sentence with a *so-what*?"

No, we are not asking you to give your *opinion*. It is important to remember the difference between an *opinion* and an *analytical judgment*:

- **Opinion** - *An opinion is a statement of preference whose grounds are wholly personal.*

- **Analytical Judgment** - *An analytical judgment is one whose grounds of support do not depend on the individual who holds them.*

Now that we have established the difference between an *opinion* and an *analytical judgment*, this is a good time to look at the Intelligence Community Analytic Standards as prescribed by the Office of the Director of National Intelligence.

ODNI: INTELLIGENCE COMMUNITY ANALYTIC STANDARDS
(For more information, please visit www.ais.dni.ic.gov)

- Objectivity
- Independent of political considerations
- Timeliness
- Based on all available sources of intelligence
- Exhibits proper standards of analytic tradecraft:
    - Properly describes quality, reliability of sources, properly caveats, and expresses uncertainties or confidence in analytic judgment
    - Properly distinguishes between underlying intelligence and analysts' assumptions/judgments
    - Incorporates alternative analysis where appropriate
    - Relevance to U.S. national security
    - Logical argumentation
    - Consistency, or highlights change
    - Accurate judgments/assessments

Not all of the above will apply to all the writing templates you will use, but it is good to keep some of them in mind even if you don't put them in your written product. For example, you should (in your mind if nowhere else) clearly distinguish when you are making a judgment versus an assumption. Remember, when you make an assumption, you have no facts or evidence on which to pin the assumption. When you make a judgment you have evidence and facts you can point to as the reason for the judgment.

Think about the gaps in your knowledge and what you need to do to fill those gaps—what requirements can you levy? This understanding of the "gaps" is particularly helpful in giving briefings. You may well be asked what evidence is lacking and what you or your organization doing to fill those gaps.

Take a closer look at some of the underlying principles of good English that should be part of all writers' tools—specifically police and intelligence officers/analysts.

PUTTING GRAMMAR AND PUNCTUATION TOGETHER

Writing is thinking on paper. By definition, police/intelligence officers/analysts are paid to use their brains—they are paid to think. When you write you give the reader a glimpse of your thinking abilities— you are saying something about yourself. Like it or not, people form images about you based on how you write. If there are a number of spelling or grammar mistakes what are you saying about yourself— careless, not well educated, lack of pride? What does sloppy writing say about you the police/intelligence officer/analyst? Writing can be easy if you remember a few simple rules:

Rule One: Think before you write. Know what you want to say before you put pen to paper or fingers to keyboard.

Rule Two: Use simple sentences wherever possible—in the active voice.

Rule Three: Pick your words carefully. Use shorter English words based on the Anglo-Saxon roots of the language. These words usually are clear and void of nuance and innuendo.

Rule Four: Economy of language—make each word count and use familiar terms.

Rule Five: Make the majority of your sentences short and to the point.

Rule Six: Organize your thoughts. If you are writing a longer paper or memorandum, take time to organize your thoughts so that you can present a logical argument.

Rule Seven: Self-edit and proofread. If you have time, have someone proofread your final product.

If you are looking for a title or name to call our type of writing, it might be best described as expository writing. Expository writing is plain talk, straight-forward and matter-of-fact communication. Expository writing is an efficient way of conveying ideas and requires precise writing and stresses clarity. A major goal of expository writing is NEVER make the reader wonder what the main point is in the paper or paragraph.

Report Writing Principles

Now, let's take a closer look at the specific types of reports you may be called upon to write.

Raw Reports

The collection of raw data or raw intelligence is the vital first step in the intelligence process. Raw data is collected in a variety of ways—the most common are observations at a crime scene, recording the words of an eyewitness, and through sources or agents.

The reporting officer at a crime scene has the duty and obligation to write down all the details and observations he or she sees. Use descriptors or precise measurements—be specific wherever possible. It is best to err on the side of too much detail, rather than too little. Subsequent reviews of the crime scene report in comparison with other evidence will help the investigating team put all the pieces together.

Accuracy and thoroughness in taking down the words of an eye witness can make or break a case. The importance of getting an eyewitness account while it is still fresh in his/her mind cannot be overestimated. Here, the reporting officer has the duty to question the witness for greater detail. If the eyewitness is not a native English speaker, the questioning may be much more extensive in order to make sure the officer accurately captures (in standard American English) what the eyewitness saw.

As time goes by witnesses' memories may fail, they become reluctant to talk, or they may want to put the incident behind them. Therefore, the clarity of the officer's initial raw report is vital and will help reduce the chances of ambiguity and misunderstanding.

It is a good idea for the officer to draft a few lines of his/her impressions. Was the eye witness reluctant to talk? Did the eyewitness look the officer in the face? Did the body language indicate the individual was telling the truth?

Raw reports are the first input into the system. The raw intelligence report is designed to do three things:

1. To convey the essentials in a readable way

2. To identify each source of data being used

3. To improve the quality of the information by putting it in a written format, rather than by keeping it in the officer's head

It is important to keep the raw intelligence report tightly focused. As new information becomes available, it is best to do new reports, rather than try to update the existing one. Do not put too many things in one report, draft separate reports—this aids in analysis, dissemination, and the review and purging of files.

The raw intelligence report (also referred to as a "field report" or an "intelligence report") may be divided into one or all of the following sections each time information is received:

- **File Number or Project Number** - This is assigned in accordance with each agency's policies and procedures.

- **Identification of Sources** - In many instances corroborating information about the same subject, activity, or event is often collected from different sources at the same time or within a very short period of time. Space should be available in each report for providing information from more than one source. Give as much information about the source as possible. For law enforcement sources, use rank/title, name, agency, city/state, and telephone number. You may use yourself as a source.

Be sure to specify what was collected from each source to will allow comparison of differing accounts. This comparison also has the benefit of identifying gaps in the overall information, which in turn will help direct resources to fill those gaps.

If it is necessary to protect someone's identity, generally the word *anonymous* is used. If someone offers to provide information on a continuing basis and wants anonymity, you can also put in *true name withheld.* Or, if it is unknown whether he/she will be used again, and you want to maintain anonymity, you can also assign an *informant number.*

- **Security Classification** - Attention to security classification is extremely important. Throughout the Intelligence Community, senior managers are repeatedly asked "what are the most frequent mistakes they encounter?" The response invariably includes a reference to incorrect security classifications.

In many instances it is necessary to protect not only the information contained in the report but the identity of the source. At the state level, classification guidelines vary from one agency to another. At the federal level there are well defined classification rules and guidelines. For example, the author of a report must justify the use of a particular classification. Management or security in the members of the IC can tell you where to find the federal guidelines.

In general there are four levels of classification:

1. Public record or "open source" information is usually unclassified. However, under certain circumstances, "open source" or public record information may carry some sort of restrictor such as "For Internal Use Only." The theory being, that because the information is being used in an intelligence report, some control or restriction is needed.

2. Information that can generally be disseminated within the law enforcement community should carry the lowest classification possible. Too high of a classification can prevent dissemination to people who need to know, or who may have information related to an investigation.

3. Active or ongoing investigations should have a mid-level classification in order to prevent the accidental disclosure of sensitive intelligence, investigative techniques, and strategy. This level of classification will probably have a designated time frame, which should be indicated. Because of the increasing cooperation between state and federal agencies, if you are working for or in a state police intelligence unit, you may want these mid-level classifications to conform to the classification guidelines of the Department of Homeland Security or the FBI—or both.

4. The highest level of classification may be used for a variety of reasons. The most common are to prevent compromising the identity of undercover personnel; when misconduct of public officials is being investigated; and when the intelligence is part of a broader national security issue such as terrorist activity, drug trafficking, and trafficking of humans.

- **Source Evaluation** - More than one source can be used in an intelligence report. It is important to identify each source and the information that each source provided. By identifying the information with the source you are taking the first vital step in the analytical process. Specifying what was collected from each source allows comparison of differing accounts can provide corroboration of facts, details, and times; and may make gaps in information readily apparent.

  For law enforcement sources, use rank/title, name, agency, city/state, and telephone number. You may use yourself as a source. Be specific about various inquiries and record's checks so that if questions arise there will be no doubt where to go to recheck the information. If information from several sources is contained in the same report, be explicit in identifying which sources corroborate which information.

  Remember to leave enough room to provide as much detail as possible; specifying what information was collected from each source. This detail is a vital part of the initial analysis and can be an invaluable aid if the same or similar information is received from other sources in other reports. The bona fides of sources can be determined early-on by paying careful attention to the "Source Evaluation" of your report.

- **Crime** - The computerized file formats that are used today allow for a text search of the narrative. This search can provide a quick summary of an individual's criminal activities. Therefore, in order to aid in future database searches, make sure that you put key words in your report related to individuals and to crimes. Many intelligence reports do not have a link to specific criminal activity; therefore, the use of key words related to crimes will aid in the future retrieval of the report.

- **Summary** - The summary or "synopsis" of the intelligence report is extremely important. This part of your report is closely tied to the uniform intelligence style of writing. This is where the conceptualization comes into play. The topic sentence of the summary needs to capture the reader's attention by telling him/her the "*what*" and the "*so-what*." This sentence—and indeed the whole summary paragraph—frames the whole report. In theory, the reader can read this portion of the report and know the significance of what follows in greater detail.

  The summary should not be a reproduction of the detailed narrative contained in the body of the report, but it should contain the salient points—what the reader needs to know. You may have heard the summary paragraph referred to as the "big picture, bottom-line" or the synthesis of the report. No matter what you call it, the important thing to remember is the summary should tell the reader quickly and concisely the main points contained in the report as well as any and all conclusions the reporting officer has about the information and the sources. The summary should not be long.

Some members of the IC use these summary paragraphs as the basis of morning briefings. Therefore, it is vital that your paragraph or paragraphs be clear and concise. Make reference to what you do not know, as well as what you know.

- **Date of Information, Date of Acquisition, and Date of Report** - The date of information is the time or period of time when the criminal activity occurred or may have occurred. The date and time span when the information was obtained (date of acquisition) is included—this information helps the reader determine the timeliness of what is being reported. You should also include the date you prepared and submitted the report.

- **Officer's/Analysts' Notes/Details—Reporting Office and Agency/Unit** - This section of the report is where you put the details and observations of the information you collected. This section requires good judgment on the part of the officer/analyst because it should not contain non-pertinent details. What is pertinent and non-pertinent is difficult to determine in a raw report, so it is better to follow the rule—if in doubt, put it in. Comments regarding the difficulty in obtaining the information should not be in this section, unless those comments reflect on the source's reliability.

  The following are examples of topics in an officers/analysts notes or details:

  - Indicate the identity of someone requesting to remain anonymous, or who may or may not be assigned a code name or number until their willingness and capability to be used as a cooperating individual is determined.

  - Report a source's motivation and willingness to provide information. This can be critical and can play a significant role in determining whether or not the source should be assigned a code name or number. (An individual who provides information once is rarely given a code name or number.)

  - Report any information you have on a source's reputation and background. This information is very important for establishing reliability. Information such as past or current substance abuse, emotional stability, prejudices, reasons for revenge, or deceptiveness should be included if known.

  - Note any conflicts in different accounts by different sources. Here, your judgment as to which version is the most reliable and why, is very important.

  - Give any information or facts about the situation or area that is not readily apparent or reported elsewhere.

  - Refer to significant information in other reports. Be careful not to provide too much linkage to material in a criminal intelligence file or report that should be protected from inadvertent disclosure.

  - Give detailed information from the source, but opinions of the drafting officer— underscoring discrepancies—should be in an addendum. Placing this information on a separate page helps prevent confusion.

Gist and Comment Reports

Gist and Comment Reports are very common and have a specific format. The format consists of two parts:

1. A gist or summary of an article, report, or activity that has occurred
2. A comment section that analyzes the report's significance

Steps to consider in preparing a Gist and Comment report include the following:

- Use a recent case, incident, or article as the basis.
- Capture and summarize salient facts in the case, incident, or article.
- Conduct background research (as much as time allows—often only files close at hand can be culled for information).
- Keep the gist and comment portions separate from one another.
- Note any omissions in the source case, incident, or article.
- Foreshadow events in the near future.

These reports may be part of a daily routine for intelligence officers/analysts. They rest on sound intelligence writing principles that are used throughout the IC at the federal and state levels—the separation of facts from analysis. These reports play a vital role in keeping police executives informed and able to make solid decisions. An example of a "Gist and Comment Report" is shown in the next section.

CRIMINAL INTELLIGENCE REPORT
Bureau of Investigation and Intelligence
California Department of Justice

Project No: | Project No. | Date of Information: | Date of Information |

Dissemination: Release Limited - Confidential

Crime:

Area: Choose an item.

Source ID Source Reliability: Choose an item. Content Validity Choose an item.

S1: | Source 1 |

S2: | Source 2 |

S3: | Source 3 |

Subject: | Subject |

Synopsis:

Details:

cc:

Writer: [Writer]   Date: [Date]   Approved: [Approved By]   Date: [Date Approved]

Note: This document contains neither recommendation nor conclusions of the Department of Justice, Bureau of Investigation and Intelligence. It is the property of the Department of Justice and is loaned to your agency for official use only. The document and its contents are not to be duplicated outside your agency.

Report Writing Principles

GIST AND COMMENT

The FBI issued an Information Bulletin on December 29, xxxx, warning of possible al-Qa'ida attacks in the United States prior to the upcoming New Year's holiday. Recent intelligence indicates that al-Qa'ida may be planning an attack, possibly targeting highly populated areas in large U.S. cities. The FBI is also investigating an increase in the smuggling of Iraqi and other Middle East nationals across the Rio Grande from Mexico.

Until recently, the United States has kept its door all but shut to the estimated two million refugees fleeing Iraq. So far, the United States has taken fewer than 800 Iraqi refugees, according to State Department officials. The administration, however, has recently agreed to take 7,000 refugees by the end of next year.

United Press International (UPI) reports unnamed FBI sources as expressing concern that al-Qa'ida may use this increase in refugees to sneak in operatives for future attacks. The FBI Information Bulletin, however, does not mention this possibility, nor does it indicate how many terrorists may have already been smuggled into the United States.

The UPI indicates that the modus operandi is to have the Iraqis and Middle East nationals meet at a safe house in Mexico, and then move across the border where contacts are waiting to drive them to train or bus stations in El Paso, Texas or Belen, New Mexico. Federal prosecutors in New Mexico told UPI they have no current cases involving illegal smuggling of Iraqis or anyone else.

Comment

Although the FBI and DHS possess no further, specific information on the smuggling or the terrorists' targets, tactics, or locations for operations, law enforcement officials should be on heightened alert to potential indicators of terrorist activity or planning. Surveillance and probing of potential targets is consistent with known practices of al-Qa'ida and other terrorist organizations that seek to maximize the likelihood of operational success through careful planning.

Law enforcement personnel should be on the lookout for any suspicious activity, and specifically for the following indicators of terrorist activity:

- Unusual or prolonged interest in security measures or personnel, entry points and access control or perimeter barriers such as fences and walls

- Unusual behavior such as staring or quick movements away from personnel or vehicles entering or leaving designated facilities or parking areas

- Observation of security reaction drills or procedures

- An increase in anonymous telephone or e-mail threats to facilities in conjunction with suspected surveillance incidents

- Foot surveillance involving two or more individuals working together

- Mobile surveillance using vehicles such as bicycles, scooters, motorcycles, cars, or trucks

- Prolonged static surveillance using operatives disguised as panhandlers, shoe shiners, food or flower vendors, news agents, or street cleaners

- Discreet use of still cameras, video recorders or note-taking at non-tourist locations

Working Intelligence Reports

For intelligence reports to be useful, they must be up-to-date and timely. Therefore, an officer/analyst should keep a "Working Intelligence Report" or a "working file" between the time the information was gathered or received, and the time a report is submitted for approval into the official file. An up-to-date "working report" will contain much more than is put in the final—official report.

Management of these files is extremely important. Non-criminal information contained in the "working file" should not be included in the official report. As the file is built, the officer/analyst should consider marking the non-criminal and other peripheral information. That way when the final report is prepared, the officer will more easily be able to determine what should be purged.

File Summaries

- **Case-Analysis Report** - At the outset of a case, an analyst compiles all available information on the topic, extracting and reassembling material from different individuals. It is also a good idea to conduct additional research at the outset of a case using the internet, commercial databases, other agencies' files, and any other sources available. Thorough research at the beginning of a case provides a solid starting point for the intelligence process.

  This case-analysis report should be as complete as possible because it may provide invaluable insights into where additional information gathering is necessary. The case-analysis report should also include any recommendations on what investigative steps might prove fruitful, given the information known.

- **Violator File Summaries (Target Identification Reports)** - A summary of all data available on an individual violator—or suspected violator—should accompany other types of analytic reports, such as the case analysis report. The violator file summaries should include as many of the following as possible:

  - Name or known aliases or other names of the violator or suspected violator
  - Physical description of the violator or suspected violator
  - Date/place of birth of the violator or suspected violator
  - The social security number of the violator or suspected violator
  - The FBI number and state and local identification numbers assigned to the violator or suspected violator
  - Any vehicles registered to the violator or suspected violator
  - The violator or suspected violator's telephone number(s)
  - Any real estate owned by the violator or suspected violator
  - The names of any known associates of the violator or suspected violator
  - Any history you have about the violator or suspected violator

- Any patterns or methods of operation associated with the violator or suspected violator
- Any geographic area where the violator or suspected violator is known to have worked, lived, or operated
- Reference to any other agencies that have an interest in the violator or suspected violator
- Supporting documents
- The driver's license number of the violator or suspected violator
- Last known address of the violator or suspected violator
- The violator's or suspected violator's employer or business
- Utilities paid by the violator or suspected violator
- Photographs of the violator or suspected violator
- Any past criminal activity which involves the violator or suspected violator
- Violence potential associated with the violator or suspected violator

Activity Reports (Security Alert-Bulletins, Security-Intelligence Reports, Warnings)

- **Security-Alert Bulletin** - A Security Alert Bulletin conveys information of a security nature to agencies or organizations that have a need to know, or may be in a position to respond to the alert.

- **Security-Intelligence Reports** - The Security-Intelligence Report should be provided to the tactical force and to senior commanders on situations with potential for violent confrontation.

- **Warnings** - There are Tactical Warnings or Strategic Warnings: A Tactical Warning reflects imminent danger; a Strategic Warning reflects long-range problems that decision makers or policymakers need to be addressing. In both warning cases, the analyst/officer may use the "gist and comment" format to describe the threat and suggest ways of dealing with the threat. Warnings and threat or vulnerability assessments go hand-in-hand. The warnings are actually the results of vulnerability or threat assessments.

Analytic Reports (Investigative Chronologies, Premonitories, Case Summaries)

- **Investigative Chronologies** - An Investigative Chronology is a report that places each event in date and time order to better understand how the activity unfolded. Think of the Investigative Chronology as an elaborate timeline where each event is summarized, and the source document from which it was obtained is referenced. Other pertinent information, such as an individual's potential as a witness, should also be included in the Investigative Chronology.

- **Premonitories** - A Premonitory is a short-term assessment that focuses on a particular crime group or criminal activity. The Premonitory looks at the most effective way of investigating and prosecuting a criminal group. Data in a Premonitory should include surveillance information, background record checks of targets, information on similar groups or activities, and informant data. The four key areas that should be covered are:

1. What illegal activities the targets are involved in?
2. What the strengths and weaknesses of the group are?
3. What the recommendations for investigative activities are?
4. What the probability of success is for those investigative activities?

The following is a suggested Premonitory format:

    I.   Introduction:
- Definition, description, and background
- Purpose of the report and intended audience
- Sources of information
- Working definitions
- Limitations of the study
- Scope of the inquiry

    II.   Collected Data:
- First topic of investigation
  - Definition
  - Findings
  - Interpretation of findings
- Second topic of investigation
  - Definition
  - Findings
- Interpretation of findings

    III.   Conclusions:
- Summary of findings
- Overall interpretation of findings
- Recommendations (adapted from a federal reporting format)

- **Case Summaries** - In the final stages of a case, the officer/analyst often assists the prosecuting attorney by providing compiled data and charts derived from intelligence analysis as aids in presenting the case. These case summaries can be, and often are, vital bridges between the investigation and the prosecution of a group of violators. In addition, the analyst can take these summaries—often in the form of charts or tables—into the grand jury or court as a summary witness. This can be followed by analytic testimony as an expert witness in a particular type of criminal activity.

Analytic Assessments (Criminal Intelligence Assessments, Threat Assessments, Estimates, Vulnerability Assessments, Encyclopedic Reports, and Forecasts)

- **Criminal Intelligence Assessments** - A good model to follow in producing Criminal Intelligence Assessments is the one used by the California Department of Justice. According to the California authorities the following eight areas should be included in all Criminal Intelligence Assessments:

CHAPTER 10

Report Writing Principles

1. **Executive Summary** - The summary should tell the busy reader exactly what he or she should know about the report. If the reader goes no further he/she will know your main conclusions about the criminal group. The summary should be concise.

2. **Capabilities** - This section of the assessment should cover the criminal groups' abilities, capabilities, and skills—and how these might grow and develop in the future. Any previous reports on the group or the group's activity should be included here.

3. **Intentions** - Here, the criminal purpose of the group, network, and criminal activities engaged in by the subject(s) or group(s) should be covered.

4. **Organization** - The organizational structure should be examined in as much detail as possible. This section should include the leadership chain of command, the names of key individuals and what positions they hold, any noted changes in organization size or leadership, and detectable "weak links," informants, members with ties outside the group, and the group's relationship to other groups. This is the section to comment, if you can, on the stability or instability of the group.

5. **Trends** - An historical overview of the development and trends of the group or organization can be very helpful. This overview can relate to changes or development in the group's size, criminal activity, propensity for violence, and past leadership changes.

6. **Forecasting** - Based on what has happened in the past, where do you see the group going? What is happening now and what may happen in the future?

7. **Charts** - Tables, graphs, charts, maps, and other graphics are highly affective in underscoring critical points. They also have the added advantage of not only removing tedious detail from the text, but being visually digestible and readily understandable for the busy consumer of your product.

8. **Conclusion** - The conclusion is usually a lengthier summary than the Executive Summary. The conclusion helps the reader understand the main points you want him/her to take away from the information he/she has just read. The conclusion also reinforces and slightly expands the Executive Summary and often refers back to the forecasts you have made. Be careful—never make over-generalizations or draw conclusions that are unsupported.

Another format for a Criminal Intelligence Assessment is:

o **Executive Summary** - The Executive Summary states the purpose of the assessment, gives the key findings, and provides policy implications.

o **Statement of Issues** - This section is intended to give the significance and fundamental issue to be explored.

o **Review of Previous Assessments** - If there are any, capture the findings of previous assessments and studies.

o **Limitations of Assessments** - Identifying the limitations of the assessment or gaps in knowledge is a critical part of the assessment. This section helps the reader put the assessment into the proper perspective. By identifying limitations, you also help managers allocate resources.

o **Methodologies** - This section should discuss the methods you used in collecting data. An explanation of any methodologies you used in analyzing the evidence should be put in this part of the assessment. The use of methodologies can buttress your credibility by underscoring the meticulous and thorough approach you took in analyzing and drafting the assessment.

o **Findings** - Empirical (experience and observation) data can be folded into this section. This data may be presented in charts, tables, graphs, and summaries.

o **Analysis and Policy Implications** - In addition to the Executive Summary, this section is one of the most important in the assessment because it contains the analysis and the implications for policy. Some of this is captured in the Executive Summary, but here you give much more detailed evidence to substantiate your conclusions.

o **Bibliography** - List all the sources you consulted in drafting the assessment.

• **Threat Assessments** - A Threat Assessment is a formal estimate in which an intelligence unit analyzes pertinent information about a new or continuing threat. If a Threat Assessment is produced it is almost always serious. In other words, the raw intelligence has met the threshold required to draw the threat to consumers' attention. There are however, Threat Assessments that are done on an annual basis to review and update the status of an ongoing threat—this is the case with al-Qa'ida.

A Threat Assessment should contain the degree of probability of a criminal or terrorist act. By definition, that probability is probably high, or you would not have decided to write. The Assessment should address the time frame of the threat and identify the possible target(s). The Assessment must contain conclusions about the probability that the threat will materialize, along with recommendations for countermeasures. For a closer look at a Threat Assessment model, see Chapter 11, Section 3 "Intelligence and Anti-terrorism."

• **Estimates** - Across the board in the IC "Estimates" are considered to be one of the premier intelligence products. At the federal level, the National Intelligence Estimate (NIE) or the Special National Intelligence Estimate (SNIE) bring together the best minds of the IC to examine problems of national security and to make projections—to give policymakers the Community's best analysis of a situation or problem and an indication of what to expect or where the problem is going.

The estimating process at the federal level bears marked similarities to the process at the state level. Indeed, the strategic estimate by the state police intelligence units is an intelligence product that requires considered judgments on an array of key intelligence problems or issues in order to provide a backdrop against which to make projections for the near future. That is parallel to what is done at the federal level.

Estimates may be produced on an annual basis, such as the Narcotics Intelligence Estimates of the National Narcotics Intelligence Consumers Committee and the National Drug Intelligence Estimate of the Royal Canadian Mounted Police.

- **Vulnerability Assessments** - Vulnerability Assessments are studies to determine the potential for harm to a person, event, or location as a result of criminal activity. The traditional use for Vulnerability Assessments is for executive protection and special events planning. However, they might also be used to determine the possible market for a new criminal product or service, or the likelihood that the jurisdiction will be impacted by a crime group or activity. The Vulnerability Assessment includes many aspects of the estimative process—the motto for most Vulnerability Assessments is "forewarned is forearmed."

- **Encyclopedic Reports** - Encyclopedic Reports give an overview of a topic such as a geographic area. These are done by such organizations as the Drug Enforcement Administration and deal with the areas of drug production and the transit routes for drug trafficking. An Encyclopedic Report would include such information as a country's population, political situation, economics, terrain, major exports and imports, and relations with other countries. The Encyclopedic Report provides a reference and basis for dealing with a given country.

- **Forecasts** - A Forecast, as its name indicates, is a prediction about what will happen in the future. Forecasts are more limited in scope than a full blown Estimate. The two share much in common, however. They both make judgments based on limited evidence; they both take risks because they are produced on fragmentary facts and information; and they often are built on speculation that the near future will be similar to the recent past. Some intelligence analysts are uncomfortable writing Estimates or Forecasts, but keep in mind the axiom that "the worst sin for an intelligence analyst/officer is to say nothing when the available evidence indicates a warning, estimate, or forecast should be issued."

The following are some guidelines to consider in the drafting of a Forecast:

- o Is the expected future trend new or a continuing development?
- o If there is some sort of change in modus operandi, leadership, strategy, or any aspect of the group, indicates what it is and the significance of the change.
- o Differentiate between mid-term and long-term change.
- o Discuss the cause of the change.
- o Point out limiting factors that may have an impact on the change.
- o Identify important contingencies or raise doubts, where appropriate.
- o Acknowledge areas of uncertainty.
- o Acknowledge assumptions that were critical to making the prediction.

Intelligence Publications (Spot Items, Weekly Reports)

- **Spot Items** - Spot Items are often prepared for intelligence periodicals—that is, regularly published and disseminated intelligence bulletins disseminated by law enforcement or security agencies. The Spot Item resembles the "Gist" part of the "Gist and Comment" publication. Your goal is to take a source or sources and pull out the key points without providing additional explanation or analysis. The following is a 125-word Spot Item on the banking crisis in Japan:

Spot Item

(Date) Japan: Finance Minister Resigns

The resignation of Finance Minister Hiroshi Mitsuzuka and his deputy in the midst of an economic crisis may open the door to badly need reforms. Mitsuzuka's departure is a blow to Prime Minister Ryutaro Hashimoto's government, but clears the way for new—and possibly stronger—financial leadership. The crisis centers on badly supervised banks. The Finance Ministry acknowledges that bad bank loans total $610 billion—three times the amount previously thought. Two senior ministry officials were arrested and charged with taking bribes in return for alerting bank's to surprise inspections. The Japanese financial markets have remained calm in part because Japanese politicians have hinted they may spend more money or cut taxes to stimulate the economy.

- **Weekly Reports** - In some agencies, the intelligence units are responsible for producing weekly reports on trends, developments, emerging patterns in crime and emergent groups to alert management and officers on the street to problems that may arise. These publications are usually a mix of "Gist and Comment" and "Spot Items."

REVIEW AND APPROVAL OF INTELLIGENCE REPORTS

It is the responsibility of a Quality Control Officer for the final approval of material to be put into a criminal intelligence file. It is not possible to file all the information received, so this officer has the unpopular task in many organizations of ensuring that rules are enforced.

The major responsibilities of this officer include ensuring that a raw intelligence report is crime-related and those criminal activities are within the current mission statement. The officer also checks to make sure that cross-referencing to all appropriate sources is critical to the subsequent retrieving of information. Giving short shrift to grammar and punctuation errors can create serious problems. Remember, an English sentence may be correct with or without a comma, but the meanings are dramatically different. Therefore, the Quality Control Officer should look at sentence structure, punctuation, and spelling. Then, after double checking the sourcing, source evaluation, and initial classification, a sequential file number is assigned by intelligence unit personnel.

One of the last steps in the approval process is to determine how long the material will be retained rather than where it should be filed. The answer to this question often hinges on the ability to verify information. Initially, the answer to this question may be unknown; therefore it is a good idea to mark the file for review in one year. Rather than keep it in a separate file, special markings can be made on the cover page and/or on index cards to indicate retention of up to one year—some organizations lump these one-year files into a "temporary file" category. File retention of five years or more is usually referred to as a permanent file. If verification of the information in the temporary file is made during the first year, the Quality Control Officer should then move the file into the permanent, five-year category.

THE ORAL REPORT

Oral briefings are very important. Some managers of intelligence and consumers prefer an oral briefing to a written report. Usually, an oral briefing is short and to the point—it is a presentation of a situation or analysis. The oral briefing often provides the audience with information needed to guide operations or make decisions about resource allocation. Traditionally the most common audiences included investigators, task force personnel, investigative managers, and prosecutors. But, as the IC has drawn closer in the wake of September 11, 2001, police intelligence officers and analysts are being called upon to brief state level officials and members of the federal IC.

Careful consideration should be given to preparing an oral briefing. Some things to consider include:

- Find out how much time is allotted for the briefing.

- Identify who will be in the audience; their backgrounds and their "need to know." If your briefing is classified, you must make sure everyone in the room has the proper clearances.

- Organize your briefing carefully. Begin by determining in your mind the main point or points you want the listeners to take away. A good rule to follow for organization is the following:

  o **Introduction** - allow 10 percent of your time to this part of your presentation. You should put your main conclusions in this section. If you have not been introduced you should lead with a short introduction of yourself and your credentials.

  o **Body** - allocate approximately 70 percent of your time to your supporting evidence and sub-points. You may want to consider organizing along one of three lines— strictly analytical, straight reporting and update, or informative and background.

  o **Conclusion** - save approximately 20 percent of your time for your conclusion. Here, you reiterate the main points made in the introduction and tie them to some of the key evidence. You also may want to end by telling the audience (if you can and if appropriate) where you see the problem going.

- Develop graphics to support the briefing and have copies ready for the audience. Be careful of Power Point! Do not hide behind Power Point slides! Visual aids should be used to support your briefing, not detract from it. The most common forms of visual aids are maps, charts, graphs, and photos. If you use visual aids well, they can:

  o Make your presentation more persuasive
  o Help the audience grasp information quickly
  o Add variety and emphasis to what you are saying
  o Reinforce your oral comments
  o Add organization to your briefing
  o Help you be concise by removing cumbersome statistics and details from your verbal presentation
  o Can help you stimulate questions

Key points to remember in using visual aids include the following:

- Do not use cluttered or complicated graphs that distract from your message
- Do not use visual aids as a filler—the audience will pick up on that immediately
- Do not use outdated visual aids
- Do not use a visual aid that does not suit your audience
- Do not use a visual aid that is interesting but irrelevant to your topic

Finally, three good rules to keep in mind about oral briefings: First know your material thoroughly; second, be succinct and to the point; and third, answer all questions—or if you cannot, get back to the individual at a later date with the answer.

A WRAP-UP OF THE PRINCIPLES OF GOOD INTELLIGENCE

Whether you are writing or briefing your intelligence there are three points to remember:

1. **Accuracy** - Distinguish between observations, quotations, rumors, hearsay, and opinions. Spell out all abbreviations if you have any concern that the reader or listener will not understand. Give full and exact names, addresses, dates, times, and amounts of money involved.

2. **Brevity** - Brevity is next to godliness in the production of intelligence. Your written and spoken sentences should be free of unnecessary words and phrases which distract from your message. Avoid information and details that are not necessary for the reader or listener to understand the point(s) you are making. Avoid repetition.

3. **Completeness** - Include all relevant information in your written or verbal intelligence that is necessary to make your point(s).

Effective intelligence writing and briefing rely on good organization, which in turn aids clarity and understanding. If drafting an outline for a paper or a briefing helps you, by all means do it—REMEMBER--conceptualize. Know what it is you want to say, know why the reader or listener should care, and take the time to make sure the intelligence reporting is easily understandable. Remember, as intelligence officers/analysts, we are paid for our brains. We are paid for our ability to take complex situations or problems and bring some sort of meaning or order to them. If your thoughts are muddled, if your writing is confusing, and if your briefings are vague, your credibility is seriously damaged.

REFERENCES

Associated Press. (2000). "Drug seizures suggest use of 'ecstasy' on a steep rise." *Trenton Times.* April 2, A 15.

Buccino, Robert J.. (1998). "the Collection of Information." *Issues of Interest to Law Enforcement—Criminal Intelligence: A Vital Police Function.* Sacramento, CA: Law Enforcement Intelligence Unit.

California Department of Justice. (1993). *The Bureau of Investigation Intelligence Operations Manual.* Sacramento, CA: Division of Law Enforcement, California Department of Justice.

Cariens, David S. Excerpts from the draft text book. *A Guide to Intelligence Analysis and Writing.* Slated for publication in late 2009 or 2010.

Department of the Army. (1967). *Investigative Reports Handbook.* Fort Holabird, MD: US Army Intelligence School. July.

Federal Bureau of Investigation. (1984). *National Crime Information Center (NCIC) Code Manual, Third Edition.* Washington, DC: U.S. Department of Justice. July.

Frost, Charles C. and Jack Morris. (1983). *Police Intelligence Reports.* Orangevale, CA: Palmer Enterprises.

Garbo, Cynthia M. (1987). *Warning Intelligence.* Association of Former Intelligence Officers.

Harris, Don R. (1976). *The Basic Elements of Intelligence-Revised.* Washington, DC: Law Enforcement Assistance Administration.

International Association of Chiefs of Police. (1985). *Law Enforcement Policy on Management of Criminal Intelligence.* Gaithersburg, MD: International Association of Chiefs of Police.

Law Enforcement Intelligence Unit. (1994-1995). *Criminal Intelligence File Guidelines.* Sacramento, CA: Law Enforcement Intelligence Unit.

Martens, Frederick T. (1983). "The Essence of the Intelligence Process: Analysis." *Issues of Interest to Law Enforcement—Intelligence—The Ultimate Managerial Tool.* Sacramento, CA: Law Enforcement Intelligence Unit.

Morehouse, Bob. (1998). "Criminal Intelligence Files." *Issues of Interest to Law Enforcement-Criminal Intelligence: A Vital Police Function.* Sacramento, CA: Law Enforcement Intelligence Unit.

Morris, Jack. (1983). *The Criminal Intelligence File.* Loomis, CA: Palmer Press.

---------(1993). "Criminal Intelligence: Gearing for the Year 2000." *IALEIA Journal.* Vol. 7, No. 2, Winter.

Petersen, Martin. Retired Deputy Executive Officer, CIA. "Making the Analytic Process Work." *Studies in Intelligence.* Vol. 44, No. 1, 2005. The Central Intelligence Agency. McLean, VA.

Peterson, Marilyn B. (1994). *Applications in Criminal Analysis: A Sourcebook.* Westport, CT: Greenwood Press.

----------(1998). "Oral Briefings." Advanced Analytic Training given in Waltham, MA. June.

Roger, Paul. (1998). "The Security of Criminal Intelligence Units." *Issues of Interest to Law Enforcement—Intelligence: A Vital Police Function.* Sacramento, CA: Law Enforcement Unit.

Schneider, Stephen R. (1995). "The Criminal Intelligence Function: Toward a Comprehensive and Normative Model." *IALEIA Journal.* Vol. 9, No. 2. June.

Wright, Richard. (1998). "Criminal Intelligence and Investigations." *Issues of Interest to Law Enforcement Criminal Intelligence: A Vital Police Function.* Sacramento, CA: Law Enforcement Intelligence Unit.

Applications of Intelligence

Section 1
Intelligence in Organized Crime
By Robert C. Fahlman

"If you know the enemy and know yourself, you need not fear the results of a hundred battles. If you know yourself but not the enemy, for every victory you will also suffer a defeat. If you know neither yourself or the enemy, you are a fool and will meet defeat in every battle."

- **Sun Tzu**, *The Art of War* (500 BC)

INTRODUCTION

Crime and criminals are no more than mirrors of the global society in which they exist. Just as the bi-polar geopolitical world has disintegrated, giving way to a new, dynamic, and volatile global environment, the nature of organized crime is in a perpetual state of evolution as well. Organized crime in itself, or linked with terrorism, poses a matrix of new challenges for the law enforcement and broader public safety communities. The business of organized crime is "business", with global illicit profits estimated at US $1,000 billion annually (United Nations, 1996). The new world order, some would say *dis*order, paints a challenging portrait of the ever-evolving nature and scope of a criminal landscape that is increasingly transnational in terms of threats and harms to urban and rural areas alike.

While there are many definitions of organized crime, it is largely accepted that its' defining characteristics – ability to corrupt, employment of violence and intimidation, wealth accumulation and multiple-enterprise scope – place this form of crime high on the agendas of law enforcement as well as government and international organizations such as the UNODC, Interpol, and Europol; to name only a few. Corruption and intimidation, arms trafficking, identity theft, environmental crime, money laundering, theft of cultural property, drug trafficking, crimes against women and children, crime over the Internet, and trafficking in body parts, provide a wide spectrum of challenges to our society today. Facing such daunting challenges, how can law enforcement, governments, and international organizations effectively control and prevent organized crime from becoming endemic in civil society around the globe?

The advent of intelligence-led policing and the more systematic employment of strategic and tactical intelligence has provided the tools with which law enforcement can level the playing field and more effectively control and prevent organized crime from gaining a stronger foothold in society. The focus of this section centers on the application of both strategic and tactical intelligence as effective tools with which to control, reduce and prevent organized crime.

STRATEGIC AND TACTICAL INTELLIGENCE: TECHNIQUES AND APPLICATIONS

Crime in the 21st century, more than in any previous era, can be characterized by two fundamental elements; it has become global and is constantly evolving. Thus, the capacity of law enforcement or government - whether at the local, national, regional, or transnational level - will, to a large extent, be dependent on its ability to adapt on a continuing basis to a constantly changing environment. In order to deal more effectively with the threats and harms posed by organized crime on society, law enforcement will need to employ more sophisticated intelligence systems and approaches to prioritize its resources aimed at dismantling criminal networks and neutralizing criminal markets. Strategic and tactical intelligence provide the necessary support for both law enforcement leaders and government policymakers to recognize emerging crime threats as well as opportunities in order to respond in a timely and proactive manner.

There are two broad, often over lapping and complementary forms of intelligence: strategic and tactical (see definitions in Figure 1: "Strategic and Tactical Intelligence Forms"). Although having different primary purposes, they should not be viewed as being totally distinct from one another. Tactical intelligence often serves as the primary base of information for strategic intelligence, and strategic intelligence in turn serves to position and often guide tactical intelligence. This interdependent and complementary relationship serves to strengthen the seven-phase intelligence process (direction/planning, collection, collation, evaluation, analysis, reporting/dissemination, and application) and, thus, better serve the operational (*tactical*) and managerial (*strategic*) requirements of law enforcement. However, whether strategic or tactical, criminal intelligence has its focus on five distinct areas in relation to organized crime or criminal market control and prevention:

(1) Capabilities

(4) Vulnerabilities

(2) Intentions

(5) Opportunities

(3) Limitations

Figure 1: Strategic and Tactical Intelligence Forms

Strategic Intelligence

Largely a management tool, strategic intelligence attempts to provide an overview of the scope and dimension of criminal activity to assist in policy development aimed at providing effective strategies to deal with the overall costs and effects of crime on society. Strategic intelligence permits the initiation of plans of action on a long-term basis against emerging crime rather than reacting – after the fact – to individual criminal acts. Strategic intelligence is able to go well beyond what tactical intelligence can provide; it takes a longer, broader view of what is, what has been, and by doing so, forecasts what might be. Strategic intelligence does not compete with tactical intelligence, rather, these two forms of intelligence complement one another, but at different levels within the law enforcement organization.

Tactical Intelligence

Principally an investigative tool, tactical intelligence is the support by analysts and intelligence officers to operational sections or investigators during the course of an investigation. Normally directed at short-term objectives, its direct application has a focus on more immediate impacts; such as arrest, seizure, and forfeiture. Its direct application to an active operation leads to better prioritization of cases for maximum enforcement effectiveness against criminal organizations and activities, as well as the efficient utilization of investigative resources.

There are a growing number of techniques employed in the tradecraft of criminal intelligence, many of which have both tactical and strategic applications (see Figure 2: "Intelligence Analysis Techniques" for a sampling of a number of frequently employed techniques). Marilyn B. Peterson, in her seminal text, *Applications in Criminal Analysis*, highlights some 65 techniques in criminal analysis (Peterson, 1994). Another valuable reference is *Successful Law Enforcement Using Analytical Methods*, published by the International Association of Law Enforcement Intelligence Analysts (IALEIA) (Peterson, Fahlman, Ridgeway, Erwin and Kuzniar - Editors, 1996).

Figure 2: Intelligence Analysis Techniques

Association Analysis	Net Worth Analysis
Bank Record Analysis	Commodity Flow Analysis
Activity Flow Analysis	Organizational Analysis
Statistical Analysis	Geo-Spatial Analysis
Business Record Analysis	Vulnerability Analysis
Telephone Record Analysis	Crime Pattern Analysis
Case Analysis	Comparative Case Analysis
Time Series Analysis	Trend Analysis
Threat Analysis	Risk Analysis
Criminal Market Analysis	Early Warning Analysis

A comprehensive understanding of organized crime and concomitant criminal markets can be gained though the development of an organized crime threat/risk assessment. The principal purpose of a threat and risk assessment is to provide decision-makers with a clear picture of key undesirable events (current and potential), the probability of those events occurring, their possible repercussions, and recommendations to minimize or address specific risks and threats (Tusikov and Fahlman, 2008).

The Royal Canadian Mounted Police (RCMP) analytical threat measurement technique known as Sleipnir[1], developed in the late 1990s, uses a numerical rank-ordered set of 19 criminogenic attributes (eg. corruption, violence, expertise, mobility, scope, etc.) to assess the relative threat posed by organized criminal groups (see Figure 3: Sleipnir – Attribute Scores and Values). Values, color-coded to visualize the threat, are assigned to each attribute: *high* (red), *medium* (orange), *low* (yellow), *nil* (green) or *unknown* (blue). In Figure 3, the color-codes have been replaced by shading in order to aid comprehension. The sum total of all the attribute scores provides the Sleipnir score for each crime group. The groups can then be rank-ordered in a matrix by threat level in order to provide a group-by-group comparison. Sleipnir is a national analytical technique employed within the Canadian law enforcement intelligence community to assess the relative threat of criminal groups. The technique has also been employed by numerous law enforcement and public safety agencies around the globe within the context of developing organized crime threat assessments (OCTAs).

---

[1] In Old Norse mythology, Sleipnir is the horse-like creature which conveys Odin between the realms of spirit and matter and is symbolic of Time. Sleipnir can gallop over land, sea, or through the air. Sleipnir has eight legs, representing eight directions and eight dimensions.

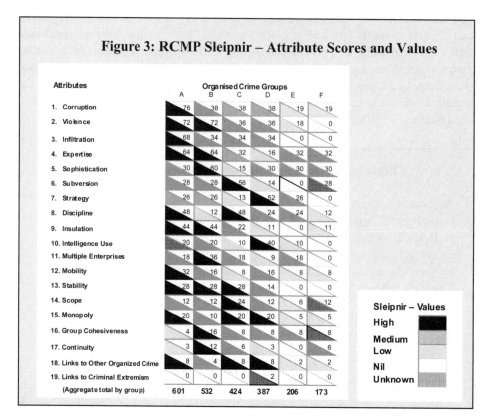

Figure 3: RCMP Sleipnir – Attribute Scores and Values

Attributes	A	B	C	D	E	F
1. Corruption	76	38	38	38	19	19
2. Violence	72	72	36	36	18	0
3. Infiltration	68	34	34	34	0	0
4. Expertise	64	64	32	16	32	32
5. Sophistication	30	60	15	30	30	30
6. Subversion	28	28	56	14	0	28
7. Strategy	26	26	13	52	26	0
8. Discipline	48	12	48	24	24	12
9. Insulation	44	44	22	11	0	11
10. Intelligence Use	20	20	10	40	10	0
11. Multiple Enterprises	18	36	18	9	18	0
12. Mobility	32	16	8	16	8	8
13. Stability	28	28	28	14	0	0
14. Scope	12	12	24	12	6	12
15. Monopoly	20	10	20	20	5	5
16. Group Cohesiveness	4	16	8	8	8	8
17. Continuity	3	12	6	3	0	6
18. Links to Other Organized Crime	8	4	8	8	2	2
19. Links to Criminal Extremism	0	0	0	2	0	0
(Aggregate total by group)	601	532	424	387	206	173

Sleipnir – Values
High
Medium
Low
Nil
Unknown

An additional benefit of an analytical threat measurement technique such as Sleipnir is in the development of intelligence Collection Plans. Through the determination of critical knowledge gaps (the category labeled "unknown" in the Sleipnir matrix) - whether in the domain of individual criminals, organized crime groups and networks, or criminal markets – a prioritized criminal intelligence Collection Plan can be developed. This type of knowledge mapping exercise permits more directed and effective collection by intelligence officers and analysts based on the critical threats and harms posed by organized crime groups and markets in any given geographical jurisdiction, whether local, regional, national, or international.

MEETING THE CHALLENGES OF THE 21ST CENTURY

The ever-evolving landscape of organized crime has brought with it many new challenges to law enforcement, government, and civil society in general in all regions of the globe. In my three decades of working within the RCMP, whether on the domestic front or on assignment internationally, the lessons learned from two of the most influential forefathers of criminal intelligence, Justin J. Dintino and Frederick T. Martens, in their guidebook *Police Intelligence Systems in Crime Control*, capture today perhaps more than ever the value of intelligence to effective crime control. "The future of law enforcement in its role against organized crime is dependent upon intelligence. Intelligence will permit an organization to meet future challenges with an awareness that allows for the development and implementation of viable crime control policies. Without intelligence there is no strategy. The intelligence process is central to the development of an effective crime control programme." (Dintino and Martens, 1983)

REFERENCES

Dintino, Justin J. and Martens, Frederick T. Police Intelligence Systems in Crime Control. Charles C. Thomas, Springfield, Illinois, USA, 1983.

Peterson, Marilyn B. Applications in Criminal Analysis: A Sourcebook. Greenwood Press, Westport, Connecticut, USA, 1994.

Peterson, Marilyn, B.; Fahlman, Robert C.; Ridgeway, R. Glen; Erwin, Phil; and, Kuzniar, Michael T. Successful Law Enforcement Using Analytic Methods. International Association of Law Enforcement Intelligence Analysts (IALEIA), South Florida, Florida, USA, 1996.

Strang, Steven. Sleipnir: An Analytical Technique for Determining Relative Levels of Threat Posed by Organized Crime Groups. Royal Canadian Mounted Police - Criminal Intelligence Directorate, Canada, 2000.

Sun-tzu. The Art of War (translation by Sawyer, Ralph D.). Barnes and Noble, Inc., USA, 1994.

Tusikov, Natasha and Fahlman, Robert C. "Threat and Risk Assessments: A Common Framework", 2008 - to be published in Ratcliffe, Jerry H., Editor; Strategic Thinking in Criminal Intelligence, updated - forthcoming in 2009.

United Nations. Crime Prevention: Seeking Security and Justice for All. The United Nations, New York, New York, USA, 1996.

Section 2
Intelligence in Narcotics Control
By James Lewis

Narcotics intelligence has been around for decades and will be around in the foreseeable future. The emphasis placed on 'zero tolerance' of drug use in the 1980s caused arrests and seizures to rise rapidly, but developing intelligence was not a top priority as narcotics arrests were "like shooting ducks in a pond" and, as a result, there was little incentive to develop complex cases (Pagano and Martens 1986:4). However, over time, the value of efficient data analysis from regional, national, and international centers combined with improved interagency cooperation has brought intelligence and its effective use to the forefront.

Several efforts in the 1980s and 1990s created an environment in which narcotics intelligence was prioritized. Among these was the work of the Regional Information Sharing System (RISS) program. One RISS program – the Western States Information Network (WSIN) – began by focusing on collecting, analyzing, and disseminating narcotic intelligence information in the five western states (Alaska, California, Hawaii, Oregon, and Washington). WSIN provided a place where member narcotics officers could send their case information to be analyzed. This included telephone-toll analysis, link analysis, and the dissemination of numerous publications on drugs and traffickers. Today however, WSIN has broadened to an "all-crimes" approach to intelligence analysis and assistance.

In the 1990s, narcotics efforts turned more toward the intelligence model, particularly with the creation of agencies such as the National Drug Intelligence Center (NDIC) in Johnstown, Pennsylvania, and the growth of the High Intensity Drug Trafficking Area (HIDTA) program intelligence centers. The HIDTAs began in fewer than a dozen locations but grew to 27 areas and 5 border regions by 2009. One of the responsibilities of the HIDTAs is to perform annual regional assessments of narcotics activity in their areas. The NDIC uses the compilation of these reports and other source information as the basis in producing a national drug threat assessment.

The HIDTA Intelligence Centers have been tasked with providing "consolidated and coordinated annual interagency drug threat assessments" in their respective areas (ONDCP 2000a:35). (See Chapter 17 for a listing of HIDTA areas.) The Arizona HIDTA Center, Intelligence Division is one example of a HIDTA. It is staffed by intelligence analysts from ten different agencies. The goal of this division is to exploit all the available and accessible information on specific narcotics suspects or organizations and to coordinate the intelligence (Martinez 1998:14).

Another agency is the U.S. Office of National Drug Control Policy (ONDCP) which, through a cooperative effort, created a General Counterdrug Intelligence Plan (GCIP), which "provides operations and investigations with timely, relevant, and actionable drug-related information and intelligence necessary to disrupt and dismantle illicit drug-trafficking infrastructures, organizations, and resources." (ONDCP 2000a:5) The GCIP includes an action plan that calls for (1) increased cooperation among federal, state, and local agencies and programs (e.g., RISS, HIDTA, Organized Crime Drug Enforcement Task Forces (OCDETF), etc.); (2) the coordination of the mission of national centers such as the NDIC, the El Paso Intelligence Center (EPIC) and the Financial Crimes Enforcement Network (FinCEN); and (3) the standardization of drug intelligence and analysis training (ONDCP 2000a:7-9). Although, the GCIP is now ten years in existence it remains the standard for counterdrug coordination within the U.S. government. It was revalidated in 2002 by the Counterdrug Intelligence Coordinating Group.

One drug intelligence methodology the GCIP highlighted is Document Exploitation (DOCEX). This technique has been heavily used by NDIC, where teams of DOCEX analysts are sent into the field to review case information, glean from it every possible lead, and organize it in a standard format (generally electronic). The phases of document exploitation include preparation, gathering all the materials and personnel to complete the DOCEX mission, immediate (on-site) review of the materials, and detailed exploitation and analysis. To improve timeliness and cost savings, numerous cases are forwarded directly to NDIC where analysis is completed internally.

Document exploitation may include, as an example, reviewing the papers and records of a drug dealer and analyzing those papers to determine the size and influence of the drug operation as well as to develop leads to other individuals and groups that may be targeted. These papers and records may be manual or computerized and may be encoded and/or in a different language. Because this document exploitation analysis is often used in tactical situations where the need for a product is immediate, the impact of this analysis is also immediate and effective (Sampson, Layton and Pohl 1999:34).

In 2008, NDIC renamed and reconfigured the DOCEX team concept to more accurately address the operations they perform. Exploitation teams are now known as Document and Media Exploitation, or (DOMEX). The DOMEX Branch of NDIC has developed a uniquely efficient approach that allows analysts to quickly organize and assimilate significant amounts of seized documentary and electronic evidence. By incorporating the talents and technology of computer forensics and the use of the Real-time Analysis Intelligence Database (RAID), mission teams have all the tools needed to successfully exploit the operations of the most complex drug organizations. For more information on the RAID database, see: *www.justice.gov/ndic/domex/raid.htm#Top.* Software and related training is available to all law enforcement agencies at no cost.

Some analysis of narcotics trends is found in U.S. drug strategy reports which have been published by the ONDCP since the 1990s and are available through the National Criminal Justice Reference Service (*www.ncjrs.gov*). The availability of narcotics, their use, price and purity, and trends relating to each are found within these publications. These reports include goals and objectives for reducing the use of drugs in the U.S. and the progress made toward those goals.

These reports also describe counter-narcotics ongoing efforts. For example, the 2009 National Drug Strategy noted, "The domestic and international partnerships forged during this Administration are creating more agile and effective responses to disrupt the illicit drug markets that threaten the health, safety, and security of the citizens of the United States." (ONCDP 2009:23)

Some counter-narcotics work has evolved into international cooperative efforts. In Afghanistan, the U.S. Drug Enforcement Administration (DEA) is the lead agency in the Afghan Threat Finance Cell, with representatives of the Departments of Defense and Treasury being co-deputy leads. In the U.K., the Joint Narcotics Analysis Centre (JNAC) brings the cooperation of U.K. expertise to U.S. counter drug efforts.

The *International Narcotics Control Strategy Report* is published by the U.S. Department of State and is a yearly summary of narcotics activity around the world. This several-hundred page report provides country-by-country detail on narcotics activity and money laundering of narcotics profits. It summarizes laws and regulations related to narcotics trafficking and money laundering by country. Each country is listed in one of the following categories: "Primary Concern," "Concern," or "Monitored." Details can be accessed on-line at: *www.state.gov/p/inl/rls/nrcrpt/2009/vol1/116523.htm.*

Narcotics strategies involving intelligence also have been evolving in the United Kingdom. "Using intelligence to identify particular targets –individuals and areas– the aim is to concentrate police resources where the greatest impact can be made, thereby reducing harm...defining drug-related crime is problematic, that intelligence around drug misuse and persistent offending is often far from adequate, and that considerable work will have to go into developing new intelligence gathering methods." (Newburn and Elliott 1998:39)

The United Nations Office on Drugs and Crime (UNODC) began publishing an annual report entitled the "World Drug Report", in 1999. This report includes statistics on cultivation and use and provides trend analysis of activity. It can be accessed at: *http://www.unodc.org/unodc/en/data-and-analysis/WDR-2009.html.*

Various forms of analysis are used in support of narcotics investigations, but the most common is link analysis. This analysis shows the cultivation, processing, and distribution networks involved. Examples of these charts can be viewed at *www.treas.gov/ofac,* the web site of the Office of Foreign Asset Control, which designates narcotics kingpins and their related businesses. Social Network Analysis, which looks at broader ranges of contacts by targeted individuals, has also increased in use.

Another narcotics intelligence methodology is post-seizure analysis. Post-seizure analysis is the review of the physical evidence and supporting documentation surrounding a seizure of narcotics or narco-currency. The types of records involved can be shipping records, travel documents, anecdotal information, and interview results. It can also provide a synopsis of the events leading up to and after the seizure. Additionally, biographical profiles of the companies or individuals involved may be prepared. The post-seizure analysis generally leads to the development of indicators related to smuggling techniques useful to detecting and deterring future attempts to smuggle drugs.

On the tactical level, drug-market analysis is used to develop knowledge of the geographic locations and spread of markets. This is done through mapping the drug locations and other relevant data including intelligence, arrest, and crime reports, calls for service, etc (Jacobson 1999:5).

The Crime and Narcotics Center (CNC), operated by the U.S. Central Intelligence Agency, prepares a report on yearly estimates of the cultivation of coca, opium poppy, and marijuana in drug-producing countries around the world. These estimates are used by decision-makers to determine the levels of support the U.S. will give to these drug-producing countries (General Accounting Office 2003). This report also analyzes the impact of the drug trade and of organized crime on U.S. national security, follows trafficking methods and routes, and monitors cooperation between organized crime groups, traffickers, and terrorists. Using targeting analysis, the CNC identifies key individuals, organizations, trends, and components in criminal organizations. Reports can be viewed at the CIA website: CIA.gov (search Crime and Narcotics Center).

Another form of these estimates was completed by the Rand Corporation in 2009 for the European Commission. Rand attempted to estimate the economic cost of drug abuse in consuming nations (Rand 2009). This document is located at: *http://www.rand.org/pubs/technical_reports/TR709/.* A final example of a drug intelligence product is the NDIC National Drug Threat Assessment. This document reflects analysis of the varied drugs and Drug Trafficking Organizations (DTOs) impacting the United States. In 2009, this assessment stated Mexican DTOs were the greatest threat to the U.S. and cocaine was the greatest threat by drug type. This report can be viewed at:
www.justice.gov/ndic/pubs31/31379/31379p.pdf.

The use of narcotics intelligence is a continuing priority in the U.S. and worldwide. As more becomes known about the nexus between narcotics and terrorism/insurgency, law enforcement and international security agencies have developed cooperative working relationships to bring a "whole of government" approach to this issue.

REFERENCES

Jacobson, Jessica. (1999) *Policing Drug Hot Spots.* London, UK: Home Office, March.

Martinez, Ritchie A. (1998) "Arizona HIDTA Intelligence Program," Intelligence Led Policing, Angus Smith, ed., Lawrenceville, NJ: IALEIA.

Newburn, Tim and Joe Elliott (1998). *Police Anti-Drug Strategies Tackling Drugs Together Three Years On.* London, UK: Police Research Group.

Office of Narcotic Drug Control Policy (2000) National Drug Control Strategy 2000. At *<www.whitehousedrugpolicy.gov/policy/ndcs00/chap3_3.html>*

Office of National Drug Control Policy (2000a) General Counterdrug Intelligence Plan. At *<www.whitehousedrugpolicy.gov/gcip>*

Pagano, Clinton L. and Frederick T. Martens. (1986) "An Enforcement Paradox: The Intelligence Dilemma in Narcotic Enforcement" *Law Enforcement Intelligence Analysis Digest*, Vol. 1, No. 2. (July).

Sampson, Stuart A., Daniel Layton and Susan Pohl. "Basic Document Exploitation" *IALEIA Journal,* Vol. 12, No. 2.

Section 3
Intelligence and Anti-terrorism
By Marilyn B. Peterson

INTRODUCTION

Anti-terrorism intelligence at all levels of the U.S. government and internationally has been a primary focus since 2001. Anti-terrorism refers to those activities that seek to prevent the execution of terrorist acts. This is different from counter-terrorism, which are those activities that respond to terrorist acts once they have occurred (Riley and Hoffman 1995:2).

There are many definitions of the term "terrorism"; however, none is universally accepted. The U.S. Department of State, which is required to report annually on terrorist activity to the public, defines it as: "premeditated, politically motivated violence perpetrated against non-combatant targets by sub-national groups or clandestine agents." (U.S. Department of State 2007: 311) Some would argue, however, that the motivation may also be social or religious—not just political. Some may also argue that terrorist acts can be committed against combatants; others would say that activity would reflect a state of asymmetrical or irregular warfare.

Key to any terrorist act is that it be seen or transmitted to a large segment of the populace in order to have some impact. While a suicide bombing in a shopping mall may only injure a dozen shoppers, it will keep thousands or millions away from malls.

Prior to 2001, there was no single U.S. Federal law that specifically made terrorism a crime. Terrorist acts were prosecuted under existing statutes (for specific crimes such as terroristic threats, extortion, bombing, arson, kidnapping, and murder). The USA PATRIOT Act of 2001, however, created new federal crimes such as one outlawing terror attacks on mass transit and instituted a longer statute of limitations on acts of terrorism (Congressional Research Service 2002:2).

Terroristic acts committed by groups of both left- and right-wing political orientations were prevalent in the United States throughout the 1960s and 1970s. Some of the active left-wing groups included the Black Guerilla Family, the Jewish Defense League, and the Weather Underground Organization. Right-wing groups included the Ku Klux Klan, the Posse Comitatus, and the Minutemen.[2]

As early as 1976, the Task Force on Disorders and Terrorism issued its report to the National Advisory Committee on Criminal Justice Standards and Goals. This report provided detailed guidelines on how to establish and run an intelligence operation that focused on violent disorders and terrorism. This report also discussed the utilization of several analytic products such as threat assessments, strategic intelligence assessments, and threat evaluations in anti-terrorism measures and in responding to terrorist acts (Task Force on Disorders and Terrorism 1976:145).

---

[2] For a detailed list of groups and terrorist acts during this time, see the 1976 report of the Task Force on Disorders and Terrorism, Appendix 6: "Chronology of Incidents of Terroristic, Quasi-Terroristic, and Political Violence in the United States: January 1965 to March 1976," by Marcia McKnight Trick.

The law enforcement response to the 2001 terror attacks was swift. The International Association of Chiefs of Police (IACP) hosted a forum on intelligence sharing in March 2002 in which 100 experts discussed how to marshal a broader and more integrated approach to intelligence across the United States. The IACP forum led to the creation of the National Criminal Intelligence Sharing Plan.[3] A few years after the terror attacks of 2001, federal, state, and local agencies began banding together in "fusion centers" that covered entire states or large metropolitan regions. While the genesis of these fusion centers was based on terrorism, a number of them became "all crime" centers in the belief that most crimes occur in concert with other crimes and should not be viewed in a vacuum. Model guidelines for fusion centers were published by the Global Justice Information Sharing Initiative.[4]

A lack of intelligence and information sharing was highlighted in the 9/11 Commission Report. It noted there was "limited intelligence collection and strategic analysis capabilities, a limited capacity to share information both internally and externally, insufficient training, perceived legal barriers to sharing information and inadequate resources." (9/11 Commission nd: 13)

ANALYTIC APPROACH TO ANTI-TERRORISM

Anti-terrorism analysis of a targeted threat group can be broken into three steps:

1. **Inventory Phase** - The inventory phase combines collecting raw data with organizing and evaluating that data. As part of this phase, potential sources of threats must be considered—both domestic and international—dependent upon the nature of the jurisdiction. The possibility of single actors (such as the Unabomber) should not be discounted. Potential targets also need to be inventoried.

   An inventory of a threat group would include all known data on the group, including its ideology, history, recruitment methods, geographic base, source(s) of funds, significant dates, propensity for violence, membership size, structure, sophistication level, criminal acts, and connections to other groups.

   An inventory of potential targets would include the critical assets, individuals, locations, or operations within the jurisdiction. Targets of opportunity should also not be ignored, such as special occasions, anniversaries, visits, etc. For each of these, their security levels, vulnerabilities, and environment should be noted.

   Another inventory could be of pre-incident indicators. Have previous threats been received? Have there been similar, smaller incidents that might lead to escalation? Are there any significant dates regarding threats or possible targets coming up?

2. **Assessment Phase** - The National Infrastructure Protection Plan 2009 defines risk as a function of consequences, vulnerability, and threat; i.e., R= f (C,V,T).

---

[3] See the Global Justice Information Sharing Initiative for a complete version of the Plan at <*www.iir.com/global/ncisp.htm*>.

[4] Guidelines can be seen at <*www.iir.com/global/fusion_center_guidelines_law_enforcement.pdf*>.

NIPP Risk Management Framework

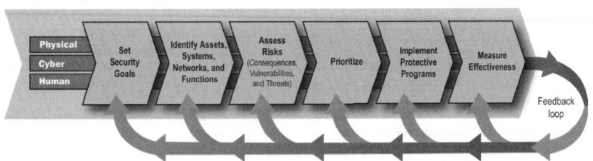

(Department of Homeland Security 2009:33)

Each of these can be looked at individually. When applying analysis in anti-terrorism efforts, the technique of providing threat assessments is critical. Peterson provided the following definition of a threat assessment: "A threat assessment is a strategic document which looks at a group's propensity for violence or criminality, or the possible occurrence of a criminal activity in a certain time or place." (1994:56-57) By collecting information on various indicators, a level of threat potential of a particular group can be estimated. Threat assessments provide an informed judgment on the intentions and capabilities of a terrorist group. Threat assessments can be used to focus investigations on those groups with the greatest propensity for violent actions. Recommendations made as part of threat assessments allow management to allocate resources and take action as necessary.

The California Department of Justice, Gang Unit utilized threat assessments to evaluate and analyze criminal extremist groups. "Threat assessments evaluate the characteristics, analyze the risks, and measure the violence potential associated with criminal extremist groups. These assessments are used for tactical and strategic purposes by law enforcement authorities to target and neutralize the groups, hopefully before they commit crimes of violence." (Marynik 1999:1)

The California Department of Justice threat assessment guide evaluated several characteristics to identify the existence and type of criminal extremist group. These characteristics are: (1) ideology (2) field of operation (3) tactics and (4) membership. Another part of this threat assessment analyzes the risks, or warning signs, posed by the group. This is accomplished by addressing these three factors: 1) the criminal predicate associated with the group, 2) the warning signs that point to potential danger, and 3) the target of the group. The guide places the characteristics and factors into a table format that provides a comprehensive threat assessment for each criminal extremist group. A written threat assessment report is prepared to document the table. The following figure represents the table in the *Threat Assessment Guide*.

COMPREHENSIVE THREAT ASSESSMENT TABLE						
	Group Characterictics Evaluation		Criminal Predicate Analysis		Target Analysis		Consequence of Intervention
Threat Level	Ideology and Operations	Tactics and Membership	Crimes and Capability	Probability and Violence	Targets and Vulnerability	Probability and Damage	
low							
medium							
high							

The following describes the assignment of the Low/Medium/High designation:

- **Low** – There is little or no threat. The groups are agitated but are not involved in focused action other than nonviolent protests. It is important to stress that in the U.S., many actions which might precede or incite violence are in fact protected by the First Amendment of the U.S. Constitution. Ensure that intelligence personnel are aware of both the law and department or agency policy when considering whether to monitor a group which may be considered a threat to public safety. Any and all reporting on such groups to evaluate if they pose such a threat should make very clear the justification for any type of collection or monitoring activities.

- **Medium** – Threat exists but does not appear imminent. The groups have a focused attention and may become violent. Law enforcement authorities need to be strategically aware of the groups' crimes and prepared to tactically respond.

- **High** – Threat is visible and distinctive. The groups have a destructive cause. All law enforcement precautionary measures need to be employed and tactical response plans activated.

Another example of the use of threat assessments in combating terrorism can be found in a 1999 report entitled *Combating Terrorism: Need for Comprehensive Threat and Risk Assessments of Chemical and Biological Attacks* by the U.S. General Accounting Office (GAO). This report recommended that the U.S. Federal Bureau of Investigation, "prepare a formal, authoritative intelligence threat assessment that specifically assesses the chemical and biological agents that would more likely be used by domestic-origin terrorists—non-state actors working outside a state-run laboratory infrastructure." (1999:22) According to the report, a threat analysis, "identifies and evaluates each threat on the basis of various factors such as its capability and intent to attack an asset and the likelihood and the severity of the consequences of a successful attack." (1999:6) This report was published after the GAO examined the technical ease or difficulty for terrorists to acquire chemical and biological agents.

The vulnerability assessment is another useful anti-terrorism tool. Vulnerability assessments focus on measuring the potential vulnerabilities of a certain targeted individual, location, or event. Locations, buildings, or installations now undergo assessments of their vulnerability to a terrorist attack. Vulnerability assessments are also performed on computer systems, public utilities, and financial networks. The *National Infrastructure Protection Plan 2009* defines vulnerability assessment as: "the evaluation of specific threats to the asset, system, or network under review to identify areas of weakness that could result in consequences of concern." (Department of Homeland Security, 2009:36)

Consequence assessment requires the knowledge of both short and long term results of a potential attack. For example, the suicide bombing in the first paragraphs of this article resulted in no more than a dozen injured, but the long-term impact could be both human (fear) and economic (loss of business). Because terrorists strive for high impact, the likelihood that an attack will occur is compounded by the possible larger consequences. Consequence assessment may be scientific (gauging the impact of a dirty bomb on an area based on size, environmental factors, etc.) or speculative (gauging the possible reactions of people to an attack).

These are most successful when done in concert with one another. The maximum impact terror attack occurs when the opportunistic nature of the terrorists successfully breach the vulnerabilities of a target to bring about maximum impact or consequences.

3. **Dissemination (Peterson 2002:1)** - The inventory and assessment phases of anti-terrorism analysis, alone, cannot prevent terror attack. The knowledge gained from these assessments must be shared with those who can make decisions which will counter the planning, preparations, or execution of a terrorist act. This may include non-traditional partners such as those serving in public health, fire, and emergency services as well as private sector security personnel responsible for critical infrastructure. State and local fusion centers in the United States are building to institutionalize these information and intelligence sharing partnerships to strengthen anti-terrorism capabilities. The knowledge gained from these assessments must be shared to forestall terror attacks on U.S. soil.

CONCLUSION

Terrorism has been seen as the most serious international issue in the first decade of this century. The threat of nuclear, biological, and chemical weapons being utilized by terrorists compounds this problem. Law enforcement authorities must recognize and deflect terrorist groups before they have the opportunity to commit violent acts. The intelligence process is an integral part of law enforcement anti-terrorism measures. Various analytical techniques and products are a part of these measures. The assessment tools described in this article are particularly useful in proactive investigations of terrorist groups.

REFERENCES

9/11 Commission. (nd). *The 9/11 Commission Report Executive Summary.* Washington, DC: The 9/11 Commission.

Congressional Research Service. (2002). *The USA PATRIOT Act: A Legal Analysis.* *<www.fas.org/irp/crs/RL31377.pdf>*.

Department of Homeland Security (2009) *National Infrastructure Protection Plan.* *<www.dhs.gov/xlibrary/assets/NIP_Plan.pdf>*.

Global Justice Information Sharing Initiative. (2003). *National Criminal Intelligence Sharing Plan.* *<www.iir.com/global/ncisp.htm>*.

------------------ (2005). *Fusion Center Guidelines.* *<www.iir.com/global/fusion_center_guidelines_law_enforcement.pdf>*.

Marynik, Jerry. (1999, August). *Threat Assessment Guide.* Sacramento, CA: California Department of Justice.

Peterson, Marilyn B. (1994). *Applications in Criminal Analysis: A Sourcebook.* Westport, CT: Greenwood Press.

------------------ (2002). "State and Local Anti-Terrorism Analysis." *Illinois Law Enforcement Executive Forum.* (March).

Riley, Kevin Jack and Bruce Hoffman. (1995). *Domestic Terrorism: A National Assessment of State and Local Preparedness.* Santa Monica. CA: RAND.

Task Force on Disorders and Terrorism. (1976, December). *Disorders and Terrorism.* Washington, DC: National Advisory Committee on Criminal Justice Standards and Goals.

United States Department of State. (2007, April). *Country Reports on Terrorism 200.* Washington, DC: U.S. Department of State.

United States General Accounting Office. (1999, September). *Combating Terrorism: Need for Comprehensive Threat and Risk Assessments of Chemical and Biological Attacks.* Washington, DC: U.S. General Accounting Office.

Section 4
Gambling Intelligence
By Richard Herrington

INTRODUCTION: UNDERSTANDING THE MISSION

One of the primary missions of the criminal intelligence unit is providing strategic intelligence to the chief executive officer of an agency. To increase effectiveness, the unit must understand and utilize all the resources from within each division of an agency. This allows a better overview of the needs of the agency as well as the individual divisions within an agency. In intelligence gathering, illegal gambling should be included, even if it is not the main mission of a particular agency or intelligence group, because it may lead to other associated crimes.

Gambling is a vice which permeates all segments of society, including law enforcement. Even in a heavily regulated geographic location, gambling intelligence can lead analysts/investigators to other criminal activities such as money laundering, organized crime, and business infiltration. In this day of the internet and specifically legal and illegal internet gambling, organized criminal elements, and terrorist organizations, can utilize this avenue to assist either as a funding resource (identity theft and credit card scams) or for passive intelligence gathering.

STRATEGIC ASSESSMENT

The agency chief executive officer should include gambling intelligence, where pertinent, in a strategic assessment or plan. This assessment should review the impact and risk of any criminal element over a period of time. This gives the administration an overview of the criminal elements' capabilities, strengths and vulnerabilities with possible trends. Gambling threat/risk assessments should include:

- Organized crime — traditional, transnational or new emergent groups
- Associated crimes — narcotics, public corruption, prostitution
- Associated White Collar Crimes — in locations which allow regulated gambling
- Internet gambling
- Legislative, economic, educational, and enforcement impacts
- Global influences
- Societal impacts

INVESTIGATIVE CHALLENGES

Outside of the obvious main priority and resource issue of the availability of personnel, an agency will find it beneficial to have experienced personnel train line officers about criminal intelligence and to recognize the elements of gambling intelligence. Human intelligence information is derived from covert undercover operations, informants, citizen sources, and the line officer. Training to recognize the language, the documentation, and the methodology of an illegal gambling operation is essential in developing criminal intelligence from these sources.

Electronic intercept intelligence is always dependent on the laws of the jurisdiction in which you work. What is applicable in the United States on a federal level is not necessarily the same as with state or local level investigators. Electronic intercepts are highly useful when a predicate act such as illegal gambling (bookmaking, numbers, lottery, horseracing) allows you the authorization to obtain electronic evidence.

Raw open source information has become a struggle, simply by the sheer volume of information available for review. The internet provides wide access to large amounts of data and brings the attendant problem of information management. Information from the local, state, and federal online services could be dated; therefore veracity of the information should be independently verified if possible.

Essential to gathering all of the above is the need to train one of the most vital resources available to an intelligence unit. The analyst-collected information is worthless unless a trained analyst can put the information together creating a meaningful assessment.

RECOGNIZING GAMBLING INTELLIGENCE

Worldwide, gross gambling earnings have been estimated at $350 billion to $500 billion per year. In 2006, legal gambling in the United States was estimated at approximately $91 billion. This is a great enticement for the criminal element. Organized crime infiltration into the legal gambling industry, game fixing, illegal bookmaking, doping, and public corruption are all byproducts of illegal gambling. Development of criminal intelligence comes from the cultivation of multiple sources—from informants in the street to the corporate boardroom.

BOOKMAKING

Without training, the first time you walk into a sports bar and overhear someone saying "I've got Philly plus 3" you might not recognize the line. Diving a little further, you might even overhear what the "juice or vig" is (cost to the loser – usually 10 percent). $110 got me $100. Betting a quarter could mean $250. The language, line sheets, tout books with numbered games, scraps of paper with a name or number (Philly +3 220), need sheets (total wagers per game which are not totally offset), parlays, are all intelligence data which must be recognized, organized, and analyzed. Beyond the ability to recognize the information, there must be a system in place in which to relay that information after it has been obtained.

Professional gamblers maintain books showing daily or weekly takes. These gambling records include the line, the day, and the wager taken. Lines are the current point spread on a certain game with each sport having a different format. A great location to find the daily line is the sports section of your local newspaper. The daily receipts and notes usually are just scraps of paper with a name or number (some bookies assign a number for individual identification), the game (Chi LA), the line (Chi +9), the amount wagered (100), and usually the result (W or L 100 or -110). Both illegitimate and legal bookmakers will take action on almost any type of event. With the Internet, you have a ready resource to find all of the bookmaking terminology that you need for inclusion into a search warrant affidavit.

ANIMAL FIGHTING

Animal fighting is a blood sport which typically involves gambling and, recently in the United States, has involved gangs. Developing a source with your local chapter of the Humane Society, veterinarians, and animal control officers can lead you to information about local chicken or dog fights. The information could include carcasses of animals that have obvious fight trauma or animals brought in for treatment. Recognizing fighting cocks with combs and waddles removed, tents with tethered roosters on someone's property, or the arenas in which the fights take place are important pieces of intelligence which can lead you to an enforcement action. In the United States animal fighting is either a felony or involves a violation of the animal cruelty statutes. The Federal Animal Welfare Act was amended under the Animal Fighting Prohibition Enforcement Act of 2007 to provide felony incarceration or fines.

CASINOS

Regulated casino gambling can provide surveillance video, player tracking, and a large pool of potential sources, i.e., card room dealers, pit bosses, card room managers, and surveillance personnel. Over the years, casinos have developed world wide distribution of information about those that attempt to cheat and steal from the casinos themselves. Some of this information is available through private investigative services such as the International Casino Surveillance Network. With Native or Tribal casinos, developing a relationship with sovereign nations could require formal compacts or agreements within the country/state in which they operate. If they have a recognized law enforcement agency, establishing contacts is extremely important for formal exchanges of intelligence information within proper guidelines.

In most regulated casinos, the employees are licensed and go through some type of background investigation. There is a great deal of background information available from the licensee files which are useful when investigating collusion, cheating, or affiliations with known criminals. A normal background check does not always come up with a criminal history.

If your jurisdiction allows legalized casino gambling, tracking currency transactions is essential. In the United States there is the Financial Crimes Enforcement Network (see Chapter 17 "Networks, Organizations, and Resources"). Your agency should obtain Currency Transaction Reports or Suspicious Activity Reports from the IRS. Canada has the Financial Transactions Reports Analysis Centre of Canada. Nationally and internationally there are Financial Action Task Forces on money laundering. Analysts should obtain the information and interpret the possible activity which might indicate money laundering.

OTHER

Illegal horseracing machines or video poker machines are another source of gambling revenue generated by criminals, some of which are gangs, and can be found in local small grocery stores, coffee shops, and pool halls. Surveillance alone can provide an insight into who is involved, especially on days of collection and payouts.

The Thai lottery originates from Thailand and is a daily numbers game. A Thai lottery based on your previous night's dreams (symbol books are available which give you the numbers to wager on) has been seen operating out of small grocery outlets. When paying for your number, you could or will receive a receipt for your wager for the numbers you are playing that day. *http://www.thailotteryresults.com*

A FEW TOOLS OF THE TRADE

One resource, which will assist in establishing a "paper trail," is through trash covers—or sometimes referred to as "dumpster diving." This can lead to the recovery of betting records, cassette tapes with the recorded wagering (just in case someone does not honor their bet), and names and addresses of the people working out of a store front. Surveillance and patience will provide you with co-conspirators, vehicles, assets, a phone room, and other targets. These targets may also prove more vulnerable allowing the investigation to focus on lower level suspects—who may provide leads up the chain of command.

Telephone toll analysis is one of the best tools to establish bookmaker involvement and show his/her pattern of communication. Once a bookmaker's telephone number is determined, a subpoena or search warrant should be obtained for the toll information. Toll analysis should be over a period of time (at least one year) not only to establish the obvious participants but also to create details regarding frequency of call pattern, times of the day, high traffic days, and discovery of co-conspirators. There are many current law enforcement computer applications which make this effort much easier. Other excellent analytical tools include link analysis, event flow analysis, and visual investigative analysis. However, remember, these are tools and do not take the place of the analytical process.

Utilize the Internet to collect information on your suspect(s) and/or their businesses. Information on younger suspects may be found on social network websites such as MySpace, Facebook, Friendster, YouTube, and Bebo. Some criminal enterprises have also used the web for recruiting and passing on information about their group. In these cases, a cold computer is better used to view any of the known criminal enterprise group's websites.

ILLEGAL INTERNET GAMBLING

Over the last 14 years, the traditional idea of what a bookmaker is or where to place your wager has changed. The most significant reason for this change is illegal internet gambling. The following provides some details regarding issues surrounding illegal Internet gambling.

Jurisdictional Issues

With the internet, learning about a country and gambling has become reasonably simple. Knowledge on how gambling began or is currently being run in a country may provide information on a possible method to infiltrate those operating illegally. Remember, with the Internet, these are snapshots in time and changes may occur in this market overnight.

Most problematic in investigating illegal Internet gambling are jurisdictional issues—which can be state to state, province to territory, country to country. The United States is not the only country with prohibitions on Internet gambling. In the European Union, most gambling is heavily regulated by the governments. This not only applies to land-based brick and mortar operations, but also on the Internet. A multitude of cases have been heard in the European Court of Justice on cases dealing with bookmaking involving the Internet: Placanica (March 2007), Gambelli (November 2003), Laara (Finland), Schindler (UK), and Zenatti (Italy). Decisions made by the World Trade Organization also have impacted the internet gambling business.

Worldwide Internet gambling began in the early 1990s and has a number of havens. Some of the countries have regulated these sites and are traded on the local stock exchanges. Regulation in other countries has been found to be lacking or at best an advertising ploy to entice bettors to come to their site.

In 2005, the Internet Gambling Task Force (IGTF) was formed. The IGTF has three primary areas of focus: Education, Legislative, and Enforcement. Fifteen U.S. states, four Federal agencies, and Canadian representatives participate in the group. Within the enforcement group, information and intelligence exchange follows the Association of Law Enforcement Intelligence Units (LEIU) guidelines. Co-operative investigations on local, state, federal, and international levels have been successfully completed by investigators whose agencies are members of this group.

Illegal Internet Gambling Investigations

As with most criminal investigations, it is preferable to have experienced investigators familiar with undercover Internet investigations participate or train those who will be investigating. It requires a cold computer with non-governmental Internet access, an undercover identification, an undercover banking account (preferably one with a credit, debit, or stored value card), and a cold e-mail account. After these preliminary steps have been completed, investigators go online and establish an account either directly or indirectly through a third party pay service. The website usually will walk you through the process.

The difficult part of the investigation comes in establishing whether or not a website is within your jurisdiction to investigate. Usually a physical location within the United States will end up being a virtual service provider with hyperlinks to the offshore site. These will be facilitators of the crime along with the technical and administrative contacts for maintaining the website. Advertisers and locations that provide servers for a fee can be included in the investigation.

Once a payment is received from the illegal site this becomes a financial investigation. Most payments are done directly through electronic money (e-money) transfers to the undercover credit card, third party pay service, or check payments directly to the undercover officer. Check payments are facilitated by automated clearinghouses which are the weak link in which search warrants will lead to extraordinary seizures of proceeds.

Criminal intelligence comes from the actual site itself along with newspapers, television, blogs, and chat rooms. Criminal intelligence will provide you with the technical background information necessary to establish the site location and the background of any companies or persons. Some locations do not provide access to customers from the United States.

NATIONAL GAMBLING INTELLIGENCE SHARING GROUP

A great resource of criminal intelligence and gambling information is available through the LEIU sponsored National Gambling Intelligence Sharing Group. Information is shared not only regarding illegal gambling operations, but also on groups of gambling con artists traveling throughout North

America, Asia, and Europe. These include dice rollers, roulette scammers, bet cappers, slot machine manipulators, and mini-baccarat and blackjack cheaters. Money laundering and organized crime topics are part of the intelligence exchange.

REFERENCES

Amending Animal Welfare Act
<http://thomas.loc.gov/cgi-bin/bdquery/z?d110:HR00137:@@@D&summ2=m&>

Directory of casinos and resorts around the world
<http://www.worldcasinodirectory.com/africa-casinos.asp>

Gambling, Law Enforcement System Issues Conference – Ontario Provincial Police
<http://gaming.uleth.ca/agri_downloads/480/moodie.pdf>

Illegal Internet Gambling Investigations: A How to Manual Washington State Gambling Commission authored by SAS Rick Herrington and SA Jim Dibble

US legal wagering *<http://www.americangaming.org/Industry/factsheets/statistics_detail.cfv?id=7>*

Section 5
Financial Intelligence
By Bethany Schussler

INTRODUCTION

The Iraq Threat Finance Cell has a motto, *"Sans argent, rien"* (without money, there is nothing). Likewise, without analysis, there is no financial intelligence, only an accounting of monetary transactions. Analyzing financial data is necessary to discern what the transactions mean.

One definition of financial intelligence within the criminal justice community is: "knowledge gleaned through the analysis of financial data which provides leads for investigations and/or supports the development of recommendations or indicators to assist in crime detection and prevention." (Peterson 2000:53)

SOURCES OF FINANCIAL DATA

The traditional sources of financial data are the transaction records generated by financial institutions including:

- Bank Statements
- Checks
- Wire Transfers
- Bank Secrecy Act reports
- Business Ledgers and Journals
- Invoices and Receipts
- Financial Statements
- Tax Records (individual and corporate income, sales, payroll)
- Credit Card Records
- Wire Remitter Records
- Money Order and Travelers' Check Seller Records
- Money Exchange Records

In today's environment, electronic records are the norm and include not only the above, but also transactions through online payment companies (PayPal, Bank Europay, eGold, eCurrency, etc.) Public records are a second major source of financial information available to the analyst/investigator. Due to the process of law, courts, federal agencies, state, county, and municipal governments have public records and filings that may be of considerable value to the analyst/investigator. Some of these records include:

- Real Estate Transactions/Mortgages

- Tax Assessment Records - The records of the county courthouse will normally contain information, by owner's name, as to the appraised values (both land and building) placed on the real estate, the tax rates, and total tax assessment.

- Plat Books - This book will outline the property owned as to size of the lot and its relation to other property in the community. This may be of considerable value to the analyst in the determination of allocated costs in subdivisions.

- <u>Registrations for Building Permits</u> - Homes and buildings to be constructed will normally require approval by the municipal or county government. These records are available and will indicate the contractor, general description of the property to be built, and the estimated cost of construction.

- <u>Chattel Mortgages</u> - The chattel mortgage books will assist in the determination of loans on equipment, furniture, automobiles, etc.

- <u>Probate Records</u> - These records will include records of deaths, births, marriages, guardianships, etc. The analyst, by the use of probate records, has access to wills, inheritances, valuations at date of death, creation of trusts by will, and similar data, all of which can be useful pieces of financial intelligence.

- <u>Brokerage Houses</u> - Like any other business, the brokerage house must maintain records of items of purchase and sale, costs and selling prices, and amounts due to and owed from customers. The analyst is able to secure information from brokerage houses in the same manner he/she may secure information from other businesses (Taylor 2001).

The aftermath of the terror attacks of 9/11 had a significant impact on the collection and retention of financial data and its availability to law enforcement in the United States. Banks have traditionally been required to maintain records to reconstruct banking activity for five years. Suspicious activity reporting in the United States, overseen by the Financial Crimes Enforcement Network (FinCEN), expanded after 9/11 to include mandatory reporting by money service businesses, casinos, and securities and commodities brokers. "Know Your Customer" requirements at banks (called "Customer Identification Programs") also became mandatory. Internationally, over 100 countries have adopted suspicious transaction reporting requirements and have agreed to gather, analyze, and share financial data to combat criminal activity.

While the best financial data is direct evidence of transactions, that is not always available. Not every financial action generates a trail which can be followed. For example, cash transactions only generate a record if they are over $10,000 in the United States. Likewise, money may move through couriers rather than financial institutions. As well, value may move rather than money. The 21st century has seen the popularity of trade-based money laundering and bartering in lieu of financial transactions. A trade-based money laundering example would be the shipment of $500,000 worth of luxury cars to Colombia to repatriate narcotics profits. In these instances, other documentation (such as trade documents, shipping records, or anecdotal data) may be all that is available. Analysts must be able to interpret a range of information to reflect all financial activity occurring in order to develop financial intelligence and prevent or detect criminal activity.

TECHNIQUES USED TO DEVELOP FINANCIAL INTELLIGENCE

The chapter on analytic techniques in this publication covers general analytic techniques, but there is no emphasis on those used to turn financial data into intelligence. Nonetheless, there are several underlying analytic techniques that can be readily applied to financial records, such as pattern analysis, indicator analysis, and inference development. These are augmented by analytic formats that had been developed to deal with specific types of financial data including bank records, Bank Secrecy Act data, business records, and net worth information.

Bank record analysis use the data found in checks, bank statements, account opening information, and transactions relating to the account (wire transfers, debit card activity, etc.) to draw conclusions about the purpose of the account and the potential presence of illegal activity (Peterson 2002). Today, bank statements include automatic debits and credits, ATM machine activity, point of sale purchases, electronic funds transfers, online banking, and other activity, providing an electronic trail on many transactions that might previously have been done using cash. An added feature to point of sale and ATM transactions is that geographic and chronologic information on the activity is provided, giving added factors (time and location) to be analyzed.

In business record analysis, business journals, tax records, legal agreements, invoices, receipts, inventories, etc. are compared to look for inconsistencies which may indicate illegal activity in the business (Peterson 2002:74-78). Money laundering may be indicated by the frequency, number, amounts, and types of transactions occurring in the business.

Net worth analysis compare assets an individual has and what he/she has spent to what he/she has declared as legal income. If the net worth plus expenses are greater than reported income, then it is unreported income and may have been garnered illegally (Nossen and Norvelle 1994). Similarly, analyzing sources and applications of funds for a series of years allows the analyst to find unreported and possibly illegal income. In either case, conclusions can then be drawn about the probability of the individual's profits from criminal activity.

Bank Secrecy Act report analysis has many possible areas to be exploited. Currency Transaction Reports (CTR), filed by banks and non-bank financial institutions—including check cashers and casinos—can show conversions to cash of substantial checks made to individuals or companies. The information from the checks as well as the information from the reports can be thoroughly analyzed.

Suspicious Activity Reports (not to be confused with the more general "suspicious activity reporting" encouraged by current U.S. Department of Justice initiatives) are filed by banks, money service businesses, casinos, and securities/futures brokers. These reports, by their nature, are indicative of some potentially criminal activity and may additionally include back-up information which can be analyzed. In some instances, financial transaction data may be accessed in bulk and a technique of "reverse engineering" in which money of unknown origin is found through review of many financial records. "When large, unexplained profits are found to be going through offshore centers, money service businesses, or financial institutions then criminal actively is strongly indicated…Following the trail of money back to the criminal source is challenging…" (Peterson 1999:238)

Currency and Monetary Instrument Reports are filed voluntarily when amounts over $10,000 are carried or shipped over the United States border. Many other countries have similar laws requiring reporting. This data can also be reviewed for patterns, locations, actors, etc.

Similar techniques may be used to analyze credit card activity. Credit card data may also provide geographic information that can be analyzed along with dates, amounts, types of purchases, etc. Credit card and debit card data can provide an overall profile of an individual's financial life if these devices are used by the person.

Trade documents such as bills of lading, letters of credit, certificates of manufacture, customs forms, and others can be analyzed and compared to one another to uncover instances of trade-based money laundering. For example, a company in the United States might ship $2 million in car parts to a company in Brazil. However, the bill of lading may document that there are only $1 million in car parts shipped and the payment made by the company in Brazil to the United States Company may only reflect $1 million. In this way, an extra $1 million in value of goods has been shipped from the United States to Brazil.

A less formal way of moving money has come into the public eye which has been in existence for centuries in countries around the world; that of hawaladars, serafi, or hundiwallas, as they are called in South Asia and the Middle East. These individuals arrange for money to be accessed at a distant point without it actually being transferred. The money is not wired from point A to point B straight away, but is physically transferred at a later time when accounts are settled between these informal money brokers. The persons wanting the money moved, however, are assured that their recipients are getting their money in a fast, trustworthy manner, without government intervention or reporting. Hawala records are believed to be informal and may be intermingled with the records of the hawaladar's shop or business. Nonetheless, if international movements of funds are occurring, there are records of it, at least in the aggregate (Peterson 2009).

APPLICATIONS OF FINANCIAL INTELLIGENCE

Financial intelligence can be of value throughout an investigation or strategic assessment. In an investigation, the initial work-up done on a potential target should include a check of activity through FinCEN. Additional names and identifiers should be checked as they emerge in the course of the investigation (Taylor 2001).

As the investigation continues, every effort should be made to identify the profits from the crime and any assets that were acquired using those profits. This includes identifying bank accounts, investment accounts, businesses, and other entities associated with each of the individuals involved in the criminal activity. If the crime occurred at a given time, records should be acquired from before the criminal activity to show the 'normal' amounts and transactions against which the criminally influenced actions can be compared. It is also important to remember that there may be a behind-the-scenes facilitator or organizer of the criminal activity who should also be identified and his/her records subpoenaed.

In any case involving profits, the analyst should work closely with the attorneys who may institute criminal or civil forfeiture proceedings against the assets held by the criminals. The government's ability to gain these assets may provide restitution to those harmed by the crime as well as funds to support future law enforcement activities.

Financial intelligence can also be used to assess the success and even predict the future of an organized crime enterprise. Peterson suggested that a "continuum of money management sophistication" be used to measure the success of an organized crime group (1998:10). The continuum stretched from "criminal profits used to obtain criminal products for self (1)" to "criminal profits used to influence major governmental policies (13)." (Peterson 1998:10-11) A number of researchers contend that organized crime is an "economic activity" and should thus be studied as one (Schelling 1967; Anderson 1979; Albanese 1994, etc.). Greco noted that "several characteristics will govern behavior patterns concerning syndicate operations and personnel. There must be a potential for large economic profit in any operation.

At times it would appear that syndicate groups are more vulnerable to a good economist, than good law enforcement." (1992:8-9) Looking at this type of information allows a holistic approach to investigation of organized crime groups that will enable enforcement to dismantle criminal operations (Peterson 1998:14).

Further, the analysis of financial data is critical to successful money laundering investigations (U.S. Department of the Treasury and U.S. Department of Justice 2000:35). Bringing charges of money laundering against those also charged with underlying criminal violations can often result in longer sentences for those convicted. A number of states now have money laundering statutes that can be used, as well as the federal legislation.

FINANCIAL INTELLIGENCE UNITS AND OTHER COOPERATIVE EFFORTS

The model of international cooperation relative to anti-money laundering and anti-financial operations is the Financial Action Task Force (FATF), established by the G-7 Economic Summit in Paris in 1989 (Savona 1998:39). Following this model have been regional groups including the Caribbean Financial Action Task Force and Moneyval. The latter was established in 1997. Moneyval is an evaluation and peer pressure mechanism that reviews the anti-money laundering measures and measures to counter the financing of terrorism in Council of Europe member States (and Council of Europe applicants which apply to join the terms of reference) which are not members of the FATF (Moneyval 2009).

In 1995, FinCEN and its Belgian counterpart coordinated a meeting of financial intelligence units which became the Egmont Group. As defined by the Egmont Group, a financial intelligence unit is "A central, national agency responsible for receiving (and, as permitted, requesting), analyzing and dissemination to the competent authorities, disclosures of financial information, (i) concerning suspected proceeds of crime, or (ii) required by national legislation or regulation, in order to counter money laundering" (FATF 2009). There are over 100 countries now with operational financial intelligence units (full list at: *www.egmontgroup.org/list_of_fius.pdf*). Some exist as governmental bodies, others as sections within the country's central bank.

CONCLUSION

Financial intelligence has become a core practice in the field of intelligence analysis as our understanding of the motivation and operation of criminal groups has grown. It is a growing field and one with which we must aggressively work to keep pace. The globalization of crime and other activities such as terrorism make it imperative for us to not only pursue financial intelligence, but to make it a priority.

REFERENCES

Financial Action Task Force 2009. Accessed 3 July, 2009 at: *<www.fatf-gafi.org>*

Greco, Joseph. (1992). "Organized Criminal Groups: A Study in Patterns of Behavior" Criminal *Organizations*, Vol. 7, No. 4, pp. 209, Winter.

Moneyval, accessed 3 July, 2009 at: *<www.coe.int/t/dghl/monitoring/moneyval>*.

Nossen, Richard and Joan Norvelle (1994). The *Detection and Investigation of Financial Crime*. Richmond, VA: Thoth Publishing.

Peterson, Marilyn B. (1998) "Assessing Criminal Organizations Through Their Management of Profits" paper for the American Criminology Society Annual Conference, Washington, DC, November.

-------------------- (1999). "Follow the Money: How to Track Criminal Profits by Using Bank and Business Records," Intersec*,* Volume 9, Issue 7/8, July August.

-------------------- (2000). "Financial Intelligence and FIUs" Intersec*,* V. 10, Issue 2, February.

-------------------- (2002). Guide *to Analyzing Business and Personal Bank Records*, Richmond, VA: National White Collar Crime Center.

-------------------- (2002b). *Guide to Understanding and Analyzing Bank Secrecy Act Data*, Quantico, VA: Federal Bureau of Investigation and National White Collar Crime Center (electronic).

-------------------- (2009). *Guide to Counter Threat Finance Intelligence.* Washington, DC. Joint Military Intelligence Training Center.

Savona, Ernesto. (1997). *Responding to Money Laundering*. The Netherlands: Harwood Academic Publishers.

Taylor, Danny L. (2001). "Financial Intelligence," in *Intelligence 2000: Revising the Basic Elements of Intelligence.* Peterson, Morehouse and Wright, editors. Sacramento, CA: LEIU.

Section 6
Gangs and Intelligence
By Dean Baratta and Melissa R. Johnson

INTRODUCTION

Organized criminal networks are a worldwide phenomenon that trouble even seasoned law enforcement officials. They extend beyond state, provincial, and country boundaries and plague entire regions and continents in the form of both traditional organized crime and street gangs. As such, analytical methods to develop intelligence and prioritize operations have become more important than ever. The Americas are struggling to monitor and suppress the expansion of the violent Mara Salvatrucha street gang; Spain initiated an investigation against the Tambov gang which had Soviet and Russian ties; and motorcycle gangs continue to be an international problem. These gangs, like many others, launder monies, traffic weapons, and perform murders.

Many countries are overwhelmed with the violence and anarchy of organized crime, extremist groups, and gangs. Kenya, Honduras, Guatemala, Mexico, and El Salvador have implemented legislation, created special task forces, and developed intelligence operations to reduce gang activity in their regions. The United Kingdom implemented a strict Intelligence-Led Policing (ILP) strategy in the 1990s to prioritize operations to battle organized crime by identifying targets, capabilities, and changes in the environment. In 2008, police reports indicated that over 169 gangs were active in London. While a majority of this article concentrates on utilizing various levels of intelligence analysis against street gang activity, it may also apply to fighting traditional organized crime, human or drug trafficking organizations, and extremist groups.

Street gangs have existed in the United States since its earliest days. However, these gangs only began to garner significant attention from law enforcement and the public as they integrated with the drug trade more than a generation ago. For more than a decade, local and state authorities have implemented specific anti-gang initiatives across the United States. These programs have absorbed millions of dollars and countless personnel hours over that time period, yet there are only superficial metrics to determine if all of those resources have had any appreciable impact upon the threat that gangs pose to our citizens. One of the reasons for our unsatisfying metrics is the varying definitions relating to gang membership or activity. How can something be measured without a definition? Part of the reason why few, if any, can say in any verifiable way if gangs today are more of a threat to the public than they were 10 or 20 years ago, is because intelligence analysis has been relegated to a relatively minor role in law enforcement operations and has not been properly incorporated into operational efforts. Although the concept of intelligence analysis has been introduced to gang investigations and operations in the United States, its application is still in its infancy and full integration faces significant challenges. This may seem counter-intuitive in the United States, especially after 2001 with the development of state and urban-area fusion centers, the increase in hiring of analysts, and the widespread adoption of the mantras of "information sharing" and "Intelligence Led Policing." Much of that effort, however, has been expended without much forethought and without any examination of its effectiveness.

It is now a cliché to say that we will not be able to arrest our way out of a gang problem, yet law enforcement has been disproportionately called upon to address gangs as simply a law enforcement problem. The law enforcement response has often been one of short-term, reactionary suppression. If we are to operate under the assumption that street gangs pose a long term organized threat to public safety, then it stands to reason that effective responses to that threat should, likewise, be organized and look beyond short-term solutions. It is therefore imperative to utilize intelligence assets to their full potential by expanding beyond traditional investigative support and providing the institutional memory and strategic forecasting needed to create long term and comprehensive anti-gang strategies.

Gang Analysis Now   **Gang Analysis in the Future**

Figure 1: The figures above highlight the percentage of analytical responsibilities associated with gang investigations presently and the direction gang analysis should move in the future.

Generally, intelligence analysis has been relegated to a support role in anti-gang efforts. Gang investigations are pursued more often because of the availability of informants or familiarity with the specific criminal organization on the part of investigators than to any systematic evaluation and prioritization of the threats posed to the public. Analysts, when used, have generally been relegated to "investigative support" which often translates to conducting the administrative tasks of searching criminal histories, conducting data entry, or producing organizational charts for prosecution, all of which are reactive in nature. Few of these tasks require much in the way of analysis which means this pseudo-intelligence becomes a "fire and forget" mentality, rarely able to put any particular set of gang activity into a larger context and derive either explanatory or predictive value from it. It is exactly that type of information that decision makers will need to allocate scarce resources if they hope to deter and prevent future criminal activity by gangs. In order to benefit from the true value that intelligence analysis can bring to anti-gang operations; it needs to be utilized at the *strategic, operational*, and *tactical* levels.

Strategic Level - The need for clear, specific direction and planning by senior leaders cannot be overemphasized when contemplating initiatives designed to make lasting impacts on the criminal activities of gangs. In order for that to occur, leaders must have a comprehensive understanding of the "big picture" or operating environment. In the case of anti-gang suppression, understanding the environment in which street gangs are operating and their intent and capacity for committing crimes are all equally important to law enforcement commanders. To reach a sufficient level of understanding, several strategic products should be assembled that outline the reach of an organization's network, capacity, and intentions. Strategic analysis would include not only the familiar analyses such as the intent and capabilities of criminal organizations (see Figure 2), but it should also include an analysis of the impact of other factors such as changes in demographics, or the economic, social, and legal environment.

Such a macro assessment of an area and gang allows law enforcement leaders to identify and prioritize the myriad of threats facing the public.

Organizational Characteristics

CAPABILITIES

Logistical	Financial	Operational	Environment
Storage, Lodging and Transportation	Donations	Supply Chain Relationships	Proximity to Members
Communications	Membership Dues	Group Cohesion	Prison
Access to Weapons or Narcotics	Illicit Enterprises	Coercive Force	Suburban, Urban and Rural
Skills, Resources	Commercial Enterprises	Social and Demographics	
Impact from Recent Policing		Governmental Influence	

Organizational Characteristics

INTENT

Explicit	Implicit
Oaths, Constitutions	Criminal Activities
Rules, Hierarchy	Non-Criminal Activities
Network	Behaviors (rewarded vs. not)
Group Folklore	

Figure 2: Sample organizational characteristics

For example, from 2004 through 2006, U.S. federal gang suppression efforts were focused against the Mara Salvatrucha (MS13) gang. After several large scale operations that resulted in the deportation of many illegal MS13 immigrants from the United States, the New Jersey State Department of Corrections conducted an internal assessment of the MS13's presence and potential influence on the state inmate population. The assessment suggested that although the state prison system did not have a substantial MS13 presence at the time, membership could increase over time if gang membership or association was expected to pass on to future generations. Further, a demographic assessment of identified MS13 members revealed that while much of the current membership was made up of illegal immigrants, many of the members could have children in the United States. The tradition of multi-generational gang membership within some gangs raised the possibility that MS13 could become increasingly resistant to deportation and immigration-related gang suppression tactics as the membership came to be dominated by citizens. These members would therefore increasingly pose a security threat within the U.S. correctional system. This strategic plan highlights that while the capabilities and intent of a criminal network may remain unchanged, the threat may still increase as a result of changes in demographics or other environmental factors. In this case, the leadership of the state prisons chose to monitor the changes in incarcerated MS13 membership and focused management efforts on a different gang.

Once the law enforcement leadership identifies specific priorities, intelligence analysis can provide assistance in the development of metrics in order to determine the success or failure of any particular course of action. While standards such as the number of arrests or the amount of contraband seized are the most common indicators of success in law enforcement, it is not clear if these statistics are always, or even often, particularly informative. As mentioned previously, these indicators are difficult to measure in relation to anti-gang suppression efforts without a clear definition of gangs, their membership, and related activity.

As priorities are developed at the strategic, operational, and tactical levels analysts can assist in the development of metrics to determine if the actions taken to achieve them are successful or not. While metrics sometimes are straightforward, it may be difficult to find metrics which directly impact upon a stated intent. How does one measure the level of public intimidation a gang imposes on a neighborhood? How much crime has a certain measure prevented? In this regard, analysts will need to recommend innovative and perhaps circuitous ways to determine success or failure. In order to increase confidence in these metrics, there should be an emphasis placed on redundancy (attempting several ways to measure each factor) and reliability (the confidence in being able to actually collect accurate data).

Examples of metrics which determine the level of fear or intimidation by a local population:
- ✓ Increased/decreased usage of public space by residents which had, until then, been the exclusive territory of gang members
- ✓ Increase/decrease of number of tips to authorities regarding criminal activity in target area
- ✓ Influx/outflow of residents from area
- ✓ Increased/decreased number of incidents of witness intimidation

---

Case Study

The following example is a sample crime/gang situation. Over the following sections this case study will outline how each level of analysis (strategic, operational, and tactical) is utilized.

In response to rising crime rates and heightened public concern, the law enforcement director commissions an analysis of recent violent crime. Specifically, the analysts are charged to determine if any causes(s) can be attributed to the recent rise in handgun shootings over the past six months. The analysts are to determine if there are clusters of such crime and how, if at all, the number of these incidents can be expected to change without law enforcement intervention over the next six months.

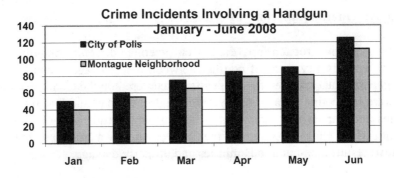

Figure 3: The frequency distribution above is often the first strategic product that highlights a change in activity over time.

The assessment revealed that a significant portion of the increased violence could be explained by the expansion of one gang (Capulets) into the territory of another (Montagues). The Montagues were recently the subject of an extensive law enforcement action and much of their leadership was incarcerated. The Capulets concluded the time was ripe to take advantage of the apparent weakness of the Montagues and make a move on their territory and criminal operations.

Most of the increased violence occurred in the city of Polis and its surrounding suburbs. Further, the founder of the Montagues was scheduled to be released from prison and had begun organizing followers to strike back at the Capulets. It was assessed that violence could be expected to increase or stay the same over the next 6 to 12 months.

Based on the analysis, the law enforcement director focused law enforcement resources in and around Polis with the goal of reducing shooting incidents involving Montagues and Capulets by 20 percent within 3 months.

Sample Strategic Priority

To reduce the number of shooting incidents between Montague and Capulet gang members by 20 percent from the 4th quarter of 2008 until the end of the 1st quarter of 2009.

Strategic analysis can be the initial and the final phase of the intelligence analysis process, assessing gang incidents at the global level for resource allocation, and changes in operational trends after the successful implementation of both tactical and operational initiatives.

Operational Level - Once the leadership has outlined clear and measurable goals through the use of an assessment of the operating environment generated by intelligence analysts, work can begin to narrow the focus more specifically. Analysis at this level should continue to refine the work of identifying and assessing physical locations and criminal networks or crime types where investigations and intelligence gathering would directly support the goals of the strategic decision makers. Additionally, analysis would be conducted which would support future tactical operations. This would include not only identifying potential targets but also trends in crime types and methods, structure, relationships, networks, and more narrow environmental factors that impact the creation and sustainment of criminal gangs within a jurisdiction.

Case Study: Operational Analysis

Taking his strategic direction from the law enforcement director, the police chief of Polis directed his staff to identify key areas of conflict between the Montagues and Capulets. An analysis of combined crime data revealed that the violence centered on the Genoa housing project where both groups were competing for a larger share of the drug market and Disco Row, a street with several nightclubs and bars where members of both groups frequented. Recently, a perceived slight against one of the female members of the Capulet gang by a Montague member resulted in a large street brawl resulting in numerous injuries and property damage.

The Capulets have actively recruited members of smaller gangs in local public schools and correctional facilities. It is believed that once they achieve a determined level of numerical superiority they will increase both the frequency and severity of their attacks upon the Montagues.

While both the Capulets and the Montagues have members throughout the region, they remain centered in their historical neighborhoods. The leadership of both groups was derived from those neighborhoods and the social networks that were established there from an early age.

The chief instructed his commanders to focus their efforts on continuing to conduct suppression operations on Disco Row while working to disrupt the activities of both groups. These suppression operations may lead to increased conflict, especially in the Genoa housing project and in the new areas of Capulet gang recruitment.

Sample Operational Priority

- Reduce opportunities for Capulet/Montague violence along Disco Row
- Concentrate anti-narcotics operations in the Genoa housing project
- Disrupt recruiting operations by the Capulets in schools and correctional facilities

Tactical Level - This is likely the most familiar level of operation for many analysts working in a law enforcement environment. Tactical operations include many of the investigative support functions that traditionally occupy the lion's share of an analyst's time and effort. However, this level also provides an opportunity to greatly expand the role of analysts and bring significant value to investigations. At the tactical level, analysts should be able to task investigators with specific questions which when combined with other information sources and completed analysis can provide insight into potential targets of interest and give greater understanding into the micro-environments in which many gangs operate.

Tactical analysis is generally limited in both time and physical space and is much more sensitive to becoming irrelevant if it is not acted upon quickly. In order to be successful, it is imperative that tactical analysts have a reliable, time sensitive mechanism in place for requesting and receiving intelligence. Given the perishable value of tactical intelligence and the large gaps of information that will plague tactical analysts, operating at this level will often require the analysts to work with more uncertainty than their operational and strategic peers. This situation makes it a necessity for agencies utilizing analysts at this level to have a well-defined process for the creation and prioritization of collection requirements.

Case Study: Tactical Analysis

Detectives and analysts, using a variety of sources ranging from confidential informants to a review of MySpace pages have further determined that Joseph Benvolio, a Montague, has been actively agitating for more violent activity by his gang. He has advocated a program of assassinating Capulet leaders along Disco Row to publicly demonstrate the strength of his gang. While his position hasn't gained much support within the gang leadership, the department of corrections has reported that a number of Benvolio's supporters have recently been released from prison and they may enact Benvolio's plan with or without the blessing of the leadership. This analysis resulted in the direct targeting of Benvolio by investigative personnel, heavy parole supervision of his recently released associates, and increased patrolling of both the Genoa housing project and Disco Row.

Two small groups of Capulets were identified as being responsible for recruitment in the schools and correctional facilities. Both groups were selected because of their access to particular facilities. It was determined that while the prison recruiters were likely to be easily replaced, the Capulets were likely to have a more difficult time identifying trusted gang members who could take over operations in the schools in the event that the existing group was incapacitated.

As a result, it was recommended that an outreach program be conducted in targeted schools; that administrators in the schools be informed of the Capulet activities; and school administrators be offered assistance in developing new anti-gang policies, develop protocols for information sharing and school resource officers, all with a focus on the Capulets rather than on a general anti-gang theme. The goal is to make membership in the Capulets appear to be too risky for prospective members.

Sample Tactical Priority:

- Increased patrolling along Disco Row and within the Genoa housing project
- Investigate Joseph Benvolio for criminal activity linked to the Montague gang
- Initiate narcotics investigations on dealers within the Genoa housing project
- Conduct outreach operations with local schools

CONCLUSION

A successful strategic plan that directs police operations, resources, and investigations highlights the beginning and end of the intelligence process. The analysis of both tactical and operational gang investigation products feeds into a strategic plan. Information regarding preliminary gang incidents, calls for service with investigative results, modus operandi, and regional changes tend to reveal organizational, geographic, and temporal trends that may also impact an overarching strategy. Additionally, a strategic plan may highlight changes in an environment as well as the intent and capability of a street gang. Network links, specific criminality and operandi are realized with operational products; while target profiles, frequency distributions and toll call analyses are appropriately conducted on the tactical level against street gang targets.

Street gangs and organized criminal groups present significant challenges to public safety and the stability of our societal institutions. While these groups have proven to be highly resistant to earlier efforts to curb their influence there is reason to believe that law enforcement possesses the tools needed to have greater success in disrupting their criminal operations. Integration of analytical resources at every level of planning and investigation will allow law enforcement leaders to not only understand their environment and deploy resources more effectively, but it also raises the possibility of quantifying success or failure to an extent that has not been previously practiced.

REFERENCES

Baratta, D. (2007). Gangs in New Jersey: Motivating Factors and Policy Implications. New Jersey State Police Strategic Intelligence Group. Unpublished assessment.

BBC News. (2005) "Mexico Seals Off Drug Gang Jail." BBC News. January 15, 2005.

Mandalit del Barco. (2005) "The International Reach of the Mara Salvatrucha." NPR. March 2005.

New Jersey State Commission of Investigation. (2008) Gangs in Prison Public Hearing. November 2008.

NJSP (2006) "NJSP Practical Guide to Intelligence-Led Policing", New Jersey State Police, Trenton, NJ. http://www.state.nj.us/njsp/divorg/invest/pdf/njsp_ilpguide_010907.pdf

Papachristos, A. (2005) "Talk of the Nation: More Gangs Going Global." NPR. February 23, 2005.

Papchristos, A. (2005) Gang World Foreign Policy. April 2005.

Reuters. (2008) "Inmates beheaded in Gauatemala prison gang brawl." CBC News. November 22, 2008.

Sheptycki, James. (2004). Organizational Pathologies in Police Intelligence Systems. European Journal of Criminology, 1 (3), 307-332

Thompson, G. (2004) "Tattooed Warriors: The Next Generation: Shuttling Between Nations, Latino Gangs Confound the Law." New York Times. September 26, 2004.

Travis, A. (2008) "Seeking Solitary: Prison gang wars force fearful inmates to plead for segregation." The United Kingdom: The Guardian. February 18, 2008.

Section 7
Suspicious Activity Reports: Shifting the Analytical Paradigm
By Rafael Brinner

INTRODUCTION

Intelligence about terrorist threats in the United States is elusive. As homeland security strategies have sought to compensate for this reality, the effort to detect threats has increasingly hinged on leveraging suspicious activity reports, or SARs.[5] In the absence of better threat intelligence, federal, state, and local agencies are allocating increasing resources to the collection, analysis, and sharing of SARs.[6] The goal is to create an environment that ensures the law enforcement, intelligence, and homeland security communities have the means to "connect the dots" and identify terrorist activity in time to prevent it.

By making SARs widely available to analysts working across a patchwork of agencies, the expectation is that pattern analysis and cross-referencing will allow analysts to develop more investigative leads and ultimately uncover threat intelligence that can prevent a future attack. Certainly an enhanced emphasis on collecting, tracking, and investigating SARs can have a positive impact on combating crime levels. But on the terrorism front, where activity is more sporadic and SARs less reliable, can SARs deliver? And how do we ensure crucial data does not get buried by an ever-growing mass of SAR data?

The key to improving analytical tradecraft with SARs lies in effectively triaging and evaluating them, enabling us to focus resources on the most promising leads and optimize our chances of recognizing the warning signs of an incipient threat. This article will explain what makes SARs distinct from traditional threat intelligence, describe the dangers of conflating SARs with threat intelligence, and offer a methodological approach for analyzing SARs in their own right.

SARs Are Not Threat Intelligence

Understanding the nature of SARs and how we relate to them is key to addressing the analytical challenges that SAR data present. SARs are perceived to varying degrees as potential indicators of threat activity, and consequently analysts tend to treat SARs as a form of threat intelligence. It may seem like splitting hairs to designate SARs as something distinct, but failure to do so can lead to a host of difficulties, as later examples will demonstrate.

Threat intelligence, broadly speaking, is information about the plans, intentions, motives, capabilities, and modus operandi of threat actors. For example, if we are concerned with detecting terrorist threats, the intelligence we are after will shed light on what some known or would-be terrorists are intending to do,

---

[5] The acronym SAR is used in this article to refer to a broad array of suspicious activity reporting, rather than the more limited reference to suspicious financial transactions, as defined in the Bank Security Act.

[6] With the December 2008 launch of the Nationwide Suspicious Activities Reporting Initiative, agencies at all levels of government are now pursuing "a coordinated effort that leverages and integrates all SAR-related activities. The NSI strategy is to develop, evaluate, and implement common processes and policies for gathering, documenting, processing, analyzing, and sharing information about terrorism-related suspicious activities. The initiative will ensure that NSI participants at all levels of government adopt consistent policies and procedures that foster broader sharing of terrorism-related SARs...", *<http://www.ise.gov/pages/sar-initiative.html>*.

how and why they are intending to do it, and – in the best case – specifics about the timing and target of an attack. Threat intelligence is often narrative in form, detailing not just activity but the rationale for it as well. For instance, a wiretap might reveal that operatives have obtained weapons and that they are intended for use in an upcoming attack. Inevitably, there will be key elements of information missing – intelligence gaps that require analysts to gather more information to fill them or make reasoned assessments to bridge them. Piecing together enough fragments of threat intelligence allows investigators and analysts to begin to trace the outline of a plot.

Analysts rarely have all the pieces of the puzzle. In the terrorism arena, reliable threat information can be extremely hard to acquire. Terrorist groups jealously guard their secrets, meaning threat intelligence is denied to all but those directly involved in or close to the activity. Though some terrorist groups may broadcast their strategic intentions and indulge in threatening rhetoric, they seldom if ever reveal any operational details for fear of jeopardizing the success of their intended plans.[7] Obtaining bona fide threat intelligence requires clandestine or surreptitious means – human or technical sources – because there is no other way to gain access to it and learn what would otherwise remain hidden. With a well-placed source, threat actors may let slip clues or actionable details about their activities or intentions, unaware that they may have compromised their own plans. As these sources gain access to denied information, a picture begins to emerge.

In contrast to threat intelligence, SARs originate as raw observation.[8] They are eyewitness accounts from security guards or law enforcement officers who notice something unusual during the course of their duties, or from vigilant members of the public concerned about something they consider out of the ordinary. Thus, a typical SAR is an anecdotal account of observed activity or behavior that the observer deemed suspicious on some level.

While SARs contain objective details to varying degrees, they tend to be full of subjective interpretation. What distinguishes SARs from threat intelligence is that in most cases the facts are mute; it is the observer who articulates what the activity signified and why it was suspicious. The observer, especially an experienced law enforcement officer intimately familiar with his or her beat, may have especially keen instincts for what is out of the ordinary;[9] but in describing the observed activity in a report, the intentions and motives ascribed to SARs are inferred, not explicitly indicated.

A subjective narrative can only get us so far. SARs frequently provide few avenues for follow-up, forcing investigators and analysts to work with an incomplete picture. Conjecture is often necessary to bind together individual SARs analytically, or to evaluate SAR data in the context of current assessments of threat and vulnerability. Here is precisely where correctly applying analytical tradecraft can mean the difference between accurate warning and crying wolf. The latter outcome is far more likely if we analyze SARs as if they were threat intelligence.

---

[7] One exception to this is terrorist groups that issue explicit warnings before attacks to minimize casualties while maximizing disruption, as the Provisional Irish Republican Army often did in the United Kingdom.

[8] The common standard promulgated by the Office of the Director of National Intelligence defines SARs as "observed behavior reasonably indicative of pre-operational planning related to terrorism or other criminal activity." Definition revised 21 May 2009. See Common Terrorism Information Sharing Standards at <http://www.ise.gov/pages/ctiss.html>.

[9] A subject matter expert may recognize anomalies by keying in on small indications that are out of place. See Malcolm Gladwell, *Blink : The Power of Thinking Without Thinking* (Little, Brown and Company, 2005).

Boxing At Shadows

If there is a single case that embodies the array of challenges SARs pose for threat analysis and response, it is the heightened alert on the Washington State Ferries system in August 2007. The alert accompanied the FBI's release of photographs of two men whom it was seeking to identify because of their unexplained behavior while riding a ferry in July. Although the FBI's Seattle office had collected hundreds of SARs involving the ferry system over the preceding five years, the photograph presented a seeming link between several reports of suspicious activity identified in summer 2007, offering what some analysts believed to be the strongest indications to date that terrorists were casing the country's largest ferry system for a terrorist attack.[10] The alert prompted a surge by multiple federal and local agencies, absent any actual threat intelligence. The manner in which this threat was assessed and later resolved illustrates the dangers of substituting SARs for threat intelligence.

FOXNEWS.COM HOME > U.S.

FBI Seeks Identity of Two Men Seen Aboard Washington State Ferries

Wednesday, August 22, 2007

E-Mail | Print

FOX NEWS

Share: F

FBI

The FBI released photographs of two men Monday who have been seen on Washington state ferries "exhibiting unusual behavior" and asked the public for help identifying them.

The agency's Seattle field office, along with the Washington Joint Analytical Center, was still seeking the men's identities and whereabouts Wednesday as ferry service was temporarily shutdown when a suspicious package was found in a ferry bathroom and taken away by authorities.

"We had various independent reports from passengers and ferry

Like most SARs, this story began with ambiguous activity that was sufficiently out of the ordinary to arouse the suspicions of those who witnessed it. In late July 2007, passengers aboard a ferry transiting from Seattle to Vashon Island became concerned when two young, "foreign-looking" men engaged in activity that, from the passengers' perspective, did not conform to typical tourist or commuter behavior.

---

[10] NPR, *All Things Considered*, 23 August 2007
<*http://www.npr.org/templates/story/story.php?storyId=13903584*>.

According to one journalist covering the story, the two men were "paying a lot more attention to the operation of the ship than to the beautiful scenery."[11] They allegedly photographed the car deck and paid undue attention to docking procedures.[12] As the FBI reportedly put it, they seemed "overly interested in the workings and layouts of the ferries."[13] Once alerted to their activity, the ferry's captain left the bridge and snapped a picture of the pair, providing visual evidence to accompany the SAR.

The photograph offered the most tangible means of assessing the SAR's significance, although almost nothing was known about the two men. The Washington Joint Analysis Center, the state's fusion center for terrorism-related information, reviewed other recent SARs from ferry passengers, identifying several more SARs that, based on witness accounts from other ferry passengers, appeared to place the two men on the ferry system on four to six occasions during the weeks before their picture was taken.[14]

The tentative linkage to other SARs lacked certainty, but when initial attempts to identify the two men failed and no further information emerged to mitigate concerns, initial threat perceptions hardened. The U.S. Coast Guard and the Transportation Security Administration joined with FBI and Washington State Patrol to search for the men and increased their coordination.[15] The prospect of pre-operational terrorist surveillance on the Washington State Ferries system was deemed sufficient to warrant an increase in security measures. In an effort to elicit information about the two men, the FBI released the photograph to local newspapers and cable news networks in late August. The publicity briefly drew media and local politics into the fray.

The Trouble With SARs

How could a single report create such a stir? Much of the fault lies with the malleability of SARs. The lack of amplifying or verifiable information in a typical SAR leaves us poorly equipped to form an accurate picture of what occurred and why. Comparing intelligence analysis to solving a jigsaw puzzle assumes that the pieces have precise contours that allow for only one correct fit and make any mismatch readily apparent. In the case of SARs, the anecdotal, incomplete nature of their information means they often lack verifiable details, leaving the contours so indistinct that they can be readily aligned with an array of other unrelated reports.

In this sense, SARs function more like LEGO® bricks than puzzle pieces. Inherent in the design of LEGO® bricks is the ability to connect any two of them in a variety of ways. To the untrained eye, SARs exhibit the same versatility. Analysts can easily leverage superficial similarities (similar color vehicle, similar non-descript, dark-haired male, etc.) to forge opportunistic linkages, but unless a good-faith effort is made to verify the hypothesis, SAR linkages too often prove to be spurious. The danger is that once one starts linking SARs, there is a tendency to perceive threats as more real than any of the constituent reports would objectively indicate. SARs, like LEGO® bricks, invite you to use your imagination.

---

[11] Seattle Times staff reporter Mike Carter quoted on National Public Radio, *All Things Considered*, 23 August 2007 <http://www.npr.org/templates/story/story.php?storyId=13903584>.

[12] ABC News, *FBI Taps Public to ID Suspicious Ferry Riders*, August 22, 2007 <http://abcnews.go.com/US/story?id=3510174&page=1>.

[13] Seattle Post-Intelligencer, *FBI seeks help identifying 2 men seen aboard ferries*, August 21, 2007 <http://www.seattlepi.com/local/328396_ferries21.html>.

[14] ABC News, *FBI Taps Public to ID Suspicious Ferry Riders*, August 22, 2007 <http://abcnews.go.com/US/story?id=3510174&page=1>.

[15] Seattle Times, *FBI asks: Who are the men in this photo from ferry?*, August 22, 2007 <http://seattletimes.nwsource.com/html/localnews/2003847538_ferries22m.html>.

It is therefore important not to mistake a SAR's narrative – i.e. the observer's *interpretation* of events – for the narrative elements (who, what, when, where, why, and how) gathered from traditional intelligence sources. An observer's judgment may be correct, but until investigation and analysis dig deeper or additional information comes to light, ascribing a motive to suspicious activity amounts to speculation. To its credit, the FBI acknowledged this dynamic when it published the photograph from the Vashon Island ferry: "what some people consider suspicious or unusual behavior actually might turn out to be something completely innocuous."[16]

As anomalous as their activity initially seemed, a thorough interview of the two men would have elicited a narrative from the subjects themselves, and given investigators a better sense of whether speculation about pre-operational terrorist surveillance was warranted or not. Indeed, when the two men eventually did come forward, investigators were able to interview them and resolve the mystery. An FBI official told the *Seattle Times*, "Their story makes sense; their story has validity…..It was perfectly normal once we learned what was going on."[17]

This is at the heart of the SAR conundrum: When imagination overtakes objective analysis, the potential for overreaction increases significantly. In the Washington State Ferries case, there was insufficient information to reach solid analytical conclusions. Without more information about the two men in the photograph, the ensuing effort to make sense of the report depended entirely on the visual recollection of witnesses who had reported other suspicious activity on the ferries, and thought they recognized one or the other of the men in the photograph. Though no one could say with certainty what the suspicious individuals in the other reports were up to, these preliminary identifications led local analysts to assert that the two men were possibly engaged in a broad casing operation for a future terrorist attack on the ferry system.

Though there were no explicit indicators, this conclusion seemed sensible in the context of recent terrorism trends. By the summer of 2007, events elsewhere had heightened threat perceptions surrounding the Washington State Ferries system. Four young men had blown themselves up among commuters on London's mass transit system in July 2005. In March of the previous year, terrorists had left cell-phone initiated explosive devices in backpacks aboard commuter trains in Madrid, killing nearly 200 passengers. More relevant still, in February 2004, just two weeks before the Madrid attacks, a terrorist smuggled a time-delayed explosive charge aboard a crowded passenger ferry in the Philippines. Although the blast was small, the ensuing fire gutted the vessel and claimed more than 100 lives. By showcasing the ease of attacking mass transit systems, these overseas attacks helped instill a perception of threat-by-analogy, whereby the inherent vulnerability of the Washington State Ferries implied that they could face the same threat that befell mass transit elsewhere.

The effort to knit together the incident on the Vashon Island ferry with other SARs from earlier that summer was logical, but given the inherent ambiguity of SAR information, the data could reasonably have suggested hypotheses other than the worst case. Not until the following April did the two subjects in the widely circulated photograph come forward to clear their names and bring closure to the story. The two men – both European, both software consultants – appeared at the U.S. Embassy in their home country and established their bona fides. In the event, the actual story was relatively simple. They

---

[16] Seattle Post-Intelligencer, *FBI seeks help identifying 2 men seen aboard ferries*, August 21, 2007 <http://www.seattlepi.com/local/328396_ferries21.html>.
    [17] Seattle Times, *Two ferry riders sought by FBI last summer were just tourists*, May 6, 2008 <http://seattletimes.nwsource.com/html/localnews/2004394642_fbi06m.html>.

confirmed that they traveled to the Seattle area in July 2007 for a business conference (precluding their involvement in earlier SARs) and admitted to riding a ferry just once, on the occasion when they were photographed. Why had they photographed the car-deck of the ferry? They were impressed by the car-carrying capacity of the ferries on Puget Sound, according to the FBI official quoted in the *Seattle Times*. "Where these gentlemen live, they don't have vehicle ferries. They were fascinated that a ferry could hold that many cars and wanted to show folks back home."[18]

But what of the other ferry incidents reported in the summer of 2007? What of the hundreds of SARs reported to the FBI's Seattle office each year? As the Washington State Ferry case helps illustrate, the ambiguous incidents that SARs describe – videotaping, unusual queries, security breaches – may not be intentionally suspicious or inherently terrorism-related.   Unless additional, clarifying information becomes available, it is premature to treat a SAR as a piece of threat intelligence solely on the basis of initial interpretations. What is missing is a model that both addresses the unique characteristics of SAR-derived information and establishes a neutral context for analyzing SARs on their individual merits.

Putting SARs In Their Place

The SAR model this article proposes builds on existing notions of how to parse terrorism-related reporting. The Intelligence Community has traditionally assessed information of this sort according to whether it reflected the perspective of threats (the intentions, capabilities, and the plans of terrorist groups) or vulnerabilities (potential targets for terrorists and exploitable gaps in their security). Much of the terrorism-related data that analysts and decision-makers regularly confront falls into one or the other of these domains (Fig. 1). The challenge has been to accurately discern from disparate, fragmentary reports, where threat indicators and vulnerabilities overlap and so present a nexus of heightened risk.

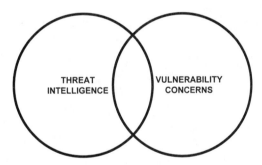

Figure 1: Threat and Vulnerability

What do the non-overlapping areas represent? Not all plans and intentions translate into action, and not all intelligence about terrorist groups relates to their operational activity. The left-hand part of the threat circle captures this sort of information. Similarly, terrorists do not assess vulnerabilities in a vacuum (as, say, a security assessment team might be asked to do). They have criteria for what makes a desirable target, as well as criteria for what is achievable in the context of their capabilities. That means that many of the things we consider vulnerabilities have likely never met the terrorists' minimum threshold for inclusion on a target list, or have been considered but struck from the list. That swath of vulnerability-related information falls in the right-hand portion of the diagram.

---

[18] Ibid.

So where do SARs factor in? To reach decisions about what targets to attack, terrorist operatives typically conduct on-scene surveillance of the target, first to assess its suitability, and later to support their plan of attack. In the threat-vulnerability model, it is tempting to seize on SARs as the key to identifying which vulnerabilities the terrorists intend to exploit (Fig. 2). As discussed earlier, SARs make this all the more tempting when we have few if any specific intelligence leads. We therefore default to treating SARs as data points existing somewhere inside this threat-vulnerability equation.

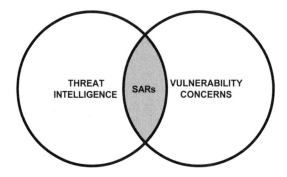

Figure 2: The presumed domain for SARs.

Regrettably this falls short of the mark. For one thing, vast amounts of SARs have no bearing on terrorist activity, or else we would expect the volume of SARs collected to be matched by commensurately high levels of terrorist activity. Adding another circle to the Venn diagram gives SARs a domain of their own, one better aligned with their role (Fig. 3). The gray circle's position illustrates how, perceptions aside, the bulk of SARs have no relationship to either the threat domain or the vulnerability domain. These SARs represent suspicious behavior that turns out to have no nexus to terrorism, or perhaps even to crime, and thus they lie outside the domain of threat intelligence.[19] These are the false positives, the innocuous activities misinterpreted by an observer, however well intentioned.

Figure 3: SARs as a domain of their own.

---

[19] These reports may still be useful in assessing activity trends – as opposed to threat trends - at a certain location or within an industrial sector, even if they have ultimately have no merit as threat indicators.

When we don't acknowledge the ambiguity of SARs, however, we run the risk of assigning them too great a significance. In theory, suspicious activity in the vicinity of a potentially vulnerable target like the Washington State Ferries should lead us to a threat. In practice however, we see plenty of suspicious activity around our critical facilities simply because that is where we have invested the resources to look.

The Venn diagram in Figure 3 above begins to convey the imbalance between spurious SARs and those that warrant concern. Pre-operational activity is sporadic in the United States; indicators are few and far between and can often resemble legitimate activity like photography. Statistically speaking, we can reasonably expect that most SARs will prove to be false positives.[20] The low threshold we tend to maintain for what is suspicious exacerbates this trend. For example, an FBI assessment in 2004 reviewed 157 SARs relating to the Washington State Ferries system. Of these, 19 SARs, or roughly 12 percent, were judged "likely" or "extremely likely" to have involved terrorist surveillance.[21] Whether or not any one of those 19 SARs was indeed terrorism-related, the assessment tacitly acknowledged that the remaining 88 percent were probably false positives. Absent any confirmation over the subsequent 5 years, it now appears that even those 12 percent judged to be probable indicators of terrorist surveillance were most likely false positives as well. Armed with this understanding of prevalence of false positives among SARs, it is easy to see that we need a means to hone in on those reports that fall in the overlapping region that constitutes the nexus between threat intelligence and suspicious activity.

Before we can take that step, we need to acknowledge that our data set is woefully incomplete. There are actually two types of incidents in the SAR domain: those incidents that become SARs, and an outer ring representing the far larger number of incidents that go unreported. To properly convey the difficulty of using SARs as terrorism indicators, we need to add another circle to this model (Fig. 4). As a result, SARs themselves only represent a small fraction of the potential data. Redrawing the SARs domain in this fashion reflects the diminished potential for any particular SAR to overlap with actual threat-related activity.

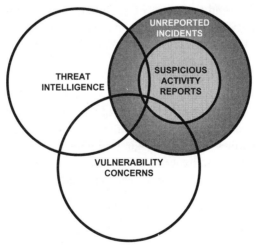

Figure 4: SARs are only a fraction of the dataset.

[20] See Jeff Jonas and Jim Harper, *Effective Counterterrorism and the Limited Role of Predictive Data Mining*, Policy Analysis No. 584, December 11, 2006, Cato Institute *<http://www.cato.org/pubs/pas/pa584.pdf>*.

[21] Seattle Times, *Why feds believe terrorists are probing ferry system*, October 10, 2004 *<http://seattletimes.nwsource.com/html/localnews/2002058959_ferry10m.html>*.

Some SARs presumably do overlap with the threat domain. In those cases where we can positively establish a nexus between a SAR and terrorist threat information, that incident certainly merits designation as a *potential* threat indicator. The purpose of this model is not to crush hopes of catching terrorists before they strike. Rather it is to ensure that we appreciate the degree of nuance that SAR analysis entails. Only then can we adequately triage the huge number of incoming SARs, divert investigative and collection resources away from the false positives, and preserve analytical and investigative capacity for those SARs we assess to be potential threat indicators. This model is about keeping our eye on the ball.

Counterintuitive Approaches to Analyzing SARs

These two factors – the incomplete data set and the high prevalence of false positives among SARs – require a cognitive shift in analytical tradecraft. Effectively analyzing SARs, means relying less on the intelligence paradigm of indicators and adopting more of a law enforcement approach of "tips and leads." Defaulting to SARs as indicators invites the twin dangers of crying wolf and engendering warning fatigue. When SARs are instead handled as leads, investigators and analysts have more room to exercise due diligence and take initial investigative steps, before threat perceptions begin to form. Only when further examination establishes a potential nexus to terrorism should a SAR merit consideration as an indicator.

The Trending Pitfall: Treating SARs as leads and not indicators has significant repercussions for SAR analysis. It imposes limitations on analytical techniques that work perfectly well for more reliable data. Trend analysis used for tracking other threats, such as crime or the spread of contagious disease, does not carry over to terrorism-related SARs: the metrics are there, we can clearly trace an increase or decrease in reporting, but these fluctuations actually reveal very little about the level of threat, or even the level of genuinely suspicious activity. For one, the incomplete dataset, coupled with the high rate of false positives, undercuts meaningful trend analysis. For another, many if not most SAR leads tend to pan out as mundane or irresolvable activity, leaving the conclusions from trending more ambiguous, not less. Perplexingly, an increase in SARs recorded may only indicate an increase in reporting, not necessarily in activity.

Meaningful trending of terrorism-related activity only works when the data discriminates between events and non-events.   SARs rarely lend themselves to quick identification as a terrorism-related event. Contrast this with an active theater of terrorist operations, such as Iraq or Afghanistan, where insurgent attacks provide a more tangible metric than ambiguous SARs.[22] An IED detonates, shots are fired: these sorts of events present unambiguous indicators of hostile activity. Lacking this fidelity, SARs offer little prospect of providing a quantitative solution to measuring threat.

A Single Incident Can Hold the Key: A single, highly suspicious incident may by itself present a more valid threat indicator than a rise or drop in the volume of SARs overall. The relative infrequency of terrorism-related SARs in the Homeland elevates the significance of *individual* reports over trends. Referring back to Figure 4, the outer ring of unreported incidents reflects that, in the realm of SARs, there is too much data missing from the equation to trust aggregate assessments. Experience suggests that drilling down into individual anomalous incidents has been a more reliable route to interdicting terrorist plots.

---

[22] "30 Days, 2,368 Attacks", William McNulty and James Glanz, New York Times, September 28, 2004 <*http://www.nytimes.com/imagepages/2004/09/28/international/29ATTACK-GRAPH.html*>.

Examples that bear this out include the state trooper who, during a traffic stop in Goose Creek, S.C., found unusual model rocketry parts in the trunk of the vehicle. One of the vehicle's occupants was found to have posted an instructional video online in which he demonstrated how to construct a detonator for an improvised explosive device.[23] The "Fort Dix Six" sought to have a video of their jihadist training activities transferred to DVD; the Circuit City technician saw fit to report the video's contents to police, who turned the investigation over to the FBI.[24] And even before 9/11, in December 1999, the Algerian al-Qaida member Ahmed Ressam aroused suspicion when he arrived at Port Angeles, Washington, from Victoria, British Columbia, by ferry rather than traveling more directly from Vancouver to Seattle via the land border.[25] The U.S. Customs agent initially suspected he was smuggling drugs, but soon discovered a carload of explosives and detonators ultimately destined for an attack on Los Angeles International Airport. What these instances suggest is that, even if we lack a quantitative measure for rating SARs, we can and should endeavor to rate them qualitatively.

Assigning Qualitative Ratings to SARs

Separating the wheat from the chaff is essential for allocating resources more effectively against a problem set as wide and as ethereal as SARs. Qualitative ratings enable this, by allowing us to filter SARs for anomalous incidents, to keep routine activity in perspective, and to apply a degree of objective rigor to an otherwise subjective process.

But what qualitative criteria should a rating system employ? The FBI's Seattle Field Intelligence Group pioneered a methodology for its Washington State Ferries assessments that rated the likelihood that a SAR represented terrorist pre-operational planning. This novel approach moved the ball in the right direction. Rather than assessing the degree of threat or nexus to terrorism that a SAR appears to present (something the foregoing discussion argues would be difficult to pin down), the rating system proposed here is designed to measure the level of suspicion a SAR arouses. The analytical criteria are intended to limit the role of analytical bias and encourage the identification of likely false positives.

Given the inherent subjectivity of most SARs, we need to tether SAR ratings to objective standards to make them meaningful. The ratings presented here, developed during the author's previous assignment, span a scale that, at its upper end, reflects the degree to which the activity conforms to known indicators of pre-operational activity. At the scale's lower end, the ratings reflect how anomalous the suspicious activity is, particularly in the context of the venue. Together, these ratings form a dynamic range that affords the flexibility to modify a rating upward or downward according to the availability of new information. This gives analysts the freedom to alter assessments in light of changing circumstances, and alert decision makers when a SAR reaches the upper end of the rating scale.

---

[23] Fred Burton and Scott Stewart, *Traffic Stops and Thwarted Plots*, STRATFOR, August 8, 2007 <*http://www.stratfor.com/traffic_stops_and_thwarted_plots*>; *The Goose Creek, South Carolina Traffic Stop*, NEFA Foundation, April 30, 2009
<*http://www.nefafoundation.org/miscellaneous/FeaturedDocs/nefagoosecreek0409.pdf*>.
[24] MSNBC, *Electronics store worker gave Fort Dix tipoff*, May 9, 2007
<*http://www.msnbc.msn.com/id/18573255*>.
[25] Seattle Times, *The Terrorist Within*, June 23, 2002
<*http://seattletimes.nwsource.com/news/nation-world/terroristwithin/chapter12.html*>.

CHAPTER 11
APPLICATIONS OF INTELLIGENCE
Section 7 – Suspicious Activity Reports: Shifting the Analytical Paradigm

Table 1: Qualitative Ratings for SARs

Suspicion Rating	Analytical Criteria
STRONG	Convergence with specific, credible threat
DEMONSTRABLE	Aggressive testing of security, evidence of pre-meditation
ELEVATED	Unusual behavior atypical for the venue
MINIMAL	Ordinary behavior or activity
NOT SUSPICIOUS	Resolved as not threat-related

Returning to the Vashon Island ferry incident, what rating did that SAR merit by these criteria? Two men photographing the car deck of a ferry, rather than the more scenic vistas above decks, would be atypical behavior for ferry passengers. But there was insufficient information to suggest the activity was premeditated or overly aggressive, so the report merited an **Elevated** suspicion rating. Unless proven, the tentative linkage to other SARs on the Washington State Ferries system would not have justified shifting the rating higher.

Although the rating methodology is a subjective tool, objective data is needed to shift ratings higher or lower. If the SAR was shown to describe behavior or activity that seemed out of place, but was in fact relatively routine, it would probably rate only **Minimal**. If law enforcement officers had met the ferry and established that the two men were legitimate tourists, the rating would drop to **Not Suspicious**. However, had the two men made persistent attempts to circumvent security, or possessed annotated maps or blueprints of the ferry, or other positive indications of possible nefarious intent, then a **Demonstrable** suspicion rating would certainly have been appropriate. In the rare event that details of a SAR converged with specific, credible threat information (the men matched the description of known operatives, or credible intelligence indicated an active threat to the ferry system), a **Strong** rating would have been warranted.

This rating methodology is not intended to provide ironclad certification either that a threat exists or that it is absent. Unlike the approach taken in FBI's Washington State Ferry assessments, these ratings are not attempting to gauge the likelihood that a SAR is threat-related. As this article has sought to establish, SARs are a weak and problematic information source. More often than not, the best that aggregate analysis of SARs can deliver is a baseline of routine activity, against which we can scan for anomalies. The ratings system proposed here is simply a tool for flagging the level of concern analysts have attached to an incident.

This methodology can be adapted to improve situational awareness by issuing alerts when analysts rate a SAR **Demonstrable** or **Strong**. At the lower end of the scale, qualitative ratings permit analysts to establish a baseline for SAR reporting and monitor what activity appears to be routine. With routine activity serving as a backdrop, the rating system highlights significant anomalies and points analysts and investigators in the direction of potentially promising leads. Finally, the lowest rating, **Not Suspicious**, ensures a degree of hygiene in SAR database holdings, keeping older, already resolved incidents from recurrently arousing concern in later database queries.

CONCLUSION

The rising volume of SARs contrasts with the continual scarcity of well-sourced intelligence about terrorist threats in the United States. This puts analysts in a quandary, tempting them to substitute SARs for more solid intelligence when too many pieces of the puzzle are missing. As this article has endeavored to show, proceeding as if SARs are threat intelligence results in faulty analysis, skewed threat perceptions, and ultimately the misallocation of finite resources. Qualitative ratings offer a means for grounding the analysis of SARs, ensuring analysts measure the suspiciousness of an incident against common thresholds.

The SAR rating methodology presented here draws on a few basic principles. To be most effective, a qualitative rating system needs to be simple and easy to apply across agencies and work groups. The ratings themselves must be distinct from one another, enabling a calibrated response. Finally, the triage process must enable analysts to demote SARs that have been cleared of suspicion and keep them from polluting analyses and information flows.

Implementing a dynamic process that allows for adjusting ratings upward or downward ensures that SAR analysis remains responsive to follow-on investigation and insights gleaned from subsequent reporting. Without such a methodology, we may connect a variety of dots, but miss the one dot that is key to unraveling a terrorist plot. In the end, it is essential that we connect the right dots, not all the dots. Qualitative ratings offer a means to isolate those singular indicators from the confusing mass of suspicious activity reporting and ensure we do not miss a crucial lead amid the information overload.

Section 8
Uses, Abuses, and Misuses of Intelligence
By Frederick T. Martens

INTRODUCTION

Crime control in a free and open society is a task fraught with all sorts of inherent and often contradictory dilemmas. There are no easy or simple answers to either the prevention of crime or containing its growth. Indeed, the simple fact of the matter is we know little about why crime rates increase and, similarly, why crime rates decline. Criminologists, with all their computer models, are loath to explain recent trends nationwide in the decline of murder and the other violent crime rates. Practitioners, on the other hand, are quick to ascribe cause and effect explanations to crime rates, with little empirical data to support their assertions. Clearly our "knowledge" of crime and its control is one of "guesswork" as opposed to "scientific revelations" (Wilson and Hernstein 1985).

Notwithstanding, the dearth of "knowledge" that pervades our (mis)understanding of crime and its control, we do know that certain law enforcement methodologies allow us to anticipate and prevent certain crimes from occurring. Intelligence is certainly a key component in any viable crime control program, particularly when addressing crime that is systematic, systemic, and organized. Terrorism, serial murders, organized crime, and gang activity all fall under the rubric of "a continuing criminal conspiracy" and are best suited for the application of the intelligence process. There is little argument for the value of intelligence in addressing conspiratorial crime; yet, there remains much debate and criticism over the role of intelligence in a free and open society (Donner 1980; Mitgang 1988; Garfinkle 2000). For when intelligence is not used or used improperly, what we have is "malpractice," which can only lead to dire consequences – not only to the law enforcement community but to society as a whole.

As we enter yet another millennium, we face a world that is no longer constrained by geography or time. Electronic media are changing the very nature of crime and crime control. Intelligence systems are essential to maintaining some sort of "knowledge" that can aid law enforcement in containing the growth of crime. We must use our resources in more creative and intelligent ways if we are to maintain the delicate balance between crime control and personal liberty and freedom. To accomplish this, we must understand and carefully constrict our use of intelligence to those threats that pose the greatest harm to our domestic tranquility and allow the traditional, reactive law enforcement methodologies to address the routine forms of crime. It is through understanding the mistakes of the past that we can avoid corrupting the intelligence process and diminishing its value in maintaining a free and open society in the future.

PRIVACY AND SECURITY ARE FUNDAMENTAL RIGHTS

The birth of this great nation was predicated on what may be one of the most diabolical theorems of any democratic society – which government is **not** to be trusted in protecting the freedom and liberty of its people. Our very theoretical foundation is that governments are designed, as a rule, to impose their will on the people and only through vigilance and citizen oversight can the instruments of repression and oppression be properly constrained. Indeed, it is an ongoing battle to protect on one hand, the right of people to "hate" their government but yet not **act** on their "hate" (Sullivan 1999:50; George and Wilcox

1996). To those not conditioned to this way of thinking, it must seem quite diabolical (to say the least) that we, as a society, protect such extremist groups as the Ku Klux Klan or the American Nazi Party, yet condemn what they stand for. We as a society are constantly struggling to maintain a balance between the fundamental **right** to promote unpopular views as a people, yet ensure that such views do not interfere with the "pursuit of happiness," which we guarantee to each and every citizen regardless of race, religion, or socio-economic status. Insofar as the preservation of individual liberty is fundamental, so too is our need to feel secure and not be terrorized by the fear that often accompanies "unpopular views" (i.e. racism, religious intolerance, sexism, discrimination based on life style, etc.). Thus, "hate" is not only protected, it enjoys a special status within our society one that shields those who exercise "unpopular views" from invasion of their views by government. Indeed, "reputation" is, in most instances, now viewed as a fundamental right and one that cannot be "searched" without proper justification (New York Times 1998a).[26] Merely opposing or advocating the end to any form of gun control is not sufficient basis for government to collect information on a person, notwithstanding the consequences of unrestricted gun ownership. Furthermore, even when such persons join together and form groups that promote views that are in opposition to that of government or its policies, invoking the intelligence process raises serious individual liberty questions that can be traced back to a dark era in American society, when the threat of Communism was seen as a threat to our very way of life: the so-called "McCarthy Era."

MCCARTHY SET THE STAGE

Post-World War II visited upon the United States a potential threat that changed in fundamental ways, the way we thought about freedom and individual liberty. Communism and all its dire manifestations caused the government of the United States to invest in a weapons arsenal that could destroy the world ten times over. Trillions of dollars were invested in this "defense" system that sought to stem the tide of Communism. In addition, lives have been spent in such far away countries as Korea, Vietnam, Guatemala, Nicaragua, and El Salvador to prevent Communism from gaining a foothold. In the United States, Congress, the federal government, state and local law enforcement agencies invested in gathering information on "suspected Communists" who would threaten our very way of life. The so-called "Red Scare" of the 50s brought about Congressional hearings chaired by the late Senator Joseph McCarthy, which sought to identify and publicly expose those who advocated Communism. The threat was real, as evidenced by the rhetoric of the late Nikita Khrushchev who prophesied "We will bury you" – a reference to the might of Russia's nuclear arsenal, which was the personification of the Communist system. McCarthy, and many others in government, joined together to bring the resources of government to bear on this public menace. Hearings were held, investigations were conducted, and prominent people were exposed – some of whom were tried and true members of the Communist Party and others who sympathized with their cause, if not their methods (Cogley 1956; Cook 1971; Weschler 1953; Roverse 1959; Anderson and May 1956; Navasky 1980). It was a time when the label "Communist Sympathizer" was sufficient to deny one the right of his or her reputation, which resulted in all forms of societal discrimination. Interestingly, many of those so labeled were members of disenfranchised ethnic or racial groups who were discriminated against in other ways by society.

---

[26] See California Constitution (Article 1, Section 1) and the Pennsylvania Constitution, both of which include a "Right to Privacy" (California) "and Protecting Property and Reputation." (Article 1, Section 1, Pennsylvania).

This period of time saw a significant investment by law enforcement agencies in "red squads," "subversive" units, and "internal security" bureaus that focused their intelligence and investigative resources toward those who chose to disrupt the operations of government. There was, of course, this fundamental contradiction for we were a democracy built on the premise that government unrestrained by law was inherently corrupt, oppressive, and repressive. Now, we were using law to rationalize the invocation of the intelligence process as a means of ensuring the security of our nation and its people. So long as we were fighting this **external** threat called "Communism" and it was being waged by those whose job it was to "protect" the people from such threats, few cared how or what methods government used to prevent domestic instability. The "McCarthy Era" proved, once again, personal liberty and freedoms protected by the Constitution can be enjoined when public discourse is muted by a government intent on suppressing our access to information. For what the "McCarthy Era" demonstrated was that raw, unevaluated, and poorly analyzed information led to the promulgation of public policy that threatened the very foundation of our democracy to a far greater extent than did the inherently corrupt ideology known as "Communism". Only when McCarthy's colleagues in the Senate finally recognized the manner in which McCarthy misused the Congressional investigatory process was he and his methods discredited. Not before, however, many lives were destroyed and careers ruined; and not before the term "McCarthyism" impugned the legitimate value of the intelligence process.

THE NIXON ERA RE-IGNITES THE DEBATE

John F. Kennedy's election to the Presidency resulted in his brother, Robert F. Kennedy, being sworn in as the Attorney General of the United States. Robert, a former counsel to the Permanent Subcommittee on Investigations, pursued organized crime and corruption with a vengeance (Navasky 1971; Schlessinger 1978; Franco and Hammer 1987). Initiating organized crime strike forces that reported directly to the Justice Department, bypassing local U.S. attorneys, Kennedy waged an unprecedented "war" which enlisted the vast resources of the FBI and a number of other Federal agencies, including the Internal Revenue Service. While Kennedy's pursuit of the late James Hoffa, President of the Teamsters Union, was legendary, it was Kennedy's reliance on intelligence that allowed his strike force program to target and prosecute the Cosa Nostra "families" that controlled vice and crime in the larger cities. With the assassination of his brother, Robert Kennedy's drive against organized crime was diminished and ultimately extinguished with the appointment of Ramsey Clark as Attorney General. Clark saw many of the methods and techniques used by Kennedy as intrusive and anti-civil libertarian and actively opposed such legislation as electronic surveillance – a central feature of any "war against organized crime."

At the same time, emphasis on civil rights was building at a federal level. The late Martin Luther King was organizing demonstrations throughout the South; some of which resulted in violent confrontations with the police. Believed by some to be a pawn of the Communist Party, King was targeted by the late J. Edgar Hoover of the FBI "Wiretaps" were placed on his phones; and "bugs" in his rooms, all of which were designed to develop information on King which would discredit his movement (Theoharis and Cos 1990; Gentry 1991; Powers 1987; Garrow 1981).

Simultaneously, black militancy was growing throughout the urban areas of the United States, as were student protests against the war in Vietnam. The late President Lyndon Johnson saw his presidency go down in tatters as the Vietnam War was escalated, and student protests turned violent. Believed to be part of a Communist plot to undermine the war effort in Vietnam, law enforcement agencies on the national, state, and local levels began collecting information on civil rights activists and Vietnam War protestors in an effort to disrupt and immobilize these groups. The now infamous COINTREL program, which introduced the term "agent provocateur" into the lexicon of law enforcement, proved just how dangerous intelligence systems could be to protest (Ungar 1976; O'Reilly 1972). What was a fundamental Constitutional right – the right to express one's views toward the actions of government – was, once again, being translated into sedition organized and funded by the Communist Party.

With Johnson stung by his mishandling of the Vietnam War, the rise of a "law and order" candidate Richard Milhouse Nixon advanced an oppressive agenda to levels heretofore publicly unknown (but perhaps with precedent). Nixon, having weathered the first four years of his term but suffering from his inability to end the war in Vietnam and contain the civil rights movement, entered into a compact with some of his advisors to obtain what was confidential information on his opponents on the Democratic Party. What is now referred to as "Watergate" was in effect the beginning of the end of the Nixon presidency, which saw offices burglarized, tax returns audited, disinformation systematically leaked to "friendly" journalists, intimate details of lives exposed, and investigations begun in order to undermine those opposed to the Nixon administration (Bernstein and Woodward 1987). It resulted in Nixon's ultimate resignation and endless inquiries into the misuse of governmental power to harass, intimidate, and sanction opponents and dissidents. While "Watergate" and its aftermath epitomized the consequences of governmental power being misused and abused, it was only a snapshot of what had enveloped our domestic intelligence apparatus.

For example, on the state and local level, intelligence units operated with no guidelines as to what conditions must exist in order to trigger a *bona fide* government "interest." Names were collected, information was gathered, and undercover operations initiated on what was the flimsiest of rationales. The concept of a "threat assessment" was non-existent, for what constituted a threat was anyone who took umbrage with a government policy or challenged the existing government ideology. Thusly, "civil rights activists" and "war protestors" were targets of governmental inquiry notwithstanding their Constitutional right to question and challenge government. This misuse and abuse of the intelligence process was predicated on the need of government to **prevent** crime from occurring – at best a dubious argument. One by one, these abuses were exposed; and law enforcement was put in the unenviable task of defending the indefensible. Some chose to fight arguing (and losing) in court that they had a right to collect such information. Others shut down their intelligence operations and returned to the practice of "burying their heads in the sand" (i.e. what we don't know won't hurt us). Still, others developed guidelines and procedures designed to provide guidance and thresholds to initiate the intelligence process. The results have been, at best, a mixed bag – with few law enforcement agencies investing in this necessary law enforcement methodology with the knowledge necessary to perform their tasks professionally as well as ethically (State of Illinois 1989).

THE DRUG WAR

It is often said that history can assure us of one thing: it will be repeated. The 80s and 90s certainly represented a return to the past. The so-called "war against drugs," while noble in its intent, has proved that intelligence-driven enforcement was merely a cliché (Martens 1986). With the abundance of drugs came a new "war;" one in which zero-tolerance would result in some questionable law enforcement practices. However, perhaps more disturbing was the failure of law enforcement administrators to use the intelligence process in ways that would enhance the efficiency of narcotic enforcement strategies. Said differently, few administrators understood the value of using intelligence in ways that measured their impact on the market. Instead, they would rely on arrest, prosecution and seizure statistics to measure success. To a large extent, these "body counts" were reminiscent of the measures that were used to measure "victories" in the Vietnam War. We know now, of course, how fallacious and self-serving these statistics were in Vietnam. The "drug war" is not much different for we are finally admitting that an "arrest and prosecution" mentality has not worked, and a more focused and selective use of resources is a more appropriate enforcement strategy.

Notwithstanding the failure of our strategic intelligence to address this issue, however, on a tactical level, we have seen civil liberties destroyed, careers ruined and the criminal justice system overwhelmed and fractured by this "war." For example, in New Jersey, the issue of "racial profiling" has engulfed the New Jersey State Police, resulting in the dismissal of its leader, counter-charges of reverse discrimination against the governor and the former attorney general, and cases being dismissed by courts because of serious constitutional and credibility issues (New York Times 1999b:1); Trenton Times 1999:1). Admittedly, this is only one case, but it has generated a national debate in other jurisdictions concerning the consequences of a zero-tolerance public policy that attributes physical characteristics to crime-control strategies.

"Racial profiling," particularly when it involves drug trafficking, has been a law enforcement methodology for decades. In the 30s, 40s and 50s, it was the Italian and French syndicates, with a smattering of Asians. By the 60s, 70s and 80s, African-Americans and Latinos were seen as the principal purveyors of lethal drugs. Through it all, intelligence has played a central role in identifying drug syndicates and networks along ethnic or racial lines. There were, of course, legitimate reasons to "target" criminal networks using ethnic/racial variables, for history has demonstrated that many (but not all) criminal organizations evolve along such lines. Nonetheless, when such generalizations become "probable cause" for "stops and searches," it is obvious that the line has been crossed – intelligence is being used to profile and stigmatize specific ethnic/racial groups. Notwithstanding the "political correctness" arguments, such methods of identifying criminal suspects, will be and must be met with serious political consequences (New York Times 2000: A-20).[27]

Of course, intelligence as a precursor to an effective drug enforcement strategy is a methodology, which has been resisted in large part by drug enforcers. As a whole, the nature of the market dictates. Intelligence is deliberate, rational, cost-conscious, and seeks measurability, at least in theory. Drug enforcement is on the whole, reactionary – taking advantage of opportunities as they occur, removing quantities of drug from the street, and arresting those who are the most visible. Seldom do these two distinct ideologies meld together (Wilson 1978; Reuss-Ianni 1983). Hence, we see little interaction between intelligence and drug units, both usually going their own separate ways. It is or likely to remain one those paradoxes in the "war against drugs" that defies any immediate or long-term resolution. When a public is inundated with a media that champions the action-oriented nature of policing, there is likely to be little if any incentives to enlist intelligence in the "drug war." Indeed, the consequences have been myriad law enforcement strategies that have exacerbated (not ameliorated) the problem (Nadelman 1998; Kaplan 1998; Reuter 1995 and 1998; Reuter, Falco and MacCoun 1993).

---

[27] In a 2000 Presidential Primary debate, Vice President Al Gore was challenged by Democratic candidate Bill Bradley to issue an Executive Order prohibiting "racial profiling." This, among other examples, demonstrates the political turmoil that has enveloped this issue.

THE MILITIAS AND TERRORISM

A most sensitive – and ultimately, the likely undoing of intelligence – is the so-called "extremist" movement in the United States. While the late Presidential candidate Barry Goldwater championed extremism –"Extremism in defense of liberty is a virtue"–today, such extremist views have been echoed by militia groups throughout the country. Insofar as gun control is the symbolic issue which many of these groups cloak themselves in, it is becoming readily apparent that the larger issues of government encroachment on personal freedoms and liberties lies at the heart of the issue. Not unlike the "left" of the 60s and 70s, the "right" of the 80s and 90s sees government as an "oppressor." They share in the belief that, unless they rise up and respond to the arrogance and oppressive nature of government, they will be smothered by a labyrinth of laws that will only enhance the power of government over those less powerful. "Ruby Ridge" was the beginning; "Waco" was the rallying call; and "Oklahoma City" was the reaction to a government out of control in the minds of some militia movements.

Indeed, in two of the events, the role of intelligence was marginalized insofar as it was never used as a means of disengaging law enforcement from what were provocative situations. For example "Ruby Ridge" – which resulted in four innocent people being killed, a $3.1 million judgment against the government, and a federal agent being indicted – need not have occurred if intelligence were used properly. The "Weavers" personal lifestyle, as well as their penchant for trading in weapons, raised the hackles of government; but they were never the threat that government contended, nor did they deserve the "force" that government used (New York Times 1997b: A-6). While hindsight is 20-20, intelligence should predict, with some degree of accuracy and certainty, the threat. In this particular case, it failed and failed miserably.

It did not, however, stop here. Several months later, "Waco" proved just how faulty our intelligence systems were – resulting in four federal agents and numerous women and children killed. A number of prominent public officials have since condemned and criticized the action of government. As a "wrongful death suit" winds its way through the federal courts, and as another federal probe seeks to determine if there was a government cover-up, one finding is certain – intelligence (or the lack thereof) was badly mishandled (New York Times 1998b:A-1). If one were to juxtapose "Waco" with that of the Japanese Embassy seizure in Peru in 1997 where intelligence was used properly and the results were far more favorable (only one person killed), the failure of intelligence in "Waco" becomes yet more startling and disturbing (New York Times 1997a:1).

Inasmuch as extremist groups may represent a threat to the public order, they also engage in free speech and allow for the expression of outrage against a "tyrannical government," or what they believe is "tyrannical." In the course of expressing their "outrage," such acts as "civil disobedience" as well as violence, may occur. The recent World Trade Organization (WTO) meeting in Seattle, Washington (1999), most vividly demonstrates the dilemma faced by law enforcement – how to allow for civil protest while preventing civil disorder? (New York Times 1999c: A-16). Intelligence is the answer providing, of course, it is understood, administered and executed properly. Collecting information on otherwise law-abiding citizens who happen to oppose a particular government policy raises an Orwellian image that only advances the cause of anti-government rhetoric. On the other hand, inadequate preparation of violent confrontation that may occur and then being placed in a position of over-reacting, only adds fuel to the fire and furthers the causes of anti-government forces. In the case of Seattle and the WTO, it is obvious that whatever intelligence was used, it was used improperly; in that, the results were not preventive or containment but rather over-reaction (New York Times 1999a; U.S. News and World Report 1999:13).

"Provocation," is, of course, a technique used by extremist and anti-government groups. It is solely designed to force an over-reaction by the police. This, in effect, exacerbates the anti-government rhetoric – accenting government's oppressive nature. Shame on the agency that permits itself to be a victim of provocation for it failed at its principal mission – the prevention of crime and public disorder. Indeed, the police must remember, "Rioters are obligated to riot, police are not."

CORRUPTION OF PUBLIC OFFICIALS

There is probably no greater or significant role intelligence can play than in uncovering corrupt alliances between organized crime and public officials. It is, by far, the most sensitive use of intelligence insofar as being wrong or "less than accurate" can and will have long-term ramifications on an agency's intelligence program. This was certainly the case in the now infamous ABSCAM probe; wherein, certain public officials were identified as "corrupt" but not subjected to prosecution (Insight 1991:26-27; New York Times 2000b). The impact on the FBI's intelligence program was felt for several decades thereafter, and never again was such an initiative pursued. While it can be debated whether or not the intelligence was inaccurate or "less than accurate," the perception was that law-abiding legislators were the "targets" of unwarranted investigations based on information the FBI "manufactured." Had it not been for FBI provocation, it was argued, the "crimes" did not exist. The "truth" may, of course, be somewhere in between.

Nonetheless, there is reason to believe that when intelligence is working properly, criminal prosecutions are more effective and productive. For example, in the investigation of the former attorney general of Pennsylvania, Ernest Preate, Jr., the now defunct Pennsylvania Crime Commission developed credible information that Preate had extorted and taken money from illegal video poker operators. Disguised as campaign funds, these monies were provided to preclude investigations of video poker operators. While the Commission was successful in forcing the attorney general to react in ways that led to a federal indictment, the Pennsylvania Legislature mobilized its forces and successfully abolished the Crime Commission, arguing it had unfairly targeted an Italian-American, Preate; it had extended its mandate beyond its legislative intent; it had engaged in a "witch-hunt" no different than that of the late Senator Joseph McCarthy; and finally, it was wrong. Of course, none of these rationales proved accurate, for Preate, in order to avoid a prosecution of his family and himself, pled guilty to one count of mail fraud and served time in federal prison (Inquirer 1995:1). If the Crime Commission did anything wrong in this case, it was not being able to use its intelligence properly to preclude the very action that resulted in its abolition. In this particular instance, knowing that the investigation of a popular and charismatic elected public official would only result in its ultimate abolition proved that even the best and most accurate intelligence cannot prevent corrupt interests from misusing and abusing their power.

Naturally, it could be argued that because of the volatility of intelligence focused on government corruption, it is better to "leave well enough alone" and address "less sensitive or more appealing" targets such as "hate groups," drug traffickers, or Cosa Nostra members. In fact, this is often the case. Unfortunately, by diverting attention away from the public officials involved in allowing the illegal activities to continue and ultimately grow, the "cause" goes unrecognized. Often, until it is too late there is a scandal. This was certainly the case in New Jersey, which precipitated the federal government to step in and clean up what was then labeled "the most corrupt state in the nation" (Hoffman 1973). In the meantime, however, the state is perceived as impotent or unable to address its organized crime problems –

adding to the public's distrust of state and local government. Cynicism sets in, and the consequence is a public policy that furthers government neglect. Chester, Pennsylvania, represents this very dilemma.
Decade after decade, the city of Chester, Pennsylvania, has suffered under one party rule (Pennsylvania Crime Commission 1991:309-322). With it, came corruption and abuse of power. Cosa Nostra members – in collusion with government officials – raped and plundered the city, making it virtually impossible to rehabilitate. The Commonwealth of Pennsylvania was well-aware of the plight of Chester, as were county officials. Nonetheless, all looked the other way, doing nothing to change the situation. Periodic intervention by the federal government resulted in some indictments and convictions, but there has never been a sustained effort to bring systemic and lasting changes. It was – and is – essentially, "America's apartheid," an example of *defacto* neglect that has led to an intractable problem of creating an underclass made up of primarily African Americans. An effective intelligence apparatus, again the Pennsylvania Crime Commission, identified the problems inherent in the government of Chester only to be castigated by the local district attorney as well as the political party in control of Chester and Delaware County for the past 100 years. It is clearly an example of "conscious neglect" by law enforcement for the most rudimentary intelligence apparatus could document the corruption and abuse of power that has undermined the administration of justice in Chester. Yet, it has chosen not to, in fear of the consequences that would befall any agency that would have the courage to expose government corruption.

There is, of course, reason to believe that Chester, Pennsylvania, and New Jersey are not unique. Other jurisdictions – such as (but not limited to) New York, Rhode Island, Louisiana, Arkansas, certain markets and industries in California – are equally as guilty of avoiding or consciously ignoring the extent of government corruption that pervades the body politic (New York Times 2000c:A-16; New York Times 1999c:A-18; Noedels Seder 1993; Providence Journal 1988:1 New York Times 1998c:A-7). It comes as no surprise that the federal government, and not state and local officials, pursued corruption probes in all these jurisdictions. There is only one conclusion that can be drawn from these examples: the systematic failure of state and local intelligence agencies to crystallize the problem of public and government corruption.

THE CHALLENGE FOR THE FUTURE

While the neglect and abuse of intelligence systems pose a serious dilemma for law enforcement administrators, they need not be seen as irresolvable. "Intelligence" must not be camouflaged in neatly packaged euphemisms that escape public attention. Intelligence – as a process – must be seen as irreplaceable, necessary, and not a luxury. It is a unique specialization that can only be performed by qualified professionals who have the capacity to discern what is and is not a proper exercise of police discretion. The ability to articulate and legitimate the intelligence function is essential to any law enforcement agency that has an organized crime control function. Perhaps before addressing the challenge inherent in promoting intelligence, we address certain misnomers that have crept into the craft of intelligence over the past decade.

- **Misnomer 1 - All Law Enforcement Agencies Can Engage in Intelligence**: Intelligence is a unique specialization that requires skills, which surpass the traditional law enforcement functions. Intelligence must be proactive but not abusive or over-intrusive. It must attract persons with the capacity to draw very sharp and critical distinctions between the illegal, improper, undesirable, and the constitutionally permitted. **Not** all law enforcement agencies have the capacity to draw upon its resources to perform such a function in a responsible manner. In fact, most traditional law enforcement agencies lack the depth or resources to properly administer the intelligence function. Indeed, when an agency decides to invest in this needed and legitimate law enforcement function, it must recognize the dangers that can beset the agency if it is executed improperly. The complexity of the tasks demands persons with unique skills and traits.

- **Misnomer 2 - Intelligence Can be Performed by Any Member of a Police Department**: The traditional police role demands with few exceptions, reactive policing skills and techniques. This is primarily a result of the police being seen as an agent of the people, responding to crime after it occurs. This restricts and confines the intrusive nature of policing to those situations where a crime occurs. It is this mindset, reactive policing that governs the law enforcement function in most police departments in the nation.

  Lately, however, the police role is seen as more preventive and proactive, intervening before a crime occurs. This is the basic premise underlying "community policing." It requires the police to increase its presence in areas where crime has been targeted for an extraordinary suppression effort. The New York City Police Department, considered the model of "target-specific enforcement policing" through its COMPSTAT program, has reported extraordinary results from this proactive method of policing (Maple 1999). However, not all police departments have the resources or the personnel to be proactive. Nor do most police agencies have the capacity to reorient the "thought processes" to a proactive way of thinking about crime. Often, the transition between "reactive" and "proactive" policing results in confusion and ill-fated attempts to prevent crime by identifying violators before they commit the crime. Particularly when it comes to translating intelligence to operational policy, an agency must be extremely careful to avoid "targeting" based on questionable criteria or indicia. It requires very skilled and experienced personnel to administer and execute the intelligence function in an ethical and constitutionally protected manner.

- **Misnomer 3 - Intelligence Systems are Essentially Information Systems**: In its quest to avoid the term "intelligence," many law enforcement agencies have renamed their intelligence systems "information systems." Intelligence is a series of definable functions that information systems need not, nor are likely, to pursue. For example, an intelligence system is required to produce a product, usable and timely. Information systems broker information – not necessarily usable, timely, or analyzed. Intelligence systems engage in analysis – the heart of intelligence. Information systems need not interpret it, leaving this task to the consumer. While intelligence systems adhere to ongoing process for transforming information into intelligence, information systems are essentially static. To confuse the two, using the terms interchangeably does a disservice to the intelligence function.

- **Misnomer 4 - Intelligence is Nothing More Than Being Prepared**: The unique nature of intelligence suggests that foreknowledge is a prerequisite of any viable intelligence program. Law enforcement administrators, in preparing for an event such as a demonstration, rely upon intelligence to gauge their response. Intelligence is a part of the planning process, which allows the police administrator to anticipate any number of options. "Being prepared" requires far more than just having intelligence, however. This was clearly illustrated in the Seattle, Washington, debacle involving the World Trade Organization. Here, the police were in receipt of accurate intelligence but responded poorly.

In as much as these examples highlight the confusion that surrounds the intelligence function, it is important that we revisit some of the basic elements of intelligence (Godfrey and Harris 1971; Harris 1976:).

  o **Intelligence Is A Specialization**: Intelligence must be viewed as a specialization in law enforcement, preferably undertaken by those who have no stake in the outcome. It cannot and should not be a proponent of any particular public policy but rather a product, supported with replicated and corroborated information.

  o **Intelligence Is Critical**: For intelligence to be accurate, it must constantly and logically challenge commonly held beliefs. To merely accept information without challenging the foundations upon which it is built, the credibility or the reliability of the source or the conclusion that is drawn undermines the true nature of the process – to challenge.

  o **Intelligence Is Measurable**: Any law enforcement activity that cannot be measured in terms of results is virtually useless. Intelligence is no exception. Whether preventing organized crime from occurring or containing or diminishing its influence, an intelligence program should always be in a position to articulate and support its results.

  o **Intelligence Seldom Seeks Publicity**: The true nature of intelligence is prevention; thus, it is seldom obligated to publicly divulge the strategies or techniques it used to prevent something from occurring. This is not to suggest that, at times, it enhances the "multiplier effect" when intelligence publicly demonstrates its preventive value. Rather, to avoid the "self-aggrandizement game" that permeates the territorial disputes in law enforcement, there is little benefit to advancing a particular preventive action publicly.

  o **Intelligence Targets Organized Crime Problems That Often are Ignored by Others**: Because intelligence has the obligation to be proactive and not reactive, it has an obligation to define organized crime problems that the traditional policing function is likely to overlook or ignore. The adage, "when you are up to your knees in alligators, you often forget your goal was to clean the swamp" should never apply to the intelligence function, for intelligence is in the enviable position to advance, its agenda beyond "making cases" or reacting to the "crisis of the moment."

o **Intelligence Requires Attention to Detail**: The intelligence function, if it is to be relevant to an organized crime initiative, must be sensitive to the details – avoiding sweeping generalization that target criminal organizations based on generic criteria. Said differently, attention to detail as to what affords one criminal organization a higher priority than yet another legitimates and advances the true value of intelligence (Dintino and Martens 1983; Andrews and Peterson 1990).

CONCLUSION

The value of criminal intelligence cannot be understated. **It is essential to the execution of the law enforcement function.** We must continue to advance its "scientific" rigor – understanding, of course, that it is an "art," which requires a solid appreciation for transforming raw data into a finished product – that product being intelligence. Developing a criminal predicate is essential to initiating the intelligence process. Perhaps more important is recognizing that the ability to prescribe **proportion** to the criminal threat is essential to ensuring a measured response and not over or under reaction. It is the issue of **proportion** that seems to have resulted in the historical abuses and misuses of intelligence. Not all criminal threats deserve an equal response. Discriminating between those that are real and those that are fleeting or transitory remains an art that can only be developed through rigorous analysis and years of experience and knowledge. Indeed, we have learned from "Ruby Ridge" and "Waco," "Watergate" and "McCarthy," to some extent. Surely, our ability to diffuse the potential for violence involving the arrest of Leroy Schweitzer, leader of the Montana Freeman, in 1996 demonstrates how intelligence can be used to appropriately measure the threat and respond accordingly. Perhaps, the abuses that emanated from the "McCarthy Era" were sufficient enough to teach us that broad based generalizations and unaccountable zealotry have no place in the criminal justice profession.

As we enter a new millennium, we can be assured that the technological revolution will create new and profound problems that will tax and challenge our ability to respond accordingly. Intelligence as a craft can allow us the ability to "measure with precision" the criminal threat. To ensure our perspective is appropriately circumscribed; understanding our past, both successes and failures, can go a long way in ensuring the viability of the intelligence function. Ignoring the past, however, is sure to result in its demise. The choice is yours.

REFERENCES

Anderson, Jack and Ronald May (1956) McCarthy: *The Man, the Senator, the Ism.* Boston: Beacon Press.

Andrews, Paul P. and Marilyn B. Peterson, eds. (1990) Criminal Intelligence Analysis. Loomis, CA: Palmer Press.

Bernstein, Carl and Bob Woodward. (1987) *All the President's Men.* New York: Simon & Schuster.

Cogley, John. (1956) *Report on Blacklisting.* New York: Fund for the Republic.

Cook, Fred J. (1971) The *Nightmare Decade: The Life and Times of Senator Joseph McCarthy.* New York: Random House.

Dintino, Justin J. and Frederick T. Martens (1983) *Police Intelligence in Crime Control.* Illinois: Charles C. Thomas.

Donner, Frank J. (1980) The *Age of Surveillance.* New York: Alfred A. Knopf.

Franco, Joseph and Richard Hammer. (1987) *Hoffa's Man.* New York: Prentice Hall.

Garfinkle, Simon (2000) Database *Nation: The Death of Privacy in the 21st Century.* New York: O'Reilly and Associates.

Garrow, David J. (1981) *The FBI and Martin Luther King.* New York: Penguin.

Gentry, Curt (1991) J. *Edgar Hoover: The Man and His Secrets.* New York: Plume.

George, John and Laird Wilcox (1996) American *Extremists.* New York: Prometheus Books.

Harris, Don and E. Drexel Godfrey (1971) (1976) *Basic Elements of Intelligence and Revised.* Washington, DC: U.S. Government Printing Office.

Hoffman, Paul (1973) Tiger *in Court.* Chicago: Playboy Press.

Insight (1991) "An Older, Wiser FBI Hesitates to Sting the Hand that Feeds" February 4.

Kaplan, John. (1998) "Taking Drugs Seriously." *The Public Interest.* No. 92. Summer.

Knodels Seder, William (1993) Stiffed. New York: Harper.

Maple, Jack. (1999) *The Crime Fighter: Putting the Bad Guys Out of Business.* New York: Doubleday.

Martens, Frederick T. (1986) "An Enforcement Paradox: The Intelligence Dilemma in Narcotics Enforcement." *Journal of Justice Issues*, Vol. 1, No. 2. Fall.

Mitgang, Herbert (1988) Dangerous *Dossiers*. New York: Donald Fine.

Nadelman, Ethan A. (1998) "The Case for Legalization" The *Public Interest*. No. 92. Summer.

Navasky, Victor S. (1980) *Naming Names*. New York: Penguin Books.

_____ (1971) Kennedy *Justice*. New York: Atheneum Press.

O'Reilly, Kenneth. (1989) *Racial Matters: The FBI's Secret File on Black America 1960-1972*. New York: The Free Press.

Pennsylvania Crime Commission (1991) "Chester Pennsylvania Racketeering at the Local Level" *A Decade of Change: 1990 Report*. Conshohocken, PA: Commonwealth of Pennsylvania.

Powers, Richard Gid. (1987) *Secrecy and Power*. New York: The Free Press.

The Providence Journal (1998) "Former Gov. Di Prete Pleads Guilty to 18 Charges of Corruption in Office" December 14.

Reuss-Ianni, Elizabeth. (1983) *Two Cultures of Policing*. New Brunswick: Transaction Books.

Reuter, Peter. (1998) "Can the Borders be Sealed?" *The Public Interest*. No. 92. Summer.

Reuter, Peter, Mathea Falco and Robert MacCoun. (1993) *Comparing Western European and North Ameican Drug Policies*. Rand Corporation.

Roverse, Richard (1959) Senator *Joe McCarthy*. New York: Harcourt, Brace.

Schlesinger, Arthur M. (1978) Robert *Kennedy and His Times*. New York: Ballentine Books.

State of Illinois. Division of Criminal Investigation. (1989) "Intelligence in Major Police Agencies." March 8.

Sullivan, Andrew (1999) "What's So Bad About Hate?" *New York Times Magazine*. September 26.

The New York Times (1999a) "John Paton Davies, Diplomat Who Ran Afoul of McCarthy, Dies at 91." December 24.

_____ (1998a) "California Weighs Release of Spying Records." April 4.

_____ (1999b) "Whitman Dismisses State Police Chief for Race Remarks." March 1.

_____ (1998b) "5 Years After Waco Standoff, the Spirit of Kouresh Lingers." April 17.

_____ (1997a) "A Signal, and Peru Hostages Opened Door to Raid; Meticulous Attack Was in the Works from the Outset." April 24.

_____ (1999c) "Seattle Police Chief Resigns in Aftermath of Protests." December 8.

_____ (1999d) "Free Trade Takes On Free Speech." December 5.

_____ (1997b) "U.S. Will Bring No More Criminal Charges Against F.B.I. Officials in Ruby Ridge Siege." August 16.

_____ (1998c) "Former Louisiana Governor is Indicted in Extortion Case" November 7.

_____ (1999) "Arkansas Lawmakers Indicted in Vast Corruption Case" April 28.

_____ (1994) "Two Year Corruption Inquiry Finds a Willful Blindness in New York's Police Dept." July 7.

_____ (2000a) "Bradley Challenges Gore" January 18.

_____ (2000b) "FBI cases a Wide Net With Plenty of Tangles Texas Suit May Bring Charges to Stings" February 9.

_____ (2000c) "Police Corruption Expands in Los Angeles" February 11.

Theoharis, Athan G. and John Stuart Cox. (1990) *The Boss: J. Edgar Hoover and the Great American Inquisition.* New York: Bantam Books.

Trenton Times (1999) "89 State Police Document: Watch Minorities." May 4.

Ungar, Sanford. (1976) *FBI.* New York: Little, Brown & Co.

U.S. News and World Report. "He Wasn't a Cop's Cop" December 28, -. 13.

Weschler, James. (1953) *The Age of Suspicion.* New York: Random House.

Wilson, James Q. (1978) *The Investigators.* New York: Basic Books.

Wilson, James Q. and Richard J. Hernstein (1985) Crime *and Human Nature.* New York: Simon & Schuster.

Intelligence Programs

Section 1
Intelligence-led Policing: Anticipating Risk and Influencing Action
By Jerry H. Ratcliffe, PhD

INTRODUCTION

Criminal intelligence work is often characterized as primarily an analysis function, a covert activity, or knowledge work. None of these views is entirely accurate. The criminal intelligence function is much broader and is primarily concerned with anticipating risks and improving public safety. The chief architects of Britain's National Intelligence Model recently wrote, "we knew that the intelligence model was in fact an ideal model for the whole business of policing that would enable police commanders to understand and *anticipate* risks and threats across the public safety domain" (Flood and Gaspar 2009: 54, emphasis added). The role of intelligence, at least within the law enforcement domain under discussion in this chapter, is thus a dual role of *anticipating* future risks to public safety and *influencing* decision-makers so that crime prevention action can be initiated.

It is worth stressing that the subject of this chapter is not intelligence, but intelligence-led *policing* (ILP). ILP is a contemporary model for situating the intelligence function within the overall mission of the police organization (Carter 2005). The dual role of anticipating risks and influencing action integrates analysis with decision-making and creates additional challenges for criminal intelligence professionals. Taking on the mantle of a more direct responsibility for public safety may make some analysts uncomfortable; however, it expands the role of analysis beyond a simple adjunct to policing and into a core function central to decision-making and the planning of public safety. It is a challenge that should be embraced.

This article begins by explaining the need within policing to manage future risks and the importance of identifying patterns of criminality to aid future crime prevention action. This all takes places within a framework of ILP. The chapter continues by defining and describing two ILP models. One is a simple conceptual model, and the second is a business model that has emerged from best practice in a police department that has many years experience with partnership models of ILP. The article concludes by summarizing the main points so that the reader can develop ILP principles into ILP practice.

THE NEED TO MANAGE AN UNCERTAIN FUTURE

The first stage of the dual role outlined in the introduction to this article (anticipating risk and influencing action) is the anticipation of risks to public safety. All crime intelligence analysis, even descriptive work of past criminal activity, makes an implicit projection of a possible future criminal environment. For this statement to be true, we have to sometimes exclude one area of activity often mislabeled as intelligence analysis; that of investigative support. Work that supports existing investigations with the aim of gathering sufficient evidence to sustain a prosecution is both laudable and invaluable to an essential police function, but it could be more accurately described as an investigative support role rather than intelligence work *per se*, irrespective of any job descriptions and titles of the individuals involved (Sheptycki 2004, Ratcliffe 2008a). This caveat in place, the activity of most crime and intelligence analysts implicitly attempts to use existing knowledge to project an image of an uncertain future. I say implicitly, because many analysts and their managers are satisfied with reports of existing crime patterns and criminal activity which make no statement of the future; however, a prediction of the future is often what decision-makers crave in their role as risk managers with responsibility to manage resource allocation.

Police commanders frequently ask the impossible. While often unable to articulate what they seek, they habitually seek 'the answer' - an unfeasible projection of the specific date, time, and place of a future criminal act. Provision of anything less is deemed failure. In reality, aiming to predict an individual crime event would be better replaced by the objective of predicting future criminal patterns and behaviors in order to be preventative rather than reactive. As I have explained elsewhere (Ratcliffe 2008a), the move to intelligence-led policing was in part driven by the desire for policing to be proactive in preventing crime instead of simply reactive to crime once it occurred. For *prevention* activity to occur, this requires that the police and crime prevention practitioners are proactive in their actions. *Proactivity* requires the criminality in question to have a component of *predictability* about it. If a crime is extremely rare we are unlikely to be able to identify future events because we require historical patterns to establish a trend and the conditions that make the event likely. Therefore *predictability* requires the identification of *patterns* of criminality. This chain (*Prevention* requires *Proactivity* requires *Predictability* requires *Patterns*) shown in Figure 1 defines the identification of patterns as a precursor to crime prevention action and is at the heart of intelligence-led policing (see Ratcliffe 2009). While some short term fluctuations sometimes exist, many crime trends and problems are long-term and ongoing until effective remedial action is taken.

Figure 1: From patterns to prevention.
Source: Ratcliffe (2009), reproduced with permission of Federation Press (Australia).

For example, most of the Philadelphia crime hotspots mapped by researchers in the 1940s (Shaw and McKay 1942) are the same problem areas that exist today. Once crime problems emerge, they linger until resolved; when organized crime groups identify a weakness they can exploit, they continue until some sort of disturbing influence is introduced; once offenders learn how to steal a particular model of vehicle, a redesign of the vehicle is often necessary; and once burglars identify a way to circumvent a security feature, they will continue to steal until new prevention mechanisms are implemented. The importance of patterns is inherent in what I call my first law of intelligence: *The most reliable indication of future criminal activity is current criminal activity.* Offenders who have identified and exploited an opportunity will continue to do so until stopped, and the upshot resulting from frequent criminal action is a pattern of events. The strategic management of patterns, in both crime events and offender behavior, will be a more effective use of enforcement energies than individual event investigations.

What does all this mean? It means that in the analytical role, the identification of patterns (both in crime and criminal behavior) is an essential first step to proactive police work geared towards crime prevention. As stated above, even descriptive analyses of past crime patterns make a comment about the future, because there is an implied suggestion that past events are indicative of future criminality. There is also the implication that some continuation of the observed patterns will continue unless action is taken. Criminal intelligence work is therefore a statement of an uncertain future, based on an often incomplete image of the present, with the aim of directing *future* police and crime prevention action to manage risk. The analytical challenges are significant.

The second stage of the dual role (anticipating risk, influencing action) is also vital within ILP; that of influencing decision-makers. Here I invoke my second law of intelligence: *intelligence that does not influence the thinking of a decision-maker is not intelligence.* This is not to denigrate the value of investigative support, background reading, or other valuable work conducted by analysts, but simply as confirmation that intelligence is "knowledge designed for action." (Grieve 2009: 29) If we are to use knowledge to drive action, then intelligence must influence decision-makers in a meaningful manner, and this means changing or initiating a course of action. The influencing of a decision-maker to take no action is even acceptable within this framework and almost inevitable given the role of crime intelligence as a pivotal tool in resource allocation: there are rarely sufficient resources to tackle all criminality. As such, *benign neglect* is a form of action, if it is taken deliberately and done such that other priorities are given explicit priority. But *meaningful* action occurs when decisions are evidence-based and intelligence-led, where the intelligence drives a course of action that aims to reduce criminality and promote public safety. As Howard Atkin noted in the first edition of this book, "ILP is predicated on the effective and efficient production AND application of intelligence." (Peterson et al. 2000: 13, emphasis in original)

Asking analytical staff to take an active role in influencing decision-makers sounds Machiavellian and it is, but not necessarily in the pejorative sense. It is more a realization that if analysts are to succeed in achieving the goal of improved public safety through ILP then they must use intelligence to drive leadership in policing. Intelligence managers and senior police staff may read this and interpret it to mean that the ability to present intelligence; to brief managers quickly, clearly and articulately; and to prepare and deliver compelling presentations and written documents are all significant skills to consider when hiring or promoting analysts. They would be right. As Mark Evans points out from his experiences as an intelligence manager in Northern Ireland and New Zealand, "The best analysts have presence, engage in effective verbal and non-verbal behavior, and have the ability to read a situation and tailor their contribution accordingly. While these may be qualities that appear intangible they can be practiced and when used successfully will contribute to the impact made." (Evans 2009: 198)

If the analytical task is to minimize uncertainty so that decision-makers are able to make wise decisions regarding prevention activity and resource allocation, what is intelligence-led policing and how is it a framework for the successful achievement of the dual role of anticipating risk and influencing action?

WHAT IS INTELLIGENCE-LED POLICING?

In a previous work, I dedicated a whole chapter to defining intelligence-led policing and providing some conceptual daylight between intelligence-led policing and Compstat, community policing, and problem-oriented policing (Ratcliffe 2008a). Space precludes that option here; however, the definition is as follows:

> *Intelligence-led policing is a business model and managerial philosophy where data analysis and crime intelligence are pivotal to an objective, decision-making framework that facilitates crime and problem reduction, disruption and prevention through both strategic management and effective enforcement strategies that target prolific and serious offenders (Ratcliffe 2008a: 89).*

I'm aware that this is considered a bit of a long-winded definition! There are other shorter and slicker characterizations of ILP that my colleagues in the intelligence community prefer; however, each phrase is grounded in research on ILP over the last decade and is explained in the following sections (for more details, see Chapter 4 of Ratcliffe, 2008a).

Intelligence-led policing is a business model and managerial philosophy... Rather than being an abstract idea to be dipped into or conceptualized in the classroom, intelligence-led policing is a philosophy of business practice that requires buy-in from all parts of the organization. Furthermore, it is a business model that prescribes, through mechanisms such as the (UK) National Intelligence Model or GMAC PBM (explained later), the way that information and crime intelligence flow around the organization to the decision-makers.

where data analysis and crime intelligence are pivotal... The term *crime intelligence* may be new to some readers. It represents a blend of crime analysis and criminal intelligence, arguing for collaboration between two strands of analysis that – in the U.S. at least – are often kept artificially separate due to organizational, cultural or technical limitations and traditions. Crime analysis can tell a decision-maker *what* is going on, and criminal intelligence, rooted as it is in understanding and explaining patterns of criminal behavior, can tell a decision-maker *why*.

to an objective decision-making framework... This part of the definition provides real challenges for intelligence staff.   What is the decision-making framework of their workplace? Where does the real power to affect change on the criminal environment lie? When analysts start asking these questions, the answer is often unexpected. Traditionally, we have sought out patrol officers, but they lack the power to control much of their own time, and often the accountability to action intelligence is missing. As an analyst in the New Zealand Police said, "There is a lack of responsibility. It is better to go through the supervisor to get *accountability*." (Ratcliffe 2005: 444)

that facilitates crime and problem reduction, disruption, and prevention...As Brian Flood and Roger Gaspar pointed out in the quote at the start of this chapter, intelligence-led policing is a model for the whole business of policing. The definition therefore recognizes that it can be used for more than crime, but also the myriad problems that police are asked to deal with, such as speeding, crash management, nuisance abatement, missing persons and public order. These risks to public safety can be anticipated with data analysis and crime intelligence and mitigated through an objective decision-making framework. When that occurs, measured responses are often more than simply arresting offenders, but include problem reduction, disruption, and prevention, as recognized by the UK Serious Organised Crime Agency: "Law enforcement efforts in the UK and overseas often lead to the *disruption* and displacement of particular drug supply chains." (SOCA 2008: 7, emphasis added)

through both strategic management...There is growing evidence that problem-oriented policing's approach of addressing the underlying causes of problems that create work for police is effective (Scott 2000; Sherman et al. 1998).   The inclusion of *strategic management* in the definition is a realization that there is an important role for more long-term strategic approaches in the search for problem prevention and reduction.   This inclusion in the definition enables police to work, for example, with street engineers to improve traffic accident black spots, with housing authorities to address crime and disorder in public housing projects, with city agencies to revoke alcohol licenses at disorderly bars, and with legislators to close financial loopholes exploited by organized crime syndicates.

and effective enforcement strategies that target prolific and serious offenders. While strategic management opens up possibilities for police to work with partners in a collaborative and 'co-production' model of crime prevention (Taylor 2006; Wood and Shearing 2007), many of the criminology-based crime control strategies of the last 30 years had no explicit role for the police: crime was to be controlled by addressing society's underlying woes. While sociological solutions to crime all have some measure of academic merit, they often lacked policy relevance to communities and the police. There is increasing evidence that specific and targeted policing strategies can help to reduce crime if targeted effectively. The key word here is *effective* (and evidence in support of this part of the definition is provided later in the chapter).

There is frequent confusion distinguishing between policing strategies. Intelligence-led policing is sometimes linked to community policing, Compstat and problem-oriented policing. When the definition is broken-down (as above), the daylight between intelligence-led policing and other approaches becomes apparent. For example, community policing has the primary aims of regaining the legitimacy of the police in the eyes of the public, moving towards a social service ethos, and allowing the community to take the lead in determining police priorities (Skogan 2006; Taylor 2006). By comparison, the primary aim of intelligence-led policing is the prevention of crime and arrest of prolific offenders, and it seeks a more objective decision-making system based on data and intelligence analysis to determine priorities.

Compstat is often mistaken as an intelligence-led policing methodology (see for example, Dannels and Smith 2001). Compstat is linked to both the order-maintenance practices of the NYPD that have been associated with the crime reduction that occurred in New York City in the late 1990s, and the 'broken windows' approach (Kelling 1999; Kelling and Bratton 2006; Sousa and Kelling 2006; Wilson and Kelling 1982). Compstat is largely focused on street-level and high volume crime, and drives short-term accountability to emerging crime problems, whereas intelligence-led policing has a long-term strategic component that is as applicable to transnational organized crime as it is to neighborhood disorder (Ratcliffe 2008a). As Scott and colleagues point out, Compstat has no theoretical basis on which to secure any short-term gains, and both "community policing and broken windows policing seem to be founded on the notion that community dysfunction can be quickly remedied by an injection of policing." (Scott et al. 2008: 243) Where Compstat is focused on crime, intelligence-led policing is focused on identifying threats (Carter and Carter 2009).

ILP seeks to employ a wider range of data sources than are found in any other policing style, with the possible exception of problem-oriented policing. Problem-oriented policing (POP) has a natural synergy with intelligence-led policing as both seek a more long-term, strategic, risk focused, and comprehensive solution to crime. Problem-oriented policing is a conceptual approach that can address a vast array of policing issues, but it requires law enforcement to delve deeper into the underlying problems that affect public safety. This requires the police to be able to scan across a range of data and information sources to identify problems, analyze these problems, and identify the underlying issue—prior to addressing the problem (Clarke 2004; Eck 2006; Goldstein 2003; Townsley et al. 2003). Both POP and ILP seek a strategic solution, but intelligence-led policing is more explicit about the role of police, supporting long-term strategic management with a clear role to bring serious, repeat offenders to justice. This enables police to be proactive and anticipate risks from organized crime and serious offenders, as well as achieve the long-term public safety gains that are sought. In summary, intelligence-led policing:

- is a management philosophy/business model
- aims to achieve crime reduction and prevention and to disrupt offender activity
- employs a top-down management approach
- combines crime analysis and criminal intelligence into crime intelligence
- uses crime intelligence to objectively direct police resource decisions
- focuses enforcement activities on prolific and serious offenders (Ratcliffe 2008a)

DECISION-MAKING AND LEADERSHIP

For intelligence-led policing to become a reality, intelligence analysis must be incorporated into the planning process of police agencies (Peterson 2005). More than this, if agencies are to anticipate risk and influence action (the theme of this chapter), then there are three requirements that Quarmby identifies as essential to proactive work: "there is an identifiable decision-making system to support; there is a will to think ahead in both the intelligence system and the decision system to be supported; and there is a will to apply the results in both the intelligence system and the decision system to be supported" (Quarmby 2009: 165-6). These three requirements pose some real challenges for both analysts *and* decision-makers.

A central issue for the adoption and success of intelligence-led policing is the level of sophistication and maturity of the decision-making environment. In reality, the problems are often quite profound. I've often been bemused by the lack of clarity regarding the decision-making process in many police departments. Mayors, police chiefs, mid-level commanders, and individual officers often appear to have free rein to make significant decisions regarding crime policy without recourse to objective analysis of the issue, or even a partial understanding or knowledge of the problem. When done in response to newspaper articles or stories on the nightly news (as appears to sometimes be the case) it is often an example of *media-led policing*. This kind of knee-jerk response to problems may have emerged as an appropriate leadership style when agencies did not have access to data, information and knowledge about the problems they faced, but it is the antithesis of intelligence-led policing.

Even when clear lines of communication and decision-making exist, they do not guarantee that decisions are strategic and evidence-based (and here the term *evidence* is used with reference to effectiveness of strategy rather than criminal evidence). For example, many police departments continue to encourage Drug Abuse Resistance Education (DARE) programs, neighborhood block watch, and low-level drug market arrests even though it has long been known that these programs and tactics do not reduce crime (Sherman et al. 1998). As Phillips (2008: 28) points out, "All too often…commanders have a strong and sometimes sorry record of relying on their preconceptions rather than a current and measured appraisal of the problem in hand. Strong leaders can be personally effective and strategically weak."

A BUSINESS MODEL FOR INTELLIGENCE-LED POLICING

Once ideas of intelligence-led policing go beyond the hermetic environment of the analyst and start to look at the business of policing, then the limitations of the intelligence cycle become apparent. Other chapters in this book will examine the intelligence cycle in depth. It is a useful training tool to conceptualize the intelligence process for new analysts, but in my view it does not address the problems of gaining traction with intelligence products. In effect, it says nothing to address my second law of crime intelligence: *intelligence that does not influence the thinking of a decision-maker is not intelligence.*

The three-i model (Figure 2) explicitly addresses the relationship between analysis and decision-makers within intelligence-led policing (Ratcliffe 2003). In the model, not only does the analyst have to actively interpret the criminal environment, but also influence a decision-maker. This requires not only identification of the appropriate person or group able to combat the crime problem, but also consideration be given to the best way to influence their thinking. This second function is always easier when the decision-maker in question is open to, and invested in, the ILP philosophy. Furthermore, as shown in Figure 2, when influencing decision-makers, analysts should also be cognizant of the need to make appropriate recommendations regarding how to have an effective *impact* on the criminal environment.

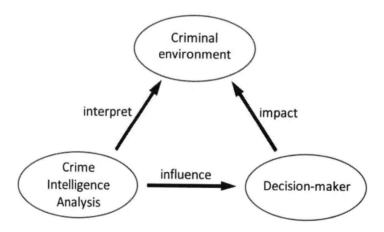

Figure 2. Three-i model of intelligence-led policing.
Source: Ratcliffe (2003, and see 2008), reproduced with permission.

While the three-i model is a conceptualization of ILP, a second model explains how it can function in practice. In the UK, Greater Manchester Against Crime (GMAC) have established a Partnership Business Model (PBM) that provides a link between strategic planning and tactical operations not only for police, but for the public safety outcomes of the health service, ambulance/paramedics, probation, community safety and drug action teams, youth offending teams and local municipal authorities (for details, see www.gmac.org.uk). The GMAC PBM is designed to allow time for the analysis of information and data from all of the partners and to feed back strategic priorities to those agencies in a coordinated sense with their planning and budget cycles (GMPA/GMP nd). The model has been independently evaluated as an example of best practice (John et al. 2006) and it is easy to see why. It incorporates both strategic and tactical cycles that integrate with each other while allowing senior staff to concentrate on long-term crime priorities, and mid-level managers to focus on tactical outcomes (Figure 3).   In effect, a strategic overview informs local targets (Flitcroft 2006).[1]

There are a number of advantages to the GMAC model from the analyst's perspective. The time frames bring a sense of predictability to the provision of the strategic assessment as well as clarity about the role of non-police partners. The tactical meetings (held either monthly or every two weeks) are not so frequent that meeting preparation consumes all the available time (compare this time frame to police departments with weekly Compstat meetings). Finally, the recognition of the difference between a strategic partnership business group and a tactical group makes clear that there is a specific role for strategic analysis in the model.

The model also has advantages for decision-makers. There is considerable capacity to include non-enforcement agencies at the strategic level resulting in an opportunity to recruit other government and non-government agencies to assist with crime prevention and disruption. With less emphasis on individual offenders at the strategic level, there are fewer privacy concerns and intelligence products can be more widely disseminated to potential crime reduction partners. The focus on a strategy set once a year (during September in the GMAC model shown) enables long-term solutions to be considered with a time frame that is more realistic regarding solution implementation. In other words, the simple fact of deciding the main priorities for a whole year (updated every 3 or 6 months) allows decision-makers to implement more considered and prevention-oriented strategies than the ubiquitous saturation or directed patrols—the short-term band-aid and favored tactic of police commanders with time pressures, limited crime prevention imagination, and a lack of other resources. Finally, the model is timed to coincide with the budget cycles of organizations that can contribute to crime reduction programs.

---

[1] Within GMAC, the business cycle actually operates on two levels, but for space and convenience only one level is shown here. The figure shown is the regional cycle; however, the district/local authority cycle is identical but simply offset earlier by three months. The purpose of the offset is to allow the strategic assessments of the local areas to be reflected in the region-wide strategic assessment (Superintendent Dave Flitcroft, Greater Manchester Police, personal communication, March 2009).

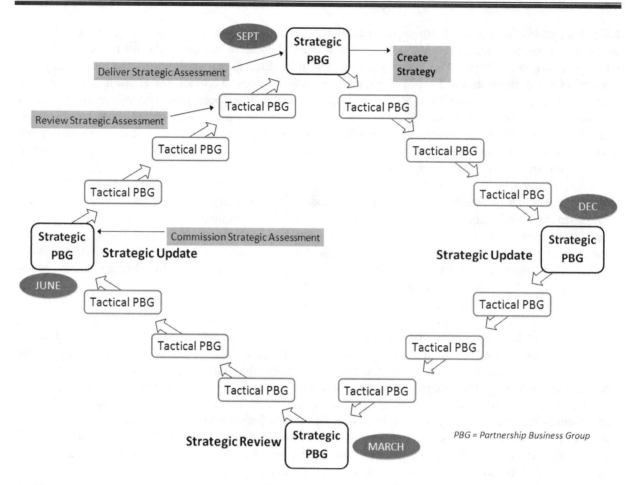

Figure 3. GMAC Partnership Business Model.
Adapted from Flitcroft (2006).

THE EVIDENCE FOR AN INTELLIGENCE-LED POLICING APPROACH

Given that intelligence-led policing is a relative newcomer to the lexicon of policing, it is not surprising that there have been fewer formal research studies than have been conducted on other policing styles. But this does not mean that we cannot make any statements regarding the effectiveness of intelligence-led policing.

Returning to the parts of the definition of intelligence-led policing as a model that reduces crime through both strategic management and effective enforcement strategies that target prolific and serious offenders; the question should arise at this point—where is the evidence that this approach is effective? There are two outcomes that have been thoroughly evaluated: *strategic management* (a broad term used here as a proxy to represent problem-oriented policing), and *enforcement strategies that target prolific and serious offenders*.

There is strong evidence to support the crime reduction effects of problem-oriented policing (Scott et al. 2008). That being said, problem-oriented policing is hard to evaluate because it is not so much a specific tactic, but rather a methodology from which a suitable crime reduction tactic can be identified. In this it is not dissimilar to intelligence-led policing. Sherman and Eck's meta-analysis of problem-oriented policing at 'hot places', in other words geographically focused, found (with one exception) substantial and statistically significant reductions in crime at targeted locations (Sherman and Eck 2002; Sherman et al. 1998). Furthermore, focused tactics to reduce the instance of gun violence and gun carrying were also evaluated as successful. Sherman and Eck summarized their findings by stating, "There is considerable evidence based on strong evaluations that problem-oriented policing is an effective way to reduce crime." (2002: 321)

The second outcome in the intelligence-led policing definition is *enforcement strategies that target prolific and serious offenders*. Again, the Sherman and Eck meta-analysis is a useful summary of the existing research, and again, this is supportive of focused police activity. Not only is there consistent scientific evidence that concentrating police patrols to high crime areas at the peak times of criminal activity is effective, but also, "the evidence on the focused proactive arrest hypothesis is generally supportive across a wide range of studies and research designs." (Sherman and Eck 2002: 312)

For example, police in Australia were able to substantially reduce burglaries in Canberra by focusing patrol activity in burglary hotspots and through the intelligence-led targeting of repeat offenders. With a weekly city average of about 146 burglaries prior to the adoption of an intelligence-led policing approach, they were able to reduce this total by over 50 burglaries a week. Furthermore, because of the incarceration of repeat offenders, the benefits extended for months after the police operation had concluded (Makkai et al. 2004; Ratcliffe and Makkai 2004).

So the strategic outcomes of conducting strategic management of crime and policing problems, and effective enforcement strategies that target prolific and serious offenders are effective; but what about the business model to deliver these outcomes? While there are potentially many different approaches, one model that has been evaluated is the Greater Manchester Against Crime Partnership Business Model (GMAC PBM) mentioned earlier. Tim John and his colleagues (2006) performed an independent evaluation of the GMAC PBM against five criteria; their data warehouse, the effective use of information technology, the role of Strategic Analytical Partnership Coordinators, the core decision making documents, and the GMAC PBM itself. Not only did they find each of the core components were fit for purpose, but their evaluation concluded that the strategic assessment documents were exemplars of best practice in the field.

The GMAC PBM has a number of key components. Firstly, there is an explicit strategic planning function. This is important because it draws police commanders into a collaborative, co-production model of crime control delivery with other key stakeholders in the field. The enumeration of long-term objectives sets goals for prioritization within intelligence-led policing. The strategic function also prevents an over-reliance on chasing unsustainable short-term gains (a criticism leveled at the Compstat process, see Scott et al. 2008).

Secondly, the model explicitly ties the role of analytical products developed by crime and intelligence analysts to a clear decision-making structure. The inclusion of decision-makers into a conceptual model of intelligence-led policing is central to the three-i model and the GMAC PBM. This is important because the GMAC PBM delivers: Over 90 percent of participants in the GMAC partnership business groups said that the delivery of crime and disorder solutions had been improved through the GMAC PBM (John et al. 2006: 49). Finally, the combination of a strategic and tactical approach demonstrates that police can successfully incorporate working with partner agencies within a framework that still allows for a focus on crime and disorder hotspots and the targeting of prolific and serious offenders.

HOLISTIC CRIME MANAGEMENT

This article has suggested that intelligence-led policing is about anticipating risk and influencing action. Increasingly, risk is being conceptualized as more than just crime, but rather as *social harm* (Hillyard and Tombs 2007). This suggests not only a broadening of the threats that the community face to include quality of life, traffic problems and financial hardships, but also a widening of the potential solutions and partners that police can work with to prevent harm. In a holistic environment, a combination of crime analysis and criminal intelligence is paramount, where the former tells a decision-maker *what* is happening, while the latter can explain *why* (Ratcliffe 2007). This combination of criminal intelligence with crime analysis is essential if decision-makers are to get a complete picture of the criminal environment (Ratcliffe 2008b). Unfortunately, resistance to merging these two important information sources runs deep in law enforcement.

With a combination of crime analysis and criminal intelligence, decision-makers can start to tackle long-term crime problems. The importance of patterns was stated at the start of this chapter, and in the first law of crime intelligence: *The most reliable indication of future criminal activity is current criminal activity.* Just to reiterate a point from earlier: this is not to say we should ignore emerging and fluctuating problems; however, a central role of intelligence-led policing is the *efficient* use of police and intelligence resources. Efficiency will come from tackling both perennial problems and hotspots, *and* serious and recidivist offenders.

There also remains a significant challenge to operationally integrate intelligence-led policing into the police organization (Carter 2004). There is still a widespread fixation with short-term tactical outcomes that traps police departments into an endless cycle of trying to rush cops from data-driven hotspot to data-driven hotspot. Irrespective of how data-informed and real-time these reflexive tactics become, in the absence of a strategic management plan they still represent old-fashioned reactive policing. This may seem contrary to my first law of crime intelligence in the preceding paragraph, but the purpose of the law is to focus strategic crime management activity, not short-term reactive policing.

The solution is for both sides (analysts and decision-makers) to come to the party. It is sometimes forgotten by some in the analytical community that the overarching aim of intelligence-led policing is for better *policing* rather than just better intelligence. Equally, decision-makers have to lift their gaze beyond immediate short-term outcomes that are frequently fleeting and Pyrrhic victories and recognize that the aim is for intelligence-led *policing* and not just intelligence-led *investigations*. There is a real need for decision-makers to view crime intelligence as valuable beyond investigative case support, and as a pivotal aid to an objective decision-making framework that strives for strategic management of crime problems. As the former Chief Constable of Kent Police noted recently, "Strategy is about making the best use of resource, time, and space. It is also about recognizing the contingencies on the wider canvas and identifying a winning formula in the prevailing context; successful operations within a losing formula avail nothing…Strategic aims are all too easily set aside for short-term advantages. Strategic oversight is therefore an ongoing responsibility." (Phillips 2008: 29)

Carter and Carter (2009) note that U.S. law enforcement agencies may have some issues regarding the adoption of intelligence-led policing. No legacy of widespread intelligence use, an ill-defined intelligence function, a lack of training and expertise, and widespread lack of police department size may all hamper intelligence capacity development. They are spot-on in their analysis, but their critique also acts as a roadmap to the challenges for agencies striving to be intelligence-led. Intelligence-led policing is not just about intelligence, but about policing. A greater integration of the intelligence function into the decision-making processes of policing will allow analysts to have the impact their contribution to crime reduction demands, and permit police leadership to escape the noxious gravitational pull of short-term crises and move towards a more holistic, strategic and, ultimately, successful crime reduction strategy.

REFERENCES

Carter, D. L. (2004). *Law Enforcement Intelligence: A Guide for State, Local, and Tribal Enforcement Agencies*. Report, Office of Community Oriented Policing Services, Washington DC.

Carter, D. L. (2005). "The law enforcement intelligence function: State, local, and tribal agencies." *FBI Law Enforcement Bulletin*, 74(6), 1-9.

Carter, D. L., and Carter, J. G. (2009). "Intelligence-Led Policing: Conceptual and functional considerations for public policy." Criminal Justice Policy Review. Forthcoming.

Clarke, R. V. (2004). "Technology, criminology and crime science." *European Journal on Criminal Policy and Research*, 10(1), 55-63.

Dannels, D., and Smith, H. (2001). "Implementation challenges of intelligence led policing in a quasi-rural county." *Journal of Crime and Justice*, 24(2), 103-112.

Eck, J. E. (2006). "Science, values, and problem-oriented policing: Why problem-oriented policing?" in D. Weisburd and A. A. Braga, (eds.), *Police Innovation: Contrasting Perspectives*. New York: Cambridge University Press, pp. 117-132.

Evans, R. M. (2009). "Influencing decision-makers with intelligence and analytical products", in J. H. Ratcliffe, (ed.), *Strategic Thinking in Criminal Intelligence*. Second edition. Sydney: Federation Press.

Flitcroft, D. (2006). "GMAC delivers: Our most complete understanding of drugs and drug markets yet". Presentation at the *4th UK National Crime Mapping Conference*. UCL Jill Dando Institute for Crime Science: London.

Flood, B., and Gaspar, R. (2009). "Strategic aspects of the UK National Intelligence Model", in J. H. Ratcliffe, (ed.), *Strategic Thinking in Criminal Intelligence*. Second edition. Sydney: Federation Press.

GMPA/GMP. (nd). *Policing Strategy 2005/8*. Greater Manchester Police Authority and Greater Manchester Police, Manchester, UK. No date.

Goldstein, H. (2003). "On further developing problem-oriented policing: The most critical need, the major impediments, and a proposal", in J. Knutsson, (ed.), *Problem-Oriented Policing: From Innovation to Mainstream*. Monsey, NJ: Criminal Justice Press, pp. 13-47.

Grieve, J. (2009). "Developments in UK criminal intelligence", in J. H. Ratcliffe, (ed.), *Strategic Thinking in Criminal Intelligence*. Second edition. Sydney: Federation Press.

Hillyard, P., and Tombs, S. (2007). "From 'crime' to social harm?" *Crime, Law & Social Change*, 48 (1-2), 9-25.

John, T., Morgan, C., and Rogers, C. (2006). *The Greater Manchester A* John, T., Morgan, C., and Rogers, C. (2006). *The Greater Manchester Against Crime Partnership Business Model: An independent evaluation*. Evaluation report, Centre for Criminology, University of Glamorgan, Glamorgan.

Kelling, G. L. (1999). *"Broken Windows" and Police Discretion*. Research Report, National Institute of Justice, Washington DC.

Kelling, G. L., and Bratton, W. J. (2006). "Policing terrorism." *Civic Bulletin*, 43, 12 pages.

Makkai, T., Ratcliffe, J. H., Veraar, K., and Collins, L. (2004). "ACT Recidivist Offenders." *Research and Public Policy Series, Australian Institute of Criminology*, No. 54, 83 pages.

Peterson, M. B. (2005). *Intelligence-Led Policing: The New Intelligence Architecture*. Bureau of Justice Assistance, Washington DC.

Peterson, M. B., Morehouse, B., and Wright, R. (2000). "Intelligence 2000: Revising the basic elements". LEIU and IALEIA: Sacramento, CA, pp. 245.

Phillips, D. (2008). "Police intelligence systems as a strategic response", in C. Harfield, A. MacVean, J. G. D. Grieve, and D. Phillips, (eds.), *The Handbook of Intelligent Policing: Consilience, Crime Control, and Community Safety*. Oxford: Oxford University Press, pp. 29-35.

Quarmby, N. (2009). "Futures work in strategic criminal intelligence", in J. H. Ratcliffe, (ed.), *Strategic Thinking in Criminal Intelligence*. Second edition. Sydney: Federation Press.

Ratcliffe, J. H. (2003). "Intelligence-led policing." *Trends and Issues in Crime and Criminal Justice*, Australian Institute of Criminology, No. 248, 6.

Ratcliffe, J. H. (2005). "The effectiveness of police intelligence management: A New Zealand case study." *Police Practice and Research*, 6(5), 435-451.

Ratcliffe, J. H. (2007). *Integrated intelligence and crime analysis: Enhanced information management for law enforcement leaders*. Police Foundation, Washington DC.

Ratcliffe, J. H. (2008a). *Intelligence-Led Policing*, Cullompton, Devon: Willan Publishing.

Ratcliffe, J. H. (2008b). "Knowledge management challenges in the development of intelligence-led policing", in T. Williamson, (ed.), *The Handbook of Knowledge-Based Policing: Current Conceptions and Future Directions*. Chichester: John Wiley and Sons, pp. 205-220.

Ratcliffe, J. H. (2009). "The structure of strategic thinking", in J. H. Ratcliffe, (ed.), *Strategic Thinking in Criminal Intelligence*. Second edition. Sydney: Federation Press.

Ratcliffe, J. H., and Makkai, T. (2004). "Diffusion of benefits: Evaluating a policing operation." *Trends and Issues in Crime and Criminal Justice*, Australian Institute of Criminology, No. 278, 1-6.

Scott, M. S. (2000). *Problem-Oriented Policing: Reflections on the First 20 Years*. COPS Office, Washington DC.

Scott, M. S., Eck, J., Knutsson, J., and Goldstein, H. (2008). "Problem-oriented policing and environmental criminology", in R. Wortley and L. Mazerolle, (eds.), *Environmental Criminology and Crime Analysis*. Cullompton, Devon: Willan Publishing, pp. 221-246.

Shaw, C. R., and McKay, H. D. (1942). *Juvenile Delinquency and Urban Areas*, Chicago: Chicago University Press.

Sheptycki, J. (2004). *Review of the influence of strategic intelligence on organised crime policy and practice*. Special Interest Series Paper, Home Office Research and Statistics Directorate, London.

Sherman, L. W., and Eck, J. E. (2002). "Policing for crime prevention", in L. W. Sherman, D. Farrington, B. Welsh, and D. L. MacKenzie, (eds.), *Evidence-Based Crime Prevention*. New York: Routledge, pp. 295-329.

Sherman, L. W., Gottfredson, D., MacKenzie, D., Eck, J., Reuter, P., and Bushway, S. (1998). *Preventing Crime: What works, what doesn't, what's promising*. National Institute of Justice, Washington DC.

Skogan, W. G. (2006). "The promise of community policing", in D. Weisburd and A. A. Braga, (eds.), *Police Innovation: Contrasting Perspectives*. Chicago: Cambridge University Press, pp. 27-43.

SOCA. (2008). *UK Threat Assessment of Serious Organised Crime 2008/9*. Serious Organised Crime Agency, London.

Sousa, W. H., and Kelling, G. L. (2006). "Of "broken windows," criminology, and criminal justice", in D. Weisburd and A. A. Braga, (eds.), *Police Innovation: Contrasting Perspectives*. New York: Cambridge University Press, pp. 77-97.

Taylor, R. B. (2006). "Incivilities reduction policing, zero tolerance, and the retreat from coproduction: weak foundations and strong pressures", in D. Weisburd and A. A. Braga, (eds.), *Police Innovation: Contrasting Perspectives*. Chicago: Cambridge University Press, pp. 98-114.

Townsley, M., Johnson, S., and Pease, K. (2003). "Problem orientation, problem solving and organizational change", in J. Knuttson, (ed.), *Problem-Oriented Policing: From Innovation to Mainstream*. Monsey, NY: Criminal Justice Press, pp. 183-212.

Wilson, J. Q., and Kelling, G. L. (1982). "Broken Windows: The police and neighborhood safety", *The Atlantic Monthly*. March 1982, pp. 29-38.

Wood, J., and Shearing, C. (2007). *Imagining Security*. Cullompton, Devon: Willan Publishing.

Section 2
Fusion Centers
By Van Godsey and Doug Frank

INTRODUCTION

It was not without some apprehension that the authors agreed they would write an article on this new phenomenon called "Fusion Centers." This apprehension was not from a lack of confidence or knowledge, but from a lack of a historical perspective to reference as well as the ever changing dynamic of the topic. How do you realistically describe and write about something that can change while you are writing? With that said, the authors discuss the current perspective of fusion centers, the developments leading up to this point, and where they believe fusion centers are heading in the future. The fusion centers are truly the new frontier in the United States in regards to information and intelligence sharing. The fusion center concept was one of many initiatives created to address the information and intelligence sharing challenges faced by the federal government after the events of September 11, 2001. In most instances, State and local agencies have taken the lead in these centers and developed them not only to assist in bridging gaps in the national information sharing effort, but to also address issues unique to their geographic areas. This article gives a brief overview of why these centers have become a focal point for state and local intelligence sharing while at the same time being leveraged in the national intelligence picture.

HISTORY

After the tragic events of September 11, 2001, there was not only an understanding that a major change in philosophy and operations had to occur to ensure "homeland security", but there was also a burning desire and urgency to see these changes implemented. Without a doubt, this tragic event was the spark that rallied American citizens as well as the law enforcement community and set in motion events and actions that would lead to the development of fusion centers as we know them today.

One of the first events was a summit held during the International Association of Chiefs of Police (IACP) conference in spring 2002. This summit was attended by law enforcement executives and intelligence experts. At this summit it was recognized that local, state, tribal, and federal law enforcement agencies had to work towards common goals, specifically the gathering of information, the development of intelligence, and the sharing of that intelligence with other law enforcement and public safety agencies.

As a result of this summit, the U.S. Department of Justice's Global Justice Information Sharing Initiative (Global) Intelligence Working Group (GIWG) was formed. One of the key documents developed by GIWG and a direct result of the summit was the *National Criminal Intelligence Sharing Plan* (NCISP).[2] The NCISP is considered a blueprint to assist law enforcement personnel in their crime fighting, public safety, and anti-terrorism efforts. It was understood and recognized that officers, investigators, and analysts working throughout the nation are the first line of

[2] *<http://it.ojp.gov/documents/National_Criminal_Intelligence_Sharing_Plan.pdf>*

prevention and defense against terrorism and crime. Specifically, the NCISP recognized the importance of local, state, and tribal law enforcement agencies as key ingredients in the nation's intelligence process.

The GIWG recognized one of the key issues that had to be addressed was the need to overcome the long-standing and substantial barriers that hinder intelligence sharing. The NCISP provides 28 recommendations to help agencies establish criminal intelligence sharing policies, procedures, standards, technologies, and training. This initial document provided action items that law enforcement executives from departments of all sizes could utilize to become a part of the solution.

In February 2003, President George W. Bush stated during a speech that information-sharing would be made an important tool in the nation's war on terror and acknowledged that local information was imperative to true homeland security. For many, this statement may have sounded somewhat mundane and quite frankly stated the obvious. However, this acknowledgement of the importance of local involvement in the information and intelligence process for homeland security highlighted a changing era. It was at this point that the seeds of change not only had been planted, but were starting to mature.

One of the major recommendations within the NCISP was the creation of a group to provide long-term oversight and assistance with the implementation and refinement of the NCISP. The Criminal Intelligence Coordinating Council (CICC) was formally established in May 2004 with the purpose of advising the U.S. Congress, the U.S. Attorney General, and the Secretary of the U.S. Department of Homeland Security (DHS) on the best use of criminal intelligence to keep the country safe. Staying consistent with the idea of local involvement, it was important that the CICC consist of representatives from local, state, tribal, and federal agencies and national law enforcement organizations.

As agencies began to digest and implement the NCISP, it became apparent to many that joint efforts would not only allow for quicker information sharing, but could also allow for leveraging of resources including space, manpower, and money. As these joint initiatives continued to mature and develop, the phrase "**Fusion Center**" was adopted. In 2004 and 2005, several states and larger cities embarked on the development of fusion centers. In many ways, these fusion centers were further developments of the Terrorism Early Warning Center concept, of which Los Angeles established one of the first.[3] As more and more of these centers were created across the nation it was obvious that some guidance should be put in place to assist in consistent and efficient operations.

It was during this time that the local, state, and tribal agencies began to see the positive effects of these fusion centers and to truly understand how these joint efforts allowed even the smallest of agencies to be involved in intelligence and information sharing. These efforts provided a mechanism for all agencies regardless of size to implement many parts of the NCISP. This was a perfect opportunity for the CICC to fulfill its role in providing oversight and implementation of the NCISP to provide leadership in the development and future of fusion centers. As part of a true joint effort between the Bureau of Justice Assistance (BJA), Office of Justice Programs, U.S. Department of Justice (DOJ), U.S. Department of Justice's Global Justice Information Sharing Initiative (Global), U.S. DHS and numerous law enforcement experts from local, state, tribal, and federal agencies, fusion center guidelines were developed. In August 2006, the *Fusion Center Guidelines - Developing and Sharing Information*

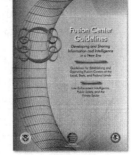

---

[3] *<http://www.lasd.org/tew/TEW2009.pdf>*

in a New Era was published.[4] It was obvious that a tremendous amount of work had been put toward the development of these initial guidelines. Without a doubt, the current and future goals of fusion centers could not and would not have been reached if not for the hard work put toward these initial guidelines.

As with any project, the guidelines—when released—had its critics. Some felt that the guidelines were too broad and not prescriptive enough while others felt they were overreaching and too restrictive. However, the majority of people involved in the actual development and operations of fusion centers felt that the guidelines were exactly what the developers had intended and provided a solid base of understanding for those already involved in the centers as well as those that would become involved. As the individuals discovered when constructing the guidelines, the simple things are sometimes the toughest. Among the questions that needed to be answered was what constituted a fusion center? Developing the basic definition of a fusion center was an accomplishment in and of itself:

> *"An effective and efficient mechanism to exchange information and intelligence, maximize resources, streamline operations, and improve the ability to fight crime and terrorism by analyzing data from a variety of sources."*[5]

It was understood by those involved with the development of these guidelines from the very beginning that although fusion centers would have unique and separate styles of operations, it was imperative for the individual centers as well as the national concept to have a consistent framework. The guidelines went past the definition of a fusion center and provided 18 overarching key elements for the establishment and effective operation of a fusion center.

CURRENT STATUS

The "Gold Rush" of fusion center creation began in 2004, and will continue beyond 2009. It is important to understand that some centers were established before this time frame and in fact some had quite mature operations even prior to 2004. Some of these developed as a result of growth in already existing law enforcement intelligence units, as experts and representatives from other agencies were brought together to provide better intelligence and contribute to the wider goal of homeland security. They may not have been called fusion centers, but they were in fact performing the same duties as are now associated with fusion centers. It also has to be understood that in some places the development of a fusion center has just begun.

There is no doubt that the expansion and growth of fusion centers can be attributed to several factors and to several groups. However, a major indicator that fusion centers were not only established but were going to thrive into the future came in 2007. In October 2007, President Bush released the administration's *National Strategy for Information Sharing*.[6] This book not only laid out the lessons learned over the previous six years after 9-11, but it also established the plan for how the exchange of information would be used in the national effort to fight terrorism. One of the foundational elements of this comprehensive strategy was that information sharing had to take place between

---

[4],*<http://it.ojp.gov/documents/fusion_center_guidelines_law_enforcement.pdf>*
[5] *<http://it.ojp.gov/documents/fusion_center_guidelines_law_enforcement.pdf>*, 2
[6] Original version available at *<http: //www.surfacetransportationisac.org/SupDocs/NSIS_book.pdf>*

the federal government and state, local, and tribal entities. One of the primary strategies provided in the report detailed how state and major urban area fusion centers "represent a valuable information sharing resource and should be incorporated into the national information sharing framework."[7]

It was understood that the fusion centers were unique and developed specifically to best fit the needs and abilities of their specific regions; however, it was also understood that to truly benefit our nation's security, there had to be some basic level of consistency in what the centers were doing and how they were doing it. The strategy was clear in detailing the efforts that both the federal government and the local, state, and tribal governments would undertake to implement this fusion center strategy, but no minimum standards had been set for fusion centers.

In September, 2008, the U.S. Department of Justice's Global Justice Information Sharing Initiative published the *Baseline Capabilities for State and Major Urban Area Fusion Centers*.[8] Understanding that many of the fusion centers were now operational and following the national strategy, it made sense to provide more specific guidance on the operations of the centers. Just as the original fusion center guidelines provided the blueprints for the establishment of the centers, the baseline capabilities would provide structure for the operations of the centers.

To provide an accurate snapshot of the current status of fusion centers is a difficult task. Because of the unique nature, individuality, and differing opinions of these centers, it is extremely difficult to provide an exact number of fusion centers with a high degree of confidence. However, the National Fusion Center Coordination Group (NFCCG) reported in August of 2009 that there were 72 fusion centers. This number includes 50 Primary Designated Fusion Centers, designated by the Governors of each state as the primary state center, and 22 Designated Fusion Centers which meet certain criteria as set out by the NFCCG. It must be kept in mind that as the fusion centers were being developed there were no hard and fast rules regarding the designation of a fusion center other than the Fusion Center Guidelines, and no accrediting agency to determine that an operation could legitimately call itself a fusion center. The DHS has developed an evaluation system in order to assign intelligence officers to state and local fusion centers, and at the time this article was written the number of officers assigned stands at 58. This number is expected to increase over the next year.

Even operating within the outline of the baseline capabilities, fusion center operations are as diverse as the agencies that comprise the centers. While there is no single formula for success in specific structure, mission, or management, each agency determines what combination of analysts and tools is best suited to the challenges it faces. As was specifically mentioned in the national strategy, it is imperative to remember the sovereignty of the state and local governments and the need to clearly define the roles and responsibilities for the federal government as well as the state and local authorities. It is understood that the fusion centers are to be owned and managed by the state and local governments. It is also understood that the centers are to support the normal public safety needs of their supporting entities while at the same time incorporating their role in national information sharing efforts.

As the centers have developed and matured, they have discovered that one consistent advantage is the synergy created when representatives from diverse fields are brought together for a common goal. The experience that intelligence analysts and officers bring to the fusion center creates a wide variety of

---

[7] *<http://www.surfacetransportationisac.org/SupDocs/NSIS_book.pdf>*, 3
[8] *<http://it.ojp.gov/documents/baselinecapabilitiesa.pdf>*

viewpoints that benefit analysis. There are no junior partners in a fusion center setting; as it can never be known from day to day when an incident may arise that requires a unique area of expertise.

With these benefits in mind, fusion centers have not developed without growing pains. Pioneers in every field face opposition and misunderstanding, and fusion centers have been no exception. Increased staffing has allowed for increased specialization, but can also contribute to information stove piping, a negative side effect that fusion centers were created to help alleviate. Communication and situational awareness is a challenge that applies not only to serious incident management but also to day-to-day operations as well. With each trial, lessons are learned, standing procedures adapted, and outreach programs implemented to educate policy makers and the general public on what fusion centers are and are not.

Regardless of the centers' missions, operations, or successes, they have critics. A legitimate concern for many is how and what the centers are doing with personal information. Fortunately for the fusion center initiative, many of the individuals and agencies involved with the initial development and implementation of the centers were also concerned with the protection of individual rights and civil liberties. When dealing with sensitive information, as fusion centers do on a daily basis, it is not only necessary but imperative that the protection of individual rights and civil liberties be at the forefront of their operation. By looking through the entire list of base documents above, it can be seen that privacy and civil liberties are and have always been one of the key concerns discussed, beginning with the original *Fusion Center Guidelines* document.

CHALLENGES

As with any project, there will be challenges and the development of Fusion Centers is no different. Although some of these issues are mentioned above, the following highlights some of the critical challenges facing fusion centers.

- It is estimated that from 2004 to 2009 the DHS has provided approximately $327 million dollars to state and local governments to support the fusion centers. This information can be quite confusing and certainly misunderstood. The DHS can and does provide funding for fusion centers; however, the funding goes to the respective state and local government entities that subsequently make decisions on how much, if any, funding will be utilized towards the operations of the fusion center. Herein lays a tremendous challenge. The challenge has been and continues to be, how does one develop consistent guidelines, training, and operations while requiring these centers meet a set of baseline capabilities when they are not provided a similar and consistent amount of funding? Much discussion has occurred over the last few years regarding direct federal funding for the fusion centers; however, at this time that has not been accomplished. What appears to be a hesitancy of the federal government to dictate to the state and local governments on how the funding should be expended, turns into a wide array of budgets for fusion centers from some receiving zero dollars to others receiving millions of dollars. Due to economic conditions in many states and the uncertainty of federal funding, the ability to meet baseline standards is sometimes the least of a fusion center's worries with the actual continued operation of some centers being the greater concern.

- The full implementation of the intelligence cycle as the backbone of fusion center operations is another obstacle that requires resolution. Through no fault of their own, many fusion center supervisors have little previous intelligence experience, making the intelligence cycle an unfamiliar novelty. Education, as well as longer "tours of duty" for fusion center supervisors, will help to alleviate this problem.

- With the rapid increase in the number of intelligence analysts assigned to the fusion centers, training (and retention of trained personnel) will need to continue to be a priority for fusion centers. While their expertise and ability to use various systems make them valuable for assisting in ongoing investigations, intelligence analysts at times will need to be specifically assigned to focus on proactive intelligence efforts, to prevent the dilution of the fusion centers' ability to predict and help prevent future incidents.

- Acquiring feedback on assistance given to partner and assisted agencies is key to the continued success of fusion centers. It is through feedback analysis that fusion center staff members discover what products are most useful to their customers. It allows them to refine their processes, products, and even their staff training. By increasing their emphasis on areas that are of most concern to them, the fusion center becomes increasingly relevant to its customers' daily operations and increases buy-in from the community. They remain flexible to the changing needs of their customers and the changing world situation, ensuring that they will remain relevant and necessary into the future.

- The challenge of working with volumes of information attempting to "connect the dots" while maintaining the integrity of the process is another issue. The only option for success is through the public understanding the fusion center's proactive role while at the same time being assured that the protection of their rights are a main stay of the fusion centers operation. Aggressive training, solid operational procedures, and continued review will allow this fine balance to occur.

- The technical challenge that the centers are facing with continued operations is substantial. Fusion centers are amassing intelligence that needs to be organized in such a manner as to be accessible, searchable, and compliant with guidelines and regulations. Dozens of products already exist that assist intelligence analysts with their work. These include public records databases, case management systems, database indexing, geographic information systems, facial recognition, organizational and timeline charting, and crime pattern analysis software, to name but a few. Continuing development will bring not only additional types of information, but also the integration of many types of databases into systems that are more user-friendly and time-efficient.

FUTURE

Fusion centers stand at a crossroads. The explosion of fusion center creation that took place following the terrorist attacks of September 11, 2001, has slowed. The absence of further successful attacks on American soil has numbed the senses of many, leading to a questioning of the continued existence of many fusion centers that were originally formed to fight terrorism. A continued effort by some civil rights groups to paint the centers as rogue agencies with no regard for individual rights remains an issue, and tightening government budgets have prevented many jurisdictions from developing or expanding their analytical capabilities.

To be successful and continue with sustained operations, the centers will certainly have to deal with many of the challenges mentioned above. In order to justify continued funding from the DHS, an emphasis will certainly be placed on quantifiable and measurable results from the fusion centers. Unlike other grants where results are easy to measure, like the number of police officers put on the street using a "COPS" grant, results from intelligence are not quite as simple. Fusion centers will need to effectively measure their capabilities to provide analytical support to outside agencies and the added value they bring to the law enforcement and intelligence communities. Additionally, fusion centers will need to continue to reach out and form partnerships with other fusion centers, law enforcement agencies that fall within their area of operations, and public and private organizations that have a viable interest and need to participate (especially critical infrastructure organizations).

In efforts to broaden their capabilities, their base of support, and funding many fusion centers have expanded their roles to include organized crime or "all crime" types. These centers are finding that many of the same tools and skills that they have acquired to combat terrorism can also be used to counter organized crime, narcotics, and street gangs. Additionally, a number of fusion centers have taken this a step further, to include intelligence related to all hazards. In parts of the country that experience natural hazards on a regular basis, such as hurricanes in the Gulf Coast states and wildfires in the West, these steps are already bearing fruit.

The way the centers have grown and developed may or may not have been envisioned in the beginning; however, the relationships between varied partners have never been better. Measuring prevention is an age old problem in law enforcement. If someone does not do something or something does not happen, how do you know if your efforts assisted in preventing that action? On the other hand, what can be measured is the amount of information and the type of information being shared amongst the partners. As mentioned in the beginning, the development of the centers truly was based on a need to fix what was perceived as a federal problem. Monumental progress has been made toward this goal while an additional benefit has been the tremendous relationship building between local and state agencies and between state agencies. In the end, it is the success of these relationships that will continue to drive the development of the centers and the critical information exchange that is required for Homeland Security. Fusion centers do face challenges from many quarters. However, they have also shown an incredible ability to adapt to circumstances and changing needs. Continued flexibility, inspired leadership, clear goals, and the hard work of intelligence analysts will allow for fusion centers to adjust, grow, and thrive.

REFERENCES

Bureau of Justice Assistance (BJA), U.S. Department of Justice. 2005. *The National Criminal Intelligence Sharing Plan.*
<http://it.ojp.gov/documents/National_Criminal_Intelligence_Sharing_Plan.pdf> (accessed January 18, 2010).

Bureau of Justice Assistance (BJA), U.S. Department of Justice. 2006. *Fusion Center Guidelines: Developing and Sharing Information in a New Era.*
<http://it.ojp.gov/documents/fusion_center_guidelines_law_enforcement.pdf> (accessed January 18, 2010).

Global Justice Information Sharing Initiative, U.S. Department of Justice. 2008. *Baseline Capabilities for State and Major Urban Area Fusion Centers: A Supplement to the Fusion Center Guidelines.*
<http://it.ojp.gov/documents/baselinecapabilitiesa.pdf> (accessed January 18, 2010).

National Strategy for Information Sharing: Successes and Challenges in Improving Terrorism-Related Information Sharing. 2007.
<http://www.surfacetransportationisac.org/SupDocs/NSIS_book.pdf> (accessed January 18, 2010).

Sullivan, John P. and Alain Bauer. 2008. *Terrorism Early Warning: 10 Years of Achievement in Fighting Terrorism and Crime. <http://www.lasd.org/tew/TEW2009.pdf>* (accessed January 18, 2010).

Section 3
Corrections Intelligence
By Melissa R. Johnson

INTRODUCTION

Corrections intelligence is produced from data retrieved from persons or sources within correctional institutions which has been analyzed to provide insights into criminal individuals, organizations, or leads in criminal investigations. Corrections intelligence is important because some offenders do not stop committing crime when they enter the prison or stop after they are released. Dismantling drug smuggling operations, taking down large gangs, and disrupting contraband networks within correctional facilities are successful examples of effective uses of corrections intelligence.

Agencies and associations around the world [9] have started projects to gather corrections data, identify its law enforcement value, and apply analytic techniques to corrections data. This article highlights why corrections intelligence is important to law enforcement and gang investigations; what corrections intelligence is, and finally, how it can be used by the criminal justice community.

THE *"WHAT"* AND THE *"SO WHAT"*: WHY IS CORRECTIONS INTELLIGENCE IMPORTANT?

Analytical work, regardless of the field, consists of two parts, the *"what"* and the *"so what."* Often times, identifying the *what (e.g.* a series of crimes) is less important than understanding the *so what.* The *so what* of the crime series is often an indication of a larger problem that could include: growing neighborhood fears, increasing high school dropout rates, gang membership shifts, closing after-school programs, changes in transportation routes, and rising unemployment rates. Unfortunately, law enforcement analysis often concentrates more on analyzing the *what*—*t*ying together the elements of crimes to prosecute the criminals more so than the *so what,* which would focus on the context, impact and root causes of the criminal activities. Instead of defining *what* corrections intelligence is, this section will first explain the *so what* of corrections intelligence or why the criminal justice field should invest in corrections intelligence. The remainder of this section describes corrections intelligence as useful for investigating crimes that current and former inmates are committing.

The sheer volume of incarcerated persons throughout the world is staggering. In 2007, almost 1% of the entire United States population, or 2.3 million people, were incarcerated at the federal, state, or local level. The Bureau of Justice Statistics (BJS) reported that this total increased by 1.5% during the year (BJS 2007). In the same report, *Prisoners in 2007*, nearly half of inmates in 2005 were in prison for violent offenses that include murder, manslaughter, rape, robbery, assault, etc. (BJS 2007) Why are these statistics important? If notable researchers and recent investigations are any indication, prisons and jails are similar to mini-cities that are ripe for flourishing crime, gang recruitment, and radicalization attempts (Public Technology 07). Even inmates who are attempting to rehabilitate themselves are in an

---

[9] Including the International Association of Chiefs of Police (IACP), the United States Department of Justice, Bureau of Justice Assistance, the Federal Bureau of Investigations, the Association of State Corrections Administrators, and American Probation and Parole Association.

environment that facilitates learning new criminal skills or methods to commit crime while they are still incarcerated or when they are released.

In June 2009, authorities in Indianapolis, Indiana, imprisoned dozens of people for drug trafficking and sales. A responding citizen's comment captures the underlying perception and intent of incarceration: "Let's get these drug dealers off the streets. They need to face the maximum sentences so they know that we are not playing with these people anymore." (Danver 2009) This view reflects a perception that incarceration prevents all inmates from committing crime. Nick Doodney, Deputy Intelligence Manager of the new Prison Intelligence Unit which links intelligence efforts between the Metropolitan Police and Prison Service in the United Kingdom, countered this sentiment saying, "The idea that once an offender is put in prison they stop committing offenses is wrong." (Public Technology 2007) Crime does not stop at the barbed wire fence, in fact, crime trends in prison mirror crimes on the streets.

In addition to the very real, serious, and everyday crimes that inmates commit or direct from inside prisons, there is a phenomenon of radicalization influencing future criminality law enforcement authorities should be wary of as well. An inmate may decide not to abide by institutional rehabilitation programs and instead focus on joining a criminal organization or to hone their criminal skills for future use. Investigations of the terrorists involved in the bombings in Madrid (2004) and London (2005) underscored the potential violence of radicalized inmates. Incarcerated since 2001, Imad al-din Barakat Yarkas, provided direction to the Madrid al-Qaeda cell to commit the Madrid bombings. In July 2005, Ibrahim Muktar Said was arrested for his involvement in the London bus bombing. Intelligence indicates that Ibrahim was in a British juvenile detention facility when he was first exposed to the radicalized ideologies. As examples, the bombings and existence of the home-grown U.S.-based cell, Jamyatt Ul-Islam Is-Saheeh (JIS) prison gang discovered in California, have shown how prison radicalization has influenced inmates looking for retribution, solace, family, and resources. Prison has become a recruiting ground for organized crime, gangs, and terrorist organizations. As radicalized or recruited offenders are released back into the community, they are given direction and support to carry out their adopted missions. Identifying radicalized and gang inmates, criminal support networks, or criminal missions are crucial to the public's safety and security.

Law enforcement's goal is to maintain public safety and reduce criminal activity. The criminal link between prisons and the streets is not a new phenomenon, however, new methods of committing criminal activity in both have evolved over time. Inmates are committing new crimes each day as they make contact with individuals on the street who are willing to smuggle contraband into a facility, launder monies for inmates, or carry out activities or assaults on the street on their behalf. Some inmate visitors smuggle drugs and other materials into the institutions or inmate family members accept monies from other inmates as payment for drugs or security.

The correctional experience is often the forgotten cog in the criminal justice wheel and is not seen as a source of intelligence, rather it is viewed as an investigatory result (Godwin 1999). However, correctional institutions are excellent resources for data and criminal intelligence for current and future crime trend analysis. Beyond the research value of inmate population data and demographic information, the corrections environment offers law enforcement partners a wealth of information that highlights an inmate's street contact network through analysis of an inmate's phone records, visit lists, and inmate accounts. Understanding the connections between inmates and people in the community is useful to law enforcement apprehending fugitives, deterring retaliation, and investigating contraband or drug smuggling.

VALUE TO GANG INVESTIGATIONS

Understanding the value of inmate data for investigations is useful, but how do gang inmates factor in? What the references and statistics previously discussed do not mention is how many gang inmates are returning to the street and at what rate? Just how large is the gang membership in prison and in the community? According to Ed Cohn, Executive Director of the National Major Gang Task Force, a survey was conducted of corrections departments throughout the United States which indicated over 113,000 inmates were identified as gang affiliates and/or members. This comprised 5-13% of the United States' inmate population depending on source information (BJS 2007; Martin 2005, NIC 2008).

According to the New Jersey State Police *Street Gang Survey* released in 2007, 43% of law enforcement agencies in the state observed a gang presence in their communities. This is a 10% increase in reports from the 2004 survey (NJSP 2007). Since 1994, The New Jersey Department of Corrections has identified over 11,000 incarcerated gang members. Before 2006, half of the total identified gang inmates were still incarcerated. However, that statistic began to decrease as more gang affiliated inmates were released after serving an average of 3 to 5 years (Johnson 2005; NJDOC 2006).

Gang activity and the number of investigations of gangs continue to rise. A common misconception is that incarcerating gang members will resolve the crime and gang problem. Godwin reports that every major street gang active in the United States receives direction from inmate gang members despite lengthy prison sentences and limited access to the outside (Godwin 1999). The gangs' reach can extend well beyond the prison bars despite the intended disconnect with the community. While inmates are directing or committing crimes with people on the street, inmates also commit crimes in prison. In 2005, 5 gang inmates serving life sentences were charged with murder and drug offenses during their incarceration at Pelican Bay Prison in California (Montgomery 2005a).

Gangs are organizing, extorting, and operating criminal enterprises behind bars while influencing operations on the streets. They are more than a localized problem and their reach has spread throughout the world to include populations that are behind bars in other regions. To reduce crime both on the streets and "behind the walls," corrections data and intelligence must be incorporated into the investigation process, similar to what has been established in the United Kingdom where the Police and Prison Services work together—bridging both the corrections and community law enforcement investigators. In a "Sharing Gang Intelligence" broadcast, Operations Manager Johnny Hawkins from the North Carolina Department of Corrections wrote that corrections intelligence is invaluable to investigations. Hawkins noted that gang prosecutions such as New Jersey's Operation 9-Connect disrupted operations between the 9-3 Blood gang members in prison and on the streets (NIC 2008).

For too long, police and corrections have unknowingly held back pieces of the intelligence puzzle from each other while gang members have increased their networking opportunities. Twenty years ago, prison officials around the world began to notice a change in prison population activity as battles between neighborhoods grew into battles between gangs that encompassed many neighborhoods, nationalities, races, genders, and ages. Gangs, sophisticated contraband schemes, money laundering attempts, and attempts to radicalize inmates into extremist activity have pushed corrections agencies into formulating comprehensive intelligence strategies. These strategies include protocols for intelligence gathering, synthesis, analysis, and dissemination. The value of corrections intelligence is nearly priceless; it impacts every facet of the criminal justice system, officer safety, violence prevention, crime solving, and contraband seizure both behind the wall and beyond.

WHAT IS INCLUDED IN CORRECTIONS INTELLIGENCE?

Researchers have concluded that corrections are the forgotten source of information, but corrections personnel may argue that corrections are not forgotten—just untapped. The plethora of useful information and criminal intelligence "hiding" in corrections are not utilized by law enforcement to its maximum potential. For example, a crime analyst working for a police department may analyze a recent spree of residential burglaries and examine links to local businesses such as jewelry and pawn shop establishments. When the analyst begins comparing eye witness reports, suspect descriptions, and video footage, what data should the descriptions be compared? Corrections data, perhaps recently released inmates with similar prior convictions, would be a good start.

In another scenario, an intelligence analyst is tasked with analyzing recent drug sale arrests and financial Suspicious Activity Reports (SAR). Some of the names listed on the recent drug arrests match transactions on the SAR reports. Perhaps there is a link between the two? The analyst could sift through corrections data to compare other pieces of information including: visit lists, phone calls, and transactions to or from inmate accounts. Accessing and analyzing all of this information is part of the data that corrections intelligence programs offer. The value of corrections data to the law enforcement community cannot be underestimated although it may be difficult to qualify and quantify.

TYPES OF CORRECTIONAL INSTITUTION DATA

In the United States most, if not all, of the federal and state prison facilities provide inmates with limited monitored phone service, visits, and financial processing depending on the individual's security classification. This means that each of the 2.3 million incarcerated persons in the United States (2007 estimate) may be permitted to have a list of phone numbers they may call and a list of people who may visit. One of the most valuable criminal intelligence resources is the many hours of recorded inmate phone conversations. Godwin noted the range of corrections data in the American Corrections Association magazine, *Corrections Today* 1999 article. The sources of information include:

- Casual Observations
- Intercepted Communications
- Recovered Organization Charts
- Gang Documents (Codes, Histories)
- Phone Monitoring
- Inmate Mail Covers
- Financial Transactions
- Visitation
- Graffiti

As Goodwin noted in the article, many of the data sources above are captured in hard copy format that makes sorting, analyzing, and dissecting the information difficult, if not impossible (Godwin 1999a). Operational and investigative reports from each satellite jail institution may also prove to be extremely valuable. The reports often highlight if an inmate had been assaulted by another inmate, if they had co-defendants, or were witnesses to other crimes. To uncover a drug smuggling syndicate an investigator or analyst could compare these reports to a visit list, inmate phone calls, or subpoenaed bank records from a known visitor.

During the 2008 public hearing on "Gangs in Prison" the New Jersey State Commission of Investigation (NJSCI) posted exhibits that showed the volume of financial transaction data available to law enforcement (NJSCI 2008). The NJSCI reported that the New Jersey Department of Corrections received over $63.8 million dollars into inmate accounts through visit and mail receipts from 2004 through 2008. The majority of that total, $54 million, was sent from persons on the street to inmates through the mail (NJSCI 2008). This is approximately $13.5 million dollars in money orders or checks per year, $1.13 million per month, or nearly $37,000 per day.

There are many layers of corrections data, mentioned above and shown in figure one, which can be analyzed and converted into actionable and useful corrections intelligence.

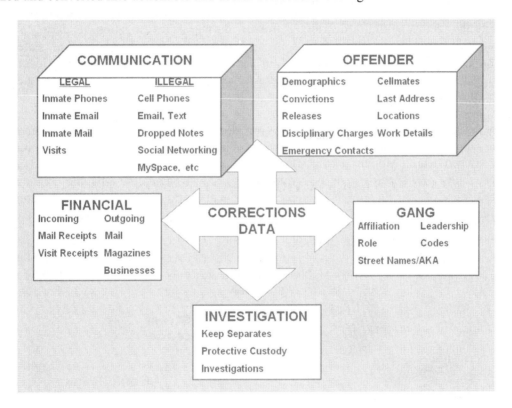

Figure 1: The chart above outlines the various points of corrections data that is used during the corrections intelligence process.

The chart in Figure 1 categorizes corrections data into five categories: communication, offender detail, financial, gang, and investigation. Within each category are fields of information which are also valuable to law enforcement authorities within the prison and on the street.

DATA EXAMPLE: GANG IDENTIFICATION

Gang management strategies are becoming a priority with the increasing percentage of gang inmates in correction facilities. The first step to any strategy is quantifying the scope of the problem. To do so, corrections intelligence personnel identify gang members, decipher codes, define structure, review correspondence, and attempt to determine membership and leadership. According to news clippings and recent multi-agency task force investigations, gangs often manage drug and contraband operations behind bars. This correctional intelligence allows us to understand who is in the gangs, how they operate, and how subsequent situational changes impact their ability to continue or enhance operations (NJSCI 2008).

While law enforcement struggles with defining gang membership and activity, corrections agencies have identified many gang members. Although identification criteria differ from department to department, evidence and documentation are almost always required to justify the identification. The following criteria are used by several agencies: self admission, possession of gang paraphernalia, possession of a gang photo, gang-related tattoo, information from an outside law enforcement agency, information from an investigation, and possession of gang correspondence (NJDOC 2006). Identification can occur when an inmate enters the facility during a debriefing process, during an investigation, or during a random gang-identification sweep when an entire facility is checked for new gang members. Law enforcement agencies working in the community are limited in the opportunities to collect gang identification documentation as readily as their corrections colleagues; as such, corrections intelligence, specifically gang identifications, can be of substantial value.

In addition to the initial gang identification data, corrections investigators also research and monitor fluctuations in gang leadership in an attempt to manage threats posed by rival gangs overpopulating a housing tier or kitchen detail. Monitoring this situational awareness about gang leadership and changes to the intent or capability of a specific gang to commit crime is just one of the valuable components that corrections intelligence offers. Figure 2 is a sample hierarchical chart. The gang members shaded in gray are identified inmates whereas the members within the white circles are currently operating on the street.

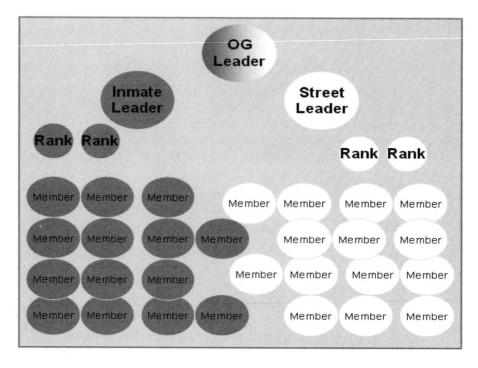

Figure 2: The figure above highlights a Street Gang structure that exists linking incarcerated persons with individuals on the street.

ANALYZING CORRECTIONS DATA

Corrections data has proved useful in operational planning, strategic prioritization, and investigations. This section reviews specific examples of the methods used to analyze corrections data. Although some agencies primarily use analysis for case support, the information in this chapter will show that corrections data analysis can be used to support and prioritize future suppression and prevention strategies and can have similar impacts on future policy changes.

Correctional institutions have been compared to small cities and many layers of data are necessary to support and direct operations within them. The institutions have citizens (inmates), have stores and libraries (laundry, kitchen, law library, gym), and have seasonal guests (visitors, mentors, contract employees). The same way citizens move through a city with checkpoints (e.g. EZ Pass and traffic lights) inmates move through a facility. Citizens receive phone bills and bank statements while an inmate has phone contacts and remits checks. Nearly every layer of data a citizen has on the street, an inmate has a similar component in the facility. The difference is that inmate data is captured for both operational and investigative needs.

The 2008 NJSCI public hearing, "Gangs in Prison," emphasized the volumes of inmate data which is collected and reported and how the data can identify relationships between inmates and their support network on the street. The financial transactions noted in that hearing were examples of how relationships can be identified. Figure 1 shows current inmates (James Jones, Ralph Rogers, and Rhonda Roads) forwarded funds to a civilian community member, Sarah Sample. Additionally, another data source was added to Figure 1—inmate contact information. This data source highlights familial relationships between Sarah Sample and two former inmates. Adding a third source of data, cellmate information, a tertiary level relationship was identified in Figure 1. One of the former inmates, Scott Stevenson, was a cellmate of a current inmate, James Jones. This information was compiled after the first report highlighted that one civilian received funds totaling only $150 from more than 1 inmate. Now imagine what the chart might look like for the $19 million worth of inmate checks forwarded to the street from 2004-2008 (NJSCI 2008).

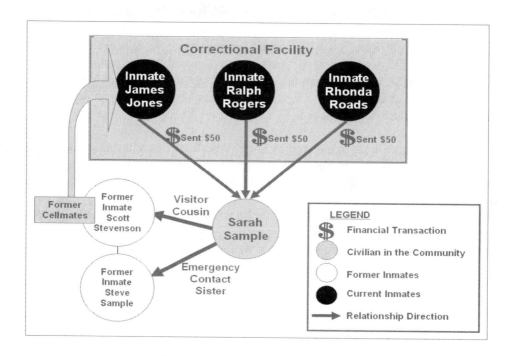

Figure 1: The diagram highlights relationships connecting inmates to a civilian in the community.

Although the example of relationships between inmates and a community member outlined in Figure 1 do not hold true in all cases, networks of similar circumstances have been uncovered in numerous criminal contraband and gang activities. To uncover these relationships, analysts must rely on access to several data elements including visitor lists and logs. The exhibit in Figure 2 was previously reported as an exhibit during the November 2008 public hearing, "Gangs in Prison." The exhibit helps put the large amount of data into context.

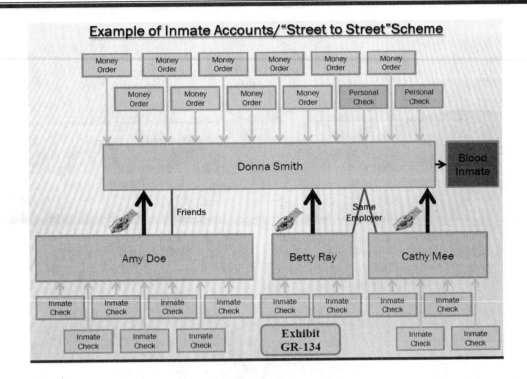

Figure 2: The exhibit above outlines a sample money laundering conspiracy involving inmates and their support network on the streets (NJSCI 2008).

In a four year period (2004-2008), New Jersey state inmates received over $63.8 million dollars in funds from street contacts. Of this amount, $54 million of money orders and checks were received in the mail during this same time (NJSCI 2008). Analysts will rapidly go into "information overload" without the necessary cutting edge technology to sift, sort, and analyze data that makes the analytical process more efficient and effective (NLECTC 2004).

Financial transactions and visitor information are not the only sources of valuable corrections data; Figure 3 outlines various methods of communication used by inmates and their support network. Communication data can be the most telling in uncovering illicit contraband networks and gang activities. The 2008 NJSCI public hearing, "Gangs in Prisons," outlines how Blood gang members use inmate accounts to transfer money to purchase drugs and phones behind bars which are smuggled into the facility by corrupt staff and visitors. During the hearing testimony an officer admitted he was paid $600 to smuggle in a phone. "The NJSCI report says it found leaders are using cell phones to run their organization and the gang controls the flow of drugs, phones, and cash in prison." (AP News 2008)

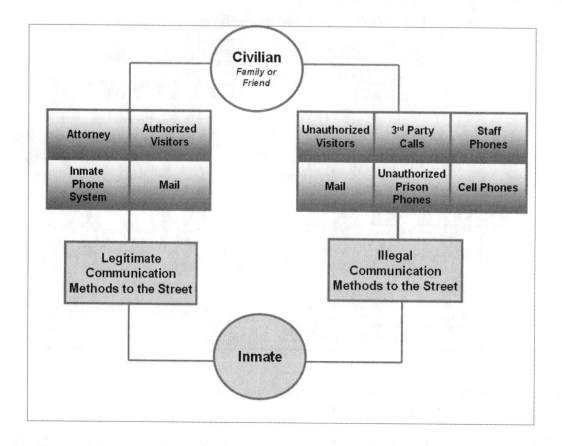

Figure 3: The flow chart above identifies the means of communication between an inmate and individuals in the community.

As stated earlier, the relationships between civilians and inmates have proved to be relevant in contraband network schemes and gang activities. Often the civilian contact receives funds from inmates wanting to "purchase" drugs or send funds to an inmate who has acted as the leader orchestrating the drug transactions. Civilian contacts can also be listed as visitors to inmates with whom they have no true relationship or have never met. These contacts, both the civilian and inmate, are considered drug mules and are the contacts who smuggle the contraband into the secured perimeter. A sample contraband conspiracy is outlined in Figure 4.

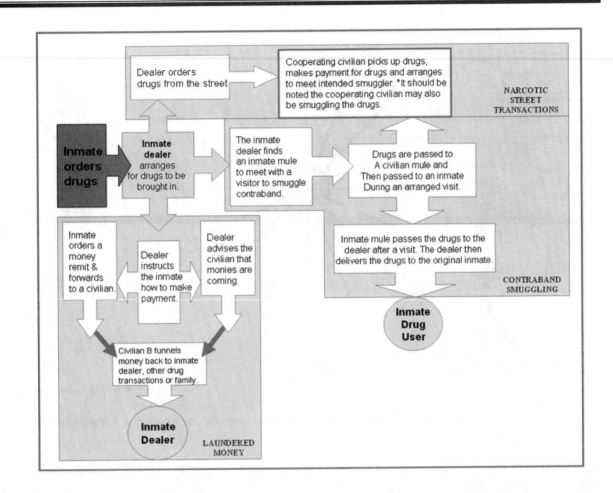

Figure 4: The event flow diagram above highlights the processes for a contraband network.

To uncover possible conspiracies, corrections analysts query data to identify persons who are contacting or visiting numerous inmates throughout the department or civilians frequently contacting or visiting a single inmate. A more extensive version of a contraband conspiracy is shown in Figure 5. In this example, there are 5 civilians and 31 inmates involved in money transfers and 1 inmate-civilian relationship determined through visit information.

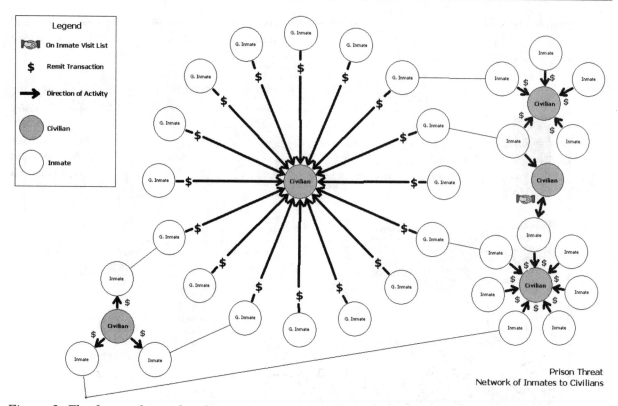

Prison Threat
Network of Inmates to Civilians

Figure 5: The figure above identifies a network of financial and visit transactions between inmates and civilians.

Civilian names appearing on visit and financial transaction data may not be the same person who is actually accepting, contacting, or visiting the inmate. Contraband networks have forwarded funds to the street in names of people who were not aware of the conspiracy or were too young or old to know the difference. Civilians also can be lured to visit someone's "friend" or "relative" to cheer them up. They may unknowingly be part of the conspiracy so a leader can "visit" with them while the leader watches contraband being smuggled by other visitors.

It is important to understand possible data discrepancies and abnormalities because of recent initiatives to warehouse all available data, including corrections intelligence, into data warehouses accessible to all law enforcement. As is the case for any information which has been collected, it is not intelligence until it has been analyzed, the validity verified, and source reliability confirmed.

STRATEGIC ANALYSIS AND ASSESSMENTS

During a 2005 National Public Radio (NPR) program, Andrew Papachristos PhD., an Assistant Professor of Sociology at the University of Massachusetts, Amherst, noted that criminal organizations are operating without concern for borders impacting efforts to combat gang activity (Papachristos 2005). By definition, incarceration implies the presence of strictly defined borders, reinforced by the visual markings of fences and walls surrounding prison facilities. Although the perception and the intention of incarceration is to sever ties, albeit temporarily, between an offender and the community, this has not been possible. Offenders, including gang members, have impacted all parts of the society, including behind prison walls.

Most inmates are still able to contact the public and receive visits—depending on the jurisdiction and institutional protocols. The impetus to stop offending based on an inmate's "residence" may be irrelevant as crime in prison is thought to mirror events on the street.

The maps in Figure 6 highlight how gang intelligence data can be compiled spatially to display the "beyond borders" phenomena. Gang identification data is shown in relation to graffiti, school, and gang incident locations. Overlapping gang data locations can highlight suppression priorities for community law enforcement agencies while providing the data support necessary to implement re-entry initiatives for corrections agencies. The same data will support funding requests for additional corrections personnel in that region as well; increasing gang incidents lead to more suppression initiatives and arrests which ultimately lead to increases in gang inmate population.

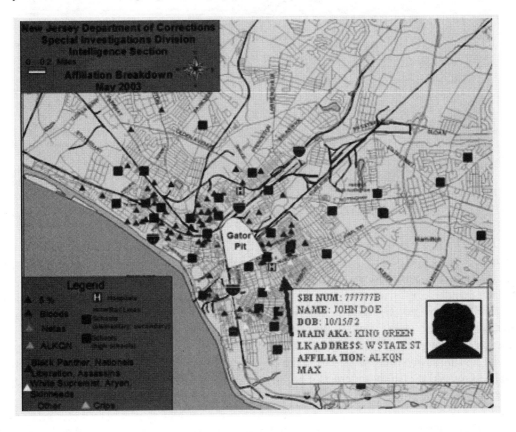

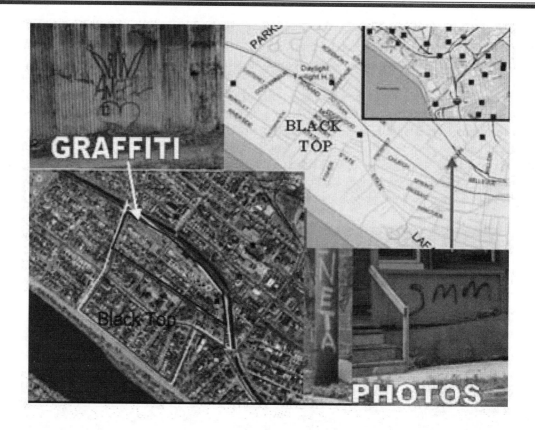

Figure 6: The Affiliation Breakdown map highlights all identified gang members who have been incarcerated. The map and graphics highlight the different methods available to incorporate information from the field and geographic information systems (Johnson 2005).

In the 2005 NPR News special, "The International Reach of the Mara Salvatrucha (MS)," MS member Ernesto Miranda, aka "Smokey," said "in this country, we were taught to kill our own people, no matter if they were from your own blood. If your father was the enemy, you had to kill him. So the training we got during the war in our country served to make us one of the most violent gangs in the United States." (Mandalit Del Barco 2005) In the interest of highlighting the applications of corrections intelligence and its impact on future crime, Figure 7 highlights a growing gang trend.

There are dozens of news articles that discuss gang violence against their own membership or family to include the violent ideology of the MS member directed to take action against their own, if warranted. Increased gang violence usually attracts a gang task force investigation targeting a specific gang with the intent to dismantle or disrupt it. As the task force investigation begins to arrest and prosecute a gang case, the leadership is interrupted and questioned. New leaders begin to ascend to new positions and the gang becomes splintered. Gang inmates begin to question the real leadership and engage in violence during the power play to prove to the new leaders that they are true to the gang. This transition that a gang can go through before and after a targeted suppression effort is highlighted in Figure 7. It illustrates that, prior to the investigation, the gang is operating in two regions with leadership in each area; whereas a new faction of the gang emerges after the investigation. This phenomenon can be identified by monitoring the same corrections communication and contact tools mentioned previously.

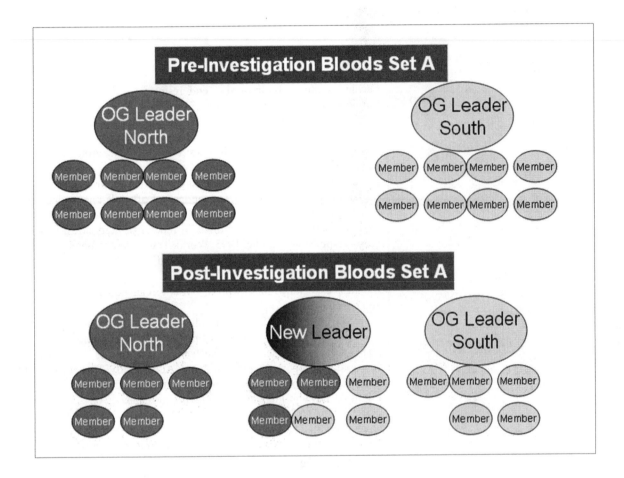

Figure 7: The figure above illustrates how one street gang was disrupted and splintered after a large take-down investigation.

Using the same visit, financial, and phone data outlined previously—analysts are able to query inmates who may have been exposed to radical influences and assemble strategic products outlining new indicators of radicalization attempts behind bars. A sample strategic product outlining potential radicalization indicators and associated threat potential is highlighted in Figure 8.

V. WARNING INDICATORS

Primary Indicators	Threat Level Status	Comments
Spread of Propaganda and Recruitment Material	ELEVATED	Outside sources continuously send re-interpreted Qurans and other religious material to the inmates promoting Islamism. Daveed Gartenstein-Ross, a former Muslim convert who said he worked for the U.S. office of Al Haramain Islamic Foundation for 9 months in the late 1990s, said that no U.S. prison ever rejected the group's literature because of its content.
Arabic Codes and Hidden Messages	ELEVATED	Documents frequently contain messages written in Arabic in a special format to conceal ideas. Due to the lack of officials knowledgeable in Arabic or other Middle Eastern languages, intervention does not happen often. Convicted terrorists in federal penitentiaries, including those responsible for the 1993 World Trade Center bombing, retain communication privileges and have had direct contact with other terrorists.
Recruitment Vulnerability	ELEVATED	Inmates, especially those who are young, can be easily manipulated and deceived.
Prison Gang Activity	ELEVATED	Jamiyyat Ul Islam Is Saheeh, a radical Islamic prison gang prominent in California, has been accused of putting forward a protocol meant to justify attacks on enemies of the Islamic faith, the U.S. government, Jews, Israel-supporters, and "infidels." Additionally, Richard Reid, the British "shoe bomber," attempted to bring down American Airlines Flight 63 through the use of explosives in his shoes on 22 December, 2001, just over 3 months after the 9/11 attacks. He was believed to have been radicalized in prison. Jose Padilla, charged with aiding terrorists and conspiracy to murder U.S. nationals overseas, is believed to have converted to Islam while in prison.
Accessibility	MODERATE	Religious services create arenas for radicalization.
Shortage of Muslim Chaplains	MODERATE	The lack of well-trained Muslim chaplains has led to a reliance on religious contractors and volunteers, especially in state and local facilities. Consequently, contracted religious leaders, volunteers, local endorsing organizations, and even Imams frequently lead prayer and do not have the appropriate experience to do so.

Figure 8: The table above is an excerpt from a strategic product that assesses indicators of prison radicalization (Bruno 2007).

It would be hard to measure the presence or absence of the radicalization indicators listed in Figure 8 for outside law enforcement authorities. However, corrections personnel could easily quantify if there is a shortage of chaplains to serve the inmate population or determine if a potentially radical influence can easily access a vulnerable inmate population. The value of corrections data and subsequent analysis cannot be compared to the value of corrections personnel on the analytical process, specifically the work products compiled by the analytical and investigative staff. Their knowledge of the subject matter, internal practices and policies, data integrity, and availability is most valuable.

CONCLUSION

Corrections intelligence data has been an area that has only recently received acknowledgement as a valuable resource for law enforcement. Corrections data and intelligence products are as important to the operational demands of operating a prison as they are to investigations and strategic planning initiatives for law enforcement as a whole. Regardless of whether an investigation targets contraband smuggling, gang activity, or radicalizing influences which threaten the safety of inmates or the public—incorporating corrections data, analysts, investigators, and intelligence products into the broader law enforcement mission is a worthwhile endeavor.

REFERENCES

Associated Press. (2008). "SCI Says Blood Leaders Rule Behind Bars." *Star Ledger and Asbury Park Press.* <http://www.nj.com>.

BBC News. (2005). "Mexico Seals Off Drug Gang Jail." *BBC News.* <http://news.bbc.co.uk/go/pr/fr/-/1/hi/world/americas/4176675.stm>.

Bruno, M. (2007). Emergence of Muslim Prison Radicalization Growth and its Growing Threat to our Global Society through Recruitment and Expansion. Strategic Early Warning Assessment. Vol. 1. No. 1. New Jersey Department of Corrections, Special Investigations Division.

Bureau of Justice Statistics. (2007). Prisoners in 2007. US Department of Justice, Office of Justice Programs, Bureau of Justice Statistics. NCJ 224280.

Danver, L. (2009). "Drug Ring Bust Nets 35 Arrests." *WishTV8.* June 30, 2009. <http://www.wishtv.com/dpp/news/crime/Drug_ring_bust_nets_35_arrests_20090630>.

Del Barco, Mandalit. (2005). "The International Reach of the Mara Salvatrucha." *NPR News.* Mar. 17 2005. <http://www.npr.org/templates/story/story.php?storyID=4539688>.

Godwin, C. (1999). "Applying Correctional Intelligence to Law Enforcement Investigations." *Correctional Compass.* Oct. 1999.

Godwin, C. (1999a). "Applying Correctional Intelligence to Law Enforcement Investigations." *Corrections Today.* Aug. 1999.

International Association of Chiefs of Police. (2009). Targeting Criminality: Successful Police-Corrections Partnerships. (Video) U.S. Department of Justice, Bureau of Justice Assistance.

Johnson, M. (2005). Using Prison Gang Intelligence from the Inside Out. NJ Department of Corrections. Presented at the 8th Annual Crime Mapping Research Conference. Savannah, GA.

Montgomery, M. (2005). "Prison Gangs Keep a Tight Rein on Members." NPR News. Mar. 12, 05. <http://www.npr.org/templates/story/story.php?storyID=4531910>.

Montgomery, M. (2005a). "Gangs Reach Out of Prison to Commit Crimes." *NPR News.* Mar. 7, 2005.

National Institute of Corrections (NIC). (2008). Sharing Gang Intelligence. Bridging the Gap: Corrections, Educators and Police. United States Department of Justice.

National Law Enforcement and Corrections Technology Center (NLECTC). (2004). Corrections Data Mining. United State Department of Justice, Office of Justice Programs, National Institute of Justice. TechBeat. Fall 2004.

New Jersey Department of Corrections. (2005). Special Investigations Division, Annual Report.

New Jersey Department of Corrections. (2006). Special Investigations Division, Annual Report.

New Jersey State Commission of Investigation. (2008). Criminal Street Gangs and New Jersey's Prison System Public Hearing. <http://www.state.nj.us/sci/index.shtm>.

New Jersey State Police. (2007). Gangs in New Jersey: Municipal Law Enforcement Response to the 2007 NJSP Gang Survey. New Jersey Department of Law and Public Safety, Division of the New Jersey State Police, Intelligence Section.

New Jersey State Police. (2007a). Arrest of Bloods gang members from North Jersey. *Operation targeted leadership of violent 'Sex Money Murder' set.* Official News Release. <http://www.njsp.org/news/pdf/pr061407-smm-arrests.pdf>.

Papchristos, A. (2005). "More Gangs Going Global." *NPR News.* Feb. 23, 2005. <http://www.npr.org/templates/story/story.php?storyID=4509988>.

Public Technology. (2007). Met Police & Prison Service to share intelligence & information. Feb. 2007. <http://www.publictechnology.net/modules.php?op=modload&name=News&file=article&sid=7686&mode=thread&order=0&thold=0>.

United States Census Bureau. (2008). Population Estimates: National and State Population Estimates. <http://www.census.gov/>.

Walmsley, R. (2005). World Prison Population List (Fifth Edition) Findings (234). United Kingdom Home Office.

Wamsley, R. (2007). World Prison Population List. Seventh Edition. King's College London, International Centre for Prison Studies.

Walmsley, R. King's College London. (2007a). The World Prison Brief. King's College London, The World Prison Brief Online. <http://www.kcl.ac.uk/depsta/law/research/icps/worldbrief/wpb_about.php>.

Evaluating the Effectiveness of the Intelligence Operation
By Gary S. Williams

INTRODUCTION

Law enforcement intelligence operations will probably meet significant headwinds in the future as budgets shrink and the memories of September 11, 2001 and the political will of local government to fund anti-terrorism efforts wane. Police departments across the country are having a difficult time dealing with local drugs and gangs, let alone international terrorism. Many in local government believe intelligence and anti-terrorism efforts are best left to the federal government. The truth is that the federal government cannot succeed in the intelligence mission in America without the assistance of state and local law enforcement intelligence efforts. However, those efforts must be effective, totally professional, and above reproach.

While many law enforcement intelligence operations missions have focused on terrorism, law enforcement intelligence is also valuable in dealing with myriad crimes. Intelligence Led Policing holds significant value to crime fighting efforts and is essential to better protect our society from terrorism, gangs, drugs, organized crime, fraud, and other serious crimes. Therefore, it behooves law enforcement leadership to continually demonstrate the value of intelligence. This requires educating government leaders and building trust and confidence to support intelligence by enhancing transparency and effectiveness of operations. Evaluating the effectiveness of intelligence operations provides an opportunity to do all these things and more.

Evaluating the overall effectiveness of the entire operation can be a time consuming and complex task. Law enforcement management must make the commitment of time, effort, and money to take advantage of the opportunity evaluation brings. While the evaluation process is complex in practice, it is rather simple in concept. However, if possible, certain ground rules for evaluation should first be accepted and understood by the CEO, political leadership and those who hold the purse strings. Those ground rules are:

- Law enforcement intelligence is not a "know all, see all" operation. To expect intelligence to always know everything about every specific criminal activity before it occurs is not realistic and is beyond the capabilities of any intelligence operation. While reliable source reporting with "eyes on", the specific potential criminal situation does occasionally occur, it does not occur routinely. Intelligence is routinely involved in making sense of a variety of bits and pieces of raw information about specific potential criminal activity so that a better understanding of it is brought to light and decision makers are better informed. Intelligence is normally a slow moving, meticulous, and complex activity that attempts to point decision makers in the right direction so that appropriate action can eventually be taken.

- Law enforcement intelligence operations generally support enforcement and normally do not directly involve enforcement action. Intelligence is primarily a crime prevention tool that cannot and should not be measured with the same criteria that traditional enforcement functions are measured. The intelligence consumer is the key element in evaluating effectiveness.

CHAPTER 13

Evaluating the Effectiveness of the Intelligence Operation

- The effectiveness of the intelligence operation should be based on documented expectations (objectives) relevant to the stated mission (terrorism or organized crime or drugs etc.) in ways that focus on quality of work and responsiveness to its consumers as well as compliance with all policies, procedures, and relevant legal and security issues.

- Only those people with sufficient training, knowledge, expertise, and background should regularly examine intelligence operations and evaluate effectiveness and compliance.

- This evaluation task should be done by way of officially sanctioned processes and a yearly documented and independent compliance and effectiveness (performance) audit, review, and evaluation.

- The results of the yearly audit, review, and evaluation should be made public without jeopardizing confidentiality issues.

The concept is simple, clearly states the mission, the expectations (objectives) as well as the policies, procedures, and relevant legal and security issues of the intelligence operation and the means by which effectiveness and compliance will be evaluated in a formal approved document. That document then establishes the official criteria for evaluating effectiveness and compliance.

Note: While complying with all the rules is not necessarily relevant to effectiveness, effectiveness and the intelligence operation may no longer be relevant if the rules are significantly violated. Therefore, compliance and effectiveness are tied together and should be examined together on a regular basis.

If possible, the document should be approved by the CEO and those relevant local or state government officials above the CEO, such as the police commissioner, city manager, mayor, state attorney general etc. and should be endorsed by the organization's legal authority, such as the city attorney or legal council etc. The document should be given to all personnel as the guidelines for performance. This guideline document, if appropriately written, could be published and made public in order to enhance transparency of operations.

The guidelines should be a living document that can change with formal approval over time as conditions or policies change. The approval issue is important because it sanctions and legitimizes the process. Relevant high- level city, county, or state leadership is telling the public they serve that this is what they expect from intelligence operations and this is how effectiveness will be measured. They are also saying that they support intelligence operations. "The bean counters" must then abide by it, but then again, so must the intelligence operation.

Note: Nothing written here suggests that management be relegated to only the methodologies and processes presented here. Obviously, management must use all the tools in the management toolbox to lead, direct and control personnel and unit performance. There are myriad important issues that must be continually examined and evaluated by direct supervision and management, on an ongoing basis, to include the expectations. And, there are numerous publications explaining how to audit and evaluate intelligence procedures, policies, processes, and security issues. The evaluation discussed here is more about the overall effectiveness of the entire operation in order to maintain accountability, a process of continuous improvement to garner support and funding and less about the technical issues of evaluating procedures, systems, and processes.

CHAPTER 13

Evaluating the Effectiveness of the Intelligence Operation

EXPECTATIONS OF EFFECTIVENESS

The following is a list of possible expectations on which effectiveness could be evaluated. In essence, the expectations define what effectiveness is and what it looks like. The expectations must be relevant to the mission and must be within the capabilities of the intelligence operation. Merely meeting the expectations equates to at least minimal effectiveness; however, as the evaluation process reveals areas of quality, and responsiveness, heightened levels of effectiveness should be realized and brought to light. This can be a significant element in a continuous improvement process. Compliance with all policies, procedures, and relevant legal and security issues are obviously desired but there may be issues of minor non-compliance and room for improvement as well. Significant abuse and/or significant non-compliance of issues such as constitutional rights, reasonable suspicion standards and/or security issues; however, are the subject of great concern and follow-up beyond this process.

The expectations listed below are very broad based examples and could be used within several different mission scenarios (terrorism, drugs, organized crime etc.) and they can be scaled and/or written to meet the potential realistic capabilities of any intelligence operation; however, they should be challenging. Relevant to the stated mission, examples of expectations are, but may not be limited to:

- Supporting decision makers by providing intelligence and information that increases the agency's ability to prevent criminal activities

- Supporting criminal investigations by providing intelligence and information that increases the agency's ability to successfully solve cases and assist in prosecutions

- Identifying suspects and groups relevant to the mission in which reasonable suspicion exists to be a potential criminal threat to the community, region and/or the country

- Supporting at least one of the agencies major objectives through effective intelligence operations (such as preventing criminal activity or solving cases etc.)

- Providing quality and responsive intelligence to the CEO, management, and other appropriate agency decision makers, regarding criminal activity in the region, state, country, and/or the world

- Complying with all stated policies, procedures, relevant legal issues, and security mandates

- Providing valuable and timely information to agency law enforcement personnel regarding relevant crime trends, threats, vulnerabilities, and potential crime related risks

- Providing valuable and timely information to agency law enforcement personnel regarding the intelligence process, the value of intelligence and information sharing systems, and processes that lead to Intelligence Led Policing

- Developing and maintaining meaningful relationships and a valuable system for communication with law enforcement personnel inside and outside the organization for the purpose of information sharing

- Developing and maintaining meaningful relationships and a valuable system for communication with relevant community members and groups such as corporate security personnel and other relevant community components, for the purpose of information sharing

- Providing valuable support to relevant federal, state, and local intelligence efforts, such as fusion centers and federal task forces

Complying with the stated expectations equates to at least a minimal level of effectiveness. It is the evaluation of all available data that then determines the level of effectiveness beyond compliance.

QUANTIFYING EFFECTIVENESS

The intelligence operation does not lend itself well to the traditional ways of measuring law enforcement effectiveness such as crime statistics, arrests, filings etc. There are intelligence activities that can be quantified but have little value in determining effectiveness. However, determining the extent that an expectation is met is the exception and could include a numeric value. Determining the extent that an expectation is met is valuable in that it helps define the value of the efforts involved and the level of effectiveness beyond mere compliance. For example, if the intelligence operation supported preventing just one criminal activity event in a year it meets the expectation, but it would require further scrutiny to determine the value of that effort and personnel time involved in that one investigation. That one investigation could have been a huge case that demanded hundreds or even thousands of personnel hours and saved lives or millions of dollars. However, if the case garnered far less than that volume of effort and results, further examination would be required to determine the real value and level of effectiveness. In essence, the number gives the evaluator an indication of the amount of work involved, as well as an indication of the level of value and operational effectiveness beyond mere compliance, but only an indication, further follow-up is always required.

Counting activities is normally used when examining productivity, if that is an issue, but the issue here is effectiveness. State and local government officials know that numbers can be used in many innovative ways. Looking productive by way of numbers may be interesting but having appropriate oversight, being accountable, being effective, and complying with all the rules are the things that government leadership should be most interested in.

Good law enforcement intelligence is a reliable and timely product of a process that makes raw information meaningful and useful to decision makers. It enables decision makers to make good judgments that prevent crime and assist in the arrest and prosecution of criminal suspects and groups. To be effective, the intelligence operation must be of high quality and responsive to the needs of those decision makers. Therefore, decision makers and other consumers of the intelligence are key in the evaluation of effectiveness, not numbers!

FOCUS OF EVALUATION

Evaluating the effectiveness of the intelligence operation is a somewhat subjective process that should focus on quality and responsiveness. Those things that equate to quality are knowledge, clarity, objectivity, and reliability. Those things that equate to responsiveness are timeliness, usability, and relevance. Quality intelligence is the reliable communication with knowledgeable insights of possible criminal activities, communicated clearly and objectively. Responsive intelligence is timely communication of relevant information that can be used to prevent crime and/or arrest and prosecute criminals and/or identify possible criminal suspects and criminal groups and/or identify possible crime trends, threats, vulnerabilities and risks. Put quality and responsiveness together and you have defined the qualities of effectiveness and the value of intelligence.

There are other expectations or objectives involved in intelligence operations, such as teaching the intelligence processes and the value of intelligence and building relationships and systems for the purpose of information sharing. They must also involve quality and responsiveness. Training or teaching requires, knowledge, clarity and reliability of the subject matter and meeting the needs of those being trained with useful, timely and relevant information. Building relationships and systems for the purpose of information sharing requires knowledge, clarity and reliability of information so that useful, timely and relevant information flows seamlessly back and forth in order to detect and prevent crime. Providing valuable support to federal, state, and local intelligence efforts involves sharing quality and responsive intelligence, information and /or resources that are valuable to their efforts.

Compliance with all stated policies, procedures, and relevant legal and security issues must also be determined. All of these issues must be flushed out in the evaluation process. Each of the expectations must be scrutinized to determine the following:

- Were the expectations met? To what extent were they met? (This is the only time a number might be appropriate but it must be tempered with the examination of quality, responsiveness and value to determine the extent of effectiveness).

- Were the products and/or communications produced knowledgeable, clear, reliable, objective, useful, timely, and relevant?

- How did the relevant decision makers and other consumers rate the overall efforts as they relate to quality, responsiveness and value?

- Were all policies, procedures and relevant legal and security issues complied with? If not, what was the extent of non-compliance? Did any non-compliance result in serious negative impact on the intelligence operation and/or the organization?

- What are the areas of needed improvement?

- Has the intelligence operation been effective relevant to the expectations?

It should be noted that there will always be room for improvement in many of the expectations. Intelligence is a human endeavor and therefore will never be perfect; however, perfection is not required to be effective. The value added component of evaluation is finding areas of needed improvement so that enhanced quality and responsiveness of operations, and therefore effectiveness, can occur on an ongoing basis.

Understanding what must be examined in order to evaluate effectiveness is the easy part, actually doing it is much more time consuming. Therefore, it is important to determine what methodologies garner the most transparency, trust, and support and at the same time get the job done in a credible and professional manner. There are two such methodologies that can be used and it is recommended that both methodologies be used in some form to maximize accountability, transparency, support, and overall effectiveness.

EXECUTIVE MANAGEMENT EVALUATION

Evaluation comes with a certain amount of subjectivity. Those closest to the work may be less able to critique the work than those somewhat removed when it comes to evaluating the effectiveness of operations. Executive management review and evaluation can be a more independent examination to determine effectiveness because it comes from those at least a step above the operation. And, they are consumers of the intelligence, so who better to evaluate it?

While one could argue that even executive management evaluation is not really independent or unbiased, it is more independent and therefore more credible than an evaluation done by those people directly involved in supervising the work. That's not to say direct supervision and management are not credible and should not be evaluating the work. It is to say that those of a higher rank and further removed, look at issues with more "unassuming and independent eyes." They may ask questions that require more fully grounded explanations. As consumers they also see areas of needed improvement and/or areas of quality and responsiveness. If executive management has established credibility with the political leadership and the public, this effort will also be seen as more credible.

Executive management review also gives the CEO, if he/she so desires, the opportunity to see and hear first hand the relevant issues, needs, strengths, and weaknesses of the operation and make his/her own evaluation. This can be critical for maintaining oversight, accountability and providing information that goes to enhance executive management's understanding, trust and support of the intelligence operation.

Executive management review and evaluation could be part of an ongoing executive management intelligence briefing process that should occur on at least a quarterly basis (monthly is most desirable). Case briefings give executive management the knowledge and intelligence it requires to make better decisions about deployment of personnel and other enforcement and/or crime prevention related issues. It is also an opportunity to ask questions about the progress of cases and determine work effort, quality, and responsiveness. It can also be part of the planning and direction process of the intelligence cycle. The briefing process lends itself well to the question and answer technique of the COMPSTAT process practiced by local law enforcement in many cities and counties throughout the country.

In essence, the executive management case briefing and review/evaluation process could be an Intelligence COMPSTAT without the traditional computerized statistics, if done appropriately. There are obvious issues of security and "need and right to know" but they can be easily overcome by limiting attendance to only "need and right to know" personnel and by appropriately dealing with the other security issues. However, this would not be the time to discuss classified intelligence unless all relevant federal security issues were dealt with.

If no other evaluation and report was going to be done, the evaluation could be documented in a confidential manner that briefly delineates relevant information for a general evaluation of effort, quality, responsiveness and overall effectiveness. It could be used later for a yearly evaluation of effectiveness report, which if written appropriately to protect sensitive sources and methods, could be made public. This would enhance transparency and public trust.

Evaluating the Effectiveness of the Intelligence Operation

NOTE: This type of evaluation is not based on a comprehensive performance and compliance audit of the entire operation but rather a snapshot of the work presented at the briefings. There would have to be some staff follow-up beyond the briefings in order to evaluate total effectiveness. There would also have to be some form of a data-capture system to show the extent of expectations achievement. Surveys or interviews of relevant intelligence consumers could be utilized in order to rate products and efforts toward the expectations. Compliance audits should be conducted on a quarterly or semi-annual schedule in order to determine if all policies, procedures, processes, relevant legal and security issues are being followed. This is normally done under the oversight of direct intelligence management or by executive management's staff auditors.

INDEPENDENT AUDIT, REVIEW, AND EVALUATION

There is another level of evaluation that could occur in addition to or instead of agency executive management evaluation. Appropriate independent yearly audits, review, and evaluation of compliance and performance are rigorous in-depth examinations of operations and bring a higher level of trust or confidence in the process and its results, particularly if they are made public. Relatively few agencies employ truly thorough and independent audits or evaluations of any aspect of its operations, let alone its intelligence operation. This usually only occurs when things go drastically wrong and the agency is forced to do it because of court action and/or public outrage. Independent evaluation may be costly and requires outside personnel that have requisite skills, knowledge, abilities, and integrity to do a truly thorough, fair, and objective job. Also, as it relates to intelligence, there are issues of security and confidentiality of concern. However, these issues can be overcome and, in fact, have been overcome by a few agencies throughout the country.

Compliance audits normally involve examining work product to determine if it meets existing standards and policies. Intelligence compliance audits normally examine intelligence files, written policies, standards, procedures, and relevant legal issues and security mandates to determine compliance. Performance audits examine work quality, productivity (if that's an issue), and goals/objectives achievement. Compliance and performance audits/evaluations are compatible because the materials being examined, along with the ability to interview or survey personnel and relevant people, allow auditors/evaluators to gain insights into compliance, quality, responsiveness, and effectiveness of work.

The aforementioned criteria (expectations) to evaluate effectiveness could be utilized in an independent performance/compliance audit and evaluation. Obviously, the people conducting the audit and evaluation must be appropriately trained, screened, and have the necessary skills and abilities. A COMPSTAT process would not be used by outside evaluators. An interview and/or a survey of consumers, if appropriately done, could gain valuable information for evaluation. The examination of classified information and/or intelligence would not occur without federal government approval and appropriate security measures, including clearances. If this process is officially sanctioned it gives those doing the evaluation and audits the "need and right to know."

Some agencies have utilized appropriately trained and vetted police commission staff or inspector general staff or other trusted and respected people to conduct independent audits. Others have utilized outside law enforcement intelligence practitioners that have already been vetted and trained as part of their present or past law enforcement assignment. One such highly trusted and respected group that can do this type of audit and evaluation is the Association of Law Enforcement Intelligence Units (LEIU). While these services come at some monetary costs, their independent audit, review, and evaluation can be highly productive in terms of enhancing accountability, building quality through continuous improvement, demonstrating effectiveness, and building trust and confidence in the intelligence operation.

CONCLUSION

Since the calamity of September 11, 2001, law enforcement authorities have devoted time and taxpayer money building numerous intelligence operations throughout the country. It must ensure itself and the public that those operations are truly professional, valuable, and effective.

Evaluating effectiveness of intelligence operations cannot be done appropriately by using traditional measurements. The evaluation of effectiveness should focus on quality and responsiveness. Users of the intelligence produced are the key elements in evaluating quality and responsiveness. Intelligence operations should define what effectiveness is by utilizing documented expectations (objectives). Its expectations of effectiveness along with its mission, policies, procedures, relevant legal and security issues, and the means by which effectiveness and compliance will be evaluated should be placed in a single officially sanctioned document. That document should then be used as the official criteria for evaluating effectiveness and compliance.

Agency executive management should be part of the evaluation process in order to enhance accountability, improve quality, and improve its knowledge of intelligence and the intelligence operation. An annual independent audit, review, and evaluation of effectiveness and compliance should be conducted and should be made public. The appropriate evaluation of intelligence operations made public brings opportunities to enhance accountability, operational effectiveness, and transparency that would garner public and political support. Large to midsize agencies with significant intelligence operations and/or state or locally managed fusion centers, with similar expectations, should consider some form of executive management and independent audit review and evaluation of effectiveness as well as compliance. One or the other will be helpful for any agency or entity, regardless of size. However, to do nothing, almost guarantees failure to maintain necessary support and funding in the long term.

Training and the Intelligence Unit
By Marilyn B. Peterson

INTRODUCTION

Training is key to any progress made by law enforcement regarding an intelligence led model of policing. Nowhere is this more true than of the training needed for intelligence and analysis to be fully integrated into the forefront of law enforcement operations. This in turn requires a re-orientation of the law enforcement agency towards an appreciation and use of intelligence as a proactive tool. Achieving this calls for a coordinated training effort directed toward non-intelligence unit personnel and command officers, as well as toward intelligence managers, officers, and analysts. Without this comprehensive approach, intelligence efforts may fail. By contrast, adopting this approach can lead to an integrated, efficient organization, staffed by committed and competent professionals, able to function both as individuals and as organizational team members.

The training given at these five levels will be somewhat different. Despite these differences, the training at each level, and for each role, needs to form a part of an integrated whole. Each individual should develop skills and appreciation not just for his/her own role, but for those of colleagues, and how these translate in the workplace to achieving real, recognizable organizational benefits. Whatever the different approaches, the goal is to make the most of information that is collected and to have informed decision-making occur based on the analyzed intelligence information.

NON-INTELLIGENCE PERSONNEL TRAINING: RECRUIT, PATROL, INVESTIGATION

The largest audience for training is non-intelligence unit personnel, including recruits, patrol officers, and investigative personnel. Training for these professionals should focus on giving them a familiarity with the intelligence process, and crucially, their role in that intelligence process, as well as what they can expect from others. It should prepare them to understand, contribute to and benefit from the intelligence process.

Recruit Training

Intelligence training should begin with an introduction to intelligence in basic recruit classes. Some police academy basic courses now spend an hour or two on intelligence. These classes may concentrate on field report writing as an input to the intelligence process rather than what the intelligence unit can do for the field officer; thus many enforcement officers believe that intelligence does not benefit them. Their image of the intelligence unit is often one of an inaccessible fortress of filing cabinets inhabited by strange officers and civilians mysteriously pushing paper instead of making arrests. The concept of intelligence guiding investigations and proactive police deployments has yet to be effectively communicated to the law enforcement community.

Intelligence should not be a mystery. Any general training program for law enforcement officers should have, as its first goal, the elimination of the mystique surrounding the concept of intelligence. There are no secrets about the process; it is simply the collection, analysis, and dissemination of information that is sensitive. Perhaps the best way to achieve this understanding is to have an intelligence staff person address recruit classes (Harris 1976:46) and explain the process.

If possible, a case study of how analysis has contributed to the unraveling of an important criminal conspiracy might be used. This kind of presentation should emphasize the laborious aspects of "making matches" between previously unconnected people, businesses, places, or groups. The actual methodology should be described--or better yet, demonstrated with students being involved in a hands-on exercise--so the students can judge for themselves how simple, yet painstaking much of intelligence work is (Harris 1976:47). The main emphasis here is raising the awareness of the recruit to the intelligence process, and to their own importance, both as future "first line" sources of raw information, and as consumers of intelligence products.

Patrol Training

Officers on patrol are an excellent, yet often unused, source of data for the intelligence section. The precinct or beat is a large source of reportable information. Patrol officers are closest to what is going on in crime and the environment in which crime exists. It is for this reason that an effort must be made to encourage police officers to observe and report their observations. This is part and parcel of the "community policing" and "problem solving policing" philosophy. Good reporting techniques have to be inspired by the knowledge that their contributions are of utmost importance.

An appropriate intelligence-oriented curriculum for the local patrol officer could be:

- Intelligence Process; officers; roles, history of intelligence, community policing, information sharing, data systems, networks and resources (50 minutes)
- Indicators of criminal activity and overview of collection methods and sharing systems, sources of information and terminology (40 minutes)
- Ethics, legal basis, liability, right to privacy (40 minutes)

(Global Intelligence Working Group 2007)

Investigations Training

The division between intelligence and investigations is non-existent in some police agencies and a large chasm in others. Ideally, officers would be assigned exclusively to intelligence and eschew investigations, but most agencies do not have the luxury of this designation. Even in those agencies with specified intelligence sections, the investigative divisions must still complete some of the same processes and methods as are used by intelligence specialists. After all, cases must be investigated and the process of gathering, collating, analyzing, and disseminating information is integral to an investigation. However, the work of intelligence in law enforcement cannot be subjugated to the more reactive investigative function if it is to be an effective tool for decision-makers at the tactical and strategic levels.

Because of the need for analysis to also support investigations, it is imperative that all personnel assigned to investigations be given some form of intelligence/analytic training. This training should be provided to personnel upon becoming a detective or investigator. Many agencies send these individuals to standard analytic training offered by a private or government vendor. This level of training may be beyond the absolute need of the officer in question as it may be more detailed than necessary, lasting for three to five days. A scaled-down version of that type of training is outlined below and would be less time-consuming and more on point to the newly assigned investigator.

- Intelligence Process (1 hour)
- Intelligence Report Writing (1 hour)
- Inference Development (1 hour)
- Crime Pattern Analysis (1 hour)
- Organized Crime (1 hour)
- Link Analysis (2 hours)
- Telephone Record Analysis (2 hours)
- Criminal Proceeds (1 hour)
- Practical Exercise (2 hours)

While one can rely on outside vendors for this type of training, it may be more economical to provide this from within, using on-staff intelligence officers and/or analysts, or leveraging relationships with organizations such as the Association of Law Enforcement Intelligence Units (LEIU) and the International Association of Law Enforcement Intelligence Analysts (IALEIA).

COMMAND OFFICER TRAINING

The main objective of command level training should be to demonstrate what intelligence led policing can do for management and what assets the intelligence unit should have at its disposal to do the necessary job of strategic support for the decision-makers. Specifically, command officers need to recognize that the intelligence process can provide administrative support for issues such as budget support, the proper allocation of personnel and awareness of potential criminal threats to the jurisdiction. Successful command training will generate an overall understanding of the command officer's role in the intelligence process and general support for the intelligence function.

The concept behind this approach is one which is reiterated throughout this volume: the component parts of the process must be understood thoroughly to appreciate the intelligence process and to be able to exploit intelligence effectively. The command-level officer who lacks a full understanding of the intelligence unit functions and needs, will be unable to grasp why he/she is being asked to provide investigators for the intelligence unit, how the overall effectiveness of the unit can be measured, or offer any reasonable resistance to the public prosecutor who wants to "let up a little on hijacking investigations and concentrate on gambling." (Harris 1976:51-52)

Command-level training must be significantly different from patrol, recruit, or investigative training. First, it is an informational or even 'infomercial' type of training; that is, the basic philosophy and concepts must be sold as well as imparted. Second, commanders respond better to their colleagues or outside 'experts.' Thus, the training programs usually cannot be put on frequently or in-house, but are rather as multi-agency endeavors that are hosted by a police association, intelligence organization, or state/federal agency. A police association may sponsor annual short programs for command-level personnel of the municipalities and counties in the region. In some states, such a training program might be given by a state police academy for the benefit of county and municipal police.

Typically, intelligence training for executives might include the following:

- National Criminal Intelligence Sharing Plan, Information Sharing Environment Implementation Plan, fusion center concept and the executives' role (1 hour)
- Intelligence led policing philosophy and practice (1 hour)
- Intelligence process and its value (2 hours)
- Legal, privacy and ethical issues relating to criminal intelligence (1 hour)
- Information on criminal information sharing networks and resources available (1 hour)

(Global Intelligence Working Group 2007)

"Command level training is the most demanding obligation of all. It will necessitate severe intellectual retooling for students and instructors alike, with all the psychic hazards this implies for the latter. The training content should have a single major theme: what intelligence can do for the command level. Minor themes would usually cluster around several topics related in some way to the main theme: breakthroughs in intelligence techniques, new strategies of the organized criminal, managing the intelligence process, recent court decisions, intelligence limitations, and so forth." (Harris 1986:51)

TRAINING INTELLIGENCE OFFICERS

Training police officers to be intelligence specialists require practical instruction on how to collect, evaluate, collate and analyze (Harris 1976:46). Of necessity, this training is much longer than that received by other officers or commanders and can be anywhere from one to three weeks in length.

The intelligence process should be at the heart of the training. "This process, which consists of a continuous series of interrelated intellectual activities, is not familiar to most people. It requires a mental discipline—a habit of mind and energy—which, although not unique to the law enforcement professional, must in great part be learned rather than developed from job experience" (Harris 1976:47). In addition to the intelligence process, training should be provided in specific types of crime that may be investigated, ethics, and other professional development topics. At this level, training should take on a 'learn by doing" approach so that the methods and techniques are integrated into the intelligence officers' skill set.

The model suggested by Harris in 1976 is shown below:

Intelligence Theory and Organized Crime (5-6 hours)

Considerable attention should be given to the role of intelligence in the battle against all forms of organized crime. The students should see intelligence as a tool to develop points of focus for intensive investigation leading to the ultimate decision that an attempt should be made to build a case. This phase of the introduction would involve exploration of both indications (or warning or danger signals) of intelligence and strategic (report on existing or potential patterns of activities) intelligence (Harris 1976:48).

CHAPTER 14

Training and the Intelligence Unit

Crime in the Jurisdiction

The intelligence officers' training should include a block devoted to the target itself—the types of crime in the jurisdiction against which intelligence will make the most effective contribution. It should concentrate on developing areas of criminal activity, white-collar and public corruption, as well as more traditional criminal areas (Harris 1976:48).

The instructor may ask the class a series of questions to stimulate thinking about crime in their jurisdictions. To what extent have street gangs grown up to be the nuclei of self-perpetuating criminal conspiracies? Do several loosely held bands of criminals cooperate with one another for specific ventures or in particular districts of the metropolitan area?

- **White Collar Crime** - Similarly, the intelligence officer must be encouraged to think beyond the traditional types of criminal activity previously associated with organized crime, such as gambling, narcotics, fencing and loan sharking. White-collar crime such as securities manipulation, credit card fraud, computer-aided fraud, new forms of extortion, and sophisticated rackets involving the physical security industry are the fields where organized crime may be moving next (Harris 1976:48).

- **Public Corruption** - Emphasis on corruption techniques of organized crime against government officials is, at this stage of training, only the first introduction of a theme that should be woven throughout the program. That theme is, clearly, the susceptibility of any law enforcement agency to penetration by organized crime. Dramatization of the impact of corruption on a city might be one approach. A discussion led by the head of the internal affairs squad—or the agency head itself—might be another (Harris 1976:49).

Ethics and Integrity

Basic ethics training should be done in every agency at the recruit and higher levels. What is under discussion here, however, is an effort to detail the devious techniques organized criminal figures use to entrap law enforcement officers, or place them unwittingly in positions from which illegal obligations can later be extracted. An audience of intelligence officers would be an excellent forum for a discussion—perhaps conducted by an attorney—of systemized approaches to anti-corruption measures (Harris 1976:49).

Analytic Techniques

The most difficult step to clarify in the intelligence process is analysis. Since almost all intelligence problems are one of a kind, no single set of re-usable guidelines can be offered to the students. A few "self testing questions" are applicable to all analysis; that is to say, there are questions the analyst should ask about all data that come his/her way that might be helpful. By asking (and answering) these questions, the new intelligence analyst does not achieve an overnight mastery of the analytic process, but he/she will be getting closer to an understanding of what is expected of an analyst (Harris 1976:49).

Training of analysts must go beyond the use of technology tools and information resources. It must include training on how to think; this includes critical and creative thinking skills. Also vital to a successful analytic product is the ability to clearly and concisely communicate the results of the analysis. This entails training in intelligence writing (which is very different from the traditional law enforcement report writing) as well as briefing skills. The best intelligence will not be acted upon if it is communicated in an ineffective manner.

Beginning with two or three scraps of raw information that point to the existence of criminal activity in a certain field, the analysts must learn to ask:

- What other information would I like to have to complete the picture?
- What other information am I likely to obtain relatively rapidly and economically—that is, what information can I get that will be worth the effort?
- Given additional information, do I perceive a new dimension in the problem?
- What is the critical element in the problem?
- Can I match any of the materials on hand with other information in storage (files or computer) to broaden my understanding of the whole problem?
- Assembling all the pieces, can I now reconstruct the problem?
- Do the results present a clearer picture than the one I had before I started the process?
- Can I draw from this new overall picture a significant judgment of some kind?
- How confident am I of my judgment; have I indicated the degree of my confidence in my judgment statement?

More sophisticated analytic techniques should be described to the class and, if possible, field exercises should be conducted using some of the techniques. Also, subjects such as the identification of real estate ownership, hidden corporate management, and gathering evidence of skimming operations, should be introduced. These subjects do involve highly technical knowledge but an introduction to these areas may stimulate the students to reach out for new techniques, or even one day to perfect analytic techniques of their own in other fields (Harris 1976:49). Harris proposed that intelligence officer training further include numerous skills including report preparation, technical training, security training and other topics (Harris 1976:50-51).

It may be desirable to "contract out" some or the entire intelligence officer training program to a private vendor or larger police agency, or assemble a staff from various agencies to teach it. The instructional staff to support these types of classes might better be arranged through a HIDTA, RISS project or organizations such as LEIU or IALEIA. (See Chapter 17 "Networks, Organizations, and Resources")

GLOBAL INTELLIGENCE WORKING GROUP MODEL

The multi-agency Global Intelligence Working Group created criminal intelligence officer training, recommending a minimum of 40 hours of training for these individuals. The breakdowns of time allotted to varied objectives were:

- Criminal Intelligence process and the role of intelligence officers (5 hours)
- Legal, ethical, and privacy issues surrounding criminal intelligence (6 hours)
- Information on resources, information sharing systems, networks and other sources of information (4 hours)
- Proper handling of criminal intelligence information, file management and information evaluation (6 hours)
- Development of tactical and strategic products and participate in that development (6 hours)

- Developing criminal intelligence through the critical thinking/inference development process (5 hours)
- Building and implementing collection plans (5 hours)
- Intelligence officer roundtable (3 hours)

(Global Intelligence Working Group 2007)

ROYAL CANADIAN MOUNTED POLICE MODEL

Another model, suggested by the Royal Canadian Mounted Police (RCMP), encompasses three weeks. Each block is four hours unless otherwise noted:

Week 1

Day 1:
    Intelligence Process (2 hours)
    History of Organized Crime (2 hours)
    Introduction to Agency Organized Crime Database
Day 2:
    Public Sources of Information
    Law Enforcement Sources of Information
Day 3:
    Physical Surveillance Techniques (8 hours)
Day 4:
    Inference Development and Logic (2 hours)
    Physical Surveillance Practical Exercise (6 hours)
Day 5:
    Criminal Intelligence and the Law
    Evaluation and Collection

Week 2

Day 6:
    Database Development
    Traditional Organized Crime
Day 7:
    Association Analysis
    Telephone Record Analysis
Day 8:
    Electronic Surveillance (8 hours)
Day 9:
    Flow Analysis
    Bank Record Analysis
Day 10:
    Electronic Surveillance Practical Exercise (8 hours)

Week 3

Day 11:
Non-traditional Organized Crime
Informant Management
Day 12:
Criminal Intelligence Report Writing
Criminal Intelligence Briefings
Day 13:
Strategic Intelligence Products (8 hours)
Day 14:
Money Laundering
Asset Forfeiture
Day 15:
Analytic Practical Exercise (6 hours)
Graduation

(116 hours total) (Peterson 1998:25-26).

This course gives officers the ability to not only act as collection officers, but also to perform rudimentary analysis and prepare basic analytic reports. This is particularly helpful in situations where analysts are at a minimum or are separated by distance from the investigations.

INTELLIGENCE MANAGER TRAINING

Intelligence managers or supervisors also require training. The individuals filling these positions are often rotated through for two or three years and may have no previous intelligence experience. They may not know what intelligence is or what to expect from those who report to them.

One model for intelligence manager or supervisor training could be accomplished in 16 hours and would include:

- Intelligence led policing and the role of the criminal intelligence manager (3 hours)
- Managing the intelligence unit (2 hours)
- Principles and regulations of handling sensitive information, informant policies and corruption prevention and recognition (2 hours)
- Legal and privacy issues (3 hours)
- Producing tactical and strategic products and the development and implementation of collection plans (4 hours)
- Information on criminal information sharing systems, networks and resources available (2 hours)

(Global Intelligence Working Group: 2007)

TRAINING INTELLIGENCE ANALYSTS

The most rigorous intelligence training must be provided to the analysts who form the lynchpin of the intelligence process. They must have the skills and models to approach any set of data regarding any type of crime and analyze the data, arriving at conclusions and recommendations for action. While in the 1980s only a handful of agencies had analysts in their employ, by 2000 thousands of analysts worked in the United States alone (Taylor 1999:6) and their number may have at least doubled after the terror attacks of 2001.

The genesis of intelligence training began in 1970 with the courses offered by Anacapa Sciences, at the request of the California Department of Justice. Both a one week and a two week course were developed by Anacapa, including topics such as:

- intelligence process
- inference development
- association matrices
- link charting

- telephone record analysis
- event flow charting
- net worth analysis
- visual investigative analysis

In addition to still offering these courses, Anacapa now also offers preliminary online courses including an introduction to intelligence analysis, collection tradeoffs, and critical thinking, (Anacapasciences.com) it has also been joined by numerous universities, agency schoolhouses and private contractors who offer basic analytic training.

The development of analytic training by Anacapa was followed by other similar courses over the next decade or so. The Drug Enforcement Administration, for example, has a ten week basic course for its analysts which include components on analysis, report writing, law, investigations, physical training, weapons training, and other topics. The Federal Bureau of Investigation, on the other hand, has a several month course for its new analysts. Through the High Intensity Drug Trafficking Areas (HIDTAs), etc. other versions of analytic training have evolved. The General Counterdrug Intelligence Plan created by the U.S. President's Council on Counter-Narcotics recommended a comprehensive drug intelligence training and education curriculum be established for analysts, including management and leadership training for federal, state and local law enforcement agencies (CNC 2000:44).

One concept of analytic training is to have levels of training; that is the basic training, followed by intermediate training, followed by more advanced training. But some agencies only provide one course to their analysts and thus prefer longer course at entry-on-duty. Some of the topics of advanced analytic training have included financial analysis, strategic intelligence, more in-depth courses on particular analytic methods and courses in specific criminal areas (counter narcotics, terrorism, organized crime, human smuggling, etc.).

One model for basic analytic two-week training might include the following components:

- Introduction to Analysis (1 hour)
- Intelligence Process (1 hour)
- Law Enforcement Sources of Information (3 hours)
- Public Sources of Information (3 hours)
- Critical Thinking (2 hours)

- Logic (2 hours)
- Inference Development & Recommendations (2 hours)
- Evidence Handling (1 hour)
- Agency Databases (3 hours)
- Crime Pattern Analysis (4 hours)
- Association Analysis (4 hours)
- Telephone Record Analysis (4 hours)
- Flow Analysis (4 hours)
- Financial Analysis (6 hours)
- Testifying in Court (2 hours)
- Organized Crime (2 hours)
- Money Laundering (2 hours)
- Asset Forfeiture (2 hours)
- Ethics (2 hours)
- Professional Development (2 hours)
- Strategic Analysis (6 hours)
- Practical Exercise (6 hours)

The Global Intelligence Working Group arrived at a consensus on a model for analytic training. It reflects at least 40 hours of training:

- Intelligence process, intelligence led policing, information sharing framework, the role of analysts (3 hours)
- Handling and collating criminal intelligence information , its management and evaluation (2 hours)
- Critical thinking, logic, inference development, and developing recommendations (4 hours)
- Developing and implementing collection and analytic plans (2-3 hours)
- Legal, privacy and ethical issues relating to intelligence (2-3 hours)
- Information on sources, information sharing systems, networks, centers, databases and other sources of information (3 hours)
- Methods, tools and techniques employed in analysis (16 hours)
- Report writing, statistics and graphic techniques (4-8 hours)

(Global Intelligence Working Group 2007)

The FIAT (Fundamentals of Intelligence Analysis Training) developed by IALEIA, LEIU and the National White Collar Crime Center in 2003 is a one-week course that is taught around the United States. It is based on the Global Intelligence Working Group analytic training standards and meets the requirements for basic training in the IALEIA certification process. Its topics include:

- Introduction to Intelligence Analysis (History of Intelligence Models, Analysis, Purpose of Intelligence Analysis, Intelligence Cycle, Legal Issues, Resources)
- Intelligence Analysis as a Thought Process (Fundamentals of Logic, Critical Thinking, Creative Thinking, Inference Development, and Recommendations Development)

- Analysis Methods & Skills (Crime Pattern Analysis, Association Analysis, Flow Analysis, Communication Analysis, Financial Analysis, Strategic Analysis, Indicator Development, Products of Intelligence, Reports and Presentations) (IALEIA 2008)

Another model for analytic training being taught in the U.K. includes a generic course of background, intelligence processes, charting, crime pattern analysis, data sources, standard products, personal skills, and legal issues followed by specialized courses including:

- Crime Pattern Analysis
- Behavioral Analysis
- Comparative Case Analysis
- Open Source Collection
- Financial Analysis
- Courtroom Skills
- Strategic Analysis
- Forensic Science Awareness
- Communications
- Law Awareness for Analysts 1

Agency-specific analytic training often includes detailed blocks on agency databases, proprietary software, agency sources of information, document exploitation, agency procedures, agency-specific report writing, sophisticated software tools, etc. These tailored blocks can add days or weeks to the analytic agenda.

INSTRUCTOR COMPETENCIES

With the growth of the analytic training 'industry,' there has been a movement toward developing instructor competencies for analytic trainers. Train-the-trainer courses have been created for courses like the IALEIA/LEIU/NW3C FIAT course so that distributed learning could occur. The IALEIA Analytic Standards suggest that persons teaching analytic courses should have practitioner experience in the field to qualify as analytic instructors.

Analytic courses are not only taught in agency schoolhouses. Several colleges and universities have taken up the challenge of teaching both undergraduates and graduate analytic skills so that they may be better qualified to apply for analytic positions. In some cases, these courses are taught by retired analytic professionals, in others they are taught by individuals who have done extensive research in this area.

Specific competencies for instructors, in some cases, include at least:

- Four year college degree
- Three years analytic experience
- Completion of a basic instructor's course

---

[1] For more information contact National Criminal Intelligence Service, UK. Website: <www.ncis.co.uk>

.

- Passing a train-the-trainer course
- Being evaluated successfully by a senior instructor
- Participating in continuing education on the subject as available.

CONCLUSIONS

Whatever the venue or topics, intelligence training is critical to an effective intelligence-led policing strategy. There should also be some care taken in finding instructors for these training blocks. Those with the most to share are naturally those with experience as intelligence officers and analysts. One additional form of training that would benefit this effort is instructor training for the intelligence professionals so they will be capable of teaching appropriately. Police agencies have methods of instruction (MOI) courses that could be tailored to work with intelligence concepts, products and exercises. Combining intelligence experience and instructional excellence is a worthy goal of an intelligence MOI.

REFERENCES

Anacapa Sciences web site, <*www.anacapasciences.com*>; accessed 12/26/2008.

Council on Counter-Narcotics (CNC) (2000) General *Counterdrug Intelligence Plan* at <*www.whitehousedrugpolicy.gov/gcip*>.

Global Intelligence Working Group (2007) *Minimum Criminal Intelligence Training Standards for Law Enforcement and other Criminal Justice Agencies in the United States Version 2.* Washington, DC: Global Intelligence Working Group

Harris, Don R. (1976) Basic *Elements of Intelligence Revised.* Washington, DC: Law Enforcement Assistance Administration.

IALEIA website, "FIAT Training", at <*www.ialeia.org*>, accessed 12/28/2008.

Peterson, Marilyn B. and R. Glen Ridgeway. (1990) "Analytical Training in Today's Law Enforcement Environment". IALEIA *Law Enforcement Intelligence Analysis Digest*. Vol. 5, No. 2. Winter. pp. 10-24.

Peterson, Marilyn B. (1998) "Criminal Intelligence Training". *Issues of Interest to Law Enforcement: Criminal Intelligence: A Vital Police Function*. February. pp. 23-26.

Taylor, Jr., Danny L. (1999) *IALEIA Journal.*Vol. 12, No. 1. February.

Security and the Intelligence Process[1]
By Paul Roger

INTRODUCTION

Law enforcement agencies have a legitimate requirement to collect and store information as a vital part of their function. This information, by its very nature will be sensitive and will be of a personal or operational nature. As such, privacy and security implications must always be at the forefront of information custodians' minds. Information that is not afforded adequate protection may be misused (either deliberately or accidentally) or alternatively it may be possible for unauthorised persons to gain access to the information and use it for unlawful purposes, or for purposes that infringe on the rights of individuals.

Misuse of law enforcement information can be damaging to an agency's operations and reputation and can also place individual's lives or reputations at risk. Complacency and lack of due attention to security and control procedures can be a major contributing factor to the misuse or unauthorised access to information. Alternatively, misuse of information may also result from corrupt behaviour within the organisation holding the information.

To ensure that opportunities for misuse are kept to an absolute minimum, it is important that an organisation has:

- Appropriate safeguards and protective measures in terms of physical storage of information, both electronic and hard copy

- Adequate internal controls governing access and use

- Suitable supervision to ensure procedures are adhered to

It is equally important that management and staff:

- Are aware of, and understand, the security needs of their organisation

- Implementing suitable checks and balances, adopt an approach that encourages both personal and corporate integrity

---

[1] This chapter has been prepared as an updated version of the chapter written by the same author and included in Intelligence 2000 – Revising the Basic Elements.

THE INTELLIGENCE UNIT AND SECURITY

While all staff of an organisation has a duty to ensure security obligations are properly met, an intelligence unit's approach to security will be more extensive, with greater emphasis on the protection of the unit's staff, assets, and information. The reasons for this are twofold.

- Firstly, the intelligence function of a law enforcement agency is, perhaps, one of the most sensitive areas in respect of the collection, storage, and use of information. Not only could the misuse or unauthorised release of intelligence information jeopardize an agency's operations, but such release could also be extremely harmful to the individuals concerned – particularly when the intelligence is yet to be confirmed or verified.

- Secondly, the very nature of an intelligence unit's work and the information it holds significantly increases the risk of the unit and its staff being targeted by organized criminal elements for infiltration and corruption.

Security – Musts

Security is a series of procedures and measures which, when combined, provide protection of:

- People from harm
- Information from improper disclosure or alteration
- Assets from theft or damage

The basic premise on which all successful security systems are based is that no single security measure is, by itself, relied upon. To be effective, a system must comprise a number of complementary "layers" that provide checks and balances and multi-level protection. This is often referred to as the "security in depth" approach.

In ensuring that intelligence information is being appropriately and securely dealt with, consideration must be given to the "security layers" that can be applied in respect of:

- **Personnel** - The intelligence unit **must** take steps to ensure that all members of the unit are of the highest possible integrity, with no personal circumstances or links to criminality that may see their integrity questioned.

- **Physical Accommodation** - The unit **must** ensure it is physically secured at all times and that only authorised personnel can gain access to the intelligence work area.

- **Information Handling** - When handling information and files, intelligence personnel **must** adopt work practices that ensure information is processed in such a way as to prevent unauthorised access to their work.

In general terms, the unit **must** take all appropriate measures to restrict knowledge of the unit's activities to as few persons as possible to avoid any compromise of those activities.

Suitable security measures relating to staff and the operational environment will ensure that intelligence material is handled, processed, and used in a manner, which is commensurate with its sensitivity and, at no time, is placed at risk. This will be achieved by ensuring that:

- The capture of intelligence material and the methods used are properly controlled
- The storage of intelligence material is secure
- The validity of intelligence material is confirmed
- The integrity of intelligence material is maintained
- The intelligence material is only available to persons deemed to have a need to know or need to access the material for authorised purposes
- Disseminated intelligence material is only used for its intended legitimate purpose
- Transmission of intelligence material is via secure means
- There is overall management control and appropriate accountability for the intelligence system and related procedures

Privacy Considerations

It is important to understand that, in addition to protecting against any compromise of the intelligence unit's activities, the security system also has an important role in protecting the right to privacy of individuals. A great deal of the information captured for intelligence purposes is drawn from allegations, unverified reports of activities and associations, and other sources where the veracity of the information has not been fully tested.

With this in mind, intelligence unit personnel and their managers **must** be fully aware of their responsibility to maintain a security system not only for protection of their own operations but also for the protection of individuals' rights, by preventing the inadvertent leakage of unsubstantiated information that might be damaging to the person, or persons, to whom the information refers.

Security – Must Nots

While the importance of security in protecting against any compromise of the intelligence unit's activities can never be overstated, it is important that security procedures are not applied to an extent where they impede the flow and use of intelligence products. Godfrey and Harris (1971:93) highlighted this fact in discussing a number of areas for which security policy should not be used to excess. These areas are still relevant today; and, in this respect, when preparing security policy and guidelines, the intelligence unit should note the following.

Security **must not** be used to exclude authorised persons with a legitimate need and right to know from accessing intelligence reports and findings. Intelligence is only of use if it is available to clients who need it in a timely way. It is of little use if retained purely for the knowledge of intelligence personnel. Once a consumer's *need to know*[2] is determined, and found appropriate, the intelligence material should

---

[2] **The concept of 'need to know'** involves not allowing access to information to those who do not need it to perform their job. For example, staff in an intelligence unit have no need to know the terms of employment of other staff within an organisation, so they are denied access. Staff working in the personnel section of the agency have no need to know details of Intelligence targets so they are not told. It is important to stress that access is by need and not solely by virtue of position, rank or level of security clearance within an agency. Even a person with

be made available. The intelligence unit may place security conditions on the intelligence material and security obligations on the recipient in respect of how the material should be handled. However, the purpose of such conditions should be to ensure the material is suitably actioned by the appropriate people with regard to its sensitivity, not to prevent it from being seen.

Security **must not** be used to conceal reports from the jurisdiction's political leadership or other representatives who are not members of the law enforcement agency. Nor should security be used to prevent documents from being used for prosecution purposes, even though the sources may be highly sensitive.

Security must not be used to conceal or cover up mistakes or corrupt activities by members of the unit or agency.

Introduction Summary

This brief introduction highlights how the sensitive nature of intelligence necessitates that security procedures must be an integral part of an intelligence unit's day to day function. The adherence to sound security procedures should enhance the morale of the agency as a whole providing strong resistance to misconduct and corruption. It should also encourage a greater flow of intelligence from within the agency due to the confidence in the security of the intelligence unit.

The main objective of security should be:

To maintain the integrity of the intelligence unit, its staff, and its information.

This objective is best achieved by applying a "security in depth" approach in respect of the following areas:

- Personnel Security to assure the personal integrity of the organisation's staff
- Physical Security to protect the organisation's accommodation and assets
- Information Security to protect information against inadvertent use or unauthorised access

These areas are discussed in more detail in the following pages in order to give readers a basic insight into the steps that should be taken to maintain the integrity of the intelligence process.

PERSONNEL SECURITY

Personnel security is the means or procedures, such as selective investigations, record checks, personal interviews, and supervisory controls, that are designed to provide reasonable assurance that people being considered for access to classified information are loyal and trustworthy (Watson, et al. 1990:435). The sensitivity of the intelligence area, and the information it handles, requires that staff engaged in intelligence work be subject to extensive background checks prior to their employment or transfer to such areas. Staff security vetting is a process that checks a person's identity and verifies his or her

---

the highest level of security clearance may be denied access to particular information on a basis that there is no 'need to know'.

background, character, and financial situation, in order to ascertain – with a degree of certainty – that the person is trustworthy, discreet and of suitable integrity for employment and access to classified material. This process goes beyond the basic pre-employment checks, as it does not necessarily follow that a person suitable for employment within the general stream of duties in an agency is automatically suitable for access to secure areas and classified material.

The integrity of a person can only be determined by probing the background of the person, his or her past employment history, associations, and lifestyle. In discussing background investigation, Godfrey and Harris (1971:94) described the process as "...not a perfect system by any means;" however, experience has shown that when done thoroughly, background security vetting does provide an effective means of establishing a person's suitability for employment.

All intelligence staff must undergo initial vetting and be security cleared before commencing employment. Security vetting is a voluntary process and the potential staff member must consent to their background being investigated for the purposes of employment. Naturally, if consent is not given, employment will not be considered further as the obtaining of an appropriate *security clearance* [3] would be a prerequisite for employment. Once employed, staff should be required to report any changes in personal circumstances, and undergo periodic security checks, to confirm continued suitability for intelligence duties.

Initial Security Vetting – Background Investigation

Initial security vetting of a potential employee is conducted by way of a background investigation that should probe all aspects of the person's professional and personal life. The investigation should seek to detect indications of lack of character or lack of integrity. Godfrey and Harris (1971:94) correctly pointed out that a person who lacks integrity in their personal life – for example, in past dealings with family or associates – should be considered a potential risk to act without integrity in a professional capacity, at some time in the future. Similarly, during a background investigation, inquires with past employers will assist considerably in judging the person's suitability for intelligence duties.

To assist in conducting the background security investigation, the person under consideration should be requested to complete a security vetting questionnaire – providing both personal and financial information. The questionnaire should require the person to provide full and accurate information in respect of the following:

- Personal details, including previous names
- Family details, including spouse and children
- Current and past residential addresses
- Education history, including places of education
- Employment history, including contact details of past supervisors
- Travel movements (if applicable)
- Details of any criminal convictions
- Details of any other adverse encounters with the law, including traffic offences
- Financial details, including savings, investments and assets

---

[3] A security clearance is an administrative determination that an individual is eligible, from a security standpoint, for access to classified information' (Watson, *et al.* 1990:505).

The questionnaire should conclude with a certification by the person as to the accuracy and completeness of the information provided. The person completing the questionnaire should also be required to provide certified copies of supporting documentation such as birth certificate, marriage certificate, passport, driver license, and education/professional qualification certificates.

Consent to Conduct Enquiries

Verification of the provided information will require the investigator to approach other agencies and third parties, such as universities. In this respect the person under vetting consideration should be requested to complete a suitable form providing consent for information to be provided to the investigator.

The background security investigation armed with the information from the questionnaire, and the consent form, the officer performing the background security investigation can then conduct independent checks to verify the information provided and explore any particular areas that require further evaluation. When appropriate the investigating officer should seek additional information by contacting persons previously associated with the person under consideration such as past educators, past employers, family members, neighbors, etc.

It is essential that the investigator carefully evaluates all information available on the subject of the investigation and that a balanced and informed assessment is made of the individual's reliability and trustworthiness[4]. An assessment of the subject's maturity, responsibility, tolerance, honesty, and loyalty in past situations will enable conclusions to be drawn regarding the suitability of the subject.

It is also essential that the investigator verify the legitimacy of any documents provided by the subject. With the ease of access to sophisticated graphic software, it is not difficult today to produce high-quality certificates and other documentation that to all intent and purpose appears genuine. Checks must, therefore, be made with the issuing authorities to confirm that the claims made by the applicant are authenticated.

Any information that casts doubt over the subject's integrity or character must be fully explored to a point where the information is either corroborated or discredited. For example, as Godfrey and Harris (1971:94) discussed, it would be of little value to simply report an allegation that a previous landlady felt the subject was an undesirable tenant because of noisy parties and wild goings-on that caused complaints from neighbors. The investigator would be duty bound to ascertain the character of the landlady and her relationship to the subject. The investigator would also have a duty to check the allegation with the neighbors and to ascertain if other information was available regarding the subject's social activities. If the investigator were simply to report that the allegation could not be substantiated, it would be open to conclude that in the absence of other evidence, there remains a possibility that the criticism reflects accurately on the subject's social life. If, on the other hand, details of the additional information gathered during evaluation are included in the investigator's report, a clearer record is created. If the additional information enables the investigator to draw a firm conclusion, the record not only facilitates

---

[4] The Commonwealth of Australia Protective Security Manual (2006) defines 'Character Assessment' as the balanced and informed estimation of an individual's reliability and trustworthiness which is derived from comprehensive checks on identity, background, personal values and behaviour.

the removal of any doubt as to whether the allegation is substantiated or discredited but also ensures that the matter is clarified once and for all.

If the investigator is unable to draw a firm conclusion regarding a particular allegation and doubt remains as to the subject's character or integrity due to the allegation, then the matter should be raised with the subject. Such a procedure is delicate and should be undertaken with care and pre-planning. A formal but friendly atmosphere is recommended for such confrontations. Often, the subject's responses will provide sufficient additional information to enable the matter to be clarified. If not, the confrontation will provide an opportunity for the investigator to observe the subject's reactions and body language, which will contribute to the investigator's assessment of the matter.

In addition to probing the personal background of a person under consideration for employment in an intelligence role, it is equally important to examine the person's financial standing. Such an examination will determine whether the subject is in any financial difficulty. A poor history of financial responsibility could cast doubts on the subject's reliability and responsibility in other areas of life. On the other hand, financial problems have the potential to place a person at risk of compromise in the form of corruption or blackmail.

The subject's financial information should be cross-referenced with other lifestyle and employment information to provide a more complete assessment of earnings and expenditure. Additionally, the recording of an employee's financial information at the commencement of employment provides a base for future comparisons should any allegations be made regarding unexplained wealth or changes in lifestyle.

On commencing employment, intelligence personnel should be briefed on the security requirements of their position. They should be advised that, during their employment they are required to report any changes in personal or financial circumstances in order that an assessment can be made as to whether the changes impact on their security clearance. They should also be advised that, in addition to any changes they report, they will also be required from time to time to undergo periodic security checks to confirm their continued suitability for intelligence duties.

Periodic security checks should involve an updating of the initial background security investigation, focusing in particular on the officer's personal life and financial status. Any significant changes to the officer's previous profile should be investigated. For example, if social activities are found to have changed and there is evidence of increased spending or substantial borrowing, explanations should be sought for the changes. While increased income may have a legitimate source, if no apparent source can be identified the subject officer may fall under suspicion of corrupt activity. Alternatively, increased borrowing could indicate the subject officer may have financial problems and may be vulnerable to corrupt approaches.

Periodic security updates should be conducted at regular intervals, for example, every two years. Personnel should be advised of these procedures and encouraged to actively participate as part of the unit's anti-corruption strategy. Pride in the integrity of the unit and its personnel should be the over-riding objective.

Notwithstanding the regular security procedures, the unit commander always retains full authority to order a background security investigation of one of the unit's staff at any time. The commander, after all, is responsible for the overall integrity of the unit. If there is any suspicion regarding the integrity or character of one of the unit's personnel, the commander should act immediately rather than wait for the next periodic security check. Any delay in acting on such suspicions would expose the intelligence unit to an unacceptable risk of serious damage.

PHYSICAL SECURITY

From a law enforcement intelligence unit perspective, physical security involves the steps taken by an agency to provide physical barriers that prevent unauthorised access to premises and information, and protect personnel from physical harm. This is best achieved by having systems that enable premises to be secure when unattended and for access to be monitored. Persons authorised to access the intelligence unit should wear appropriate ID passes at all times when in the unit, and any visitors should be issued with ID passes that clearly show their visitor status, and they should be escorted. The security system should include electronic keys and audit logs of all access. In addition to secure access to the unit, all information and related documents should be stored in secure containers such as safes, strong rooms or secure lockable cabinets, when not in use.

With appropriate physical security in place, personnel within the intelligence unit should have confidence that they can work freely without fear of compromising their material.

The Physical Environment

The location of the intelligence unit should be given careful consideration in order that the unit may be given the optimum protection. If at all possible, an area that handles extremely sensitive information should not be located on the ground floor of the agency's accommodation. Nor would it be wise to locate such an area close to a main entrance or busy corridors. To reduce the risk of unauthorised persons accessing the intelligence area, it is wiser to locate the unit above the ground floor and in a quieter part of the agency accommodation where there is less passing traffic.

The physical work environment of the intelligence unit must be secure at all times, with access restricted to authorised personnel only. This is best achieved by issuing all unit personnel with identification passes, which must be worn in a visible manner at all times while working in the unit and by utilising a single controlled access point, which requires unit personnel to use individual unique security pass keys to move through secure doors. Modern technology provides numerous access security systems, ranging from simple electronically coded keys and proximity cards, to the more sophisticated biometric systems that recognize individual attributes such as voice, fingerprint and retina. By using electronic security systems, a security audit log can be generated for all movement into and out of the unit. Where there is a necessity for visitors to enter the unit for legitimate work-related reasons, there must be a physical method of identifying the visitor and recording their access. A common method of recording visitors is to use a register, which can be completed with the following details:

- Date of visit
- Name of visitor
- Agency or organisation the visitor represents
- Name of the officer to be visited
- Time of the visitor's arrival
- Time of the visitor's departure
- Signature of the visitor

On completion of the register, visitors should be issued with, and instructed to visibly display, a temporary visitor's pass while within the intelligence unit.

During normal working hours, the responsibility for recording access to the unit by non-unit personnel should rest with a specific staff member. Outside of normal working hours, the unit should be secured to the extent that only unit personnel using their security pass keys may gain access. Movement detectors and internal surveillance cameras can provide additional levels of protection for the unit when unattended. If such devices are installed, they must be linked to an alarm system, which is monitored on a 24-hour basis; for example, in the agency's main operational control room.

Building regulations and work place safety requirements usually require that offices have more than one exit in case of fire or other emergency. Within a secure intelligence unit such exits should be designed for "emergency flight from the unit only." All emergency exits should be alarmed so that, if they are opened at any time, attention is immediately drawn to the fact that the security of the unit may be at risk.

Secure Hard Copy Storage

Physical (hard copy) Intelligence files and source documents, when not in use, should be centrally stored in a separately secured dedicated area. This provides for a further level of security and also enables additional controls to be placed on the movement of material.

The build for the central storage room should ensure the walls are slab to slab, rather than floor to ceiling, as many modern ceilings are in fact a false ceiling with open cavities above for air-conditioning and fire sprinkler systems, etc. The walls and door should also be constructed from fire resistant/fire proof materials.

Access to the file room should be restricted to a small number of staff, usually those with designated registry of filing roles. Access should be through a single door which has the same access control system as that used for the unit as a whole. All movement of files to and from the file room must be recorded by the registry/file room staff to maintain an audit trail of access and to maintain a record of the location of files at any given time, should the same material be required by other staff.

With modern technology, and dependent on the needs of the unit, technology such as RFID (Radio Frequency Identification) tracking and management tags can be affixed to files and documents and their location recorded by the use of suitable RFID readers.

Secure Storage Containers

When in day-to-day use, it is sometimes impracticable to return all material to the central storage repository. In such cases, intelligence personnel must have access to their own secure storage containers. In seeking to protect documentary information, the storage container in which the information is contained is the last line of defense. Storage containers must provide an adequate level of protection commensurate with the sensitivity of the material to be stored.

Various types of secure containers are available ranging from high-security containers-such as a fireproof combination and key safes - through mid security containers such as a key lock safe or a metal filing cabinet with additional locking bar and padlock to the lower level secure filing cabinet with key.

A risk assessment should be conducted regarding the sensitivity of the material requiring storage to identify the appropriate type of container required.

Clear Desk Policy

An additional security measure to prevent unauthorised access or knowledge of information is to ensure that all staff practices a "clear desk policy"[5] when absent from their work desk for an extended period of time. This will include securing material in appropriate containers as discussed above, and either logging off computer systems or implementing a password-protected screen saver. This type of security practice is particularly important in work areas that have open plan accommodation and where compartmentalization is difficult. It is also an important practice, on occasions, where an intelligence officer is seconded to assist another investigation unit, at a location outside of the intelligence unit that may not be afforded the same level of security as the intelligence unit.

Physical Security Checks

To ensure compliance with the above requirements and the clear desk policy, regular physical inspections should be conducted of the intelligence unit's work areas. Unattended desks should be checked to ensure no classified material has been left unattended, security cabinets should be checked to ensure that when unattended they are locked. A regular security check should also be conducted at the end of normal office hours. Where breaches of security procedures are discovered, the officer discovering the breach should take immediate action to secure any material appropriately and a breach notice should be issued and the unit commander advised in order that follow up action can be taken. Such breach notices are often referred to as Security Infringement Notices, or SINS. Serious breaches, or frequent minor breaches by the same officer, would necessitate disciplinary action.

INFORMATION SECURITY

Information security is the process of protecting information and safeguarding it against unauthorised disclosure. When handling information and files, intelligence staff must adopt work practices that ensure information is processed in such a way as to prevent unauthorised access. Information security systems are based on the principles of accountability and protection. It is axiomatic that, in order to be able to account for information, there must be a record of its existence. It is also axiomatic that, some items of information are more sensitive than others and therefore require a greater level of protection. These principles are recognized by the use of a system that not only records information but also allocates security classifications and restrictions to differing levels of information sensitivity.

Classification Systems

Information should be allocated a security classification dependent on its sensitivity and the level of protection it requires. The criteria for assessing the sensitivity of files or information are, at best, subjective. That is to say, a personal judgment factor enters into most decisions as to whether a file, or particular piece of information, requires special treatment and protective handling. When making such

---

[5] "Clear desk" and "clean desk" can be used interchangeably with the same meaning.

assessments, consideration should be given to the amount of damage that could result at the time or in the future from any unauthorised disclosure, alteration or destruction of the information.

Commonly used classification systems usually employ four distinct categories of classification, for example:
- Un-classified, Restricted, Confidential, Secret
- Un-classified, In-confidence, Protected, Highly Protected
- Unclassified, Confidential, Secret, Top-Secret

Such classifications are a form of caveat that warns the recipient/user of their responsibility and liability with regard to the security of the information. As a general rule, the level of classification should be kept to a minimum -consistent with affording adequate protection to the information. The urge to apply a higher classification when in doubt should be resisted. Over-classifying can result in expensive storage and auditing measures and ultimately bring the system into disrepute.

In addition to utilizing a classification system, similar to those described above, the intelligence unit can also introduce a range of subject indicators that provide for additional categorisation of information. The use of technology and various computer software packages enables subject categories to be an integral part of the intelligence unit's database. The database records should clearly indicate the various subject matters covered in each document and also indicate any restrictions that are placed on the use of the material. For example an un-classified piece of information may be marked 'for [Agency name] use only' or 'not for further dissemination'. Current operationally sensitive information may be marked 'not to be disseminated to other units without owner permission' (the owner being the operation manager). In this way, personnel accessing the database should be able to quickly identify not only the classification level of the material, but also the matters the material relates to and whether there are additional restrictions placed on the material's use. Such restriction may be removed at a later date when a period of operational sensitivity passes.

An additional level of security used by some agencies is to use special security paper in addition to other caveats. Such paper makes each particular hard copy document unique, should there be more than one copy of the document. This approach is particularly relevant to the more highly classified material that cannot be passed electronically and requires to be disseminated as secure hard copy material.

IT System Security

To ensure appropriate and secure use of IT systems for the processing and analysis of intelligence data, the following minimum level of controls should be considered:

- Each staff member should be issued with a unique user ID and password.
- Staff should be required to keep their password confidential and to change it regularly.
- User profiles should permit various actions within the IT system, and restrict others. For example, read only access, or read and write access, etc.
- Access to systems should be regularly reviewed, to ensure user profiles remain current.
- User access should be cancelled immediately on the transfer of a staff member or on cessation of employment.

- IT Systems should have appropriate security layers and store all transactions, providing an audit trail.
- Data should be stored on central secure servers and not on individual desk tops (PCs /notebooks, etc).
- Computer screens should have timed log outs or screen locks when screen remains inactive for a period of time (say 5 minutes).
- A comprehensive backup regime for all data should be in place.
- If the system allows access to the internet, suitable firewalls and intruder detection procedures must be in place, and up-to-date virus software installed.
- Rules regarding the use of e-mail must be clearly articulated and system procedures in place to prevent the transmission of classified material via e-mail, or as an attachment to an e-mail.
- The use of portable data recording devices, such as thumb dives/USBs, discs, MP3 players and mobile phones, must be strictly controlled.

Storage of Intelligence Material

Intelligence information should be stored in both hard-copy and electronic format. Hard-copy source documents must be retained in order to verify data recorded electronically. In addition to providing for secure storage of documents, as discussed under the heading of "Physical Security", the intelligence unit must also have procedures in place to provide for appropriate backup copies of electronic data.

Backup copies of electronic data should be created on a regular basis and stored at a separate secure location. Backup procedures provide a full record of the data at any given time in the past. This can be useful if an allegation is made that the data has been tampered with. The existence of a full backup of electronic data also ensures a minimal amount of data is lost should a disaster of some type (for example a total system failure or fire) strike the intelligence unit. Collation methods and appropriate storage procedures-for both electronic and hard copy material-should be detailed in written procedural instructions. The procedures should provide for appropriate security and specifically nominate who is responsible for such material.

Access to electronically stored data should be subject to strict authorisation, with appropriate procedures in place to ensure security is maintained. Authorised access should only be granted on a need-to-know basis and each user uniquely identifiable through secure user ID's and personal passwords. Individual user ID's coupled with appropriate structuring of data storage procedures, will restrict access to only that data to which that user has a need to access. All access transactions should be logged, and procedures should exist for audits to be conducted in this respect. Such procedures should cover both reactive and proactive auditing. Audits should be documented and available for inspection.

Included within access controls are any facilities that allow extraction/transfer of electronic data (for example, downloading from a central database to other applications such as a PC database or software graphics package). Any such facilities must be subject to strict control procedures, as access to such extracted data must also be maintained for audit purposes.

Although seen by some as inconvenient, the use of disks and portable drives (such as thumb drives) should be strictly controlled. This type of additional security approach will not only help to prevent unauthorised copying of electronic records but will also help to guard against damage by computer viruses or malicious code that may be imported electronically through the use of disks or direct downloads/electronic transfers of data. Suitable security precautions against this type of threat should include:

- Strict control over who has the ability to change the operating system and applications software
- Strict procedures controlling the import of software or documents from external sources
- Compulsory use of virus checking software for all imported software and documents before being loaded onto the unit's main system
- A suitable decontamination plan should damage occur

Integrity of Intelligence Material – Quality Control

In additional to preventing unauthorised access to intelligence data, it is equally important that procedures are in place to ensure that the integrity of intelligence data is maintained. Relevance, accuracy, and reliability are major considerations in respect of integrity. These factors are particularly important in respect of electronic databases, which are accessed and relied upon more frequently than hard-copy material. As such, intelligence databases should be subject to a specified process of quality control, with a dedicated member of the intelligence unit being responsible for checking new data after collation to verify if it is free from error and that it has been correctly classified and stored.

Dissemination of Intelligence

The security of the intelligence unit and its information systems also extends to the dissemination of intelligence material, either at the unit's own initiative or in answer to requests from other units or agencies. Intelligence information should, under no circumstances, be provided to non-law enforcement agencies. When disseminating to a law enforcement agency, care should also be taken to ensure that the receiving agency has appropriate procedures in place to ensure that the security of the information is maintained at an appropriate level.

It should be clear to all staff within the intelligence unit who has the authority to authorise the dissemination of intelligence material. This authority will ordinarily rest with the commander/officer in charge and/or one or more of the senior managers of the unit if the unit is large. Procedures should provide for a record to be kept of all disseminations; highlighting the data disseminated the reason for dissemination, to whom and by whom it was disseminated, and how the information was disseminated.

Where a request for information is received from outside of the unit, procedures should detail how an individual intelligence officer should receive and respond to the request. The identity of the requesting officer and the reason for the request should be carefully considered in order to verify if the request satisfies the need and right to know principles. Records of all disseminations should be available for auditing.

In respect of the actual physical transmission of intelligence material, the intelligence unit should have clear procedures regarding how intelligence material - both hard-copy and electronic copy - should be dispatched. Such procedures should provide for appropriate security through the use of suitable packaging such as double enveloping, receipt books, and methods of transmission. Electronic dissemination should only be made via closed inter-agency systems where encryption is available. Classified intelligence material should never be disseminated as part of, or an attachment to, an email via the public internet. Extremely sensitive material should only be dispatched via a secure "safe-hand" system. All records and receipts should be retained and available for inspection.

RESPONSIBILITY OF THE UNIT COMMANDER/OFFICER IN CHARGE

While all staff members have an obligation to maintain security, the intelligence unit commander or officer in charge has a particular responsibility for the effectiveness of an intelligence unit's security system and related policies and practices[6]. The unit commander must take steps to ensure that appropriate procedures and guidelines are in place to ensure the integrity of the unit and its information is not placed at risk. In this respect the commander must ensure that all unit staff is of the highest integrity and that they have a thorough awareness of the procedures and guidelines governing their work particularly in respect of the collection, storage, and use of intelligence and the requirement for appropriate security safeguards. The commander must also ensure that the unit's accommodation is suitably located and physically secured to prevent unauthorised access or misuse of the unit's information.

To assist in meeting security obligations, the unit commander should appoint a specific security officer who has responsibility for the development of security policies and procedures and ensuring security policies and procedures are implemented and adhered to. All personnel within the intelligence unit should be afforded ready access to the security policies and procedures under which they are required to operate (Commonwealth of Australia, 2006). The security officer should also be responsible for educating and training staff in respect of their security responsibilities. It is useful to conduct initial security awareness training of all new staff on commencement of employment in the unit, and have the staff member sign an acknowledgement of their understanding of the security responsibilities. Further training should be conducted on a regular basis to ensure currency. Where a breach of security is identified or suspected the unit security officer should take initial responsibility for any preliminary investigation, reporting to the unit commander.

Security Risk Review and Protective Security Plan

To ensure a rational approach is taken to identify security threats, risks and vulnerabilities, the unit commander should develop a *protective security plan* [7] appropriate to the unit's functions and the security risks it faces. This is best achieved by requiring that a Security Risk Review be undertaken at regular intervals, at least annually. The outcome of this review process and the resulting protective security plan will ensure the commander is in a position to effectively deploy appropriate resources to counter any perceived threats.

---

[6] See for example – The Commonwealth of Australia "Protective Security Manual", 2006. While this publication discusses security responsibilities from an organisation perspective, the responsibilities are equally applicable to unit and section heads, particularly in areas such as intelligence units, where sensitive information is processed and stored.

[7] Protective Security is a term used to describe an organised system of defensive measures that are instituted and maintained with the aim of maintaining the safety of people, information and assets (Watson, *et al.* 1990:466).

CHAPTER 15

Security and the Intelligence Process

SUMMARY

The uniqueness of the intelligence unit's function requires that the unit adopt additional security precautions to those practiced by other units within its parent agency. These requirements will require additional budget and will, therefore, require the unit commander to justify the expenditure. In some instances, a lack of understanding on the part of other areas within the agency may result in some resistance to the intelligence unit commander's security requirements. However, perseverance on the part of the unit commander should succeed in demonstrating that adherence to sound security procedures will not only protect the agency against compromise but should also enhance the morale of the agency as a whole by providing strong resistance to misconduct and corruption.

If appropriate policies and procedures are in place and understood by intelligence personnel and by the agency as a whole, the opportunity for misuse of information – either intentionally or accidentally – is considerably reduced. By limiting opportunity and providing appropriate accountability through audit trails and designated lines of responsibility, these procedures not only prevent misuse but also provide for a suitable investigatory tool to assist in detecting any breach, should one occur.

CHAPTER 15

Security and the Intelligence Process

REFERENCES

Commonwealth of Australia, 2006. Protective Security Manual. Commonwealth Government Printer, Canberra.

Godfrey E & Harris, D, 1971. Basic Elements of Intelligence. U.S. Government Printing Office, Washington DC.

Roger P, 2000, Chapter 12 in Intelligence 2000: Revising the Basic Elements. Joint publication of LEIU & IALEIA.

Watson B, Watson S, & Hopple G, (Eds). 1990. United States Intelligence, an Encyclopedia. Garland Publishing, New York.

Criminal Intelligence Software Applications
By Chris Rogers

INTRODUCTION

In October 2002, the Markle Foundation Task Force issued its first report, *Protecting America's Freedom in the Information Age*. The report articulated the need for an information-sharing network consisting of information collection, analysis, communications, and sharing—a network empowering those participating in the information-sharing network to contribute, access, use, analyze, and disseminate information in a manner that protects and preserves privacy and civil liberties. Follow-on reports not only detailed how the information sharing network should be created, but offered recommendations to enhance information access and improve cooperation to ensure people have the right information, at the right time, under the right conditions.

While the nation scrambles to step up its information collection and analysis efforts and attempts to use information more effectively, the quantity and types of information available to analysts continues to increase dramatically. Information technology advances, the proliferation of the use of computers, and the Internet, has made it possible to collect, store, and collate huge quantities of information. Improvements in software and standardization of architectures, technology, and communications, have made it possible for organizations, cities, counties, and states alike, to provide access to literally millions of records in dozens of databases. The physical nature of raw data has continued to change too, e.g., surveillance video, wiretap audio and transcripts, and phone records, email messages, global positioning system (GPS) trackers, etc., and almost every piece of data is either readily available in digital format or it can be easily converted. With all of this comes total information overload.

In light of the changing nature of information and its analysis, it is critical that intelligence units are equipped to handle the analytical challenges of the next decade. The analysts' tools and technologies must become more intelligence-oriented, quickly locating only relevant information so actionable information can surface quickly. A number of emerging technologies developed in the areas of defense, homeland security, and others areas have great potential for use in law enforcement. The key is to recognize which of these technologies are relevant, and those that can be easily incorporated into daily intelligence operations without disrupting other systems and processes.

Providing a comprehensive overview of all aspects of criminal intelligence applications and systems design would be beyond the scope of a single chapter. In short, a criminal intelligence system should be able to capture, index, summarize, retrieve, analyze, disseminate, and manage data and information regardless of its nature or source. The criminal intelligence system should be able to perform these functions in such a way as to logically emulate the flow of intelligence operations and work seamlessly with other applications, meaning the information within the criminal intelligence system should be available to analytical and reporting tools and vice versa without the need for re-entry of data or data conversion. Finally, the criminal intelligence system should utilize technologies that make it possible to share information with any other system, person, or persons in a secure and trusted manner.

CHAPTER 16

Criminal Intelligence Databases and Applications

THE CRIMINAL INTELLIGENCE SYSTEM

The phrase "criminal intelligence system" refers to the interaction between business processes and the technology that supports the criminal intelligence function. These interactions can occur within or across organizational boundaries. Information systems not only represent the technology used by an organization, they are also prescriptive of the way in which the organization interacts with the technology. Most organizations, particularly those that perform a variety of functions, use a variety of different technologies. Some technologies work together, some do not. Some vendors bundle together multiple applications, e.g., a word processor, a spreadsheet, etc., to be marketed as an application suite. Application suites usually have related functions, features, and user interfaces that are able to interact with each other, e.g. import data from one to the other.

As such, rather than thinking of a criminal intelligence system as one application, or database, that does everything, consider it a collection of databases, applications, and analytical tools that operate together to achieve a common purpose—supporting the intelligence function. There is no single vendor that can provide all applications and tools an intelligence analyst could possibly need, nor would it be prudent for an intelligence unit to purchase all software products from a single vendor. In reality, vendors specialize in software applications that perform particular tasks such as geographic information systems (GIS), link analysis, or analysis of other types of communications whether it be telephone, email, etc. In a traditional sense then, a criminal intelligence database could be considered the "core" database—a repository, primarily for evaluated raw data for intelligence purposes, purging, and dissemination control. Simply stated, the core database receives input, processes data, and delivers processed information as output.

For these reasons and more, design and software considerations, in addition to the definition of internal business requirements, are requisite to begin the quest for the criminal intelligence system that best suits your intelligence operation.

Design

"Database design" is the formal process of analyzing details about the real world into a suitable database structure, e.g., determining the appropriate tables, attributes, and relationships, that satisfy a given set of requirements. In contrast, software design is the process of problem solving and planning for a software solution. It is the discipline concerned with the construction of efficient, reliable, robust, and easy to maintain software.

Although labeled as a noun, design is not a thing; design is more appropriately defined by the activity of designing. An object is deemed "well-designed" whenever it is well suited to its environment. Complex systems can evolve without a coherent master design; for example, the Internet, but even in this case, conscious design is at work in creating the individual pieces and relationships that make up the whole (Winograd, 1996).

Basic database design and compatibility are, perhaps, the most often overlooked aspects of software in general, even though they are fundamental to the success of an application. Moreover, as security is fast becoming a non-negotiable business requirement, it too warrants consideration throughout the design of an intelligence system. Effective information safeguards and security measures accompany greater sharing of sensitive information, such as we are discussing.

Software

A "database" is a structure that stores information about multiple types of things, known as entities, the characteristics of those entities, and the relationships among the entities, in a structure that ensures the data are stored in a way as to minimize the cost of processing and storage (Awad & Gotterer, 1992).

A database management system (DBMS), sometimes referred to as the "database engine", is the software product that handles the actual manipulation of the underlying database, e.g., store and retrieves functions, as well as other database-related functions and tasks. Users of the system access data by going to the DBMS or through another program that goes to the DBMS, but should never be permitted to access the data by going directly to the database.

When evaluating the suitability of a product, some capabilities to consider include:

- Support for storing different types of data that includes video, audio, word processing documents or other multimedia, an important capability because the source and type of raw intelligence varies greatly.

- The ability to respond to requests for data from other types of application software, typically through open database connectivity (ODBC) standards—a feature that provides for maximum interoperability with other applications by means of a common interface; for example, importing or exporting data from, or to, another application, such as spreadsheets or statistical packages. Without this capability, it may mean that standardized tools for reporting and analysis may not be available for use within your intelligence system.

- Support for multiple, concurrent users—critical if more than one person will use the system at any one time. This implies that the DBMS supports table and record locking, preventing two users from updating the same record at the same time.

- Scalability—essential for an organization that has large volumes of data or one that anticipates the amount of information they will accumulate will increase significantly.

- Audit and logging capabilities that provides a trace or history of who was logged onto the system and when, which records were accessed, and actions taken, if any. The drawback of audit trails is that they require lots of disk space and frequent archiving which is to back up the audit trail logs and remove them to make room for new ones.

- Automated backups that provide for the backups to occur without intervention and without affecting daily operations. This means backups occur in the background, largely without user intervention and without affecting daily operations. Ideally, the backed-up information should be stored off-site in a location other than where the database sits.

THE CORE APPLICATION

No matter how much thought goes into the database design or how good the underlying database engine is, a well-designed criminal intelligence system "core" must be able to support daily intelligence operations, not an easy task, primarily because intelligence database applications are very different from traditional database applications due to the nature of the area of application. Developing a criminal intelligence application can be very challenging and time consuming and requires a considerable amount of expertise in intelligence operations. Before beginning a discussion of application characteristics and features, a distinction must be made between the applications used to analyze raw data, the supporting analytical applications, and the core intelligence application used to collect previously evaluated data. There may also be more than one type of database to consider, e.g., a case management database designed to manage law enforcement activities and store fact-based information.

Criminal intelligence systems are process driven. The status of each piece of information in the system depends on a variety of factors. In the criminal intelligence world, captured information or a report may be based on hearsay or conjecture. Data may or may not be correct. In addition, information can have varying degrees of sensitivity. Highly sensitive information may not be available to all personnel.

Perhaps the hardest part in designing a criminal intelligence application is the fact that laws and guidelines governing the use and storage of intelligence information can vary widely across organizations. Although the principles of information collection and collation are the same everywhere, what may be perfectly legal in one state could be a violation of the law in another. In addition, law enforcement agencies receiving federal funds to support their computer systems must adhere to the guidelines governing federally grant-funded multijurisdictional criminal intelligence systems, outlined in the Criminal Intelligence Systems Operating Policies, 28 Code of Federal Regulations (CFR) Part 23 (28 CFR Part 23). 28 CFR Part 23 provides guidance for electronically stored intelligence information and how it must be treated by law enforcement agencies in five primary areas including 1) information submission or collection, 2) secure storage, 3) inquiry and search capability, 4) controlled dissemination, and 5) the review and purge process. Regardless of the funding source, 28 CFR Part 23 is a best practice for all criminal intelligence systems.

Designing an application that conforms to the law, is intuitive and useful, and emulates the intelligence gathering and evaluation process, can be very difficult indeed. For these reasons, it is impossible to describe the ideal criminal intelligence application that would work for every law enforcement agency. Therefore, this section focuses on the core application. The guidelines listed above have implications on design, but the best way to approach the discussion of application design is to focus on the main aspects of the core intelligence application: data entry, search and retrieval, dissemination, and purge control.

Data Entry

Data entry can be the most time consuming of all tasks involving the database, but it is one of the most important tasks. After all, the old adage, "garbage in, garbage out" is especially true for intelligence systems. The more time spent entering, collecting, and ensuring data is accurate and properly linked together, the easier it will be to later to search and find what you are looking for.

Data entry in a criminal intelligence system differs from other systems in that it is recommended a criminal intelligence supervisor first approve the information before it can be viewed or queried by others. This means that all information entered must be kept separate or tagged appropriately until it has been approved. It also implies that an approval process must be an integral part of data entry.

Another data entry issue directly related to design is that, to avoid duplicate entries of things such as persons and addresses, the application should notify the user of any previous entries with similar attributes. For example, as a first and last name is entered, the application would automatically check whether the person already exists in the database. If there is a match on the first and last name, the user should be presented with a list of persons with the same attributes and allow them to confirm if the entry is indeed a new person even though the name is the same.

Part of the data entry process should include establishing connections between entities, e.g., person, address, organization, vehicle, vehicle, report narratives, etc., and denoting the known relationship(s) between them. Establishing these linkages up front will enhance searching capabilities down the road. For example, asking the question if there is a connection between two subjects.

An application that makes full use of today's multimedia capabilities e.g., spreadsheets, word processing documents, and other third party products, can support the capture and storage of other data types including audio, video, images, and unformatted text, etc., including surveillance video, wiretap audio, scanned handwriting samples, pictures of tattoos, etc.

Search and Retrieval

One of the most frequent complaints of law enforcement personnel is that their criminal intelligence systems are "black holes". Data entered is either impossible to retrieve, or the process is so complex and time-consuming, many people just give up.

It is essential that data be retrievable in as many ways as possible, regardless of variations including phonetics, transcription or keyboarding errors, nicknames, abbreviations, missing words, extra words, and noise and sequence variations. It is simply not enough to retrieve information by filling in blank data screens and searching the database for things such as a last name or a date of birth. A simple search, known as an exact match search, that returns database entries exactly matching a character or number string, are useful only if the user knows exactly what s/he is looking for. In general, a good search mechanism will help an analyst find out what he or she does not already know.

Name recognition/resolution is particularly challenging given predictable name variations due to diminutives, phonetics, similarities of names, typos, concatenation and truncation errors, acronyms, cultural variations, errors in supporting identifying information, e.g., addresses, dates, identification numbers, telephone numbers, etc., not to mention the number of identities one person alone may use, e.g. maiden names, aliases, professional names, nicknames, etc. To add to the confusion, some names are even represented differently or abbreviated, e.g., Tenth Street, 10th St., 10th Ave., etc.

Closely related to an exact match search, is a partial search, sometimes referred to as a "string" search. Partial searches, search for a string of text or numbers, returning database entries that contains the string of text or numbers entered.

A search more commonly used, particularly when the exact spelling of a name is unknown, the soundex search, uses a "sound-alike" algorithm to encode the last name of a person based upon phonetics and certain classes of typical spelling and typing errors. It consists of a simple set of rules to convert a last name word into a four, five, or six digit numbers that have a high probability of being the same. All names that meet the soundex criterion are returned.

Similar in concept to a soundex search, a phonetic search breaks a word down into an approximation of its English phonetic pronunciation, but is much more comprehensive in its approach. A diminutive search, which searches for nicknames and diminutives of names, would return Jim, Jimmy, Jimmie, Jamie, Jimbo, Jamey, among others, for the name James.

Since much of the information today contains at least one reference to a specific geographical location; combining text and geographic search capabilities allows an analyst to find relevant information faster based on spatial references and addresses. For example, an advanced search capability combining geographic search capabilities with full-text keyword search, document categorization, and temporal filtering, could accelerate the delivery of intelligence; allowing analysts to see geographic trends as they emerge, improve situational awareness, and enable instant corroboration between disparate sources concerned with proximate locations. Geographic-based queries can be a very powerful tool, especially if it is not exactly known where a crime occurred or if the exact address of someone, something, or an event is unknown.

Another analytical trend is the examination and analysis of patterns found in the underlying structure and associations of a group of entities. Although there will likely be unrealistic assumptions, irrelevant links, or missing associations when looking at the relationships of one entity to another, the motivation for understanding the underlying relationships between people in an organization is the ever-increasing, particularly because of massive amounts of data available. Consider the implications using the capability in relation to an individual caught transporting illegal materials and law enforcement needing to rapidly deduce who the possible accomplices are (Kubica).

Dissemination

The dissemination of information and reports, including notifying the contributor of the release of the information, is the step after querying the system for information. Criminal information stored in a database for intelligence purposes by its very nature, is highly sensitive, and unlike other applications where information can be freely printed out and given to others, intelligence-related information requires different procedures. Guidelines and, in some states, state law, govern the use and dissemination of criminal intelligence-related information which requires agencies to maintain a log of each disseminated record, the date, the recipient of the information, and the reason the information was released. There are also laws that prohibit the secondary dissemination of information to ensure those agencies disseminating information are legally protected from the actions of those who would violate those laws.

Not only must the requisite controls be in place to ensure information does not fall into the hands of those who do not have a right or need to know, the intelligence system itself must also ensure that the controlling agency or "owner" of any information disseminated is notified of its release. Known as notification, the process dictates that information contributors (owners) are made aware, not only that their information was released, but also of who received the information. An agency may also want to consider an approval process for dissemination, similar to the one used in data entry. As such, the intelligence system may also have a review and tracking mechanism to support dissemination requests.

Purge Review

Purging is the final stage in the lifecycle of criminal intelligence information or a criminal intelligence report. All information in the criminal intelligence system must be reviewed and validated for continuing compliance with submission criteria within a 5-year retention period. Any information not validated within that period must be purged. The review ensures the accuracy of the criminal intelligence information and that it is as up-to-date as reasonably possible. Once a record has been reviewed and validated, the system must provide for notations, including an explanation of any decisions to retain the information (28 CFR 23.20(h)). Naturally, the specific reasons for retaining or purging criminal intelligence reports or information will differ from jurisdiction to jurisdiction.

Ideally, a criminal intelligence system would automatically identify any information due for purge review. For example, each time an analyst signs onto the system, a check would be made by examining the amount of time elapsed since the information was submitted or collected or last validated. The system would notify the analyst of any information she/he is responsible for that needs to be reviewed.

As with dissemination requests, the purge review should be forwarded to a supervisor for review and approval. If the criminal intelligence information or report is to be retained, it must be marked as such and updated with additional information that would extend the "life" of the information for another 5-years; to be reviewed again during the next purge cycle. If the information is to be purged, all criminal intelligence information is deleted from the database, with the exception of an entry effectively creating an audit trail noting any report number(s) and the date the information was purged from the system.

SUPPORTING APPLICATIONS

Database decisions that dictate compliance with standards, provide for maximum interoperability with other applications, and ensure that standardized or specialized reporting and analytical tools can be used to complement the core criminal intelligence application.

Today there are a variety of standardized analytical and reporting tools available. In addition to word processing and spreadsheet packages, there are packages for gathering and analyzing crime data for crime trends, patterns, or series detection. There are analytical tools such as telephone toll analysis, flow analysis, link analysis, visual investigative analysis, and time event charting; crime analysis statistics enabling forecasting and predicting crime trends, and packages supporting crime and intelligence analysis functions and presentation of information in the form of maps, bulletins, and charts. In terms of system design, integration is key, which means being able to use an array of tools without time consuming data exports, address matching, or having to manually assemble link charts. These tools can provide a quick overview of intelligence information, a case or an intelligence report, not only providing a way to visualize the information entered, but also an excellent way to generate presentations. After all, it is much easier to understand a picture, e.g., a map or chart, than to ask someone to go through pages of data and other information.

There are many vendor packages available on the market today, although most of these commercial packages comply with standards that allow them to connect to the majority of database engines, it cannot be stressed enough that the ability to utilize these types of applications and tools depends on a good design and software that can connect without additional data entry.

OTHER CONSIDERATIONS

Information Sharing

One of the biggest challenges that face those with criminal intelligence systems is ensuring that authorized individuals have access to the authorized resources they need. The Global National Criminal

Intelligence Sharing Plan (NCISP), the Markle reports, and the 9/11 Commission each recognized the urgent need to share information, intelligence information included, in a secure manner between federal, state, and local organizations. Ensuring that your criminal intelligence system does not fall into the category of isolated data storage, commonly referred to as an "information silo", is a technical challenge easily overcome today, not only through design and software decisions but also through a commitment to make your information resources "sharable."

Solutions and best practices designed to improve information across the country have come about as a result of the U.S. Department of Justice Global Justice Information Sharing Initiative (Global), a federal advisory Committee which serves to advise the U.S. Attorney General and the Department of Homeland Security on justice information sharing and integration initiatives *http://www.it.ojp.gov.* The Global mission is the efficient sharing of data among justice and homeland security entities and several practices and standards that have emerged from this consortium that include:

- The National Information Exchange Model (NIEM) framework which offers a standard to exchange data with agreed-on meaning and format *<http://niem.gov>*,

- The GLOBAL Federated Identity and Privilege Management (GFIPM) security framework, a rapidly maturing technology that allows a user's roles, rights, and privileges to be communicated securely without manual intervention *<http://www.it.ojp.gov>*, and

- The Justice Reference Architecture (JRA), a "services-oriented architecture" (SOA) which prescribes a way of building applications tailored for technology systems in the justice environment *<http://www.it.ojp.gov/documents/JRA_Specification_1-7.doc>*.

The intent of these work products is that the frameworks can be used to develop flexible and cost-effective technical capabilities for secure, instantaneous sharing of information. The good news is that private industry vendors have not only partnered with the justice community in the definition of these emerging standards, they are embracing the solutions and aligning their commercial products which can only serve to address potential compatibility factors within your own intelligence systems.

Information Security

Information security, as defined in the U.S. C. Title 44, Section 3502, means protecting information and information systems from unauthorized access, use, disclosure, disruption, modification or destruction in order to provide integrity, confidentiality, and availability. In addition to guaranteeing information is not tampered with or altered, ensuring information is protected from indiscriminate viewing, and making sure data is available when and as expected, other principles of information security include:

- Verifying the identity of those accessing the data, which can be as simple as the use of a personal identification number (PIN) or password, or as complex as biometrics, e.g., fingerprints,

- ensuring only those users who are allowed to view and/or manipulate the data, known as authorization,

- controlling access to those who have been authorized to access the information within the system, and

- maintaining a record of system and/or user activity, e.g., when and where a transaction took place, such that the action is indisputable.

Information security involves much more than technology though. A comprehensive approach to information security includes the rules and procedures that ensure an environment of trust. Information security is also an ongoing process that consists of exercising due care and due diligence to protect data, information, and information system itself, from unauthorized access, use, disclosure, destruction, modification, or disruption or distribution.

Whether or not it is a technical exchange, information sharing is founded upon trust between two parties. This trust is usually formed on a personal level, such as what happens when law enforcement task force as personnel from different agencies come together for a common purpose. In the case of the task force, information sharing can either flourish or falter due to changes in personnel, personality differences, or real or perceived issues. Trust among task force participants is further ensured by setting standards for participation.

In much the same way as the task force, achieving technical information sharing objectives requires that information-sharing partners establish electronic trust between systems, accomplished by ensuring the protections listed above are in place. Criminal intelligence analysts can then, collect, collate, analyze, and share criminal intelligence information electronically in a secure, trusted environment.

CONCLUSION

Designing or implementing criminal intelligence database applications or systems is by no means a straightforward process. Criminal intelligence systems can be quite complex. Application software suitable for one organization may not be suitable for another. It is unlikely the ideal criminal intelligence application, or system, exists, and as a result, a distinction should be made between the applications used to analyze raw data, the supporting analytical applications, and the core criminal intelligence application.

Utilizing the latest technologies and leveraging the work products of national collaborative efforts, e.g., Global will ensure your criminal intelligence system and your criminal intelligence operation is poised to be an empowered partner in the national information sharing system.

For most agencies, the decision to go with a particular criminal intelligence database application is a long-term commitment. Not only is it often not economically feasible to switch to a new application every few years, but the process of switching software can be quite disruptive to daily operations and is very time consuming. The goal of this chapter is to aid those in the process of deciding which criminal intelligence applications to use, to ask the right questions, and make decisions that are more informed.

REFERENCES

A. Ramesh Babu, Y. P. Singh, and R.K. Sachdeva, *Chapter 18 - Establishing a Management Information System*.

A Report of the Markle Foundation Task Force, *Creating a Trusted Network for Homeland Security*, October 2002.

Bureau of Justice Assistance, *National Criminal Intelligence Sharing Plan*, October 2003, <*http://it.ojp.gov/documents/ncisp/National_Criminal_Intelligence_Sharing_Plan.pdf*>.

Bureau of Justice Assistance, *Criminal Intelligence System Operating Policies* (28 Code of Federal Regulations Part 23.20). 1993.

Elias M. Awad, Malcolm H. Gotterer (1992): Database Management, 1st Edition, Course Technology Press, Boston, MA.

Jeremy Kubica, Andrew Moore, David Cohn, Jeff Schneider (2003) Finding Underlying Connections: A Fast Graph-Based Method for Link Analysis and Collaboration Queries, Robotics Institute, Carnegie Mellon University, Pittsburgh, PA.

Kroenke, D.M. and Dolan, K.A. (1988): Database Processing: Fundamentals, Design, Implementation, 3rd Edition, Science Research Associates, Chicago.

National Information Exchange Model (NIEM) <*http://www.niem.gov*>.

Randy Ridley, Jeffrey Sauder, and John Frank (2003) MetaCarta, Inc., Can Geography Rescue Text Search? Where is Your Information About?

Second Report of the Markle Foundation Task Force, *Creating a Trusted Network for Homeland Security*, December 2003.

Silberschatz, A., Korth, H.F. and Sudarshan, S. (1996): Database System Concepts, 3rd Edition, McGraw-Hill, Boston.

Terry Winograd (1996): Bringing Design to Software, Addison-Wesley.

Networks, Organizations, and Resources
By Chuck Boschert

INTRODUCTION

Government and private sector agencies offer a number of resources to the law enforcement intelligence community. These resources vary from general public information databases to classified networks focusing solely on counterterrorism. While the number of available resources is extensive, this chapter provides an overview of some of those more commonly utilized by law enforcement intelligence professionals.

REGIONAL INFORMATION SHARING SYSTEM (RISS) PROGRAM

The Regional Information Sharing System (RISS) was developed in 1974 as a means to provide investigative support and share secure information among law enforcement agencies. The mission of RISS is to enhance the ability of state and local law enforcement nationwide to combat illegal drug trafficking, identity theft, human trafficking, violent crime, and terrorist activity, as well as to promote officer safety. RISS is comprised of six regional, multi-state centers designed to offer support services that are tailored to the needs of member agencies while fostering interagency cooperation and criminal intelligence products that are of nationwide significance. Among the services offered to member agencies is information sharing resources, analytical services, loans of specialized investigative equipment, confidential funds, training conferences and technical assistance. RISS membership includes over 8,100 local, state, tribal and federal criminal justice agencies in all fifty states, the District of Columbia, U.S. Territories, Australia, Canada and England.

RISS operates a secure intranet site, RISSNET, which was designed to facilitate law enforcement information sharing nationwide in an effort to combat criminal activities spanning jurisdictional boundaries. Through RISSNET, members can access a number of online resources relating to intelligence, gangs, critical infrastructure, etc.:

- **RISSIntel** - RISS maintains a centralized, secure database containing information concerning known or suspected criminals, businesses, organizations, and their related identifying information. RISSIntel functions as a pointer system where member agencies may submit information and make queries.

- **RISSGang** - The RISS National Gang Intelligence Database offers law enforcement agencies easy access to gang information – including suspects, organizations, weapons, locations, and vehicles - as well as visual imagery of gang members, gang symbols, and gang graffiti. RISSGang provides gang-specific news, documents, and publications organized by specific areas of gang activity.

- **RISSSafe** - RISS has also developed an officer safety event de-confliction system. The purpose of the RISSafe application is to store and maintain information on planned law enforcement activities. Used in conjunction with a mapping system, upcoming events are posted and monitored for potentially dangerous conflicting law enforcement operations.

- **RISS ATIX** - Having recognized that the need to exchange information extends beyond law enforcement and traditional users of intelligence, RISS has created the Automated Trusted Information Exchange (ATIX). ATIX is a communication system that allows local first responders, critical infrastructure personnel, and other public safety personnel—including public utility and school personnel, firefighters, and local, state, and federal law enforcement—to share terrorism and homeland security information in a secure, real-time environment.

RISS INTELLIGENCE CENTERS

MAGLOCLEN
Middle Atlantic-Great Lakes Organized Crime Law Enforcement Network® MAGLOCLEN
140 Terry Road, Suite 100
Newtown, Pennsylvania 18940

Phone: 800-345-1322 / E-mail: info@magloclen,riss.net

Web: http://magloclen.rissinfo.com/
Serving Delaware, Indiana, Maryland, Michigan, New Jersey, New York, Ohio, Pennsylvania, and the District of Columbia, as well as Australia, parts of Canada, and England.

MOCIC
Mid-States Organized Crime Information Center®
P.O. Box 1250
Springfield, Missouri 65801

Phone: 800-846-6242 / E-mail: info@mocic.riss.net

Serving Illinois, Iowa, Kansas, Minnesota, Missouri, Nebraska, North Dakota, South Dakota, and Wisconsin, as well as parts of Canada.

NESPIN
New England State Police Information Network®
124 Grove Street, Suite 305
Franklin, Massachusetts 02038

Phone: 800-343-5682 / E-mail: info@nespin.riss.net

Serving Connecticut, Maine, Massachusetts, New Hampshire, Rhode Island, and Vermont, as well as parts of Canada.

RMIN
Rocky Mountain Information Network®
2828 N. Central Avenue, Suite 1000
Phoenix, Arizona 85004

Phone: 800-821-0640 / E-mail: info@rmin.riss.net

Web: http://rmin.rissinfo.com/
Serving Arizona, Colorado, Idaho, Montana, Nevada, New Mexico, Utah, and Wyoming, as well as parts of Canada.

ROCIC
Regional Organized Crime Information Center®

545 Marriott Drive, Suite 850
Nashville, Tennessee 37214
Phone: 800-238-7985 / E-mail: info@rocic.riss.net

Web: http://www.rocic.com

Serving Alabama, Arkansas, Florida, Georgia, Kentucky, Louisiana, Mississippi, North Carolina, Oklahoma, South Carolina, Tennessee, Texas, Virginia and West Virginia, as well as Puerto Rico, and the U.S. Virgin Islands

WSIN
Western States Information Network

P.O. Box 903198
Sacramento, CA 94203-1980
Phone: 800-952-5258
E-mail: info@wsin.riss.net
Serving Alaska, California, Hawaii, Oregon, Washington, as well as parts of Canada and Guam.

Each of these regional RISS projects has established an oversight group composed of representatives from state and local member agencies in the project's multistate region. These oversight groups develop policy and provide direction regarding project operations and administration. For additional information regarding the RISS Projects, please visit *www.riss.net.*

HIGH INTENSITY DRUG TRAFFICKING AREAS (HIDTA)

Authorized by the Anti-Drug Abuse Act of 1988, the director of the Office of National Drug Control Policy (ONDCP) has designated areas within the United States exhibiting serious drug trafficking problems as High Intensity Drug Trafficking Areas (HIDTAs). The HIDTA program provides additional federal resources to state and local law enforcement agencies in those areas. Participating agencies, as a condition to joining the program, must agree to work together in multi-agency initiatives, share intelligence and information, and provide data to measure their performance. Law enforcement organizations within HIDTAs assess drug trafficking problems and design specific initiatives to reduce or eliminate the production, manufacture, transportation, distribution and chronic use of illegal drugs and money laundering.

The key priorities of the program are:

- Assess regional drug threats
- Design strategies to focus efforts that combat drug trafficking threats
- Develop and fund initiatives to implement strategies
- Facilitate coordination between federal, state and local efforts
- Improve the effectiveness and efficiency of drug control efforts to reduce or eliminate the harmful impact of drug trafficking

CHAPTER 17

Networks, Organizations, and Resources

As of January 2009, there are 28 HIDTAs and 5 Southwest Border Regions. In 2006, the HIDTA program provided support to law enforcement in 45 States, Puerto Rico, the U.S. Virgin Islands, and the District of Columbia. Each HIDTA is governed by its own executive board comprised of approximately 16 members—8 federal members and 8 state or local members. These boards facilitate interagency drug control efforts to eliminate or reduce drug threats. The executive boards ensure threat specific strategies and initiatives are developed, employed, supported, and evaluated. The following 28 areas were designated as HIDTAs as of the dates listed:

- **1990** - Houston, Los Angeles, New York/New Jersey, South Florida and Southwest Border (California, Arizona, New Mexico and Texas)

- **1994** - Washington/Baltimore (Maryland, Virginia and District of Columbia) and Puerto Rico/U.S. Virgin Islands

- **1995** - Atlanta, Chicago and Philadelphia/Camden

- **1996** - Rocky Mountain (Colorado, Montana, Utah and Wyoming), Gulf Coast (Alabama, Louisiana and Mississippi), Lake County (Indiana), Midwest (Iowa, Kansas, Missouri, Nebraska, North Dakota and South Dakota) and Northwest (Washington State)

- **1997** - Southeastern Michigan (subsequently, portions of western Michigan) and Northern California

- **1998** - Appalachia (Kentucky, Tennessee and West Virginia), Central Florida, Milwaukee and North Texas (Texas and Oklahoma)

- **1999** - Central Valley California, Hawaii, New England (Connecticut, New Hampshire, Maine, Massachusetts, Rhode Island and Vermont), Ohio and Oregon

- **2001** - North Florida and Nevada

The HIDTA Program helps improve the effectiveness and efficiency of drug control efforts by facilitating cooperation between drug control organizations through resource and information sharing, co-locating, and implementing joint initiatives. HIDTA funds help federal, state, and local law enforcement organizations invest in infrastructure and joint initiatives to confront drug-trafficking organizations. Funds are also used for demand reduction and drug treatment initiatives.

<http://www.whitehousedrugpolicy.gov/HIDTA/>

HIGH INTENSITY FINANCIAL CRIME AREAS (HIFCA)

High Intensity Financial Crime Areas (HIFCAs) were first announced in the 1999 National Money Laundering Strategy and were conceived in the Money Laundering and Financial Crimes Strategy Act of 1998 as a means of concentrating law enforcement efforts at the federal, state, and local levels in high intensity money laundering zones. HIFCAs may be defined geographically or they can also be created to address money laundering in an industry sector, a financial institution, or group of financial institutions.

298

The HIFCA program is intended to concentrate law enforcement efforts at the federal, state, and local level to combat money laundering in designated high-intensity money laundering zones. In order to implement this goal, a money-laundering action team is created or identified within each HIFCA to spearhead a coordinated federal, state, and local anti-money laundering effort. Each action team will be composed of all relevant federal, state, and local enforcement authorities, prosecutors, and financial regulators.

Factors from three general categories of information are considered when designating a HIFCA:

1. Patterns of Bank Secrecy Act (BSA) filings
2. Descriptive information identifying trends
3. Patterns in money laundering activity and the level of law enforcement response to money laundering in the region

The following is a list of HIFCA Regions and the counties encompassed within those regions:

- **California, Northern District** - Monterey, Humboldt, Mendocino, Lake, Sonoma, Napa, Marin, Contra Costa, San Francisco, San Mateo, Alameda, Santa Cruz, San Benito, Monterey, Del Norte

- **California, Southern District** - Los Angeles, Orange, Riverside, San Bernardino, San Luis Obispo, Santa Barbara, Ventura

- **Southwest Border** - Arizona - All Counties, Texas - Counties Bordering, and adjacent to those bordering, the US and Mexico Boundary

- **Chicago** - Cook, McHenry, Dupage, Lake, Will, Kane

- **New York** - New York - All Counties, New Jersey - All Counties

- **Puerto Rico** - Puerto Rico - All Areas, U.S. Virgin Islands - All Areas

- **South Florida** - Broward, Miami-Dade, Indian River, Martin, Monroe, Okeechobee, Palm Beach, and St Lucie

<http://www.fincen.gov/law_enforcement/hifca/index.html>

NATIONAL DRUG INTELLIGENCE CENTER (NDIC)

Established in 1993 by the Department of Defense Appropriations Act, the National Drug Intelligence Center (NDIC) was created to "coordinate and consolidate drug intelligence from all national security and law enforcement agencies, and produce information regarding the structure, membership, finances, communications, and activities of drug trafficking organizations." The mission of NDIC is to provide strategic drug-related intelligence, document and computer exploitation support, and training assistance to the drug control, public health, law enforcement, and intelligence communities of the United States in order to reduce the adverse effects of drug trafficking, drug abuse, and other drug-related criminal activity.

NDIC supports national-level policymakers and the Intelligence Community by preparing strategic analytical studies on the trafficking of illegal drugs and on related illegal activities that pose a threat to the national security of the United States. In addition, NDIC partners with the Department of Homeland Security Office of Counternarcotics Enforcement to provide critical intelligence to identify, track, and sever the nexus between drug trafficking and terrorism. NDIC also produces strategic money laundering reports that help policymakers and senior law enforcement decision makers implement national-level anti-money laundering initiatives. NDIC reports address the methods high-level traffickers use to launder drug proceeds. NDIC supports the National Money Laundering Threat Assessment and the National Money Laundering Strategy-interagency projects that enhance the nation's ability to counter international money laundering.

The NDIC mission emphasizes the identification, collection, organization, and analysis of large amounts of information and intelligence. To accomplish this, NDIC accesses commercial and governmental databases and uses available technology to search for and extract useful information. NDIC also uses technology developed in-house to reveal patterns in the information contained in records seized by law enforcement agencies during drug investigations and subsequent prosecutions. NDIC obtains information from a diverse array of activities that include directly surveying local and state law enforcement agencies, obtaining information from other federal law enforcement and intelligence agencies, and extracting information from documents and electronic media seized by law enforcement agencies and prosecutors. NDIC also uses open-source information from news providers and public health agencies.

NDIC employs more than 120 analysts who are assisted by detailees from the Department of Defense, DEA, FBI, and the Federal Bureau of Prisons (BOP). NDIC analysts represent diverse fields of study with a number having foreign language capabilities and advanced degrees.

<http://www.usdoj.gov/ndic/>

EL PASO INTELLIGENCE CENTER (EPIC)

The El Paso Intelligence Center (EPIC) was established in 1974 to create an Intelligence Service Center focused on the United States/Mexico border with an emphasis on Mexico's heroin traffickers and illegal alien smugglers. With increased use of aircraft and seagoing vessels, and the proliferation of global drug trafficking networks, EPIC's focus broadened and became international in scope. EPIC is currently staffed by representatives from the Drug Enforcement Administration, the U.S. Department of Homeland Security, Customs and Border Protection, the Bureau of Alcohol, Tobacco, Firearms and Explosives, the U.S. Secret Service, the U.S. Marshals Service, the National Drug Intelligence Center, the Internal Revenue Service, the U.S. Department of the Interior, the National Geospatial Intelligence Agency, the U.S. Department of Defense, the Joint Task Force – North, the Joint Interagency Task Force – South, the Texas Department of Public Safety, the Texas Air National Guard, and the El Paso County Sheriff's Office.

EPIC now serves U.S. federal agencies, all 50 States, the District of Columbia, Puerto Rico, the U.S. Virgin Islands, and Guam. It also supports law enforcement efforts conducted by foreign counterparts throughout the world. EPIC currently has Memorandas of Understanding (MOUs) with Canada, Australia, and the Netherlands. Responding to increased multiagency needs, EPIC has developed into a fully coordinated, tactical intelligence center supported by databases and resources from member agencies.

In 2001, immediately after the terrorist attacks in New York and Washington, D.C., the multiagency environment of EPIC was called upon to support investigations to find those responsible. EPIC's mission evolved from its experience in supporting interdiction efforts and investigations regarding drug trafficking, alien and weapon smuggling, and other criminal activities, by adding counterterrorism to its efforts.

As one of the nation's foremost tactical intelligence centers, EPIC's vision is to continue to provide timely and expeditious support to federal, state, local, tribal, and international law enforcement agencies.

<http://www.usdoj.gov/dea/programs/epic.htm>

FINANCIAL CRIMES ENFORCEMENT CENTER (FinCEN)

The Financial Crimes Enforcement Network (FinCEN) was established in 1990 by the U.S. Department of the Treasury to provide a government-wide multisource financial intelligence and analysis network. The organization's operation was broadened in 1994 to include regulatory responsibilities for administering the Bank Secrecy Act, one of the nation's most potent weapons for preventing corruption of the U.S. financial system.

FinCEN's mission is to enhance U.S. national security, deter and detect criminal activity, and safeguard financial systems from abuse by promoting transparency in the U.S. and international financial systems. FinCEN supports law enforcement investigative efforts and fosters interagency and global cooperation against domestic and international financial crimes, providing U.S. policy makers with strategic analysis of domestic and worldwide money laundering developments, trends, and patterns.

FinCEN controls millions of reports filed under the Bank Secrecy Act (BSA) and other similar law. These reports are accessed by federal, state, and local law enforcement agencies, which are provided with information regarding large currency transactions in banks, casinos, and money service businesses, large international currency movements, foreign bank accounts, and any suspicious transactions generally over $5,000. This information is not readily available elsewhere.

The USA PATRIOT Act of 2001, enacted shortly after the 9/11 terrorist attacks, broadened the scope of the Bank Secrecy Act to focus on terrorist financing as well as money laundering. The Act also gave FinCEN additional responsibilities and authorities in these important areas, and established the organization as a bureau within the Treasury Department.

On March 8, 2004, the organization became a part of the Department of the Treasury's new Office of Terrorism and Financial Intelligence. This is the lead office in the Treasury Department for fighting the financial war on terror, combating financial crime, and enforcing economic sanctions against rogue nations.

<http://www.fincen.gov/>

STATEWIDE INTELLIGENCE SHARING SYSTEMS

A number of states have developed mechanisms for the statewide collection and exchange of criminal intelligence information among law enforcement agencies. One of the original and most successful programs is the Iowa Law Enforcement Intelligence Network (LEIN). Established in 1984, LEIN's mission is to develop and disseminate knowledge about significant criminal conditions that affect the state of Iowa. LEIN uses this information to conduct cooperative multi-agency investigations. Information is reported by members to LEIN, and is then disseminated to participating agencies throughout the state. These agencies subsequently use the information to identify and evaluate criminal activity in their area. Due to its success, the LEIN program has been implemented in several other states.

Another example of a robust statewide information sharing system is the California Joint Regional Information and Exchange System (CAL JRIES). This portal is a powerful and versatile solution that is highly adaptable to changing requirements and supportive of national information sharing / collaboration strategies and is currently available for use. CAL JRIES is composed of two main components: a web portal for storing information such as documents, photos, alerts, warnings, secure information sharing, and collaboration environment using Microsoft's Groove Virtual Office software. The Portal provides an area for users to post and search data that may assist in law enforcement activities. Groove is desktop collaboration software that allows users to share information and activities in secure workspaces. This site hosts the Association of Law Enforcement Intelligence Units (LEIU) – 'team site' on this secure information-sharing portal. LEIU also houses and maintains its membership roster on this site. Additionally, LEIU uses this site to post other items such as training, member bulletins and other membership information. Application to access CAL JRIES can be accomplished at the link below.

Partly as a reaction to the terrorist attacks of 2001, and partly due to advances in technology, several additional states have developed joint data sharing mechanisms. Many jurisdictions have incorporated these information-sharing systems as primary components of their state and regional fusion centers.

< http://www.dps.state.ia.us/intell/lein/index.htm>
<https://cal-jries-reg.doj.ca.gov/CJRegistration/default.aspx>

LAW ENFORCEMENT ONLINE (LEO)

Operated by the Federal Bureau of Investigation's Criminal Justice Information Services (CJIS), Law Enforcement Online (LEO) is a secure, internet-based communications portal for law enforcement, first responders, criminal justice professionals, and anti-terrorism and intelligence agencies around the globe. LEO catalyzes and strengthens collaboration and information sharing by providing access to sensitive but unclassified information and various state-of-the-art communications services and tools. It is available to vetted users anywhere in the world around the clock and is offered free of charge to members.

LEO started in 1995 as a small dial-up service with just 20 members. Now, it has more than 100,000 members across the world and a host of features and capabilities offered through a Virtual Private

Network on the Internet. Among the services offered by LEO are:

- A national alert system directing members to the LEO site for information on emergencies

- Over 500 Special Interest Groups (SIGs) that allow members who share expertise or interests to connect with each other, including sections on terrorism, street gangs, and bombs

- Access to important and useful databases, like those run by the National Center for Missing and Exploited Children

- A Virtual Command Center (VCC)—an information sharing and crisis management tool that allows the law enforcement community to use LEO at local and remote sites as an electronic command center to submit and view information and intelligence

- A multimedia library of publications, documents, studies, research, technical bulletins, and other reports of interest to LEO users

LEO membership is available to law enforcement, criminal justice, and public safety personnel.

<http://www.fbi.gov/hq/cjisd/leo.htm>

HOMELAND SECURITY INFORMATION NETWORK (HSIN)

Hosted by the U.S. Department of Homeland Security, the Homeland Security Information Network (HSIN) is a computer-based counterterrorism communications system connecting all 50 states, 5 territories, Washington, D.C., and 50 major urban areas. HSIN allows all states and major urban areas to collect and disseminate information between federal, state, and local agencies involved in combating terrorism. The mission of HSIN is to:

1. Provide situational awareness
2. Facilitate information sharing and collaboration with homeland security partners throughout the federal, state and local levels
3. Provide advanced analytical capabilities
4. Enable real-time sharing of information

This communications capability delivers to states and major urban areas real-time interactive connectivity with the National Operations Center. This collaborative communications environment was developed by state and local authorities.

As a component of HSIN, the Homeland Security State and Local Intelligence Community of Interest (HS SLIC) has become a vital tool for state and major urban area fusion centers. The connectivity of the fusion centers within this portal is extremely effective and allows members to exchange information within a secure environment.   Through the HS SLIC, intelligence analysts across the country collaborate via weekly threat conference calls, analytic conferences, and a secure web portal for intelligence information sharing at the sensitive-but-unclassified level. HS SLIC members have secure access to an extensive library of intelligence documents, online briefings, forum discussions, and a variety of other intelligence and information sharing tools.

<http://www.dhs.gov/index.shtm>

HOMELAND SECURITY STATE AND LOCAL INTELLIGENCE COMMUNITY OF INTEREST (HS SLIC)

The Homeland Security State and Local Intelligence Community of Interest is the nationwide forum for homeland security intelligence information sharing and collaboration among intelligence analysts at all levels of government (Federal, State, Local, Tribal, Territorial). The HS SLIC uses many mechanisms for communicating and collaborating on intelligence issues in securing the homeland. These include:

- Posting Sensitive, but, unclassified intelligence reports and products and communicating in real time via HSIN Intelligence

- Participating in weekly teleconferences to discuss relevant threats

- Participating in bi-weekly threat secure video teleconferences (via Secret level Homeland Secure Data Network)

- Conducting quarterly, in-person analytical conferences across the country

The HS SLIC was formalized and has been successful in building and maintaining community trust among members due to a comprehensive governance structure founded on business processes that define information handling and use, and also defining the individual criteria for membership. Individuals interested in joining HS SLIC must be able to assert that they are:

- US citizens,
- Engaged in intelligence analysis functions,
- Employed by law enforcement, criminal justice or homeland security agency,
- Engaged in detecting, defeating, or deterring terrorist acts,
- Have a government email address (fed, state or local), and
- Associated with a Fusion Center (for State & Local participants and Feds in the field)

For additional information please e-mail Homeland Security at: *hs.slic@hq.dhs.gov.*

CRIMINAL INTELLIGENCE COORDINATING COUNCIL (CICC)

Recognizing the importance of local, state, and tribal law enforcement agencies as a key ingredient in the nation's intelligence process, the National Criminal Intelligence Sharing Plan (NCISP) recommended the establishment of the Criminal Intelligence Coordinating Council (CICC). The NCISP acknowledged that officers, investigators, and analysts working throughout the country are the first line of detection and prevention of terrorism and crime, and the CICC was formed to create the linkage needed to improve intelligence and information sharing among all levels of government.

Composed of members from law enforcement agencies nationwide, the CICC was formally established in May 2004 to provide advice in connection with the implementation and refinement of the NCISP. Members of the CICC serve as advocates for local law enforcement and support their efforts to develop and share criminal intelligence for the purpose of promoting public safety and securing our nation.

The CICC is in the unique position, because of the makeup of its membership and its function within the nation's intelligence landscape, to serve as a voice for all levels of law enforcement agencies, which it does by advising the U.S. Attorney General on the best use of criminal intelligence to keep our country safe. The Council works to ensure that every chief, sheriff, and law enforcement executive has a stake in this effort so that all law enforcement and homeland security agencies gain an understanding of their role in the development and sharing of information and intelligence. The advice of members of the CICC has also been sought by the Secretary of the U.S. Department of Homeland Security (DHS), members of Congress, and representatives of state government.

<http://www.iir.com/global/council.htm>

INTERAGENCY THREAT ASSESSMENT AND COORDINATION GROUP (ITACG)

The Interagency Threat Assessment and Coordination Group (ITACG) facilitates increased information sharing between the National Intelligence Community and its state, local, tribal, and private sector (SLTP) partners. The ITACG was established at the direction of the President and Title 6, U.S. Code 210D as part of the Implementing Recommendations of the 9/11 Commission Act of 2007. Consisting of state, local, tribal, and federal homeland security, law enforcement, and intelligence officers, the ITACG is housed within the National Counterterrorism Center (NCTC) near Washington, D.C.

The ITACG serves as the NCTC focal point to guide the development and dissemination of federal counterterrorism intelligence products through DHS and FBI to their SLTP partners. ITACG members inform and help shape National Intelligence Community products by providing advice, counsel, and subject-matter expertise to better meet the needs of SLTP entities. The ITACG supports the production of the following products:

- Alerts, warnings, notifications, and updates of time-sensitive information related to terrorism threats to locations within the United States

- Situational awareness reporting regarding significant events or activities occurring at the international, national, state, or local levels

- Strategic and foundational assessments of terrorist threats to the United States.

The ITACG does not originate reporting or analysis, but instead relies on reporting and analysis produced by agencies within the Intelligence and Law Enforcement communities to ensure that relevant information is made available to SLTP agencies via established UNCLASSIFIED and SECRET level reporting mechanisms.

The ITACG complements and supplements existing analysis and production, and facilitates product dissemination to appropriate SLTP entities through established DHS and FBI mechanisms. In the event of conflicting reporting, or as the need arises, the ITACG facilitates federal coordination to ensure that reporting on threat information is clear and actionable to the greatest extent possible.

The ITACG is overseen by an Advisory Council that is tasked with setting policy, recruiting members, and developing processes for the integration, analysis, and dissemination of federally coordinated information. The 9/11 Commission Act requires that at least fifty percent of the ITACG Advisory Council members are from state, local, and tribal governments.

<http://www.ise.gov/Pages/ITACG.aspx>

CLASSIFIED INFORMATION SHARING SYSTEMS

A variety of systems exist or are under development which are designed to make classified terrorism-related information available to state and local law enforcement. The Homeland Secure Data Network (HSDN) allows the federal government to move information and intelligence to the states at the SECRET level, and is designed for deployment at fusion centers. State and local law enforcement and other public safety partners who have the appropriate clearances can establish accounts through the fusion centers and have direct access to classified information. The Secret Internet Protocol Router Network (SIPRNet) is a system of interconnected computer networks used by the U.S. Department of Defense and the U.S. Department of State to transmit classified information in a secure environment. The FBI's centralized network management system, FBINet, provides access to various financial and investigative systems. It is worth noting that SIPR and FBInet are not currently available to most state and local law enforcement agencies, however, this is a topic of ongoing discussions at the national level.

The National Counterterrorism Center (NCTC) enables the sharing of a wide spectrum of terrorism intelligence and related information among users in the counterterrorism community through its production of comprehensive, "federally coordinated" analytical products, which are available on its secure website, NCTC Online – SIPRNet (NOL-S). NOL-S provides access to all of the U.S. government's counterterrorism information approved for the SECRET level. It also provides a forum for sharing counterterrorism information with military, state, and local law enforcement partners. NOL-S is delivered through SIPRNet, FBINet, and HSDN.

Access to these systems (not FBInet, not SIPRnet) is available to state and local law enforcement personnel who have the appropriate clearance, and are operating within federally approved secure systems and facilities, usually state or major urban area fusion centers. While only a limited number of fusion centers currently meet these requirements, it is expected that the number will increase as these centers continue to develop.

INTERPOL

Established in 1923, INTERPOL – short for International Police – is the world's largest international police organization, with 187 member countries. It facilitates cross-border police cooperation, and supports and assists all organizations, authorities, and services whose mission is to prevent or combat crime. The General Secretariat is located in Lyon, France. INTERPOL operates seven regional offices –

in Argentina, Cameroon, Côte d'Ivoire, El Salvador, Kenya, Thailand and Zimbabwe – and a representative office at the United Nations in New York. Each member country maintains a National Central Bureau (NCB) staffed by highly trained law enforcement officers. The NCB is the designated contact point for the General Secretariat, regional offices and other member countries requiring assistance with overseas investigations and the location and apprehension of fugitives. Within the United States, INTERPOL also uses a system of state-level coordinators, often through state police agencies.

INTERPOL has identified four core functions on which to concentrate its efforts and resources:

1. Secure global police communications services - INTERPOL manages a global police communications system known as I-24/7, which enables police in all of its member countries to request, submit, and access vital police data instantly in a secure environment.

2. Operational data services and databases for police – INTERPOL manages a range of databases with information on names and photographs of known criminals, wanted persons, fingerprints, DNA profiles, stolen or lost travel documents, stolen motor vehicles, child sex abuse images, and stolen works of art. INTERPOL also disseminates critical, crime-related data through its system of international notices. There are seven kinds of notices, the most well-known of which is the "Red Notice," an international request for the provisional arrest of an individual.

3. Operational police support services – INTERPOL has six priority crime areas: corruption, drugs and organized crime, financial and high-tech crime, fugitives, public safety and terrorism, and human trafficking. INTERPOL operates a 24-hour Command and Coordination Center to assist any member country faced with a crisis situation, coordinate the exchange of information, and assume a crisis management role during serious incidents.

4. Police training and development – INTERPOL provides focused police training initiatives for national police forces and also offers on-demand advice, guidance, and support in building dedicated crime-fighting components. The aim is to enhance the capacity of member countries to effectively combat serious transnational crime and terrorism. This includes sharing knowledge, skills, and best practices in policing, and the establishment of global standards for combating specific crimes.

INTERPOL aims to facilitate international police cooperation, even where diplomatic relations do not exist between particular countries. Action is taken within the limits of existing laws in different countries and in the spirit of the Universal Declaration of Human Rights. INTERPOL's constitution prohibits 'any intervention or activities of a b.

<http://www.interpol.int/>

EUROPOL

Europol is the European Union law enforcement organisation that handles criminal intelligence. Its aim is to improve the effectiveness and cooperation between the competent authorities of the member states in preventing and combating serious international organised crime and terrorism. The mission of Europol is to make a significant contribution to the European Union's law enforcement action against organised crime and terrorism, with an emphasis on targeting criminal organisations.

Europol supports the law enforcement activities of the member states against:

- Illicit drug trafficking
- Illicit immigration networks
- Terrorism
- Forgery of money (counterfeiting of the Euro) and other means of payment
- Trafficking in human beings (including child abuse)
- Illicit vehicle trafficking
- Money laundering

In addition, other main priorities for EUROPOL include crimes against persons, financial crime and cybercrime. This applies where an organised criminal structure is involved and two or more member states are affected.

Europol provides support by:

- Facilitating the exchange of information between member states via their liaison officers assigned to Europol as representatives of their national law enforcement agencies

- Providing operational analysis in support of operations

- Generating strategic reports (e.g. threat assessments) and crime analysis on the basis of information and intelligence supplied by member states and third parties

- Providing expertise and technical support for investigations and operations carried out within the EU, under the supervision and the legal responsibility of the member states concerned

Europol is also active in promoting crime analysis and harmonization of investigative techniques within the member states.

NATIONAL WHITE COLLAR CRIME CENTER (NW3C)

The National White Collar Crime Center (NW3C) is a non-profit corporation funded through the Bureau of Justice Assistance (BJA). NW3C provides a national support network for state and local enforcement agencies involved in the prevention, investigation, and prosecution of economic and high-tech crime.

The NW3C is a member affiliated organization comprised of law enforcement agencies, state regulatory bodies, and state and local prosecution offices. Neither individuals nor private companies are eligible for membership. NW3C is a national program with a presence in all 50 states. Support services are offered to state and local law enforcement agencies in 5 main categories:

1. Economic and computer crime training
2. Intelligence and analytical services
3. Case funding for designated cases
4. Research
5. Fraud complaint referral and analysis

A cooperative effort between NW3C and the FBI, the Internet Crime Complaint Center (IC3) is a single location that receives internet-related criminal complaints and refers them to appropriate federal, state, local, or international law enforcement and/or regulatory agencies for the level of investigation they deem appropriate. A component of the IC3, the Internet Complaint Search and Investigation System (ICSIS) is a tool developed by NW3C for member agencies with criminal investigative authority. ICSIS allows member agencies to access information about current internet crimes and open investigations in their areas. Users can search through the vast amount of data in the IC3 database, organize pertinent data into cases and collaborate with other agencies. ICSIS also allows for the development of statistics from Internet complaint data.

Headquartered in Richmond, Virginia, NW3C is staffed by computer crime specialists, curriculum developers, enforcement analysts, intelligence technicians, researchers, and training coordinators. NW3C services are coordinated by an elected board of directors comprising a chairman and seven regional directors from across the United States.

<http://www.nw3c.org/>

AUSTRALIAN INSTITUTE OF PROFESSIONAL INTELLIGENCE OFFICERS

Founded in 1990, the Australian Institute of Professional Intelligence Officers (AIPIO) is an organization dedicated to promoting intelligence as a recognized profession in Australia.

The AIPIO publishes a quarterly newsletter - AIPIO News - as an informal channel to highlight people and events, as well as short articles addressing matters of interest to AIPIO members as well as publishing a referenced journal on a quarterly basis. The AIPIO also hosts an annual conference and exhibition to promote the intelligence profession in Australia. The conference features national and international speakers, as well as training workshops. The Institute is governed by an elected Board of Management and a number of co-opted members to strengthen regional support for the wider intelligence community.

<http://www.aipio.asn.au/>

INTERNATIONAL ASSOCIATION OF LAW ENFORCEMENT INTELLIGENCE ANALYSTS (IALEIA)

The International Association of Law Enforcement Intelligence Analysts (IALEIA) was founded in 1980 by leaders in the U.S. and Canadian analytic communities. The mission of IALEIA is to professionalize analysis in law enforcement, the military, and in private industry. IALEIA strives to advance high standards of professionalism in law enforcement intelligence analysis at the local, state/provincial, national and international levels. Its aim is to enhance general understanding of the role of intelligence analysis, encourage the recognition of intelligence analysis as a professional endeavor, develop international qualification and competence standards, reinforce professional concepts, devise training standards and curricula, furnish advisory and related services on intelligence analysis matters, conduct analytic-related research studies and provide the ability to disseminate information regarding analytical techniques and methods.

Based in the United States, IALEIA is managed by an international Board of Directors made up of nine elected IALEIA members. Several board members are also supported by volunteer committees. IALEIA has a paid administrator and Executive Director, as well as an Executive Advisory Board appointed by the President. IALEIA supports regional chapters throughout the world in accordance with a policy manual. IALEIA has a certification program for analysts, a code of ethics, and bylaws providing structure for the organization. The organization represents law enforcement analysts in a variety of venues, and provides an environment of community by establishing regional chapters.

IALEIA publishes a peer-reviewed journal twice a year. The Journal is a scholarly publication that strives to "bridge the gap" between academic research and the practical techniques employed by criminal intelligence professionals and experts worldwide. Additionally, IALEIA has published a number of booklets on analysis in law enforcement including *Law Enforcement Analytic Standards, Intelligence Led Policing – Getting Started, Guidelines for Starting an Analytic Unit, Successful Law Enforcement Using Analytic Methods, and Intelligence Models and Best Practices*. These booklets have been made available to law enforcement managers around the world and have helped to develop an appreciation for the role analysis plays. IALEIA also publishes a newsletter, the INTELSCOPE, three times a year, featuring news from the local chapters, information regarding available training and articles of interest to law enforcement analysts. The IALEIA website provides current information on varied training programs, conferences, and bibliographical materials.

IALEIA partners frequently with the Association of Law Enforcement Intelligence Units (LEIU) on publications such as Intelligence 2000 and Criminal Intelligence in the 21st Century. This partnership also extends to the deployment of the Foundations of Intelligence Analysis Training (FIAT) and annual training conferences for law enforcement intelligence analysts and officers worldwide. IALEIA is also affiliated with the Australian Institute of Professional Intelligence Officers, a sister organization in Australia.

<http://www.ialeia.org/>

ASSOCIATION OF LAW ENFORCEMENT INTELLIGENCE UNITS (LEIU)

In the mid 1950s, local and state law enforcement agencies in the United States recognized that no single agency or organization was responsible for receiving, collating, maintaining, and disseminating information on persons involved in organized crime. These law enforcement agencies surmised correctly that organized crime would exploit advancing technologies in transportation and communications, become more mobile, and increase their spheres of influence and criminal activities. As a result, twenty-six law enforcement agencies met in San Francisco, California on March 29, 1956 to discuss problems and possible solutions. The most important result of that meeting was the creation of LEIU, the Law Enforcement Intelligence Unit, and the development of an organizational purpose that survives to this day.

CHAPTER 17

Networks, Organizations, and Resources

The mission of LEIU is to provide leadership and promote professionalism in the criminal intelligence community. LEIU's purpose is to gather, record, and exchange confidential information not available through regular police channels concerning organized crime and terrorism. LEIU is an association of law enforcement agencies, similar in many respects to numerous other professional associations serving doctors, attorneys, journalists, and educators. LEIU members have exclusive access to a secure, online database containing criminal intelligence information on organized crime, terrorism, and street gangs. Members also have access to an automated gaming index to assist with gaming license background investigations. An LEIU analyst is available to respond to members' inquiries for information on suspected criminals and their activities.

LEIU is divided geographically into four zones: Eastern, Central, Northwestern and Southwestern. Each Zone elects a Chairperson and Vice Chairperson to serve as Zone Officers. LEIU elects a General Chairperson and Vice General Chairperson. The General Chairperson appoints a Secretary-Treasurer, a legal advisor, a Federal Agency Representative and an Executive Director who, along with the Past General Chairperson and two representatives from the Central Coordinating Agency (CCA) serve as National Officers. The National Officers and the Zone Officers make up the Executive Board. The CCA acts as the administrative arm for LEIU and is housed in the California Department of Justice in Sacramento, California. The CCA has been located at the California Department of Justice since LEIU was founded in 1956. Comprising approximately 240 law enforcement agencies in the United States, Canada, and South Africa, LEIU membership is limited to law enforcement organizations having an intelligence function. Because of the rapport established at the annual training seminars and through multi-agency investigations, representatives of member agencies have established a highly professional relationship of trust and respect. This facilitates the exchange of confidential criminal information between agencies.

In 2008, in order to more accurately reflect its structure, the organization officially changed its name to the Association of Law Enforcement Intelligence Units, while still retaining the acronym "LEIU." In addition, LEIU recently expanded its membership classification to accommodate federal law enforcement agency membership, and created a position on the Executive Board for a Federal Agency Representative.

LEIU strives to be a voice for information sharing and criminal intelligence issues at the national level. LEIU leaders assisted in the development of the National Criminal Intelligence Sharing Plan, and serve on several national-level committees, including the Criminal Intelligence Coordinating Council (CICC), the Global Intelligence Working Group, the National Fusion Center Coordination Group, the Interagency Threat Assessment and Coordination Group (ITACG) Advisory Council, The Homeland Security Information Network (HSIN) Advisory Council, the Homeland Security State and Local Community of Interest (HS SLIC) Advisory Board, and the Controlled Unclassified Information (CUI) Council.

Since 1956, LEIU has been on the forefront of establishing professional standards for law enforcement intelligence units. Through these well defined standards, the Association of Law Enforcement Intelligence Units seeks to create a balance between protecting our constitutional liberties and protecting society against those involved in criminal or terrorist activity.

<http://leiu.org>

INTERNATIONAL ASSOCIATION FOR INTELLIGENCE EDUCATION (IAFIE)

The International Association for Intelligence Education (IAFIE) was founded in 2005 to support colleges, universities and schoolhouses dedicated to providing intelligence education. It was an outgrowth of the Mercyhurst College Colloquium series, but has expanded to over 400 members.

IAFIE holds annual conferences at which law enforcement, intelligence community, military, and competitive intelligence educational professionals meet to share programs and ideas about teaching intelligence. Its website includes a calendar of events, a member listing and documents shared on intelligence. It has local chapters in Washington, DC and the Great Lakes area and has members in the U.S., Canada, Australia, Europe and South Africa.

<http://www.iafie.org>

Challenges Facing Law Enforcement Intelligence
By Lisa Palmieri

INTRODUCTION

Looking ahead into the 21st century after almost 20 years of working with police agencies, I believe there are clear challenges facing law enforcement regarding the production and consumption of intelligence. My background is defined not only by my years working as an analyst in law enforcement, but also from my experience working in military intelligence as a collector, and as a current member of the intelligence community. It is a unique perspective, and I was asked to share some of my observations, many from my view at the executive level of the International Association of Law Enforcement Intelligence Analysts (IALEIA).

Background

In the years since 9/11, there have been two significant advancements related to improving and expanding criminal intelligence in the United States. The first involved creating the National Criminal Intelligence Sharing Plan (NCISP). This effort, led by the International Association of Chiefs of Police and the U.S. Department of Justice brought together experts in law enforcement and criminal intelligence to create a plan that would correct the inadequacies and barriers that impeded information and intelligence sharing among law enforcement and national security agencies. The resulting document subsequently outlined a number of recommendations for local, state, tribal, and federal law enforcement agencies regarding effective intelligence sharing. These recommendations encompassed all aspects of building or enhancing a model intelligence system including; principles and policies, training, protecting privacy and civil rights, technology, and promoting intelligence-led policing. In essence, the NCISP provided law enforcement with appropriate standards for establishing or upgrading their intelligence function.

The second significant advancement in recent years involves the establishment of a national integrated network of state and major urban area fusion centers. These centers are designed to include federal, state, and local agency personnel in one location to gather, process, analyze, and share information and intelligence related to public safety. Many of these 72 centers are still adapting to their new role and working to train staff and obtain consistent funding for their operations. In any event, the fusion center concept certainly provides the potential for enhanced intelligence sharing in the United States.

Challenges

In spite of these two positive improvements to law enforcements' criminal intelligence efforts, much remains to be done. Approximately 75% of the law enforcement agencies in the United States are too small to assign full time personnel to the intelligence function, and have not been trained to participate in the intelligence cycle at the regional or state level. Many other agencies of sufficient size either lack the desire, training, or funding to participate in the intelligence function.

CHAPTER 18

Challenges Facing Law Enforcement Intelligence

A third group of law enforcement agencies includes those that have intelligence units in place but have yet to establish or maintain appropriate standards or provide useful intelligence products for their jurisdiction. The following perspectives address some of the issues that should be recognized and acted upon in order to bring law enforcement agencies up to acceptable criminal intelligence standards.

Many law enforcement agencies continue to focus training and evaluate performance only on reactive capabilities: arrests, seizures, prosecutions. If the intelligence function is to be effectively integrated into the public safety field, there needs to be a methodology to quantify the benefit of informed decision making, deterrence, disruption, and prevention of criminal activity. Most, if not all of the challenges to implementing the intelligence cycle in support of decision making, in both tactical and strategic environments are surmountable. However, in order to accomplish this, intelligence training must be built into policing at all levels, from patrol to executive, and developed to a national or even international standard.

The most important adjustment needed across the board in the law enforcement community is the understanding of what intelligence is, and how it can benefit decision-makers. Decision-makers may be patrol officers on the street, investigators, or executive officers. They need to be able to make informed decisions based on analysis of all relevant information by trained personnel. Law enforcement agencies collect and store massive amounts of information about criminal activity, whether it is arrests, calls for service, or various reports during the course of business. Generally speaking, this knowledge is not sufficiently shared to support policing objectives beyond those involved in specific investigations. Police executives, patrol officers and investigators should receive a consistent flow of intelligence products to help identify, understand, and respond to trends of criminal activity in their jurisdictions.

At this point in the evolution of law enforcement intelligence, too many consumers are being ill-served by "intelligence" products which merely provide information regarding arrests made in a given time period, or a rehash of current events taken straight from their own systems, or worse, internet media sites. Most of this can be attributed to a lack of training, and the inability to quantify the value of intelligence in support of law enforcement objectives.

The most common use of intelligence in most countries is in the national security field. In this context, there are clearly defined collection requirements which are set by the needs of the decision makers based on questions or problems posed by decision makers. These information needs, or requirements are understood by and guide the work of operators and analysts who are knowledgeable in their given fields. The analytic function pieces together the information gathered (which is much more complex than the connection of "dots" referred to in current lexicon) and interprets what it means in a structured, logical manner. National security officials expect to hear the "what" and the "so what" from analysts who have accessed information from all available sources, not merely what the agency currently has on hand.

Law enforcement has lagged far behind the national security Intelligence Community in focusing collection on priorities. Decision makers should not be satisfied to have analysts try to interpret only what has been collected routinely, whether it resides in databases or is collected as part of an investigation. There is a lack of understanding and emphasis on the need for trained and professional analysts as an integral component of an intelligence unit. In order to qualify as intelligence, a product (which could be anything from a 5 minute briefing to a 30 page assessment) must communicate the "what" (e.g., "there has been an uptick in violent assaults between the red and the blue gangs"), the "so what" (e.g., "this violence threatens to endanger innocent people and may dissuade investors from

Challenges Facing Law Enforcement Intelligence

participating in a rehabilitation project for the local commercial district"), and depending on the situation, the "what now," which would provide recommendations to deter further deterioration of public safety in the area.

A major challenge to law enforcement intelligence as a discipline is that it is not a recognized professional track for sworn officers. There is a lack of academy based intelligence training to complement other standards such as weapons training, interview techniques, or report writing. Very few police officers graduate from their training academies with even a basic understanding of the intelligence cycle, intelligence requirements, intelligence products, or their role in the process. Intelligence commanders and officers are often posted to intelligence units with no specialized training at all, and are expected to learn on the job. This often results in a reliance on the collection of information from limited sources with little analysis or production to support customers. Those commanders and officers who do take the initiative to learn about intelligence and do their best within their jurisdictions to provide true intelligence support to their agencies are rarely left in place long enough to make institutional changes; promotional considerations or rotational policies usually mandate transfers after a few years.

Until intelligence becomes a standardized and recognized field in policing with available training for all levels within law enforcement agencies, an alternate way to address this challenge would be to develop a cadre of professional civilian intelligence analysts to manage the intelligence function in police agencies. This would support the more traditional policing structure as it exists, and could also build depth into the intelligence unit, encourage and reward professionalization, and mitigate the effects of leadership changes every two or three years. Institutional knowledge would be preserved and could better support the intelligence needs of the agency and jurisdiction. A professional cadre would also support more appropriate tasking of intelligence analysts and provide consistent management of the analytic function, and soften the learning curve for new police officers regarding what intelligence is, and how it can be used to support policing priorities.

The incorporation of intelligence as an element of policing culture would also address the challenge of evaluating intelligence analysts in police agencies. Many analyst positions do not have a specific job definition because of the limitations of the civil service system. The job descriptions which exist can be generic, and unless someone has been committed to driving the process of creating an accurate job description, the evaluation criteria is also like fitting a square peg in a round hole. Development of a professional analytic cadre within the organization will further support evaluation processes which will be suited to the tasks and responsibilities of the unit.

This leads to the topic of the training, integration, and professionalization of law enforcement analysts. For many years, the individual referred to as an "analyst" was the person who knew how to extract specific information from the myriad of disjointed databases available to support law enforcement. While this was, and continues to be, a pressing need for law enforcement due to the byzantine information systems which continue to proliferate, it limited the role of an analyst in a police agency. Instead of accessing and analyzing disparate data resulting in a product to support the intelligence needs of the consumer, the "analyst" became more of a "computer person," finding and disseminating data upon request, or a computer graphics specialist providing visual aids to support prosecutions. There has been little demand for proactive analysis to support the customer. Over the past several years, this has been changing in some agencies due to the vigilance of individuals, but has not been institutionalized. As law enforcement officers become more familiar with true intelligence by way of exposure to national security intelligence methodologies, some are making an effort to recreate this function in their agencies. The challenge is to now institutionalize this trend and make it the rule, not the exception.

Analytic support to investigations has become increasingly recognized in law enforcement, and provides a true advantage to police investigators who are trying to make arrests for complex and sophisticated crimes. It provides excellent training to newer analysts, and exercises their ability to think in a structured way which must be substantiated and documented in preparation for testifying in court. However, this does not exercise the full potential for analysis in law enforcement. The intelligence cycle can be implemented in the context of a criminal investigation, but information collected during investigations and prosecutions is often disregarded if it is peripheral to proving the elements of the crime. What needs to be done to take this a step beyond the individual investigation is to take all the information learned across investigations and jurisdictions to support the more strategic efforts to detect, deter and prevent criminal activity on a grand scale. This implementation of the intelligence cycle would support decisions which would have an impact on the broader criminal environment, and make a tangible difference to the communities affected by it. Achieving and measuring this level of effectiveness will be a formidable challenge, but with the appropriate training of personnel at all levels within law enforcement, it is certainly an attainable goal.

Aside from investigative information, there is an enormous volume of structured data available to law enforcement. This information is collected and stored in dozens of databases, but for the most part, is only used for specific queries targeting individuals, incidents, addresses, or other structured data points. Use of this information to become better informed about the criminal environment is the exception, not the rule, and there are many reasons for this. One is that technology used by law enforcement over the past few decades has not been developed to support analysis of the information stored within. In general, technology acquisition has not been guided by a needs assessment which includes utilization of data by analysts supporting an intelligence mission. This weakness in information systems makes holistic analysis of criminal information challenging, and limits the efficiency of the intelligence process.

The focus of the intelligence unit is also a challenge, in that many intelligence units are not proportionately resourced to serve their agencies or properly address their assigned mission. Setting priorities can be a difficult thing to do politically, because someone must make a decision on what the priorities are, and then maintain focus on them despite emergence of the "issue of the moment." Intelligence Led Policing, as defined by IALEIA is *"Executive implementation of the INTELLIGENCE CYCLE to support proactive decision making for resource allocation and crime prevention."* It goes on to state that *"Executives responsible for and supported by any type of intelligence unit must take on a leadership role in engaging stakeholders and setting priorities if they are to succeed using Intelligence Led Policing as a tool for deterring, preventing and solving crimes in their communities."* Setting of priorities which lead to developing information requirements is a major part of the planning and direction step of the intelligence cycle and intelligence units will not be effective without it.

CONCLUSION

The law enforcement community has made significant progress in the past ten years as far as understanding the importance of the intelligence function and the need to share information. However, there are many improvements that can and should be made to enhance our intelligence efforts. If these improvements are addressed and if we can focus and overcome the challenges discussed here, we will continue to strengthen our capability to keep our communities safe.

Appendix I

"Guidelines and Regulations"

- *LEIU's Criminal Intelligence File Guidelines*
- *28 CFR Part 23.20*
- LEIU's *"Criminal Intelligence Unit Guidelines for First Amendment Demonstrations"*

LEIU's CRIMINAL INTELLIGENCE FILE GUIDELINES

I. CRIMINAL INTELLIGENCE FILE GUIDELINES

These guidelines were established to provide the law enforcement agency with an information base that meets the needs of the agency in carrying out its efforts to protect the public and suppress criminal operations. These standards are designed to bring about an equitable balance between the civil rights and liberties of citizens and the needs of law enforcement to collect and disseminate criminal intelligence on the conduct of persons and groups who may be engaged in systematic criminal activity.

II. CRIMINAL INTELLIGENCE FILE DEFINED

A criminal intelligence file consists of stored information on the activities and associations of:

A.   Individuals who:

1.   Are suspected of being involved in the actual or attempted planning, organizing, financing, or commission of criminal acts; or

2.   Are suspected of being involved in criminal activities with known or suspected crime figures.

B. Organizations, businesses, and groups that:

1.   Are suspected of being involved in the actual or attempted planning, organizing, financing, or commission of criminal acts; or

2.   Are suspected of being operated, controlled, financed, or infiltrated by known or suspected crime figures for use in an illegal manner.

III. FILE CONTENT

Only information with a criminal predicate and which meets the agency's criteria for file input should be stored in the criminal intelligence file. Specifically excluded material includes:

A.   Information on an individual or group merely on the basis that such individual or group supports unpopular causes.

B.   Information on an individual or group merely on the basis of ethnic background.

C.   Information on any individual or group merely on the basis of religious or political affiliations.

D.   Information on an individual or group merely on the basis of non-criminal personal habits.

E.   Criminal Offender Record Information (CORI) should be excluded from an intelligence file. This is because CORI may be subject to specific audit and dissemination restrictions which are designed to protect an individual's right to privacy and to ensure accuracy.

F.   Also excluded are associations with individuals that are not of a criminal nature.

State law or local regulations may dictate whether or not public record and intelligence information should be kept in separate files or commingled. Some agencies believe that separating their files will prevent the release of intelligence information in the event a subpoena is issued. This belief is unfounded, as all information requested in the subpoena (both public and intelligence) must be turned over to the court. The judge then makes the determination on what information will be released.

The decision to commingle or separate public and intelligence documents is strictly a management decision. In determining this policy, administrators should consider the following:

A.   Records relating to the conduct of the public's business that are prepared by a state or local agency, regardless of physical form or characteristics, may be considered public and the public has access to these records.

B.   Specific types of records (including intelligence information) may be exempt from public disclosure.

C.   Regardless of whether public record information is separated from or commingled with intelligence data, the public may have access to public records.

D.   The separation of public information from criminal intelligence information may better protect the confidentiality of the criminal file. If a request is made for public records, an agency can release the public file and leave the intelligence file intact (thus less apt to accidentally disclose intelligence information).

E.   Separating of files is the best theoretical approach to maintaining files; however, it is not easy to do. Most intelligence reports either reference public record information or else contains a combination of intelligence and public record data. Thus, it is difficult to isolate them from each other. Maintaining separate public and intelligence files also increases the amount of effort required to index, store, and retrieve information.

IV. FILE CRITERIA

All information retained in the criminal intelligence file should meet file criteria prescribed by the agency. These criteria should outline the agency's crime categories and provide specifics for determining whether subjects involved in these crimes are suitable for file inclusion.

File input criteria will vary among agencies because of differences in size, functions, resources, geographical location, crime problems, etc. The categories listed in the suggested model below are not exhaustive.

A. Permanent Status

1. Information that relates an individual, organization, business, or group is suspected of being involved in the actual or attempted planning, organizing, financing, or committing of one or more of the following criminal acts:

   - Narcotic trafficking/manufacturing
   - Unlawful gambling
   - Loan sharking
   - Extortion
   - Vice and pornography
   - Infiltration of legitimate business for illegitimate purposes
   - Stolen securities
   - Bribery
   - Major crime including homicide, sexual assault, burglary, auto theft, kidnapping, destruction of property, robbery, fraud, fencing stolen property, and arson
   - Manufacture, us of, or possession of explosive devices for purposes of fraud, intimidation, or political motivation

2. In addition to falling within the confines of one or more of the above criminal activities, the subject/entity to be given permanent status must be identifiable-- distinguished by a name and unique identifying characteristics (e.g., date of birth, criminal identification number, driver's license number, address). Identification at the time of file input is necessary to distinguish the subject/entity from existing file entries and those that may be entered at a later time. NOTE: The exception to this rule involves modus operandi (MO) files. MO files describe a unique method of operation for a specific type of crime (homicide, fraud) and may not be immediately linked to an identifiable suspect. MO files may be retained indefinitely while additional identifiers are sought.

B. Temporary Status:

Information that does not meet the criteria for permanent storage but may be pertinent to an investigation involving one of the categories previously listed should be given "temporary" status. It is recommended the retention of temporary information not exceed one year unless a compelling reason exists to extend this time period. (An example of a compelling reason is if several pieces of information indicate that a crime has been committed, but more than a year is needed to identify a suspect.) During this period, efforts should be made to identify the subject/entity or validate the information so that its final status may be determined. If the information is still classified temporary at the end of the one-year period, and a compelling reason for its retention is not evident, the information should be purged. An individual, organization, business, or group may be given temporary status in the following cases:

1. **Subject/entity is unidentifiable** - subject/entity (although suspected of being engaged in criminal activities) has no known physical descriptors, identification numbers, or distinguishing characteristics available

2. **Involvement is questionable** - involvement in criminal activities is suspected by a subject/entity which has either:

   - **Possible criminal associations** - individual, organization, business, or group (not currently reported to be criminally active) associates with a known criminal and appears to be jointly involved in illegal activities

   - **Criminal history** - individual, organization, business, or group (not currently reported to be criminally active) that has a history of criminal conduct, and the circumstances currently being reported (i.e., new position or ownership in a business) indicates they may again become criminally active

3. **Reliability/validity unknown** - the reliability of the information sources and/or the validity of the information cannot be determined at the time of receipt; however, the information appears to be significant and merits temporary storage while verification attempts are made

V. INFORMATION EVALUATION

Information to be retained in the criminal intelligence file should be evaluated and designated for reliability and content validity prior to filing.

The bulk of the data an intelligence unit receives consists of unverified allegations or information. Evaluating the information's source and content indicates to future users the information's worth and usefulness. Circulating information which may not have been evaluated, where the source reliability is poor or the content validity is doubtful, is detrimental to the agency's operations and contrary to the individual's right to privacy.

To ensure uniformity with the intelligence community, it is strongly recommended that stored information be evaluated according to the criteria set forth below.

Source Reliability:

(A) **Reliable** - The reliability of the source is unquestioned or has been well tested in the past.

(B) **Usually Reliable** - The reliability of the source can usually be relied upon as factual. The majority of information provided in the past has proven to be reliable.

(C) **Unreliable** - The reliability of the source has been sporadic in the past.

(D) **Unknown** - The reliability of the source cannot be judged. Its authenticity or trustworthiness has not yet been determined by either experience or investigation.

Content Validity:

(1) **Confirmed** - The information has been corroborated by an investigator or another independent, reliable source

(2) **Probable** - The information is consistent with past accounts.

(3) **Doubtful** - The information is inconsistent with past accounts.

(4) **Cannot Be Judged** - The information cannot be judged. Its authenticity has not yet been determined by either experience or investigation.

VI. INFORMATION CLASSIFICATION

Information retained in the criminal intelligence file should be classified in order to protect sources, investigations, and the individual's right to privacy. Classification also indicates the internal approval which must be completed prior to the release of the information to persons outside the agency. However, the classification of information in itself is not a defense against a subpoena duces tecum.

The classification of criminal intelligence information is subject to continual change. The passage of time, the conclusion of investigations, and other factors may affect the security classification assigned to particular documents. Documents within the intelligence files should be reviewed on an ongoing basis to ascertain whether a higher or lesser degree of document security is required to ensure that information is released only when and if appropriate.

Classification systems may differ among agencies as to the number of levels of security and release authority. In establishing a classification system, agencies should define the types of information for each security level, dissemination criteria, and release authority. The system listed below classifies data maintained in the Criminal Intelligence File according to one of the following categories:

Sensitive

1. Information pertaining to significant law enforcement cases currently under investigation

2. Corruption (police or other government officials), or other sensitive information

3. Informant identification information

4. Criminal intelligence reports which require strict dissemination and release criteria

Confidential

1. Criminal intelligence reports not designated as sensitive

2. Information obtained through intelligence unit channels that is not classified as sensitive and is for law enforcement use only

Restricted

1. Reports that at an earlier date were classified sensitive or confidential and the need for high-level security no longer exist

2. Non-confidential information prepared for/by law enforcement agencies

Unclassified

1.   Civic-related information to which, in its original form, the general public had direct access (i.e., public record data)

2.   News media information - newspaper, magazine, and periodical clippings dealing with specified criminal categories

VII. INFORMATION SOURCE

In all cases, source identification should be available in some form. The true identify of the source should be used unless there is a need to protect the source. Accordingly, each law enforcement agency should establish criteria that would indicate when source identification would be appropriate.
The value of information stored in a criminal intelligence file is often directly related to the source of such information. Some factors to consider in determining whether source identification is warranted include:

- The nature of the information reported

- The potential need to refer to the source's identity for further or prosecutorial activity

- The reliability of the source

Whether or not confidential source identification is warranted, reports should reflect the name of the agency and the reporting individual. In those cases when identifying the source by name is not practical for internal security reasons, a code number may be used. A confidential listing of coded sources of information can then be retained by the intelligence unit commander. In addition to identifying the source, it may be appropriate in a particular case to describe how the source obtained the information (for example "S-60, a reliable police informant heard" or "a reliable law enforcement source of the police department saw" a particular event at a particular time).

VIII. INFORMATION QUALITY CONTROL

Information to be stored in the criminal intelligence file should undergo a thorough review for compliance with established file input guidelines and agency policy prior to being filed. The quality control reviewer is responsible for seeing that all information entered into the criminal intelligence files conforms with the agency's file criteria and has been properly evaluated and classified.

IX. FILE DISSEMINATION

Agencies should adopt sound procedures for disseminating stored information. These procedures will protect the individual's right to privacy as well as maintain the confidentiality of the sources and the file itself.

Information from a criminal intelligence report can only be released to an individual who has demonstrated both a "need-to-know" and a "right-to-know."

"Right-to-know" - Requestor has official capacity and statutory authority to the information being sought.

"Need-to-know" - Requested information is pertinent and necessary to the requestor agency in initiating, furthering, or completing an investigation.

No "original document" which has been obtained from an outside agency is to be released to a third agency. Should such a request be received, the requesting agency will be referred to the submitting agency for further assistance.

Information classification and evaluation are, in part, dissemination controls. They denote who may receive the information as well as the internal approval level(s) required for release of the information. In order to encourage conformity within the intelligence community, it is recommended that stored information be classified according to a system similar to the following.

Security Level	Dissemination Criteria	Release Authority
Sensitive	Restricted to law enforcement personnel having a specific need-to-know and right-to-know	Intelligence Unit Commander
Confidential	Same as for sensitive	Intelligence Unit Manager or designee
Restricted	Same as for Sensitive	Intelligence Unit Supervisor or designee
Unclassified	Not restricted Personnel	Intelligence Unit

The integrity of the criminal intelligence file can be maintained only by strict adherence to proper dissemination guidelines. To eliminate unauthorized use and abuses of the system, a department should utilize a dissemination control form that could be maintained with each stored document. This control form would record the date of the request, the name of the agency and individual requesting the information, the need-to-know, the information provided, and the name of the employee handling the request. Depending upon the needs of the agency, the control form also may be designed to record other items useful to the agency in the management of its operations. This control form also may be subject to discovery.

X. FILE REVIEW AND PURGE

Information stored in the criminal intelligence file should be reviewed periodically for reclassification or purge in order to: ensure that the file is current, accurate, and relevant to the needs and objective of the agency; safeguard the individual's right of privacy as guaranteed under federal and state laws; and, ensure that the security classification level remains appropriate.

Law enforcement agencies have an obligation to keep stored information on subjects current and accurate. Reviewing of criminal intelligence should be done on a continual basis as agency personnel use the material in carrying out day-to-day activities. In this manner, information that is no longer useful or that cannot be validated can immediately be purged or reclassified where necessary.

To ensure that all files are reviewed and purged systematically, agencies should develop purge criteria and schedules. Operational procedures for the purge and the method of destruction for purged materials should be established.

A. Purge Criteria:

General considerations for reviewing and purging of information stored in the criminal intelligence file are as follows:

1. Utility

How often is the information used?
For what purpose is the information being used?
Who uses the information?

2. Timeliness and Appropriateness

Is this investigation still ongoing?
Is the information outdated?
Is the information relevant to the needs and objectives of the agency?
Is the information relevant to the purpose for which it was collected and stored?

3. Accuracy and Completeness

Is the information still valid?
Is the information adequate for identification purposes?
Can the validity of the data be determined through investigative techniques?

B. Review and Purge Time Schedule:

Reclassifying and purging information in the intelligence file should be done on an ongoing basis as documents are reviewed. In addition, a complete review of the criminal intelligence file for purging purposes should be undertaken periodically. This review and purge schedule can vary from once each year for documents with temporary status to once every five years for permanent documents. Agencies should develop a schedule best suited to their needs and should contact their legal counsel for guidance.

C. Manner of Destruction:

Material purged from the criminal intelligence file should be destroyed. Disposal is used for all records or papers that identify a person by name. It is the responsibility of each agency to determine that their obsolete records are destroyed in accordance with applicable laws, rules, and state or local policy.

XI. FILE SECURITY

The criminal intelligence file should be located in a secured area with file access restricted to authorized personnel.

Physical security of the criminal intelligence file is imperative to maintain the confidentiality of the information stored in the file and to ensure the protection of the individual's right to privacy.

Glossary

PUBLIC RECORD

Public record includes any writing containing information relating to the conduct of the public's business prepared, owned, used, or retained by any state or local agency regardless of physical form or characteristics.

"Member of the public" means any person, except a member, agent, officer, or employee of a federal, state, or local agency acting within the scope of his or her membership in an agency, office, or employment.

For purposes of these guidelines, public record information includes only that information to which the general public normally has direct access, (i.e., birth or death certificates, county recorder's information, incorporation information, etc.)

CRIMINAL OFFENDER RECORD INFORMATION (CORI)

CORI is defined as summary information to arrests, pretrial proceedings, sentencing information, incarcerations, parole and probation.

    a.   Summary criminal history records are commonly referred to as "rap sheets." Data submitted on fingerprint cards, disposition of arrest and citation forms and probation flash notices create the entries on the rap sheet.

Code of Federal Regulations
Title 28, Volume 1
Revised as of July 1, 2009
From the U.S. Government Printing Office via GPO Access
CITE: 28 CFR 23.20
Page 433-435

Title 28—Judicial Administration
Chapter 1—Department of Justice
Part 23--Criminal Intelligence Systems Operating Policies--Table of Contents

Sec. 23.20 Operating Principles.

    (a) A project shall collect and maintain criminal intelligence information concerning an individual only if there is reasonable suspicion that the individual is involved in criminal conduct or activity and the information is relevant to that criminal conduct or activity.

    (b) A project shall not collect or maintain criminal intelligence information about the political, religious or social views, associations, or activities of any individual or any group, association, corporation, business, partnership, or other organization unless such information directly relates to criminal conduct or activity and there is reasonable suspicion that the subject of the information is or may be involved in criminal conduct or activity.

    (c) Reasonable Suspicion or Criminal Predicate is established when information exists which establishes sufficient facts to give a trained law enforcement or criminal investigative agency officer, investigator, or employee a basis to believe that there is a reasonable possibility that an individual or organization is involved in a definable criminal activity or enterprise. In an interjurisdictional intelligence system, the project is responsible for establishing the existence of reasonable suspicion of criminal activity either through examination of supporting information submitted by a participating agency or by delegation of this responsibility to a properly trained participating agency which is subject to routine inspection and audit procedures established by the project.

    (d) A project shall not include in any criminal intelligence system information which has been obtained in violation of any applicable Federal, State, or local law or ordinance. In an interjurisdictional intelligence system, the project is responsible for establishing that no information is entered in violation of Federal, State, or local laws, either through examination of supporting information submitted by a participating agency or by delegation of this responsibility to a properly trained participating agency which is subject to routine inspection and audit procedures established by the project.

[Page 434]

(e) A project or authorized recipient shall disseminate criminal intelligence information only where there is a need to know and a right to know the information in the performance of a law enforcement activity.

(f)(1)Except as noted in paragraph (f)(2) of this section, a project shall disseminate criminal intelligence information only to law enforcement authorities who shall agree to follow procedures regarding information receipt, maintenance, security, and dissemination which are consistent with these principles.

(2) Paragraph (f)(2) Paragraph (f)(1) of this section shall not limit the dissemination of an assessment of criminal intelligence information to a government official or to any other individual, when necessary, to avoid imminent danger to life or property.

(g) A project maintaining criminal intelligence information shall ensure that administrative, technical, and physical safeguards (including audit trails) are adopted to insure against unauthorized access and against intentional or unintentional damage. A record indicating who has been given information, the reason for release of the information and the date of each dissemination outside the project shall be kept. Information shall be labeled to indicate levels of sensitivity, levels of confidence, and the identity of submitting agencies and control officials. Each project must establish written definitions for the need to know and right to know standards for dissemination to other agencies as provided in paragraph (e) of this section. The project is responsible for establishing the existence of an inquirer's need to know and right to know the information being requested either through inquiry or by delegation of this responsibility to a properly trained participating agency which is subject to routine inspection and audit procedures established by the project. Each intelligence project shall assure that the following security requirements are implemented:

(1) Where appropriate, projects must adopt effective and technologically advanced computer software and hardware designs to prevent unauthorized access to the information contained in the system

(2) The project must restrict access to its facilities, operating environment and documentation to organizations and personnel authorized by the project

(3) The project must store information in the system in a manner such that it cannot be modified, destroyed, accessed, or purged without authorization

(4) The project must institute procedures to protect criminal intelligence information from unauthorized access, theft, sabotage, fire, flood, or other natural or manmade disaster

(5) The project must promulgate rules and regulations based on good cause for implementing its authority to screen, reject for employment, transfer, or remove personnel authorized to have direct access to the system

(6) A project may authorize and utilize remote (off-premises) system data bases to the extent that they comply with these security requirements.

(h) All projects shall adopt procedures to assure that all information which is retained by a project has relevancy and importance. Such procedures shall provide for the periodic review of information and the destruction of any information which is misleading, obsolete or otherwise unreliable and shall require that any recipient agencies be advised of such changes which involve errors or corrections. All information retained as a result of this review must reflect the name of the reviewer, date of review and explanation of decision to retain. Information retained in the system must be reviewed and validated for continuing compliance with system submission criteria before the expiration of its retention period, which in no event shall be longer than five (5) years.

(i) If funds awarded under the Act are used to support the operation of an intelligence system, then:

(1) No project shall make direct remote terminal access to intelligence information available to system participants, except as specifically approved by the Office of Justice Programs (OJP) based on a determination that the system has adequate policies and procedures in place to insure that it is accessible only to authorized systems users; and

[Page 435]

(2) A project shall undertake no major modifications to system design without prior grantor agency approval.

(ii) [Reserved]

(j) A project shall notify the grantor agency prior to initiation of formal information exchange procedures with any Federal, State, regional, or other information systems not indicated in the grant documents as initially approved at time of award.

(k) A project shall make assurances that there will be no purchase or use in the course of the project of any electronic, mechanical, or other device for surveillance purposes that is in violation of the provisions of the Electronic Communications Privacy Act of 1986, Public Law 99-508, 18 U.S.C. 2510-2520, 2701-2709 and 3121-3125, or any applicable State statute related to wiretapping and surveillance.

(l) A project shall make assurances that there will be no harassment or interference with any lawful political activities as part of the intelligence operation.

(m) A project shall adopt sanctions for unauthorized access, utilization, or disclosure of information contained in the system.

(n) A participating agency of an interjurisdictional intelligence system must maintain in its agency files information which documents each submission to the system and supports compliance with project entry criteria. Participating agency files supporting system submissions must be made available for reasonable audit and inspection by project representatives.   Project representatives will conduct participating agency inspection and audit in such a manner so as to protect the confidentiality and sensitivity of participating agency intelligence records.

(o) The Attorney General or designee may waive, in whole or in part, the applicability of a particular requirement or requirements contained in this part with respect to a criminal intelligence system, or for a class of submitters or users of such system, upon a clear and convincing showing that such waiver would enhance the collection, maintenance or dissemination of information in the criminal intelligence system, while ensuring that such system would not be utilized in violation of the privacy and constitutional rights of individuals or any applicable state or federal law.

Association of

LAW ENFORCEMENT INTELLIGENCE UNITS

Founded in 1956

Your Voice at the National Level!

Criminal Intelligence Unit Guidelines

for First Amendment Demonstrations

Revised: July 29, 2009

Acknowledgment

The LEIU Executive Board is acknowledging the significant contribution of Mr. John Gordnier to this product. At the request of the Executive Board, John voluntarily undertook researching, drafting, and finalizing this document with input from members of the Executive Board. John has been a long-time friend and advisor to the LEIU Executive Board, many of its members, and to other law enforcement entities around the nation. He has advised us on issues ranging from changes in the Code of Federal Regulations (relating to criminal intelligence) to our published criminal intelligence file guidelines. Many of you may have also attended his workshops on legal issues in criminal intelligence at our annual conferences.

John received his BA degree from the University of Washington in 1966. His JD was earned at the University of Wyoming in 1969. In January 1970 he was sworn in as a member of the California bar. From 1970 until 1972 John worked as a Deputy District Attorney in the County of San Bernardino. In October 1972 he became a Deputy Attorney General in the Criminal Law Division of the California Attorney General's Office. During his time in the Criminal Law Division he tried cases involving public officials, served as the head of the Political Reform Act Enforcement Unit, and was in charge of the Attorney General's Legislative/Lobbyist Task Force. When the Special Prosecutions Unit was created to handle organized crime cases in 1979, John was one of the attorneys assigned to a team consisting of an attorney and two special agents. In 1983 he was named the Senior Assistant Attorney General in charge of the Special Prosecutions Unit, a position he held until the Unit was disbanded in 1991. During his tenure in the Special Prosecutions Unit, John not only prosecuted cases and supervised prosecutions by the unit he also was responsible for the creation and enactment of laws penalizing money laundering, allowing for asset forfeiture, and permitting prosecution under a state RICO provision. From 1991 to 1998 John was a Senior Assistant Attorney General in the Trials and Special Projects Unit. In this capacity he served as the legislative liaison for the Criminal Law Division, prosecuted certain cases such as the Mark Furman perjury case, implemented the Attorney General's response to the Medical Marijuana initiative and successfully defended California's Assault Weapons Law. From 1998 until his retirement in 2007, John was assigned to act as the attorney for the California Department of Justice's intelligence systems, serve as the legal advisor to the CalGANG intelligence system, and teach intelligence law for both basic level and executive level courses sponsored by the Attorney General's Advanced Training Center. Since retiring from public service, John has acted as a consultant and instructor on criminal intelligence law.

Please join the LEIU Executive Board in expressing our thanks to John for his significant support, wise counsel, and professional and personal assistance. It is through friends like John that allow us to develop products such as this.

LEIU Demonstration Guidelines for Intelligence Units

The LEIU Board has received a number of requests from membership asking that we provide guidelines which address interaction between a law enforcement intelligence entity and citizens engaged in a public demonstration. In this context the word "demonstration" means any effort by a citizen or citizens to express a point of view by lawful means in a public space normally open to use by all citizens. Such a model is provided in the main portion of this paper. Several caveats are appropriate with respect to these suggested guidelines.

First, the only demonstrations to which these guidelines ought to be applied are those which fall under the freedoms granted by the First Amendment of the United States Constitution (which freedoms are contained in the constitutions of the states). Other types of demonstrations may be subject to other, specific rules. If, as an example, a labor demonstration is involved these rules should not be applied and the agency should consult with knowledgeable counsel before acting.

Second, it is important to stress that these guidelines assume that there has been no judicial action that has resulted in a consent decree or other order that directs how law enforcement shall respond to such events.

Third, in all cases, no policy should be adopted by an agency without legal review which assures that the legal advisor for that agency is satisfied that it is based on the appropriate controlling legal authorities for that jurisdiction. In some jurisdictions such legal review may require approval by the governing body of the agency as well as the legal advisor.

Fourth, once a policy has been adopted there should be proper, ongoing training directed at the goal of providing the officers who will be tasked with implementing the policy, with a clear understanding of the proper manner in which to discharge their responsibilities.

Last, each event which requires application of all or any part of the policy should be treated as an opportunity to evaluate and, if necessary, modify the policy based on the lessons learned from the event.

When appropriate, under the LEIU Criminal Intelligence File Guidelines or Code of Federal Regulations, Title 28, Part 23, information obtained while following the policy adopted in the particular jurisdiction may be used for creating temporary files, intelligence files, or both.

MODEL GUIDELINES

Statement of Need

It is the responsibility of law enforcement agencies to provide for the safety of the public at public events, including events which are for the purpose(s) of exercising First Amendment privileges. The purpose of these guidelines is to assist in establishing the proper balance between the needs of law enforcement to secure the public's safety and the right of citizens to exercise First Amendment privileges.

It is always the case that an agency has an obligation to respect First Amendment freedoms. Those citizens who participate in a demonstration have an expectation that they will be permitted to lawfully make their point safely and without disruption from persons within the demonstration or disruption by persons not participating in the demonstration. Citizens not participating in a demonstration have an expectation that the demonstration will not be conducted in a manner that will endanger the safety of their persons or property. Law enforcement does not have an obligation to enable the exercise of constitutional rights; rather it has an obligation to provide for the safety of all citizens, demonstrators and non-demonstrators, in a manner that honors constitutional rights.

Right to Access Information

A law enforcement agency may seek information from all legal sources with regard to the question of whether the group(s) or any member(s) of the group(s) to be involved in the demonstration have been involved in unlawful behavior which would present a threat of harm to persons or property within the jurisdiction of the law enforcement agency or would prevent other citizens from exercising their First Amendment Rights.

Information, which a law enforcement agency may access, shall include all materials that have been gathered by the authority that has or shares approval responsibility for demonstrations if that authority is not the law enforcement agency. Such information may be used by the law enforcement agency in its planning with respect to the demonstration.

Observation

In all cases, law enforcement intelligence officers/agents may observe the demonstration to the same extent as any member of the public who is invited to observe the demonstration. This "same as any member of the public" rule applies to demonstrations that occur in any location to which there is no limitation on which members of the public are invited.

A law enforcement intelligence officer does not have to identify himself or herself as a law enforcement officer while observing a demonstration.

Photography/Recording

Law enforcement intelligence personnel may take photographs, videotape, make audio recordings or otherwise record a demonstration. If the demonstration is conducted peaceably and in accordance with the permit issued for the demonstration, the recordings may be retained for a reasonable period of time not to exceed 60 days, and then destroyed. If the demonstration is not conducted peaceably or in accordance with the permit issued for the demonstration, the recordings may be retained and may be used for identification and prosecution and/or for intelligence purposes.

Unless law enforcement intelligence personnel have a legal justification to detain a person involved in a demonstration, no person shall be detained for the purpose of making a visual record of his/her presence at the demonstration.

If credible, reliable information has been received that persons, groups or organizations participating in the demonstration have, in the past, been involved in unlawful behavior in connection with demonstrations, then law enforcement intelligence personnel may record such persons, groups or organizations and the persons, groups or organizations with whom or which they interact at the demonstration. Such recordings shall be made for the purpose of protecting the rights of those persons whose goals are within the proper exercise of their First Amendment privileges and the safety of members of the public present at the demonstration.

Recordings made for the purposes stated in the preceding paragraph may be retained for a reasonable period of time not to exceed 60 days, and then destroyed unless unlawful conduct has occurred. If unlawful conduct has occurred, the recordings may be used to identify those persons reasonably suspected of engaging in, instigating or aiding/abetting the unlawful conduct. Images of persons reasonably suspected of engaging in unlawful conduct may be retained for the purpose of prosecution and/or may be retained in intelligence files for the appropriate period of retention governing such files. Any images that do not assist in identifying persons reasonably suspected of involvement with the unlawful conduct should be destroyed within a reasonable period of time not to exceed 60 days.

Documentation

All observations of demonstrations by law enforcement intelligence personnel may be used for the purpose of improving security procedures in connection with public demonstrations.

When a demonstration has been peaceful and conducted as required by the permit issued for the demonstration, the head of the law enforcement agency (or his/her designee) with jurisdiction may notify the permitting agency(s) that there were no incidents. In the event the law enforcement agency is the sole permitting agency, it may place such a notice in the public records pertaining to the demonstration.

When there has been unlawful behavior in the demonstration a report should be filed. This report may be used for prosecution purposes and/or any other legitimate law enforcement purpose including intelligence purposes.

Participation

A law enforcement intelligence officer may participate in a demonstration in an undercover capacity when the level of approval required by the policies and procedures of his/her department has been met and:

1. there is documented credible, reliable information that a person(s) lawfully participating in the demonstration is in danger of harm; or

2. that an officer already acting in an undercover capacity needs to participate in the demonstration to preserve his/her undercover credibility; or

3. there is a legitimate investigative or public safety need for an officer(s) to participate in the demonstration, such as monitoring the activities of the demonstrators and spectators, to prevent any unlawful activity or disruption of the demonstration; or

4. to further an intelligence or criminal investigation.

If a law enforcement intelligence officer participates to maintain undercover credibility, the participating officer should not assume any leadership or organizational role in the planning or execution of the demonstration plan other than participation.

In any of the situations mentioned above occur; the participating officer(s) should file a complete report of his/her actions and observations within the shortest reasonable time after the demonstrations. Such reports shall not be open to the public unless state or local law requires that they be open to the public.

DEMONSTRATION GUIDELINES AUTHORITIES

These case authorities were relied on in the construction of the Demonstration Guidelines document. While they were persuasive in the mind of the Guidelines author, it is always prudent to have legal counsel for your agency examine them in light of the controlling legal authorities in your jurisdiction.

1. Access to Permit Information:

    - *Sullivan and Dansinger v. City of Augusta* 511 F.3d 16 (1st. Cir. ME. 2007) – The issue in this case was the application of a city ordinance which dealt with parades and "mass outdoor gatherings". Useful rules from this case are: (a) although the First Amendment protects protest marches there is no absolute right to stage a protest march; (b) the standard applied is whether the permit requirements are reasonable in light of the other regulations governing the streets; (c) the mere existence of a regulation that applies to street marches does not "chill" the exercise of First Amendment rights; (d) if a party asserts that the regulation "chills" or otherwise impinges on the exercise of the First Amendment right the burden is on that party to show (i) a concrete and particularized invasion of a legally protected interest which (ii) is actual or imminent rather than hypothetical or conjectural; (e) an advance notice requirement of up to 30 days is reasonable provided there is a provision for spontaneous demonstrations; and (f) law enforcement may review the permit information in those cases in which it is not the primary entity with which the permit must be vetted, such review may require face to face meetings so long as reasonable exceptions are provided.

      The case also contains most of the provisions of the ordinance that was upheld against the various challenges and can serve as a useful source of language for jurisdictions which are creating permit ordinances.

    - *Green v. City of Raleigh* 523 F.3d 377 (4th Cir. NC. 2008) – The city ordinance at issue in this case requires persons who wish to picket or demonstrate on public sidewalks or other public thoroughfares to give advance notice and comply with certain restrictions. Useful rules from this case are: (a) a city has a legitimate interest in maintaining the "safety, order and accessibility of its streets and sidewalks"; (b) an advance notice requirement which doesn't interfere with the speech interest more than necessary is constitutionally proper; and (c) the advance notice requirement allows the police to assign those personnel necessary "to protect the safety, order and First Amendment right of both demonstrators and bystanders."

Obviously law enforcement has a right to the information so it can carry out its duties. A copy of the city code sections upheld as constitutional is attached to the case as an appendix.

- *Long Beach Area Peace Network v. City of Long Beach*
  522 F.3d 1010 (9th Cir. CA. 2008) – A municipal ordinance governing demonstrations was challenged on various constitutional grounds. While the case – not surprisingly since it is the 9th Circuit – found some parts of the ordinance to be acceptable and others to be unacceptable, it upheld and applied the general rules that: (a) permit requirements are appropriate when an event would likely pose a threat to public safety and (b) law enforcement has a legitimate need to have access to permit information.

  The case does provide a good review of the First Amendment issues and discussion of authorities in the issue area.

2. Observation of the First Amendment Activity:

- *Laird, Secretary of Defense v. Tatum* 408 U.S. 1 (1972) held that the mere surveillance of First Amendment activity by government authorities does not "chill" the exercise of such rights. While this case arose out of the 1967 Detroit riots it is the standard for this proposition. Obviously the cases cited above which endorse law enforcement involvement in First Amendment event control for public safety and related purposes assume that law enforcement will observe the events.

3. Photography/Recording of First Amendment Activity:

- *Handshu v. Special Services Division* 475 F.Supp.2d 331 (U.S.D.C., Southern Dist. N.Y. 2007) – Although this case arose and relates to a jurisdiction which was under a judicial consent decree it is useful on the photography issue. Here there were two contrasting situations. In one, photographs had been taken of persons who were committing infractions of the law (running stop signs) in connection with a sanctioned demonstration. In the other, photographs were taken of persons who were engaged in a demonstration but no legal or permit violations occurred (a subsequent factual submission would show that there were permit violations).

  In the first instance the court found that there was a "legitimate law enforcement purpose" (a reasonable suspicion or belief) for the photography, in the second it found no such purpose. Of importance is the fact that this ruling was a "tightening" of an order entered immediately after 9/11/01, which allowed photography when documentation was deemed "potentially beneficial or useful."

  Further, this case applied the *Laird* rule that law enforcement observation of demonstrations did not "chill" the exercise of the First Amendment rights. It also commented on the use of infiltration and/or undercover operations as constitutionally permissible, so long as the infiltrating/undercover person does not encourage the unlawful exercise of these rights (the infiltration issue is discussed more extensively in a subsequent section of these authorities).

- _Piscottano v. Murphy_ 511 F.3d 247 (2nd Cir. Conn. 2007) involved a disciplinary action against state correctional officers who were members of the Outlaws M.C. This case made several helpful findings: (a) it is proper to rely on information from an intelligence system, criminal prosecution records and expert analysis/opinion based on such sources to determine/establish that an organization engages in unlawful activities; (b) when an association with an organization which engages in unlawful activity poses a threat which the government needs to address the association can be the basis for acting as to the associated individual provided there is credible evidence that the individual supports the unlawful goals and/or methods.

4. Infiltration/Undercover:

- _U.S. v. Mayer_ 490 F.3d 1129 (9th Cir. Cal. 2007), _cert.den._ 128 S. Ct. 1105 (2008) is a very helpful case. An FBI agent infiltrated NAMBLA initially in connection with an ongoing investigation. After the investigation was closed, the agent continued to belong to and participate in activities of the organization. The agent was not entirely passive in his association.

  The helpful findings in this case are: (a) the test here is whether the actions undertaken are unreasonable in light of the values of free expression; (b) rejected the concept that introduction of an "agent provocateur" into an organization was forbidden by the First Amendment (had this concept been accepted it would essentially eliminate undercover operations with respect to First Amendment situations); (c) measured the undercover operator's conduct by the standard whether it interfered with the organization's expressive/associational interests finding that because there was no assumption of leadership or published misstatements of the organization's goals no interference occurred; (d) applied the "invited informer" doctrine which sustains an undercover investigation if (i) it is undertaken in "good faith" (not for the purpose of interfering with exercise of First Amendment rights) and (ii) the investigator acts strictly within the limits of the invitation which has been extended. In other words, the court concluded that the invitation extended determines the extent of the privacy expectation which is reasonable.

  With respect to "good faith" the court held "…good faith…requires that an investigation threatening First Amendment rights, like any government investigation, be justified by a legitimate law enforcement purpose that outweighs any harm to First Amendment interests.". In this connection, then, so long as there is a legitimate law enforcement purpose there is no need for reasonable suspicion or probable cause before an investigation can occur.

5. Counter-Demonstration Issues:

- While this matter is not covered as part of the model a recent case is worth noting because it provides a good example of measured and appropriate conduct by law enforcement. In *Startzell v. City of Philadelphia* F.3d (3rd Cir. PA. 2008) a gay pride group had obtained a permit for a street celebration open to the public. A counter belief group had announced its intention to attend and protest the event. When the permitted group learned of the intentions of the counter belief group, it requested that the police prevent the counter belief group from attending. The helpful rulings from the case are: (a) that a private sponsored event open to the public in a public forum is just that, and the police will not be required to bar admission of any member of the public; (b) issuance of a permit to conduct an event in a public place does not transform the nature of the place – it is still public; (c) the state may take reasonable action to maintain public order when the exercise of First Amendment freedoms would threaten public order; and (d) that "**The right to free speech does not encompass the right to cause disruption...**"

- It would also be useful for counsel to read *ACLU of Colorado v. City and County of Denver* 2008 U.S. Dist. LEXIS 59591 (8/6/08). Although this case was not certified as citable, it contains a very good and complete constitutional analysis of the steps taken to provide for safety and provide for the exercise of First Amendment rights at the recent political convention in Denver. Of greatest importance is the point that it is the purpose of the government regulation that will be the focus of the legal analysis. Thus, the better the articulation of the reasons for the action proposed or taken, the more likely that the regulation will be permitted.

- Undercover operations involving groups, organizations or associations active in the areas protected by the associational freedoms umbrella have generated discussion. Some comments are in order.

  o "Agents provocateur" is the concept arising out of the ConIntelPro era during which some law enforcement entities not only infiltrated groups but became actively involved in advocating that the groups engage in unlawful acts. The initial *Handshu* case involved such activities. In the *Mayer* case the court rejected the argument that any infiltration by an undercover operator ought to be viewed as the introduction of an "agent provocateur", which would lead to the conclusion that such infiltration could never occur, period. Thus, the issue turns to an examination of the conduct of the infiltrator.

  o Leadership positions ought to be avoided by an undercover operator simply because the exercise of leadership will be construed as setting the policy and/or actions of the group, association or organization. Any basis for the argument that the infiltrator was able to set policy is the predicate for the argument that, but for the undercover agent's assumption of the leadership position, the unlawful activity would not have occurred. Put another way, the organization would never have expressed its beliefs in an unlawful manner had it not been for the "agitation" of the infiltrating law enforcement agent.

o   This leads to the wisdom of the application of the "invited informer" rule. As the discussion in Mayer makes clear, so long as the infiltrator does not assume a leadership role and does not act beyond the role he/she is "invited" to play, there is not going to be a finding that the infiltration "chilled" the exercise of associational freedom. Obviously, this will allow the use as intelligence and/or evidence of the information gathered by the infiltrator.

Appendix II

"Standards"

- *CALEA Standards*
- *IACP Policy*
- *CPOA Standards*
- Global's *"Minimum Criminal Intelligence Training Standards"*
- IALEIA's *"Standards for Analysts"* and
- IALEIA's *"The Addendum – Law Enforcement Intelligence Analysis Definitions"*
- Fusion Center Standards *"Executive Summary"* and
- Fusion Center Standards *" Summary of Guidelines and Key Elements"*

42.1.6 *A written directive addresses the collection, processing, and sharing of suspicious incidents and criminal intelligence relating to criminal and homeland security activities (including information detailed in 43.1.1 and 46.3.2) with appropriate entities, to include:*

a) *a description of the function*

b) *the responsibilities of all agency personnel*

c) *training of personnel*

d) *procedures for safeguarding, securing, and storing information*

e) *procedures for ensuring that information collected is limited to criminal conduct or relates to activities that present a potential threat to the jurisdiction*

f) *legal and privacy requirements*

g) *documentation, reporting, and dissemination of information*

h) *procedures for purging out-of-date or incorrect information*

i) *an annual review of procedures and processes*

Commentary: The intent of this standard is to document agency accountability for the collection and sharing of suspicious incidents and criminal intelligence information.

Intelligence-gathering activities are important in all agencies. All agencies, regardless of size, must have a criminal intelligence function. The need to develop and share information and criminal intelligence across all levels of government is imperative. Each agency has a stake in the development and exchange of suspicious incidents, information, and criminal intelligence.

Law enforcement agencies should operate under specific guidelines to ensure that no abuses occur. The sensitive nature of criminal intelligence files requires that they be maintained separately from other agency records to prevent compromise and protect the integrity of the file system. If the intelligence function is performed by an individual with other responsibilities (e.g., CEO, deputy chief) or as an activity of a larger function (criminal investigations), the separation and security intentions of this standard still apply. It is recommended that agencies utilize file procedures (i.e., Association of Law Enforcement Intelligence Units (LEIU) *Criminal Intelligence File Guidelines*) as a check and balance against inappropriate activities. The collection/submission, access, storage, and dissemination of criminal intelligence information must respect the privacy and constitutional rights of individuals, groups, and organizations.

Law enforcement personnel should be trained and encouraged to document information gleaned from a variety of sources. Training should emphasize that all personnel, regardless of their jobs, have a role in criminal intelligence and the sharing of information. Training can range from roll-call to more advanced training and is frequently available at little or no agency cost.

The *National Criminal Intelligence Sharing Plan* (NCISP) identifies a wide array of suggested accountability mechanisms, such as periodic review by management on decision making throughout the criminal intelligence function; audit trails within criminal intelligence processes and computer systems; staff surveys and questionnaires; effective training on department policies, procedures, and professional criminal intelligence practices; and periodic audits of criminal intelligence operations and files.

Agencies should leverage a number of resources, including existing information sharing initiatives—such as INTERPOL, the Homeland Security Information Network (HSIN), the Regional Information Sharing Systems (RISS), and Law Enforcement Online (LEO)—and reference materials such as *Fusion Center Guidelines: Law Enforcement Intelligence, Public Safety, and the Private Sector*, LEIU *Criminal Intelligence File Guidelines*, the *Justice Information Privacy Guideline* document, and the NCISP. (M M M M)

43.1.1 *The agency has a written directive for investigating vice, drug, and organized crime activities, to include:*

a) *specifying procedures for receiving and processing complaints*
b) *maintaining a record of complaints received*
c) *maintaining a record of information conveyed to and received from outside agencies*
d) *specifying procedures for advising the agency's CEO of activities*

Commentary: The agency should establish procedures ensuring that each complaint received is recorded and investigated to the fullest extent possible. The directive should include a listing of complaint forms used, information needed, and preliminary actions to be taken. The agency should establish procedures for conducting preliminary and follow-up investigations of vice, drug, and organized crime offenses. Every complaint received should be recorded and entered in a complaint filing system with provision for purging after a specified period of time.

It is recognized that some agencies may not have functional responsibility for the investigation of vice, drug, or organized crime activities. Notwithstanding, the agency should have procedures for meeting the standard, even if only in the normal course of the agency's reporting mechanism. (M M M M)

46.3.2 *A written directive establishes procedures for reporting and relaying terrorism related intelligence/information to the proper task force or agency.*

Commentary: None. (M M M M)

International Association of Chiefs of Police (IACP)
National Law Enforcement Policy Center
Criminal Intelligence
February 1, 1998

Purpose

It is the purpose of this policy to provide law enforcement officers in general, and officers assigned to the intelligence function in particular, with guidelines and principles for the collection, analysis, and distribution of intelligence information.

Policy

Information gathering is a fundamental and essential element in the all-encompassing duties of any law enforcement agency. When acquired, information is used to prevent crime, pursue and apprehend offenders and obtain evidence necessary for conviction. It is the policy of this agency to gather information directed toward specific individuals or organizations reasonably suspected of criminal activity, to gather it with due respect for the rights of those involved, and to disseminate it only to authorized individuals as defined. While criminal intelligence may be assigned to specific personnel within the agency, all members of this agency are responsible for reporting information that may help identify criminal conspirators and perpetrators.

Definitions

- *Criminal Intelligence*: Information compiled, analyzed and/or disseminated in an effort to anticipate, prevent, or monitor criminal activity.

- *Strategic Intelligence*: Information concerning existing patterns or emerging trends of criminal activity designed to assist in criminal apprehension and crime control strategies, for both short- and long-term investigative goals.

- *Tactical Intelligence:* Information regarding a specific criminal event that can be used immediately by operational units to further a criminal investigation, plan tactical operations and provide for officer safety.

Procedures

Mission: It is the mission of the intelligence function to gather information from all sources in a manner consistent with the law in support of efforts to provide tactical or strategic information on the existence, identities, and capabilities of criminal suspects and enterprises generally and, in particular, to further crime prevention and enforcement objectives /priorities identified by this agency.

1. Information gathering in support of the intelligence function is the responsibility of each member of this agency although specific assignments may be made as deemed necessary by the Officer-In-Charge (OIC) of the intelligence authority.

2. Information that implicates, suggests implication or complicity of any public official in criminal activity or corruption shall be immediately reported to this agency's chief executive officer or another appropriate agency.

Organization

Primary responsibility for the direction of intelligence operations; coordination of personnel; and collection, evaluation, collation, analysis, and dissemination of intelligence information is housed in this agency's intelligence authority under direction of the intelligence OIC.

1. The OIC shall report directly to this agency's chief executive officer or his designate in a manner and on a schedule prescribed by the chief.

2. To accomplish the goals of the intelligence function and conduct routine operations in an efficient and effective manner, the OIC shall ensure compliance with the police, procedures, mission, and goals of the agency.

I. Professional Standards

The intelligence function is often confronted with the need to balance information-gathering requirements for law enforcement with the rights of individuals. To this end, members of this agency shall adhere to the following:

1. Information gathering for intelligence purposes shall be premised on circumstances that provide a reasonable indication that a crime has been committed or is being planned.

2. Investigative techniques employed shall be lawful and only so intrusive as to gather sufficient information to prevent the criminal act and/or to identify and prosecute violators.

3. The intelligence function shall make every effort to ensure that information added to the criminal intelligence base is relevant to a current or on-going investigation and the product of dependable and trustworthy sources of information. A record shall be kept of the source of all information received and maintained by the intelligence function.

4. Information gathered and maintained by this agency for intelligence purposes may be disseminated only to appropriate persons for legitimate law enforcement purposes in accordance with law and procedures established by this agency. A record shall be kept regarding the dissemination of all such information to persons within this or another law enforcement agency.

APPENDIX II - STANDARDS

International Association of Chiefs of Police (IACP)

Compiling Intelligence

1. Intelligence investigations/files may be opened by the intelligence OIC with sufficient information and justification. This includes but is not limited to the following types of information:

   a. Subject, victim(s) and complainant as appropriate
   b. Summary of suspected criminal activity
   c. Anticipated investigative steps to include proposed use of informants, photographic, or electronic surveillance
   d. Resource requirements, including personnel, equipment, buy/flash monies, Ravel costs, etc
   e. Anticipated results
   f. Problems, restraints or conflicts of interest

2. Officers shall not retain official intelligence documentation for personal reference or other purposes but shall submit such reports and information directly to the intelligence authority.

3. Information gathering using confidential informants as well as electronic, photographic, and related surveillance devices shall be performed in a legally accepted manner and in accordance with procedures established for their use by this agency.

4. All information designated for use by the intelligence authority shall be submitted on the designated report form and reviewed by the officer's immediate supervisor prior to submission.

Receipt/Evaluation of Information

Upon receipt of information in any form, the OIC shall ensure that the following steps are taken:

1. Where possible, information shall be evaluated with respect to reliability of source and validity of content. While evaluation may not be precise, this assessment must be made to the degree possible in order to guide others in using the information. A record shall be kept of the source of all information where known.

2. Reports and other investigative material and information received by this agency shall remain the property of the originating agency, but may be retained by this agency. Such reports and other investigative material and information shall be maintained in confidence, and no access shall be given to another agency except with the consent of the originating agency.

3. Information having relevance to active cases or that requires immediate attention shall be forwarded to responsible investigative or other personnel as soon as possible.

4. Analytic material shall be compiled and provided to authorize sources as soon as possible where meaningful trends, patterns, methods, characteristics or intentions of criminal enterprises or figures emerge.

File Status

Intelligence file status will be classified as either "open" or "closed," in accordance with the following:

1. Open - Intelligence files that are actively being worked will be designated as "Open." In order to remain open, officers working such cases must file intelligence status reports covering case developments at least every 180 days.

2. Closed - "Closed" intelligence files are those in which investigations have been completed, where all logical leads have been exhausted, or where no legitimate law enforcement interest is served. All closed files must include a final case summary report prepared by or with the authorization of the lead investigator.

Classification/Security of Intelligence

1. Intelligence files will be classified in order to protect sources, investigations, and individual's rights to privacy, as well as to provide a structure that will enable this agency to control access to intelligence. These classifications shall be reevaluated whenever new information is added to an existing intelligence file.

    a. Restricted - "Restricted" intelligence files include those that contain information that could adversely effect an ongoing investigation, create safety hazards for officers, informants or others and/or compromise their identities. Restricted intelligence may only be released by approval of the intelligence OIC or the agency chief executive to authorized law enforcement agencies with a need and a right to know.

    b. Confidential - "Confidential" intelligence is less sensitive than restricted intelligence. It may be released to agency personnel when a need and a right to know have been established by the intelligence OIC or his designee.

    c. Unclassified - "Unclassified" intelligence contains information from the news media, public records, and other sources of a topical nature. Access is limited to officers conducting authorized investigations that necessitate this information.

2. All restricted and confidential files shall be secured, and access to all intelligence information shall be controlled and recorded by procedures established by the intelligence OIC.

    a. Informant files shall be maintained separately form intelligence files.

b. Intelligence files shall be maintained in accordance with state and federal law.

c. Release of intelligence information in general and electronic surveillance information and photographic intelligence, in particular, to any authorized law enforcement agency shall be made only with the express approval of the intelligence OIC and with the stipulation that such intelligence not be duplicated or otherwise disseminated without the approval of this agency's OIC.

d. All files released under freedom of information provisions or through disclosure shall be carefully reviewed.

Auditing and Purging Files

1. The OIC is responsible for ensuring that files are maintained in accordance with the goals and objectives of the intelligence authority and include information that is both timely and relevant. To that end, all intelligence files shall be audited and purged on an annual basis as established by the agency OIC through an independent auditor.

2. When a file has no further information value and/or meets the criteria of any applicable law, it shall be destroyed. As record of purged files shall be maintained by the intelligence authority.

The development of this IACP policy was supported by Grant No. 95-DD-BX-K014 awarded by the Bureau of Justice Assistance, Office of Justice Programs, U.S. Department of Justice.

California Peace Officers' Association Intelligence Committee (CPOA)

Suggested Criminal Intelligence Standards and Guidelines

Every local and state enforcement agency engaged in the collection, retention, and dissemination of intelligence-related information should consider implementing the following standards and guidelines.

1. **Standard – Every agency should implement a mission statement dictating the existence and function of its intelligence operations program.**

   <u>Guidelines</u> – The mission statement should contain a concise, well-defined mandate describing the program; the use of the intelligence process in support of the program; and the programs expected results. The statement should clearly delineate the program's focus on specific criminal activities and emphasize the use of intelligence as a crime prevention tool dedicated to the concept of community-oriented policing. The statement should specify the program's primary function is to help the agency's chief executive officer (CEO) make rational choices regarding unanticipated criminal threats and the deployment of resources in response to those threats. At the very least, the statement should contain the following:

   Sample Mission Statement

   The Department's Intelligence Operations Program will collect and analyze information on individuals and groups suspected of being—or known to be—involved in the following criminal activities: _____, _____, _____, _____, _____, and provide this information to the CEO for crime prevention and decision-making purposes.

   ---

2. **Standard – Every agency should recognize that active management and supervision of the criminal intelligence function are necessary to provide appropriate direction and control, staffing, and logistical support.**

   <u>Guidelines</u> – Management and supervision of an intelligence operations program are responsible for providing proper direction, guidelines and procedures, staffing, equipment, training, and direct access to the agency CEO.

3. **Standard – Every agency should implement a policy and procedures manual detailing its intelligence operations program, mission, methods of operation, file guidelines, and security procedures.**

   <u>Guidelines</u> – The manual should depict the program's operational policy and procedures; protocol for creating an intelligence-related record on a subject; entering the record into a file and/or database; and/or opening an investigation on a subject. The protocol should be based on the subject's involvement, or suspected involvement, in the specific criminal activities

focused upon the agency's mission statement. A criminal predicate is required for all file entries.

4. **Standard – Every agency should implement a set of guidelines that regulate the contents of its intelligence-related file.**

   <u>Guidelines</u> – The guidelines should conform to state and federal regulations and prescribe the criteria for the retention and purge of intelligence-related records contained in file. The information must be evaluated for its validity and the source assessed for reliability. Access to the information should be restricted to protect the source, investigation, and a subject's right to privacy.

5. **Standard – Every agency should implement a process for systematically exploiting intelligence-related information that is intended to prevent and reduce crime.**

   <u>Guidelines</u> – That exploitation should consist of the following intelligence process:

   - Collection – A planned effort focused on obtaining information identifying suspected or known criminal activity that impacts the jurisdiction.

   - Evaluation – A determination regarding the validity of obtained information and an assessment of the reliability of the source.

   - Collation – An orderly arrangement of information that systematically connects elated activities in the file.

   - Analysis – Conversion of information into intelligence that results in useful knowledge and appropriate recommendations to the CEO and the agency.

   - Dissemination – The intelligence product is provided to personnel who have a "need to know" and a "right to know."

6. **Standard – Every agency should implement appropriate training for all personnel assigned to, impacted by, or overseeing the intelligence operations program.**

   <u>Guidelines</u> – Personnel assigned to the agency's intelligence operations program should be trained in all aspects of the intelligence process, along with the guidelines and liability issues pertaining to the collection, retention and dissemination of intelligence-related information. An understanding of intelligence, how it works and why it is important—with a distinction between intelligence and information—should be part of the training foundation. The training should emphasize analysis and clearly explain the terminology and definitions pertaining to intelligence. The agency's CEO, the rest of the agency's personnel, the agency's legal advisor, and appropriate elected and public officials should also be trained or briefed in the intelligence process and the role it plays in the agency's community-oriented policing program.

7. **Standard – Every agency should provide the intelligence operations program with secure quarters and allow the program to be a separate entity within the law enforcement agency.**

   <u>Guidelines</u> – Criminal intelligence is a pro-active crime prevention function that operates differently than an enforcement unit. It frequently deals with sensitive information obtained from diverse sources with various levels of credibility. This information must be handled differently than routine investigative information. The intelligence process involves evaluation and analysis and requires that the needs of law enforcement are balanced against the individual's right to privacy. The dissemination of this intelligence must be in conjunction with established "right to know" and "need to know" standards. These requirements support the need to assign the intelligence function to a separate unit and to maintain the intelligence file in a secure location.

8. **Standard – Every agency should implement security precautions for their intelligence-related database and information.**

   <u>Guidelines</u> – A directive should be written to govern the security precautions of the agency's intelligence database and to protect the confidential storage of information in that database. The directive should also declare the files retained by the intelligence operations program are kept separate from the agency's other files.

9. **Standard – Every agency should hold the intelligence operations program accountable for producing both strategic and tactical products and for maintaining appropriate liaison with local, state, and federal law enforcement agencies.**

   <u>Guidelines</u> – The CEO should expect a high level of accountability from personnel assigned to the intelligence operations program and require both tactical and strategic products on a regular basis. The CEO should require the program to liaison with neighboring agencies and participate in regional and state networks so information of mutual interest can be shared and exchanged.

10. **Standard – Every agency should implement a procedure for evaluating the effectiveness of its intelligence operations program.**

    <u>Guidelines</u> – Objectives should be established by an agency so the management and operations of the intelligence program can be evaluated on a regular schedule.

11. **Standard – Every CEO with a criminal intelligence function should actively champion it and describe it as a pro-active crime prevention tool that supports community oriented policing.**

    <u>Guidelines</u> – The CEO should actively support the intelligence operations program and ensure it receives the political and budgetary commitment it deserves. The support should extend to obtaining community support for this pro-active law enforcement effort at preventing crime.

Global's
"Minimum Criminal Intelligence Training Standards"

For Law Enforcement and other
Criminal Justice Agencies in the United States

Findings and Recommendations
October 2007 Version 2

INTRODUCTION

The intent of this document is to provide perspective and guidance for the development and delivery of law enforcement intelligence training. It is recognized that any type of "standard" can be debated based on an individual's personal philosophy, professional priorities, and life experiences. In order to minimize bias or atypical context, the development process for these standards used a consensual approach reflecting the cumulative judgment of law enforcement intelligence practitioners, managers, executives, trainers, and scholars from all levels of government.

The standards reflect the collective judgment of these subject-matter experts (SMEs) with respect to the minimum training needed in each noted classification to provide the basic knowledge, skills, and abilities for personnel in each classification in order for them to perform their intelligence duties. In particular for the intelligence analyst, those duties would be at the entry level.

This document should be viewed as a "living document" because supplements may be developed in the future. Future supplements may address additional training classifications or other specialized training needs based on threats that, although not criminal, have implications for homeland security. Individuals and organizations are invited to submit recommendations for future versions of this document via the National Criminal Intelligence Resource Center (http://www.ncirc.gov) e-mail address: information@ncirc.gov.

PHILOSOPHY

These minimum standards were created within the context of the following statement of philosophy as applied to all training categories:

> *This training is designed to develop a culture of information analysis and information sharing within the law enforcement communities for the purpose of safeguarding America's communities while protecting citizens' privacy and civil rights.*

UNDERSTANDING MINIMUM STANDARDS

The SMEs who developed these standards expressed the need to reinforce the fact that these are <u>minimum</u> training standards. Personnel who attend training that meets these standards will possess core competencies to perform their duties lawfully and effectively. Of course, effectiveness and efficiency will both increase with experience and additional training.

Program developers are urged to expand the modules' content and times as practicable. This is particularly true as new laws, issues, trends, and best practices emerge. Standards are dynamic, reflecting the best knowledge at the time they are written; monitoring changes within the training environment is a critical responsibility of training program developers.

- Permeating each component of the training should be the consideration of issues related to fusion centers, the Information Sharing Environment (ISE), privacy issues, and community policing, as applicable to each component of the training.

The <u>minimum</u> standards outlined in this document are recommendations for core <u>minimum</u> criminal intelligence training standards for each training classification:

- Intelligence Analyst
- Intelligence Manager/Commander
- Law Enforcement Executive
- General Law Enforcement Officer—Basic Criminal Intelligence
- General Law Enforcement Officer—Criminal Intelligence Refresher
- Criminal Intelligence Officer
- Train-the-Trainer

The recommendations include objectives, standards, and suggested curriculum/sources of information, as well as time allocations. Standards are defined as specific courses or topics of instruction required to meet the training objective.

CURRICULA

Program developers are reminded that the <u>minimum</u> standards are not curricula. The standards represent topics for which curricula are developed. A suggested curriculum and sources of information are included for each standard. The SMEs who developed these standards made one overarching recommendation regarding curricula.

Curricula content should include the latest iteration of national standards for law enforcement intelligence (e.g., the *National Criminal Intelligence Sharing Plan* (NCISP) and the *Information Sharing Environment Implementation Plan*) as well as the most current developments in the field (e.g., new regulations, emerging privacy guidelines and/or state-specific requirements, new technologies, and intelligence resources).

Curricula structure should be based on accepted principles of adult learning. These include methods to evaluate learning, such as pre- and posttests; problem-solving exercises; and/or demonstration of learning objective mastery.

ADDITIONAL CRIMINAL INTELLIGENCE TRAINING

The training categories contained in this document are drawn from those articulated in the NCISP and are dependent largely on a person's specific assignment in a law enforcement organization. It is recognized there are important and relevant intelligence training programs that are not covered by the standards; for example, programs for developing an intelligence capacity in a law enforcement agency, new programs focused specifically on intelligence-led policing, or a program on public/private partnerships for the intelligence process and the ISE. Similarly, new programs may target specific issues, such as gang intelligence or drug intelligence. These programs are important and have value despite the lack of specifically defined minimum standards. Collaborative efforts with other criminal justice agencies, such as corrections and parole and probation, may also result in additional topics in the future.

Program developers are urged to explore the diverse applications of law enforcement intelligence where training voids exist. In those programs, developers are also urged to adopt the same philosophy and curricular issues described above.

INTELLIGENCE ANALYST

Time Allotment: 40 hours minimum
Time Allotment per Objective:

3 hours	**Objective I:**	Intelligence analysts will understand the criminal intelligence process, intelligence-led policing, the information sharing framework, and their roles in enhancing public safety.
2 hours	**Objective II:**	Analysts will gain an understanding of the proper handling and collation of criminal intelligence information, including file management and information evaluation.
4 hours	**Objective III:**	Analysts will experience the development of intelligence through the processes of critical thinking, logic, inference development, and recommendation development.
2–3 hours	**Objective IV:**	Analysts will understand the methodical process of developing and implementing collection and analytic plans, to include the reevaluation of that process/product.
2–3 hours	**Objective V:**	Analysts will be familiar with the legal, privacy, and ethical issues relating to intelligence.
3 hours	**Objective VI:**	Analysts will be provided with information on sources, including the Internet, information sharing systems, networks, centers, commercial and public databases, and other sources of information and their limitations.
16 hours	**Objective VII:**	Analysts will be able to demonstrate a practical knowledge of the methods, tools, and techniques employed in analysis.
4–8 hours	**Objective VIII:**	Analysts will be familiar with the skills underlying analytic methods, including report writing, statistics, and graphic techniques.

Globals' "Minimum Criminal Intelligence Training Standards"

* It is recommended that the most current developments in the field (e.g., fusion centers, *Information Sharing Environment* (ISE) *Implementation Plan* (IP), and updated terminology) be referenced in the curriculum for each training objective.

SUMMARY

The role of the intelligence analyst is more critical than ever as we move to a systemic model involving the ISE. Analysts have more diverse information and are required to produce more explicit tactical and strategic intelligence products. There are demands for threat assessments and the need to prepare intelligence reports that are in a form easily consumed, not only by intelligence professionals but also by line-level law enforcement officers. The Minimum Criminal Intelligence Training Standards for the Intelligence Analyst must incorporate these elements if the conceptual model for intelligence fusion and the Information Sharing Environment (see appendix) is going to reach fruition. Thus, these standards include new and emerging responsibilities for the intelligence analyst that are necessary throughout the law enforcement intelligence community.

Objective I: Intelligence analysts will understand the criminal intelligence process, intelligence-led policing, the information sharing framework, and their roles in enhancing public safety.

	Standards	Topics to Be Considered for Curriculum/Sources of Information
3 hours	Introduction to intelligence	
	Intelligence process/cycle	Collection, analysis, dissemination/production, collation, evaluation, assessment Origin/history of intelligence Roles and responsibilities of the analyst Intelligence-led policing
	Networking	Liaise with peers, other agencies, organizations, and professional memberships for dissemination of information
	Importance of the *National Criminal Intelligence Sharing Plan* (NCISP)	Information sharing/information sharing initiatives (LEISP, Global, N-DEx) (Curriculum developers should include current initiatives and those of local and/or regional importance.) Threats facing community, state, nation Terrorism/topical materials Intelligence-led policing Community policing

Globals' "Minimum Criminal Intelligence Training Standards"

Professional standards/certification program for analysts	International Association of Law Enforcement Intelligence Analysts *Law Enforcement Analytic Standards* International Association of Crime Analysts
Information sharing framework	Fusion centers, ISE IP, and local/regional initiatives

Objective II: Analysts will gain an understanding of the proper handling and collation of criminal intelligence information, including file management and information evaluation.

Standards	Topics to Be Considered for Curriculum/Sources of Information
Security	LEIU *Criminal Intelligence File Guidelines* http://www.ioss.gov/
Information management	Electronic Archives (storage) Files (hard copy)
Evaluation	Reliability/source validity
Markings and using confidential information	Classified Sensitive But Unclassified (SBU) Proposed Controlled Unclassified Information (CUI) framework State-authorized markings

(2 hours)

Objective III: Analysts will experience the development of intelligence through the processes of critical thinking, logic, inference development, and recommendation development.

Standards	Topics to Be Considered for Curriculum/Sources of Information
Critical thinking	
Logical/fallacies of logic	
Inference development	Carter, David L. (1994). *Law Enforcement Intelligence: A Guide for State, Local, and Tribal Law Enforcement Agencies.* Washington, DC; U.S. Department of Justice.

(4 hours)

Globals' "Minimum Criminal Intelligence Training Standards"

	Crime indicators	
	Crime patterns/analysis	

Objective IV: Analysts will understand the methodical process of developing and implementing collection and analytic plans, to include the reevaluation of that process/product.

	Standards	Topics to Be Considered for Curriculum/Sources of Information
2–3 hours	Needs of the consumer (strategic, tactical)	Does the intelligence product meet the needs of its intended purpose?
	Intelligence requirements/collection	Intelligence gaps Intelligence requirements Global's state, local, and tribal intelligence requirements
	Effective planning of intelligence products	Development of collection and investigative plans
	Infusing consumer feedback into the intelligence cycle	

Objective V: Analysts will be familiar with the legal, privacy, and ethical issues relating to intelligence.

	Standards	Topics to Be Considered for Curriculum/Sources of Information
2–3 hours	Law and legal aspects	Adhering to policies/procedures 28 CFR Part 23 Possible resources include U.S. Attorneys' Offices, District Attorneys' Offices, and local prosecutors
	Privacy, civil liberties, and civil rights	Include privacy issues/examples
	Ethics	Provide scenario to illustrate importance

Globals' "Minimum Criminal Intelligence Training Standards"

	Civil liability	Overview of liability issues in the intelligence process

Objective VI: Analysts will be provided with information on sources, including the Internet, information sharing systems, networks, centers, commercial and public databases, and other sources of information and their limitations.

	Standards	**Topics to Be Considered for Curriculum/Sources of Information**
3 hours	Sources of information/available resources	Law enforcement and intelligence information systems, such as RISS, HSIN, and LEO Corrections and other criminal justice information systems Open-source information Demonstration of selected systems

Objective VII: Analysts will be able to demonstrate a practical knowledge of the methods, tools, and techniques employed in analysis.

	Standards	**Topics to Be Considered for Curriculum/Sources of Information**
16 hours	Analytical techniques	Threat assessments Crime pattern analysis Association analysis Telephone record analysis Flowchart analysis (event/commodity) Financial analysis Strategic analysis
	Analytical tools	Spreadsheets Flowcharting applications Analytic software Presentation software, etc.

Objective VIII: Analysts will be familiar with the skills underlying analytic methods, including report writing, statistics, and graphic techniques.

Globals' "Minimum Criminal Intelligence Training Standards"

	Standards	Topics to Be Considered for Curriculum/Sources of Information
4–8 hours	Report writing	Principles of good report writing Differences between intelligence/investigative reports, briefs, etc.
	Presentation of information	Oral and written briefings

INTELLIGENCE MANAGER/COMMANDER

Time Allotment: 16 hours minimum
Time Allotment per Objective:

3 hours	Objective I:	Managers will understand the criminal intelligence process, intelligence-led policing, and their roles in enhancing public safety.
2 hours	Objective II:	Managing the Intelligence Unit. Managers will understand the personnel and policy considerations when establishing or assuming command of the intelligence function within an agency.
2 hours	Objective III:	Managers will understand the principles and practices of handling sensitive information, informant policies, and corruption prevention and recognition.
3 hours	Objective IV:	Managers will understand the legal and privacy issues surrounding the criminal intelligence environment.
4 hours	Objective V:	Managers will understand the processes necessary to produce tactical and strategic intelligence products and will understand the development process and implementation of collection plans.
2 hours	Objective VI:	Managers will be provided with information on criminal information sharing systems, networks, and resources available to their agencies.

* It is recommended that the most current developments in the field (e.g., fusion centers, *Information Sharing Environment* (ISE) *Implementation Plan* (IP), and updated terminology) be referenced in the curriculum for each training objective.

SUMMARY

Law enforcement managers/commanders are often assigned to a new position without having any experience or substantive knowledge of the new area of responsibility. There is an old administrative adage from the auto industry that an effective manager does not have to know how to build a car but must know how others build a car. Although there is some truth to this, lessons learned have shown us that when managers have substantive knowledge of the processes under their supervision, they are even more effective managers. Law enforcement intelligence is a politically and constitutionally sensitive area that requires a manager to understand the responsibilities, hazards, and challenges of the intelligence process. The Minimum Criminal Intelligence Training Standards for Intelligence Managers/Commanders are not designed to teach management; rather, they are designed to give managers critical knowledge of the law enforcement intelligence process to not only maximize their leadership capabilities but also prepare them for the unique challenges faced by personnel under the manager's command.

Objective I: Managers will understand the criminal intelligence process, intelligence-led policing, and their roles in enhancing public safety.

	Standards	Topics to Be Considered for Curriculum/Sources of Information
3 hours	Intelligence purpose/mission	Where does intelligence fit in your agency? Roles/responsibilities of intelligence function Provide examples of intelligence function missions Write a mission for your intelligence function
	Importance of the NCISP	Information sharing/information sharing initiatives (LEISP, Global, N-DEx) (Curriculum developers should include current initiatives and those of local and/or regional importance.) Threats facing community, state, nation Terrorism/topical materials Intelligence-led policing Community policing
	Definition of "intelligence"	Examples of what it is/what it is not Do not rely on one definition
	General intelligence process/cycle	Include impediments to the intelligence process/cycle
	Why intelligence is important to managers, analysts, executives	Focus on why intelligence is important for the agency and community you serve
	Intelligence-led policing	Brief overview/definitions of "intelligence-led policing" Community-oriented policing
	Information sharing network	Fusion centers, ISE IP, and local/regional initiatives

Objective II: Managing the Intelligence Unit. Managers will understand the personnel and policy considerations when establishing or assuming command of the intelligence function within an agency.

	Standards	Topics to Be Considered for Curriculum/Sources of Information
2 hours	Personnel selection	Background process consistent with NCISP
	Personnel training	Informative component; include what executives, analysts, and officers should be trained on and where training is available
	Personnel evaluation	Evaluate personnel unique to the intelligence function to the extent possible
	Evaluating intelligence unit performance	Does the mission/scope of the unit match the products produced? Is there effective communication within the law enforcement organization and with consumers? CALEA and other applicable national and state standards Provide handout/checklist; include: Production of bulletins Analysis of threats Information regarding performance metrics Training of unique measures related to criteria unique to the intelligence process Evaluation tied to the mission
	Operating policies and procedures—mechanics of an intelligence function	Physical security File management Informants Ethics Handouts/CDs (e.g., glossary)

Objective III: Managers will understand the principles and practices of handling sensitive information, informant policies, and corruption prevention and recognition.

	Standards	Topics to Be Considered for Curriculum/Sources of Information
2 hours	Handling and storing of information (security, e-mail)	Internet, networks/systems, firewalls

Globals' "Minimum Criminal Intelligence Training Standards"

	Classifications	Secret, top secret, national security issues (pamphlets from FBI, etc.)
	Operational security processes	Protecting methods and sources Policies/rules (i.e., dissemination) Disclosure of sensitive information to media, other law enforcement entities, citizens, public safety agencies, etc.
	Markings and using confidential information	Classified Sensitive But Unclassified (SBU) Proposed CUI framework State-authorized markings

Objective IV: Managers will understand the legal and privacy issues surrounding the criminal intelligence environment.

	Standards	Topics to Be Considered for Curriculum/Sources of Information
3 hours	Legal and historical perspectives	Historical abuses of civil rights due to antiquated law enforcement practices Provide examples or scenarios that illustrate the importance of legal/privacy issues Include issues/examples regarding privacy Possible resources include U.S. Attorneys' Offices, District Attorneys' Offices, and local prosecutors
	Current regulations	Regulations/resources on CD (28 CFR Part 23)
	Application	Question-and-answer session How to put this information into practice
	Ensuring accountability	Provide a checklist to gauge compliance (LEIU Checklist copies)
	Privacy	Privacy policy development Global Privacy and Civil Liberties Policy Development Guide and Implementation Templates
	Ethics	Review IACP code of conduct and agency-specific or recognized code of ethics

Globals' "Minimum Criminal Intelligence Training Standards"

Objective V: Managers will understand the processes necessary to produce tactical and strategic intelligence products and will understand the development process and implementation of collection plans.

	Standards	Topics to Be Considered for Curriculum/Sources of Information
4 hours	Defining the customers	Understand the needs of the customer and what is important to the customer
	Methods of collection	Identifying gaps
	Competing hypotheses	Reliability/validity—ensure that analysis is reliable; do not follow a blind alley
	Types of intelligence products and analytic techniques	Discuss the various intelligence products available to the agency Planning for intelligence products Threat assessments Strategic, tactical, operational, data visualization Discuss the value of products
	Principles of good report writing	Provide differences between intelligence/investigative projects/reports, briefs, etc.
	Feedback	Does the intelligence product meet the needs of its intended purpose?

Objective VI: Managers will be provided with information on criminal information sharing systems, networks, and resources available to their agencies.

	Standards	Topics to Be Considered for Curriculum/Sources of Information
2 hours	Sources of information/available resources	Provide overview, resource CD Law enforcement and intelligence information systems Open-source information (inclusive of criminal history, RISS) Demonstration of selected systems
	Networking/relationship building	Discuss how intelligence is not only technical, it is a human effort Provide information on associations/networking opportunities

LAW ENFORCEMENT EXECUTIVE

Time Allotment: 6 hours
Time Allotment per Objective:

1 hour	Objective I:	Executives will understand the National Criminal Intelligence Sharing Plan (NCISP), Information Sharing Environment Implementation Plan (ISE IP), fusion center concept, and their own roles in each.
1 hour	Objective II:	Executives will understand the philosophy and practices of intelligence-led policing.
2 hours	Objective III:	Executives will understand the criminal intelligence process and its role in enhancing public safety.
1 hour	Objective IV:	Executives will understand the legal, privacy, and ethical issues relating to criminal intelligence.
1 hour	Objective V:	Executives will be provided with information on existing criminal information sharing networks and resources available in support of their agencies.

* It is recommended that the most current developments in the field (e.g., fusion centers, *Information Sharing Environment* (ISE) *Implementation Plan* (IP), and updated terminology) be referenced in the curriculum for each training objective.

SUMMARY

The intelligence function will not be successful without support from the agency's chief executive. Rather than knowing the processes of law enforcement intelligence, the chief executive needs to know what value the intelligence function will provide to the agency, the resources needed for the intelligence function to be effective, and the challenges—as well as potential liabilities—that are inherent in the intelligence process. Since many chief executives have minimal experience in contemporary law enforcement intelligence, they also need insight on new and changing roles and responsibilities of the intelligence function. For example, law enforcement executives will no doubt have some impression of fusion centers and the Information Sharing Environment, but they are not likely to have sufficient detailed information to understand the role of their agency in these new developments and the changes in law enforcement intelligence philosophy. The Minimum Criminal Intelligence Training Standards for Law Enforcement Executives are designed to address these needs.

Objective I: Executives will understand the *National Criminal Intelligence Sharing Plan* (NCISP), *Information Sharing Environment Implementation Plan* (ISE IP), fusion center concept, and their own roles in each.

Globals' "Minimum Criminal Intelligence Training Standards"

Standards	Topics to Be Considered for Curriculum/Sources of Information
Overview of the NCISP	National Criminal Intelligence Sharing Plan
Impediments to information sharing	Community-oriented policing
Information sharing framework	Fusion centers, ISE IP, and local/regional initiatives

(1 hour)

Objective II: Executives will understand the philosophy and practices of intelligence-led policing.

Standards	Topics to Be Considered for Curriculum/Sources of Information
Overview of the philosophy of intelligence-led policing	The intelligence function Using intelligence to support and develop policy Executive leadership roles and responsibilities
Overview of best practices in intelligence-led policing	Elements of Community policing Problem-oriented policing CompStat Other initiatives

(1 hour)

Objective III: Executives will understand the criminal intelligence process and its role in enhancing public safety.

Standards	Topics to Be Considered for Curriculum/Sources of Information
Why intelligence is important to the law enforcement executive	Types of intelligence (strategic/tactical) Available products (briefs, reports/charts)
Intelligence process/cycle	Evaluating progress/performance Demonstrate translation from intelligence to operational
Policies and procedures	Overview of the need for policies and procedures for intelligence officers and intelligence units Provide glossary/common language as a handout

(2 hours)

The following are recommended to be included in the curriculum, but not as specific standards	Impediments to the intelligence process/cycle Building a successful intelligence unit Managing/maximizing intelligence resources

Objective IV: Executives will understand the legal, privacy, and ethical issues relating to criminal intelligence.

	Standards	Topics to Be Considered for Curriculum/Sources of Information
1 hour	Overview of legal and liability issues, intelligence audits/integrity, accountability, 28 CFR Part 23, and standards for protecting information	Provide model policy/guidelines as a handout Possible resources include U.S. Attorneys' Offices, District Attorneys' Offices, and local prosecutors
	Overview of community trust and communication with citizens and media (briefing city and community leaders on local ordinances)	Ethics Public relations (handling difficult situations)

Objective V: Executives will be provided with information on existing criminal information sharing networks and resources available in support of their agencies.

	Standards	Topics to Be Considered for Curriculum/Sources of Information
1 hour	Sources of information/available resources	Law enforcement and intelligence systems Open sources Demonstration of selected systems
	Overview of support materials	Resource guide, contacts, standards, etc.
	Strategies to build relationships/networking	Discuss how intelligence is not only technical, it is a human effort Provide information on associations/ networking opportunities
	Public/private partnerships	Networking and information sharing

Globals' "Minimum Criminal Intelligence Training Standards"

GENERAL LAW ENFORCEMENT OFFICER— BASIC CRIMINAL INTELLIGENCE

Time Allotment: 2 hours
Time Allotment per Objective:

40 minutes	Objective I:	Law enforcement officers will understand the criminal intelligence process and its ability to enhance their contributions to the criminal justice system.
10 minutes	Objective II:	Law enforcement officers will be provided with information on available data systems, networks, and resources.
40 minutes	Objective III:	Law enforcement officers will be able to identify key signs of criminal activity and procedures for collecting data on and reporting such activity.
30 minutes	Objective IV:	Law enforcement officers will gain an understanding of the legal, privacy, and ethical limitations placed on the collection of criminal intelligence information.

* It is recommended that the most current developments in the field (e.g., fusion centers, *Information Sharing Environment* (ISE) *Implementation Plan* (IP), and updated terminology) be referenced in the curriculum for each training objective.

SUMMARY

One of the more significant changes in law enforcement intelligence in the post-9/11 era deals with the philosophy of information sharing. Previously, a critical part of the intelligence philosophy was to maintain operations security of intelligence reports. Inherently, this also meant that information sharing was minimal. The line-level officer rarely saw intelligence reports. The current philosophy, however, is that information sharing must be maximized—as much information about threats should be placed in as many law enforcement hands as possible. The reason: the more personnel who have information about threats, the greater the likelihood of stopping or mitigating the threats. However, because of the sensitive nature of intelligence, the information must be shared in an "informed manner." That is, general law enforcement officers must understand the difference between intelligence records and criminal records, how to handle intelligence reports, and how raw information must be shared with the intelligence function. They must also understand the critical nature of their role in the entire intelligence process. The Minimum Criminal Intelligence Training Standards are designed to incorporate these critical issues.

Objective I: Law enforcement officers will understand the criminal intelligence process and its ability to enhance their contributions to the criminal justice system.

APPENDIX II - STANDARDS

Globals' "Minimum Criminal Intelligence Training Standards"

	Standards	Topics to Be Considered for Curriculum/Sources of Information
40 minutes	Officers' roles and responsibilities in the intelligence process/cycle	Ensure that officers understand the steps of the intelligence cycle Discuss impediments to the process Provide a copy of the intelligence policy or model intelligence policy Provide a glossary of intelligence terms
	Types of intelligence (strategic, tactical)	Define "strategic intelligence" Define "tactical intelligence" Provide examples of products
	Origins/history of intelligence	Overview of the NCISP
	Importance of intelligence for the law enforcement officer	Provide case examples of why intelligence is important for the agency and community served
	Community policing and its relationship to the intelligence function	Maintaining community relations Define "community-led policing" Relationship between intelligence-led policing and community-oriented policing Case examples
	Information sharing framework	Fusion centers, ISE IP, and local/regional initiatives
	Sources of information/available resources	Law enforcement and intelligence systems Open sources Demonstration of selected systems

Objective II: Law enforcement officers will be provided with information on available data systems, networks, and resources.

	Standards	Topics to Be Considered for Curriculum/Sources of Information
10 minutes	Provide overview of the types of systems available	Explain the significance of different programs Types of systems (pointer systems, intelligence systems, etc.) Discuss systems unique to participants Provide a list or summary of available resources and systems

Objective III: Law enforcement officers will be able to identify key signs of criminal activity and procedures for collecting data on and reporting such activity.

	Standards	Topics to Be Considered for Curriculum/Sources of Information
40 minutes	Importance of recording and submitting raw information	Provide a copy of agency communication process/procedures Case examples
	Information collection methods, reporting procedures, and use of law enforcement sharing systems	Provide examples of the intelligence process and how it can be a success Provide instruction for understanding current threats Provide techniques to recognize and report behavior related to criminal threats (Include use of field interview cards.) Provide information on local/state/regional/federal systems and networks Provide information on resources local officers might use to collect information (including open sources) Case examples, videos (as time allows)
	Understanding terminology	Define "intelligence"—what is and what is not intelligence; provide examples of products Define "intelligence-led policing" Develop glossary in form of pocket guide

Objective IV: Law enforcement officers will gain an understanding of the legal, privacy, and ethical limitations placed on the collection of criminal intelligence information.

	Standards	Topics to Be Considered for Curriculum/Sources of Information
30 minutes	Ethics	Explain why ethics is pertinent to information handling
	Legal basis, limitations, and liability issues	Use legal advisor, if available Include current regulations and provide copies of key regulations
	28 CFR Part 23	General overview of 28 CFR Part 23 Provide copy of regulation

■	Right to privacy and protection of personal liberties—current privacy initiatives/concerns	Include issues/examples regarding privacy Video—immigrant interview contrasting rights in the United States and their country of origin, particularly the First and Fourth Amendment rights

GENERAL LAW ENFORCEMENT OFFICER— CRIMINAL INTELLIGENCE REFRESHER

Time Allotment: 2 hours
Time Allotment per Objective:

40 minutes	Objective I:	Law enforcement officers will understand the criminal intelligence process and its ability to enhance their contributions to the criminal justice system.
10 minutes	Objective II:	Law enforcement officers will be provided with information on available data systems, networks, and resources.
40 minutes	Objective III:	Law enforcement officers will be able to identify key signs of criminal activity and procedures for collecting data on and reporting such activity.
30 minutes	Objective IV:	Law enforcement officers will gain an understanding of the legal, privacy, and ethical limitations placed on the collection of criminal intelligence information.

*It is recommended that the most current developments in the field (e.g., fusion centers, *Information Sharing Environment* (ISE) *Implementation Plan* (IP), and updated terminology) be referenced in the curriculum for each training objective.

SUMMARY

One of the more significant changes in law enforcement intelligence in the post-9/11 era deals with the philosophy of information sharing. Previously, a critical part of the intelligence philosophy was to maintain operations security of intelligence reports. Inherently, this also meant that information sharing was minimal. The current philosophy, however, is that information sharing must be maximized—as much information about threats should be placed in as many law enforcement hands as possible. The reason: the more personnel who have information about threats, the greater the likelihood of stopping or mitigating the threats. However, because of the sensitive nature of intelligence, the information must be shared in an "informed manner." That is, general law enforcement officers must continue to understand the difference between intelligence records and criminal records, how to handle intelligence reports, and how raw information must be shared with the intelligence function. They must also understand the critical nature of their role in the entire intelligence process. The Criminal Intelligence Refresher standards are designed to incorporate these critical issues. These standards serve to reinforce the importance of information collection and the officers' role in the intelligence process.

Globals' "Minimum Criminal Intelligence Training Standards"

Objective I: Law enforcement officers will understand the criminal intelligence process and its ability to enhance their contributions to the criminal justice system.

40 minutes	Standards	Topics to Be Considered for Curriculum/Sources of Information
	Officers' roles and responsibilities in the intelligence process/cycle	Ensure that officers understand the steps of the intelligence cycle Discuss impediments to the process Provide a copy of the agency intelligence policy or model intelligence policy Provide a glossary of intelligence terms
	Types of intelligence (strategic, tactical)	Define "strategic intelligence" Define "tactical intelligence" Provide examples of products
	Origins/history of intelligence	Overview of the NCISP
	Importance of intelligence for the law enforcement officer	Provide case examples of why intelligence is important for the agency and community served
	Community policing and the criminal intelligence collection function	Maintaining community relations Define "community-led policing" Relationship between intelligence-led policing and community-oriented policing Case examples
	Information sharing framework	Fusion centers, ISE IP, and local/regional initiatives

Objective II: Law enforcement officers will be provided with information on available data systems, networks, and resources.

10 minutes	Standards	Topics to Be Considered for Curriculum/Sources of Information
	Provide overview of the types of systems available	Explain the significance of different programs Types of systems (pointer systems, intelligence systems, etc.) Discuss systems unique to participants Provide list or summary of available resources and systems

Globals' "Minimum Criminal Intelligence Training Standards"

Objective III: Law enforcement officers will be able to identify key signs of criminal activity and procedures for collecting data on and reporting such activity.

	Standards	Topics to Be Considered for Curriculum/Sources of Information
40 minutes	Review importance of recording and submitting intelligence information	Provide a copy of agency communication processes/procedures Case examples
	Update on information collection methods, reporting procedures, and use of law enforcement sharing systems (RISS, HIDTA, LEO, ATAC, JTTF)	Provide techniques to recognize key intelligence and criminal activity Include use of field interview cards Provide examples of the intelligence process and how it can be a success
	Review the identification of sources of information	Case examples, videos Provide instruction in understanding current threats Provide information on local/state/regional/ federal systems and networks Online resources Public/commercial data
	Review and update of terminology	Define "intelligence" — what is and what is not intelligence; provide examples of products Define "intelligence-led policing" Develop glossary in form of pocket guide

Objective IV: Law enforcement officers will gain an understanding of the legal, privacy, and ethical limitations placed on the collection of criminal intelligence information.

	Standards	Topics to Be Considered for Curriculum/Sources of Information
30 minutes	Ethics	Explain why ethics is pertinent to information handling
	Update on legal basis, limitations, and liability issues	Use legal advisor, if available Include current regulations and provide copies of key regulations
	Update on 28 CFR Part 23	General overview of 28 CFR Part 23 Provide copy of regulation

	Review right to privacy and protection of personal liberties—current privacy initiatives/concerns	Include issues/examples regarding privacy Video—immigrant interview contrasting rights in the United States and their country of origin, particularly the First and Fourth Amendment rights

CRIMINAL INTELLIGENCE OFFICER

Time Allotment: 40 hours minimum
Time Allotment per Objective:

5 hours	Objective I:	Intelligence officers will understand the criminal intelligence process and their critical role in the process.
6 hours	Objective II:	Intelligence officers will understand the legal, ethical, and privacy issues surrounding criminal intelligence and their liability as intelligence information collectors.
4 hours	Objective III:	Intelligence officers will be provided with information on Internet resources, information sharing systems, networks, and other sources of information.
6 hours	Objective IV:	Intelligence officers will gain an understanding of the proper handling of criminal intelligence information, including file management and information evaluation.
6 hours	Objective V:	Intelligence officers will understand the processes of developing tactical and strategic products and experience the development of some products.
5 hours	Objective VI:	Intelligence officers will experience the development of criminal intelligence from information through the critical thinking/ inference development process.
5 hours	Objective VII:	Intelligence officers will understand the tasks of building and implementing collection plans.
3 hours		A 3-hour roundtable discussion is recommended.

* It is recommended that the most current developments in the field (e.g., fusion centers, *Information Sharing Environment* (ISE) *Implementation Plan* (IP), and updated terminology) be referenced in the curriculum for each training objective.

SUMMARY

For the law enforcement professional assigned as an intelligence officer, there are several critical issues that emerge: the lawful basis for collecting raw information for an intelligence inquiry, maintaining operational security of collected information, and the proper method of submitting collected information to ensure that it provides the information needed by an analyst. The issue of civil rights as well as the ability to distinguish between behaviors that are "unusual" and those "which have a criminal nexus beyond mere suspicion" are intricately tied together. The intelligence officer must, at a minimum, have a clear understanding of these issues. Finally, the intelligence officer must understand the concept of "intelligence requirements" in order to effectively perform this function.

Objective I: Intelligence officers will understand the criminal intelligence process and their critical role in the process.

	Standards	Topics to Be Considered for Curriculum/Sources of Information
5 hours	Introduction to intelligence	Discuss the origin/history of intelligence Provide a glossary of intelligence terms Provide an overview of the NCISP
	Intelligence officers' roles and responsibilities in the intelligence process/cycle	Ensure that intelligence officers understand the steps of the intelligence cycle Discuss impediments to the process Provide a copy of the agency intelligence policy or model intelligence policy
	Importance of intelligence for the intelligence officer	Provide case examples of why intelligence is important for the agency and community served
	Community policing and its relationship to the intelligence function	Maintaining community relations Define "community-led policing" Relationship between intelligence-led policing and community-oriented policing Case examples
	Networking	Liaise with peers, other agencies, organizations, and professional memberships for dissemination of information Allow participants to discuss the way their agency networks
	Information sharing framework	Fusion centers, ISE IP, and local/regional initiatives

Objective II: Intelligence officers will understand the legal, ethical, and privacy issues surrounding criminal intelligence and their liability as intelligence information collectors.

Globals' "Minimum Criminal Intelligence Training Standards"

Standards	Topics to Be Considered for Curriculum/Sources of Information
Legal basis and limitations	Use legal advisor, if available Include current regulations and provide copies of key regulations, as appropriate Possible resources include U.S. Attorneys' Offices, District Attorneys' Offices, and local prosecutors
28 CFR Part 23	General overview of 28 CFR Part 23 Provide copy of regulation
Privacy, civil liberties, and civil rights	Include issues/examples regarding privacy Video—immigrant interview contrasting rights in the United States and their country of origin, particularly the First and Fourth Amendment rights
Ethics	Explain why ethics is pertinent to information handling Provide scenario to illustrate importance
Civil liability	Provide an overview of liability issues in the intelligence process

(6 hours)

Objective III: Intelligence officers will be provided with information on Internet resources, information sharing systems, networks, and other sources of information.

Standards	Topics to Be Considered for Curriculum/Sources of Information
Sources of information/available resources	Law enforcement and intelligence information systems, such as RISS, HSIN, and LEO Open-source information Demonstration of selected systems Human source development
Research methods	Research methods versus investigative methods

(4 hours)

Objective IV: Intelligence officers will gain an understanding of the proper handling of criminal intelligence information, including file management and information evaluation.

Globals' "Minimum Criminal Intelligence Training Standards"

<table>
<tr><th></th><th>Standards</th><th>Topics to Be Considered
for Curriculum/Sources of Information</th></tr>
<tr><td rowspan="7">6 hours</td><td>Handling evidence/intelligence</td><td></td></tr>
<tr><td>Markings and confidential information</td><td>Classified
Sensitive But Unclassified (SBU)
Controlled Unclassified Information (CUI)
State-authorized markings</td></tr>
<tr><td>Operational security processes</td><td>Protecting methods and sources
Policies/rules
Disclosure of sensitive information to media, other law enforcement entities, citizens, public safety agencies, etc.</td></tr>
<tr><td>Information management</td><td>Electronic
Archives (storage)
Files (hard copy)</td></tr>
<tr><td>Evaluation</td><td>Reliability/source validity</td></tr>
<tr><td>Courtroom testimony</td><td>Include short role-playing session
Provide "dos" and "don'ts"</td></tr>
<tr><td>Marking and using confidential information</td><td>Classified
Sensitive But Unclassified (SBU)
Proposed CUI framework
State-authorized markings</td></tr>
</table>

Objective V: Intelligence officers will understand the processes of developing tactical and strategic products and experience the development of some products.

<table>
<tr><th></th><th>Standards</th><th>Topics to Be Considered
for Curriculum/Sources of Information</th></tr>
<tr><td rowspan="3">6 hours</td><td>Types of intelligence products</td><td></td></tr>
<tr><td>Principles of good report writing</td><td>Provide differences between intelligence/investigative projects/reports, briefs, etc.</td></tr>
<tr><td>Uses of intelligence products</td><td>Strategic, tactical, operational, data visualization, and value of products
Threat assessments</td></tr>
</table>

Globals' "Minimum Criminal Intelligence Training Standards"

	Feedback	Does the intelligence product meet the needs of its intended purpose?

Objective VI: Intelligence officers will experience the development of criminal intelligence from information through the critical thinking/inference development process.

	Standards	Topics to Be Considered for Curriculum/Sources of Information
5 hours	Critical thinking	
	Logic/fallacies of logic	Analysis of competing hypotheses
	Inference developments	
	Recommendations development	
	Crime indicators	

Objective VII: Intelligence officers will understand the tasks of building and implementing collection plans.

	Standards	Topics to Be Considered for Curriculum/Sources of Information
5 hours	Developing collection and investigative plans	Class exercise—develop a collection plan Matching intelligence collection strategies to requirements
	Needs of the consumer	Does the information meet the needs of its intended purpose?
	Infusing consumer feedback into the intelligence cycle	

*A three-hour roundtable discussion is recommended as part of this 40-hour training.

TRAIN-THE-TRAINER

Time Allotment: 16 hours minimum
Time Allotment per Objective:

Globals' "Minimum Criminal Intelligence Training Standards"

2 hours	Objective I:	Trainers will understand the intelligence process and how it functions.
1 hour	Objective II:	Trainers will understand the National Criminal Intelligence Sharing Plan (NCISP), intelligence-led policing, and other national information sharing initiatives and the role they play in reducing crime and violence throughout the country.
5 hours	Objective III:	Trainers will be provided with information regarding intelligence systems; other sources of information; current criminal threats, trends, and patterns; and strategies to access and apply information.
2 hours	Objective IV:	Trainers will understand the processes and uses of tactical and strategic intelligence products.
3 hours	Objective V:	Trainers will be familiar with the latest innovations in training and will be aware of appropriate topical resources for criminal intelligence instruction.
1 hour	Objective VI:	Trainers will be knowledgeable of existing course materials and their use.
1 hour	Objective VII:	Trainers will be aware of the legal, privacy, and ethical issues relating to intelligence.
1 hour	Objective VIII:	Trainers will prepare and present a short module on intelligence.

* It is recommended that the most current developments in the field (e.g., fusion centers, *Information Sharing Environment* (ISE) *Implementation Plan* (IP), and updated terminology) be referenced in the curriculum for each training objective.

SUMMARY

The NCISP states that all law enforcement officers should have training on the criminal intelligence process. The intent of this training is to ensure that an agency may effectively develop an intelligence capacity and participate in the Information Sharing Environment. One of the most efficient ways to provide widespread intelligence awareness training to America's police officers is through a Train-the-Trainer program. The intent of a Train-the-Trainer program is that an agency would send personnel to this program in order to receive the knowledge and curricula needed to develop the necessary foundation of information on intelligence processes required so that an effective intelligence capacity could be built in an agency. The Minimum Criminal Intelligence Training Standards for a Train-the-Trainer program are designed to ensure that the critical information needed for the new trainer is incorporated into the curriculum.

Objective I: Trainers will understand the intelligence process and how it functions.

Globals' "Minimum Criminal Intelligence Training Standards"

Standards	Topics to Be Considered for Curriculum/Sources of Information
2 hours	
Intelligence process/cycle	Ensure that trainers fully understand and can apply the steps of the intelligence cycle Include the roles and responsibilities of intelligence personnel Impediments to the process Case examples; videos
Origin/history of intelligence	
Why intelligence is important	Provide examples of why intelligence is important to different people/groups— executives, policymakers, investigators, analysts, etc. Case examples

Objective II: Trainers will understand the *National Criminal Intelligence Sharing Plan* (NCISP), intelligence-led policing, and other national information sharing initiatives and the role they play in reducing crime and violence throughout the country.

Standards	Topics to Be Considered for Curriculum/Sources of Information
1 hour	
Overview of the *National Criminal Intelligence Sharing Plan* (NCISP) and information sharing initiatives and systems	Information sharing/information sharing initiatives (LEISP, Global, N-DEx) (Curriculum developers should include current initiatives and those of local and/or regional importance.) Threats facing community, state, nation Terrorism/topical materials Intelligence-led policing Community policing
Information sharing framework	Fusion centers, ISE IP, and local/regional initiatives
Intelligence-led policing, community policing, and their relationship to intelligence	Define "intelligence-led policing" Discuss benefits of intelligence-led policing

Objective III: Trainers will be provided with information regarding intelligence systems; other sources of information; current criminal threats, trends, and patterns; and strategies to access and apply information.

Standards	Topics to Be Considered for Curriculum/Sources of Information
Intelligence sharing systems	Law enforcement and intelligence information systems Open-source information (inclusive of criminal history, RISS) Demonstration of selected systems
Applying intelligence to current threats	Motives, methods, targets

(5 hours)

Objective IV: Trainers will understand the processes and uses of tactical and strategic intelligence products.

Standards	Topics to Be Considered for Curriculum/Sources of Information
Understanding terminology	Define "intelligence"—what is and what is not intelligence; provide examples of products Define "intelligence-led policing" Develop glossary in form of pocket guide
Types of intelligence	Define "strategic intelligence" Define "tactical intelligence" Provide examples of products
Intelligence products (intelligence reports, data/link analysis, etc.)	Understanding reports, differences between strategic and tactical intelligence

(2 hours)

Objective V: Trainers will be familiar with the latest innovations in training and will be aware of appropriate topical resources for criminal intelligence instruction.

Standards	Topics to Be Considered for Curriculum/Sources of Information
Current innovations and instructional techniques	
Audiovisual aids, instructional media, and their use	Familiarity with a variety of audiovisual aids Troubleshooting technical issues Training materials package

(3 hours)

Objective VI: Trainers will be knowledgeable of existing course materials and their use.

Globals' "Minimum Criminal Intelligence Training Standards"

	Standards	Topics to Be Considered for Curriculum/Sources of Information
1 hour	Familiarity with existing curricula, lesson plans, tests, and exercises	Handouts with lesson plans, materials, and exercise demonstrations Understand what types of training are offered and by whom

Objective VII: Trainers will be aware of the legal, privacy, and ethical issues relating to intelligence.

	Standards	Topics to Be Considered for Curriculum/Sources of Information
1 hour	Legal basis and limitations	Current regulations and how they apply to intelligence Intelligence audits/integrity
	Liability issues	Standards for protecting information
	28 CFR Part 23	Provide copy of regulation
	Right to privacy and protection of personal liberties (examples of privacy issues/initiatives)	Provide scenarios illustrating privacy issues Discuss strategy to protect personal information
	Ethics	

Objective VIII: Trainers will prepare and present a short module on intelligence.

	Standards	Topics to Be Considered for Curriculum/Sources of Information
1 hour	Trainers will provide participants with topics or allow students to choose topics for presentation. Participants may use multimedia. The length of the presentation is dependent on the number of participants and remaining time available.	

APPENDIX

CRIMINAL INTELLIGENCE GLOSSARY OF TERMS—OCTOBER 2007

Law enforcement agencies at all levels are working together more than ever to support information sharing. It is important to note that there is a tremendous effort under way to streamline intelligence terms to facilitate information sharing. As a result, criminal intelligence terminology is changing. It is recommended that organizations stay abreast of emerging intelligence-related terminology.

The definitions contained herein are provided from the perspective of criminal intelligence. Further, it is recognized that some words and phrases will have alternate or additional meanings when used in the context of national security intelligence, the military, or business. The definitions are intended to be merely descriptive of an entity, issue, or process that may be encountered by those working with the criminal intelligence function. Definitions may differ according to state statutes or local rules.

Access (to sensitive information)

Sensitive information and/or intelligence may be released by a law enforcement agency when at least one of the following four prescribed circumstances applies to the person(s) receiving the information:

Right to Know

Based on having legal authority, one's official position, legal mandates, or official agreements, allowing the individual to receive intelligence reports.

Need to Know

As a result of jurisdictional, organizational, or operational necessities, intelligence or information is disseminated to further an investigation.

Investigatory Value

Intelligence or information is disseminated in the law enforcement community for surveillance, apprehension, or furtherance of an investigation.

Public Value

Intelligence or information can be released to the public when there is a need to know and a right to know the information because of the value that may be derived from public dissemination to (1) aid in locating targets/suspects and (2) for public safety purposes (i.e., hardening targets, taking precautions).

Actionable

Intelligence and information with sufficient specificity and detail to implement explicit responses to prevent a crime or terrorist attack.

Administrative Analysis

The analysis of economic, geographic, demographic, census, or behavioral data to identify trends and conditions useful to aid administrators in making policy and/or resource allocation decisions.

Allocation

Collection and analysis of information that shows relationships among varied individuals suspected of being involved in criminal activity that may provide insight into the criminal operation and which investigative strategies might work best.

Analysis

That activity whereby meaning, actual or suggested, is derived through organizing and systematically examining diverse information and applying inductive or deductive logic for the purposes of criminal investigation or assessment.

Globals' "Minimum Criminal Intelligence Training Standards"

Archiving (Records)

The maintenance of records in remote storage after a case has been closed or disposed of, as a matter of contingency, should the records be needed for later reference.

Association Analysis

The entry of critical investigative and/or assessment variables into a two-axis matrix to examine the relationships and patterns that emerge as the variables are correlated in the matrix.

Automated Trusted Information Exchange (ATIX)

Operated by the Regional Information Sharing Systems®, ATIX is a secure means to disseminate national security or terrorist threat information to law enforcement and other first responders via the ATIX electronic bulletin board, secure Web site, and secure e-mail.

Bias/Hate Crime

Any criminal act directed toward any person or group as a result of that person's race, ethnicity, religious affiliation, or sexual preference.

C3

An intelligence application concept initially used by military intelligence that stands for command, control, and communication as the hallmark for effective intelligence operations.

Clandestine Activity

An activity that is usually extensive and goal-oriented, planned, and executed to conceal the existence of the operation. Only participants and the agency sponsoring the activity are intended to know about the operation. "Storefront" operations, "stings," and certain concentrated undercover investigations (such as ABSCAM) can be classified as clandestine collections.

Classified Information/Intelligence

A uniform system for classifying, safeguarding, and declassifying national security information, including information relating to defense against transnational terrorism, to ensure that certain information is maintained in confidence in order to protect citizens, U.S. democratic institutions, U.S. homeland security, and U.S. interactions with foreign nations and entities.

Top Secret Classification

Applied to information, the unauthorized disclosure of which reasonably could be expected to cause exceptionally grave damage to the national security that the original classification authority is able to identify or describe (Executive Order 12958, March 25, 2003).

Secret Classification

Applied to information, the unauthorized disclosure of which reasonably could be expected to cause serious damage to the national security that the original classification authority is able to identify or describe (Executive Order 12958, March 25, 2003).

Confidential Classification

Applied to information, the unauthorized disclosure of which reasonably could be expected to cause damage to the national security that the original classification authority is able to identify or describe (Executive Order 12958, March 25, 2003).

Collation (of information)

A review of collected and evaluated information to determine its substantive applicability to a case or problem at issue and placement of useful information into a form or system that permits easy and rapid access and retrieval.

Collection (of information)

The identification, location, and recording/storing of information, typically from an original source and using both human and technological means, for input into the intelligence cycle for the purpose of meeting a defined tactical or strategic intelligence goal.

Collection Plan

The preliminary step toward completing an assessment of intelligence requirements to determine what type of information needs to be collected, alternatives for how to collect the information, and a timeline for collecting the information.

Command and Control

Command and control functions are performed through an arrangement of personnel, equipment, communications, facilities, and procedures employed by a commander in planning, directing, coordinating, and controlling forces and operations in the accomplishment of a mission.

Commodity (Illegal)

Any item or substance that is inherently unlawful to possess (contraband) or materials which, if not contraband, are themselves being distributed, transacted, or marketed in an unlawful manner.

Commodity Flow Analysis

Graphic depictions and descriptions of transactions, shipment, and distribution of contraband goods and money derived from unlawful activities in order to aid in the disruption of the unlawful activities and apprehend those persons involved in all aspects of the unlawful activities.

Communications Intelligence (COMINT)

The capture of information, either encrypted or in "plaintext," exchanged between intelligence targets or transmitted by a known or suspected intelligence target for the purposes of tracking communications patterns and protocols (traffic analysis), establishing links between intercommunicating parties or groups, and/or analysis of the substantive meaning of the communication.

Conclusion

A definitive statement about a suspect, action, or state of nature based on the analysis of information.

Confidential

See Classified Information/Intelligence, Confidential Classification.

Continuing Criminal Enterprise

Any individual, partnership, corporation, association, or other legal entity and any union or group of individuals associated in fact, although not a legal entity, that are involved in a continuing or perpetuating criminal activity.

Controlled Unclassified Information (CUI)

This is a proposed term to replace the term "Sensitive But Unclassified." It has not been officially adopted.

Coordination
The process of interrelating work functions, responsibilities, duties, resources, and initiatives directed toward goal attainment.

Counterintelligence
Information compiled, analyzed, and/or disseminated in an effort to investigate espionage, sedition, or subversion that is related to national security concerns. A national security intelligence activity that involves blocking or developing a strategic response to other groups, governments, or individuals through the identification, neutralization, and manipulation of their intelligence services.

Covert Intelligence
A covert activity is planned and executed to conceal the collection of information and/or the identity of any officer or agent participating in the activity.

Crime Analysis
The process of analyzing information collected on crimes and police service delivery variables in order to give direction for police officer deployment, resource allocation, and policing strategies as a means to maximize crime prevention activities and the cost-effective operation of the police department.

Crime-Pattern Analysis
An assessment of the nature, extent, and changes of crime based on the characteristics of the criminal incident, including modus operandi, temporal, and geographic variables.

Criminal History Record Information (CHRI)
Information collected by criminal justice agencies on individuals, consisting of identifiable descriptions and notations of arrests, detentions, indictments, information, or other formal criminal charges and any disposition arising therefrom, including sentencing, correctional supervision, and/or release. The term does not include identification information, such as fingerprint records, to the extent that such information does not indicate involvement of the individual in the criminal justice system.

Criminal Informant
See Informant.

Criminal Intelligence
See Intelligence (Criminal) and Law Enforcement Intelligence.

Criminal Investigative Analysis
An analytic process that studies serial offenders, victims, and crime scenes in order to assess characteristics and behaviors of offender(s) with the intent to identify or aid in the identification of the offender(s).

Criminal Predicate
Information about an individual or his/her behavior that may only be collected and stored in a law enforcement intelligence records system when there is reasonable suspicion that the individual is involved in criminal conduct or activity and the information is relevant to that criminal conduct or activity.

Cryptanalysis
The process of deciphering encrypted communications of an intelligence target.

Globals' "Minimum Criminal Intelligence Training Standards"

Cryptography
The creation of a communications code/encryption system for communication transmission with the intent of precluding the consumption and interpretation of one's own messages.

Cryptology
The study of communications encryption methods that deal with the development of "codes" and the "scrambling" of communications in order to prevent the interception of the communications by an unauthorized or unintended party.

Data Element
A field within a database that describes or defines a specific characteristic or attribute.

Data Owner
The agency that originally enters information or data into law enforcement records system.

Data Quality
Controls implemented to ensure that all information in a law enforcement agency's records system is complete, accurate, and secure.

Deconfliction
The process or system that is used to determine whether multiple law enforcement agencies are investigating the same person or crime and that provides notification to each agency involved of the shared interest in the case, as well as providing contact information. This is an information and intelligence sharing process that seeks to minimize conflicts between agencies and maximize the effectiveness of an investigation.

Deductive Logic
The reasoning process of taking information and arriving at conclusions from within that information.

Deployment
The short-term assignment of personnel to address specific crime problems or police service demands.

Designated State and/or Major Urban Area Fusion Center
The fusion center in each state designated as the primary or lead fusion center for the information sharing environment.

Dissemination (of Intelligence)
The process of effectively distributing analyzed intelligence utilizing certain protocols in the most appropriate format to those in need of the information to facilitate their accomplishment of organizational goals.

Due Process
Fundamental fairness during the course of the criminal justice process, including adherence to legal standards and the civil rights of the police constituency; the adherence to principles that are fundamental to justice.

El Paso Intelligence Center (EPIC)
A cooperative intelligence center serving as a clearinghouse and intelligence resource for local, state, and federal law enforcement agencies. Its primary concern is drug trafficking; however, intelligence on other crimes is also managed by EPIC.

Globals' "Minimum Criminal Intelligence Training Standards"

Enterprise
Any individual, partnership, corporation, association, or other legal entity and any union or group of individuals associated in fact, although not a legal entity.

Estimate
See Intelligence Estimate.

Evaluation (of Information)
All information collected for the intelligence cycle is reviewed for its quality with an assessment of the validity and reliability of the information.

Event Flow Analysis
Graphic depictions and descriptions of incidents, behaviors, and people involved in an unlawful event, intended to help understand how an event occurred as a tool to aid in prosecution as well as prevention of future unlawful events.

Exemptions (to the Freedom of Information Act)
Circumstances wherein a law enforcement agency is not required to disclose information from a Freedom of Information Act (FOIA) request.

Field Intelligence Group (FIG)
The centralized intelligence component in a Federal Bureau of Investigation (FBI) field office that is responsible for the management, execution, and coordination of intelligence functions within the field office region.

Field Intelligence Report (FIR)
An officer-initiated interview of a person believed by the officer to be acting in a suspicious manner that may be indicative of planning or preparing to conduct criminal activity.

Financial Analysis
A review and analysis of financial data to ascertain the presence of criminal activity. It can include bank record analysis, net worth analysis, financial profiles, source and applications of funds, financial statement analysis, and/or Bank Secrecy Act record analysis. It can also show destinations of proceeds of crime and support prosecutions.

Flow Analysis
The review of raw data to determine the sequence of events or interactions that may reflect criminal activity. Flow analysis includes timelines, event flow analysis, commodity flow analysis, and activity flow analysis and may show missing actions or events that need further investigation.

For Official Use Only (FOUO)
A designation applied to unclassified sensitive information that may be exempt from mandatory release to the public under the FOIA.

Forecast (as related to Criminal Intelligence)
The product of an analytic process that provides a probability of future crimes and crime patterns based on a comprehensive, integrated analysis of past, current, and developing trends.

Freedom of Information Act (FOIA)

The Freedom of Information Act, 5 U.S.C. 552, enacted in 1966, statutorily provides that any person has a right, enforceable in court, to access federal agency records, except to the extent that such records (or portions thereof) are protected from disclosure by one of nine exemptions.

Fusion Center

The physical location of the law enforcement intelligence fusion process.

Fusion Center Guidelines

A series of nationally recognized standards developed by law enforcement intelligence subject-matter experts designed for the good practice of developing and managing an intelligence fusion center.

Fusion Process

The overarching process of managing the flow of information and intelligence across levels and sectors of government.

Granularity

Considers the specific details and pieces of information, including nuances and situational inferences that constitute the elements on which intelligence is developed through analysis.

Guidelines

See Intelligence Records Guidelines.

Homeland Security Advisory System

An information and communications structure designed by the U.S. government for disseminating information to all levels of government and the American people regarding the risk of terrorist attacks and for providing a framework to assess the risk at five levels: Low, Guarded, Elevated, High, and Severe.

Human Intelligence (HUMINT)

Intelligence-gathering methods that require human interaction or observation of the target or targeted environment. The intelligence is collected through the use of one's direct senses or the optical and/or audio enhancement of the senses.

Hypothesis (from Criminal Intelligence Analysis)

An interim conclusion regarding persons, events, and/or commodities based on the accumulation and analysis of intelligence information that is to be proven or disproved by further investigation and analysis.

Imagery

The representation of an object or locale produced on any medium by optical or electronic means. The nature of the image will be dependent on the sensing media and sensing platform.

Indicator

Generally defined and observable actions that, based on an analysis of past known behaviors and characteristics, collectively suggest that a person may be committing, may be preparing to commit, or has committed an unlawful act.

Inductive Logic

The reasoning process of taking diverse pieces of specific information and inferring a broader meaning of the information through the course of hypothesis development.

Globals' "Minimum Criminal Intelligence Training Standards"

Inference Development
The creation of a probabilistic conclusion, estimate, or prediction related to an intelligence target based on the use of inductive or deductive logic in the analysis of raw information related to the target.

Informant
An individual not affiliated with a law enforcement agency who provides information about criminal behavior to a law enforcement agency. An informant may be a community member, a businessperson, or a criminal informant who seeks to protect himself/herself from prosecution and/or provide the information in exchange for payment.

Information
Pieces of raw, unanalyzed data that identify persons, evidence, or events or illustrate processes that indicate the incidence of a criminal event or witnesses or evidence of a criminal event.

Information Classification
See Classified Information/Intelligence.

Information Evaluation
See Evaluation (of Information).

Information Sharing Environment
A trusted partnership among all levels of government, the private sector, and foreign partners to detect, prevent, preempt, and mitigate the effects of terrorism against territory, people, and interests of the United States of America. This partnership enables the trusted, secure, and appropriate exchange of terrorism information, in the first instance, across the five federal communities; to and from state, local, and tribal governments, foreign allies, and the private sector; and at all levels of security classifications.

Information Sharing System
An integrated and secure methodology, whether computerized or manual, designed to efficiently and effectively distribute critical information about offenders, crimes, and/or events in order to enhance prevention and apprehension activities by law enforcement.

Information System
An organized means, whether manual or electronic, of collecting, processing, storing, and retrieving information on individual entities for purposes of record and reference.

Intelligence (Criminal)
The product of the analysis of raw information related to crimes or crime patterns with respect to an identifiable person or group of persons in an effort to anticipate, prevent, or monitor possible criminal activity.

Intelligence Analyst
A professional position in which the incumbent is responsible for taking the varied facts, documentation of circumstances, evidence, interviews, and any other material related to a crime and organizing them into a logical and related framework for the purposes of developing a criminal case, explaining a criminal phenomenon, describing crime and crime trends and/or preparing materials for court and prosecution, or arriving at an assessment of a crime problem or crime group.

Intelligence Assessment
A comprehensive report on an intelligence issue related to criminal or national security threats available to local, state, tribal, and federal law enforcement agencies.

Globals' "Minimum Criminal Intelligence Training Standards"

Intelligence Bulletins

A finished intelligence product in article format that describes new developments and evolving trends. The bulletins are typically Sensitive But Unclassified (SBU) and available for distribution to local, state, tribal, and federal law enforcement.

Intelligence Community

Those agencies of the U.S. government, including the military that have the responsibility of preventing breeches to U.S. national security and responding to national security threats.

Intelligence Cycle

An organized process by which information is gathered, assessed, and distributed in order to fulfill the goals of the intelligence function. It is a method of performing analytic activities and placing the analysis in a useable form.

Intelligence Estimate

The appraisal, expressed in writing or orally, of available intelligence relating to a specific situation or condition with a view to determining the courses of action open to criminal offenders and terrorists and the order of probability of their adoption. Includes strategic projections on the economic, human, and/or quantitative criminal impact of the crime or issue that is subject to analysis.

Intelligence Function

That activity within a law enforcement agency responsible for some aspect of law enforcement intelligence, whether collection, analysis, and/or dissemination.

Intelligence Gap

An unanswered question about a cyber, criminal, or national security issue or threat.

Intelligence Information Reports (IIR)

Raw, unevaluated intelligence concerning "perishable" or time-limited information about criminal or national security issues. Although the full IIR may be classified, local, state, and tribal law enforcement agencies will have access to Sensitive But Unclassified information in the report under the tear line.

Intelligence-Led Policing

The dynamic use of intelligence to guide operational law enforcement activities to targets, commodities, or threats for both tactical responses and strategic decision making for resource allocation and/or strategic responses.

Intelligence Mission

The role that the intelligence function of a law enforcement agency fulfills in support of the overall mission of the agency; it specifies in general language what the function is intended to accomplish.

Intelligence Mutual Aid Pact (IMAP)

A formal agreement between law enforcement agencies designed to expedite the process of sharing information in intelligence records.

Intelligence Officer

A law enforcement officer assigned to an agency's intelligence function for purposes of investigation, liaison, or other intelligence-related activity that requires or benefits from having a sworn officer perform the activity.

Intelligence Products

Reports or documents that contain assessments, forecasts, associations, links, and other outputs from the analytic process that may be disseminated for use by law enforcement agencies for prevention of crimes, target hardening, apprehension of offenders, and prosecution.

Intelligence Records (Files)

Stored information on the activities and associations of individuals, organizations, businesses, and groups who are suspected (reasonable suspicion) of being involved in the actual or attempted planning, organizing, financing, or commissioning of criminal acts or are suspected of being or having been involved in criminal activities with known or suspected crime figures.

Intelligence Records Guidelines

Derived from the federal regulation 28 CFR Part 23, these are guidelines/standards for the development of records management policies and procedures used by law enforcement agencies.

International Criminal Police Organization (INTERPOL)

INTERPOL is a worldwide law enforcement organization established for mutual assistance in the prevention, detection, and deterrence of international crimes. It houses international police databases, provides secure international communications between member countries for the exchange of routine criminal investigative information, and is an information clearinghouse on international criminals/fugitives and stolen properties.

Key Word In Context (KWIC)

An automated system that indexes selected key words that represent the evidence or information being stored.

Law Enforcement Intelligence

The end product (output) of an analytic process that collects and assesses information about crimes and/or criminal enterprises with the purpose of making judgments and inferences about community conditions, potential problems, and criminal activity with the intent to pursue criminal prosecution or project crime trends or support informed decision making by management.

Law Enforcement Sensitive (LES)

Sensitive But Unclassified information specifically compiled for law enforcement purposes that, if not protected from unauthorized access, could reasonably be expected to 1) interfere with law enforcement proceedings, 2) deprive a person of a right to a fair trial or impartial adjudication, 3) constitute an unwarranted invasion of the personal privacy of others, 4) disclose the identity of a confidential source, 5) disclose investigative techniques and procedures, and/or 6) endanger the life or physical safety of an individual.

Methods

These are the methodologies (e.g., electronic surveillance or undercover operations) of how critical information is obtained and recorded.

Micro-Intelligence

Intelligence activities focusing on current problems and crimes for either case development or resource allocation.

Money Laundering

The practice of using multiple unlawful transactions of money and/or negotiable instruments gained through illegal activities with the intent of hiding the origin of the income, those who have been "paid" from the income, and/or the location of the unlawful income.

National Central Bureau (NCB or USNCB)

The United States headquarters of INTERPOL is located in Washington, DC.

National Criminal Intelligence Resource Center (NCIRC)

An Internet Web site that contains information regarding law enforcement intelligence operations and practices and provides criminal justice professionals with a centralized resource information bank to access a multitude of criminal intelligence resources to help law enforcement agencies develop, implement, and retain a lawful and effective intelligence capacity.

National Criminal Intelligence Sharing Plan (NCISP)

A formal intelligence sharing initiative, supported by the U.S. Department of Justice, Office of Justice Programs, that securely links local, state, tribal, and federal law enforcement agencies, facilitating the exchange of critical intelligence information. The Plan contains model policies and standards and is a blueprint for law enforcement administrators to follow when enhancing or building an intelligence function. It describes a nationwide communications capability that will link all levels of law enforcement personnel, including officers on the street, intelligence analysts, unit commanders, and police executives.

National Security Intelligence

The collection and analysis of information concerned with the relationship and equilibrium of the United States with foreign powers, organizations, and persons with regard to political and economic factors, as well as the maintenance of the United States' sovereign principles.

Network

A structure of interconnecting components designed to communicate with each other and perform a function or functions as a unit in a specified manner.

Open Communications (OPCOM)

The collection of open or publicly available communications, broadcasts, audio or video recordings, propaganda, published statements, and other distributed written or recorded material for purposes of analyzing the information.

Open-Source Information (or Intelligence)

Individual data, records, reports, and assessments that may shed light on an investigatory target or event that do not require any legal process or any type of clandestine collection techniques for a law enforcement agency to obtain. Rather, it is obtained through means that meet copyright and commercial requirements of vendors, as well as being free of legal restrictions to access by anyone who seeks that information.

Operational Analysis

An assessment of the methodology of a criminal enterprise or terrorist organization that depicts how the enterprise performs its activities, including communications, philosophy, compensation, security, and other variables that are essential for the enterprise to exist.

Operational Intelligence

Information is evaluated and systematically organized on an active or potential target, such as groups of or individual criminals, relevant premises, contact points, and methods of communication. This process is developmental in nature, wherein there are sufficient articulated reasons to suspect criminal activity. Intelligence activities explore the basis of those reasons and newly developed information in order to develop a case for arrest or indictment.

Outcome Evaluation

The process of determining the value or amount of success in achieving a predetermined objective through defining the objective in some qualitative or quantitative measurable terms, identifying the proper criteria (or variables) to be used in measuring the success toward attaining the objective, determination and explanation of the degree of success, and recommendations for further program actions to attain the desired objectives/outcomes.

Planning

The preparation for future situations, estimating organizational demands and resources needed to attend to those situations, and initiating strategies to respond to those situations.

Pointer System or Index

A system that stores information designed to identify individuals, organizations, and/or crime methodologies with the purpose of linking law enforcement agencies that have similar investigative and/or intelligence interests in the entity defined by the system.

Policy

The principles and values that guide the performance of a duty. A policy is not a statement of what must be done in a particular situation. Rather, it is a statement of guiding principles that should be followed in activities that are directed toward the attainment of goals.

Prediction

The projection of future criminal actions or changes in the nature of crime trends or a criminal enterprise based on an analysis of information depicting historical trends from which a forecast is based.

Preventive Intelligence

Intelligence that can be used to interdict or forestall a crime or terrorist attack.

Privacy (Information)

The assurance that legal and constitutional restrictions on the collection, maintenance, use, and disclosure of personally identifiable information will be adhered to by criminal justice agencies, with use of such information to be strictly limited to circumstances in which legal process permits use of the personally identifiable information.

Privacy (Personal)

The assurance that legal and constitutional restrictions on the collection, maintenance, use, and disclosure of behaviors of an individual—including his/her communications, associations, and transactions—will be adhered to by criminal justice agencies, with use of such information to be strictly limited to circumstances in which legal process authorizes surveillance and investigation.

Privacy Act

Legislation that allows an individual to review almost all federal files (and state files under the auspices of the respective state privacy acts) pertaining to him/her, places restrictions on the disclosure of personally identifiable information, specifies that there be no secret records systems on individuals, and compels the government to reveal its information sources.

Proactive

Taking action that is anticipatory to a problem or situation with the intent to eliminate or mitigate the effect of the incident.

Procedural Due Process
Mandates and guarantees of law that ensure that the procedures employed during the course of the criminal justice process to deprive a person of life, liberty, or property meet constitutional standards.

Procedure
A method of performing an operation or a manner of proceeding on a course of action. It differs from policy in that it directs action in a particular situation to perform a specific task within the guidelines of policy. Both policies and procedures are goal-oriented. However, policy establishes limits to action, whereas procedure directs responses within those limits.

Profile/Criminal Profile
An investigative technique used to identify and define the major personality and behavioral characteristics of the criminal offender based on an analysis of the crime(s) he or she has committed.

Protocol (of Intelligence Collection)
Information collection procedures employed to obtain verbal and written information, actions of people, and physical evidence required for strategic and tactical intelligence analysis.

Purging (Records)
The removal and/or destruction of records because they are deemed to be of no further value or because further access to the records would serve no legitimate government interest.

Qualitative (Methods)
Research methods that collect and analyze information that is described in narrative or rhetorical form, with conclusions drawn based on the cumulative interpreted meaning of that information.

Quantitative (Methods)
Research methods that collect and analyze information that can be counted or placed on a scale of measurement that can be statistically analyzed.

Racketeer Influenced and Corrupt Organizations (RICO) Act or Similar State Statutes
Title IX of the Organized Crime Control Act of 1970 (18 U.S.C. Sections 1961-1968) provides civil and criminal penalties for persons who engage in a pattern of racketeering activity or collection of an unlawful debt that has a specified relationship to an enterprise that affects interstate commerce.

Racketeering Activity
State felonies involving murder, robbery, extortion, and several other serious offenses and more than 30 serious federal offenses, including extortion, interstate theft offenses, narcotics violations, mail fraud, and securities fraud.

Reasonable Suspicion
When information exists that establishes sufficient facts to give a trained law enforcement or criminal investigative agency officer, investigator, or employee a basis to believe that there is a reasonable possibility that an individual or organization is involved in a definable criminal activity or enterprise

Recommendations
Suggestions for actions to be taken based on the findings of an analysis.

Records (Intelligence)
See Intelligence Records (Files).

Records System
A group of records from which information is retrieved by reference to a name or other personal identifier, such as a social security number.

Red Team
A technique for assessing vulnerability that involves viewing a potential target from the perspective of an attacker to identify its hidden vulnerabilities and to anticipate possible modes of attack.

Regional Information Sharing Systems® (RISS)
RISS is composed of six regional intelligence centers that provide secure communications, information sharing resources, and investigative support to combat multijurisdictional crime and terrorist threats to over 8,000 local, state, tribal, and federal member law enforcement agencies in all 50 states, the District of Columbia, U.S. territories, Australia, Canada, and England.

Regional Intelligence Centers
Multijurisdictional centers cooperatively developed within a logical geographical area that coordinate federal, state, and local law enforcement information with other information sources to track and assess criminal and terrorist threats that are operating in or interacting with the region.

Reliability
Asks the question, "Is the source of the information consistent and dependable?"

Reporting
Depending on the type of intelligence, the process of placing analyzed information into the proper form to ensure the most effective consumption.

Requirements (Intelligence)
The types of intelligence operational law enforcement elements need from the intelligence function within an agency or other intelligence-producing organizations in order for law enforcement officers to maximize protection and preventive efforts as well as identify and arrest persons who are criminally liable.

Responsibility
Responsibility reflects how the authority of a unit or individual is used and determines whether goals have been accomplished and the mission fulfilled in a manner that is consistent with the defined limits of authority.

Risk Assessment
An analysis of a target, illegal commodity, or victim to identify the probability of being attacked or criminally compromised and to analyze vulnerabilities.

Risk Management-Based Intelligence
An approach to intelligence analysis that has as its object the calculation of the risk attributable to a threat source or acts threatened by a threat source; a means of providing strategic intelligence for planning and policymaking, especially regarding vulnerabilities and countermeasures designed to prevent criminal acts; a means of providing tactical or operational intelligence in support of operations against a specific threat source, capability, or modality; can be quantitative if a proper database exists to measure likelihood and impact and calculate risk; can be qualitative

and subjective and still deliver a reasonably reliable ranking of risk for resource allocation and other decision making in strategic planning and for operations in tactical situations.

Rules

A specific requirement or prohibition that is stated to prevent deviations from policy or procedure. A violation of a rule typically results in an internal investigation and may result in disciplinary action.

Sensitive Compartmented Information (SCI)

Classified information concerning or derived from intelligence sources, methods, or analytical processes that is required to be handled within formal access control systems.

Sensitive Compartmented Information Facility (SCIF)

An accredited area, room, group of rooms, buildings, or an installation where SCI may be stored, used, discussed, and/or processed.

Sealing (Records)

Records are stored by an agency but cannot be accessed, referenced, or used without a court order or statutory authority based on a showing of evidence that there is a legitimate government interest to review the sealed information.

Security

A series of procedures and measures that, when combined, provide protection of people from harm, information from improper disclosure or alteration, and assets from theft or damage. (Criminal Justice Commission, 1995.)

Sensitive But Unclassified (SBU) Information

Information that has not been classified by a federal law enforcement agency that pertains to significant law enforcement cases under investigation and criminal intelligence reports that require dissemination criteria to only those persons necessary to further the investigation or to prevent a crime or terrorist act.

Sensitive Homeland Security Information (SHSI)

Any information created or received by an agency or any local, county, state, or tribal government that the loss, misuse, unauthorized disclosure, modification of, or the unauthorized access to could reasonably be expected to impair significantly the capabilities and/or efforts of agencies and/or local, county, state, and tribal personnel to predict, analyze, investigate, deter, prevent, protect against, mitigate the effects of, or recover from acts of terrorism. SHSI does not include any information that is:

1. Classified as national security information pursuant to Executive Order 12958, as amended, or any successor order.

2. Designated by Executive Order 12951, any successor order, or the Atomic Energy Act of 1954 (42 U.S.C. § 2011), to require protection against unauthorized disclosure.

3. Protected Critical Infrastructure Information (PCII) as defined in 6 Code of Federal Regulations (CFR) § 29.2.

4. Sensitive Security Information (SSI) as defined in 49 CFR Part 1520.

Globals' "Minimum Criminal Intelligence Training Standards"

Signal Intelligence (SIGINT)

The interception of various radio frequency signals, microwave signals, satellite audio communications, nonimagery infrared and coherent light signals, and transmissions from surreptitiously placed audio microtransmitters in support of the communications intelligence activity.

Sources

From an intelligence perspective, these are persons (human intelligence or HUMINT) who collect or possess critical information needed for intelligence analysis.

Spatial Analysis

The process of using a geographic information system in combination with crime-analysis techniques to assess the geographic context of offenders, crimes, and other law enforcement activity.

Statistical System

An organized means of collecting, processing, storing, and retrieving aggregate information for purposes of analysis, research, and reference. No individual records are stored in a statistical system.

Strategic Intelligence

An assessment of targeted crime patterns, crime trends, criminal organizations, and/or unlawful commodity transactions for purposes of planning, decision making, and resource allocation; the focused examination of unique, pervasive, and/or complex crime problems.

Substantive Due Process

Guarantees persons against arbitrary, unreasonable, or capricious laws, and it acts as a limitation against arbitrary governmental actions so that no government agency may exercise powers beyond those authorized by the Constitution.

Surveillance

The observation of activities, behaviors, and associations of a LAWINT target (individual or group) with the intent to gather incriminating information, or "lead" information, that is used for the furtherance of a criminal investigation.

Tactical Intelligence

Evaluated information on which immediate enforcement action can be based; intelligence activity focused specifically on developing an active case.

Target

Any person, organization, group, crime or criminal series, or commodity being subject to investigation and intelligence analysis.

Target Profile

A profile that is person-specific and contains sufficient detail to initiate a target operation or support an ongoing operation against an individual or networked group of individuals.

Targeting

The identification of crimes, crime trends, and crime patterns that have discernable characteristics that make collection and analysis of intelligence information an efficient and effective method for identifying, apprehending, and prosecuting those who are criminally responsible.

Tear-Line Report

A report containing classified intelligence or information that is prepared in such a manner that data relating to intelligence sources and methods are easily removed from the report to protect sources and methods from disclosure. Typically, the information below the "tear line" can be released as Sensitive But Unclassified.

Telemetry

The collection and processing of information derived from noncommunications electromagnetic radiations emitting from sources such as radio navigation systems (e.g., transponders), radar systems, and information/data signals emitted from monitoring equipment in a vehicle or device.

Telephone Record (Toll)/Communications Analysis

An assessment of telephone call activity associated with investigatory targets to include telephone numbers called and/or received, the frequency of calls between numbers, the dates of calls, length of calls, and patterns of use.

Third Agency Rule

An agreement wherein a source agency releases information under the condition that the receiving agency does not release the information to any other agency—that is, a third agency.

Threat Assessment

An assessment of a criminal or terrorist presence within a jurisdiction integrated with an assessment of potential targets of that presence and a statement of probability that the criminal or terrorist will commit an unlawful act. The assessment focuses on the criminal's or terrorist's opportunity, capability, and willingness to fulfill the threat.

Threat Inventory

An information and intelligence-based survey within the region of a law enforcement agency to identify potential individuals or groups that pose a criminal or terrorist threat without a judgment of the kind of threat they pose. The inventory is simply to determine their presence.

Undercover Investigation

Active infiltration of or an attempt to infiltrate a group believed to be involved in criminal activity and/or the interaction with a LAWINT target with the intent to gather incriminating information or lead information that is used for the furtherance of a criminal investigation.

Validity

Asks the question, "Does the information actually represent what we believe it represents?"

Variable

Any characteristic on which individuals, groups, items, or incidents differ.

Vet

To subject a proposal, work product, or concept to an appraisal by command personnel and/or experts to ascertain the product's accuracy, consistency with philosophy, and/or feasibility before proceeding.

Violent Criminal Apprehension Program (VICAP)

A nationwide data information center operated by the FBI's National Center for the Analysis of Violent Crime, designed to collect, collate, and analyze specific crimes of violence.

Vulnerability Assessment

An assessment of possible criminal or terrorist group targets within a jurisdiction integrated with an assessment of the target's weaknesses, likelihood of being attacked, and ability to withstand an attack.

Warning

To notify in advance of possible harm or victimization as a result of information and intelligence gained concerning the probability of a crime or terrorist attack.

IALEIA's
"Law Enforcement Analytic Standards"

Following are summaries of the International Association of Law Enforcement Intelligence Analysts (IALEIA) *"Law Enforcement Analytic Standards"* published by IALEIA. For a complete version of this publication please contact IALEIA at admin@ialeia.org.

STANDARDS FOR ANALYSTS

#1 Education Standard

Analysts hired should have four-year college degrees or commensurate experience. Commensurate experience is defined as no less than five years of previous research/analysis/intelligence- oriented experience with a two-year degree, or no less than ten years of previous research/analysis/ intelligence-oriented experience with less than a two-year degree. This experience can come from the private, public, or military sector. The experience can be documented through job descriptions and/or examples of work products. Appropriate college degree areas include those with research and writing components, including social sciences, English, journalism, and criminal justice. The areas may also include business or science degrees if the knowledge gained will assist in the types of analysis needed to be completed.

#2 Training Standard

Initial analytic training shall be a minimum of 40 hours and shall be provided by instructors with law enforcement analytic experience. Training shall incorporate, but not necessarily be limited to, the following topics:

- Intelligence cycle/process Intelligence-led policing NCISP
- File management Information evaluation Critical thinking
- Logic
- Inference and recommendation development
- Collection plans
- Research methods and sources Crime-pattern analysis Association/network analysis
- Telephone record analysis/communication analysis
- Flow analysis Spatial/geographic analysis Financial analysis
- Strategic analysis
- Analytic writing Presentation skills Statistics
- Graphical techniques
- Computerized programs to assist analysis
- Ethics Professionalism Court testimony

#3 Continuing Education

Continuing analytic education of at least eight hours per year shall be received by those performing the analytic function, to be accomplished through a combination of formal education, training classes, distance learning, or self-directed study efforts. The training provider should have professional association or academic credentials in the subject matter. Continuing education may include topics as listed in Analytic Standard #2.

#4 Professional Development Standard

Analysts shall maintain a program of professional development throughout their career and be supported in this process by their employer. Employers should ensure that analysts provide maximum benefit to operations by implementing professional development programs for their analytic staff, whether analysts or sworn officers are performing the intelligence duties.

#5 Certification Standard

Analysts should be certified by an agency or organization (governmental, professional association, or institution of higher learning) specifically developed for intelligence analysts. These analytic certification programs shall reflect experience, education, training, and proficiency testing.

#6 Professional Liaison Standard

Analysts and their organizations shall be encouraged to maintain links to and seek available support from recognized professional bodies and associations.

#7 Analytic Attributes Standard

Analysts shall be hired and evaluated based on their work and attributes, including strong:

- Subject-matter expertise Analytic methodologies customer-service ethics
- Information handling and processing skills
- Communication skills Critical-thinking skills computer literacy
- Objectivity and intellectual honesty

#8 Planning Standard

Analysts shall understand the objective of their assignment, define the problem, and plan for the necessary resources. This shall be done through the use of a collection or investigative plan or through intelligence requirements. Specific steps to be taken to complete the assignment, including potential sources of information and a projected timeline, shall be included. The needs of the client (requirements) shall be reflected in the plan.

#9 Direction Standard

Analysts shall be involved in planning and direction. Law enforcement agencies shall use analytic expertise to develop both short - and long-term investigative priorities and plans. Analytic expertise may also be used to develop intelligence requirements as a driving force to determine investigative priorities and for incorporation into investigative plans to drive operations.

#10 Collection Standard

Analytic research shall be thorough and use all available sources. An analytic product shall contain all relevant data available through sources and means available to the analyst.

#11 Collection Follow-Up Standard

In the course of collection by investigators and others, analysts shall evaluate the progress of the collection to determine if the collection plan/requirements are being met and shall identify additional sources of information, as well as identify information that may be useful to other cases or activities. Where possible, analysts shall relay that information to an appropriate body for follow- up.

#12 Legal Constraints Standard

Raw data that has been obtained in violation of any applicable local, state, or federal law or ordinance shall not be incorporated into an analytic product.

#13 Evaluation Standard

Information collected from all sources shall be evaluated and designated for source reliability, content validity, and relevancy. Effective evaluation is important not only to the validity of the intelligence product but also to officer safety, investigative effectiveness, and solidity of evidence in prosecutions.

#14 Collation Standard

Raw data shall be organized and formatted so the analyst can retrieve; sort; identify patterns, anomalies, and information gaps; and store the data. When possible, this shall be done in a computerized format using the most appropriate software available to the analyst.

#15 Analytic Accuracy Standard

An analytic product shall be an accurate representation of the data. In cases where exculpatory data has been found along with proofs, both should be included.

#16 Computerized Analysis Standard

Analyses shall utilize the best and most current computerized visualization and analytic tools available to the analyst.

#17 Analytic Product Content Standard

Analytic products shall always include analysis, assessments, integrated data, judgments, conclusions, and recommendations. Forecasts, estimates, and models shall be developed, where appropriate

#18 Analytic Outcomes Standard

Analyses shall include alternative scenarios and avoid single-solution outcomes where appropriate, especially when the outcomes could have significant consequences. Analyses shall indicate the most likely hypothesis, but this hypothesis shall be arrived at through the analysis of competing hypotheses. Those hypotheses not chosen shall also be noted.

#19 Dissemination Plan Standard

Analysts shall develop a dissemination plan to encourage sharing of the product with applicable agencies. This plan shall indicate the security level of the document.   It shall be reviewed and approved by supervisory personnel.

#20 Analytic Report Standard

Reports shall be written clearly and facts documented thoroughly. A precise, analytic bottom line should be provided. A tight, logical organization of facts shall show how the analyst arrived at conclusions. Objective and dispassionate language shall be used, emphasizing brevity and clarity of expression.

#21 Analytic Product Format Standard

Analytic product formats shall be tailored to the consumer's need. Products shall include, but are not limited to:

- Strategic and tactical assessments
- Problem and target profiles Crime-pattern analysis Criminal business profiles Network analysis
- Demographic/social trend analysis
- Risk analysis Market profiles Results analysis
- Communication analysis
- Flow analysis Financial analysis Indicator analysis Geographic analysis

#22 Analytic Testimony Standard

Analysts shall be capable of giving testimony as fact/ summary and expert witnesses. They shall be able to present and defend their qualifications as witnesses and explain and defend the material they present.

#23 Data Source Attribution Standard

Every intelligence product shall clearly distinguish which contents are public domains or general unclassified information, what information is restricted or classified, and what contents are the judgments or opinions of analysts and/or other professionals.

#24 A nalytic Feedback Standard

The analytic product shall be reviewed, if appropriate, by peers and evaluated by customers. Peer review may be limited to factual content accuracy or may encompass collaborative comments concerning content and recommendations.

#25 Analytic Product Evaluation

Analytic products shall be evaluated based on the standards set forth in this document.

Addendum - Law Enforcement Intelligence Analysis Definitions

Analytic Writing – Written communication that focuses on distilling and summarizing factual information for the purpose of providing concise and clear reports for managers and other customers.

Analysis – The evaluation of information and its comparison to other information to determine the meaning of the data in reference to a criminal investigation or assessment.

Assessments – Strategic and tactical assessments are completed to assess the impact of a crime group or a criminal activity on a jurisdiction, now or in the future. These may include threat assessments, vulnerability assessments, or risk assessments.

Association Analysis/Network Analysis – Collection and analysis of information that shows relationships among varied individuals suspected of being involved in criminal activity that may provide insight into the criminal operation and which investigative strategies might work best.

Collation – The process whereby information is assembled together and compared critically.

Collection – The directed, focused gathering of information from all available sources.

Collection Plan – A plan that directs the collection of data on a particular topic with a specific objective, a list of potential sources of that data, and an estimated time frame.

Crime-Pattern Analysis – A process that looks for links between crimes and other incidents to reveal similarities and differences that can be used to help predict and prevent future criminal activity.

Criminal Analysis – Criminal analysis is the application of analytical methods and products to raw data that produces intelligence within the criminal justice field.

Criminal Business Profile – A product that details how criminal operations or techniques work, including how victims are chosen, how they are victimized, how proceeds of crime are used, and the strengths and weaknesses in the criminal system.

Criminal Intelligence – Information compiled, analyzed, and/or disseminated in an effort to anticipate, prevent, or monitor criminal activity.

Critical Thinking – The objective, open, and critical cognitive process applied to information to achieve a greater understanding of the data, often through developing and answering questions about the data.

Communication Analysis – See Telephone Record Analysis.

IALEIA's "Addendum – Law Enforcement Intelligence Analysis Definitions"

Content Validity – An evaluation scale generally represented from 1 to 5 or 1 to 4 that reflects the level of accuracy of the content of a raw data report. The scale ranges from known to be true to truthfulness unknown.

Customers – Consumers of intelligence products who may be within the agency of the analyst or in other agencies or organizations.

Demographic/Social Trend Analysis – An examination of the nature of demographic changes and their impact on criminality, the community, and law enforcement.

Dissemination – The release of information, usually under certain protocols.

Dissemination Plan – A plan that shows how an intelligence product is to be disseminated, at what security level, and to whom.

Estimate – A numeric forecast of activity based on facts but not able to be verified or known.

Evaluation – An assessment of the reliability of the source and accuracy of the raw data.

Feedback/Reevaluation – A review of the operation of the intelligence process and the value of the output to the consumer.

Financial Analysis – A review and analysis of financial data to ascertain the presence of criminal activity. It can include bank record analysis, net worth analysis, financial profiles, source and application of funds, financial statement analysis, and/or bank secrecy record analysis. It can also show destinations of proceeds of crime and support prosecutions.

Flow Analysis – The review of raw data to determine the sequence of events or interactions that may reflect criminal activity. It can include timelines, event-flow analysis, commodity-flow analysis, and activity-flow analysis. It may show missing actions or events that need further investigation.

Forecast – A look at what has happened or what may happen, based on what is known and verifiable, suspected and not verifiable, and unknown. Likelihoods or probabilities of future activity are usually included, with suggested steps to protect against criminal activity.

Geographic Analysis – A look at the locations of criminal activity or criminals to determine if future criminal activity can be deterred or interdicted through forecasting activity based on historical raw data.

Hypothesis – A tentative assumption that is to be proven or disproved by further investigation and analysis.

Indicator Analysis – A review of past criminal activity to determine if certain actions or postures taken can reflect future criminal activity. It can result in the development of "flagging" systems in computerized environments or behavioral profiles.

APPENDIX II - STANDARDS

IALEIA's "Addendum – Law Enforcement Intelligence Analysis Definitions"

Intelligence – The product of systematic gathering, evaluation, and synthesis of raw data on individuals or activities suspected of being, or known to be, criminal in nature. Intelligence is information that has been analyzed to determine its meaning and relevance. Information is compiled, analyzed, and/or disseminated in an effort to anticipate, prevent, or monitor criminal activity.

Intelligence Cycle – Consists of planning, collection, collation, evaluation, analysis, dissemination, and feedback.

Intelligence-led Policing – The collection and analysis of information to produce an intelligence end product, designed to inform police decision making at both the tactical and strategic levels.

Market Profile – An assessment that surveys the criminal market around a particular commodity in an area for the purpose of determining how to lessen that market

Models – Hypothetical sets of facts or circumstances that are developed to test the likelihood of a hypothesis.

Network Analysis – See Association Analysis.

Problem Profile – Identifies established and emerging crimes or incidents for the purpose of preventing or deterring further crime.

Raw Data – Data that is collected by officers or analysts that has not yet been subjected to the intelligence process and thus is not intelligence.

Results Analysis – An assessment of the effectiveness of police strategies and tactics as used to combat a particular crime problem. May include suggestions for changes to future policies and strategies.

Requirements – The details of what a customer needs from the intelligence function.

Risk Analysis/Assessment – Assesses the scale of risks posed by individual offenders or organizations to individual potential victims, the public at large, and law enforcement agencies. Generally includes preventative steps to be taken to lessen the risk.

Source Reliability – A scale that reflects the reliability of information sources; often shown as A–D or A–E. It ranges from factual source to reliability unknown.

Spatial Analysis – See Geographic Analysis.

Strategic Intelligence – Most often related to the structure and movement of organized criminal elements, patterns of criminal activity, criminal trend projections, or projective planning.

Tactical Intelligence – Information regarding a specific criminal event that can be used immediately by operational units to further a criminal investigation, plan tactical operations, and provide for officer safety.

Target Profile – A person- or organization-specific report that provides all that is known on the individual or organization that may be useful as the investigation is initiated. Based on the data, a best course of action regarding the investigation may be recommended.

IALEIA's "Addendum – Law Enforcement Intelligence Analysis Definitions"

Telephone Record Analysis/Communication Analysis – The review of records reflecting communications (telephone, e-mail, pager, text messaging, etc.) among entities that may be reflective of criminal associations or activity. It may recommend steps to take to continue or expand the investigation or study.

Threat Assessment – A report that looks at a criminal group or criminal activity and assesses the threat that activity or group poses to a jurisdiction, either at present or in the future, and recommends ways to lessen the threat.

Vulnerability Assessment – A report that looks at an individual, location, or event and assesses the vulnerability of that individual, location, or even to a criminal act and recommends ways to lessen or eliminate the vulnerability.

Fusion Center Standards
"Executive Summary"

EXECUTIVE SUMMARY

The need to develop and share information and intelligence across all levels of government has significantly changed over the last few years. The long-standing information sharing challenges among law enforcement agencies, public safety agencies, and the private sector are slowly disappearing. Yet, the need to identify, prevent, monitor, and respond to terrorist and criminal activities remains a significant need for the law enforcement, intelligence, public safety, and private sector communities.

Through the support, expertise, and knowledge of leaders from all entities involved, the fusion center concept can become a reality. Each official has a stake in the development and exchange of information and intelligence and should act as an ambassador to support and further this initiative. It is the responsibility of leadership to implement and adhere to the *Fusion Center Guidelines*.

The development and exchange of intelligence is not easy. Sharing this data requires not only strong leadership, it also requires the commitment, dedication, and trust of a diverse group of men and women who believe in the power of collaboration.

How can law enforcement, public safety, and private entities embrace a collaborative process to improve intelligence sharing and, ultimately, increase the ability to detect, prevent, and solve crimes while safeguarding our homeland? Recently, an initiative has emerged that incorporates the various elements of an ideal information and intelligence sharing project: fusion centers (or "center"). This initiative offers guidelines and tools to assist in the establishment and operation of centers. The guidelines are a milestone in achieving a unified force among all levels of law enforcement agencies; public safety agencies, such as fire, health, and transportation; and the private sector. Fusion centers bring all the relevant partners together to maximize the ability to prevent and respond to terrorism and criminal acts. By embracing this concept, these entities will be able to effectively and efficiently safeguard our homeland and maximize anticrime efforts.

What Is The Fusion Center Guidelines Initiative?

In 2004 and 2005, many states began creating fusion centers with various local, state, and federal funds. At the time, no standards or guidelines were in existence to assist with interoperability and communication issues with other centers at the state, regional, and federal levels. As a result, centers designed to share information were actually silos of information, incapable of information exchange. In response, the U.S. Department of Justice (DOJ), at the request of its Global Justice Information Sharing Initiative's (Global) Criminal Intelligence Coordinating Council (CICC), formed the Law Enforcement Intelligence Fusion Center Focus Group (FCFG).[1]

---

[1] Previously named the Fusion Center Intelligence Standards Focus Group.

Concurrently, the U.S. Department of Homeland Security's (DHS) Homeland Security Advisory Council (HSAC or Council) Intelligence and Information Sharing Working Group was focusing on prevention and information sharing by developing guidelines for local and state agencies in relation to the collection, analysis, and dissemination of terrorism-related intelligence (i.e., the fusion process). The recommendations resulting from DOJ's initiative and HSAC's efforts laid the foundation for the expansion of the *Fusion Center Guidelines* to integrate the public safety and private sector entities.

Subsequent to publishing Version 1 of the *Fusion Center Guidelines* and the HSAC's *Intelligence and Information Sharing Initiative: Homeland Security Intelligence and Information Fusion* report, DOJ and HSAC established two additional focus groups—the Public Safety FCFG and the Private Sector FCFG—in an effort to develop a comprehensive set of guidelines for fusion centers. Participants in the three focus groups[2] included experts and practitioners from local, state, and federal law enforcement agencies; public safety agencies; and the private sector as well as representatives from currently operating fusion centers.[3] In addition, representatives from national law enforcement, public safety, and private sector organizations participated in the focus groups.

These guidelines should be used to ensure that fusion centers are established and operated consistently, resulting in enhanced coordination efforts, strengthened partnerships, and improved crime-fighting and antiterrorism capabilities. The guidelines and related materials will provide assistance to centers as they prioritize and address threats posed in their specific jurisdictions for all crime types, including terrorism. In addition, the guidelines will help administrators develop policies, manage resources, and evaluate services associated with the jurisdiction's fusion center.

The guidelines should be used for homeland security, as well as all crimes and hazards. The full report contains an in-depth explanation of the guidelines and their key elements. Also included in the report are additional resources, model policies, and tools for guideline implementation.

What Is the Fusion Process?

The concept of fusion has emerged as the fundamental process to facilitate the sharing of homeland security-related and crime-related information and intelligence. For purposes of this initiative, fusion refers to the overarching process of managing the flow of information and intelligence across all levels and sectors of government and private industry. It goes beyond establishing an information/intelligence center or creating a computer network. The fusion process supports the implementation of risk-based, information-driven prevention, response, and consequence management programs. At the same time, it supports efforts to address immediate or emerging threat-related circumstances and events.

Data fusion involves the exchange of information from different sources—including law enforcement, public safety, and the private sector—and, with analysis, can result in meaningful and actionable intelligence and information. The fusion process turns this information and intelligence into actionable knowledge. Fusion also allows for relentless reevaluation of existing data in context with new data in order to provide constant updates. The public safety and private sector components are integral in the

---

[2] A complete listing of participants from each of the focus groups can be found in Appendix A.

[3] Information on currently operating fusion and intelligence centers can be accessed via the National Criminal Intelligence Resource Center at <www.ncirc.gov>.

fusion process because they provide fusion centers with crime-related information, including risk and threat assessments, and subject-matter experts who can aid in threat identification. Because of the privacy concerns that attach to personally identifiable information, it is not the intent of fusion centers to combine federal databases containing personally identifiable information with state, local, and tribal databases into one system or warehouse. Rather, when a threat, criminal predicate, or public safety need is identified, fusion centers will allow information from all sources to be readily gathered, analyzed, and exchanged, based upon the predicate, by providing access to a variety of disparate databases that are maintained and controlled by appropriate local, state, tribal, and federal representatives at the fusion center. The product of this exchange will be stored by the entity taking action in accordance with any applicable fusion center and/or department policy, including state and federal privacy laws and requirements.

What Is a Fusion Center?

A fusion center is an effective and efficient mechanism to exchange information and intelligence, maximize resources, streamline operations, and improve the ability to fight crime and terrorism by analyzing data from a variety of sources. In addition, fusion centers are a conduit for implementing portions of the *National Criminal Intelligence Sharing Plan* (hereafter, NCISP or Plan).[4] The NCISP is the blueprint for law enforcement administrators to follow when enhancing or building an intelligence function. The Plan contains over 25 recommendations that were vetted by law enforcement officials and experts from local, state, tribal, and federal agencies. It embraces intelligence-led policing, community policing, and collaboration and serves as the foundation for the *Fusion Center Guidelines*.

A *fusion center* is defined as a "collaborative effort of two or more agencies that provide resources, expertise, and information to the center with the goal of maximizing their ability to detect, prevent, investigate, and respond to criminal and terrorist activity." Among the primary focuses of fusion centers are the intelligence and fusion processes, through which information is collected, integrated, evaluated, analyzed, and disseminated. Nontraditional collectors of intelligence, such as public safety entities and private sector organizations, possess important information (e.g., risk assessments and suspicious activity reports) that can be "fused" with law enforcement data to provide meaningful information and intelligence about threats and criminal activity. It is recommended that the fusion of public safety and private sector information with law enforcement data be virtual through networking and utilizing a search function. Examples of the types of information incorporated into these processes are threat assessments and information related to public safety, law enforcement, public health, social services, and public works. Federal data that contains personally identifiable information should not be combined with this data until a threat, criminal predicate, or public safety need has been identified. These processes support efforts to anticipate, identify, prevent, monitor, and respond to criminal activity. Federal law enforcement agencies that are participating in fusion centers should ensure that they comply with all applicable privacy laws when contemplating the wholesale sharing of information with nontraditional law enforcement entities.

Ideally, the fusion center involves every level and discipline of government, private sector entities, and the public—though the level of involvement of some of these participants will vary based on specific circumstances. The fusion process should be organized and coordinated, at a minimum, on a statewide level, and each state should establish and maintain a center to facilitate the fusion process. Though the

---

[4]   The *National Criminal Intelligence Sharing Plan* is available at <www.it.ojp.gov>.

foundation of fusion centers is the law enforcement intelligence component, center leadership should evaluate their respective jurisdictions to determine what public safety and private sector entities should participate in the fusion center. To aid in this assessment, functional categories have been developed, in which similar entities are grouped. These categories are not comprehensive but represent a starting point for fusion center leadership to begin assessing what agencies and organizations should be involved in the center's operations.

The functional categories include:

- Agriculture, Food, Water, and the Environment
- Banking and Finance
- Chemical Industry and Hazardous Materials
- Criminal Justice
- Education
- Emergency Services (non-law enforcement)
- Energy
- Government
- Health and Public Health Services

- Hospitality and Lodging
- Information and Telecommunications
- Military Facilities and Defense Industrial Base
- Postal and Shipping
- Private Security
- Public Works
- Real Estate
- Retail
- Social Services
- Transportation

The *Fusion Center Guidelines* report contains an appendix describing the functional categories and provides examples of the types of information that the entities can provide to fusion centers.

Why Should Fusion Centers Be Established?

The ultimate goal is to provide a mechanism through which government, law enforcement, public safety, and the private sector can come together with a common purpose and improve the ability to safeguard our homeland and prevent criminal activity. It is critical for government to accomplish more with less. Fusion centers embody the core of collaboration, and as demands increase and resources decrease, fusion centers will become an effective tool to maximize available resources and build trusted relationships. It is recommended that fusion centers adhere to these guidelines and integrate the key elements of each guideline to the fullest extent, in order to enhance information and intelligence sharing.

Fusion Center Standards
"Summary of Guidelines and Key Elements"[5]

<u>Adhere to the tenets contained in the *National Criminal Intelligence Sharing Plan* (NCISP) and other sector-specific information sharing plans, and perform all steps of the intelligence and fusion processes.</u>

Consult the tenets of the NCISP, and use model standards and policies as a blueprint for establishing or enhancing the intelligence function within the center.

Consult the Homeland Security Advisory Council's (HSAC) *Intelligence and Information Sharing Initiative: Homeland Security Intelligence and Information Fusion* report when incorporating the fusion process in the center.

<u>Collaboratively develop and embrace a mission statement, and identify goals for the fusion center.</u>

Develop the center's mission statement and goals collaboratively with participating entities.

Identify customer needs, define tasks, and prioritize functions.

Ensure the mission statement is clear and concise and conveys the purpose, priority, and role of the center.

Include the name and type of the center, what the center does, and whom the center serves in the mission statement.

<u>Create a representative governance structure that includes law enforcement, public safety, and the private sector.</u>

Ensure all participating agencies have a voice in the establishment and operation of the fusion center.

Ensure participating entities are adequately represented within the governance structure.

Compose the governing body with officials who have authority to commit resources and make decisions.

<u>Create a collaborative environment for the sharing of intelligence and information among local, state, tribal, and federal law enforcement agencies, public safety agencies, and the private sector.</u>

Maintain a diverse membership to include representatives from local, state, tribal, and federal law enforcement, public safety, and the private sector.

Conduct regular meetings with center personnel, and participate in networking groups and organizations.

Educate and liase with elected officials and community leadership to promote awareness of center operations.

---

[5] Electronic versions of the documents, products, and reports referenced in the following guidelines can be found at <www.it.ojp.gov>.

APPENDIX II - STANDARDS

Fusion Center Stardards "Summary of Guidelines and Key Elements"

Utilize Memoranda of Understanding (MOUs), Non-Disclosure Agreements (NDAs), or other types of agency agreements, as appropriate.

Educate and consult legal advisors early in the fusion center development process.

Utilize an NDA for fusion center personnel and participants to aid in the security of proprietary information.

Ensure awareness of local, state, and federal public records laws as they relate to NDAs, including the Freedom of Information Act (FOIA).

Use an MOU as the foundation for a collaborative initiative, founded on trust, with the intent to share and exchange information.

At a minimum, consider including the following elements in fusion center MOUs:

- Involved parties
- Mission
- Governance
- Authority
- Security
- Assignment of personnel (removal/rotation)
- Funding/costs
- Civil liability/indemnification issues
- Policies and procedures
- Privacy
- Terms

- Integrity control
- Dispute resolution process
- Points of contact
- Effective date/duration/modification/ termination
- Services
- Deconfliction procedure
- Code of conduct for contractors
- Special conditions
- Protocols for communication and information exchange

Leverage the databases, systems, and networks available via participating entities to maximize information sharing.

Obtain access to an array of databases and systems. At a minimum, consider obtaining access to driver's license information, motor vehicle registration data, location information, law enforcement and criminal justice systems or networks, and correctional data.

Become a member of a regional or state secure law enforcement network, such as the Regional Information Sharing Systems® (RISS)/Federal Bureau of Investigation's (FBI) Law Enforcement Online (LEO) system, the U.S. Department of Homeland Security's (DHS) Homeland Security Information Network (HSIN), or the FBI's Law Enforcement Regional Data Exchange (R-DEx) and National Data Exchange (N-DEx).

Create an environment in which participants seamlessly communicate by leveraging existing systems and those currently under development, and allow for future connectivity to other local, state, tribal, and federal systems. Use the U.S. Department of Justice's (DOJ) Global Justice Extensible Markup Language (XML) Data Model and the National Information Exchange Model (NIEM) standards for future database and network development, and consider utilizing the Justice Information Exchange Model (JIEM) for enterprise development.

Establish formal communications protocols, and ensure effective and efficient information exchange.

Develop and implement a communications plan, and ensure secure and redundant communications.

Ensure communications and systems access policies, including consequences for noncompliance.

Consider utilizing the Organization for the Advancement of Structured Information Standards (OASIS)-ratified Common Alerting Protocol (CAP) to enable the exchange of emergency alert and public warning information over data networks and computer-controlled warning systems.

Develop, publish, and adhere to a privacy and civil liberties policy.

Develop, display, adhere to, and train personnel on the center's privacy policy.
Consult the Fair Information Practices when developing a privacy policy.
Ensure all other policies and internal controls are consistent with the center's privacy policy.
Establish a process for tracking and handling privacy complaints or concerns.
Develop rules on the use of privately held data systems information.
Adhere to applicable state and federal constitutional and statutory privacy and civil liberties provisions.
Specify that public safety and private sector databases should not be combined with any federal databases that contain personally identifiable information.
Fusion center participants should comply with all local, state, tribal, and federal privacy laws, when applicable.

Ensure appropriate security measures are in place for the facility, data, and personnel.

Develop, publish, and adhere to a security plan, and ensure proper safeguards are in place.
Ensure security plans are marked, handled, and controlled as sensitive but unclassified (SBU) information.
Obtain appropriate security clearances for personnel within the center and key decision makers who need access.
Conduct background checks on personnel.
Train personnel on the center's security protocols.
Consult Global's *Applying Security Practices to Justice Information Sharing* document and resource materials when developing a security plan.
Consult the Homeland Security Information Act of 2002: Critical Infrastructure Information Act when collecting and storing critical infrastructure-related information.
Consult private industry security personnel when obtaining and storing industry-specific information (e.g., building security plans).
Ensure state laws allow for the security and confidentiality of public and private sector data.

Integrate technology, systems, and people.

Colocate personnel and/or utilize virtual integration to bring technology, systems, and people together.
Base the selection of a site on the functional needs of the center.
Plan, identify, design, train, implement, and adhere to a physical security plan and a contingency plan.

Achieve a diversified representation of personnel based on the needs and functions of the center.

Maintain a 24-hour-a-day/7-day-a-week operation when feasible.
Require a minimum term commitment for full-time center personnel.
Identify subject-matter experts from the private sector for utilization when industry-specific threats or crimes are identified (e.g., cyber threats).

APPENDIX II - STANDARDS

Fusion Center Stardards "Summary of Guidelines and Key Elements"

Adhere to the *Law Enforcement Analytic Standards* booklet and other relevant analytic publications available through the International Association of Law Enforcement Intelligence Analysts (IALEIA) when hiring personnel to perform the analytic function.

Ensure personnel are properly trained.

Adhere to the training objectives outlined in the *National Criminal Intelligence Sharing Plan*.

Ensure center personnel meet the minimum training standards outlined in the report *Minimum Criminal Intelligence Training Standards for United States Law Enforcement and Other Criminal Justice Agencies.*

Ensure center personnel receive training on facility and information security, operations, policies, and procedures.

Include cross-educational training regarding the fusion centers and the applicable functional categories, including the types of information that entities can provide to the fusion center and what the center does with the information, once received.

Provide a multitiered awareness and educational program to implement intelligence-led policing and the development and sharing of information.

Ensure appropriate noncenter personnel involved in the intelligence process are aware of the center's functions, including policymakers, agency heads, and private sector executives.

Develop and disseminate outreach and educational materials to officers, analysts, policymakers, and others.

Offer a variety of intelligence services and products to customers.

Produce strategic and tactical products to support the mission and priorities of the center.

Consult the *Law Enforcement Analytic Standards* booklet to ensure development of professional quality analytic products.

Ensure that feedback from participating agencies and organizations occurs when products are created and distributed.

Develop, publish, and adhere to a policies and procedures manual.

Use a standardized format to allow for easy reading, filing, retrieving, and correcting.

Implement an annual review of center directives, and purge or revise outdated policies and procedures.

Ensure that personnel have access to the latest policies and procedures manual.

Define expectations, measure performance, and determine effectiveness.

Design performance measures based on the center's core mission, goals, and objectives.

Ensure performance measures are valid, reliable, measurable, and quantifiable.

Develop an evaluation process to gauge the adequacy, appropriateness, and success of center services.

Use performance measures and an evaluation process to make decisions and allocate resources.

Utilize performance measures to track progress and ensure accountability.

Inform center personnel of performance and progress on a regular basis.

417

Fusion Center Stardards "Summary of Guidelines and Key Elements"

Establish and maintain the center based on funding availability and sustainability.

Identify center needs and available funding sources, to include local, state, tribal, federal, and nongovernmental sources.

Establish an operational budget and adhere to reporting requirements.

Develop and implement a communications plan among fusion center personnel; all law enforcement, public safety, and private sector agencies and entities involved; and the general public.

Determine primary and secondary modes of communication between the fusion center and participating entities.

Incorporate regular testing of the plan to ensure its functionality.

Include a mechanism to alert fusion center participants of new information and intelligence.

A companion CD has been developed in conjunction with the Fusion Center Guidelines report. This CD contains sample policies, checklists, resource documents, and links to Web sites that are referenced throughout the report. For copies of the resource CD, contact DOJ's Global at (850) 385-0600. The fusion center resources are also available at DOJ's Global Web site, >www.it.ojp.gov/fusioncenter<, DHS's Web site, and the Homeland Security Information Network (HSIN).

Appendix III

"Resources"

- *Collections* - Chapter 6 by Paul Coambs

COLLECTION – Chapter 6
BY PAUL COAMBS

Listed below are a wide variety of information resources. If there is no web address provided, use a search engine to locate the specific site of interest. Some of the resources require a fee-based subscription.

<u>U.S., State Government & Law Enforcement</u>-use an Internet search engine to identify specific web site addresses not listed herein.

- Agriculture, U.S. Department of *http://www.usda.gov/wps/portal/usdahome*
- Alcohol Beverage Control, State
- Alcohol, Tobacco and Firearms, U.S. Bureau of *http://www.atf.gov/*
- Association of Law Enforcement Intelligence Units (LEIU) *http://leiu.org*
- Boards of Equalization, State
- Census Bureau, U.S. *http://www.census.gov/*
- Central Intelligence Agency, U.S. *https://www.cia.gov/*
- Civil Service, U.S. Commission *http://www.opm.gov/*
- Consumer Affairs, State
- Corporations, State Department of
- Corrections, State
- Courts, Municipal and Superior, County
- Defense Intelligence Agency *http://www.dia.mil/*
- District Courts, U.S. *http://www.uscourts.gov/districtcourts.html*
- Drug Enforcement Administration, U.S. *http://www.usdoj.gov/dea*
- El Paso Intelligence Center (EPIC) *www.usdoj.gov/deal/programs/epic.htm*
- FBI Law Enforcement Online *http://www.leo.gov/*
- Federal Aviation Administration *http://www.faa.gov/*
- Federal Bureau of Investigation *www.fib.gov*
- Federal Election Commission, U.S. *http://www.fec.gov/*
- Federal Emergency Management Agency *http://www.fema.gov/*
- Financial Crimes Enforcement Network (FINCEN) *www.fincen.gov*
- High Intensity Drug Trafficking Area (HIDTA) Investigative Support Centers *www.whitehousedrug policy.gov/HIDTA*
- High Intensity Financial Crimes Areas (HIFCA) *www.fincen.gov/law_enforcement/hifca*
- Homeland Security, U.S. Department of *http://www.dhs.gov/index.shtm*
- Immigration and Customs, U.S. *http://www.ice.gov/*
- Institute for Intergovernmental Research *www.iir.com*
- Interior, U.S. Department of *http://www.doi.gov/*
- International Association of Law Enforcement Intelligence Analysis (IALEIA) *www.ialeia.org*
- Labor, U.S. Department of *http://www.dol.gov/*
- Law Enforcement Agencies, State, County, Municipal
- Maritime, U.S. Administration *http://www.marad.dot.gov/*
- Marshals Service, U.S. *http://www.usmarshals.gov/*

- Middle Atlantic-Great Lakes Organized Crime Law Enforcement (MAGLOCLEN) *http://magloclen.rissinfo.com*
- Mid-States Organized Crime Information Center (MOCIC) *http://riss.net*
- Motor Vehicle, State
- National Archives and Records Administration, U.S. *http://www.archives.gov/*
- National Crime Information Center (NCIC) *http://www.fbi.gov/hq/cjisd/ncic.htm*
- National Criminal Justice Reference Service *http://www.ncjrs.gov/*
- National Drug Intelligence Center (NDIC) *http://www.usdoj.gov/ndic/*
- National White Collar Crime Center (NW3C) *www.nw3c.org*
- New England State Police Information Network (NESPIN) *http://riss.net*
- Organized Crime Drug Enforcement Task Forces (OCDETF) *http://www.usdoj.gov/criminal/links/ocdetf.html*
- Personnel Management, U.S. Office of *http://www.opm.gov/*
- Prisons, Federal Bureau of *http://www.bop.gov/*
- Public Debt, U.S. Bureau of *http://www.publicdebt.treas.gov/*
- Regional Information Sharing System (RISS) *http://riss.net*
- Regional Organized Crime Information Center (ROCIC) *www.rocic.com*
- Rocky Mountain Information Network (RMIN) *http://riss.net*
- Secret Service, U.S. *http://www.secretservice.gov/*
- Secretary of State, State
- Securities and Exchange, U.S. Commission *http://www.sec.gov/*
- Social Security, U.S. Administration *http://www.ssa.gov/*
- State Law Enforcement Intelligence Networks (LEIN) *http://www.dps.state.ia.us/commis/intell/lein/index.htm*
- State, U.S. Department of *http://www.state.gov/*
- Transportation Security Administration, U.S. *http://www.tsa.dhs.gov/*
- Treasury, U.S. Department of *http://www.ustreas.gov/*
- United States Intelligence Community *http://www.intelligence.gov/1-members.shtml*
- U.S. Postal Service, U.S. *http://www.usps.com/*
- Veterans Affairs, U.S. Department of *http://www.va.gov/*
- Western States Information Network (WSIN) *http://riss.net*

Foreign Government and Law Enforcement

- Australian Crime Commission *http://www.crimecommission.gov.au/*
- Canadian Security Intelligence Service *www.csis-sers.gc.ca*
- Drugs and Crime, U.N. Office on *http://www.unodc.org/*
- Embassies and Consuls
- Europol *www.europol.europa.eu*
- Financial Action Task Force *http://www.fatf-gafi.org*
- Interpol *www.interpol.int*
- National Criminal Intelligence Service U.K. *www.ncis.co.uk*
- Royal Canadian Mounted Police *http://www.rcmp-grc.gc.ca/*
- American Samoa Government *http://www.americansamoa.gov/departments/agencies/spicin.htm*
- United Nations *www.un.org/terrorism*

APPENDIX III - RESOURCES

Non-Governmental

- Anti-Defamation League *http://adl.org/*
- Anti-Drug Network (ADNET) *http://fas.org/irp/program/disseminate/adnet.htm*
- Bar Associations, State
- Better Business Bureau *http://us.bbb.org*
- Center for the Study and Political Violence *http://www.st-andrews.ac.uk/~wwwir/research/cstpv/*
- Chamber of Commerce, U.S. *http://www.uschamber.com*
- Debka File *http://www.debka.com*
- Congressional Research Service-Federation of American Scientists *http://fas.org/irp/crs/*
- Federation of American Scientists *http://fas.org*
- International Association for the Study of Organized Crime *http://www.iasoc.net/*
- International Policy Institute for Counter-Terrorism *http://www.ict.org.il/*
- Jane's Information Group *http://www.janes.com/*
- Memorial Institute for the Prevention of Terrorism *http://www.mipt.org/*
- National Association of Securities Dealers (NASD) *http://www.investopedia.com/terms/n/nasd.asp?viewed=1*
- Rand *http://rand.com/*
- Southern Poverty Law Center *http://www.splcenter.org*
- Stratfor *www.stratfor.com*
- Terrorism Research Center *http://terrorism.com/*
- Yorke University Nathanson Centre on Transnational Human Rights, Crime and Security *http://www.yorku.ca/nathanson*
- Wall Street Journal *http://online.wsj.com*
- Washington Institute for Near East Policy *http://www.washingtoninstitute.org*

Commercial Databases and Internet Resources-some subscription

- Accurint *http://www.accurint.com/*
- Choice Point *http://www.choicepoint.com/*
- CNN *http://www.cnn.com/*
- Dataquick *http://www.dataquick.com/*
- DataTimes Newspaper Index *http://www.virtualref.com/_verifier/85.htm*
- Dow Jones Newswire *http://dowjonesnews.com*
- Drudge Report *http://drudgereport.com/*
- Dun and Bradstreet *http://www.dnb.com/us/*
- Equifax *http://www.equifax.com*
- Fox News *http://www.foxnews.com/*
- Google News *http://www.google.com/*
- Investopedia *http://www.investopedia.com*
- LEXIS/NEXIS *http://www.lexisnexis.com/*
- Merlin *http://merlindata.com/*
- MSNBC *http://www.msnbc.msn.com/*
- New York Times *http://nytimes.com/*
- Standard and Poor's *http://www2.standardandpoors.com*

- The Huffington Post *http://www.huffingtonpost.com/*
- Townhall.com *http://townhall.com/*
- Virtual Reference Desk *http://www.virtualref.com*
- Yahoo *http://www.yahoo.com/*
- You Tube *http://www.youtube.com/*
- Wikipedia *http://www.wikipedia.org/*
- ZabaSearch *http://www.zabasearch.com*

Social Networks

- List of social networks *http://en.wikipedia.org/wiki/List_of_social_networking_websites*
- Craigslist *http://www.craigslist.org*
- Facebook *http://www.facebook.com/*
- My Space *http://www.myspace.com/*
- Twitter *http://twitter.com/*

Directories

- AnyWho (businesses and people) *http://www.anywho.com/*
- AT&T Telephone Directory *http://www.corp.att.com/directory/*
- Google Reference Directories *http://www.google.com/Top/Reference/Directories/*
- MedlinePlus (health related) *http://www.nlm.nih.gov/medlineplus/directories.html*
- Subject Directories *http://www.lib.berkeley.edu/TeachingLib/Guides/Internet/SubjDirectories.html*

Search Engines

- About *http://www.about.com/*
- AOL *http://www.aol.com*
- Ask *http://www.ask.com/*
- Dogpile *http://www.dogpile.com/*
- Google *http://www.google.com/*
- Live Search *http://www.live.com*
- Lycos *http://lycos.com/*
- Search Engine Guide *http://www.searchengineguide.com/searchengines.html*
- Yahoo *http://yahoo.com/*

Compliance Audits/Surveys

- Evaluations by Paul Rogers
- LEIU's Audit Checklist

Evaluations

1. Possible Questions to be Included in Compliance Audits/Surveys for Intelligence Units – Paul Roger

Personnel Security

- What personnel security vetting procedures exist in respect of personnel working within the intelligence area?

- Are periodic security updates conducted for intelligence personnel on a regularly basis?

- Are guidelines in place for disclosure by members should their personal circumstances change?

- What measures are taken by the intelligence unit and its personnel to guard against subversion or other risks to the intelligence unit?

- (In the context of personnel security, subversion is the altering of a person's loyalties, or changing a person's moral standards, by the application of some form of coercion. This coercion normally takes the form of bribery, blackmail, psychological pressure or physical threats. Subversion, as a general threat, is best countered by education of staff as to methods, thus allowing individuals to recognize and counter it.)

Physical Security

- Is the intelligence unit physically secure? (If yes, how?)

- Does the security prevent access by unauthorised persons?

- Is access and egress of authorized personnel monitored and recorded?

- Is access ability terminated when personnel are on leave or cease to work in the intelligence unit?

- Are there guidelines on staff taking intelligence material home or out of the building?

- Are there guidelines for transferring material to or from floppy disks?

Capture of Intelligence Material

- Do you have a data capture plan? (Attach copy of relevant documents)

- Does this plan detail procedures/guidelines that govern what intelligence is to be collected and the methods for collection?   (Attach copy of relevant documents)

- What procedures are practiced to ensure that only designated data is captured and entered onto the intelligence database?

- Who is responsible for collecting data?

- Who is responsible for ensuring correct procedures are followed in respect of collection?

Storage of Intelligence Material

Hard Copy Storage

o What procedures are in place to govern the storage, handling and security of hard copy source material?   (Give details or attach copies of relevant documents.)

o Do you retain hard copy source documents regarding intelligence information?

o Where are they stored?

o Who has access to these documents?

o How is access controlled?

o Electronic Storage

Electronic Storage

o Are there guidelines for recording intelligence material on electronic (IT) systems? (Give details or attach copies of documents.)

o Are there adequate access checks and scrutiny, e.g. Passwords, etc?

o How often are passwords changed?

o Is facility access deleted when personnel are on leave or cease to work in the intelligence unit?

o Is the IT system capable of producing an audit trail for any system interrogation?

o Is access graded on a 'need to access' basis?

o Are files adequately safeguarded through back-up and recovery routines, and off-site storage of critical files, programs and systems?

o Is the IT system isolated from other networks and, if not, are appropriate "firewalls" in place?

Integrity of Intelligence Material

Quality Control

o What quality control procedures are in place to ensure quality of data is maintained?

o In respect of electronic databases, what procedures are in place to ensure quality of data?

o Is there a clear responsibility in a particular position for the continued development, maintenance and implementation of quality control systems?

Culling and Destruction

o Do you have procedures for the culling and destruction of intelligence material?

o What criteria is used during the culling process?

o Who is responsible for culling and the subsequent destruction?

o Are staff aware of any relevant Archive or related legislation?

o When hard copy material is culled, is corresponding electronic data also culled? (If yes, who is responsible for culling electronic data?)

o Are records maintained of culling and destruction exercises? (If yes, are they available for inspection?)

Availability of Intelligence Material

Access

o What electronic databases are maintained that contain intelligence material?

o Who has access to these databases?

o What level of access do officers possess (e.g. read/write etc.)?

o Who is responsible for controlling access?

o Who audits access?

o How often are audits conducted?

o How are audits performed (e.g. reactively, proactively, regularly, randomly etc.)?

o What records are maintained in respect of audits of access?

o Is access immediately deleted when personnel leave or transfer?

o Are regular reviews undertaken to determine the continued necessity for current personnel to have intelligence system access?

Dissemination of Intelligence Material

At Own Initiative

o Are there procedures covering the dissemination of intelligence material? (If yes, attach procedures.)

o Who may authorize dissemination of intelligence material?

o What records are kept of dissemination of intelligence material?

o Are these records audited?

o If audits are conducted, who by?

o Are records kept of such audits for inspection purposes?

Responses to Requests

o Do you have procedures that govern the way intelligence personnel will respond to a request for information? (If yes, attach procedures.)

o What criteria is used in reaching a decision regarding the need and right of the requesting person to receive information?

o What records are kept of requests and responses?

o Are these records audited?

o If yes, by whom and how frequently?

o Are records kept of such audits?

Transmission of Material

o Do you have procedures which govern the methods of enveloping, dispatching and recording of such dispatch of classified material from the intelligence unit? (If yes, attach procedures.)

o What methods of dispatch are used for intelligence documents dispatched from your unit (e.g. courier, safe hand, internal dispatches, postal services etc.)?

o What criteria is used in reaching a decision as to which method of dispatch to use?

o Are there appropriate mechanisms in place to identify the non-receipt of classified material? (If yes, attach procedures.)

Accountability and Management of System

Responsibilities

o Is there regular assessment of the purposes and goals of the intelligence system and an evaluation of the extent and effectiveness of the achievement of these goals?

o Are there clear lines of responsibility and accountability for the functions of the intelligence unit?

o Are individual responsibility statements regularly reviewed and updated?

o Are there adequate resources to meet the responsibilities in a practical way?

o Is a regular Security Risk Review of the intelligence unit and its systems carried out?

o Are managers and those responsible for the effective operation of the intelligence system adequately trained and kept up to date in the required operation of the system?

o Are delegations and authority limits regularly reviewed?

Awareness

o Are staff generally aware of the security and privacy implications of the intelligence function and the collection and storage of intelligence material?

o Is there an adequate system to ensure any amendments or updates to procedures are read and understood?

o Are staff aware of actions they should take and procedures to follow should they encounter any departures from approved policy and procedures in the operation of the intelligence system?

o Does unit management clearly demonstrate that it insists on the highest standards of ethical and professional behavior?

2. Numeric Intelligence Evaluation System from Harris (1976:134-138)

This approach is based on an evaluation in terms of questions relating to the major elements of the functions within the intelligence process. On the basis that each function is essential to the process, each is assigned a value of 100 as follows:

Collection/flow of information	100
Processing/collation of information	100
Analysis	100
Production/dissemination of information	100
Management procedures	100

Points are then assigned based on the following breakdown of each function.

a. Collection

(1) Intelligence unit receives as part of normal flow of information, copies of all (the bulk of) investigator reports (except in large units where reports relating to known or suspected persons associated with organized crime and major criminal activity would be sufficient).　　30

(2) Intelligence unit has its own investigators or can task the department's investigative unit to probe areas determined to be important as a result of the intelligence unit's assessment. A procedure exists for the tasking of non-intelligence unit personnel on the basis of agreement between the intelligence and operational unit commanders or orders of the department chief.　　25

(3) Department has an effective procedure operating whereby the officer on patrol can report on specified subjects directly to the intelligence unit.　　20

(4) Intelligence unit receives (or at least records information contained in) sensitive reports from undercover units, informants, or other specialized sources.　　15

(5) Intelligence unit has a plan of action to gain information from other law enforcement agencies—local in area, state, and federal.　　10

Total　　100

b. Processing/Collation

(1) Information, once filed, can be quickly and correctly retrieved　　25

(2) The information filing system has a capability to focus data received by major crime figures, area/location, type of crime, and other subjects the analysts find useful.　　25

(3) Unit has an information flow system that causes reports to be reviewed distributed, and earmarked for filing in a manner that ensures the analysts (or other persons responsible for performing analyst functions) reads important reports relating to his/her area of responsibility. 20

(4) There is an efficient and effective operating system for updating biographies (abstracts or biographic forms) of known or suspected major criminals in the area (not necessarily restricted to persons residing within the boundaries of the jurisdiction). 20

(5) There is an operational plan for purging the files of outdated and non-pertinent material. 10

Total 100

c. **Analysis**

(1) The intelligence unit has one or more persons tasked to analyze information received to develop/project/estimate: 50

  - patterns of organized crime by type of crime
  - patterns of association among persons believed to be part of organized crime
  - interrelationships among criminals and types of organized crimes in which they are suspected of being involved.

(2) The intelligence unit has a procedure whereby the person or persons responsible for analysis are available to assist departmental investigators, in person or by phone, by applying information in the intelligence file and his/her own expertise to a current investigation. 50

Total 100

d. **Production/Dissemination**

(1) The intelligence unit is responsive to requirements of on-going investigations, including having a procedure to keep its members aware of major cases. 40

(2) The intelligence unit produces periodically and/or on order reports on major trends in criminal activity in its jurisdiction, emphasizing new or developing types of organized crime activities. 30

(3) Intelligence reports are disseminated as widely as possible within limits set by need-to-know and sensitivity of information (the rule should be positive, giving the benefit of dissemination to those who need and can use the information). 30

Total 100

e. **Management Procedures**

    (1) The intelligence unit has a procedure for obtaining the reactions of consumers   25
        to its products.

    (2) The intelligence unit has a collection plan to assist it in focusing its efforts   20
        on the most important of the crime problems. The plan is periodically
        updated (monthly) and is coordinated with the chief of investigations and
        approved by the department head.

    (3) There is an element in the department's training program to prepare   20
        personnel for the specialized activities of the intelligence unit, especially analysis
        and intelligence investigation.

    (4) Security guidelines are in existence and observed, especially in limiting access   20
        to the files to analysts and file clerks, distributing intelligence reports only to those
        with a need-to-know within the organization and only to other law enforcement
        agencies on the outside with whom there is an agreement for the protection of the
        intelligence material.

    (5) There is a procedure for evaluation of the effectiveness of the intelligence unit's   <u>15</u>
        operation.

                                    Total   100

In evaluating performance, each element will be graded in terms of the following scale:

1. The element is being implemented effectively 1.0

2. The unit is organized to accomplish the element but the operation is only partially effective .80/.70/.60

3. The unit is in the process of organizing to accomplish the element but is not yet operational .50

4. The unit has been organized to accomplish the element but the operation is ineffective .30

5. The unit has not/does not recognize the requirement to accomplish the element 0

An example of how this system would apply follows:

A. *The intelligence unit is responsive to investigations including having a procedure to keep its members aware of major cases.* The evaluator found there was no procedure to keep its members aware of major cases; thus he gave the unit .60 of the total value of the item or .60 times 40 which equals 24 points.

B. *The intelligence unit produces periodically and/or on order reports on major trends in criminal activity in its jurisdiction, emphasizing new or developing types of organized crime activities. The evaluator, after reviewing reports, found that they were being produced, but only infrequently highlighted new and developing organized crime activity. Thus, he gave the unit only .70 of this value, or .70 times 30 which equals 21 points.*

C. *Intelligence reports are disseminated as widely as possible within limits set by need-to-know and sensitivity of dissemination. The evaluator finds that the unit stresses dissemination and gives the unit full value, or 1.00 times 30 which equals 30 points.*

Total for this portion of evaluation: 75 points

LEIU's Audit Checklist
for the Criminal Intelligence Function

INTRODUCTION

"The protection of individuals' privacy and constitutional rights is an obligation of government officials and is crucial to the long-term success of criminal intelligence sharing. Protecting the privacy and constitutional rights of individuals, while at the same time providing for homeland security and public safety, will require a commitment from everyone in the system – from line officers to top management."

– National Criminal Intelligence Sharing Plan, p. 10

The criminal intelligence function is an effective tool for deterring, preventing, and protecting the public from serious crime. However, the information-gathering activities associated with the criminal intelligence process could also pose significant threats to the constitutional rights of individuals.

Serious consequences arise when an agency fails to protect the individual rights of those who may be the subject of the criminal intelligence process. In addition to the direct harm caused to the individuals whose civil liberties may be infringed upon, these serious consequences include a loss of public trust and confidence in the police, the inhibition of legitimate and lawful political activity, costly and time-consuming civil litigation, disbanding of the criminal intelligence function, and other harms.

Law enforcement agencies can effectively use a combination of accountability mechanisms to prevent these serious consequences from arising. As mentioned in the *National Criminal Intelligence Plan*, these accountability mechanisms help *eliminate* the unnecessary discretion in police decision-making processes, *guide* (or structure) the discretion that is needed, and *audit* (or check) the processes to ensure conformance with overall goals.

Clear policies and effective training, for example, can be used to prohibit improper practices (i.e., eliminating the unnecessary discretion), and to provide authorization and guidance to agency personnel for those actions that are necessary to carry out their duties (i.e., structuring the necessary discretion). Periodic audits and reviews serve as useful checks to ensure that the criminal intelligence function is being carried out in accordance with established ethical standards, regulations, and laws.

The attached checklist titled "Audit Checklist for the Criminal Intelligence Function" can assist law enforcement executives with conducting a review of their agency's criminal intelligence function. Using this checklist, law enforcement agencies demonstrate their commitment to protecting the constitutional rights and the privacy of individuals, while ensuring the operational effectiveness of their criminal intelligence function.

ABOUT THE DEVELOPMENT OF THIS CHECKLIST

This checklist was developed by the Law Enforcement Intelligence Unit (LEIU), in support of the National Criminal Intelligence Sharing Plan. Founded in 1956, LEIU is the oldest law enforcement association dedicated to the sharing of criminal intelligence and the advancement of professional criminal intelligence standards and practices. LEIU has led the way in establishing professional standards for the collection, maintenance, and dissemination of intelligence among law enforcement agencies.

In the 1970s, LEIU first developed a set of guidelines, known as the *LEIU File Guidelines*, for establishing and maintaining criminal intelligence files in law enforcement agencies. These guidelines were developed to provide protection of citizens' privacy and other constitutional rights, promote professionalism, and provide guidance to law enforcement agencies when collecting information in the pursuit of preventing and solving crimes. Over the years, the *LEIU File Guidelines* have been modified to reflect the most current standards for lawful and ethical criminal intelligence practices. Civil liberties groups, citizens, and government and police officials have agreed that the standards embodied by the *LEIU File Guidelines* are proper for collecting, maintaining, and disseminating criminal intelligence information.

In recent years, LEIU has worked closely with the International Association of Law Enforcement Intelligence Analysts (IALEIA), the International Association of Chiefs of Police (IACP), the Global Justice Information Sharing Initiative, and others to develop the National Criminal Intelligence Sharing Plan (NCISP). In fact, members of the LEIU Executive Board helped plan and conduct the IACP Criminal Intelligence Sharing Summit, served on Global's Intelligence Working Group, and contributed to the final publications from both initiatives (IACP's *Criminal Intelligence Sharing* report and Global's *NCISP*).

The NCISP recommends that law enforcement agencies use the *LEIU File Guidelines* as a model for criminal intelligence file maintenance. Additionally, the NCISP recommends periodic audits of criminal intelligence operations and files to ensure that these guidelines and other regulations are put into practice. LEIU has previously assisted local and state law enforcement agencies in conducting audits of their criminal intelligence function, and has now developed the attached checklist to assist agencies in conducting a self-assessment of their criminal intelligence function. With 240 member agencies in four countries, LEIU remains a leader in promoting the professional trust, training, and communication required to facilitate the lawful and ethical sharing and use of criminal intelligence among law enforcement agencies.

The purpose of this checklist is to provide law enforcement executives and senior- to mid-level law enforcement managers with a tool for conducting an audit or evaluation of their agency's criminal intelligence function. Specifically, this audit tool can help an agency ensure that it is carrying out the criminal intelligence function in accordance with applicable laws, regulations, and guidelines. The principles found in the checklist apply most directly to municipal, county, and state law enforcement agencies. Several introductory comments are appropriate.

This checklist should be applied only to criminal intelligence files – not to other types of law enforcement records. Some law enforcement officials fail to make the distinction between criminal intelligence files and other types of law enforcement records (e.g., investigative files). In the law enforcement context, however, these differences are important and must be recognized.

Investigation generally refers to the systematic examination of facts to determine if a crime has occurred and, if so, develop a case for prosecution. Generally, the term "investigative files" refers to information collected in the course of an investigation where there are reasonable grounds to suspect that a person has committed specific criminal acts.

On the other hand, the criminal intelligence process is an ongoing activity, and is not necessarily triggered by the investigation of any specific offense. While investigation tends to be reactive in nature, criminal intelligence is proactive and used to identify and understand criminals operating in a particular area. Once individuals or groups are identified and their habits known, law enforcement authorities may begin to assess current trends in crime and to forecast, and possibly prevent, future criminal activities. Intelligence provides the knowledge on which to base decisions, and select appropriate targets (subjects, criminal groups or businesses) for investigations. Although criminal intelligence may be used to assist in investigations, surveillance operations, and prosecution of cases, it also provides law enforcement agencies with the ability to effectively manage resources, budget, and meet their responsibility to forecast community threats to prevent crime.

Criminal intelligence consists of pieces of raw information that when collected, evaluated, collated, and analyzed form meaningful and useful judgments that are both accurate and timely. Taking this raw information and turning it into intelligence can be described as a sequential process with multiple distinct phases. Following appropriate planning, the first phase is collection, which is obtaining raw information from various sources. Evaluation then occurs, which is determining the reliability of the source and the validity of the information. The third phase is collation and involves indexing, cross-referencing and filing of information. The fourth phase is analysis, which identifies trends, future developments and case building. The fifth phase is dissemination, which involves the actual dispensing of the intelligence information. A unit that does not complete each of these phases is not a criminal intelligence unit.

Ideally, this checklist is designed to be utilized by senior law enforcement managers who are not directly involved in the day-to-day operations of the agency's criminal intelligence function. This helps ensure that the audit is objective, and accurately identifies the function's strengths and weaknesses. However, the checklist can also be used as a self-assessment tool by personnel who are directly involved with the agency's criminal intelligence function. This type of an effort will help determine if the unit is acting in accordance with the standard practices and procedures established by LEIU.

Historically, criminal intelligence units have experienced problems in the area of unit operating procedures, collection, collation, and dissemination; therefore, this checklist focuses on these four areas.

Operating Procedures

Item	Question		
1	Does the criminal intelligence unit have a mission statement? If no, go to question 10.	❑ Yes	❑ No
2	Does the mission statement contain a concise, well-defined mandate describing the criminal intelligence unit?	❑ Yes	❑ No
3	Does the mission statement describe the use of the intelligence process in support of the criminal intelligence unit?	❑ Yes	❑ No
4	Does the statement focus toward criminal predicate?	❑ Yes	❑ No

Item	Question		
5	Does the statement indicate that the criminal intelligence unit will provide the Chief Executive with criminal information and resulting analysis to counter and control criminal activities?	❑ Yes	❑ No
6	Does the statement identify the criminal intelligence unit's expected results?	❑ Yes	❑ No
7	Is the criminal intelligence unit staying within its mission?	❑ Yes	❑ No
8	Is the criminal intelligence unit assuming work beyond the authorized crime areas?	❑ Yes	❑ No
9	Is the statement reviewed on a periodic basis to insure that it is meeting the needs of the agency/organization?	❑ Yes	❑ No
10	Does the criminal intelligence unit have policy and procedures and guidelines? If no, go to question 18.	❑ Yes	❑ No
11	Do the guidelines describe the criminal intelligence unit's operations?	❑ Yes	❑ No
12	Do the guidelines provide the criminal intelligence unit's mission statement?	❑ Yes	❑ No
13	Do the guidelines detail the criminal intelligence unit's methods of operation?	❑ Yes	❑ No
14	Do the guidelines outline the criminal intelligence unit's file guidelines?	❑ Yes	❑ No
15	Do the guidelines establish the criminal intelligence unit's security procedures?	❑ Yes	❑ No

Item	Question		
16	Do the guidelines describe personnel responsibilities and assigned duties?	❑ Yes	❑ No
17	Have the guidelines been provided to personnel?	❑ Yes	❑ No
18	Are periodic security updates conducted for intelligence personnel on a regular basis?	❑ Yes	❑ No
19	Is the criminal intelligence unit located in a physically secure location?	❑ Yes	❑ No
20	Are unauthorized persons prevented from accessing the criminal intelligence unit's location?	❑ Yes	❑ No
21	Is access terminated when personnel are on leave or cease to work in an intelligence capacity?	❑ Yes	❑ No
22	Are there guidelines for transferring material to or from floppy disks?	❑ Yes	❑ No
23	Does the criminal intelligence unit have access to the Chief Executive?	❑ Yes	❑ No
24	Does the unit provide the Chief Executive with recommendations?	❑ Yes	❑ No
25	Does the unit provide the agency with valuable strategic and tactical products?	❑ Yes	❑ No
26	Do personnel receive appropriate training?	❑ Yes	❑ No
27	Are there clear lines of responsibility and accountability for the functions of the intelligence unit?	❑ Yes	❑ No
28	Is a regular security risk review of the intelligence unit and its systems conducted?	❑ Yes	❑ No
29	Are procedures in place governing the criminal intelligence unit's use of special funds?	❑ Yes	❑ No

Item	Question		
30	Is the criminal intelligence unit's mission achievable with the number of assigned staff?	❑ Yes	❑ No

Collection

Item	Question		
31	Does a collection effort begin with the development of a written plan?	❑ Yes	❑ No
32	Does the collection plan include a set of information requirements that specifies what data is needed by the agency or investigator (s)?	❑ Yes	❑ No
33	Does the collection plan comply with applicable local, state, and federal statutes and case law?	❑ Yes	❑ No
34	Is the collection plan focused on identifying the nature and extent of criminal activity?	❑ Yes	❑ No
35	Does the collection plan utilize all known available sources?	❑ Yes	❑ No
36	Are the plan's objectives and requirements communicated to criminal intelligence unit staff?	❑ Yes	❑ No
37	Has the Criminal Intelligence Function encouraged the development of a close working relationship between analysts and investigators?	❑ Yes	❑ No
38	Have those assigned to the Criminal Intelligence Function received training in the right to privacy?	❑ Yes	❑ No
39	Does the state in which your agency resides have laws that address the collection of criminal intelligence data? If no, go to question 41.	❑ Yes	❑ No
40	If yes to question 39, are your criminal intelligence personnel trained in these legal applications?	❑ Yes	❑ No
41	Have your criminal intelligence personnel been trained legal collection methods?	❑ Yes	❑ No

Item	Question		
42	Does your agency have informant guidelines in place? If no, go to question 44.	❑ Yes	❑ No
43	Do these guidelines address informant control and management?	❑ Yes	❑ No
44	Do these guidelines address the maintenance of informant files?	❑ Yes	❑ No

Collation

Item	Question		
45	Does the unit have criminal intelligence file guidelines?	❑ Yes	❑ No
46	Is the criminal intelligence unit operating within the guidelines?	❑ Yes	❑ No
47	Are files kept ONLY on individuals who are suspected of being involved in actual or attempted acts; or suspected of being involved in criminal activities with known or suspected crime figures?	❑ Yes	❑ No
48	Are files kept ONLY on organizations, businesses, and groups that are suspected of being involved in actual or attempted acts; or are suspected of being operated, controlled, financed, or infiltrated by known or suspected crime figures?	❑ Yes	❑ No
49	Do the guidelines clearly delineate criteria for determining if information should be entered and retained in the files?	❑ Yes	❑ No
50	Is the information stored in criminal intelligence files evaluated according to source reliability and content validity before it is included in a criminal intelligence file?	❑ Yes	❑ No
51	Is there a clearly articulated system for assessing source reliability and content validity?	❑ Yes	❑ No
52	Is a distinction made between permanent, temporary, and working files along with appropriate retention periods?	❑ Yes	❑ No

Item	Question		
53	Is the information stored in criminal intelligence files classified in order to protect sources, investigators, and the individual's right to privacy?	❑ Yes	❑ No
54	Are files clearly marked with appropriate classification?	❑ Yes	❑ No
55	Is information maintained in the criminal intelligence file reviewed for reclassification or purge on a periodic basis to ensure that it is current, has utility, is accurate, safeguards an individual's right to privacy, and is classified at an appropriate security level?	❑ Yes	❑ No
56	Do the criminal intelligence unit's purge policies comply with local, and/or state law regarding records retention?	❑ Yes	❑ No
57	Is there a specific staff member(s) who is responsible for purging files?	❑ Yes	❑ No
58	Are procedures in place to govern the storage, handling, and security of hard copy source material?	❑ Yes	❑ No
59	Does the criminal intelligence unit retain hard copies of source documents? If no, go to question 63.	❑ Yes	❑ No
60	Are these documents stored in a safe and secure location?	❑ Yes	❑ No
61	Is access to these documents restricted?	❑ Yes	❑ No
62	Are procedures in place to govern the storage, handling, and security of source material in an electronic database?	❑ Yes	❑ No
63	Is access to the file database restricted?	❑ Yes	❑ No
64	Is a specific employee(s) responsible for controlling automated access?	❑ Yes	❑ No

Item	Question		
65	Are automated access audits conducted periodically?	❑ Yes	❑ No
66	Is a record of audits maintained?	❑ Yes	❑ No
67	Is automated access immediately deleted when personnel leave or transfer?	❑ Yes	❑ No
68	Are files adequately safeguarded through back up and recovery routines, and off-site storage of critical files, programs, and systems?	❑ Yes	❑ No
69	Is the system isolated from other networks or protected by a firewall to restrict unauthorized access?	❑ Yes	❑ No
70	Are files (either hard or electronic copy) indexed in an organized fashion?	❑ Yes	❑ No
71	Is a file locator system in place?	❑ Yes	❑ No
72	Is a particular employee(s) responsible for overseeing the criminal intelligence file system so that it is operating within the guidelines of all applicable laws?	❑ Yes	❑ No
73	Are purged documents destroyed in a secure and appropriate manner according to all applicable laws?	❑ Yes	❑ No
74	Is information regarding political, religious, or social views of an individual or group prohibited from inclusion in a criminal intelligence file unless it directly relates to criminal conduct or activity?	❑ Yes	❑ No

Dissemination

Item	Question		
75	Are procedures in place for responding to requests for information?	❑ Yes	❑ No
76	Are records kept of requests for information and responses? If no, go to question 78.	❑ Yes	❑ No

Item	Question		
77	Are these records audited periodically?	❑ Yes	❑ No
78	Are there procedures in place governing the dissemination of law enforcement sensitive material?	❑ Yes	❑ No
79	Is criminal intelligence information released only to those who have demonstrated a right-to-know and a need-to-know?	❑ Yes	❑ No
80	Is there an audit trail to determine who has accessed criminal intelligence files?	❑ Yes	❑ No
81	Has the criminal intelligence unit established a policy prohibiting third-party dissemination?	❑ Yes	❑ No
82	Has the agency identified legal resources that are familiar with criminal intelligence issues and procedures that can adequately represent the agency in legal matters?	❑ Yes	❑ No

National Criminal Intelligence Sharing Plan (NCISP)

"Executive Summary"

Executive Summary

The need for a National Criminal Intelligence Sharing Plan ("Plan") was recognized as critical after the tragic events of September 11, 2001, when nearly 3,000 innocent lives were lost as a result of terrorist attacks against the United States. This event initiated a concerted effort by American law enforcement agencies to correct the inadequacies and barriers that impede information and intelligence sharing—so that future tragedies could be prevented.

In spring 2002, law enforcement executives and intelligence experts attending the International Association of Chiefs of Police (IACP) Criminal Intelligence Sharing Summit recognized that local, state, tribal, and federal law enforcement agencies and the organizations that represent them must work towards common goals—gathering information and producing intelligence within their agency and sharing that intelligence with other law enforcement and public safety agencies. Summit participants called for the creation of a nationally coordinated criminal intelligence council that would develop and oversee a national intelligence plan.[1] In response

to this crucial need, the Global Justice Information Sharing Initiative (Global) Intelligence Working Group (GIWG) was formed. Local, state, and tribal law enforcement representatives were key participants in the development of the National Criminal Intelligence Sharing Plan.

Many state law enforcement agencies and all federal agencies tasked with intelligence gathering and assessment responsibilities have established intelligence functions within their organizations. However, approximately 75 percent of the law enforcement agencies in the United States have less than 24 sworn officers, and more often than not, these agencies do not have staff dedicated to intelligence functions. Officers in these smaller, local agencies interact with the public in the communities they patrol on a daily basis. Providing local agencies with the tools and resources necessary for developing, gathering, accessing, receiving, and sharing intelligence information is critically important to improving public safety and homeland security.

During a February 2003 speech, President George W. Bush pledged to make information sharing an important tool in the nation's war on terror. "All across our country we'll be able to tie our terrorist information to local

---

[1] Additional information on the IACP Summit can be located in *Recommendations from the IACP Intelligence Summit, Criminal Intelligence Sharing: A National Plan for Intelligence-Led Policing at the Local, State, and Federal Levels.* This document is available at: http://www.theiacp.org/documents/pdfs/Publications/intelsharingreport.pdf.

information banks so that the front line of defeating terror becomes activated and real, and those are the local law enforcement officials. We expect them to be a part of our effort; we must give them the tools necessary so they can do their job." The National Criminal Intelligence Sharing Plan is a key tool that law enforcement agencies can employ to support their crime fighting and public safety efforts.

Whether it is the officer on the street, the intelligence manager, or the agency executive—having access to the information that will help them do their job is essential. As law enforcement officials begin reviewing this Plan, they should ask themselves the questions, "What is my responsibility?" and "What can I do to get involved?" They should assess what type of intelligence functions are currently being performed in their agency, and utilize the guidelines in this Plan to determine how they can improve their intelligence process.

This report outlines specific "action steps" that can be taken immediately by almost any agency and what can be expected by performing those steps. The portion of the report titled "The Rationale for the National Criminal Intelligence Sharing Plan" should be carefully reviewed, as it provides an in-depth discussion of the issues and recommendations presented in the National Criminal Intelligence Sharing Plan.

GIWG Vision

The GIWG membership articulated a *vision* of what the National Criminal Intelligence Sharing Plan should be to local, state, tribal, and federal law enforcement agencies:

- A model intelligence sharing plan.
- A mechanism to promote intelligence-led policing.
- A blueprint for law enforcement administrators to follow when enhancing or building an intelligence system.
- A model for intelligence process principles and policies.
- A plan that respects and protects individuals' privacy and civil rights.
- A technology architecture to provide secure, seamless sharing of information among systems.
- A national model for intelligence training.
- An outreach plan to promote timely and credible intelligence sharing.
- A plan that leverages existing systems and networks, yet allows flexibility for technology and process enhancements.

The GIWG focused their efforts on developing an intelligence sharing plan that emphasized better methods for developing and sharing critical data among all law enforcement agencies.

The GIWG identified several issues that were viewed as inhibitors of intelligence development and sharing. The GIWG expressed these issues as needs when formulating recommendations for the national plan. One of the key issues acknowledged by the GIWG was the need to **overcome the long-standing and substantial barriers that hinder intelligence sharing**. Examples include the "hierarchy" within the law enforcement and intelligence communities and deficits in intelligence. Overcoming the barriers that impede information and intelligence sharing is a continuous endeavor that will require a firm commitment by all levels of government, and the implementation of the National Criminal Intelligence Sharing Plan will most certainly assist in this undertaking.

The following additional issues were recognized and addressed by the GIWG:

♦ **The need to develop minimum standards for management of an intelligence function.**

♦ **The need to establish a Criminal Intelligence Coordinating Council, composed of local, state, tribal, and federal entities that will provide and promote a broadly inclusive criminal intelligence generation and sharing process.**

♦ **The need to ensure institutionalization of the National Criminal Intelligence Sharing Plan.**

♦ **The need to ensure that individuals' constitutional rights, civil liberties, civil rights, and privacy interests are protected throughout the intelligence process.**

♦ **The need to develop minimum standards for all levels of the intelligence process: Planning and Direction, Information Collection, Processing/Collation, Analysis, Dissemination, and Reevaluation (feedback).**

♦ **The need to increase availability of information, from classified systems to local and state law enforcement agencies, for the prevention and investigation of crime in their jurisdictions.**

♦ **The need to develop minimum criminal intelligence training standards for all affected levels of law enforcement personnel to include training objectives, missions, number of hours, and frequency of training.**

♦ **The need to identify an intelligence information sharing capability that can be widely accessed by local, state, tribal, and federal law**

enforcement and public safety agencies.

From the issues identified above, the GIWG developed recommendations for the National Criminal Intelligence Sharing Plan. Following are the action items and steps that local, state, tribal, and federal law enforcement agencies should use as a road map to ensure that effective intelligence sharing becomes institutionalized throughout the law enforcement community nationwide.

This report represents the first version of the Plan that is intended to be a "living document" and will be periodically updated. Those charged with developing and implementing the Plan will continue to solicit the involvement of the law enforcement and intelligence communities, national organizations, and other government and public safety entities, in order to ensure that the Plan is responsive to their needs for information and intelligence development and sharing.

Action Items/Recommendations

The primary purpose of intelligence-led policing is to provide public-safety decision makers the information they need to protect the lives of our citizens. The following recommendations detail the essential elements of the National Criminal Intelligence Sharing Plan.

Recommendation 1: In order to attain the goals outlined in this Plan, law enforcement agencies, regardless of size, shall adopt the minimum standards for intelligence-led policing and the utilization and/or management of an intelligence function as contained in the National Criminal Intelligence Sharing Plan. The standards focus on the intelligence process and include elements such as mission of the function, management and supervision, personnel selection, training, security, privacy rights, development and dissemination of intelligence products, and accountability measures.

The agency chief executive officer and the manager of intelligence functions should:

- Seek ways to enhance intelligence sharing efforts and foster information sharing by participating in task forces and state, regional, and federal information sharing initiatives.

℘ Implement a mission statement for the intelligence process within the agency.

℘ Define management and supervision of the function.

℘ Select qualified personnel for assignment to the function.

℘ Ensure that standards are developed concerning background investigations of staff/system users to ensure security (of the system, facilities, etc.) and access to the system/network.

℘ Ensure appropriate training for all personnel assigned to or impacted by the intelligence process.

℘ Ensure that individuals' privacy and constitutional rights are considered at all times.

℘ Support the development of sound, professional analytic products (intelligence).

℘ Implement a method/system for dissemination of information to appropriate components/entities.

℘ Implement a policies and procedures manual. The intent of the manual is to establish, in writing, agency accountability for the intelligence function. The manual should include policies and procedures covering all aspects of the intelligence process.

℘ Implement an appropriate audit or review process to ensure compliance with policies and procedures.

℘ Promote a policy of openness when communicating with the public and all interested parties regarding the criminal intelligence process, when it does not affect the security and integrity of the process.

Recommendation 2: In order to provide long-term oversight and assistance with the implementation and refinement of the National Criminal Intelligence Sharing Plan, a Criminal Intelligence Coordinating Council (CICC) should be established as contemplated in the IACP *Criminal Intelligence Sharing Report*. The purpose of the CICC is to advise the Congress, the U.S. Attorney General, and the Secretary of Homeland

Security on the best use of criminal intelligence to keep our country safe. The CICC should operate under the auspices of the Global Advisory Committee (GAC). The CICC should consist of representatives from local, state, tribal, and federal agencies and national law enforcement organizations. The GIWG will act as the interim CICC until such time as the CICC is operational.

Recommendation 3: The CICC should monitor the implementation of the National Criminal Intelligence Sharing Plan, in order to gauge the success of the Plan. A report on the progress of the Plan will be submitted to the Office of Justice Programs (OJP) beginning December 31, 2004, and annually thereafter.

Recommendation 4: This Plan is designed to strengthen homeland security and foster intelligence-led policing. There is a critical need for more national funding to accomplish these goals. Without adequate funding, many of the recommendations contained herein, such as improving training and technical infrastructure, will not occur, and the country will remain at risk. The CICC, the GAC, and the U.S. Departments of Justice and Homeland Security should partner to identify and fund initiatives that implement the recommendations contained in this report.

Recommendation 5: In order to publicly recognize the creation of the Plan and demonstrate a commitment by all parties involved, a National Signing Event should be held where law enforcement and homeland security agency heads, from all levels, and other relevant groups come together to "sign on" to the National Criminal Intelligence Sharing Plan. The National Signing Event should be held before December 31, 2003.

Recommendation 6: All parties involved with implementing and promoting the National Criminal Intelligence Sharing Plan should take steps to ensure that the law enforcement community protects individuals' privacy and constitutional rights within the intelligence process.

Recommendation 7: Local, state, tribal, and federal law enforcement agencies must recognize and partner with the public and private sectors in order to detect and prevent attacks to the nation's critical infrastructures. Steps should be taken to establish regular communications and methods of information exchange.

Recommendation 8: Outreach materials prepared by the CICC should be utilized by law enforcement agency officials to publicize and promote the concepts of standards-based intelligence sharing and intelligence-led policing, as contained within the National Criminal Intelligence Sharing Plan, to their agency personnel and the communities that they serve.

Recommendation 9: In order to ensure that the collection/submission, access, storage, and dissemination of criminal intelligence information conforms to the privacy and constitutional rights of individuals, groups, and organizations, law enforcement agencies shall adopt, at a minimum, the standards required by the Criminal Intelligence Systems Operating Policies federal regulation (28 CFR Part 23),[2] regardless of whether or not an intelligence system is federally funded.

Recommendation 10: Law enforcement agencies should use the IACP's *Criminal Intelligence Model Policy* (2003 revision)[3] as a guide when implementing or reviewing the intelligence function in their organizations.

Recommendation 11: In addition to federal regulation 28 CFR Part 23, law enforcement agencies should use the Law Enforcement Intelligence Unit (LEIU) *Criminal Intelligence File Guidelines* as a model for intelligence file maintenance.[4]

Recommendation 12: The International Association of Law Enforcement Intelligence Analysts (IALEIA) should develop, on behalf of the CICC, minimum standards for intelligence analysis to ensure intelligence products are accurate, timely, factual, and relevant and recommend implementing policy and/or action(s).   These minimum standards should be developed by June 30, 2004. Law enforcement agencies should adopt these standards as soon as developed and approved by the CICC.

Recommendation 13: To further enhance professional judgment, especially as it relates to the protection of individuals' privacy and constitutional rights, the National Criminal Intelligence Sharing Plan encourages participation in professional criminal intelligence organizations and supports intelligence training for all local, state, tribal, and federal law enforcement personnel.

Recommendation 14: To foster trust among law enforcement agencies, policymakers, and the communities they serve, the National Criminal Intelligence Sharing Plan promotes a policy of openness to the public regarding the criminal intelligence function, when it does not affect the security and integrity of the process.

Recommendation 15:   The National Criminal Intelligence Sharing Plan promotes effective accountability measures, as expressed in 28 CFR Part 23, the LEIU *Criminal Intelligence File Guidelines*, and the *Justice Information Privacy Guideline*,[5] which law

---

[2] This 28 CFR Part 23 regulation is included on the companion CD and is also available at www.it.ojp.gov.
[3] The IACP Criminal Intelligence Model Policy is included on the companion CD and is also available at www.theiacp.org.
[4] The March 2002 update of the LEIU *Criminal Intelligence File Guidelines* is included on the companion CD.
[5] This document is included on the companion CD and is also available at: http://www.ncja.org/pdf/privacyguideline.pdf.

enforcement agencies should employ to ensure protection of individuals' privacy and constitutional rights and to identify and remedy practices that are inconsistent with policy.

Recommendation 16: Law enforcement agencies involved in criminal intelligence sharing are encouraged to use, to the extent applicable, the privacy policy guidelines provided in *Justice Information Privacy Guideline—Developing, Drafting and Assessing Privacy Policy for Justice Information Systems.*[6] The goal of the *Justice Information Privacy Guideline* is to provide assistance to justice leaders and practitioners who seek to balance public safety, public access, and privacy when developing information policies for their individual agencies or for integrated (multiagency) justice systems.

Recommendation 17: The CICC, in conjunction with federal officials, should identify technical means to aid and expedite the production of unclassified "tear-line" reports. These reports are the declassification of classified data needed for law enforcement purposes, with the sensitive source and method-of-collection data redacted, yet retaining as much intelligence content as feasible. The technical means for production of these reports should be identified by June 30, 2004.

Recommendation 18: Training should be provided to all levels of law enforcement personnel involved in the criminal intelligence process. The training standards, as contained within the National Criminal Intelligence Sharing Plan, shall be considered the minimum training standards for all affected personnel.[7] Additionally, recipients of criminal intelligence training, as recommended in the National Criminal Intelligence Sharing Plan, should be recognized and awarded certificates for successful completion of training.

Recommendation 19: The CICC shall foster a working relationship with the International Association of Directors of Law Enforcement Standards and Training (IADLEST) organization, the IACP State and Provincial Police Academy Directors Section (SPPADS), and other relevant training organizations, in order to obtain their assistance with implementing the recommended National Criminal Intelligence Sharing Plan training standards in every state.

Recommendation 20: In order to support agency tactical, operational, and strategic needs, law enforcement agencies are encouraged to consider an automated, incident-based criminal records tracking capability, in addition to traditional case management

---

[6] This document is available at http://www.ncja.org/pdf/privacyguideline.pdf.

[7] The recommended training standards for each level, including roles and missions, core training objectives, and length of training, are included in the appendix of this report and on the companion CD.

and intelligence systems, to use as an additional source for records management and statistical data. These systems should be Web-based and configured to meet the internal reporting and record-keeping needs of the component, in order to facilitate the exportation of desired data elements—without the need for duplicate data entry or reporting—to relevant statewide and federal criminal information programs.

Recommendation 21: The Regional Information Sharing Systems™ (RISS) and the Federal Bureau of Investigation (FBI) Law Enforcement Online (LEO) systems, which interconnected September 1, 2002, as a virtual single system, shall provide the initial sensitive but unclassified secure communications backbone for implementation of a nationwide criminal intelligence sharing capability. This nationwide sensitive but unclassified communications backbone shall support fully functional, bidirectional information sharing capabilities that maximize the reuse of existing local, state, tribal, regional, and federal infrastructure investments. Further configuration of the nationwide sensitive but unclassified communications capability will continue to evolve in conjunction with industry and the development of additional standards, and the connection of other existing sensitive but unclassified networks.

Recommendation 22: Interoperability with existing systems at the local, state, tribal, regional, and federal levels with the RISS/LEO communications capability should proceed immediately, in order to leverage information sharing systems and expand intelligence sharing.[8]

Recommendation 23: The CICC shall work with Global's Systems Security Compatibility Task Force to identify and specify an architectural approach and transitional steps that allow for the use of existing infrastructures (technology, governance structures, and trust relationships) at the local, state, tribal, regional, and federal levels, to leverage the national sensitive but unclassified communications capabilities for information sharing. This strategic architectural approach shall ensure interoperability among local, state, tribal, regional, and federal intelligence information systems and repositories.

Recommendation 24: All agencies, organizations, and programs with a vested interest in sharing criminal intelligence should actively recruit agencies with local, state, tribal, regional, and federal law enforcement and intelligence systems, to connect to the nationwide sensitive but unclassified communications capability. Such agencies, organizations, and programs are encouraged to leverage the nationwide sensitive but

---

[8] The GIWG conducted a preliminary survey of systems/initiatives that are operational or being developed at the local, state, federal, and regional levels. Several systems/initiatives were identified. Refer to the companion CD for a list of the systems identified, as well as summary information obtained during the survey.

unclassified communications capability, thereby expanding collaboration and information sharing opportunities across existing enterprises and leveraging existing users. Moreover, participant standards and user vetting procedures must be compatible with those of the currently connected sensitive but unclassified systems, so as to be trusted connections to the nationwide sensitive but unclassified communications capability.

Recommendation 25: Agencies participating in the National Criminal Intelligence Sharing Plan are encouraged to use *Applying Security Practices to Justice Information Sharing*[9] as a reference document regarding information system security practices. The document was developed by the Global Security Working Group to be used by justice executives and managers as a resource to secure their justice information systems and as a resource of ideas and best practices to consider when building their agency's information infrastructure and before sharing information with other agencies.

Recommendation 26: Agencies are encouraged to utilize the latest version of the Global Justice Extensible Markup Language (XML) Data Model (GJXDM) and its component Global Justice XML Data Dictionary (GJXDD)[10] when connecting databases and other resources to communication networks. The GJXDM and GJXDD were developed to enable interoperability through the exchange of data across a broad range of disparate information systems.

Recommendation 27: In order to enhance trust and "raise the bar" on the background investigations currently performed, law enforcement agencies must conduct fingerprint-based background checks on individuals, both sworn or nonsworn, prior to allowing law enforcement access to the sensitive but unclassified communications capability. Background requirements for access to the nationwide sensitive but unclassified communications capability by law enforcement personnel shall be consistent with requirements applied to the designation and employment of sworn personnel, as set by the participating state or tribal government, so long as, at a minimum, those requirements stipulate that a criminal history check be made through the FBI and the appropriate local, state, and tribal criminal history repositories and be confirmed by an applicant fingerprint card. Additionally, a name-based records check must be performed on law enforcement personnel every three years after the initial fingerprint-based records check is performed.

---

[9] This document is available at: http://www.it.ojp.gov/global/.

[10] The latest version of the Global Justice XML Data Model and the Global Justice XML Data Dictionary is included on the companion CD and can be found at: http://www.it.ojp.gov/jxdm.

<u>Recommendation 28</u>: The CICC, in conjunction with the OJP and the connected sensitive but unclassified systems, shall develop an acquisition mechanism or centralized site that will enable law enforcement agencies to access shared data visualization and analytic tools. The CICC shall identify analytical products that are recommended for use by law enforcement agencies in order to maximize resources when performing intelligence functions, as well as a resource list of current users of the products. The CICC will submit a report on these tools to OJP by June 30, 2004.

Author Biographies

AUTHOR BIOGRAPHIES

AUTHOR BIOGRAPHIES

Baratta, Dean

Dean Baratta has served as an intelligence analyst with the U.S. Army for 18 years and with the New Jersey State Police for 6 years. He began working with law enforcement as part of the Pennsylvania National Guard Counter Drug Program where he focused on narcotics and street gang investigations. He has since developed products to support tactical, operational, and strategic level operations as well as training and operational guidelines for analysts within the New Jersey State Police. While supporting Operation Enduring Freedom in Afghanistan from 2003-2004, he began exploring similarities between successful responses to organized criminal networks and insurgencies.

He may be contacted at *dean.baratta@gmail.com*

Bochert, Chuck

Lieutenant Chuck Boschert graduated from Central Missouri State University in 1983 with a Bachelor's Degree in Criminal Justice Administration and has been a commissioned member of the St. Louis County Police Department since that time. In addition to assignments in the department's West County, North County, and Central County Precincts, he previously spent ten years assigned to the Bureau of Drug Enforcement as both a detective and sergeant, including a five-year detachment to the Federal DEA Task Force in St. Louis. Lieutenant Boschert also spent 11 years as commander of the St. Louis County Police Intelligence Unit supervising investigations into organized crime, public corruption, and terrorism. During that time, he oversaw the development of the St. Louis Terrorism Early Warning Group and served as director of this regional intelligence fusion center.

Lieutenant Boschert has served as a member of the U.S. Attorney's Anti-Terrorism Advisory Council, the U.S. Attorney's Hate Crimes Task Force, the Mid-Missouri Domestic Terrorism Working Group, and the national Interagency Threat Assessment and Coordination Group (ITACG) Advisory Council. He is a graduate of the U.S. Secret Service's National Threat Assessment Center and is a former Vice General Chairman of the Association of Law Enforcement Intelligence Units (LEIU). Lieutenant Boschert is a member of the St. Louis Area Regional Response System (STARRS) Advisory Council and the St. Louis Regional Resource Coordination Plan development committee.

Lieutenant Boschert currently serves as the Deputy Commander of the St. Louis County Multi-jurisdictional Drug Task Force.

Brinner, Rafael

Rafael Brinner serves with the U.S. Department of Homeland Security's Office of Intelligence and Analysis. He has advised federal, state, and local agencies on best practices for analyzing suspicious activity reports and has presented his ideas to law enforcement and intelligence community audiences at national and international conferences. In 2008, Mr. Brinner received a Distinguished Analysis Award from the Deputy Director of National Intelligence for Analysis in recognition of his pioneering efforts in this area. Mr. Brinner is a graduate of the University of California at Berkeley and holds master's degrees from Northwestern University and the Monterey Institute of International Studies.

Cariens Jr., David

Dave Cariens was born in Columbus, Ohio, and holds a B.A. and M.A. from Ohio State University in German and Polish history. Cariens served in the CIA for 31 years before retiring in 1997. During his career he was a political analyst for 22 years in the Directorate of Intelligence, specializing in Balkan affairs. In this capacity he produced finished intelligence for all levels of the U.S. government, from the President to working level counterparts throughout the Community. He headed the training unit teaching all new CIA analysts in the writing and briefing skills needed to produce finished intelligence. He has designed intelligence analysis/writing courses and taught them throughout the Intelligence Community. He has trained foreign intelligence services in the writing skills needed to produce finished intelligence.

Following the collapse of the Soviet Union, he designed and taught the basic analytic/writing course currently used by one former member of the Warsaw Pact to train its new intelligence analysts. Cariens also served on the CIA's Inspector General's staff. Since retiring, he continues to design and teach intelligence writing and briefing courses throughout the Intelligence Community—including the CIA, the FBI, the Intelligence Community Staff, the National Counterterrorism Center, the Department of Homeland Security, the Department of Justice, all branches of military intelligence, the Colorado Bureau of Investigation, and the Massachusetts State Police Fusion Center. He has given writing workshops at the International Association of Law Enforcement Intelligence Analysts (IALEIA) in Alexandria in 2005, in Mexico City in 2006, in Vancouver, Canada in April, 2007, in Boston in 2008, and in Las Vegas in 2009. He has conducted intelligence analysis training for the Criminal Intelligence Service of Canada and for the Royal Canadian Mounted Police.

Cariens is a victims' rights advocate and is currently working with the families of the shooting at Virginia Tech University. He is the author of *A Question of Accountability: The Murder of Angela Dales*, an examination of the killing rampage at the Appalachian School of Law on January 16, 2002

www.aquestionofaccountability.com

Coambs, Paul

Paul Coambs' career includes 30 years in California Law Enforcement with the last 20 years as a Criminal Intelligence Detective for the Simi Valley Police Department. He holds a BA and MS from the University of the Pacific in Stockton, CA. He has instructed law enforcement recruits at the Ventura County Criminal Justice Training Center and lectured to both law enforcement and public audiences on the subjects of criminal intelligence, terrorism, outlaw motorcycle gangs, ritual crime, hate crime, and victimization. He has held board positions for the Southern California Outlaw Motorcycle Gang Investigators Association, the California Ritual Crimes Investigator Association, and the Ventura County Intelligence Unit.

Fahlman, Robert C.
Director General, Criminal Intelligence, RCMP

Robert C. Fahlman, a career professional intelligence officer with the Royal Canadian Mounted Police (RCMP), was promoted to Director General, Criminal Intelligence (CI), RCMP effective May 30, 2008. In his new position he is responsible for CI policy, governance and doctrine; professional standards and training; domestic and international partnerships; research, development, and innovation.

From August 2002 through to May 2008, Robert was detached to Criminal Intelligence Service Canada (CISC) as Deputy Director General, Intelligence Analysis and Knowledge Development, CISC. He was responsible for launching the CISC National Threat Assessment, Sentinel Strategic Early Warning methodology, National Intelligence Requirement and Canadian Criminal Intelligence Model (CCIM). Prior to August 2002, Robert was seconded by the RCMP to Interpol General Secretariat in Lyon, France (May 1999 to August 2002) where he was Assistant Director responsible for Interpol's Criminal Intelligence Program. Prior to May 1999, Robert was the Officer-in-Charge of the RCMP's Criminal Analysis Branch, Criminal Intelligence Directorate in Ottawa, Canada.

Mr. Fahlman is a member of the Council of Advisors, Canadian Centre of Intelligence and Security Studies, Carleton University, Ottawa and a member of the Canadian Association for Security and Intelligence Studies. Robert is also a member of the Executive Advisory Board, International Association of Law Enforcement Intelligence Analysts (IALEIA), and was Executive Director, IALEIA from 2002 to 2004. He has also served as the Chancellor, Society of Certified Criminal Analysts (SCCA) from 1995 to 1999 and holds the title of Lifetime Certified Criminal Analyst (CCA). Robert was a founding member of the Board of Governors of the SCCA and was the recipient of the 1997 SCCA Lifetime Achievement Award.

Robert has worked in over 30 countries as a consultant in the field of intelligence systems with a focus on intelligence analysis development. He has written numerous articles in this field and conducted training seminars for both practitioners and executive. He currently serves on a number of advisory boards, both in the governmental and private sectors. Robert has a Bachelor of Applied Arts (Journalism) from Canadian Police College, Ottawa; the RCMP Training Academy, Regina; Queen's University, Kingston; and, Georgetown University, Washington, D.C., USA.

Fowler, Robert D.
Lieutenant, Garden Grove (CA) Police Department

Lieutenant Robert Fowler is currently the Vice General Chairman for LEIU and has served in that capacity since June 2010. He previously served as Southwestern Vice Zone Chairperson from August 2004 to April 2008. Robert Fowler is a 23-year veteran of law enforcement. He has spent the last 19 years with the Garden Grove Police Department, located in Southern California. He is currently assigned as a lieutenant in the Community Policing Bureau. Within that capacity, he oversees the Department's Terrorism Liaison Officer Program, Mounted Enforcement Unit, and Resort Services Team. Previously, as a sergeant, Lieutenant Fowler supervised the Department's Criminal Intelligence Unit. Previous assignments include Intelligence, Patrol, Juvenile Investigations, and Resort Services. Lieutenant Fowler holds a bachelors degree in Business Management and a Master's Degree in Public Administration.

Frank, Doug

Criminal Intelligence Analyst, Missouri Information Analysis Center (MIAC)
Missouri State Highway Patrol

Mr. Frank received his BS degree in Military History and a commission as a lieutenant in the U.S. Army in 2000 from the United States Military Academy at West Point, New York. For the next five years, Mr. Frank served as an armor officer in Georgia and Kentucky. He then joined the Missouri Army National Guard, and in 2005 was deployed as an executive officer for a provincial reconstruction team in

Afghanistan. In 2007, Mr. Frank joined the Missouri Information Analysis Center as a criminal intelligence analyst. He is a member of the International Association of Law Enforcement Intelligence Analysts (IALEIA) and the International Association of Crime Analysts (IACA).

Godsey, Van
Assistant Director, Division of Drug and Crime Control
Missouri State Highway Patrol

Mr. Godsey received his BA degree in Business and Political Science in 1984 from Drury University in Springfield, Missouri. In 1986 Mr. Godsey graduated from the Tennessee Law Enforcement Academy and for the next 4 years he worked as a police officer in Southeast Tennessee. In 1990, Mr. Godsey went to work at the Missouri Attorney General's Office in the special prosecution unit. Mr. Godsey left the Attorney General's Office in 1995 as the Chief Criminal Investigator and assumed the role of Violent Crime Support Unit Supervisor at the Missouri State Highway Patrol (MSHP). In 1998, the MSHP combined the Violent Crime Support Unit and the Criminal Intelligence/Crime Analysis Unit and Mr. Godsey was promoted to supervisor of both units. Over the next seven years, Mr. Godsey supervised the Criminal Intelligence/Crime Analysis unit and became involved in several information and intelligence sharing initiatives. Some of these efforts include the Missouri Statewide Police Intelligence Network (MoSPIN), the Midwest HIDTA, the National Virtual Pointer System (NVPS), and many others. Mr. Godsey is a member of the International Association of Law Enforcement Intelligence Analyst (IALEIA), International Association of Crime Analyst (IACA) and is the General Chairman for the Association of Law Enforcement Intelligence Units (LEIU). In December 2005, Mr. Godsey was appointed as Director of the Missouri Information Analysis Center (MIAC), the State of Missouri's designated Fusion Center. In April of 2009, Mr. Godsey assumed his current position as Assistant Director to the Division of Drug and Crime Control. Mr. Godsey has been involved as a Subject Matter Expert (SME) on numerous initiatives for the Department of Homeland Security (DHS) and the Department of Justice (DOJ) and served as the Central Region Vice Chair for the Homeland Security-State and Local Intelligence Community (HS-SLIC).

Gordnier, John

John received his BA degree from the University of Washington in 1966. His JD was earned at the University of Wyoming in 1969. In January 1970 he was sworn in as a member of the California bar. From 1970 until 1972 John worked as a Deputy District Attorney in the County of San Bernardino. In October 1972 he became a Deputy Attorney General in the Criminal Law Division of the California Attorney General's Office. During his time in the Criminal Law Division he tried cases involving public officials, served as the head of the Political Reform Act Enforcement Unit, and was in charge of the Attorney General's Legislative/Lobbyist Task Force. When the Special Prosecutions Unit was created to handle organized crime cases in 1979, John was one of the attorneys assigned to a team consisting of an attorney and two special agents. In 1983 he was named the Senior Assistant Attorney General in charge of the Special Prosecutions Unit, a position he held until the Unit was disbanded in 1991. During his tenure in the Special Prosecutions Unit, John not only prosecuted cases and supervised prosecutions by the unit he also was responsible for the creation and enactment of laws penalizing money laundering, allowing for asset forfeiture, and permitting prosecution under a state RICO provision. From 1991 to 1998 John was a Senior Assistant Attorney General in the Trials and Special Projects Unit. In this capacity he served as the legislative liaison for the Criminal Law Division, prosecuted certain cases such as the Mark Furman perjury case, implemented the Attorney General's response to the Medical Marijuana initiative and successfully defended California's Assault Weapons Law. From 1998 until his retirement in 2007, John was assigned to act as the attorney for the California Department of Justice's intelligence systems, serve as the legal advisor to the CalGANG intelligence system, and teach intelligence law for both basic level and executive level courses sponsored by the Attorney General's Advanced Training Center. Since retiring from public service, John has acted as a consultant and instructor on criminal intelligence law.

Herrington, Richard

Richard L. Herrington is a graduate from the University of Portland, Portland, Oregon with a B.S. in Life Sciences and is a 31 year veteran of Law Enforcement. Currently he is a Special Agent Supervisor for the Washington State Gambling Commission (WSGC). He is assigned to the WSGC Criminal Intelligence Unit as a supervisor and has supervised the Criminal Investigations Undercover Unit as well as being a Special Agent in the regulatory and enforcement of the WSGC. He was a narcotics detective, major crimes investigator, and a detective with the Lewis County Sheriff's Office for fifteen years prior to becoming a commissioned Special Agent with the WSGC in 1992. He is part of the informal national Illegal Internet Gambling Task Force, currently head of the enforcement group and authored the investigative plan for the task force. He has co-authored a training manual for illegal internet gambling investigations. He has been an instructor training law enforcement officers on illegal internet gambling investigations on a local, national and international level.

Johnson, Melissa R.

Ms. Johnson has worked as an Intelligence Analyst for state corrections for the last six years. She analyzes intelligence data, identifies criminal activity and contraband networks, monitors gang member identifications and releases, prepares intelligence briefs, and threat assessments. Ms. Johnson worked for the NJ State Police as a Crime Analyst prior to her current employment and has a wide range of analytical experience to include spatial analysis, crime pattern identification, next-hit probabilities, gang migration trends, and threat assessment analysis. Ms. Johnson is a Certified Criminal Analyst and Certified Gang Professional and she participates in several professional, law enforcement Organizations, to include: the International Association of Law Enforcement Intelligence Analysts, East Coast Gang Investigators Association, and the International Association of Crime Analysts.

Larm, Doug

Doug Larm, a retired US Army military intelligence officer, is a Strategic Advisor for Seattle Police Department's Criminal Intelligence Section and is assigned as a senior intelligence analyst at the Washington State Fusion Center. In his military career, Doug served in programs with the Defense Intelligence Agency and the Central Intelligence Agency. He is a graduate of the US Army War College's Defense Strategy Course and the Department of Defense's advanced intelligence training course at Goodfellow Air Force Base in Texas. Doug has worked with the Seattle Police Department since 2006 and with the Washington State Fusion Center since 2009. He concurrently serves as an adjunct professor teaching graduate students "Data and Intelligence Analysis" at Seattle University for the Master in Criminal Justice program. Doug completed his Master in Project Management and is the 2010 Distance Education and Training Council's Outstanding Graduate of the Year.

Lewis, James

Mr. James Lewis is an Intelligence Analyst at the U.S. Department of Justice, National Drug Intelligence Center; Johnstown, Pennsylvania. NDIC's primary mission is production of domestic strategic drug intelligence. In his 15 years with NDIC he has worked on a variety assignments ranging from Collections Management to National Threat Assessments. He is currently assigned to the Special Projects Unit focusing on the connection between street, prison, and outlaw motorcycle gangs and the illegal drug trade in the United States.

Martens, Frederick T.

Frederick T. Martens is the former Executive Director of the Pennsylvania Crime Commission. He 'retired' from the New Jersey State Police, having worked in an undercover capacity conducting organized crime and narcotics investigations. He is on the faculty of the College of New Jersey and has lectured extensively on organized crime, intelligence systems, money laundering, and terrorism. He currently conducts investigations for the corporate sector.

Morehouse, Bob

LEIU Executive Director Bob Morehouse worked with the California Department of Justice (CA DOJ) for over 34 years and in the criminal intelligence environment for over 31 years. He is currently a retired annuitant working in the Bureau of Investigation and Intelligence (BII) of the CA DOJ as the LEIU Executive Director. Mr. Morehouse has written several professional law enforcement publications, and was a contributing author and editor to Intelligence 2000: Revising the Basic Elements. He is a member of the International Association for Law Enforcement Intelligence Analysts (IALEIA), and has been awarded a Lifetime Certification in the Society of Certified Criminal Analysts. Prior to his half-time assignment as LEIU's Executive Director, Mr. Morehouse managed BII's Intelligence Support Unit and the Situation and Group Analysis Units of the California Anti-Terrorism Information Center (CATIC). These units are responsible for such diverse activities as the Bureau's automated criminal intelligence file and maintaining a current overall statewide strategic perspective on terrorism-related events and investigations. CATIC's Situation Unit is also responsible for the dissemination of tactical terrorism-related information to local, state, and federal agencies in California. Analysts in this unit also support eight CA DOJ task forces. Mr. Morehouse received his bachelor's degree in public administration from California State University, Sacramento.

Palmieri, Lisa

Lisa Palmieri works for the Department of Homeland Security's Office of Intelligence and Analysis as an Intelligence Officer assigned to the Commonwealth Fusion Center (CFC) in Massachusetts. She has also served as Acting Regional Director for the Northeast since 2009. Her duties include ensuring that homeland security threat information and intelligence flow bi-directionally between public and private sector entities at the state and local level and the Department of Homeland Security. Previously, Ms. Palmieri was a Supervisory Intelligence Analyst for the Massachusetts State Police at the CFC. Her previous experience includes work as both analyst supervisor and an investigative analyst working on complex white collar crime investigations at the Insurance Fraud Bureau of Massachusetts, and as a Criminal Intelligence Analyst at the New England State Police Information Network (NESPIN). Ms.

Palmieri started her career in military intelligence with the U.S. Army after graduating from Plymouth State College in New Hampshire, and was later a civilian debriefer for the British Ministry of Defense in West Berlin. She served as President of the International Association of Law Enforcement Intelligence Analysts (IALEIA) from 2004-2009, and in that position served on both the Criminal Intelligence Coordinating Council and the International Chiefs of Police Investigative Operations Committee.

Peterson, Marilyn B.
C.C.A., C.F.E., CAMS

Marilyn B. Peterson is a Senior Instructor with the Defense Intelligence Agency, Joint Military Intelligence Training Center in Washington, DC. She retired as an intelligence management specialist with the Division of Criminal Justice, New Jersey Department of Law and Public Safety, in December 2005. Her assignments in law enforcement included organized crime, narcotics, fraud, money laundering, and intelligence.

Ms. Peterson is a noted author who wrote *Applications in Criminal Analysis: A Sourcebook* (1994) and co-edited *Criminal Intelligence Analysis* (1990). She also wrote A *Guide to the Financial Analysis of Personal and Corporate Bank Records*, published by the National White Collar Crime Center (1996, 1998 and 2002). In 2001, she was the managing editor for *Intelligence 2000: Revising the Basic Elements*. She authored *A Guide to Understanding and Analyzing Bank Secrecy Act Data* in 2002 published by the National White Collar Crime Center and the Federal Bureau of Investigation. Her work, *Intelligence Led Policing: The New Intelligence Architecture* was published by the US Department of Justice, Bureau of Justice Assistance. In 2009, she wrote *A Guide to Counter Threat Finance Intelligence*. She has been qualified as an expert in detecting patterns of money laundering in financial transactions and has testified both in State Grand Jury and in the New Jersey Superior Court.

She received a Lifetime Achievement Award from the Society of Certified Criminal Analysts in 1996. She is the winner of seven analytic awards, six of which were for her written contributions to the field. In 2005, she received the LEIU 2005 Chairman's Award for her work in the intelligence community. She is the current Chair of the International Association for Intelligence Education (IAFIE), is past president of the International Association of Law Enforcement Intelligence Analysts (IALEIA); past Chancellor of the Society of Certified Criminal Analysts (SCCA) and is a Regent Emeritus and Fellow of the Association of Certified Fraud Examiners. She is also a Certified Anti-Moneylaundering Specialist (CAMS).

Ratcliffe PhD, Dr. Jerry

Dr Jerry Ratcliffe is a Professor with the Department of Criminal Justice at Temple University, Philadelphia, Pa, USA. Prior to academia, Professor Ratcliffe served for eleven years with the Metropolitan Police in London (UK), leaving after a severe winter mountaineering accident. For a number of years he coordinated Australia's National Strategic Intelligence Course, and he has conducted research, training and consulting on intelligence-led policing around the world. In 2007, Dr Ratcliffe was awarded the Professional Service Award for outstanding contributions to criminal intelligence analysis by the International Association of Law Enforcement Intelligence Analysts (IALEIA).

He has published over 50 research articles and four books: "Intelligence-Led Policing" (Willan, 2008); "Strategic Thinking in Criminal Intelligence" (Federation Press, 2004 and 2009); "GIS and Crime Mapping" (Wiley, 2005) and "Policing Illegal Drug Markets" (Criminal Justice Press, 2005). Recent research articles have examined shooting patterns in Philadelphia, the effectiveness of CCTV, and drug gang investigations by the New Jersey State Police. He was lead researcher on the Philadelphia Foot Patrol Experiment.

Jerry was an officer in the British Army Reserves (Royal Engineers), has climbed the three highest mountains in Africa, led an expedition down the Selenga river in Siberia, and was the first non-Iban tribesman to successfully navigate (with a traditional boat) the rapids of the Temburong River in Borneo. He likes to scuba dive, fly his ultralight seaplane, and drink single malt whiskey…just not at the same time.

Rogers, Chris

Chris Rogers began her career with the California Department of Justice (DOJ) in January, 1989 in the Division of Criminal Justice Information Systems (DCJIS). Throughout her tenure in DCJIS she earned the trust and recognition of criminal justice professionals throughout the state and country, committed to the advancement of information sharing through emerging technologies.

In 2008, she accepted a position with the DOJ Division of Law Enforcement, Bureau of Investigation and Intelligence where she works as an Assistant Bureau Chief overseeing the programs and activities of the bureau's Intelligence Operations Program. Assistant Chief Rogers is a member of the Global Security Working Group (GSWG) and the Global Infrastructure/Standards Working Group (GISWG), working groups under the umbrella of the Global Justice Information Sharing Initiative (Global). She holds a bachelors degree in Management Information Systems.

Roger, Paul
FAIM, FAIPIO, CCA

Paul Roger has over 30 years of management experience in the law enforcement, national security, and compliance fields.

Paul is currently a Senior Associate with Booz & Company where he leads the Public Safety, Law Enforcement and Justice Account for Australia, New Zealand and South East Asia. Prior to joining Booz & Company, Paul was a Senior Executive with the Queensland Crime and Misconduct Commission where he had responsibility for the management of the Commission's Intelligence, Information Management and Security resources in support of a multi-disciplined approach to investigating corruption and organised crime. Prior to this Paul was a Senior Officer with the Royal Hong Kong Police Force.

Paul is a Fellow of the Australian Institute of Management, a Fellow, and past President of the Australian Institute of Professional Intelligence Officers (AIPIO), and a past Governor with the Society of Certified Criminal Analysts (SCCA). Paul is also a recipient of the Society of Certified Criminal Analysts' Lifetime Achievement Award in recognition of his contribution to the law enforcement profession over three decades as an analyst, trainer, author, manager, and international advisor.

Paul has published several papers on intelligence, security and organised crime related subjects, and has lectured at graduate and post graduate level. He holds a Master of Justice (Strategic Intelligence), and a Bachelor Justice Studies, from Queensland University of Technology.

Schussler, Bethany

Bethany Schussler is a nine-year veteran of a state-level investigative agency, primarily working in its money laundering section and insurance fraud bureau. She has taught financial investigations, open source research and how to analyze FinCEN records. Ms. Schussler is an IALEIA member, a Certified Criminal Analyst, and past Treasurer of the IALEIA Mid-Atlantic Chapter. She possesses a Bachelor of Science degree in Business Administration, with a major in finance from Bryant College. She is also a member of the Association of Certified Fraud Examiners and wrote an article for the *IALEIA Journal*, titled "Getting the Most Out of the Internet." Prior to coming into law enforcement, she worked as a bankruptcy fraud specialist, a senior treasury assistant, and on Wall Street in the Commodities Exchange.

Wells, Ian

Ian Wells has had a long career in intelligence analysis and intelligence education. He currently holds a leadership role with the Centre for Policing, Intelligence and Counter Terrorism at Macquarie University in Sydney, Australia. Prior to this he spent over ten years as a senior academic working in intelligence education. He has held a wide range of intelligence appointments, including Principal Intelligence Analyst with the Queensland Criminal Justice Commission and Coordinator Intelligence and Manager Asia Branch (Analysis) within the Australian Security Intelligence Organisation. Ian also served two terms as senior South Asia analyst with the Office of National Assessments. Ian was a senior policy officer in the Australian Department of Defense in international relations and capability development, at various times heading up the areas responsible for developing peacekeeping policy, counter terrorism policy and major capability investment.

Williams, Gary S.

Captain Gary Williams retired from the Los Angeles Police Department after nearly 40 years of service. He was formerly the Commanding Officer of the Major Crimes Division, which included the anti-terrorism and organized crime intelligence sections. Captain Williams is a graduate of the University of Redlands (BSBM), and a graduate of the FBI National Academy. He was one of the original architects of the Los Angeles Joint Regional Intelligence Center (JRIC), the founder of the LAPD Terrorism Threat Assessment Center and the Regional Public/Private Information Collaboration System (RPICS) now used at the JRIC. He is also the former Secretary-Treasurer of the Association of Law Enforcement Intelligence Units (LEIU) and is now the Chief Financial Officer for the LEIU Foundation, a 501 C (3) organization supporting law enforcement intelligence efforts throughout the country.

Wright, Richard

Richard Wright began his law enforcement career with the Los Angeles Police Department in 1965 and worked a variety of uniformed, detective, and specialized assignments as an Officer, Sergeant and Lieutenant during 21 years of service. During the last six years at LAPD, he was assigned as a section leader in the Organized Crime Intelligence Division. In 1986, he joined the Simi Valley Police Department as a Captain and served as commanding officer of each of the Department's divisions as well as interim Chief of Police.

Captain Wright co-authored the California Peace Officers' Association's publication, *Criminal Intelligence Program for the Smaller Agency* and several other criminal intelligence articles. He also is a co-editor and contributing author of LEIU/IALEIA's *Intelligence 2000: Revising the Basic Elements.* Captain Wright has taught numerous criminal intelligence classes for the California Department of Justice and other law enforcement organizations as well as having served on the California Attorney General's Organized Crime Advisory Committee.

Captain Wright was a two-term LEIU General Chairperson beginning in May 2001. Before becoming General Chairperson, he served on the Executive Board for ten years as Southwestern Vice Zone Chairperson, Zone Chairperson and LEIU's Vice General Chairperson. Captain Wright retired from the Simi Valley Police Department in 2005, but remains active on LEIU's Executive Board as the Past General Chairperson. He currently consults and has a company specializing in internal administrative investigations for government agencies.

Richard Wright is a graduate of the 122nd session of the Federal Bureau of Investigation's National Academy and holds a bachelor's degree in Public Management and a master's degree in Public Communication from Pepperdine University.

INDEX

2021 release

Adobe® Illustrator®
The Professional Portfolio

AGAINST THE CL CK
mastering graphic technology

Managing Editor: Ellenn Behoriam
Cover & Interior Design: Erika Kendra

10   9   8   7   6   5   4   3   2   1

Print ISBN: 978-1-946396-58-7
Ebook ISBN: 978-1-946396-59-4

4710 28th Street North, Saint Petersburg, FL 33714
800-256-4ATC • www.againsttheclock.com

About Against The Clock

Against The Clock, long recognized as one of the nation's leaders in courseware development, has been publishing high-quality educational materials for the graphic and computer arts industries since 1990. The company has developed a solid and widely respected approach to teaching people how to effectively use graphics applications, while maintaining a disciplined approach to real-world problems.

Having developed the *Against The Clock* and the *Essentials for Design* series with Prentice Hall/Pearson Education, ATC drew from years of professional experience and instructor feedback to develop *The Professional Portfolio Series*, focusing on the Adobe Creative Suite. These books feature step-by-step explanations, detailed foundational information, and advice and tips from professionals that offer practical solutions to technical issues.

About the Author

Erika Kendra holds a BA in History and a BA in English Literature from the University of Pittsburgh. She began her career in the graphic communications industry as an editor at Graphic Arts Technical Foundation, and has been a full-time professional graphic designer since 1999.

Erika is the author or co-author of more than forty books about Adobe graphic design software. She has also written several books about graphic design concepts such as color reproduction and preflighting, and dozens of articles for industry online and print journals. Working with Against The Clock for almost twenty years, Erika was a key partner in developing *The Professional Portfolio Series* of software training books.

Contributing Editors and Artists

A big thank you to the people whose comments and expertise contributed to the success of these books:

- **Roger Morrissey,** technical editor
- **Gary Poyssick,** technical editor
- **Andrew Clark,** copy editor

Images used in the projects throughout this book are in the public domain unless otherwise noted. Individual artists' credit follow:

Project 5:
Einstein mural photo by Sidney Perry on Unsplash.com
DNA image by vitstudio on Publicdomainpictures.net

Project 7:
Artwork by Chance Hoffman

Project 8:
Guitar photo used to create the header background illustration by Dark Rider on Unsplash.com

Project Goals

Each project begins with a clear description of the overall concepts that are explained in the project; these goals closely match the different "stages" of the project workflow.

The Project Meeting

Each project includes the client's initial comments, which provide valuable information about the job. The Project Art Director, a vital part of any design workflow, also provides fundamental advice and production requirements.

Project Objectives

Each Project Meeting includes a summary of the specific skills required to complete the project.

Real-World Workflow

Projects are broken into logical lessons or "stages" of the workflow. Brief introductions at the beginning of each stage provide vital foundational material required to complete the task.

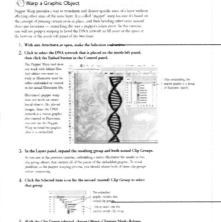

Step-By-Step Exercises

Every stage of the workflow is broken into multiple hands-on, step-by-step exercises.

Visual Explanations

Wherever possible, screen shots are annotated so students can quickly identify important information.

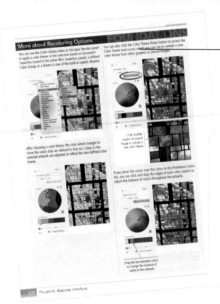

Illustrator Foundations

Additional functionality, related tools, and underlying graphic design concepts are included throughout the book.

Advice and Warnings

Where appropriate, sidebars provide shortcuts, warnings, or tips about the topic at hand.

Project Review

After completing each project, students can complete these fill-in-the-blank and short-answer questions to test their understanding of the concepts in the project.

Portfolio Builder Projects

Each step-by-step project is accompanied by a freeform project, allowing students to practice skills and creativity, resulting in an extensive and diverse portfolio of work.

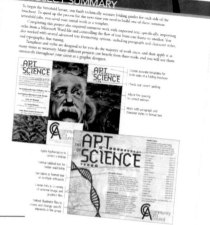

Visual Summary

Using an annotated version of the finished project, students can quickly identify the skills used to complete different aspects of the job.

The Against The Clock *Portfolio Series* teaches graphic design software tools and techniques entirely within the framework of real-world projects; we introduce and explain skills where they would naturally fall into a professional workflow. For example, rather than an entire chapter about printing (which most students find boring), we teach printing where you need to do so — when you complete a print-based project.

The project-based approach in *The Professional Portfolio Series* allows you to get in depth with the software beginning in Project 1 — you don't have to read several chapters of introductory material before you can start creating finished artwork.

Our approach also prevents "topic tedium" — in other words, we don't require you to read pages and pages of information about text (for example); instead, we explain text tools and options as part of larger projects (in this case, beginning with placing text on corporate identity pieces).

Clear, easy-to-read, step-by-step instructions walk you through every phase of each job, from creating a new file to saving the finished piece. Wherever logical, we also offer practical advice and tips about underlying concepts and graphic design practices that will benefit students as they enter the job market.

The projects in this book reflect a range of different types of Illustrator jobs, from creating a series of icons to designing a corporate identity to building a web page interface. When you finish the eight projects in this book (and the accompanying Portfolio Builder exercises), you will have a substantial body of work that should impress any potential employer.

The eight Illustrator projects are described briefly here; more detail is provided in the full table of contents (beginning on Page viii).

project 1

Campground Icons

❑ Setting up the Workspace

❑ Drawing with Basic Shapes

project 2

Regatta Artwork

❑ Drawing Complex Artwork

❑ Coloring and Painting Artwork

❑ Creating the Finished Poster

project 3

Identity Package

❑ Working with Gradient Meshes

❑ Working with Type

❑ Working with Multiple Artboards

❑ Combining Text and Graphics

As you complete the projects in this book, our goal is to familiarize you with the tool set so you can be more productive and more marketable in your career as a graphic designer.

It is important to keep in mind that Illustrator is an extremely versatile and powerful application. The sheer volume of available tools, panels, and features can seem intimidating when you first look at the software interface. Most of these tools, however, are fairly simple to use with a bit of background information and a little practice.

Wherever necessary, we explain the underlying concepts and terms that are required for understanding the software. And we're confident that these projects provide the practice so that you'll be able to create sophisticated artwork by the end of the very first project.

Prerequisites

To use *The Professional Portfolio Series,* you should know how to use your mouse to point and click, as well as how to drag items around the screen. You should be able to resize and arrange windows on your desktop to maximize your available space. You should know how to access drop-down menus, and understand how check boxes and radio buttons work. It also doesn't hurt to have a good understanding of how your operating system organizes files and folders, and how to navigate your way around them. If you're familiar with these fundamental skills, then you know all that's necessary to use the Portfolio Series.

Resource Files

All the files you need to complete the projects in this book — except, of course, the Illustrator application files — are on the Student Files Web page at againsttheclock.com. See the inside back cover of this book for access information.

Each archive (ZIP) file is named according to the related project (e.g., **Studio_AI21_RF.zip**). At the beginning of each project, you must download the archive for that project and expand it to access the resource files that you need to complete the exercises. Detailed instructions for this process are included in the Interface chapter.

Files required for the related Portfolio Builder exercises at the end of each project are also available on the Student Files page; these archives are also named by project (e.g., **Triumph_AI21_PB.zip**).

ATC Fonts

You must download and install the ATC fonts from the Student Files Web page to ensure that your exercises and projects work as described in the book. You should replace older (pre-2013) ATC fonts with the ones on the Student Files Web page.

Software Versions

This book was written and tested using the original release of Adobe Illustrator 2021 (version 25.0) from October 2020. You can find the specific version number in the Splash Screen that appears while your application is launching, or by choosing About Illustrator in the Illustrator/Help menu.

Because Adobe releases periodic upgrades throughout the year, some features and functionality might have changed since publication. Please check the Errata section of the Against The Clock website for any significant issues that might have arisen from these periodic upgrades.

System Requirements

The Professional Portfolio Series was designed to work on both Macintosh or Windows computers; where differences exist from one platform to another, we include specific instructions relative to each platform. One issue that remains different from Macintosh to Windows is the use of different modifier keys (Control, Shift, etc.) to accomplish the same task. When we present key commands, we always follow the same Macintosh/Windows format — Macintosh keys are listed first, then a slash, followed by the Windows key commands.

Adobe Illustrator is the industry-standard application for creating digital drawings or **vector images** (graphics composed of mathematically defined lines instead of pixels). Our goal in this book is to teach you how to use the available tools to create different types of work that you might encounter in your professional career. Some projects in this book focus on creating graphics and illustrations — the true heart of the application. You can also use the tools in Illustrator to combine type, graphics, and images into a cohesive design — as you will do in several projects to create posters, flyers, package design, and even a website interface.

The simple exercises in this introduction are designed for you to explore the Illustrator user interface. Whether you are new to the application or upgrading from a previous version, we highly recommend that you follow these steps to click around and become familiar with the basic workspace.

Explore the Illustrator Interface

The first time you launch Illustrator, you will see the default user interface (UI) settings as defined by Adobe. When you relaunch after you or another user has quit, the workspace defaults to the last-used settings — including open panels and the position of those panels on your screen. We designed the following exercise so you can explore different ways of controlling panels in the Illustrator user interface.

1. **Create a new empty folder named WIP on any writable disk (where you plan to save your work).**

2. **Download the InterfaceAI_AI21_RF.zip archive from the Student Files web page.**

3. **Macintosh users: Place the ZIP archive in your WIP folder, then double-click the file icon to expand it.**

   Windows users: Double-click the ZIP archive file to open it. Click the folder inside the archive and drag it into your primary WIP folder.

   The resulting **InterfaceAI** folder contains all the files you need to complete the exercises in this introduction.

Macintosh: Double-click the archive file icon to expand it.

Windows: Open the archive file, then drag the InterfaceAI folder from the archive to your WIP folder.

4. **Macintosh users: While pressing Command-Option-Shift, launch Illustrator. Hold down the modifier keys until Illustrator opens.**

   Windows users: While pressing Control-Alt-Shift, launch Illustrator. Hold down the modifier keys until Illustrator opens.

   This step resets Illustrator to the preference settings that are defined by Adobe as the application defaults. This helps to ensure that your application functions in the same way as what we show in our screenshots.

5. **If you get a warning message about GPU Performance, click OK.**

    GPU Performance enables faster on-screen rendering if your hardware meets the
    feature requirements. If you do not have the appropriate hardware, you will still
    be able to use all of the Illustrator toolset, but rendering will be processed by your
    computer's Central Processing Unit (CPU).

6. **Macintosh users: Open the Window menu and make sure the Application
    Frame option is toggled on.**

    Many menu commands and options in
    Illustrator are **toggles**, which means they
    are either on or off; when an option is
    already checked, that option is toggled
    on (visible or active). You can toggle an
    active option off by choosing the checked
    menu command, or toggle an inactive option on by choosing the unchecked menu
    command.

    This option should
    be checked.

Note:

*On Windows, the Ap-
plication Frame menu
command is not avail-
able; you can't turn off
the Application Frame
on the Windows OS.*

Understanding the Application Frame

On Windows, each running application is contained within
its own frame; all elements of the application — including
the Menu bar, panels, tools, and open documents — are
contained within the Application frame.

Adobe also offers the Application frame to Macintosh users as
an option for controlling the workspace. When the Application
frame is active, the entire workspace exists in a self-contained
area that can be moved around the screen. All elements of

the workspace (excluding the Menu bar) move when you
move the Application frame.

The Application frame is active by default, but you can toggle
it off by choosing Window>Application Frame. If the menu
option is checked, the Application frame is active; if the
menu option is not checked, it is inactive. (On Windows, the
Application Frame menu command is not available; you can't
turn off the Application Frame on the Windows OS.)

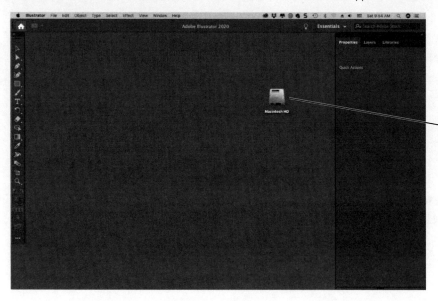

When the Application
frame is not active, the
desktop is visible behind
the workspace elements.

7. Review the options in the Home screen.

The default user interface shows a stored "Home" workspace. No panels are visible in this workspace. When you first launch the application, you have "quick start" access to several common file sizes. After one or more files have been opened, those buttons are replaced with icons for recently opened files.

Macintosh

Menu bar

Application bar

Link to your Adobe Creative Cloud account.

Windows

Menu bar

The Home workspace appears whenever Illustrator is running, but no file is open. As soon as you open or create a file, the interface reverts to show the last-used workspace arrangement.

The Macintosh and Windows workspaces are virtually identical, with a few primary exceptions:

- On Macintosh, the application bar appears below the Menu bar; the Close, Minimize, and Restore buttons appear on the left side of the application bar, and the Menu bar is not part of the Application frame.

- On Windows, the Close, Minimize, and Restore buttons appear at the right end of the Menu bar, which is part of the overall Application frame.

- Macintosh users have two extra menus (consistent with the Macintosh operating system structure). The Apple menu provides access to system-specific commands. The Illustrator menu follows the Macintosh system-standard format for all applications; this menu controls basic application operations such as About, Hide, Preferences, and Quit.

Note:

When a file is open, you can return to the Home workspace by clicking the Home icon in the left side of the Application/Menu bar.

8. Choose Window>Workspace>Essentials.

Saved **workspaces** provide one-click access to a defined group of panels.

9. Choose Window>Workspace>Reset Essentials.

If you or someone else changed anything, and then quit the application, those changes

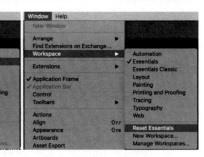

are remembered when Illustrator is relaunched. Because we can't be sure what your default settings show, completing this step resets the user interface to the built-in, default Essentials workspace so that your screen will match our screenshots.

Note:

If a menu or dialog box option is grayed out, it is not available for the active selection.

10. Macintosh users: Choose Illustrator>Preferences>User Interface.

Windows users: Choose Edit>Preferences>User Interface.

Remember that on Macintosh systems, the Preferences dialog box is accessed in the Illustrator menu; Windows users access the Preferences dialog box in the Edit menu.

Preferences customize the way many of the program's tools and options function. When you open the Preferences

Macintosh

Windows

dialog box, the active pane is the one you chose in the Preferences submenu. Once open, however, you can access any of the Preference categories by clicking a different option in the left pane; the right side of the dialog box displays options related to the active category.

In the User Interface preferences, you control the overall appearance of the workspace:

- **Brightness.** You might have noticed the rather dark appearance of the interface background. Illustrator uses the medium-dark "theme" as the default.

- **Canvas Color.** This setting determines the color of the space around the artboard.

- **Auto-Collapse Iconic Panels.** When panels are iconic/iconized (only the panel name and icon are visible), clicking a panel button opens that panel to the left of the icon. When this option is active, iconic panels automatically collapse as soon as you click away from the panel.

- **Open Documents As Tabs.** Checked by default, each open file appears as a separate tab below the Application/Menu bar. If you uncheck this option, each file appears in its own separate floating window.

- **Large Tabs.** Checked by default, this setting enlarges the text in the various panel tabs; this is part of Adobe's overall efforts to reduce eyestrain throughout the Creative Cloud suite. If you uncheck this option, the panel tabs revert to the smaller text of previous versions.

- **UI Scaling.** When you launch Illustrator the first time (or after clearing the preferences, as you did at the beginning of this exercise), Illustrator identifies your screen resolution and adjusts the application scale so that measurements on your screen mirror real-life measurements as accurately as possible. Scale Cursor Proportionately, which is checked by default, scales cursor icons in proportion to the UI Scaling that you have selected.

Note:

We use the Light UI brightness option throughout this book because text in the interface elements is easier to read in printed screen captures.

Note:

Changes to the UI Scaling options do not take effect until you relaunch the application.

11. In the Brightness menu, choose any option that you prefer.

12. Check the Auto-Collapse Iconic Panels option.

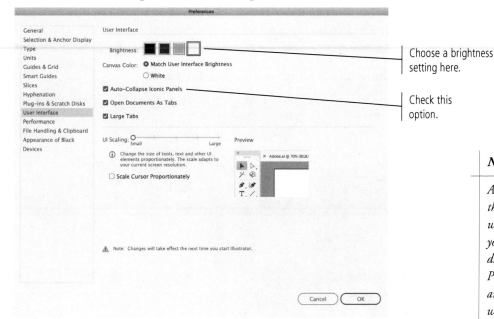

Choose a brightness setting here.

Check this option.

Note:

*As you work your way through this book, you will learn not only what you can do with these different collections of Preferences, but also **why** and **when** you might want to adjust them.*

We also changed the UI Scaling option to use the smallest setting. If you change this option, you see a warning that your changes take effect when you restart the application. Clicking OK automatically quits and relaunches Illustrator so that the UI Scaling change takes effect.

13. Click OK to close the Preferences dialog box.

14. Continue to the next exercise.

Explore the Arrangement of Illustrator Panels

Illustrator includes a number of options for arranging and managing the numerous panels, so you can customize and personalize the workspace to suit your specific needs. We designed the following exercise to give you an opportunity to explore different ways of controlling Illustrator panels.

Note:

Because workspace preferences are a matter of personal taste, the projects in this book instruct you to use certain tools and panels, but where you place those elements within the interface is up to you.

1. **With Illustrator open, review the options available in the user interface.**

   The default Essentials workspace includes the Tools panel on the left side of the screen and a set of expanded panels attached to the right side of the screen. (The area where the panels are stored is called the **panel dock**.)

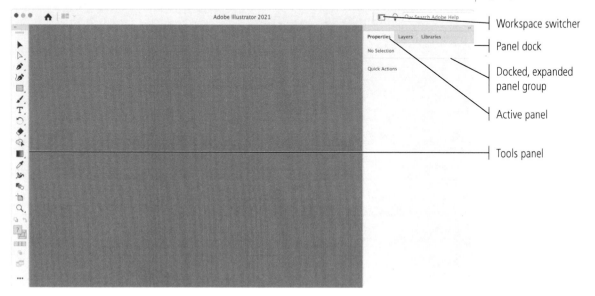

- Workspace switcher
- Panel dock
- Docked, expanded panel group
- Active panel
- Tools panel

2. **Review the panel dock on the right side of the interface.**

The active panel is lighter than others in the same panel group.

The area behind the panel tabs is called the **drop zone**.

Each panel in the group is represented by a tab.

3. **Click the Properties panel tab and drag it away from the docked group.**

   You can click an individual panel tab to drag it to another location, or click the panel group drop zone to move an entire group. If you drag a panel (group) away from the dock, it **floats** freely in the workspace.

Macintosh   **Windows**

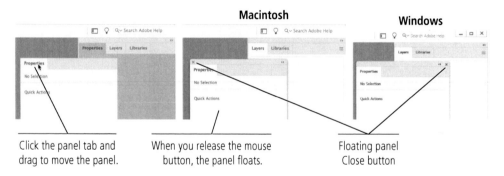

Click the panel tab and drag to move the panel.

When you release the mouse button, the panel floats.

Floating panel Close button

4. Click the floating Properties panel tab and drag until a blue highlight appears to the left of the docked panel group.

You can create multiple columns of panels in the dock. This can be very useful if you want easy access to a large number of panels, and if you have a monitor with enough available screen space.

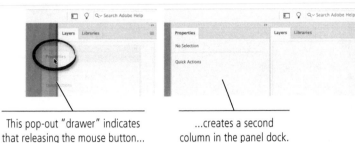

This pop-out "drawer" indicates that releasing the mouse button...

...creates a second column in the panel dock.

Note:

Most screenshots in this book show floating panels so we can focus on the most important issue in a particular image. In our production workflow, however, we make heavy use of docked and iconized panels and take full advantage of saved workspaces.

5. Choose Window>Artboards.

All Illustrator panels are available in the Window menu.

- If you choose a panel that is open but iconized, the panel expands left of its icon.

- If you choose a panel that is open in an expanded group, that panel comes to the front of the group.

- If you choose a panel that isn't currently open, it opens in the same position as when it was last closed.

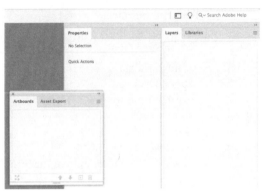

You can press the Tab key to temporarily hide all panels at one time. (Press the Tab key a second time to restore the same panels that were visible when you first pressed Tab.)

6. In the floating panel group, Control/right-click the Asset Export panel tab and choose Close from the contextual menu.

As we explained in the Getting Started section, when commands are different for the Macintosh and Windows operating systems, we include the different commands in the Macintosh/ Windows format. In this case, Macintosh users who do

Control/right-click the panel tab to access that panel's contextual menu.

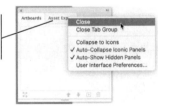

not have right-click mouse capability can press the Control key and click to access the contextual menu. You do not have to press Control *and* right-click to access the menus.

Control/right-clicking opens a contextual menu, where you can change a variety of behaviors or properties of the specific object you Control/right-click. Many elements in Illustrator have contextual menus, which make it easy to access item-specific options.

In this contextual menu, you can use the Close option to close a single panel or choose Close Tab Group to close all panels in the same group. (When a panel group is floating, you can also use the floating group's Close button to close an entire floating group.)

Note:

If you're using a Macintosh with a mouse that doesn't have right-click capability, we highly recommend that you purchase one that does. They're inexpensive, available in most retail stores, and will save you significant amounts of time when accessing contextual options.

7. **Click the Artboards panel tab (in the floating panel group) and drag until a blue highlight appears below the docked panel group in the right column.**

Individual panels can be dragged to different locations (including into different groups) by dragging the panel's tab. The target location — where the panel will be located when you release the mouse button — is identified by the blue highlight.

- If the highlight surrounds an existing panel group, the dragged panel will become part of the highlighted group.

- If the highlight appears between existing panel groups (or at an edge of the dock), the dragged panel will create a new group at the location of the highlight.

The highlight shows where the panel will be placed if you release the mouse button.

The dragged panel is moved into the dock, in its own group.

8. **Hover the mouse cursor over the bottom edge of the Layers/Libraries panel group (in the right column of the dock) until you see a two-facing arrow icon, then click and drag up.**

When you drag the bottom edge of a docked group, other variable panels in the same column expand or contract to fit the available space. By "variable panels," we mean any panel that has an undefined number of options. Some panels, such as the Stroke panel, have a fixed number of options so they do not expand or contract. The Layers panel, on the other hand, can list a variable number of items so it can be made larger or smaller.

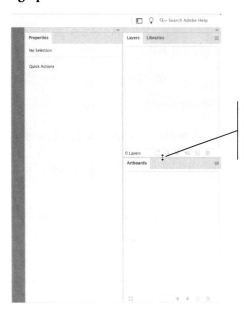

Dragging the bottom edge of a docked panel group changes the height of that group.

Note:

You can drag the left edge of a column to change the width of any docked column.

9. **Double-click the dock title bar above the docked icons to collapse the docked panels to icons.**

    You can independently iconize or expand each column of docked panels and each floating panel group.

Double-click the title bar at the top of the dock column to collapse or expand it.

Each column in the dock can be iconized independently.

Note:

You can double-click the panel tab in an expanded group to minimize that group, or collapse it down to show only the panel tabs.

10. **Hover the mouse cursor over the left edge of the iconized dock column until you see a two-facing arrow icon, then click and drag right.**

    When panels are iconized, each panel is represented by a button that defaults to show the icon and panel name. Narrowing the iconized dock column reduces the panel buttons to show only the related icons.

Icons that are grouped together in the dock represent a panel group.

Dragging the left edge of a dock column changes the width of all panels in that column.

11. **Control/right-click the title bar above either column of docked panel icons. Make sure the Auto-Collapse Iconic Panels option is toggled on (checked), then click away from the contextual menu to dismiss it.**

    Because you turned on the Auto-Collapse option in the User Interface preferences, this toggle is already checked. You can use either option — preference or contextual menu command — to toggle the option on or off at any time.

Dock title bar

This option should be checked (active).

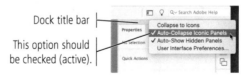

12. **In the panel dock, click the top button (Layers).**

    Clicking a collapsed panel icon expands that panel to the left of the icon. If you expand a panel that is part of a group, the entire group expands; the icon you click is the active panel in the group.

The icon you clicked is the active panel in the expanded group.

The panel name appears in a tool tip when the cursor hovers over the icon.

13. Click away from the expanded panel, anywhere in the workspace.

Because the Auto-Collapse option is active, the expanded panel group collapses back to an icon when you click away from the panel.

14. On the left side of the workspace, review the Tools panel.

The default Tools panel in the built-in Essentials workspace includes a limited set of the dozens of tools that are available in Illustrator. The More button at the bottom of the Tools panel provides quick access to the complete set, so that you can add the hidden tools into the Tools panel (see Customizing Tools Panels on Page 12).

15. Choose Window>Toolbars>Advanced.

This command restores all tools, including the nested variations, to the Tools panel.

Note:

Throughout this book, we assume you are using the Advanced Tools panel.

16. If you don't see all of the panel options, double-click the Tools panel title bar.

The Tools panel can be displayed as either one or two columns; double-clicking the Tools panel title bar toggles between these two modes.

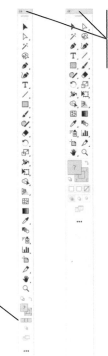

Double-click the Tools panel title bar to toggle between the one- and two-column layouts.

If your monitor cannot show all options, use the panel in two-column mode.

Note:

You can also single-click the double-arrow icon in the Tools panel title bar to switch the panel between one- and two-column formats.

Note:

Some monitors — especially laptops — are not high enough to display the large number of tools that are available in Illustrator's Tools panel. If this is the case, you should use the two-column mode.

17. Continue to the next exercise.

Identifying and Accessing Illustrator Tools

In the Illustrator Tools panel, tool icons that show a small black arrow in the lower-right corner have **nested tools**. You can access nested tools by clicking the primary tool and holding down the mouse button until a pop-up menu shows the nested variations (you can release the mouse button once the nested tools appear), or Control/right-clicking the tool in the panel.

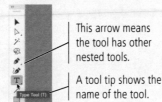

This arrow means the tool has other nested tools.

A tool tip shows the name of the tool.

If you hover your mouse over a tool, a pop-up **tool tip** shows the name of the tool, as well as the associated keyboard shortcut if one exists. If a tool has a defined shortcut, pressing that key activates the associated tool. (If you don't see tool tips, check the Show Tool Tips option in the General pane of the Preferences dialog box.)

If you click the bar on the right of the nested-tool menu, the nested-tool options separate into their own floating toolboxes, so you can more easily access the nested variations. (The primary tool is not removed from the main Tools panel.)

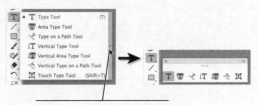

Click here to tear off a separate panel with all the related tools.

The chart below offers a quick reference of nested tools, as well as the keyboard shortcut, if any, for each tool. Nested tools are shown indented. This chart shows the tool arrangement in the Advanced (complete) toolbar.

- ► Selection tool (V)
- ▷ Direct Selection tool (A)
  - ▷⁺ Group Selection tool
- ⅋ Magic Wand tool (Y)
- ⅋ Lasso tool (Q)
- ⅋ Pen tool (P)
  - ⁺⅋ Add Anchor Point tool (+)
  - ⅋ Delete Anchor Point tool (-)
  - ⋀ Anchor Point tool (Shift-C)
- ⅋ Curvature tool (Shift-`)
- T Type tool (T)
  - Ⓣ Area Type tool
  - ⅋ Type on a Path tool
  - ↓T Vertical Type tool
  - ↓Ⓣ Vertical Area Type tool
  - ⅋ Vertical Type on a Path tool
  - Ⓣ Touch Type tool (Shift-T)
- / Line Segment tool (\)
  - ⌒ Arc tool
  - ◎ Spiral tool
  - ▦ Rectangular Grid tool
  - ⊕ Polar Grid tool

- ▢ Rectangle tool (M)
  - ▢ Rounded Rectangle tool
  - ◯ Ellipse tool (L)
  - ⬡ Polygon tool
  - ☆ Star tool
  - ◉ Flare tool
- ✎ Paintbrush tool (B)
  - ✎ Blob Brush tool (Shift-B)
- ⅋ Shaper tool (Shift-N)
  - ✏ Pencil tool (N)
  - ⅋ Smooth tool
  - ✎ Path Eraser tool
  - ⅋ Join tool
- ◆ Eraser tool (Shift-E)
  - ✂ Scissors tool (C)
  - ✎ Knife tool
- ↻ Rotate tool (R)
  - ▷◀ Reflect tool (O)
  - ⊡ Scale tool (S)
  - ⅋ Shear tool
  - ⅋ Reshape tool

- ⅋ Width tool (Shift-W)
  - ◤ Warp tool (Shift-R)
  - ⅋ Twirl tool
  - ⅋ Pucker tool
  - ⅋ Bloat tool
  - ◤ Scallop tool
  - ⅋ Crystallize tool
  - ⅋ Wrinkle tool
- ⅋ Free Transform tool (E)
  - ⅋ Puppet Warp tool
- ⅋ Shape Builder tool (Shift-M)
  - ⅋ Live Paint Bucket tool (K)
  - ⅋ Live Paint Selection tool (Shift-L)
- ⅋ Perspective Grid tool (Shift-P)
  - ⅋ Perspective Selection tool (Shift-V)
- ⅋ Mesh tool (U)
- ▊ Gradient tool (G)
- ✎ Eyedropper tool (I)
  - ⅋ Measure tool
- ⅋ Blend tool (W)

- ⅋ Symbol Sprayer tool (Shift-S)
  - ⅋ Symbol Shifter tool
  - ⅋ Symbol Scruncher tool
  - ⅋ Symbol Sizer tool
  - ⅋ Symbol Spinner tool
  - ⅋ Symbol Stainer tool
  - ⅋ Symbol Screener tool
  - ⅋ Symbol Styler tool
- ⅃⅃⅃ Column Graph tool (J)
  - ⅋ Stacked Column Graph tool
  - ⅋ Bar Graph tool
  - ⅋ Stacked Bar Graph tool
  - ⅋ Line Graph tool
  - ⅋ Area Graph tool
  - ⅋ Scatter Graph tool
  - ⅋ Pie Graph tool
  - ⊗ Radar Graph tool
- ⅋ Artboard tool (Shift-O)
- ⅋ Slice tool (Shift-K)
  - ⅋ Slice Selection tool
- ✋ Hand tool (H)
  - ⅋ Print Tiling tool
- 🔍 Zoom tool (Z)

The Tools panel can be customized to show only certain tools, making it easier and quicker to find what you need to complete a given task. The built-in Essentials workspace, for example, includes only the more commonly used drawing tools.

The Find More Tools button ⋯ at the bottom of the Tools panel provides access to the entire toolset, regardless of which tools are currently available in the Tools panel.

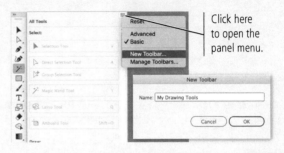

Tools that are already in the Tools panel appear grayed out in the pop-up menu. You can drag additional tools into the Tools panel from the menu. You can also drag to reposition existing tools within the panel.

You can remove a tool from the Tools panel by simply dragging it away from the primary Tools panel into the pop-up edit panel.

Drag a tool from the pop-up menu between existing tools to add it to the Tools panel:

Drag a tool onto another tool to add it as a nested tool in that location:

Drag a tool away from the primary Tools panel (into the pop-up edit panel) to remove it:

In addition to modifying the built-in Tools panels, you can also create custom Tools panels that you can recall at any time.

The New Toolbar option in the Find More Tools panel menu opens a dialog box where you can name the new panel. (You can also choose Window>Toolbars>New Toolbar.)

Click here to open the panel menu.

Clicking OK creates a new empty Tools panel; the large plus-sign icon indicates that you have not yet added any tools to it. You can click the Find More Tools button at the bottom of the new panel to add tools. The process is the same as adding, reorganizing, and removing tools from the basic Tools panel.

Changes to a custom Tools panel are saved automatically. If you close a custom panel (by clicking the panel's Close button), the same tools appear in the same position when you reopen it. Existing custom Tools panels can always be opened in the Window>Toolbars submenu.

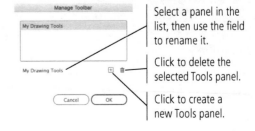

Choosing Window>Toolbars>Manage Toolbars opens a dialog box where you can rename or delete custom panels.

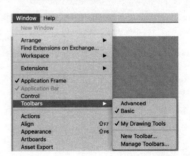

Select a panel in the list, then use the field to rename it.

Click to delete the selected Tools panel.

Click to create a new Tools panel.

Customizing Keyboard Shortcuts

In addition to positioning specific panels in precise locations, you can also add to or modify the keyboard shortcuts used for different functions in the application.

Choosing Edit>Keyboard Shortcuts opens a dialog box where you can modify the shortcuts for menu commands and tools. If you assign a shortcut that isn't part of the default set, you have to save a custom set of shortcuts (Illustrator won't let you modify the default set of keyboard shortcuts).

When more than one set of shortcuts exists (i.e., if you or someone else has added to or changed the default settings), you can switch between the different sets using the menu at the top of the dialog box.

 Create a Saved Workspace

By now you should understand that you have virtually unlimited control over the appearance of your Illustrator workspace — what panels are visible, where and how they appear, and even the size of individual panels and panel groups.

Over time you will develop personal preferences based on your work habits and project needs. Rather than re-establishing every workspace element each time you return to Illustrator, you can save your custom workspace settings so you can recall them with a single click.

1. **Click the Workspace switcher on the right side of the Application/Menu bar and choose New Workspace.**

    Again, keep in mind that we list differing commands in the Macintosh/Windows format. On Macintosh, the Workspace switcher is in the Application bar; on Windows, it's in the Menu bar.

Workspace switcher

2. **In the New Workspace dialog box, type Portfolio and click OK.**

Note:

Because workspace preferences are largely a matter of personal taste, the projects in this book instruct you regarding which panels to use, but not where to place those elements within the interface.

Note:

The Manage Workspaces option opens a dialog box where you can rename or delete user-defined custom workspaces. You can't alter the default workspaces that come with the application.

3. **Click the Workspace switcher and choose Essentials from the list of available workspaces.**

   Calling a saved workspace restores the last-used state of the workspace. You have made a number of changes since calling the Essentials workspace at the beginning of the previous exercise, so calling the Essentials workspace restores the last state of that workspace — in essence, nothing changes from the saved Portfolio workspace.

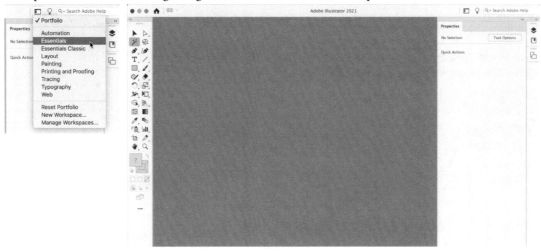

4. **Open the Workspace switcher and choose Reset Essentials (or choose Window>Workspace>Reset Essentials).**

   Remember, saved workspaces remember the last-used state; calling a workspace again restores the panels exactly as they were the last time you used that workspace. For example, if you close a panel that is part of a saved workspace, the closed panel will not be reopened the next time you call the same workspace. To restore the saved state of the workspace, including opening closed panels or repositioning moved ones, you have to use the Reset option.

5. **Continue to the next exercise.**

Explore the Illustrator Document Window

There is much more to using Illustrator than simply arranging panels around the workspace. In this exercise, you open several Illustrator files and explore interface elements that will be important as you begin creating digital artwork.

Before completing this exercise, you should download and install the ATC fonts from the Student Files web page.

1. **In Illustrator, choose File>Open and navigate to your WIP>InterfaceAI folder.**

2. **Click to select butterfly.ai in the list of available files, then press Shift and click tiedye.ai.**

   The Open dialog box is a system-standard navigation dialog box. This is one area of significant difference between Macintosh and Windows users.

   On both operating systems, this step selects all files including and between the two you click. Pressing Shift allows you to select multiple consecutive files in the list. You can also press Command/Control and click to select multiple non-consecutive files.

Note:

Press Command/ Control-O to access the Open dialog box.

Macintosh   Windows

3. **Click Open. If you see a pop-up window with an introductory tour, click the Okay button to dismiss the window.**

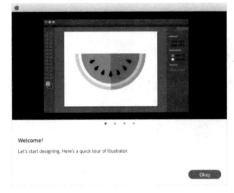

Welcome!

Let's start designing. Here's a quick tour of Illustrator.

Okay

4. **Click the document tab for tiedye.ai if it is not already active.**

    Illustrator files open in the document window. Across the top of the document window, each open document is represented by a separate tab; the document tabs show the file name, current view percentage, color space, and current viewing mode.

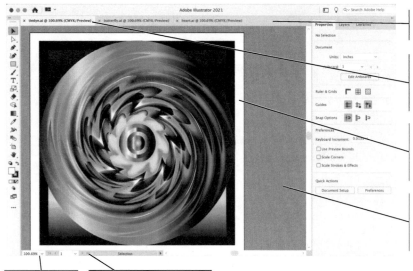

Open files appear in a document window.

The **document tab** shows the active file name, view percentage, color space, and current viewing mode.

The **artboard** is essentially the digital page, or the area where artwork should be created or placed.

The **canvas** (sometimes called the **pasteboard**) around the artboard defaults to a gray color.

View Percentage menu/field

Use these options to navigate from one artboard to another within a single file.

5. **Open the View Percentage menu in the bottom-left corner of the document window and choose 200%.**

    Different people prefer different view percentages, depending on a number of factors, such as eyesight, monitor size, and so on. You can zoom an Illustrator document from 3.13% to 64000%.

    As you complete the projects in this book, you'll see our screen shots zoom in or out as necessary to show you the most relevant part of a particular file. In most cases, we do not tell you what specific view percentage to use for a particular exercise unless it is specifically required for the work being done.

Note:

Files open in the order you select them in the Open dialog box. Don't worry if they appear on your screen in a different order than what you see in our screen captures.

Note:

Macintosh users: If you turn off the Application frame (Window>Application Frame), the new document will have its own title bar.

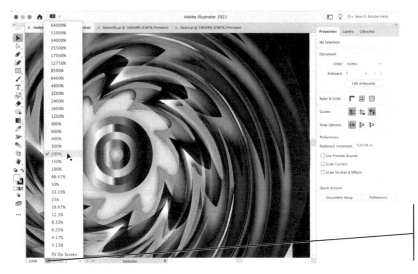

Type a specific percentage in the field or choose one of the predefined percentages from the menu.

6. Choose View>Fit Artboard in Window.

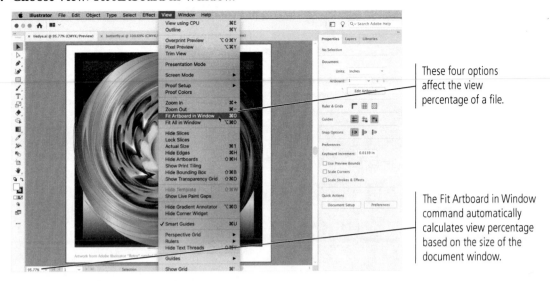

These four options affect the view percentage of a file.

The Fit Artboard in Window command automatically calculates view percentage based on the size of the document window.

7. Review the options in the Properties panel.

The Properties panel is context sensitive, which means it provides access to different options depending on which tool is active and what is selected in the document.

When nothing is selected in the file, you can use the Properties panel to change a number of settings related to the overall file. The most important options open the Document Setup dialog box and the Preferences dialog box (more about these specific elements in the projects).

Document and application-specific options are available when nothing is selected.

Note:

Most of the options in the Properties panel duplicate options in other panels or menu commands.

8. **Click the Selection tool at the top of the Tools panel to make that tool active, then click the purple square at the edge of the artwork to select that object.**

The Selection tool (the black arrow) is used to select entire objects in the file. The Control panel shows the attributes of the selected object (in this case, a path).

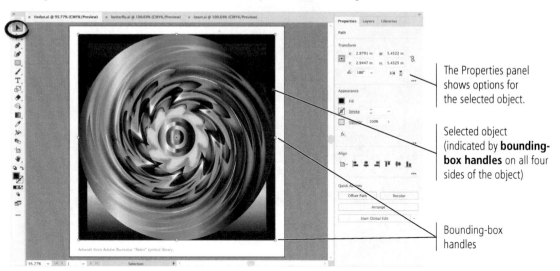

The Properties panel shows options for the selected object.

Selected object (indicated by **bounding-box handles** on all four sides of the object)

Bounding-box handles

9. **Choose Window>Control to open the Control panel.**

The Control panel, which appears at the top of the interface, is another context-sensitive tool that shows options related to the selected object.

10. **Click the text near the bottom of the artwork to select the type object.**

Like the Properties panel, the Control panel changes to show options related to type objects.

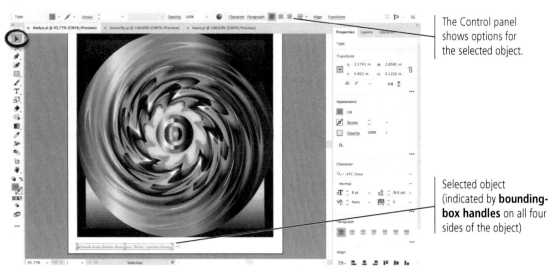

The Control panel shows options for the selected object.

Selected object (indicated by **bounding-box handles** on all four sides of the object)

11. **Continue to the next exercise.**

What you see in the Control panel depends on the size of your monitor (or the size of your Application frame if you've made it smaller than your monitor). When working with a smaller space, some options are not available directly in the panel; instead, you have to use the hot-text links (identified by an underline) to open pop-up versions of the related panel.

In the images below, for example, you have to click the Paragraph hot-text link in the top version to open the pop-up panel and access the paragraph alignment options. In the wider version, you can access three paragraph alignment options directly in the Control panel.

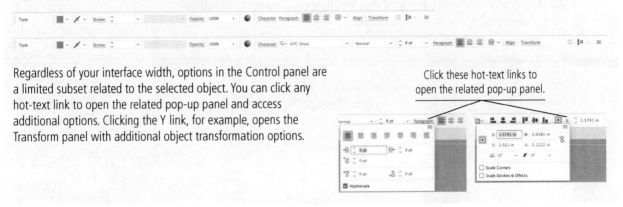

Regardless of your interface width, options in the Control panel are a limited subset related to the selected object. You can click any hot-text link to open the related pop-up panel and access additional options. Clicking the Y link, for example, opens the Transform panel with additional object transformation options.

Click these hot-text links to open the related pop-up panel.

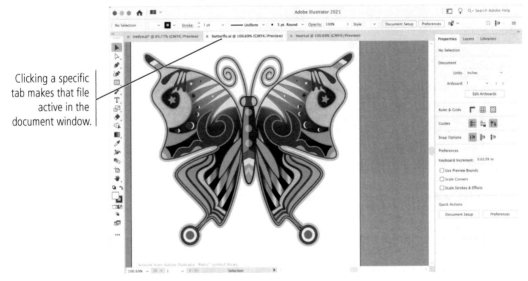

Explore the Arrangement of Multiple Documents

Because designers frequently need to work with more than one Illustrator file at once, Illustrator incorporates a number of options for arranging multiple documents. We designed the following simple exercise to allow you to explore these options.

1. Click the butterfly.ai tab at the top of the document window.

Clicking a specific tab makes that file active in the document window.

2. **Choose Window>Arrange>Float in Window.**

Floating a document separates the file into its own document window.

The title bar of the separate document window shows the same information that was in the document tab.

> **Note:**
>
> *You can separate all open files by choosing Window>Arrange> Float All In Windows.*

> **Note:**
>
> *You can drag document tabs to rearrange their order. You can also drag a floating window back to the document tab bar, or use the Consolidate All option to restore the floating document to a tabbed file.*

3. **In the Application/Menu bar, click the Arrange Documents button to open the menu of defined arrangements.**

   The Arrange Documents menu includes a number of tiling options for arranging multiple open files in the workspace.

   On Macintosh systems, the Application bar must be visible to access the Arrange Documents button. On Windows, the Arrange Documents menu appears to the right of the Help menu in the Menu bar.

   Consolidate All button

   The appearance of each icon suggests the result of each option.

   Rolling your mouse cursor over an icon shows the arrangement name in a tool tip.

4. **Click the Consolidate All button (top-left) in the Arrange Documents panel.**

   The Consolidate All button consolidates all floating documents into a single tabbed document window (just like the default arrangement).

> **Note:**
>
> *When multiple floating document windows are open, two options in the Window>Arrange menu allow you to cascade or tile the different document windows.*

   The remaining buttons in the top row separate all open files into individual document windows, and then arrange the different windows as indicated.

   The lower options use a specific number of floating documents (2-Up, 3-Up, etc.); if more files are open than an option indicates, the extra files are consolidated as tabs in the first document window.

5. **Click the button at the bottom of the Tools panel to show the screen mode options.**

   Illustrator has four different **screen modes**, which change the way the document window displays on the screen. The default mode, which you saw when you opened these three files, is called Normal Screen mode.

   Presentation Mode ⇧F
   ✓ Normal Screen Mode
   Full Screen Mode with Menu Bar
   Full Screen Mode

6. **Choose Full Screen Mode with Menu Bar from the Screen Mode menu.**

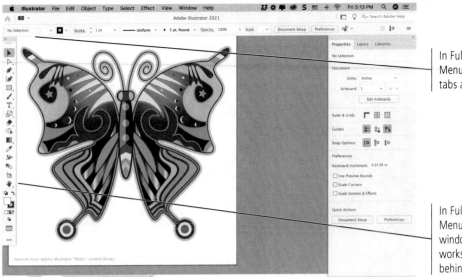

In Full Screen Mode with Menu Bar, the document tabs are hidden.

In Full Screen Mode with Menu Bar, the document window fills the entire workspace and extends behind the docked panels.

7. **Click the Screen Mode button at the bottom of the Tools panel and choose Full Screen Mode.**

All open files are listed at the bottom of the Window menu. You can use those menu options to navigate from one file to another, which is particularly useful in Full Screen Mode with Menu Bar because the document tabs are not visible in this mode.

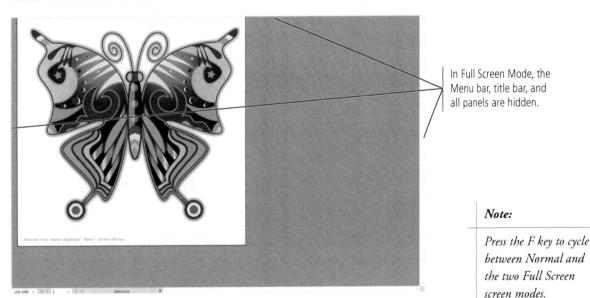

In Full Screen Mode, the Menu bar, title bar, and all panels are hidden.

Note:

Press the F key to cycle between Normal and the two Full Screen screen modes.

8. **Press the Escape key to exit Full Screen Mode and return to Normal Screen Mode.**

9. Press Shift-F to enter Presentation mode.

Presentation mode fills the entire screen with the active spread; the area around the page is solid black.

In Presentation mode, the page, surrounded by solid black, fills the entire screen.

10. Press ESC to exit Presentation mode.

11. Click the Close button on the butterfly.ai tab. If asked whether you want to save changes, click Don't Save.

Closing the Application frame closes all files open in that frame.

Clicking the Close button on a document tab closes only that file.

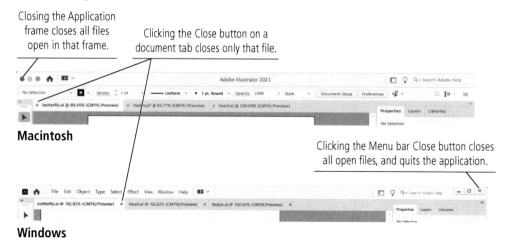

Macintosh

Clicking the Menu bar Close button closes all open files, and quits the application.

Windows

12. Macintosh: Click the Close button in the top-left corner of the Application bar. If asked, click Don't Save for all files.

Closing the Macintosh Application frame closes all open files, but does not quit the application.

Windows: Click the Close button on each document tab to close the files. If asked, click Don't Save for all files.

Clicking the Close button on the Windows Menu bar closes all open files *and* quits the application. To close open files *without* quitting, you have to manually close each file using the document tabs.

As we show you how to complete different stages of the workflow, we usually won't tell you when to change your view percentage because that's largely a matter of personal preference. However, you should understand the different options for navigating around an Illustrator file so you can efficiently get to what you want.

To change the file view percentage, you can type a specific percent in the **View Percentage field** of the document window or choose from the predefined options in the menu.

You can also click with the **Zoom tool** to increase the view percentage in specific, predefined intervals (the same intervals you see in the View Percentage menu in the bottom-left corner of the document window). Pressing Option/Alt with the Zoom tool allows you to zoom out in the same defined percentages.

Animated Zoom is active by default when GPU Preview is enabled; clicking and dragging with the Zoom tool dynamically changes the view percentage depending on which way you drag (right to enlarge or left to reduce).

If you turn off Animated Zoom in the Performance pane of the Preferences dialog box, you can drag a marquee with the Zoom tool to zoom in to a specific location; the area surrounded by the marquee fills the available space in the document window.

The **View menu** also provides options for changing view percentage. (The Zoom In and Zoom Out options step through the same predefined view percentages as clicking with the Zoom tool.)

Zoom In	Command/Control-plus (+)
Zoom Out	Command/Control-minus (-)
Fit Artboard in Window	Command/Control-0 (zero)
Fit All in Window	Command-Option-0/ Control-Alt-0 (zero)
Actual Size (100%)	Command/Control-1

Whatever your view percentage, you can use the **Hand tool** to drag the file around in the document window. The tool changes what is visible in the window; it has no effect on objects in the file. If the insertion point is not flashing, you can press the Spacebar to temporarily access the Hand tool; when the insertion point is placed, you can press the Option/Alt key to temporarily access the Hand tool.

Using the Navigator Panel

The **Navigator panel** (Window>Navigator) is another method of adjusting what you see, including the view percentage and the specific area that is visible in the document window. The Navigator panel shows a thumbnail of the active file; a red rectangle (called the Proxy Preview Area) represents exactly how much of the document shows in the document window. You can drag the proxy in the panel to change the visible portion of the image in the document window.

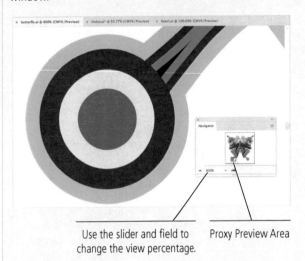

Use the slider and field to change the view percentage.   Proxy Preview Area

Working with Saved Views

Named views can be helpful if you repeatedly return to the same area and view percentage. By choosing View>New View, you can save the current view with a specific name.

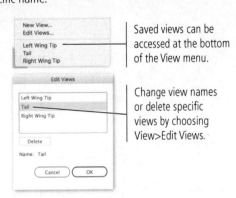

Saved views can be accessed at the bottom of the View menu.

Change view names or delete specific views by choosing View>Edit Views.

Campground Icons

Cooper's Lake Campground is a family-oriented campground that hosts individual camping, as well as large planned events at their grounds. The owner has hired you to create a digital collection of icons that they can use to create signs, print on a variety of collateral, and place on their website.

This project incorporates the following skills:

❑ Placing raster images into an Illustrator file to use as drawing templates

❑ Creating and managing simple shapes and lines

❑ Using various tools to transform objects' color, position, and shape

❑ Cloning objects to minimize repetitive tasks

❑ Using sublayers and groups to organize and manage artwork

❑ Drawing complex shapes by combining simple shapes

We have a set of icons on our website, but we need to use the same artwork in other places as well — signs throughout the park, flyers that we hand out to new guests, and so on.

Our printer told us that the symbols on our website are "low res," so they can't be used for print projects. The printer also said he needs vector graphics that will scale larger and still look good. The printer suggested we hire a designer to create digital versions of the icons so we can use them for a wide variety of purposes, from large signs to small cards, to anything else that might come up.

We need you to help us figure out exactly what we need, and then create the icons for us.

Basically, we have the icons, but they're low-resolution raster images, so they only work for the web, and they can't be enlarged. The good news is that you can use the existing icons as templates and, more or less, trace them to create the new icons.

The client needs files that can be printed cleanly and scaled from a couple of inches up to several feet. Illustrator vector files are perfect for this type of job. In fact, vector graphics get their resolution from the printer being used for a specific job, so you can scale them to any size you want without losing quality.

To complete this project, you will:

❑ Use a variety of tools and techniques to create, align, and transform basic shapes

❑ Control objects' fill and stroke attributes

❑ Import raster images to use as artwork templates

❑ Use sublayers and groups to manage complex artwork

❑ Use the Line Segment tool to create a complex object from a set of straight lines

❑ Edit properties of Live Shapes to create finished icon artwork

❑ Draw and combine basic Live Shapes using the Shaper tool

❑ Draw complex artwork with the Pencil tool

STAGE 1 / Setting up the Workspace

There are two primary types of digital artwork: raster images and vector graphics. (**Line art**, sometimes categorized as a third type of image, is actually a type of raster image.)

Raster images are pixel-based, made up of a grid of individual **pixels** (**rasters** or **bits**) in rows and columns (called a **bitmap**). Raster files are **resolution dependent**; their resolution is determined when you scan, photograph, or create the file. As a professional graphic designer, you should have a basic understanding of the following terms and concepts:

- **Pixels per inch (ppi)** is the number of pixels in one horizontal or vertical inch of a digital raster file.

- **Lines per inch (lpi)** is the number of halftone dots produced in a linear inch by a high-resolution imagesetter, which simulates the appearance of continuous-tone color.

- **Dots per inch (dpi)** or **spots per inch (spi)** is the number of dots produced by an output device in a single line of output.

Drawing objects that you create in Illustrator are **vector graphics**, which are composed of mathematical descriptions of a series of lines and points. Vector graphics are **resolution independent**; they can be freely scaled and are output at the resolution of the output device.

Create a New Document

In this project, you work with the basics of creating vector graphics in Illustrator, using a number of different drawing tools, adding color, and managing various aspects of your artwork. The first step is to create a new document for building your artwork.

1. **Download Camping_AI21_RF.zip from the Student Files web page.**

2. **Expand the ZIP archive in your WIP folder (Macintosh) or copy the archive contents into your WIP folder (Windows).**

   This results in a folder named **Camping**, which contains all of the files you need for this project. You should also use this folder to save the files you create in this project.

   If necessary, refer to Page 1 of the Interface chapter for specific information on expanding or accessing the required resource files.

3. **In Illustrator, choose File>New.**

   You have several options for creating a new file:

   - Choose File>New;
   - Use the associated keyboard shortcut, Command/Control-N; or
   - Click the Create New button in the Home workspace.

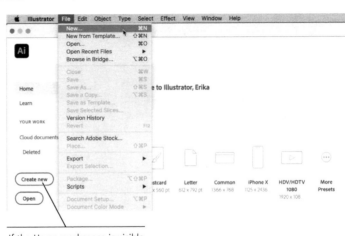

If the Home workspace is visible, click the Create New button.

4. **Click the Print option at the top of the resulting New Document dialog box.**

The New Document dialog box offers a number of preset sizes and prebuilt starter templates, broken into categories based on the intended output.

When you choose the Print category, you see common page sizes such as Letter and Legal. The Print presets automatically default to the CMYK color mode and 300 ppi raster effects, which are required for commercial printing applications. For all other categories of presets (Mobile, Web, Film & Video, and Art & Illustration), the new document defaults to the RGB color mode and 72 ppi raster effects. (You will learn more about the importance of those options in later projects.)

Note:

You can change the color mode and raster effects settings by expanding the Advanced Options in the right side of the New Document dialog box.

Click a category name to show related presets.

Click to select an existing preset or template.

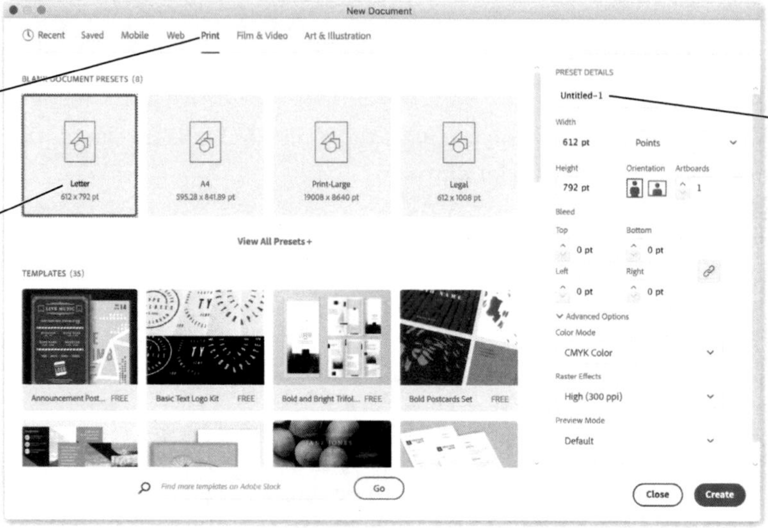

Click here to define a new file name.

5. **On the right side of the dialog box, type `icons` in the Name field.**

6. **Choose Points in the Units menu, and choose Portrait Orientation.**

Although inches is the standard unit of measurement in the United States, the default **points** option is a standard unit of measurement for graphic designers. There are 72 points in an inch. Don't worry, though, about being able to define everything in points; Illustrator can make the calculations for you.

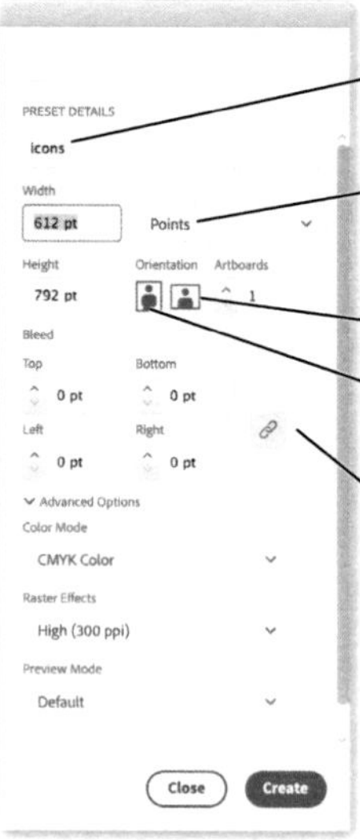

File name

Default unit of measurement

Landscape

Portrait

When linked, all four Bleed fields will have the same value.

7. **Make sure the Number of Artboards field is set to 1.**

Options on the right side of the dialog box, such as artboard orientation and units of measurement, default to the last-used settings.

Illustrator includes the ability to create multiple **artboards** (basically, Illustrator's version of "pages"). For this project, you need only a single artboard.

8. **Set all four bleed values to `0`.**

Bleed is the amount an object needs to extend past the edge of the artboard or page to meet the mechanical requirements of commercial printing.

9. Click Create to create the new file. Immediately choose View>Fit Artboard in Window.

In the resulting document window, the letter-size "page" (or artboard) is represented by a dark black line.

The color of the pasteboard (the area around the artboard) defaults to match the brightness of the user interface. You can change this setting to show a white pasteboard in the User Interface pane of the Preferences dialog box.

As we explained in the Interface chapter, the panels you see depend on what was done the last time you (or someone else) used the application. Because workspace arrangement is such a personal preference, we tell you what panels you need to use, but we don't tell you where to place them.

Note:

Our screenshots show the Macintosh OS using the Application frame.

The name you defined appears in the document tab.

This is the artboard edge.

The artboard area is white.

The area outside the artboard is gray.

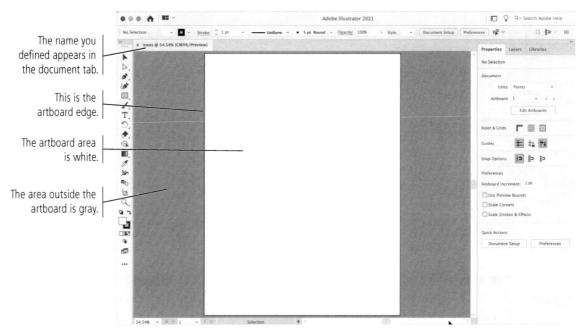

10. Choose File>Save As. In the resulting dialog box, click the Save on Your Computer button.

When you save a file in Illustrator, you now have a choice to save the file as an Illustrator Cloud document, or a regular Illustrator file on your desktop. If you choose the Save to Cloud Documents button, the file is saved in your Creative Cloud account with the special extension ".aic".

Note:

Press Command/ Control-S to save a document, or press Command/Control-Shift-S to open the Save As dialog box.

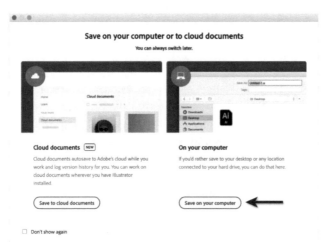

11. Navigate to your WIP>Camping folder as the target destination.

If you assign a name in the New Document dialog box (as you did in Step 5), that name becomes the default file name in the Save As dialog box.

The dialog box defaults to Adobe Illustrator (.ai) format, and the extension is automatically added to the name you defined.

12. Click Save in the Save As dialog box. Review the options in the resulting Illustrator Options dialog box.

This dialog box determines what is stored in the resulting file. The default options are adequate for most files.

- Use the **Version** menu to save files to be compatible with earlier versions of the software. (Keep in mind that many features are not supported by earlier versions; if you save a file for an earlier version, some file information will probably be lost.)

- **Subset Fonts when Percent of Characters Used Is Less Than** determines when to embed an entire font instead of just the characters that are used in the file. Embedding the entire font can significantly increase file size.

- Make sure **Create PDF Compatible File** is checked if you want to use the file with other Adobe applications (such as placing it into an InDesign layout). This does not create a separate PDF file; it simply includes PDF preview data in the file.

- **Include Linked Files** embeds files that are linked to the artwork.

- **Embed ICC Profiles** stores color information inside the file for use in a color-managed workflow.

- **Use Compression** compresses PDF data in the Illustrator file.

- **Save Each Artboard to a Separate File** saves each artboard as a separate file; a separate master file with all artboards is also created.

- **Transparency** options determine what happens to transparent objects when you save a file for Illustrator 9.0 or earlier. Preserve Paths discards transparency effects and resets transparent artwork to 100% opacity and Normal blending mode. Preserve Appearance and Overprints preserves overprints that don't interact with transparent objects; overprints that interact with transparent objects are flattened.

13. Click OK to save the file, and then continue to the next exercise.

Define Smart Guide Preferences

Adobe Illustrator provides many tools to help you create precise lines and shapes. **Smart Guides** are dynamic snap-to guides that help you create, align, and transform objects. Smart Guides also show you when the cursor is at a precise angle relative to the original position of the object or point you're moving. In this exercise, you will make sure the correct Smart Guides are active.

1. **With `icons.ai` open, make sure the Control panel is visible (Window>Control).**

2. **Click the Preferences button in the Control panel or Properties panel.**

    When nothing is selected in the file, you can access the Preferences dialog box directly from either panel. If something is selected in the file, you have to choose from the Illustrator>Preferences (Macintosh) or Edit>Preferences (Windows) submenu.

3. **Choose Smart Guides in the list of categories on the left.**

4. **In the Display section, check all but the Construction Guides option.**

    The Display options determine what is visible when Smart Guides are active:

    - When **Alignment Guides** is active, Smart Guides show when a new or moved object aligns to the center or edge of a nearby object.

    - When **Object Highlighting** is active, moving the mouse over any part of an unselected object shows the anchors and paths that make up that object.

    - When **Transform Tools** is active, Smart Guides display when you scale, rotate, or shear objects.

    - When **Anchor/Path Labels** is active, Smart Guides include labels that show the type of element (path or anchor) under the cursor.

    - When **Measurement Labels** is active, Smart Guides show the distance and angle of movement.

    - When **Construction Guides** is active, Smart Guides appear when you move objects in the file at or near defined angles (0°, 45°, 90°, and 135° are the default angles). A number of common angle options are built into the related menu, or you can type up to six specific angles in the available fields.

5. **Click OK to close the Preferences dialog box.**

6. **Choose View>Smart Guides to make sure that option is toggled on (checked).**

    If the option is already checked, simply move your mouse away from the menu and click to dismiss the menu without changing the active option.

    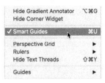

7. **Continue to the next exercise.**

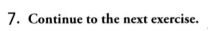

Draw Rounded Rectangles

Illustrator includes a number of tools that make it easy to create basic shapes — rectangles (or squares), ellipses (or circles), and so on.

Using any of the basic shape tools, you can click and drag with the tool cursor to create a shape of any size. Pressing Shift while dragging constrains the shape to equal height and width — for example, an exact square or circle. Pressing Option/Alt while you drag creates the shape so that the center appears where you first click. In the images to the right, the red dot identifies where we first clicked to create the new shape; the yellow circle identifies the current location of the cursor.

You can also single-click using a basic shape tool to open a dialog box, where you can define settings specific to the shape. In this case, the top-left corner of the new shape will be positioned at the place where you click.

In this exercise, you are going to draw a set of simple rectangles with rounded corners to contain the icon artwork that you create throughout this project. We introduce you to a number of techniques for creating these shapes so you can be better aware of the options as you continue your professional career using Illustrator.

Click and drag

Shift-click and drag

Option/Alt-click and drag

1. **With icons.ai open, choose Window>Toolbars>Advanced.**

   This command shows the entire Illustrator toolset, including all nested variations. Throughout this book, we assume you are using the Advanced Tools panel.

2. **Click the Rectangle tool in the Tools panel and hold down the mouse button until the nested tools appear. Choose the Rounded Rectangle tool from the list of nested tools.**

   When you choose a nested tool, that variation becomes the default option in the Tools panel. You don't need to access the nested menu to select the Rounded Rectangle tool again as long as the application remains open.

Note:

Feel free to work with whatever workspace settings you are most comfortable using as you complete the projects in this book.

3. **Click the Default Fill and Stroke button at the bottom of the Tools panel.**

   In Illustrator, the default fill is white and the default stroke is 1-pt black. The button appears in a slightly different location depending on whether your Tools panel is in one- or two-column mode.

One-Column mode

Default Fill and Stroke | Swap Fill and Stroke

Two-Column mode

Default Fill and Stroke | Swap Fill and Stroke

Note:

You can also press D to restore the default fill and stroke colors.

4. **With the Rounded Rectangle tool active, click anywhere on the artboard.**

   In the case of the Rounded Rectangle tool, you can define the size of the shape you want to create, as well as the corner radius. The default measurement system is points, which you defined when you created this file.

The Width field is highlighted when the dialog box opens.

   When the dialog box first opens, the Width field is automatically highlighted. You can simply type to replace the highlighted value.

5. Type 1.75″ in the Width field, then press Tab to move to the Height field.

Regardless of which unit of measurement you see in the dialog box, you can enter values in whatever system you prefer, as long as you remember to type the correct unit in the dialog box fields (use ″ for inches, mm for millimeters, and pt for points). Illustrator automatically translates one unit of measurement to another.

When you move to the next field, Illustrator calculates the conversion of 1.75 inches (the value you typed) to 126 pt (the value that automatically appears in the Width field after you move to the Height field).

The value in inches is converted to the default measurement (points).

Pressing Tab automatically highlights the next field value.

6. Type 1.75″ in the Height field.

Because you are making a shape with the same height and width, you could also click the Constrain icon (the broken chain) on the right side of the dialog box to make the Height field match the modified Width field.

7. Make sure the corner radius field is set to 12 pt.

A rounded-corner rectangle is simply a rectangle with the corners cut at a specific distance from the end (the corner radius). The two sides are connected with one-fourth of a circle, which has a radius equal to the amount of the rounding.

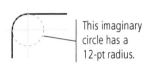

This imaginary circle has a 12-pt radius.

8. Click OK to create the new shape.

A shape appears on the artboard with its top-left corner exactly where you clicked with the Rounded Rectangle tool. (If you Option/Alt-click with any of the shape tools, the place where you click becomes the center of the new shape.)

9. Zoom in so you can clearly see the entire rectangle.

As a general rule, we don't tell you what view percentage to use unless we want to highlight a specific issue. As you work through the projects in this book, we encourage you to zoom in and out as necessary to meet your specific needs.

10. Click the Selection tool (the black arrow) at the top of the Tools panel. If the rounded rectangle is not already selected, click to select the shape.

The Selection tool is used to select entire objects.

When the object is selected, the rectangular **bounding box** marks the outermost edges of the shape. **Bounding-box handles** mark the corners and exact horizontal and vertical center of the shape. (If you don't see the bounding box, choose View>Show Bounding Box.) Because this shape has rounded corners, the corner bounding-box handles actually appear outside the shape edges.

Four small circles inside each corner of the shape are Live Corner widgets, which allow you to click and drag to change the shape of object corners.

Note:

You can choose View>Hide Corner Widget to toggle the visibility of live corner widgets.

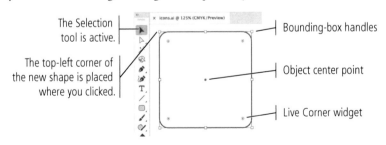

The Selection tool is active.

The top-left corner of the new shape is placed where you clicked.

Bounding-box handles

Object center point

Live Corner widget

11. Click the Rounded Rectangle tool in the Tools panel and hold down the mouse button until the nested tools appear. Choose the Rectangle tool from the list of nested tools.

12. Move the cursor to the right of the top edge of the existing shape. When you see a guide line connected to the top edge of the first shape, click, hold down the mouse button, and drag down and right.

The line is a function of the Smart Guides feature, which provides instant feedback while you draw.

13. When cursor feedbacks show both Width and Height values of 126 pt, release the mouse button to create the second shape.

As you drag, cursor feedback shows the size of the new shape. Smart Guides identify when the new shape's bottom edge aligns with the bottom of the previous shape. The diagonal guide identifies when the shape has equal height and width, making it easy to draw a perfect square. (You can also press Shift while dragging to create a shape with equal height and width.)

Note:

If you do something wrong, or aren't happy with your results, press Command/Control-Z to undo the last action you took.

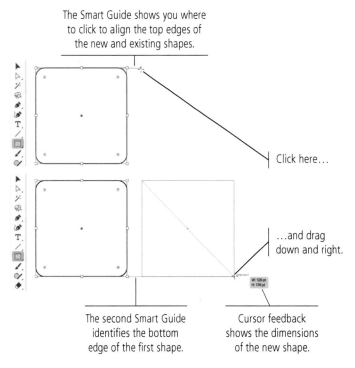

The Smart Guide shows you where to click to align the top edges of the new and existing shapes.

Click here...

...and drag down and right.

The second Smart Guide identifies the bottom edge of the first shape.

Cursor feedback shows the dimensions of the new shape.

Because you are using the Rectangle tool instead of the Rounded Rectangle tool, the second shape does not have rounded corners; the bounding-box handles match the actual shape corners.

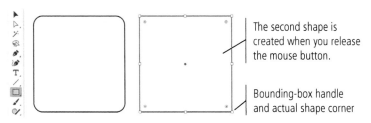

The second shape is created when you release the mouse button.

Bounding-box handle and actual shape corner

14. Click one of the Live Corner widgets and drag toward the center of the shape. When cursor feedback shows a corner radius of approximately 12 pt, release the mouse button.

The Live Corner widgets allow you to manually adjust the corner radius for all corners on the selected shape. Dragging in toward the shape center increases the corner radius; dragging out toward the corner decreases the corner radius.

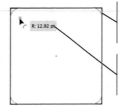

Dragging the Live Corner widget affects the shape of all selected corners.

Cursor feedback shows the corner radius as you drag.

Because the entire object is selected, dragging any of the widgets applies the same change to all corners on the shape. To change only certain corners, you can use the Direct Selection tool to select the corner points you want to affect before dragging a Live Corner widget.

More about Working with Live Corners

If a shape is an actual rectangle (with all 90° corners), the Live Corner widgets appear whenever the shape is selected with either Selection tool. For any other shape, including a four-cornered polygon with different-angled corners, the widgets appear only when the shape is selected with the Direct Selection tool.

Select the shape with the Direct Selection tool to access the Live Corner widgets.

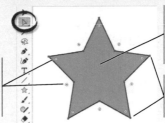

Click inside the shape to select the entire object (and all shape corners).

Click specific corner points to select only those corners.

If the entire object is selected, dragging any one Live Corner widget affects all corners on the same shape (below left). If you want to affect only specific corners, you can select those points first, and then drag any of the visible widgets to change only the selected corners (below right).

Option/Alt-clicking a Live Corner widget toggles through the available corner shapes — round, inverted round, and chamfer/beveled. Again, only selected corners are affected by the shape change.

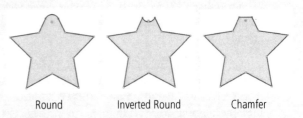

Round   Inverted Round   Chamfer

If you have a wide enough application frame, you can also access the Corner options in the Control panel.

Click the Corners hot-text link to access options for the selected shape.

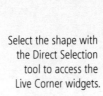

15. **With the adjusted shape still selected, open the Transform panel (Window>Transform).**

    When a rectangle is selected, the Transform panel shows the corner radius of all four corners on the shape. If you find it difficult to achieve an exact radius by dragging, you can always use these fields to adjust the corner radius to specific values.

16. **Make sure the Constrain icon between the Corner Radius fields is active (highlighted). Highlight any of the Corner Radius fields and type 12. Press Return/Enter to finalize the change.**

    Because you are using the default unit of measurement (points), you don't need to type the unit.

    Corner radius fields are only available in the Transform panel if the shape is a rectangle (with four 90° corner angles).

    Corner Radius fields can also be accessed by clicking the Shape hot-text link in the Control panel, or by clicking the More Options button in the Transform section of the Properties panel.

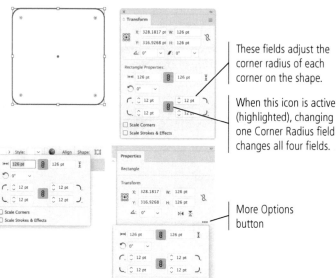

These fields adjust the corner radius of each corner on the shape.

When this icon is active (highlighted), changing one Corner Radius field changes all four fields.

More Options button

17. **Choose the Selection tool in the Tools panel.**

18. **Using the Selection tool, press Option/Alt, then click the second shape and drag right.**

    When you drag an object with the Selection tool, you move it to another location. If you press Option/Alt while dragging, you clone (make a copy of) the original object and move the clone.

    Again, Smart Guides make it easy to align objects. You can see the horizontal guide connecting the center of the original object to the center of the one you are cloning. Smart Guides also identify distances between objects, so you can place multiple objects at the same distances from one to the next. (Don't worry about the exact spaces between the objects; you will define precise object spacing in a later exercise.)

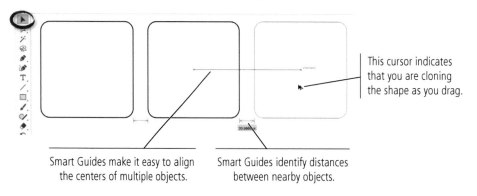

This cursor indicates that you are cloning the shape as you drag.

Smart Guides make it easy to align the centers of multiple objects.

Smart Guides identify distances between nearby objects.

19. **Save the file and continue to the next exercise.**

Understanding Selection Basics

Most Illustrator objects (including shapes like rounded-corner rectangles) contain two basic building blocks: anchor points and paths. You don't need to worry about the geometric specifics of vectors because Illustrator manages them for you — but you do need to understand the basic concept of how Illustrator works with anchor points and paths. You should also understand how to access those building blocks so you can do more than create basic shapes.

Path (line) segment

Curve handle controls the shape of the path

Anchor point

If you select an object with the **Selection tool** (the black arrow), you can see the bounding box that identifies the outermost dimensions of the shape. Bounding-box handles, which you can use to resize the shape, appear at the edges of the bounding box. (Press Command/Control-Shift-B to show or hide the bounding box of selected objects.)

When you select an object with the **Direct Selection tool** (the white arrow), you can see the anchor points and paths that make up the selected object. As you work with Illustrator, keep this distinction in mind: use the Selection tool to select an entire object; use the Direct Selection tool to edit the points and paths of an object.

Selection tool

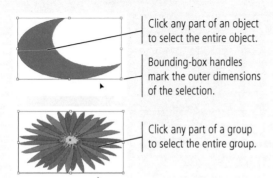

Click any part of an object to select the entire object.

Bounding-box handles mark the outer dimensions of the selection.

Click any part of a group to select the entire group.

Direct Selection tool

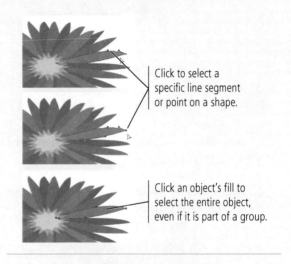

Click to select a specific line segment or point on a shape.

Click an object's fill to select the entire object, even if it is part of a group.

Clicking and dragging to draw a marquee with the Selection tool...

...selects any object touched by the marquee.

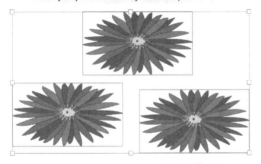

Clicking and dragging to draw a marquee with the Direct Selection tool...

...selects only points within the marquee.

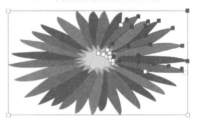

Control Fill and Stroke Attributes

At the beginning of the previous exercise, you clicked the Default Fill and Stroke button in the Tools panel to apply a white fill and 1-pt black stroke to the objects you created. Obviously, most artwork requires more than these basic attributes.

As you complete the projects in this book, you will learn about styles, patterns, gradients, effects, and other attributes that can take an illustration from flat to fabulous. In this exercise, you learn about a number of options for changing the basic fill, stroke, and color attributes for objects on the page.

1. **With icons.ai open, choose the Selection tool in the Tools panel. Click the left rectangle on the artboard to select it.**

2. **Choose View>Hide Corner Widget.**

   These widgets can be distracting, so it's useful to turn them off when they are no longer needed.

Live Corner widgets are no longer visible.

Bounding-box handles are still visible.

3. **Choose Window>Swatches to open the Swatches panel. If the panel is docked, float it away from the dock.**

   If the panel shows a list of items including the color names, open the Swatches panel Options menu and choose Small Thumbnail View.

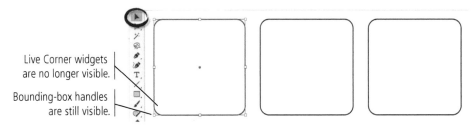

Click here to open the panel Options menu.

Choose this option.

Note:

Remember, panels can always be accessed in the Window menu.

The Swatches panel includes a number of predefined and saved colors, which you can use to change the color of the fill and stroke of an object. You can also save custom swatches to more efficiently apply specific colors as you create artwork.

4. At the top of the Swatches panel, click the Stroke icon to bring it to the front of the stack.

The fill and stroke icons in the Swatches panel are used to determine which attribute is active — in other words, which would be changed by clicking a swatch in the Swatches panel. Clicking one of these buttons brings it to the front of the stack, making it active, so you can change the color of that attribute.

You can also use the same icons at the bottom of the Tools panel to change the active attribute.

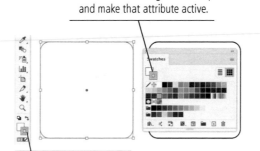

Click an icon to bring it to the top and make that attribute active.

The same options are available in the Tools panel.

Note:

You can press the X key to switch the active attribute between Stroke and Fill.

5. In the Swatches panel, click the light brown swatch in the third row.

Because the Stroke icon is active in the Tools panel, the color of the selected object's stroke (border) changes to light brown.

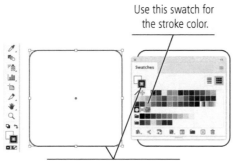

Use this swatch for the stroke color.

The top icon determines what attribute will be changed when you click a swatch in the panel.

Note:

It is very easy to forget to check which icon (fill or stroke) is on top of the stack. If you forget and accidentally change the color of the wrong attribute, simply undo the change (press Command/Control-Z), and then bring the correct attribute to the front before changing colors.

6. In the Tools or Swatches panel, click the Fill icon to bring it to the front of the stack. In the Swatches panel, click the black swatch in the first row.

Because the Fill icon is the active attribute, clicking the black color swatch changes the fill color of the selected object.

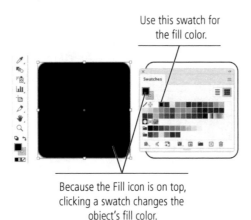

Use this swatch for the fill color.

Because the Fill icon is on top, clicking a swatch changes the object's fill color.

7. **With the rounded rectangle selected, highlight the current value in the Stroke Weight field. Type 3 pt as the new value, and press Return/Enter to apply the change.**

The Stroke icon in the Tools panel does not need to be active to change the stroke weight. The Tools panel icons relate only to color changes made with the stand-alone Swatches or Color panels.

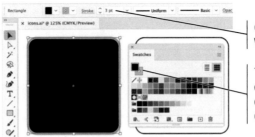

Change the Stroke Weight field to 3 pt.

The Stroke icon doesn't need to be on top to change an object's stroke weight.

8. **With the rectangle still selected, click the Swap Fill and Stroke button in the Tools panel.**

This button makes it easy to reverse the fill and stroke colors of an object; the stroke weight remains unaffected when you swap the colors.

Swap Fill and Stroke button

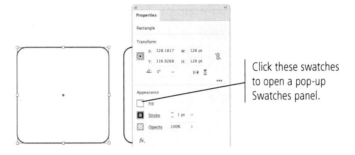

Note:

You can press Shift-X to swap the active Stroke and Fill colors.

9. **Using the Selection tool, click the second rectangle on the artboard.**

The Fill and Stroke icons change to reflect the colors of the selected objects.

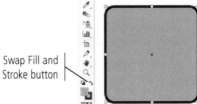

Click these swatches to open a pop-up Swatches panel.

Note:

Fill Color, Stroke Color, and Stroke Weight fields are also available in the Control panel.

10. **In the Appearance section of the Properties panel, change the Stroke Weight value to 3 pt.**

11. **Click the Fill color swatch to open the pop-up Swatches panel. Choose the light brown swatch in the third row to change the fill color for the selected object.**

When an object is selected with the Selection tool, the Properties panel provides quick access to the stroke and fill colors for the selected object; you don't need to worry about which icon is active in the Tools panel.

Clicking the Fill color swatch opens an attached Swatches panel so you can change the fill for the selected object without opening the separate Swatches panel.

12. **Using the Selection tool, click the third rectangle on the artboard.**

    Again, the Fill and Stroke icons in the Tools panel change to reflect the colors of the selected object.

13. **Select the Eyedropper tool in the Tools panel, and then click the first or second rectangle on the artboard.**

    The Eyedropper tool copies fill and stroke attributes from one object (the one you click) to another (the one you first selected).

Note:

You can double-click the Eyedropper tool in the Tools panel to define which attributes are picked up and applied by clicking with the tool.

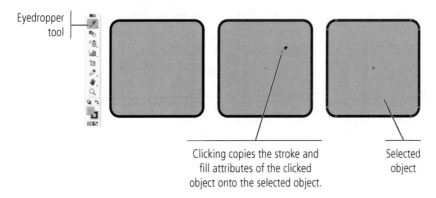

Eyedropper tool

Clicking copies the stroke and fill attributes of the clicked object onto the selected object.

Selected object

14. **Press and hold the Command/Control key, and click anywhere on the artboard away from the three rectangles.**

    Pressing Command/Control temporarily switches to the last-used Selection tool (Selection or Direct Selection). By clicking on the empty artboard area while holding down the modifier key, you can quickly deselect the selected object(s). When you release the Command/Control key, the tool reverts to the one you last used — in this case, the Eyedropper tool.

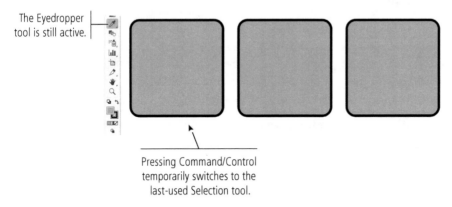

The Eyedropper tool is still active.

Pressing Command/Control temporarily switches to the last-used Selection tool.

15. **Release the Command/Control key.**

16. **Choose the Rounded Rectangle tool in the Tools panel.**

17. **To the right of the third shape on the artboard, draw a fourth rounded rectangle that is 126 pt square.**

The Fill and Stroke swatches remember the last-used options, so the new rectangle has the same heavy black stroke and brown fill as the others. Don't worry if your shapes aren't entirely on the artboard; you will define their precise positions in the next exercise.

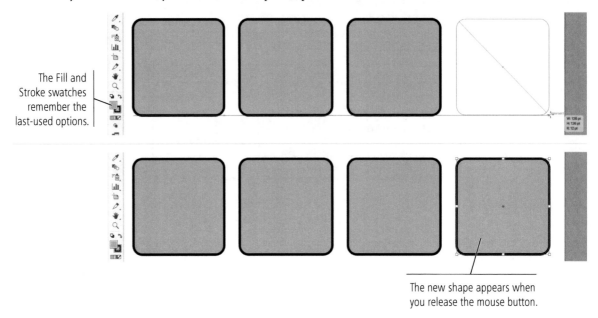

The Fill and Stroke swatches remember the last-used options.

The new shape appears when you release the mouse button.

18. **Save the file (File>Save or Command/Control-S) and continue to the next exercise.**

Control Object Positioning

The ability to move objects around on the artboard is one of the advantages of digital drawing. On paper, you have to manually erase items and then redraw them in their new locations. Illustrator offers a number of tools that make it easy to move objects around the artboard, either as isolated objects or in relation to other elements on the page. In this exercise, you learn several techniques for moving objects on the artboard.

1. **With icons.ai open, change your zoom percentage so you can see all four shapes and the entire top of the artboard.**

2. **Choose View>Rulers>Show Rulers to show the rulers at the top and left edges of the document window.**

Because you created this file using points as the default unit of measurement, the rulers — and fields in dialog boxes and panels — show measurements in points.

Note:

The Change to Global Rulers option is only relevant when you work with multiple artboards.

3. **Control/right-click the top ruler and choose Inches from the contextual menu.**

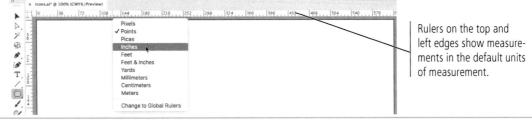

Rulers on the top and left edges show measurements in the default units of measurement.

4. **Choose the Selection tool at the top of the Tools panel, then click the left rectangle on the artboard to select it.**

5. **In the Properties panel, review the Transform options for the active selection.**

Transform options in the Properties panel are the same as those that are available in the stand-alone Transform panel (Window>Transform).

The **reference points** correspond to the bounding box handles of the selected object. The selected square in this icon identifies which point of the object is being measured.

Reference point
around which numeric transformations are based

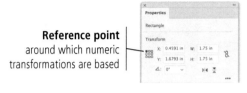

Note:

If you have a wide monitor, the reference point proxy and the X, Y, W, and H fields are available directly in the Control panel.

If you have a smaller application frame, the Control panel includes a hot-text link to a pop-up Transform panel.

If you use the W or H fields to resize an object, you can constrain the object's height-to-width aspect ratio by clicking the chain icon (to the right of the W and H fields in the Transform panel, or between the W and H fields in the Control panel).

In Illustrator, the default **zero point** (the source of measurements) is the top-left corner of the artboard; the X and Y positions of an object are measured relative to that location. The X axis is the horizontal value and the Y axis is the vertical value. You can change the zero point by clicking where the horizontal and vertical rulers meet, and dragging to a new position; if you do reposition the zero point, you can double-click the intersection of the rulers to restore the default zero point.

Keep these ideas in mind when you move something in an Illustrator file:

- Moving up requires subtracting from the Y value.
- Moving down requires adding to the Y value.
- Moving left requires subtracting from the X value.
- Moving right requires adding to the X value.

6. **Click the top-left reference point to select it.**

The X and Y fields now show the exact position of the top-left bounding box handle for the selected object.

7. **Highlight the X field and type .25. Press Return/Enter to apply the change.**

You don't need to type the measurement unit (″) or the preceding zero (0). Because the rulers are showing inches, Illustrator automatically applies inches as the unit of value.

The top-left reference point is selected.

Measurements correspond to this point of the selected shape.

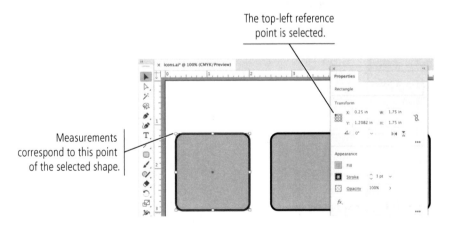

8. Highlight the Y field and type .25. Press Return/Enter to apply the change.

The top-left handle of the selected object is now 1/4″ from the top and left edges. The numbers you typed correspond to the measurements you see on the rulers.

Rulers show that the selected point of the object is at the position you just defined.

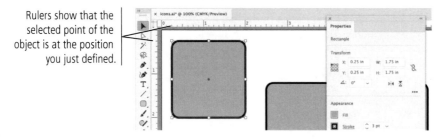

9. Using the Selection tool, click the second rectangle and drag until a guide line appears, connecting the center points of the first and second shapes.

As you drag, the cursor feedback shows the relative position of the object. In other words, you can see the change (<u>d</u>ifference) in the object's position, both horizontally (<u>X</u>) and vertically (<u>Y</u>) — hence the "dX" and "dY" values.

As we explained previously, Smart Guides can be very useful for aligning objects on the artboard. Illustrator identifies and highlights relative alignment as you drag, and snaps objects to those alignment points.

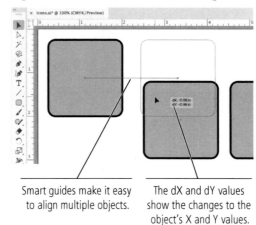

Smart guides make it easy to align multiple objects.

The dX and dY values show the changes to the object's X and Y values.

Note:

The X position is an object's horizontal position on the artboard; the Y position is the object's vertical position.

10. Release the mouse button while the center Smart Guide is visible.

If you don't see the alignment guides as you drag, make sure that option is checked in the Smart Guides preferences.

Note:

When a field value is highlighted in a panel or dialog box, you can use the Up Arrow and Down Arrow keys to increase or decrease (respectively) the highlighted value.

11. Click the fourth shape on the page. Select the top-right reference point, type 8.25 in the X field, and type .25 in the Y field.

Because you changed the reference point, you defined the X/Y position for the top-right bounding-box handle of the fourth rectangle.

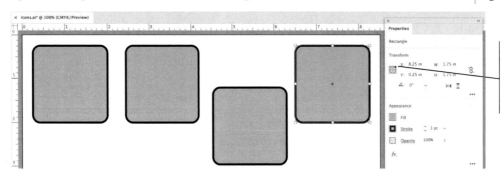

The top-right reference point means the X and Y values refer to the top-right corner of the selected shape.

12. Save the file and continue to the next exercise.

Understanding Alignment Options

As you have already seen, there is almost always more than one way to accomplish a specific task. Although Smart Guides make alignment very easy, the Align panel is useful for certain functions that are not enabled by Smart Guides. You can use the Align panel to align multiple objects relative to one another within a selection, to a specific object in the selection, or to the active artboard.

The **Align Object options** are fairly self explanatory; when multiple objects are selected, the objects align based on the edge(s) or center(s) you click. Icons on the various buttons indicate the function of each.

- Align Left Edges
- Align Horizontal Centers
- Align Right Edges
- Align Top Edges
- Align Vertical Centers
- Align Bottom Edges

You can use the Align To menu to determine how selected objects will align. If you don't see the Align To menu, open the panel Options menu and choose Show Options.

The **Align To Selection** option aligns selected objects to one another based on the outermost edge of the entire selection. In other words, aligning the top edges moves all objects to the same Y position as the highest selected object.

If you use the **Key Object** option, you can click any object in the selection to designate it as the key. (The key object shows a heavier border than other objects in the selection.)

Because you can align objects relative to the document, the align buttons are also available when only one object is selected, allowing you to align any single object to a precise location on the page or spread.

By default, Align options apply based on the outermost edge of the active selection. In the following image, dashed lines indicate the original top edges of the objects:

Using the **Align To Key Object** option, the middle image was selected as the key. The Align options apply to the edges of the defined key object:

The **Distribute Objects options** enable you to control the positions of multiple objects relative to each other. By default, objects are equally distributed within the dimensions of the overall selection.

- Distribute Top Edges
- Distribute Vertical Centers
- Distribute Bottom Edges
- Distribute Left Edges
- Distribute Horizontal Centers
- Distribute Right Edges

The following images show the original placement, followed by the result of applying the Distribute Vertical Centers and Distribute Horizontal Centers options to evenly space the three fish.

You can use the Distribute Spacing option to align objects to one another by a specific amount based on the selected key object. To access the measurement field for these options, you must first click one of the selected objects to define the key. You can then type a value in the field, then click the Horizontal or Vertical options (or both, as we did in the following image):

If you don't see the Distribute Spacing options, open the panel Options menu and choose Show Options.

Align and Distribute Objects

In addition to dragging objects around the artboard, the Illustrator Align panel makes it very easy to align and distribute selected objects relative to one another, to a specific key object in the file, or to the overall artboard. In this exercise, you learn how to use the Align panel to align shapes.

Note:

When multiple objects are selected, you can access the basic Align options in the Properties panel. Click the More Options button to access the full pop-up panel.

More Options

1. **With icons.ai open, click and drag with the Selection tool to draw a marquee that touches some part of all four objects on the artboard.**

   The Selection tool selects objects, so the selection marquee only needs to touch the objects you want to select. The marquee doesn't need to surround the objects entirely.

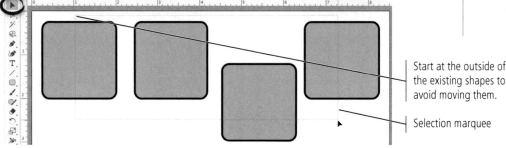

Start at the outside of the existing shapes to avoid moving them.

Selection marquee

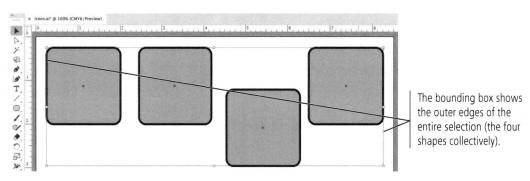

The bounding box shows the outer edges of the entire selection (the four shapes collectively).

2. **Open the Align panel (Window>Align) and click the Vertical Align Top button.**

   By default, alignment and distribution functions occur relative to the selected objects. In other words, when you click the Vertical Align Top button, Illustrator determines the topmost edge of the selected objects, and then moves the top edges of all other selected objects to that position.

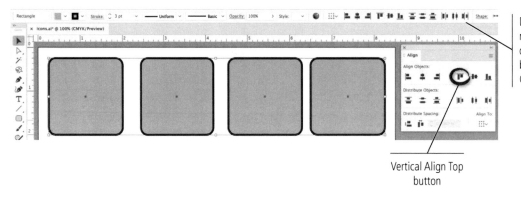

Depending on your monitor width, Align options might also be available in the Control panel.

Vertical Align Top button

3. **With all four objects selected, click the Horizontal Distribute Center button.**

By default, the distribution functions create equal distance between the selected point of the selected objects. In this case, Illustrator distributes the center points along the horizontal axis by determining the center positions of the outermost selected objects, and then moving the middle two objects to create equal distance between the centers of all four selected objects; the positions of the two outer objects remain unchanged.

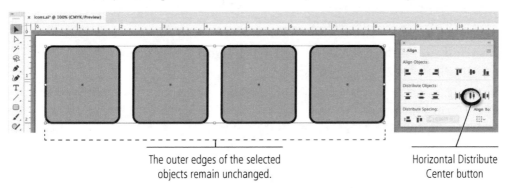

The outer edges of the selected objects remain unchanged.

Horizontal Distribute Center button

4. **Click inside any of the selected objects. While still holding down the mouse button, press Option/Alt and drag down.**

5. **Use the Smart Guides and cursor feedback to drag exactly vertical (the dX value should be 0). When the dY value in the cursor feedback is 2 in, release the mouse button.**

Remember, pressing Option/Alt while you drag clones the original selection.

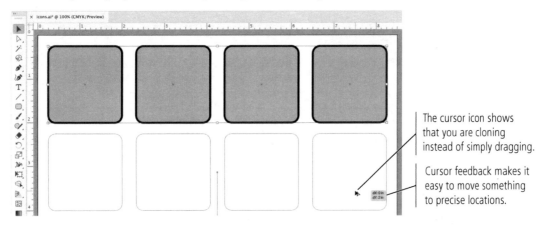

The cursor icon shows that you are cloning instead of simply dragging.

Cursor feedback makes it easy to move something to precise locations.

6. **Click anywhere outside the selected shapes to deselect all objects.**

7. **Save the file and continue to the next exercise.**

Import Template Images

Many Illustrator projects require you to start with something that has already been captured — a sketch, for example, or low-resolution image (which is the case in this project). In this exercise you will place files to use as templates for your new artwork.

1. **With icons.ai open, choose File>Place. Navigate to your WIP>Camping folder and click picnic.jpg to select that file.**

2. **Macintosh users: If you don't see a series of check boxes across the bottom of the dialog box, click the Options button.**

    The dialog box button remembers the last-used state, so the actual options might already be visible. We do not repeat the instruction to click the Options button whenever you place a file throughout the projects in this book.

3. **At the bottom of the Place dialog box, check the Link and Template options.**

    When you check the Link option, the placed file does not become a part of the actual file where you're working; for the file to output properly, Illustrator must be able to locate the linked file in the same location (hard drive, flash drive, etc.) as when you placed it. If the Link option is *not* checked, the placed file is **embedded** — it becomes part of the file where it's placed; the original external file is not necessary for the artwork to output properly.

    In the case of this project, you are going to delete the template images after you create the artwork; it doesn't matter if the images are embedded.

Macintosh users: Click the Options button to reveal the actual options.

Make sure this option is checked.

4. **Click Place.**

    When you place an object into Illustrator as a Template, it is automatically centered in the current document window. In our example, you can see that the placed image is mostly hidden by the background shapes; regardless of where your template images appear, you will correct this issue in the next exercise.

The Control panel shows information about the placed image.

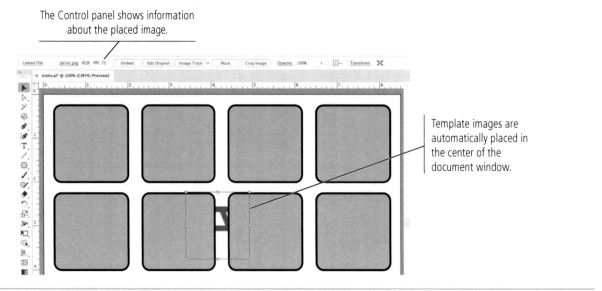

Template images are automatically placed in the center of the document window.

5. **Choose File>Place a second time. Select hiking.jpg in the list, check the Template option, and click Place.**

The Place dialog box remembers the last-used location, so you don't have to re-navigate to the Camping folder. The Link option also remembers the last-used settings. The Template option, however, always defaults to off, so you have to manually check this box for each template object.

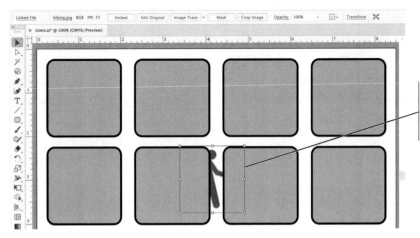

This image is also placed in the center of the document window, directly on top of the first placed image.

6. **Repeat Step 5 to place campfire.jpg and tents.jpg into your file as template images.**

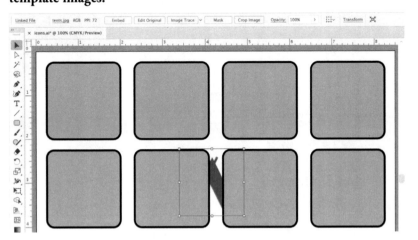

Note:

If you change the view percentage or scroll the document in the window before placing the second image, the second file will not be centered over the first. Instead, it will be centered in the document window based on the current view.

7. **Click an empty area of the artboard to deselect the last-placed template image.**

8. **Save the file and continue to the next exercise.**

Manage Multiple Layers

When you create artwork in Illustrator, you almost always end up with more than one object on the artboard. In many cases, a completed file has dozens or hundreds of objects, arranged in specific order on top of one another. As files become more and more complex, it can be difficult to find and work with exactly the pieces you need. Illustrator layers are one of the most powerful tools available for solving this problem.

1. **In the open `icons.ai` file, open the Layers panel.**

   By default, all files have a single layer, named Layer 1.

   When you place an object as a template, it's added to the file on a separate, non-printing layer that is partially grayed, making it easier to work with. Below Layer 1, your file has four additional layers — the template layers. Template layers are locked by default, which means you can't select or modify objects on those layers.

Note:

If you don't see all four locked template layers, you forgot to check the Template option when you placed one of the images. You can select and delete the placed file from the artboard, and then replace the necessary image as a template.

2. **In the Layers panel, click the Layer 1 name and drag it below all four template layers in the stack.**

   The top-to-bottom position of objects or layers is called the **stacking order**. Objects and layers typically appear in the stack based on the order in which they are created — the first-created is at the bottom, the last-created is at the top, and so on, in between.

Click and drag a layer to move it in the stacking order.

   Placed template objects are the exception; these layers are placed *below* the currently selected layer (i.e., lower in the stacking order). In this case, the rectangle shapes are filled with a color, which obscures the template images on the underlying layers. To see the template images, you need to move the template object layers above the layer containing the background shapes. Rather than moving four layers above Layer 1, you can save a few clicks by moving Layer 1 below all of the template layers.

Note:

If you can't see the entire layer names, click and drag either edge of the Layers panel to show more of the layer names.

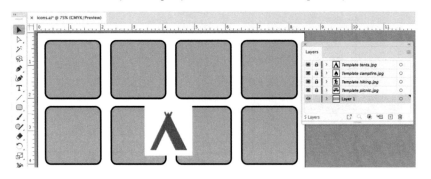

3. **In the Layers panel, click the icon in the left column for the Template tents.jpg, Template campfire.jpg, and Template hiking.jpg layers to hide those layers.**

Because you need to move the placed template object into the correct position, you first need to unlock the layer where that object resides.

Click here to hide the template layers.

Note:

For a template layer, the Visibility icon is a small square instead of an eye.

4. **In the Layers panel, click the Lock icon for the Template picnic.jpg layer to unlock that layer.**

Because you need to move the placed template object into the correct position, you first need to unlock the layer where that object resides.

Click here to unlock the template layer.

5. **Using the Selection tool, click the top-left rounded rectangle to select it.**

6. **With the Selection tool active, press Shift and click anywhere inside the area of the visible template image.**

7. **With both objects selected, click the Align To button in the Control panel.**

The Align and Distribute options in the Control panel are the same as the options in the Align panel.

Click this button to access the Align To options.

The rectangle and template image are both selected.

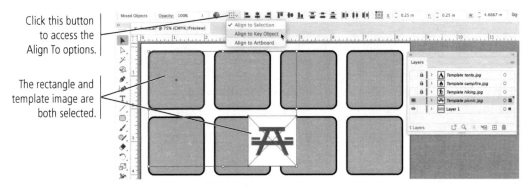

8. **Choose Align to Key Object in the menu.**

The default key object is identified with a heavy border.

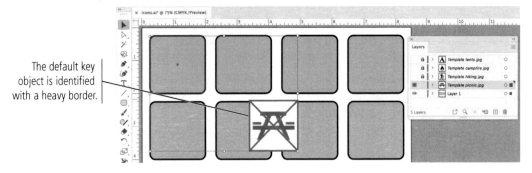

9. **Click the selected rounded rectangle on the artboard.**

   Key Object alignment allows you to define where you want other objects to align. By selecting the key object, you're telling Illustrator which object to use as the basis for alignment.

Click any selected object to define the key object for the alignment.

The border colors match the defined layer colors.

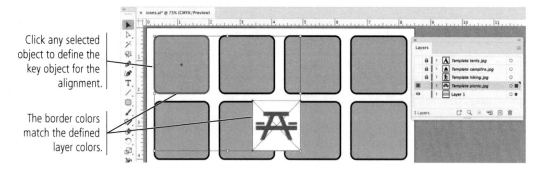

10. **Click the Horizontal Align Center and Vertical Align Center buttons in the Control panel.**

    Because you selected the rounded rectangle as the key object, the placed template image moves to the horizontal and vertical center of the rounded rectangle; the rectangle — the key object — remains in the same place.

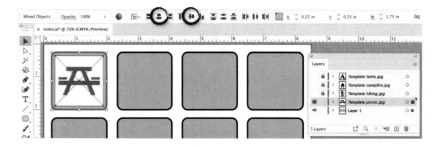

11. **In the Layers panel, click the empty space to the left of the Template picnic.jpg layer to relock that layer.**

    Now that the template object is in place, it's a good idea to lock it again so you don't accidentally move the object.

12. **Double-click the layer thumbnail of the Template picnic.jpg layer.**

    Double-clicking a layer thumbnail opens the Layer Options dialog box for that layer, where you can change a number of attributes for the selected layer.

13. **Change the Dim Images To field to 30, and then click OK to close the Layer Options dialog box.**

    Dimming the template image will make it easier to see your artwork when you draw.

Note:

The Color menu in the Layer Options dialog box determines the color of bounding box handles and other visual indicators for objects on a layer.

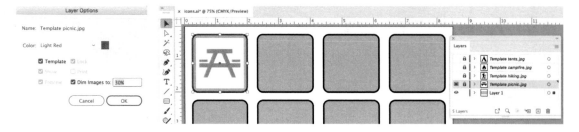

14. In the Layers panel, click the left column for the Template hiking.jpg layer to show that layer.

15. Repeat the process from Steps 4–14 to align the hiking template image to the second rounded rectangle in the top row.

16. Show the Template campfire.jpg template layer, then use the process from Steps 4–14 to align the campfire image to the third rounded rectangle in the top row.

17. Show the Template tents.jpg template layer, then use the process from Steps 4–14 to align the tent image to the fourth rounded rectangle in the top row.

18. In the Layers panel, double-click the Layer 1 name to highlight it. Type **Backgrounds** to change the layer name, then press Return/Enter.

Whenever you have more than one working layer, it's a good idea to use names that tell you what is on each layer. Doing so prevents confusion later when you or someone else needs to change a particular item.

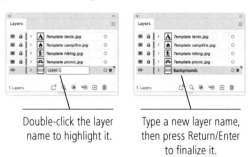

Double-click the layer name to highlight it.

Type a new layer name, then press Return/Enter to finalize it.

19. **In the Layers panel, click the empty space immediately left of the Backgrounds layer.**

Lock the Backgrounds layer to protect the objects on that layer.

This step (locking the Backgrounds layer) is a safeguard to avoid accidentally changing the background rectangles while you're drawing the icon artwork.

20. **In the Layers panel, click the Create New Layer button.**

Create New Layer button

In the next stage of the project, you will start tracing the objects in the templates. The completed icon will be a series of black icons on top of the rounded rectangles with the brown background color.

At this point, the background shapes are mostly obscured by the placed images, because the template layers are above the layer containing the rectangles. If you tried to draw the icon shapes on the existing non-template layer, you would be drawing *behind* the template — in other words, you wouldn't be able to see what you were drawing. Instead, you need a layer above the template layers, where you can create the icon artwork.

21. **In the Layers panel, drag Layer 6 to the top of the layer stack.**

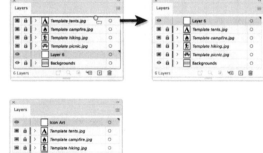

New layers are placed immediately above the selected layer. You need this new layer to be above the template layers so you can see what you're drawing.

22. **Double-click the Layer 6 name in the Layers panel. Type Icon Art and press Return/Enter to finalize the new layer name.**

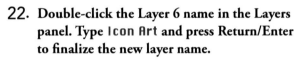

23. **Save the file and continue to the next stage of the project.**

A number of tools and utilities can be used to create complex Illustrator artwork. Creating the icons in this project gives you an opportunity to experiment with some of these options. As you complete the other projects in this book, you will dig deeper into complex drawing techniques.

 ## Numerically Transform Drawing Objects

Basic shapes, such as rectangles, can be used as the basis for a wide variety of drawings. In the next two exercises, you will use basic rectangles to create the picnic table art.

1. **With icons.ai open, make sure the Icon Art layer is active, and then zoom in to the picnic table template image.**

2. **Choose the Rectangle tool in the Tools panel.**

3. **With nothing selected on the artboard, change the fill color to black and the stroke color to None.**

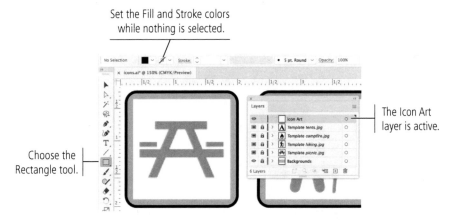

Set the Fill and Stroke colors while nothing is selected.

Choose the Rectangle tool.

The Icon Art layer is active.

4. **Click and drag to create the shape that represents the top of the picnic table.**

5. **Click and drag again to create the second horizontal shape in the artwork.**

6. **Using the Selection tool, click the top rectangle to select it.**

7. **Open the Transform panel (Window>Transform). Make a note of the H (height) field in the Transform panel.**

   We use the stand-alone Transform panel in this exercise because it eliminates the need to constantly reopen the panel using the Control panel hot-text link.

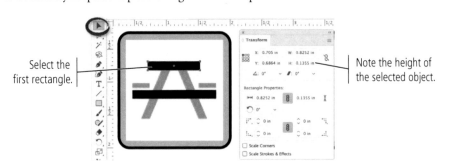

Select the first rectangle.

Note the height of the selected object.

Note:

We changed the layer color of the Icon Art layer to magenta so that the visual indicators on the layer will be more visible in our printed screen captures.

8. **Click to select the second shape (from Step 5).**

9. **If necessary, click the Constrain Width and Height Proportions button in the Transform panel to turn off that option.**

    When this button is active, changing the height or width field makes a proportional change to the other dimension. When it is inactive, you can change one dimension of a shape without affecting the other dimension.

    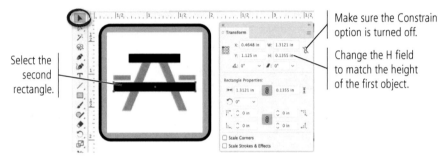

    W: 1.3121 in H: 0.128 in — The Constrain option is turned on.

    W: 1.3117 in H: 0.128 in — The Constrain option is turned off.

10. **With the second shape selected, change the H (height) field to the same value that you noted in Step 7.**

    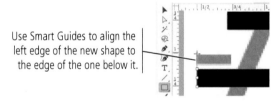

    Select the second rectangle.

    Make sure the Constrain option is turned off.

    Change the H field to match the height of the first object.

11. **Using the Rectangle tool, click and drag to create the seat shape on the left side of the template.**

    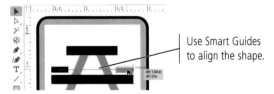

    Use Smart Guides to align the left edge of the new shape to the edge of the one below it.

12. **Choose the Selection tool. Press Option/Alt, then click the new shape and drag right to clone it.**

13. **Continue dragging until Smart Guides show the right edge of the cloned shape aligned to the right edge of the bottom rectangle (as shown here).**

    Use Smart Guides to align the shape.

14. **Save the file and continue to the next exercise.**

Shear and Reflect Drawing Objects

Illustrator includes four transformation options — Rotate, Reflect, Scale, and Shear. Each of these transformations can be applied either by hand, using the related tool in the Tools panel; or numerically, using either the fields in the Transform panel or the appropriate dialog box from the Object>Transform menu. In this exercise, you will use these methods to finish the picnic table artwork.

1. **With icons.ai open, choose the Rectangle tool in the Tools panel.**

2. **Draw a vertical rectangle beginning at the bottom of the artwork and ending at the bottom edge of the top horizontal shape (as shown after Step 3).**

   Illustrator recognizes certain basic shapes, including rectangles, ellipses, and lines. When one of these shapes — called Live Shapes — is selected, the lower half of the Transform panel includes properties specific to the type of shape. For a rectangle, you can change the height, width, rotation angle, and corner radius for each corner.

3. **With the Constrain option turned off, change the W field in the Transform panel to the same value you used for the height of the horizontal shapes in the previous exercise.**

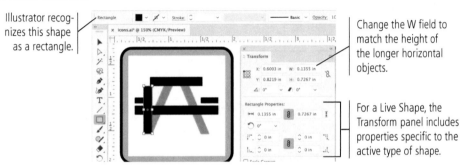

Illustrator recognizes this shape as a rectangle.

Change the W field to match the height of the longer horizontal objects.

For a Live Shape, the Transform panel includes properties specific to the active type of shape.

4. **Select the Shear tool (nested under the Scale tool) in the Tools panel.**

   When you select one of the transformation tools, an **origin point** appears by default at the center of the selected object. This origin point acts as an anchor when using the transformation tools; it is the point around which transformations occur. You can single-click anywhere to define a different origin point.

5. **Move the cursor to the bottom-right anchor point of the vertical rectangle. When you see the word "anchor" in the cursor icon, click to reposition the origin point.**

   The word "anchor" is another function of Illustrator's Smart Guides. When you move the cursor near an existing anchor point, Illustrator identifies that point so you can click exactly on the existing point.

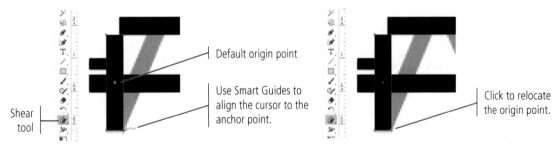

Shear tool

Default origin point

Use Smart Guides to align the cursor to the anchor point.

Click to relocate the origin point.

6. **Click the top edge of the selected shape and drag right until the shape matches the table leg shape in the template image.**

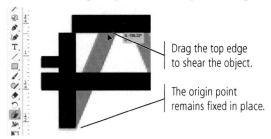

Drag the top edge to shear the object.

The origin point remains fixed in place.

Note:

The Illustrator transformation tools all use this same origin point concept as the basis for transformations. You can click without dragging to reposition the origin point before applying the transformation.

After you shear a Live Shape, it is no longer recognized as the original Live Shape; the specific shape properties are no longer available in the Transform panel.

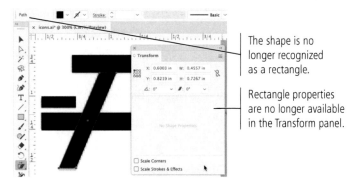

The shape is no longer recognized as a rectangle.

Rectangle properties are no longer available in the Transform panel.

7. **Choose the Reflect tool (nested under the Rotate tool) in the Tools panel.**

8. **Double-click the Reflect tool in the Tools panel.**

   Double-clicking a transformation tool in the Tools panel opens a dialog box, where you can numerically define the transformation. (This dialog box is the same one you would see by choosing Object>Transform>Reflect.)

9. **Check the Preview option at the bottom of the dialog box.**

   When the Preview option is active, you can see the result of your choices before finalizing them.

10. **Choose the Vertical option in the Axis section.**

   Reflecting vertically flips the object around the Y axis. Reflecting horizontally flips the object around the X axis.

Note:

Transformation dialog boxes default to the last-used settings for that transformation.

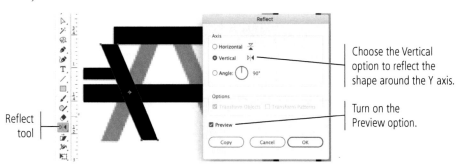

Reflect tool

Choose the Vertical option to reflect the shape around the Y axis.

Turn on the Preview option.

11. **Click Copy.**

If you simply clicked OK, the original object would have been reflected. By clicking Copy, you create the second table leg shape; the original remains in place.

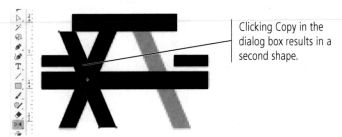

Clicking Copy in the dialog box results in a second shape.

12. **Using the Selection tool, click the reflected shape and drag right. Use Smart Guides to keep the dragged shape aligned to the original.**

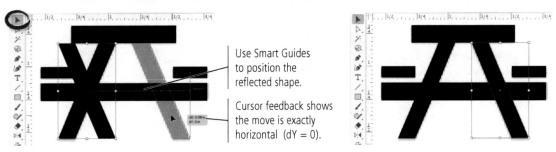

Use Smart Guides to position the reflected shape.

Cursor feedback shows the move is exactly horizontal (dY = 0).

13. **Save the file and continue to the next exercise.**

 ## Manage Artwork with Groups

The artwork for this icon consists of six separate shapes (seven, if you count the background rectangle). Because these distinct objects make up one piece of artwork, you should create a group so that all pieces can be treated as a single unit.

1. **With icons.ai open, select the Template picnic.jpg layer in the Layers panel.**

2. **Click the panel's Delete Selection button. When asked to confirm the deletion, click Yes.**

Since the picnic table artwork is complete, you no longer need the template image.

Delete Selection button

3. **In the Layers panel, click the arrow to the left of the Icon Art layer.**

When you expand a layer in the panel, you can see the individual objects that exist on that layer (called **sublayers**). You drew six shapes in the previous exercise; the expanded Icon Art layer lists each of those objects separately.

Objects are listed in the order you created them; the first object you create appears at the bottom of the list and the last object appears at the top. This bottom-to-top arrangement is called **stacking order**.

4. With the Selection tool active, choose Select>All.

This command selects all unlocked objects in the file.

If you have more than one artboard in the file, the Select>All on Artboard command selects unlocked objects only on the active artboard.

Click these arrows to expand a layer.

Each separate object is listed individually.

These squares identify selected objects.

Because the Backgrounds layer is locked, the rectangle behind the artwork is not selected.

5. With all the objects selected, choose Object>Group.

The six individual objects are components of a single thing — the "picnic" icon. Grouping them allows all the pieces to be treated as a single object on the artboard.

Grouping allows you to treat the icon artwork as a single object.

6. Click the arrow to the left of the Backgrounds layer to expand that layer.

Because you locked the entire layer, all objects on that layer are also locked.

Because the parent layer is locked, all objects on that layer are also locked.

7. Click the Lock icon for the Backgrounds layer to unlock it.

When you unlock a layer, all objects on that layer are also unlocked.

8. Using the Selection tool, Shift-click the brown background shape to add it to the active selection.

If you used the Select All method, you would select all eight background shapes because the Backgrounds layer is now unlocked. Manually clicking is a better choice to select only the one you want.

Objects on multiple layers can be selected at the same time.

9. **Choose Object>Group.**

10. **In the Layers panel, click the arrow to the left of the resulting group.**

    When you group objects that exist on different layers, all objects in the group are moved to the top-most layer in the selection. In this case, the background rectangle is moved from the Backgrounds layer to the group on the Icon Art layer.

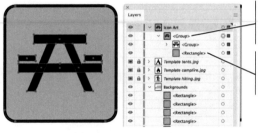

The parent group contains the icon group and the background rectangle.

All grouped objects are moved to the top-most layer in the selection.

11. **Click the arrow to collapse the Backgrounds layer, and then click the empty space to the left of the Backgrounds layer to relock that layer.**

12. **With the group on the Icon Art layer selected, choose Object>Lock> Selection.**

    The lock icon in the Layers panel shows that the group is locked, but the parent Icon Art layer is not. You can draw more artwork on the same layer without accidentally affecting the existing artwork.

Note:

You can choose Object>Ungroup, or press Command/Control-Shift-G, to ungroup objects in a group.

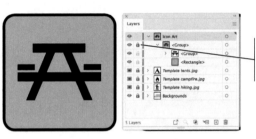

Click this space to lock or unlock only a specific sublayer.

13. **In the Layers panel, double-click the parent <Group> name to highlight it.**

14. **Type Picnic Table, then press Return/Enter to finalize the new name.**

    You can assign specific names to sublayers, just as you do to regular layers. Meaningful names for each group will make it easier to manage the various icons if you need to make changes at a later date.

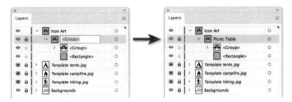

15. **Click the arrows to collapse the Picnic Table sublayer and the Icon Art layer.**

16. **Save the file and continue to the next exercise.**

Using the Group Selection Tool

You can create more than one level of group, called **nesting**, by selecting an existing group, and then grouping it with other objects or groups. You can use the **Group Selection tool** to help navigate complex levels of nested groups.

The first click with the Group Selection tool selects an individual object in a group. The second click selects that object's containing group. The third click adds the next containing group to the selection, and so on, until the entire parent group is selected.

Group Selection tool

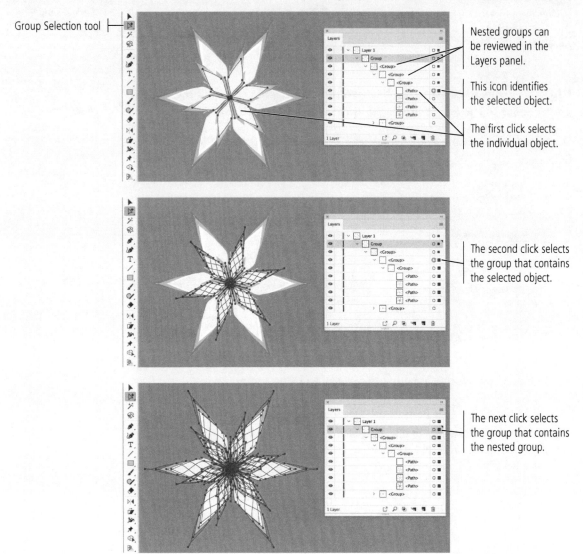

Nested groups can be reviewed in the Layers panel.

This icon identifies the selected object.

The first click selects the individual object.

The second click selects the group that contains the selected object.

The next click selects the group that contains the nested group.

Create Artwork with Lines

The Hiker icon is a perfect candidate for drawing with lines — which makes it ideal for introducing the Line Segment tool. In this exercise, you combine simple lines with other basic shapes to create the final icon.

1. **With icons.ai open, make sure the Icon Art layer is active. Make the hiker template art prominent in the document window.**

2. **Choose the Line Segment tool in the Tools panel. Using the Control panel, set the Fill to None and the Stroke to 1-pt Black.**

3. **Click near the top of the figure's neck, hold down the mouse button, and drag down to the bottom of the figure's back leg (as shown in the following image).**

   As you drag, the cursor feedback shows the distance (D) or length, as well as the angle of the line you're drawing.

Note:

If you don't see the cursor feedback, choose View>Smart Guides to toggle on that option.

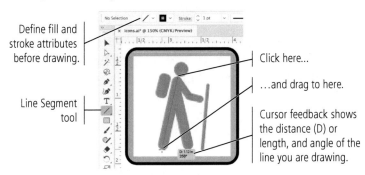

Define fill and stroke attributes before drawing.

Line Segment tool

Click here...

...and drag to here.

Cursor feedback shows the distance (D) or length, and angle of the line you are drawing.

   When you release the mouse button, the line appears with the 1-pt black stroke that you defined in Step 2. The Control panel shows that Illustrator recognizes this object as a Line — a function of Live Shapes capability. The Transform panel includes Line Properties of length and rotation.

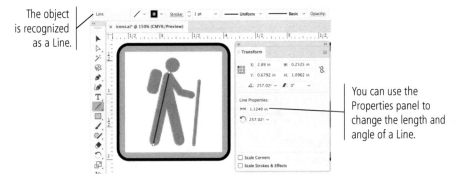

The object is recognized as a Line.

You can use the Properties panel to change the length and angle of a Line.

4. **Using the Control panel, change the Stroke Weight field to 12 pt.**

5. **Open the Stroke panel (Window>Stroke). If you only see the Stroke Weight field, open the panel's Options menu and choose Show Options.**

   Stroke properties are not limited to simply the stroke weight. The panel includes a number of options for customizing the appearance of a line.

Click here to open the panel Options menu.

6. **With the line selected on the artboard, choose the Round cap style in the Stroke panel.**

By default, lines have flat ends that stop at the anchor points that mark the ends of the lines. If you choose the Round or Square cap styles, the caps extend beyond the ending anchor points by one half the defined stroke weight.

In this case, you defined a 12-pt stroke, so the caps extend 6 points beyond the ending anchor points. Because the round caps essentially make the line longer, you have to change the line length to match the icon artwork.

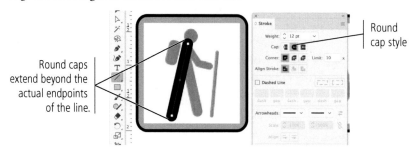

Round caps extend beyond the actual endpoints of the line.

Round cap style

The Stroke Panel in Depth

The **Cap** options define the appearance of a stroke beyond the endpoint of the line.

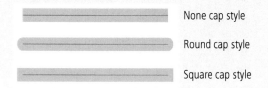

None cap style

Round cap style

Square cap style

The **Corner** options define the appearance of corners where two lines meet. When Miter Join is selected, you can define a miter limit in the Limit field. A miter limit controls when the corner switches from a pointed joint to a beveled joint as a factor of the stroke weight. If you define a miter limit of 2 for a 2-point line, the corner is beveled if the pointed corner extends beyond 4 points (2 × 2).

Miter join   Round join   Bevel join

The **Align Stroke** options determine where the stroke is placed relative to the actual path.

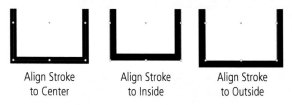

Align Stroke to Center   Align Stroke to Inside   Align Stroke to Outside

When the **Dashed Line** option is checked, you can define a specific pattern of dashes and gaps in the related fields. The two buttons to the right of the check box determine how a dash pattern is stretched (or not) so that line ends or object corners have the same appearance.

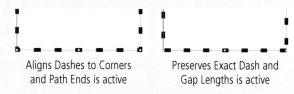

Aligns Dashes to Corners and Path Ends is active   Preserves Exact Dash and Gap Lengths is active

The **Arrowheads** options can be used to control end treatments on each end of a line. You can choose an arrowhead shape from the menus, and change the scale of applied arrowheads (relative to the applied stroke weight).

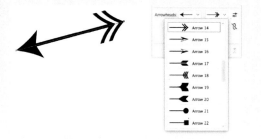

The Align [Arrowheads] options determine how arrowhead treatments are positioned relative to the path endpoint.

Place Arrow Tip at End of Path   Extend Arrow Tip Beyond End of Path

7. **Using the Transform panel, change the Line Length field to 1 in. Press Return/Enter to finalize the change.**

When you use the Line Properties options, the change always orients around the center of the line. The selected reference point at the top of the panel has no effect on the change.

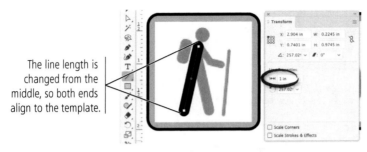

The line length is changed from the middle, so both ends align to the template.

8. **Press Command/Control to temporarily access the Selection tool and click away from the active line to deselect it.**

If you don't deselect the first line, clicking at the same spot as an existing, selected anchor point would actually drag the existing point instead of drawing a new line. This function of Live Shapes means you can edit existing line points and properties without switching tools, but it also means you can't begin a new line at the same point without first deselecting the original line.

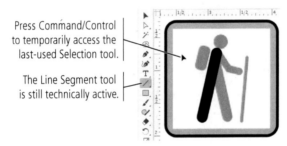

Press Command/Control to temporarily access the last-used Selection tool.

The Line Segment tool is still technically active.

9. **With the Line Segment tool still active, move the cursor over the top end of the existing line until you see the word "anchor" in the cursor.**

The "anchor" label, a function of Smart Guides, indicates that clicking will create a new point at the same location as the existing one. Because you are using the Line Segment tool, the two lines will remain separate; they are not connected at the overlapping anchor points.

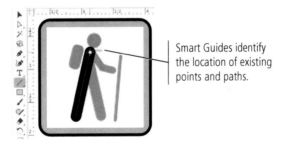

Smart Guides identify the location of existing points and paths.

10. **Click and drag down to the bottom of the front leg in the template artwork. When the cursor feedback shows the line is 1 in long, release the mouse button.**

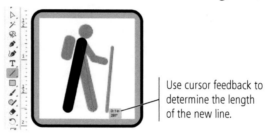

Use cursor feedback to determine the length of the new line.

11. **Command/Control-click away from the selected line to deselect it.**

12. **Click again at the point where the lines meet, and drag to create the figure's top arm segment.**

The new line uses the same stroke attributes as the previous ones unless you change those settings before drawing. In this case, the 12-pt stroke is too heavy, so you need to reduce it.

13. **Using the Control panel or the Stroke panel, change the line weight to 8 pt.**

14. **Deselect the new line, then draw the lower segment of the figure's arm.**

15. **Using the Line Segment tool, click and drag to create the walking stick. Define the line to have a 4-pt stroke with round caps.**

16. **Save the file and continue to the next exercise.**

Draw with Live Shapes

In addition to using the Transform panel to edit the properties of Live Shapes, you can also use the tool cursor to edit those shapes without the need to constantly switch tools. In this exercise, you will create and edit two more live shapes to complete the Hiking icon artwork.

1. **With icons.ai open, deselect everything on the artboard.**

2. **Choose the Rectangle tool, and define a 1-pt black stroke with no fill.**

Note:

Zooming in to the artwork can be helpful for completing the next two exercises.

3. **Click and drag to create a rectangle that is approximately the same size as the backpack in the template art.**

The shape is recognized as a Rectangle.

4. **Click the object's center point and drag to move the shape until its center approximately matches the center of the shape in the template art.**

    Because this is a Live Shape, you do not need to change tools to rotate, move, or transform the shape.

Click the center point and drag to move the Live Shape.

The Rectangle tool is still active.

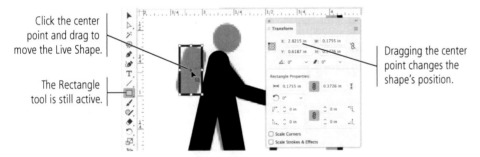

Dragging the center point changes the shape's position.

5. **Move the cursor near the corner of the resulting shape. When you see the rotation cursor, click and drag to rotate the shape to match the angle of the same shape in the template art.**

Click just outside a corner point and drag to rotate the Live Shape.

The Rectangle tool is still active.

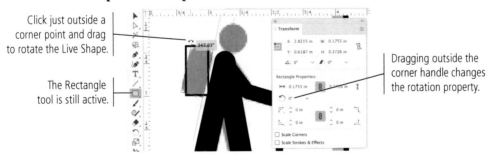

Dragging outside the corner handle changes the rotation property.

6. **Click and drag any of the bounding-box handles until the shape's height and width matches the template art.**

Click and drag any of the bounding-box handles to resize the Live Shape.

The Rectangle tool is still active.

Dragging the bounding-box handles changes the shape's size properties.

7. **In the Transform panel, make sure the link between the Corner Radius fields is active, then change any of the fields to 0.05 in.**

   Remember, you hid the Corner Widgets in an earlier exercise. If they were visible, you could drag the live widgets to change the shape's corner radius.

Note:

To show corner widgets, choose View>Show Corner Widgets.

The Rectangle tool is still active.

Use these fields to change the corner radius if the on-screen widgets are not visible.

8. **With the object selected, click the Swap Fill and Stroke button at the bottom of the Tools panel.**

Swap Fill and Stroke button

9. **Choose the Ellipse tool (nested under the Rectangle tool).**

10. **Press Option/Alt, then click at the center of the figure's head and drag out. Use the Smart Guides to create a shape with equal height and width.**

   Pressing Option/Alt while you draw creates the new shape with its center at the point where you click. You can press Shift to constrain the new shape to a circle, or simply use the Smart Guides.

   Again, ellipses are recognized by Illustrator's Live Shapes functionality. The Transform panel shows options that are relative to an ellipse.

Option/Alt-click the center of the figure's head to draw out from the center.

Ellipse tool

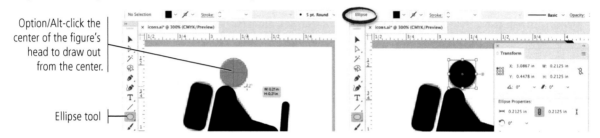

11. **If necessary, adjust the circle's size and position until you are satisfied with the results.**

12. **Save the file and continue to the next exercise.**

Transforming Objects with the Bounding Box

Bounding-box handles make it easy to transform an object on the artboard. When the Selection tool is active, you can resize an object by dragging any handle, and even rotate an object by placing the cursor directly outside a corner handle. If Smart Guides are active, cursor feedback helps if you want to make specific transformations, or you can work freestyle and drag handles until you're satisfied with the results.

Drag a left- or right-center handle
to change the object's width.

Shift-drag to maintain an object's original
height-to-width aspect ratio as you transform it.

Drag a top- or bottom-center handle
to change the object's height.

Option/Alt-drag a handle to transform
the object around its center point.

Drag a corner handle to change both the
height and shape of an object at once.

Click directly outside an object's
corner handle to rotate the object.

Artwork used in these examples is taken from the built-in Adobe symbol libraries.

The Free Transform tool allows you to change the shape of selected objects by dragging transformation handles.

The **Touch widget**, which you can use to change the active transformation mode, appears when the Free Transform tool is active. To move the Touch bar in the workspace, click away from the three buttons and drag to another location.

Transformation handles

When the cursor is over a transformation handle, the icon shows which distortions can be made.

Constraint

Free Transform

Perspective Distort

Free Distort

Moving the cursor over a handle shows the transformation that can be made by dragging that handle. Clicking one of the handles shows a larger icon to indicate the possible transformation.

When you first select the Free Transform tool, the widget shows that the **Free Transform** mode is active. Larger transformation handles appear over all eight of the selected object's bounding-box handles. In this case, most of the available transformations are the same as those you can make when the Selection tool is active.

Drag a corner handle diagonally in or out to scale the selection horizontally and vertically at the same time.

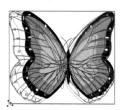

Drag a center handle perpendicular to the bounding box edge to scale the selection in one direction.

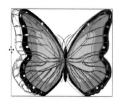

Drag a center handle parallel to the bounding box edge to skew the selection.

Click a corner handle and drag around to rotate the selection.

Press Option/Alt to apply the transformation around the center point.

Press Shift, or activate the Constraint option, to transform the selection proportionally (maintaining the original height-to-width aspect ratio).

If you activate the **Perspective Distort** option in the Touch widget, you can drag the object's corner transformation handles to change the object's perspective. (The Constraint option is not available when Perspective Distort is active.)

When the Free Transform mode is active, you can accomplish the same goal by clicking a corner handle, then pressing Command-Option-Shift/Control-Alt-Shift and dragging.

If you activate the **Free Distort** option, you can drag the corner transformation handles to distort the selection. When Constraint is active, you can only drag the corner exactly horizontal or vertical from its previous position.

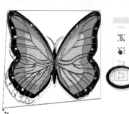

When the Free Transform mode is active, you can accomplish the same goal by clicking a corner handle, then pressing Command/Control and dragging.

Explore Artwork Outlines

As you develop complex artwork, it can be helpful to view the basic artwork structure without applied fill and stroke attributes. Illustrator's Outline mode makes this possible.

1. **With icons.ai open, deselect everything in the file.**

2. **Choose View>Outline.**

    Regardless of the defined stroke weight, lines are still just lines. Outline mode shows you a wireframe of your artwork; fill and stroke attributes are not visible.

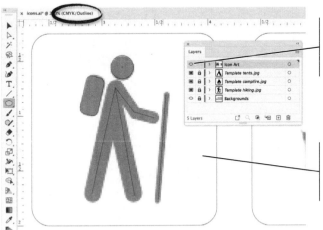

In Outline viewing mode, the Layers panel shows a hollow eye icon for non-template layers.

In Outline mode, you can't see the objects' fill or stroke attributes.

Note:

By default, objects on template layers remain visible in outline mode. You can convert a template layer to outlines by Command/Control-clicking the template layer icon.

3. **Choose the Join tool in the Tools panel (nested under the Shaper tool).**

    The Join tool is an easy way to connect open line segments.

4. **Click and drag with the Join tool to paint an area over the point where the figure's elbow meets.**

    Because these lines have rounded caps, outline mode makes it easier to see the actual ends of the lines.

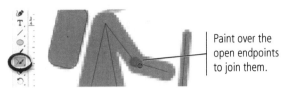

Paint over the open endpoints to join them.

Note:

You can also select open endpoints and choose Object>Path>Join. If the selected points overlap, as in this exercise, the two points are simply combined into a single corner endpoint. If the selected endpoints do not overlap, this command creates a straight, connecting segment between the points.

5. **Choose the Selection tool in the Tools panel, and click either of the arm segments to select them.**

    You can now see the bounding box of the selected object — both angled lines, which have been joined into a single Path object (as you can see in the Control panel). After joining the endpoints of the two lines, they no longer function independently.

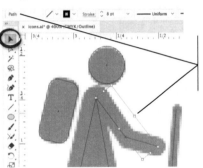

Joining the endpoints combines the two separate lines into a single path with multiple segments.

6. **With the new Path object selected, choose Object>Lock>Selection.**

   When an object is locked, you can't select or change it — just as locking a layer protects the objects on that layer.

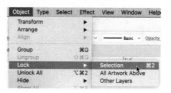

7. **Choose the Join tool again. Click and drag over the top endpoints of the lines that make up the figure's legs.**

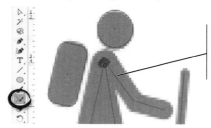

   This shape is locked, so the upper endpoint of this line segment is not affected.

Note:

The Join tool works even when the line's endpoints do not overlap — simply paint from one endpoint to another. If lines overlap and the endpoints do not connect, you can paint to remove extra line segments past where the lines overlap.

8. **Choose View>Preview or View>GPU Preview.**

   On Macintosh, choosing View>Preview restores the full-color preview to either the GPU or CPU preview, whichever was enabled before choosing the Outline view. On Windows, you have to choose which preview to use when you return from Outline mode.

   When Outline mode is turned off, you can see the result of joining the endpoints. By default, connected line segments use the Miter Join method. This is obviously not appropriate for the icon artwork in this exercise.

Note:

If your computer supports the technology, GPU Preview is enabled by default.

9. **Click either unlocked line with the Selection tool to select the Path object.**

   Again, joining the open endpoints combined the two Lines into a single Path object.

10. **With the Path object selected, click the Round Join Corner option in the Stroke panel.**

11. **In the Layers panel, expand the Icon Art layer.**

As you can see, the Picnic Table artwork group is locked from the earlier exercise. The second path object that makes up the figure's arm is also locked from Step 6.

These five objects make up the Hiker artwork.

12. **Click the Lock icon for the Path object to unlock only that object.**

The Object>Unlock All menu command unlocks all individually locked objects on unlocked layers (it does not affect objects on locked layers). When a layer is expanded, however, you can use the Lock column in the Layers panel to lock and unlock individual objects without unlocking everything.

Use this column to lock or unlock specific objects on a layer.

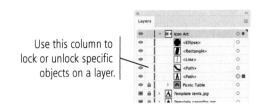

13. **Use what you learned in the previous exercise to finalize the icon artwork:**

- **Delete the Template hiking.jpg layer**
- **Choose Select>All**
- **Choose Object>Group**
- **Unlock the Backgrounds layer**
- **Press Shift, then click the background shape to add it to the active selection**
- **Choose Object>Group**
- **Lock the Backgrounds layer**
- **Rename the parent group** Hiker **in the Layers panel**
- **Lock the Hiker sublayer**

14. **Save the file and continue to the next exercise.**

Working with GPU Preview

The Graphics Processing Unit (GPU) is a specialized processor that can quickly execute image display commands, which allows faster rendering in Illustrator.

If your computer meets the hardware and software requirements*, GPU Performance is enabled by default. You can temporarily disable Illustrator's GPU Preview mode by choosing View>View using CPU. You can also permanently disable the feature in the Performance pane of the Preferences dialog box.

When GPU Performance is enabled and the Zoom tool is active, you can also use the animated zoom feature:

- Hold down the mouse button to dynamically zoom in on the spot where you click.
- Click and drag right to dynamically zoom in.
- Click and drag left to dynamically zoom out.

*A complete list of requirements can be found at https://helpx.adobe.com/illustrator/kb/gpu-performance-preview-improvements.html

Draw with the Shaper Tool

The Shaper tool allows you to easily create basic shapes, almost as you would with a pencil on paper. The software automatically translates your drawing into rectangles, polygons with other than four sides, ellipses, or straight lines. In this exercise, you use this tool to create the tent artwork.

1. **With icons.ai open, expand the Icon Art layer, and then zoom in to the tent template artwork.**

2. **Make sure the Icon Art layer is active, then choose the Shaper tool in the Tools panel.**

    If you continued directly from the previous exercise, the tool is nested under the Join tool.

3. **If you see a window appear with advice on using the Shaper tool, click the window's Close button.**

    Illustrator includes a number of these pop-up "helper" dialog boxes that explain certain features. Feel free to explore those dialog boxes when they appear.

4. **Click and drag to draw a triangle that represents the outer shape of the tent.**

    For some reason, the Shaper tool always defaults to a light gray fill, even if you define a different fill color before drawing.

Shaper tool

Objects created with the Shaper tool are recognized as Live Shapes.

5. **Click and drag again to draw the inner triangle.**

6. **Click and drag again to draw two straight lines that represent the tent poles.**

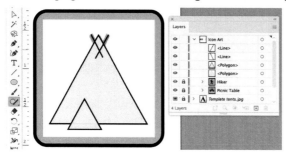

7. **Using the Shaper tool, scribble a path that begins below both rectangles and touches the overlapping area of the two triangles.**

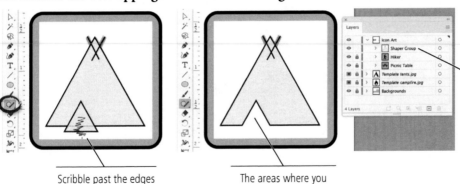

The four objects you drew with the Shaper tool are combined into a special Shaper Group object.

Scribble past the edges of both triangles.

The areas where you scribbled is knocked out.

8. **In the Layers panel, expand the Shaper Group sublayer.**

Scribbling over an area of overlapping objects converts those objects into a Shaper Group. All overlapping objects become part of the group, even it they were not affected by the scribbling motion.

All overlapping shapes are included in the Shaper Group.

How you scribble with the tool determines what will happen:

- Scribble past the outer edges of the shapes to remove (knock out) both the fill and stroke attributes of the area.

- Scribble entirely within an overlap area to knock out that area.

- Scribble from an overlap area to a non-overlap area to merge the shapes where you scribble. The resulting shape is the color of the front shape in the stacking order.

- Scribble from a non-overlap area to an overlap area to create shapes that depend on where you start to scribble:

  – Start in the back object to create a merged shape with the same color as the back shape.

  – Start in the front object to knock out the areas where you scribble.

9. **Move the Shaper tool cursor over overlapping shapes to reveal the overlapping paths.**

10. **Click the group to select it.**

Clicking inside a Shaper Group selects the entire group object. It is surrounded by a single bounding box, and an arrow widget appears on the right edge. When the entire Shaper Group is selected, changes to the fill or stroke attributes affect all visible elements of the group.

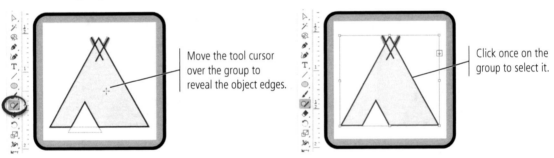

Move the tool cursor over the group to reveal the object edges.

Click once on the group to select it.

11. In the Control panel, change the Stroke color to None.

Because the entire group is selected, this affects all objects in the group — including the two lines that are supposed to represent the tent poles.

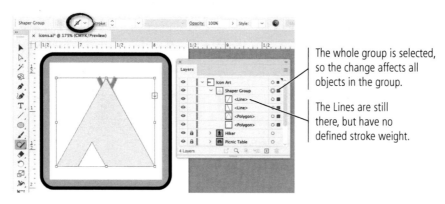

The whole group is selected, so the change affects all objects in the group.

The Lines are still there, but have no defined stroke weight.

12. Click once on the surface of the visible (back) triangle shape.

Clicking any of the filled shapes in the Shaper Group enters into Face Selection mode, in which the selected surface is identified with a crosshatch overlay. You can use this method to edit the fill color — but not the stroke color — of only the selected element within the group.

13. Using the Control panel, change the selected shape's fill color to Black.

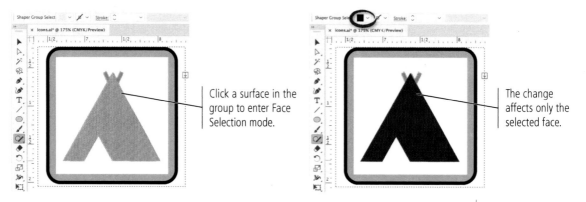

Click a surface in the group to enter Face Selection mode.

The change affects only the selected face.

14. Click the arrow icon in the top-right corner of the shaper group's bounding box to enter Construction mode.

Clicking the arrow widget on the Shaper Group bounding box enters Construction mode, in which you can access and edit the individual shape properties of the component shapes of a shaper group.

Note:

If the arrow on the group's bounding box is pointing up, you are in Construction mode.

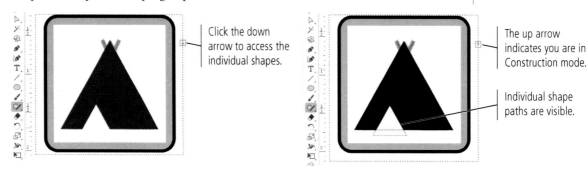

Click the down arrow to access the individual shapes.

The up arrow indicates you are in Construction mode.

Individual shape paths are visible.

15. Click the black filled area again to reveal the triangle's bounding box. Adjust the bounding-box handles until it approximately matches the outer shape in the template image.

It is important to realize that Shaper Groups maintain the original shapes, even after you knock out or merge specific areas of those shapes.

Use Construction mode to edit individual shapes in the group.

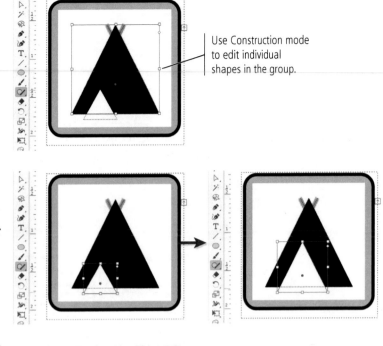

16. Click the edge of the inner triangle to select that element of the group. Adjust the bounding-box handles until you are satisfied with the inner shape's size and position relative to the template artwork.

Because that shape has no fill, you have to click the edge to select it.

17. Select each of the tent pole lines and define a 4-pt black stroke.

You can edit the lines individually, or Shift-click to select both before changing the stroke weight.

18. Click away from the Shaper Group to exit Construction mode and deselect the group.

19. Delete the Template tents.jpg layer from the file.

20. Use what you learned in previous exercises to create a final locked group named Campsites for the tent artwork and its background.

In this case you do not need to create a separate group for the icon because it is already combined in a special Shaper Group.

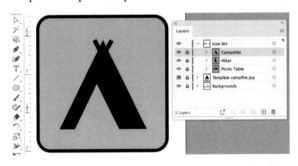

21. Save the file and continue to the next exercise.

Note:

You can also single-click an object's stroke or double-click an object's fill to enter into Construction mode.

Note:

To remove an object from a Shaper Group, enter into Construction mode for that group. Click the center point of the shape you want to remove, then drag it out of the Shaper Group's bounding box.

Draw with the Pencil Tool

As you might already realize, not all artwork can be created from basic shapes and lines. Illustrator includes everything you need to create artwork in any form, including irregular shapes. The Pencil tool is one method for creating custom shapes. Like a regular pencil on a piece of paper, the Pencil tool creates lines that follow the path of your cursor.

Note:

If you have a digital drawing tablet, the Pencil tool can be particularly useful for drawing custom artwork.

1. **With icons.ai open, make sure the Icon Art layer is selected in the Layers panel. Zoom in to the campfire template artwork.**

2. **Choose the Pencil tool (nested under the Shaper tool) in the Tools panel, and click the Default Fill and Stroke button in the Tools panel.**

Pencil tool

3. **Double-click the Pencil tool in the Tools panel.**

   Double-clicking certain tools in the Tools panel opens an Options dialog box, where you can control the behavior for the selected tool. The Pencil tool options include:

   - **Fidelity.** This option determines how far apart anchor points are added as you drag. Smooth results in fewer points and smoother curves, but also less accuracy matching the path you draw. More accurate means more anchor points and a path closer to what you draw (this can make the lines appear choppy).

   - **Fill New Pencil Strokes.** By default, pencil paths are not filled, regardless of the fill color defined in the Tools panel.

   - **Keep Selected.** If this option is checked, the line you draw is automatically selected when you release the mouse button.

   - **Option Key Toggles to Smooth Tool.** As the name suggests, this allows you to quickly and temporarily switch to the Smooth tool while drawing with the Pencil tool. The Smooth tool can be used to remove unnecessary points along a pencil-drawn path, removing small or jagged jumps in the path.

   - **Close Paths when Ends are within __ Pixels.** When this option is active, dragging back near the original starting point creates a closed path when you release the mouse button. If this option is not checked, dragging near the original point does not create a closed path.

   - **Edit Selected Paths.** If this option is checked, drawing near a selected path (based on the Within value) can change the existing path. This is an important distinction — especially when Keep Selected is checked — because you can accidentally edit the first path instead of creating a second shape.

4. Define the following settings in the Pencil Tool Options dialog box:
    - Set the Fidelity slider to the midpoint.
    - Check the Close Paths... option
    - Uncheck all other options

5. Click OK to apply your changes and return to the artboard.

6. Click at the bottom-left point of the fire icon. Hold down the mouse button and begin dragging around the shape of the fire.

7. When you get near your original starting point and a hollow circle appears in the cursor icon, release the mouse button.

    As you drag, a colored line indicates the path you're drawing. Don't worry if the path isn't perfect; when you release the mouse button, Illustrator automatically smooths the path.

    When you release the mouse button, the shape shows the defined stroke color, but not the fill color because you unchecked the Fill New Pencil Strokes option in Step 4.

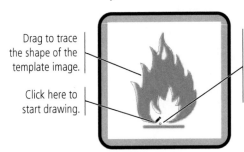

Drag to trace the shape of the template image.

Click here to start drawing.

The hollow circle in the cursor icon indicates that releasing the mouse button will create a closed shape.

8. Click near the top point of the white flame area (inside the first path) and drag to create the white inner shape in the fire icon.

Use the Pencil tool to draw this shape.

9. Using the Rectangle tool, draw the bar below the fire shape.

10. In the Layers panel, delete the Template campfire.jpg layer.

11. Expand the Icon Art layer if necessary.

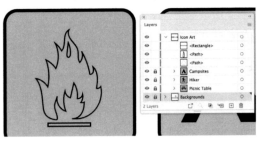

Note:

Pressing the Option/Alt key while you drag with the Pencil tool places an anchor point at the location of the cursor when you press the key.

If you hold down the Option/Alt key while dragging, you can draw a straight line. When you release the modifier key, an anchor point ends the straight segment; continuing to drag resumes drawing a path in whatever shape you drag.

12. Use the Selection tool to select all three shapes of the icon art. Change the fill color to black and the stroke color to None.

When all three objects are filled, you can't see the inner shape at the top of the flame.

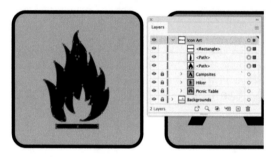

13. Choose Object>Compound Path>Make.

A **compound path** is a single shape made up of more than one path. Compound paths usually have inner "empty" areas, such as the letter O or Q.

This option combines all three selected shapes into one; the area of the smaller top shape is removed from the larger shape behind it.

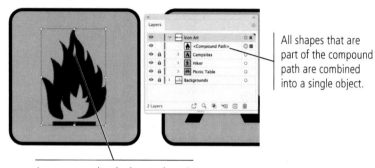

All shapes that are part of the compound path are combined into a single object.

As a compound path, the top shape is knocked out from the bottom shape.

14. Use what you learned in previous exercises to create a locked group named Campfire **for the final icon artwork.**

In this case you do not need to create a separate group for the icon because it is already combined in the Compound Path object.

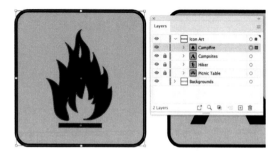

15. Save the file and continue to the final exercise.

Edit Individual Grouped Elements

The client has decided that the icons should be white artwork on green backgrounds, so the final step in this exercise requires changing the colors of both the background shapes and the icon artwork. This is a fairly easy process, but because each of the icons are grouped, it will require a few extra steps.

1. **With icons.ai open, change your view percentage so you can see all the artwork in the file.**

2. **In the Layers panel, unlock all layers and sublayers in the file.**

3. **Choose the Selection tool, then click the picnic table artwork.**

   Because the artwork is grouped, the Selection tool selects the entire group. You need to use a different method to select only certain elements within the group.

The smaller icon indicates that only some objects on the layer (or in the group) are selected.

The large icon indicates that the entire group is selected.

Clicking with the Selection tool selects the entire group.

4. **Click anywhere outside the rectangle shapes to deselect the group, then choose the Direct Selection tool in the Tools panel.**

   The Direct Selection tool selects pieces of an object — specific paths, anchor points, or individual elements in a grouped object.

5. **Click the brown fill of the background shape behind the picnic table artwork to select it.**

   Because you clicked the fill, you selected the entire object. If you had clicked along the object's stroke, you would have selected that particular segment of the shape's edge.

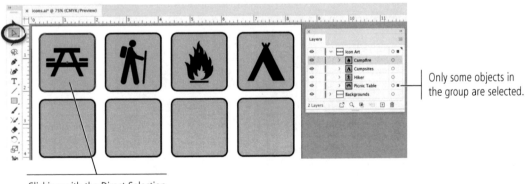

Only some objects in the group are selected.

Clicking with the Direct Selection tool selects only that object.

6. **Choose Select>Same>Fill Color.**

    The options in this menu are very useful for finding objects that share specific attributes. They select all similar unlocked objects on the entire artboard. The Select>Same menu options select objects regardless of which layer they occupy.

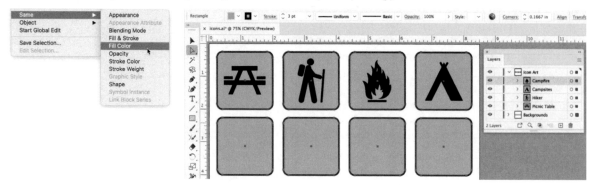

7. **With all eight brown shapes selected, use the Control panel to change the Stroke color to None and the Fill color to a medium green.**

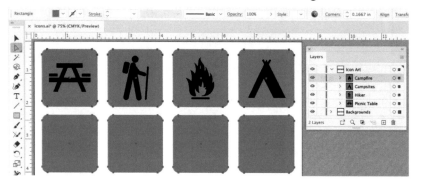

Note:

You can also use the Select Similar Objects menu in the Control panel to select objects with like attributes.

8. **Using the Direct Selection tool, click any of the black shapes that make up the picnic table icon.**

9. **Choose Select>Same>Fill Color.**

10. **With all the black-filled objects selected, change the Fill color to White.**

    As you can see, there are two problems. First, the lines in the Hiker icon are still black because they are lines and not filled shapes. Second, the elements in the Campsite icon are still black because the Select>Same commands cannot access individual pieces of a Shaper Group.

11. Choose the Selection tool in the Tools panel, and click away from all artwork to deselect everything.

12. Double-click the Hiker artwork. In the Layers panel, expand the Hiker group.

Double-clicking a group enters into **Isolation mode**, where only objects within the selected group are available. Basically, Isolation mode provides access to objects in the group without ungrouping the objects on the main artboard. Other elements outside the group are dimmed and visible, but you can't access or edit them.

13. Using the Selection tool, click to select the Hiker artwork.

Remember, you created a group from the icon artwork, and then grouped that with the background shape. Because there are two levels of grouping, you have to enter into Isolation mode for the second (nested) group to access the individual paths that make up the actual icon artwork.

The Edit bar shows the path to the group you are editing (called "breadcrumbs").

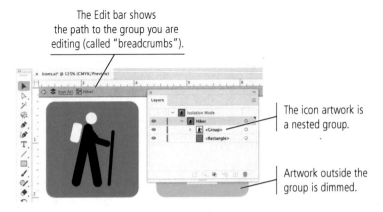

The icon artwork is a nested group.

Artwork outside the group is dimmed.

14. Double-click the icon artwork on the artboard to enter into the nested group. In the Layers panel, expand the Group sublayer.

15. Shift-click to select the two Path objects and the Line object.

Layer Parent Group Nested Group

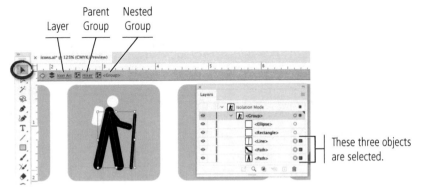

These three objects are selected.

16. Choose Object>Path>Outline Stroke.

This command converts lines to filled shapes. You can no longer access the actual paths that made up the original Line or Path objects.

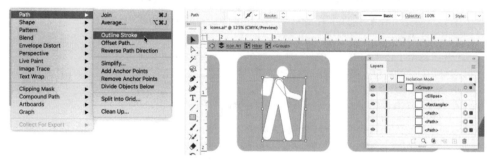

17. With all three shapes selected, change the Fill color to White.

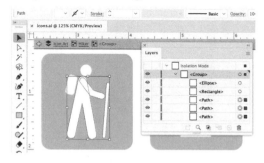

18. At the top of the document window, click the arrow button three times to return to the main artboard.

The first click closes the nested group. The second click closes the Hiker group. The third click exits the layer and returns to the main artboard.

19. Using the Shaper tool, click to select the Campsite icon artwork.

The Shaper tool selects the Shaper Group, even though it is grouped with the background rectangle.

20. Using the Control panel, change the Fill and Stroke colors to White.

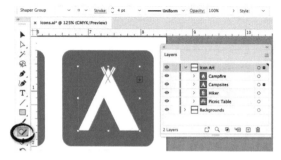

21. Save the file and close it.

Note:

You can also press the ESC key, or double-click an area outside the group, to exit Isolation mode.

Editing Similar Shapes with Global Edit

In this project, you used the Select>Similar menu to select and edit all shapes with the same fill color at one time. Illustrator includes a related option to identify similar shapes based on their appearance, size, or both.

Start Editing Similar Shapes Together

Click the arrow button to define the parameters of the search.

When an object is selected on the artboard, you can click the Start Global Edit button in the Quick Actions section of the Properties panel, or click the Start Editing Similar Shapes Together button in the Control panel to find other objects that match the current selection.

Clicking the arrow button to the right of either button opens a pop-up panel of preferences, where you can define the attributes you want to include in the search.

Appearance refers to attributes listed in the Appearance panel — fill and stroke, opacity, effects, and so on. Size refers to the physical dimensions (height and width) of the object. You can also determine which artboards to include in the search, as well as whether to include objects on the canvas (pasteboard) outside the artboard boundaries.

When you enter the Global Edit mode, the software highlights other shapes that match the attributes of the original selection. (The highlight can be difficult to see, depending on the actual artwork you are building.) Changes to the selected object are also reflected in the highlighted shapes.

When you are finished editing, you can click the Stop Global Edit button or simply click away from the original selection to exit this mode.

In this example, we selected Shape 1 and chose the Match Appearance option. Five objects are not highlighted:

Shapes 2 and 6	Different fill color
Shape 7	Different stroke weight
Shape 9	Different shape
Shape 11	Applied drop shadow

Note that Shape 5 is selected even though it is a different size than Shape 1.

Shape 9 is not selected because different types of objects are not considered to match; a 1" × 1" ellipse will not be identified if the original selection is a 1" × 1" rectangle.

Changing the fill color of the selected shape also changes the fill color of all highlighted shapes.

Match Appearance is active

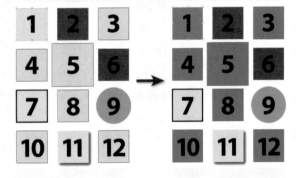

In this second example, we selected Shape 1 and chose the Match Size option. Only Shapes 5 and 9 are not highlighted.

Because some of the identified objects have different style attributes (the drop shadow), a warning notes that attributes of the selected item will be copied to all highlighted objects.

After changing the fill color of Shape 1 and dismissing the warning message, all highlighted objects now have a green fill color. The drop shadow effect that was previously applied to Shape 11 has been removed because Shape 1 has no applied drop shadow.

Adobe Illustrator

The style attributes will be copied from the original artwork to the highlighted artwork. Do you wish to continue?

No   Yes

Match Size is active

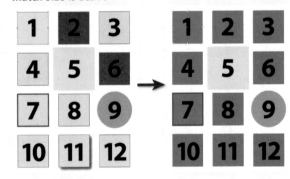

1. _____ are composed of mathematical descriptions of a series of lines and points; they are resolution independent, can be freely scaled, and are automatically output at the resolution of the output device.

2. _____ are pixel-based, made up of a grid of individual pixels (rasters or bits).

3. The _____ is a rectangle that marks the outermost edges of an object, regardless of the actual object shape.

4. _____ is the relative top-to-bottom order of objects on the artboard, or of layers in the Layers panel.

5. The _____ is used to select entire objects or groups.

6. The _____ is used to select individual paths and points of a shape, or to select component pieces within a group.

7. The _____ is used to draw freeform paths defined by dragging the mouse cursor.

8. Press _____ to temporarily access the Selection tool; releasing the modifier key restores the previously selected tool.

9. A(n) _____ combines multiple Live Shapes, but maintains the original shapes in a special group.

10. A(n) _____ is a single object that is made up of more than one shape.

1. Briefly explain the difference between vector graphics and raster images.

2. Briefly explain the difference between the Selection tool and the Direct Selection tool.

3. Briefly explain how the Fill and Stroke icons at the bottom of the Tools panel affect your work.

Use what you have learned in this project to complete the following freeform exercise.
Carefully read the art director and client comments, then create your own design to meet the needs of the project.
Use the space below to sketch ideas. When finished, write a brief explanation of the reasoning behind your final design.

art director comments

The client is pleased with the first four icons, and they want you to complete the rest of the set. They also want you to create an additional set of icons for athletic activities that they offer during their special holiday weekend events.

To complete this project, you should:

❑ Complete the remaining campsite icons. The bitmap versions are in your WIP>Camping folder.

❑ Carefully consider the best approach for each icon and use whichever tool (or tools) you feel is most appropriate.

❑ Create a second Illustrator file for the five new tournament icons.

client comments

Holidays are one of our busiest times, and we host a number of family-oriented special events during those weekends. To help keep everyone happy, we always set up organized tournaments for families with children of all ages, and we want to be able to post signs directing guests to those activities.

Since you did such a good job on the first four icons, we would like you to finish those first.

For the second set, we need icons for badminton, bocce, relay races, horseshoes, and volleyball. We don't have the images for these ones, so we would like you to come up with something. Remember, icons need to be easily recognizable, so they should clearly convey each activity.

project justification

_____
_____
_____
_____
_____
_____
_____
_____
_____
_____
_____
_____
_____
_____
_____

The skills that you learned in this project will serve as the foundation for most work you create in Illustrator. You learned how to place raster images as templates, from which you created scalable vector graphics that will work in virtually any printed application. You learned a number of techniques for selecting objects and component pieces of objects, as well as various options for aligning objects relative to one another and to the artboard.

You learned how to draw primitive geometric shapes, and how to control the color of objects' fill and stroke attributes. You used a number of transformation options, including cloning methods to copy existing objects. Finally, you learned how to draw freeform shapes to suit more complex needs. As you move forward in this book, you will build on the basic skills you learned in this project to create increasingly complex artwork.

Draw, shear, reflect, and clone basic shapes

Use stroke properties to create unique artwork

Create and align basic rectangles with rounded corners

Use various techniques to select objects, groups, and the component pieces of those objects and groups

Use the Shaper tool to combine and manage Live Shapes

Use the Pencil tool and compound paths to draw complex shapes

Regatta Artwork

2

Your client is the marketing director for the Long Beach Regatta, which attracts tens of thousands of visitors to the beach community throughout the four-day event. You have been hired to create the primary artwork for this year's event, which will be used in a variety of different products (ads, posters, etc.).

This project incorporates the following skills:

❏ Drawing complex custom shapes with the Pen tool

❏ Editing points and handles to control the position of vector paths

❏ Drawing irregular shapes by painting with the Blob Brush tool

❏ Creating a custom color scheme using saved swatches

❏ Adding interest and depth with color gradients

❏ Adjusting color, both globally and in specific selections

❏ Saving a PDF file for print distribution

The poster to promote the Regatta is basically the "play bill," and we will place it in store windows, public sites, and on bulletin boards all over the city. It will also be placed in local newspapers and entertainment magazines, and used as the cover for the souvenir program that we produce for the event.

We want the artwork to be very colorful and vivid, so the main focus — and most of the poster real estate — should be on the graphics. The only text for the poster is the event name, date, and location.

I sketched a mock-up of a sailboat that you can use as the basis for the artwork. You should use the Pen tool to draw the necessary paths because simple shapes won't work and the Pencil tool doesn't provide fine enough control to efficiently achieve what you need.

I assigned the ocean background artwork to another designer, so you will have to incorporate your artwork into that file. This is going to be a complex piece of artwork, so you should pay close attention to the layer content when you organize the various pieces. That will make it far easier to edit specific components as necessary if the client decides to make changes.

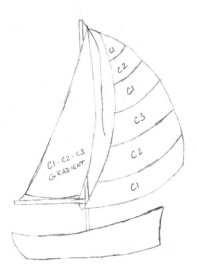

To complete this project, you will:

- ❏ Use the Pen tool to draw precise curves
- ❏ Adjust anchor points and handles to precisely control the shape of vector objects
- ❏ Reshape line segments with the Anchor Point tool
- ❏ Use the Blob Brush tool to "paint" the area of vector shapes
- ❏ Define custom color swatches to allow easy universal changes
- ❏ Create color gradients to blend multiple colors in a single object
- ❏ Adjust gradients in context on the artboard
- ❏ Manage artwork with sublayers
- ❏ Save the file as a PDF

Much of the artwork you create will require far more complexity than simple lines and geometric shapes. When you need to produce custom artwork — whether from scratch or by tracing a hand-drawn sketch or photo — Illustrator includes a powerful set of tools to create and manipulate every point and path in the illustration. In the first stage of this project, you begin exploring the Pen tool, as well as other options for building and controlling custom shapes.

Prepare the Drawing Workspace

As with any project, setting up the workspace is an important first step. This project requires a single artboard to contain the entire illustration.

1. Download **Regatta_AI21_RF.zip** from the Student Files web page.

2. Expand the ZIP archive in your WIP folder (Macintosh) or copy the archive contents into your WIP folder (Windows).

   This results in a folder named **Regatta**, which contains the files you need for this project. You should also use this folder to save the files you create in this project.

3. In Illustrator, choose File>New. Choose the Print option at the top of the dialog box, and choose the Letter document preset.

   Remember, using the Print category of presets automatically applies the CMYK color mode and 300 ppi raster effects.

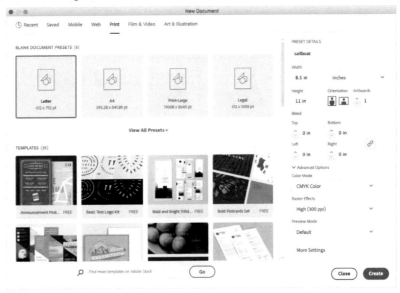

4. Define the following settings in the Preset Details section:

Name:	**sailboat**
Units:	**Inches**
Orientation:	**Portrait**
Artboards:	**1**

5. Click Create to create the file.

6. Choose View>Fit Artboard in Window.

   On Macintosh, the artboard of a new file is automatically centered in the document window. On some Windows systems, the artboard might be slightly off-center. The Fit Artboard in Window command centers the artboard in the document window, so the template image you place in the next step will be automatically centered on the artboard.

7. **Choose File>Place. Navigate to the file `sketch.jpg` in your WIP>Regatta folder. Check the Link and Template options at the bottom of the dialog box, and then click Place.**

   Macintosh users: remember, you might have to click the Options button to reveal the options check boxes at the bottom of the Place dialog box.

   You will use this client-supplied sketch to create the primary artwork for this illustration.

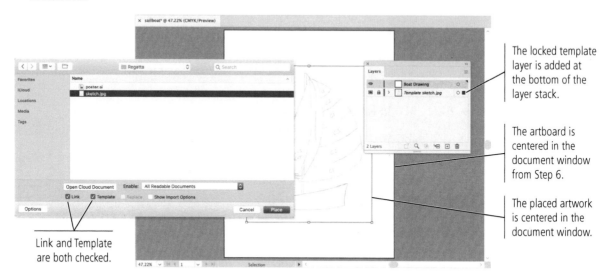

The locked template layer is added at the bottom of the layer stack.

The artboard is centered in the document window from Step 6.

The placed artwork is centered in the document window.

Link and Template are both checked.

8. **Double-click the template layer icon in the Layers panel to open the Layer Options dialog box. Uncheck the Dim Images option and click OK.**

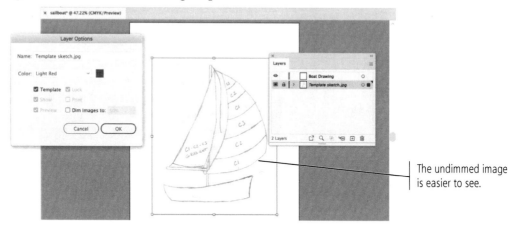

The undimmed image is easier to see.

9. **Double-click the Layer 1 name in the Layers panel to highlight it. Rename the layer `Boat Drawing`, then press Return/Enter to finalize the new name.**

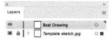

10. **Click away from the placed sketch image to deselect it.**

11. **Save the file as an Illustrator file named `sailboat.ai` in your WIP>Regatta folder using the default Illustrator options, and then continue to the next exercise.**

Use the Pen Tool to Trace the Sketch

In this project, you use the Pen tool, which provides far more power to control the precise position of every line in a drawing. In fact, many believe the Pen tool is the most powerful and important tool in the Illustrator Tools panel.

An **anchor point** marks the end of a line **segment**, and the point **handles** determine the shape of that segment. That's the basic definition of a vector, but there is a bit more to it than that. Fortunately, you don't need to be a mathematician to master the Pen tool because Illustrator handles the underlying geometry for you.

Note:

The lines you create by connecting anchor points and pulling handles are called ***Bézier curves***.

Understanding Anchor Points and Handles

Each segment in a path has two anchor points, and can have two associated handles.

You can create corner points by simply clicking with the Pen tool instead of clicking and dragging. Corner points do not have their own handles; the connected segments are controlled by the handles of the other associated points. (Using the Convert Direction Point tool, click a smooth point to convert it to a corner point; click and drag from a corner point to add handles, converting it to a smoother point.)

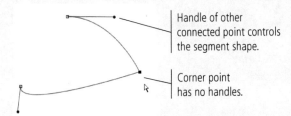

Handle of other connected point controls the segment shape.

Corner point has no handles.

In the image to the right, we clicked to create Point A and dragged (without releasing the mouse button) to create Handle A1. We then clicked and dragged to create Point B and Handle B1; Handle B2 was automatically created as a reflection of B1 (Point B is a **symmetrical point**).

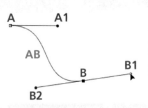

The next image shows the result of dragging Handle B1 to the left instead of to the right when we created the curve. Notice the difference in the curve here and the curve above. When you drag a handle, the connecting segment arcs away from the direction you drag.

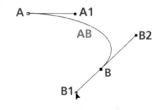

It's important to understand that every line segment is connected to two handles. In this example, Handle A1 and Handle B2 determine the shape of Segment AB. Dragging either handle affects the shape of the connected segment.

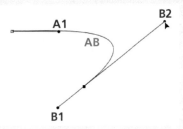

When you use the Pen tool, clicking and dragging a point creates a symmetrical (smooth) point; both handles start out at equal length, directly opposite one another. Changing the angle of one handle of a symmetrical point also changes the opposing handle of that point. In the example here, repositioning Handle B1 also moves Handle B2, which affects the shape of Segment AB. You can, however, change the length of one handle without affecting the length of the other handle.

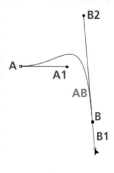

1. **With sailboat.ai open, open the Selection and Anchor Display pane of the Preferences dialog box.**

   Remember, on Macintosh, preferences are accessed in the Illustrator menu. On Windows, they are accessed in the Edit menu.

2. **In the lower half of the dialog box, change the Size slider to one of the larger settings.**

   By default, anchor points and handles are rather small, and can be difficult to distinguish. You can use the Size slider to make the points and handles appear larger, which makes them easier to work with.

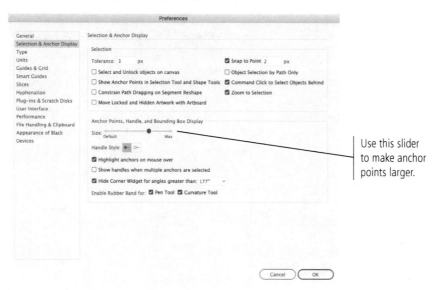

Use this slider to make anchor points larger.

3. **Click OK to apply the change.**

4. **Zoom in so you can clearly see the shape of the boat in the sketch.**

   As you draw, zoom in as necessary to view different parts of the sketch.

5. **Open the View menu. If the menu command near the bottom of the menu says "Hide Corner Widget," choose that option.**

   This menu command toggles between "Show" and "Hide." If the command already says "Show Corner Widget," then these widgets are already hidden; you can simply click away from the menu to dismiss it.

   Live Corner widgets can be distracting when you don't need them; turning them off allows you to focus on only what you need to see to complete these exercises.

6. **Choose the Pen tool in the Tools panel. Using the Control panel, set the stroke to 1-pt black and the fill to None.**

7. Click with the Pen tool to place the first anchor point on the top-left corner of the boat shape.

We typically find it easier to start drawing at a corner (if one exists).

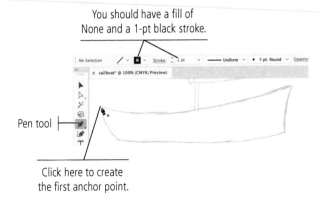

You should have a fill of
None and a 1-pt black stroke.

Pen tool

Click here to create
the first anchor point.

Note:

If you are not able to draw, make sure the Boat Drawing layer is selected in the Layers panel.

8. Click again at the bottom-left corner of the boat shape and immediately drag down and right to create handles for the second point. When the preview of the connecting segment matches the sketch, release the mouse button.

When you click and drag without releasing the mouse button, you create symmetrical handles, which determine the shape of the segment that connects the two points.

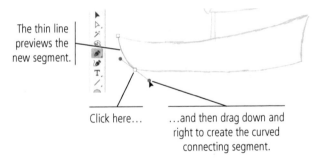

The thin line previews the new segment.

Click here...   ...and then drag down and right to create the curved connecting segment.

Note:

When we say "click and drag," you should hold down the mouse button until the end of the step.

9. Click and drag again from the bottom-right corner of the boat shape.

Again, clicking and dragging creates a smooth, symmetrical point. Equal-length, exactly opposing handles are created on both sides of the point.

Note:

Don't worry if the connecting segment doesn't exactly match the sketch. The bottom of the boat will be obscured by other artwork in the final poster.

Project 2: Regatta Artwork   95

10. Click again on the third anchor point and release the mouse button without dragging.

Clicking a smooth point as you draw converts it to a corner point, removing the outside handle from the point; the inside handle that defines the shape of the connecting segment remains in place. This allows you to change direction as you draw.

Note:

While drawing with the Pen tool, you can Option/Alt-click an anchor point, hold down the mouse button, and drag to add a non-symmetrical handle to one side of a corner point.

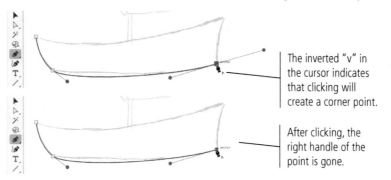

The inverted "v" in the cursor indicates that clicking will create a corner point.

After clicking, the right handle of the point is gone.

11. Click and drag to create a new point (with handles) from the top-right corner of the boat shape. Drag the handles until the connecting segment matches the shape of the sketched line.

Click here and drag up and right until the connecting segment matches the shape of the sketched line.

12. Click the original point without dragging to close the shape.

When you return to the original point, the cursor shows a small hollow circle. This indicates that clicking the existing point will close the shape.

Note:

The words "anchor" and "path" near the cursor icon are a function of Illustrator Smart Guides.

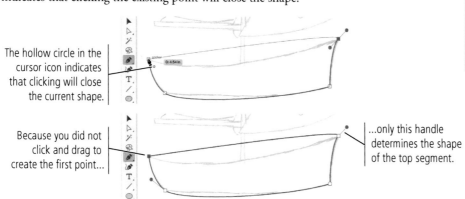

The hollow circle in the cursor icon indicates that clicking will close the current shape.

Because you did not click and drag to create the first point...

...only this handle determines the shape of the top segment.

13. **Using the Direct Selection tool, click the top-right point on the shape to select only that anchor point.**

You can use the Direct Selection tool to edit any specific anchor point or segment.

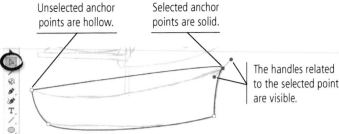

Unselected anchor points are hollow.

Selected anchor points are solid.

The handles related to the selected point are visible.

14. **Press Option/Alt, then click and drag the top handle of the selected point. Drag the handle left until the top segment matches the line in the sketch.**

Remember, the Direct Selection tool allows you to adjust individual anchor points and handles. Option/Alt-dragging one handle of a smooth point converts the point to a corner point, but leaves both handles in place. This method allows you to change the direction of an existing point, but leaves the opposite curve intact.

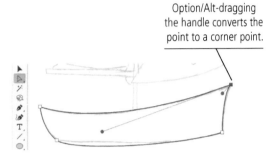

Option/Alt-dragging the handle converts the point to a corner point.

Note:

A diagonal line in the Pen tool cursor icon indicates that clicking will connect to an open endpoint so you can continue drawing the shape.

15. **Save the file and continue to the next exercise.**

Understanding Anchor Point and Bézier Curve Tools

Keep the following points in mind as you work with the Pen tool (and its nested variations) and Bézier curves.

Using the Direct Selection tool:

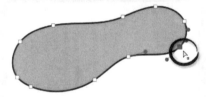

Click a specific anchor point to select it and show all handles that relate to that point.

Option/Alt drag a handle of a smooth point to convert it to a corner point.

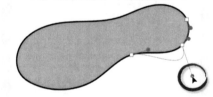

Click a segment on a selected path and drag to bend the path; connected segments might also be affected.

Using the Pen tool:

Place the cursor over an existing point to temporarily access the Delete Anchor Point tool.

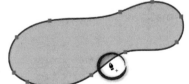

Place the cursor over an existing segment to temporarily access the Add Anchor Point tool.

Press Option/Alt and place the cursor over an existing point to temporarily access the Anchor Point tool.

Reshape Line Segments

In Illustrator, you have numerous options to create, select, and modify shapes — or parts of shapes — so you can create exactly what you need, regardless of what is already on the artboard. In this exercise you use a convenient method to easily bend line segments into the shapes you need.

1. **With sailboat.ai open, make the right sail in the sketch visible in the document window.**

2. **Using the Pen tool, click to place three connected anchor points at the corners of the sail.**

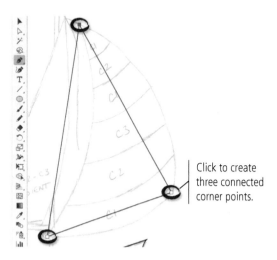

Click to create three connected corner points.

Note:

As a general rule, use as few points as necessary to create a shape with the Pen tool.

3. **Press the Option/Alt key to temporarily access the Anchor Point tool.**

The Anchor Point tool, nested under the Pen tool, can be used to change anchor points from corner to smooth (or vice versa):

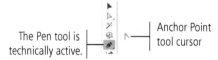

The Pen tool is technically active.

Anchor Point tool cursor

- Click a smooth point to convert it to a corner point.

- Click and drag a corner point to convert it to a smooth point with symmetrical handles.

- Option/Alt-click a handle to move only that handle, even if the point has an opposing handle; a smooth point is converted to a corner point as you drag.

4. **While holding down the Option/Alt key, click the right segment of the sail and drag until the segment matches the sketch.**

You can click and drag a segment to bend it into a different shape; handles are added to, or adjusted as necessary for the related points. This method of reshaping a line segment makes it very easy to edit your artwork without manually manipulating anchor points or handles.

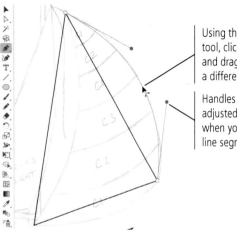

Using the Anchor Point tool, click a segment and drag to push it into a different shape.

Handles are added or adjusted as necessary when you reshape a line segment.

5. **Still holding down the Option/Alt key, adjust the other two lines that make up the sail shape.**

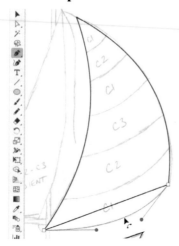

6. **Repeat Steps 2–5 to create the shape of the left sail.**

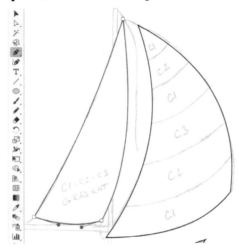

7. **Using the Pen tool, click to place a new anchor point to the left of the bottom horizontal line in the right sail, then click again past the right side of the sail shape (as shown in the following image).**

These two clicks create a straight line, connecting the two points you create by clicking.

You are going to use the Shape Builder tool to divide the sail into the necessary shapes. For this process to work properly, the dividing lines need to be at least on top of the outside shape; to be sure, you should extend the lines farther than they need to be.

The Pen tool preview shows that clicking again will create another connected segment.

When you move the mouse cursor away from the last point you created, a thin line previews the segment that would be created by clicking again. You can turn this preview on and off using the Enable Rubber Band for Pen Tool option in the Selection and Anchor Display pane of the Preferences dialog box.

8. **Press Option/Alt, then use the Anchor Point tool to reshape the segment to match the line in the sketch.**

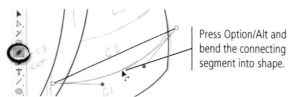

Press Option/Alt and bend the connecting segment into shape.

9. **While the Pen tool is still active, press Command/Control to temporarily access the Selection tool and click away from the line to deselect it.**

You can simply click away from selected objects with the Selection or Direct Selection tool to deselect the current selection. You can also press Command/Control-Shift-A to deselect the current selection.

Pressing Command/Control while drawing temporarily switches to the last-used Selection tool. This technique allows you to easily deselect the current path, and then continue to draw another unconnected path, all without manually switching tools.

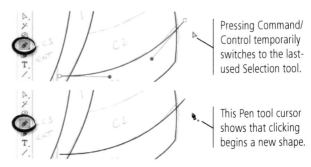

Pressing Command/Control temporarily switches to the last-used Selection tool.

This Pen tool cursor shows that clicking begins a new shape.

10. **Still using the Pen tool, draw the second horizontal line on the sail.**

If you don't deselect the previous path before clicking to draw the next line, the third click would create a segment that is connected to the last place you clicked (on the first line). In the context of this exercise, a single line with multiple anchor points is much more difficult to control than two separate lines with open endpoints.

11. **Press Option/Alt, then use the Anchor Point tool to reshape the segment to match the line in the sketch.**

Editing Anchor Points with the Control Panel

When you are working with Bézier paths, the Control panel provides options for editing selected anchor points.

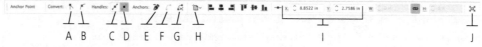

A B   C D E F G H   I   J

A **Convert Selected Anchor Points to Corner** removes direction handles from both sides of the selected point(s).

B **Convert Selected Anchor Points to Smooth** adds symmetrical handles to both sides of the selected point(s).

C **Show Handles for Multiple Selected Anchor Points.** If this option is toggled on, direction handles display for all selected points.

D **Hide Handles for Multiple Selected Anchor Points.** If this option is toggled on, direction handles are not visible when more than one point is selected.

E **Remove Selected Anchor Points** removes the selected point from the path. If the removed point was between two other points, the connecting segment is not removed.

F **Connect Selected End Points** has the same effect as the Object>Path>Join command.

G **Cut Path at Selected Anchor Points** results in two overlapping, open endpoints where the selected point was previously a single point.

H **Align To.** Use this menu to align a selected point to the active selection or relative to the artboard.

I **Point Position.** Use the X and Y fields to define a specific position for the selected point. You can also use mathematical operations to move a point relative to its current position (e.g., move it left by typing "-1" after the X value).

J **Isolate Selected Object** enters isolation mode with the object containing the selected point(s). If points are selected on more than one object, this button is not available.

12. Move the cursor away from the existing line, then press the ESC key.

When drawing with the Pen tool, this key disconnects your drawing from the current shape. You can then click to begin a new shape that is not part of the previously suggested shape.

Pressing the ESC key disconnects the tool from the previous shape.

13. Repeat Steps 10–12 to draw the rest of the curved horizontal lines on the sail.

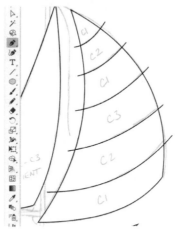

14. Save the file and continue to the next exercise.

Drawing with the Curvature Tool

The Curvature tool can be used to create and edit complex paths without manually manipulating anchor points.

Using the Curvature tool, begin by clicking to place points in a new path. As you drag after creating the first two points, the software shows a rubber-band preview of the path that will be created by clicking again. (You can turn this preview behavior off in the Selection and Anchor Display pane of the Preferences dialog box.)

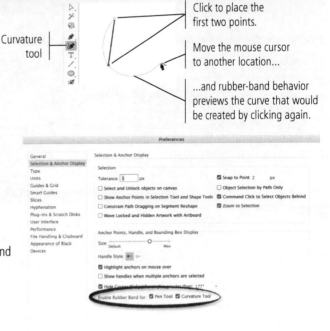

Click to place the first two points.

Move the mouse cursor to another location...

...and rubber-band behavior previews the curve that would be created by clicking again.

As long as the Curvature tool is active, you do not need to change tools to edit the path:

• Option/Alt-click to create a corner point.

• Click anywhere along an existing path to add a new anchor point.

• Double-click any point to toggle it between a smooth and corner point.

• Click a point to select it.

• Drag a selected point to move it.

• Press Delete to remove the selected point; the existing curve is maintained.

• Press the ESC key to stop drawing the current shape.

Build Shapes from Overlapping Paths

The Shape Builder tool makes it easy to break apart overlapping objects into component pieces. This tool offers similar functionality as the Pathfinder, but on a piece-by-piece basis, rather than for entire selected shapes. In this exercise, you will use the Shape Builder tool to break the sail into the individual strips that are shown on the sketch.

1. **With sailboat.ai open, use the Selection tool to draw a marquee that selects all lines that make up the right sail.**

2. **Choose the Shape Builder tool in the Tools panel, and then reset the default fill and stroke colors.**

3. **Move the cursor over the bottom section of the sail.**

   The Shape Builder tool identifies overlapping areas of selected objects, which is why you had to select the pieces in Step 1.

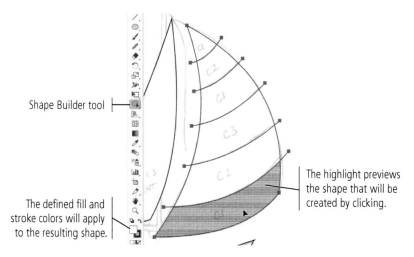

Shape Builder tool

The defined fill and stroke colors will apply to the resulting shape.

The highlight previews the shape that will be created by clicking.

4. **Click the highlighted area to create the new shape.**

   Clicking with the Shape Builder tool changes the fill of the resulting shape to the active fill color — white, in this case, because you reset the default fill and stroke colors in Step 2. The resulting shape now obscures the sketch behind it; this helps to identify which pieces you have already created.

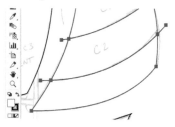

5. **Repeat Steps 3–4 for the remaining five strips on the sail.**

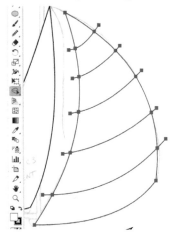

Note:

When the Shape Builder tool divides the objects into separate shapes, it creates anchor points as necessary at the intersections, and also maintains the original points.

6. **Press Option/Alt, and move the cursor over the bottom line segment outside the right sail edge. When the line segment is highlighted and the cursor shows a minus sign in the icon, click the segment to remove it.**

The Shape Builder tool can be used to both create and remove shapes. Pressing Option/Alt switches the tool into Erase mode so you can remove paths or shapes.

The area that will be removed is highlighted.

After clicking, the segment is gone.

7. **Repeat Step 6 to remove the remaining extraneous line segments.**

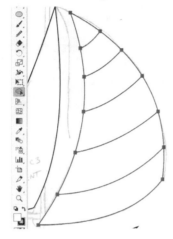

8. **Command/Control-click away from the sail to deselect everything.**

9. **Using the Direct Selection tool, click the right edge of the top shape to select that segment. Click the selected segment and drag slightly out to create a slightly bulged appearance.**

When the Direct Selection tool is active, you can click and drag a selected segment on a closed path to access the same path-reshaping functionality as you have using the Anchor Point tool.

10. **Repeat Step 9 to adjust the right edges of the other shapes in the sail.**

11. **Save the file and continue to the next exercise.**

Click and drag with the Shape Builder tool to combine multiple pieces into a single shape:

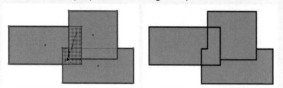

Option/Alt-click and drag with the Shape Builder tool to remove multiple pieces at once:

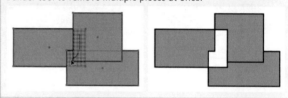

When In Merge Mode, Clicking Stroke Splits the Path is active, click a path to cut apart the path at the nearest anchor points:

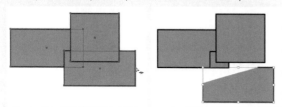

When Cursor Swatch Preview is active, three available swatches appear above the tool cursor. Use the Left and Right Arrow keys to move through those swatches:

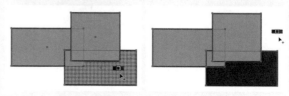

Double-clicking the Shape Builder tool in the Tools panel opens the Shape Builder Tool Options dialog box, where you can change the tool's behavior.

If a small opening exists in a path, you can activate **Gap Detection** settings to overlook small, medium, large, or custom-sized gaps in open paths. This option is especially useful if the Consider Open Filled Paths as Closed option is not checked.

The **Pick Color From** menu determines whether the tool recognizes all swatches in the file or only colors that are actually used in the artwork.

The **Selection** option defines how you can click and drag to connect shapes. The default option (Freeform) means you can drag in any direction to select objects to join. If Straight Line is active, you can only drag a straight path to combine shapes.

You can also use the **Highlight** options to determine what, if anything, is highlighted when you move the tool cursor over a shape.

 ## Use the Draw Behind Mode

Illustrator's three drawing modes allow you to create new shapes in different ways relative to other existing shapes. In the Draw Normal method (the default), new objects are simply created on top of one another in sequential order; you can rearrange them using commands in the Object>Arrange submenu, or drag them in the Layers panel. Alternatively, you can use the Draw Behind mode to automatically create new shapes behind existing objects, which eliminates a few steps in reaching the accurate object stacking order.

1. **With sailboat.ai open, use any method you prefer to fill the left sail with white and fill the boat shape with black.**

2. **Deselect everything on the artboard.**

3. **Choose the Pen tool in the Tools panel. In the Control panel, set the fill color to a dark brown from the built-in swatches and the stroke to None.**

4. **At the bottom of the Tools panel, choose the Draw Behind option.**

   If your Tools panel is in one-column mode, the Drawing Mode options are available in a pop-up menu. If your Tools panel is in two-column mode, the Drawing Mode options are presented as three buttons (from left to right: Draw Normal, Draw Behind, and Draw Inside).

   When you use the Draw Behind mode, new objects are automatically placed behind the selected object(s), or at the bottom of the stacking order if nothing is selected.

5. **Using the sketch as a guide, use the Pen tool to click four times without dragging to create the mast shape (use the following image as a guide).**

   Remember, when you see a small round circle in the cursor icon, clicking creates a closed shape. Because you aren't dragging when you click to place the anchor points, you are creating four corner points and a closed polygon shape.

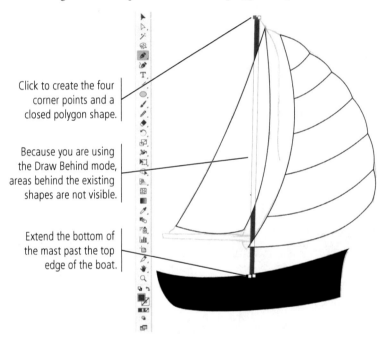

Click to create the four corner points and a closed polygon shape.

Because you are using the Draw Behind mode, areas behind the existing shapes are not visible.

Extend the bottom of the mast past the top edge of the boat.

6. **Use the Pen tool to create the boom (the horizontal pole sticking out from the mast).**

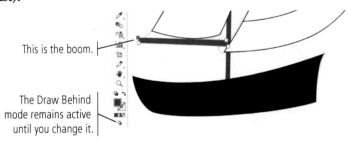

This is the boom.

The Draw Behind mode remains active until you change it.

7. **Deselect the shape you just created.**

8. **At the bottom of the Tools panel, choose the Draw Normal option.**

   The drawing mode remains at the last-used setting. To draw the rope shapes in font of the sails and mast, you need to restore the Draw Normal mode.

9. **Choose the Pencil tool in the Tools panel. In the Control panel, change the fill color to None, choose a medium brown swatch as the stroke color, and define a stroke weight of 2 pt.**

10. **Use the Pencil tool to draw the ropes on the sketch.**

11. **If necessary, adjust the anchor points of the ropes until you are satisfied with the results.**

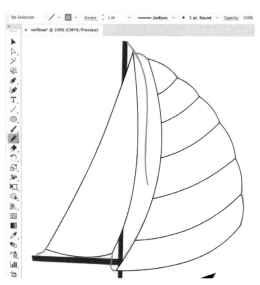

12. **Save the file and continue to the next stage of the project.**

Using the Draw Inside Mode

The Draw Inside mode, which is only available when an existing object is selected, is an easy way to create new objects inside a **clipping path** (a shape that defines areas of other objects that will be visible; anything outside the area of the clipping path is not visible).

If you select the clipped object with the Selection tool, you can use the Edit Clipping Path and Edit Contents buttons in the Control panel to edit either shape without ungrouping and without entering isolation mode.

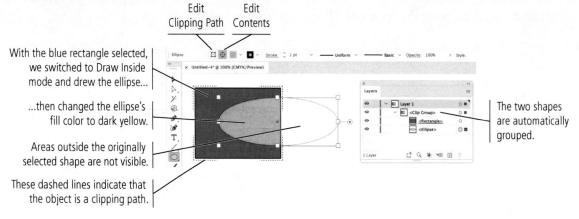

Edit Clipping Path   Edit Contents

With the blue rectangle selected, we switched to Draw Inside mode and drew the ellipse...

...then changed the ellipse's fill color to dark yellow.

Areas outside the originally selected shape are not visible.

These dashed lines indicate that the object is a clipping path.

The two shapes are automatically grouped.

STAGE 2 / Coloring and Painting Artwork

The CMYK color model, also called "process color," recreates the range of printable colors by overlapping layers of cyan, magenta, yellow, and black inks in varying (0–100) percentages.

Using theoretically pure pigments, a mixture of equal parts of cyan, magenta, and yellow would produce black. Real pigments, however, are not pure; the actual result of mixing these three colors usually appears as a muddy brown. The fourth color, black (K), is added to cyan, magenta, and yellow to extend the range of printable colors and allow purer blacks to be printed. Black is abbreviated as "K" because it is the "key" color to which others are aligned on the printing press. Using K for black also avoids confusion with blue in the RGB color model, which is used for digitally distributed files.

In process-color printing, each of the four process colors — cyan, magenta, yellow, and black — is imaged, or separated, onto an individual printing plate. Each color separation is printed on a separate unit of a printing press. When printed on top of each other in varying percentages, the semi-transparent inks produce the range of colors in the CMYK **gamut**. Other special colors (called spot colors) are printed using specifically formulated inks as additional color separations.

Different color models have different ranges or gamuts of possible colors. A normal human visual system is capable of distinguishing approximately 16.7 million different colors; color reproduction systems, however, are far more limited. The RGB model has the largest gamut of the output models. The CMYK gamut is much more limited; many of the brightest and most saturated colors that can be reproduced using light (in the RGB model) cannot be reproduced using CMYK inks.

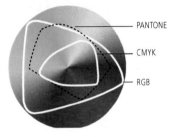

PANTONE

CMYK

RGB

 ## Create Global Custom Color Swatches

As you saw in the original sketch, the sail in this project will be filled using three different colors (indicated as C1, C2, and C3). In this exercise, you are going to create these colors and then save them as swatches that can be changed at any time to dynamically modify the colors in the artwork.

1. **With sailboat.ai open, deselect everything on the artboard.**

2. **Open the Color and Swatches panels.**

   If you don't see four color fields/sliders in the Color panel, open the panel options menu and choose Show Options.

   We dragged both panels out of the panel dock so we could work with both panels at once.

   Because you defined CMYK as the color mode for this document, the Color panel shows ink value sliders for those four primary colors.

Click here to open the panel Options menu.

Choose Show Options to see the individual color sliders.

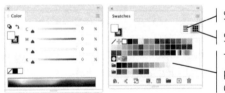

Show List View

Show Tile View

The default Swatches panel includes a number of default swatches.

3. Open the Swatches panel Options menu and choose Select All Unused.

The default Swatches panel includes a number of basic swatches that provide a good starting point for some artwork; you already used two of these to color the mast, boom, and rope shapes. When you build custom swatches, it can be a good idea to delete any default swatches that you don't need so your panel isn't too cluttered.

Note:

The default swatches appear in every new file you create, even if you delete them from a specific file.

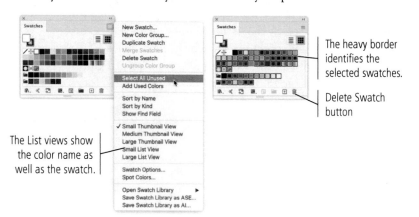

The List views show the color name as well as the swatch.

The heavy border identifies the selected swatches.

Delete Swatch button

4. Click the Swatches panel Delete button, and then click Yes in the resulting warning dialog box.

You used two of the built-in swatches to create the mast and ropes, so those swatches remain in the panel and file.

Note:

If you delete a swatch that you applied to objects in a project, there is no effect on the existing objects; you simply can't apply that color to any new objects in the project.

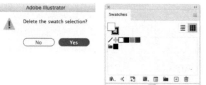

5. Using the Selection tool, click to select any of the white-filled shapes and then choose Select>Same>Fill Color.

Alternatively, you can Shift-click each white-filled object to select them individually.

6. With all the white shapes selected, change the Opacity field in the Control panel to 50%.

Opacity defines the transparency of the selected object. In this case, you're reducing the opacity from 100% (entirely solid or opaque) so you can see the color indicators on the original sketch.

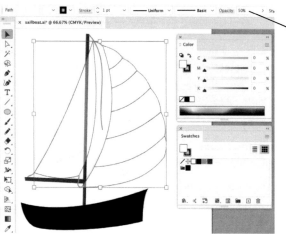

Change the shapes' opacity to 50%.

7. Deselect everything, and then use the Selection tool to select only the top stripe in the sail (labeled C1 in the sketch).

8. **Press Shift and click the other two C1 shapes to add them to the selection.**

By pressing Shift, you can click to add other objects to the current selection. Shift-clicking an object that is already selected removes it from the active selection.

9. **In the Color panel, make sure the Fill icon is on top of the Stroke icon.**

Like the options in the Tools panel, the Fill and Stroke icons determine which attribute you are currently changing. Whichever icon is on top will be affected by changes to the color values.

10. **In the Color panel, click a green area in the color spectrum bar.**

All three selected objects fill with the green color you clicked. They seem lighter because they are still semi-transparent.

Note:

Press Shift while dragging any of the sliders in the Color panel to drag all four sliders at once. Their relative relationship to each other remains the same while you drag.

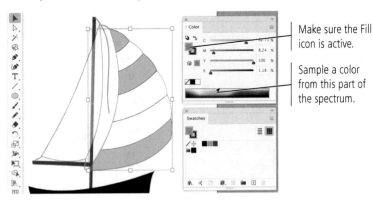

Make sure the Fill icon is active.

Sample a color from this part of the spectrum.

11. **With the Fill icon still active in the Swatches panel, click the New Swatch button at the bottom of the panel.**

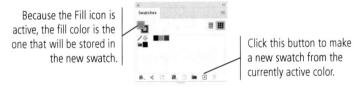

Because the Fill icon is active, the fill color is the one that will be stored in the new swatch.

Click this button to make a new swatch from the currently active color.

12. **Check the Global option in the New Swatch dialog box.**

13. **Uncheck the Add to My Library option, then click OK.**

Note:

If you have an individual user account for the Adobe Creative Cloud, CC Libraries are a way to share assets between Adobe applications. They are explained in Project 4: Ski Resort Map.

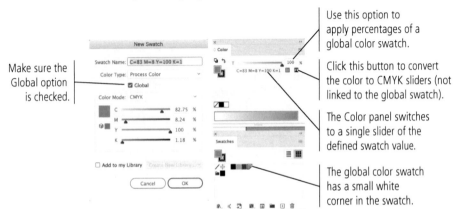

Make sure the Global option is checked.

Use this option to apply percentages of a global color swatch.

Click this button to convert the color to CMYK sliders (not linked to the global swatch).

The Color panel switches to a single slider of the defined swatch value.

The global color swatch has a small white corner in the swatch.

14. Select the two shapes marked C2 in the sketch.

15. Repeat the process from Steps 9–13 to fill the C2 shapes with a blue color and then create a global swatch from the color.

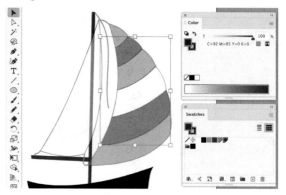

16. Select the shape marked C3 in the sketch, fill it with a purple color, and then create a third global swatch from the color.

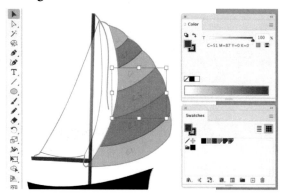

17. With the purple shape still selected, choose Select>Same>Opacity. Return the selected objects' opacity to 100%.

    You no longer need to see the color markers on the sketch, so you can return these objects to full opacity.

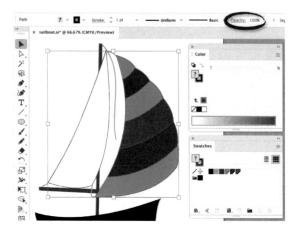

18. Deselect all objects in the file, save the file, and then continue to the next exercise.

Add a Color Gradient

Illustrator supports three types of gradient fills. When an object is selected, clicking one of the gradient types at the top of the Gradient panel (Window>Gradient) applies the default gradient to the active attribute (fill or swatch). The Gradient panel remembers the last-used gradient as the default sample, so that gradient is applied to the selected object when you apply a gradient.

Note:

A fourth type, called a gradient mesh, is explained in Project 3: Identity Package.

Linear gradient

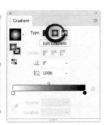

Radial gradient

Freeform gradient

Default gradient   Fill is the active attribute

When a linear or radial gradient is applied, you can use the Gradient panel to change the gradient colors. Defined stops appear as large circles below the ramp. You can change the stop colors, move stops along the gradient, change the midpoints between adjacent stops, and add new stops. To remove a stop, simply drag it off the gradient ramp. You can also use the Gradient panel to change the angle of the applied gradient, as well as the aspect ratio of radial gradients.

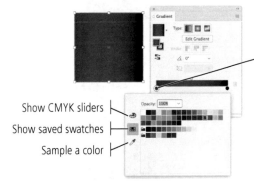

Double-click a gradient stop to change its color.

Show CMYK sliders

Show saved swatches

Sample a color

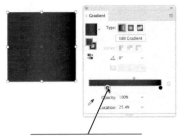

Drag a stop to move the color along the gradient.

Drag these markers to move the midpoint between stops.

Click below the ramp to add a new stop.

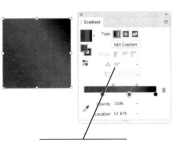

Change the angle of a linear gradient.

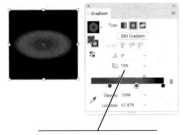

Change the aspect ratio to make a radial gradient oval instead of perfectly round.

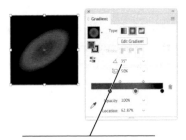

When the aspect ratio is less than 100%, you can change the angle of the radial gradient.

When a linear or radial gradient is applied, you can click the Edit Gradient button in the Gradient panel to automatically activate the Gradient tool and show the Gradient Annotator controls. You can use this on-screen widget to dynamically change the applied gradient in immediate relation to the selected object.

When the Gradient tool is active, you can click and drag to change the position and angle of the gradient. The place where you first click is the beginning of the gradient, or the left end of the ramp in the Gradient panel; the end color of the gradient, or the right end of the ramp, exists where you release the mouse button.

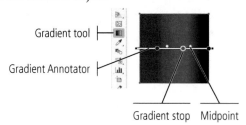

Gradient tool

Gradient Annotator

Gradient stop   Midpoint

The same color stop controls you see on the ramp in the Gradient panel appear on the Gradient Annotator. You can also change the gradient angle and aspect ratio (for radial gradients) by dragging the annotator handles.

Note:

You can also click the Edit Gradient button in the Gradient panel to access the Gradient Annotator.

Click and drag to define the gradient.

Drag the Annotator endpoint to change the gradient length.

Move the cursor slightly away from the endpoint to rotate the gradient.

Note:

You can turn off the Gradient Annotator in the View menu (View>Hide Gradient Annotator).

Drag the aspect ratio handle to change a radial gradient away from round.

Drag either endpoint to change the size of a radial gradient.

Drag the radial gradient boundary to rotate the gradient.

The original sketch shows that the left sail needs to be a gradient of the three colors in the other sail. Because the sketch shows the look of a sail billowing in the wind, a straight linear gradient would not accurately reflect the way blended colors would appear in a real sail. Instead, you will use the third type of gradient— a freeform gradient — to create the necessary effect.

1. **With sailboat.ai open, use the Selection tool to select the left sail shape.**

2. **Open the Gradient panel (Window>Gradient). If you see only a gradient sample in the panel, open the panel Options menu and choose Show Options.**

3. **If you see a pop-up window about working with Gradients, click the Skip Tour button.**

4. **With the left sail shape selected, click the Freeform Gradient button at the top of the Gradient panel.**

Freeform gradients use color points to define the location of various colors in the gradient. When you first apply a freeform gradient, the software automatically adds at least one color point to the shape.

By default, freeform gradients are created in [Draw] Points mode, which means the individual color points in the gradient are not connected.

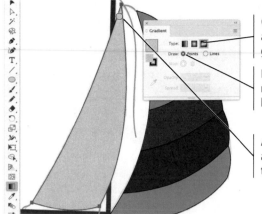

Click here to apply a freeform gradient.

Draw Points mode is active by default.

A color point is automatically added to the selected shape.

5. **Click to select the color point in the sail shape.**

When a color point is selected, you can drag it to a new location, or press the Delete key to remove it from the gradient. You can also click the Delete button in the Gradient panel to remove the selected point.

If you move the cursor over a selected point, the dotted line identifies the spread of that point's color within the overall gradient. You can click the dotted line and drag to change the spread percentage.

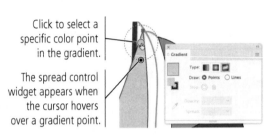

Click to select a specific color point in the gradient.

The spread control widget appears when the cursor hovers over a gradient point.

6. **Click the selected color point and drag it to the bottom-left corner of the shape.**

7. **Double-click the selected stop to open the pop-up color selector for that stop.**

You can change the color of stops by double-clicking the circles, which opens the color panel for that stop (the same as when you change the color for a linear or radial gradient).

8. **If the pop-up panel shows CMYK sliders, click the Swatches button to show the swatches that are saved in the file.**

9. **Choose the custom green swatch, then press Return/Enter to dismiss the panel.**

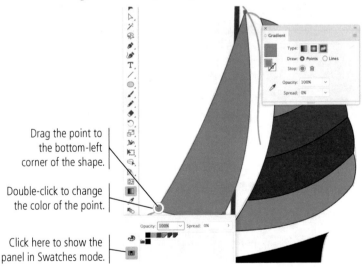

Drag the point to the bottom-left corner of the shape.

Double-click to change the color of the point.

Click here to show the panel in Swatches mode.

Note:

You can change the opacity of the selected gradient point in the Gradient panel.

10. Choose the Lines option in the Gradient panel.

The Lines option allows you to draw a path that defines the precise shape of a gradient, rather than simply blending from one point to another.

11. Click the existing color point to connect to it, then move the cursor halfway up the left edge of the sail. Click near the left edge of the shape to place a new color point.

Although it can be difficult to see on the green background, a thin blue line connects each color point on the same line. This preview shows the curve that will be created when you click to place a new point.

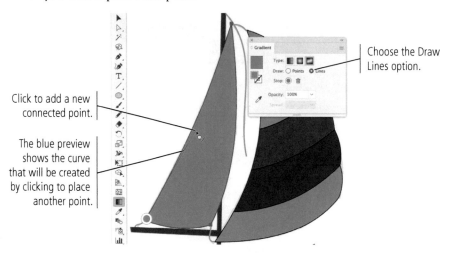

Choose the Draw Lines option.

Click to add a new connected point.

The blue preview shows the curve that will be created by clicking to place another point.

12. Move the cursor to the top of the sail shape. Click just inside the sail shape to place a third color point on the same line.

Color points in a gradient line are automatically created with smooth points; you can Option/Alt-click a point on the gradient line to convert it to a corner point.

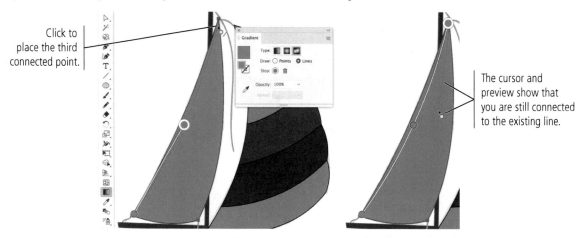

Click to place the third connected point.

The cursor and preview show that you are still connected to the existing line.

13. Press the ESC key to disconnect from the current gradient line.

As with the Pen tool, the cursor remains connected to the existing line until you intentionally disconnect.

The cursor shows that clicking creates a new point not connected to the previous line.

14. **Click near the middle of the bottom line in the sail shape to create a new color point.**

15. **Double-click the new point to open the color selector. Choose the custom blue swatch as the stop color, then press Return/Enter to dismiss the panel.**

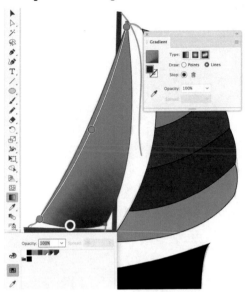

16. **Move the cursor to the middle of the shape, then click to place a new point.**

17. **Move the cursor near the top of the shape, then click to place a third point on the middle line.**

    Make sure you don't click directly on top of the top point of the left line; doing so would actually connect to the existing line, which is not what you want.

    You can always use the Undo command (Command/Control-Z) to undo the last click if you accidentally connect to another existing point.

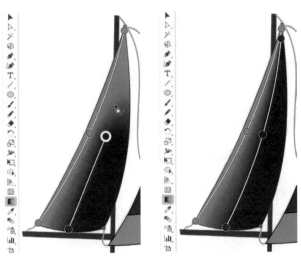

18. **Press the ESC key to disconnect from the current gradient line.**

19. **Repeat Steps 14–18 on the right side of the shape to add a third gradient line, using the custom purple swatch as the color for the stops.**

20. **Save the file and continue to the next exercise.**

Edit Global Color Swatches

Global swatches offer a particular advantage when you need to change the colors used in your artwork. In the case of this project, you are going to place this artwork into a stylized ocean illustration, in which blues are the predominant color. To make the boat more prominent in the final poster, you are going to use a yellow-orange scheme — complementary colors to blue — for the boat sails.

1. **With sailboat.ai open, deselect all objects on the artboard.**

2. **In the Swatches panel, double-click the green custom swatch.**

3. **In the resulting Swatch Options dialog box, make sure the Preview option is checked.**

4. **Change the color values to C=0 M=75 Y=75 K=10, and then click OK to change the swatch definition.**

   Because this is a global color swatch, any objects that use the color (including the gradient) reflect the new swatch definition. Locked objects are also affected by the change.

Note:

Complementary color *refers to opposing colors on a color wheel.*

Everything that was colored with the green swatch is now orange.

5. Repeat Steps 2–4 to change the blue swatch definition to C=0 M=10 Y=100 K=0.

6. Repeat Steps 2–4 to change the purple swatch definition to C=0 M=60 Y=100 K=0.

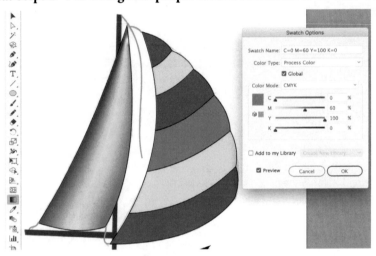

7. Save the file and continue to the next stage of the project.

FOUNDATIONS

Many vague and technical-sounding terms are mentioned when discussing color. Is hue the same as color? The same as value? As tone? What's the difference between lightness and brightness? What is chroma? And where does saturation fit in?

This problem has resulted in several attempts to normalize color communication. A number of systems have been developed to define color according to specific criteria, including Hue, Saturation, and Brightness (HSB); Hue, Saturation, and Lightness (HSL); Hue, Saturation, and Value (HSV); and Lightness, Chroma, and Hue (LCH). Each of these models, or systems, plots color on a three-dimensional diagram, based on the elements of human color perception — hue, intensity, and brightness.

Hue is what most people think of as color — red, green, purple, and so on. Hue is defined according to a color's position on a color wheel, beginning at red (0°) and traveling counterclockwise around the wheel.

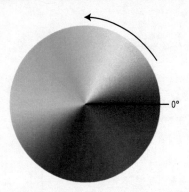

Saturation (also called "intensity") refers to the color's difference from neutral gray. Highly saturated colors are more vivid than those with low saturation. Saturation is plotted from the center of the color wheel. Color at the center is neutral gray and has a saturation value of 0; color at the edge of the wheel has the most intense saturation value (100) of that hue.

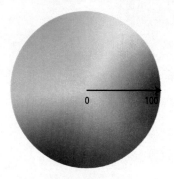

If you bisect the color wheel with a straight line, the line creates a saturation axis for two complementary colors. A color is dulled by the introduction of its complement. Red, for example, is neutralized by the addition of cyan (blue and green). Near the center of the axis, the result is neutral gray.

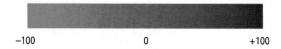

−100   0   +100

Chroma is similar to saturation, but chroma factors in a reference white. In any viewing situation, colors appear less vivid as the light source dims. The process of chromatic adaptation, however, allows the human visual system to adjust to changes in light and still differentiate colors according to the relative saturation.

Brightness is the amount of light reflected off an object. As an element of color reproduction, brightness is typically judged by comparing the color to the lightest nearby object (such as an unprinted area of white paper).

Lightness is the amount of white or black added to pure color. Lightness (also called "luminance" or "value") is the relative brightness based purely on the black-white value of a color. A lightness value of 0 means there is no addition of white or black. Lightness of +100 is pure white; lightness of −100 is pure black.

All hues are affected equally by changes in lightness.

The final step in the process is to place your finished sailboat in the background illustration that was created by a colleague; this type of collaborative workflow is common in the graphic design world. Although there are many ways to accomplish this task, you are going to use the most basic — copying and pasting — in this project. When all of the pieces are together in the same file, you will make necessary adjustments to make all pieces of the file work together as a single composition.

 ## Manage Artwork with Sublayers

In the first stage of this project you created the entire sailboat on a single layer. When you paste it into the background artwork, you need to be able to manage the sailboat as a single object. In this exercise, you work with sublayers to accomplish this goal.

1. **With sailboat.ai open, make the Section tool active and make sure nothing is selected on the artboard.**

2. **In the Layers panel, click the arrow to the left of the Boat Drawing layer to reveal the sublayers.**

   Individual objects are listed as sublayers in the Layers panel. Because you created all of the artwork in this file on a single layer, every object appears as a sublayer of the Boat Drawing layer.

   Click this arrow to expand the layer.

   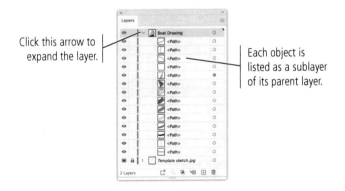

   Each object is listed as a sublayer of its parent layer.

3. **Click the empty space to the right of any of the available sublayers.**

   You can use sublayers to select individual objects on a specific layer; the Selected Art icon (the larger rectangle) identifies selected objects. The parent layer of selected art shows a smaller Selected Art icon, which makes it easier to identify which layer contains a specific object.

   This technique also works to select individual components of a group.

   The smaller rectangle indicates that one or more (but not all) objects on the layer are selected.

   Click this space to select a specific sublayer.

   This icon identifies a selected object.

   Target icon

   You can also click the Target icon for a specific layer or sublayer to select specific objects.

4. Choose Select>All.

This command selects all unlocked objects on the artboard. The Layers panel now shows a Selected Art icon for all objects on the Boat Drawing layer. The Selected Art icon for the parent layer is now larger, which means all objects on that layer are selected.

Note:

Press Command/Control-A to select all objects in the file.

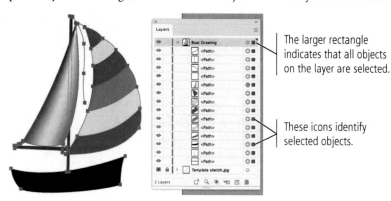

The larger rectangle indicates that all objects on the layer are selected.

These icons identify selected objects.

Note:

You can click the space to the right of a specific layer name to select all objects on that layer.

5. Choose Object>Group. In the Layers panel, click the arrow to expand the Group.

Grouping multiple objects creates a second level of nesting: the Boat Drawing layer is the parent of the Group, which is the parent of the individual objects in the artwork. You can use the Selected Art icons in the Layers panel to select individual objects in a group, just as you can to select those objects when they are not grouped.

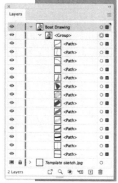

6. In the Layers panel, double-click the <Group> name to highlight it. Type Sailboat to rename the group, then press Return/Enter to finalize the new name.

You can rename sublayers — including groups and individual objects — just as you would rename actual layers. This type of descriptive naming can help you to better organize and manage the elements in a complex file.

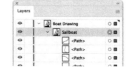

7. With the group selected on the artboard, choose Edit>Copy.

8. Save the sailboat.ai file, then choose File>Open. Navigate to **poster.ai** in the WIP>Regatta folder and click Open.

9. Choose View>Fit Artboard in Window.

This command not only shows you the entire artboard, but also centers the artboard in the active document window.

Note:

You can press Command/Control-C to copy the selected objects.

10. **Choose Edit>Paste.**

The group you copied in Step 7 is pasted into the poster file, in the center of the document window.

11. **In the Layers panel, click the arrow to the left of Layer 1 to expand that layer.**

Because you grouped the sailboat objects before you copied them, they are pasted as a group. If you had not grouped them, each object that makes up the sailboat artwork would be pasted as a separate sublayer in the poster file.

12. **Click the arrow to the left of the Sailboat sublayer to collapse it (if necessary).**

13. **Using the Selection tool, drag the selected group into the empty space at the top-right section of the poster (use the following image as a guide).**

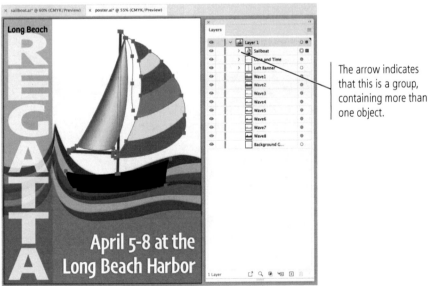

The arrow indicates that this is a group, containing more than one object.

14. **In the Layers panel, drag the Sailboat sublayer down. When a heavy line appears below the Wave6 sublayer, release the mouse button.**

    When you use the Edit>Paste command, the pasted objects are placed at the top of the stacking order on the active layer. You can use this method to easily reorder sublayers as necessary.

Changing the stacking-order position of the sublayer means the bottom of the Sailboat group is hidden by sublayers higher in the stack.

15. **If necessary, adjust the position of the sailboat artwork so the entire bottom edge is hidden by the third wave from the top.**

16. **Save the file and continue to the next exercise.**

Lock and Hide Artwork

The final required adjustment for this poster is to change the shape of the highest wave so it looks like a splash. If you review the existing artwork and Layers panel, you can see that the wave nearest the top of the artboard is also the lowest in the sublayer stacking order — Wave8, according to the object names assigned in the Layers panel. To make this task easier, you are going to lock and hide certain sublayers to avoid accidentally changing elements that you don't want to change.

1. **With poster.ai open, click the empty space to the left of the Date and Time sublayer. Hold down the mouse button and drag down the same column to lock all other sublayers.**

    Individual objects in a file can be locked by clicking the empty space immediately left of the object name in the Layers panel. If a Lock icon already appears in that space, you can click the lock icon to unlock a specific object.

    You can also select an object on the artboard and choose Object>Lock.

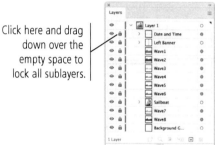

Click here and drag down over the empty space to lock all sublayers.

2. **Click the Lock icon to the left of the Wave8 sublayer to unlock only that element.**

The Object>Unlock All menu command is an all-or-nothing option; it unlocks all locked objects on all layers. The Layers panel allows you to unlock only certain objects, which provides better control over your workflow.

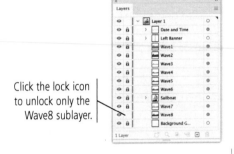

Click the lock icon to unlock only the Wave8 sublayer.

Because all other objects in the file are locked, you can now edit the Wave8 shape without affecting the other elements.

3. **In the Layers panel, click the Eye icon for the Left Banner sublayer.**

The Eye icons identify visible layers and sublayers. You can click any Eye icon to hide an entire layer, or hide only specific sublayers. If an element is already hidden, you can click the empty space in the Layers panel to show that element.

Note:

When an object is locked, you can't select it, which means you also can't change it.

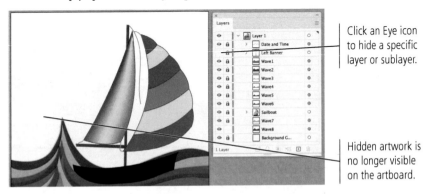

Click an Eye icon to hide a specific layer or sublayer.

Hidden artwork is no longer visible on the artboard.

You can also select an object on the artboard and choose Object>Hide>Selection. The Object>Show All command, however, shows all hidden objects on all layers in the file. As with locking and unlocking objects, it is often better to use the icons in the Layers panel to show and hide exactly (and only) the elements you need.

4. **Choose Select>All.**

Because all the other sublayers are locked and/or hidden, you selected only the artwork on the Wave8 sublayer.

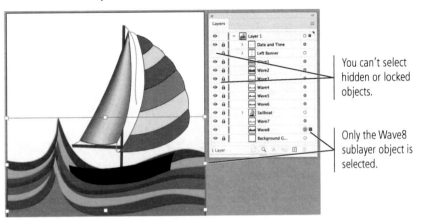

You can't select hidden or locked objects.

Only the Wave8 sublayer object is selected.

5. **Save the file and continue to the next exercise.**

Create Shapes with the Blob Brush Tool

The Blob Brush tool is used to paint filled shapes, which you can manipulate just as you would any other shape made up of anchor points and handles. In this exercise, you use the Blob Brush tool to paint a splashing wave shape, which you will then merge with the top wave shape to create a single object.

1. **With sailboat.ai open, deselect everything on the artboard.**

2. **Choose the Blob Brush tool (nested under the Paintbrush tool).**

3. **Double-click the Blob Brush tool in the Tools panel to open the Blob Brush Tool Options dialog box.**

4. **Check the Keep Selected option and uncheck Merge Only with Selection.**

   Overlapping Blob Brush strokes merge to create a single object. If Merge Only with Selected is active, overlapping strokes will not merge unless the previous strokes are selected.

   Blob Brush tool ⊢

5. **Set the Fidelity slider to the halfway point (if it is not already there).**

   Like the Pencil tool, the Blob Brush tool Tolerance options determine the accuracy of the resulting shape. Fidelity settings nearer the Accurate end of the scale result in more points to better match the path you drag with the tool; a setting closer to the Smooth end of the scale results in fewer points and smoother edges on the shape you draw.

6. **Leave the remaining options at their default values, then click OK.**

   The lower half of the dialog box defines the size, angle, and roundness of the brush cursor.

7. **Reset the default fill and stroke colors, then move the Blob Brush tool cursor near the peak of the top wave shape. Align the right side of the brush to the right side of the wave peak, as shown here:**

Reset the default fill and stroke colors.

When you draw with the Blob Brush tool, the cursor shows the size and shape of the defined brush.

Align the right edge of the cursor to the right edge of the wave shape.

Note:

Press the right bracket key ( ]) to increase the brush size by one point. Press the left bracket key ([ ) to decrease the brush size by one point.

8. **Click and drag to create an arch shape that approximately matches the curve of the existing wave.**

You are essentially painting a shape that matches the brush stroke you see while you drag. As you paint, the path might look a bit sketchy; however, the resulting path is smoothed based on the Fidelity setting defined in the tool options.

When you release the mouse button, the result is a single shape that fills the entire area where you drew. The shape is still selected because you activated the Keep Selected option in the tool options.

It is important to note that the resulting path is filled with the default *stroke* color you defined in Step 7. When you "paint" with the Blob Brush tool, the defined fill color has no effect on the resulting shape unless the stroke color is set to None.

The previous Stroke color becomes the Fill color of the resulting shape.

When you release the mouse button, the result is a filled shape based on where you dragged the brush cursor.

Anchor points are automatically created to define the outside edge of the shape.

9. **With the path still selected, click and drag to create another path near the top of the splash, using a slightly different arch.**

As you complete the rest of this exercise, use our images as a guide. You do not have to match the exact shape you see in our images, but your end result should be similar.

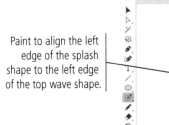

Draw a second arched shape that branches off of the first shape.

The second path is merged with the previous (selected) path.

10. **Continue adding brush strokes to the selected path to create more branches off the splash shape.**

As you draw, you can press the right bracket key ( ]) to increase the brush size by one point; press the left bracket key ([ ) to decrease the brush size by one point. Feel free to enlarge or reduce the brush size to create different thicknesses throughout the shape.

11. **Where the splash shape meets the top wave, make sure the left edge of the splash shape matches the left edge of the wave shape.**

Paint to align the left edge of the splash shape to the left edge of the top wave shape.

12. Paint several shapes that do not overlap the main splash shape.

When you paint a shape that does not overlap the existing selection, it is created as a new, separate shape.

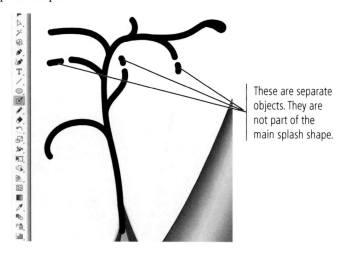

These are separate objects. They are not part of the main splash shape.

13. Deselect everything in the layout.

14. Save the file and continue to the next exercise.

 ## Combine Shapes with the Pathfinder

Using the Illustrator Pathfinder panel, you can combine multiple shapes in a variety of ways, or you can use one object as a "cookie cutter" to remove or separate one shape from another. As you work with more complicated artwork in Illustrator, you will find many different ways to use the Pathfinder functions, alone or in combination.

1. With poster.ai open, open the Pathfinder panel (Window>Pathfinder).

2. In the Layers panel, click the top <Path> sublayer to select it in the panel. Press Shift and click the bottom <Path> object to add it, and all in-between sublayers, to the previous selection.

Selecting an element in the Layers panel is not the same as selecting it on the artboard. The right side of the panel shows no Selected Art icons, which means nothing is selected on the artboard.

Note:

You can Command/Control-click to select multiple, nonconsecutive layers or sublayers in the Layers panel.

3. In the Layers panel, click any of the selected elements and drag them below the Wave8 sublayer.

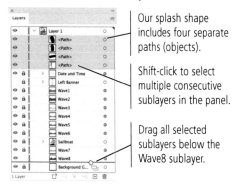

Our splash shape includes four separate paths (objects).

Shift-click to select multiple consecutive sublayers in the panel.

Drag all selected sublayers below the Wave8 sublayer.

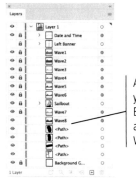

All the path objects you created with the Blob Brush tool should appear below the Wave8 layer.

4. Choose Select>All.

Because most objects are locked, only the top wave and splash shapes are selected.

5. In the Pathfinder panel, click the Unite button.

Options in the Pathfinder panel allow you to cut shapes out of other shapes and merge multiple shapes into a single shape.

The Unite function merges overlapping shapes into a single object; non-overlapping objects are grouped with the merged shape. All elements affected by the unification adopt the appearance attributes (fill color, opacity, etc.) of the top-most selected object — which is why you reordered the sublayers in Step 3.

Unite button

The resulting group contains all objects in the wave shape.

6. Choose Select>Deselect to turn off any active selection.

7. In the Layers panel, click the empty space to the left of the Left Banner sublayer to show that layer.

Click here to reshow the Left Banner sublayer.

8. Save the file and continue to the final exercise.

In the Pathfinder panel, the top row of buttons — the Shape Modes — create complex shapes by combining the originally selected shapes. You can press Option/Alt and click a Shape Mode to maintain the paths from the original objects.

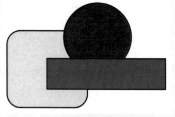

Original objects

Unite combines all selected objects into a single shape. By default, the Shape options result in a single new object.

If you Option/Alt-click a shape mode button, the result maintains the original paths unless you manually expand it.

Minus Front removes overlapping areas from the backmost shape in the selection.

Intersect creates a shape of only areas where all selected objects overlap.

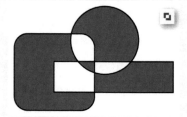

Exclude removes any areas where two objects overlap.

The second row of options — the Pathfinders — do exactly that. The resulting shapes are some combination of the paths that made up the originally selected objects.

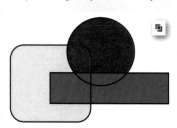

Divide creates separate shapes from all overlapping areas of selected objects.

Trim removes underlying areas of overlapping objects. Objects of the same fill color are not combined.

Merge removes underlying areas of overlapping objects. Objects of the same fill color are combined.

Crop returns the areas of underlying objects that are within the boundary of the topmost object.

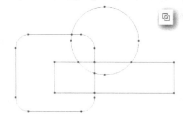

Outline divides the selected objects, then returns unfilled, open paths.

Minus Back removes the area of underlying objects from the front object.

Save the File as PDF

Adobe PDF (or simply PDF, for Portable Document Format) has become a universal method of moving files to virtually any digital destination. One of the most important uses for the PDF format is the ability to create perfectly formatted digital documents, exactly as they would appear if printed on paper. You can embed fonts, images, drawings, and other elements into the file so all the required bits are available on any computer. The PDF format can be used to move your artwork to the web as a low-resolution RGB file or to a commercial printer as a high-resolution CMYK file.

1. **With `poster.ai` open, choose File>Save As.**
   If necessary, navigate to your WIP>Regatta folder as the target location.

2. **Choose Adobe PDF in the Format/Save As Type menu and click Save.**

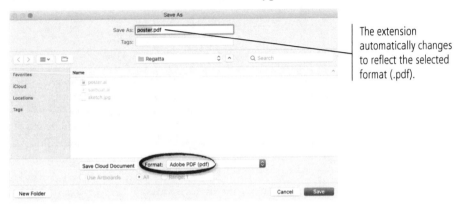

The extension automatically changes to reflect the selected format (.pdf).

3. **Choose Illustrator Default in the Adobe PDF Preset menu.**

4. **Review the options in the General pane.**

   Read the description area to see what Adobe has to say about these options.

Use this menu to call a group of saved settings (called a preset).

Choose a category from this menu to see related options.

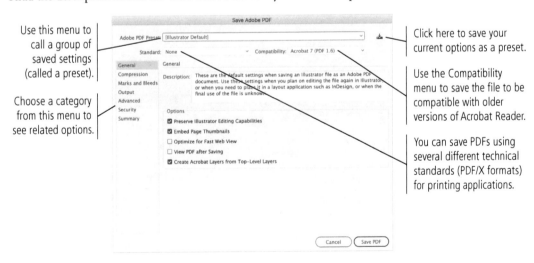

Click here to save your current options as a preset.

Use the Compatibility menu to save the file to be compatible with older versions of Acrobat Reader.

You can save PDFs using several different technical standards (PDF/X formats) for printing applications.

5. **Click Compression in the list of categories on the left and review the options.**

These options allow you to reduce the resulting file size by compressing color, grayscale, and/or monochrome bitmap (raster) images. You can also compress text and line art by clicking the check box at the bottom.

6. **Review the Marks and Bleeds options.**

These options add different marks to the output page:

- **Trim marks** indicate the edge of the page, where a page printed on a larger sheet will be cut down to its final size. You can also define the thickness (weight) of the trim marks, as well as how far from the page edge the lines should appear (offset).

- **Registration marks** resemble a small crosshair. These marks are added to each ink unit on a printing press to make sure the different inks are properly aligned to one another.

- **Color bars** are rows of small squares across the sheet, used to verify press settings for accurate color reproduction.

- **Page information** adds the file name, date, and time of output.

- **Bleeds** define how much of elements outside the page boundaries will be included in the final output. Most printers require at least a 0.125″ bleed on each side, but you should always ask before you create the final file.

Note:

Most printers require trim marks to be created outside the bleed area. Always check with your service provider when saving a PDF for commercial output.

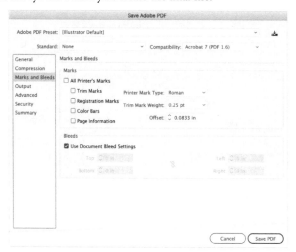

Note:

The other categories of options are explained in later projects that discuss transparency and color management.

7. **Click Save PDF.**

8. **Close any open Illustrator files.**

1. The _____ tool is used to place anchor points that are connected by line segments.

2. The _____ tool is used to change a smooth anchor point to a corner anchor point (and vice versa).

3. The _____ tool is used to edit individual anchor points (and their related handles) on a vector path.

4. _____ is the range of possible colors within a specific color model.

5. _____ are the four component colors in process-color output.

6. The _____ panel includes value sliders for each component in the defined color model.

7. The _____ is used to paint shapes of solid color based on the defined brush size and the area you drag with a single mouse click.

8. The _____ appears over a gradient-filled object when selected with the Gradient tool; you can use it to control the position and direction of color in the gradient-filled object.

9. Changes made to a _____ color swatch are reflected in all elements where that color is applied.

10. Individual objects on a layer appear as _____ in the Layers panel.

1. Describe three ways to deselect the current selection on the artboard.

2. Briefly explain the significance of "process color" related to Illustrator artwork.

3. Briefly explain the advantage of using the PDF format for creating printable files.

Use what you have learned in this project to complete the following freeform exercise.
Carefully read the art director and client comments, then create your own design to meet the needs of the project.
Use the space below to sketch ideas. When finished, write a brief explanation of the reasoning behind your final design.

art director comments

Your local animal shelter hosts an annual fundraising gala on the first Saturday in October. You have been hired to create a poster advertising this year's theme — a classic, black-tie masquerade ball.

❏ Design an 11″ × 17″ poster to promote the event in local storefronts and public venues.

❏ Develop a creative type treatment for the event name: "Barking Mad for the Masquerade."

❏ Find or create imagery and graphics to support the event theme.

❏ Include the event date (look at this year's calendar to find the exact date) prominently in the poster design.

❏ Include the contact information (phone number and web address) for your local animal shelter.

client comments

We raise a considerable portion of our annual operating budget during this annual event. This year, the theme is a very classic masquerade in the style of Victorian-England opulence — think "Phantom of the Opera," the state dining room on the Titanic, that sort of thing. Men in tuxes and women in flowing gowns, everyone masked in some fashion until the traditional "reveal" at midnight.

Every year, the event includes a silent auction with some incredible prizes that are donated by local businesses, as well as a gourmet four-course meal prepared by a celebrity chef.

If there is any way you could tastefully incorporate a couple of animal photos in the poster, we would like that. However, it isn't really a requirement as long as the shelter's name and contact information is clearly displayed.

project justification

This project incorporated more advanced drawing techniques that allow you to exercise precise control over every point and path in a file. The Pen tool is arguably one of the most important tools you will use throughout your career as an illustrator; although it can be challenging at first, practice is the best way to master this skill.

This project also explored working with color in Illustrator: applying color, saving global color swatches to make changes more efficiently, and using gradients to add visual interest.

Finally, you saved your artwork in a file format that is commonly used to share Illustrator artwork with other applications. The PDF format is an invaluable part of design workflows using software applications that can't import native Illustrator files.

Use the Pen tool to create custom artwork based on lines in a hand-drawn sketch

Use the Anchor Point tool to reshape specific line segments

Use the Blob Brush tool to paint the outline of custom shapes

Use the Shape Builder tool to divide overlapping objects into individual shapes

Create a freeform gradient to blend colors in a non-linear shape

Use global swatches to allow universal changes to all objects where that color is applied

Use layers and sublayers to manage the various elements in a complex file

Long Beach

April 5-8 at the Long Beach Harbor

Identity Package

3

Your client is rebranding and relaunching a local cafe that has been open since 1982. She has hired you to create a logo for the establishment's new name, as well as stationery that can be used for various purposes throughout the business operations.

This project incorporates the following skills:

❑ Developing custom logo artwork based on an object in a photograph

❑ Using a gradient mesh to create realistic color blends

❑ Manipulating letter shapes to create a finished logotype

❑ Using layers to easily manage complex artwork

❑ Creating multiple artboards to contain specific projects and layouts

❑ Building various logo versions to meet specific output requirements

❑ Printing desktop proofs of individual artboards

PROJECT MEETING

client comments

In six weeks, Home Town Diner will officially become Cafe Limon. First, we need a logo for the new name. I want the words to be clearly styled — not just regular type — using a lemon in place of the letter "o."

We want to have everything in place for the Grand Reopening, so we need to make things as versatile as possible. Once the logo is created, we need a letterhead-style page that we're going to have printed in large quantities. We'll use those preprinted blanks for everything, including daily menus, invoices, and correspondence.

The printer I spoke with said I could do this for less money if I go "four-color" for the letterhead, but "two-color" for the envelope; I really don't know what that means — I'm hoping you do.

art director comments

The logo is the first part of this project because you will use it on the other two pieces. The client told you exactly what she wants, so that part is done. I had our photographer take a good picture of a lemon; use that as the basis for the one you draw in the logo art.

The client wants to print the letterhead in four-color and the envelope in two-color, so you will have to create two different versions of the logo. Since logos are used on far more than just these two jobs in this one application, you should also create a one-color version because the client will inevitably ask for it at some point.

project objectives

To complete this project, you will:

- ❑ Use the Pen tool to trace the outline of a photograph
- ❑ Create a gradient mesh
- ❑ Use Smart Guides to manage a gradient mesh
- ❑ Use effects to add object highlights
- ❑ Create and control point-type objects
- ❑ Convert text to outlines so you can manipulate the letter shapes
- ❑ Use the Appearance panel to revert gradient mesh objects back to regular paths
- ❑ Apply spot-color inks for special printing applications
- ❑ Create versions of the final logo for one-color, two-color, and four-color printing
- ❑ Print desktop proofs of the completed identity pieces

STAGE 1 / Working with Gradient Meshes

There are several important points to keep in mind when you design a logo. First, logos need to be scalable. A company might place its logo on the head of a golf tee or on the side of a building. Vector graphics — the kind you typically create in Illustrator — can be scaled as large or small as necessary without losing quality. Photographs are raster images, and they typically can't be greatly enlarged or reduced without losing quality. That's why you're converting a photograph (a raster image) into a vector graphic in this project.

Second, you almost always need more than one version of a logo. Different kinds of output require different formats (specifically, one set of files for print and one for the web), and some types of jobs require special options saved in the files, such as the four-color, two-color, and one-color versions that you will create in this project.

Set up the Workspace

Illustrator includes a number of tools ideally suited for creating lifelike illustrations. In this project, you will work from a photograph to create a vector-based lemon graphic that will be part of your client's logo. You will start with the full-color version, and then work from there to create variations that are part of a typical logo package.

1. Download `Cafe_AI21_RF.zip` from the Student Files web page.

2. Expand the ZIP archive in your WIP folder (Macintosh) or copy the archive contents into your WIP folder (Windows).

   This results in a folder named **Cafe**, which contains the files you need for this project. You should also use this folder to save the files you create in this project.

3. In Illustrator, choose File>New. Choose the Print option at the top of the dialog box, and then choose the Letter document preset.

   Remember, using the Print category of presets automatically applies the CMYK color mode and 300 ppi raster effects.

   Because the CMYK gamut is smaller than the RGB gamut, you are starting with the smaller gamut to avoid the color shift that could occur if you started with RGB and converted the colors to CMYK. You are also creating the file to meet the high-resolution requirements of commercial printing.

4. Define the following settings in the Preset Details section:

Name:	cafe-logo
Units:	Inches
Orientation:	Portrait
Artboards:	1

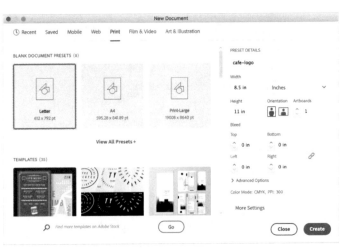

   You are simply using this artboard as a drawing space, so you only need to make it large enough to draw. Later, you will adjust the artboard to meet the specific needs of the finished logo. You will also add multiple artboards to hold various versions of the logo.

5. **Click Create to create the file.**

6. **Choose View>Fit Artboard in Window.**

    The Fit Artboard in Window command centers the artboard in the document window, so the template image you place in the next step will be automatically centered on the artboard.

7. **Choose File>Place. Navigate to lemon.jpg in your WIP>Cafe folder. Make sure the Template option is checked, and then click Place.**

    Macintosh users might need to click the Options button to access the actual Options at the bottom of the dialog box.

8. **In the Layers panel, double-click the template layer icon to open the Layer Options dialog box. Uncheck the Dim Images option, then click OK.**

    Choosing the Template option places an image onto a template layer that is automatically dimmed. You want the photograph to appear at full visibility so you can extract colors from the photo.

Uncheck this option.

    For most of the drawing process, you will use the lemon photo as the basis of your artwork. You will draw on other layers, and then delete the template layer when your lemon graphic is complete. You're starting with a letter-size artboard. After you finish the logo graphic, you will resize the artboard to fit the artwork.

9. **Save the file as a native Illustrator file named cafe-logo.ai in your WIP>Cafe folder, and then continue to the next exercise.**

Note:

Whenever you save an Illustrator file throughout this book, use the default Illustrator options.

Create a Gradient Mesh

A gradient mesh is basically a special type of fill. Each point in the mesh can have a different color value. Areas between mesh lines are gradients of the surrounding point colors; connecting lines between mesh points control the shape of related gradients.

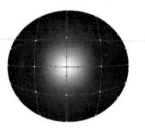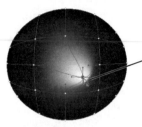

Moving a mesh point or changing its handles affects the position and shape of the associated gradient areas.

1. **With cafe-logo.ai open, double-click the Layer 1 name and type Lemon. Press Return/Enter to finalize the new layer name.**

2. **Using the Pen tool with a 1-pt black stroke and no fill, draw the outline of the lemon in the template image.**

3. **If necessary, use the Direct Selection tool to adjust the anchor points and handles until the outline matches the lemon shape.**

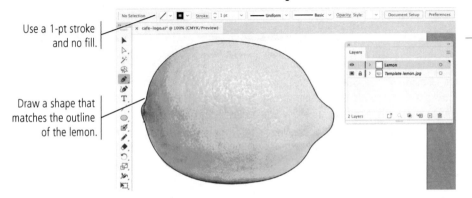

Use a 1-pt stroke and no fill.

Draw a shape that matches the outline of the lemon.

Note:

Refer back to Project 2: Regatta Artwork for details about drawing and editing Bézier curves.

4. **Using the Selection tool, select the outline shape on the Lemon layer.**

5. **Using the Eyedropper tool, click a medium-yellow color in the template image to fill the selected shape with the sampled color.**

   You can add a gradient mesh to a path without filling it with color first, but if you don't choose a color, the mesh will automatically fill with white.

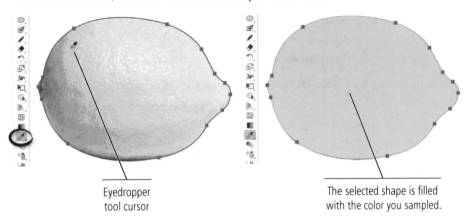

Eyedropper tool cursor

The selected shape is filled with the color you sampled.

6. **Choose Object>Create Gradient Mesh.**

7. **In the Create Gradient Mesh dialog box, activate the Preview option. Set the Rows value to 8 and the Columns value to 7, and make sure the Appearance menu is set to Flat.**

    The Rows and Columns settings determine how many lines make up the resulting mesh.

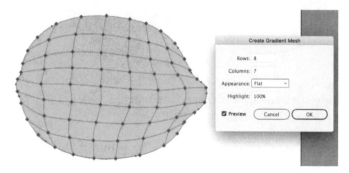

Note:

When you convert a path to a mesh, the shape is no longer a path. You cannot apply a stroke attribute to a gradient mesh object.

8. **Click OK to create the mesh.**

9. **Save the file and continue to the next exercise.**

Understanding Gradient Mesh Options

The Appearance option in the Create Gradient Mesh dialog box determines how colors affect the mesh you create.

Flat spreads a single color to all points in the mesh. If you don't fill the shape with a color before creating the mesh, the mesh object will fill with white.

To Center creates a white highlight at the center and spreads the highlight color outward toward the object edges. The Highlight (%) field controls the strength of white in the resulting mesh.

To Edge is essentially the opposite of the To Center option; the white highlight appears around the edges of the mesh, blending to the solid color in the center of the mesh object.

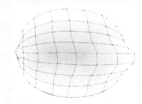

Work in Outline Mode

Outline mode allows you to see the points and paths of an object without the colors and fills. This viewing mode can be very useful when you need to adjust anchor points of one shape while viewing the underlying objects.

Note:

When using Smart Guides, make sure the Snap to Point option is toggled off. If Snap to Point is active, Smart Guides will not work (even if you have the command selected in the menu).

1. **With `cafe-logo.ai` open, choose View>Smart Guides to make sure that option is turned on.**

    When Smart Guides are active, you can see the entire mesh wireframe as soon as your cursor touches any part of the object —even if that object is not selected. The cursor feedback also identifies specific points along the mesh.

Turn on Smart Guides.

Turn off Snap to Point.

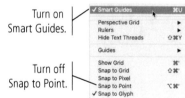

2. **Make sure the Snap to Point option is toggled off in the View menu.**

3. Choose View>Outline.

In Outline mode, you see only the edges, or **wireframes**, of the objects in the file.

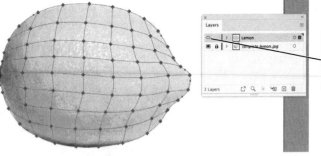

The iris in the icon is missing when a layer displays in Outline mode.

Template layers are not affected when you view the file in Outline mode. You can now see the mesh wireframe and the actual pixels of the lemon image, enabling you to sample colors directly from the lemon image, and then use those colors to paint the mesh points.

4. Using the Direct Selection tool, click the left anchor point on the bottom horizontal mesh line to select only that mesh point.

Your mesh might appear different than ours, based on where you placed your anchor points on the shape edges. You will still be able to achieve the same overall effect as what you see in our examples.

5. With the mesh point selected, choose the Eyedropper tool in the Tools panel, and then click next to the selected mesh point to sample the color from the lemon photo.

Because the mesh object is still displayed in Outline mode, you can't see the effect of the color sampling.

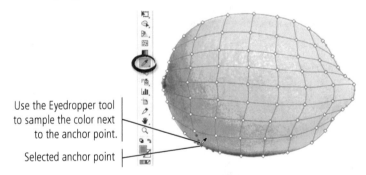

Use the Eyedropper tool to sample the color next to the anchor point.

Selected anchor point

6. Press and hold the Command/Control key to temporarily access the Direct Selection tool, and then click to select the next point along the bottom line of the mesh.

Remember, pressing Command/Control with another tool selected temporarily accesses the last-used Selection tool.

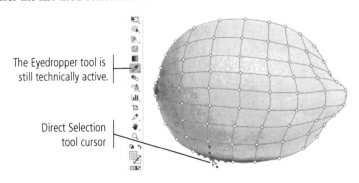

The Eyedropper tool is still technically active.

Direct Selection tool cursor

Note:

In our screen shots, we have the bounding box turned off to better show only the mesh points. You can turn off the bounding box by choosing View>Hide Bounding Box.

7. **Release the Command/Control key to return to the Eyedropper tool, and then click to sample the color next to the selected mesh point.**

   When you release the Command/Control key, you return to the previously active tool.

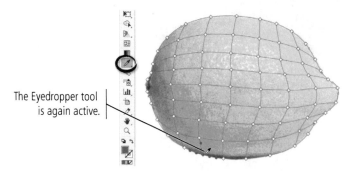

The Eyedropper tool is again active.

8. **Continue this process to change the color of all mesh points on the bottom three rows of points on the mesh.**

9. **Command/Control-click the eye icon for the Lemon layer to change only that layer back to Preview mode.**

   When working in Outline mode, Command/Control-clicking a layer's visibility icon (the eye icon) returns only that layer to Preview mode.

10. **Deselect the mesh object and review your progress.**

    When you change the color of a mesh point, you change the way surrounding colors blend into that point's color. After painting only the bottom three rows of mesh points, you can already see how the shadows and highlights are starting to blend naturally.

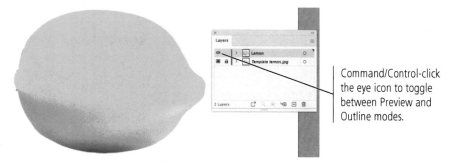

Command/Control-click the eye icon to toggle between Preview and Outline modes.

11. **Command/Control-click the eye icon for the Lemon layer to change that layer back to Outline mode.**

12. **Using the same technique from the previous steps, finish painting all the mesh points in the mesh object.**

    This task might seem tedious because there are so many points in the mesh, but with this process, you can create realistic depth in a flat vector object in a matter of minutes. To accomplish the same result using manual techniques would require many hours of time and a high degree of artistic skill.

13. **Deselect the mesh object. Command/Control-click the Lemon layer eye icon to return that layer to Preview mode, then review your results.**

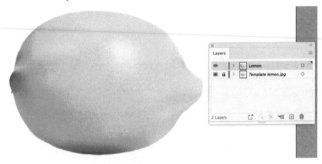

14. **Select the template layer in the Layers panel, then click the Delete Selection button at the bottom of the panel to remove the template layer. When asked to confirm the deletion, click Yes.**

Delete Selection button

15. **Save the file and continue to the next exercise.**

 ## Edit the Gradient Mesh Lines

In addition to simply painting the points that were created when you defined the mesh, you can add to or remove lines from the mesh, move existing points, and even adjust the point handles to change the blending direction. In this exercise, you will adjust the mesh to manipulate the shadows that appear in the lemon artwork.

1. **With cafe-logo.ai open, make sure the Direct Selection tool is active.**

2. **Click to select the center point along the bottom internal mesh line (as shown in the following image).**

   You are going to add a new mesh line to the bottom of the lemon shape to minimize the shadow that appears on the shape's bottom edge.

   Selecting a point changes the Fill color to match the color of the selected point. This color will become the color for the new point you add in the next few steps.

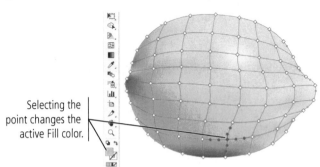

Selecting the point changes the active Fill color.

3. **Click away from the shape to deselect it, then choose the Mesh tool in the Tools panel.**

   The Mesh tool adds new gridlines to an existing mesh, or it creates a mesh if you click inside a basic shape that doesn't currently have a mesh. You can also press Option/Alt and click an existing gridline to remove it from the mesh.

4. **Move the cursor over the center vertical gridline, between the bottom edge and the first internal horizontal gridline.**

Because Smart Guides are active, you can see the mesh lines as soon as the tool cursor enters the shape area.

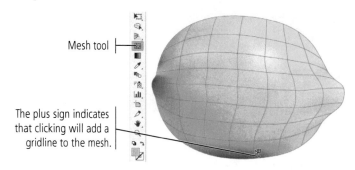

Mesh tool

The plus sign indicates that clicking will add a gridline to the mesh.

Note:

If you don't see the plus sign in the Mesh tool cursor, clicking simply selects an existing point or handle on the mesh.

5. **When you see a plus sign in the tool cursor, click to add a new gridline to the mesh.**

When you see the plus sign in the cursor, clicking adds a new line to the mesh. Clicking a horizontal gridline adds a new vertical one; clicking a vertical gridline adds a new horizontal one.

The point where you click uses the fill color you defined in Step 2. The darker color on the bottom edge now only extends as far as the new line; you have effectively reduced the shadow area in half by adding the new gridline.

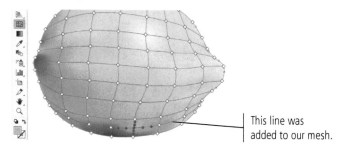

This line was added to our mesh.

6. **Using the Eyedropper method from the previous exercise, change the color of each mesh point on the new row to match the point immediately above it.**

7. **Using the Direct Selection tool, move down the points in the new horizontal mesh line to further reduce the shadow distance on the shape's bottom edge.**

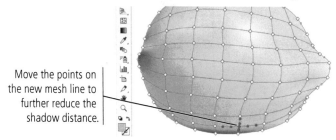

Move the points on the new mesh line to further reduce the shadow distance.

8. **Continue adjusting the positions and colors of the mesh points until you are satisfied with the result.**

9. **Save the file and continue to the next stage of the project.**

STAGE 2 / Working with Type

In this stage of the project, you will use some of Illustrator's basic type formatting options to set your client's company name. You will also use illustration techniques to manipulate the individual letter shapes in the company name to create the finished logotype.

Before you begin the exercises in the second stage of this project, you should understand the terms that are commonly used when people talk about type. Keep the following terms in mind as you work through the next exercises.

Baseline ├ Never tell people how to do things. ┤ Serif font
Tell them what to do and they will ┤ Body clearance
Leading ├ surprise you with their ingenuity.

– George Smith Patton, *War as I Knew It*, 1947 ┤ Sans-serif font

Type is typically divided into two basic categories: serif and sans serif. **Serif type** has small flourishes on the ends of the letterforms; **sans-serif** has no such decorations (*sans* is French for "without"). There are other categories of special or decorative fonts, including script, symbol, dingbat, decorative, and image fonts.

The actual shape of letters is determined by the specific **font** you use; each character in a font is referred to as a **glyph**. Fonts can be monospaced or proportionally spaced. In a monospace font, each character takes up the same amount of space on a line; in other words, a lowercase i and m occupy the same horizontal space. In a proportionally spaced font, different characters occupy different amounts of horizontal space as necessary.

The **x-height** of type is the height of the lowercase letter x. Elements that extend below the baseline are called **descenders** (as in g, j, and p); elements that extend above the x-height are called **ascenders** (as in b, d, and k).

The size of type is usually measured in **points**; there are approximately 72 points in an inch. When you define type size, you determine the distance from the bottom of descenders to the top of ascenders (plus a small extra space above ascenders called the **body clearance**).

Ascender

explore ┤ x-height

Descender

When you set type, it rests on a non-printing line called the **baseline**. If a type element has more than one line in a single paragraph, the distance from one baseline to the next is called **leading** (pronounced "ledding"). Most applications set the default leading as 120% of the type size.

Create Point-Type Objects

Creating type in Illustrator is fairly simple; just click with the Type tool and begin typing. Many advanced options are also available, such as importing type from an external file, using type areas to control long blocks of text, and so on. In this project, you concentrate on the basic type formatting controls.

1. **With `cafe-logo.ai` open (from your WIP>Cafe folder), lock and hide the Lemon layer.**

2. **Create a new layer named `Type` at the top of the layer stack, and make sure the new layer is selected.**

3. **Choose the Type tool in the Tools panel, and then click an empty area of the artboard to create a new point-type object.**

When you single-click with the Type tool, you create **point type**. The type object is automatically filled with placeholder text, which is highlighted. The type automatically defaults to black fill and no stroke, set with the last-used character and paragraph formatting options.

Depending on the width of your application frame, basic character and paragraph formatting options might be available in the Control panel. If not, you can use the Character and Paragraph hot-text links to open the pop-up panels.

You can also access character and paragraph formatting options in the Properties panel whenever a type object is selected.

Note:

You can turn off the automatic placeholder text in the Type Preferences dialog box by unchecking the Fill New Type Objects with Placeholder Text option.

Highlighted placeholder text

The Control panel might include basic text formatting options.

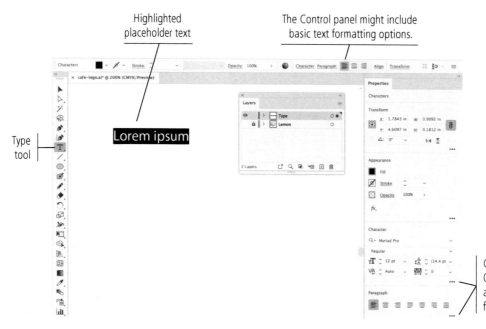

Type tool

Click the More Options button to access additional type formatting options.

4. **With the placeholder text highlighted, type cafe.**

When the type tool is active and text is not highlighted, the insertion point flashes in the type object. This insertion point marks the location where text will be added if you continue typing.

Insertion point

Note:

Hot text *is any text in the user interface that appears underlined in a panel. Clicking these hot-text links opens a panel or dialog box where you can change the related settings.*

5. **Choose the Direct Selection tool in the Tools panel.**

When selected with the Direct Selection tool, you can see the point and path that make up the type object.

6. **Open the Character panel (Window>Type>Character).**

The Character panel provides access to all character formatting options that can be applied in Illustrator. Character formatting options can also be accessed in the Properties panel, or by clicking the Character hot-text link in the Control panel.

You can create two basic kinds of type (or text) objects in Illustrator: **point-type objects** (also called **path type**), where the text usually resides on a single line or path, and **area-type objects**, where the text fills a specific shape (usually a rectangle).

Clicking with the Type tool creates a point-type object. Clicking and dragging with the Type tool creates an area-type object.

Point type (or path type) starts at a single point and extends along or follows a single path. **Area type** fills up an area (normally a rectangle).

The difference between the two kinds of type becomes obvious when you try to resize them or otherwise modify their shapes using the Selection tool. Area type is contained within an area. If you resize that area, the type doesn't resize; it remains within the area but simply flows (or wraps) differently. If you scale or resize point type by dragging a bounding box handle, the type within the object resizes accordingly.

Point-Type Objects

When selected with the Direct Selection tool, you can see the paths that make up the type object.

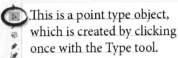

When selected with the Selection tool, you can see the object's bounding-box handles.

This is a point type object, which is created by clicking once with the Type tool.

Using the Selection tool, resizing the bounding box resizes the text in the point-type object.

This is a point type object, which is created by clicking once with the Type tool.

Area-Type Objects

When selected with the Direct Selection tool, you can see the edges of the type object, but no bounding-box handles appear.

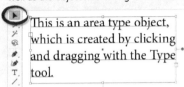

You can see the edges of the type object, as well as the object's bounding-box handles.

This is an area type object, which is created by clicking and dragging with the Type tool.

Using the Selection tool, resizing the bounding box resizes the object; the text rewraps inside the new object dimensions.

This is an area type object, which is created by clicking and dragging with the Type tool.

Path Alignment

Another consideration is where the "point" sits on the type path. When you change the paragraph alignment of point type, the point remains in the same position; the text on the point moves to the appropriate position, relative to the fixed point.

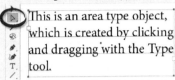

Point (path) type — Left-aligned text

Point (path) type — Center-aligned text

Point (path) type — Right-aligned text

The point for path type is determined by where you click to place the object.

Converting Type Objects

When the Selection tool is active, the handle on the right side of the type-object bounding box indicates whether that object contains point type or area type. A hollow handle identifies a point-type object; a solid handle identifies an area-type object. When you move the cursor over a type object, an icon in the cursor indicates that double-clicking will convert the object to the other kind of type object.

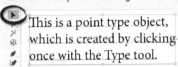

This is a point type object, which is created by clicking with the Type tool.

Double-click the hollow handle to convert to an area-type object.

This is an area type object, which is created by clicking and dragging with the Type tool.

Double-click the solid handle to convert to a point-type object.

7. **Click the Font Family field to highlight the active font. Type `atc`.**

When you type in the Font Family field, a menu shows all fonts that include the letters you type. By default, the menu includes any font containing those letters, regardless of the position of the letters within the font name. In other words, typing "gar" would show fonts named both "Garamond" and "Adobe Garamond."

If you click the Magnifying Glass icon to the left of the field, you can choose Search First Word Only. In that case, the letters you type automatically scroll the Font Family list to the first font with the typed letters at the beginning of the name; typing "gar" would scroll to Garamond and skip over Adobe Garamond.

8. **Move your mouse cursor over various fonts in the menu.**

You can use this method in the font menu to show a live preview of various fonts before actually applying them to the selected text.

Individual characters do not need to be selected to change text formatting. Changes made while a type *object* is selected apply to all text in that type object.

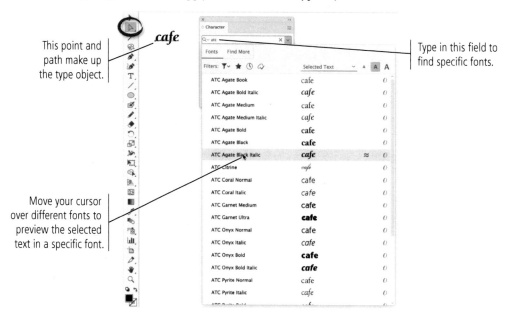

This point and path make up the type object.

Type in this field to find specific fonts.

Move your cursor over different fonts to preview the selected text in a specific font.

9. **Click ATC Garnet Medium in the Font menu to select that font.**

After you select the font, you should notice that the Font Family menu shows "ATC Garnet" and the secondary Font Style menu shows "Medium." When you use the Font Search option (as in Step 7), the resulting menu shows all font variations that include the letters you type — including different styles within the same family.

Font Family

Font Style

10. **Click the Selection tool in the Tools panel.**

When the Selection tool is active, you can see the bounding-box handles of the type object. (If you don't see the bounding box, choose View>Show Bounding Box to toggle it on.) Like any other object, you can use the handles to stretch, scale, or rotate the type object.

11. Click any of the type object's corner handles and drag out to make the type larger. When the type object is approximately three times its original size, release the mouse button (use the following image as a guide).

You can press Shift after you begin dragging to constrain the object's original proportions.

In the initial 2021 release, there is a bug that prevents cursor feedback from showing accurate measurements while you are resizing a type object. You might see the W and H measurments as 0 instead of the accurate dynamic size.

Note:

We turned Smart Guides on (View>Smart Guides) to show the cursor feedback in our screen shots.

12. If you only see four fields below the Font Style menu in the Character panel, open the panel Options menu and choose Show Options.

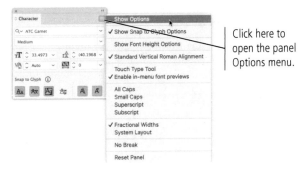

Click here to open the panel Options menu.

13. Review the extended character formatting options in the Character panel.

The Size menu shows the new size that results from resizing the object by dragging its bounding-box handles. If you do not constrain the resizing, you might have a horizontal or vertical scale other than 100%.

14. In the Character panel, change the Size field to 72. Make sure both the horizontal and vertical scale values are set to 100%.

Pressing Tab moves through the panel fields; as soon as you move to a new field, your changes in the previous field are reflected in the document. You can also press Return/Enter to finalize a change.

15. **Using the Type tool, double-click the word "cafe" to select all the letters in the word.**

16. **In the Character panel, change the Tracking field to -10 to tighten the space between all selected letters.**

Tracking and kerning are two terms related to the horizontal spacing between characters in a line of text. **Kerning** is the spacing between two specific characters; **tracking** refers to the spacing between all characters in a selection.

Smaller type does not usually pose tracking and kerning problems; when type is very large, however, spacing often becomes an issue. To fix spacing problems, you need to adjust the kerning and/or tracking values.

You can change the field manually, choose a pre-defined value from the Tracking menu, or click the up- or down-arrow button to change the tracking by 1 unit with each click.

Note:

Kerning and tracking are largely matters of personal preference. Some people prefer much tighter spacing than others.

17. **Click with the Type tool to place the insertion point between the "c" and the "a".**

This is a good example of a **kern pair** that needs adjustment. The Auto setting built into the font leaves a little too much space between the two characters, even after you have tightened the tracking considerably.

18. **Change the Kerning value to -20.**

Like tracking, you can change this value manually, choose a value from the pop-up menu, or use the Kerning field buttons to change kerning by 1 unit.

Insertion point

These slight modifications to tracking and kerning improve the overall appearance and readability of the logo. Later in the project, you will use a different technique to adjust letter spacing. For now, however, you should become familiar with making this type of manual adjustment.

19. **Save the file and continue to the next exercise.**

The Character panel includes all the options you can use to change the appearance of selected text characters.

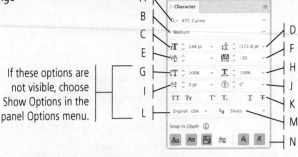

A **Font Family** is the general font that is applied, such as Minion or Warnock Pro.

B **Font Style** is the specific variation of the applied font, such as Italic, Bold, or Light.

C **Font Size** is the size of the type in points.

D **Leading** is the distance from one baseline to the next. It is important to realize that leading is a character attribute, and applies only to selected characters.

If you change the leading for only certain characters in a line, keep in mind that the adjusted leading applies to the entire line where adjusted characters exist; for example:

> In this sentence, we changed the leading
> for only the underlined word; all text in
> the same line moves to accommodate the
> adjusted leading of the characters.

E **Kerning** increases or decreases the space between pairs of letters. Kerning is used in cases where particular letters in specific fonts need to be manually spread apart or brought together to eliminate a too-tight or too-spread-out appearance. Manual kerning is often necessary in headlines or other large type elements. Many commercial fonts have built-in kerning pairs, so you won't need to apply much hands-on intervention. Adobe applications default to the kerning values stored in the **font metrics**.

F **Tracking**, also known as "range kerning," refers to the overall tightness or looseness across a range of characters. Tracking and kerning are applied in thousandths of an **em** (or the amount of space occupied by an uppercase "M," which is usually the widest character in a typeface).

G **Vertical Scale** artificially stretches selected characters top to bottom.

H **Horizontal Scale** artificially stretches selected characters left to right.

Character scaling is a quick way of achieving condensed or expanded type if those variations of a font don't exist. Type that has been artificially condensed or expanded too much looks bad because the scaling destroys the type's metrics. If possible, use a condensed or expanded version of a font before resorting to horizontal or vertical scaling.

I **Baseline Shift** moves the selected type above or below the baseline by a specific number of points. Positive numbers move the characters up; negative values move the characters down.

If these options are not visible, choose Show Options in the panel Options menu.

J **Character Rotation** rotates only selected letters, rather than rotating the entire type object.

K Type Styles — **All Caps**, **Small Caps**, **Superscript**, **Subscript**, **Underline**, and **Strikethrough** — change the appearance of selected characters.

L **Language Dictionary** defines the language that is used to check spelling in the story.

M **Anti-aliasing** can be used to help smooth the apparent edges of type that is exported to a bitmap format that does not support vector information.

N **Snap to Glyph** options. When Smart Guides are active and Snap to Glyph is checked in the View menu, these button enable guides to identify various parts of live text when you move or draw another object near the characters (glyphs) in a type object.

You can use the buttons at the bottom of the Character panel to turn specific glyph measurements on or off. From left to right:

— **Baseline** snaps to the base of glyphs.

— **x-height** snaps to the height of a lowercase glyph.

— **Glyph Bounds** snaps to top, bottom, left, and right bounds of a glyph.

— **Proximity Guides** snaps to guides generated near the baseline, x-height, and glyph bounds.

— **Angular Guides** snaps to the angular guides that appear when you select a glyph with angular segments, or on rotating a type object.

— **Anchor Points** snap to the anchor points of glyphs.

Manipulate Type Objects

Note:

When the insertion point is flashing in a type object, you can't use the keyboard shortcuts to access tools; instead, pressing a key adds that letter to the current type object, at the location of the insertion point.

When you work with type in Illustrator, you need to be aware of a few special issues that can affect the way you interact with the application. This exercise explores some common problems that can arise when you work with type, as well as some tricks you can use to work around them.

1. **With `cafe-logo.ai` open, select the Type tool in the Tools panel. Click anywhere in the existing type object to place the insertion point.**

2. **Move the Type tool cursor away from the existing type object. Click to deselect the existing type object.**

When the insertion point is already flashing in a type object, the exact position of the cursor determines what happens if you click. When the cursor is within the bounds of the existing type object, clicking simply places the insertion point where you click. If you move the cursor outside the bounds of the active type object (where the insertion point is flashing), clicking deselects the previously active type object; you can then click again to create a new point-type object.

This cursor moves the insertion point.

This cursor deselects the current type object.

3. **With the Type tool active, click to create a new point-type object.**

When you add a new type object, the placeholder text is automatically set using the last formatting options that you defined in the Character panel. (Settings that were altered by scaling the type object, such as font size and horizontal scale, are not maintained.)

4. **With the placeholder text highlighted, type `Limon`.**

Note:

You can press the ESC key to switch to the Selection tool, which effectively removes the insertion point and selects the type object.

5. **With the insertion point flashing, press Command/Control.**

   As you know, this modifier key temporarily switches the active tool to the last-used Selection tool. The bounding box of the type object remains visible as long as you hold down the Command/Control key. If you release the Command/Control key, you return to the previously active tool (in this case, the Type tool).

6. **While still holding down the Command/Control key, click within the bounding box of the type object.**

   When you click, you select the actual type object. The point and path become active, and the insertion point no longer flashes. You can use this method to move or modify a type object without switching away from the Type tool.

   Pressing Command/Control temporarily accesses the last-used Selection tool and reveals the type object's bounding box.

7. **Press Command/Control. Click the second type object and drag it until the "i" in Limon aligns with the "f" in cafe.**

   You might want to zoom in to better align the two type objects. Use the image here as a guide.

   The layer color previews the new position of the type object.

8. **Release the mouse button to reposition the type object.**

9. **Press the Command/Control key again, click the type object, then press Shift and drag up or down until there is only a small space between the bottom of the "e" in cafe and the top of the "m" in Limon.**

   Note:

   When you're working with type, it can be easier to work with bounding boxes turned off. You can turn off the bounding boxes for all objects — including type objects — by choosing View>Hide Bounding Box.

10. **Release the Command/Control key to return to the Type tool.**

11. **Save the file and continue to the next exercise.**

You can click the arrow to the right of the Font Family menu to open the Font panel, which provides a number of options for finding fonts you want to use in your design. (The same options are available wherever you see a Font Family menu — the Character panel, the Control panel, and the Properties panel.)

The top section of the menu lists up to ten most recently used fonts. These appear in the order in which they were used, with the most recent at the top of the menu. You can change the number of displayed fonts in the Type pane of the Preferences dialog box.

The second lists variable fonts. The third section lists picture fonts at the top, and then all other fonts that are available to Illustrator.

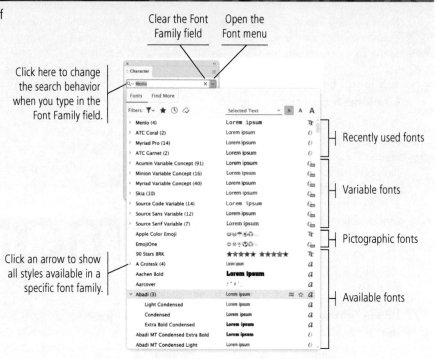

Clear the Font Family field

Open the Font menu

Click here to change the search behavior when you type in the Font Family field.

Click an arrow to show all styles available in a specific font family.

Recently used fonts

Variable fonts

Pictographic fonts

Available fonts

The font family names in each section appear in alphabetical order. An arrow to the left of a font name indicates that a specific font family includes more than one style. You can click the arrow to show all possible styles in the panel.

If you apply a font that includes more than one style, the style you choose appears in the Font Style menu. You can open the Font Style menu to change the style without changing the font family.

Each font in the panel includes a sample of the font, which defaults to show the currently selected text. If no text is selected, the sample text simply shows the word "Sample." You can choose a different sample text from the menu at the top of the panel. You can also change the size of the sample text using the three icons to the right of the menu.

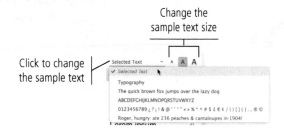

Change the sample text size

Click to change the sample text

The right column in the Font menu shows an icon to identify the type of font:

a **PostScript (Type 1) fonts** have two file components (outline and printer) that are required for output.

Tт **TrueType fonts** have a single file, but (until recently) were primarily used on the Windows platform.

O **OpenType fonts** are contained in a single file that can include more than 60,000 glyphs (characters) in a single font. OpenType fonts are cross-platform; the same font can be used on both Macintosh and Windows systems.

*O*ᵥₛᵥᵍ **OpenType SVG fonts** allow font glyphs to be created as SVG (scalable vector graphics) artwork, which means glyphs can include multiple colors and gradients. These fonts, which are relatively new, are most commonly used for emojis.

*O*ᵥₐᵣ **OpenType Variable fonts**, introduced in 2016, were developed jointly by Adobe, Apple, Google, and Microsoft to allow a single font file to store a continuous range of variants. If you apply a variable font, you can adjust the width and weight of the applied font without the need for different font files for variations such as Bold, Black, Condensed, or Extended.

⌂ **Adobe fonts** are those that have been activated in your Creative Cloud account.

Above the list of fonts in the Font panel, you can use the Filters options to show only certain fonts in the panel. Clicking the Filter Fonts by Classification button opens a menu where you can find fonts of a certain style (serif, sans serif, etc.), as well as fonts with specific properties:

▼˅ Filter Fonts by Classification

★ Show Favorite Fonts

🕐 Show Recently Added Fonts

☁ Show Activated (Adobe) Fonts

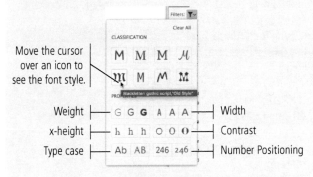

Move the cursor over an icon to see the font style.

Weight ├— G G **G** A A —┤ Width

x-height ├— h h h O O O —┤ Contrast

Type case ├— Ab AB 246 246 —┤ Number Positioning

- Weight, or the thickness of strokes in the letterforms
- Width of the individual letterforms
- x-height, or the ratio of lowercase letter height compared to uppercase
- Contrast, or the ratio of thin strokes compared to thick strokes in individual letterforms
- Type case, or whether a font includes both upper- and lowercase, or all capitals/small caps and all caps
- Number positioning, which refers to whether numbers all align to the baseline or extend above or below the baseline

When you use any of the filtering options, the Font panel shows only fonts that match the selected filter. You can click the Clear All link in the top-right corner of the panel to restore the default font list.

When the mouse cursor hovers over a font in the list, two additional icons appear on the right side of the panel for the highlighted font.

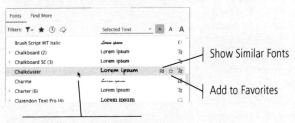

Show Similar Fonts

Add to Favorites

Move the cursor over a font to reveal additional options.

You can click the Show Similar Fonts ≈ button to show only fonts similar to the one you selected; clicking the Back hot-text link returns to the full Font panel.

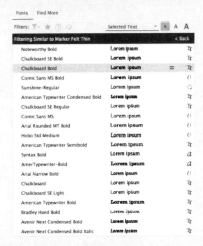

Clicking the Add to Favorites ☆ button designates a font as a Favorite. Favorite fonts are identified by a solid star icon even when the cursor is not hovering over that particular font. You can also use the Filtering option at the top of the panel to show only Favorite fonts.

Working with Adobe Fonts

Adobe Fonts (formerly called Typekit) is an online library of high-quality fonts that are available to anyone with a Creative Cloud subscription.

The Find More option at the top of the Font panel provides a link to Adobe Fonts directly from the InDesign interface.

When you find a font you want to use, move your mouse over that font to show the Activate icon ; click that icon to activate it in your Creative Cloud account. (A separate icon shows that a particular font is currently being activated .) Synced fonts will be available for use in any application on your device.

If only certain fonts in a family are active, you can click the Active Remaining icon to activate all fonts in that family.

If a font is already active, move your mouse over the Active icon to access the Deactivate icon ; click that icon to unsync that font.

Verifying your Adobe ID

To use Adobe fonts in an Adobe application, you must first verify that you are signed in using the username and password that is associated with your individual user subscription. (Adobe Font functionality is not available if you are working on a computer that has an Adobe software Device license instead of an individual user subscription.)

If you open the Help menu, you will see an option to either Sign In or Sign Out. If you see the words "Sign Out," the menu option also shows the email address (username) that is currently signed in.

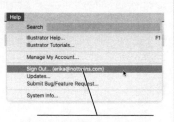

This is the Adobe ID email that is currently signed in to the Adobe Creative Cloud.

If you see your own username, you are already signed in, and can use the Adobe Font functionality. If you see a different username, you should choose the Sign Out option, and then sign in with your own username. If you see the words "Sign In," you should choose that menu option and follow the on-screen directions to sign in with your own username.

Managing Missing Fonts

It is important to understand that fonts are external files of data that describe the font for the output device. The fonts you use in a file need to be available on any computer that opens the file. Illustrator stores a reference to used fonts, but it does not store the actual font data.

When you open a file that uses fonts you don't have installed on your computer, a Missing Fonts dialog box shows which fonts should be installed. The software scans the Adobe Font library to locate missing fonts; those that exist in the library are automatically checked. Clicking the Activate Fonts button syncs the required Adobe Fonts in your Creative Cloud account, making them available in your desktop version of Illustrator.

You can also use the Find Font dialog box (accessed by clicking the Find Fonts button in the Missing Fonts dialog box or by choosing Type>Find Font) to replace one font with another throughout a layout.

The top half of the dialog box lists every font used in the file; missing fonts are identified by a warning icon in the list. If a missing font is available in the Adobe Font library, it is automatically checked in the top list. You can click the Activate Fonts button to sync those fonts in your CC account.

The lower half shows fonts that can be used to replace fonts in the top list. Document shows only fonts used in the file. Recent shows fonts you have recently used in Illustrator. System shows all fonts that are active on your computer.

If you click the Change or Change All button, the font selected in the top list will be replaced with the font selected in the bottom list. You can also use the Find button to locate instances of the selected font without making changes.

Convert Type to Outlines

In Illustrator, fonts — and the characters that compose them — are like any other vector objects. They are made up of anchors and paths, which you can modify just as you would any other vector object. To access the anchor points, however, you must first convert the text to outlines.

1. **With `cafe-logo.ai` open, expand the Type layer in the Layers panel.**

   Each type object exists as a separate sublayer.

2. **Use the Selection tool to select both type objects in the file.**

3. **Choose Type>Create Outlines.**

   When you convert the type to outlines, the anchor points and paths that make up the letter shapes appear. Each type object (in this case, one for "cafe" and one for "Limon") is a separate group of letter shapes.

Note:

Press Command/Control-Shift-O to convert type to outlines.

Selected objects are identified by solid squares.

4. **In the Layers panel, click the arrow to the left of each group on the Type layer to expand them.**

   By expanding the individual layers and sublayer groups, you can use the Layers panel to access and work with individual objects in a group without ungrouping the objects.

Note:

If the Properties panel is open, you can also click the Create Outlines button in the Quick Actions section of the panel.

5. In the Layers panel, click the space to the right of the Target icon of the "m" to select only that object.

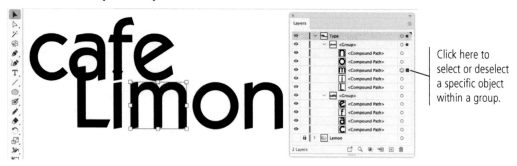

Click here to select or deselect a specific object within a group.

6. With the Selection tool active, press the Left Arrow key three times to nudge the selected object left, narrowing the space between the letter shapes.

You can open the General pane of the Preferences dialog box to change the distance an object moves when you press the arrow keys (called the **keyboard increment**). Press Shift and an arrow key to move an object 10 times the default keyboard increment.

You could have fine-tuned the letter spacing with tracking and kerning before you converted the letters to outlines. Since you're working with these letters as graphics, you are nudging individual pieces of a group to adjust the spacing in the overall logotype.

7. Repeat Steps 5–6 to move the "o" and "n" shapes closer to the other letters in the same word.

As mentioned previously, letter spacing is largely a matter of personal preference. You might prefer more or less space between the letters than what you see in our images.

8. **Repeat Steps 5–6 to move the "e" closer to the "f" in the word cafe.**

9. **In the Layers panel, click the space to the right of the Target icon of the "a" to select only that object.**

10. **Press Shift, and click the same space for the "c" to add that object to the active selection.**

    You can Shift-click the icons in the panel to add or subtract sublayers from the active selection. In this case, however, Shift-clicking does not select all in-between sublayers when you add more than one object to the selection.

    You can also Shift-click the icon for a selected object to remove it from the active selection.

11. **Press the Right Arrow key one time to nudge both selected objects closer to the "f" in the same word.**

Shift-click to select multiple sublayers.

12. **Use the Layers panel to select only the "L" in Limon, then drag it until the vertical section appears immediately below the vertical line in the "a" (use the following image as a guide).**

    Although the individual letter shapes are parts of various groups, selecting sublayers in the Layers panel means you don't need to switch to the Direct Selection tool to move only the selected objects.

13. **Save the file and continue to the next exercise.**

Create Custom Graphics from Letter Shapes

Because you converted the letter shapes to outlines, the logo text no longer behaves as type. You can now apply your drawing skills to adjust the vector shapes and create a unique appearance for your client's logotype. Remember, you can use the Add Anchor Point tool to add points to a vector path, use the Delete Anchor Point tool to remove points from a vector path, and use the Anchor Point tool to convert smooth points to corner points (and vice versa). All three of these tools are nested below the Pen tool in the Tools panel.

1. **With cafe-logo.ai open, click the Eye icon to hide the "cafe" sublayer.**

2. **Select only the "i" object, and then choose Object>Compound Path>Release.**

    A compound path is simply a single object that is made up of more than one path. Where multiple objects overlap, the top object knocks out (removes) underlying objects without destructively changing the underlying shapes.

    In this case, releasing the compound path simply breaks the two shapes that make up the "i" into separate objects.

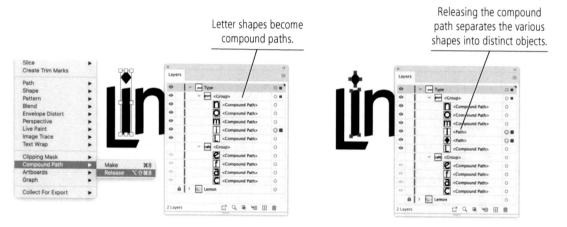

Letter shapes become compound paths.

Releasing the compound path separates the various shapes into distinct objects.

3. **Using what you know about anchor points, edit the dot over the "i" to resemble a leaf character.**

    We converted the bottom, left, and right points to smooth points, then adjusted the position of the top point to achieve the leaf shape.

4. **Change the fill color of the selected object to a medium green from the built-in swatches.**

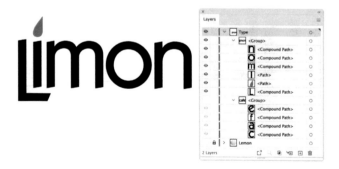

5. Show the "cafe" sublayer, then edit the bottom of the "f" to align with the leaf shape you just created, leaving a small white space between the two shapes (as shown in the following image).

6. Using the Direct Selection tool, select the two right anchor points on the "L" shape. Drag them right until the shape creates an underline below all the other letters in the word "Limon."

7. Select and delete the "o" object from the "Limon" sublayer.

8. Show and unlock the Lemon layer. Transform the gradient-mesh object and move it to fill the space left by deleting the "o" letter shape.

Note:

Your W and H values might be slightly different than what you see in our screenshots, but they should be in the same general ballpark.

9. Save the file and continue to the next stage of the project.

For all intents and purposes, the Cafe Limon logo is now complete. However, you still need to create the alternate versions that can be used in other applications. You need a two-color version for jobs that will be printed with spot colors, and you need a one-color version for jobs that will be printed with black ink only.

Rather than generating multiple files for individual versions of a logo, you can use Illustrator's multiple-artboard capabilities to create a single file that manages the different logo variations on separate artboards.

In this stage of the project, you adjust the artboard to fit the completed logo. You then duplicate the artwork on additional artboards, and adjust the colors in each version to meet the specific needs of different color applications.

 Adjust the Default Artboard

When you place an Illustrator file into another file (for example, a page-layout file in InDesign or even another Illustrator file) you can decide how to place that file — based on the artwork boundaries (the outermost bounding box), on the artboard boundaries, or on other specific dimensions. To make the logo artwork more placement-friendly, you should adjust the Illustrator artboard to fit the completed logo artwork.

1. **With cafe-logo.ai open, make the Selection tool active, then choose Select>All to select all elements on the artboard.**

2. **Using the Properties panel, choose the top-left reference point in the Transform section. Change the X and Y positions to 0.125 in.**

Position the selection based on the top-left reference point.

3. **Make sure the W and H fields are linked, then type 250% in the W field.**

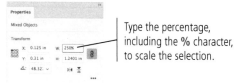

Type the percentage, including the % character, to scale the selection.

4. **Press Return/Enter to finalize the transformation.**

When you press Return/Enter (or simply click away from the panel field), the selection is scaled proportionally to 250% of its original size.

5. **Select the Artboard tool in the Tools panel.**

   When the Artboard tool is active, the artboard edge is surrounded by marching ants; you can drag the side and corner handles to manually resize the artboard in the workspace.

Drag the handles to manually resize the artboard.

Artboard tool

6. **Click the bottom-right handle of the artboard, then drag up and left until the artboard is approximately 1/8″ larger than the artwork on all four sides.**

7. **Click the Selection tool to exit the Artboard-editing mode.**

8. **Save the file and continue to the next exercise.**

When the Artboard tool is active, the Control panel presents a number of options for adjusting the active artboard.

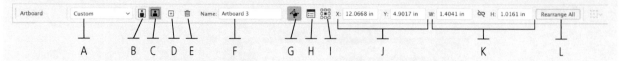

A B C D E F G H I J K L

A   Use this menu to change the artboard to a predefined size (letter, tabloid, etc.).

B   Click to change the artboard to portrait orientation.

C   Click to change the artboard to landscape orientation.

D   Click to add a new artboard at the currently defined size. The cursor is "loaded" with the new artboard; you can click to place the new artboard in the workspace.

E   Click to delete the active artboard.

F   Type here to define a name for the active artboard.

G   Click to toggle the Move/Copy Artwork with Artboard option. When active, objects on the artboard move along with the artboard being moved (or cloned).

H   Click to open the Artboard Options dialog box.

I   Choose a registration point for changes in size or position.

J   Use these fields to define the position of the artboard. (The first artboard always begins at X: 0, Y: 0.)

K   Use these fields to change the size of the artboard. If the link icon is active, the height and width will be constrained.

L   If a file includes more than one artboard, you can click this button to open a dialog box in which you can define a grid pattern for all existing artboards. You can determine the number of columns in the grid, as well as the exact space between individual artboards.

Clicking the Artboard Options button opens a dialog box where you can further manage and control the selected artboard. Most of these options (Preset, Width, Height, Orientation, and Position) are the same as those available in the Control panel.

The remaining choices are explained here:

- **Constrain Proportions** maintains a consistent aspect ratio (height to width) if you resize the artboard.
- **Show Center Mark** displays a point in the center of the crop area.
- **Show Cross Hairs** displays lines that extend into the artwork from the center of each edge.
- **Show Video Safe Areas** displays guides that represent the areas inside the viewable area of video.

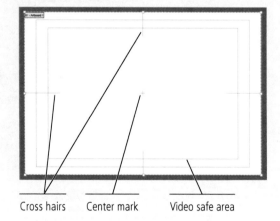

Cross hairs   Center mark   Video safe area

- **Video Ruler Pixel Aspect Ratio** specifies the pixel aspect ratio used for artboard rulers.
- **Fade Region Outside Artboard** displays the area outside the artboard darker than the area inside the artboard.
- **Update While Dragging** keeps the area outside the artboard darker as you move or resize the artboard.

Use the Layers Panel to Organize Artwork

Your goal is to create three separate versions of the logo — the four-color version that's already done, a two-color version for spot-color applications, and a one-color version that will be used in jobs that are printed black-only.

As you created the artwork, you used two layers and a variety of sublayers to manage the arrangement and stacking order of the various elements. Now that the drawing is complete, however, you will use layers for a different purpose — to create, isolate, and manage multiple versions of the logo in a single file.

Note:

You might want to zoom out so you can see the entire original artboard and the empty space below it.

1. **With `cafe-logo.ai` open, make the Selection tool active.**

2. **Choose Select>All to select all objects on the artboard.**

3. **Choose Object>Group. In the Layers panel, expand the resulting group.**

   When you group objects, the resulting group is placed on the top-most layer in the active selection. All objects in the group are moved to the same layer containing the group. The original stacking order is maintained, so the mesh object from the Lemon layer still appears at the bottom of the list in the resulting group

The new group exists on the top-most layer in the previous selection.

The mesh object is moved from its original layer into the group.

The mesh object is still below other objects in the stacking order.

4. **Collapse the Type layer in the panel to hide the sublayers.**

5. **Double-click the Type layer name to highlight it. Type Four-Color Logo, then press Return/Enter to finalize the new name.**

6. **Select the Lemon layer in the Layers panel, then click the Delete Selection button.**

   Because this layer no longer has any artwork, you are not asked to confirm the deletion.

Delete Selection button

7. **Save the file and continue to the next exercise.**

Copy the Artboard and Artwork

The final step in this project is to create the two alternate versions of the logo. This process is largely a matter of cloning the existing artboard and artwork — but you need to complete a few extra steps to convert the mesh objects to standard filled paths.

1. **With cafe-logo.ai open, choose the Artboard tool in the Tools panel.**

2. **With the only artboard currently active, highlight the contents of the Name field in the Control panel and type Four Color.**

3. **Make sure the Move/Copy Artwork with Artboard option is toggled on.**

The Artboard name appears in the Name field and in the artboard tag.

The Move/Copy Artwork with Artboard option should be toggled on.

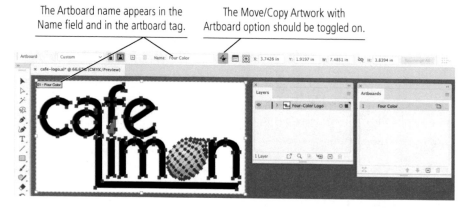

4. **Place the cursor inside the artboard area. Press Option/Alt and then click and drag down to clone the existing artboard.**

Pressing Option/Alt clones the existing artboard, just as you would clone a regular drawing object.

Because Move/Copy Artwork with Artboard is toggled on, the logo artwork and the artboard are cloned at the same time.

5. **When the new artboard/artwork is entirely outside the boundaries of the first artboard, release the mouse button.**

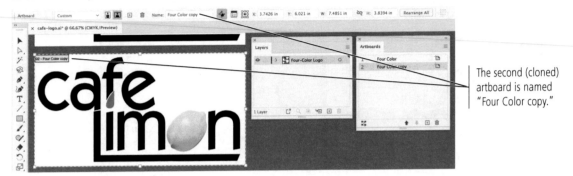

The second (cloned) artboard is named "Four Color copy."

6. **With the second artboard active, change the Name field to Two Color.**

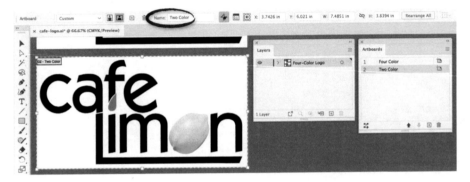

7. **In the Layers panel, click the Create New Layer button.**

New layers are added above the previously selected layer. Because the Four Color layer was the only layer in the file, the new layer is added at the top of the layer stack.

Create New Layer button

8. **Double-click the new layer name in the panel, then type Two-Color Logo to rename the layer.**

9. **Using the Selection tool, drag a marquee to select all the objects on the second artboard.**

10. **In the Layers panel, drag the Selected Art icon from the Four-Color Logo layer to the Two-Color Logo layer.**

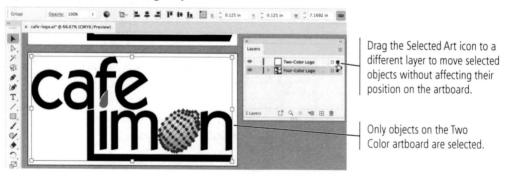

Drag the Selected Art icon to a different layer to move selected objects without affecting their position on the artboard.

Only objects on the Two Color artboard are selected.

When you release the mouse button, the selected objects are moved to the Two-Color Logo layer.

11. **Save the file and continue to the next exercise.**

Convert Mesh Objects to Regular Paths

When you created the gradient meshes in the first stage of this project, you saw that adding the mesh removed the original path you drew. When you worked on the mesh, you might have noticed that the Control panel showed that the selected object was transformed from a path object to a mesh object.

To create the flat two-color version of the logo, however, you need to access the original paths you drew to create the mesh objects. There is no one-step process to convert the mesh object back to a flat path object, so you need to take a few extra steps to create the flat version of the logo.

Because the black-only version of the logo is also flat, you are going to create the flat two-color version first, and then clone it. Doing so avoids unnecessary repetition of the process presented in this exercise.

1. **With cafe-logo.ai open, deselect everything in the file and then open the Artboards panel (Window>Artboards).**

   The Artboards panel can be used to access and arrange the various artboards in a file.

2. **In the Artboards panel, double-click the Two Color artboard (away from the artboard name).**

   This forces the selected artboard to fill the space available in the document window.

3. **Expand the Two-Color Logo layer in the Layers panel. If necessary, expand the first group so you can see the three sublayers in the group.**

4. **Use the Layers panel to select the mesh object on the Two-Color Logo layer.**

5. **Open the Appearance panel (Window>Appearance).**

6. **With the mesh object selected, click the Add New Stroke button at the bottom of the Appearance panel.**

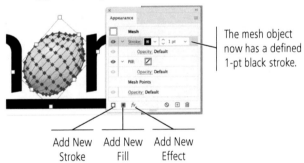

The mesh object now has a defined 1-pt black stroke.

Add New Stroke   Add New Fill   Add New Effect

7. **With the mesh object still selected, choose Object>Expand Appearance.**

   This command converts the selected object into separate constituent objects — one path for the shape's stroke attribute and one for the object's mesh fill — which are automatically grouped together.

8. **In the Layers panel, expand the new group.**

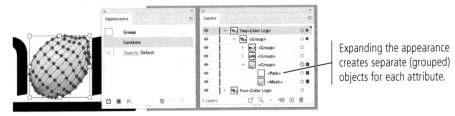

Expanding the appearance creates separate (grouped) objects for each attribute.

9. **Use the Layers panel to select only the mesh object in the group.**

10. **Press Delete/Backspace to remove the selected mesh object.**

    You now have a simple path object that is essentially the lemon shape. However, you need to complete one more step because the path is still part of the group that was created by the Expand Appearance command.

After deleting the mesh, the remaining path is still part of the group.

11. **Use the Layers panel to select the path in the group, and then choose Object>Ungroup.**

After ungrouping, the selected path is a regular sublayer (it is not grouped).

12. **Save the file and continue to the next exercise.**

The Appearance Panel in Depth

The Appearance panel allows you to review and change the appearance attributes of objects, including stroke, fill, transparency, and applied effects.

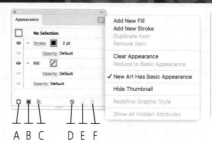

A Add New Stroke
B Add New Fill
C Add New Effect
D Clear Appearance
E Duplicate Selected Item
F Delete

A B C   D E F

As you know, the last-used settings for fill color, stroke color, and stroke weight are applied to new objects. Other attributes, such as the applied brush or effects, are not automatically applied.

If you need to create a series of objects with the same overall appearance, you can turn off the **New Art Has Basic Appearance** option in the Appearance panel Options menu.

Clicking the **Clear Appearance** button reduces the selected object to a fill and stroke of None.

Choosing **Reduce to Basic Appearance** in the panel Options menu resets an object to only basic fill and stroke attributes; fill color and stroke weight and color are maintained, but all other attributes are removed.

You can use the **Duplicate Selected Item** button to create multiple versions of the same attribute for an object, such as two stroke weights/colors, allowing you to compound the effect without layering multiple objects.

New appearance attributes are created on top of the currently selected appearance. You can drag the appearance names in the panel to change their stacking sequence, which can have a significant impact on the end result.

If you want to remove a specific attribute, simply select that item and click the panel's **Delete** button.

Add Spot Color to the Two-Color Logo

Spot colors are created with special premixed inks that produce a certain color with one ink layer; they are not built from the standard CMYK process inks. Each spot color appears on its own separation. Spot inks are commonly used to reproduce colors you can't get from a CMYK build, in two- or three-color documents, or as additional separations when exact colors are needed.

You can choose a spot color directly from the library on your screen, but you should look at a printed swatch book to verify that you're using the color you intend. Special inks exist because many of the colors can't be reproduced with process inks, nor can they be accurately represented on a monitor. If you specify spot colors and then convert them to process colors later, your job probably won't look exactly as you expect.

Note:

In the United States, the most popular collections of spot colors are the Pantone Matching System (PMS) libraries. TruMatch and Focoltone are also used in the United States. Toyo and DICColor (Dainippon Ink & Chemicals) are used primarily in Japan.

1. **With `cafe-logo.ai` open, choose Window>Swatch Libraries>Color Books>Pantone+ Solid Coated.**

   Illustrator includes swatch libraries of all the common spot-color libraries. You can open any of these libraries to access the various colors available in each collection.

   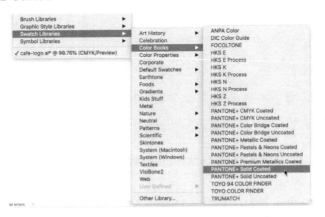

2. **In the Pantone+ Solid Coated library Options menu, choose Small List View to show the color names for each swatch.**

   It is often easier to view swatches with their names and samples, especially when you need to find a specific swatch (as in this exercise).

Note:

The View options in the panel Options menu are available for all swatch panels, including colors, patterns, and brushes.

3. **On the Two Color artboard/layer, select the path that represents the lemon.**

4. **In the Find field of the color library panel, type `102`.**

   You could simply scroll through the panel to find the color you want, but typing a number in the Find field shows only colors that match what you type.

Note:

To restore all spot color to the panel, simply delete the characters from the panel's Search field.

5. **Make sure the Fill icon is active in the Tools panel, and then click Pantone 102 C in the swatch Library panel.**

   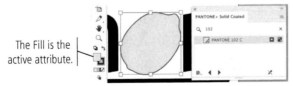

   The Fill is the active attribute.

6. **Review the Swatches panel (Window>Swatches).**

   When you apply a color from a swatch library, that swatch is added to the Swatches panel for the open file.

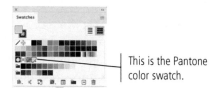

   This is the Pantone color swatch.

7. **Using whichever method you prefer, change the stroke color of the selected object to None.**

8. **Select only the leaf shape that you created from the dot over the "i."**

   Use the Direct Selection tool or the icons in the Layers panel to select only that shape.

9. **Change the fill color to None and change the stroke to 2-pt Black.**

10. **Choose the Artboard tool. With the Move/Copy Artwork with Artboard option still active, press Option/Alt and then click and drag down to clone the flat version. Rename the new artboard One Color.**

11. **Move the artwork on the third artboard to a new layer named One-Color Logo. Change the lemon shape to a fill of None with a 2-pt Black stroke.**

12. **Save the file, close it, and then continue to the next stage of the project.**

STAGE 4 / Combining Text and Graphics

The final stage of this project requires two additional layouts: a letterhead and a business envelope. Rather than adding more artboards to the logo file, you are going to create a new file that will contain both pieces of stationery. This means you must place the logos from the original cafe-logo.ai file, and understand how to work with objects that are placed from external files.

 ## Work with Placed Graphics

Some production-related concerns dictate how you design a letterhead. In general, there are two ways to print a letterhead: commercially in large quantities, or one-offs on your desktop laser or inkjet printer. The second method includes a letterhead template, which you can use to write and print your letters from directly within a page-layout program; while this method is common among designers, it is rarely done using Illustrator.

If your letterhead is being printed commercially, it's probably being printed with multiple copies on a large press sheet, from which the individual letterhead sheets will be cut. Most commercial printing happens this way. This type of printing typically means that design elements can run right off the edge of the sheet; this is called **bleeding**. If you're using a commercial printer, always ask the output provider whether it's safe (and cost-effective) to design with bleeds, and find out how much bleed allowance to include.

If you're designing for a printer that can only run letter-size paper, you need to allow enough of a margin area for your printer to hold the paper as it moves through the device (called the **gripper margin**); in this case, you can't design with bleeds.

1. **Open the New Document dialog box (File>New). Define the following settings:**

Intent:	**Print**
Preset:	**Letter**
Name:	stationery
Units:	**Inches**
Orientation:	**Portrait**
Artboards:	**1**
Bleed:	**0.125 in (all four sides)**

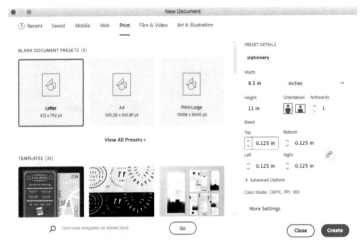

2. Click Create to create the new file.

The red line indicates the defined bleed (1/8″ outside the artboard edge).

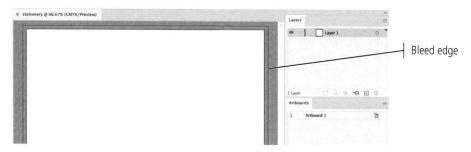

Bleed edge

3. Choose File>Place. Navigate to the file cafe-logo.ai in your WIP>Cafe folder, and make sure Link and Template are both unchecked. Check the Show Import Options box, then click Place.

Until now, you have placed raster images in the JPEG format. Different types of files, however, have different options that determine what is imported into your Illustrator file.

4. Review the options in the Place PDF dialog box.

Although you're placing a native Illustrator (.ai) file, the dialog box shows options for placing PDF files. Illustrator files use PDF as the underlying structure (which is what enables multiple artboard capability), so the options are the same as those you would see if you were placing a PDF file.

The **Crop To** option determines exactly what is placed into an Illustrator file. (If you are placing an Illustrator file, many of these options produce the same result.)

Use these arrows to select which artboard you want to place.

- The **Bounding Box** setting places the file's bounding box, or the minimum area that encloses the objects on the page or artboard.

- The **Art** setting crops incoming files relative to the size and position of any objects selected at the time of the cropping. For example, you can create a frame and use it to crop an incoming piece of artwork.

- Use the **Crop** setting when you want the position of the placed file to be determined by the location of a crop region drawn on the page; when placing an Illustrator file, this refers to the defined artboard.

- The **Trim** setting identifies where the page will be physically cut in the production process, if trim marks are present.

- The **Bleed** setting places only the area within bleed margins (if a bleed area is defined). This is useful if the page is being output in a production environment. The printed page might include page marks that fall outside the bleed area.

- The **Media** setting places the area that represents the physical paper size of the original PDF document (for example, the dimensions of an A4 sheet of paper), including printers' marks.

Note:

If Show Import Options is not checked in the Place dialog box, the Illustrator file is placed based on the last-used Crop To option.

5. **Choose Bounding Box in the Crop To menu, and then click OK to place the four-color logo.**

6. **If you get a warning about an unknown image construct, click OK to dismiss it.**

For some reason, gradient mesh objects *created in Illustrator* are unrecognized *by Illustrator*, which is the case with this logo file. Gradient meshes are imported into the new file as "non-native art," objects that can't be edited in the new file unless you use the Flatten Transparency command to turn them into embedded raster objects.

After dismissing the warning message, the selected file is loaded into the Place cursor.
A small preview of the loaded file appears in the cursor.

The selected file is loaded into the Place cursor.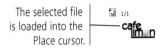

7. **Click near the top-left corner of the artboard to place the loaded image.**

8. **Open the General pane of the Preferences dialog box. Make sure the Scale Strokes & Effects option is checked, and then click OK.**

Note:

On Macintosh, open the Preferences dialog box in the Illustrator menu. On Windows, open the Preferences dialog box in the Edit menu.

If this option is checked, scaling an object also scales the applied strokes and effects proportionally to the new object size. For example, reducing an object by 50% changes a 1-pt stroke to a 0.5-pt stroke. If this option is unchecked, a 1-pt stroke remains a 1-pt stroke, regardless of how much you reduce or enlarge the object.

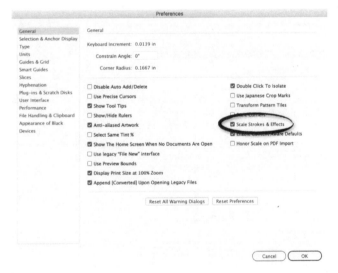

9. **With the placed artwork selected, use the Properties panel to scale the artwork to 3 in wide (constrained). Using the top-left reference point, position the artwork 0.25 in from the top and left edges (as shown in the following image).**

Constrain the width and height before changing the object size.

10. **Using the Type tool, click to create a new point-type object. Type 47653 Main Street, Pittsburgh, PA 05439. Format the type as 9-pt ATC Coral Normal.**

11. **Using the Selection tool, position the type object directly below the stylized L (use the following image as a guide).**

Note:

Remember, your original artwork might be a slightly different size than ours, so your resized height might also be slightly different than what is shown here.

12. **Activate the Selection tool, then choose File>Place. Navigate to the file leaves.ai in your WIP>Cafe folder and click Place.**

The Show Import Options check box remembers the last-used setting, so it should still be checked. After clicking Place, the Place PDF dialog box automatically appears.

The Place PDF dialog box also defaults to the last-used option, so Bounding Box should already be selected in the Crop To menu.

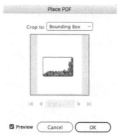

13. **Click OK to close the Place PDF dialog box.**

Again, the selected file is loaded into the Place cursor.

14. **Click the loaded Place cursor to place the leaves.ai file.**

15. **Using the Selection tool, drag the placed graphic so the edges of the artwork align with the bottom and right bleed guides.**

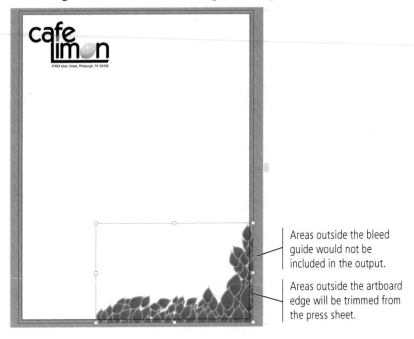

Areas outside the bleed guide would not be included in the output.

Areas outside the artboard edge will be trimmed from the press sheet.

16. **Choose View>Trim View.**

The Trim view hides any elements that extend beyond the artboard edge. This allows you to more accurately preview the finished job as it will appear when output.

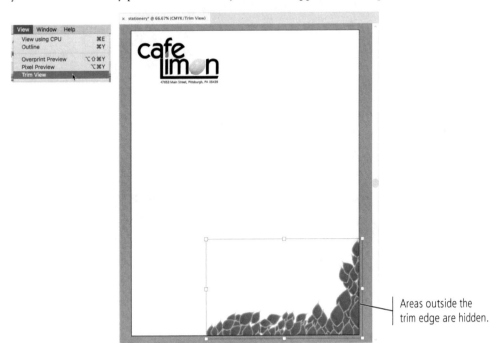

Areas outside the trim edge are hidden.

17. **Choose View>Trim View to toggle off that option.**

18. **Save the file as an Illustrator file named** stationery.ai **in your WIP>Cafe folder, and then continue to the next exercise.**

Create the Envelope Layout

In general, printed envelopes can be created in two ways. You can create and print the design on a flat sheet, which will be specially **die cut** (stamped out of the press sheet), and then folded and glued into the shape of the finished envelope. Alternatively (and usually at less expense), you can print on pre-folded and -glued envelopes.

Both of these methods for envelope design have special printing requirements, such as ensuring no ink is placed where glue will be applied (if you're printing on flat sheets), or printing far enough away from the edge (if you're printing on pre-formed envelopes). Whenever you design an envelope, consult with the output provider that will print the job before you get too far into the project.

In this case, the design will be output on pre-folded #10 business-size envelopes (4-1/8″ by 9-1/2″). The printer requires a 1/4″ gripper margin around the edge of the envelope where you cannot include any ink coverage.

Note:

*The **live area** is the "safe" area inside the page edge, where important design elements should remain. Because printing and trimming are mechanical processes, there will always be some variation, however slight. Elements too close to the page edge run the risk of being accidentally trimmed off.*

1. With **stationery.ai** open, zoom out until you can see the entire artboard and an equal amount of space to the right.

2. Choose the Artboard tool. With the current artboard active, type **Letterhead** in the Name field of the Control panel.

3. Place the cursor to the right of the existing artboard, then click and drag to create a new artboard.

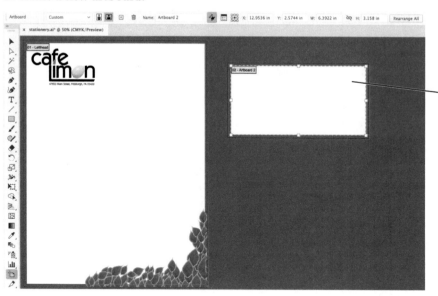

Click and drag to create a new artboard.

4. With the second artboard active, type **Envelope** in the Name field of the Control panel.

5. **With the second artboard active, use the fields in the Control panel to change the artboard dimensions to W: 9.5 in, H: 4.13 in.**

If the W and H fields are not visible in your Control panel, click the Artboard Options button in the Control panel and use the resulting dialog box to change the artboard size.

Depending on where you created the second artboard, and which reference point was active when you changed the artboard size, your two artboards might end up overlapping.

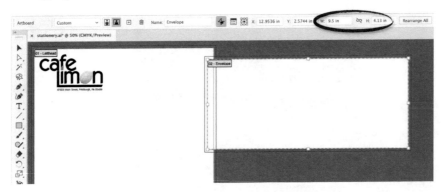

6. **Click the Rearrange All button in the Control panel.**

This dialog box allows you to align multiple artboards to one another in a specific, defined grid.

The Grid-by-Row (▨) option aligns the top edge of each artboard in a single row. If the number of artboards is greater than the allowed number of columns (in the Columns field), additional rows of artboards are created as necessary to accommodate all artboards in the file.

The Grid-by-Column (▧) option aligns the left edge of each artboard in a single row. If the number of artboards is greater than the allowed number of rows (in the Rows field), additional columns of artboards are created as necessary to accommodate all artboards in the file.

The Spacing field determines how much space appears between individual artboards in a row or column.

The Arrange by Row (↔) and Arrange by Column (↕) options place all artboards in a single row or column, respectively.

The Layout Order defaults to use the Left-to-Right (→) option, which places artboards left-to-right (for example, Artboard 1, then 2, then 3). If you select the Change to Right-to-Left Layout option (←), artboards are placed in reverse order (for example, Artboard 3, then 2, then 1).

Grid by Row   Grid by Column

7. **Change the Spacing field to 0.25 in and click OK.**

The top edges of the two artboards are aligned, with 0.25″ between the two artboards.

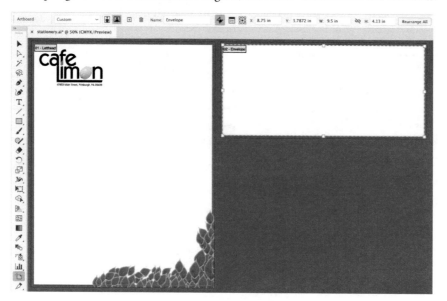

Note:

Press Shift and drag a marquee to select multiple artboards in the document window.

8. **Choose File>Place. Navigate to the file `cafe-logo.ai` in your WIP>Cafe folder. Make sure Show Import Options is checked, then click Place.**

9. **In the Place PDF dialog box, click the right-arrow button to show 2 of 3, then click OK.**

Use these buttons to determine which artboard (or page) to place.

10. **Click with the loaded Place cursor to place the loaded file on the Envelope artboard.**

11. **Make the Selection tool active. If rulers are not visible in your document window, choose View>Rulers>Show Rulers.**

12. **Choose View>Rulers and make sure the menu option reads "Change to Global Rulers."**

When Artboard rulers are active — which you want for this exercise — the menu command reads "Change to Global Rulers."

Artboard rulers show all measurements from the zero-point of the active artboard. Global rulers show all measurements from the zero-point of Artboard 1 (unless you reset the zero-point when a different artboard is active).

Note:

You can't switch between Artboard and Global rulers while the Artboard tool is active.

13. **Select the placed object with the Selection tool. Scale it to 2.5 in wide (constrained) and place it 0.25 in from the top and left edges of the envelope artboard.**

Because Artboard rulers
are active, each artboard
has its own zero point.

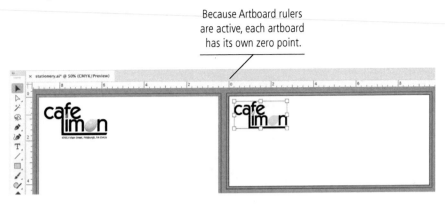

14. **Copy the type object from the letterhead and paste it onto the envelope layout. Change the size of the type in the pasted object to 7.5 pt.**

15. **Save the file and continue to the next exercise.**

Print Desktop Proofs of Multiple Artboards

Before you send a file to a commercial output provider, it's a good idea to print a sample to see how the artwork looks on paper. Illustrator provides a large number of options for outputting files.

There are two important points to remember about using inkjet and laser proofs. First, inkjet printers are usually not PostScript driven. Because the commercial output process revolves around the PostScript language, proofs should be created using a PostScript-compatible printer, if possible. Second, inkjet and laser printers typically do not accurately represent color.

1. **With stationery.ai open, choose File>Print.**

The Print dialog box is divided into eight sections or categories, which display in the window on the left side of the dialog box. Clicking one of the categories in the list shows the associated options on the right side of the dialog box.

Note:

A print preset is a way to store many different settings in a single menu choice. You can create a print preset by making your choices in the Print dialog box, and then clicking the Save Preset button.

2. **In the Printer menu, choose the printer you want to use, and then choose the PPD for that printer in the PPD menu (if possible).**

    If you are using a non-PostScript printer, complete as much of the rest of this exercise as possible based on the limitations of your output device.

    The most important options you'll select are the Printer and PPD (PostScript printer description) settings at the top of the dialog box. Illustrator reads the information in the PPD to determine which of the specific print options are available for the current output.

3. **With the General options showing, choose the Range radio button and type 1 in the field.**

    By default, all artboards in the file are output when you click Print.

    If your printer can only print letter-size paper, you need to tile the letterhead artboard to multiple sheets, so you can output a full-size proof. Tiling is unavailable when printing multiple artboards, so in this exercise you are printing each artboard separately.

4. **In the Options section, make sure the Do Not Scale option is selected.**

    As a general rule, proofs — especially final proofs that would be sent to a printer with the job files — should be output at 100%.

5a. **If your printer is capable of printing oversize sheets, choose Tabloid/A3/11×17 in the Media menu. Choose the Portrait orientation option.**

5b. **If you can only print to letter-size paper, turn off the Auto-Rotate option and choose the Landscape orientation option. Choose Tile Full Pages in the Scaling menu and define a 1 in Overlap.**

    To output a letter-size page at 100% on letter-size paper, you have to tile to multiple sheets of paper. Using the landscape paper orientation allows you to tile to 2 sheets instead of 4 (as shown in the preview area).

Note:

The Auto-Rotate option is useful if you are printing multiple artboards; when this option is active, the application automatically positions each artboard to take best advantage of the available paper.

Note:

The Tile options are not available if you are printing multiple artboards at one time.

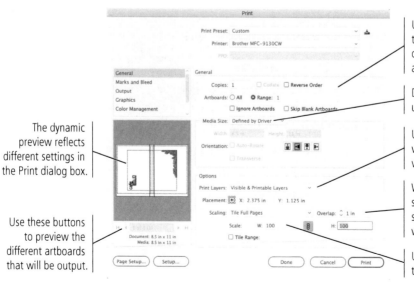

Use these options to print more than one copy and reverse the output order of the multiple artboards (last to first).

Define the paper size used for the output.

The dynamic preview reflects different settings in the Print dialog box.

Use this menu to output visible and printable layers, visible layers, or all layers.

When tiling a page to multiple sheets, you can define a specific amount of space that will be included on both sheets.

Use these buttons to preview the different artboards that will be output.

Use these options to scale the output (if necessary).

6. **Click the Marks and Bleed option in the list of categories on the left. Activate the All Printer's Marks option, and then change the Offset value to 0.125 in.**

If you type the value in the Offset field, Illustrator rounds up to the nearest two-decimal value. Since 0.13″ is larger than the 0.125″ bleed, this offset position is fine.

7. **In the Bleeds section, check the Use Document Bleed Settings option.**

When you created the stationery file, you defined 1/8″ bleeds on all four sides of the artboard. Checking this box in the Print dialog box includes that same 1/8″ extra on all four sides of the output.

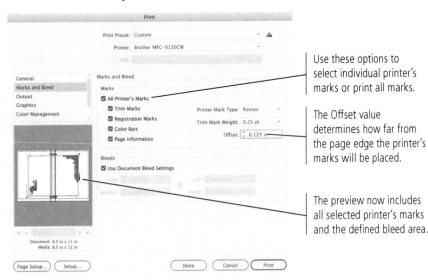

Use these options to select individual printer's marks or print all marks.

The Offset value determines how far from the page edge the printer's marks will be placed.

The preview now includes all selected printer's marks and the defined bleed area.

Note:

Some output providers require printer's marks to stay outside the bleed area, which means the offset should be at least the same as or greater than the defined bleed area.

8. **Click the Output option in the list of categories on the left.**

Depending on the type of output device you are using, you can print all colors to a single sheet by choosing Composite in the Mode menu, or print each color to an individual sheet by choosing Separations (Host-based). The third option — In-RIP Separation — allows the file data to be separated by the output device instead of by the software.

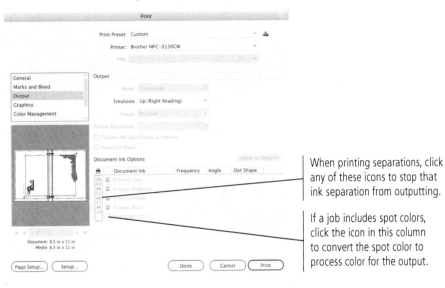

When printing separations, click any of these icons to stop that ink separation from outputting.

If a job includes spot colors, click the icon in this column to convert the spot color to process color for the output.

Note:

The other options in this dialog box (Emulsion and Image) are reserved for high-end commercial output to a filmsetter or imagesetter.

9. **Click Print to output the artwork.**

10. **Choose File>Print again. Choose the Range radio button and type 2 in the field to print the envelope layout.**

11. **Choose US Letter in the Size menu and choose the Landscape orientation option. Choose Do Not Scale in the Scaling menu.**

    In this case, a letter-size sheet is large enough to print the envelope artboard without scaling. Some of the printer's marks might be cut off by the printer's gripper margin, but that is fine for the purpose of a desktop proof.

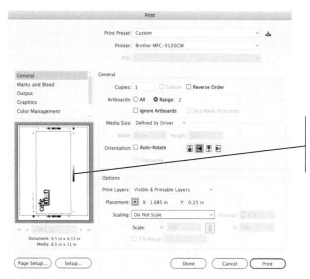

The preview area shows that the envelope artboard will fit on a letter-size page at 100% if you use landscape orientation.

12. **Click Print to output the envelope proof.**

13. **When the document comes back into focus, save and close it.**

1. The _____ provides access to handles that you can use to manually resize the artboard in the workspace.

2. Press _____ and click the eye icon on a specific layer to switch only that layer between Preview and Outline mode.

3. When _____ are active, moving your cursor over an unselected object reveals the paths that make up that object.

4. The _____ tool is used to sample colors from an object already placed in the file.

5. The _____ is used to monitor and change the individual attributes (fill, stroke, etc.) of the selected object.

6. The _____ is the imaginary line on which the bottoms of letters rest.

7. _____ is the spacing between specific pairs of letters (where the insertion point is placed).

8. The _____ command makes the vector shapes of letters accessible to the Direct Selection tool.

9. A _____ is a special ink used to reproduce a specific color, typically used for one- or two-color jobs.

10. Click the _____ in the Layers panel to select a specific sublayer.

1. Explain the advantages of using a gradient mesh, compared to a regular gradient.

2. Briefly explain two primary differences between point-type objects and area-type objects.

3. Explain the potential benefits of using multiple artboards rather than different files for different pieces.

Use what you have learned in this project to complete the following freeform exercise.
Carefully read the art director and client comments, then create your own design to meet the needs of the project.
Use the space below to sketch ideas. When finished, write a brief explanation of the reasoning behind your final design.

art director comments

The Cincinnati Zoo has hired you to create a series of graphics that will be used to rebrand the facility at next spring's Grand Reopening. Your work will be used for everything from printed collateral and park signage, to the zoo's website, and even embroidery on clothing.

❑ Create a new logo to identify the redesigned zoo.

❑ Create a series of icons for each of the zoo's seven main sections: Tropics, Desert, Arctic, Forest, Ocean, Sky, and Kids Kingdom.

❑ Create an invitation for the Grand Reopening celebration incorporating the new logo. Research the best size for a printed invitation that will be sent through the U.S. Postal Service. Include placeholder text for the date and time of the event, as well as the zoo's phone number and web address.

client comments

Our facility received a significant grant from an anonymous donor to update the entire facility — everything from the animal enclosures and guest facilities, to the walking paths and water fountains. Basically, we've rebuilt from the ground up, and are very excited to reveal our efforts to the public next spring at the Grand Reopening.

Since everything is new, we felt it was also time to update our corporate identity. The previous logo was designed more than 20 years ago and is little more than the words, "Cincinnati Zoo." We want something fresh that incorporates more than just two words in a fancy typeface. Remember though, it has to look good on a 15-foot sign or embroidered on the pocket of a T-shirt.

For the section icons, try to keep them simple. We don't want visitors to have to work to figure out what they mean. You can include the actual words, but we're an international facility, so not everyone will be able to read the English explanations.

project justification

_____
_____
_____
_____
_____
_____
_____
_____
_____
_____
_____
_____
_____
_____

Logos are one of the most common types of artwork that you will create in Illustrator. These can be as simple as text converted to outlines, or as complex as a line drawing based on an object in a photograph. Most logos will actually be some combination of drawing and text-based elements. As you learned throughout this project, one of the most important qualities of a logo is versatility. A good logo can be used in many different types of projects, and output in many different types of print processes. To accomplish this goal, logos should work equally well in grayscale, four-color, and spot-color printing.

By completing this project, you worked with complex gradients to draw a realistic lemon, then added creative type treatment to build the finished logotype. After completing the initial logo, you converted it to other variants that will work with different output processes (two-color and one-color). Finally, you incorporated the logo artwork into completed stationery for your client's communication needs as he expands his business.

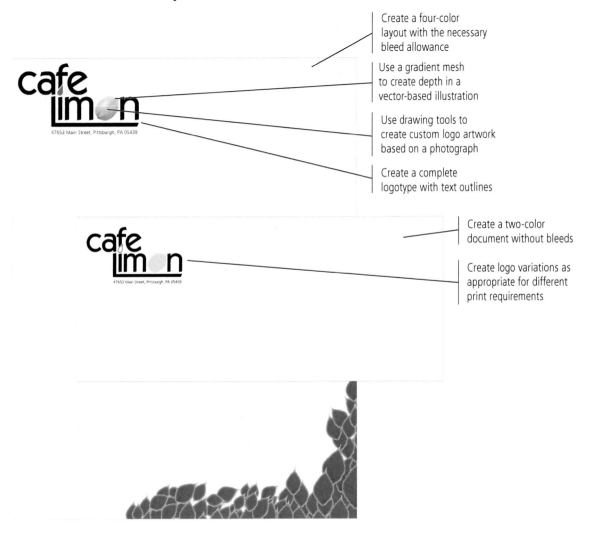

Create a four-color layout with the necessary bleed allowance

Use a gradient mesh to create depth in a vector-based illustration

Use drawing tools to create custom logo artwork based on a photograph

Create a complete logotype with text outlines

Create a two-color document without bleeds

Create logo variations as appropriate for different print requirements

Ski Resort Map

Your client manages a ski resort. He wants to create a basic map of the resort to show the locations of various resort features and amenities. The map will be printed independently, but also placed into other projects, such as the local entertainment magazine and local restaurant menus.

This project incorporates the following skills:

❑ Managing built-in libraries of swatches, brushes, and symbols

❑ Defining custom art and pattern brushes for specific applications

❑ Saving user-defined libraries of custom assets

❑ Understanding and creating symbols and symbol instances

❑ Transforming symbol instances and editing symbol artwork

❑ Replacing symbols in placed instances

❑ Creating a clipping mask

This map will be available on kiosks around the resort, but it is also going to be used in advertising and cross-promotional marketing. We'll be placing it in the local entertainment magazine and papers, along with some coupons, and we also have some interest from local restaurants to print the map on their placemats and menus.

I started to create the map I want, but I need you to finish it. I did find some nice graphics for the resort lodge, but I realized that I don't have the time or skills to create something that looks good.

When you see what he gave us, you can see what needs to be done. He didn't get any further than different colored lines and some text telling where a few things are.

I already showed the client some ideas for icons instead of text to identify different amenities. He approved those, so I created a library for you to use when you build the completed file. You'll need to include the icons both in the legend and wherever they are indicated by the existing text.

To complete this project, you will:

- ❏ Open and use built-in swatch libraries
- ❏ Define custom gradient swatches
- ❏ Modify a stroke width profile
- ❏ Create a new custom pattern swatch based on existing artwork
- ❏ Define custom art and pattern brushes
- ❏ Save a custom brush library
- ❏ Open and use an external symbol library
- ❏ Place and control symbol instances
- ❏ Edit symbols to change all placed instances
- ❏ Break the link from placed instances to the original symbols
- ❏ Replace symbols in placed instances
- ❏ Spray multiple symbol instances
- ❏ Create a clipping mask to hide unwanted parts of the artwork

STAGE 1 / Working with Custom Swatches

The default Swatches panel (Window>Swatches) includes a seemingly random collection of swatches from various built-in libraries. Illustrator also includes a large number of built-in swatch libraries, many of which contain thematic color schemes (such as Earthtone, Metal, and Nature). These libraries are accessed by choosing Window>Swatch Libraries, or by opening the Swatch Libraries menu at the bottom of the Swatches panel.

If you open more than one swatch library from the Window>Swatch Libraries menu, each library opens as a new panel, grouped with other open swatch libraries. Library panels open in the same location and state as the last time they were used. If a panel is not automatically grouped with other library panels, it was already used and repositioned.

If you open a different library using the Swatch Libraries menu at the bottom of an open panel, the new library replaces the one that was active when you opened the new library. You can drag a panel out of the group to manage it independently.

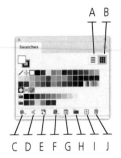

A Show List View
B Show Thumbnail View
C Swatch Libraries menu
D Open Color Themes panel
E Add to Current Library
F Show Swatch Kinds menu
G Swatch Options
H New Color Group
I New Swatch
J Delete Swatch

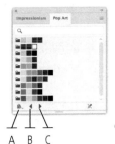

A Swatch Libraries menu
B Load Previous Swatch Library
C Load Next Swatch Library

Manage the Swatches Panel

In this project, your client created the basic elements, but was unable to complete the entire map. The first logical step in any project where you are provided with an existing file is to review the supplied artwork.

1. **Download Skiing_AI21_RF.zip from the Student Files web page.**

2. **Expand the ZIP archive in your WIP folder (Macintosh) or copy the archive contents into your WIP folder (Windows).**

    This results in a folder named **Skiing**, which contains the files you need for this project. You should also use this folder to save the files you create in this project.

3. **Open the file summit-map.ai from your WIP>Skiing folder.**

    The file includes a very basic map, with mostly plain text, basic solid lines, and a few graphics that have been placed by the client. Your job is to add visual interest using a variety of methods, including custom gradients, patterns, brush strokes, and symbols.

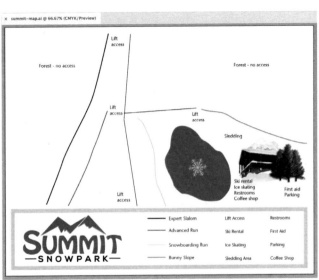

4. Open the Swatches panel (Window>Swatches).

The default Swatches panel (Window>Swatches) includes a seemingly random collection of swatches from the various built-in libraries. Every new file includes these swatches, plus any custom swatches that have been created in the file.

The file you were provided for this project also includes four custom global swatches.

5. Open the Swatches panel Options menu and choose Select All Unused.

Note:

We recommend using floating panels through-out this project to avoid problems created by auto-collapsing docked panels.

6. Click the Delete Swatch button at the bottom of the panel. When asked, click Yes to confirm the deletion.

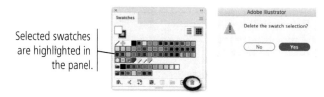

Selected swatches are highlighted in the panel.

Note:

Deleting a used swatch does not affect objects where the color is applied.

7. Click the Show List View button at the top of the Swatches panel. Click the bottom-right corner of the panel and drag until you see the entire list of swatches.

The Swatches panels appear by default in Thumbnail mode. In the list view, you see the name of the color, as well as an icon that indicates the type of the color. You can also choose Small List View or Large List view in the panel's Options menu.

CMYK color icon

Click here and drag to resize the panel.

Note:

When a library displays in Thumbnail mode, you can roll the mouse over a specific swatch to see the swatch name in a tool tip. The same option is available for brush libraries, graphic style libraries, and symbol libraries.

8. Click the Grays folder in the panel and drag to the Delete Swatch button.

The only swatch in this color group is 100% Black — the same as the basic Black swatch that is not in the group; there is no reason to maintain two swatches with the same color make-up, so you are deleting the extra black swatch.

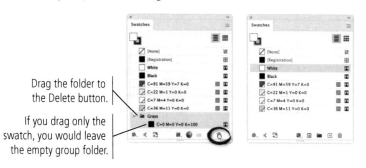

Drag the folder to the Delete button.

If you drag only the swatch, you would leave the empty group folder.

Note:

The Registration swatch, which can't be deleted, is a special color that outputs at 100% of all inks. It is typically used for file information on a printing plate, outside the trim area. You should never use the registration color inside the artboard boundaries.

9. Save the file and continue to the next exercise.

Define Gradient Swatches

A gradient smoothly merges one color into another. Illustrator supports both linear gradients, which move in a line from one color to another, and radial gradients, which move from one color at the center of a circle to another color at the outer edges.

Illustrator includes a number of built-in pattern and gradient swatch libraries, which can be accessed in the Window>Swatch Libraries>Gradients or >Patterns submenus. You can also create your own gradient and pattern swatches, which are stored in the file's Swatches panel. In this exercise, you will create two custom gradient swatches that you can apply to any object in the file.

1. **With summit-map.ai open, open the Gradient panel (Window>Gradient).**

2. **Choose the Radial option at the top of the Gradient panel.**

3. **Drag the C=7 M=4 Y=0 K=0 swatch from the Swatches panel onto the left stop of the gradient ramp (in the Gradient panel).**

   The gradient-stop color changes from white to blue, and the sample swatch now shows the effect of the new stop color.

Note:

Several gradient swatches are also available in the default Swatches panel. If you use a gradient or pattern swatch from one of the built-in library collections, it is automatically added to the file's Swatches panel.

Drag this swatch onto the left gradient stop.

Choose the radial type of gradient here.

The swatch shows a sample of the gradient with the current settings.

4. **Drag the C=36 M=11 Y=0 K=0 swatch from the Swatches panel onto the right stop of the gradient ramp.**

Drag this swatch onto the right gradient stop.

5. **Drag the C=22 M=1 Y=0 K=0 swatch from the Swatches panel to the middle of the gradient ramp.**

6. **With the new stop selected, change the Location field to 67%.**

Note:

Delete specific stops from the gradient by dragging the stops down and away from the gradient ramp.

Drag this swatch to the midpoint of the gradient ramp to add a new stop...

...then change the Location to 67%.

7. **Drag the C=36 M=11 Y=0 K=0 swatch in the Swatches panel to the 33% location on the gradient ramp.**

8. **Double-click the new stop to open the options for that stop. Change the tint slider to 70%.**

If the pop-up panel shows swatches instead of the tint slider, click the Color button on the left side of the panel.

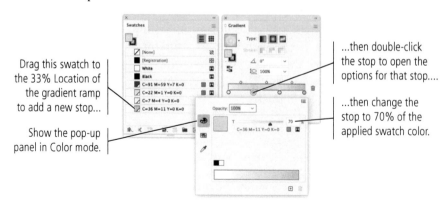

Drag this swatch to the 33% Location of the gradient ramp to add a new stop...

Show the pop-up panel in Color mode.

...then double-click the stop to open the options for that stop....

...then change the stop to 70% of the applied swatch color.

9. **Click the sample swatch in the Gradient panel and drag it into the main Swatches panel.**

Drag this sample into the Swatches panel.

10. **Double-click the new swatch name in the Swatches panel. Type Ice Radial to rename the swatch, then press Return/Enter to finalize the new name.**

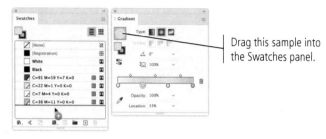

Double-click the swatch name to highlight it so you can rename it.

Note:

You can also double-click the swatch thumbnail to open the Swatch Options dialog box, where you can rename the swatch.

11. **In the Gradient panel, click the Linear button to change the Gradient type.**

Changing the type of gradient does not change the color-stop settings.

12. **Repeat Steps 9–10 to create a new gradient swatch named Ice Linear.**

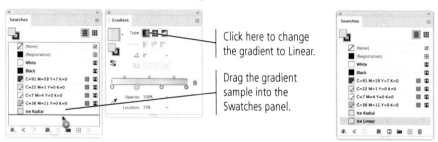

Click here to change the gradient to Linear.

Drag the gradient sample into the Swatches panel.

13. **Save the file and continue to the next exercise.**

If you create a gradient that blends from a spot color to a process-color build, the results will be unpredictable at best, and disastrous at worst. In short, we strongly discourage this practice. It is possible, however, to create a gradient that blends from a spot color to white; doing so just requires a simple trick to avoid output problems.

The images to the right show the components of a basic linear gradient that blends from white to Pantone 2582C. By default, the White stop is actually a CMYK build, with all four ink components set to zero. When a Pantone color blends into the CMYK white, the intermediate steps of the gradient will be created with CMYK builds instead of shades of the Pantone color.

To solve the problem, apply the spot color to both stops, and define the white stop as 0% of the spot color. When both stops are tints of a Pantone color, the intermediate shades of the gradient will be created as shades of the Pantone color instead of CMYK percentages.

Color makeup of the first gradient stop:

Color makeup of the second gradient stop:

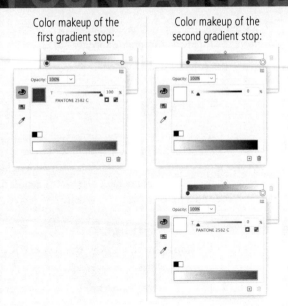

Apply and Control Gradients

Once you have created gradient swatches, you can apply them by simply selecting an object, selecting the target attribute (fill or stroke), and then clicking the appropriate swatch. You can then use the Gradient panel and Gradient tool to control the position of an applied gradient.

1. **With summit-map.ai open, use the Selection tool to select the lake shape on the artboard.**

2. **Open the Fill Color panel from the Control panel, and click the Ice Radial swatch.**

   The Fill and Stroke Color panels include the same swatches that are available in the document's Swatches panel. Because you deleted the unused swatches from the default set, you see only the few colors that were part of the original file and the two gradient swatches that you defined in the previous exercise.

The same swatches in the Swatches panel are available in the Control panel's pop-up panels.

The applied radial gradient is centered in the selected object.

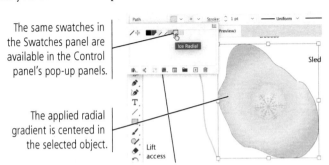

Note:

You can Shift-click the Fill or Stroke icons in the Control panel to show an alternate color panel UI:

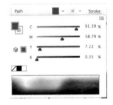

3. Using the Gradient tool, click near the top area of the lake object and drag to the bottom area.

When you first choose the Gradient tool, the Gradient Annotator appears; by default, it is exactly horizontal. After you complete this step, the Gradient Annotator matches the line you drag with the Gradient tool.

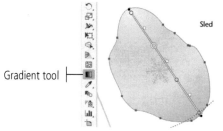

Gradient tool

Sled

Note:

If you are not satisfied with the length and angle of your gradient, simply click and drag again to change it.

When you are using a radial gradient, the first place you click with the Gradient tool defines the center point (the starting color) of the applied gradient. The location where you release the mouse button marks the outer edge of the radial gradient. The area beyond the outer edge of the gradient fills with the end-stop color of the gradient. The direction to drag defines the angle of the gradient.

4. In the Gradient panel, change the Aspect Ratio field to 45%.

Changing the aspect ratio of a radial gradient converts the gradient shape to an ellipse instead of a circle. A 45% aspect ratio means the gradient's height is 45% of its width.

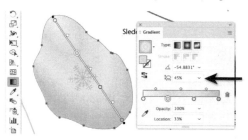

5. Using the Selection tool, select the rectangle shape around the logo.

6. Open the Stroke Color panel from the Control panel, then click the Ice Linear swatch.

When you apply a gradient to a stroke, the default option (Apply Gradient within Stroke) basically "fills" the stroke with the gradient.

By default, gradients are applied within the stroke.

7. In the Gradient panel, bring the Stroke attribute to the front of the stack.

8. **Click the Apply Gradient Along Stroke button.**

Using the Apply Gradient Along Stroke option, the gradient is applied in a linear fashion. Depending on the shape of the path, this option might not make a noticeable difference. For this rectangle, however, you can see that the starting point of the gradient is located at the bottom-right corner of the stroke; the gradient then travels around the shape, until the ending point of the gradient meets the same corner.

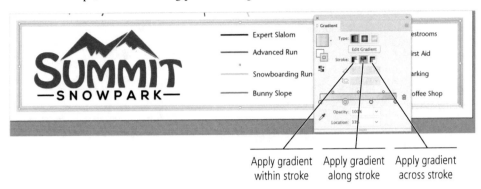

Apply gradient within stroke   Apply gradient along stroke   Apply gradient across stroke

9. **Click the Apply Gradient Across Stroke button.**

Using the Apply Gradient Across Stroke option, the gradient begins at the outside edge of the path and ends on the inside edge.

10. **Save the file and then continue to the next exercise.**

 Edit a Path Profile

In addition to simply applying stroke attributes to a path, you can use the Width tool to adjust the shape of a stroke at any point along a specific path. This moves beyond the ability to manipulate the points and segments that make up a shape. In this exercise, you will modify the path that surrounds the legend.

1. **With summit-map.ai open, choose the Width tool in the Tools panel.**

2. **Move the cursor over the top-left corner of the legend box.**

It might help to zoom in so you can more clearly see the anchor points that make up the shape.

3. **When you see the word "anchor" in the cursor feedback, click and drag away from the point. When the overall width is approximately 0.28 in, release the mouse button.**

When a path is selected, clicking the path with the Width tool adds a width point. You can drag out from the width point to add symmetrical width handles, which change the stroke width at that point along the path. If you click and drag an existing width handle, the opposite handle is also affected.

When the Width tool cursor is over an existing stroke, the cursor feedback shows the overall width of the stroke at that point, as well as the width of each side of the stroke.

Clicking and dragging with the Width tool adds symmetrical handles on both sides of the path. Cursor feedback shows the width of each side, and the overall width of the point.

Click and drag to add symmetrical width handles on both sides of the path.

Width tool

Cursor feedback shows the width of the stroke, and each side of the stroke.

4. **Move the cursor along the path until the feedback shows an "intersect" with the center of the placed logo.**

5. **Press Option/Alt, then click and drag down until cursor feedback shows that Side 2 is approximately 0.08 in.**

If you press Option/Alt while dragging from a width point, you add non-symmetrical width handles. You can also Option/Alt-click an existing width handle and drag to adjust it independently of the opposing handle.

Option/Alt-click and drag to create non-symmetrical handles.

Don't worry if the measurements are not exact; you will learn how to define precise side widths in the next few steps.

Note:

To remove a width point from a stroke, click with the Width tool to select a particular point, then press Delete/Backspace.

6. **About halfway across the stroke, click and drag down slightly to initiate the width points, then drag up until the overall width of the point is slightly less than 0.1 in.**

In this case, the two sides of the stroke are already different because you created non-symmetrical handles on the previous point. Dragging the handles of this point maintains the proportional relationship between the two sides.

7. **Double-click the new point from Step 6. In the resulting Width Point Edit dialog box, activate the link icon to force the Side 1 and Side 2 fields to symmetrically proportional lengths.**

You can numerically manipulate the length of width handles by double-clicking a particular width point. When the link icon is active, changing one side has a proportional effect on the other side.

Note:

If multiple points are selected when you double-click, this dialog box will include fields for each point.

8. **Change the Side 1 field to 0.04 in, then press Tab to highlight the Side 2 field.**

Because you linked the two fields, the width of Side 2 is also changed proportionally (from 0.032 to 0.0239 in our example).

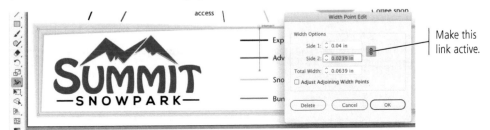

Make this link active.

9. **Click OK to close the Width Point Edit dialog box.**

10. **Click the point you added in Step 6 (the one in the middle of the top edge) and drag right until that point is approximately two-thirds of the way across the frame edge.**

You can move a specific width point by clicking and dragging; other width points are not affected.

Note:

If you Shift-click and drag a width point, other points on the path adjust proportionally.

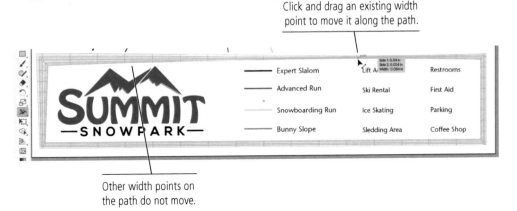

Click and drag an existing width point to move it along the path.

Other width points on the path do not move.

When you release the mouse button, you can see the effect of moving one width point on the overall path shape.

11. Double-click the width point above the logo on the top of the frame edge. Unlink the two Side fields, change the Side 2 field to 0.07 in, then click OK.

Because you did not link the two Side fields, changing one does not affect the other. In this case, you are modifying the width on only Side 2 — the side nearest the logo.

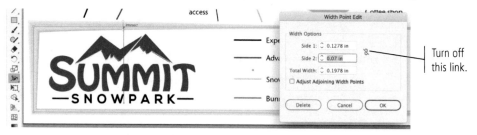

12. Add and adjust width points along the bottom path of the shape until you are satisfied with the overall result.

13. Save the file and continue to the next exercise.

Creating Variable-Width Stroke Profiles

Once you have edited the shape of a path, you can save your work as a custom stroke profile so you can apply that same stroke appearance to other paths.

The Variable Width Profile menu is available in both the Control and Stroke panels. Stroke profiles do not include the initial stroke width; the profile is applied proportionally based on the defined width of the stroke where you apply the profile.

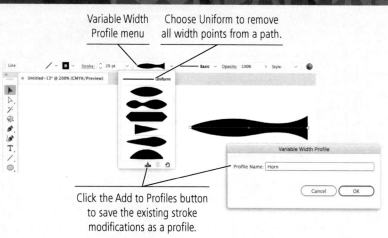

Variable Width Profile menu

Choose Uniform to remove all width points from a path.

Click the Add to Profiles button to save the existing stroke modifications as a profile.

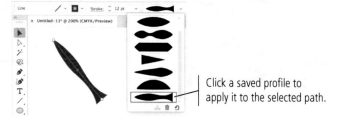

Click a saved profile to apply it to the selected path.

Create a Custom Pattern

Illustrator includes a Pattern Options panel, which makes it very easy to create a custom pattern from any artwork. In this project, you will create a snowflake pattern that fills the background of the entire artboard.

1. **With summit-map.ai open, make sure nothing is selected on the artboard.**

2. **Using the Selection tool, click the snowflake artwork and drag it to the Swatches panel.**

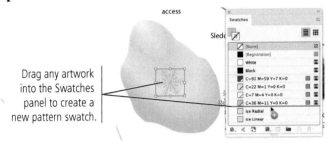

Drag any artwork into the Swatches panel to create a new pattern swatch.

3. **Double-click the new swatch name in the panel. Type Snowflake, then press Return/Enter to finalize the new name.**

4. **Choose View>Fit Artboard in Window.**

    This command changes the view percentage to match the available space, and centers the current artboard in the document window.

    When you enter Edit Pattern mode in the next step, the pattern artwork appears in the center of the document window. If the artboard is not centered in the document window before you enter Edit Pattern mode, the pattern artwork might not appear entirely within the artboard boundary.

    It doesn't matter where the pattern artwork appears relative to the artboard; however, it can be confusing if the pattern appears partially inside and partially outside the artboard edge. Using the View>Fit Artboard in Window command works around this problem.

    Note:

    Do not move the artboard (with the Artboard tool) when working in Edit Pattern mode.

5. **Double-click the Snowflake swatch thumbnail to enter into Edit Pattern mode.**

    Edit Pattern mode is a special interface where you can define specific parameters of the pattern. The Pattern Options panel includes a number of options that make it easy to define a custom pattern from any artwork. You can define the repeating area (the "tile") and the manner in which it is repeated, and see an instant on-screen preview of each change you define.

    Artboards in the active file are also visible in the document window while working in Edit Pattern mode. The pattern artwork defaults to appear in the center of the document window. However, the actual pattern has no relation to the artboard.

    Note:

    You can also click the Edit Pattern button at the bottom of the Swatches panel.

6. **If necessary, zoom in so you can more clearly see the pattern.**

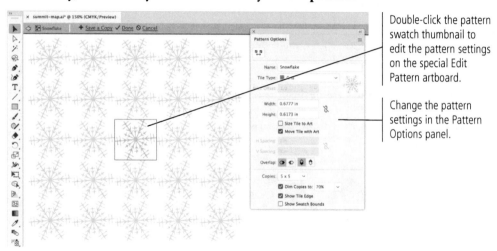

Double-click the pattern swatch thumbnail to edit the pattern settings on the special Edit Pattern artboard.

Change the pattern settings in the Pattern Options panel.

7. **At the bottom of the Pattern Options panel, uncheck the Show Swatch Bounds option (if necessary).**

The Copies menu defines how many copies of the pattern artwork appear in the pattern preview. The Dim Copies To field reduces the opacity of the copies so you can more easily distinguish the actual pattern artwork.

The Tile Edge, which appears as a solid black line on the artboard, is the area that is repeated when you apply the pattern. The Swatch Bounds is simply the storage space surrounding the pattern artwork. If you change the tile size, the swatch boundary grows or shrinks to accommodate the new tile size.

When you first create a pattern, the tile size matches the size of the pattern artwork. You can use the Width and Height fields in the Pattern Options panel to change the tile size, or click the Pattern Tile tool at the top of the panel to manually resize the tile on the artboard.

Note:

Don't confuse changing the tile size with changing the artwork size.

8. **Activate the link icon to link the Width and Height fields. Change the Width field to 0.5 in, then press Return/Enter.**

If you use the fields in the panel to change the tile size, you can activate the link icon to maintain the original aspect ratio of the tile; changing one field applies a proportional change to the other field.

Changing the tile size changes the way individual objects interact when the pattern is repeated. Artwork outside the tile area is still included in the pattern, overlapping the other repeating objects.

If you change the size of the artwork, you can check the Size Tile to Art option to force the tile to match the resized artwork. When this option is active, you can use the H Spacing and V Spacing fields to add or remove a specific amount of space around the artwork when it is repeated in the panel. You can also use the Overlap options to determine how individual objects affect others in the repeated pattern, which is useful if pattern artwork has applied effects or transparency.

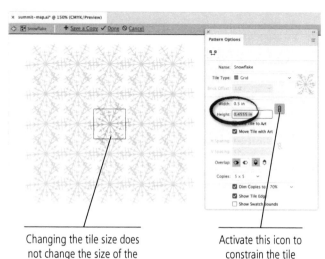

Changing the tile size does not change the size of the actual pattern artwork.

Activate this icon to constrain the tile size aspect ratio.

9. **In the Tile Type menu, choose Brick by Row. Choose 1/3 in the Brick Offset menu.**

The Tile Type menu determines how the pattern artwork repeats. When you choose one of the Brick options, you can use the Brick Offset menu to determine how the "bricks" are stacked in the repeating pattern.

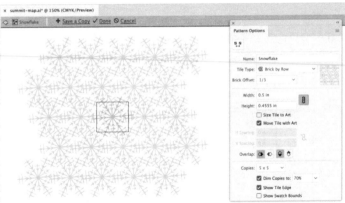

10. **Click the Done option at the top of the document window.**

Clicking Done saves the changes to the existing pattern. If you had already applied the pattern anywhere in the file, those objects would reflect the new pattern.

You can also click Save a Copy to save your changes as a new pattern; in this case, the changes would not be reflected in any objects where the original pattern had been applied.

If you click Cancel, the changes are not saved and the existing pattern is not affected.

11. **Select and delete the snowflake from the middle of the lake.**

12. **Using the Rectangle tool, create a shape that fills the entire artboard. Apply a 6-pt black stroke, then apply the Snowflakes pattern as the shape's fill.**

13. **In the Layers panel, expand Layer 1 and locate the pattern-filled rectangle.**

Note:

You can double-click a specific object in the layers panel to name it, just as you name specific layers. For example, you could rename the "Rectangle" item as "Background filled rectangle."

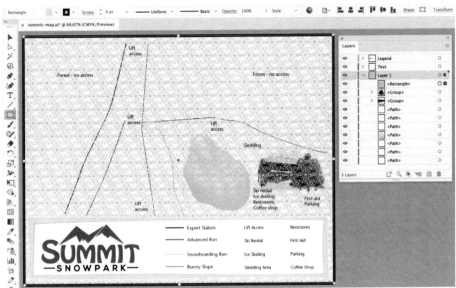

14. **Create a new layer named** `Background`, **and move it to the bottom of the layer stack.**

15. **Click the Selected Art icon and drag to the Background layer.**

    The pattern now appears behind the other artwork, but it is still too strong compared to other objects in the file.

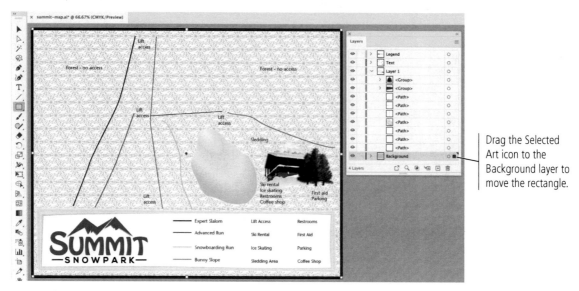

Drag the Selected Art icon to the Background layer to move the rectangle.

16. **Deselect everything on the artboard.**

17. **In the Swatches panel, double-click the Snowflakes pattern swatch to re-enter Edit Pattern mode.**

18. **Using the Selection tool, click to select the snowflake artwork in the pattern tile. Change the fill tint to 25% in the Color panel.**

    Pattern artwork is still artwork, which means you can modify it just as you would any other artwork.

Because the fill is a global swatch, you can apply a percentage of the swatch.

19. Click the Done link at the top of the document window.

When you click Done, the changes are reflected anywhere the pattern has been applied. As you can see, lightening the color in the pattern artwork makes the overall background pattern much more subtle.

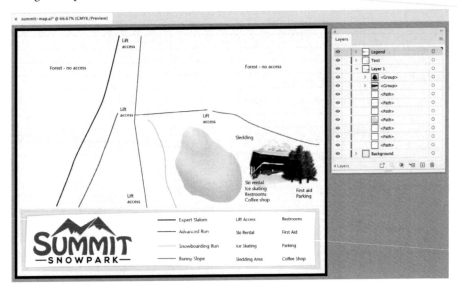

20. Save the file and then continue to the next stage of the project.

STAGE 2 / Working with Brushes

Brushes enhance or (as Adobe puts it) decorate paths. The default Brushes panel (Window>Brushes) includes several basic brushes of different types. You can use the Brushes panel Options menu to change the panel display, manage brushes, and load different brush libraries.

The Brushes panel appears by default in Thumbnail mode. If you choose List View in the panel Options menu, you see the name of the brush, as well as an icon that indicates the type of brush.

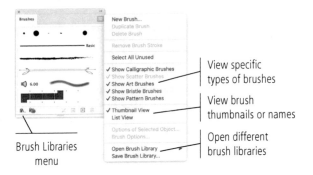

- **Art brushes** apply a brush stroke or object shape across the length of a path.

- **Bristle brushes** create strokes that mimic the behavior of a real artist's brushes.

- **Calligraphic brushes** create strokes that resemble what you would draw with the angled tip of a calligraphic pen.

- **Pattern brushes** paint a pattern of defined tiles along the length of a path, on inner and outer corners, and the beginning and end of a path.

- **Scatter brushes** scatter copies of an object along a path.

Beyond the few brushes in the default Brushes panel, you can also open a number of built-in brush libraries using the Brush Libraries menu at the bottom of the Brushes panel or at the bottom of the Window menu.

Note:

Brush libraries open in the same position as when they were last used. If you open more than one brush library, the new library opens as a separate tab in the existing panel group unless it has already been moved into a different panel group.

Create a New Art Brush

An art brush applies an object along the length of a path. You will use this type of brush to create the ski lift paths. To create an art brush, you must first create the object(s) you want to use as the brush stroke.

1. **With summit-map.ai open, create a new layer named Ski Lift immediately above Layer 1.**

2. **Select the two ski-lift paths on the artboard.**

   The ski-lift paths are the two black lines that meet in a "T" near the middle of the map.

3. **In the Layers panel, click the Selected Art icon for Layer 1, then drag it to the Ski Lift layer.**

   If you dragged the Selected Art icon for any specific path, only that path would be moved to the new layer. Because you dragged the Selected Art icon for the active layer that contained both paths, both are moved to the new layer.

The smaller square indicates that some (but not all) objects on that layer are selected.

Larger squares identify specific selected objects.

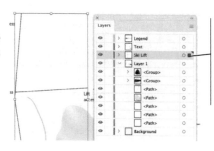

Drag the Selected Art icon from Layer 1 to the Ski Lift layer to move selected objects to the new layer.

4. **Option/Alt-click the eye icon for the Ski Lift layer to hide all but that layer.**

5. **Click away from the two paths to deselect everything.**

6. **Anywhere on the artboard, create a 5-pt horizontal black line that is approximately 1″ long. Change the stroke color to 75% black.**

7. **With the line selected, choose Edit>Copy.**

8. **Choose Edit>Paste in Front to paste a copy of the line directly on top of the original.**

   The Paste options are very useful for positioning copied objects.

   - **Paste** puts the copy in the center of the document window.

   - **Paste in Front** puts the copy in the same place as the copied object, one level higher in the object stacking order than the current selection.

   - **Paste in Back** puts the copy in the same place as the copied object, one level lower in the object stacking order than the current selection.

   - **Paste in Place** puts the copy on the selected artboard in the same position as it was on the original artboard.

   - **Paste on All Artboards** puts a copy on all artboards in the document, in the same position as the original artboard. A copy is also placed on the original artboard, so you might want to remove the duplicate copy from the original active artboard.

9. **With the pasted line still selected, change the stroke weight to 2.5 pt and change the stroke color to 30%.**

10. **Select both lines, then choose Object>Path>Outline Stroke.**

    This command converts a path stroke to a filled object. The original stroke color becomes the fill color of the resulting shape.

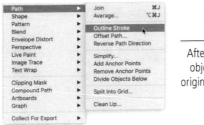

After outlining the strokes, the two objects are now filled shapes. The original paths are no longer available.

11. **Select both rectangles and group them (Object>Group or Command/Control-G).**

12. **Make sure the basic Brushes panel is open (Window>Brushes), and then drag the grouped rectangles into the Brushes panel.**

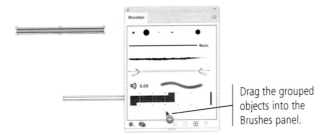

Drag the grouped objects into the Brushes panel.

Note:

Depending on what you (or other users) did before beginning this project, your Brushes panel might have fewer or more default brushes than what you see in our screenshots. It doesn't matter in this case, because you will only use the brushes that you create.

13. **In the resulting New Brush dialog box, choose the Art Brush radio button and then click OK.**

14. **Type Ski Lift in the Name field of the resulting dialog box, and then click OK.**

After you click OK in the dialog box, the new brush appears in the Brushes panel.

There's the new art brush.

15. **Delete the grouped lines from the artboard, save your work, then continue to the next exercise.**

Understanding Art Brush Options

The Art Brush Options dialog box opens automatically when you create a new art brush. You can also double-click an existing art brush to change its options.

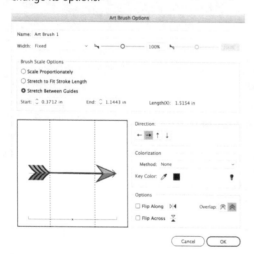

The **Width** field defines the width of the brush stroke relative to the applied stroke weight. For example, a 200% Width value would result in a 2-pt apparent stroke if the path has a 1-pt defined stroke weight.

The **Fixed** menu can be used to allow a variable stroke width based on a number of factors, including pressure and tilt from drawing tablet hardware.

In the Brush Scale Options, **Scale Proportionally** stretches the artwork both horizontally and vertically to match the stroke length.

Stretch to Fit Stroke Length stretches the brush artwork horizontally across the entire length of the stroke (in only the direction of the stroke).

Stretch Between Guides can be used to define areas of the brush artwork that do not stretch. Areas between the defined Start and End guides (dashed lines in the Preview) will stretch across the stroke length.

Direction controls the direction of brush artwork relative to the path. The active button matches the direction of the arrow in the preview; both of these indicate which side of the original artwork will be the end of the stroke.

Colorization options determine how colors in the paths are affected by colors in the brush artwork.

Flip Along and **Flip Across** reverse the orientation of art relative to the path.

Overlap controls how the artwork is treated on corners.

Control an Art Brush Stroke

Applying a brush stroke is simple — draw a path (or select an object), then click the brush you want to apply (either in the Brushes panel or in the Control panel menu). Once a brush stroke is applied, however, you should also understand how to control it.

1. **With summit-map.ai open, select the two paths that represent the ski lifts.**

2. **Click the Ski Lift brush in the Brushes panel.**

    The paths immediately take on the appearance of the brush you created earlier. You created the original darker-line stroke as 5 pt. When you created a brush from the grouped rectangles, you left the Width field (in the Art Brush Options dialog box) at 100%.

    The width of the path stroke is important when using brushes. When you apply artistic brush strokes, the width of the path's stroke actually defines the percentage of the brush width that will be applied. In this case, the width of the path stroke is 1 pt, so the applied brush stroke is 100% of the brush size. In other words, applying the brush to a 1-pt path results in a brush stroke with a 5-pt width.

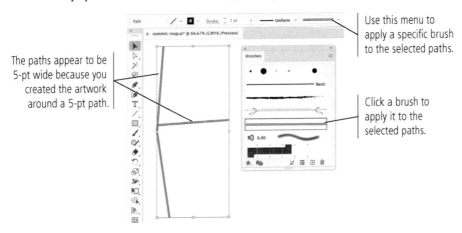

The paths appear to be 5-pt wide because you created the artwork around a 5-pt path.

Use this menu to apply a specific brush to the selected paths.

Click a brush to apply it to the selected paths.

3. **With the brushed path selected, double-click the Ski Lift brush in the Brushes panel to open the Art Brush Options dialog box.**

4. **In the Art Brush Options dialog box, change the Width field to 200% and then click OK.**

    The Width field defines brush stroke width as a percentage of the applied stroke weight.

    You could accomplish the same result by changing the path strokes to 2 pt. Every job has different requirements, so it's important to understand your options.

Note:

You can also click the Options of Selected Object button at the bottom of the Brushes panel to edit the brush options.

5. In the resulting dialog box, click Apply to Strokes.

When you change the options for a specific brush, you can determine what to do for strokes where the brush has already been applied.

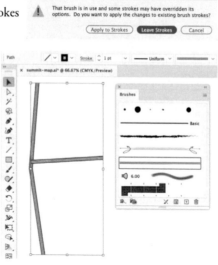

- If you click Apply to Strokes, the changes will be applied to any path where the brush has been applied.
- If you click Leave Strokes, existing paths are unaffected; a copy of the changed brush is added to the Brushes panel.
- If you click Cancel, the Brush Options dialog box closes without applying the new brush options.

6. Save the file and continue to the next exercise.

Expand Brush Strokes into Objects

If you look at the map as it is now, you might notice a problem where the ski lift paths connect — the dark gray of the horizontal path overlaps the light gray of the vertical path. To more accurately reflect the appearance of a single path that branches off in a different direction, you need to convert the path strokes to regular objects so you can manipulate selected parts of the paths (i.e., where the lines intersect).

1. With summit-map.ai open, zoom in so you can more clearly see where the two paths meet.

2. Select both paths, then choose View>Hide Bounding Box.

When the bounding box is hidden, you can better see the selected paths without the bounding box that marks the outer bounds of the active selection.

3. Open the Appearance panel (Window>Appearance).

The Appearance panel shows the properties of the selected objects, including the applied stroke and fill attributes. You can see here that the stroke attribute is Ski Lift.

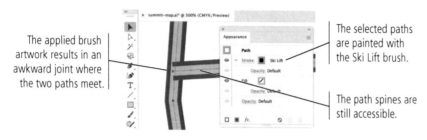

The applied brush artwork results in an awkward joint where the two paths meet.

The selected paths are painted with the Ski Lift brush.

The path spines are still accessible.

Note:

If you try to delete a brush that has been used in the open file, you must decide what to do with strokes where the brush has been applied.

If you click Expand Strokes, the applied brush strokes are converted to filled objects.

If you click Remove Strokes, objects that include the deleted brush strokes are reduced to their basic appearance (fill color, stroke color, and weight).

If you click Cancel, your artwork is unaffected and the brush remains in the Brushes panel.

4. **With the paths still selected, choose Object>Expand Appearance.**

In the Appearance panel, you now see that the selection is a group. When you expand the appearance of a selection, Illustrator simplifies the selection (as much as possible) into basic filled and stroked shapes; the resulting shapes are grouped.

Objects that make up the brush patterns are accessible and the path spines are gone.

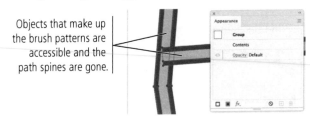

5. **In the Layers panel, expand the Ski Lift layer.**

As a result of expanding the strokes, each path is now a group.

6. **Click the arrows to expand each group.**

Each group contains the two paths in the artwork that made up the brush stroke.

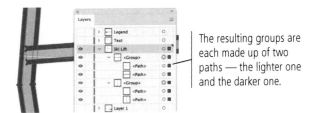

The resulting groups are each made up of two paths — the lighter one and the darker one.

7. **With the expanded paths still selected, choose Object>Ungroup.**

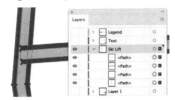

8. **Deselect everything, and then select the lighter path of the horizontal ski lift.**

9. **Choose Select>Same>Fill Color to select the other object that has the lighter fill.**

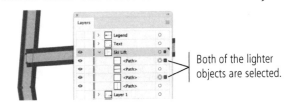

Both of the lighter objects are selected.

10. **In the Pathfinder panel (Window>Pathfinder), click the Unite button.**

All the selected shapes are now a single object. When you use the Pathfinder, the merged objects move to the stacking-order position of the highest object in the original selection, as you can see in the Layers panel. This is unlike the Shape Builder tool, which moves the merged object to the stacking-order position of the first object you click.

The combined object moves to the highest stacking-order position of the original component objects.

11. Repeat Steps 8–10 to unite the darker objects into a single shape.

You don't need to send the combined object to the back of the stacking order because it is already behind the lighter object.

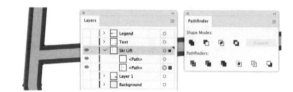

12. In the Layers panel, collapse the Ski Lift layer.

13. Save the file and continue to the next exercise.

Create Pattern Brush Tiles

While an art brush stretches a specific piece of artwork along a path, a pattern brush repeats specific artwork along the path. You can even define different artwork to use for sides, corners, and endpoints of a specific path. In this exercise, you will use an art brush to define the four different ski runs at the resort.

1. With summit-map.ai open, hide the Ski Lift layer and show Layer 1.

2. Create a new layer named Ski Runs immediately above the Ski Lift layer.

3. Select the four ski-run paths on the artboard. In the Layers panel, click the Selected Art icon for Layer 1, then drag it to the Ski Runs layer.

4. Hide Layer 1, then deselect everything on the artboard.

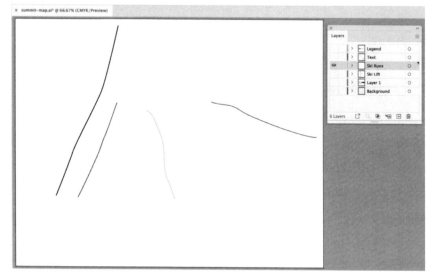

5. **Choose the Rectangle tool, then click and drag anywhere on the page to create a rectangle that is 0.4" square. Fill the new rectangle with black and apply a stroke of None.**

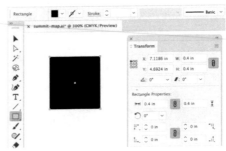

Depending on which selection tool was last used, the shape might appear differently on your screen than what you see here. If you last used the Selection tool, you will see eight bounding-box handles surrounding the shape (as in our screen shots). If you last used the Direct Selection tool, you will only see the new shape's anchor points.

6. **Rotate the rectangle 45°.**

When you rotate the object, the bounding box remains attached to the original object dimensions.

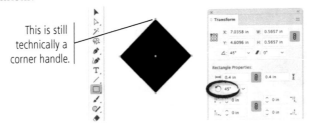

This is still technically a corner handle.

7. **In the Transform panel, make sure the W and H fields are not linked, then change the H field to 0.35 in.**

This icon should show broken links before you change the H field value.

8. **With the object still active, click the Selection tool in the Tools panel to reveal the shape's bounding-box handles.**

If you don't see all eight bounding-box handles on the shape, choose View>Show Bounding Box.

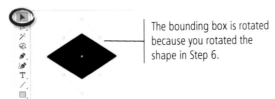

The bounding box is rotated because you rotated the shape in Step 6.

9. **Choose Object>Transform>Reset Bounding Box.**

When you rotated the shape in Step 6, the bounding box rotated along with the shape; the corners are still the corners. If you drag what appears to be the top handle, you would change the height and width of the shape.

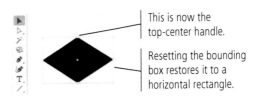

This is now the top-center handle.

Resetting the bounding box restores it to a horizontal rectangle.

The Reset Bounding Box command restores the bounding box to a horizontal rectangle. If you drag the top-center handle, you will affect only the height of the shape.

10. **Using the Selection tool, press Option/Alt, then click and drag the shape to the right to clone it.**

11. **Using the Line Segment tool with the default stroke weight, draw a vertical line that bisects the second diamond.**

    Smart guides make it easy to create a path that exactly aligns to the center of the diamond.

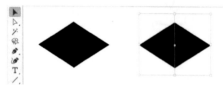

12. **Using the Selection tool, press Shift and click the diamond shape to add it to the selection.**

13. **In the Pathfinder panel, click the Divide button.**

14. **With the group still selected, transform the selected artwork to 140% proportionally.**

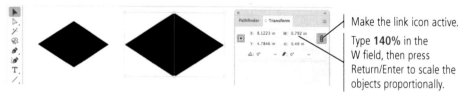

Make the link icon active.

Type **140%** in the W field, then press Return/Enter to scale the objects proportionally.

15. **In the Layers panel, expand the Ski Runs layer, then expand the group at the top of that layer.**

    When a pathfinder option results in more than one shape, the resulting shapes are automatically grouped together. You are going to use the halves individually, so you need to ungroup them.

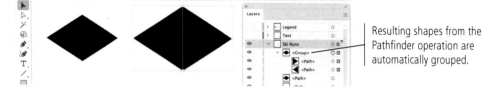

Resulting shapes from the Pathfinder operation are automatically grouped.

16. **With the entire group selected, choose Object>Ungroup.**

17. **Save the file and continue to the next exercise.**

Create a New Pattern Brush

Now that you have the three objects you need to create the pattern brush, you have to convert those objects to patterns, and then define the pattern brush.

1. With **summit-map.ai** open, deselect all objects on the artboard.

2. Using the Selection tool, drag the right-facing triangle shape into the Swatches panel.

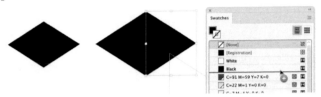

3. In the Swatches panel, double-click the new swatch to highlight the name. Type **Run Start** and press Return/Enter.

4. Delete the right-facing triangle from the artboard.

5. Repeat Steps 2–4 to create a pattern swatch named **Run End** from the left triangle shape, and a swatch named **Run Path** from the diamond shape.

   Make sure you delete the shapes from the artboard after you create the necessary pattern swatches.

6. Use the Show Swatch Kinds menu at the bottom of the panel to show only pattern swatches.

7. If the panel changes to thumbnail view, click the Show List View button at the top of the panel to restore the panel to Small List view.

8. With nothing selected on the artboard, click the New Brush button at the bottom of the Brushes panel.

   If anything is selected when you click the New Brush button, Illustrator tries to create a new brush based on the current selection.

9. In the New Brush dialog box, select the Pattern Brush option and click OK.

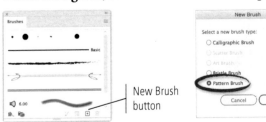

New Brush button

Note:

On some Windows systems, there is a bug that prevents some custom swatches from appearing in the Pattern Brush Options dialog box until you save the file where you created the swatches.

10. **In the Pattern Brush Options dialog box, name the brush Ski Runs.**

11. **Click the menu for the Side Tile icon, and then choose Run Path from the list of available pattern swatches.**

    Pattern brush tiles must be saved as pattern swatches (as you did in Steps 2–5) before you can access them in the Pattern Brush Options dialog box.

    After you choose the Side Tile pattern, the preview area shows how the pattern tile will appear along a path.

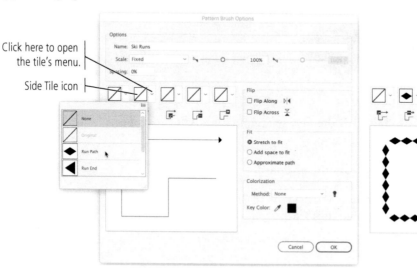

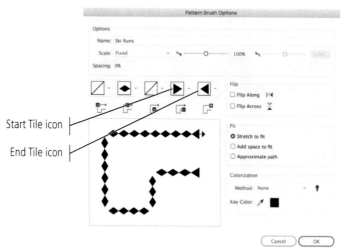

Note:

Pattern brushes can consist of five possible tiles: side, outer corner, inner corner, start, and end. You can define different patterns for any or all of these tiles.

12. **Open the Start Tile menu, and then click Run Start in the list of patterns.**

13. **Open the End Tile menu, and then click Run End in the list of patterns.**

Note:

The end tile of a pattern brush should be created with the path end pointing to the right. If the "end" of the end tile points left, you could end up with unexpected results such as this:

14. **Click OK to create the brush.**

15. **Select all four of the paths on the visible layer and click the Ski Runs pattern brush in the Brushes panel.**

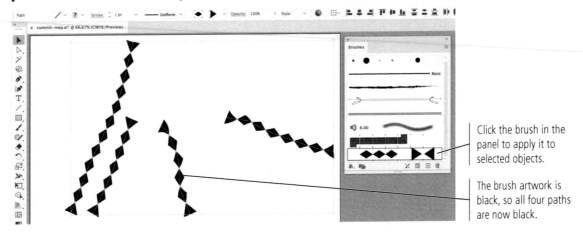

Click the brush in the panel to apply it to selected objects.

The brush artwork is black, so all four paths are now black.

Understanding Pattern Brush Options

As with art brushes, you can control the settings for pattern brushes when you first create them or by double-clicking an existing pattern brush in the Brushes panel.

Scale adjusts the tiles relative to their original size.

Spacing adjusts the space between tiles in the stroke.

The **Tile buttons** allow you to apply different patterns to different parts of the line.

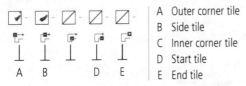

A Outer corner tile
B Side tile
C Inner corner tile
D Start tile
E End tile

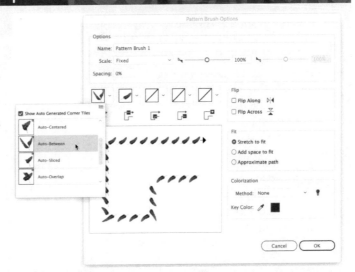

After you define the side tile, Illustrator automatically generates four options for the inner and outer corner tiles. This means you do not need to manually create separate corner artwork (although you can if you choose).

- **Auto-Centered.** The side tile is stretched around the corner and centered on it.
- **Auto-Between.** The side tiles extend all the way into the corner, with one copy on each side.
- **Auto-Sliced.** The side tile is sliced diagonally; the pieces are reassembled similar to the corners of a picture frame.
- **Auto-Overlap.** The side tiles overlap at the corner.

Flip Along and **Flip Across** reverse the orientation of the art in relation to the path.

In the Fit options, **Stretch to Fit** adjusts the length of the pattern tiles to fit the path.

Add Space to Fit adds blank space between pattern tiles to maintain proportions in the applied pattern.

Approximate Path fits tiles to the closest approximate path without changing the tiles.

Colorization methods determine how colors in the paths are affected by colors in the brush stroke artwork.

16. With all four paths selected, change the stroke weight to 0.5 pt.

As we explained earlier, changing the stroke size for the applied art brush and changing the stroke width of the path achieves the same result. The 0.5-pt stroke weight means the applied stroke is half the width of the defined brush.

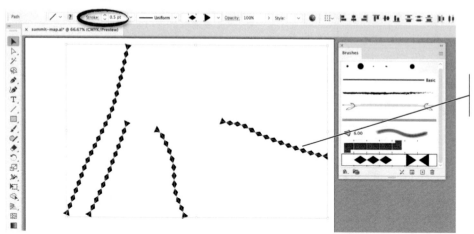

The width of the brush artwork is relative to the applied stroke weight.

17. In the Brushes panel, double-click the Ski Runs brush to open the Pattern Brush Options dialog box.

18. Choose Tints in the Colorization menu, then click OK.

Note:

Click the Tips button to the right of the menu to see a preview of colorization options.

The Colorization menu controls how colors in an art, scatter, or pattern brush interact with the defined stroke color.

- Select **None** to use only the colors defined in the brush.

- Select **Tints** to apply the brush stroke in tints of the current stroke color. Black areas of the brush become the stroke color, other areas become tints of the stroke color, and white remains white.

- Select **Tints and Shades** to apply the brush stroke in tints and shades of the stroke color. Black and white areas of the brush remain unaffected; all other areas are painted as a blend from black to white through the stroke color.

- Select **Hue Shift** to change the defined key color in brush artwork to the defined stroke color when the brush is applied; other colors in the brush artwork are adjusted to be similar to the stroke color. Black, white, and grays are unaffected. The key color defaults to the most prominent color in the brush art. To change the key color, click the eyedropper in the brush preview to select a different color.

19. In the resulting dialog box, click Apply to Strokes.

Using the Tint colorization method, black in the brush artwork is reproduced as 100% of the applied stroke color.

Note:

Don't forget to delete the triangles you used to create the pattern swatches that are used in the brush.

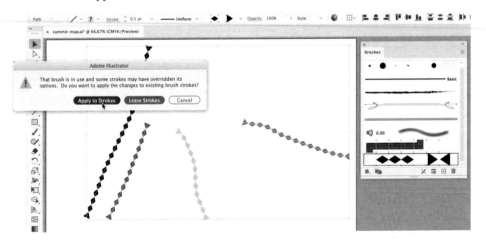

20. Save the file and continue to the next exercise.

Save Custom Brushes

When you create custom brushes, swatches, or other elements, they are only available in the file where you create them. To access those assets in other files, you have to save your own custom libraries.

1. With summit-map.ai open, show the Brushes panel. Open the panel Options menu and choose Select All Unused.

Everything but the Basic brush and the Ski Runs pattern brush should be selected. (Remember, you expanded the appearance of the ski lift paths, so the Ski Lift art brush is not currently applied in the file.)

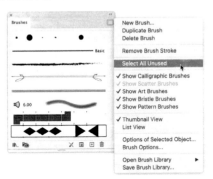

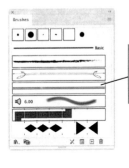

The Ski Lift art brush is selected because it is not technically in use.

2. Command/Control-click the Ski Lift art brush to deselect it, and then click the panel's Delete button. Click Yes in the dialog box asking if you want to delete the brush selection.

You are not permanently deleting the brushes from the application; you are only deleting them from the Brushes panel for this file. However, Illustrator still asks you to confirm the deletion.

Command/Control-click to remove the Ski Lift brush from the active selection...

...then click the panel Delete button.

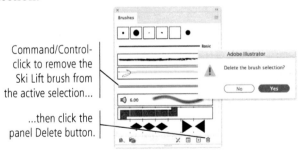

3. **Open the panel Options menu and choose Save Brush Library.**

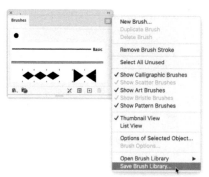

Note:

The Basic option is an application default, which effectively removes any applied brush stroke and reverts a path to a simple 1-pt stroke.

4. **In the resulting dialog box, navigate to your WIP>Skiing folder as the target location.**

If you're working on your own computer, the dialog box defaults to the application's Brushes folder when you save a custom brush library. If you are using a shared computer, you might not be able to save files in the application's default location. Saving the file directly to your WIP folder makes it readily available whenever you need it.

5. **Change the file name to map-brushes.ai and click Save.**

6. **Close the Brushes panel.**

7. **Choose Window>Brush Libraries>Other Library.**

Note:

Brush, symbol, and swatch libraries are saved with the ".ai" extension.

8. **In the resulting dialog box, navigate to your WIP>Skiing folder. Select the map-brushes.ai file and click Open.**

If you save a custom brush library in the application's default location, you can access it in the Window>Brush Libraries>User Defined submenu.

The map-brushes panel opens; it contains only the brushes that were available when you saved the library. The Basic brush and Touch Calligraphic options are not included; they are, however, available in the Brushes panel of any file you open in Illustrator.

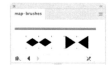

9. **Save the summit-map.ai file and continue to the next stage of the project.**

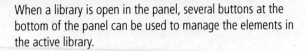
Managing Libraries

If you have an individual-user subscription to the Adobe Creative Cloud, you have access to CC Library functionality, which allows you to easily share assets across various Adobe applications. This technology makes it very easy to maintain consistency across a design campaign — for example, using the same color swatches for all pieces, whether created in Illustrator, InDesign, or Photoshop.

When you first open the Libraries panel you see a list of all libraries that exist in your Adobe account. You can:

- Click an existing library name to open it in the panel.
- Click the Create New Library button to add a new one to your account.
- Click Browse Shared Libraries to view libraries that other users have shared with you.
- Click Find Public Libraries to find assets that have been created by other users and shared publicly.

You can access these same options by clicking the + button in the bottom-right corner of the panel.

Once you create a library, it is stored in your Creative Cloud account so you can access the same assets in other Adobe applications.

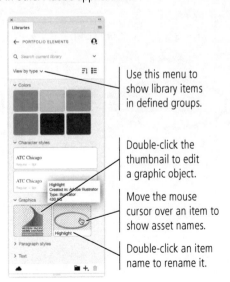

Use this menu to show library items in defined groups.

Double-click the thumbnail to edit a graphic object.

Move the mouse cursor over an item to show asset names.

Double-click an item name to rename it.

When a library is open in the panel, several buttons at the bottom of the panel can be used to manage the elements in the active library.

- Library Sync Status shows whether the active library is currently synced to your Adobe account.
- Create New Group adds a folder to the library, which you can use to manually group elements based on whatever criteria you determine.
- Add Elements opens a menu that you can use to add various types of library items. The options here depend on the selected objects in active file; if a type object is selected, for example, this menu would also include options to add character and/or paragraph styles based on the type formatting applied to that object.
- Delete removes the selected element(s) from the active library.

Sharing and Collaboration

Libraries also offer a powerful opportunity to communicate assets with other users.

You can click the Invite People button at the top of the Libraries panel to share a library with specific other users. Clicking this button navigates to your online Adobe account in the Creative Cloud desktop application, and automatically asks for the email addresses of those you want to share with.

You can click the arrow to the left of the "Can Edit" text to determine whether invited users can edit the library or simply view it.

Creating Library Items

In addition to the Add Elements button at the bottom of the Libraries panel, you can also drag and drop items from the layout into the panel.

The Swatches, Paragraph Styles, and Character Styles panels also provide an easy method for adding existing assets to the active library. Clicking the Add Selected... button adds the selected assets to the active Library.

You can also add new elements to a Library when you define a new color swatch, paragraph style, or character style by checking the Add to my Library option in each dialog box.

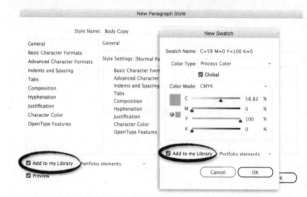

Working with Library Items

Graphics in Libraries maintain a dynamic link between the library item and placed instances of that library item.

If you double-click a graphic in the Libraries panel, the object opens in the application where it was created. If you edit the library item and save it, the changes are automatically reflected in any placed instances.

In the example here, we placed an instance of the Highlight graphic from our library onto the artboard:

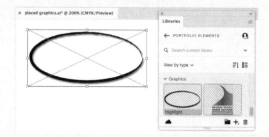

We then double-clicked the Highlight item in the Libraries panel to open it, and changed the object's stroke color:

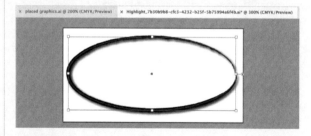

After saving the file and closing it, the placed instance in the first file reflects the new blue stroke color:

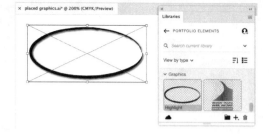

Important Note: Although you can add specific text to a library as a "Text" item, at the time of this writing, placed instances of synced text in Illustrator do not accurately reflect changes made to the synced object. If you make changes to the synced text, you have to manually replace the text in placed instances.

STAGE 3 / Using Symbols

In many cases, you will need to use multiple copies of a specific graphic in a complex illustration like the one in this project. You can create any element and define it as a **symbol**, which you can then use as many times as necessary in a drawing. All placed **instances** of a symbol are linked dynamically to the saved definition of the symbol; this means that you can change all instances simultaneously by changing the saved definition of the symbol. You can also isolate specific instances of a symbol, which effectively breaks the link to the saved definition of the symbol (and its other instances). Once the link is broken, changes to the original saved symbol no longer affect the isolated instances.

As with brushes and swatches, symbols are managed in panels. The default Symbols panel (Window>Symbols) has a few randomly selected symbols from various built-in libraries. You can also open other symbol libraries by choosing from the menu at the bottom of the Window menu, or in the Symbol Libraries menu at the bottom of the Symbols panel.

If you open a symbol library from the Window menu, the first library opens in its own panel. Successive panels open as separate tabs that are automatically grouped with other open symbol libraries, unless they have been intentionally moved out of the panel group and positioned elsewhere in the workspace. If you open a symbol library using the Symbol Libraries menu at the bottom of the Symbols panel, the new library replaces the active library.

Open Custom Symbol Libraries

Several elements of this project will benefit from the use of symbols. Many of the symbols for this project have already been created and saved in a custom library, which you can easily load so you don't have to recreate work that has already been completed.

1. **With summit-map.ai open, open the Symbols panel (Window>Symbols).**

2. **Click the Symbol Libraries menu button at the bottom of the default Symbols panel, and choose Other Library at the bottom of the menu.**

   If you create a custom library on your computer using the default Save location, the library appears in the User Defined submenu of the main Libraries menu. If a custom library was created on another computer, you have to choose Other Library from the menu and navigate to the file that contains the library you want to use.

Note:

As with the Brushes panel, your default Symbols panel might have more options than what you see in our screenshots. Again, you will only be using the symbols you create (or import), so the default symbols don't matter in this project.

Note:

The same options are also available for loading swatch libraries and brush libraries that were created on another computer.

3. **Navigate to `map-symbols.ai` in your WIP>Skiing folder and click Open.**

The new symbol library appears in its own panel (possibly grouped with other library panels if other symbol libraries are also open).

Symbols in loaded libraries are not connected to the current file unless you place an instance of a symbol from the loaded library into the file. When you place a symbol instance from a loaded library, the symbol is added to the default symbol library for the file. The same is true when working with brush libraries.

4. **Continue to the next exercise.**

 ## Control Symbol Instances

In addition to loading built-in or custom symbol libraries, you can also create new symbols by drawing the art and dragging it into the default Symbols panel. In this exercise, you create a custom symbol to identify the different ski runs on the map — a simple road sign. You need four different signs to label the various runs.

1. **With `summit-map.ai` open, show and lock all layers. Create a new layer named `Signs` at the top of the layer stack and make sure it is selected.**

2. **Click and drag the Sign symbol from the Map-Symbols panel to the artboard.**

Note:

Simply clicking a symbol in an external panel copies that symbol into the file's Symbols panel.

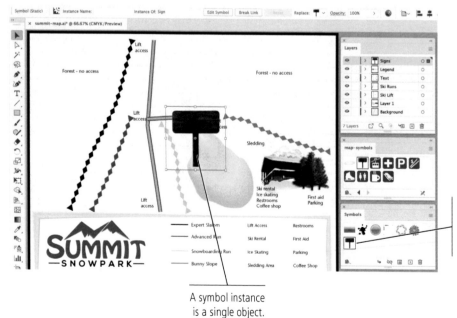

A symbol instance is a single object.

Symbols placed from other libraries are added to the default Symbols panel for the file.

3. **Using the Transform panel, scale the placed instance to 1″ wide (proportionally).**

You can transform the instance as you would any other object, by dragging the bounding-box handles. This has no effect on the original symbol, nor on other placed instances of the same symbol.

When you transform a symbol instance, the Transform/Control panel does not offer the reference point proxy option. The symbol's registration point position, around which transformations will be applied, is defined when you create the symbol.

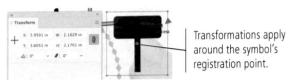 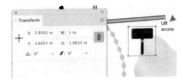

Transformations apply around the symbol's registration point.

4. **Using the Selection tool, drag the resized symbol instance near the top of the black-diamond ski path.**

5. **Clone (Option/Alt-drag) the sign symbol instance three times. Place each clone near the top of each ski run path.**

Each symbol instance is an object, which means it can be modified — transformed, rotated, stretched, etc. — as you would modify any other object. Transforming a placed instance has no effect on other placed instances of the same symbol.

Cloning an instance results in an additional instance of the symbol. All instances are linked to the original symbol.

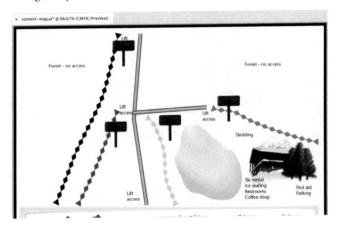

6. **Choose View>Fit Artboard in Window.**

As with the Edit Pattern mode, the symbol artwork is centered in the document window when you edit the symbol artwork. This command centers the artboard in the document window, so the artboard edges will not interfere with symbol artwork.

7. **In the Symbols panel, double-click the Sign symbol to enter into Symbol Editing mode.**

Make sure you double-click the symbol in the regular Symbols panel and not the Map-Symbols panel.

This opens **Symbol Editing mode**, which shows the symbol artwork centered in the active document window. The symbol artwork is the only visible item; other artwork in the file is not visible.

8. **Drag the snowdrift symbol from the Map-Symbols panel onto the artboard. Place it over the bottom edge of the signpost.**

Note:

*Double-clicking a placed instance allows you to edit the symbol in the context of the surrounding artwork, called **editing in place**.*

Editing in place shows the symbol at full size, not the scaled dimensions of the placed instance. When you exit Symbol Editing mode, the placed instance returns to its scaled size.

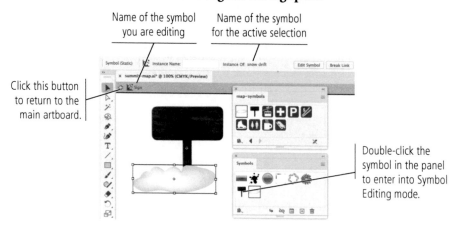

Name of the symbol you are editing

Name of the symbol for the active selection

Click this button to return to the main artboard.

Double-click the symbol in the panel to enter into Symbol Editing mode.

9. **Choose the Type tool in the Tools panel.**

10. **Click anywhere outside the sign area to create a new point-type object. With the placeholder text highlighted, type:**

    SNOSURF [Return/Enter]
    SLOPE

11. **Choose the Selection tool.**

    When you change from the Type tool to the Selection tool, the type object where the insertion point was placed is automatically selected.

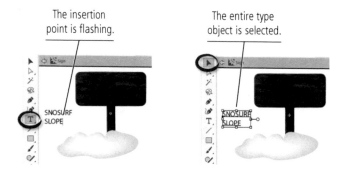

The insertion point is flashing.

The entire type object is selected.

12. **With the type object selected, change the type formatting to 23-pt ATC Garnet Ultra with 21-pt leading, filled with white, with centered alignment.**

13. **Move the type object to be centered in the horizontal area of the sign.**

14. **In the top-left corner of the screen, click the left arrow button to exit Symbol Editing mode and return to the main artboard.**

The new type element has been added to all four placed instances. As we mentioned, the advantage of using symbols is that you can change all linked instances — whether there are 4 or 400 — by making changes once to the saved symbol definition.

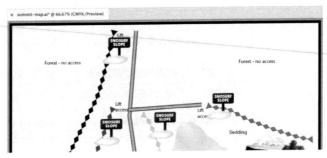

The problem, of course, is that the ski runs are not all named "Snosurf Slope." Although changing the symbol definition allowed you to add, format, and align the type object, you still need to edit it separately on each instance. To change the text on each individual sign, you have to break the link from each instance to the original symbol.

15. **Select all four instances of the Sign symbol and click the Break Link button in the Control panel.**

Once the links are broken, all the elements of the symbol artwork become a group in the main file. Editing the actual symbol will have no effect on instances that are no longer linked to the symbol.

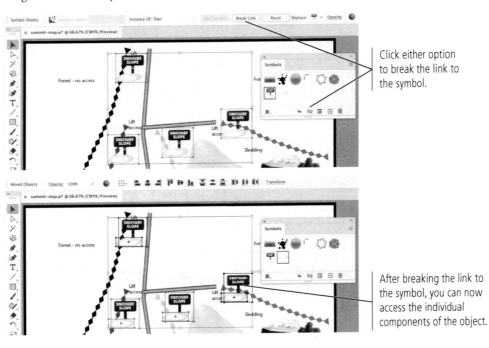

Click either option to break the link to the symbol.

After breaking the link to the symbol, you can now access the individual components of the object.

16. **Change the text of each former symbol instance as follows. Use the Return/Enter key to place each word in the titles on a separate line:**

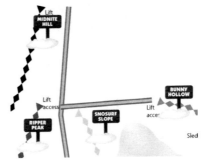

Black run: MIDNITE HILL

Cyan run: RIPPER PEAK

Pink run: BUNNY HOLLOW

17. **Save the file and continue to the next exercise.**

Replace Symbols

The next step of this map project involves placing icons around the map to identify different services. The symbols were provided in the supplied library, so this is a relatively simple process of placing symbols in the right place.

1. **With summit-map.ai open, lock the Signs layer. Create a new layer named Amenities at the top of the layer stack and make sure it is selected.**

2. **Drag the Lift Access symbol from the Map-Symbols panel to the artboard. Place the instance on top of the matching words near the top of the artboard.**

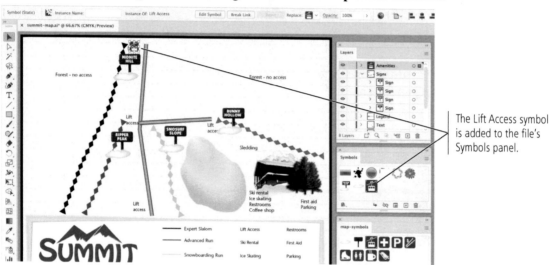

The Lift Access symbol is added to the file's Symbols panel.

3. **Place three more instances of the Lift Access symbol according to the text on the original map.**

4. **Continue dragging symbols from the Map-Symbols panel to the artboard, using the text as a guide.**

   Skip the legend for now; you will create that later in this exercise.

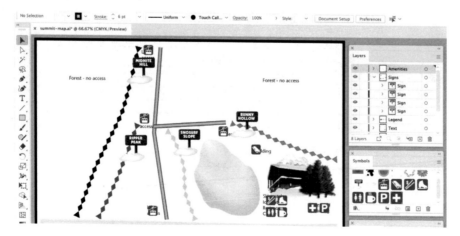

5. **Delete the Text layer from the file.**

6. **Lock the Amenities layer. Unlock the Legend layer and make it active.**

7. **Drag an instance of the Lift Access symbol from the main Symbols panel to the artboard. Place it to the left of the words "Lift Access," centered vertically with the text object.**

8. **Drag additional instances of the Lift Access symbol to appear before each label in the legend.**

   Use any method — the Align panel, Smart Guides, etc. — to align the instances to one another, as shown here:

9. **Select the symbol instance next to the Ski Rental text. Open the Replace menu in the Control panel and choose the Ski Rental symbol.**

   As soon as you select the new symbol, the selected instance changes to the new symbol.

   The Replace With menu includes all symbols that are available in the file's Symbols panel.

10. **Repeat Step 9 for the remaining symbols in the legend, choosing the correct symbol to match the text.**

11. **Save the file and continue to the next exercise.**

Spray Symbols

The next task is to create the forest around the ski runs. The supplied file already has a perfectly good group of trees near the lodge graphic; you are going to use those trees to create a new symbol, then spray a forest around the map.

1. **With summit-map.ai open, lock the Legend layer and unlock Layer 1.**

2. **Using the Selection tool, select the trees on the right side of the artboard.**

3. **Drag the selected group onto the main Symbols panel.**

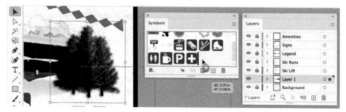

4. **In the resulting dialog box, define the following settings, then click OK:**

    Name: Trees

    Export Type: Movie Clip

    Symbol Type: Static Symbol

    Registration: Center

    When you create a symbol from objects on the artboard, the original objects are automatically converted to an instance of the new symbol.

The selection is now an instance of the new Trees symbol.

5. **Lock Layer 1, then create a new layer named Forest at the top of the layer stack. Make the Forest layer active.**

6. Double-click the Symbol Sprayer tool in the Tools panel.

The Symbol Sprayer tool is used to spray multiple symbol instances onto the artboard. Other tools nested under the Symbol Sprayer in the Tools panel can be used to squeeze, spread, pinch, and otherwise modify the sprayed symbol instances.

Double-clicking the tool in the Tools panel opens the Symbolism Tools Options dialog box, where you can change settings that apply when you use the symbolism tools.

- **Diameter** reflects the tool's current brush size. The Symbol Sprayer tool defaults to the last-used size.
- **Method** determines how the symbol modifier tools (all but the Symbol Sprayer and Symbol Shifter) adjust symbol instances:
  - **Average** smoothes out values in symbol instances.
  - **User Defined** adjusts instances in relation to the position of the cursor.
  - **Random** modifies instances randomly under the cursor.
- **Intensity** determines the rate of change for modifying instances.
- **Symbol Set Density** creates more tightly packed (higher values) or loosely packed (lower values) instances in the symbol set.

If the Symbol Sprayer tool is selected in the middle of the dialog box, you can control a variety of options related to how new symbol instances are added to symbol sets. Each option has two possible choices:

- **Average** adds new symbols with the average value of existing symbol instances within the brush radius. For example, in an area where the average existing instance is rotated by 10°, new instances will be rotated by the same amount.
- **User Defined** applies specific values for each parameter, primarily based on the original symbol size, mouse direction, and current color settings.

If the Symbol Sizer is selected, you have two additional options:

- **Proportional Resizing** maintains a uniform shape for each instance as you resize.
- **Resizing Affects Density** moves symbol instances away from each other when they are scaled up, and moves symbol instances toward each other when they are scaled down.

If the **Show Brush Size and Intensity** option is checked, the cursor reflects the tool diameter.

7. Change the Diameter field to 1.5 in, and the Symbol Set Density to 5. Click OK to apply the change.

Diameter determines the tool's current brush size. Symbol Set Density determines how tightly symbol instances are sprayed; higher values create more instances (spaced closely together) in the symbol set.

Note:

Press the left bracket key ([ ) to decrease or the right bracket key ( ]) to increase the size of the tool (and its cursor).

8. **Click outside of the artboard to the left of the black ski path and drag down, following the ski path as a rough guide.**

   When you click and drag with the Symbol Sprayer tool, you create a **symbol set** — multiple instances of a single symbol that are treated as a single, cohesive unit.

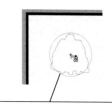

As you spray the symbols, you can see wireframe outlines of the shapes that will be added.

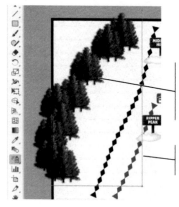

When you release the mouse button, the full-color symbol instances appear on the artboard.

This boundary shows the edge of the symbol set.

Note:

The slower you drag, the more instances will build up in a single place. We dragged at a moderate pace to place this first set of trees.

If you click and hold the mouse button without dragging, symbol instances pile on top of one another, just as spray paint builds up if you hold the can in one place.

9. **Without deselecting the symbol set, click again and drag to fill in the entire top-left corner of the artboard.**

   Each click of the tool adds more instances to the set, but can also affect the position of existing instances in the set. Don't worry if your trees cover other objects on the map; you will fix that problem shortly.

   By leaving the set selected, the new instances are added to the existing set.

The set expands to include the new instances.

10. **Press Command/Control to temporarily access the Selection tool and click away from the symbol set to deselect it.**

    Pressing Command/Control temporarily switches to the Selection tool; when you release the Command/Control key, the Symbol Sprayer tool is again active.

    If you don't deselect the active symbol set, clicking again adds more instances to the selected symbol set. In this case, you want to create a second symbol set, so you have to deselect the first set before clicking again with the Symbol Sprayer tool.

Modifying Symbol Sets

When using sprayed symbols, many designs call for adjustments to individual components or instances within a symbol set. Without breaking the links between individual instances and the original symbol, you can use a number of tools (nested under the Symbol Sprayer tool) to modify symbols within a set.

The **Symbol Shifter** tool ( ) pushes instances around the artboard. The tool only affects instances touched by the tool cursor.

The **Symbol Scruncher** tool ( ) causes the cursor to act as a magnet; all instances in the set are drawn toward the cursor when you click. Pressing Option/Alt reverses the effect, pushing instances away from the cursor.

The **Symbol Sizer** tool ( ) changes the size of instances within a set. Clicking causes instances under the cursor to grow. Option/Alt-clicking causes instances under the cursor to shrink.

The **Symbol Spinner** tool ( ) rotates instances under the cursor where you click. Dragging indicates the direction of the rotation.

The **Symbol Stainer** tool ( ) changes the hue of instances under the cursor using the defined fill color.

The **Symbol Screener** tool ( ) increases the opacity of instances under the cursor. Press Option/Alt to decrease instance opacity.

The **Symbol Styler** tool ( ) allows you to apply a graphic style to symbol instances.

11. **Click the Symbol Sprayer tool above the horizontal ski lift path and drag to create the second forested area.**

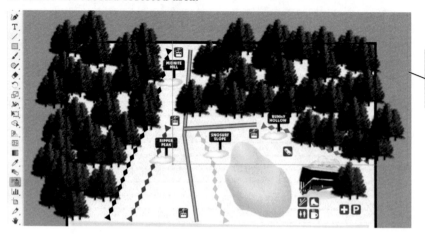

Because you deselected the first set of trees, this group is a separate symbol set.

12. **Select the Symbol Shifter tool (nested under the Symbol Sprayer tool).**

13. **Click and drag within the selected set to move all the trees away from the important objects on the map.**

14. **Press Command/Control to temporarily access the Selection tool and click the forest on the left side of the map to select that symbol set.**

15. **Use the Symbol Shifter tool to adjust the position of trees so that no objects on the map are obscured.**

Using the Symbol Shifter tool, you can click and drag within the selected symbol set to move individual instances.

Note:

Press Option/Alt and drag with the Symbol Sprayer tool to delete symbol instances from a symbol set.

Note:

Although you can't use the Direct Selection tool to access individual instances within a set, you can use the Selection tool to move the entire set all at once.

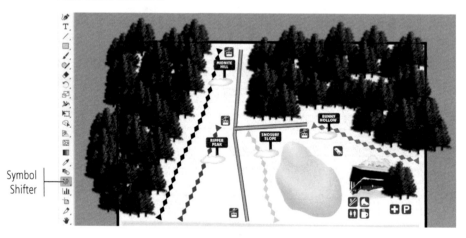

Symbol Shifter

16. **Save the file and continue to the next exercise.**

Understanding Dynamic Symbols

The symbols you used in this project are static; you can edit the master symbol to change each placed instance, but you can't access or change the individual elements of symbol artwork in specific placed instances.

Dynamic symbols, identified by a + in the symbol thumbnail, offer a more versatile alternative. If you choose the Dynamic option when you create a symbol (or open the Symbol Options dialog box using the button at the bottom of the Symbols panel), you will be able to modify certain attributes of symbol artwork without detaching the instances from the master symbol.

Using the Direct Selection tool, you can select individual elements of a placed symbol instance and change their fill and stroke attributes. Those changes do not affect the original symbol artwork or other placed instances of the same symbol.

If you do edit individual instances of a dynamic symbol, you can use the Reset button in the Control panel to restore the original symbol artwork.

Unfortunately, dynamic symbols are fairly limited at this time. You can't, for example, edit the text of a type object in an individual symbol instance. To accomplish the goal of this project, for example, you would still have to break the links to the master symbol to change the name on each sign.

Each graphic is an instance of a dynamic symbol named Book-Title. We used the Direct Selection tool to change the fill color of each instance.

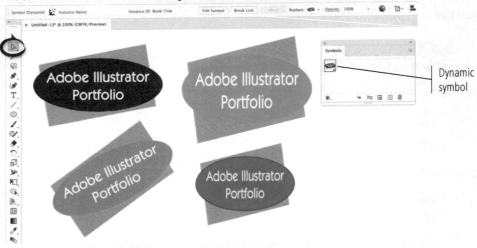

Changes to the master symbol are reflected in placed instances; transformations applied to the placed instances are not overridden.

Create a Clipping Mask

The final step of this project is to save the file so it can be used in other applications. Part of this process requires "finishing off" the edges so that no objects, such as trees, hang past the artwork edges. Rather than manually cutting your artwork, you can square off the design by creating a **clipping mask** to hide the elements you don't want to see.

In this exercise, you are going to perform a few small clean-up tasks, and then create a clipping mask to show only parts of the forest inside the artboard area.

1. **With summit-map.ai open, make all layers unlocked and visible.**

2. **Rename Layer 1 as Lodge.**

   Remember, it's always a good idea to use descriptive names.

3. **Drag the Legend layer to the top of the layer stack.**

   Rearranging the layer order makes more logical sense, and prevents the legend from being obscured by the forest.

4. **Using the Selection tool, click to select the four lines in the legend. Drag the left-center bounding-box handle until the width of the selection is 1.15".**

   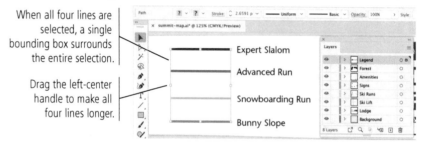

   When all four lines are selected, a single bounding box surrounds the entire selection.

   Drag the left-center handle to make all four lines longer.

5. **In the Control panel, apply the Ski Runs brush, and then change the stroke weight to 0.5 pt.**

   Use this menu to apply a different brush stroke to the selected paths...

   ...then change the stroke weight to 0.5 pt to reduce the size of the applied brush strokes.

   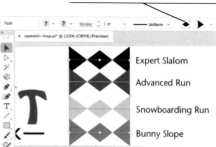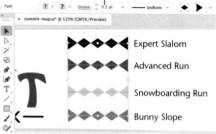

6. **Deselect everything on the artwork.**

7. **In the Layers panel, click the Forest layer to select it. Press Command/Control and click the Background layer to add it to the selection.**

8. **Open the Layers panel Options menu and choose Collect in New Layer.**

Note:

Clipping masks do not permanently affect the artwork. You can remove the mask by selecting the mask shape and choosing Object> Clipping Mask>Release.

9. **Rename the new layer Clipped Forest, then expand it in the panel.**

This option maintains the layered integrity of your finished artwork by collecting the individual layers into sublayers of the new one, allowing you to treat the finished layers as a single unit by selecting the containing layer.

The Collect in New Layer command maintains the original layer names as sublayers in the new layer.

Note:

*To create a clipping mask, all the objects you want to clip should be part of the same layer as the masking object. If you create a clipping mask for objects on different layers, all affected objects are copied to the layer that contains the mask object (called **flattening**).*

10. **Drag the Background sublayer above the Forest sublayer.**

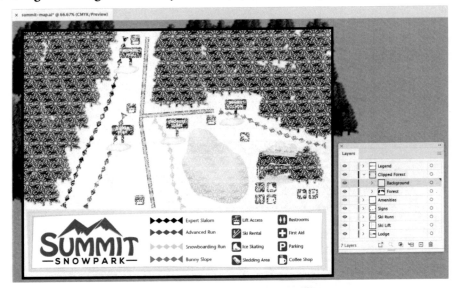

11. **Click the Selected Art icon for the Clipped Forest layer to select all objects on that layer (including the objects on both sublayers).**

12. **Choose Object>Clipping Mask>Make.**

A **clipping mask** is an object that masks other artwork; only those areas within the clipping mask shape remain visible.

This option converts the topmost selected object into a clipping path; other underlying (selected) objects are clipped by the shape of the topmost object.

Once an object is converted to a clipping mask, the defined fill and stroke attributes are removed. However, you can reapply fill or stroke attributes to any clipping mask shape, just as you would to any other object.

13. **Expand the Background sublayer in the layers panel, then expand the clip group.**

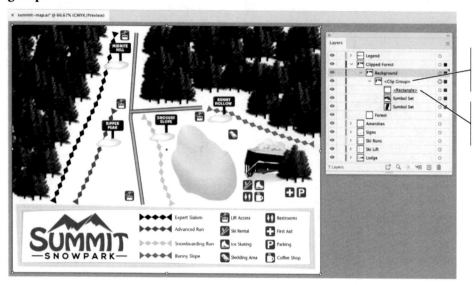

All selected objects are now part of a clip group.

The topmost selected object is converted to a clipping path.

14. **Click the Selected Art icon for only the Rectangle object at the top of the Clip Group.**

15. **Using the Control panel, change the object's fill to the Snowflakes pattern and change the stroke to 6-pt black.**

The fill attributes of a clipping path object — in this case, the snowflakes pattern — are applied behind the clipped objects. Objects on underlying layers, however, are still obscured by the clipping object's fill attribute.

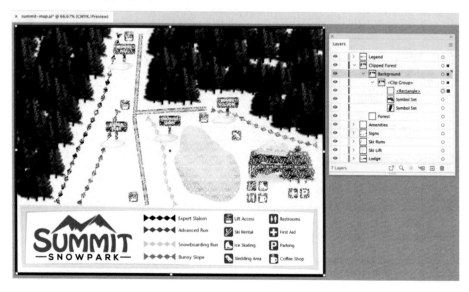

16. Drag the Clipped Forest layer to the bottom of the layer stack.

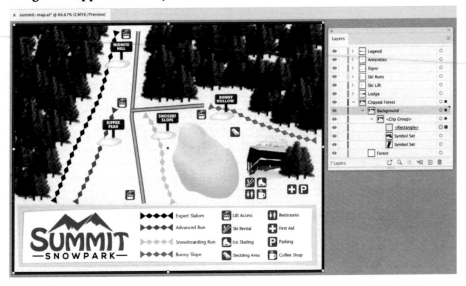

17. Save the file and close it.

1. The _____ panel provides access to colors, patterns, and gradients that have been saved in the active file.

2. _____ brushes scatter copies of an object along a path.

3. _____ brushes apply a brush stroke or object shape across the length of a path.

4. _____ brushes paint a pattern of defined tiles along a path. You can define different tiles for straight edges, inner and outer corners, and the beginning and end of a path.

5. After choosing _____ in the Object menu, you can no longer access a path spine, but you can access the outlines of the resulting shapes.

6. The _____ is used to add multiple copies of a symbol with a single mouse click. When you release the mouse button, added symbol instances are contained within a group.

7. Use the _____ format to export an Illustrator swatch library for use in Photoshop.

8. After clicking the _____ button for a specific symbol instance, editing a symbol's content has no effect on that instance.

9. Double-clicking a symbol instance on the artboard, or double-clicking a symbol in the Symbols panel, enters into _____.

10. A(n) _____ is an object that masks other artwork; only those areas within the _____ shape remain visible.

1. Briefly explain the potential problem caused by using spot colors in gradients.

2. Briefly explain the differences between an art brush and a pattern brush.

3. Briefly explain two advantages of using symbols.

Use what you have learned in this project to complete the following freeform exercise.
Carefully read the art director and client comments, then create your own design to meet the needs of the project.
Use the space below to sketch ideas. When finished, write a brief explanation of the reasoning behind your final design.

The Los Angeles parks and recreation director has hired you to create an illustrated, user-friendly map of the Griffith Park recreation complex.

❏ Download the park map from the park website (https://www.laparks.org/sites/default/files/griffith/pdf/GriffithParkMap.pdf).

❏ Use drawing techniques to create the basic park layout, including roads, trails, and defined paths.

❏ Create or find symbols to identify the different facilities and services.

❏ Add artwork, images, and color however you prefer to identify the different venues and attractions throughout the park.

Griffith Park is one of the largest public green spaces in the western United States. The park is home to a number of famous attractions, including the Griffith Observatory, Greek Theater, and the L.A. Zoo. It also offers equestrian trails, bike and hiking trails, and golf courses, as well as swimming, camping, concerts, and a host of other activities.

As you can guess from all of these available activities and attractions, the park is a very large place. We currently have a detailed topographic map from our master plan document, but I'd like something that is more attractive to tourists. I want to create an appealing, colorful, printed brochure that visitors can purchase for a nominal fee at park entrances and facilities so they can easily find what they're looking for.

As you completed this map project, you learned a wide range of important new skills, including managing many types of assets (swatches, patterns, and brushes), accessing built-in and custom libraries, and creating your own custom assets. You can apply these skills at any stage of an Illustrator project, saving significant amounts of time and effort.

Some of the planning work for this project was completed by the art director — including creating the icons for different elements of the artwork — and approved by the client in an earlier project meeting. Rather than taking the time to recreate those elements, you streamlined the design process by accessing that artwork as symbols that can be easily updated as necessary.

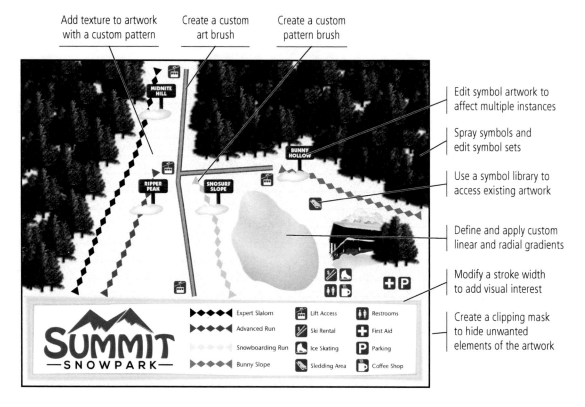

Add texture to artwork with a custom pattern

Create a custom art brush

Create a custom pattern brush

Edit symbol artwork to affect multiple instances

Spray symbols and edit symbol sets

Use a symbol library to access existing artwork

Define and apply custom linear and radial gradients

Modify a stroke width to add visual interest

Create a clipping mask to hide unwanted elements of the artwork

Letterfold Brochure

Your client is a non-profit artists' cooperative in San Francisco that coordinates and hosts special events throughout the year. This year they are launching a new "Art of Science" program, which will be a month-long series of special events all over the city to promote the city's artistic community. You have been hired to create the first brochure to begin advertising the new program.

This project incorporates the following skills:

❑ Creating a folding template that meets production requirements

❑ Placing and managing links to external graphics and images

❑ Importing text and controlling the flow of text across multiple frames

❑ Working with styles to automate repetitive text-formatting tasks

❑ Correcting typographic problems, such as widows

❑ Checking for and correcting spelling errors

❑ Exporting PDF files of specific artboards for print

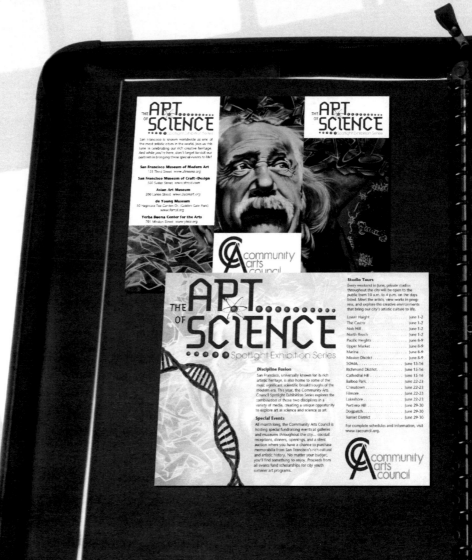

PROJECT MEETING

I really don't have that much input on what the flyer should look like — I am relying on your expert opinion to produce an effective, functional brochure. I have the text, two logos, and several images that I want to include; you can modify those pictures as necessary to better fit the overall project.

A lot of people design folding documents incorrectly. Some people use a six-page layout with each page the size of the final folded job. Other people use two pages, each one divided into three equal "columns." In both cases, all panels on the job are the same width, which is wrong.

Paper has inherent thickness; any panel that folds "in" to the other panels needs to be smaller than the other panels. In the case of a folding brochure, the inside panel needs to be 1/16″ smaller than the other panels.

Different types of folding documents also have different facing- or non-facing-page requirements. For a letterfold, the job needs to be set up on two separate "pages" with guides and margins that mirror each other. One page has the front panel, back panel, and the outside of the folding flap; the other page has the three inside panels.

To complete this project, you will:

- ❑ Define folding guides and margins as required for a folding document
- ❑ Create an Illustrator template file so you can access a common layout again later
- ❑ Place images based on the panel position in the final folded piece
- ❑ Import and format client-supplied copy
- ❑ Manage the flow of copy across multiple text frames
- ❑ Define paragraph and character styles to simplify formatting across multiple text elements
- ❑ Control hyphenation and line spacing
- ❑ Format tabs to improve readability
- ❑ Check spelling in a layout
- ❑ Save artboards as PDF files for commercial print output

When you design entire pages, you need to be aware of several important measurements. **Trim size** is the size of the flat page (for example, a letter-size piece of paper has a trim size of 8.5″ × 11″). When pages are printed on a commercial output device, they are typically combined with other pages (possibly multiple copies of the same page) on a large press sheet. After the ink is dry, the individual pages are cut or trimmed from the press sheets to end up with the final job.

Because commercial printing is a mechanical process, there is inherent variation in the output from one page to another and in the accuracy of any given device (including the cutters that cut apart pages). **Bleed allowance** is the distance objects should extend beyond the trim. Using a bleed ensures that no unwanted white space appears around the edges of the final trimmed output (if there is variation in the cutting process). Most printers require at least a 1/8″ bleed allowance, but you should always check with the output provider who is producing a specific job.

Live area is the space within the trim area where it is safe to place important content. Live area is essentially the opposite of bleed allowance; content within the live area remains untouched during the trimming process.

Folding Document Considerations

There are several common types of folds:

Letterfolds have two folds and three panels to a side. These are often incorrectly called "trifold" because they result in three panels. The panel that folds in should be 1/16″ to 1/8″ narrower than the two outside panels. Ask your service provider how much allowance is required for the paper you're using.

Accordion folds can have as many panels as you prefer. When it has six panels (three on each side), it's often referred to as a **Z-fold** because it looks like the letter Z. Because the panels don't fold into one another, an accordion-fold document has panels of consistent width.

Double-parallel folds are commonly used for eight-panel rack brochures (such as those often found in a hotel or travel agency). Again, the panels on the inside are narrower than the outside panels. This type of fold uses facing pages because the margins need to line up on the front and back sides of the sheet.

Barrel folds (also called **roll folds**) are perhaps the most common fold for 14″ × 8.5″ brochures. The two outside panels are full size, and each successive panel is narrower than the previous one. You can theoretically have as many panels as you want, but at some point the number of fold-in panels will become unwieldy.

Gate folds result in a four-panel document. The paper is folded in half, and then each half is folded in half toward the center, so the two ends of the paper meet at the center fold. The panels that fold in are narrower than the two outside panels. This type of brochure allows two different spreads: the first revealed when you open the outer panels, and the second revealed when you open the inner flaps.

Note:

Some service providers give their clients folding templates to use for building a layout. You should ask your service provider if these templates are available before you waste time and effort reinventing the wheel.

It is important to understand that the mechanics of commercial printing require allowances for cutting and folding.

There are two basic principles to remember when designing documents that fold. First, paper sometimes shifts as it moves through a folding machine (most are accurate to about 0.0125″). Second, paper has thickness. Because of these two principles, any panel that folds into the other panels needs to be smaller than the other panels — typically at least 1/16″ smaller, but greater allowance might be required depending on variables such as paper thickness.

It is also important to understand the relationship between the front and back (or "inside" and "outside") of a folding document. If your job requires different-size panels, the position of panels on the front needs to mirror the position of those same panels on the back.

You should note that these issues have nothing to do with the subjective elements of design. Page geometry is governed by specific mechanical variables in the production process. These principles are rules, not suggestions.

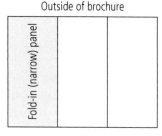

Use Artboards to Create the Panel Layout Structure

On the outside of a letterfold brochure, the left panel is the fold-in panel; it is slightly narrower than the other two panels. On the inside of the brochure, the right panel is the fold-in panel. In this exercise, you create a single Illustrator file with multiple artboards to manage both sides of the brochure.

1. **Download Science_AI21_RF.zip from the Student Files web page.**

2. **Expand the ZIP archive in your WIP folder (Macintosh) or copy the archive contents into your WIP folder (Windows).**

   This results in a folder named **Science**, which contains the files you need for this project. You should also use this folder to save the files you create in this project.

3. **In Illustrator, choose File>New. Choose the Print option at the top of the dialog box, and choose the Letter document preset.**

   Remember, using the Print category of presets automatically applies the CMYK color mode and 300 ppi raster effects.

4. **Define the following settings in the Preset Details section:**

Name:	Rack 4x9
Units:	Inches
Orientation:	Portrait
Width:	4 in
Height:	9 in
Artboards:	6

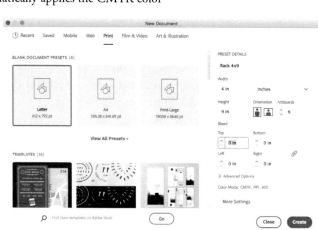

   The brochure has 6 panels, and you are going to create each panel as a separate artboard. You are setting the dimensions of each artboard as the defined flat size of the folded brochure. Once the file is created, you will use the Artboard tool to change the size of the fold-in panels to meet print requirements.

5. Click the More Settings button at the bottom of the Preset Details section.

6. In the resulting More Settings dialog box, make the following choices:

Arrangement: **Grid by Row**

Spacing: **0 in**

Columns: **3**

Bleed: **0 in**
(all four sides)

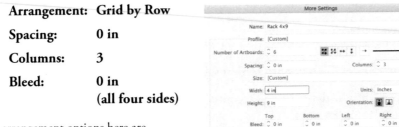

- Grid by Row
- Grid by Column
- Arrange by Row
- Arrange by Column
- Change to Right-to-Left Layout

Make this button active to force all four fields to the same value.

The arrangement options here are the same as those you used when you arranged the two artboards in Project 3: Identity Package.

The Grid options place multiple artboards left-to-right, top-to-bottom, based on the defined number of rows. The Arrange options place all artboards in a single row or column. The Spacing value defines how much space will be created between each artboard.

With the Chain icon active, the bleed fields are constrained. In other words, changing one bleed value changes all four bleed values to the same measurement.

7. Click Create Document to create the file.

8. Open the Artboards panel (Window>Artboards).

Each artboard in the file is listed in the panel, numbered according to its position in the file — left-to-right across the first row and then the second row, as you defined in the New Document dialog box when you created the file.

Note:

Note:

Although you need bleed allowance for each side of this brochure as a whole, you do not need bleeds for each panel. You will use a different method to create bleed guides later.

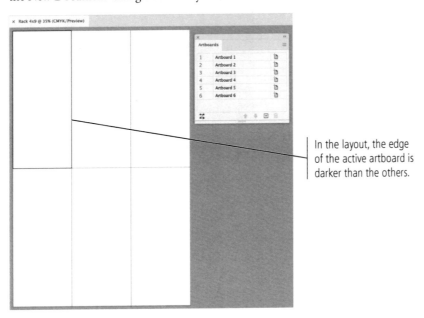

In the layout, the edge of the active artboard is darker than the others.

9. Save the file as **Rack 4x9.ai** in your WIP>Science folder, and then continue to the next exercise.

Control Artboard Size and Position

As you know, you need one panel on each side of this brochure to be narrower than the other panels. When you create a file, all artboards adopt the size that you define in the New Document dialog box. You can use the Artboard tool and panel to control the size and position of individual artboards within the file.

1. **With Rack 4x9.ai open, choose the Artboard tool in the Tools panel.**

2. **With Artboard 1 active, highlight the existing artboard name in the Control panel and type Outside Fold In.**

    Artboard labels do not appear in the file output; they only appear in the document window when the Artboard tool is active. Meaningful artboard names are far more useful than the default numbered names.

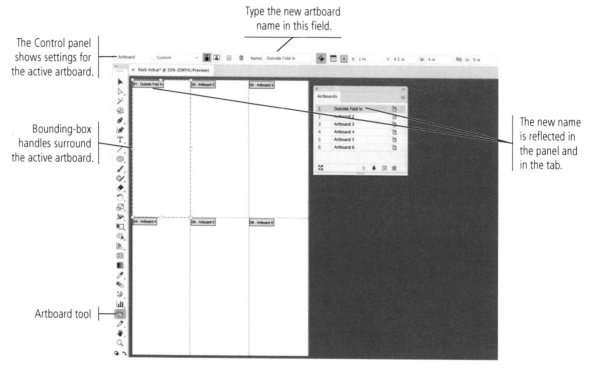

Type the new artboard name in this field.

The Control panel shows settings for the active artboard.

Bounding-box handles surround the active artboard.

The new name is reflected in the panel and in the tab.

Artboard tool

3. **Choose the right-center reference point in the Control panel.**

4. **Make sure the W and H fields are not linked. Click after the existing W (width) value and type -.125, then press Return/Enter.**

If your Control panel does not show the W and H fields, you can use the same fields in the Properties panel, or click the Artboard Options button in the Properties panel and use the Artboard Options dialog box to change the artboard width.

Because you know the fold-in panel needs to be 1/8″ smaller than the other panels, it is easy to simply subtract that amount from the original artboard width. By selecting one of the right reference points, you make sure the two panels remain aligned with no space in between the left and center panels.

Note:

Illustrator recognizes standard mathematical operators in most panel and dialog box fields.
* *Use + to add*
* *Use – to subtract*
* *Use / to divide*
* *Use * to multiply*

Note:

Unfortunately, Illustrator's Properties panel only shows two decimal places for the size of an artboard. After you subtract 0.125″ from the existing 4″ width, the software rounds the new artboard width to 3.88″. However, the software does store the accurate measurement of 3.875″, as you see in the Control panel.

Select the right-center reference point...

...then type **–.125** after the existing value and press Return/Enter.

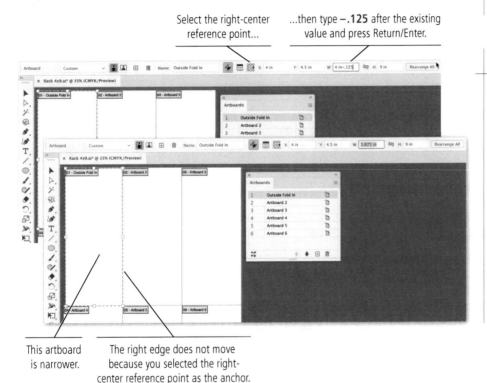

This artboard is narrower.

The right edge does not move because you selected the right-center reference point as the anchor.

5. **With the Artboard tool active, click inside the bounds of Artboard 2 to select that artboard. Use the Control panel to change the artboard name to Outside Center.**

As we stated previously, meaningful names are more useful than generic ones. This name reminds you that this panel needs to contain self-mailer information.

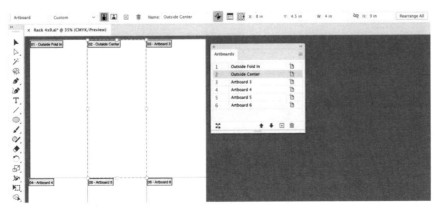

6. **Repeat Step 5 to name the remaining artboards as follows:**

Artboard 3	Outside Right – Front
Artboard 4	Inside Left
Artboard 5	Inside Center
Artboard 6	Inside Fold In

Note:

As with layers, you can double-click the art-board name in the panel to rename an artboard.

7. **With the Inside Fold In artboard active, select one of the left reference points in the Control panel, and then subtract 0.125″ from the current width.**

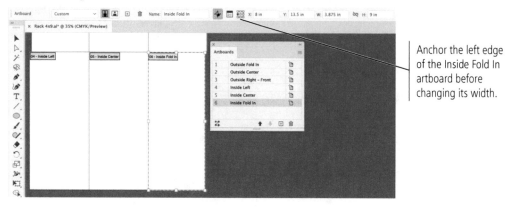

Anchor the left edge of the Inside Fold In artboard before changing its width.

8. **With the Artboard tool active and the Inside Fold In artboard active, press Shift and click the other two inside artboards.**

Pressing Shift allows you to select multiple artboards at one time. You can also press Shift and then drag a marquee to select multiple artboards.

9. **Click inside any of the selected artboard areas, then drag down and slightly right until the Smart Guides show the left edge aligning to the left edge of the Outside Fold In artboard, with at least 1/2-inch of space between the two rows.**

Make sure you click inside the artboard area to move the artboard. If you click too close to the artboard edges, you might accidentally resize the artboard instead.

Note:

You might want to zoom in to better see the smart guides when you drag the artboard.

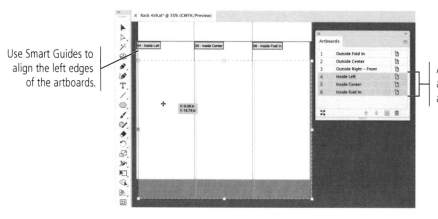

Use Smart Guides to align the left edges of the artboards.

All three selected artboards move at one time.

10. **Using the Artboard tool, click and drag a new artboard that overlaps all three of the outside-panel artboards.**

You are creating two more artboards that identify each "side" of the brochure. When the layout work is complete, you will use these two artboards to output each side of the brochure as a single PDF file.

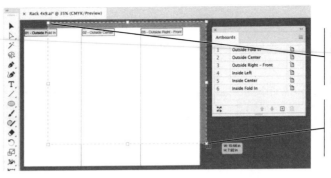

Click outside the existing artboard areas to begin drawing the new artboard.

Click and drag to create a new artboard that overlaps the three "outside" artboards.

11. **Still using the Artboard tool, adjust the corners of the new artboard to match the entire spread formed by the first three artboards.**

If you click the corner of an existing artboard, you will change the shape of that artboard instead of creating a new one. Instead, you have to create the new artboard, and then adjust its size by snapping the handles to the underlying artboards.

12. **In the Control panel, change the new artboard name to Outside.**

The new artboard is automatically added at the bottom of the list of artboards, numbered according to its top-to-bottom position.

Align the new artboard corners with the corners of the outside-panel artboards.

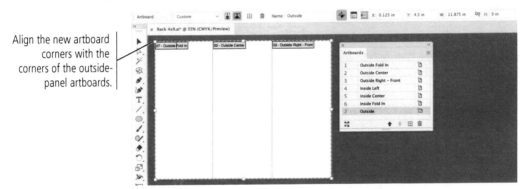

13. **Repeat Steps 10–12 for the Inside artboards and name the new artboard Inside.**

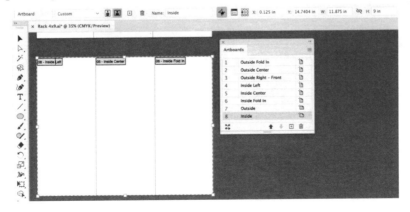

14. **In the Artboards panel, Shift-click to select Artboards 7 and 8 (Outside and Inside).**

15. **Click either selected artboard and drag to the top of the panel.**

    You can rearrange the order of artboards by simply dragging in the panel, or selecting a single artboard in the panel and using the Move Up and Move Down buttons at the bottom of the panel. Moving the artboards up changes the numbers associated with each artboard in the file.

16. **Save the file and continue to the next exercise.**

 ## Create Margin and Bleed Guides

A few more elements are required in your folding layout to make the actual implementation easier. First, you need to define the bleed area for each side of the brochure (not for each panel). Unfortunately, you can't define different bleed settings for individual artboards, so you have to define this area manually. Second, you need to define margin guides for each panel because Illustrator does not include an automatic margin guide option.

1. **With Rack 4x9.ai open, choose the Selection tool and make sure the Outside artboard is active.**

    You can't change the artboard rulers when the Artboard tool is active.

2. **If rulers are not already visible, choose View>Rulers>Show Rulers (Command/Control-R).**

3. **Control/right-click the top ruler. If the bottom option in the menu shows "Change to Artboard Rulers," choose that option.**

    When Global rulers are active, the zero point remains in place relative to the overall file. After you changed the width of the Outside Left panel, the left edge of that panel no longer aligns to the file's original zero point.

    When using Artboard rulers, the zero point automatically defaults to the top-left corner of the active artboard.

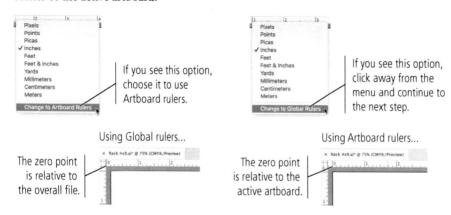

4. **Choose the Rectangle tool in the Tools panel and click the Default Fill and Stroke button.**

Note:

You can also change from Global to Artboard rulers (and vice versa) in the View>Rulers submenu.

5. **Using the Smart Guides to snap to the existing artboard edges, create a rectangle that exactly matches the size of the Outside artboard.**

Remember, the Outside artboard width is the sum of the three individual panel widths: 4 + 4 + 3.875 = 11.875″. This should be the width of the rectangle you create.

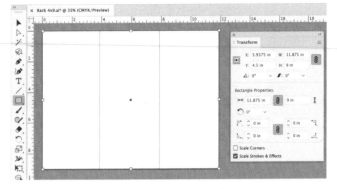

Note:

Remember: The software only shows two decimal places for the artboard dimensions. This Outside artboard is actually 11.875″ wide.

As you drag the rectangle, the cursor feedback shows the two-digit decimal places of 11.88″. Remember, this is a flaw in the software — the same flaw that rounded the artboard width to two decimal places. However, when you release the mouse button, the Transform panel shows the accurate three-digit decimal measurement of 11.875″.

6. **Using the Control or Transform panel, choose the center reference point.**

7. **Break the link between the W and H fields. After the existing W value, type +.25, and then press Return/Enter to apply the change.**

Again, mathematical operators make it easy to add the required 0.125″ bleed to the rectangle. Because you anchored the rectangle at the center reference point, half of the 0.25″ is added to each side of the shape.

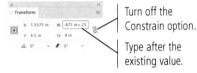

Turn off the Constrain option.

Type after the existing value.

Note:

Remember, if you have a small monitor or Application frame, the X and Y fields in the Control panel might be condensed into a "Transform" hot-text link that opens the Transform panel where you can define the guide positions.

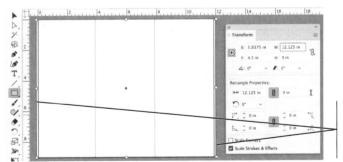

The rectangle is now 1/4″ wider than the artboard, with 1/8″ on either side.

8. **Repeat Step 7 to add 0.25″ to the rectangle height, half on each side.**

You don't need to reselect the reference point because it retains the last-used option.

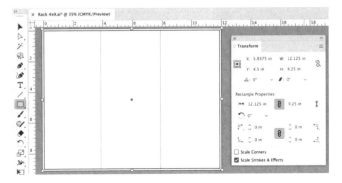

9. **With the resized rectangle selected, choose View>Guides>Make Guides.**

   You can use this command to turn any regular object into a nonprinting guide.

10. **Command/Control-click away from the selected rectangle to deselect it, then release the Command/Control key to return to the Rectangle tool.**

    When converted to a guide, the object loses its defined fill and stroke attributes.

Note:

Press Command/Control-5 to create a guide from any selected object. Add the Shift key to release all guides that have been created from objects.

11. **Repeat Steps 3–8 to add a bleed guide around the Inside artboard.**

12. **Using the Rectangle tool, create a rectangle that aligns with the edge of the Outside Fold In artboard (the top left artboard).**

    Remember, this is the fold-in panel; its width is 3.875″. The rectangle should exactly match the existing panel width.

13. **With the center reference point active in the Transform or Control panel, use mathematical operators to subtract 0.5 from the height and width of the rectangle, then convert it to a guide.**

    This rectangle defines 0.25″ margins on each side of the panel.

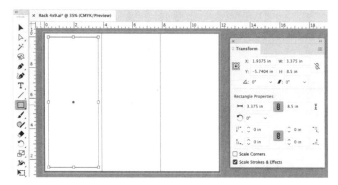

Note:

When you create the rectangle in Step 12, it should properly snap to the artboard edges. However, depending on exactly how far you drag before releasing the mouse button, the middle artboard might become the active one, indicated by the heavier artboard edge. It doesn't affect your work here, but it is something to be aware of in case you need to change an object's X/Y position based on the active artboard.

14. Repeat Steps 10–11 to add 0.25″ margin guides to all panels in the layout.

The margin-guide rectangles on the full-size panels should be 3.5″ wide by 8.5″ high.

On the fold-in panels, the margin-guide rectangles should be 3.375″ wide by 8.5″ high.

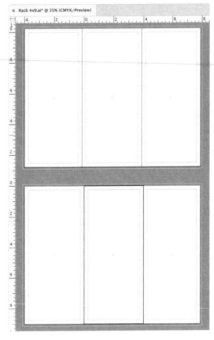

Note:

Choose View>Guides> Release Guides to convert a guide object into a regular object; the object's original fill and stroke (before you converted it to a guide) are restored. This is an all-or-nothing action. You can't release a single custom guide; you have to release all of them at once.

Note:

View>Guides>Clear Guides removes all guides from the page. If you want to remove only a single guide, you can select it (as long as it's unlocked) and press Delete.

15. Choose View>Guides, and make sure guides are locked.

If the submenu shows Lock Guides, choose that option to lock guides in the file. If the submenu shows "Unlock Guides," guides are already locked; you can click away from the menu to dismiss it.

16. Save the file and continue to the next exercise.

Create Folding Marks

The final step in establishing your folding grid is marking the location of folds. Once you have done so, you should then save your work as a template because this is a common project size and you can reuse the template whenever you need to build a new folding rack brochure.

1. With Rack 4x9.ai open, make the Outside Fold In artboard active.

You can click the artboard name in the Artboard panel, or simply click inside the target artboard with either Selection tool.

2. Choose the Line Segment tool in the Tools panel.

3. Create a vertical line that is 0.5″ high anywhere in the pasteboard area above the Outside artboard.

Use Smart Guides to create the line exactly vertical, or simply press Shift while you drag up or down with the Line Segment tool. It doesn't matter exactly where you create the line, because you will place it numerically in the next few steps.

4. **Using the Transform, Properties, or Control panel, select the top-center reference point. Change the line's X position to 3.875 in and Y position to -0.5 in.**

The line should appear to blend in with the black line that marks the artboard edges.

Because Artboard rulers are active, the zero point relates to the active artboard.

5. **With the line still selected, open the Stroke panel and change the stroke weight of the active line segment to 0.5 pt.**

6. **If you only see the Weight field in the Stroke panel, open the panel Options menu and choose Show Options.**

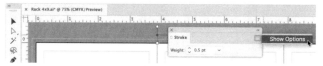

7. **In the middle of the Stroke panel, check the Dashed Line option. Type 3 in the first Dash field, press Tab, and type 3 in the first Gap field.**

The dash and gap fields define the specific appearance of dashed lines.

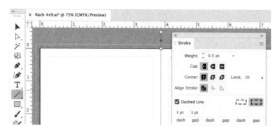

8. **Double-click the Selection tool to open the Move dialog box.**

This opens the Move dialog box, which is an easy way to move or clone the selected object(s) by exact measurements.

9. **Change the Horizontal field to 4, the Vertical field to 0, and click Copy.**

   You know the center panel is 4″ wide, so copying the line 4″ to the right places the copy exactly over the panel edge. The software automatically calculates the angle of 0° because you are moving the object exactly right, horizontally.

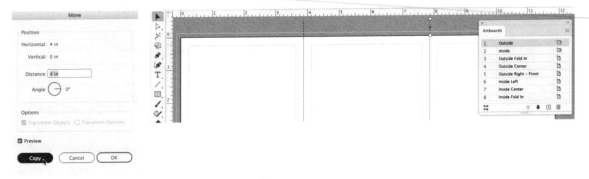

10. **Select both lines above the outside spread, then double-click the Selection tool. Change the Position Horizontal field to 0, the Vertical field to 9.5, and click Copy.**

    You are moving the copy by 9.5″ because the marks are 0.5″ and the panels are 9″ high. The total movement places the copied lines immediately below the bottom of the Outside artboard. The software automatically calculates the angle of −90° because you are moving the object exactly down, vertically.

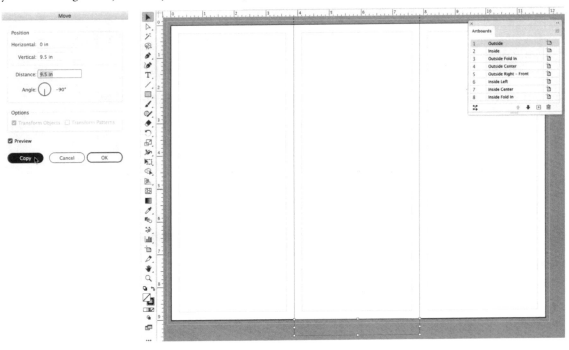

11. **With the Selection tool active, choose Select>All to select all four folding marks. Press Option/Alt, then click and drag any of the selected marks to clone all four in the same position relative to one another.**

    Although the fold marks will occupy a different X position on the Inside artboard, the center panels are the same width, so the relative position of the marks is the same on both "pages" of the brochure. Rather than recreating the marks, you are cloning the existing ones, which you will precisely place in the next few steps.

12. **In the Artboards panel, activate the Inside artboard.**

Because you are using Artboard rulers, measurements for the selected objects are now relative to the Inside Center artboard.

13. **Choose the top-left reference point, then change the selection's position to X: 4 in, Y: –0.5 in.**

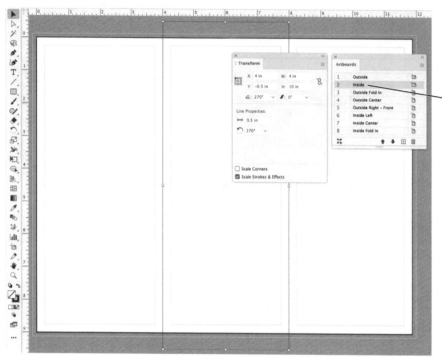

When Artboard rulers are active, measurements relate to the active artboard.

14. **In the Layers panel, rename the active layer Guides and Marks, then lock the layer.**

15. **Choose File>Save As Template. Navigate to your WIP>Science folder as the target location, and click Save.**

Since you have taken the time to properly set up these folding guides, you are saving your work as a template so you can access these same folds whenever you need them.

When you use the Save As Template command, the Save As dialog box defaults to the application's default "Templates" folder. Illustrator Template (ait) is automatically selected in the Format/Save As Type menu, and the file extension is changed to ".ait".

16. **Close the file and continue to the next stage of the project.**

Most page-layout jobs incorporate a number of different elements, including images and graphics that exist in external files. Although Illustrator does not include the sophisticated link-management options of a dedicated layout application, such as Adobe InDesign, you can place and work with a variety of common image formats. The key to creating a successful job is understanding a job's output requirements so that you use only the types of graphics that are suitable for the project you are building.

Place Layout Images

Both sides of the brochure require images that were already created — some in Illustrator and some in Photoshop. When you place external images into a file, you need to understand the concept of file linking, so you can create a complete file with all of the information necessary for high-quality, commercial print output.

1. Choose File>Open. Navigate to Rack 4x9.ait in your WIP>Science folder and click Open.

You could also use the File>New From Template menu command. However, that option defaults to the application's built-in Templates folder, so you would have to navigate to your WIP>Science folder to find your template file.

Make sure you choose the template file and not the regular Illustrator file.

When you open a template file, you are actually opening a copy of the template with the name "Untitled." This prevents you from accidentally overwriting the original template.

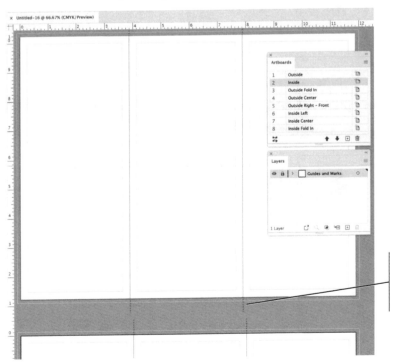

The file created from the template includes all elements in the template.

Note:

You can overwrite a template by manu-ally typing the same file name as the original template when you save the file. You will be asked to confirm that you're sure you want to replace the existing file.

2. **Add a new layer named** Graphics **above the existing Guides and Marks layer.**

3. **With the Graphics layer selected, choose File>Place.**

4. **Click** aos-logo.ai **in the WIP>Science folder to select that file.**

5. **Press Command/Control, then click** cac-logo.ai **and** einstein.jpg **to add those files to the active selection.**

   You can press Shift to select multiple consecutive files in the Place dialog box, or press Command/Control to select non-consecutive files.

Note:

If more than one file is selected in the Place dialog box, you cannot choose the Template option.

6. **At the bottom of the dialog box, check the Link and Show Import Options, then click Place.**

   Macintosh users: Remember, you might have to click the Options button to reveal the check boxes.

   When the Link option is checked, the placed graphic will be a link to the original file. When Show Import Options is checked, placement options will appear for native Illustrator files.

Press Command/Control to select multiple, non-consecutive files in the dialog box.

7. **In the resulting Place PDF dialog box, choose Art in the Crop To menu and click OK.**

   Because you checked the Show Import Options box in Step 6, the Place PDF dialog box shows options related to the first selected Illustrator file.

Note:

No further import options are available for placed JPEG or TIFF files.

8. **Review the Place PDF dialog box for the second file, then click OK again.**

   The second dialog box shows the options for the second selected Illustrator file (cac-logo.ai); the dialog box defaults to the last-used option.

   After clicking OK, all three of the selected files from the Place dialog box are loaded into the Place cursor at one time. The cursor icon shows a preview of which file will be placed if you click, as well as the total the number of loaded files (e.g., "1/3").

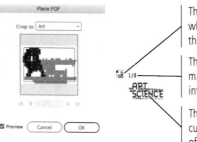

This number shows which file is active in the cursor.

This number shows how many files are loaded into the Place cursor.

The loaded Place cursor shows a preview of the active file.

9. **With the first image in the loaded Place cursor, click and drag to place that file at the top of the Outside Fold In artboard, inside the margin guides of the panel (as shown in the following image).**

If you click and drag with the loaded Place cursor, you can define the area in which the loaded file is placed. This area retains the original aspect ratio of the file being placed.

Use Smart Guides to begin the placement marquee at the top-left guide corner and end the marquee at the right margin guide on the Outside Fold In artboard.

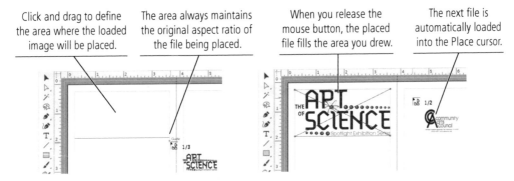

Click and drag to define the area where the loaded image will be placed.

The area always maintains the original aspect ratio of the file being placed.

When you release the mouse button, the placed file fills the area you drew.

The next file is automatically loaded into the Place cursor.

10. **With the second image loaded in the Place cursor, click and drag to place the second image within the margin guides on the Outside Center artboard.**

11. **Press Command/Control to temporarily access the Selection tool, then drag the placed image to align with the bottom and left margin guides.**

When you release the Command/Control key, you return to the loaded Place cursor. The third loaded file automatically becomes active in the cursor after you place the second file.

Press Command/Control to access the Selection tool and reposition the placed image.

12. **With the third image loaded in the Place cursor, click at the top-left corner of the bleed guide for the Outside artboard.**

Clicking without dragging places the loaded image at 100% of its original size. The top-left corner of the image is placed at the location you click.

13. Make the Inside artboard active in the document window, then choose File>Place.

14. Press Command/Control, then click to select **aos-logo.ai**, **cac-logo.ai**, **dna.ai**, and **einstein-light.jpg**.

With the Link option still checked, uncheck the Show Import Options box and then click Place.

The Link and Show Import Options boxes remember the last-used value. If you do not show import options, the last-used Crop To option will be applied to any selected Illustrator files.

15. With four images loaded in the Place cursor, press the Right Arrow key until the cursor shows the fourth image (4/4) as the active one.

When more than one image is loaded in the cursor, the images are loaded in the order in which they appear in the containing folder. You can use the arrow keys to make a different loaded image the active one.

Note:

You can press the ESC key to remove the active loaded image from the Place cursor.

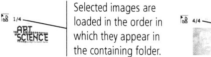

Selected images are loaded in the order in which they appear in the containing folder.

Use the arrow keys to make a different image active in the loaded Place cursor.

16. Click the top-left bleed guide of the Inside artboard to place the active loaded image.

After you place the active image, the next image is active in the Place cursor. Because the one you just placed was image 4, image 1 is the next one to become active.

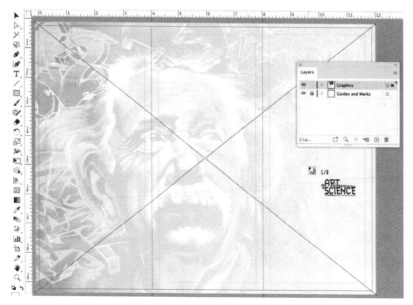

17. **Using the click-drag method, place the loaded image (the aos-logo file) across the top of the Inside Left and Inside Center artboards.**

    Use the panel margin guides to define the left and right edges of the image.

18. **Using the click-drag method, place the loaded image (the cac-logo file) at the bottom of the Inside Right artboard.**

19. **Click to place the final loaded image at 100%. Drag it until it snaps to the bottom bleed guide and the right margin guide of the Inside Left artboard.**

20. **Save the file as a native Illustrator file named aos-brochure.ai in your WIP>Science folder, and then continue to the next exercise.**

Manage Linked and Embedded Files

As you have seen, you have the option to place a link to an external file, or embed the external file directly into your Illustrator file. There are advantages and disadvantages to each method, so you should consider what you need to accomplish before you choose.

When you link to an external file, that file needs to be available when the Illustrator file is output. If the linked file is moved or changed after being placed into the Illustrator file, you have to locate or update the linked file before output. Missing and modified images are both identified in the Links panel.

If you embed the external file into the Illustrator file, the physical file data becomes part of the file. This eliminates the potential problem of missing required files, but it can add significantly to the size of your Illustrator file.

This icon means a linked file has been modified since being placed.

This icon means a file has been embedded into the Illustrator file.

This icon means a linked file is missing; it has been moved or deleted since being placed.

Linked files make it easier to update multiple placed instances of the same file. By editing the original file, all placed and linked instances will reflect the changes when the links are up to date. If you embed specific placed instances, they are no longer linked to the original file data; any changes in the original file are not reflected in the placed and embedded instances. This means you can independently edit the embedded instances without affecting other linked instances.

1. **With `aos-brochure.ai` open, open the Layers panel (if necessary) and expand the Graphics layer.**

   As you can see, the Graphics layer includes a number of <Linked File> items. Although each linked file appears as a separate sublayer in the panel, the way each is listed depends on the type of file that you place:

   - TIFF and native Photoshop (PSD) files are listed by file name.
   - Native Illustrator (AI), PDF, and JPEG files are listed as <Linked File> items.

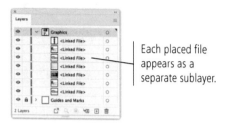

   Each placed file appears as a separate sublayer.

2. **Open the Links panel (Window>Links). If the bottom half of the panel is not visible, click the Right-Arrow icon to show the information section of the panel.**

   Every file that has been placed with the Link option is listed in this panel. You can use the panel to navigate to selected images.

   - **Relink from CC Libraries** allows you to create a dynamic link to a graphic that is stored in one of your CC libraries.
   - **Relink** opens a navigation dialog box, which you can use to replace the selected file image with a different one. If a linked file is missing, you can also use this button to locate the missing file.
   - **Go To Link** selects the linked file in the layout, and changes the document view to center the selected object in the document window.
   - **Update Link** updates a modified link to show the most current version of the linked file.
   - **Edit Original** opens the linked file in its native application (for example, a placed AI file opens in Illustrator and a placed PSD file opens in Photoshop).

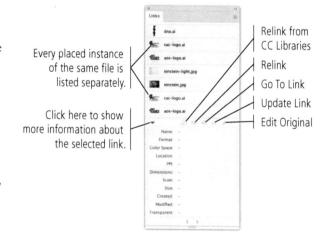

   Every placed instance of the same file is listed separately.

   Click here to show more information about the selected link.

   Relink from CC Libraries
   Relink
   Go To Link
   Update Link
   Edit Original

3. **Select einstein.jpg in the Links panel list and click the Go To Link button in the middle of the panel.**

The einstein.jpg file is a raster image, which means it has a defined resolution. If you resize a raster image, the number of pixels per inch is stretched or reduced to fit into the new object dimensions; the result of factoring physical size into an image's resolution is called **effective resolution**.

The Control panel shows a number of useful data points for placed raster images, including the file name, color model, and resolution. The same information is also available in the bottom half of the Links panel.

The Control panel shows the name, color mode, and resolution of the linked file.

The file you selected in the Links panel is selected and centered in the workspace.

Linked files are identified with crossed diagonal (nonprinting) lines.

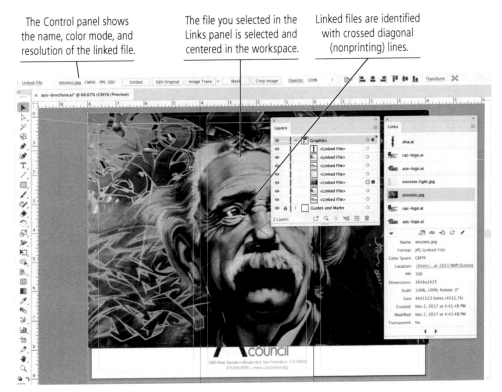

4. **Navigate to the Inside artboard. Using the Selection tool, select the CAC logo on the Inside Fold In artboard.**

As you can see in the Links panel, there are several placed instances of the same file. The panel, however, does not identify the location of each link. When you select a placed file in the layout, it is automatically selected in the Links panel as well.

You want to remove the address information from this instance, but not from the instance that is placed on the Outside artboard.

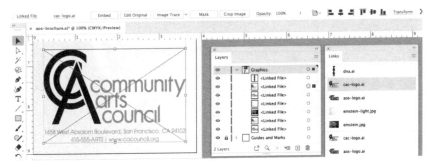

5. In the Control panel, click the Embed button.

Rather than affecting all instances, you can embed this instance of the placed Illustrator file directly into the layout. Because the placed file is an Illustrator file, the Illustrator objects become a native part of the layout file.

When you embed a previously linked Illustrator file, it is converted to a group of artwork objects. The Layers panel now shows the group, which you can expand to view the individual objects that make up the embedded artwork.

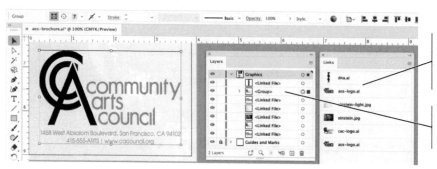

After being embedded, one instance of the Illustrator file is no longer listed in the Links panel.

The embedded artwork is automatically converted to a group.

6. In the Layers panel, click the arrow icon to the left of the new <Group> sublayer, then click the arrow icon to the left of the <Clip Group> sublayer to expand it.

Any embedded Illustrator file results in a somewhat messy stack. When you expand the group, you first see a secondary sublayer called <Clip Group>. That group contains a <Clipping Path> object and another <Clip Group> object. If you expanded the secondary Clip Group, you would see another <Clipping Path> object at the top of the stack of objects that make up the logo artwork.

Note:

*A **clipping path** defines the visible area of underlying objects in the clip group; areas outside the clipping path are hidden.*

*A **clip group** is a group comprising the clipping path object and the objects being clipped.*

7. Using the Selection tool, double-click the group on the artboard to enter into Isolation mode for the group.

8. Using the Direct Selection tool, draw a selection marquee around the address information. Drag from the top-left to the bottom-right, past the bottom-right corner of the artboard.

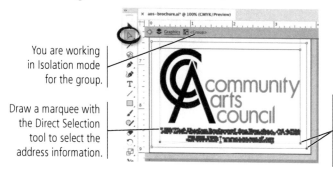

You are working in Isolation mode for the group.

Draw a marquee with the Direct Selection tool to select the address information.

Dragging past the artboard corner will select part of all clipping path objects that were created when this file was placed.

9. **Press Delete/Backspace to remove the selected objects.**

Because your selection included the bottom-right corner of the clipping-path shapes, you have also deleted those points. The remaining parts of the clipping-path shapes, however, still apply to the underlying objects in the Clip Groups, which is why half of the group appears to be missing.

The clipping paths that are created by embedding other Illustrator files are almost always unnecessary, but you should be aware of their existence.

Deleting the selected points leaves only the unselected top paths of the previous selection.

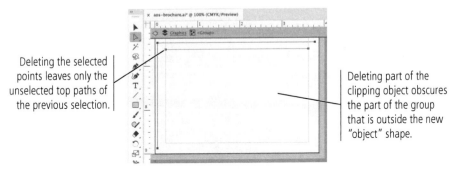

Deleting part of the clipping object obscures the part of the group that is outside the new "object" shape.

10. **Press Delete to remove the remaining portion of the clipping-path objects.**

After you deleted the selected points in Step 9, the remaining points of the clipping-path shape are automatically selected. Pressing Delete in this step removes those points and effectively removes the clipping path.

11. **In the Edit bar (at the top of the document window), click the arrow button two times to exit Isolation mode.**

You can also press the ESC key, or double-click away from the artwork, to exit Isolation mode.

12. **Using the Selection tool, drag the logo down to snap to the bottom margin guide on the Inside Fold In panel.**

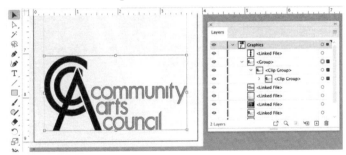

13. **Save the file and continue to the next exercise.**

Warp a Graphic Object

Puppet Warp provides a way to transform and distort specific areas of a layer without affecting other areas of the same layer. It is called "puppet" warp because it's based on the concept of pinning certain areas in place, and then bending other areas around those pin locations — mimicking the way a puppet's joints pivot. In this exercise, you will use puppet warping to bend the DNA artwork to fill more of the space at the bottom of the inside left panel of the brochure.

1. **With `aos-brochure.ai` open, make the Selection tool active.**

2. **Click to select the DNA artwork that is placed on the inside left panel, then click the Embed button in the Control panel.**

The Puppet Warp tool does not work with linked files. Any object you want to warp in Illustrator must be either embedded or created in the actual Illustrator file.

Illustrator's puppet warp does not work on raster-based objects, like placed images. Since the DNA artwork is a vector graphic also created in Illustrator, you can use the Puppet Warp to bend the graphic after it is embedded.

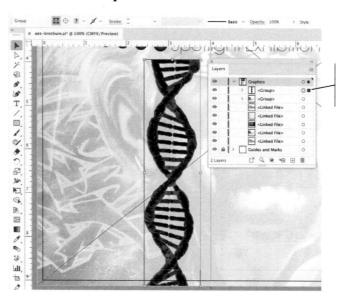

After embedding, the placed graphic is a group of Illustrator objects.

3. **In the Layers panel, expand the resulting group and both nested Clip Groups.**

As you saw in the previous exercise, embedding a native Illustrator file results in two clip group objects that contain all of the pieces of the embedded graphic. To avoid problems in the puppet warping process, you should release both of these clip groups before continuing.

4. **Click the Selected item icon for the second (nested) Clip Group to select that group.**

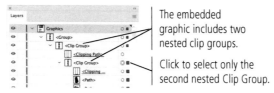

The embedded graphic includes two nested clip groups.

Click to select only the second nested Clip Group.

5. **With the Clip Group selected, choose Object>Clipping Mask>Release.**

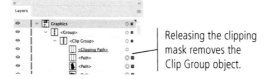

Releasing the clipping mask removes the Clip Group object.

6. **Repeat Steps 4–5 to release the remaining Clip Group.**

Select the remaining Clip Group and release it.

7. **Click the Selected Item icon for the top Path object, then Shift-click the Selected Item icon for the second Path object to add it to the selection.**

These two paths defined the clipped areas in the two clip groups you just released. The paths are unnecessary after releasing the clipping masks; they can now be deleted.

8. **Press the Delete/Backspace key to remove the two selected objects from the artboard.**

Remember, these icons select objects on the artboard, so you delete them as you would any other object from the layout. If you try to use the panel's Delete button you will remove the entire layer and all objects on that layer instead of only the two selected paths.

Select and delete the top two Path objects.

9. **Using the Selection tool, click to select the DNA graphic on the artboard.**

10. **Choose the Puppet Warp tool (nested under the Free Transform tool).**

When you select the Puppet Warp tool, the software scans the selected object and automatically places pins in key locations. A mesh appears over the entire object; this represents the joints in the shape that can bend when you warp it.

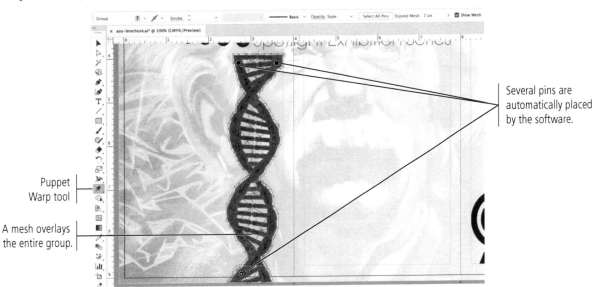

Several pins are automatically placed by the software.

Puppet Warp tool

A mesh overlays the entire group.

11. **With the mesh group selected, click the Select All Pins button in the Control panel.**

    Important note: There is a bug in the software that might cause the pins to disappear after a brief pause. You can still select the pins even when they are not visible.

12. **If you don't see the pins in the mesh, move the mouse cursor over the selected object to reveal the selected pins.**

13. **Press the Delete/Backspace key to delete the selected pins.**

    The software automatically placed these pins based on its analysis of the graphic, but automatic options do not always meet your specific goals. In this case, it is better to remove the automatic pins, and then place your own.

14. **With the Puppet Warp tool active, click the bottom-left corner of the DNA graphic group.**

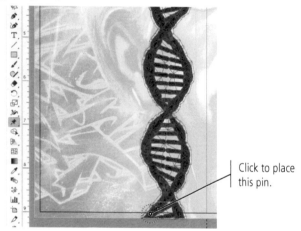

Click to place this pin.

> **Note:**
>
> *You can toggle the mesh visibility using the Show Mesh checkbox in the Control or Properties panel.*

15. **Click to place a second pin at the bottom-right corner of the object.**

    These two pins anchor the bottom edge in place so that they do not move away from the bleed guide when you warp the upper portion of the graphic.

16. **Click near the top-left corner of the graphic to place a third point.**

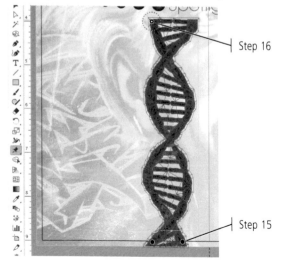

Step 16

Step 15

17. Click the third point and drag left to the left bleed guide.

You can't click and drag to create a pin and move it at the same time. You must first place the pin, then click the existing pin and drag to move it.

As you drag a pin, you can see a slight bend occur near the bottom of the graphic. The two bottom pins remain anchored in place, so the bend at this point is very slight.

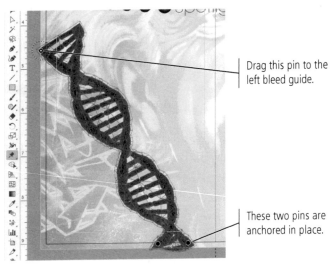

Drag this pin to the left bleed guide.

These two pins are anchored in place.

Note:

The mesh disappears while you are dragging the pin.

18. Move the cursor away from the third point until a dotted circle appears around the pin.

19. Click and drag counterclockwise to rotate the mesh and the underlying graphic. Release the mouse button when the entire top edge of the group extends beyond the left bleed guide.

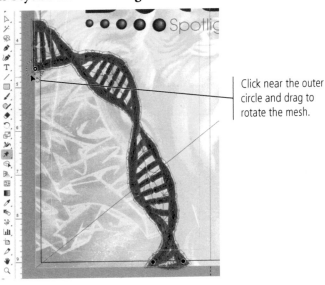

Click near the outer circle and drag to rotate the mesh.

20. Click to select the first pin, then press Shift and click the second point to select both bottom pins.

21. Click the right selected pin and drag right until the second point aligns to the right panel edge.

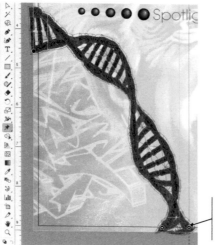

Shift-click to select both bottom points, then drag them right.

22. Save the file and continue to the next exercise.

 ## Crop Images in Illustrator

The outside of the brochure you are building requires breaking the Einstein painting image into three separate pieces. Although you can't cut a raster image apart in Illustrator, you can use image cropping, along with duplication, to accomplish the same goal.

1. With **aos-brochure.ai** open, make the Outside artboard visible in the document window.

2. Choose the Einstein image with the Selection tool, then click the Embed button in the Control panel.

Illustrator's image-cropping functionality requires the image data to be embedded in the Illustrator file. If you try to crop a linked image, you are warned that the linked file must be embedded and the cropping will not affect the original placed file.

3. In the Layers panel, expand the Graphics layer (if necessary).

4. With the embedded image selected, choose Object>Arrange>Bring To Front.

Commands in this submenu affect the stacking order of selected objects:

- **Bring to Front** moves selected objects to the top of the stacking order, above all other objects on the same layer.

- **Bring Forward** moves selected objects up one place in the stacking order.

- **Send Backward** moves selected objects down one place in the stacking order.

- **Send to Back** moves selected objects to the bottom of the stacking order, below all other objects on the same layer.

When you paste objects — as you will do in the next step — the pasted objects are placed at the top of the layer stack. Although not strictly necessary, this step moves the original embedded image to the top of the stack on the Graphics layer, so that all three copies will appear in sequential order in the Layers panel.

5. **With the embedded image still selected, choose Edit>Copy, and then immediately choose Edit>Paste In Place two times.**

This step results in three copies of the same image in the exact same position, which you need to show different areas of the image on each of the three outside panels. The Layers panel shows each instance of the image as a separate sublayer.

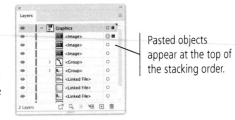

Pasted objects appear at the top of the stacking order.

6. **In the Layers panel, rename the three instances of the image as follows:**

Einstein Left

Einstein Middle

Einstein Right

After embedding and duplicating the image, all three sublayers have the name <image>, which can become confusing. Renaming the individual sublayers makes it easier to understand which image is in which place.

7. **In the Layers panel, click the Eye icon for the Einstein Middle and Einstein Right sublayers to hide them.**

8. **Click to select the still-visible image on the artboard, then drag it down until it snaps to the bottom bleed guide.**

9. **With the image selected, click the Crop Image button in the Control panel.**

In cropping mode, the image's bounding-box handles turn into crop handles, which you can drag to define the portion of the image you want to keep.

Crop handles replace the regular bounding-box handles.

10. **Click the top-right crop handle on the image, then drag down and left until cursor feedback shows the image dimensions to 4″ wide and 3.1″ high.**

As you drag the crop handles, areas outside the bounding box are screened back. The area inside the bounding box remains at full strength to identify the area that will be maintained when you finalize the crop.

Note:

You can press the ESC key to exit the cropping process without cropping the image.

Dragging the handles changes the crop area.

Areas outside the crop are screened back.

11. **Press Return/Enter to finalize the crop.**

After cropping, pixels outside the crop area are permanently removed from the file. You can use the Undo command to reverse the process, but you cannot change the visible portion of the image at a later time after you finalize the crop.

Before image cropping was enabled in Illustrator, you had to use a clipping mask to hide areas you wanted to remove. Although a clipping mask allows you to change the visible portion of the image at a later date, the entire embedded file data is still included in the layout, which can significantly increase processing time.

After cropping, the object in the Layers panel is renamed <Image> because the cropping process essentially creates a new image.

12. **Rename the <Image> object Einstein Left.**

13. **In the Layers panel, hide the Einstein Left sublayer and show the Einstein Middle sublayer.**

14. **Select the visible image on the artboard and click the Crop Image button in the Control panel.**

15. Drag the bottom-center crop handle up until the image height is 6.5″. Drag the left-center crop handle to the left edge of the center artboard, and drag the right-center crop handle to the right edge of the center artboard.

16. Press Return/Enter to finalize the crop, then rename the resulting <Image> object Einstein Middle.

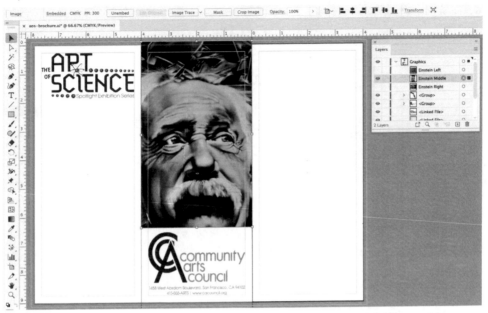

17. In the Layers panel, hide the Einstein Middle sublayer and show the Einstein Right sublayer.

18. Drag the visible image down until it snaps to the bottom bleed guide, then crop it to leave only the area on the right panel with a height of 7.15″.

19. Press Return/Enter to finalize the crop, then rename the resulting <Image> object Einstein Right.

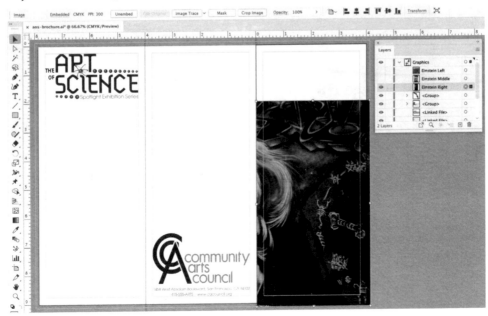

20. **Show all three Einstein sublayers.**

21. **Clone the "Art of Science" logo from the left panel and place the clone into the empty space at the top of the right panel.**

22. **Save the file and continue to the next stage of the project.**

Unembedding Images

When an embedded image is selected the Control panel offers an Unembed button. Clicking that button opens a dialog box, where you can define a file name and choose the location where you want to save the resulting file.

JPEG and TIFF files are automatically converted to native Photoshop files (using the .PSD extension).

After you unembed an image, the placed instance in the layout becomes a linked instance to the unembedded file.

Click Unembed to convert the embedded image to a separate Photoshop image file.

After unembedding, the placed instance is linked to the resulting PSD file.

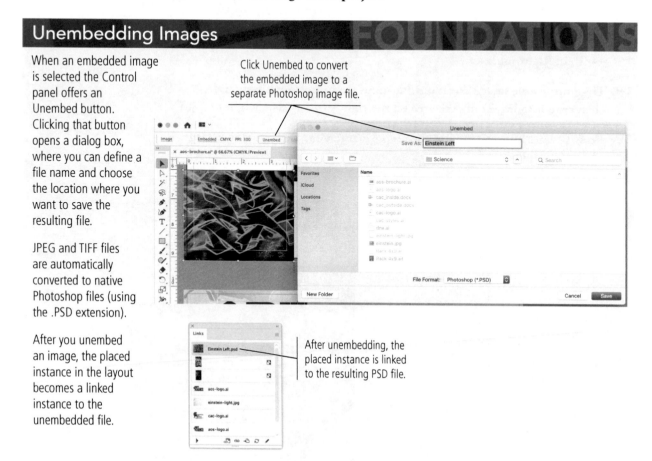

Depending on how much text you have to work with, you might place all the layout text in a single frame; you might cut and paste different pieces of a single story into individual text frames; or you might thread text across multiple frames — maintaining the text as a single story, but allowing flexibility in frame size and position. In many cases — including this project — you will use more than one of these methods within a single file.

 Import Text for the Inside Panels

Illustrator provides a number of tools and options for formatting text, from choosing a font, to automatically formatting paragraphs with styles. The first step in this project, however, requires importing the client-supplied text into the brochure layout.

1. **With aos-brochure.ai open, make the Inside artboard visible.**

2. **Collapse and lock the Graphics layer, then create a new layer named Text at the top of the layer stack.**

3. **With the Text layer active, choose File>Place. Navigate to cac_inside.docx in the WIP>Science folder and click Place.**

   When you import a Microsoft Word file into Illustrator, the application asks how you want to handle formatting in the file. In addition to the basic text, you can also choose to include special options such as a table of contents, footnotes, and an index.

4. **In the Microsoft Word Options dialog box, make sure the Remove Text Formatting option is not checked and click OK.**

   This dialog box appears even when the Show Import Options box is not checked in the Place dialog box.

   If the Remove Text Formatting option is checked, the imported copy will be formatted with the Illustrator default type settings only. Although you will typically reformat most imported text, it's a good idea to import text with formatting so you can review the editorial priority of the copy (i.e., where titles and headings are intended to appear).

5. **If you see a missing font warning, click OK.**

   For the text to display properly with the formatting that was applied in the Word file, Illustrator needs access to the same fonts that were used in the Word file. If you don't have the same fonts available on your system, you might see a Font Problems dialog box listing the missing fonts. In most cases, you can simply dismiss it because you will replace the original fonts with ones more suited to professional graphic design.

Note:

The Font Problems dialog box frequently appears when you import a Microsoft Word file.

6. **With the Word file loaded in the Place cursor, move the cursor over the left margin guide on the center panel, below the placed logo.**

The Smart Guides show the word "intersect" when the cursor is over the left margin guide.

The gray line on the vertical ruler shows the Y position of the cursor.

Smart Guides show when the cursor is over the margin guide.

The gray line on the ruler shows the position of the cursor.

The cursor shows that a text file is loaded into the Place cursor.

7. **When the cursor is at the 4.125″ mark, click and drag to create a type area that fills the space in the margin guides below the logo.**

When a text file is loaded into the Place cursor, clicking and dragging creates an area-type object (also simply called a type area and commonly referred to as a text frame) with the text in the file you selected to import.

The small red symbol at the bottom of the area-type object is called the **overset text icon**; this indicates that the story includes more text than will fit in the available space.

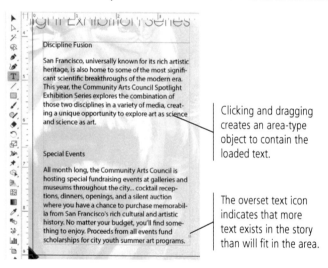

Clicking and dragging creates an area-type object to contain the loaded text.

The overset text icon indicates that more text exists in the story than will fit in the area.

8. **Save the file and continue to the next exercise.**

Thread Multiple Type Areas

When a story includes more text than the current type area can accommodate, you have to decide how to solve the problem. In some cases, when only one or two words are overset, minor changes in formatting will create the additional space you need. If you can edit the text (although graphic designers are typically not permitted to do so), changing a word or two might also help.

When you can't edit the client-supplied text and you have a considerable amount of overset text (as in this project), the only solution is to add more space for the leftover text. Here again, you have two alternatives: cut some of the text and paste it into another type area, or link the existing area to one or more additional type areas (called **threading**) so the story can flow through multiple frames.

1. **With aos-brochure.ai open, choose the Selection tool and click to select the area-type object you created in the previous exercise.**

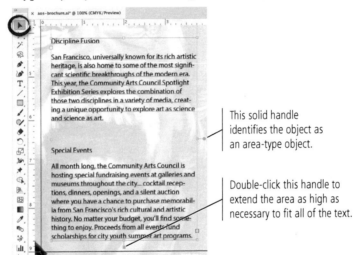

This solid handle identifies the object as an area-type object.

Double-click this handle to extend the area as high as necessary to fit all of the text.

Note:

Click and drag with the Type tool to create a new, empty area-type object.

2. **Click the Overset Text icon once with the Selection tool.**

The Overset Text icon appears in a small rectangle, which is the **out port** of the selected text frame. By clicking the out port of an area (regardless of whether overset text exists), you can direct the flow of text into another type area.

When you click an out port with an Overset Text icon, the cursor changes to the loaded text cursor.

Loaded text cursor

Clicking the out port loads the rest of the story into the cursor.

You can use that cursor to click any other text frame, or click and drag to create a new frame in the same thread.

3. Click the top-left margin guide on the right panel to create another area-type object.

The new frame automatically fills with more of the text from the first frame, which had been loaded into the cursor.

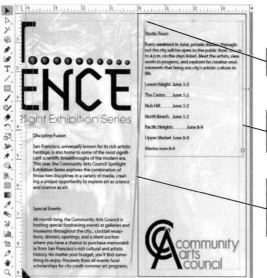

Click here with the loaded text cursor.

The new area is the same size as the first frame in the story.

The thread path is identified by a line connecting the out port of one frame to the in port of the next frame.

4. Using the Selection tool, click the bottom-right corner of the area-type object and drag to the bottom-right margin guide on the right panel.

Dragging a handle on an area-type object resizes the object; text inside the area reflows to match the area's new dimensions. Until you release the mouse button, the text appears in the same color as the layer on which the text object is placed.

Don't worry about the text overlapping the logo; you will fix that problem later when you format the text.

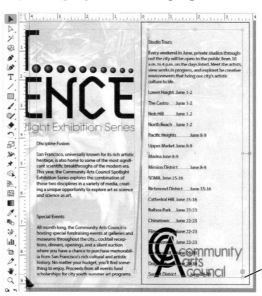

Use the Selection tool to resize the type area.

Note:

You can use the out ports to link empty frames; when you eventually place text into the frame, it automatically flows from one to another in the chain.

5. Save the file and continue to the next exercise.

Work with Hidden Characters

Your layout now includes a story that threads across two separate text frames. The only obvious formatting is extra space between paragraphs. You can identify the intended headings (the short paragraphs), but the layout lacks the polish of professional design.

1. With aos-brochure.ai open, choose Type>Show Hidden Characters.

Hidden characters identify spaces, paragraph returns, and other non-printing characters. It can be helpful to view these hidden characters, especially when you are working with long blocks of text.

When you work with client-supplied text, you will frequently find each paragraph separated by two (or more) paragraph returns. Because Illustrator's typographic controls allow you to easily change the spacing of paragraphs, these double paragraph returns are unnecessary and should be deleted.

Unfortunately, Illustrator's Find and Replace function is very limited. Unlike InDesign, you can't use the utility to search for a paragraph return character — you have to manually delete the extra paragraph returns.

This is the hidden character for a paragraph return.

Using the Find and Replace Dialog Box

Finding and replacing text is a function common to many applications. Illustrator's Find and Replace utility (Edit>Find and Replace) is fairly straightforward, offering the ability to search for and change text in a layout, including a limited number of special characters and options. The menus associated with the Find and Replace With fields list the special characters that can be identified and replaced.

The check boxes below the Replace With field are toggles for specific types of searches:

- When **Match Case** is active, a search only finds text with the same capitalization as the text in the Find field. For example, a search for "Illustrator" does not identify instances of "illustrator" or "ILLUSTRATOR."

- When **Find Whole Word** is active, a search only finds instances where the search text is not part of another word. For example, a search for "old" as a whole word does not include the words "gold" or "embolden."

- When **Search Backwards** is selected, Illustrator searches from the insertion point to the beginning of the story.

- When **Check Hidden Layers** is active, the search includes text frames on layers that are not visible. In this case, the hidden layer remains visible until you close the Find and Replace dialog box.

- When **Check Locked Layers** is active, the search locates text on locked layers.

2. **Using the Type tool, click to place the insertion point in the first empty paragraph in the text, and then press Delete/Backspace.**

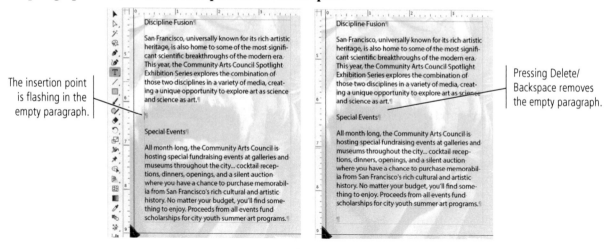

The insertion point is flashing in the empty paragraph.

Pressing Delete/Backspace removes the empty paragraph.

3. **Using the same method, remove all extra empty paragraphs in the story.**

You might need to use the arrow key to move the insertion point into the second frame. You can also press Command/Control to select the second frame, then click with the Type tool to place the insertion point in the empty paragraph in that frame.

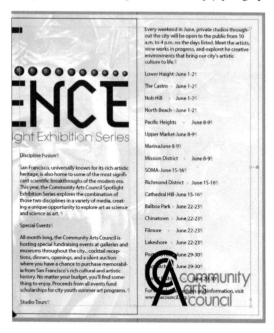

4. **Save the file and continue to the next exercise.**

Define Paragraph Styles

When you work with long blocks of text, many of the same formatting options are applied to different text elements throughout the story (such as headings).

To simplify the workflow, you can use styles to store and apply multiple formatting options in a single click. Styles also have another powerful benefit: when you change the options applied in a style, any text formatted with that style reflects the newly defined options. In other words, you can change multiple instances of non-contiguous text in a single process, instead of selecting each block and making the same changes repeatedly.

1. **With `aos-brochure.ai` open, click with the Type tool to place the insertion point anywhere in the text and choose Select>All.**

   When you use the Select All command, you select the entire story in all threaded frames.

2. **Open the Paragraph Styles panel (Window>Type>Paragraph Styles).**

   Text imported from a Microsoft Word file is commonly formatted with styles in the native application; those styles are imported into Illustrator when you place the text.

   The Paragraph Styles panel shows that the selected text is formatted with the Body Copy style. The plus sign (+) next to the style name indicates that some formatting is applied other than what is defined by the style. This is a quirk of importing formatted text. Although you imported the text and chose to include formatting, Illustrator doesn't recognize something in the style, resulting in the plus sign. This will occur in almost all text you import into Illustrator.

Note:

Not every instance of a plus sign (+) next to a style name is an error, but you should always be sure that what you have is really what you want.

3. **With the text selected, open the Paragraph Styles Options menu and choose Clear Overrides.**

This is an issue that you should be aware of; if you do not clear the overrides, later changes to the style might not correctly reflect in text formatted with the style. When you work with styles — whether they are imported styles or styles that you create — check the applied styles to see if a plus sign appears where you know it shouldn't.

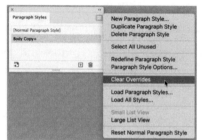

Note:

You can also click the plus sign in the style name to clear overrides.

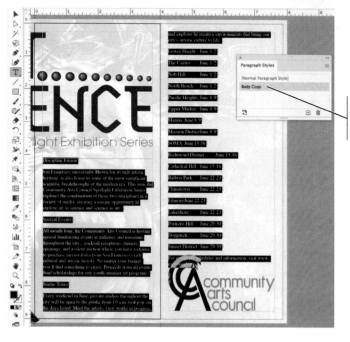

After choosing Clear Overrides, the plus sign is gone.

4. **Command/Control-click away from the text frame to deselect the text (and the containing frames).**

5. **In the Paragraph Styles panel, double-click the Body Copy style item away from the style name.**

If you double-click the actual style name, you will highlight the name so you can rename it. If you want to edit the style, double-click the style *away* from the style name.

You can also edit a style by single-clicking it in the panel, and then choosing Paragraph Style Options in the panel Options menu.

6. **In the resulting dialog box, make sure the Preview option is checked.**

Double-clicking a style opens the Paragraph Style Options dialog box for that style, where you can edit the settings stored in the style.

Checking the Preview option allows you to immediately see the effects of your changes in the layout before you finalize them.

7. **Click Basic Character Formats in the left list to show the related options. Choose ATC Onyx in the Font Family menu and Normal in the Font Style menu. Change the Size to 12 pt and the leading to 15 pt.**

Different options are available in the right side of the dialog box, depending on what is selected in the list of categories.

To see the effects of your changes, you have to click away from the active field to apply the new value. You can either tab to another field or click an empty area of the dialog box to preview the results.

Note:

You do not have to select text to change the definition of a style. In fact, you don't even need to select a text frame for this process to work.

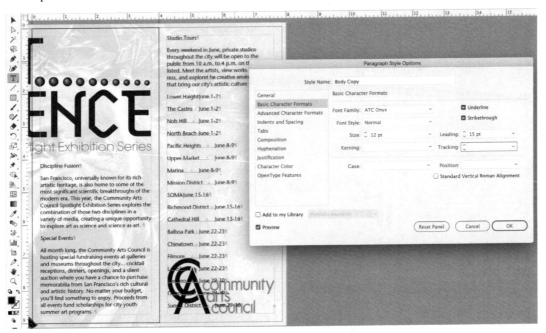

8. **Click Indents and Spacing in the category list. Change the Space Before field to 0 pt and the Space After field to 10 pt.**

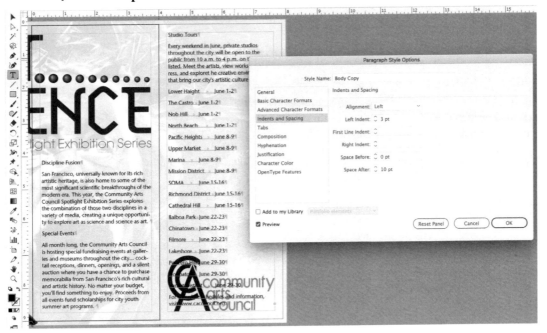

9. **Click Hyphenation in the category list. Click the Hyphenate check box twice to turn off automatic hyphenation.**

   When you work with styles that are imported from Microsoft Word, some style settings will be ambiguous, indicated by a dash in the check box. You might have to click a check box more than once to completely disable that option.

Note:

Later in this project you will apply hyphenation only in specific locations.

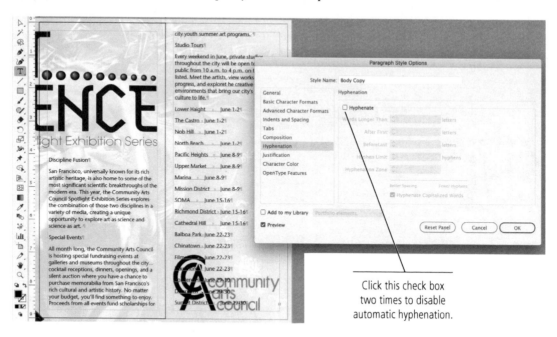

Click this check box two times to disable automatic hyphenation.

10. **Click OK to finalize the new style definition.**

11. **In the layout, use the Type tool to highlight the first paragraph in the story ("Discipline Fusion"). Using the Control or Character panel, change the formatting to ATC Onyx Bold and the type size to 13 pt.**

Note:

To open the Character panel, choose Window> Type>Character, or click the Character hot text in the Control panel.

To open the Paragraph panel, choose Window> Type>Paragraph, or click the Paragraph hot text in the Control panel.

12. **Using the Paragraph panel, change the Space After Paragraph field to 3 pt.**

   Unlike character formatting, paragraph formatting applies to the entire paragraph in which the insertion point is placed. If text is selected, paragraph formatting applies to any paragraph that is entirely or partially selected.

   If you don't see the Space Before Paragraph and Space After Paragraph fields in the Paragraph panel, open the panel Options menu and choose Show Options.

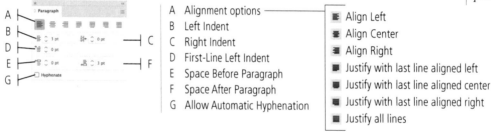

A Alignment options
B Left Indent
C Right Indent
D First-Line Left Indent
E Space Before Paragraph
F Space After Paragraph
G Allow Automatic Hyphenation

- Align Left
- Align Center
- Align Right
- Justify with last line aligned left
- Justify with last line aligned center
- Justify with last line aligned right
- Justify all lines

13. With the same type selected, click the Create New Style button in the Paragraph Styles panel.

When you create a new style, it defaults to include all formatting options applied to the currently selected text (or to the location of the insertion point, if no characters are selected).

The altered Body Copy style is still applied to the selected paragraph.

The new style is created.

Create New Style

Note:

By default, every Illustrator document includes the [Normal Paragraph Style] option. The formatting applied in this style is the default formatting for new text areas created in the file. You can edit this style to change the default settings for new text areas in the existing file.

14. With the heading selected, click Paragraph Style 1 to apply the new style to the selected text.

Clicking the style name applies that style to the active/selected paragraph.

15. In the Paragraph Styles panel, double-click the Paragraph Style 1 name. Type Heading, then press Return/Enter to finalize the change.

16. Place the insertion point in the second heading (Special Events) and click the Heading style in the Paragraph Styles panel.

Applying a paragraph style is as simple as placing the insertion point and clicking a style. You do not need to select the entire paragraph to apply the paragraph style.

17. Using the same method, apply the Heading style to the Studio Tours heading.

Note:

You can delete a style by dragging it to the panel Delete button. If the style had been applied, you would see a warning message, asking you to confirm the deletion. You do not have the opportunity to replace the applied style with another one, as you do in Adobe InDesign.

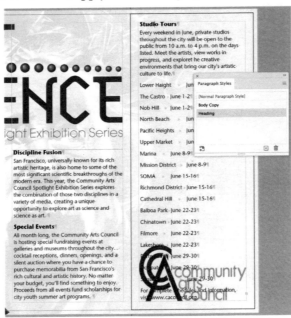

18. If necessary, use the Selection tool to adjust the height of the first text frame so the third heading is forced into the second frame.

Unfortunately, you can't use the Transform panel to change the height of the type area. If you do, you will artificially scale the height of the text within the area to match the new dimensions. This is counter to what you might expect (especially if you are familiar with working in Adobe InDesign). However, you can drag the type area's handles to resize the area. In this case, the text is not scaled; it reflows to fit the new dimensions of the area.

19. Select the first paragraph in the story (the heading "Discipline Fusion"). Using the Fill Color menu in the Control panel, change the text color to one of the darker red swatches.

Remember, everything between paragraph return characters (¶) is considered a paragraph, even if that text occupies only a single line.

We applied this swatch as the text fill color.

Note:

If you don't see the default color swatches, you can access them by opening the Default Swatches>Basic CMYK swatch library.

20. With the same text still selected, open the Paragraph Styles panel Options menu and choose Redefine Paragraph Style.

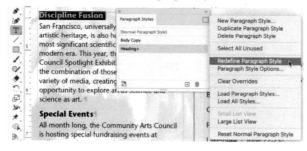

This option changes the selected style formatting to match the formatting of the current text selection in the document.

All text formatted with the Heading style reflects the new text color.

21. Save the file and continue to the next exercise.

Import Styles from Other Files

Once you create styles, you can apply them to any text in the file, on any artboard. You can also import styles from other Illustrator files so those styles can be used for different projects.

1. With **aos-brochure.ai** open, make the Outside artboard visible in the document window and make the Selection tool active.

2. Place the file **cac_outside.docx** into a type area on the Outside Fold In artboard (the one on the left). Include formatting in the placed file, and click OK if you see the Font Problems dialog box.

3. Using the Selection tool, drag the new text area's handles so its top edge begins approximately 1/8″ below the logo and the other edges align with the panel's margin guides.

   Don't worry about the text overlapping the bottom image. You will correct this problem as you apply type-formatting options in the remainder of this project.

4. Use the Type tool to place the insertion point in the placed text, then choose Select>All. Use the Paragraph Styles panel Options menu to clear the style overrides in the selected text.

   When the insertion point is placed, the Select All command selects all text in the active story. Text in other (non-threaded) type areas is not selected.

Note:

If the Paragraph Styles panel is closed before you select all the text, the applied style does not appear highlighted when you first open the panel. To work around this bug, open the panel, and then select the text that you want to format. The applied style (in this case, Body Copy+) is highlighted so you can use the Clear Overrides option.

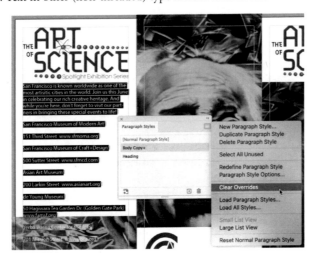

5. Open the Paragraph Styles panel Options menu and choose Load Paragraph Styles.

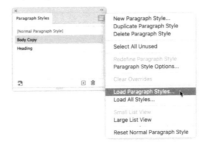

6. **Navigate to the file `cac-styles.ai` (in your WIP>Science folder) and click Open.**

If styles of the same name exist in the open and imported files, Illustrator maintains the definition from the active file. Unlike other applications, Illustrator does not allow you to control the import process for individual styles.

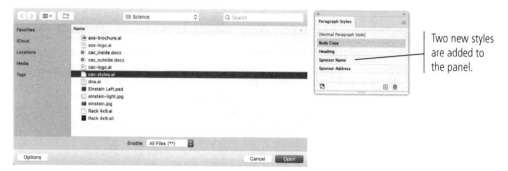

Two new styles are added to the panel.

7. **Using the Layers panel, hide the Graphics layer.**

Since the type objects are now in the proper position, hiding the underlying graphics makes it easier to focus on the type formatting without distraction.

8. **Select any part of all but the first paragraph in the text area, and click the Sponsor Address style.**

Paragraph styles relate to entire paragraphs — anything between two paragraph return (¶) characters.

Paragraph styles apply to any paragraph that is even partially selected.

9. **Place the insertion point in the first paragraph you just formatted, and then click the Sponsor Name style to apply it.**

10. **Apply the Sponsor Name style to every other paragraph in the list.**

Make sure you pay attention to where paragraphs begin and end. Don't apply the style to every other *line*.

11. **Save the file and continue to the next exercise.**

Define a Character Style

As with paragraph styles, a character style can be used to store and apply multiple character formatting options with a single click. The primary difference is that character styles apply to selected text only, such as italicizing a specific word in a paragraph or adding a few characters in a different font.

1. **With aos-brochure.ai open, highlight the web address in the first sponsor listing.**

2. **Using the Control or Character panel, change the font to ATC Onyx Italic.**

3. **Open the Character Styles panel (Window>Type>Character Styles).**

4. **Click the Create New Style button at the bottom of the panel.**

    The process of creating a character style is basically the same as creating a paragraph style. The new style is created, but it is not yet applied to the selected text.

Create New Style

Note:

You can Option/Alt-click the Create New button in most panels to automatically open the Options dialog box for the asset you are creating.

5. **Double-click the new style name in the panel. Type Web Address, then press Return/Enter to finalize the new name.**

    Because you double-clicked the style to rename it, the first click of that double-click applied the selected style. Like a paragraph style, new character styles adopt the formatting of the current selection.

6. **Highlight each web address in the list and apply the Web Address character style.**

    Unlike paragraph styles, character styles apply only to selected text.

7. **Save the file and continue to the next stage of the project.**

STAGE 4 / Fine-Tuning Text

There are still a number of typographic issues in the brochure text that should be addressed so the layout looks professional and well-polished, instead of appearing just "good enough." Although some problems will require manual intervention, many can be solved using Illustrator's built-in utilities.

Apply Smart Punctuation

When you import text from an external text file, it is possible that you are importing a number of typographic errors — both typing errors and errors of typography.

From a typography standpoint, some problems, such as straight quotes, have to do with the way text is encoded in the file you import. Other issues, such as double spaces after a period, are intentionally (but incorrectly) created by the author. In any case, Illustrator includes a utility to find and fix these common issues.

1. **With aos-brochure.ai open, make sure nothing is selected in the layout.**

2. **Choose Type>Show Hidden Characters to toggle those characters off.**

3. **Zoom in to the Inside artboard so you can clearly see the text.**

4. **Choose Type>Smart Punctuation.**

   This dialog box makes it very easy to search for and change common characters to their typographically correct equivalents. You can affect selected text only, or you can affect the entire document at once.

   - **ff, fi, ffi Ligatures** converts these combinations to the replacement ligatures.

   - **ff, fl, ffl Ligatures** converts these combinations to the replacement ligatures.

   - **Smart Quotes** converts straight quote marks into true (curly) quotes.

   - **Smart Spaces** eliminates multiple space characters after a period.

   - **En, Em Dashes** converts a double keyboard dash to an en dash and a triple keyboard dash to an em dash.

   - **Ellipses** converts three periods to a single-character ellipsis glyph.

   - **Expert Fractions** converts separate characters used to represent fractions to their single-character equivalents.

5. **In the Replace Punctuation area, check all options but Expert Fractions.**

6. **Choose the Entire Document option, make sure the Report Results box is checked, and then click OK.**

7. **Review the information in the report dialog box, and then click OK.**

8. **Save the file and continue to the next exercise.**

Note:

Two spaces after a period is a relic from a time when manual typewriters placed every character in the same amount of space (called monospace type). To more clearly identify a new sentence, the typist entered two spaces after typing a period. This convention still survives today, even though most people never use manual typewriters.

Control Hyphenation and Justification

The text on both sides of the brochure shows a problem called a **widow**, which is a short line at the end of a paragraph (typically one word, or two very short words). Whenever possible, these should be corrected. One way to do so is to adjust the hyphenation and justification settings in a paragraph.

Note:

*A **widow** is a very short line — usually one or two words — at the end of a paragraph.*

*An **orphan** is a heading or the first line of a paragraph at the end of a column, or the last line of a paragraph at the beginning of a column.*

1. **With `aos-brochure.ai` open, use the Type tool to place the insertion point in the paragraph after the Studio Tours heading.**

2. **Open the Paragraph panel Options menu and choose Hyphenation.**

Large, uneven gaps appear at the right side of the column.

This is a widow.

3. **In the Hyphenation dialog box, activate the Preview check box.**

4. **Check the Hyphenation option to allow automatic hyphenation based on the settings defined in the lower part of the dialog box.**

Allowing hyphenation fixes the widow.

The Hyphenation options allow you to control the way Illustrator applies hyphenation.

- **Words Longer Than _ Letters** defines the minimum number of characters that must exist in a hyphenated word.

- **After First** and **Before Last** defines the minimum number of characters that must appear before or after a hyphen.

- **Hyphen Limit** defines the maximum number of hyphens that can appear on consecutive lines. Remember, you are defining the *limit*, so zero means there is no limit, allowing unlimited hyphens.

- **Hyphenation Zone** defines the amount of white space allowed at the end of a line of unjustified text before hyphenation begins.

- The slider allows Illustrator to determine the best spacing. Dragging left allows more hyphens; dragging right reduces the number of hyphens in a paragraph, but might produce less-pleasing results in line spacing.

- If **Hyphenate Capitalized Words** is checked, capitalized words (proper nouns) can be hyphenated.

5. **Click OK to apply the change and return to the layout.**

6. **Navigate to the Outside Fold In artboard and place the insertion point in the first paragraph.**

7. **Using the Paragraph panel, apply the Justify All Lines alignment option.**

8. **Open the Paragraph panel Options menu and choose Justification.**

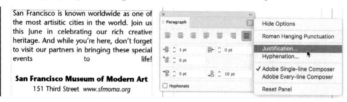

9. **Activate the Preview option, and then change the Minimum Word Spacing field to 50%.**

Note:

Issues such as paragraph and word spacing are somewhat subjective. Some of your clients will break all other typographic rules to reduce loosely fitted lines, while others will absolutely refuse to allow widows, and still others will disallow hyphenation of any kind.

The specific way you solve problems will be governed by your client's personal typographic preferences.

The Justification dialog box allows you to control the minimum, desired, and maximum spacing that can be applied to create justified paragraph alignment.

- **Word Spacing** defines the space that can be applied between words (where spaces exist in the text). At 100% (the default Desired amount), no additional space is added between words.

- **Letter Spacing** defines the space that can be added between individual letters within a word. All three values default to 0%, which allows no extra space between letters. At 100%, an entire space would be allowed between characters, making the text very difficult to read.

- **Glyph Scaling** determines how much individual character glyphs can be scaled (stretched or compressed) to justify the text. At 100%, the default value for all three settings, characters are not scaled.

- In narrow columns, single words sometimes appear on a line by themselves. If the paragraph is set to full justification, a single word on a line might appear to be too stretched out. You can use the **Single Word Justification** menu to center or left-align these single words, instead of leaving them fully justified.

By reducing the Minimum Word Spacing value, the spaces between words in the second line are reduced. Basically, you are telling Illustrator, "Reduce the amount of word spacing down to 70% of the normal spacing that would be applied by pressing the spacebar." This setting results in smaller word spaces throughout the paragraph, and corrects the widow at the end of the paragraph.

10. **Click OK to apply the change and return to the layout.**

11. **Save the file and continue to the next exercise.**

Format Tabbed Text

On the inside of the brochure, the list of dates was created with tab characters separating the locations from the dates. Rather than leaving the list as it is — more or less unformatted and messy — you can adjust tab formatting to present a well-ordered, easy-to-read list.

1. **With `aos-brochure.ai` open, select any part of each list paragraph (the lines listing the event dates) on the Inside Fold In artboard.**

   Tab positions are technically paragraph formatting attributes, so your changes will apply to any paragraph that is even partially selected.

2. **Open the Tabs panel (Window>Type>Tabs).**

   If the top edge of the active text frame is visible, the Tabs panel will automatically appear at the top of the frame. If the top edge of the frame is not visible, the panel floats randomly in the workspace. Because these two frames are linked, the left side of the Tabs panel appears above the left text frame — the first frame in the thread.

   If the Tabs panel does not automatically open above the active type area, you can adjust the file in the document window, and then click the Position Panel Above Text button to position the panel above the active type area. Keep in mind, there must still be enough room above the frame for the panel to fit in the workspace.

Position Panel Above Text

3. **Click the Right-Justified Tab marker at the top of the panel.**

   This defines the type of tab stop you are going to create. If an existing tab marker is already selected on the ruler, clicking a different type of marker changes the type of the selected stop.

4. **Click the ruler in the Tabs panel above the left frame to place a tab stop, then drag that stop to about the middle of the left frame.**

Left-Justified Tab
Center-Justified Tab
Right-Justified Tab
Decimal-Justified Tab

This line marks the location of the tab stop that you are dragging. It extends down both linked frames in the story.

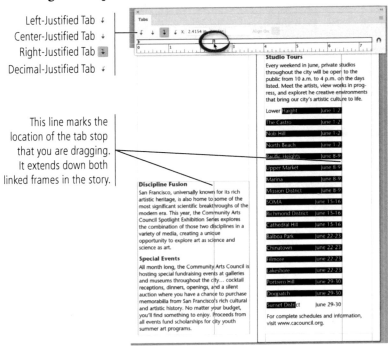

Note:

If you use a Decimal-Justified Tab stop, you can use this field to determine which character is the alignment key.

5. **Click the existing tab stop and drag right until the line shows the tab located just short of the right edge of the right frame.**

Remember, these two frames are slightly different sizes due to the size difference of the artboards. You have to watch the line in the right frame to make sure the tab will be aligned properly.

6. **With the tab stop still selected, type period-space in the Leader field, and then press Return/Enter to apply the change.**

Whatever you type in the Leader field will occupy the space between tab stops.

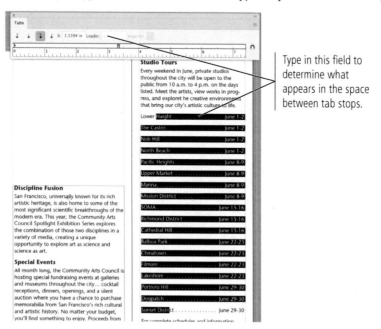

Type in this field to determine what appears in the space between tab stops.

7. **Select any part of all but the last list item, then use the Paragraph panel to change the Space After Paragraph value to 3 pt.**

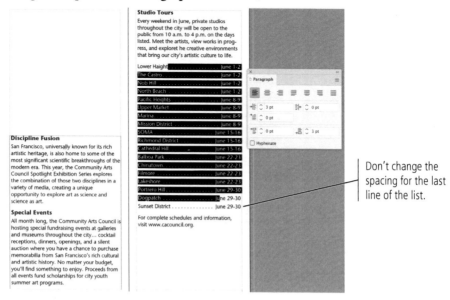

Don't change the spacing for the last line of the list.

8. **Save the file and continue to the next exercise.**

Check Spelling

Misspellings and typos creep into virtually every job, despite numerous rounds of content proofs. These errors can ruin an otherwise perfect job. As with most desktop applications, Illustrator allows you to check the spelling in a document. It's all too common, however, to skip this important step, which could result in spelling and typing errors in the final output.

You probably won't create the text for most design jobs, and you aren't technically responsible for the words your client supplies. However, you can be a hero if you find and fix typographical errors before a job goes to press; if you don't, you will almost certainly hear about it after it's too late to fix. You simply can't brush off a problem by saying, "That's not my job" — at least, not if you want to work with that client again.

Note:

Keep in mind that spell-check is not infallible; it does not check for incorrect usage or grammar — for example, incorrectly using "two many copies" instead of "too many copies."

1. **With aos-brochure.ai open, make sure nothing is selected in the layout.**

2. **Choose Edit>Check Spelling.**

3. **In the resulting Check Spelling dialog box, click Start.**

   As soon as you click Start, Illustrator locates the first potential problem and highlights it in the layout.

   This error ("exploret he") is a typo, but it presents a spell-checking problem: "exploret" is an error, but the second half of the typo ("he") will not be identified as a misspelling. In this case, you have to use the upper field to make the necessary correction to both words.

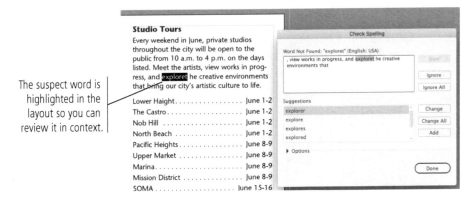

The suspect word is highlighted in the layout so you can review it in context.

4. **In the upper window of the Check Spelling dialog box, change "exploret he" to explore the.**

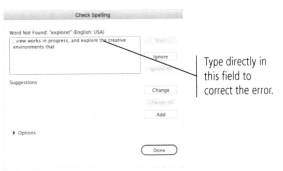

Type directly in this field to correct the error.

5. Click Change.

As soon as you click Change to correct the first error, Illustrator automatically highlights the next suspect word.

Your change from the previous step is applied.

The next suspected error is highlighted.

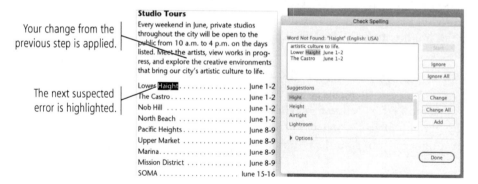

6. Click Ignore in the Check Spelling dialog box and review the next flagged word.

In this case, the suspect word is the name of a street in San Francisco, and it is spelled correctly.

Keep in mind that Illustrator checks spelling based on the language defined for the text. (You can change the default language in the Hyphenation pane of the Preferences dialog box, or you can assign a specific language to selected text using the Character panel.) Some words, although spelled correctly, are not included in the built-in dictionaries, so they are flagged as errors when you check spelling.

As soon as you click Ignore, Illustrator automatically highlights the next suspect word.

Note:

Never simply click Change when you check spelling. Carefully evaluate the suspect word in the context of the layout.

7. Continue reviewing any potential problems, making any necessary changes to words that are not place names or web addresses.

Many of the suspected problems in this file are either place names or web addresses; both are commonly flagged as potential errors, even when they are spelled correctly.

For the sake of this project, you can assume place names and web addresses are correct. In a professional environment, those are common sources of typos; always check the accuracy of these words carefully.

The only other actual spelling error is the word "artisitic" on the Outside artboard.

Note:

If you expand the Options section at the bottom of the Check Spelling dialog box, you see a number of choices to refine the evaluation.

The Find section allows the spell checker to identify repeated words (e.g., "the the") and non-capitalized beginnings of sentences (i.e., lowercase words immediately following a period and space).

In the Ignore section, you can force Illustrator to skip words that are all uppercase, words with numbers, and Roman numerals.

8. Click Done to close the Check Spelling dialog box.

When Illustrator can't find any more potential problems, the dialog box shows that the Spell Checker utility is complete.

9. Save the file and continue to the next exercise.

Create a Job Package

As we have already stated, the images and fonts used in a layout must be available on the computer used to output the job. Now that your file is complete, you can package it to send to an output provider, or to create an archive for later use. Illustrator now includes a Package utility that makes this process very easy.

1. **With aos-brochure.ai open, show the Graphics layer.**

2. **Choose File>Package. In the resulting dialog box, change the Folder Name field to Finished Culture Brochure.**

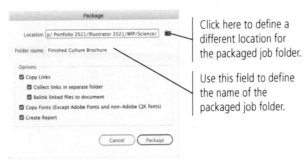

Click here to define a different location for the packaged job folder.

Use this field to define the name of the packaged job folder.

3. **Make sure all options are checked at the bottom of the dialog box, then click Package.**

    These options determine what will be included in the packaged job folder.

    • **Copy Links.** When checked, this option copies all linked files into the resulting job package folder. The original linked file is not affected.

    • **Collect Links in Separate Folder.** When checked, the packaged job folder includes a secondary Links folder to contain all of the link files. If this option is not checked, the linked files will be placed in the main job package folder.

    • **Relink Linked Files to Document.** When checked, links in the Illustrator file are changed to refer to the new copied link files. If this option is not checked, the links still point to the original placed file, which might cause a missing-file warning when you send the job package to another user (or open the file at a later time).

    • **Copy Fonts (Except Adobe Fonts and non-Adobe CJK fonts).** When checked, this option results in a secondary Fonts folder to contain the font files that are used in the Illustrator file.

        As the name of this item suggests, Adobe and CJK (Chinese/Japanese/Korean) fonts are not copied into the job package. If you send a file to other users, they will have to license the required CJK fonts, or sync the required Adobe fonts using their own Creative Cloud subscriptions.

    • **Create Report.** When checked, this option creates a text file that includes information about the Illustrator file (color mode, linked files, etc.).

Note:

CJK (Chinese/Japanese/Korean) fonts contain a large number of picto-graphic characters.

4. **Read the resulting warning, then click OK.**

    As with any software, you purchase a license to use a font — you do not actually own the font. It is illegal to distribute fonts freely, as it is illegal to distribute copies of your software. Most (but not all) font licenses allow you to send your copy of a font to a service provider, as long as the service provider also owns a copy of the font. Always verify that you are not violating font copyright before submitting a job.

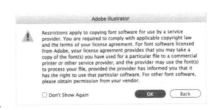

5. **In the resulting dialog box, click the Show Package button.**

   If you don't see this dialog box, it is possible someone else has checked the Don't Show Again option. (If someone has disabled the dialog box, you can open the General pane of the preferences dialog box and click the Reset All Warning Dialogs button.) In this case, you can use your desktop Finder to view the contents of the packaged job folder.

   When the process is complete, all of the necessary job elements appear in the job folder (in your WIP>Science folder).

6. **Continue to the next exercise.**

Export a PDF File for Print

The Portable Document Format (PDF) was created by Adobe to facilitate cross-platform transportation of documents, independent of the fonts used, linked files, or even the originating application. The format offers a number of advantages for commercial printing workflows:

- PDF files can contain all of the information needed to successfully output a job.

- Data in a PDF file can be high or low resolution, and it can be compressed to reduce file size.

- PDF files are device-independent, which means you don't need the originating application or the same platform to open and print the file.

- PDF files are also page-independent, which means a PDF document can contain rotated pages and even pages of different sizes.

1. **With aos-brochure.ai open in Illustrator, choose File>Save As. Choose Adobe PDF in the Format/Save As Type menu.**

2. **Navigate to the Finished Culture Brochure folder (in your WIP>Science folder) as the target location for saving the PDF file.**

3. **Choose the Range option, type 1-2 in the related field, then click Save.**

When you save a file as PDF in Illustrator, the software automatically uses artboards that are defined in the file as the "pages" that will be created in the PDF. The Use Artboards checkbox is automatically selected and grayed out.

Because you created separate artboards to contain each composite side of the brochure, you are using the Range option to output only those two artboards in the PDF file.

Macintosh   Windows

4. **In the Save Adobe PDF dialog box, choose Press Quality in the Adobe PDF Preset menu.**

The Adobe PDF Preset menu includes six PDF presets (in brackets) that meet common industry output requirements. Other options might also be available if another user created custom presets in Illustrator or another Adobe application.

Because there are so many ways to create a PDF — not all of them optimized for commercial printing — the potential benefits of the file format are often negated. The PDF/X specification (defined in the Standard menu) was created to help solve some of the problems associated with bad PDF files entering the prepress workflow. PDF/X is a subset of PDF, designed to ensure that files have the information necessary for, and available to, the digital prepress output process. Ask your output provider whether you should apply a PDF/X standard to your files, and if so, which version to use.

The Compatibility menu determines which version of PDF you will create. This is particularly important if your layout uses transparency. PDF 1.3 does not support transparency, so the file will require flattening. If you save the file to be compatible with PDF 1.4 or later, the transparency information will be maintained in the PDF file; it will have to be flattened later in the output process (after it leaves your desk).

Note:

Since you chose the High Quality Print preset, these options default to settings that will produce the best results for most commercial printing applications.

5. Review the Compression options.

The Compression options determine what — and how much — data will be included in the PDF file. This set of options is one of the most important when creating PDFs, since too-low resolution results in bad-quality printing, and too-high resolution results in long download times.

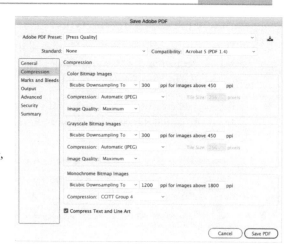

Before you choose compression settings, you need to consider your final goal. If you're creating a file for commercial printing, resolution is more important than file size. If your goal is a PDF for posting on the web for general consumption, file size is equally as important (if not more so) as image quality.

You can define a specific compression scheme for color, grayscale, and monochrome images. Different options are available, depending on the image type:

- ZIP compression is lossless, which means all file data is maintained in the compressed file.

- JPEG compression options are lossy, which means data is discarded to create a smaller file. When you use one of the JPEG options, you can also define an Image Quality option (from Low to Maximum).

If you don't compress the file, your PDF file might be extremely large. For a commercial printing workflow, large file size is preferable to poor image quality. If you don't have to submit the PDF file via modem transmission, large file size is not an issue. If you must compress the file, ask your service provider what settings they prefer you to use.

Note:

The Output options relate to color management and PDF/X settings. Ask your output provider if you need to change anything for those options.

6. In the Marks and Bleeds options, check the Trim Marks option, and change the Offset field to 0.125 in.

Most printers prefer trim marks to appear outside of the bleed area, which is 0.125″ for this project; this requires a 0.125″ offset.

7. In the Bleeds section, make sure the four fields are not linked. Change the Top and Bottom values to 0.5 in, and change the Left and Right values to 0.125 in.

Because you did not define a specific bleed setting for the artboards in this file, the Use Document Bleed Settings option won't work.

You have to manually define the area on each side to include in the exported file. You're including more space on the top and bottom so the folding marks will be visible in the resulting PDF file.

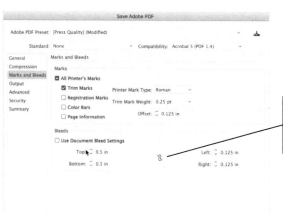

If this button shows a linked chain, click to unlink the four Bleed fields.

8. Click Save PDF. When the process is finished, close the aos-brochure.ai file.

1. _____ is the size of a flat page before folding, and after it has been cut from a press sheet.

2. _____ is the area where it is safe to place important content.

3. _____ is the amount you must extend objects beyond the actual artboard edge for them to safely appear at the cut edge of the final job.

4. For a folding document, panels that fold in need to be at least _____ smaller than outside panels.

5. The _____ command can be used to convert any object into a nonprinting guide.

6. Using _____ rulers, measurements relate to the first artboard in the file.

7. Using _____ rulers, measurements relate to the currently active artboard.

8. The _____ icon indicates that more text exists in the story, but does not fit into the current text area or chain.

9. You can use the _____ dialog box to change all instances of a selected font in the active file.

10. You can choose the _____ command to show visible, nonprinting indicators of spaces and paragraph return characters.

1. Briefly explain how the mechanics of printing affect the layout for folding documents.

2. Briefly explain two advantages of using styles for text formatting.

3. Briefly explain the difference between linked and embedded files.

Use what you have learned in this project to complete the following freeform exercise.
Carefully read the art director and client comments, then create your own design to meet the needs of the project.
Use the space below to sketch ideas. When finished, write a brief explanation of the reasoning behind your final design.

art director comments

The Painted Turtle is a camp for children with serious medical conditions. It is run entirely by donations, and children are not charged to attend the camp.

Last spring the camp was heavily damaged by fire, so the camp directors and organizers are launching a fundraising campaign to raise the funds to rebuild.

❏ Create a letterfold brochure that can be mailed, placed in stand-up rack-card holders, and handed out at community events.

❏ Look at the camp's website for inspiration (www.thepaintedturtle.org).

❏ Include a "Donate Now" section with a form to gather the donor's name, contact information, amount of donation, and method of donation (check or credit card). Be sure to include space to gather the donor's credit card information if necessary.

client comments

Our camp is one of the largest of its kind, catering to the special needs of children (and their families) who would not normally be able to experience the joy of attending summer camp. Our largely volunteer staff gives its time and expertise to make this a positive experience for every child who comes through the gates.

We estimate that it costs about $1,600 per child to attend the camp, but we never turn away a sick child whose family can't afford it. Our fundraising efforts are vitally important to provide as many children as possible with memories they will cherish. The fire last spring was devastating, and we need more funds now than ever to help rebuild.

We want the fundraising pamphlet to be happy and colorful, and reflect the overall spirit of our camp. You can find a lot of text and images on our website; use anything you want from the site as FPO images. Once you know which ones you want to use, we'll provide you with high-resolution versions for print.

project justification

To begin the letterfold layout, you built technically accurate folding guides for each side of the brochure. To speed up the process for the next time you need to build one of these common letterfold jobs, you saved your initial work as a template.

Completing this project also required extensive work with imported text, specifically, importing styles from a Microsoft Word file and controlling the flow of text from one frame to another. You also worked with several advanced text-formatting options, including paragraph and character styles, and typographic fine-tuning.

Templates and styles are designed to let you do the majority of work once, and then apply it as many times as necessary. Many different projects can benefit from these tools, and you will use them extensively throughout your career as a graphic designer.

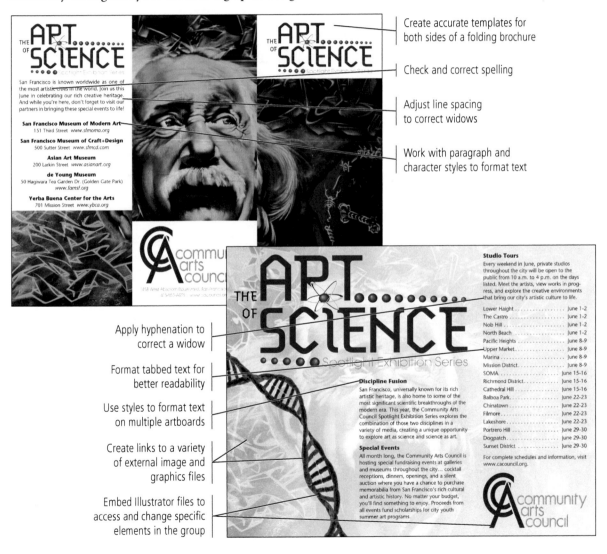

Create accurate templates for both sides of a folding brochure

Check and correct spelling

Adjust line spacing to correct widows

Work with paragraph and character styles to format text

Apply hyphenation to correct a widow

Format tabbed text for better readability

Use styles to format text on multiple artboards

Create links to a variety of external image and graphics files

Embed Illustrator files to access and change specific elements in the group

Candy Packaging

Your client, a candy manufacturer, has hired you to design and build the packaging for a new product launch at its anniversary party, which will be held at the annual candy expo. You will incorporate client-supplied elements and create custom graphics as you develop an attractive, modern box design.

This project incorporates the following skills:

- ❑ Using Image Trace to create a complex illustration
- ❑ Sampling colors to create custom swatches
- ❑ Using warp and 3D effects to add depth to artwork
- ❑ Creating type on an irregular path
- ❑ Controlling object blending modes and opacity
- ❑ Understanding and defining raster effect settings
- ❑ Previewing 3D artwork

We're celebrating our company's 75th anniversary this year. For the annual candy expo, we are introducing SmartTarts™ — a new product that combines different flavor profiles and textures into a single candy. Response at early focus groups has been very positive, so we're excited about the potential.

We would like to create a fun, colorful box to hand out product samples at our reception following the first day of the show. We'd like to give a larger sample size to the VIP guests who are invited to the party, so we need a box that is a 4-inch cube. Later we'll need to create a smaller box that we can use for show-floor samples, as well as final packaging that will be used for the retail product.

We have a template from the printer with the package structure already laid out, based on an existing die that's used to cut the flat box from the press sheet. There's no need to reinvent the wheel, so use this template to build the finished box artwork.

The only thing they said they want is "fun, colorful" packaging, so we have complete artistic freedom for this project. They did send some components that need to be included: a background image, an anniversary logo, and some copy. They didn't send a company logo, so I think we'll try something creative with their company name.

Illustrator has all the tools you need to make this package technically accurate and aesthetically pleasing. When you finish the layout, you can even use built-in tools to create a comp of the final folded box.

To complete this project, you will:

- ❏ Create the package file from a template
- ❏ Sample colors to create custom swatches
- ❏ Create warp and 3D effects
- ❏ Create type on an irregular path
- ❏ Change object blending modes and opacity
- ❏ Apply raster effects to vector objects and placed images
- ❏ Apply effects to pieces of a group
- ❏ Define raster effect settings
- ❏ Preview transparency flattening
- ❏ Flatten transparency in a PDF file
- ❏ Preview a 3D representation of the completed box artwork

When you work on a package design, it's important to realize that many types of packages have a standard size and shape. Although there is something to be said for standing out in a crowd, package design is often governed by the space allowed on store shelves, which means you probably won't have any choice regarding the size and shape of the package.

You also need to understand that packages are typically designed and printed as a flat layout, using a template to indicate edges and folds. They are then diecut, folded, and glued. The next time you finish a box of cereal, tear it apart along the glue flaps to see how the package was designed. Because many packages share common sizes, printers often have existing templates you can use.

 Create the Package File from a Template

The printer for this package has provided you with a template file that includes the die-cut layout and folding guides. You will use this file as the basis for the entire project.

1. Download **Candy_AI21_RF.zip** from the Student Files web page.

2. Expand the ZIP archive in your **WIP folder (Macintosh) or copy the archive contents into your WIP folder (Windows).**

   This results in a folder named **Candy**, which contains the files you need for this project. You should also use this folder to save the files you create in this project.

3. Create a new file by opening the **square-box.ait** template file from your **WIP>Candy folder. Resize the view so you can see the entire artboard.**

   The file has three layers: one has guides indicating the location of the folds, one has guides that define margins and bleeds for each panel, and one has the die lines for the box shape. The box's top and bottom panels are identified, as well as the flap where glue will be applied in the converting process to create the finished box shape.

4. Save the new file as a native Illustrator file named **candy-box.ai** in your **WIP>Candy folder, then continue to the next exercise.**

Note:

You should notice that the red bleed guide does not extend to the end of the glue flap. The printer for this job has recommended that ink should not be printed in the gluing area — a common requirement for package printing.

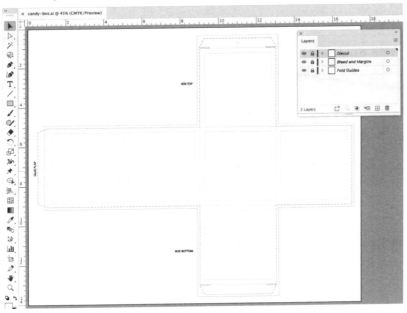

Use Image Trace to Create a Complex Image

If you have completed the other projects in this book, you should have a solid foundation for creating basic and complex vector graphics, whether based on a sketch or photograph, or from scratch.

Another option — Image Trace — makes it very easy to create vector graphics directly from an image, using a variety of options to determine how realistic the resulting illustration will be.

1. **With `candy-box.ai` open, create a new layer named `Background`.**

2. **In the Layers panel, drag the Background layer below the Diecut layer.**

   The Diecut layer shows the location of the cut lines. Although it will not be printed in the final output, this layer needs to be visible while you create the basic package.

   Be careful how you drag the layer to reposition it. If you accidentally move the layer to the wrong place in the stack, or move it to be a sublayer of another layer, simply drag it again to the top of the layer stack.

   Note:

   Even though the panel layers are above the guide layers, guides always appear in front of artwork.

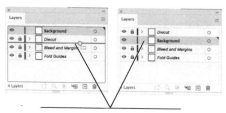

   The heavy line identifies where the layer will be positioned when you release the mouse button.

3. **With the Background layer selected in the Layers panel, choose File>Place.**

4. **Select the file `background.tif` in your WIP>Candy folder. Make sure none of the options at the bottom of the dialog box are checked, then click Place.**

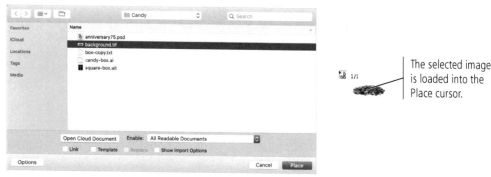

   The selected image is loaded into the Place cursor.

5. **Click the loaded Place cursor to place the selected image.**

6. **Using the Selection tool, position the placed file so the pile of candy extends across all four side panels, but does not extend into the top panel. (Use the following image as a guide.)**

As you can see in the Control panel, the placed image is only 72 ppi, which is insufficient resolution for commercial printing. Because you are going to use this image as the basis for a vector illustration, the low resolution will not be a problem.

Click to apply the Image Trace function to the selected image.

Open this menu to choose a specific Image Trace preset.

7. **Hide all but the Background layer.**

You don't need these layers for this stage of the process; hiding them allows you to better see the effect of the Image Trace process.

8. **With the placed background image selected, click the Image Trace button in the Control panel.**

By clicking this button, Illustrator automatically traces the image using the default black-and-white preset.

The result is a special type of object called an **image tracing object** (which you can see in the Control panel). As long as you don't expand the tracing object, you can change the settings to produce different results from the same picture.

9. **Open the Image Trace panel (Window>Image Trace).**

When you trace an image, the original photo is hidden and the illustrated version appears in its place.

Note:

In the Layers panel, Option/Alt-clicking the Eye icon for a layer hides all other layers in the file.

Note:

You can also apply the default Image Trace settings by choosing Object>Image Trace>Make.

Choose a defined tracing preset.

Open the Image Trace panel.

Use this menu to change the visibility of the original traced image.

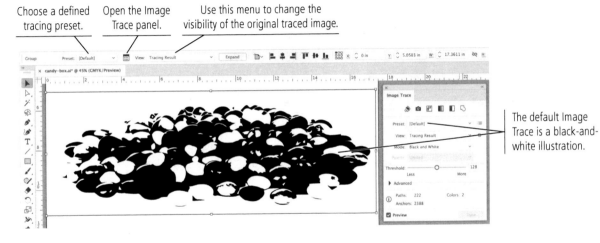

The default Image Trace is a black-and-white illustration.

10. Open the Preset menu and choose Low Fidelity Photo.

Illustrator includes a number of Image Trace presets that you can apply to any image. These can be accessed in the Image Trace panel or Control panel when a tracing object is selected.

Use this menu to access one of the built-in presets.

As long as you don't expand the tracing object, you can change the settings that generate the illustration. However, when the Preview option is checked at the bottom of the panel, every change requires Illustrator to reprocess the image to generate the correct curves. Because this is a rather large image, processing each change could take considerable processing power and time (depending on your computer).

Using the current settings, the resulting illustration will include 1050 distinct colors.

11. Open the Palette menu and choose Limited.

Using a limited color palette can reduce the complexity of the file. The Image Trace panel shows that you have reduced the tracing from 1000+ colors (from Step 10) to 30, which is the default option when using the Limited palette option. You can use the Colors slider to reduce the number of colors even further.

By allowing only a small number of colors, you force Illustrator to create larger objects of solid colors, ultimately resulting in more of a "paint-by-numbers" effect.

Note:

Increasing the number of possible colors creates a more realistic result, and a more complex illustration.

When you use a Limited palette, you can define the specific number of colors to allow in the illustration.

12. At the bottom of the panel, uncheck the Preview option.

Rather than waiting to preview each change, it's a better idea to activate the preview after defining your initial choices; you can then toggle the preview on and off as necessary to reduce the time you spend sitting and waiting.

13. Click the arrow to the left of the Advanced heading to expand the panel.

14. Change the Paths option to 75%.

This controls how tightly the tracing conforms to the original image; a higher number means more tightly fitting paths.

15. Change the Corners option to 25%.

This controls how corners in the original image are represented in the tracing; a higher number results in more corners instead of rounded paths.

Click here to show or hide the advanced options.

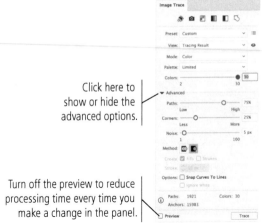

16. Change the Noise option to 5 px.

This controls the smallest-size area that is ignored in the tracing result; higher values mean fewer small spots of color in the tracing.

Turn off the preview to reduce processing time every time you make a change in the panel.

Understanding Image Trace Options

With so many options and sliders, the Image Trace panel might seem intimidating at first. As with any tool, it's easier to get the desired results if you understand the options.

Buttons at the top of the panel apply specific color modes to the illustration (from left): Auto Color, High Color, Low Color, Grayscale, Black and White, or Outline.

- **Preset** includes a number of built-in groups of settings that produce specific results, such as Sketched Art or Technical Drawing.

- **View** changes what is visible in the document. You can show the tracing result with or without outlines, the source image with or without outlines, or only the source image.

- **Mode** defines the color mode (color, grayscale, or black and white) of the resulting illustration.

- **Palette**, which is available when the Mode is set to Color, defines the specific colors that can be used. The default Full Tone option allows Illustrator to use an unlimited palette to create the illustration.

- **Threshold**, which is available when the Mode is set to Black and White, defines the maximum tonal value that will remain white before an area is filled with black.

- **Colors.** When Full Tone or Automatic is selected in the Palette menu, this option defines the accuracy of illustration colors as a percentage; higher values result in a larger number of colors being used.

  When the Limited palette is selected, this option defines the specific number of colors Illustrator can use to trace the image. More colors create more depth, but also increase the complexity and number of points in the illustration.

- **Paths** adjusts how closely traced paths will follow the pixels of the original image.

- **Corners** defines the minimum angle that can be traced as a sharp corner instead of a smooth curve.

- **Noise** adjusts the smallest color area (in pixels) that can be drawn as a path.

- **Method** determines whether shapes in the illustration are created as abutting (left) or overlapping (right).

- When you use the Black and White color mode, you can use the **Create** options to define whether the illustration is created as fills, strokes, or a combination.

  - **Fills** results in solid-filled paths.

  - **Strokes** results in paths with an applied stroke color and weight. The Stroke Width field defines the maximum stroke weight that can be applied before a stroke will be recreated as a fill object.

- **Snap Curves to Lines** replaces slightly curved lines with straight lines.

- **Ignore White** does not create shapes to represent white areas in the image.

17. **Check the Preview option at the bottom of the panel to review the results of your choices.**

The change is subtle, but you should notice slightly more accurate path shapes (Step 14), fewer sharp corners (Step 15), and fewer small areas of isolated color (Step 16).

18. **Open the View menu in the Image Trace panel and choose Tracing Result with Outlines.**

By default, vector outlines that make up the image-tracing object are not visible in the document. Without expanding the image tracing object, these preview options allow you to view the resulting paths based on your current Image Trace settings.

When Tracing Result with Outlines is selected, you can see the vector paths that will make up the resulting illustration.

Note:

To access the individual anchors and paths, you have to expand the image-tracing object.

19. **Choose Tracing Result in the View menu.**

This turns off the path outlines and restores the illustration to full opacity.

20. **Click the Eye icon to the right of the View button and hold down the mouse button.**

You can click and hold this button to show the original image that is used to make the Image Trace. This provides a quick method for reviewing the original image, while still experimenting with the Image Trace options.

21. **Save the file, and then continue to the next exercise.**

Sample Colors and Create Custom Swatches

Using the Eyedropper tool, you can select colors from other objects in the file, which makes it easier to create a cohesive package design. In this exercise you will sample three colors from the tracing image; you will use those swatches later for other elements of the design.

1. **With `candy-box.ai` open, deselect everything in the file.**

   In many instances, sampling a color with the Eyedropper tool automatically changes the attributes of any selected objects. Although this is not the case for a tracing object, you should get into the habit of deselecting objects before sampling new colors, unless you want to purposefully change the color of a selected object.

2. **Display the Swatches and Color panels, and then choose the Eyedropper tool in the Tools panel.**

   If you don't see the color sliders in the Color panel, choose Show Options in the panel's Options menu.

3. **Click the Eyedropper tool in a dark red color of the tracing object.**

   Clicking with the Eyedropper tool changes the color in the Color panel; this method is called **sampling** color.

We clicked here to sample the dark red color.

Eyedropper tool

The template includes only four color swatches: Registration, White, Black, and CMYK Green.

Sampled color values appear in the Color panel.

4. **With the Fill icon on top (the active attribute) in the Swatches and Color panels, click the New Swatch button at the bottom of the Swatches panel.**

5. **In the resulting New Swatch dialog box, activate the Global check box and uncheck the Add to My Library option. Click OK to accept the default swatch name and color values.**

   The sampled color is saved as a swatch, so you can access it again later.

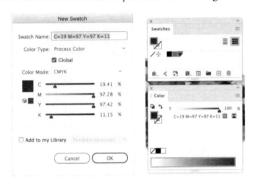

Note:

If your Color and Swatches panels are docked, drag them out of the dock so you can use them both at once.

Note:

You could also simply click the New Swatch button in the Swatches panel to create a custom color swatch.

6. **Use the Eyedropper tool again to sample a light pink color, and then add the sampled color as a second global swatch.**

We sampled the light pink color in this area.

7. **Use the Eyedropper tool again to sample a light yellow color, and then add the sampled color as a third global swatch.**

We sampled the light yellow color in this area.

8. **Save the file and continue to the next stage of the project.**

STAGE 2 / Working with Styles and Effects

When you design a complex project, such as this package, it helps to decide on a logical approach to accomplish the task. Rather than jumping around in the layout, it makes more sense to work on one panel at a time. In this stage of the project, you are going to use a number of tools and techniques to create the various pieces that are required, primarily using advanced type options and Illustrator effects.

Illustrator includes a number of effects for enhancing objects in a layout. Effects in Illustrator are live and non-destructive, which means they can be edited or removed from an object without destroying the original object.

When you work with effects, you should be aware that many of these options eventually result in rasterized elements, even when you apply them to vector objects.

Some of the Illustrator Effects — specifically Drop Shadow, Inner Glow, Outer Glow, and Feather options in the Stylize submenu — all utilize some form of graded transparency, and they all result in objects that reproduce as pixels (rasters) instead of vectors. For example, a drop shadow creates a soft-edge shadow object that blends from the shadow color to fully transparent. To achieve this effect on output, the shadow has to be rasterized into pixels that reproduce the visual effect.

In this stage of the project, you use effects and transparency controls to add visual interest to different elements of the box artwork. In Stage 3 of this project, you will learn how to control transparent objects that need to be rasterized before they can be successfully output.

Transform and Warp Design Elements

The first two side panels in this box require a banner-type object that highlights the product name. Rather than simply creating a flat banner, you're going to use built-in effects to create a three-dimensional banner that appears to wave around the box corner. You're also going to create the banner in two separate pieces so that the content for each side can be easily isolated later.

1. **With candy-box.ai open, lock and hide the Background layer. Show the Diecut, Bleed and Margins, and Fold Guides layers.**

2. **Create two new layers, named Side 1 and Side 2, immediately above the Background layer. Make Side 1 the active layer.**

3. **Create a rectangle in the center of the left panel that is 3.75″ wide and 1″ high. Fill the rectangle with the dark red custom swatch and set the stroke to None. Position it so the shape's right edge aligns to the right edge of the left panel.**

   Use the image after Step 4 as a guide for positioning this object.

4. **Using the Add Anchor Point tool, add an anchor point to the left edge of the rectangle, halfway between the corners. Use the Direct Selection tool to drag the point right, creating the basic banner shape.**

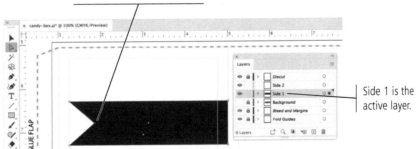

We added an anchor point to a basic rectangle to create the left side of the banner shape.

Side 1 is the active layer.

5. **Click the object's fill to select the entire shape, then choose the Reflect tool (nested under the Rotate tool).**

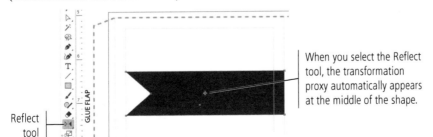

Reflect tool

When you select the Reflect tool, the transformation proxy automatically appears at the middle of the shape.

Note:

The small blue x in the middle of the panel area is a remnant of the object that was used to create the margin guide. Its visibility on the artboard seems to be a minor bug in the software, but it has no effect on the final outcome of your file.

6. **Click the right edge of the selected shape to move the transformation point.**

7. **Press Option/Alt-Shift, then drag right to clone and reflect the selected shape.**

   Pressing Option/Alt allows you to clone the object while you reflect it. Pressing Shift constrains the reflection to 45° angles.

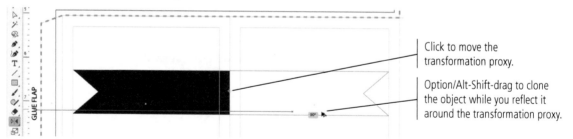

Click to move the transformation proxy.

Option/Alt-Shift-drag to clone the object while you reflect it around the transformation proxy.

8. **In the Layers panel, expand the Side 1 layer. Drag the Selected Art icon to the Side 2 layer, then expand the Side 2 layer.**

   Remember, expanding a layer shows the objects contained on the layer (called sublayers). You can further expand sublayer groups so that you can show — and select — the individual elements in a group, if necessary.

Expanding the layer shows the objects (sublayers) on that layer.

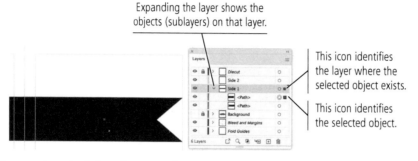

This icon identifies the layer where the selected object exists.

This icon identifies the selected object.

You can drag the Selected Art icon from the layer or from the actual selected object. If more than one object is selected, dragging from the actual layer name moves all selected objects to the new target layer.

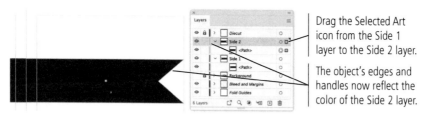

Drag the Selected Art icon from the Side 1 layer to the Side 2 layer.

The object's edges and handles now reflect the color of the Side 2 layer.

9. **With Side 1 as the active layer, use the Type tool to create a point-type object near the center of the banner shape on the left panel.**

   Be sure the cursor is not near the existing shape edge when you click with the Type tool. If you click too close to the edge of the existing shape, clicking with the Type tool will convert the existing shape into an area-type object. Use the shape of the cursor as a guide for when you can click to create a new type area.

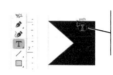

When you see this cursor, clicking will convert the existing shape to a type area.

   To work around this potential problem, you could also click to create a type object somewhere else, then drag it into position later.

If the cursor is far enough away from the edges of existing shapes, you can click and drag to create a new type object.

10. Type **Smart** to replace the default placeholder text, and then format the text as 60-pt ATC Garnet Ultra with a white fill and right paragraph alignment.

11. Position the type object so the text is centered vertically in the banner shape, 1/8″ from the right panel edge (as shown in the following image).

Side 1 is the active layer.

12. Using the Selection tool, press Option/Alt-Shift and drag the type object right until the bounding box is 1/8″ from the left edge of the second side panel.

The cloned object automatically appears on the same layer as the original. Because these objects exist on Side 1, which is lower than Side 2, the red shape on Side 2 obscures the text in the cloned type object.

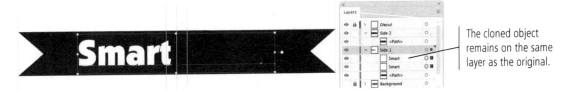

The cloned object remains on the same layer as the original.

13. In the Layers panel, drag the Selected Art icon to the Side 2 layer.

When you move objects from one layer to another using the Selected Art icon, the objects are automatically moved to the top of the object stacking order on the target layer.

14. Using the Control or Paragraph panel, change the selected object to left paragraph alignment. Use the Selection tool to reposition the type object to be 1/8″ from the left edge of the Side 2 panel area.

You might want to reset the zero point to the left edge of this panel, or you can simply use the artboard rulers to place the second type object properly.

15. Change the type in the second object to **Tarts**.

16. Apply kerning as necessary for each type object until you are satisfied with the result.

Note:

Feel free to toggle rulers on and off (View>Rulers>Show/Hide Rulers, or Command/Control-R) as necessary to complete the exercises in this project.

17. **Place the insertion point at the end of the second type object, then open the Glyphs panel (Window>Type>Glyphs).**

18. **Scroll through the panel to find the trademark symbol (TM). Double-click that glyph to add it at the location of the insertion point.**

    The trademark symbol is a single character (glyph) even though it has two letters.

Double-click a glyph to add it at the location of the insertion point.

19. **Highlight the trademark character. In the Character panel, change the type size to 40 pt and change the baseline shift to 10 pt.**

    If you don't see the Baseline Shift field, choose Show Options in the panel Options menu.

Note:

On Macintosh:

Type Option-2 to enter the trademark glyph ™.

Type Option-R to add the registration glyph ®.

Type Option-G to add the copyright glyph ©.

20. **In the Layers panel, click the empty space to the right of the Side 1 layer to select all objects on that layer.**

Click here to select all objects on a layer.

21. **With both shapes on the panel selected, choose Object>Group.**

22. **Repeat Steps 20–21 for the Side 2 panel.**

23. **Save the file and continue to the next exercise.**

Understanding the Glyphs Panel

FOUNDATIONS

The Glyphs panel (Window>Type>Glyphs or Type>Glyphs) provides access to all glyphs in a font. Using the panel is simple: place the insertion point where you want a character to appear, then double-click the character you want to place.

A Show the entire font or access specific character sets

B Double-click a glyph in the chart to add it at the current insertion point

C Change the font family that is displayed in the panel

D Change the font style that is displayed in the panel

E Zoom out (make glyphs in the panel grid smaller)

F Zoom in (make glyphs in the panel grid larger)

By default, the panel shows the entire active font, but you can show only specific character sets using the Show menu.

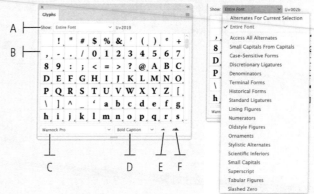

ASCII is a text-based code that defines characters with a numeric value between 001 and 256. The standard alphabet and punctuation characters are mapped from 001 to 128. Extended ASCII characters are those with ASCII numbers higher than 128; these include symbols (copyright symbols, trademark symbols, etc.) and some special formatting characters (en dashes, accent marks, etc.).

OpenType fonts offer the ability to store more than 65,000 glyphs (characters) in a single font — far beyond what you could access with a keyboard (even including combinations of the different modifier keys). The large glyph storage capacity means that a single OpenType font can replace separate "Expert" fonts that contain variations of fonts.

Unicode fonts include two-bit characters common in some foreign language typesetting (e.g., Cyrillic, Japanese, and other non-Roman or pictographic fonts).

Apply a Warp Effect

The Warp effect allows you to easily distort objects in predefined shapes, based on the selected style, direction, bend, and distortion values. The Warp effect, like most Illustrator effects, is non-destructive, which means you can change the applied settings at any time to change the resulting shape.

1. **With `candy-box.ai` open, select the group on the Side 1 layer.**

   You can use the Layers panel to select the group, or simply click the group on the artboard with the Selection tool.

2. **With the group selected, choose Effect>Warp>Arc. In the resulting Warp Options dialog box, activate the Preview check box.**

The bounding box and paths reflect the original objects without the warp.

The icon for each warp style suggests the result that will be created.

The Bend value determines how much warping will be applied.

Distortion values change the horizontal and vertical perspectives.

3. Choose Arch in the Style menu.

As the Arch icon suggests, the object's left and right edges are unaffected by an Arch warp.

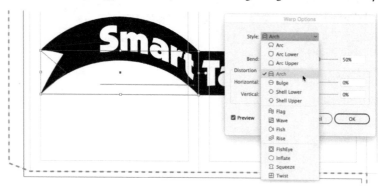

Note:

You can choose from any of the 15 styles in the Style menu (these are the same as the options listed in the Effect>Warp submenu).

4. Change the Bend value to -32 and click OK to apply the warp.

The warp effect is treated as an appearance attribute. When the warped object is selected, you can see the original object shape.

Note:

Effects dialog boxes remember the last-used settings.

5. In the Layers panel, expand the Side 1 and Side 2 layers if necessary so you can see both groups.

6. Press Option/Alt, then click the Target icon for the group in Side 1 and drag to the target icon of the Side 2 group.

The filled target icon indicates that effects and/or transparency attributes have been applied to a specific object. You can move those attributes to a different object by dragging from the filled icon to the hollow icon of another object.

By pressing Option/Alt, you are actually cloning the appearance attributes of the original object and applying those same attributes to another object.

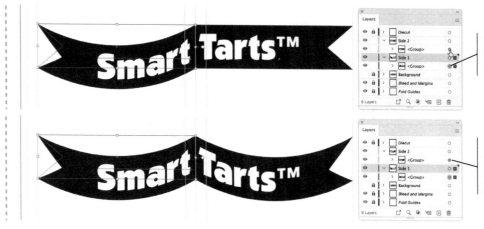

This icon indicates that an appearance attribute has been applied.

Option/Alt-drag the filled target icon to clone the appearance attributes to another object.

7. **Select the group on the Side 2 layer, then open the Appearance panel.**

Remember, effects in Illustrator are non-destructive. You can use the hot-text links in the Appearance panel to change an effect's settings at any

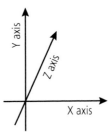

time. You can hide a specific effect by clicking the Eye icon in the Appearance panel, or permanently remove an effect by dragging that listing to the panel's Delete button.

8. **Click the Warp:Arch hot text to reopen the dialog box for the applied effect.**

Choosing the same option more than once in the Effect menu actually applies a second instance of that effect to the selected object. Use the Appearance panel to modify the settings of an applied effect.

9. **Change the bend value to 32% and click OK.**

10. **Save the file and continue to the next exercise.**

Create a 3D Effect

3D effects allow you to create three-dimensional objects from two-dimensional artwork. You can simulate depth by changing an object's rotation along three axes, or use extrusion settings to basically "pull" an object in three directions. You can also control the appearance of 3D objects with lighting, shading, and other properties.

1. **With candy-box.ai open, use the Selection tool to select the banner group on the Side 1 panel.**

2. **Choose Effect>3D>Extrude & Bevel and activate the Preview option.**

In the 3D Extrude & Bevel Options dialog box, the cube/preview shows the approximate position of the original object (the blue surface) in relation to the object created by the settings in this dialog box.

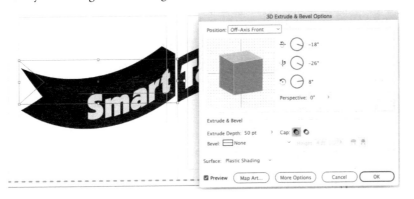

Note:

The X Axis value rotates an object around an invisible horizontal line.

The Y Axis value rotates an object around an invisible vertical line.

The Z Axis value rotates an object around an invisible line that moves from the front of an object to the back.

3. Click the preview icon and drag it around.

As you drag the preview cube, the values in the three fields change, based on how and where you drag. In the layout, the selected group also changes because the Preview option is active.

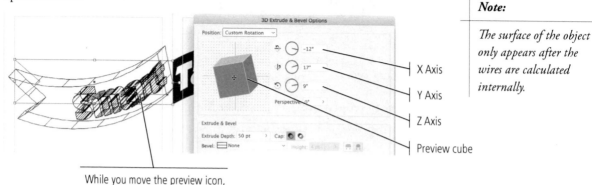

X Axis

Y Axis

Z Axis

Preview cube

Note:

The surface of the object only appears after the wires are calculated internally.

While you move the preview icon, the object appears as a wire frame (the basis of 3D artwork).

4. When you're done experimenting with the preview, specify the following values:

X Axis = 20°

Y Axis = 0°

Z Axis = 0°

Extrude Depth = 50 pt

5. Click OK to apply the effect.

6. Select the banner group on Panel 2, then choose Effect>Apply Extrude & Bevel.

The top menu option shows the last-used effect. If you use this menu command, the effect will be applied with the last-used settings. You will not see the effect's dialog box.

Note:

Illustrator remembers the last-used effect, and the specific settings you used to apply that effect. The top of the Effect menu includes the option to apply the last-used effect without opening the related dialog box, or to open the dialog box for the last-used effect.

7. Using the Arrow keys, nudge the second banner group up or down until the two objects align to each other.

The Extrude & Bevel effect can slightly shift objects on the artboard. To restore the appearance of a single banner extending across both box panels, you have to nudge the extruded banners back into the correct position.

8. Save the file and continue to the next exercise.

Create Type on a Path

You can create unique typographic effects by flowing text onto a path. A text path can be any shape you can create in Illustrator, whether it's a simple shape created with one of the basic shape tools, a straight line drawn with the Line Segment tool, or a complex graphic drawn with the Pen tool.

1. **With candy-box.ai open, lock the groups on the Side 1 and Side 2 layers.**

   You can use the Lock icon for individual sublayers to lock those objects without locking entire layers.

2. **With the Side 1 layer active, choose the Pen tool. Change the fill to None and the stroke to 1-pt black.**

3. **Draw a curve above the banner shape, extending across both panels (as shown in the following image).**

4. **Double-click the Eraser tool in the Tools panel.**

   The Eraser tool erases parts of a shape, whether from an open or closed path. When you use this tool, Illustrator automatically adds anchor points as necessary based on what you erase.

5. **In the resulting dialog box, change the Size field to 8 pt, then click OK.**

   You can also use this dialog box to change the angle and roundness (shape) of the Eraser tool cursor.

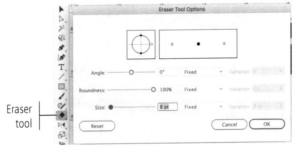

Eraser tool

Note:

The Eraser tool erases from the fill and stroke of the object. The Path Eraser tool only erases from the selected path; an object's fill is not affected.

6. **Place the cursor over the panel fold line between the first and second panels.**

The tool cursor indicates the brush size.

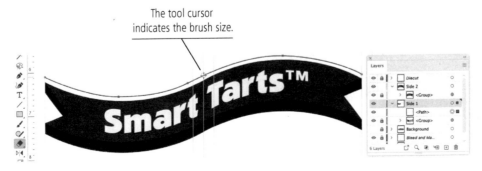

7. **Click to erase 8 points of space from the path you created in Step 3.**

Anchor points are added to the now-open ends of the path where you erased the previous line segment. The Layers panel shows that the result is two separate paths, each of which ends before the fold guide that separates the two panels.

8. **Using the Selection tool, click away from the selected objects to deselect them, then select only the right path (in the second panel).**

9. **In the Layers panel, drag the Selected Art icon from the Side 1 layer to the Side 2 layer.**

Move the right path to the Side 2 layer.

Note:

If you choose Panel Options in the Layers panel Options menu, you can change the size of thumbnails so you can better see the contents of each layer and sublayer.

10. **Select the Type tool in the Tools panel, and then click near the left end of the path on the left panel.**

Clicking an existing path with the Type tool converts the path to a type path. You could select the Type on a Path tool (nested under the Type tool), but it's not necessary because when the Type tool cursor is near an existing path, it automatically switches to the Type on a Path tool cursor.

When the Type tool cursor is near an existing path, it switches to the Type on a Path tool cursor.

The location where you click defines the starting point for text along the path.

11. **Type A sweet, fruity trip to replace the highlighted default placeholder text.**

12. **Select all the text on the path (Select>All) and format it as 24-pt ATC Coral Normal, with 0 pt baseline shift and right paragraph alignment. Change the text color to the dark red swatch.**

The 1-pt black stroke attribute is automatically removed when you convert the stroke to a type path.

The text is aligned to the right end of the type path.

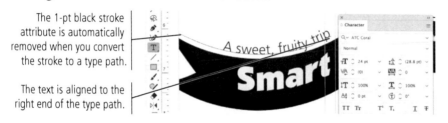

Note:

If you continued directly from the previous exercises, the adjusted baseline shift from the trademark character is still applied. You need to reset the baseline shift to 0 for the type on these paths.

13. **With the Type tool still active, press Command/Control and click away from the active object to deselect it.**

14. **Using the Type tool, click anywhere on the right path to convert it to a type path. Type with a sour zip!.**

    The Type tool remembers the last-used settings, so the second path also uses 24-pt ATC Coral Normal with right paragraph alignment. For some reason, however, the new type is filled with black instead of the custom red swatch.

15. **Change the paragraph alignment to left, and change the type fill color to the custom red swatch.**

Type on a Path Options

You can control the appearance of type on a path by choosing Type>Type on a Path>Type on a Path Options. You can apply one of five effects, change the alignment of the text to the path, flip the text to the other side of the path, and adjust the character spacing around curves (higher Spacing values remove more space around sharp curves).

The **Align options** determine which part of the text (baseline, ascender, descender, or center) aligns to which part of the path (top, bottom, or center).

The **Flip** check box turns type onto the other side of the path. This option is useful for putting text inside shapes.

The **Rainbow** (default) effect keeps each character's baseline parallel to the path.

The **Skew** effect maintains the vertical edges of type, while skewing the horizontal edges around the path.

The **3D Ribbon** effect maintains horizontal edges of type, while rotating vertical edges to be perpendicular to the path.

The **Stair Step** effect aligns the left edge of each character's baseline to the path without rotating any characters.

The **Gravity** effect aligns the center of each character's baseline to the path, keeping vertical edges in line with the path's center.

16. Choose the Direct Selection tool in the Tools panel.

When the insertion point is placed in type on a path (or type on a path is selected), switching to the Direct Selection tool reveals the start and end points of the type path. Modifying those points is the same basic concept as changing the left and right indents for text in a regular type area.

You can also click a type path with the Selection tool, or click the type on the path with the Direct Selection tool, to reveal the start and end points of the type.

17. Click the start bar and drag near the left end of the path, until the "w" is approximately 1/8″ from the left panel edge.

The start bar automatically appears at the point where you first click to create the type path (Step 14). Dragging the start bar repositions the starting point for text on the path.

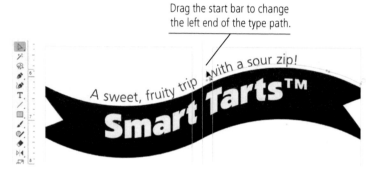

Drag the start bar to change the left end of the type path.

Note:

The start bar's original location is based on where you click to convert the path to a type path.

Note:

Make sure you click the start bar and not the white square that represents the in port of the text path.

18. Unlock the groups on both Side layers, then show the Background layer.

19. Choose Select>All, then move all the selected objects up until the text is not obscured by any object on the Background layer.

Because the Background layer is still locked, the Select>All command selects only the banner groups and type paths.

20. Collapse the Side 1 and Side 2 layers in the Layers panel.

21. Save the file and continue to the next exercise.

Place a Native Photoshop File

Native Photoshop files offer a number of advantages over other formats, including the ability to store multiple layers and even, in some cases, maintain editability directly on the Illustrator artboard.

1. **With `candy-box.ai` open, create a new layer named `Side 3` immediately above the Side 2 layer.**

2. **Lock all but the Side 3 layer, and make sure Side 3 is the active layer.**

3. **Make the third side panel prominent in the document window.**

4. **Using the Rectangle tool, create a white-filled rectangle that fills the third side panel area.**

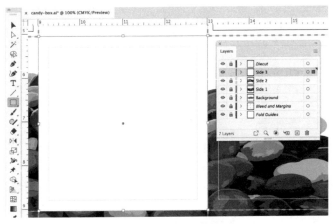

5. **Choose File>Place. Select `box-copy.txt` and click Place. In the resulting dialog box, click OK to accept the default text import options.**

   The TXT extension identifies a text-only file, which is a text file that has been saved without any formatting. These files can be generated in any text-editing software, from full word-processing suites to basic text apps on mobile devices.

Note:

The Text Import Options dialog box appears even if Show Import Options is not checked in the Place dialog box.

6. **Click and drag to create an area-type object that fills the margin guides on the Side 3 panel (as shown in the following image).**

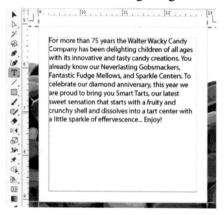

7. **Select all the text in the type area, then change the type formatting to 12.5-pt ATC Coral Normal with 17-pt leading.**

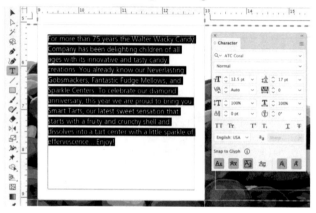

8. **Choose File>Place and select anniversary75.psd (in your WIP>Candy folder). Make sure Link is _not_ checked and Show Import Options _is_ checked, then click Place.**

Note:

*Learn more about Adobe Photoshop in the companion book of this series, **Adobe Photoshop: The Professional Portfolio**.*

9. **In the resulting dialog box, make sure the Show Preview option is checked.**

The Photoshop Import Options dialog box allows you to control how Photoshop elements are translated into Illustrator:

- Use the **Layer Comp** menu to import a specific layer comp saved in the file.

- If you link to the file instead of embedding it, you can use the **When Updating Link** menu to control what happens if you update the linked image.

- **Convert Layers to Objects** converts Photoshop layers to Illustrator objects. This option preserves type layers as editable type objects in Illustrator. It also preserves masks, blending modes, transparency, and slice information. Adjustment layers and layer effects are flattened into the placed objects.

- **Flatten Layers to a Single Image** combines all Photoshop layers into a single layer. The appearance of the image is preserved, but you can't edit the layers.

- **Import Hidden Layers** can be checked to include layers that are not visible in the Photoshop file.

- **Import Slices** is only available if the Photoshop file includes slices for web layouts. If this option is checked, the slices will be maintained in the imported file.

10. **Choose the Convert Layers to Objects option (if necessary) and click OK.**

This image has only one layer, which you will not edit, so this option has the same result as converting Photoshop layers to Illustrator objects.

11. **Click to place the loaded image on the artboard. Using the Selection tool, move the placed file to the top-right corner of the third side panel. Leave approximately 1/8″ between the placed art and the panel edges.**

12. **With the placed object selected, choose Object>Text Wrap>Make.**

Applying a **text wrap** to an object forces surrounding text to flow around that object instead of directly in front of or behind it.

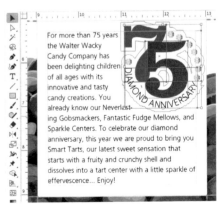

13. Choose Object>Text Wrap>Text Wrap Options.

14. In the resulting dialog box, change the Offset field to 12 pt and click OK.

The **Offset** value defines the distance at which text will wrap from the object.

If you check the Invert Wrap option, the surrounding text will flow into the wrap shape instead of flowing around it.

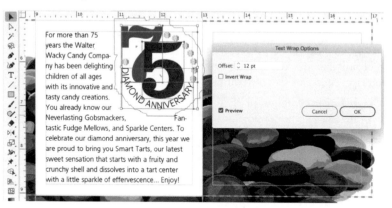

15. Use the Arrow keys to nudge the placed logo group until all text in the story is visible, and you are happy with the position of text.

16. Save the file and continue to the next exercise.

Apply Transparent Effects

Many Illustrator options allow you to add dimension and depth to virtually any design element. You can apply creative effects (such as drop shadows) that incorporate transparency, apply different blending modes so objects blend smoothly into underlying objects, and change the transparency of any object.

1. With candy-box.ai open, expand the Side 3 layer in the Layers panel and then expand the anniversary75.psd sublayer.

Because you chose to convert layers to objects when you placed the native Photoshop file, the resulting object is a group. Each layer in the original file becomes a separate sublayer within the group.

2. Click the Selected Art icon to select only the Seven object in the sublayer.

Select only the Seven object.

3. **Choose Effect>[Illustrator Effects] Stylize>Drop Shadow.**

    Make sure you choose the option in the Illustrator Effects section and not the Photoshop Effects section.

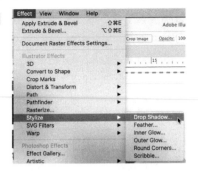

4. **Activate the Preview check box, then change the drop shadow settings to the following:**

Mode:	**Multiply**
Opacity:	**50%**
X Offset:	**0.02 in**
Y Offset:	**0.02 in**
Blur:	**0.03 in**
Color:	**Black**

5. **Click OK to apply the drop shadow.**

6. **Open the Appearance panel (Window>Appearance).**

    The drop shadow is treated as an appearance attribute. You can edit the applied settings by clicking the effect hot text in the Appearance panel. You can remove the effect by dragging it to the Appearance panel's Delete button.

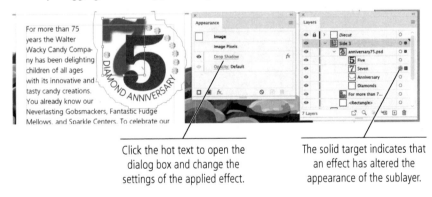

Click the hot text to open the dialog box and change the settings of the applied effect.

The solid target indicates that an effect has altered the appearance of the sublayer.

7. **In the Layers panel, click the target icon to select the Five sublayer in the anniversary75.psd object.**

8. **Choose Effect>Apply Drop Shadow.**

    This command reapplies the listed effect with the last-used settings.

9. **With the Five object still selected, open the Blending Mode menu in the Transparency panel (Window>Transparency) and choose Multiply.**

   After changing the blending mode, the text is a blend of the original black text color and the blue gradient color of the badge object.

10. **Select the white-filled rectangle at the bottom of the Side 3 layer stack.**

11. **In the Transparency panel, change the Opacity field to 80%.**

    The Opacity value determines how much of the underlying colors show through the affected object. If an object is 80% opaque, 20% of the underlying colors are visible.

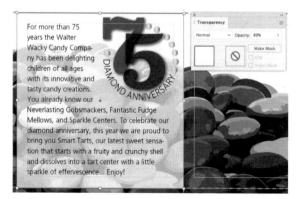

12. **Collapse the Side 3 layer in the Layers panel.**

13. **Save the file and continue to the next exercise.**

Blending Modes

Blending modes control how colors in an object interact with colors in underlying objects. Objects are set to Normal by default, which simply overlays the top object's color onto underlying objects (i.e., the "base").

- **Darken** returns the darker of the blend or base color. Base pixels that are lighter than the blend color are replaced. Base pixels that are darker remain unchanged.

- **Multiply** multiplies (hence, the name) the base color by the blend color, resulting in a darker color. Multiplying any color with black produces black. Multiplying any color with white leaves the color unchanged.

- **Color Burn** darkens the base color by increasing the contrast. Blend colors darker than 50% significantly darken the base color by increasing saturation and reducing brightness. Blending with white has no effect.

- **Lighten** returns the lighter color (base or blend). Base pixels that are darker than the blend color are replaced. Base pixels that are lighter remain unchanged.

- **Screen** is basically the inverse of Multiply, always returning a lighter color. Screening with black has no effect. Screening with white produces white.

- **Color Dodge** brightens the base color. Blend colors lighter than 50% significantly increase brightness. Blending with black has no effect.

- **Overlay** multiplies or screens the blend color to preserve the original lightness or darkness of the base color.

- **Soft Light** darkens or lightens base colors, depending on the blend color. Blend colors lighter than 50% lighten the base color (as if dodged). Blend colors darker than 50% darken the base color (as if burned).

- **Hard Light** combines the Multiply and Screen modes. Blend colors darker than 50% are multiplied, and blend colors lighter than 50% are screened.

- **Difference*** inverts base color values according to the brightness value in the blend layer. Lower brightness values in the blend layer have less effect on the result. Blending with black has no effect.

- **Exclusion*** is similar to Difference, except mid-tone values in the base color are completely desaturated.

- **Hue*** results in a color with the luminance and saturation of the base color and the hue of the blend color.

- **Saturation*** results in a color with the luminance and hue of the base color and saturation of the blend color.

- **Color*** results in a color with the luminance of the base color, and the hue and saturation of the blend color.

- **Luminosity*** results in a color with the hue and saturation of the base color, and the luminance of the blend color (basically, the opposite of the Color mode).

*To prevent problems in the output process, avoid applying these blending modes to objects with spot colors.

Options at the bottom of the Transparency panel allow you to control transparency settings relative to grouped objects. In the examples shown here, the letter and blue shape are grouped. The yellow shape at the back of the object stacking order is not part of the group. If you don't see these check boxes, choose Show Options in the panel Options menu.

Choose Show Options in the panel Options menu to show these check boxes.

If **Isolate Blending** is checked for the group, blending changes only apply to other objects in the same group. The group effectively knocks out the underlying shapes. In this example, we applied the Multiply blending to the purple letter. When Isolate Blending is checked for the group (bottom), the blending mode does not affect the underlying yellow shape.

If **Knockout Group** is checked, transparency settings for elements within the group do not apply to other elements in the same group. The transparent effects are only applied to objects under the entire group. In this case, elements within the group knock out other objects in the same group. In the images here, the opacity of the purple letter has been reduced to 50%. When Knockout Group is checked (bottom), the opacity only affects underlying objects that are not part of the group.

If **Opacity and Mask Define Knockout Shape** is checked, the mask object's opacity creates a knockout effect. Where the mask is 100% opaque, the knockout effect is strong. In areas of lower opacity, the knockout is weaker.

An opacity mask defines the transparency of selected artwork. In Illustrator, you can create an opacity mask by selecting two or more shapes and clicking the Make Mask button in the Transparency panel. The topmost selected object (or group) becomes the masking object. Underlying objects in the selection are the masked artwork.

The best way to explain the concept of opacity masks is through example. The first image shows two separate objects: the top object (the word "OK" converted to outlines) and the gradient-filled rectangle.

When you define an opacity mask, shades in the masking (top) object determine the degree of transparency in the masked (underlying) artwork.

- Where the mask is white, the masked object is 100% visible.
- Shades of gray in the mask allow some of the underlying object to be visible.
- Black areas of the mask completely obscure underlying areas.

Masked artwork thumbnail   Mask thumbnail

When the **Invert Mask** option is checked, tones in the masking object are reversed (black becomes white and white becomes black). Transparency of the masked artwork is also effectively reversed.

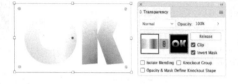

When the **Clip** option is checked, the masking object also determines which parts of the masked artwork are visible; any areas outside the mask object are not visible. In this image, we turned off the Clip option to allow the gradient-filled rectangle to be visible beyond the edges of the masking lettershapes.

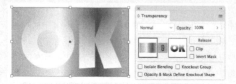

By default, the masking object and masked artwork are linked, which means you can't move one without the other. If you click the Link icon between the masked artwork and the mask thumbnails, you can move the two elements independently.

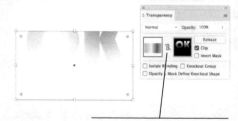

Turn off the Link option to move either object independently.

Use the Touch Type Tool

If you have completed the previous projects in this book, you've already learned a number of ways for manipulating type in an Illustrator file. As you know, you can highlight any characters and change their formatting using the Character panel options. You can also convert type to outlines, and then transform it as you would any other drawing object (using the Selection tool, Free Transform tool, etc.).

In this exercise, you learn how to use the Touch Type tool, which allows you to dynamically transform a selected character using transformation handles, all while maintaining the character as live text. This means you can simply drag in the artboard to experiment with character size and position, but still maintain the ability to edit the actual text in the type object.

1. **With candy-box.ai open, create a new layer named Box Top above the Side 3 layer. Lock all other layers, and make the Box Top layer active.**

2. **Make the Box Top area of the artboard prominent in the document window.**

3. **Using the Type tool, create a new point-type object with the following text:**
   alter [Return/Enter]
   Wacky

4. **Format the type as 56-pt ATC Pyrite Heavy with 50-pt leading, with right paragraph alignment.**

5. **Position the type object so it is centered near the top of the Box Top panel area.**

6. **Choose the Touch Type tool (nested below the regular Type tool).**

Note:

This tool is called the "Touch Type" tool because its options work on a touch-enabled screen.

7. **Click the W in the point-type object to select it.**

When you select a character with the Touch Type tool, you can use the resulting handles to modify the selected character in much the same way as you would transform an object that is selected with the Free Transform tool.

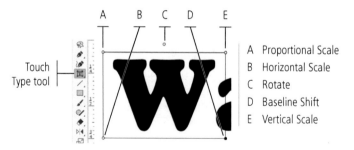

Touch Type tool

A B C D E

A Proportional Scale
B Horizontal Scale
C Rotate
D Baseline Shift
E Vertical Scale

8. **Click inside the character's bounding box and drag down until the bottom is slightly below the baseline of the second line.**

We aligned the top of the uppercase W with the top of the lowercase a.

Note:

You can also click the Baseline Shift handle to reposition the selected character.

Click inside the bounding box and drag to reposition the character.

Baseline Shift:-8.1 pt

9. **Click the Proportional Scale handle and drag up and left until the top of the W is higher than the tops of the letters in the first line.**

H.Scale:272.21 %
V.Scale:272.21 %

BOX TO

10. **Click the Horizontal Scale handle and drag right to make the scaled character slightly narrower.**

X TO

H.Scale:214.8 %

11. **Choose the Type tool in the Tools panel, then click to place the insertion point before the "a" in the second line of the type object.**

When you place the insertion point in a type object where characters have been manipulated with the Touch Type tool, it can be very helpful to use the Arrow keys to move the insertion point to the location you need.

12. **Using the Character panel, reduce the kerning between the W and the a.**

Remember, kerning adjusts the space between two specific letters. Although you modified the W with the Touch Type tool, it is still a live character, which means you can still use kerning to adjust the spacing between the characters.

13. **Continue adjusting the kerning for all letter pairs in the type object until you are satisfied with the results.**

14. **Place the insertion point at the beginning of the first line. Increase the kerning until the entire letter "a" is visible past the modified character.**

When the insertion point is at the beginning of a line, kerning moves the first character left or right relative to the end of the type path; all other letters in the line also move.

15. **Save the file and continue to the next exercise.**

Apply a Built-In Graphic Style

In addition to the numerous effects that you can apply, Illustrator includes a number of graphic style libraries, which are simply stored groups of appearance attributes that can be applied in a single click. In this exercise you will use a built-in style to create a custom logotype for the top and bottom of the box.

1. **With `candy-box.ai` open, select the logotype object (on the Box Top layer) with the Selection tool.**

2. **Move the type object to be approximately centered in the box-top panel area.**

3. **Choose Window>Graphic Style Libraries>Scribble Effects.**

   Graphic styles are managed in much the same way as swatches and other libraries.

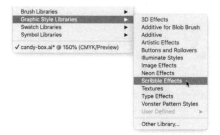

4. **With the logotype object selected, click the top-left style in the Scribble Effects panel.**

5. **Open the Appearance panel and review the options.**

   Built-in styles are basically a combination of attributes and effects that can be applied in Illustrator. They are all non-destructive, which means the logotype object is still live text.

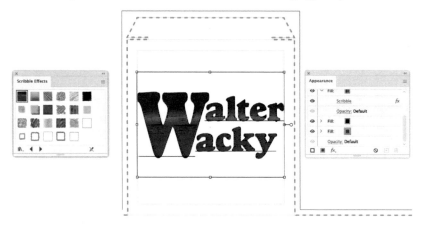

6. **Create another point-type object with the words Candy Company. Format the type in this object as 15-pt ATC Coral Normal, and change the type fill color to the custom pink swatch.**

7. **Move the second type object until it appears as shown in the following image:**

8. **Select the two objects on the top panel and group them.**

9. **Create a new layer named Box Bottom above the Box Top layer.**

10. **Select the group on the Box Top layer. In the Layers panel, Option/Alt-click the Selected Art icon, then drag to the Box Bottom layer.**

    By this point, you should realize that this clones the selected art, placing the cloned copy on the Box Bottom layer.

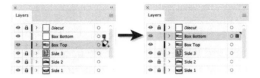

11. **Lock the Box Top layer.**

12. **On the artboard, drag the art on the Box Bottom layer so it is centered in the box-bottom panel area.**

13. **Using the Layers panel, select only the logotype object in the group. Apply a 1-pt white stroke to the selected object.**

    This helps the logotype to stand out from the background object.

Click here to add a new stroke to the selected object...

...then use these menus to change the stroke color and weight.

14. **Save the file and continue to the next stage of the project.**

Because object opacity, blending modes, and some effects relate to transparency, you should understand what transparency is and how it affects your output. Transparency is the degree to which light passes through an object, so that objects in the background are visible. In terms of graphic design, transparency means being able to "see through" objects in the front of the stacking order to objects in the back of the stacking order.

Because of the way printing works, applying transparency in print graphic design is a bit of a contradiction. Commercial printing is, by definition, accomplished by overlapping a mixture of (usually) four semi-transparent inks in different percentages to reproduce a range of colors (the printable gamut). In that sense, all print graphic design requires transparency.

But *design* transparency refers to the objects on the page. The trouble is, when a halftone dot is printed, it's either there or it's not. There is no "50% opaque" setting on a printing press. This means that a transformation needs to take place behind the scenes, translating what we create on screen into what a printing press produces.

When transparent objects are output, overlapping areas of transparent elements are actually divided into individual elements (where necessary) to produce the best possible results. Ink values in the overlap areas are calculated by the application based on the capabilities of the mechanical printing process. The software converts our digital designs into the elements that are necessary to print.

Although some output devices can accurately translate transparent elements to printed elements, older equipment might have problems rendering transparency. Similarly, if the file you're creating will be placed into another layout — for example, as an ad in a magazine or newspaper — you also need to consider the capabilities of the software being used to create the larger project. Older versions of software might not be able to interpret transparent elements correctly.

For transparent elements to output properly in these workflows, the transparent elements must be converted, or **flattened**, into information that can be rendered.

The following exercises explain the concept of flattening so you will understand what to do if your file needs to work with older equipment that does not support transparent design elements.

Note:

Don't assume everyone has the most recent version of a software application or output device. For one reason or another, many professional environments still use older versions of software or older output device drivers.

Define Raster Effect Settings

Flattening means dividing transparent elements into the necessary vector and raster objects to properly output the file. In some cases, flattening results in the creation of new rasterized objects (for example, where transparent text overlaps a raster image).

If you are going to create raster objects — either manually or allowing Illustrator to manage the process — you need to be able to control the resolution of those elements. For high-quality print jobs, you should use at least 300 pixels per inch.

This white text has been set to 80% opacity.

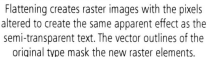

Flattening creates raster images with the pixels altered to create the same apparent effect as the semi-transparent text. The vector outlines of the original type mask the new raster elements.

This text has a drop shadow applied.

Flattening the text object results in a separate raster object to create the drop shadow.

1. **With `candy-box.ai` open, choose Effect>Document Raster Effects Settings.**

2. **Review the settings in the resulting dialog box.**

   These settings, applied in the printer's original template, are already optimized for high-quality output. However, it's a good idea to check the settings when you work.

   The **Color Model** menu determines the mode that will be used for new rasterized objects (CMYK, Grayscale, or Bitmap for a document in CMYK mode; an RGB option replaces CMYK if the file uses the RGB color mode).

   The **Resolution** options include three basic settings: 72 ppi for low-resolution screen display, 150 ppi for medium-resolution desktop printers, or 300 ppi for high-resolution print output. You can also assign a custom resolution in the Other field.

   The **Background** options determine how unfilled areas of the file will be handled when placed into another file. If White is selected, underlying objects will not be visible through empty areas of the file.

   In the **Options** area:

   - **Anti-alias** helps to create smooth transitions, reducing stair-stepping around the edges of rasterized objects.

   - **Create Clipping Mask** creates a vector mask that makes the background of the rasterized image appear transparent.

   - **Add _ Around Object** creates a specific-sized border around a rasterized image. If you use the White Background option, this area will be filled with white.

   - **Preserve Spot Colors** allows spot-color objects to be maintained as spot colors instead of being converted to CMYK.

3. **Click OK to close the dialog box.**

4. **Continue to the next exercise.**

Note:

Note the warning at the bottom of the dialog box that says, "Changing these settings may affect the appearance of currently applied raster effects."

 Preview Transparency Flattening

If you are designing with transparency, it's a good idea to know exactly what elements will be affected when the file is flattened for output. Illustrator provides a Flattener Preview panel that you can use to review the file for potential problems.

1. **With `candy-box.ai` open, choose Window>Flattener Preview.**

2. **If nothing appears in the white space of the panel, click the Refresh button.**

Drag this corner to make the panel larger, and then click Refresh to enlarge the preview image.

3. **In the Highlight menu, choose All Affected Objects.**

The red areas in the preview show all objects that are affected by transparency in the file; all of these objects will somehow be affected by flattening. You can use the Flattener Preview to highlight different kinds of areas to determine which settings are best for the entire file or for a specific object.

- **None (Color Preview)** displays the normal layout.
- **Rasterized Complex Regions** highlights areas that will be rasterized based on the Raster/Vector Balance defined in the applied preset.
- **Transparent Objects** highlights objects with opacity of less than 100%, blending modes, and/or transparency effects (such as drop shadows).
- **All Affected Objects** highlights all objects affected by transparency, including the transparent objects and the objects overlapped by transparent objects. All of these objects will be affected by flattening.
- **Affected Linked EPS Files** highlights all EPS files that are linked (not embedded) in the file.
- **Expanded Patterns** highlights patterns that will be expanded by flattening. Pattern effects must be expanded if they are affected by transparency; this takes place automatically when you output the file.
- **Outlined Strokes** highlights all strokes that will be converted to filled objects when flattened. For example, a 5-pt stroke with the Screen blending mode will be converted to a 5-pt-high rectangle filled with the underlying object when the file is flattened.

4. **In the Highlight menu, choose Transparent Objects.**

The highlighted areas reduce to only the objects where transparency is actually applied.

5. **Choose Show Options in the panel Options menu, and then click Refresh.**

The options show the specific settings that will be used to flatten the artwork, based by default on a flattener preset.

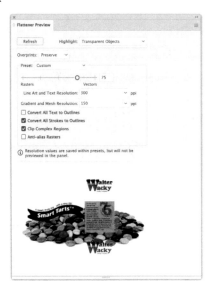

6. **Close the Flattener Preview panel, and then continue to the next exercise.**

More About Outputting Complex Files

Expanding Appearance Attributes

If you select an object and choose Object>Expand Appearance, the object is permanently altered to mimic the appearance of applied effects. Raster effects are converted to raster objects, which are grouped with the converted vector objects.

After expanding effects, the file will output faster, but you won't be able to change the effect settings. We highly recommend saving the original and expanded versions as separate files so you can make changes if necessary.

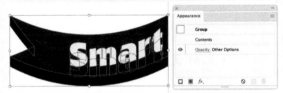

Two effects have been applied to this object:
Warp (Arch) and 3D Extrude & Bevel.

The paths show the new objects created by expanding the effects. The effects are no longer editable.

Flattening Individual Objects

Although flattening is typically managed for you when you output a file, you can also flatten selected objects manually. Flattening is a permanent action — you can no longer edit any effect or setting that caused the transparency. Again, we recommend maintaining your original file and saving a new version with the manually flattened artwork.

When a transparent object is selected, you can choose Object>Flatten Transparency to define settings that will be used to create the necessary raster object.

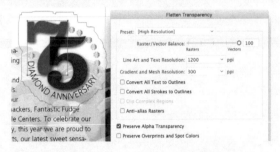

Flattening the object created a new raster object to reproduce the Drop Shadow effect. (If Preserve Alpha Transparency is not checked, the flattened artwork will have a white background; the effect will not blend into the background color.)

Understanding Flattener Presets

Illustrator includes four default flattener presets. You can also choose Edit>Transparency Flattener Presets to create your own presets or load presets that might be provided by others (e.g., an output service provider).

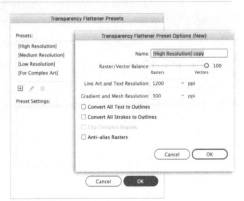

- **Raster/Vector Balance** determines how much vector information will be preserved after flattening, from 0 (all vectors will be rasterized) to 100 (maintains all vector information).

- **Line Art and Text Resolution** defines the resulting resolution of vector elements that will be rasterized, up to 9600 ppi.

- **Gradient and Mesh Resolution** defines the resolution for gradients that will be rasterized, up to 1200 ppi.

- **Convert All Text to Outlines** converts all type to outlines. The text will not be editable or selectable in a PDF file.

- **Convert All Strokes to Outlines** converts all strokes to filled paths.

- **Clip Complex Regions** forces boundaries between vector objects and rasterized artwork to fall along object paths, reducing potential problems that can result when only part of an object is rasterized.

- **Anti-Alias Rasters** helps to create smoother edges in the raster images that are created from vector graphics.

Export a PDF File for Proofing

Although packaging such as this box is commonly printed directly from the Illustrator file, you should still create a proof that your client can review either on screen or printed. The PDF format is ideal for this use because the client doesn't need Illustrator to open or print the proof file.

1. **With `candy-box.ai` open, choose File>Save As.**

2. **Navigate to your WIP>Candy folder as the destination and choose Adobe PDF in the Format/Save As Type menu.**

3. **Click Save.**

4. **Choose High Quality Print in the Adobe PDF Preset menu.**

   The Adobe PDF Preset menu includes six PDF presets that meet common industry output requirements.

5. **Choose Acrobat 4 (PDF 1.3) in the Compatibility menu.**

   The Compatibility menu determines which version of the PDF format you will create. Not all clients will have the latest versions of technology, so you should consider saving all proof-quality PDFs to be compatible with the earliest version of PDF possible.

6. **Click Advanced in the list of options.**

   PDF 1.3 does not support transparency, so the file will require flattening. If you save the file to be compatible with PDF 1.4 or later, the transparency information will be maintained in the PDF file; it will have to be flattened later in the process.

7. **Choose High Resolution in the Preset menu.**

Even though this PDF is for proofing purposes, high-resolution produces better results. If file size is not a concern, it's a good idea to use the high-resolution flattener even for proofs.

8. **Click Save PDF to output the file.**

9. **Close the PDF file, then continue to the final stage of the project.**

STAGE 4 / Previewing the Box in 3D

In Stage 2, you used the 3D Extrude & Bevel feature to add depth to the banners on the front of the box. This effect can also be used to create a box shape, and preview your flat box artwork in three dimensions, which is especially useful for showing a client how the art will look when the final piece is printed and folded.

Export Artboards for Screens

As you know, the background image for the box artwork currently extends across multiple panels in the folding template. To map artwork to a 3D box mock-up, you need to cut that background image into separate pieces for each box panel. Although there are many ways to accomplish this goal, the easiest is to use artboards to define the different sides of the box.

1. **Open candy-box.ai from your WIP>Candy folder. Zoom out so you can see the entire artboard.**

Make sure you open the Illustrator file and not the PDF file that you created at the end of the last stage.

2. **Show all layers except the Diecut and Bleed and Margins layers, then lock all layers.**

3. **Choose the Artboard tool in the Tools panel. Click to the right of the existing artboard and drag to create a new artboard.**

If you click inside the existing artboard area, dragging will move the existing artboard instead of creating a new one. Instead, you are using the pasteboard to create the new artboard; you can then move it into the correct position overlapping the existing artboard.

4. **In the Control panel, change the new artboard name to box-top.**

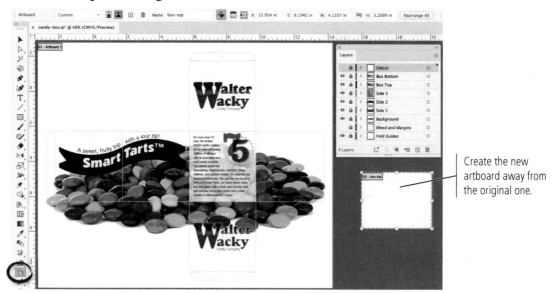

Create the new artboard away from the original one.

5. **Move the Artboard tool cursor inside the new artboard area and drag it to be on top of the box top area in the layout.**

Click inside the artboard boundary and drag to reposition it.

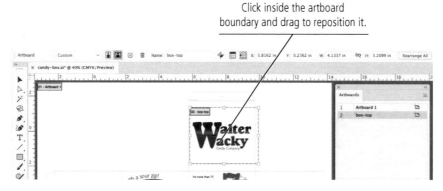

6. **Drag the artboard corner handles to snap to the guides that mark the box top area in the layout.**

After adjusting the handles, the box-top artboard should be 4″ wide × 4″ high.

Snap the artboard edges to the guides that mark the box panel sides.

The artboard should be 4″ wide and 4″ high.

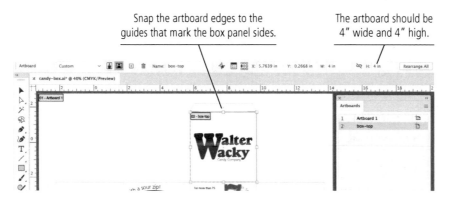

7. **In the Control panel, turn off the Move/Copy Artwork with Artboard option.**

8. **Click the box-top artboard and hold down the mouse button, then press Option/Alt-Shift and drag down to clone the artboard. Place the cloned artboard over the box-bottom area of the layout.**

Clone the artboard and position it over the box-bottom panel.

Move/Copy Artwork with Artboard is toggled off.

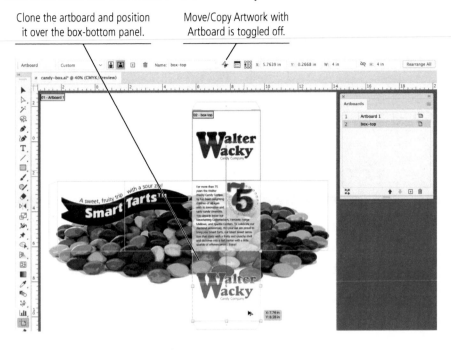

9. **Change the selected artboard's name to** box-bottom.

10. **Using the same general process outlined in the previous steps, create new artboards for the remaining four sides of the box. Use the names shown in the following image.**

You can draw new artboards, or simply clone the existing ones and drag them into place for each side of the box.

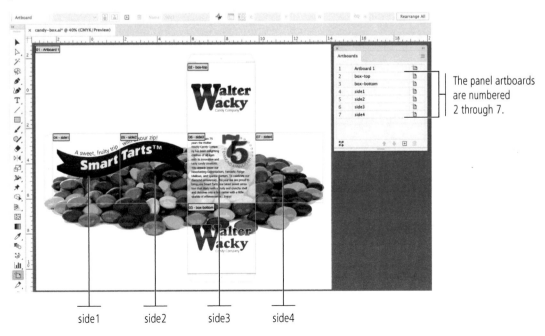

The panel artboards are numbered 2 through 7.

side1   side2   side3   side4

11. **Choose File>Export>Export As.**

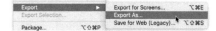

12. **In the resulting dialog box, create a new folder named `side-panels` in your WIP>Candy folder.**

13. **Choose JPEG in the Format/Save As Type menu.**

    Illustrator can export a number of different formats. The JPEG format creates a single flat file with a white background for each artboard you choose to export.

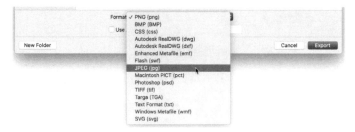

14. **At the bottom of the Export dialog box, choose the Use Artboards option. Choose the Range radio button, and type `2-7` in the attached field.**

    You do not need to export the overall artboard with the diecut layout (Artboard 1). You need to export each of the artboards you just created as a separate file, which you will later use to create the 3D box preview.

Check the Use Artboards option...

...then type **2-7** in the Range field.

15. **Click Export. In the resulting dialog box, define the following settings:**

Color Model:	CMYK
Quality:	10 (Maximum)
Resolution:	High (300 ppi)

16. **Click OK to export the necessary files.**

17. **When the export process is complete, save and close the candy-box.ai file.**

18. **On your desktop, review the contents of your WIP>Candy folder.**

    Six new files, one for each side of the box, should appear in the side-panels folder. The file names are made up of the original file name (which appeared in the Save As field of the Export dialog box) and the artboard name (which you defined earlier).

19. **Continue to the next exercise.**

 Create Symbols for Box Panels

For this process to work, you first have to do a bit of setup work. The artwork for each panel has to be saved as a symbol before it can be applied to the 3D box shape. This means you have to do some cutting and cleanup work so that you have the exact shapes you need before you create the 3D box preview.

1. **Create a new file for print that uses Inches for the unit of measurement and contains two letter-sized artboards. Save it as box-folded.ai in your WIP>Candy folder.**

2. **Choose File>Place. Navigate to your WIP>Candy>side-panels folder. Select all six images in the folder. Make sure none of the options at the bottom of the box are checked, then click Place.**

3. **When the images are loaded into the Place cursor, click to place each loaded image onto the artboard.**

    Don't worry if all the files don't fit into the artboard. You are only using them to create symbols, after which you will delete the original images from the artboard.

4. **Open the Symbols panel (Window>Symbols) and float it away from the panel dock if necessary.**

5. **Open the panel's Options menu and choose Large List View so you can see the symbol names.**

6. **Open the Symbols panel Options menu and choose Select All Unused.**

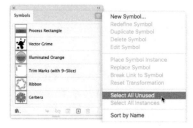

7. **With all the default symbols selected, click the panel's Delete button. Click Yes when asked to confirm the deletion.**

    Although this is not strictly necessary, removing the unnecessary pieces makes it easier to manage the remaining symbols.

8. **Select the box-bottom image on the artboard, then click the New Symbol button in the Symbols panel.**

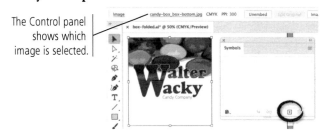

The Control panel shows which image is selected.

9. **In the resulting dialog box, name the symbol `box-bottom` and click OK.**

The other options in this dialog box have no effect on this project, so you can leave them at the default settings.

10. **Repeat Steps 8–9 for the remaining five images on the artboard, naming each symbol appropriately.**

11. **Select all of the placed images on the artboard and delete them.**

12. **Save the file and continue to the next exercise.**

Map the Art to a 3D Box

Now that you have symbols for each side of the box, you have to create a shape that you can turn into a three-dimensional box. This shape needs to be the correct size for the existing artwork, so you will again use the panel folding guides to build the shape.

1. **With `box-folded.ai` open, use the Rectangle tool to create a shape that is 4″ wide by 4″ high, with a white fill and no stroke.**

Each panel on the box template is 4″ square. A shape of this size will be the basis for your three-dimensional box sample.

2. **With the new rectangle selected, choose Effect>3D>Extrude & Bevel. Make sure the Preview option is checked.**

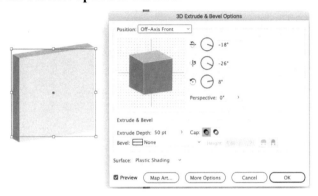

3. In the Extrude Depth field, type 4" and press Tab to apply the change.

Because the shape is 4″ square, you are using this measurement as the depth to create a cube with equal height, width, and depth. Illustrator automatically makes the necessary conversion to points.

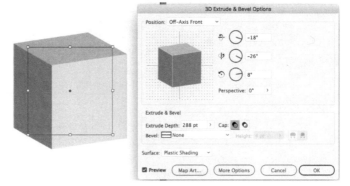

4. Define the following parameters in the Position area:

X axis:	**70°**
Y axis:	**40°**
Z axis:	**-13°**

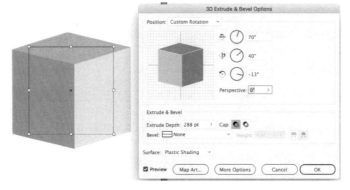

5. Uncheck the Preview box, and then click the Map Art button.

When the Map Art dialog box is open, the object in the layout displays as a 3D wireframe preview, even when the Preview option is unchecked. The red line around the preview shows which side (surface) of the shape is being mapped.

The red line indicates the side where art is being mapped.

Use this menu to choose which symbol to place on the active surface.

Use these options to navigate the surfaces that can have mapped art.

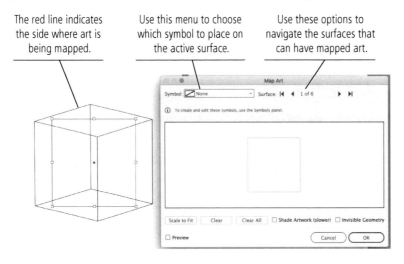

6. **Choose box-top in the Symbol menu, then turn on the Preview option in the Map Art dialog box.**

Illustrator renders a preview of the symbol on the 3D box shape (this might take a few seconds to complete).

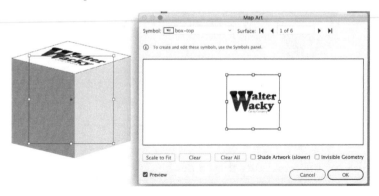

7. **Click the right Next Surface arrow, then choose box-bottom in the Symbol menu.**

The preview shows the box-bottom panel is selected. No other change is apparent because the bottom of the box is not visible using the existing shape position.

The box-bottom surface is not visible in this position.

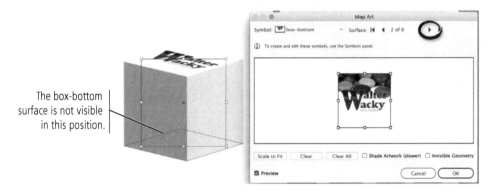

8. **Click the right Surface arrow to select the next side, then choose side4 in the Symbol menu.**

The thumbnail is placed in the wrong orientation, so you need to rotate it. You can click an object in the Map Art preview and drag to move the symbol artwork, or you can use the bounding-box handles to resize or rotate the symbol until it fits the gray surface shape.

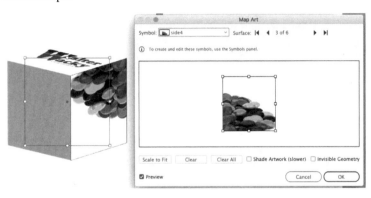

Note:

Rendering 3D artwork takes time and must be redone every time you make a change in the dialog box. If you prefer, you can turn off the Preview option while you're making changes, and then turn it on only when you want to review your progress.

9. **Place the cursor near one of the top corner handles. Click when you see the rotate cursor, press Shift, and drag around to rotate the artwork 180°.**

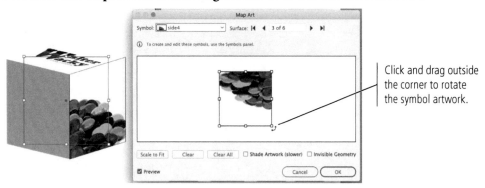

Click and drag outside the corner to rotate the symbol artwork.

10. **Repeat Steps 8–9 to add the artwork for the remaining three sides.**

Make sure you place the symbols in the correct order. Because the side4 artwork is on the first side panel, you should place side3 on the next panel, then side2, then side1.

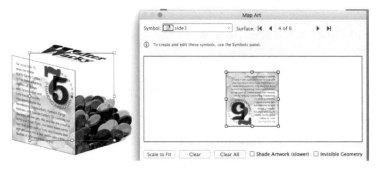

You won't see any difference in the artboard for surfaces 5 and 6 because they are not visible in this position. You will create another object to show those sides in the next few steps.

11. Click OK to close the Map Art dialog box, and then click OK again to finalize the 3D box preview.

12. Using the Selection tool, clone the existing shape and place the clone on the second artboard.

13. In the Appearance panel, click the 3D Extrude & Bevel hot-text link to open the dialog box for that effect.

14. Check the Preview option at the bottom of the dialog box. In the preview proxy, place the cursor over one of the vertical lines and drag until the other two sides of the box are visible.

Dragging one of the vertical lines in the proxy changes only the Z rotation.

  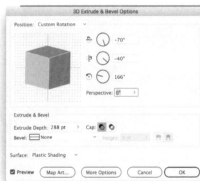

15. Click OK to apply the change.

16. Save the file and close it.

1. You can use the _____ tool to sample colors from placed images.

2. The _____ can be used to review all the available characters in a font.

3. Checking the _____ option when you place a native Photoshop file results in a single object on a single layer in the Illustrator file.

4. The _____ determines the left-indent position of type on a path.

5. You can use the _____ panel to review and edit applied effects.

6. Applying a(n) _____ to an object forces surrounding text to flow around that object instead of directly in front of or behind it.

7. The _____ is the specific method used to blend the color of one object into the colors of underlying objects.

8. _____ refers to the degree to which light passes through an object.

9. A(n) _____ can be used to restrict opacity to selected objects; colors in the topmost object determine which areas of the underlying object are visible.

10. The _____ effect can be used to preview a box 3D shape.

1. Briefly explain how the concept of a diecut relates to package design in Illustrator.

2. Briefly explain the concept of sublayers, including at least one example of their potential benefit.

3. Briefly explain how transparency settings relate to Illustrator files created for commercial printing.

Use what you have learned in this project to complete the following freeform exercise.
Carefully read the art director and client comments, then create your own design to meet the needs of the project.
Use the space below to sketch ideas. When finished, write a brief explanation of the reasoning behind your final design.

art director comments

You have been hired to create a label design for a new energy water called triUMPH. It is going to be marketed throughout the United States, so it must incorporate the required elements for food packaging and retail sales.

❑ Use the label template that has been provided in the **Triumph_AI21_PB.zip** archive on the Student Files web page.

❑ Create a compelling type treatment for the product name. Find or create imagery as necessary to support the overall package design.

❑ Include the nutrition information and the barcode that have been provided by the client. Also include the package size (16.9 FL OZ/500 mL) somewhere in the label design.

❑ Include the "Recycle" logo in the design.

❑ Include the following text in the design: ME-HI-5¢ CA CRV

client comments

The energy drink market is huge in the United States, so we've decided to branch out from our traditional soda manufacturing. We need you to create an energetic logotype for the new product, as well as a complete label design for the bottles.

Our printing company has provided us with a template that is standard for this type of packaging. The pressroom manager wanted me to make sure to remind you to keep important design elements away from the glue area that is indicated on the template.

Because this is a consumable product, there are a lot of elements that must be incorporated in the package design. Make sure nothing important is left out, or we won't be able to meet our ship date.

project justification

The flexible artboard size and layer controls, coupled with the extensive set of creative tools, make Illustrator ideally suited to meet the complex needs of packaging design. You can design sophisticated artwork that can be wrapped or folded into virtually any shape to package virtually any product.

This project combined the technical requirements of packaging design — specifically using a custom diecut template supplied by the output provider — with the artistic capabilities necessary to create the final design for a custom candy package. You composited a number of existing elements and created others, then used a number of features to modify artwork, adding interest and depth to unify the different pieces into a single, cohesive design.

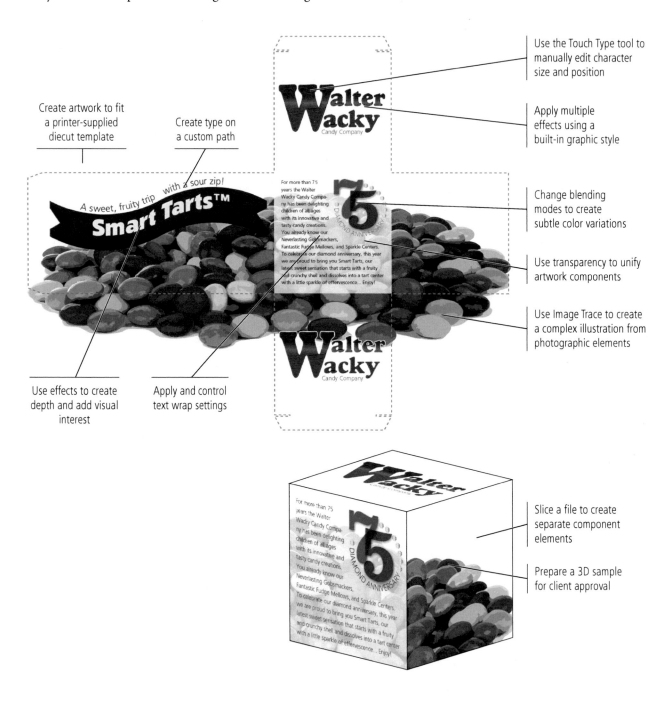

Use the Touch Type tool to manually edit character size and position

Apply multiple effects using a built-in graphic style

Create artwork to fit a printer-supplied diecut template

Create type on a custom path

Change blending modes to create subtle color variations

Use transparency to unify artwork components

Use Image Trace to create a complex illustration from photographic elements

Use effects to create depth and add visual interest

Apply and control text wrap settings

Slice a file to create separate component elements

Prepare a 3D sample for client approval

Consumer Infographics

As the illustrator for a magazine publisher, it's your job to create interesting graphics for articles in a variety of magazines. Next month's feature article is about trends in the food and beverage industry. You need to create several graphs and one illustration to accompany the article.

This project incorporates the following skills:

❑ Creating graphs to present data in a visual format

❑ Editing graph data to change the appearance of a graph

❑ Importing data from an external file

❑ Managing fills, legends, and labels to make graphs more visually appealing

❑ Defining a perspective grid

❑ Putting objects into the correct perspective

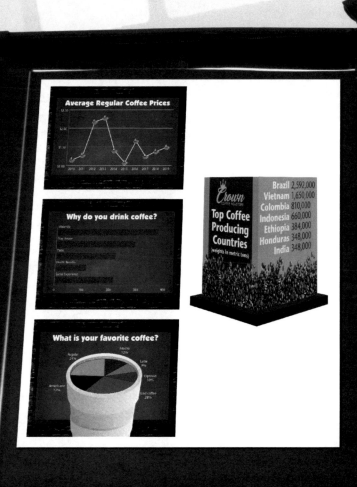

PROJECT MEETING

One feature article in next month's trade magazine for the food and beverage industry is about trends in coffee production and drinking.

We need three different graphs:

- Historical coffee pricing data
- Coffee-drinking habits as reported by consumers (from a long-term survey)
- Coffee preferences (from the same survey)

This is a general interest consumer magazine and not a financial report. I'd like something more than just a set of plain graphs. I'd like you to put the graphs into some kind of context, or overall illustration, to make the presentation more interesting.

Finally, we want some kind of illustration showing the seven top coffee producing countries in the world. I don't want just a boring table of numbers.

Before you start creating the graphs, you should evaluate the kinds of data you have; that way, you can determine which type of graph will best suit the data. Illustrator's graphing tools support many graph types, but you probably won't need more than a few. Bars and pies are the most common types, but the others have important uses, too.

You might want to look at some other consumer and personal financial magazines to see how different kinds of graphs and charts are typically used, and how they are incorporated into illustrations to make the data appear more attractive and interesting.

I sketched a "coffee dispenser" idea that I think will be a good container for the final illustration. I already put it into an Illustrator file and created the pieces I want you to use in the perspective artwork.

To complete this project, you will:

- ❑ Create line, bar, and pie graphs to present different types of data
- ❑ Edit live graph data to change the segment breakdown in a graph
- ❑ Import data from an external file to create a graph
- ❑ Edit fills, legends, and labels to create aesthetically pleasing, technically accurate graphs
- ❑ Create a perspective grid for complex, three-dimensional artwork
- ❑ Draw new objects on different perspective planes
- ❑ Move and transform perspective objects
- ❑ Create type objects in perspective
- ❑ Place existing artwork and symbols in perspective

STAGE 1 / Creating Charts and Graphs

The first stage of this project revolves around one of the more powerful, but least-used functions in Illustrator — the ability to generate graphics based on data. Information graphics (referred to as "infographics") are illustrations that deliver information; bar graphs, pie charts, and area charts are all examples of information provided in a visual format that makes it easier to understand.

Successfully designing infographics requires knowing which kind of chart best shows which type of information. Once you know what kind of chart you need, Illustrator provides the tools to generate the chart.

Distinguishing Types of Graphs

Column graphs compare values across several categories using vertical columns.

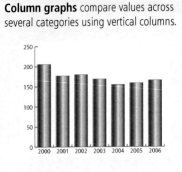

Bar graphs compare values over several categories using horizontal bars.

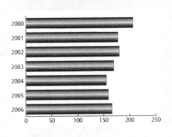

Line graphs plot a series of points across the graph, connecting those points with a line. These graphs show a progressive change in values, such as different prices over time.

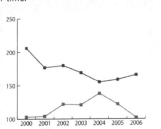

Stacked column graphs divide each column into segments to show the relationship between pieces of the total value.

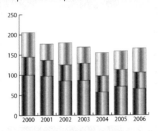

Stacked bar graphs are horizontal versions of stacked column graphs.

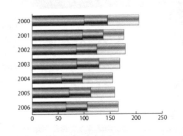

Area graphs are modified line graphs. The space below the line is filled to emphasize the plotted values.

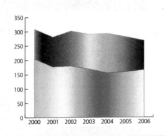

Scatter graphs plot multiple data points along the horizontal and vertical axes. These graphs are used to show trends or clusters in the data points.

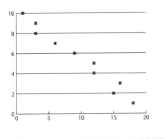

Pie graphs show categorical values as percentages of the whole.

Radar graphs compare sets of values in a circular format. These graphs are useful for displaying cyclical data, such as annual sales by month.

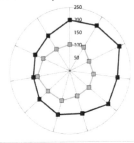

Create a Line Graph

The first graph for this project is based on historical data of coffee prices. Because this data tracks a change in value over time, a line graph is the best way to represent this information visually.

1. **Download Coffee_AI21_RF.zip from the Student Files web page.**

2. **Expand the ZIP archive in your WIP folder (Macintosh) or copy the archive contents into your WIP folder (Windows).**

   This results in a folder named **Coffee**, which contains the files you need for this project. You should also use this folder to save the files you create in this project.

3. **Create a new file by opening the file chalkboard.ait in your WIP>Coffee folder.**

   You will use this artwork as the "frame" for each of the graphs you build in this project.

4. **In the Tools panel, choose the Line Graph tool (it might be nested under one of the other graph tools).**

   When you choose a specific graph tool, it becomes the default tool in the Tools panel. Depending on what was previously done in your version of the application, your default graph tool might be different than ours.

5. **Click and drag an area that snaps to the guides on the artboard.**

   The size you define here represents the size of the graph shape only; it does not include the legend or axis labels. If you know the amount of space available for the entire graph (including labels and legend), you should define a smaller graph size so the labels and legend fit within the available space.

Note:

If you click once with a graph tool, a dialog box opens where you can define the height and width of the new graph, just as when you single-click with one of the basic drawing tools.

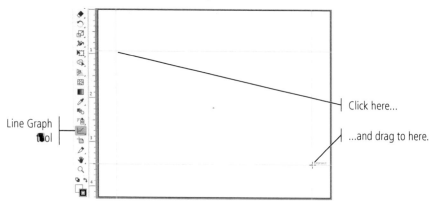

Line Graph tool

Click here...

...and drag to here.

When you create a new graph, a spreadsheet-like window opens. This is the Illustrator Data panel, where you enter the data that will make up your graph. You can simply type in the various data cells, but many graphing projects will involve importing data from an external file, as you will do in this project.

6. **In the Data panel, click the Import Data button. Navigate to the file prices.txt in the WIP>Coffee>Data folder and click Open.**

This data was originally a Microsoft Excel file, but it was exported as a tab-delimited text-only file. You cannot directly import an Excel file into Illustrator; if you try, you will see either an error message or incomprehensible data that is useless for making a graph.

Import Data button

7. **Click the Apply button in the Data panel.**

As you can see, there is clearly a problem in the resulting graph. The imported data has two columns of numbers, but the first column actually shows the years associated with the data in the second column. By default, Illustrator's Data panel treats all numbers as parts of the data. In cases like this — when you want certain numbers to be treated as regular text, rather than actual data — you have to enclose those numbers within quotes in the Data panel.

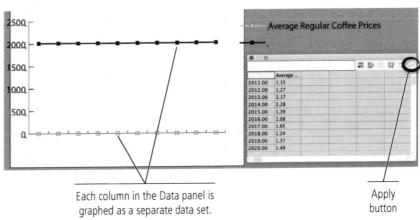

Each column in the Data panel is graphed as a separate data set.

Apply button

8. **Click the 2011.00 cell in the Data panel to select it.**

9. **In the text field at the top of the panel, add quote characters on both sides of the number.**

You can't use the arrow keys on your keyboard to move the insertion point within the Data panel text field. You have to click in the appropriate location to add a new character.

Enclosing the years in quotation marks enables Illustrator to properly translate the numbers as data labels.

Note:

Unlike traditional spreadsheet applications, you can't drag data cells to a new location in the panel. You can, however, cut cells and paste them into a new position if you need to add new data between existing data.

10. Press Return/Enter to highlight the next cell down, and then add quote characters around the 2012 text.

Pressing Tab moves to the next cell in the row. Pressing Return/Enter moves to the next cell down in the column. You can also use the arrow keys to move through the cells.

11. Repeat this process for all years in the table, then click the Apply button at the top of the Data panel.

Unfortunately, there is no way to speed up this process. You simply have to type the quotes for each year in the data.

After clicking apply, you can see the effects of revising the graph data. Because the first column is now treated as labels, the graph has only one data set (one line).

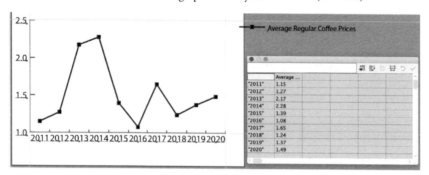

Note:

Pressing the Enter key on your numeric keypad has the same effect as clicking the Apply button.

12. Click the Cell Style button at the top of the Data panel. In the resulting dialog box, change the Number of Decimals field to 3, then click OK.

By default, the Illustrator Data panel shows the first two decimal points in the imported data. The Number of Decimals option changes the number of digits that are visible after the decimal point. If the data does not include as many decimals as you allow, Illustrator adds zeros at the end of the existing values.

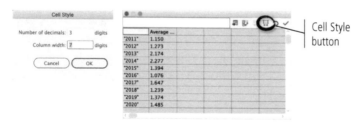

Cell Style button

Note:

The Column Width field can be changed to make longer data points visible in the Data panel cells.

13. Click the Data panel Close button to close the panel. When asked if you want to save changes to the data, click Save/Yes.

Adding the extra decimal is technically a change, even though you won't see a significant change in the actual graph.

Panel Close button

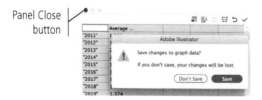

14. Save the file as price-graph.ai in your WIP>Coffee folder and then continue to the next exercise.

Change Graph Formatting Options

When you create a graph in Illustrator, all of the elements within the graph are grouped together in a special graph object. If you ungroup the graph, the data is no longer editable, which means you can no longer replot data points in the graph design. As a general rule, you should maintain a graph object as a graph object as long as possible in case you need to change some aspect of the graph data, which happens far more often than you might expect.

1. **With price-graph.ai open, click any part of the graph object with the Selection tool.**

2. **In the Character panel, change the character formatting to 9-pt ATC Onyx Normal with 90% horizontal scale.**

   Type objects in a graph object are originally formatted with Illustrator's default type settings. When a graph object is selected, changes to type formatting options apply to all type elements within the graph object.

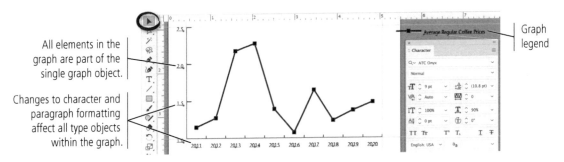

All elements in the graph are part of the single graph object.

Changes to character and paragraph formatting affect all type objects within the graph.

Graph legend

3. **Control/right-click the graph and choose Type in the contextual menu.**

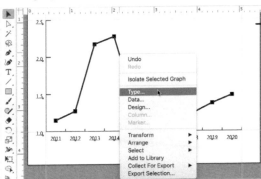

4. **Choose Value Axis in the menu at the top of the resulting dialog box.**

   This dialog box has different options depending on the type of graph you are creating. The value axis (in this case, the vertical axis on the left) is the one that marks the range of values that are depicted in the data. The current axis labels are automatically generated based on the data in the table. This graph shows prices in dollars, so you are going to change the axis labels to more accurately reflect those prices.

5. **Choose Full Width in the Tick Marks Length menu.**

    By default, tick marks are short lines on the inside of the graph area. You can choose Full Width to extend the tick marks across the full width of the graph, or you can choose None to turn off the value axis divisions.

6. **In the Add Labels area, type $ in the Prefix field and type 0 [zero] in the Suffix field.**

    The prefix will be added before the existing axis labels; the suffix will be added at the end of the existing axis labels.

Note:

You can access the same graph-editing options in the Object>Graph submenu.

Note:

Unfortunately, the Graph Type dialog box does not include a Preview check box. You can't see the results of your choices until you click OK. As long as the graph object remains a graph object, you can always make changes.

7. **Choose Category Axis in the top menu and change the corresponding Tick Marks Length menu to None.**

    By default, categories are separated by tick marks (just as values are).

Note:

If you are including divisions in your graph, you can add subdivisions using the Draw _ Tick Marks Per Division option.

8. **Click OK to apply your changes.**

The value labels now include the prefix and suffix, clearly showing that they are prices.

Value-axis tick marks now extend the full width of the graph.

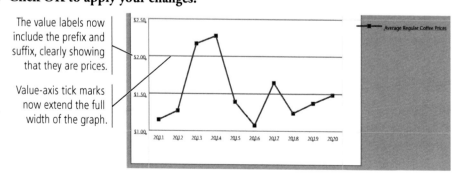

9. **Save the file and continue to the next exercise.**

Transform Graph Objects and Graph Components

The special nature of a graph object makes changing the individual elements a bit tricky, but you can change the formatting of various pieces within the graph as long as you understand how to access them.

You cannot resize a graph object by dragging bounding-box handles or using the Transform panel. You can, however, use the transformation tools (Scale, Rotate, Reflect, and Shear) or the transformation dialog boxes that are available in the Object>Transform submenu. You can also use the Direct Selection tool to access and edit individual elements within a graph.

1. **With price-graph.ai open, use the Selection tool to select the graph object on the artboard.**

   Remember, the Selection tool selects entire objects.

2. **With the graph object selected on the artboard, double-click the Scale tool in the Tools panel.**

   Double-clicking a transformation tool opens the related dialog box, where you can numerically define the transformation. This is the same dialog box you would access by choosing Object>Transform>Scale; double-clicking the tool provides a faster method for accessing the dialog box.

3. **Choose the Uniform Scale option and type 90% in the field.**

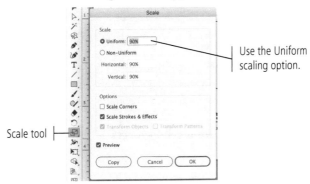

Scale tool

Use the Uniform scaling option.

4. **Click OK to return to finalize the change.**

   Transformations applied to a graph object apply to every element of the graph, including the type. By reducing the graph size to 90%, you also changed the type to 90% of the 9 pt you defined in the previous exercise.

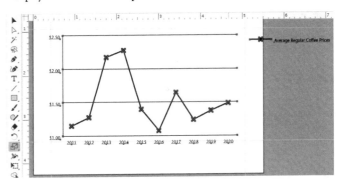

5. **Choose the Selection tool again. With the graph object selected, change the type size back to 9 pt.**

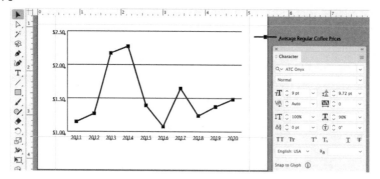

6. **With the graph object still selected, use the arrow keys to nudge the graph until it fits entirely within the guides.**

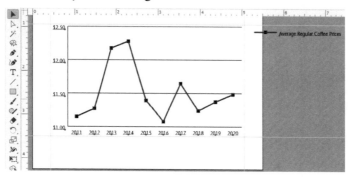

7. **Choose the Direct Selection tool in the Tools panel.**

The Direct Selection tool is the key to changing individual elements within a graph. You can't double-click to "enter into" the graph, as you can with a regular group. The Direct Selection tool can be used to select the individual components of a graph.

8. **Drag a selection marquee that selects only the three legend objects (including the type object).**

Make sure your selection marquee selects all anchor points of all three objects.

When the first row of your data defines labels for each column, the graph automatically includes a legend with a marker of the assigned color and the related label.

9. **Using the Direct Selection tool, drag the legend objects entirely outside the artboard area.**

Because this graph has only a single line, you don't really need a legend. However, you can't delete the legend icon objects because they are technically part of the graph object.

Drag the selected objects entirely outside the artboard boundary.

Anything entirely outside the artboard area is excluded when an Illustrator file is placed into another file. This technique effectively removes the legend icon, without breaking apart the graph.

10. **Save the file and continue to the next exercise.**

Note:

In a later exercise, you will add a title to the graph using a type object that is built into the template file.

Format Graph Markers

Rather than using plain squares to mark data points on a graph, you can use any existing artwork in place of the default data-point markers. In this exercise, you will use artwork provided in the template to plot data on your line graph.

1. **With price-graph.ai open, use the Direct Selection tool to select the first square on the data line.**

   Be careful when you use the Direct Selection tool to select these small squares. You have to click the fill to select the entire object instead of an individual anchor point on the shape. It can be helpful to zoom in to complete this part of the project.

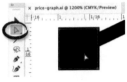 

   Click inside the shape's fill to select the entire object.

   Make sure you don't select only one point of the shape.

2. **Double-click the Scale tool to open the Scale dialog box. Change the Uniform Scale field to 300%, then click OK.**

   When you replace the default markers with custom artwork, the artwork defaults to the same size as the marker it is replacing. You are enlarging the markers now so that the custom markers will be more easily distinguishable on the graph.

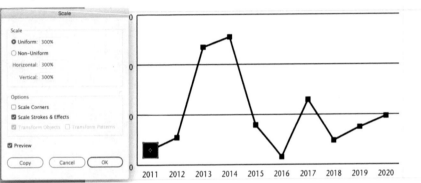

3. **Press Command/Control to access the Direct Selection tool, and click to select the second square on the line.**

4. **Release the Command/Control key, then double-click the Scale tool to reopen the Scale dialog box.**

5. **With the Scale Uniform field still set to 300%, click OK to apply the change to the second data point.**

   You might have noticed that the dialog box remembers the last-used settings when it is reopened. These steps provide a faster method of accomplishing the repetitive task of scaling each graph marker.

Note:

Unfortunately the Transform Again command does not work correctly on graph markers.

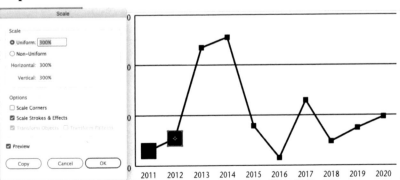

6. Repeat Steps 3–5 for each data point on the line.

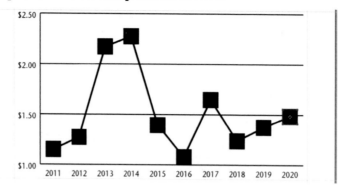

7. Choose the Selection tool, then click away from the graph to deselect it.

8. Show the Design Elements layer. Using the Selection tool, click to select the small coffee cup artwork to the right of the artboard.

You want to select the entire group, so you need to use the Selection tool and not the Direct Selection tool.

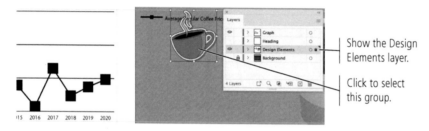

Show the Design Elements layer.

Click to select this group.

9. With the artwork selected, choose Object>Graph>Design.

Nothing appears in the Graph Design dialog box until you intentionally define one or more designs.

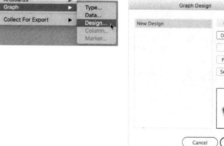

10. Click New Design in the Graph Design dialog box.

The artwork that was selected is added to the list of available graph designs.

11. Click Rename. Type `Coffee Cup` in the dialog box and click OK, then click OK to close the Graph Design dialog box.

12. Using the Selection tool, click to select the graph object. Control/right-click the selected graph object on the artboard and choose Marker in the contextual menu.

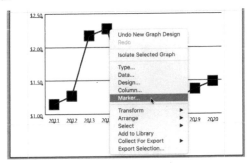

13. Choose Coffee Cup in the Graph Marker dialog box, then click OK.

The selected design replaces the squares that mark data points on the graph. The design you choose as the marker is the same size as the original square.

Remember, you have to use the Direct Selection tool to select individual pieces of a graph (including the markers). If you tried to select the cup artwork instances after they become the graph markers, you would only be able to select individual elements that make up the cup artwork instead of the entire marker instance. Scaling the markers before defining the design works around this problem.

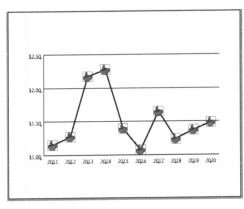

14. Save the file and continue to the next exercise.

Unify Template and Graph Elements

For all intents and purposes, your line graph is complete. However, the provided template includes a background image reminiscent of a chalkboard menu that you might see at a local coffee shop. In this exercise, you will modify individual graph elements to appear clearly on the provided background.

1. **With price-graph.ai open, make sure guides are locked (in the View>Guides submenu).**

2. **Deselect the entire graph object and then use the Direct Selection tool to click and drag a marquee around the vertical line at the left side of the graph.**

   It can be helpful to zoom in to the line to make this selection, so that you select exactly (and only) the elements you want. Make sure none of the type objects are selected.

   Because you dragged the marquee, you also selected the left endpoints of the four horizontal tick-mark lines; those lines are now also selected.

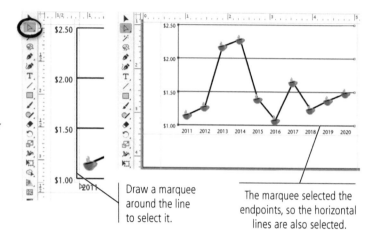

Draw a marquee around the line to select it.

The marquee selected the endpoints, so the horizontal lines are also selected.

3. **Use any method you prefer to change the selected lines to 0.5-pt stroke weight, using 20% black as the stroke color.**

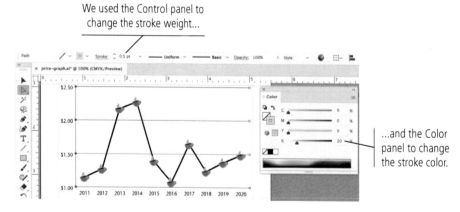

We used the Control panel to change the stroke weight...

...and the Color panel to change the stroke color.

4. **Repeat this process to select the type objects on the left and bottom edges of the graph, then change the type fill color to white.**

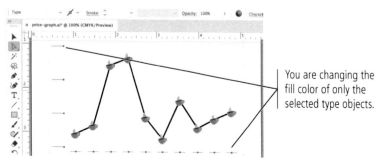

You are changing the fill color of only the selected type objects.

5. **Using the Direct Selection tool, click to select the first connecting line on the graph. Press Shift and click the other connecting lines to add them to the selection.**

6. **Use any method you prefer to change the selected lines to 1.5 pt using white as the stroke color.**

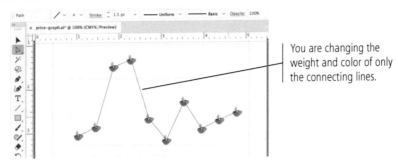

You are changing the weight and color of only the connecting lines.

7. **Click away from the graph to deselect everything.**

8. **In the Layers panel, delete the Design Elements layer, then show the Background and Heading layers.**

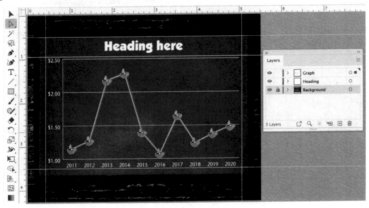

9. **Click the Heading layer to make it active.**

10. **Using the Type tool, replace the placeholder text on the Heading layer with the text from the graph legend.**

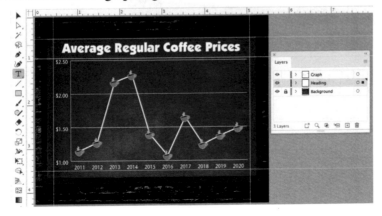

11. **Save the file and close it.**

Create a Bar Graph

The second required graph is based on data from a survey that asked 500 people why they drink coffee. Respondents were allowed to select one or more answers. Because this data shows a comparison of values for different categories, a bar graph will accurately represent the data.

Orientation is the only real difference between a bar graph and a column graph. Bar graphs represent each data set as a horizontal bar, while column graphs use vertical columns. Because the chalkboard you're using as a background is horizontally oriented, a bar graph is more appropriate for this project.

1. **Create a new file by opening chalkboard.ait from the WIP>Coffee folder.**

2. **Choose the Bar Graph tool in the Tools panel, then click and drag an area that snaps to the guides on the artboard.**

3. **Click the Import Data button in the Data panel. Navigate to reasons.txt in your WIP>Coffee>Data folder and click Open.**

Bar Graph tool

4. **Click the Apply button in the Data panel to generate the graph.**

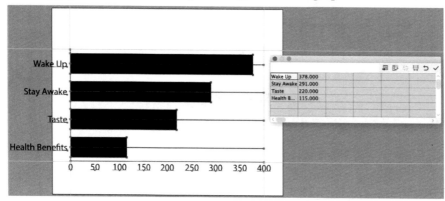

5. **Close the Data panel, clicking Save if asked.**

6. **Double-click the Scale tool. Change the Scale Uniform field to 90%, then click OK.**

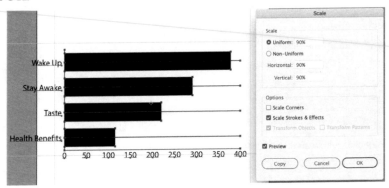

7. **With the graph object selected, change the type formatting to 9-pt ATC Onyx Normal with 90% Horizontal Scale.**

8. **Choose the Selection tool, then nudge the graph object as necessary until it fits inside the sign area (excluding the category labels on the left).**

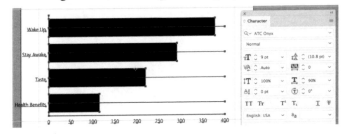

9. **Control/right-click the graph object with the Selection tool and choose Type in the contextual menu.**

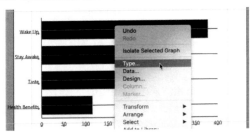

10. **Choose Value Axis in the Graph Options menu. Check the Override Calculated Values box, then type 4 in the Divisions field.**

For bar graphs, Illustrator uses a range, beginning with 0 and extending in increments as necessary, to show all of the defined data. You can use the Min and Max fields to define the values of a specific axis, such as always extending to 100 instead of ending at 70, or any other lower value.

The Divisions field determines how many labels are added to the value axis (the horizontal axis for this bar graph). The number of labels will always be one more than the number of divisions you define.

11. **Choose None in the Tick Marks Length menu.**

12. **Choose Category Axis in the Graph Options menu, and choose none in the Tick Marks Length field.**

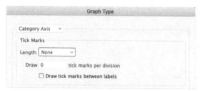

13. **Click OK to close the Graph Type dialog box and apply your changes.**

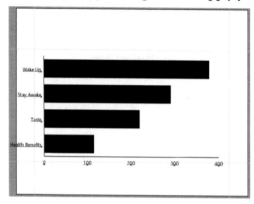

14. **Save the file as `reasons-graph.ai` in your WIP>Coffee folder, then continue to the next exercise.**

Define Graph Column Graphics

When you created the line graph, you defined a graph design object to use in place of the data markers. Those markers can be applied to any graph that plots individual data points (line, scatter, and radar). You can use a similar technique to apply custom graphics as the fill for bar and column graphs, as you will do in this exercise.

1. **With `reasons-graph.ai` open, use the Layers panel to show the Design Elements layer.**

2. **Using the Selection tool, click to select the coffee-bean artwork, then choose Object>Graph>Design.**

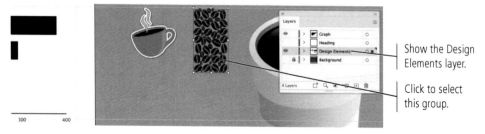

Show the Design Elements layer.

Click to select this group.

3. **Click New Design in the Graph Design dialog box.**

This is the same process you used to define an available graphic for the data markers. You have to define the graphic first before you can apply it to the fills on a bar or column graph.

4. **Click the Rename button, then type Coffee Beans in the Graph Design field. Click OK to return to the primary Graph Design dialog box.**

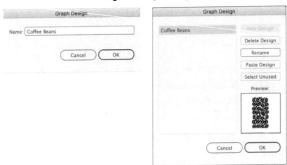

5. **Click OK to return to the artboard.**

6. **Using the Selection tool, click to select the graph. Control/right-click the selected graph on the artboard and choose Column in the contextual menu.**

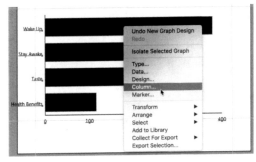

7. **In the Graph Column dialog box, choose Coffee Beans in the list of designs.**

8. **Make the following choices in the lower half of the dialog box:**

Column Type:	**Repeating**
Each Design Represents:	**50**
For Fractions:	**Chop Design**

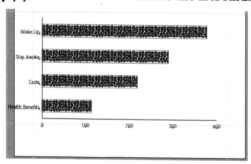

The Column Type menu determines how the graph will be extended across the length of the bar or height of the column.

- **Vertically Scaled** stretches a single instance of the graphic across the length of the entire column. The graphic is distorted to exactly fit the space defined by the bar or column.

- **Uniformly Scaled** places a single instance of the graphic, scaled as necessary to fit proportionally across the entire height of the bar or length of the column. Although the graphics are not distorted, the scaling can enlarge individual bars so that they overlap other bars.

- **Repeating** creates a pattern from the graphic, based on additional settings defined below the Column Type menu:

  – **Each Design Represents** determines the amount of space that will be occupied by each instance of the graphic.

  – **For Fractions** determines how the last instance of the graphic will appear in the column. If you choose Scale Design, the last instance will be disproportionally scaled to fit into the space defined by the bar or column. You can choose Chop Design to simply cut off the unscaled graphic at the end of the bar or column.

- **Sliding** places a single instance of the graphic in the bar or column. The ends of the graphic are not affected. The middle is stretched or compressed to fit the defined space.

9. **Click OK to apply your choices and return to the artboard.**

10. **Delete the Design Elements layer from the file.**

11. **Save the file and continue to the next exercise.**

Edit Graph Data

As long as you maintain a graph object without ungrouping it, you can edit both the parameters and the data that make up the graph. Any changes in the data are automatically reflected in the graph object on the artboard.

1. **With `reasons-graph.ai` open, select the graph object with the Selection tool.**

2. **Control/right-click the graph object and choose Data in the contextual menu.**

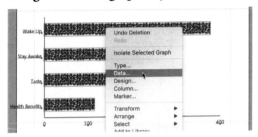

3. **Click the cell below the "Health Benefits" cell and type Social Experience.**

4. **Press Tab to highlight the cell to the right and type 215.**

5. **Click the Apply button in the Data panel.**

    The graph automatically changes to include the new data. The height of existing bars changes to accommodate the new fifth category in the defined space of the graph.

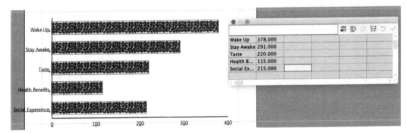

6. **Close the Data panel.**

7. **Using the Direct Selection tool, select the two lines at the left and bottom edges of the graph. Using any method you prefer, change the selected lines to 0.5 pt with a 20% black stroke.**

    Dragging a small marquee around the area where the two lines meet is the easiest way to select only the two lines.

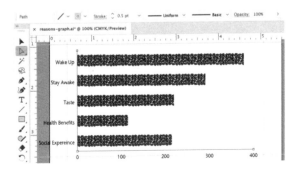

8. **Select only the type objects at the bottom edge of the graph. Change the type fill color to white.**

9. **Select only the type objects on the left side of the graph. Change the type formatting to left paragraph alignment.**

10. **Drag the selected type objects so they appear immediately above each bar on the graph.**

   It is easier to position the type objects while you can still see the actual text.

11. **Change the fill color of the selected type objects to white.**

12. **Show the Background and Heading layers.**

13. Change the heading placeholder text to **Why do you drink coffee?**.

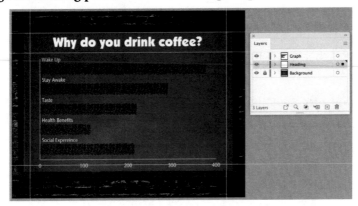

14. Save the file and close it, then continue to the next exercise.

Create a Pie Graph

The final required graph is based on data from a survey of 500 people who were asked their favorite type of coffee. Each person gave a single response to the question, so the combined percentages of responses will equal 100%. A pie graph is the best way to show values as percentages of the whole.

1. Create a new file by opening **chalkboard.ait** from the WIP>Coffee folder.

2. Choose the Pie Graph tool in the Tools panel, then click and drag an area that snaps to the guides on the artboard.

    Regardless of the shape you draw, pie graphs are always circles.

3. Click the Import Data button in the Data panel. Navigate to **favorites.txt** in your WIP>Coffee>Data folder and click Open.

Note:

Pie graphs always present numbers as percentages of the whole. If data is provided as actual numbers instead of percentages, Illustrator calculates the necessary percentages based on the entered data.

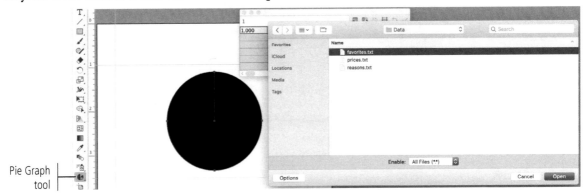

Pie Graph tool

4. Click the Apply button in the Data panel.

Mocha	Latte	Espresso	Iced coffee	Americano	Regular
12.000	9.000	10.000	28.000	17.000	24.000

5. **Close the Data panel.**

6. **Choose the Direct Selection tool, then click away from the graph to deselect it.**

7. **Using the Direct Selection tool, click to select only the top-left wedge in the graph.**

8. **Open the Swatches panel. Make sure the Fill Color icon is active, then click the lightest brown swatch to change the selected wedge's fill color.**

   This template file includes six different built-in swatches, which you will use to format the graph elements in this exercise.

   Changing the wedge color does not affect the color of the related legend object. You would have to manually select the legend object and change its fill color to match. In the following steps, however, you will create a different type of legend, so you don't need to worry about the legend objects.

Note:

You can create more than one pie graph by entering additional sets of values in subsequent rows of the Data panel.

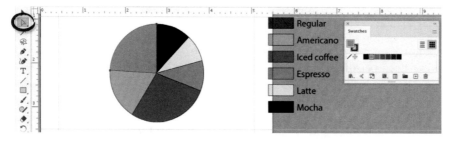

9. **Change the fill color of each wedge, using a different built-in swatch for each.**

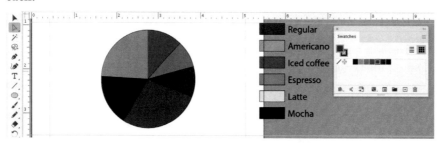

10. **Choose the Selection tool in the Tools panel, then click to select the entire graph object.**

11. **Control/right-click the graph and choose Type in the contextual menu.**

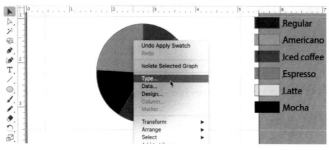

12. In the Options area of the Graph Type dialog box, choose Legends in Wedges in the Legend menu.

You can use the Legend menu to remove the legend completely, create a standard stacked legend (the default), or place the legend labels inside the associated wedges.

Note:

If you check Add Legend Across Top when the Standard Legend option is selected, the legend appears as a row above the graph.

13. Click OK to return to the document.

Using the Legends in Wedges option, the legend type objects move into the related wedges. The color-filled squares are removed.

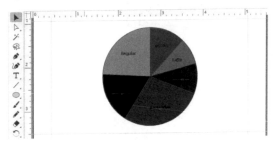

14. Save the file as `favorites-graph.ai` in your WIP>Coffee folder, then continue to the next exercise.

Edit Pie Graph Elements

Pie graphs are very common, but they present several unique formatting challenges and opportunities. In this exercise, you manipulate the graph legend to add information, and then apply gradients to the wedges to add visual interest.

1. With `favorites-graph.ai` open, Control/right-click the graph and choose Data from the contextual menu.

2. Select the first label field in the Data panel, then place the insertion point at the end of the existing text (Mocha) in the field at the top of the panel.

3. Type |12%, then click the Apply button.

The pipe character (Shift-Backslash) is used to create a new line in the graph label.

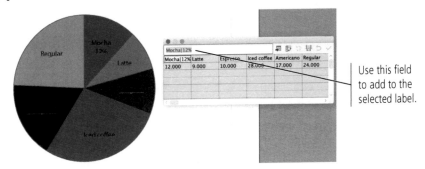

Use this field to add to the selected label.

4. Using the same method, add the appropriate values to each label in the Data panel, click the Apply button, and then close the Data panel.

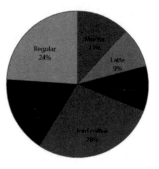

The point of infographics is to make data easy to view and understand. The labels now reflect the actual data that was used to create the graph wedges.

5. Using the Layers panel, show the Design Elements layer.

6. Drag the large coffee-cup artwork onto the artboard. Position the bottom edge of the cup at the bottom edge of the artboard, and center it horizontally (as shown here).

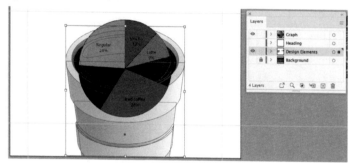

7. Lock the Design Elements layer.

8. Using the Selection tool, drag the graph object so its top center aligns with the top center of the "coffee" in the cup artwork.

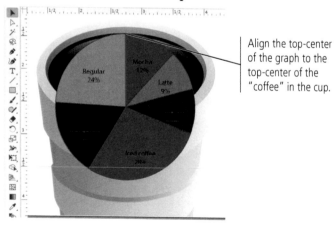

Align the top-center of the graph to the top-center of the "coffee" in the cup.

Note:

We zoomed in to complete the scaling process outlined in the next few steps.

9. Choose the Scale tool in the Tools panel, then click the top-center point of the graph to reposition the transformation point.

Remember, when you use the transformation tools, the transformation point is the "anchor" around which transformations are made.

10. Click the bottom-center of the graph and drag up to scale the graph vertically. Release the mouse button when you see a pink horizontal smart guide.

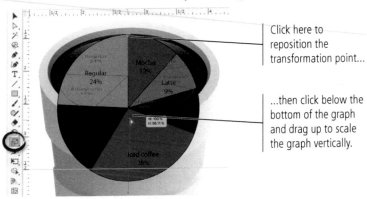

Click here to reposition the transformation point...

...then click below the bottom of the graph and drag up to scale the graph vertically.

11. Click the right edge of the graph and drag out until the graph fills the area that represents the coffee in the cup artwork (as shown here).

Because the top-center of the graph is anchored, dragging the right side out applies an equal change to the left side of the graph.

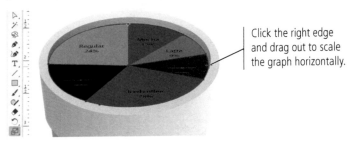

Click the right edge and drag out to scale the graph horizontally.

12. With the graph object selected, open the Character panel.

As you can see, the disproportionate scaling you applied to the graph had a significant effect on type objects within the graph.

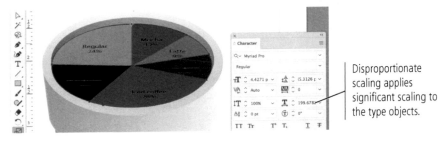

Disproportionate scaling applies significant scaling to the type objects.

13. With the entire graph selected, change the type formatting to 9-pt ATC Onyx Normal with 100% vertical and horizontal scaling.

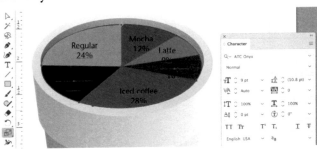

14. Deselect the graph, then choose the Direct Selection tool.

15. Click each legend in the graph and drag it just outside the cup artwork, as shown here:

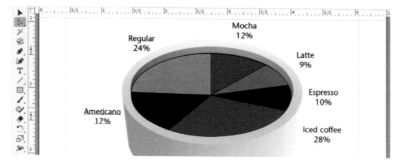

16. Shift-click to select all 6 legend type objects, then change the type fill color to white.

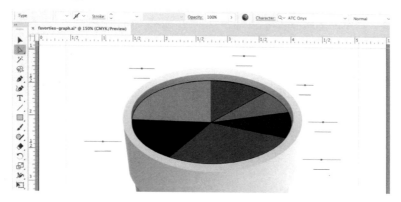

17. Show the Background and Heading layers. Change the heading placeholder text to What is your favorite coffee?.

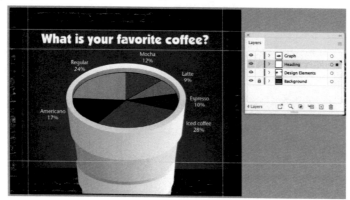

18. Save the file and close it, then continue to the next stage of the project.

STAGE 2 / Drawing in Perspective

The second half of the word "infographics" means adding visual elements that make data more attractive and accessible. The graphs from the first half of this project use a "chalkboard" background to present data in a visual manner that makes sense with the magazine article they illustrate.

Infographics can be as basic as graphs and charts, or as complex as any type of art you can conceive. In the second half of this project, you will create a coffee-dispenser box like you might see at a meeting or volunteer event. One side of the box will display the infographic heading, while the other will show the data being presented.

Define the Perspective Grid

In this series of exercises, you will create artwork based on a flat pencil sketch. Objects in the real world have depth, which means the box you are drawing should reflect that same level of dimension.

To recreate this effect using two-dimensional drawing tools, you need to understand the basic artistic principle of perspective. The concept of perspective means that all lines on the same surface (or plane) eventually appear to meet at a single point in the distance, called the **vanishing point**. Lines move closer together as they approach the vanishing point, creating the illusion of depth.

Illustrator includes a Perspective Grid tool that makes it very easy to define the perspective planes that will guide your drawing.

1. **Open the file box.ai from your WIP>Coffee folder.**

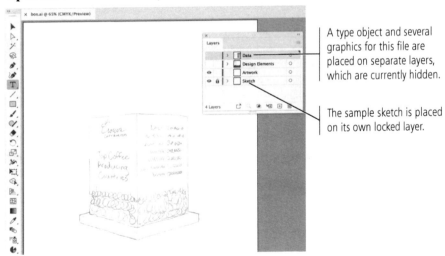

A type object and several graphics for this file are placed on separate layers, which are currently hidden.

The sample sketch is placed on its own locked layer.

2. **Choose the Perspective Grid tool in the Tools panel.**

    When you first choose this tool, the default two-point perspective grid appears in the file. You can change the grid to one- or three-point perspective by choosing the appropriate option in the View>Perspective Grid menu.

Note:

Press Shift-P to access the Perspective Grid tool.

3. If you can't see all handles of the perspective grid, zoom out slightly.

In two-point perspective, there are two vanishing points — left and right — and three planes — left, right, and ground. Illustrator's perspective grid shows the left plane in blue, the right plane in orange, and the ground plane in green.

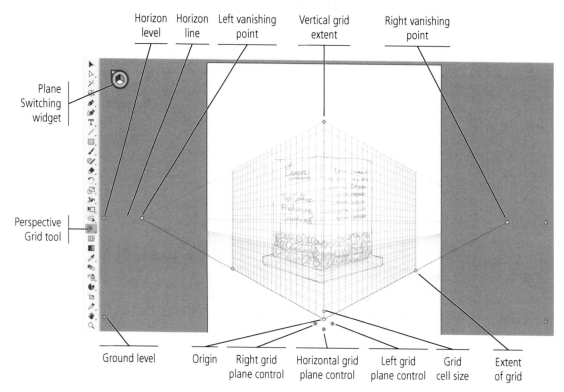

If you have never worked with perspective drawing, the grid might seem intimidating at first. However, once you understand the various elements, you will see how this grid makes it very easy to draw in correct perspective. To begin, you should also understand several basic terms related to dimensional drawing:

- A **plane** is a flat surface (even if it is only theoretical).

- A **vanishing point** is the location where all lines on a plane appear to converge.

- The **horizon line** is the height of the theoretical viewer's eye level.

- The **origin** is the zero point for perspective objects. For objects on the horizontal plane, the origin point is X: 0, Y: 0. For objects on the left or right plane, the origin point is X: 0.

- The **ground level** is the position of the theoretical ground in relation to the planes in the perspective grid.

> **Note:**
>
> *You can change the position of the Plane Switching widget by double-clicking the Perspective Grid tool to open the Perspective Grid Options dialog box.*

4. **With the Perspective Grid tool active, click either Ground Level handle and drag until the origin aligns with the corner in the sketch (as shown here).**

You can use the Ground Level handles to move the grid without affecting the perspective.

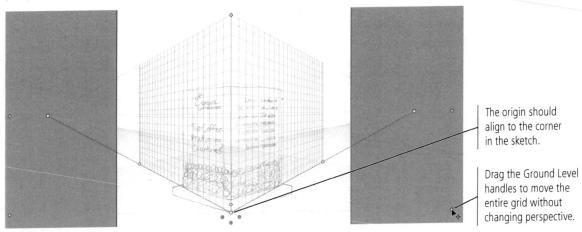

The origin should align to the corner in the sketch.

Drag the Ground Level handles to move the entire grid without changing perspective.

5. **Click either Horizon Level handle and drag up until the horizon line matches the top-left and -right corners of the box in the sketch.**

Changing the horizon line changes the height of both vanishing points. All three perspective planes are affected by the change.

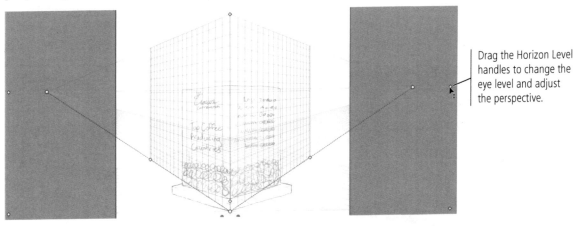

Drag the Horizon Level handles to change the eye level and adjust the perspective.

6. **Zoom out if necessary to show more area around the perspective grid.**

7. Click the Right Vanishing Point handle and drag right until the bottom line of the orange grid aligns with the bottom line in the sketch.

Keep in mind that you're working from a sketch, which is probably not exact. The ultimate goal is to create accurate perspective artwork, using the sketch as a *rough* guide.

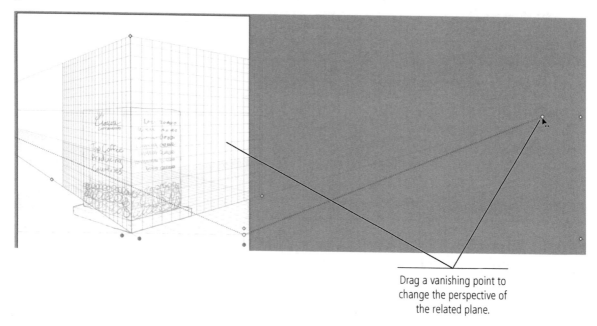

Drag a vanishing point to change the perspective of the related plane.

8. Click the Left Vanishing Point handle and drag left until the bottom line of the blue grid aligns with the bottom line in the sketch.

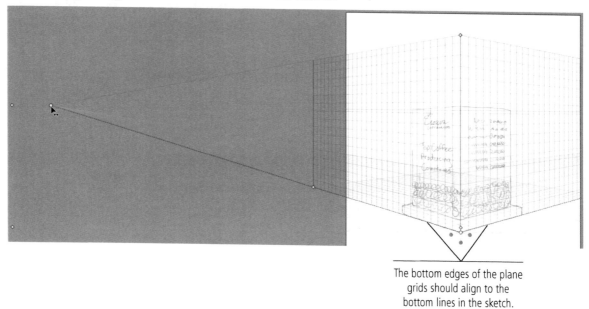

The bottom edges of the plane grids should align to the bottom lines in the sketch.

If you choose View>Perspective Grid>Lock Station Point, both vanishing points move when you drag either. They are effectively locked in position relative to each other. The origin point becomes a pivot, around which the vanishing points rotate.

9. **Click the Extent of Grid handle for the right plane and drag left until the right-most orange gridline aligns with the right edge of the box.**

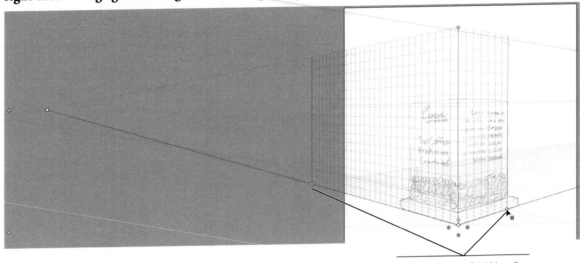

Drag the Extent of Grid handles to change the horizontal area that displays gridlines.

10. **Click the Extent of Grid handle for the left plane and drag right until the left-most blue gridline aligns with the left edge of the box.**

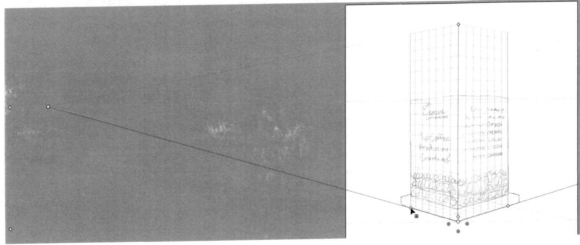

11. **Click the Vertical Grid Extent handle and drag down until the handle aligns to the corner of the box on the sketch.**

It is important to realize that the perspective grid is only a visual guide; the extent of the grid planes does not limit the location of the planes. Each plane is theoretically infinite.

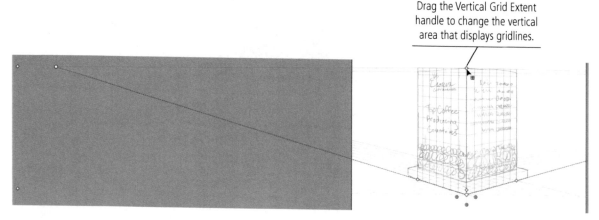

Drag the Vertical Grid Extent handle to change the vertical area that displays gridlines.

12. **Zoom in to the sketch. Click the Grid Cell Size handle and drag up until the first row of the grid appears to match the height of the box's platform.**

The grid cell size is the same for all planes on the grid. Although you are basing the grid size on the right plane, all three grids change to reflect the new grid size.

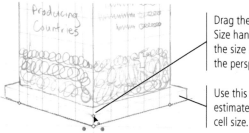

Drag the Grid Cell Size handle to change the size of squares in the perspective grid.

Use this surface to estimate the grid cell size.

13. **Choose View>Perspective Grid>Define Grid.**

You can use this dialog box to define very specific, numeric grid settings, which can be useful for precise technical illustration.

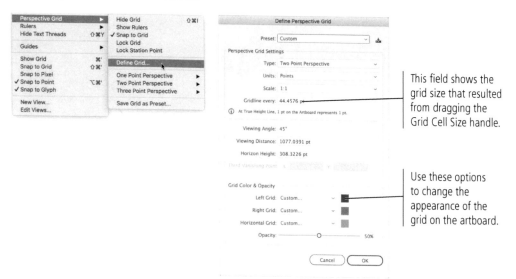

This field shows the grid size that resulted from dragging the Grid Cell Size handle.

Use these options to change the appearance of the grid on the artboard.

Understanding Default Perspective Grids

UNDATIONS

Illustrator supports one-, two-, and three-point perspective grids, all of which can be accessed in the View>Perspective Grid submenus.

Only one perspective grid can exist in a single file regardless of the number of artboards in the file. If you choose a different preset from one of the submenus, you replace any grid that already exists in your file.

If you have established a grid that you think you might need again, you can save it as a preset by choosing View>Perspective Grid>Save Grid As Preset. The resulting dialog box has most of the same options as the Define Perspective Grid dialog box, but you can type a name in the top field for easier recognition. Your saved grid presets will then be available in the View>Perspective Grid submenus.

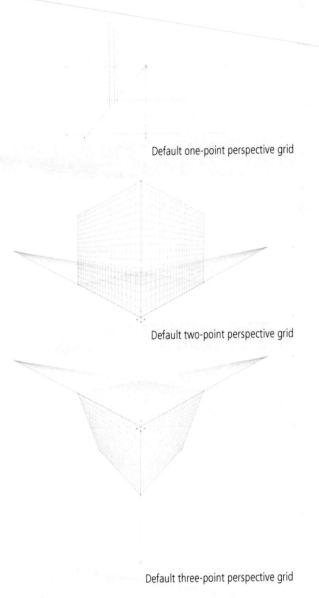

Default one-point perspective grid

Default two-point perspective grid

Default three-point perspective grid

14. **Change grid Opacity to 30%, then click OK to apply your change.**

    Reducing the grid opacity makes it easier to see what you're building.

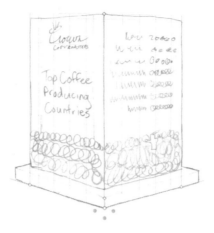

Note:

Some users report a bug that causes the perspective grid to disappear after defining the grid properties. If this is the case, simply choose View>Perspective Grid>Show Grid.

Note:

If you choose View>Perspective Grid>Show Rulers, the Y position of gridlines appears near the edge of each vertical perspective plane.

15. **Save the file as `coffee-producers.ai` in your WIP>Coffee folder and then continue to the next exercise.**

Draw in Perspective

Once you have defined a perspective grid, creating objects in perspective is a fairly simple process. The most important issue is determining which plane you should draw on, and making sure that plane is active when you draw.

1. **With `coffee-producers.ai` open, choose the Rectangle tool in the Tools panel and reset the default fill and stroke attributes.**

2. **In the Layers panel, make the Artwork layer active.**

3. **In the Plane Switching widget, click the Right Grid proxy to make it the active plane.**

4. **Using the Rectangle tool, click near the corner of the sketch, then drag right to create a shape that represents the right-front edge of the box platform.**

    Although you are drawing with the basic Rectangle tool, the new shape automatically adopts the perspective defined by the active plane in the grid.

Click the Right Grid proxy in the widget to change the active plane.

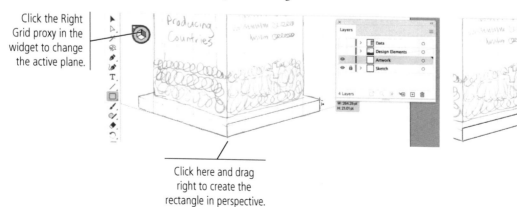

Click here and drag right to create the rectangle in perspective.

5. **Click the Left Grid proxy in the Plane Switching widget.**

6. **Starting at the top-right corner, draw another rectangle representing the left-front edge of the platform.**

   Smart guides work in perspective drawing mode just as they do in regular drawings. You can snap to existing objects to align edges and corners when you draw new objects. However, the perspective grid also acts magnetic by default, so it might be difficult to snap to exactly the right location.

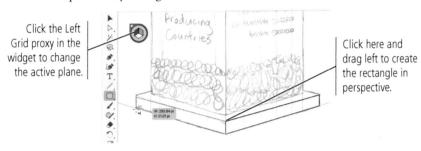

Click the Left Grid proxy in the widget to change the active plane.

Click here and drag left to create the rectangle in perspective.

Note:

It might be helpful to turn off the snapping behavior by choosing View>Perspective Grid>Snap to Grid.

7. **Click the Horizontal Grid proxy in the Plane Switching widget.**

8. **Using the Rectangle tool with the default fill and stroke attributes, draw another rectangle representing the top surface of the platform.**

   Start at the left corner and drag to the right corner, snapping to the existing points to create the top surface of the sign platform.

Note:

Click the background area in the Plane Switching widget to select No Active Grid if you want to draw objects that aren't attached to the perspective grid.

 No Active Grid(4)

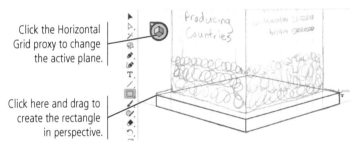

Click the Horizontal Grid proxy to change the active plane.

Click here and drag to create the rectangle in perspective.

9. **Use the Layers panel to hide the Sketch layer, and then choose View>Perspective Grid>Hide Grid.**

10. **Using the Selection tool, select the top-surface shape.**

11. **Use any method you prefer to change the object's stroke weight to 0 and the fill color to the CCR Brown1 swatch provided in the file's Swatches panel.**

    To move or resize a perspective object within the perspective grid, you have to use the Perspective Selection tool (nested under the Perspective Grid tool). This is a very important distinction, and one that is easy to forget. If you move or resize a perspective object with the regular Selection tool, the object's perspective is not maintained in the transformation.

    In this case, you are only changing a property of the object — not its actual dimensions — so you do not need to use the Perspective Selection tool.

12. Using any method you prefer, change the fill and stroke properties of the other two objects as follows:

> **Right-front surface:**
> Fill: CCR Brown2
> Stroke: 0 pt
>
> **Left-front surface:**
> Fill: CCR Brown3
> Stroke: 0 pt

13. Click the Perspective Grid tool in the Tools panel.

When you choose the Perspective Grid tool, the grid automatically reappears. You can also choose View>Perspective Grid>Show Grid.

14. Show the Sketch layer, save the file, then continue to the next exercise.

 ## Moving Objects in Perspective

One of the most powerful advantages of drawing in Illustrator's perspective grid is the fact that it is mostly nondestructive. Perspective objects can be moved around on their planes, and even moved to different planes, without degrading their quality.

Note:

A perspective drawing object is still a drawing object. You can use the Control panel, Swatches panel, or Color panel to change the fill and stroke colors of the selected shape.

1. With **coffee-producers.ai** open, choose the Perspective Selection tool (nested under the Perspective Grid tool).

Remember, to move or resize a perspective object within the perspective grid, you have to use the Perspective Selection tool.

2. Press Option/Alt-Shift, then click the rectangle on the right-front face of the platform and drag up until the top edge aligns with the top edge of the sketched box.

The same keyboard shortcuts for transforming objects work for transforming objects in perspective. Press Shift to constrain an object's movement to 45° angles (including exactly horizontal or vertical). Press Option/Alt to clone the object that you are dragging.

As you move the clone, you can see how the object adopts the appropriate shape based on the active perspective plane.

Note:

Press Shift-V to access the Perspective Selection tool.

Note:

The perspective grid does not need to be visible to transform objects in perspective; in fact, it is sometimes easier to make fine changes when the grid is not visible.

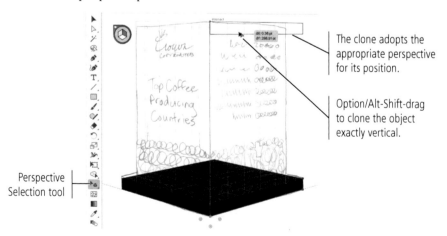

The clone adopts the appropriate perspective for its position.

Option/Alt-Shift-drag to clone the object exactly vertical.

Perspective Selection tool

3. **Change the selected object's fill color to the CCR Box1 swatch.**

4. **Using the Perspective Selection tool, click the bottom-center handle of the rectangle, and drag down until it meets the top edge of the first shape.**

   Remember, to resize an object in perspective, you have to use the Perspective Selection tool and not the regular Selection tool.

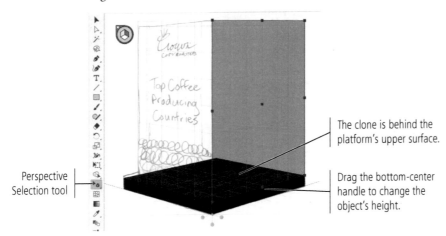

Perspective Selection tool

The clone is behind the platform's upper surface.

Drag the bottom-center handle to change the object's height.

5. **Choose Object>Arrange>Bring To Front to move the second rectangle above the top edge of the platform.**

   Object stacking order in perspective drawing follows the same rules as in regular drawing. New objects are automatically created at the top of the stacking order on the active layer. When you clone an object, the new clone is stacked immediately above the object you cloned.

6. **Press and hold the 5 key, then click the light-brown rectangle and drag approximately 1/4″ left.**

   Pressing the 5 key while dragging an object moves the object perpendicular to the plane on which it sits. In other words, the object moves nearer or farther away without changing its horizontal (X) position on that plane.

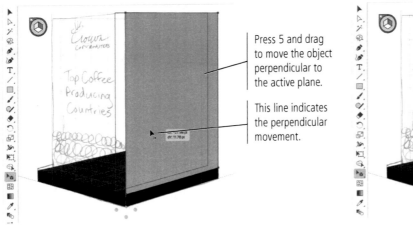

Press 5 and drag to move the object perpendicular to the active plane.

This line indicates the perpendicular movement.

7. **Choose Object>Arrange>Bring To Front to move the second rectangle back in front of the top edge of the platform.**

   When you move an object perpendicularly on its plane, a bug in the software might move that item to the back of the stacking order.

8. **Using the Perspective Selection tool, drag the left-center handle until the left edge aligns with the left edge of the lower-right shape.**

   The sketch appears to show the exact corner of the box, so the corners of the two surfaces should appear to align.

9. **Drag the right-center handle left to bring the box edge in slightly from the platform edge.**

Note:

When the Perspective Selection tool is active, arrows in the cursor icon remind you which plane is active.

⊙ *·· Left Grid*

⊙ *··Right Grid*

⊙ *·· Horizontal Grid*

⊙ *· No Grid*

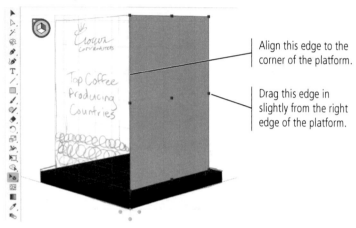

Align this edge to the corner of the platform.

Drag this edge in slightly from the right edge of the platform.

10. **Press Option/Alt, then click and drag the rectangle to clone it to the left. While still holding the Option/Alt key and the mouse button, press 1 to move the clone to the left perspective plane.**

    You can move an object to a different plane by pressing the appropriate shortcut key while you drag the object:

    - Left plane: 1
    - Horizontal (ground) plane: 2
    - Right plane: 3
    - No plane: 4

    These keyboard shortcuts relate only to the main numbers on the keyboard; the numeric keypad numbers do not work for switching planes.

Note:

On Windows, you have to be actively dragging the clone to move the object to another plane.

Option/Alt-drag the object to clone it...

... then press 1 to move the clone to the left plane.

11. **Using the Perspective Selection tool, resize the object to the appropriate shape by dragging the object handles.**

    If necessary, turn off the Snap to Grid feature to resize the object appropriately.

12. **Change the selected object's fill color to the CCR Box2 swatch.**

Note:

Using the Perspective Selection tool, you can only select and group multiple objects if they exist on the same plane.

Using the regular Selection tool, you can select and group objects on different perspective planes. If you do, selecting an object in the group with the Perspective Selection tool only affects the object you click. You can't move or transform objects on different planes at the same time.

13. **With the left-plane object selected, choose Edit>Copy, then immediately choose Edit>Paste in Place.**

14. **Using the Perspective Selection tool, drag in the left- and right-center handles of the pasted shape. Leave approximately 1/4″ between the edges of the front and back shapes.**

15. **Change the color of the selected object to the CCR Box3 swatch.**

16. **Save the file and continue to the next exercise.**

Work with Type in Perspective

Most drawing objects can be placed in perspective, with a few exceptions (notably, graphs). Adding existing artwork to the perspective grid is a fairly simple process.

1. With **coffee-producers.ai** open, show the Design Elements layer.

2. Using the regular Selection tool, click to select the group of coffee beans to the right of the artboard.

3. Choose the Perspective Selection tool and choose the Left Grid proxy in the Plane Switching widget.

4. Click the group of coffee beans to the right of the artboard, then drag the group into perspective on the left surface of the box.

Drag with the Perspective Selection tool to place the object onto the active plane.

5. Using the Perspective Selection tool, drag the group so its bottom edge appears to sit on top of the upper surface. Adjust the group's corner and side handles so it fits into the box area, as shown here:

Note:

Some users, especially on Windows, have noted problems switching an object to a different perspective plane. You might need to hold down the 3 key, or press it several times, for the cloned object to accurately change planes.

6. Press Option/Alt, then click and drag the group to clone it to the right. While still holding the Option/Alt key and the mouse button, press 3 to move the clone to the right perspective plane.

7. Using the Perspective Selection tool, drag the group so its bottom edge appears to sit on top of the upper surface. Adjust the group's corner and side handles so it fits into the box area, as shown here:

8. Choose the Left Grid proxy in the Plane Switching widget.

9. Click the group that includes the client's logo (to the right of the artboard) and drag it into perspective on the left surface of the box. Adjust the group's handles so it fits into the darker brown area above the coffee beans.

10. Show the Data layer.

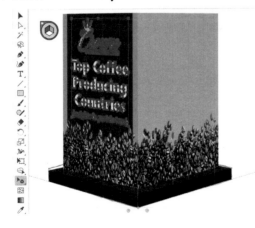

11. **Choose the Perspective Selection tool and choose the Right Grid proxy in the Plane Switching widget.**

12. **Click the type object to the right of the artboard and drag until it appears on the right face of the box.**

   Both point-type and area-type objects can be applied to a perspective grid. The text remains editable unless you release the object from the perspective grid.

13. **Drag the left- and right-center handles to fit all the text into the width of the box face.**

14. **With the type object selected, click the Edit Text button in the Control panel.**

   When a perspective type object is selected, you have to enter into the text to change the color of the text. Unlike other objects, you can't change the fill or stroke attributes of a perspective type object without first entering Edit Text mode.

15. **In Edit Text mode, use the Type tool to change the word "Idia" to "India."**

In Edit Text mode, type options are available in the Control panel.

Changes dynamically reflect on the main artboard.

Note:

You can also double-click the type object to enter the Edit Text mode.

16. **Click the arrow button at the top of the document window two times to exit Edit Text mode.**

17. **Deselect everything on the artboard, delete the Sketch layer, then choose View>Perspective Grid>Hide Grid.**

Note:

You might want to zoom in and check the corners and edges of the various elements. Be sure to use the Perspective Selection tool if you need to adjust any of the shapes.

18. **Save the file and close it.**

Transforming Perspective Type Objects

Make sure you use the Perspective Selection tool and not the regular Selection tool to transform perspective type objects.

If you try to resize a perspective type object with the regular Selection tool, the object is detached from the perspective grid and expanded into a group of shapes that represent the letters. The appearance of perspective is maintained, but the object is no longer attached to the perspective grid; the text is no longer editable.

The warning you see does not have a Cancel button, so you have to simply click OK. If the action was an error, you can use the Undo command to restore the perspective type object.

Other Perspective Grid Options

Attaching Objects to the Perspective Grid

If you create a regular drawing object that is not attached to a perspective plane, you can attach it to a specific plane by selecting it with the Perspective Selection tool and choosing Perspective>Attach to Active Plane in the object's contextual menu (or by choosing Object>Perspective>Attach to Active Plane). The object's shape is maintained, but the bounding box changes to reflect its new perspective boundaries.

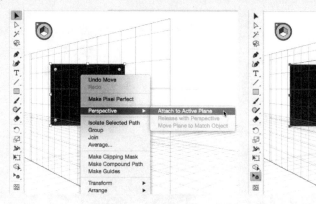

Releasing Objects from the Perspective Grid

To convert an object from a perspective object to a regular object, you can choose Perspective>Release with Perspective in the object's contextual menu (or choose Object>Perspective>Release with Perspective). The selected shape becomes a regular drawing object. The apparent perspective is maintained, but the object is no longer attached to a plane. The object's bounding box reveals the outermost edges of the flat artwork.

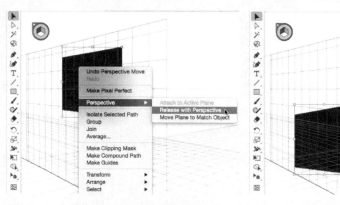

Moving the Plane to Match Perspective

If you have moved objects perpendicularly away from the active plane, you can adjust the grid plane to meet the position of the selected object by choosing Perspective>Move Plane to Match Object in the object's contextual menu (or by choosing Object>Perspective>Move Plane to Match Object). The active plane snaps to the face of the selected object, which makes it easier to create or place new objects along the same plane as the existing object.

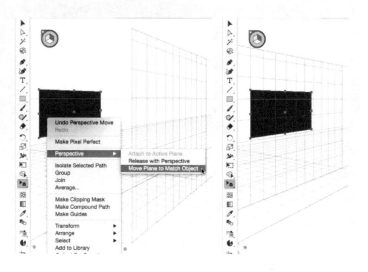

1. A _____ graph shows values as percentages of the whole.

2. A _____ graph plots values as a series of connected points, showing progressive change in value.

3. You must use _____ to enter numbers as text in the Data panel.

4. You must use the _____ to select one segment of a graph without ungrouping the entire graph.

5. You can click the _____ button in the Data panel to increase the number of decimals that are included in each data cell.

6. The _____ is the height of the theoretical viewer's eye level.

7. The _____ is the spot at which multiple lines on the same perspective converge.

8. The _____ tool is used to define the position of various attributes of the perspective grid.

9. The _____ is used to determine which perspective plane is active.

10. The _____ tool is used to move or resize objects in perspective.

1. Briefly explain what is meant by the term "infographics."

2. Briefly explain the concept of two-point perspective.

3. Briefly explain the difference between the Selection tool and the Perspective Selection tool.

Use what you have learned in this project to complete the following freeform exercise.
Carefully read the art director and client comments, then create your own design to meet the needs of the project.
Use the space below to sketch ideas. When finished, write a brief explanation of the reasoning behind your final design.

art director comments

The main theme for next month's magazine is "Living Green." The main articles all focus on some aspect of environmental conservation, such as renewable energy, recycling strategies, and landfill reduction. Your job is to create infographics for data that will accompany the cover story.

To complete this project, you should:

❏ Download the **Info_AI21_PB.zip** archive from the Student Files web page.

❏ Use the supplied data to create three infographics that present the data in a visually interesting way.

❏ Create illustrations for each set of data that support the overall theme of the article.

client comments

The main focus of next month's cover story is the different methods that are being explored to supply affordable electricity in large metropolitan areas, such as New York City and Los Angeles.

The author has compiled three different sets of data about renewable energy — wind power, water power, and so on — that will support the ideas and facts in the article. We need some type of illustrated graph for each of these data sets.

We want our readers to see the graphs even if they only flip through and skim the article. Create a compelling illustration for each one, so they are more than just graphs. However, keep in mind that the data is the most important element — it needs to be clear and understandable.

Use a consistent color scheme in all three graphs; green should play a prominent role because people naturally associate that color with environmentalism and natural resources.

project justification

Infographics like the ones you created in this project are frequently used in newspapers, magazines, and presentations to visually represent complex statistics or other numerical data. Infographics range from simple pie charts and line graphs to elaborate full-color images.

When you create this type of illustration, keep in mind that the information or data being presented is always the priority. Although aesthetic appeal is a primary concern of most graphic designers, the integrity of the information is the most important aspect of creating infographics.

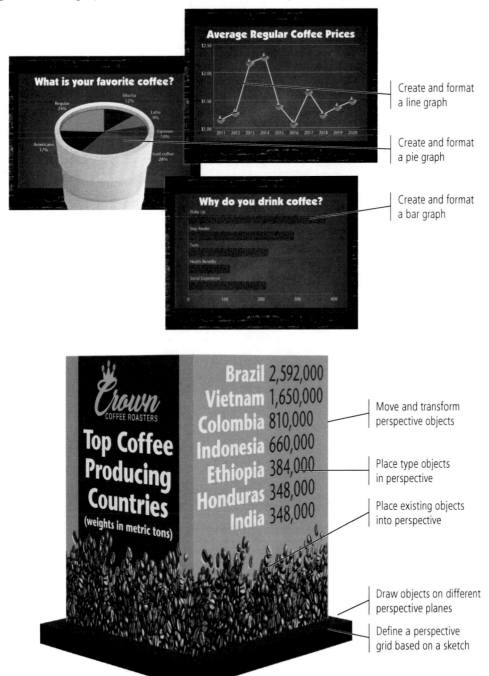

Website Interface

As an in-house designer for a multimedia services company, your job is to create the pieces that are required for a client's new home page. The basic site structure has already been designed; you need to make changes that were requested by the marketing manager, and then export the necessary pieces and information that is required for the HTML page to function properly.

This project incorporates the following skills:

☐ Working with color groups to unify the overall composition

☐ Using Live Color to edit vector elements

☐ Preparing page elements for export to use in a web page

☐ Defining cascading style sheets (CSS) to properly format various page elements in the final HTML file

client comments

We are very happy with the overall site layout. There are just a few things we'd like to change.

The guitar illustration in the original comp was a bit overpowering. We like the idea, but can you darken the colors in that illustration a bit so that the logo stands out more?

The blue color from the old site doesn't really work with the new illustration behind the navigation links. Can you change all the blue to something that works better with the guitar illustration?

Finally, can you change the bottom-half of some of the squares in the focus illustration? We're aiming for something that looks like the digital bars on a mixing board, but we want all the pieces to work together better.

art director comments

Illustrator color groups should make it fairly easy to meet all three of the client's requests. You can use them to universally lighten the illustration, change blue objects to red in just a few clicks, and even cut apart squares and paint only certain areas of vector shapes.

While you're making the aesthetic changes, I'll have the Dreamweaver developer start working on the web page code. By the time you get to that point, you will have an HTML page that you can use as a reference when you define names in Illustrator to create the necessary CSS and image files.

project objectives

To complete this project, you will:

- Create color groups to manage the color swatches in the file

- Adjust global color attributes in all selected artwork

- Adjust individual colors in a group to change all objects where the color is applied

- Work with Live Paint groups

- Explore HTML page code

- Examine the pixel grid

- Define object names to create CSS class selectors

- Create a gradient page background

- Define character styles to create CSS tag selectors

- Export CSS and image files

STAGE 1 / Using Color Groups and Live Color

As you should already know, you can use Illustrator to create virtually any type of illustration — from a basic vector drawing to a complex, realistic illustration. You can also use Illustrator to design an entire composition, whether a letterfold brochure that will be printed or a website interface that will be used as the map for an HTML page. In the first stage of this project, you are going to use color groups and Live Color to adjust global and specific colors to unify various elements of the existing site design.

Use a Color Group to Change Multiple Swatches

Color groups are useful for organizing color swatches into logical and manageable collections. You can make changes that affect all colors within a group; this takes the concept of global color swatches one step further. In this exercise, you create a group from the tracing object swatches, so you can make changes that affect the entire illustration.

1. Download **Studio_AI21_RF.zip** from the Student Files web page.

2. **Expand the ZIP archive in your WIP folder (Macintosh) or copy the archive contents into your WIP folder (Windows).**

   This results in a folder named **Studio**, which contains the files you need for this project. You should also use this folder to save the files you create in this project.

3. **Open the file site-design.ai from the WIP>Studio folder.**

4. **In the Layers panel, expand all five layers (if necessary) and review the various elements.**

   The basic site layout follows a structure that is fairly common in website design. Four layers — Navigation, Header, Main, and Footer — represent the various sections of a basic HTML page. A fifth layer, named Background, contains a single path with a solid gray fill, representing the background color of the entire page.

Note:

As you work through the exercises in this project, the importance of the structure used in this file will become apparent.

5. **In the Layers panel, click to the right of the Target icon to select the bottom group on the Header layer.**

Remember, clicking in this area reveals the Indicates Selected Art icon.

The selected group was created by applying the Image Trace function to a photograph of a flaming guitar; this results in a group of vector objects that can each be selected and manipulated individually to achieve the designer goal.

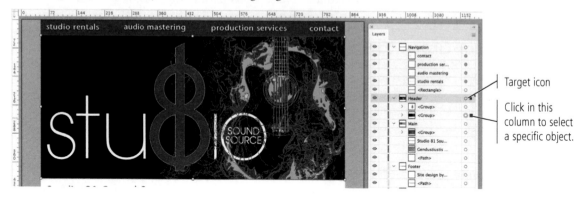

Target icon

Click in this column to select a specific object.

6. **With the group selected, click the New Color Group button at the bottom of the Swatches panel.**

New Color Group button

7. **In the resulting dialog box, type Guitar Colors in the Name field, then define the following settings:**

- **Choose the Create From Selected Artwork radio button.**
- **Check the Convert Process to Global option.**
- **Turn off the Include Swatches for Tints option.**

8. **Click OK to create the new color group.**

By checking the Selected Artwork option, every color used in the selection is added as a separate swatch in the group. Each is a global swatch, which means editing the swatch will affect the appearance of any object where that swatch is applied.

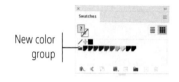

New color group

Note:

It is helpful to view the Swatches panel in Swatch view instead of list view.

9. **With the artwork still selected, click the color group folder icon to select the entire group.**

If you click a swatch instead of the group folder, you will change the fill/stroke attribute (whichever is active) of the selected objects.

10. **Click the Edit or Apply Color Group button at the bottom of the Swatches panel.**

Click the folder icon to select the color group.

Edit or Apply Color Group button

11. **Change the Recolor Artwork dialog box to Edit mode, and make sure the Recolor Art option is checked in the bottom-left corner.**

12. **Make sure the Link Harmony Colors button is active. Drag the Brightness slider (below the color wheel) slightly right to lighten all colors in the image.**

The Link Harmony Colors button is a toggle. When it is already active, the tool tip for the button shows "Unlink Harmony Colors" (and vice versa).

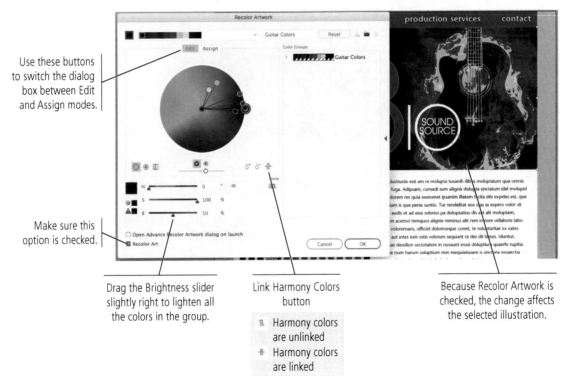

Use these buttons to switch the dialog box between Edit and Assign modes.

Make sure this option is checked.

Drag the Brightness slider slightly right to lighten all the colors in the group.

Link Harmony Colors button

⅋ Harmony colors are unlinked

⅋ Harmony colors are linked

Because Recolor Artwork is checked, the change affects the selected illustration.

13. **Click OK to apply the change.**

14. **Save the file and continue to the next exercise.**

Use a Color Group to Manage File Colors

In addition to managing universal changes to all swatches in a group, color groups can also be useful for simplifying a design and managing the individual colors included in specific areas of a file. In this exercise, you use a color group to combine similar colors into tints of a single color swatch.

1. **With site-design.ai open, use the Layers panel to lock the guitar illustration group.**

   The blue accent color in the rest of the site elements does not suit the predominant reds in the guitar illustration. You are going to use another color group to manage the site colors, changing the blue to a red color that better suits the new main image.

2. **Choose Select>All to select all unlocked artwork.**

   The color group you create in the next few steps will only include colors in the selected objects. Because the guitar-illustration group is locked, you can't select that group; colors in that illustration will not be included in the second color group.

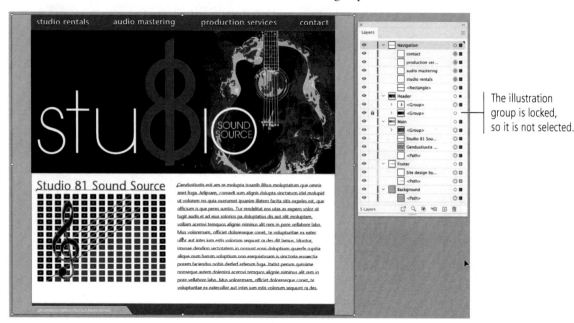

The illustration group is locked, so it is not selected.

3. **With the artwork selected, click the Recolor button in the Quick Actions section of the Properties panel.**

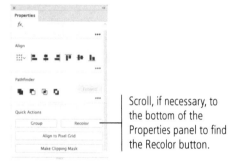

Scroll, if necessary, to the bottom of the Properties panel to find the Recolor button.

4. Review the options in the Recolor panel.

Many of the options here are the same as those you saw in the full Recolor Artwork dialog box. This panel presents a more condensed version, as well as several new options for dynamically recoloring artwork on the artboard.

The prominent colors in the selection appear as spokes on the color wheel, which defaults to show the Saturation and Hue of colors. You can use the buttons in the bottom left section of the panel to switch between Saturation and Brightness.

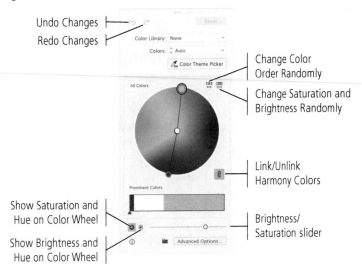

Undo Changes
Redo Changes

Change Color Order Randomly

Change Saturation and Brightness Randomly

Link/Unlink Harmony Colors

Show Saturation and Hue on Color Wheel

Show Brightness and Hue on Color Wheel

Brightness/ Saturation slider

5. Click the Link/Unlink Harmony Colors button to the right of the color wheel to unlink the color spokes.

When Harmony Colors are linked, the button is highlighted and the links in the icon appear to be connected ( ). When they are unlinked, the button is not highlighted, and a diagonal line appears over the icon ( ).

6. Click the blue spoke on the wheel and drag to a red hue.

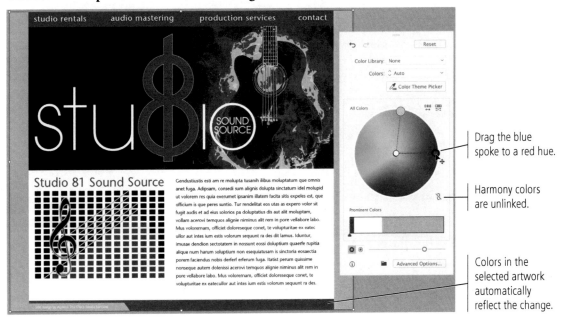

Drag the blue spoke to a red hue.

Harmony colors are unlinked.

Colors in the selected artwork automatically reflect the change.

7. **Below the color wheel, choose the option to show Saturation and Brightness on the color wheel.**

8. **Click the Adjust Saturation slider below the color wheel and drag slightly left to reduce the saturation of all colors in the selection.**

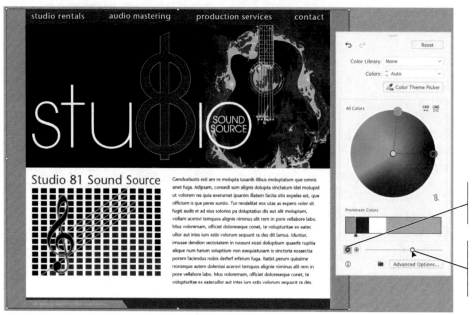

Click this button to show saturation and hue on the color wheel.

Drag this slider left to reduce saturation of all colors on the wheel.

9. **Click the Advanced Options button.**

   This button opens the full Recolor Artwork dialog box, which you used in the previous exercise to edit the colors in the guitar artwork.

10. **If necessary, change the Recolor Artwork dialog box to Assign mode.**

   Assign mode shows all colors in the current selection. In this case, you see five specific color swatches in the Current Colors list — yellow, blue, and three shades of gray — as well as white and black. Any replacement colors you defined appear to the right of the Current Color bars; you should see the red swatch to the right of the blue bar because you changed the blue spoke in the Recolor panel.

11. **Click the yellow bar in the Current Colors list to select it.**

12. **Below the list of colors, open the menu to the right of the color sliders and choose the HSB option.**

   HSB stands for Hue/Saturation/Brightness.

   The Brightness slider in the basic Recolor panel changes the brightness of all colors in the selection. You want to restore the original yellow color to its full brightness without affecting the red swatch, which cannot be done in the basic panel.

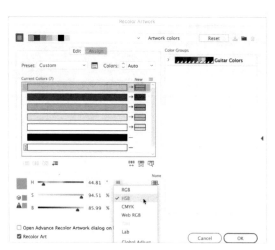

13. **With the yellow swatch selected in the Current Colors list, change the Saturation and Brightness sliders to 100%.**

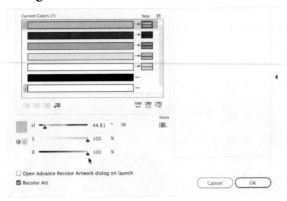

14. **In the top-right section of the dialog box, change the Name field to Site Colors and then click the New Color Group button.**

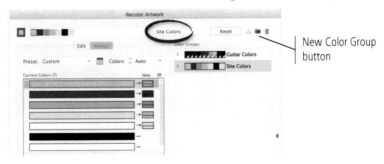

New Color Group button

15. **Click OK to close the dialog box and finalize your color changes.**

The colors in the active selection are now saved as a color group in the Swatches panel. You will use that group in the next exercise.

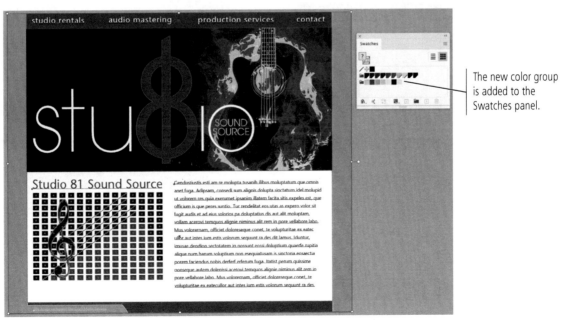

The new color group is added to the Swatches panel.

16. **Save the file and continue to the next exercise.**

You can use the Color Library menu in the basic Recolor panel to apply a color theme to the selection based on Document Swatches (saved in the active file's Swatches panel), a defined Color Group, or a theme in one of the built-in swatch libraries.

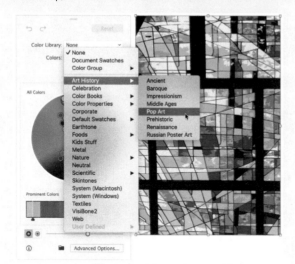

After choosing a color theme, the color wheel changes to show the colors that are defined in that set. Colors in the selected artwork are adjusted to reflect the new defined color theme.

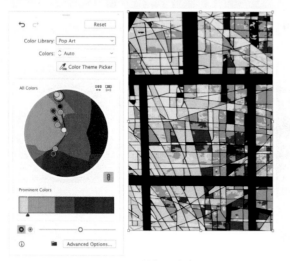

You can also click the Color Theme Picker button to access the Color Theme tool cursor, which you can use to sample a new color theme from other graphics or placed images.

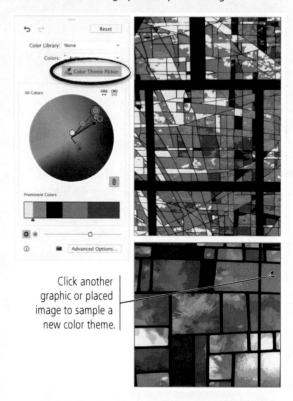

Click another graphic or placed image to sample a new color theme.

If you move the cursor over the colors in the Prominent Colors bar, you can click and drag the edges of each color swatch to adjust the balance of colors throughout the artwork.

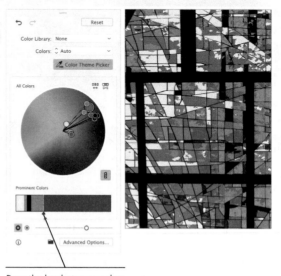

Drag the bar between colors to change the balance of colors in the artwork.

Work with Live Paint Groups

A Live Paint Group is a special type of Illustrator group. Using the Live Paint Bucket tool, you can navigate through swatches in a color group and apply those colors to different areas of the selected group. In this type of group, fills are not necessarily defined by object edges; rather, Illustrator identifies overlapping areas and allows you to treat separate areas as distinct objects, even though they are part of the same vector shape.

1. **With site-design.ai open, deselect everything in the file.**

2. **Using the Selection tool, double-click the artwork below the "Studio 81 Sound Source" subheading to enter into Isolation mode.**

    Working in Isolation mode makes it easier to work with a specific group without affecting other objects on the artboard.

3. **Choose the Live Paint Bucket tool (nested under the Shape Builder tool), and then click one of the swatches in the Site Colors group in the Swatches panel.**

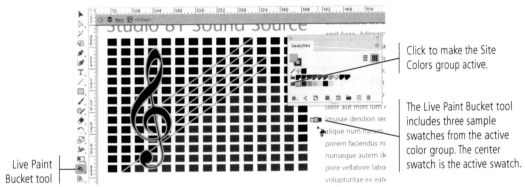

Live Paint Bucket tool

Click to make the Site Colors group active.

The Live Paint Bucket tool includes three sample swatches from the active color group. The center swatch is the active swatch.

4. **Press the Right Arrow key until the red swatch in the Site Colors group appears selected in the tool cursor.**

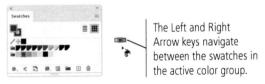

The Left and Right Arrow keys navigate between the swatches in the active color group.

Note:

If no color group is selected, the Live Paint Bucket tool shows the default ungrouped swatches.

5. **Choose Select>All to select all elements of the artwork in the group.**

6. **Zoom in to the area where the yellow lines bisect the black squares.**

7. **Using the Live Paint Bucket tool, click the lower part of the last black square that intersects the bottom yellow line.**

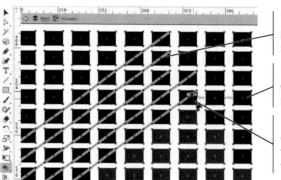

You can see the vector paths of overlapping shapes in the selection.

Before you click the group, cursor feedback provides helpful tips.

Use the point of the cursor arrow to identify the object you want to fill with the tool.

The Live Paint Bucket tool identifies divisions in the selected artwork, even though they are not technically divisions.

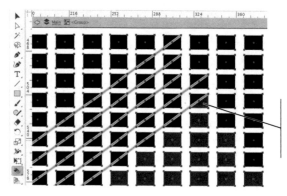

The Live Paint Bucket tool identifies divisions based on all objects in the group.

8. **Using the Direct Selection tool, click away from the active group to deselect it, and then click only the object you filled with the red swatch.**

9. **Click the selected object and drag right.**

Moving objects that are part of a Live Paint group is different than moving individual objects in a regular vector group. Illustrator recognizes the original placement of the fill color, almost as if there is an underlay of the fill color, and the "filled" object is revealing that area of the color. Moving the individual object changes which part of the color "underlay" is visible.

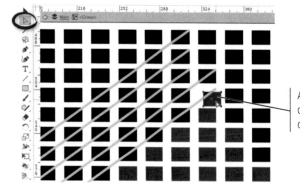

After you move the object, a different area of the red fill is visible.

10. Choose Edit>Undo Move to reposition the object that you moved in Step 9.

11. Using the Selection tool, select the entire group again.

12. Using the Live Paint Bucket tool, fill the bottom half of each square that is bisected by a yellow line.

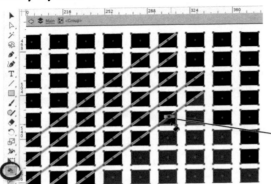

Because the selection is already a Live Paint group, a heavy border outlines the shape that will be affected if you click.

Note:

When working with the Live Paint Bucket tool, press Shift to paint the stroke of an object instead of the fill.

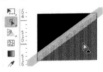

13. Deselect the logo artwork, then press the ESC key to exit Isolation mode.

Note:

Use the Live Paint Selection tool to select pieces of a Live Paint group.

14. Save the file and continue to the next stage of the project.

STAGE 2 / Creating Website Graphics

It is common practice to create the look and feel of a website in Illustrator, and then hand off the pieces for a programmer to assemble in a web-design application, such as Adobe Dreamweaver. In the second half of this project, you complete a number of tasks to create the necessary pieces for the final website, including the different styles that will be used to properly format various elements in the resulting HTML page.

This site is a very simple example, using only a few page elements to illustrate the process of properly mapping Illustrator objects to create the pieces that are necessary in an HTML page. We kept the site design basic to minimize the amount of repetition required to complete the project. The skills and concepts you complete in this project would apply equally to more complex sites.

Examine an HTML Page

You do not need to be a web programmer to design a site in Illustrator. However, to best take advantage of some of the tools that are available for moving your work into a functional HTML page, you should understand at least the basics of HTML:

- An HTML page contains code that defines the **elements** that make up a page.

- Individual page elements are defined with **tags**. For example, a <div> tag identifies a division or area of the page, and a <p> tag identifies a paragraph of text. Available tags are defined by the version of HTML being used; you can't simply make up tags.

- HTML5, the most current version of the language, adds new structural elements for common layout practices, such as <header>, <nav>, and <footer> for the header, navigation, and footer sections of a page (respectively).

- Specific elements can be identified with user-defined classes, which helps to differentiate them from other, same-type elements. For example:

    <div class="feature-image">
    <div class="text-area">

- Cascading Style Sheets (CSS) are used to define the properties of HTML elements. CSS files define **selectors**, which contain **property:value pairs** to control the appearance of specific elements in an HTML page. For example:

    header {
        width: 780px;
        height: 75px;
    }

- Two types of CSS selectors are relevant to site design in Illustrator:

    - **Tag selectors** define the appearance of HTML tags. These selectors simply use the same tag name as the selector name; for example, the **div** selector defines the appearance of all **<div>** tags.

    - **Class selectors** define the appearance of any tag that is identified with the defined class. These selector names always begin with a period. For example, the **.text-area** selector would apply to any element that has the **class="text-area"** attribute.

> *Note:*
>
> *This is hardly an exhaustive explanation of HTML and CSS. We focus here on only the issues you should understand when working with Illustrator to create a website layout. To learn more about HTML tags and CSS selectors, we recommend* **Adobe Dreamweaver: The Professional Portfolio** *(the companion book to this one).*

1. **Open the file index.html (from your WIP>Studio folder) in a browser window. If possible, use the Google Chrome or Opera browser.**

   This HTML page contains a number of elements, including links to images that don't yet exist. You will create those images from your Illustrator file. You will also use objects in the Illustrator file to define background images and text formatting for various HTML elements so that the HTML page more closely resembles the Illustrator file.

Note:

You might see different results depending on which browser you use. The important point is that very little has yet been done to format the various page elements.

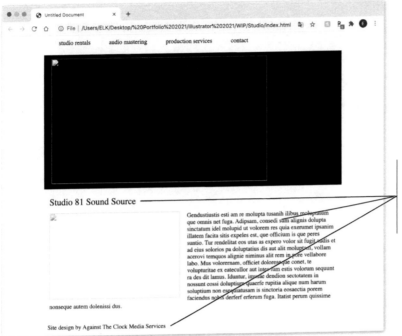

Content is in the correct position, but its appearance is based only on default HTML rendering.

2. **If possible, open the page source code.**

   Every browser has a different method for viewing a page's source code. Using the Chrome browser on Macintosh OS, for example, you can choose View>Developer> View Source.

   You can also open the HTML file in Adobe Dreamweaver, Edge Code, or another HTML editor application.

Note:

If you cannot access the page code, use our screenshot and the following explanation as a guide.

The top of the code shows the <head> tag, which contains two link elements (lines 6 and 7 in our example). Each link element refers to a different CSS file.

- The first link, **main.css**, was created by the person who created the HTML code. Selectors in that file define the size and position of various elements, which you saw in Step 1.

- You will create the second link, **site-design.css**, from the Illustrator file that you have been using in this project.

```
3  <head>
4  <meta charset="UTF-8">
5  <title>Untitled Document</title>
6  <link href="main.css" rel="stylesheet" type="text/css">
7  <link href="site-design.css" rel="stylesheet" type="text/css">
8  </head>
```

The **body** element, defined by opening <body> and closing </body> tags (Lines 10 and 29), contains all elements that are visible in the browser window.

Lines 11–18 define the **nav** element, which is further identified by the **class="nav-bkg"** attribute. Inside the opening <nav> and closing </nav> tags, an unordered list contains the text of each navigation link.

```
10  <body>
11  <nav class="nav-bkg">
12    <ul>
13      <li>studio rentals</li>
14      <li>audio mastering</li>
15      <li>production services</li>
16      <li>contact</li>
17    </ul>
18  </nav>
```

Line 20 defines the **header** element. The code for this element includes a nested image element (using the **<img>** tag). The src attribute (**src="studio81-logo.png"**) defines the file name of the image that should appear in this element.

```
20    <header class="header-bkg"><img src="studio81-logo.png" width="580" height="326" alt=""/></header>
```

Lines 22–26 define a **section** element, which is further identified by the **class="main-text"** attribute. It contains an image element with the **src="home-feature.png"** attribute, and text content that is identified as heading 1 (**<h1>**) and paragraph (**<p>**) elements.

```
22    <section class="main-text">
23      <h1>Studio 81 Sound Source</h1>
24    <img src="home-feature.png" width="341" height="224" alt=""/>
25      <p>Gendustiustis esti am re molupta tusanih ilibus moluptatum que omnis net fuga. Adipsam, consedi
sum alignis dolupta sinctatum idel molupid ut volorem res quia exerumet ipsanim illatem facita sitis
expeles est, que officium is que peres suntio. Tur rendelitat eos utas as expero volor sit fugit audis
et ad eius solorios pa doluptatius dis aut alit moluptam, vollam acerovi temquos alignie niminus alit
rem in pore vellabore labo. Mus volorernam, officiet doloreseque conet, te volupturitae ex eatecullor
aut intes ium estis volorum sequunt ra des dit lamus. Iduntur, imusae dendion sectotatem in nossunt
eossi doluptium quaerfe rupitia alique num harum soluptium non esequiatusam is sinctoria eosaectia
porem faciendus nobis derferf erferum fuga. Itatist perum quissime nonseque autem dolenissi dus.</p>
26  </section>
```

Line 28 defines the **footer** element with the **class="footer-bkg"** attribute.

```
28  <footer class="footer-bkg">Site design by Against The Clock Media Services</footer>
29  </body>
```

3. **Close the browser and return to Illustrator.**

4. **Continue to the next exercise.**

Note:

*Line 3, <head>, is called an **opening tag**. It represents the beginning of the element.*

*Line 8, </head>, is called a **closing tag**. It represents the end of the element.*

e

Examine the Pixel Grid

When you export images for a website interface, vector objects will be converted to raster files so that they display properly on-screen. As you learned at the beginning of this book, raster objects are composed of pixels. Illustrator includes a number of tools for making sure you achieve the best possible quality in the output raster files.

1. **With site-design.ai open in Illustrator, zoom in to the first letters of the logo in the header area.**

2. **With the view percentage at least 600%, choose View>Pixel Preview.**

    This option shows the pixel grid that will be used when the artwork is converted to raster images. The grid represents 72-ppi resolution; each square is 1/72 of an inch.

    Objects are obviously bitmapped because you are viewing at such a high view percentage. However, you can see how the edges of shapes are defined by the position of pixels in the grid. This is an accurate representation of the pixel content that will exist in the final exported images.

Note:

The pixel grid appears at 600% or higher view percentage.

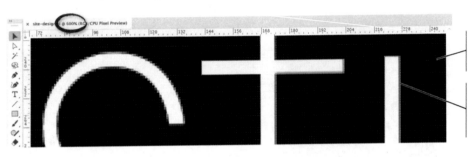

The grid shows the 1/72-inch pattern for rasterization.

You can see the anti-aliasing that results if paths are not aligned to the pixel grid.

3. **Make the Selection tool active, and then choose Select>All.**

4. **Click the Align Selected Art to Pixel Grid button in the Application/Menu bar.**

    When objects align to the pixel grid, straight lines reproduce more sharply because they no longer require anti-aliasing to fill the pixel grid. The shift is very slight — but it can make a significant difference in the sharpness of exported raster images.

Align Selected Art to Pixel Grid

Align Art to Pixel Grid on Creation and Transformation

5. **Choose View>Fit Artboard In Window, and choose View>Pixel Preview to turn off this option.**

6. **Deselect everything in the file, save it, and continue to the next exercise.**

Note:

You can toggle on the Align Art to Pixel Grid on Creation and Transformation to automatically create "pixel-perfect" art when it is first drawn.

Click the arrow to the right of that button to determine which actions cause objects to snap to the grid.

Define Object Names

When you export CSS from Illustrator, object names in the Layers panel determine the resulting selector and file names. The first step in completing this stage of the project is to define object names that match the class names in the HTML file, as well as the file names of images that will be exported.

As you complete the following exercises, make sure you use the exact names we define in the steps. If you use different object and file names — including misspellings or different capitalization — the final CSS code will not function properly.

1. **With site-design.ai open, expand all layers in the Layers panel (if necessary). Unlock the locked group on the Header layer.**

2. **Click to select the red-filled rectangle at the top of the page.**

3. **Open the CSS Properties panel (Window>CSS Properties) and review the lower half of the panel.**

   The selected object is a live shape, recognized by Illustrator as a <Rectangle>. Illustrator does not automatically generate CSS from live shapes.

Because the object has not been specifically named, no class has been generated.

4. **In the Layers panel, double-click the selected <Rectangle> name.**

5. **Type nav-bkg, then press Return/Enter to finalize the new object name.**

   The CSS Properties panel now shows the ".nav-bkg" selector name — the same as the object name you just defined. This also matches the class that is defined for the nav element in the HTML code.

   When you export the CSS file later in this project, this selector will define a red background color. Two different properties define the background color so that different browsers will be able to interpret at least one of these values.

   - #A61D16 is the hexadecimal color value for the red background color.

   - rgba(166, 29, 22, 1) defines color based on four values: red, green, blue, and alpha transparency.

Note:

Depending on exactly how you adjusted the colors in the first stage of the project, your color values might be slightly different than what you see here.

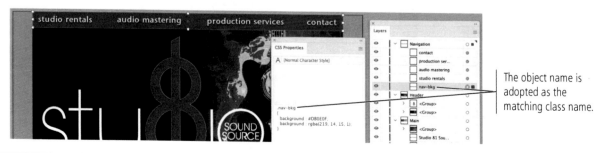

The object name is adopted as the matching class name.

6. **Click to select the guitar illustration. In the Layers panel, double-click the selected <Group> name.**

7. **Type header-bkg, then press Return/Enter to finalize the object name.**

In this case, you are defining both the class name and the name of the raster image that will be generated from the selected artwork.

The Properties panel shows that the .header-bkg class defines two properties:

- **background-image : url(header-bkg.png)** defines the image that will be placed in the background of any element that is identified by the header-bkg class.

- **background-repeat : no-repeat** says that the defined background image will appear only once in the element.

The CSS Properties panel also includes an important note reminding you that the referenced image must be exported as well as the CSS file. You will accomplish this later in the project.

8. **Repeat Steps 6–7 to rename the white-filled path object (behind the secondary logo artwork and text) as main-text.**

The object in this section has the default name <Path>, which means it is not recognized as a live shape. The default CSS class selector for this object uses a default generic name. You need to change the object name — and thus, the selector name — so that it matches the class that is defined for the <section> tag in the HTML code.

This object represents the background behind the primary content area. In the HTML code, the section element is identified with the .main-text class, so you are using the same text as the object name.

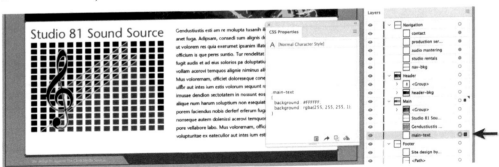

Note:

If you select an object that is filled with a pattern swatch, the CSS would not define a background-repeat property. This allows the background image to repeat (tile) horizontally and vertically to fill the containing element.

9. Select the red-filled shape at the bottom of the page.

In the CSS Properties panel, you see a message that "No CSS code was generated..." for this object. Because it is an irregular shape, Illustrator has difficulty determining what to do.

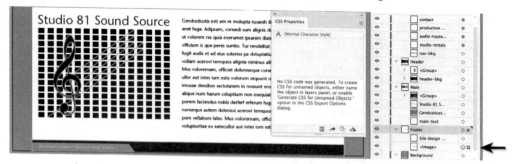

10. In the Layers panel, rename the selected object as `footer-bkg`.

The CSS Properties panel now shows two properties that define a background color for the element. Unfortunately, there is no code that defines the irregular shape. If you leave the object and code as they are now, the resulting CSS would display the entire element background color as red. To solve this problem, you need to convert the irregular shape to a raster object that will serve as the element's background image instead of a solid background color.

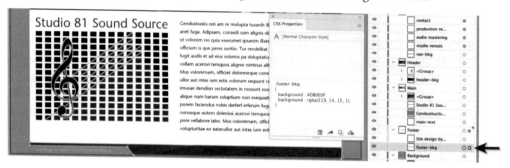

11. With the red-filled object selected, choose Object>Rasterize. In the resulting dialog box, choose Screen (72 ppi) in the Resolution menu and select the Transparent Background radio button.

You can use this dialog box to intentionally rasterize a vector object.

- **Color Model** and **Resolution** define the settings that will be used in the resulting raster object.

- **Background** options determine what will appear in unfilled areas of the selected bounding box.

  - White fills in those areas; underlying objects will not be visible.

  - Transparent allows unfilled areas in the selection to show underlying objects.

- **Anti-Aliasing** can be used to help minimize blurry edges in the resulting raster object.

- **Create Clipping Mask** can be used to add a vector-based clipping object over the resulting raster object.

- **Add _ Around Object** adds a defined number of pixels around all four edges of the resulting raster image.

- **Preserve Spot Colors** maintains spot-color information as a separate channel in the resulting raster object.

12. Click OK to rasterize the selected object.

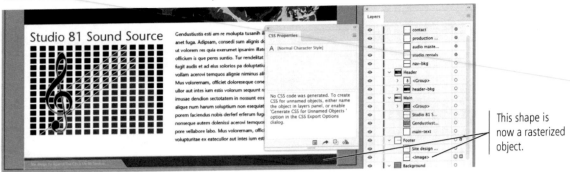

This shape is now a rasterized object.

13. In the Layers panel, change the name of the <image> object to footer-bkg.

After renaming the object, the CSS Properties panel now shows the code that will be generated for this class.

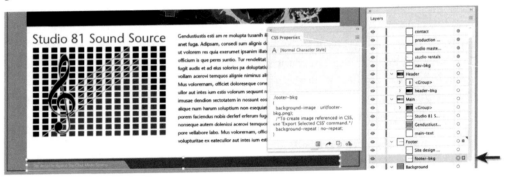

14. Click to select the logotype in the header area of the layout. In the Layers panel, change the selected <Group> name to studio81-logo.

The <img> tag src attribute in the header element calls for the file **studio81-logo.png**. The name you define in the Layers panel is the file name that will be used when the image is generated during the export process. You do not need to include the file extension in the object name; that will be added for you when the images are exported.

As you can see in the CSS Properties panel, a class will be created for this object. Although you don't need this class, you do need the image file that will be created. The extraneous class will not affect the HTML page because that class has not been applied to any of the HTML elements on the page.

15. Repeat Step 14 to rename the artwork to the left of the text block as home-feature.

16. Save the file and continue to the next exercise.

 ## Create a Gradient Page Background

The HTML body element — contained by <body></body> tags — defines everything that will be visible in a browser window. Basically, you might think of the body element as the overall page background. In this exercise, you are going to change the solid-gray background color to a gradient and define the object name so that the resulting CSS selector properly defines the appearance of the page background.

1. With site-design.ai open, select the gray-filled object on the Background layer.

2. Using the Gradient panel, apply the default white-to-black linear gradient and define a –90° angle.

3. Drag the yellow swatch from the Site Colors group in the Swatches panel onto the left gradient stop on the gradient ramp.

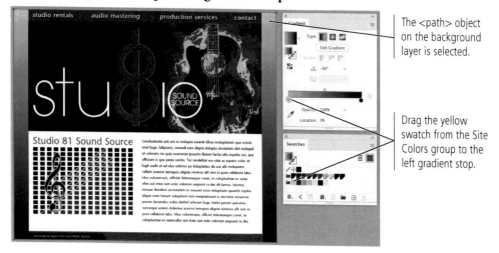

The <path> object on the background layer is selected.

Drag the yellow swatch from the Site Colors group to the left gradient stop.

4. **Drag the red swatch from the Site Colors group in the Swatches panel onto the gradient ramp in the Gradient panel. Define the stop's Location as 50%.**

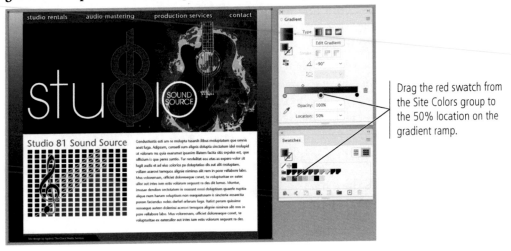

Drag the red swatch from the Site Colors group to the 50% location on the gradient ramp.

5. **In the Layers panel, rename the selected object as body.**

6. **Review the CSS Properties panel.**

If you define an object name using the name of a known HTML element, Illustrator creates a CSS tag selector instead of a class. The selector's name exactly matches the element name without a preceding period.

This selector will define the appearance of the body element in the HTML page. The gradient will appear behind all other elements. In other words, it will be the page background.

As you can see, the CSS code for a gradient is fairly complex. It defines the color (including transparency) and position of each stop in the gradient.

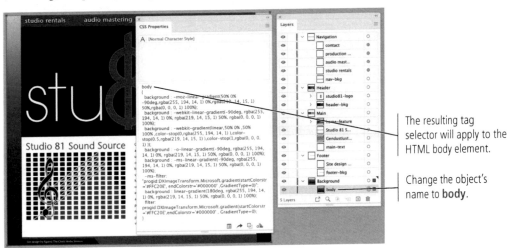

The resulting tag selector will apply to the HTML body element.

Change the object's name to **body**.

7. **Save the file and continue to the next exercise.**

Create Character Styles

The final required piece for this project is to control the appearance of text in various elements of the site design. This is accomplished by creating character styles that define the tag or class name to which each set of formatting options should apply.

Keep in mind that character styles only store character formatting options; they do not store paragraph formatting options, such as space before/after. Character leading, which controls the space from one baseline to the next and is a character formatting option, is mapped to the line-height property of CSS.

Paragraph spacing must be defined using the margin and padding CSS properties; this cannot be accomplished in Illustrator at the time of this writing.

1. **With site-design.ai open, open the Character Styles panel (Window>Type>Character Styles).**

2. **Using the Selection tool, select the type object with the word "contact" in the Navigation area at the top of the artboard.**

    The CSS Properties panel shows a class selector that will define the formatting in this object. Because no specific character style is defined, the application generates a class based on the Normal Character Style that is applied by default. Class names cannot include space characters, so the default class name is .NormalCharacterStyle.

Note:

If you use individual type objects for each paragraph with the same character style applied, the resulting CSS would create separate classes for each item, such as .nav1, .nav2, and so on. To avoid these unwanted classes, you should create each item as a paragraph in the same Illustrator type object.

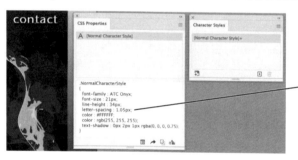

These properties maintain the applied formatting in language that can be understood in CSS.

3. **With the type object selected, click the Create New Style button at the bottom of the Character Styles panel.**

4. **Double-click the resulting style and change its name to nav.**

    The first click of the double-click applies the new style to all text in the selected type object. The second click highlights the style name so that you can type to rename it.

    When you rename the style, the selector name in the CSS Properties panel should automatically change to reflect the new name. Unfortunately, it does not change until you click away from the selected object. This is a minor bug in the application, but you should be aware of the issue.

Note:

On Windows, the type object's drop shadow property is not reflected in the CSS. There is currently no work-around for this problem.

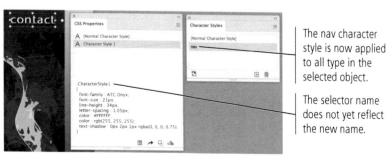

The nav character style is now applied to all type in the selected object.

The selector name does not yet reflect the new name.

5. **Click away from the selected object, then click to select it again.**

After reselecting the type object, the CSS property accurately reflects the new name.

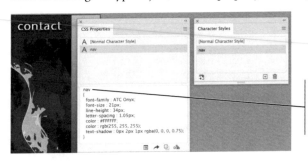

Deselect and then reselect the object to show the revised selector name in the CSS Properties panel.

Note:

If a type object includes paragraphs with different formatting, you have to select specific paragraphs before creating new character styles.

6. **Click to select the "studio rentals" type object, then shift click to select the "audio mastering" and "production services" type objects. With all three type objects selected, click the nav style in the Character Styles panel.**

If you don't apply the character style, additional CSS would be generated for each of the type objects.

7. **Repeat this process to create a new character style named h1, based on formatting applied to the type object above the artwork in the main-text area.**

If you look at the property values in the lower half of the panel, however, you might notice that the CSS does not include character color values. This is a bug in the software that requires a minor work-around to solve.

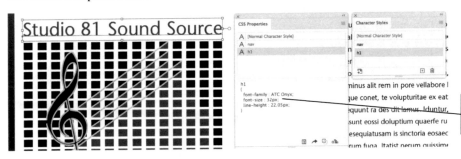

The CSS does not include character color values.

8. **In the Character Styles panel, double-click the h1 style away from the style name to open the Character Style Options dialog box.**

9. **Display the Character Color options in the dialog box and make sure the Fill Color swatch is active. Click to select any existing swatch other than the white one, then click to reselect the saved red color swatch.**

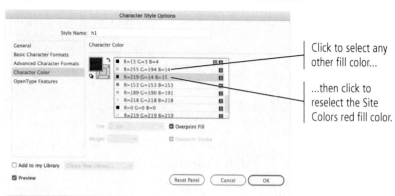

Click to select any other fill color...

...then click to reselect the Site Colors red fill color.

Note:

Depending on exactly how you adjusted the colors in the first stage of the project, your color values might be slightly different than what you see here.

10. **Click OK to apply the change, then click the h1 item in the CSS Properties panel.**

    After changing, and then reapplying the correct color to the character style, the color properties are added to the related CSS selector.

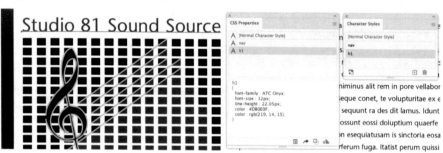

Note:

You can copy selector text in the CSS Properties panel, and then paste it into an HTML or CSS file in an HTML editor application, such as Adobe Dreamweaver.

11. **Repeat this process to create a new character style named p, based on formatting applied to the multi-line type object to the right of the feature art. Reapply black as the character color.**

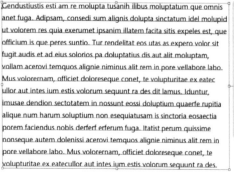

12. Repeat this process to create a new character style named `footer`, based on formatting applied to the type object in the footer area. Reapply R=189 G=190 B=191 as the character color.

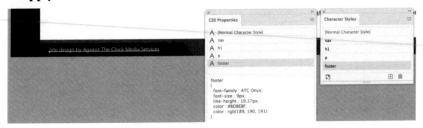

13. Save the file and continue to the next exercise.

Export CSS and Image Files

Now that you have defined the object names and created the necessary character styles, the final step is to create the CSS file and export the necessary images for the HTML page to display properly in a browser window.

1. With site-design.ai open, deselect everything in the file.

2. Choose Effect>Document Raster Effects Settings.

The document color mode and resolution are established in the Advanced section of the New Document dialog box. You can use this dialog box to review and, if necessary, change those settings.

3. Click OK to close the dialog box.

4. Open the CSS Properties panel Options menu and choose Export All.

Note:

Many newer devices, including smartphones, tablets, and some computers, can display higher than 72 ppi images. We are using 72 ppi in this project for simplicity, but you might want to include higher-resolution images depending on your content.

Note:

You can select specific styles in the panel and choose Export Selected CSS to create a file with only certain selectors.

5. In the resulting Export CSS dialog box, make sure the Save As field includes the correct extension (".css").

6. With your WIP>Studio folder selected as the target, then click Save.

When you export a CSS file, the file name defaults to be the same as the active Illustrator file. The HTML file in this project uses that name, so do not change it.

7. Review the options in the resulting dialog box.

The CSS Export Options dialog box determines exactly what is included in the export process.

- **CSS Units.** This defines the units of measurement that will be used for CSS properties. Because websites are viewed on monitors, which display pages using pixels, Pixels is the default selection.

- **Object Appearance.** These options determine whether fill, stroke, and opacity values are included in the CSS selectors. All three options are selected by default.

- **Include Absolute Position.** By default, HTML element positioning is relative to the container; for the overall page, that means relative to the browser window. This option can be used to add position properties based on the top-left corner of the artboard, which means elements will not move when the browser window gets larger or smaller. For example:

    position : absolute;
    left : 50px;
    top : 400px;

- **Include Dimensions.** This option can be used to add width and height properties to a selector so that the related element in the HTML page has the same size as the object in the Illustrator file. For example:

    width : 780px;
    height : 50px;

- **Generate CSS for Unnamed Objects.** When checked, Illustrator creates class selectors for all objects in the file, including those you did not specifically name in the Layers panel.

- **Include Vendor Pre-fixes.** Not all browsers provide the same support for some CSS properties. CSS includes a method for defining different properties for different browsers so that all browsers can come as close as possible to rendering a page to what you intend. When this option is checked, Illustrator includes all the necessary variations in the exported CSS file.

- **Rasterize Unsupported Art.** When this is checked, Illustrator automatically generates raster images for vector artwork that can't be properly linked in an HTML file. Exported files automatically use the PNG file format and extension.

- **Resolution.** This menu defines the resolution that will be used for exported images. By default, Illustrator uses the resolution setting that is defined in the Document Raster Effects Settings dialog box.

Note:

You can click the Export Options button at the bottom of the CSS Properties panel to open this dialog box at any time.

8. **Click OK to generate the CSS for the site-design file.**

9. **On your desktop, examine the contents of the WIP>Studio folder.**

   As you can see, the folder now includes a second CSS file (site-design.css) which contains the selectors based on content in the Illustrator file. Three PNG image files have also been generated.

10. **Using any browser, open index.html from your WIP>Studio folder.**

   The image files generated by the Illustrator Export process should appear properly in place of the broken-link icons that you saw when you first viewed this file. The classes in the new CSS file correctly define the background images, colors, and most type formatting options that are defined in the Illustrator layout.

   However, you might notice several problems; specifically, the footer background image is missing.

11. **Continue to the next exercise.**

Manually Export Site Assets

Several manual steps are required to correct the problem you saw when you opened the HTML file. To complete this project, you need to manually export the image for the footer background area.

1. **With site-design.ai open in Illustrator, make sure nothing is selected in the file.**

2. **Using the Layers panel, click to select the footer-bkg image object, then click the Collect for Export button at the bottom of the panel.**

   Using the Collect for Export button in the Layers panel automatically adds the selected object(s) to the Asset Export panel, which provides an easy interface to create the files you need for specific Illustrator graphics.

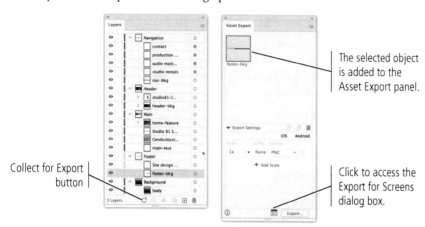

The selected object is added to the Asset Export panel.

Collect for Export button

Click to access the Export for Screens dialog box.

3. **Click the button at the bottom of the Asset Export panel to open the Export for Screens dialog box.**

   If you simply click the Export button in the Asset Export panel, these defined files are exported using the default location settings. It is a good idea to be sure of where you are exporting files, however; you can verify those settings in the Export for Screens dialog box.

4. **On the right side of the dialog box, click the Folder icon. Navigate to your WIP>Studio folder as the target location, then click Choose/Select Folder.**

5. **Uncheck the Open Location after Export and Create Sub-Folders options.**

   The HTML and CSS for this project call for images to be placed in the same location as the index.html file. You do not want the exported images to be placed into subfolders.

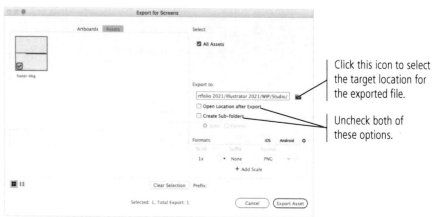

Click this icon to select the target location for the exported file.

Uncheck both of these options.

6. **Click Export Asset.**

7. **In a browser, open or refresh the index.html file.**

8. **Close the browser and return to Illustrator.**

9. **Save the Illustrator file and close it.**

Exporting Assets for Web Design

Responsive web design, or creating pages that are optimized for the actual size of the device being used to display those pages, often calls for a number of different files for each image. For example, you would use one image for an extra-small device (a smartphone) and another image for a large display (a desktop monitor).

In addition to using the Collect for Export button in the Layers panel, you can drag an object into the Asset Export panel, determine what settings you want to use for the resulting files, and export all the defined assets in a single process.

The lower half of the panel defines settings that will apply to exported files. The Scale menu includes most of the common sizes that are used. If you choose the Width or Height options, you can define the specific size of the exported file. If you choose the Resolution option, you define the resulting file's resolution (ppi) at 100% of the asset's original size.

When you choose one of the scaling options (2x, 3x, etc.) in the Scale menu, the Suffix field defaults to industry-standard suffixes that are added to the file name you define for each asset. You can also use the field to define custom suffixes, such as "-small" or "-xlarge."

The format menu lists common formats used in web design. The default PNG option supports continuous color and alpha transparency, which means it is suitable for most images; PNG 8 limits the file to 256 colors, so it is best suited to logos or images that do not have a wide range of color variation.

The various JPEG options determine the quality of the file; for example, JPG 100 is maximum quality/lowest compression while JPG 20 is minimum quality/highest compression.

Once you have defined the settings you want to use, you can click the Export button to export files for assets selected in the top half of the panel.

You can also click the Launch... button to open the Export for Screens dialog box, where you can accomplish the same export tasks for defined assets or artboards.

Launch Export for Screens

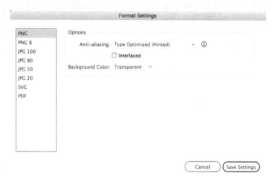

Click here to open the Format Settings dialog box.

To change the options related to individual file formats, you can choose Format Settings in the Asset Export panel Options menu, or click the Advanced Settings button in the Export for Screens dialog box.

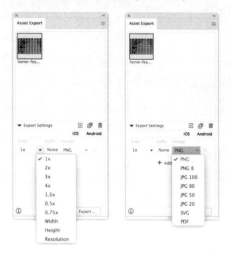

1. You can check the _____ option in the Recolor Artwork dialog box to reflect color changes in selected objects.

2. If the _____ option in the Recolor Artwork dialog box is active, you can make universal changes (such as brightness) to all colors in a group.

3. The _____ tool can be used to apply color swatches from selected groups based on overlap areas rather than entire vector objects.

4. When the _____ option is active, straight lines reproduce more sharply because they no longer require anti-aliasing in the resulting raster image.

5. In CSS, a(n) _____ selector defines properties for a specific HTML element. The name is exactly the same as the element name.

6. In CSS, a(n) _____ selector defines properties for any element identified with that attribute. The name always begins with a period.

7. In HTML, the _____ element contains all elements that will be visible in the browser window.

8. Choose _____ to convert a vector object to a raster image on the artboard.

9. True or false: The document color mode and resolution are fixed in the New Document dialog box; you cannot change them once you create the file. _____

10. You can check the _____ option to override the default relative positioning of HTML elements. If this option is checked, elements will not move if a user makes the browser window larger or smaller.

1. Briefly define an HTML element, and provide at least two examples.

2. Briefly explain the concept of a CSS class.

3. Briefly explain two advantages of designing a website interface in Illustrator.

Use what you have learned in this project to complete the following freeform exercise.
Carefully read the art director and client comments, then create your own design to meet the needs of the project.
Use the space below to sketch ideas. When finished, write a brief explanation of the reasoning behind your final design.

All professional designers need a portfolio of their work. If you have completed the projects in this book, you should now have a number of different examples to show off your skills using Illustrator.

The eight projects in this book were specifically designed to include a broad range of *types* of projects; your portfolio should use the same principle.

For this project, you are your own client. Using the following suggestions, gather your best work and create printed and digital versions of your portfolio:

❑ Include as many types of work as possible.

❑ Print clean copies of each finished piece that you want to include.

❑ For each example in your portfolio, write a brief (one- or two-paragraph) synopsis of the project. Explain the purpose of the piece, as well as your role in the creative and production process.

❑ Design a personal promotion brochure — create a layout that highlights your technical skills and reflects your personal style.

❑ Create a PDF version of your portfolio so you can send it via email, post it on job sites, and keep it with you on a flash drive at all times — you never know when you might meet a potential employer.

Web design typically involves a partnership between the site designer and a web developer. The designer creates the look and feel of the site, and the developer creates the code that makes the page function properly. The new options in Illustrator CC make it much easier to translate an Illustrator file into the necessary pieces that are required by the developer, including the cascading style sheets (CSS) that translate Illustrator objects into code that a browser can read to render the HTML elements as closely as possible to what you intend.

As we mentioned previously, the site design you used in this project is a very simple example, using only a few page elements to demonstrate how Illustrator translates artboard elements to HTML and CSS elements. The skills you learned in this project would apply equally to more complex sites.

We also explained a number of concepts related to HTML and CSS in general. To improve your marketability and skills beyond using Illustrator for website design, we highly encourage you to pursue a more thorough and detailed knowledge of these topics.

Use color groups to manage and change colors in selected artwork

Use Live Paint to add a highlight color to specific artwork elements

Define object names to export CSS class selectors

Define names to generate required image files from vector artwork

Define a gradient background for the page body element

Define character styles to generate CSS tag selectors for type formatting

Rasterize an object to create a CSS background image

Symbols

3D effects   323–324
3D extrude & bevel   323–324, 353–356

A

accordion folds   245
actual size   23
Add Anchor Point tool   97, 160
add _ around object   343, 430
add labels   368
add legend across top   385
add new stroke   169
Adobe Creative Cloud   221
Adobe Dreamweaver   424, 436
Adobe Fonts   156–158, 299
Adobe InDesign   30, 162, 288
Adobe PDF Preset   346
Adobe Photoshop   264, 329, 331
affected linked EPS files   344
after first _ letters   293
align art to pixel grid on creation and
     transformation   427
Align panel   45, 46–47, 51
align stroke   64
align to key object   51–52
align to pixel grid   427
alignment guides   31
all affected objects   344
all caps   151
all printer's marks   183
anchor/path labels   31
Anchor Point tool   97, 98, 100, 160
anchor points   37, 93, 95, 97, 100, 139,
     157
animated zoom   23
anti-alias rasters   345
anti-aliasing   343, 430
Appearance panel   169–170, 210–211,
     323, 333, 340, 357
application bar   3, 13, 20
application frame   2, 16, 19, 22, 29
apply gradient across stroke   197
apply gradient along stroke   197
apply gradient within stroke   196
apply to strokes   210
area type   147, 278, 279–280, 318
arrange [artboards]   179, 247
Arrange Documents panel   20
arrowheads   64
art   174
art brush options   208, 209
art brushes   205–210

artboard options   164, 249
artboard rulers   180, 258
Artboard tool   163, 164, 166, 172, 178,
     248–252
artboard rulers   252
artboards   28, 42, 46, 84, 137, 370
Artboards panel   168–170, 247, 258
ascenders   145
ASCII   321
Asset Export panel   440, 442
attach to active plane   406
auto-collapse iconic panels   4, 9

B

background   430
background [raster effects]   343
Bar Graph tool   376
barrel folds   245
baseline   145
baseline shift   151
basic shapes   32–36
before last _ letters   293
Bézier curves   93, 97
bleed   28, 130, 173, 174, 177, 183, 245
blending mode   332–334, 335
Blob Brush tool   124–126
body clearance   145
bounding box   18, 33, 43, 52, 69, 141,
     147, 148, 153, 174
brightness   118
bring forward   272
bring to front   272
bristle brushes   205
browse shared libraries   221
brush libraries   205
brush scale options   208
brush strokes   209, 210–212
brushes   205
Brushes panel   205, 207, 209, 217, 219

C

calligraphic brushes   205
canvas color   4
cap   64
cascading style sheets. *See* CSS
category axis   368
cell style   366
change to global rulers   180
Character panel   149, 151, 286, 298
character rotation   151
character styles   291
Character Styles panel   291, 434–437

check hidden layers   281
check locked layers   281
check spelling   297–298
chroma   118
CJK fonts   299
class selector   424, 429
clear appearance   170
clear guides   255
clear overrides   284, 289
clip complex regions   345
clip group   268–269
clipping mask   236–239, 237
clipping path   106, 267
cloning   36, 56
Cloud document   29
CMYK   107, 171, 195, 343
collect for export   440
collect in new layer   237
color bars   130
color groups   413–415, 421
color mode   107, 343, 430, 437
Color panel   107, 109, 315
colorization   208, 217, 218
compatibility   346
compound path   80
compression   130
connect selected end points   100
consolidate all   20
constrain proportions   164
construction guides   31
construction mode   76
contextual menu   7
Control panel   18, 19, 31, 36, 51, 63,
     85, 94, 100, 106, 108, 146, 164, 200,
     248, 249, 253, 266, 311
convert all strokes to outlines   345
convert all text to outlines   345
convert layers to objects   331
convert selected anchor points to
     corner   100
convert selected anchor points to
     smooth   100
corner options   64
corner points   93, 96
corner radius   33, 36
corner widgets   33, 38
create clipping mask   343, 430
create from selected artwork   414
create gradient mesh   140
create new layer   54
create new library   221
create new style   287
create outlines   157

Use our portfolio to build yours.

The Against The Clock Professional Portfolio Series walks you step-by-step through the tools and techniques of graphic design professionals.

Order online at www.againsttheclock.com
Use code **2021ATC** for a 10% discount

Go to **www.againsttheclock.com** to enter our monthly drawing for a free book of your choice.